AFRICAN HISTORICAL DICTIONARIES
Edited by Jon Woronoff

1. *Cameroon,* by Victor T. Le Vine and Roger P. Nye. 1974. *Out of print. See No. 48.*
2. *The Congo,* 2nd ed., by Virginia Thompson and Richard Adloff. 1984. *Out of print. See No. 69.*
3. *Swaziland,* by John J. Grotpeter. 1975.
4. *The Gambia,* 2nd ed., by Harry A. Gailey. 1987.
5. *Botswana,* by Richard P. Stevens. 1975. *Out of print. See No. 70.*
6. *Somalia,* by Margaret F. Castagno. 1975.
7. *Benin (Dahomey),* 2nd ed., by Samuel Decalo. 1987. *Out of print. See No. 61.*
8. *Burundi,* by Warren Weinstein. 1976. *Out of print. See No. 73.*
9. *Togo,* 3rd ed., by Samuel Decalo. 1996.
10. *Lesotho,* by Gordon Haliburton. 1977.
11. *Mali,* 3rd ed., by Pascal James Imperato. 1996.
12. *Sierra Leone,* by Cyril Patrick Foray. 1977.
13. *Chad,* 3rd ed., by Samuel Decalo. 1997.
14. *Upper Volta,* by Daniel Miles McFarland. 1978.
15. *Tanzania,* by Laura S. Kurtz. 1978.
16. *Guinea,* 3rd ed., by Thomas O'Toole with Ibrahima Bah-Lalya. 1995.
17. *Sudan,* by John Voll. 1978. *Out of print. See No. 53.*
18. *Rhodesia/Zimbabwe,* by R. Kent Rasmussen. 1979. *Out of print. See No. 46.*
19. *Zambia,* 2nd ed., by John J. Grotpeter, Brian V. Siegel, and James R. Pletcher. 1998.
20. *Niger,* 3rd ed., by Samuel Decalo. 1997.
21. *Equatorial Guinea,* 3rd ed., by Max Liniger-Goumaz. 2000.
22. *Guinea-Bissau,* 3rd ed., by Richard Lobban and Peter Mendy. 1997.
23. *Senegal,* by Lucie G. Colvin. 1981. *Out of print. See No. 65.*
24. *Morocco,* by William Spencer. 1980. *Out of print. See No. 71.*
25. *Malawi,* by Cynthia A. Crosby. 1980. *Out of print. See No. 54.*
26. *Angola,* by Phyllis Martin. 1980. *Out of print. See No. 52.*
27. *The Central African Republic,* by Pierre Kalck. 1980. *Out of print. See No. 51.*
28. *Algeria,* by Alf Andrew Heggoy. 1981. *Out of print. See No. 66.*
29. *Kenya,* by Bethwell A. Ogot. 1981. *Out of print. See No. 77.*
30. *Gabon,* by David E. Gardinier. 1981. *Out of print. See No. 58.*
31. *Mauritania,* by Alfred G. Gerteiny. 1981. *Out of print. See No. 68.*

32. *Ethiopia*, by Chris Prouty and Eugene Rosenfeld. 1981. *Out of print. See No. 56.*

33. *Libya*, 3rd ed., by Ronald Bruce St John. 1998.

34. *Mauritius*, by Lindsay Riviere. 1982. *Out of print. See No. 49.*

35. *Western Sahara*, by Tony Hodges. 1982. *Out of print. See No. 55.*

36. *Egypt*, by Joan Wucher King. 1984. *Out of print. See No. 67.*

37. *South Africa*, by Christopher Saunders. 1983. *Out of print. See No. 78.*

38. *Liberia*, by D. Elwood Dunn and Svend E. Holsoe. 1985. *Out of print. See No. 83.*

39. *Ghana*, by Daniel Miles McFarland. 1985. *Out of print. See No. 78.*

40. *Nigeria*, 2nd ed., by Anthony Oyewole and John Lucas. 2000.

41. *Côte d'Ivoire (The Ivory Coast)*, 2nd ed., by Robert J. Mundt. 1995.

42. *Cape Verde*, 2nd ed., by Richard Lobban and Marilyn Halter. 1988. *Out of print. See No. 62.*

43. *Zaire*, by F. Scott Bobb. 1988. *Out of print. See No. 76.*

44. *Botswana*, 2nd ed., by Fred Morton, Andrew Murray, and Jeff Ramsay. 1989. *Out of print. See No. 70.*

45. *Tunisia*, 2nd ed., by Kenneth J. Perkins. 1997.

46. *Zimbabwe*, 3rd ed., by Steven C. Rubert and R. Kent Rasmussen. 1998.

47. *Mozambique*, by Mario Azevedo. 1991.

48. *Cameroon*, 2nd ed., by Mark W. DeLancey and H. Mbella Mokeba. 1990.

49. *Mauritius*, 2nd ed., by Sydney Selvon. 1991.

50. *Madagascar*, by Maureen Covell. 1995.

51. *The Central African Republic*, 2nd ed., by Pierre Kalck; translated by Thomas O'Toole. 1992.

52. *Angola*, 2nd ed., by Susan H. Broadhead. 1992.

53. *Sudan*, 2nd ed., by Carolyn Fluehr-Lobban, Richard A. Lobban, Jr., and John Obert Voll. 1992.

54. *Malawi*, 2nd ed., by Cynthia A. Crosby. 1993.

55. *Western Sahara*, 2nd ed., by Anthony Pazzanita and Tony Hodges. 1994.

56. *Ethiopia and Eritrea*, 2nd ed., by Chris Prouty and Eugene Rosenfeld. 1994.

57. *Namibia*, by John J. Grotpeter. 1994.

58. *Gabon*, 2nd ed., by David E. Gardinier. 1994.

59. *Comoro Islands*, by Martin Ottenheimer and Harriet Ottenheimer. 1994.

60. *Rwanda,* by Learthen Dorsey. 1994.
61. *Benin,* 3rd ed., by Samuel Decalo. 1995.
62. *Republic of Cape Verde,* 3rd ed., by Richard Lobban and Marlene Lopes. 1995.
63. *Ghana,* 2nd ed., by David Owusu-Ansah and Daniel Miles McFarland. 1995.
64. *Uganda,* by M. Louise Pirouet. 1995.
65. *Senegal,* 2nd ed., by Andrew F. Clark and Lucie Colvin Phillips. 1994.
66. *Algeria,* 2nd ed., by Phillip Chiviges Naylor and Alf Andrew Heggoy. 1994.
67. *Egypt,* 2nd ed., by Arthur Goldschmidt, Jr. 1994.
68. *Mauritania,* 2nd ed., by Anthony G. Pazzanita. 1996.
69. *Congo,* 3rd ed., by Samuel Decalo, Virginia Thompson, and Richard Adloff. 1996.
70. *Botswana,* 3rd ed., by Jeff Ramsay, Barry Morton, and Fred Morton. 1996.
71. *Morocco,* 2nd ed., by Thomas K. Park. 1996.
72. *Tanzania,* 2nd ed., by Thomas P. Ofcansky and Rodger Yeager. 1997.
73. *Burundi,* 2nd ed., by Ellen K. Eggers. 1997.
74. *Burkina Faso,* 2nd ed., by Daniel Miles McFarland and Lawrence Rupley. 1998.
75. *Eritrea,* by Tom Killion. 1998.
76. *Democratic Republic of the Congo (Zaire),* by F. Scott Bobb. 1999. (Revised edition of *Historical Dictionary of Zaire,* No. 43)
77. *Kenya,* 2nd ed., by Robert M. Maxon and Thomas P. Ofcansky. 2000.
78. *South Africa,* 2nd ed., by Christopher Saunders and Nicholas Southey. 2000.
79. *The Gambia,* 3rd ed., by Arnold Hughes and Harry A. Gailey. 2000.
80. *Swaziland,* 2nd ed., by Alan R. Booth. 2000.
81. *Republic of Cameroon,* 3rd ed., by Mark W. DeLancey and Mark Dike DeLancey. 2000.
82. *Djibouti,* by Daoud A. Alwan and Yohanis Mibrathu. 2000.
83. *Liberia,* 2nd ed., by D. Elwood Dunn, Amos J. Beyan, and Carl Patrick Burrowes. 2000.

Historical Dictionary of Equatorial Guinea

Third Edition

Max Liniger-Goumaz

African Historical Dictionaries, No. 21

The Scarecrow Press, Inc.
Lanham, Maryland, and London
2000

SCARECROW PRESS, INC.

Published in the United States of America
by Scarecrow Press, Inc.
4720 Boston Way, Lanham, Maryland 20706
www.scarecrowpress.com

4 Pleydell Gardens, Folkestone
Kent CT20 2DN, England

British Library Cataloguing in Publication Information Available

Library of Congress Cataloging-in-Publication Data

Liniger-Goumaz, Max.
  Historical dictionary of Equatorial Guinea / /Max Liniger-Goumaz. — 3rd ed.
    p. cm. — (African historical dictionaries ; no. 21)
    Includes bibliographical references.
    ISBN 0-8108-3394-8 (alk. paper)
      1. Equatorial Guinea—History—Dictionaries.   I. Title. II. Series.

DT620.15 L57 2000
967.18—dc21
                                                    00-059546

❖ CONTENTS ❖

❖ EDITOR'S FOREWORD ❖

Few of Africa's many new nations are as completely unknown in most circles, including even those which are generally familiar with Africa, as Equatorial Guinea. Its origin in the more restricted and less penetrable colonial empire of Spain is partly at fault. More so, unfortunately, is the fact that not long after becoming independent the country was bottled up by its new rulers, most foreigners were encouraged to leave or were expelled, and few people were let in. The reasons for this are not hard to find and, as in the case of Libya, Rwanda, and some others which avoid inquisitive eyes, they reside largely in the regimes and leaders.

Equatorial Guinea, however, was far from poorly endowed upon independence in 1968 and showed signs of joining the African community as a reasonably prosperous and successful member. Its economy, although modest, had a good foundation. Its elite, although small, was well trained. Some of its leaders showed promise. Today, over thirty years later, there is little evidence of this promise. The economy is decaying, education has fallen off, and most serious of all, many of the intellectual and political elite have been jailed, executed, or gone into voluntary exile. The Macías regime was strong enough to withstand the few attacks that were made on it; for no one showed any particular concern. After the overthrow of this regime by his nephew, Obiang Nguema, the Nguemist regime lived on unabashed, using the same team to carry out the same policies. Equatorial Guinea remains one of the least visited countries on the African continent despite the initiation of oil production by American companies.

We are thus particularly grateful to the author of this dictionary both for providing extremely hard-to-find information and for showing concern for what has happened. Nowhere in the English-language literature and scarcely even in Spanish sources could one find a more comprehensive guide to Equatorial Guinea. There is certainly no more complete "who's who," although sadly enough many of the figures are no longer alive. And finally the only other good bibliography is the one by the author of this book himself. Dr. Max Liniger-Goumaz, an international expert and consultant on Africa, who has worked on numerous assignments all over the continent since 1962, is also a writer on African and European issues and has recently completed a ten-volume general bibliography on Equatorial Guinea in Spanish for the Swiss National Commission for UNESCO and the Editions du Temps (Geneva). He is also a professor at the Swiss Federal Institute of Technology and the School of Economics and Business Administration in Lausanne, Switzerland, and was recently named an honorary member of the Spanish Association of Africanism. The present dictionary, giving the essential background information, will go far toward filling the huge gaps that exist in our knowledge of probably the least-known African state.

Jon Woronoff
Series Editor

❖ ACKNOWLEDGMENTS ❖

I am indebted to various persons whose help was indispensable in researching, compiling, and checking the information presented here. Many Equato-Guineans living in the country or refugiated abroad have shared their knowledge of the country, its peoples, and recent events, but because of the present political situation in their country, they cannot be named.

It is unfortunate that the internal situation of Equatorial Guinea impeded normal research in the country; as a consequence, some distortions may unavoidably have escaped my notice.

I owe special gratitude to Mrs. Re'sy Oguey-Frommes, who kindly read and criticized the first manuscript, to Professor John Wood, an Africanist well acquainted with Equatorial Guinea, for his valuable advice as to both form and content of the second edition, and to Mrs. Ranganayaki Venugopal and Fabienne Trippini Pagano for this third edition.

Finally, this book would not exist without the solicitude of my family, both during our stay in Equatorial Guinea and while this information was collected.

Max Liniger-Goumaz
Swiss Federal Institute of Technology, Lausanne
School of Economics and Business Administration, Lausanne

❖ A NOTE ON PLACE NAMES ❖

At the August 1973 Congress of the Partido Unico Nacional de Trabajadores (PUNT), one year after President Macías Nguema Biyogo appointed himself "President for Life" and "Tireless and Unique Miracle of Equatorial Guinea," various place names were changed. For the continental province of Río Muni—occupied by Spain in 1926 and therefore exposed to little Spanish impact—only the name of Río Benito has been changed, to Mbini; the people of the town of Río Benito were most atrociously massacred by Macías Nguema. Macías Nguema tried especially to change the names of the Insular Province composed of the two islands of Fernando Po and Annobón, without consulting the Bubi, Creoles, and Ambú populations concerned. The most important changes are the following:

Fernando Po — renamed *Macías Nguema Biyogo Island* after the dictator Macías Nguema, even though he had no ethnic connection with the island or its inhabitants. In 1979 Obiang Nguema renamed it *Bioko*.

San Fernando — renamed *Ela Nguema* after Macías Nguema's nephew who was his private secretary and later aide-de-camp. This suburb of Santa Isabel was absorbed into the capital in 1979.

Santa Isabel — renamed *Malabo* (named after the Bubi king, 1904-1937), accomplice of the Spanish occupation, capital.

San Carlos — renamed *Luba* (named after the Bubi chief who fought the excesses of Spanish occupation), town in western Fernando Po.

Concepción — renamed *Riaba* (named after a Bubi chief), town in eastern Fernando Po.

Punta Fernanda — renamed *Punta de la Unidad Africana* (renamed at the very time when the Organization of African Unity [OAU] was virtually expelled), easternmost tip of the sunken crater around which Santa Isabel is built.

A typical example of the Nguemist orientation of these name changes is that of Annobón (island), which was supposed to become "Pagalu," which in the local Portuguese creole (ambú) means "Papa Galo," or Father Cock, the name given to Macías Nguema after his 1968 presidential campaign during which he had adopted the rooster as a symbol. This new name came at the time when Macías Nguema refused international assistance to save a large part of the island's population stricken with cholera; the remaining inhabitants were later deported into forced labor in the cocoa plantations of Fernando Po (or "Macías Nguema"or "Bioko") that had been abandoned by the Nigerian agricultural workers repatriated from

Equatorial Guinea by their government. In 1979, the islanders forced the Obiang Nguema regime to revert to the name Annobón.

The toponymic fantasies of 1973 were unanimously rejected by the 110,000 Equatorial Guinean exiles (the total intelligentsia of the country) who, before amending any of the goals reached at independence, called for a democratic consultation, impossible in the present tragic situation.

❖ ACRONYMS AND ABBREVIATIONS ❖

Also see entry for political parties for additional acronyms and abbreviations.

ADB	African Development Bank
ADP	Alianza Democrática Progresista (Democratic Progressive Alliance)
AI	Amnesty International
AIF	African Investment Fund
ALENA	Compañía Nacional de Colonización Africana
ANALIGE	Acción Nacional de Liberación de Guinea Ecuatorial
ANRD	Alianza Nacional para la Restauración Democrática (National Alliance for Democratic Restoration)
AP	Acción Popular, Alianza Popular
ASEA	Anglo-Spanish Employment Agency
ASODAGE	Asociación de Amigos de Guinea Ecuatorial
ASODEGUE	Asociación para la Solidaridad Democrática con Guinea Ecuatorial
BADEA	Arab Bank for the Economic Development of Africa
BADEAC	Banco de Desarrollo de los Estados de Africa Central
BEAC	Banque des Etats de l'Afrique centrale (franc zone) (Bank of Central African States)
BEAO	Bank of the West African States
BIAO	International Bank of West Africa
BNDD	Banco Nacional de Depósito y Desarrollo
BRGM	Bureau de Recherches géologiques et minières (France)
CAHIS	Circulo Afro-Hispano
CCCE	Cairsse centrale de coopération économiques (France)
CCDC	Caisse centrale de dépôt et de consignation (France)
CDE	Centro de Desarrollo de la Educación
CEGUI	Compañía Española del Golfo de Guinea
CEIA	Comunidad de Españoles con Intereses en Africa
CEMAC	Communauté Économique et monétaire d'Afrique centrale
CFA	African Financial Community (France oriented)
CFAO	Compagnie Française de l'Afrique Occidentale
CICIBA	Centre International des Civilisations Bantu, Libreville (Gabon)
CIPSA	Compañía Ibérica de Prospección, S.A.
CLD	Liberal Democratic Convergency
CMS	Consjo Militar Supremo (Supreme Military Council)

CNPGE	Congreso Nacional de los Pueblos de Guinea Ecuatorial (National Peoples Congress of Equatorial Guinea)
CNLGE	Cruzada Nacional de Liberación de la Guinea Ecuatorial
COGUISA	Colonizadora de la Guinea Continental, S.A.
COMAGE	Compañia Marítima de Guinea Ecuatorial (Navigation Company of Equatorial Guinea)
CPDS	Convergencia para la Democrácia Social (Convergency for Social Democracy)
CSCE	Conference for Security and Cooperation in Europe
CSD	Coalición Social Democrática
CSDP	Convergencia Social Demócrata y Popular (Social Democratic and Popular Convergency)
EC	European Community
ECA	Economic Commission for Africa (UN)
EDF	European Development Fund
EGA	Sociedad Ecuato-Guineana de Aviación
ENPGE	Empreosa Nacional de Peasca de Guinea Ecuatorial (National Fishing Company of EG)
EP	European Parliament
EU	European Union
FAC	Fonds d'aide et de coopération (France)
FAM	Frente Anti-Macías
FAO	Food and Agriculture Organization
FC	Football Club (soccer)
FCFA	Franc of the African Financial Community (French franc zone)
FDR	Fuerza Democrática Republicana
FERBUBLANC	Fernandino—Bubi-—Blancos
FERE	Federación Española de Religiosos de Enseñanza
FF	French Franc
FIEU	Fonds International d'Echanges Universitaires
FINGUINEA	Sociedad Financiera de Guinea
FRELIGE	Frente de Liberación de Guinea Ecuatorial
FRELINAGE	Frente de Liberación del Pueblo Guineano
FRENAPO	Frente Nacional y Popular de Liberación de Guinea Ecuatorial
GEMSA	Joint Spanish-Guinean Mining Company Limited
GEPSA	Joint Spanish-Guinean Petroleum Company Limited
IBRD	International Bank for Reconstruction and Development (World Bank)
ICJ	International Commission of Jurists
ICRC	International Committee of the Red Cross
IDA	International Development Agency

IDEA	Instituto de Estudios Africanos
IDEP	Instituto de Estudios Políticos
IFES	International Foundation for Electoral Systems
ILO	International Labor Organization
IMF	International Monetary Fund
INFOGE	Instituto de Fomento de Guinea Ecuatorial
INSESO	Instituto Nacional de Seguridad Social
INSO	Instituto Nacional de Seguro Social (National Institute for Social Security)
IPGE	Idea Popular de Guinea Ecuatorial
IRI	Instituto per la Reconstruzzione Industriale (Italy)
ITU	International Telecommunications Union
LAGE	Lineas Aéreas de Guinea Ecuatorial
MAIB	Movimiento para la Autodeterminación de la Isla de Bioko
MLSTP	Movimiento de Liberação de São Tomé e Príncipe
MOLIFUGE	Movimiento de Liberación y Futuro de Guinea Ecuatorial
MONALIGE	Movimiento Nacional de Liberación de Guinea Ecuatorial
MPIGE	Movimiento Pro-Independencia de Guinea Ecuatorial
MSG	Movimiento Socialista Guineano
MUN	Movimiento de Unión Nacional
MUNGE	Movimiento de Unión Nacional de Guinea Ecuatorial
NGO	Non-Governmental Organization
OAU	Organization of African Unity
OMGE	Organización de la Mujer de Guinea Ecuatorial
ONORGE	Organización Nacional de la Oposición de Guinea Ecuatorial en el Exilio
ONUDI	United Nations Organization for Industrial Development
PANDECA	Partido Nacional para Democracia, Desarrollo y Educación Cívica
PCSD	Partido de la Coalición Social-Democrata (Social Democratic Party of Equatorial Guinea)
PDGE	Partido Democrático de Guinea Ecuatorial (Democratic Party of Equatorial Guinea)
PDP	Partido Democrático Popular (Popular Democratic Party)
PL	Partido Liberal (Liberal Party)
POC	Plataforma de la Oposición Conjunta (Joint Opposition Platform)
PP	Partido del Progreso (Progress Party)
PSAGE	Partido Socialista Africano (African Socialist Party)
PSD	Partido Socialosta Africano (Social Democratic Party)
PSGE	Partido Socialista (Socialist Party)
PSOE	Partido Socialista Obrero de España

PUN   Partido Unico Nacional
PUNT   Partido Unico Nacional de Trabajadores

RDF   Republican Democratic Force
RDPLGE   Reunión Democrática para la Liberación de Guinea
            Ecuatorial (Democratic Union for the Liberation of
            Equatorial Guinea)

SEGESA   Sociedad Eléctrica de Guinea Ecuatorial
SEMU   Servicio Eléctrico Municipal
SOCOGUI   Sociedad Colonial de Guinea

UAP   Union des Assurances de Paris
UDC   Unión Couanierè del Centro (Democratic Union of the
            Centre, Spain)
UDEAC   Union Democratica des Etats de l'Afrique centrale
            (Customs Union of the Central African States)
UDS   Unión Democrática y Social (Democratic and Social Union)
UFER   Mouvement pour l'Union Fraternele entre les Races et les
            Peuples
UGTGE   Unión General de Trabajadores de Guinea Ecuatorial
UN   United Nations
UNDEMO   Unión Democrática Fernandina (Creole Democratic Union)
UNDP   United Nations Development Program
UNED   Universidad Nacional de Educación a Distancia (Spanish
            Univeristy-level Distance Education Service)
UNESCO   United Nations Educational, Scientific and Cultural
            Organization
UNHCR   United Nations High Commissionate for Refugees
UNICEF   United Nations International Infants and Children Fund
UP   Unión Popular (Popular Union)
UPU   Universal Postal Union
URGE   Unión Revolucionaria de Guinea Ecuatorial

WFP   World Food Program (United Nations)
WHO   World Health Organization (United Nations)

❖ CHRONOLOGY OF MAJOR EVENTS ❖

500 BC

First (disputed) discovery by the Carthaginian navigator Hannon, described in "Hannon's Journey" where he mentions a volcano on the "Libyan coast" (Mt. Cameroon?).

1469-74

Explorations in the Bight of Biafra by Lope Gonsalvez and Fernáo do Poo, Portuguese seafarers.

1471

Discovery and naming of the island of Annobón on January 1st by Juan de Santarem and Pedro Escobar, Portuguese seafarers.

1472

Discovery of the island of Fernando Po, named "Formosa."

1493

Governor of São Tomé assigned jurisdiction over Fernando Po.

1641

Establishment of de facto control over Fernando Po by Dutch slavers.

1642-48

Corisco used by the Dutch as a slave-trading station.

1700?

Arrival of the Benga people on the Guinean coast.

1740

De facto control over Fernando Po resumed by Portugal.

1777

Treaty of San Ildefonso between Spain and Portugal.

1778

Treaty of El Pardo, Portugal ceding to Spain their rights over Annobón, Fernando Po, and the Guinea Coast in exchange for restoration of the Colonia del Sacramento and Santa Catalina Island in Río de la Plata to Portuguese sovereignty. Spanish suzerainty over Fernando Po and Guinea Coast proclaimed at San Carlos Bay by Conde de Argelejos, commander of a colonizing expedition sent from Montevideo. Death of Argelejos.

1780

Failed attempt at settling in Concepción.

1781

The Spanish Expedition returns to America.

1783

Return to Montevideo of the 26 survivors (of 150) of the Argelejos expedition. First attempt by Bullon and Lawson, British seafarers, to enlist the sympathy of the Bubi of Fernando Po towards England.

1810

Six English soldiers killed by Bubi after landing at San Carlos.

1817

Anglo-Spanish agreement to establish a port for the suppression of the slave trade in Fernando Po.

1827

Headquarters of the Mixed Commission for the Suppression of the Slave Traffic transferred from Sierra Leone to Fernando Po by the English without formal Spanish consent. Founding of Clarence Port by William D. Owen on December 25.

1829

Protestant chapel established at Port Clarence (Santa Isabel).

1830

Failure of English colonization attempt at San Carlos Bay.

1831-34

Explorations along the Guinean Coast by Dr. Marcelino de Andrés. British Slave Trade Commissioners withdrawn.

1832

E. Nicolls is ordered by the British government to abandon Clarence.

1835

A new Anglo-Spanish treaty against slave trading.

1836

Morós Morellón's scientific-cum-commercial expedition.

1837?

Fang invasion of the Cameroon-Guinean region, as a consequence of military defeat by the Fulbé.

1839

£60,000 offered by Britain for the purchase of Fernando Po and Annobón. The French settle in Gabon and begin colonizing Spanish territories.

1841

On January 1, John Clarke arrives at Fernando Po. Spanish Government withdraws agreement for sale.

1843

Formal reassertion of Spanish sovereignty over Fernando Po by Lerena. Port Clarence renamed Santa Isabel. John Beecroft named first Governor of Fernando Po by the Spaniards.

1845

Remaining English place names supplanted by Spanish names. Nicolás de Monterola's expedition, following which the traders of the Catalan company Montagut y Vidal y Rivas establishes factories. The traders of Menorca Baltasar Simón and

Francisco Vicente also settled. The expedition of Guillemar de Aragón arrives on December 25.

1854

Death of Governor Beecroft.

1858

First Organic Act for Guinea promulgated by Spanish Overseas Minister, O'Donnell. Chacón appointed first Spanish Governor. One hundred twenty-eight levantine settlers arrived. Establishment of tobacco and sugar cane plantations. Establishment of import and export tax.

1859

Arrival of two expeditions of Spanish settlers.

1860

Pontifical decree attributing Cape San Juan, Corisco, and Elobeyes to Spanish prefecture (January 4).

1860-61

French claims of sovereignty over the Corisco Bay Islands rejected by Spain.

1862

Arrival at Santa Isabel of 250 deported emancipated Cuban Negroes.

1870

Document showing Spanish rights over Guinea coast sent to the French Government.

1875

Iradier's 834-day expedition in the Gulf of Guinea, including southern part of Río Muni.

1878

Gold medal for the tobacco of Fernando Po at the Amsterdam Exhibition. Decree organizing the colony (December 26).

1880

Founding of the "Consejos de Vecins" [municipalities]. Decree on a Fiscal Law.

1881

Arrival of 165 political deportees from Cuba.

1883

Arrival of the first Claretian missionaries in Fernando Po. Iradier, Ossorio, and Montes de Oca expedition to Rio Muni.

1884

Responsibility for all primary school education granted to Claretian missionaries. Emilio Bonelli draws the first map of the region, published by d'Almonte.

1885

Hispano-german protocol on the utilization of Fernando Po.

1886

Spain claims all continental land as far as Ubangui River. Sea link with Fernando Po alotted to the Compañia Trasatlántica.

1888
Arrival of the first Spanish small steamer in Fernando Po.
1892
Establishment of Spanish settlers of Algerian origin from Valencia at Basilé.
1893
First telephone connecting Santa Isabel and Basilé. Construction of the Basilé sanitarium. Protectionist customs duty in Fernando Po.
1897
Arrival in Fernando Po of a company of Spanish marines and Cuban deportees.
1898
Bubi insurrection in San Carlos. Treaty of Paris ending Spanish sovereignty in Cuba, Puerto Rico, and the Philippines.
1900
Treaty of Paris signed on June 27, after several months of negotiation between France and Spain, establishing the definitive boundaries of Spanish Guinea and Spanish Sahara.
1901
Continental borders determined by Franco-Spanish delimitation commission. Creation of the Curaduría Colonial.
1902
Establishment of the first Court of First Instance in Santa Isabel.
1903
Exclusive Spanish ecclesiastical authority over Continental Guinea and offshore islands decreed by the Holy See. Patronato de Indígenas created to promote "morality and culture" among the Guineans, as well as their adherence to Spain.
1904
Fernando Po raised to the status of Apostolic Vicariate, with Armengol Coll as Bishop. Detention and imprisonment of the Bubi leader Ebuera (from Balacha), last dynastic Bubi. Application of the statutes of the Colonial Administration. Publication of basic norms of property.
1906
Regulations on indigenous work. Creation of the colonial Curaduría.
1907
First regulation on teaching by Governor Angel Barrera. Use of money made compulsory.
1908
Colonial Guard created to garrison the colony, replacing marines; lower-rank Spanish soldiers replaced by Africans.
1910
Second Bubi insurrection in southern Fernando Po.
1912
Beginning of radio-telegraph service on Fernando Po.

1914

Treaty signed between Spain and Liberia providing for unlimited recruitment of Liberians for labor in Fernando Po.

1914-18

Approximately 50,000 refugee German troops and Africans interned in Río Muni, transferred to Fernando Po and repatriated.

1919

The French missionaries of the Holy Ghost (Spiritans) leave Bata.

1920

Start of the establishment of sawmills and factories within Río Muni, with 15-20 colonial guards in each locality.

1924-25

Forced shipments of 330 and 700 Liberians to Fernando Po.

1926

Governor Nuñez de Prado makes Spanish compulsory.

1926-27

Construction of the road from Bata to Mikomeseng and control of borders.

1928

Status of Patronato de Indígenas, expected since 1904. Creation of the Instituto colonial Indígena (high school).

1930

League of Nations investigation into alleged Liberia-Fernando Po slave trading; termination of labor shipment to Fernando Po recommended.

1932

One hundred twenty-one trade unionists from Barcelona deported to Annobón.

1935

Government of Luis Sanchez Guerra, a road engineer; start of work at the port of Bata by the Forest Surveillance Service.

1936

Census: 157,881 natives.

1937

Comité Sindical de Cacao created to market Guinean cocoa.

1938

Reform of the Patronato de Indígenas.

1940

Great encouragement to the cooperative movement.

1942

Spanish annexation of Calabar and Gabon proposed by different authors. Hispano-Nigerian agreement regulating recruitment of Nigerians for labor in Fernando Po.

1943

Promulgation of the new Teaching Statutes in the Spanish Territories of the Gulf of Guinea.

1944

Decree deciding the status of the "Emancipados" and the "no Emancipados." The Instituto Colonial Indígena becomes Escuela Superior Indígena.

1946

First neolithic remains unearthed in Fernando Po.

1947

Project for the installation of "Radio Atlantic" at San Jorge.

1948

Laws on family lumbering concessions. First nationalist demonstrations. During his first visit, Carrero Blanco receives a protestation manifest against political movements: MONALIGE, IPGE.

1949

The colony becomes Spanish Province.

1950

First territory-wide census.

1951

Creation of the Hispano-English Employment Agency for the enlistment of the Nigerian maneuvers.

1954

Revision of 1942 Hispano-Nigerian labor agreement. First production unit for abaca, in Fernando Po.

1955

Founding of the Bata School for Agriculture and the Professional Institute of Fernando Po.

1957

New Hispano-Nigerian Labor agreement providing higher wages and social security. Spain began awarding the silver medal of the Order of Africa to Equato-Guineans in the administration and to planters.

1958

Murder of nationalist leaders Enrique Nró and Acacio Mañe; hundreds of Equato-Guineans exiled to Cameroon and Gabon.

1959

Fernando Po/Annobon and Río Muni declared Spanish Provinces. Founding of the first nationalist parties (MONALIGE, IPGE) by exiled Guineans. Suppression of Patronato de Indígenas. Equatorial Guinea produces 2.15% of the world's cocoa. Creation in exile of the Unión General de Trabajadores de Guinea Ecuatorial.

1960

W. Jones Niger elected first African mayor in Santa Isabel. Africans named Procuradores en Cortes. Best coffee and banana production. Municipal elections.

1961

Macías Nguema named Commander of the Order of Africa by Spain.

1962

Visit of Spanish head of government, Carrero Blanco. Best year for cattle count (237,984), for the production of palm oil and abaca fibers. The future vice-president, E. Bosio Dioco, received the silver medal of the Order of Africa.

1963

Foundation of Escuela de Magisterio. Autonomy status granted. Founding of MUNGE. New Hispano-Nigerian labor agreement.

1964

Town-council elections. Civil governors named in both provinces. Beginning of the regime of Autonomy, whose President was Bonifacio Ondó.

1965

UN insists on the independence of Equatorial Guinea. R.M. Nzé Abuy is the first native bishop.

1966

United Nations special committee recommends Guinea's independence after visiting the country. Best year for the production of timber (375,645 t.).

1967

Foundation of Unión Democrática Fernandina and Unión Bubi. Constitutional Conference (October-November) in Madrid, with 41 Guinean representatives, interrupted by ideological disputes between individuals.

1968

Second Constitutional Conference (April-June). Constitution submitted to Cortes. Constitution approved by the people (August 11). Presidential and parliamentary elections (September 22 and 29). President Macías Nguema announces first government. Proclamation of independence (October 12). Best year for the production of cocoa (39,262 t.) and for fisheries (5,600 t.). Inauguration of television in Santa Isabel.

1969

January: Ondo Edu, President of former autonomous government assassinated. February: Spanish troops occupy airports and strategic points in Bata and Santa Isabel. March: Government proclaims emergency. March 5, failure of a coup d'Etat prepared by the Minister of Foreign Affairs, Ndongo Miyone, who is killed. End of March about 7,000 Spanish civilians and troops leave the country. October: Inauguration of the Banco Central; the Equato-Guinean peseta is put into circulation and the country admitted to the IMF.

1970

Constitution of the Youth Movement "Juventud en Marcha con Macías" used as a terror instrument (February 12). Founding Congress of the PUN (July 7). Macías Nguema departs from the democratic constitution. Abolition of political parties and creation of the Partido Unico Nacional de Trabajadores (PUNT).

1971

Information on Equatorial Guinea declared "Materia reservada" (censored) by the Spanish Government (March 30). French Company "Dragages" begins major works, and French Forestal Company of Río Muni starts activities. October: Legalization of the death penalty. Cooperation agreement with Cuba. Agreement for technical assistance with Spain.

1972

May: all students abroad compelled to spend their holidays in the country, under the threat of losing their scholarship in case of refusal. Fisheries agreement with the USSR. Transfer of territories to Gabon. Substitution of the inconvertible ekwele by the peseta. Bishop of Bata, Nzé Abuy, goes into exile. Beginning of Unesco project of Centro de Desarrollo de la Educación. Macías Nguema proclaims himself President for Life (July 14). Signing of economic, cultural and technical assistance agreements with the USSR, Cuba, and other countries. Gabonese forces occupy Guinean islands. OAU commission tries conciliation.

1973

New constitution in force. Change of place names. United Nations Development Program Representative expelled with personnel and family (July). One tenth of population fled abroad.

1974

Various opposition groups constituted abroad: FRELIGE, ANALIGE, URGE, MOLIFUGE, and ANRD. Failure of coup d'Etat attempt in Bata with 118 killed (June). UNDP Coordinator and Unesco expert declared persona non grata. Approval of the last budget of the State.

1975

New deterioration of diplomatic relations with Spain and Nigeria. Numerous assassinations. January: Nigerian Army withdraws about 26,000 Nigerians by an air and sea operation. Expulsion of the chief expert of the World Bank.

1976

March 5: Occupation of Equatorial Guinean Embassy in Madrid by Guinean students in support of political claims. Departure of the last expert of the WHO. May 9: First plenary meeting between the different opposition groups. June: End of Cuban civil assistance; militiamen remain for presidential guard (about 500). ANRD presents the García Trevijano file, causing the lawyer's elimination from the Spanish opposition group Coordinación Democrática (winner of the 1977 elections). October 20: Cancelation of "Materia reservada" in Spain. December 6: More than 100 high officials arrested by Obiang Nguema after presenting a petition for a change in economic policy. Most of them eliminated.Numerous murders in Bata.

1977

Various books on Equatorial Guinea published, especially by Equato-Guineans (Ndongo Bidyogo, Mitogo, Boriko Lopeo) and the publication of ANRD's bulletin (La Voz del Pueblo) and newsletters.

January: Students of Centro de Desarrollo de la Educación sent to compulsory labor (cocoa plantation) before end of training; some of them in exile in Cameroon and Gabon.

September: Official visit by Macías Nguema to Vietnam and China. Hua Kuo Feng announces limitation of Chinese assistance.

October: Spanish government publishes a decree permitting Guinean refugees to take Spanish nationality. November: According to the Spanish press, Gabon's President Bongo seeks Spain's help to occupy Guinean Islands as a trade-off for recognition by Gabon of Canary Islands as Spanish Territory. Spanish royal decree offering Spanish nationality to the Equato-Guineans of Spain.

December: Unesco experts withdrawn from Centro de Desarrollo de la Educación by decision of the Director General of Unesco.

1978

January: Macías' wife and nephew (a cabinet minister) reported as having fled to Spain with Macías' funds, but the news proved incorrect as both returned to Santa Isabel via Libya.

March: The last Spanish teachers leave.

April: French helicopter of Elf-Erepca Co (Cameroon) makes forced landing on Fernando Po with five passengers; returned to France after a payment of a $25,000 ransom.The ANRD publishes special number (4) of La Voz del Pueblo protesting against Gabon's, Spain's, and France's policy toward Equatorial Guinea.

May: Macías Nguema declares Equatorial Guinea an atheistic state.

June: Macías Nguema forbids the practice of Roman Catholicism.

July: Equatorial Guinea joins nonaligned countries in Belgrade Conference; six Spanish priests expelled after payment of a ransom.

August: ANRD representative accused, by Macías Nguema's envoy at UN Subcommission for Prevention of Discrimination, of being subversive (the Subcommission rejects the accusation). The ANRD organizes a Conference of Equato-Guinean refugees in Geneva.

December: The International Commission of Jurists accuses the Macías Nguema regime of flagrant violations of human rights.

1979

March: The UN Commission on Human Rights decides to make an inquiry into violation of human rights in Equatorial Guinea.

May: The Panafrican Youth Movement condemns in Algiers the "neo-facist" regime of Macías Nguema.

June: The ANRD organizes a protest movement of civil servants. Macías Nguema liquidates a number of army officers for claiming arrears of salaries.

August: On August 3, the Supreme Military Council, presided by Obiang Nguema, strips Macías Nguema of his powers. After a week-long confrontation between the two factions, Macías Nguema is arrested with the help of the Gabonese army. On August 25, a military government is established. Most of its members are Esangui from Mongomo. On August 30, a new Spanish ambassador takes up his post in Santa Isabel. From August 1979 to April 1980 external reserves ($20 million and 2,500 pieces of gold) placed in banks in Europe and the United States disappeared.

September: Arrival of 180 Moroccan Soldiers, Spanish police officers and antiriot gear. September 24-29—trial of Macías Nguema. On September 29, the first Nguemist dictator and six others are executed by Moroccans.

October: On the occasion of the 11th Independence Day celebrations, Obiang Nguema is proclaimed President of the Republic, becoming the second Nguemist dictator. An amnesty is proclaimed for all exiles. France and the European Economic Community begin making overtures toward the new government.

November: A UN Human Rights Commission team spends the first half of the month in the country. The reports of the ICJ on the trial of the Macías Nguema show that only a few of the Nguemist clique were brought to trial.

December: On December 2, Ela Nseng, the second Vice-President is received by President Giscard d'Estaing in Paris. King Juan Carlos of Spain, pays and official visit. The ANRD points out that there has been no let-up in the dictatorship. Ela Nseng is removed from the vice-presidency and sent as ambassador to China.

1980

January: Suspension of the fisheries agreement with Russia. Obiang Nguema visits Cameroon.

February: The report of the UN Human Rights Commission alludes to the continued existence of the dictatorship and violations of basic human rights. The UN High Commission for Refugees indicates that it stands ready to assist refugees to return. On February 25, Obiang Nguema pays an official visit to Gabon. There he inadvisedly signs agreements giving Gabon advantageous territorial (oil?) concessions. The African Development Bank provides experts to Equatorial Guinea.

April: A Soviet vice-consul is expelled. On April 24, the ANRD protests Obiang Nguema's official visit to Madrid.

May: The Mauritanian Press Agency objects to Obiang Nguema's pro-Moroccan declarations. A joint venture company with Spanish participation (GEMSA) is founded to further mining development.

June: Obiang Nguema pays official visit to Morocco. June 25, the ANRD roundly condemns the dictator's declarations.

July: The ANRD objects to the pressure put on refugees in Spain by the UN High Commission for Refugees to persuade them to return home. The government demands a review of the oil agreements signed by Obiang Nguema in January.

October: Obiang Nguema pays an official visit to Paris and France promises aid. On October 24, Morocco and Equatorial Guinea decide to strengthen their cooperation.

November: King Juan Carlos of Spain pays a second visit to Santa Isabel on November 10, en route to Gabon and the Cameroon. This despite Equatorial Guinea's decision earlier in the month to join the Customs Union of the Central African States (UDEAC).

1981

March: The UN Human Rights Commission again reports flagrant violations of basic human rights. The Spanish right-wing parties criticize the aid provided to Obiang Nguema's government.

April: Spain is granted oil concessions. Maye Ela visits Latin America. A carefully stage-managed insurrection paves the way for the arrest of a number of officers and civil servants loyal to Maye Ela. The Nguemist government demands a reduction in the staff of the Soviet Embassy, which refuses the request.

June: The "insurgents" of April are put on trial and one of them is sentenced to death. The wife of the ambassador to Spain is implicated in a drug scandal; the ambassador is recalled as a result and is made Secretary for Foreign Affairs.

July: Mbá Oñana, Inspector-General of the Armed Forces, visits Madrid. While Obiang Nguema continues to complain about delays in the provision of Spanish assistance, the Spanish press reveals that he had derived considerable financial benefits from the April "insurrection" that Mbá Oñana had helped to stage-manage.

August: On August 3, Obiang Nguema mentions the possibility of elections being held, followed soon afterwards by the announcement of a constitutional referendum. On August 25, he pardons 29 Nguemists involved in the April "insurrection." On

August 23, Spanish newspapers are banned. Negotiations entered into with Nigeria bring no results.

September: The UN Human Rights Commission condemns the press censorship. Madrid denies that Spanish troops have been sent to their former colony, but that they had offered to train soldiers and officers from Equatorial Guinea. On September 12, the exiled cousin of Obiang Nguema, Oyono Ayingono, tries to set up a pseudo-opposition movement in Paris.

October: Former teachers of the Spanish overseas assistance program in Equatorial Guinea claim 27 million pesetas in back pay from both governments.

November: The United States reopens the embassy in Santa Isabel. Several international oil companies complain about the special privileges granted to the Spanish company Hispanoil.

December: In an important ministerial reshuffle, Maye Ela is outposted as ambassador to the UN in New York. On December 22, Calvo Sotelo, the Spanish Prime Minister, begins an official visit to Santa Isabel.

1982

January: 1982 is proclaimed a "Year of Work" and is met with passive resistance from the population. The Spanish diplomatic pouch is violated by the authorities in Santa Isabel and a senior local official takes refuge in Spain. The first civilian government is named (it includes former members of the Supreme Military Council and of the Esangui Clan from Mongomo).

February: On February 16, Pope John Paul II visits Bata. The ANRD complains about his silence regarding human rights issue.

March: The Prime Minister, Seriche Bioco Dougan, pays an unfruitful visit to Madrid. However, on December 14, he is followed by Obiang Nguema himself, who succeeds in drawing up a new statute for Spanish experts in Equatorial Guinea.

April: The population of Santa Isabel experiences food shortages. Co-operation with Morocco is increased. Shots are fired at a Spanish aircraft over Bata. On April 18, Mbá Oñana is received by Kim Il-Sung in North Korea. A conference of donor countries to assist Equatorial Guinea is organized by the UNDP in Geneva, Switzerland from April 16 to 22. Pledges totalling US$ 92 million were made. Conflicting reports circulat as to the worth of the country's oil resources.

May: Despite strained relations with Spain (national funds blocked by Spain and Spanish vessel blocked at Santa Isabel), Obiang Nguema goes to Madrid on May 12 and grants Most Favored Nation treatment to Spain. A Spanish businessman is jailed in Santa Isabel.

August: On August 15, the constitutional referendum is held. It is passed by a majority of voters, most of whom did not know that they were really voting for a presidential constitution that had been elaborated at Akonibé by stalwarts of the regime. Its text consolidates the second Nguemist dictatorship. Obiang Nguema is confirmed as President by virute of an article added to the constitution without public knowledge. Obiang Nguema denies French vessels fishing rights in territorial waters, but reverses this decision in the course of a visit to Paris on August 26.

September: On September 23, Obiang Nguema again visits Paris and dines with President Mitterrand. On September 27, he is received in Madrid.

October: The Vice-President of Nigeria attends the 13th Independence Day celebrations (October 12) in Santa Isabel.

November: Equatorial Guinea is invited to the summit meeting of the Customs Union of Central African States (UDEAC) in an observer capacity.

December: The Supreme Military Council is dissolved. The only change, however, is that its members changed into civilian clothing. The UDEAC agrees in principle to Equatorial Guinea's membership.

1983

February: Equatorial Guinea's bank accounts are again frozen in Spain. The ambassador of Equatorial Guinea in France is arrested for fraud.

March: The European Economic Community offers food aid.

April: Two ministers are implicated in fraud. The opposition requests France to suspend all aid to the dictatorship. The former ambassador to France is sentenced to hard labor, but succeeds in escaping to France. The opposition threatens to resort to armed struggle. The Spanish Prime Minister Felipe González is invited to Equatorial Guinea, but the visit does not take place.

May: On May 20 there is an attempted coup. One soldier seeks sanctuary in the Spanish embassy. To defuse a tense situation, the Spanish Minister of Foreign Affairs, Moran, stops over in Santa Isabel for three hours and releases the soldier to the authorities after receiving a formal guarantee that he would not be executed.

June: The joint Spanish/Equatorial-Guinean commission reviews the Spanish assistance program in Madrid. The Nguemists take a strong line.

July: The soldier released from the Spanish embassy is sentenced to death, but the sentence is then commuted to life imprisonment. On July 28, Obiang Nguema arrives in Madrid and his bodyguards insist on landing with their arms. The opposition reports further violations of human rights.

August: A Spanish TV team is detained at Santa Isabel and their equipment is confiscated. Minister of Health Buale Borico takes refuge in Spain and reveals how Obiang Nguema enriches himself. The first "legislative" elections are held based on a single party list on which there are over forty Nguemists for the sixty available seats.

September: A Spanish missionary is murdered at Ebebeyin. A U.S. naval vessel pays a courtesy call to Santa Isabel. The official responsible for Spanish assistance resigns.

October: A new embargo on information from Equatorial Guinea is imposed by Spain.

November: France increases her trade with Equatorial Guinea.

December: Equatorial Guinea becomes the fifth member of the French oriented Customs Union of Central African States (UDEAC) and the Bank of the Central African States (BEAC).

1984

January: The Secretary of State for Foreign Affairs and the Minister of Justice are removed from office.

February: The International Commission of Jurists denounces the Nguemist regime. Financial agreements are reached with France for cooperation and culture. A fisheries agreement is made with the HEC. A Presidential decree orders the confiscation of immovable assets of the Spanish who had fled during the Macías Nguema period.

March: There is an outbreak of cholera.

April: Hispanoil discovers oil and gas in the north of Fernando Po. The cholera epidemic abates.

July: On July 27, Equatorial Guinea signs the agreement of accession to the French African franc (CFA) zone.

December: The Spanish press voices concern over Equatorial Guinea's surrender to French interests. The embassy of Equatorial Guinea in Libreville, Gabon, arranges the kidnapping of one of their citizens in exile there. The publication of daily newspapers in Equatorial Guinea comes to an end.

1985

January: On January 2 the CFA franc becomes the official currency, replacing the Equato-Guinean ekuele.

February: A Spanish citizen dies at the Santa Isabel airport due to obstruction by the authorities in providing medical attention. The Spanish ambassador receives various threats. The International Union of Christian Democrats protests the violation of human rights in Equatorial Guinea.

March: Nigeria demands indemnities on behalf of its citizens evacuated in 1976 before any new labor agreement can be envisaged.

May: Obiang Nguema goes to France for a working visit. The People's Assembly accepts the creation of a single-party system. Christina Onassis is rumored to be considering buying the island of Corisco.

June: The local press voices fears of Gabonese aggression against the country and point to the increase in the cost of living since the introduction of the CFA franc. Obiang Nguema again visits France.

July: The International Monetary Fund (IMF) extends substantial credits to Equatorial Guinea and the Club de Paris agrees to reschedule the country's debt. A report of the UN Human Rights Commission accuses the country of committing acts of genocide.

October: The Prime Minister, Seriche Bioco Dougan visits Yugoslavia and the Minister of Finance goes to Seoul, South Korea, for the IMF and World Bank meeting there.

November: French business interests press for the opening of agencies of the International Bank of West Africa (BIAO) and of French insurance companies. The Spanish Secretary of State for External Aid comes to Santa Isabel for the meeting of the Joint Commission and remarks on the "fluid" state of the relationship between the two countries. An overall plan of mutual co-operation is however accepted. The dictatorship requests Spain to safeguard the country's interests vis-à-vis the EC.

1986

January: The monthly periodical Potopoto, printed in Bata, becomes the sole remaining local publication. A number of ministerial posts are reshuffled on January 17. Obiang Nguema takes over the Defense portfolio and Mbá Oñana moves to Public Works. ObiangNguema's cousin, Nguema Ela, loses the Finance portfolio.

February: In a rapid air and naval exercise, Nigeria evacuates 200 of their workers from Fernando Po, after one of their number had been murdered. The Nigerian Press speaks of slavery-like conditions in Equatorial Guinea.

April: A protocol of agreement is signed with the (French oriented) International Bank of West Africa (BIAO).

June: A delegate of the Spanish University-level Distance Education Service expresses his fears that Spanish may well disappear in Equatorial Guinea by the end of the century. The French Press refers to Gabonese territorial ambitions on Equatorial Guinea.

July: On July 14, Obiang Nguema attends the National Day celebrations in Paris. During his absence there is an attempted coup, between July 17 and 19, led by Mbá Oñana and some of Obiang Nguema's relatives. The attempt was foiled by the Moroccan guards. Obiang Nguema returns on July 19. A score of military personalities are arrested along with some ministers and former ministers as well as Mbá Oñana himself, Nguema Ela, Mbá Ondo, Mañe Abeso and others.

August: An unpublicized court martial is held. It passes one death sentence and a number of long prison terms for participants in the July coup attempt. Obiang Nguema's relatives, however, get off with mere two-year sentences.

October: Obiang Nguema is promoted to Brigadier General during the 18th Independence day celebrations in Bata. He is awarded decorations by the general commanding the Spanish Military Academy in Saragossa, "in the name of the King of Spain." The U.S. State Department circulates a "Post Report" on living conditions in Equatorial Guinea which substantiates the dictatorial character of the Nguemist regime.

December: On December 2, Obiang Nguema is forced to borrow five million naira from Nigeria to finance the Conference of the UDEAC in Bata that is due to be held within two weeks. His soldiers, however, have not been paid for over two months. On December 8, Mary of the Immaculate Conception is declared Patron Saint of Equatorial Guinea. The Spanish Order of Franciscan Contemplative Sisters opens a convent in Akonibé.

1987

January: On January 2, a Spanish military transport aircraft crashes on take-off from Bata airport, with 18 deaths. The Ambassador to Spain, Ndong Ela Nzang, accuses the Spanish pilots of responsibility for the accident. On January 10, Obiang Nguema announces his intention to create the "Democratic Party of Equatorial Guinea." The journal Africa Confidential mentions the opening of a large cattle ranch with a landing strip in Fernando Po (by a South African company).

February: The UN Human Rights Commission asks the Economic and Social Council to remind Obiang Nguema that he has not given any reply to the Secretary-General's notes about human rights violations since 1981. Obiang Nguema pays an official visit to Nigeria, during which a mutual defense and nonaggression treaty is signed.

March: The Spanish Press makes allusion to a "Mitterrand Plan" designed to turn Equatorial Guinea into a province of "French" Gabon or Cameroon. The Minister of Finance of Equatorial Guinea announces that the Guinextebank had a deficit of 1,500 million pesetas due to "political" loans granted to members of the Mongomo Clan, including Obiang Nguema's wife. Spain agrees to bail out the bank with 700 million pesetas. A relay station for TV transmissions from Santa Isabel is installed in Bata.

April: A meeting of the governing board of the Development Bank of the Central African States (BDEAC) is held in Santa Isabel. In Spain a number of pro-Guinean activities are organized, such as a lecture series on the history of the country, the creation of an Association of Friends of Equatorial Guinea, a proposal for an automobile rally in the country, etc. Spain begins a detailed analysis of the 16 billion pesetas of technical and capital assistance that had been granted to Equatorial Guinea since 1979. The London-based *Index on Censorship* reports that nothing had changed since the demise of Macías Nguema.

May: Amnesty International publishes a damning report on the operation of military tribunals, used also for civilian cases, on the passing of death sentences, and on the lack of fundamental rights in Equatorial Guinea.

July: The French petroleum company Total announces a profit from their operations in Equatorial Guinea. The international press mentions an increase in South African interests on Fernando Po.

August: On August 3, Obiang Nguema forcefully imposes a "democratic" single-party system on the country. An aircraft of the Equato-Guinean Airlines (EGA) is involved in another accident. Obiang Nguema appoints his wife Constancia Mangue cousellor to the president.

September: The United States closes its embassy in Santa Isabel.

October: The senior officials of the Spanish technical assistance program are relieved of their function for fraud. The bankruptcy of the Guinextebank is confirmed. The French forestry company Roussel is granted a new concession. A telecommunications station is opened in Bata, connected with Paris. Creation of the BIAO of Equatorial Guinea. Telecommunications are put into the hands of France Cable.

November: The Catholic Church complains about the shortage of Equato-Guinean priests. On November 2, the ambassador to the UN, and former vice-president, F. Maye Ela, signs a secret contract of $1.6 million with British arms dealers for toxic deposits on the island of Annobón.

December: Four non-Esangui ministers are arrested while Obiang Nguema is on a visit to France.

1988

January: Beginning of an Amnesty International mission.

February: Decision is taken to close Guinextebank. The Association of Friends of Equatorial Guinea in Madrid is reactivated. Creation of the aviation company EGA. Beginning of a news bulletin in French on national radio. Moto Nsá announces his candidacy in the elections for the post of President of the Republic.

March: The Human Rights Commission of the United Nations again denounces the Nguemist regime.

May: Criticism of the OUA against relations of the Nguemists with South Africa.

June: The contract with two British enterprises to allow toxic deposits is confirmed. Refusal to legalize the Partido de Progreso. On June 21, dissolution of the Parliament. Ultimatum from the IMF for the modification of the economic policy, but granting of a loan of $16 million.

August: The Human Rights Commission publishes a report on toxic deposits in Annobón. On the 13th an attempted military coup d'Etat is aborted.

September: Wave of arrests of members of the opposition. Two soldiers executed. In Paris, Obiang Nguema declares his intention to rejoin Francophone countries. On the September 24, the First Secretary of the embassy in Madrid is expelled for drug trafficking. A mission of nine Spanish deputies is rejected by Obiang Nguema.

October: The former chief of the UNED in Equatorial Guinea accuses the Spanish embassy of manipulation of funds.

November: The ANRD denounces the Nguemist regime before the UNDP.

1989

January: France financially supports the regime. Obiang Nguema negotiates in Madrid for economic aid. Spain writes off 30% of the debt. The Spanish opposition condemns Spanish laxism. The report of the Human Rights Commission denounces the Nguemists.

March: Constitution of the Pacto de Madrid.

June: On the 25th, Obiang Nguema, sole candidate, is reelected president for seven years, with 99.96% of the votes. Compulsory voting, closed borders. Obiang Nguema asks the opposition to return.

September: French becomes compulsory in schools.

October: Amnesty International denounces the killings.

December: The IMF grants a loan of $16 million. Yona (Israel) buys the Semge lumbering concession (France).

1990

January: The report of the Human Rights Commission speaks of the need for pressure.

February: Conference on the violation of Human Rights in Equatorial Guinea (King's College, Cambridge).

April: The ANRD accuses the Spanish Cooperation of being too soft.

September: The opposition demands democratization with the help of Spain. AI *Report on Torture* states torture is a common practice.

October: Equatorial Guinea refuses to recognize dual nationality holders and proceeds to arrest them.

1991

March: Admission to the ILO.

May: The leaders of Convergency for Social Democracy are arrested and tortured. Founding of the Social Democratic Coalition Party. Adolfo Suarez tries to mediate between the opposition and the regime. It is a failure.

July: Death of Archbishop Nze Abuy. Refusal to allow a second mission by Suarez.

October: Obiang Nguema accepts the idea of multipartism.

November: The opposition recommends the boycott of the constitutional referendum. The new constitution is voted. Presentation of the Joint Opposition Platform (POC) in Madrid.

December: Founding of the Unión Democrática y Social (UDS) in Lisbon. AI denounces the increase in the number of prisoners of opinion.

1992

January: Obiang Nguema promulgates the amnesty law, the law on political parties, and the law on meetings and demonstrations. The opposition demands negotiations. On the 18th, the government is dissolved. Presentation of a "transitional" government on the 23rd, without opposition participation.

February: Obiang Nguema and the Italian Mafia found a bank. A number of detractors are arrested.

April: The EC demands that the return of opponents be facilitated. AI denounces new violence. The Interparliamentary Conference strongly denounces the arrest of the Vice President of the Parliament.

May: Popular Union is legalized. The EU demands the observance of human rights.

June: Legalization of the satellite party Liberal Democratic Convention.

July: A new rejection of a visit by A. Suarez. He qualifies Obiang Nguema as mentally ill, unscrupulous, and cowardly.

August: On the 31st, effective inauguration of the POC at Santa Isabel.

September: The EU demands the release of political prisoners.

October: Arrest of two Spanish traders. Members of the opposition are arrested and beaten in Mikomeseng. Obiang Nguema accepts a multiparty project.

November: Budgetary aid from France (customs and security forces). The POC asks Spain to send mediating forces. The Spanish Prime Minister arrives on an official visit (June 22-24), without results. Forty students arrested are and beaten in Bata (one dies).

December: The Spanish opposition force the government to revise cooperation. About a hundred arrests and incidents of torture of professors, priests and students by relatives of Obiang Nguema. AI raises an alarm. Talks with Gabon on the dispute over the islands of Río Muni. Strict Report of the Human Rights Commission.

1993

January: Obiang Nguema invites the police to use "more democratic" means. New electoral law excluding the Diaspora. The Ambassadors of Spain, the United States, and the EC receive a verbal note calling them "agitators," along with threats, for "hostile attitude." Spanish diplomatic bags blocked. The EP votes for the suppression of aid. Spain cuts off a part of its program. The Association for Human Rights in Equatorial Guinea (exiled) protests against the French and the Nguemists.

February: About fifty members of Popular Union detained and beaten. A French volunteer for cooperation preparing a book on the Nguemists assassinated. Obiang Nguema rejects observers. Spain reiterates partial suspension of its aid. On the 19th, the ambassadors of Spain and the United States and the resident representative of the UNDP receive death threats. The United States withdraws its Peace Corps volunteers.

March: Ambassador Bennett is recalled to Washington for consultation. The Human Rights Commission formulates fresh condemnations. On the 16th, signing of the National Pact. On the 31st, presidential decree for the release of political prisoners.

April: Mission of the EU for application of the National Pact. Seven members of the Partido del Progreso imprisoned and tortured. Donor countries and organizations demand "political guarantees" for aid for the elections. AI denounces hundreds of arbitrary arrests. Obiang Nguema spends fifteen days in France. On the 19th, the ANRD expells Carmelo Mokong Onguene; Luis Ondo Ayang becomes Secretary General. The government protests the Report on aid for elections. A habitual criminal according to French justice, Llansol, Obiang Nguema's Counsellor, is expelled from Switzerland.

July: Dissolution of the Chamber. The editors of *La Verdad* imprisoned and tortured. United States support for Ambassador Bennett. Obiang Nguema rejects Spanish and American observers for the elections. France breaks the international boycott and finances the electoral campaign. The corruption of Ambassadors Engonga Motulu and Llansol is made public. On the 14th, Obiang Nguema announces the "temporary" withdrawal of the Moroccan guards (under United States pressure). They are replaced by the Jovenes Antorchas Ninjas trained by French counsellors. On the 20th, bloody operation by 200 Ninjas in Annobón. Spain is accused of spreading disorder. Madrid denounces Obiang Nguema's calumny. A Spanish evacuation plan is announced. Following the boycott called by the POC, the elections are postponed to November 21. On the 22nd, ritual assassination of Motu Mamiaga by Obiang Nguema's cronies. On the 30th, the wife of the ambassador to Spain is arrested in Brazil for drug trafficking. AI speaks of the increase in political oppression.

September: Considering the boycott of the POC, the government begins to "buy" small opposition groups. Renewed attempts to confiscate Spanish diplomatic bags. An opponent is shot in public by a brother of Obiang Nguema. An employee of the UN is beaten and incarcerated. The POC proposes a "Government of national concentration" for democratic transition. On the 29th, prohibition of La Verdad (the CPDS defied the ban).

October: The leaders of the opposition are forbidden from moving about. Six Spanish tourists are incarcerated and then expelled. On the 12th, at the 25th anniversary of independence, Switzerland expels the "ambassador" Engonga Motulu, who leaves $700,000 in debts. The UN refuses to send observers for elections.

November: The Human Rights Commission condemns Equatorial Guinea. The Spanish press connects Llansol to the Medellin Cartel. The Spanish socialist party qualifies the elections as "illegitimate"; Washington speaks of an "electoral farce." The boycott of the elections results in 70% abstentions in Río Muni and 80% in Fernando Po. 85% of the votes go to the PDGE. United States Ambassador Bennett is accused of sorcery.

December: On the 3rd, the persecution of detractors, professors, and students of the UNED begins; 29 students are tortured. The consul of Spain in Bata is expelled. Madrid expels the Secretary of the Equato-Guinean embassy and reduces its aid by half. The Nguemists close Radio Africa 2000. On the 22nd the new government is named, with 38 appointed ministers, but including no opposition member.

1994

January: Le Monde Diplomatique suggests that Obiang Nguema be considered the bane of humanity. Washington refuses an official visit by Obiang Nguema to the United States. La Verdad is again banned; death threats are made against its editors. Reporters Sans Frontières protest. The franc CFA is devalued 50% by France. Spain confirms an aid-budget cut of 50%. The European Parliament demands the end of all cooperation with the Nguemists. Yet another agreement is signed with the IMF.

February: On the 15th, at Dakar, Obiang Nguema calls Spanish an obstacle to the development of the country. The U.S. State Department, AI, and the human rights Commission report grave deterioration in the Human Rights situation.

March: AI denounces the detentions after the November 1993 elections. On March 9, the Human Rights Commission votes for strict denunciation of the Nguemist regime. Spain withdraws its two Aviocars.

April: The broadcasts of Radio Exterior de España are jammed. Obiang Nguema promises revision of the constitution and the electoral law.

May: The geopolitical drug observatory places Obiang Nguema at the center of the traffic. Some Bubis again claim their right to autonomy.

July: Spain plans another convention on cooperation. *Le Monde Diplomatique* (Paris) speaks of "Equatorial Guinea under the thumb of a clan. With a background of Franco-Spanish rivalry." Repression and torture are the work of a milita trained by France.

September: Announcement of the second national census; the opposition recommends a boycott.

November: Renewed arrests and torture of opponents. Constitutive Congress of the CPDS: Placido Miko, Secretary General.

December: The French press raises an outcry over the murder of two French experts.

1995

January: Freedom House (USA) cites Equatorial Guinea among the countries where political and civil liberties are violated the most. The Human Rights Commission speaks of phony progress and of serious violations. The POC considers democratization as being blocked. The United States replaces its ambassador with a chargé d'affaires; the Nguemists protest. According to the Spanish press, Teodorin, the elder son of Obiang Nguema, is arrested at Orly airport (Paris) for carrying drugs; Obiang Nguema denies this. The periodical *El Sol* is suspended and fined. Spain prepares a new treaty for cooperation. The General Secretary of the ANRD explains in Geneva that the expulsion is due to José D. Dougan Beaca's attempts to divide the party. Mobil Oil reports the discovery of two new oil deposits. Moto Nsá, President of the Partido del Progreso, is placed under house arrest. The Public Prosecutor, Elo Nve Mbengono, denounces corruption among court personnel.

February: CMS Nomeco buys the totality of Walter's (Alba) shares.

March: The publisher of *El Sol,* Nvo Mbolio, is attacked by presidential guards.

May: The International Federation of Liberal and Radical Youth (IFIRY) asks the EU and Spain to stop their financial assistance to Obiang Nguema. UNICEF reports that there is an average of 112 children in first-year classes; 70% of the classes do not have chalk; 99% of the pupils do not have books. There is an epidemic of hemorrhagic dysentry in Fernando Po (104 deaths).

July: The American public affairs company of Black, Manafort, Stone & Kelly is in charge of improving the nguemist image until December 14.

November: The US embassy is closed.

1996

January: The UN publishes a report on torture with a list of victims.

September: 1-3, Obiang Nguema visits Beijing. Reporters Without Borders rates Obiang Nguema as one of the "Top 25 enemies of Press Freedom," on a scale based on the 185 members of the UN.

October: 8, Ange-Félix Patassé, president of the Central African Republic, visits Equatorial Guinea.

November: Cameroonians are arrested and expelled. The IFLIRY condemns, once more, the nguemist dictatorship. On the 25th, Reporters Without Borders say that a Canadian journalist and his Cameroonian colleague were arrested and that a ransom was demanded. They manage to escape to Gabon.

December: Seventeen churches and sects are present in the country. The 1996 Report of the International Conference of Free Unions describes Equatorial Guinea as one of the countries that paralyse union structures by preventing their existence. Mobil's oilfield of Zafiro produces 40,000 b/d, but should go up to 80,000 b/d.

1997

January: The Chinese vice-prime minister visits Equatorial Guinea and signs an economic and technological agreement. An explosion occurs due to gas on a drilling platform. CMS announces it will open a factory for the liquefaction of gas. The problems with Nigeria concerning borders will be administrated by the Multilateral Investment Guarantee Agency of the World Bank. Eight biologists from Beaver College (Glenside, PA) arrive to research primates on the island of Bioko and proceed to a census. There are about thirty Americans in the county.

February: The 1997 Report of the International Narcotics Control Board says that Equatorial Guinea is one of the nine African states involved in drug dealing.

April: Mobil says it has reached its production goal of 80,000 b/d. On the 15th, vice-prime minister Ngomo Mbengono, in front of the UN Human Rights Commission in Geneva, says that his country "has successfully learned to be a democracy and to respect human rights" and that human rights are one of the government's priorities. The special rapporteur of the commission reports numerous violations of human rights; the nguemists demand he be replaced. With UMC, many promising drillings are announced.

May: On the 16th, Moto Nsá attempts a coup and fails, in Angola (Cabinda), with Russian, Italian, Spanish, and Angolan mercenaries. On the walls of the capital one may read, "Kabila, come." The US Overseas Security Advisory Council warns that Ninjas are dangerous because they are often drugged and heavily armed.

June: A wave of repression hits the opposition after the announcement of Moto Nsá's failed attempted coup. The government dissolves the PP. The dictatorship blackmails Bubi planters, saying they will only get fertilizers and phytosanitarian products if they join Obianag Nguema's party (PDGE). The EU announces that 1,650 tons of meat were exported to EG (during the boycott against mad cow disease). On the 11th, the Permanent Council of the PP destitutes Moto Nsá. On the 16th, the spokesman for the ZS State Department tells journalists that "in two and a half years working as a spokesman, never was I asked a single question about Equatorial Guinea." The US State Department states that the airline EGA does not meet international standards of security. On the 17th, a note of protest from the Armed Forces to Obiang Nguema is handed over to the dictator. Moto Nsá publishes a list of Obiang Nguema's men in the Spanish government. According to AI, nguemists cannot tolerate the opposition. Militants of the PDGE beat the mayor of Baney. The nguemists start changing traditional chiefs for the legislative elections in 1998. On the 24th, the coordinator of the Spanish Committee for Assistance to Refugees declares, "Equatorial Guinea is not a country, but the possession of Obiang Nguema and his clan, who have no respect whatsoever for human rights." UMC Corp. increases its capital by $50 million.

July: Many arrests. Seven people are tortured by the police in Bata; a soldier dies in prison. On the 6th, the former minister of sports, Obama Bikomo, is arrested in Madrid with 15 kg of heroin. Among the 22 people arrested are a niece of Obiang Nguema and her husband. On the 15th, US customs officers report they have stopped two Lithuanians attempting to sell Soviet missiles to the Colombian mafia aboard a ship registered in Equatorial Guinea.

August: The Court of Malabo condemns Moto Nsá (refugied in Spain) to 101 years imprisonment for "high treason." From the end of August through September, numerous ritual crimes, with severe multilations, are reported throughout the country. Borders are closed due to pressure from Cameroon, which assets that Nigerians transit through Equatorial Guinea and arrive in Cameroon to destabilize it.

September: *Gaceta de Guinea Ecuatorial* reports that thefts are increasing. Spain confirms that it will continue the refugee status of Moto Nsá, The minister of Foreign Affairs accuses Radio Exterior de España of "harassment." Obiang Nguema interrupts his relations with Spain and on the 22nd decides that French will be the second national language. Western Atlas Int. is ready to start drilling the seabed of the country for three months. On the 28th, Obiang Nguema decides to close the borders without an explanation. About twenty ritual crimes occur in Rio Muni while an economic conference is being held in Bata. The opposition says it is just a bluff. The Nigerian community complains about being persecuted: coast guards kill two Nigerian traders. Sccording the former minister Moto Nsá, Obiang Nguema is the head of an African narco-traffic network.

October: Spanish ambassador Otero de León is replaced by Jacobo González Arnau Campos.

November: IU accuses the Aznar government of collaborating with Obians Nguema. The PSOE and Moto Nsá even say that the Spanish PP is financed by Obiang Nguema. A UN mission of technical evaluation arrives on the 17th, as well as the rapporteur of the Human Rights Commission. The prime minister participates in the Conference of Francophony in Hanoi.

December: On the 1st, Obiang Nguema declares that the coalition of political opposition parties is forbidden. On the 17th, the army forbids fishing and night transports in waters under Equato-Guinean jurisdiction to foreign or national boats, in order to "guarantee national security."

1998

January: The PSOE blames the Aznar government for its "rambled and incoherent" behavior with regard to Equatorial Guinea. In Kogo, the main leaders of the CPDS are arrested, along with militants accused of practising the forbidden Bwiti cult. The first and second vice presidents of the PP join the governing party. On the 15th, the government resigns. On the 17th, Obiang Nguema appoints Angel Serafin Dougan prime minister. On the same day, the crew of the *Acacio Mañe* is arrested in order to carry out an investigation related to the fact that the ship burned down. On the 20th, young Bubi attack police and army quarters in Luba and the suburbs of the capital and kill four soldiers. Moka and Baho Grande are also attacked. The government accuses the MAIB; they deny the charge. On the 21st, Obiang Nguema appoints a few new ministers, among then his eldest son, Teodorín, who becomes minister of Ennvironment and Forests. On the 23rd, the army "neutralizes" nine "terrorists" and holds prisoner a Nigerian who is said to have led the rebels. On the 27th, the police arrest and torture more than 200 Bubi. The press in Gabon talks of "the growing insecurity at the border with Equatorial

Guinea" due to "the numerous exactions by soldiers of that country on our territory."

February: Negotiations between Mobil and the government take place in London concerniing the increase of national profits. On the 10th, the Lagos press announces that 700 Nigerians are said to have been killed on Bioko and buried in a communal grave, but the Nigerian consul denies this. On the 13th, Moto Nsá is dismissed as president of the PP. On the 17th, the US declares it intends to reopen its embassy. On the 18th, the Council of the Elderly Bisio and Ndowe denounce the confiscation of ancestral lands by the government. On the 23rd, Obiang Nguema goes to Paris to meet Jacques Chirac. On the 24th, the dictator changes the electoral law. On the 25th, the French company ELF is granted an offshore area of 8,800 km^2 to carry out investigations. On the same day it is announced that France will organize a summit of Central African countires in Equatorial Guinea.

March: Atlantic Methanol Production Company (AMPCO) is founded by CMS and Samedan. During the first three months of 1998, thirty ritual crimes are committed. On the 25th, the government and the opposition sign an agreement to set up a mixed commission in view of the elections.

April: On the 5th, UP and CPDS denounce "serious violations" of the March agreement. The US says it sent to Bara, on April 20, hundreds of tons of rice, vegetable oil, and pinto beans. Breton is the new French ambassador. On the 19th. Obiang Nguema goes to Morocco. Ocean Energy merges with the United Meridia Corp. The revolving light buoy at the Zafiro platform is replaced by a radar buoy.

May: Between the 18th and the 22nd, Bata holds a subregional conference on "Democratic Institutions and Peace in Central Africa." On the 25th, more than 100 Bubi are tried. Five Spanish journalists (plus technicians working for TV) are authorized to attend the trial. A weekly flight from Zurich to Malabo is opened by Swissair. On the 31st, the Spanish journalists, accused of insulting Obiang Nguema and the government, are expelled.

June: On June 1, fifteen death sentences are issued, as well as 55 imprisonment sentences. The European Parliament asks for revision of the trial. Miguel Oyono, minister of Foreign Affairs, talks of "unbearable harassment on a sovereign state." On the 8th, in the UN at New York, Obiang Nguema says that the weapons used by Moto Nsá in his failed coup in January 1998 were purchased with money coming from drugs. Total-Equatorial Guinea buys 80% of the capital to consolidate its position in Africa. Nguema asks for numerous votes during the elections of 1998.

July: The nguemists reject the European request concerning the revision of the Bubi trial. The BAD grants $3 million for a project to improve the health sector. On July 8, UP denounces the preparation of massive electoral frauds because 50 of its agents working in voting locations have been expelled. On the 14th, the nguemists denouce "the lack of maturity shown by the leaders of the opposition." Miguel Oyono, minister of Foreign Affairs, asserts that only those sentenced to death can ask for pardon. On the 21st, the US appoints a new ambassador, John Melvin Yates. On the 25th, after the Bubi trial, and while the trial regarding the leaders of Fuerza Democrática is taking place, Archbishop Ildefonso Obama denounces the fact that "priests and Catholic nuns and monks are victims of persecutions and bad treatment in all of Equatorial Guinea." One of the lawyers of the Bubi trial is arrested. Foreign Minister M. Oyono goes to Iran to establish diplomatic relations and cooperation ties. Lucas Nguema Esono, Minister of Information, Tourism, and Culture, goes on a visit to Mexico.

August: It is announced that twelve solder members of opposition parties, who are refugees in Cameroon, will be sent to Argentina. Mobil announces an increase in oil production. Ocean Energa says there are many new active wells.s The minister of Foreign Affairs, M. Oyono, threatens in a disguised way, the Spanish cooperation. A permanent representative for the Francophony is appointed, and soon after a Commission for Francophony is created, run by the presidency. Four employees of a Spanish company are arrested for ten days, falsely accused of terrorism, and a ransom is demanded. Negotiations are held concerning the maritime border with São-Tomé-Principe. On the 21st, Equatorial Guinea protests concerningnonauthorized activities done by ELF on its territorial waters. On the 25th, Obiang Nguema asks for a ceasefire in the Democratic Republic of Congo. Violent rains flood and damage Malabo and Luba.

September: On the 9th, Obiang Nguema commutes the fifteen death sentences of the Bubi trial. On the 13th, Equatorial Guinea pays its overdue dues to the UN to recover its right to vote. On the 14th, the mixed Spanish/Equato-Guinean Commission starts working. Between the 14th and 16th, Obiang Nguema goes on an official visit to Ghana. On the 18th, the dictator goes on a work trip to Nigeria; the vice-minister of Education finishes a mission in Cuba. Beginning of the construction of INSESO headquarters. Asian companies destroy the forest of Rio Muni. On the 23rd, Spain says it is ready to increase its cooperation with its former colony if the country becomes a true democracy.

October: on the 4th, the creation of a new Central Bank is announced. On the 9th, the opposition accuses the government of dismissing mayors who are members of the opposition. On the 12th, the thirtieth anniversary of independence is celebrated. Obiang Nguema sends a message to the King of Spain but does not invite an official delegation. On the 13th, the democratic opposition announces a transition pact, in view of the legislative elections. On the 20th, Obiang Nguema ends his official visit to São-Tome-Principe without having signed an agreement on maritime borders. On the 26th, the parties of the opposition end their participation in the making of the electoral lists. On the 28th, the government withdraws 65,000 electors from the lists (opponents). On the 30th, the government accuses the democratic opposition of wanting to sabotage the elections. The next day, the government annouces that the legislative elections will be held within legal deadlines. Numerous opponents are arrested. The prison of Playa Negra still holds numerous political prisoners.

November: On November 4, Obiang Nguema calls for international tenders for oil. On the 15th, the opposition accuses Obiang Nguema of not holding the legislative elections within the legal deadline. More opponents are arrested. The nguemists accuse the democratic opposition of "spreading confusion." On the 18th, Moto Nsá files a denunciation of Obianag Nguema and two ministers in the Spanish Audiencia Nacional, for various crimes and offenses. From the 23rd to the 24th, a delegation of from the CPDS participates in the Socialist International meeting in Geneva.

December: Terror increases. On the 1st, the opposition reports the death of Nguema Ela Angue Ndong, one of the leaders of the RDF, after being tortured to death in the prison at the capital. While the UN special rapporteur on Human Rights is on assignment, the mixed commission of the government and the opposition fails. On the 3rd, in Paris, TV3 reports nguemist torture. The date for the legislative elections, overdue since September, has not yet been set.

❖ INTRODUCTION ❖

Except for some booklets dating back to 1920, this book is the first general presentation about Equatorial Guinea (the former Spanish Guinea) in English. It fills an important gap that can be explained by the small size of the young republic and the fact that it is the only sub-Saharan African state having Spanish as its official language.

The degradation of the internal situation since independence, with an increasingly despotic form of government, and the fact that one-third of the population fled in exile, render all research difficult. Censorship (even in Spain) and border controls were relentlessly enforced. Except for France, only the Communist countries and Equatorial Guinea's immediate neighbors maintained embassies in Santa Isabel. After the dictator Macías Nguema had been eliminated by his nephew Obiang Nguema, the country apparently turned to the West. However, it was still very difficult to find out what was actually going on. This was apparent in a 1985 report of the Spanish Ministry of Education and Science and the 1987 report of Amnesty International. Furthermore, certain business interests, especially French ones, misleadingly presented the regime as having all the trappings of a democracy. Ever since, the only new element is the fact that the United States entered the list with, on the one hand, the government criticizing the dictatorship and, on the other, the friendly optimism of the oil companies.

A number of articles and pamphlets consulted by the author, mostly in Spanish, appear in four volumes of his *Bibliographía general de Guinea Ecuatorial* published between 1974 and 1988 with the assistance of the Swiss National Commission for UNESCO. Volumes five to ten were published between 1985 and 1998 by Les Editions du Temps in Geneva. An eleventh volume will be published in 1999 by the same press.

Equatorial Guinea's 28,110 sq. km. (Maryland: 27,394 sq. km., Haiti: 27,750 sq. km.) represents less than 0.1 percent of Africa's surface. The country, situated slightly north of the equator in the Gulf of Guinea, is divided into an insular province (Fernando Po, Annobón) and a continental one (Río Muni), the latter covering about 26,000 sq. km. (10,000 sq. miles). Except for the São Tomé-Príncipe Republic, all other neighboring countries have an area ten to thirty times that of Equatorial Guinea.

The insular province is formed with the volcanic mass that characterizes the large West African rift, stretching out from Tibesti in northern Chad to the island of Annobón in the South Atlantic. The Río Muni province occupies a slice of the large African platform with metamorphic rocks in its center, covered with thick layers of ferrogenous sands and cretaceous deposits that contain oil fields along the coast. The climate, except for Annobón, where it is tropical, is equatorial: warm and humid all year long. The area of Ureka, south of Fernando Po, with yearly rainfalls of 10 meters (approximately 390 inches), is one of the most humid places of the world. Only Río Muni has large waterways, most of them oriented east-west: in the north, Río Campo; in the south, the Utamboni river; and in the center, Río Benito, hinge of the province. The country is covered with thick humid forests, where mahogany, ebony, and okoumea trees are found. Elephants, gorillas, manatees, and whales, once abundant, have suffered from overhunting and fishing and are dying out.

While the first occupiers of the country seem to have been the Pygmies, of whom only isolated pockets exist, Bantu migrations between the 13th and the 19th centuries brought Ndowe people (erroneously called Playeros), then Fang; elements of the latter appear to have generated the Bubi of Fernando Po who succeeded former neolithic populations. The Annobón population is native to Angola and was introduced to Fernando Po by the Portuguese via São Tomé.

Ceded by Portugal to Spain at the end of the 18th century, the territories of the Gulf of Guinea, which then covered about 800,000 sq. km. (30,000 sq. miles), were first the favorites of the slave traders, as well as of British, German, Dutch, and French merchants. Fernando Po was even administered by the British from 1827 to 1858 before being taken over by the Spanish authorities. However, effective occupation of Río Muni only started in 1926, once Spain at the end of the 19th century had been dispossessed of a large part of its colonial territories in Asia and the Americas by the United States, and in Africa by the United Kingdom, France, and Germany.

From 1904 to independence in 1968, Spanish Guinea was exposed to the paternalism of the Spanish state and of the Roman Catholic church, most of the natives being considered mentally unprepared for emancipation. Thanks to the contribution of foreign workers (Liberia, Cameroon, Nigeria), the Spanish colony became an important cocoa, coffee, and timber producer. Beginning in 1948 the first claims for independence were voiced but were strongly repressed by Spain. Having become a member of the United Nations in 1955, Spain had to mitigate its position, specially under Afro-Asian pressures which in 1960-63 led to the "provincialization" of Equatorial Guinea, and in 1964-68 to autonomous status. A constitutional conference (1967-68) prepared the country's independence with an elected president, Macías Nguema. Shortly after October 12, 1968, with the rapid hardening of President Macías personal power, 7,000 out of 8,000 Spaniards living in Equatorial Guinea hastily left the country, followed in early 1976 by 25,000 of the 45,000 Nigerians. Despite international assistance from the UN, OAU, People's Republic of China, and Cuba, a state of terror and economic chaos rapidly overcame the country. With the despotic power of President Macías Nguema and his clan from Mongomo, gross income per capita, previously the highest of West-Central Africa, fell to the level of the poorest African countries ($170 per year per capita). Thousands of educated people and farmers unable to flee abroad were slaughtered.

In August 1979, a palace revolution was led by Obiang Nguema, the nephew of Macías Nguema who had held the post of Commander-in-Chief of the Armed Forces for a number of years. Following this successful coup, Macías Nguema was arrested, tried by court martial, and sentenced to death. The sentence was carried out on September 28, 1979. On October 12, Obiang Nguema proclaimed himself president and with the backing of 600 Moroccan soldiers became the second Nguemist dictator. There was no change in the prevailing corruption, but the country came progressively under Western influence, particularly French, to become in 1984 a member of the France-oriented Customs Union of the Central African States (UDEAC). At the beginning of 1985 the French African franc (CFA), in use in neighboring Gabon and Cameroon, became the official currency. Despite these changes, the economy continued to stagnate through 1988 with levels of production no better than those achieved in 1945.

Various political movements created by the exiles—of which the Alianza Nacional para la Restauración Democrática (ANRD) is the most active—have fought for recognition of refugee status for some 110,000 Equato-Guineans outside the country, trying to alert the world to the dramatic events that their young country is facing. In mid-March 1979, the Commission on Human Rights of the United Nations decided to organize a study concerning the violation of human rights in Equatorial Guinea, and every year since then their reports have condemned the regime for violation of these rights.

In 1987, Obiang Nguema reinstated the PUNT set up by his uncle Macías through the creation of a "democratic" single-party system. Due to the army's control of the country (posing as civilians), coups, as under Macías Nguema, often fictitious, began to reccur, together with rivalries among Esangui members of the Mongomo clan. These conditions brought about the attempted coup in July 1986, led by another uncle, Colonel Mbá Oñana. The non-Esangui were condemned to death or twenty years in prison, while Obiang's relatives were out by October 12, 1987, the date of the announcement of Guinextebank's collapse due to the "political loans" made to the clique in power since 1968. France's hold over Equatorial Guinea increased at this time. On October 12, 1988, Equatorial Guinea celebrated the 20th anniversary of her independence.

From 1988 onwards, the second dictatorship was courted more and more earnestly by foreign powers. France was responsible for a French news bulletin on the national radio, while the United Kingdom increased its contracts for American waste deposits, all of which brought Obiang Nguema great revenues. Thus the BIAO/Equatorial Guinea was born in October and thus the nation's telecommunications were controlled by France Cable. The dictator named his first wife as the president's adviser, while his cousin Maye Ela made a secret deal with the British for huge deposits of toxic wastes in Annobón. In the meanwhile, the regime was again denounced, not only by the UN Human Rights Commission—which reported the deposits granted on Annobón—but also by the OUA, as a result of the Nguemists courting of South Africa. The opposition was subject to a number of arrests; outside the country, it denounced, through the ANRD, the dictatorship before international organizations.

In Spain, the opposition parties tried to come together under a rather fragile and short-lived Pact of Madrid. As for Paris, it gave its financial support to the Nguemists. In September, French became compulsory in schools. On June 25, 1989, Obiang Nguema had just been elected president for another term of seven years, by 99.96 percent of the votes. While the dictator boasted that he was the savior of the country, Amnesty International again denounced the killings regularly practiced by the regime. Economic and financial circles paid no attention to this terrorism. The IMF loaned $16 million and the Israeli lumbering company

Yona bought the largest concession in the country. This dichotomy between the business world and those preoccupied with the observance of fundamental freedoms continued until Amnesty International's *Report on Torture* in September, 1990.

In the ninties, numerous governmetal and nongovernmental institutions and organizations denounced the oppressive regime of Teodoro Obiang Nguema and his civil and military accomplices:

Amnesty International (London)
Asociación Pro-Derechos Humanos (Madrid)
ASODEGUE (Madrid)
Christus für alle Nationen (Germany)
Commission Française Justice et Paix (Paris)
Congressional Human Rights Causus (Washington)
Doctors without Borders (Paris)
Economic Intelligence Unit (London)
Ensemble luttons contre la Torture–AGAT (Paris)
European Union (Brussels)
Freedom House (New York)
Human Rights Internet (Ottawa)
International Demo-Christian
International Commission of Jurists (Geneva)
International Committee of the Red Cross (Geneva)
International Federation of Human Rights (Paris)
International Federation of Jurists (Geneva)
International Federation of Journalists (Brussels)
International Federation of Young Liberals and Radicals
International Labour Organization (Geneva)
International Service for Human Rights (Geneva)
International Socialist (London)
Interparlamentarian Union (Geneva)
Interpueblos, Santander (Spain)
Izquierda Unida (IU, Madrid)
Landesjugendwerk (Baden-Würtemberg)
Lawyer-to-Lawyer
Observatiore Géopolitique de la Drogue (Paris)
Partido Socialista Obrero Popular (PSOE, Madrid)
Radio Exterior de España (Madrid)
Radio France (Paris)
Reporters without Borders (Paris)
U.N. Commission for Human Rights (Geneva)
Union Fraternelle pour l'Entente entre les Races et les Peuples (Geneva)
U.S. State Department (Washington)
Veterinarians without Borders (Spain)
Voice of America (Washington)
World Confederation of Labour (Brussels)

In 1991, Obiang Nguema's electoral farce began with his proposal for multipartism. But in spite of the efforts of A. Suarez (ex-Prime Minister of Spain) to mediate a reconciliation between opposition parties and the regime, the arrests and the torture of opponents continued. Despite a boycott called by the opposition on the occasion of the Constitutional Referendum in November, the Fundamental Law ensuring the victory of the clan from Mongomo was voted. Faced with manipulation by the Nguemists, the various non-domesticated opposition parties founded the Joint Democratic Coalition (JDC).

In January 1992, Obiang Nguema promulgated a law on political parties and a law on meetings and demonstrations, apart from a dishonest amnesty law, aimed at the refugees who had fled his regime. A "transitional" government—which was, like the previous ones, dominated by the clan from Mongomo—was named, involving zero participation from the opposition members who were increasingly being arrested. The involvement of France increased, and Prime Minister Siale Bilekia was also simultaneously the minister for the francophony and culture. Faced with continued terror tactics, Amnesty International and the International Interparliamentary Commission reminded the dictator of the need to observe human rights.

While Obiang Nguema seemed to accept the idea of multipartism, the arrests, especially of secondary school students, their teachers, and Spanish traders increased, until Madrid threatened to cut off aid. These threats were effective with Obiang Nguema, who asked the police to be more moderate in its actions. But the dictator recovered from this momentary lapse from his normal behavior by refusing, through legislation, all dialogue with exiled compatriots. Meanwhile, he launched tirades against the United States, Spain, the United Nations, and the European Union for their alleged interference in the internal affairs of the country. The concurrent 1992 report published in 1993 by the EU explained that "Continual serious violations of human rights have made it difficult to develop cooperation with Equatorial Guinea. As a result, excepting humanitarian aid, no significant cooperation operation has been implemented since mid-1992."

Soon after, some ambassadors received death threats. The European Parliament and the Spanish government responded by cutting off aid to Nguemist Equatorial Guinea. While the United States recalled its Peace Corps volunteers as well as Ambassador Bennet for consultations, France continued to aid the dictatorship and received Obiang Nguema in Paris, in spite of the assassination of two of its volunteers. On March 16, the internal situation seemed to clear up with the conclusion of a National Pact between opposition parties and Nguemists, but this Pact was violated almost at once, mainly with the arrests of a number of opposition militants, in spite of the overtures of a special mission for the European Commission. In Europe, the National Alliance for Democratic Restauration (ANRD), under its new Secretary General Luis Ondo Ayang, expelled some of its members, accused of striking deals with the regime. At the same time, Switzerland expelled Obiang Nguema's French economic counsellor, who was soon followed by the ambassador to the United Nations in Geneva, Engonga Motulu, notorious for his crooked behavior and deals. While Ambassador Bennet returned to Santa Isabel (Malabo) with renewed support from Washington, the parties constituting the POC announced their boycott of the legislative elections schedular for autumn.

The arrests and torture of opponents, particularly of journalists of *La Verdad,* began anew. An expedition of 200 Ninjas on the Island of Annobón spread terror, assassinations, and deportations of young men to Bata. Donor countries refused to provide observers for the elections, which were judged as having been rigged. France was the only country to break this unanimous decision. Under pressure from the United States, Morocco withdrew its 600 guards. The oppression intensified. In the capital, one of the pillars of the Unión Popular, P. Motu Mamiaga was assassinated in the prison of Playa Negra (the Nguemists alleged suicide), and his viscera were used for Esangui ritual celebrations. Soon after, another opponent was shot by a brother of Obiang Nguema and an employee of the UN arrested. In Río Muni, Spanish tourists were arrested and leaders of the opposition prevented from campaigning. During the month of September, the wife of the Nguemist Ambassador to Spain was arrested in Brazil with 30 kgs of cocaine. Subsequently, the Geopolitical Drug Observatory (Paris) declared that Equatorial Guinea was a narco-state under the direct authority of Obiang Nguema and the protection of France. The legislative elections set for September were postponed to November; all the observers deemed them illegal. In spite of nearly 70 percent absenteeism, the PDGE, the dictator's party, won the elections. Immediately, the tracking down of opponents (including a number of high school students and teachers) began again, and the diplomatic corps was abused. U.S. Ambassador Bennet was accused of sorcery and the consul of Spain in Bata was expelled. On December 22, a government of 38 ministers was appointed, with no opposition participation.

In early 1994 *Le Monde Diplomatique* condemned France's official policy of compromise with the regime and demanded that Obiang Nguema be declared an outlaw from humankind. Washington and the European Union seemed to take steps in this direction by refusing to receive him in the United States and by confirming the suppression of all cooperation. The U.S. State Department, the Human Rights Commission of the UN, and Amnesty International severely criticized the Nguemist regime. Following the 50 percent devaluation of the CFA (declared by Obiang Nguema as a "disaster for the economy"), the IMF signed a financial agreement with the dictatorship. The international press began to inform the world of French involvement and the training of the Nguemist militia and the political police of Obiang Nguema, the Jóvenes Antorchas (Young Torches) and the Ninjas.

It didn't bother the mediocre *Afrique Business Magazine* to publish in the summer of 1994 a ludicrous issue dedicated to the "exemplary transition" of Equatorial Guinea, with a glorification of the Obiang Nguema regime.

In 1995, there had clearly been an infiltration of the democratic opposition and the muzzling of rather opportunistic political parties. At a press conference in Geneva, Luis Ondo Ayang, the General Secretary of the National Alliance for Democratic Restoration, publicly exposed attempts to sabotage the ANRD by men such as Jose Dougan Beaca and Carmelo Mokong. The Second Convention of the PDGE (a replica of the PUNT) was attended by a delegation of the opposition parties muzzled by the Nguemists (CLD, PSD, PCSD, PSGE, UDENA), which had signed documents supporting the dictatorship. The parties forming the Joint Opposition Platform (POC) were absent.

An increasing number of articles and programs in the French media, the press, and even Radio France, denouncing the terror in Equatorial Guinea, expressed disapproval and repudiation of the Nguemist regime, thus confirming the revelations of Radio Exterior de España, which had been highly vilified by the Nguemist dictatorship. Each year, the United States reacted through its State Department *Report on Human Rights Violations to the Congress*. In the report published in April 1996, it was stated that:

> Equatorial Guinea is nominally a multiparty constitutional republic, but in reality power has been exercised by the President Teodoro Obiang [Nguema] through a small subclan of the majority Fang tribe which has ruled since the country's independence in 1968. Despite the formalities of a multiparty form of government, President Obiang, in power since 1979, together with his associates, dominates the government. The President's Democratic Party of Equatorial Guinea (PDGE) controls the judiciary and the legislature, the latter through fraudulent elections.

It is therefore hardly surprising that in October 1995, the United States decided to replace their ambassador with a chargé d'affaires, in spite of Nguemist protests. However, while the official policy of the United States was to maintain its distance, the large petroleum interests in America, dominated by Mobil Oil Corporation, grew to be highly accommodative of the dictatorship.

In 1995 and 1996 the entire history of Nguemist Equatorial Guinea during the last quarter century was repeated.

- The ineptitude of the Spanish diplomacy in African political affairs.
- The Machiavellian African policy of Paris, which was willing to curry favor with all autocrats, including Obiang Nguema.
- The hypocritical behavior of the United States, which officially condemned the dictatorship, but privately benefited from the petroleum resources, without giving a thought to the criminal regime.
- The huge increase in arbitrary arrests, especially for crimes of freedom of expression.
- The continuation of torture and violence towards various groups.
- The allegation of so-called coups d'état by civilians and army personnel to eliminate potential rivals of the dictator in future elections.
- Special military courts made up of members of the dictator's family.
- Electoral law reform preventing the candidacy of confirmed political leaders.
- Use by the dictatorship of a tame opposition.
- Continued flights into exile, etc.

All of these events go to prove that the so-called "Coup for Liberty" of August 1979 was little more than a Nguemist (or Macist) lure. Nothing has changed, fundamentally, with Obiang Nguema, and the Equato-Guinean people remaining under the grip of the clan from Mongomo.

Not unlike his uncle Macías Nguema, ever fearful of elimination, Obiang Nguema is distrustful of his army. In May 1995, he managed the return of a 600 man contingent of Moroccan mercenaries. Mobil announced its simultaneous discovery of two petroleum deposits, which assure enormous royalties to the dictatorship. This encouraged various groups favorable to the installation of democracy to request the American company to pressure the dictator in that direction, without results.

In July 1995, Amnesty International published a *Review of Unkept Promises,* in which it showed that ever since the adoption of a multiparty system in 1992, the government's promises were little more than empty gestures meant to distract international attention and to silence the qualms of donor countries. Once the aid had been given, the regime recommenced repressive measures against the opposition. On August 2, 1995, under international pressure—Obiang Nguema pardoned 33 political prisoners. In preparation for the November 1995 visit of the special rapporteur to the Human Rights Commission, M.A. Artucio, other political prisoners were released. But shortly after M. Artucio's mission, the arrests and violence began again. The municipal elections, which the opposition as well as the Spanish observers claimed had been manipulated, were held in September. At this time, a number of assassinations were committed under the orders of executives of the regime (mainly in the Woleu-Ntem, province of Ebebiyin). Other atrocities occurred in Niefang, Akurenam, and the capital. In spite of the observers recording the victory of the Joint Opposition Platform (POC) and the European Parliament's demand of resect for the election results, the Nguemists declared themselves victorious in 18 out of 27 municipalities. However, the capital went to the opposition, with a Bubi mayor.

Nguemism began to undergo growing internal dissent. A former vice president of the republic and ex-president of the Parliament, although members of the clan from Mongomo, have fled to Gabon, fearing for their lives. Corruption, all kinds of extortions, lies, unkept promises, and violations of human rights remain the bane of the country. The failure of the second dictatorship is also expressed by the continued voluntary, needless, to say clandestine, emigration. The United States, France, and others maintain a policy of silence on Nguemist Equatorial Guinea, due to economic and strategic interests, or even because of fears that a third dictatorship could be even worst than the previous ones. Meanwhile, the country is falling further and further into a state of decay, but this does not prevent Obiang Nguema and his ministers from reporting to any party that will listen that Spain and others are interfering in the internal affairs of Equatorial Guinea with their demands for democratization. Also starting in 1996, agents of the dictator's party pressured the population to sign a PDGE form, through which they promised, under oath and in the name of "God, honor, and respect" never to speak against the decisions of the party. All of whose decisions they accept by giving the party an irreversible vote. In December 1995, the Spanish missionary journal *Mundo Negro* expressed the sad reality thus: "Equatorial Guinea. After the fraud, the reprisals." A study (under pseudonyms) by two Equato-Guinean economists, on petroleum extraction, spoke of the almost clandestine nature of these operations and of the pilfering of the national heritage that it represents.

On January 8, 1996, there was a minor reshuffle of ministers. Three new ministers, including a counsellor to the dictator, a member of the clan from Mongomo, were appointed. Of 22 ministers, half were from Mongomo or from its district (Wele-Nzas); among the others, there was a majority of confirmed Nguemists. In the guise of a democratic rearrangement of the executive, the dictatorship made arrangements for presidential elections. In mid-January, to everybody's surprise, the election date was set for February 25, 1996, without consultations with the opposition parties. A series of decrees prevented opposition members from participating: stay in the country during the five years preceding the elections (against Moto Nsá); age limit of at least forty years (against Placido Miko), etc. The opposition denounced the unconstitutionality of these elections, criticized the so-called electoral census which eliminated all sympathizers of the opposition and the fact that the national electoral commission only included supporters of Obiang Nguema. The six parties forming the POC coalition (UP, CPDS, PP, AP, ADP, FDR) agreed to participate in the presidential elections with a single candidate. The Ministry for the Interior published a document criticizing and condemning the position of the clergy over human rights matters, and therefore over politics. In late January, the Bishop of Bata, Anacleto Sima Nguema wrote to the dictator in protest against the measures and to justify the position of the clergy by arguments quoting the Apostles; he threatened to reduce the number of places of worship to 5 percent. Remembering the closure of churches under Macías Nguema, Sima Nguema demanded the cancellation of measures violating the constitution and the international commitments of the regime.

The dictatorship created a "shock troop" of 300 men, charged with supervising the polling stations. The POC chose architect Amancio G. Nzé, of the CPDS (the only candidate fulfilling the criteria of the electoral law), as its candidate for presidency. Moto Nsá, who had been speaking for years of his destiny as a national leader was upset and withdrew the Progress Party from the POC. This attitude made Mba Ada, the president of Popular Union (UP) decide to stand for election too, and to leave the POC. The Electoral Commission rejected the candidacy of the POC under the pretext that it did not exist anymore and shut down his offices but accepted the candidacy of Moto Nsá, Mba Ada, and two other minor candidates, to whom the dictator alloted $30,000 for the campaign. Obiang Nguema wished to give a democratic facade to his regime. The UN and the EU, especially Spain and France, demanded that fair elections be held.

Toward the end of January 1996, the Nguemist extortions started again. Opponents, including mayors and municipal councillors, were tortured, and a Spanish doctor with leanings toward the opposition was expelled from Kogo. Priests were prevented from all movement between January 25 and February 28. A large number of them were arrested, tortured, and even threatened with death. The first democratically elected mayor of the capital and president of the Democratic and Progressive Alliance, Victorino Bolekia Bolay, was arrested with his deputies, including C. Bakale, chief editor of the POC's periodical, *La Verdad,* during a French lesson on the premises of the French Cooperation. Illiterate agents of the Seguridad accused them of plotting a coup d'état. All of them were tortured. Bolekia Bolay was injured from head to toe and was seen leaving the Criminal Investigation Department with his clothes all bloody and unable to walk. The Nguemist regime accused Radio Exterior de España of dividing the Equato-Guinean people with its daily broadcast toward the Gulf of Guinea. In mid-February Mgr. Sima Ngua denounced the torture of a priest, Carlos Esono, and the campaign of intimidation and terror. Obiang Nguema restricted the freedom of action of international observers, especially by assigning them to specific polling stations. This restriction led to the refusal of the UNDP, the EU, France, and Spain to send observers. The United States observers from the Carter Foundation also decided against going to Equatorial Guinea. Cameroon and Gabon were the only countries to send observers. They were joined by four Americans sent in by petroleum companies. Faced with the impossibility to campaign, three of the four opposition candidates withdrew from the race, but the Nguemists refused to take into account their decision. Secundino Oyono, the president of the Social Democratic and Popular Convergency (CSDP) was the only one to face Obiang Nguema, who declared to the population that "Those who do not vote for me are of low birth."

Obiang Nguema announced that the embassy of Equatorial Guinea in the United States was being financed by Mobil. At the same time, it was learned that the company, with the help of others, was financing the election campaign of the dictator. The dictator contracted the services of a well-known public relations firm in the United States to edit and produce pamphlets to attract investors to Equatorial Guinea. In France, *Jeune Afrique Economie,* run by Cameroonians, brought out a 434-page special issue, with 72 photos of the dictator. There are frequent references to the author of this book, carefully leaving out his criticisms of the Nguemist dictatorship. To ensure the electoral victory of Obiang Nguema, the South African company Strategic Concepts was called in. Four American observers from Electoral Systems were offered by Strategic Concepts. These experts could observe the effect of the torture that the mayor of the capital, Victorino Bolekia, and his deputies had been subject to.

On February 25, there was a marked absence of crowds before the polling stations indicating a low level of voter participation, Obiang Nguema was reelected with 99 percent of the votes and with the Nguemist Electoral Commission speaking of a participation of 75 percent of the registered voters. The Fang journalist and historian Donato Ndongo Bidyogo observed in *Mundo Negro* (Madrid) that the only thing the African dinosaurs ever learned from the Bible was that "He who is not with me is against me." This attitude, he said, led to the imprisonments, tortures, and murders, "in the name of African authenticity, a concept which has caused more deaths and misery than colonization itself." In *Las Provincias* (Valencia), the Bubi Djongele Bokokó Boko called the reelection of Obiang Nguema, the sole candidate, an official coup d'état.

The victory of Obiang Nguema is mainly testimony to the failure of the regime. *El País* (Madrid) expressed the view that Obiang Nguema was ruling since January 25, 1996, "with the same level of legality as before, which was nil." According to the dictator, this election brought the process of democratization to a culmination point. From then on, those who pursued political activities would be prosecuted. During all future elections, citizens will have to publicly declare their choice. While one of the American observers sent in by Strategic Concepts declared that he had never seen such a high level of vote rigging, the African Committee of the International Socialist, in Uagadugu (Burkina Faso), asked the international community not to recognize the polls. *Diari Avui* (Barcelona) stated that after the dubious "reelection" of Obiang Nguema, French President Jacques Chirac hurried to congratulate the Nguemist dictator. The article stressed that successive French governments, whatever their ideology, were quick to call Equatorial Guinea a real democracy.

After his reelection, Obiang Nguema formed a new government on April 8, 1996, after negotiations with parties of the domesticated opposition. The new government of 41 members included five Bubi, one Ndowe, one Annobónese, and 33 Fang, of whom 11 were natives of the district of Wele-Nzas (Mongomo). The executive remained under the yoke of the clan from Mongomo and of the dictator's family. Out of 41 posts, 6 were given to the tame opposition; all the important ministries remained with noted Nguemists. The so-called "government of national unity" included one ministerial post for 277 government employees and for 10,000 inhabitants.

The well-informed French periodical *Marchés Tropicaux* noted on April 1, 1996, that "the victory of Obiang Nguema Mbasogo was testimony to the helplessness of the foreign sponsors (Spain, United States, the European Union, and the United Nations), who had pleaded with the dictator for democratization. . . . In order to justify the size of their investments, they stated that the petroleum companies needed political stability" even if the regime was no more than a democratorship.

In Geneva, the special rapporteur to the UN Human Rights Commission, A. Artucio, stressed in his 1996 report that military courts continue to judge civil cases, that torture and mistreatment are common occurrences, and that the government is not responding sufficiently to the recommendations of the commission. The report concludes that the presidential election was not credible. The Nguemists protested, claiming that Artucio was only expressing the opposition's point of view. But in April 1996, the U.S. State Department's *Report on Human Rights in the World* (1995), submitted to the Congress, refuted the claims of the Nguemist dictatorship with a terrifying description of the situation in Equatorial Guinea.

President Obiang exercises control over the police and security forces through the Minister of Interior. The security forces committed serious human rights abuses. . . . Serious human right abuses continue. After some progress in 1994, the human rights situation deteriorated in 1995. Citizens do not have the right to change government.

It also provided a terrifying list of the

principal abuses by the security forces: arrests and physical abuses of prisoners in their custody, several extrajudicial killings, torture, beatings of detainees, arbitrary arrests and detention.... The judicial system does not ensure due process and is subject to executive influence.... The Government severely restricts freedom of speech and the press and effectively limits the right of assembly....Torture and Other Cruel, Inhuman or Degrading Treatment or Punishment.... are serious, frequent and widespread...The judiciary is not independant; the judges serve at the pleasure of the President....The government withould ever minimal access to broadcasting from opposition parties.... While there is an elected Chamber of Deputies, it is not representative and is dominated by the Government. . . .

Amnesty International's 1996 report confirms all the items of this deplorable list, including the violence practiced on some political detractors, and denounces the systematic repression and the violence practiced with impunity by the Nguemist security forces, including the Moroccans.

It is this sad reality that led the Swiss Minister for Foreign Affairs and acting President of the Conference for Security and Cooperation in Europe (CSCE), Flavio Cotti, during the 1996 session of the UN Human Rights Commission, to warn of "extremely serious problems" that were to be observed in Equatorial Guinea. He thus confirmed the statements of the 1996 report of the American nongovernmental organization *Freedom House,* which categorizes Nguemist Equatorial Guinea among "the most repressive regimes." In the Madrid daily *ABC,* F. Jiminez Losantos joked that next Equatorial Guinea could be called "Mongomo Guinea."

But that won't stop the oil from running in this practically stateless country which the dictator runs as his own personal property. To give the impression of change, Obiang Nguema convened a meeting of the 14 legally recognized parties in the beginning of August 1996 to discuss the National Pact which he violates and tears up since 1993. Soon after, in Madrid at the initiative of the ANRD, a dozen political groups met to decide on common action aimed at relaunching and reforming the National Pact that Obiang Nguema had violated. It was then that the annual report of the UNDP came out. It clearly stated that the Nguemist Equatorial Guinea was going through a serious economic crisis, with a sky-high foreign debt. This report also confirmed that the money made from the oil had not gone into the National Treasury.

In November 1966, the democratically elected mayor of the capital, teacher Victorino Bolekia, described in an interview the way the Nguemist government worked.

In Equatorial Guinea nothing is respected; life, home, the smallest freedom of expression or movement. Prisoners are tortured, people are put in jail arbitrarily, people are thrown out of their houses by means of violence....The repressive strategy of the police consists in arresting someone at 8:00 PM, torturing him throughout the night, and releasing him the next day at 6:00 AM as if nothing had happened. But some of these people have died of their wounds. Yet, they keep on arresting, they keep on torturing, but in a hidden way.

Professor Douglas Yates, of the American University in Paris, declared in *Panafrica* (London, 11/96) that due to the Franco-American lust for the resources of Equatorial-Guinea, and particularly to the clandestine nature of the oil industry, the Equato-Guinean people will have to wait for the international pressures they had hoped for. "For anyone who has the remotest idea of the relationship between oil and power, the prospect of the United States interfering in Equatorial Guinea seems highly unlikely."

At the end of 1996, the tension between Nigeria and Equatorial Guinea started again. One must not forget that along with the Equato-Guinean offshore oilfields, exploited by Mobil, there are Nigerian offshore oilfields exploited by the French Elf Aquitaine.

In January 1997, the U.S. Corporate Council on Africa organized a tour in Equatorial Guinea, sponsored by Equator Bank and Occidental Petroleum. Meanwhile numerous arrests of opponents of the regime occurred throughout the country.

The 1997 report of the *Observatoire des fransferts d'armement,* published in Paris in 1998, gives details concerning France's military engagement as well as a clear description of the methods used by the nguemist regime. The promises concerning the respect of human rights "have not been kept" and "are a simple devise used when the international community examines the country's situation with regards to human rights or when the countries that provide assistance threated to stop their help. As soon as a country has committed itself to providing additional assistance, repression starts again. Violation of human rights occur daily and lead to an atmosphere of fear and insecurity. . . . The government uses imprisonment and bad treatment to prevent human rights and political activists from carrying out their activities, and to interrupt the democratic process." A few improvements concerning the freedom of expression have been reported, "but the respect of human rights will not be at its best as long as security forces continue to misuse their power with impugnity."

In April 1998, Yates underlined in *West Africa* that with the increase of oil revenues, the political situation was worsening. "The arrival of [oil] revenues in Malabo has been a catastrophe for Equato-Guineans. Oil allows Obiang Nguema to remain in power. Not only does it make him rich, it provides him with money to pay his soldiers and police and to pay munitions. It gives him the resources needed to buy off political rivals. It allows him to produce the spectacle of elections. . . . As long as the international press continues to report on oil production without investigating the cycles of accumulation and violence to which Obiang Nguema has harnessed his power, it acts in complicity with his continuing dictatorship."

In Evinayong, on the 30th anniversary of Independance, October 12, 1998, Obiang Nguema accused the Western world of looking for new ways of dominating African peoples. Under the pretexts of democracy and governance, "the colonial powers want to create linguistic and cultural areas that protect hidden interests and aims." Equatorial Guinea will maintain the relations of friendship and co-operation with all countries, "within the context of a scrupulous respect of the sovereignty and independance." He did not give a date for the legislative elections. The CPDS released a statement in which it underlined that after Macías Nguema's tyranny, "Obiang Nguema and his family have transfomed the county into a private property," adding that not only laymen but the clergy also is a victim of Nguemist terror. The men in power at the end of 1998 are those of the days of Macías Nguema, which proves the continuity of the dictatorship.

Equatorial Guinea remains of one the 45 least developed countries of the world. The best definition to describe the failure of the two nguemist dictatorships is the well-known joke: "What existed before candles in Equatorial Guinea?" The answer is: "Electricity." The outlook for 1998-99 of the *British Economic Intelligence Unit* (3rd quarter, 1998) forecasts that "the ruling PDGE will win legislative elections scheduled to take place in 1998, but the electoral process will fail to win international approval. President Obiang Nguema is, therefore, likely to remain isolated by key donors, while diplomatic relations with the region will continue to be strained. Growing oil wealth will contribute to drive high growth rates, and a new round of licensing for exploration blocks is expected to be offered in the near future." But "popular resentment towards the government is high and growing. The absence of any material benefits from the oil boom for the majority of the population and continuing political repression are the main contribution factors."

In his book *Iboga: La sociedad secreta del Bueti. Guinea Ecuatorial (Iboga: The secret society of Bueti*. Madrid, 1998), J. M. Novoa Ruiz explains that "the characters in this novel are real and presently living in Equatorial Guinea. Due to the regime of terror that prevails in this African country, the names of some of the characters have been replaced by fictious names to preserve their physical integrity." This makes research concerning this country particularly difficult: either one works there incognito or under an assumed name (several researchers have done that), or one has to rely on information given by people who are in the country, thus endangering their lives. This did not stop beginning in December 1998: death of one of the leaders of the FDR, owing to tortures; arrest and torture of 35 Bubi; failure of the negotiations opposition/dictatorship.

Equatorial Guinea remains a country without book-shops.

Exchange rate: FCFA/$US

1992	165
1993	273
1994*	555
1995 (4th Quarter)	490
1996 (4th Quarter)	524
1997 (4th Quarter)	599
1998 (2nd Quarter)	618

*On January 12, 1994, the FCFA was devaluated from 50 FCFA per FF to 100 FCFA per FF.

❖ THE DICTIONARY ❖

❖ A ❖

ABAGA EDJANG, F. Fang of Mikomeseng. Born December 20, 1956. Elemental studies in Bata and Mikomeseng. High Schools Carlos Lwanga (Bata, 1972-74) and Rey Malabo (Malabo, 1974-81).

University studies in the USA (Western Illinois University): Certificate of English as a Second Language (1983), Bachelor of Science (Agricultural Economics, 1987), Master of Arts in Economy (1988).

In 1989, he starts as collaborator of the UNDP in Malabo. Since 1996, professor of the UNED.

In 1998 he was vice resident representative of UNDP.

Abaga Edjang has published several studies on African and Equato-Guinean Economy.

ABAGA NDONG, Francisco. He was vice-minister of Employment and Social Security in the January 21, 1998, government.

ABAGA ONDO BINDANG, Alberto. From Mongomo. General Secretary of the Ministry of the Interior from 1982 onwards. In 1987 he became general secretary of the Nguemist "Democratic" Party of Equatorial Guinea.

ABAGA ONDO MAYE, Eusebio. An Esangui from Mongomo. TV technician. Married to Concepcíon Nguema, a cousin of President Obiang Nguema. Was director of the television service from 1968 to 1969. After the 1979 coup, he became adviser to the Supreme Military Council for Information and Tourism. In March 1981 he was accused of association with a conspiracy led by Mbá Ada and dismissed. However, in December 1981 he was made presidential adviser of information, and at the end of 1982 promoted to Secretary of State for Information.

From 1988 to 1991, he was ambassador to the U.S.S.R. Arrested in 1991, along with notables of the Macías Nguema period, as part of the controversy over multipartism. His brother, A. Ondo Maye, a priest, was arrested for expressing his protest.

From 1992 onwards, he was a militant in Popular Union and was arrested in December along with students and professors of the capital, and tortured. Upon release, he described torture involving rubber whips applied to prisoners made to lie on the bare floor. He denounced Armengol Nguema and Manuel Nguema, brother and uncle to the dictator Obiang Nguema. He sought refuge in Gabon.

ABAYAK. Obiang Nguema's surname, as child. Soon after his coup d'etat in August 1979, Obiang Nguema bought, at a ridiculously low price, a cocoa plantation located on the road to the airport of the capital (3 km). He called this property Aabayak, and transformed it into a large housing estate. Teodorín Nguema Obiang lives in this compound, where are also located the offices and accomodations of the Mobil Oil Staff and other American companies. The Abayak estate is guarded by the Ninjas.

ABESO, Acacio see Evinayong

ABESO FUMA, Faustino (alias Tito Garriga). From Bata. Did not complete his baccalaureate. Trained to be an airplane mechanic in the Soviet Union. Upon his return, he married one of Obiang Nguema's daughters. A member of the presidential escort and security. Upon promotion to captain, he took part in the repression and torture. On May 8, 1995, with the back-up generator of the presidential palace out of fuel during a general failure of the electrical network, he was the one sent to beg the American petroleum company Walter Int. for fuel.

In December 1998, he was still aide-de-camp of his father-in-law.

ABESCO ONDO, Andrés. From Niefang. Born in Añisok. Holds a degree in law (Soviet Union). In January 1994, he became a judge in the Court of First Instance in the continental region.

ABIA BITEO BORICO, Miguel. Born in 1961. Became vice-minister under Juan Olo Mba, minister for mines and petrochemicals in the January 8, 1996, government. He holds a seat in the administrative council of APEGESA and LITOR-WELE. On April 8, 1996, he became secretary of state for mines and Energy. He hoped that petroleum production will reach 500,000 b/d by the year 2000.

In the government of January 21, 1998, he was minister delegate of economic affairs and finance.

A.B.M. (Astimex, Bisa, Matransa). In 1992, Obiang Nguema signed the founding contract for the A.B.M. Lumber Company, along with M. M. Varona and Bartolome Llompart Coro. These companies owed the public treasury CFA Fr 3,000 million; the contract erased these debts. A.B.M. was permitted to import petrol free of duty. See also Mafesa; Nzambi Machinde, F.; Obiang Nguema, T.; Timber; Vilarrasa Balanza, S.

ABRIL CASTELLON, Santos see Vatican

ABUY, Indalecio see Convergency for Social Democracy; Niefang

ACCION NACIONAL DE LIBERACION DE GUINEA ECUATORIAL (ANALIGE) (National Action for the Liberation of Equatorial Guinea). Movement set up in Andorra in August 1972 by Esteban Nsué Ngomo, J. Mbá Nsué, and E. Bodipo. Two years before, Nsué Ngomo had founded another reactionary movement, the Frente de Liberación de Guinea Ecuatorial (FRELIGE), connected with the former Spanish interests in Equatorial Guinea. While Nsué Ngomo's faction attended the founding Congress of Alianza Nacional de Restauración Democrática (ANRD), held in Geneva August 17-19, 1974, Mbá Nsué's faction joined Mariano Nsué Nguema, Antonio Masogo, and Antonio Ondo Mondo. ANALIGE is a strongly conservative group working in close cooperation with the Spanish extreme right (known as "Bunker"). It has not been active at all since the 1979 coup d'etat.

ACCION POPULAR (AP) see Popular Action

ADARO (National mineral prospecting company, Spain). Affiliated with the Spanish group INI. On May 28, 1980, this enterprise, founded in cooperation with the Nguemist dictatorship, the prospecting company GEMSA (a joint Spanish, Equatorial Guinean mining company). ADARO contributed 45% of the capital. The company's activities did not cover the exploration of petroleum resources or of radioactive ores. In 18 months of prospecting, ADARO collected 8,000 samples and drew up a geophysical map of the country. According to ADARO's chairman, the company invested 340 million pesetas. It seems that they purchased, together with the French company BRGM, the geological data belonging to the Spanish lawyer Garcia Trevijano, former economic adviser to Macías Nguema.

ADDAX BV ROTTERDAM. Dutch Company for the commercialization of petroleum products with its headquarters in Geneva (Switzerland). It buys concentrates extracted by Walter Int. from the deposits at Alba. Also present in Ivory Coast. See also Petroleum.

ADEEYAH (Pop.) see Bubi

ADJIA LIFIDA. Fulbé chief of Ngaoundéré (Cameroon) sought refuge in Fernando Po with the German troops in 1916, and settled at Pequeño-Bokoko. In 1919, together with Chief Atangana and other chiefs, he signed a petition to the king of Spain appealing for a return to a German-administered Cameroon.

ADMINISTRATION. After Owen's expedition in 1827, the island of Fernando Po was placed completely under British administration until 1843, when Beecroft became governor of the island with Spain's consent. A decree of December 13 settled the administrative and organic status of the colony for the first time. Another decree dated November 12, 1868, recorded the failure of this first effort and announced the granting of concessions for Spanish colonists as well as suppression of taxes on foreign trade. Infantry troops were sent to Santa Isabel, the island capital, and the chief of the naval station of this town became gobernador general (governors-general) of the colony. In 1969 a consultative "Junta de Autoridades" (Council of Local Authorities) was set up; because of the failure of colonization efforts, a Consejo de Gobierno (Government council) composed of navy officers, the Santa Isabel parish priest, and others was set up in 1872 to assist the governor. The Overseas Ministry was responsible for Spanish Guinea. In 1899 this ministry was abolished, and the Spanish possessions of the Gulf of Guinea came under the direct authority of the head of government; then, from 1901 to 1925, under the State Ministry. In 1925 the Dirección General de Marruecos y Colonias (Directorate General for Morocco and Colonies) was founded to deal with the granting of concessions at the very time the Spanish government was determined to fully occupy Río Muni, Bata becoming the headquarters of the local government. The colonial guard was in charge of maintaining order and administering the territories.

The lack of interest shown by Spain for its Guinean Gulf possessions is best expressed in the succession of the 65 gobernadores general (governors general) between 1865 and 1910. With the beginning of the 20th century, Spanish Guinea became an exploitation colony rather than a settlement one. During the dictatorship of Primo de Rivera (and under Governor General Nuñez de Prado), Río Muni was fully occupied. Whereas the Curador Colonial and the Patronato de Indígenas had chaperoned the natives since 1905, the "Dirección General de Marruecos y Colonias" started distributing concessions in 1928. Thanks to a special budget in 1926, various roads, schools, and medical facilities appeared. But the setting up of the Spanish Republic in 1931 slowed down this development. A new administrative distribution was introduced with three districts in Fernando Po and 10 in Río Muni. In 1938 the colony came under the full authority of the head of "Direccion General de Marruecos y Colonias," under the supervision of the head of state, taking the name of Spanish Territories of the Gulf of Guinea. After Franco's victory, the districts were reorganized and the administrators' tasks clarified. With provincialization from 1960 to 1964, two provinces appeared: Río Muni (with Corisco, Elobeyes, and other islands) and Fernando Po (with Annobón). The "Dirección General de Marruecos y Colonias" became "Dirección General de Plazas y Provincias Africanas" (General Department for African Towns and Provinces), directed by the head of the Spanish government. The governor general, placed directly under the head of government's authority, was the highest authority in the colony. He was assisted by two gobernadores civiles (civil governors) and a secretary ggeneral. Ayuntamientos (District Councils) and Diputaciones Provinciales (Provincial Assemblies) replaced the "Patronato de Indígenas." In the provinces, the Guinean administration became an exact copy of the metropolitan one, with all Spanish staff members remaining in their offices. The year 1964 marked the beginning of autonomy with a greater administrative and economic freedom, but without the right to political self-government. Spanish Guinea was at that time headed by a Consejo de Gobierno (Governmental Council), assuming the principal tasks of the ex-governor general who became commissioner general. The legislative power was vested in an interprovincial Asamblea General (General Assembly).

After independence, in October 1968, a Consejo de Ministros (Cabinet), an Asamblea de la República (House of Representatives), and a Consejo de la República (Senate) were set up. However, administration remained highly centralized, all authority coming from the president of the republic and the two provinces being placed under the authority of the Civil Governors. The administrative apparatus rapidly became too large because of its growing politicization, which led to an important budget deficit starting in 1969. In 1971, 6,692 civil servant positions were budgeted, half of which went to the presidency, the assemblies, foreign and domestic affairs, and defense, and the other half to technical ministries. The provinces had their own staff (2,700 civil servants). No staff member had any guarantee of employment. Salaries have remained unchanged since 1968.

Since the 1979 coup d'etat, a Cameroonian, Mesa Bill Congue, has been in charge of the administration in the post of secretary general. By virtue of Decree 12/1980, civil servants are forbidden to engage in commercial activities, but agricultural production is tolerated.

In March 1980 a number of internal boundaries were changed, including an enlargement of the Mongomo district, which was renamed Wele-Nzas. Eighty percent of the leading members of the Nguemist dictatorship come from this district. The newly formed districts were as follows:

A. Continental region: Coastal district (capital Bata), with four wards; South-Central district (capital Evinayong), three wards; Kie-Ntem (capital Ebebiyin), three wards; Wele-Nzas (capital Mongomo), four wards.

B. Island region: Fernando-Po North, two wards; Fernando-Po South, San Carlos commune; Annobón, Palé commune.

Under the terms of a decree of April 20, 1980, the number of civil servants was limited to 3,000. Effective May 1981, Obiang Nguema decided to move the capital for four months every year to Bata, but in reality he remained confined to his palace in Santa Isabel protected by Moroccan soldiers. In May 1980 also, the village councils (consejos de poblados) were reinstated and the Martin Luther King School of Public Administration was reopened with L. Madiba as director and P. Mbomio as director of studies. All the available information points to the corruption in the Nguemist administration as well as to the dominance of the Esangui from the Wele-Nzas district.

In 1985, the number of officials in the central government was reduced from 4,500 to 2,500 (salary: CFA Fr 15,000). S. Muñoz Ylata was named minister for the interior and communications in October 1990. The reform of the administration failed. In 1991, out of 5,349 civil servants, only 196 (3.7%) were university graduates.

The following individuals figured in the January 24, 1992, "transitional" government: minister for public administration and administrative coordination, Ciriaco Tamarite Burgos; minister for the interior, J. Ndong Ela Mangue, who retained the post he had occupied since the December 22, 1993, government. Following the November elections, the government officials who were unable to produce their stamped election card were deprived of their December salary.

In 1994, Morocco trained territorial administration executives. In May, the government announced that at the insistence of the IMF and the IBRD it was going to reduce the number of central government officials (5,600) by 10%. With some reluctance, the Parliament accepted a 14% increase in salaries (the effective devaluation of the CFA Fr was 50%). Obiang Nguema benefited from the demands for structural adjustments to liquidate government officials who were also political adversaries (especially from UP), including Hilario Nsue Alene, ex-minister for planning and development; Enrique Matogo, ex-minister for civil service; Manuel Nse Nsogo, ex-director of presidential protocol; as well as a number of professors and doctors, mostly Bubis.

Angel Serafin Seriche Dougan became the secretary of state for public administration in the new government which came into power on January 8,1996. In the April 8, 1996, government, he was also entrusted with the post of prime minister. Francisco-Javier Ngomo Mbengono was simultaneously vice-prime-minister and minister for public administration and administrative reform. He was aided by Fernando Mabale Mba Nomo as minister with special responsibilities for public administration and administrative reform. Just as the government is dominated by the Mongomo clan, the majority of posts of general secretaries and general directors, in all of the administrations, are entrusted to people coming out of Mongomo or its province (Wele-Nzas). In the ministerial reshuffle of January 21,

1998, Mba Mabale was named minister of civil service and administrative reforms. Julio Ndong Ela Mangue is minister of territorial administration and local government.

According to the UNDP, the administration suffers from constant changes in the governmental structure. See also Salaries.

ADOUAL. Commercial firm with headquarters in the Canary Islands, managed by the Lebanese Juan Cecin. As of 1975 the company benefited from the collaboration of D. Oyono Ayingono, nephew of Macías Nguema. Adoual was in direct competition with Garcia Trevijano's Simed S. A.

ADVENTISTS see Protestantism

AFFAIR MARCEAU LOUIS see Louis, Marceau

AFFAIR OF SENIOR OFFICIALS see Senior Officials Affair

AFRICAN COMPANY FOR COASTAL NAVIGATION (Sociedad Africana de Cabotage) see Belgium

AFRICAN DEVELOPMENT BANK (ADB). Granted a $650,000 loan in October 1979, to be repaid over a period of 10 years, for the renovation of Bata Airport. Financed various projects (cocoa, Bata Airport) in 1982. The African Development Fund contributed to the construction of the National Institute for Agriculture in Santa Isabel. The ADB declared its support for the development of food crops, an animal farm in Moka, and a poultry farm. It looked into projects for the construction of a primary school and a teachers training college, the renovation of the Bata hospital, nonindustrial fisheries, regeneration of palm groves, softening of water, and road maintenance.

In 1985, the ADB granted loans for improvements to the Bata and Santa Isabel Airports, the electrification of 10 towns and for health projects. See also Aviation.

AFRIPESCA. Affiliated firm of Spanish company Frigopesquera. The company owns two cold warehouses (Santa Isabel and Bata) kept at -20° C. In 1966 deep-frozen stocks included a thousand metric tons of fish from Spanish Guinea. Under Macías Nguema this installation was ruined. The enterprise was brought back into being in 1980 by Ramon Vizcaino Company.

See also Fisheries; Ndong Ela Nzang, E.

AGGOR. Company connected with the Banco Exterior de España, owning a 500-hectares (approximately 1,240-acre) oil palm plantation at Río M'Bañe (Río Muni), producing 7,500 ton-clusters a year. The factory is inoperative. Aggor also owned a forest exploitation near Río Benito, and coffee plantations.

AGIP. An Italian petroleum company. It was part of a drilling consortium in Río Muni, towards the end of 1983, along with Elf Aquitaine, Ultramar, and Murphy.

AGRICULTURE, Ministry of. Called Ministry of Soil Cultivation since 1973. See also specific entries such as Coffee; Oil Palms, etc., and Camara Oficial Agrícola.

After the 1979 coup, the responsibility for agriculture was entrusted to Obiang Enama. In 1980, forced recruitment of labor for cocoa plantations began in Río

Muni. Peasants were given a booklet making it possible to check on their activities and movements. The African Development Bank planned to start 5,000 hectares of cocoa plantations. The European Development Fund wanted to help small peasants with market gardening and animal husbandry at Moca. USaid brought in $1 million for the cooperatives (tractors) and for the poultry farm in Basile. The FAO delivered 5,000 chicks. The Spanish planters preferred receiving compensation, rather than return. The Supreme Military Council intended to launch an Agricultural Development Bank.

In 1981 the first civilian in the military government, Emiliano Buale, an agricultural engineer, was named the minister for agriculture. In October 1982, Miguel Oyono Ndongo Mifumu became minister, and Angel Alogo Nchama, secretary of state, when E. Buale sought refuge in Spain. Towards the end of 1984, the country enjoyed the benefits of $45 million in agricultural projects (IBRD, BAD, EEC, Spain, France, Fida, ILO, GDR, North and South Korea, FAO, FENU).

The new minister in 1986 was Alfredo Abeso Nvono Onguene. The National Institute for Agriculture was inaugurated at the outskirts of the capital. In October 1990 Anatolio Ndong Mba became minister. An agricultural diversification project aimed at liberating the country from its dependence on cocoa was launched.

The school of agriculture was managed by Trinidad Morgades Besari from 1993 onwards. Alfred Mukudi Nnanga became the minister for agriculture, fisheries, and food. There were measures, such as the suspension of a part of the Spanish aid in late 1993, which affected the experimental farms, the teachers in the School for Agriculture, and grants in favor of the establishment. Equatorial Guinea was ignored by the FAO statistics. According to the FAO, in 1994, on a total national area of 2,805,000 hectares, only 230,000 ha are cultivated. The rural population represents 71% of the entire population.

In 1996, 8.1% of the land was cultivated; 78% of the working population was involved in agriculture. The agricultural balance was always positive. Sixty percent of the national product comes from agriculture. In June the first twenty students of the National Institute for Agriculture graduated. In June 1997, the dictatorship blackmailed Bubi planters in Fernando Po: you will get sulphate and lime only if you sign a document proving your support of Obiang Nguema. The French agricultural project of Niefang was stopped at the end of 1997, and represents yet another failure of the nguemist regime.

In the government of January 21, 1998, Constantino Ekong Nsue is Minister of Agriculture, Fishing and Cattle-rearing. At the end of 1998, agricultural production was dropping and food producing agriculture only responds to domestic comsumtion. See also African Development Bank; Alogo Nchama, A.; Buale Borico, E.; Cattle; Choni Bekoba, V.; Cocoa; Coffee; Dirección de Agricultura; Education; European Union; Fisheries; Germany; Mba Ndemensogo, D.; Missions; Modu Akuse Bindang, C.; Mokudi Nanga, A.; Nculu Asumu, A.; Ndong Mba, A.; Nepotism; Niefang; Nvono Nka Manene, C.; Oyono Ndong Mifumu, M.; Salaries; Siale Bilekia, S.; Timber; Toro, G.; United Nations; University; World Council of Churches.

AGROFORESTAL see Timber

AGRUPACION DEMOCRATICA Y SOCIAL (ADSOGE) see Social and Democratic Group

AIDS. Between 1979 and 1990, five cases had been counted; in 1993, there were 12. In 1994 WHO estimated about 2,000 cases (0.5% of total population), Cameroon 1.3%, Gabon 1%, Nigeria 1%. Towards the middle of 1995, there were 157 medically diagnosed cases of AIDS, mostly in Bata and Santa Isabel, but the authorities officially acknowledged only 74 cases. The national program to fight AIDS is directed by Dr. Manuel Nsué.

AKALAYONG. Locality to the southwest of Río Muni, occupied by Gabon in 1985 for petroleum drilling. Loud protests from Obiang Nguema helped avoid its annexation. There is a boat connecting Akalayong to Kogo and Cocobeach. The EDF proposes to restore the Akalayong-Río Benito road. At Easter 1994, the army made a violent foray into Akalayong for unknown reasons. In early October, upon their return from a conference in Libreville, three opposition party executives (Mikó Abogo, Bolekia Bonay, and Mecheba Ikaka) were arrested in Akalayong, taken to Bata, and tortured. See also Benito; Bolekia Bonay, V.; Borders; Convergency for Social Democracy; Gabon; Kogo; Mecheba Ikaka, J.; Miko Abogo, P.; Navigation; Río Benito; Transports.

AKOAKAM. A locality of Río Muni, near Mongomo, where Macías Nguema and Obiang Nguema were born and where Obiang Nguema has a palace. Secondary school students from Akoakam were urged, at the end of October 1993, by the threats of the general secretary of the Ministry of Mines and Petrochemicals, to become members of the PDGE.

In 1987, seven Franciscan Conceptionist nuns from Benicarlo (Spain) started the country's first convent for a meditative life. In January 1989, a monastery was inaugurated by the Franciscans of Toledo.

In 1993, the priest Job Nze Obiang was evicted from the locality by the Nguemists. On October 4, Mgr. Juan Matogo anointed the first Equato-Guinean Contemplative nun. Members of the opposition were terrorized by Nicolas Obama Owono, a nephew of Obiang Nguema (with two years of secondary school education followed by failure at the Military Academy of Nigeria), who had been appointed representative of the government.

In March 1994, Amnesty International denounced the violent torture inflicted on Norberto Mba Nze, Akonibe representative of the Convergency for Social Democracy. In April 1995, Mba Nze was again arrested in the Moto Nsá case.

See also Convergency for Social Democracy; Garcia Barleycorn, F.; Matogo Oyana, J.; Mba Ondo, C.; Missions; Ndong Ela Mangue, J.; Nguema Ndong, A.; Nkogo Ondo, E.; Nsue Nchama, J. M.; Nve Nzeng, A. F.; Parliament; Rono Macoso; Rufina, Maria; Siale Bilekia, S.; Si Ondo, S.; Sitoko Buiyaban, T.; Torture; Victims.

AKONIBE. A community of 1,700 inhabitants. Some Nguemist ministers were involved in a 400-million-peseta fraud in a nearby pineapple plantation belonging to the Spanish company PEDASA. It was here that the Constitutional Commission held its meeting in May 1982, which led to the Constitution that was submitted to popular vote in August and which served to consolidate the power base of the dictator Obiang Nguema.

In 1997, Hipólito Mba Sima, a government delegate, tortured members of the CPDS there.

AKURENAM. Located in south-central Río Muni, close to the Gabonese border, 45 km from Evinayong. In 1941 a large manioc plantation was started. The town had a military garrison, a hospital, a secondary boarding school run by Oblate Sisters, and an English Evangelist Mission; the school and mission were closed in 1973. After Pope John Paul II's visit to Santa Isabel in February 1982 it was decided to reopen the missionary center.

In 1992, Eulalia Mangue, an agent of the presidential security force, became the mayor of this town. Captain Obama Nsue (alias Ncoa-Bidoló), of Akurenam, was the government's representative. Having taken refuge in Gabon under Macías Nguema, he returned after Obiang Nguema's coup d'etat and joined the presidential escort, of which he remained a member until he became the Commissioner for presidential security. He participated in brief training sessions in Morocco and in the United States. At age 17, his daughter Celestine was delivered of Obiang Nguema's child.

During the municipal elections of September 1995, the offices of Esculape and Calasancra priests were broken into and ransacked under the order of the provincial governor who was attempting to locate an alleged antigovernment radio transmitter. In spite of the strength of the opposition, it was the PDGE that emerged victorious in the elections. There are important amounts of colubite-tantalite in the veins of pegmatite in the area of Akonibe. See also Elections; Mabala Mba Nomo, F.; Nguema Esono Nchama, B.; Nsue Nguema Nsuga, M.; Obiang Nguema, T.; Parliament; Progress Party; Victims.

ALAR AYONG. "Unity of the clans" in Fang. A Ntumu Fang movement. The Ntumu Fangs were educated by American Presbyterian missionaries during the 1930s. The movement aimed at reuniting the Fangs (*lato sensu*) by resisting the colonial yoke. The colonizers, especially France, tried to stop the movement, which has now, towards the end of the 20th century, been revived. See also Bwiti.

ALADA. Spanish incorporated company with a monopoly of sales of oil products in Equatorial Guinea. Since 1985 replaced by the French Total-Equatorial Guinea.

ALBA OIL FIELD see Petroleum

ALEN, Mount. Located in Río Muni, 50 km. away from the Atlantic Ocean, Mt. Alen is part of the Niefang mountain ranger, south-west of Mr. Chocolate. Mt. Alen National Park covers 1,400 km^2 of dense and humid forest, at an altitude of 300 m. to 1,200 m. (900 ft. to 3,600 ft.). It is characterized by an uneven ground with many rapids and wateralls; these waterfalls could be used to produce electricity. The forest shelters a flora and wildlife that are typical of the forest area of Atlantic Guinea, rich in plants belonging to the Caesalpiniaceai family. The wildlife offers more than 105 species of mammals, 16 of which are primates. Toward the south, Mt. Alen National Park joins Mt. Mitra National Park by means of a large 600 m^2 forest corridor. Ten percent of the country's surface is a protected area.

ALENA (Compañía Nacional de Colonización en Africa) (National Company for Colonization in Africa). Company connected with the Banco Exterior de España, of which the former president of the Spanish government, Carrero Blanco, was the main stockholder. Established in Guinea in the second half of the 19th century, ALENA owned important timber and agricultural concessions in Río Muni (Río Utonde, Etembue, etc.). In Fernando Po, ALENA owned coffee plantations and a large cattle ranch of 3,000 hectares (approximately 7,400 acres) near Moka. In 1926 ALENA purchased the Trasatlántica shipping company which, at that time, monopolized all communications with the colony. In March 1969 ALENA's activities were interrupted by order of Macías Nguema. In Gabon, ALENA is connected with the Song consortium (Société de l'Okoume de la Ngoumé S.A.). The company began limited operations again in 1980.

ALENE MBA, Margarita. In the April 8, 1996, government, she became minister of social affairs and the condition of women. She retains this function of the Government of January 21, 1998.

ALIANZA DEMOCRATICA PROGRESISTA (ADP) see Democratic Progressive Alliance

ALIANZA NACIONAL PARA LA RESTAURACION DEMOCRATICA (ANRD) see National Alliance for the Restoration of Democracy

ALLEN, William, 1792-1864. British naval commander who participated in an expedition of the Niger River in 1832 (Lander-Oldfield). He left a series of six engravings of Santa Isabel and Mount Cameroon, as well as an account of a second mission to Fernando Po in 1841.

ALMONTE Y MURIEL, Enrique, 1858-1917. An explorer and cartographer; he was in charge of determining the Río Muni and Cameroon border in 1906. He planned a transafrican railway with Río Muni as the possible starting point.

ALOBARI. Brother of King Bubi Malabo, whom he succeeded to the throne in 1937.

ALOGO NCHAMA, Angel. Fang from Akurenam. Agricultural engineer trained in Spain. Appointed director of agriculture in 1980. Promoted to secretary of state for rural development in October 1982 and appointed minister of forestry and water resources in January 1986.
   Condemned in 1989 for corruption. Pardoned in August 1990. Favors discussions with the opposition.
   Minister of forestry and agriculture in the "transition government" of January 1992. Dropped from the government in December 1993. Named counsellor to the president's civil cabinet for economic and financial affairs of January 19, 1994. In 1998, he was counselor of the government for Water Resources and Forestry.
   See also Coup d'etat of December 1987; Mongomo; Redondo; Timber.

ALONSO ALONSO, Mariano. Governor general from 1942 to 1943. After attempting to become king of the Bubi, he was dismissed.

ALVAREZ CORUGEDO, Juan. Spanish economist, responsible for the 1964-66 development plan of Equatorial Guinea.

ALVAREZ GARCIA, Heriberto. Inspector general of education in Spanish Guinea and director of the Instituto Colonial Indígena (secondary school) from 1944 to 1955. Thanks to him, teachers' training programs were extended from six months to five years. For having proposed an alignment of teachers' salaries with those of other servants, he was dismissed in 1948 along with Governor General Bonelli Rubio.

AMBAM. Town in south Cameroon where the IPGE had its headquarters before independence. Since 1969, Ambam had a refugee camp of Equato-Guineans, which moved further north in 1974.

AMNESTIES. On October 12, 1979, two months after taking power, Obiang Nguema declared an amnesty for all citizens who had fled from the Nguemist dictatorship, of which he was one of the founders. The Equatorial Guinean diaspora accused the regime of hypocrisy. Only a few hundred political refugees returned, mainly members of the Obiang and Nguema families.

On October 12, 1991, Obiang Nguema decreed a verbal amnesty similar to the one in October 1979. According to article 1, "All Equato-Guinean nationals who, having sought political asylum abroad, now wish to return of their own free will, may do so without fear of persecution or punishment for having abandoned the Republic of Equatorial Guinea." This article is in violation not only of the Universal Declaration of Human Rights: "All individuals have the right to leave any country, including his own, and to return to his country," but also of the International Agreement on Civil and Political Rights: "No one may be arbitrarily deprived of his right to enter his own country." A number of Equato-Guinean nations who have taken the risk of returning have become victims of violence and have returned to exile.

On August 2, 1995, Obiang Nguema decreed a general amnesty for political prisoners including Moto Nsá. See also Benito; Motu Mamiaga, P.; Obiang Nguema, T.; Río Benito (Mbini); UNICEF; Volio-Jimenez, F.

AMNESTY INTERNATIONAL. In April 1975 this organization asked Macías Nguema to cease tortures and atrocities. The 1977 report of Amnesty International on Equatorial Guinea confirms the existence of torture and other atrocities.

After Equatorial Guinea came into the Western orbit, interests have taken advantage of this silence, interpreting it as proof of the absence of violations of human rights by the regime. Nevertheless, the Amnesty International report of 1986 gave details of the arrest in 1985 of parliamentarians while carrying out their official duties, on charges of having "insulted the Head of State."

In May 1987 Amnesty International circulated a very detailed report on the military tribunals and the death sentences in Equatorial Guinea. The document stresses concern about the illegal application of death sentences; the lack of impartiality and independence of these tribunals—which are usually composed of officers with concurrent political tasks; the lack of even minimal guarantees for defense; the denial of the right of appeal; the sentencing of civilians by military tribunals; and the absence of any right of protection against self-incrimination.

In 1992 and 1993, Amnesty International denounced cases of arbitrary arrests and torture of members of the Convergency for Social Democracy. It expressed its concern at the torture, the unfair trials, death sentences, and routine assassinations. In March 1994, it published a document on "Detentions since the holding of elections in November 1993."

In 1994-96, Amnesty International was forced to publish several *Urgent Actions* concerning the regime's arrest of several civilians and military personnel, most of whom were exposed to torture. The 1996 AI report stated that hundreds of opponents were detained for several days or weeks; a number of them were political prisoners. Two obviously unfair political trials were held; those condemned were however released upon presidential amnesty. Recourse to the torture of political prisoners was widespread. Two persons were said to have been executed. The report stressed the "systematic repression of the militants and violence exercised with impunity by security forces."

In the capital, in Bata and throughout Río Muni, repressive measures were taken against the opposition after the announcement of Moto Nsá's attempted coup in June 1997. Amanacio Gabriel Nze, head of the CPDS, is arrested along with a dozen other members. According to AI, the government cannot bear the opposition. Many members of the FDR were also arrested, among whom were relatives of Eloy Olo Nvo Mbengono.

Two members of Amnesty International were allowed to attend the trial of more than 100 Bubi on May 25, 1998. AI asked for clemency toward the 15 people condemned to the death penalty, underlying that torture had been used and that the trial lacked credibility. On July 10, while reporting the prisoners' pitiful conditions of detention, AI described it as "slow execution." In September, AI was happy to find out that Obiang Nguema had commuted the death sentence. But AI had to protest several times against the inhuman conditions of imprisonment in the jail of Playa Negra, and the total lack of medical care.

See also Bubi; Ngomo Ndumu, A.; Nguemism; Public Health; Victims.

ANDEME see Ekong Andeme, Pedro

ANDEME ELA, María del Carmen. Born 1958. Esangui from Nzang-Along. Daughter of Pedro Ela Nguema, chief of Macías Nguema's civil house. Nurse training in Cuba. In the April 8, 1996 ministerial reshuffle, she became director general for medical assistance and coordination.

ANDOMBE BUANGA, Gabriel. Fang, born 1938. An economist from Añisok. Appointed director of the Banco de Credito y Desarrollo in September 1979. Arrested in April 1981 for participation in an alleged conspiracy and sentenced to six years in jail, he was pardoned by Obiang Nguema on August 3, 1981. Shortly afterwards he took refuge in Spain, where he joined the Junta Civica de Salvación Nacional.

Envisions a Social Union of Equatorial Guinea with a development project and a plan for a transition to democracy involving the aid of Spain and avoiding French influence, a project that led nowhere.

In 1992, Andombe Buanga was forced to close down his pub in Valencia (Spain) due to drug peddling on the premises. In May 1995, he founded the Foro Social de Reconciliación Nacional, which later became the Foro para la Democrácia and enjoyed the support of a number of Spanish people. This project never dame through. Andombe works as a tradesman between Valencia (Spain) and Cameroon.

See also Civil Junta for National Salvation; Elema Borengue, J.

"ANGABI" see Navigation Company of Equatorial Guinea

ANGLO-SPANISH EMPLOYMENT AGENCY (ASEA). Agency in charge of recruiting Nigerian workers, located at Calabar, under the supervision of a Board of Directors since 1953.

ANGOLA. Between 1975 and 1976, 9,000 Cubans passed through the port of San Carlos on their way to Angola. In 1989, a military agreement was signed for a possible replacement of the Moroccan presidential guards and for possible cooperation between the air forces. The agreement remained nonoperational. An Angolan delegation was present at the first convention of the PDGE held in the spring of 1995 at Bata.

In August 1998, four days of discussion were held between ministers of the interior, the issue being the reinforcement of co-operation and friendship. A visit of Cabina was scheduled.

ANGUE ONDO, Purificación. Born 1943. Obiang Nguema's sister-in-law. From Angong-Obug (Mongomo), the native village of Obiang Nguema's wife. A highly pro-Spanish school teacher trained in Santa Isabel. Nicknamed "la Huevera" (prolific child-bearer) by the public for her numerous half-breed daughters and son (Miguelin). Lived in Gabon under Macías Nguema's regime. Returned to the country after Obiang Nguema's coup d'etat. Close to Carmelo Modu Akuse.

Secretary of state for women's rights from 1982. Responsible for the creation of the new single party, she participated in the formation of the PDGE. Became vice-minister for women's rights in 1989 but lost the post in 1992.

In 1995, upon becoming minister for social welfare and national delegate for the Women's Wing of the PDGE, she was elected to the Central Committee at the 2nd Convention. The POC journal, *La Verdad,* alleged that she was guilty of the torture inflicted in 1995 on Primo José Esono, who was then receiving medical treatment in Spain. See also Esono Miko, P. J. E.; Olo Mba Nseng, J.; Torture.

AÑISOK. Small town in north-central Río Muni, close to Mikomeseng, formerly called Bimbiles. Many inhabitants of this town and surrounding districts were victims of the Nguemist terror, including Deputies Ebang Masié and Ebang Mbele. The prison still holds political detainees.

In 1979, local chiefs confirmed the practice of forced labor. In late 1992, an Argentinean priest was threatened with expulsion for opposing the practice of polygamy. The government's representative was Florentino Cogo Ndong (alias Nkoke) from Mongomo (a member of the Youth Marching with Macías) who used to torture his schoolmates in Bata. After the 1979 coup d'etat, he became an agent of the presidential security force in the educational buildings of Bata. In spite of having abandoned his studies, he became chief of the presidential security force and was then transferred to Añisok.

In the September 1995 municipal elections, Eduardo Ebang Mesie (PDGE) was elected mayor. In July 1996 several members of the CPDS were arrested and sentenced to hard labor.

The hospital has been modernized with the help of Nigeria. On July 23, 1998, three Catholc missionaries were expelled from Añisok.

See also Abeso Ondo, A.; Andombe Buanga, G.; Bengono Miko, R.; Bivini Mangue, S.; Catholicism; Ela Abeme, F. J.; Esono Abaga, A.; Kogo; Mafesa; Ndong Micha Mia, A.; Nguema Owono, S.; Nsobeya Efuman Nsue, S.; Nsue Obama Engono, P.; Obiang Abogo, V.; Parliament; Timber; Victims.

AÑISOK MONGOLA see Timber

ANNOBON. Volcanic island located 160 km off São Tomé-Principe and 355 km west of Cape López (Gabon) 940 km from Corisco and 680 km from Fernando Po; the area is 18 sq km (i.e., 7 sq miles). It is a volcanic peak emerging from a deep base (4,000 m below sea level) with four summits, among which are Pico de Fogo (600 m) and Mazofín (831 m) of recent basaltic origin. Its coastline is abrupt, except in the north where the chief town San Antonio de Palé is located. The island has two rain seasons: April to July and October to November and is covered with rich equatorial type of vegetation. The island counts 17 endemic species (8 plants, 3 reptiles). The population (about 1,500) is formed of Bantu of Angola and São Tomé/Príncipe, and Bubi. The language is Portuguese Creole.

The island was seen for the first time in 1471-72 by João de Santarem and Pedro Escobar, two Portuguese navigators, but it is Ruy Sequeiro who first set foot on it on January 1, 1474, thus the name "Anno Bon" (New Year). At the end of the 16th-century, a governor, a teacher, and some Africans from São Tomé were sent to Annobón. At first the property of Jorge de Melo, the island was sold later to Luis de Almeida, who extended its population. The Dutch "Nassau" expedition reached Annobón in 1623. During the 17th century vain evangelization attempts were made among the population. Missionary expeditions in 1757 and 1770 also failed. In 1778 the island became a Spanish possession under the Pardo Treaty. Spain sent out the Argelejos/Primo de Rivera expedition, which failed because of Argelejos's death (believed to have been killed by the Annobónese) and the sailors' rebellion. In 1827 the Spanish government offered to sell Annobón and Fernando Po to the British, who accepted the offer in 1839, but Spanish public opinion was strongly opposed and brought about the failure of the transaction in 1841. The effective possession of the island took place with the Lerena expedition (1843). In 1856 the French hoisted their flag on Annobón, which led to complaints to the French ambassador in Madrid. The schooner Santa Teresa arrived in Annobón, in September 1859. Its aim was to recruit workers, but it failed because the population made it very difficult. Only in 1885 at the time when the Germans attempted to occupy the island did the first missionary school open (Claretians). The only Europeans on the island before independence were six Spanish missionaries and a detachment of the Guardia Civil (Civil Guard). In 1902, Leonardo Fa collected ants (Strumienys Zandala). In 1932, 121 trade-unionists from Barcelona were deported to Annobón. From 1907 to 1942, Annobón had a separate administrative district; then it became integrated in the Bata district. Since 1960, it has been attached to the insular province of Fernando Po.

The inhabitants live off whaling (see Fisheries). But since the beginning of the 20th century, the British and Norwegians have practically depleted the whale stock in the region. For lack of work on the island, many Annobonese work on foreign fishing boats or as soldiers in the Guardia Nacional (National Guard).

At the Constitutional Conference of 1967-68, Annobón was represented by Castellón Ntayo and S. Mun. During Autonomy, Guinea was represented in Spain by the Annobónese Castillo Barril (assassinated in 1973). The same year the island suffered from a cholera epidemic, which the government refused to control. In 1976, all sound men of Annobón were sent to forced labor in the Fernando Po cocoa plantations. In the same year the island seems to have become a supply base for the Soviet navy.

After the 1979 coup, a lower secondary school was established in Annobón as well as a radio-telephone link with the capital. A medical doctor was provided by the Spanish aid program. The Claretine Father Doce died there in 1975.

Under the regime of Macías Nguema the island was renamed Pagalu, partly in memory of a local chief named Mana Bizga, meaning "Father Rooster," and partly in honor of Macías Nguema whose electoral symbol was a rooster. After the fall of the Macías dictatorship, Annobón saw the construction of a middle school in 1980. The island received a visit from Vice-President Oyo Riqueza who was accompanied by Capitular Vicar J. T. Bosari. Under popular pressure, a decree decided that the island was to return to its name of Annobón.

From June to September 1981, the ORSTOM center located in Pointe-Noire measured power supplies around Annobon.

Since 1990, the island is considered as one of the Marine ptotected areas of the country.

Spain's plan for the conservation of nature accorded total protection to the island in 1986. An open letter signed by 11 citizens denounced criminal acts by the prisoners brought over to the island as well as the Nguemist troops.

In June 1988, Obiang Nguema signed a ten-year contract with a British firm for 2 million barrels of unsorted toxic waste deposits to be buried on Annobón, under an area of 200 hectares, for a payment of $1.6 million. Members of a UN delegation dated the first consignment August 1988. According to doctors, the island has the highest rate of skin infection and the highest percentage of lepers and tuberculosis patients in the world. Feliciano Obama Nsue (Mbato) who was sent to Annobón made his presence felt through acts of violence and the raping of little girls.

The population received a number of promises (airport, roads, etc.) during the presidential elections of 1989. In 1990, Segundo Muñoz Ylata, from Annobón, became minister for territorial administration and the president's counsellor on security matters.

Marcos Ondo Nze, a member of the central committee of the PDGE, was the island's governor in 1992-93. Anger at the government's unkept promises led the people to tear up the PDGE flag and swear that they would obey no president until the 1996 elections. The authorities were helpless in spite of the arrival of Muñoz Ilata to the island. Between March and April 1993, Marike Port, linguist of the University of Amsterdam, stayed on the island for Creole studies. Her report warned of total malnutrition. A Spanish cooperative mission confirmed the report, having found 3% of the children suffering from kwashiorkr and an infant mortality rate of 68%; 9.3% of the babies had low birth weight (4.5% before 1993). Extraordinary food aid and an agricultural project were proposed. The mission stressed the fact that the island was being punished by Obiang Nguema.

In May 1993, the Council of Elders signed a communiqué reiterating its refusal to participate in the elections. In June, the Nguemists prohibited all flights to Annobón and blocked Spanish planes carrying food and medicines. In August, the population mobbed the soldiers garrisoned at Annobón. Two hundred men and members of the Jovenes Antorchas and Ninjas were sent, under the command of Lt Col. Agustin Ndong Ona (Mongomo) and Gabriel Mbá Bela; they went about murdering and torturing people under the pretext of putting down an uprising in which they claimed there was Spanish involvement. Twenty-two young men were brought over to Bata, and several were condemned to long prison terms. At the end of August, the Council of Elders published a second letter stressing the decayed state of the only line that carried water to Palé, constructed between 1946-49. In Santa Isabel, several people from Annobón were arrested upon the denunciation of Muñoz Ylata. Obiang Nguema pardoned them on the occasion of the 25th anniversary of the country and decorated the military personnel who had participated in the operation of August 1993. At the November 21 elections, the government claimed a participation of 63% in Annobón, glossing over the fact that not more than 19 persons had been registered.

In June 1994, the cultural association VIYIL formed by Annobónese refugees in Spain became an NGO and organized a day of discussions on Annobón in Barcelona. On September 17, 1995, the PDGE declared it was the winner of the municipal elections, in spite of Annobón's extreme hostility to the party. In the September 1995 municipal elections, Anselmo Aguilar Menejal (PDGE) was elected mayor. The April 8, 1996, government of "national unity" included Hilario Sisa Tores, an Annobónian.

Spanish radio amateurs who had arrived on the island in October 1997 reported that no plane had landed on the island in the last eight years. See also Spanish radio amateurs.

See also Argelejo de Santos; Army; Benin; Canary Islands; Castellon; Ntayo Erimola, V.; Children; Convergency for Social Democracy; Elections; Fisheries; Government of National Unity; International Bank for Reconstruction and Development; Jesuits; Juanola, J.; Civil Junta for National Salvation; Micha Nsue Nfumu, J.; Muñoz Ylata, S.; Navigation; Navigation Company of Equatorial Guinea; Ndong Ona, A.; Obama Nsue Mangue, F.; Obiang Nguema, T.; Madrid Pact; Palacios, J.; Parliament; Popular Union; Portugal; Public Health; Radio; Ronda, S.; Segu, R.; Sisa Tores, H.; National Security; Tamarite Burgos, C.; Telecommunications; Torture; Toxic Wastes; United Kingdom; Zamora, F.

ANTORCHAS, Jovenes see Young Torches

APEGESA. A Nguemist company charged with the recruitment of staff for petroleum companies. It has the status of a private employment agency. It deducts 55% from the salaries paid by the petroleum companies. On its administrative councils are several Nguemists: Juan Olo Mba Nseng, Pastor Micha, Miguel Abia Biteo, Carlos Nsé Nsuga.

In May 1996, the minister of labor, Carmelo Modo Akuse, announced that recruitment of labor for the petroleum industry would be conducted by his ministry. This measure did not become effective.

APEGESA's competitors are the nguemist companies ATGE and Armengol Nguema. See also Petroleum.

ARAB BANK FOR AFRICAN DEVELOPMENT (BADEA). An agreement for a loan of $4.7 million payable over 16 years was signed with the BADEA in 1983 for the renovation of the Bata Airport and the modernization of (road and sea) transport. In 1986, the BADEA granted ECU 3.3 million for the restoration of cocoa plantations.

ARGELEJOS DE SANTOS Y FREIRE, Brigadier Felipe José, Count of, 1721–1778. Shortly after the signature of the Pardo Treaty, Argelejos was sent from Montevideo to take possession of Fernando Po and Annobón, as well as the Río Muni coasts, in order to set up a base for the slave trade. The expedition reached Fernando Po on October 21, 1778; three days later it left for Annobón, but Argelejos died during the trip and his lieutenant Primo de Rivera took over command. A rebellion and several casualties doomed the expedition to failure.

See also Annobón.

ARGENTINA. As a result of Minister of Foreign Affairs Maye Ela's mission to Argentina in April 1981, the government of the colonels granted a credit of $5 million (US) to the Nguemist dictatorship for the purchase of equipment, as well a grant of 5,000 tons of wheat. Two agreements were signed relating to cooperation in the fields of agriculture and petroleum.

In October 1985 Argentina agreed to the rescheduling of the Equatorial Guinean debt. However, the restoration of democracy in Argentina seems to have put an end to their economic cooperation with Obiang Nguema.

It received Equato-Guinean students for training, including C. Tamarite Burgos, who became the minister for public administration in 1992. The Argentinean project for an agro-industrial complex (for US $5 million), which was to have been built in Mongomo, the stronghold of the Nguemists, failed due to various instances of fraud. The same fate befell the associated craft-fishing project.

In early 1996, Ebang Mbele (ex-member of the PDGE and vice-president of Parliament, president of the Democratic and Progressive Alliance from 1992) and his Nigerian girlfriend, both holders of Equato-Guinean diplomatic passports, were arrested at Buenos Aires for cocaine trafficking.

At the end of 1997, there were 20 Equatorial-Guinean scholarships in Argentina. In August 1998 it is announced that the 12 officers opposed to the regime and refugiated in Cameroon will be sent to Argentina, Spain and France having refused to welcome them.

In July 1998, an Argentinian 69-year-old Claretin missionary/doctor has been expelled from Añisok.

See also Catholics; Corruption; Drugs; Economy; Finances.

ARMENGOL COLL. Claretian Father, first bishop of the Apostolic Vicariate of Fernando Po in 1904; he was appointed chairman of the Patronato de Indígenas in the same year. He left his ministry in 1918. See Missions.

ARMENIA. Diplomatic relations were established in 1992.

ARMIJO GONZALEZ, Francisco. Spaniard. Until independence he worked for AUCONA (subsidiary company of Transmediterránea), then became a civil servant in the Ministry of Labor in Madrid. A Spanish member of the Monalige, he was not allowed to take trips to Guinea for some time. He is assumed to be the author, together with Novais, of Macías Nguema's Independence Speech, having substituted his text for the one written by García Trevejano and a member of the Profinanco Group, who in 1969–1970 attempted to persuade Macías Nguema to create a central bank with private capital. The venture failed because of the Emergencia and the foundation of a bank with the help of Spain. In 1971 Macías Nguema accused Armijo of having left the country with 20 million pesetas ($320,000).

ARMS DEALING. On July 5, 1997, the *Sun-Sentinel* of Ft. Lauderdale (Florida, U.S.A.) reports that two Soviets (in fact Ukrainians), Alexander Progrebeshki and Alexander Darichev (respectively age 28 and 36) were arrested by American customs because they were suspected of dealing arms. They had organized the sales of missile for a drug mafia boss in Colombia. These missiles were loaded on a ship stationed in Equatorial Guinea and transported from Bulgaria to Puerto Rico. See Drugs; Navigation.

ARMY. In 1960, a wave of Equato-Guineans underwent military training in Spain. Among them were Obiang Nguema and those belonging to the Grupo de Saragoza. Between 1969 and 1976, Equatorial Guinea had the highest soldier-density: 10 out of every 1,000 inhabitants were soldiers. In 1977, military expenditure rose per capita to $22 per year and to $1,000 per soldier per year. In 1978, 290 Equato-Guinean nationals were abroad (Europe, Cuba, China, North Korea) for military training.

After his coup d'etat of August 3, 1979, Obiang Nguema recalled the professional members of the military who had been sidelined by him and Macías Nguema and startedruling the country with a Suprme Military Council. He abolished by decree the terms Guardia Nacional, Milicia Popular, Marina de Guerra, Policía armada, Guardia municipal. Capt. Melanio Ebendeng Nsomo (Zaragoza group) has been the chief of headquarters staff since the coup. Maye Ela declared that the Youth Marching with Macías had been incorporated into the army.

The army was reorganized in 1980 with three military regions: the island, the coast, and the eastern region. The Russians sent two amphibian troop carriers, four P-6 gunboats, one patrol boat, and a helicopter. National defense was in the charge of Melchor Ndong Mba Obono from October onwards. The 1977 Soviet-Equato-Guinean agreement for military assistance remained in effect.

In 1981, Mba Oñana Nchama was named inspector-general of the armed forces. In December, Equato-Guinean nationals, trained in Spain to be presidential close guards (GEOs), returned to the country accompanied by the Spanish commander. ou presidential orders, the latter was prevented from disembarking while the GEOs were arrested by the Moroccan mercenaries. Three GEOs were tortured and accused of plotting to kill the president. Frightened by their technical know-how, Obiang Nguema disbanded the unit. A number of GEOs sought asylum in Gabon.

The first Equato-Guinean air force unit trained in Spain; "Apoyo del 4 de Agosto 1979" was established in 1982. Mba Oñana became vice-prime minister in charge of defense in October of that year with Melchor Ndong Mba as vice-minister.

In early 1983, Equato-Guinean officers carried out joint maneuvers with Spanish officers in the Canaries. There were 1,400 men in the army in 1986, 100 in the navy, and 100 in the air force (with no fighter planes or armed helicopters, but with one Yak 40 and one C-212 lent by Spain). A 2nd class soldier was paid $40 a month. There were 2,000 more troops in paramilitary units and in two civil security companies. A fee for the PDGE is deducted from the soldiers' wages, regardless of their rank. Some officers are trained in Nigeria.

In December 1990, Melanio Ebendeng Nsomo became minister of defense. Between 1991 and 1993, the Moroccan guards arrested and tortured a number of people. In the "transition" government brought to power on January 24, 1992, the army was still under the charge of Ebendeng Nsomo. In Bata the armed forces were led by Antonio Mba, one of Obiang Nguema's brothers, who is known for his ferocity. A military academy was started in Musola.

In early 1993, a number of military personnel recalled by Obiang Nguema in 1979 were again dismissed because they belonged to opposition parties. In March, seven soldiers who belonged to the PP were arrested and tortured in Evinayong. Observers spoke of the Jovenes Antorchas being trained by French counsellors and of the wooing of the population by French military volunteers through the distribution of military rations. In August, a semi-military operation was directed against Annobón as a punitive measure. In Libreville on September 4, the 11 member countries of the CEEAC signed a mutual nonaggression pact involving a subregional peacekeeping force to resolve any existing conflicts. The men who took part in the Annobón operation were decorated on the occasion of the 25th anniversary of Equatorial Guinea.

In 1994, Capt. Gabriel Nse Obiang became director-general for military cooperation, in the Ministry of Defense. At that time the national defense employed 1,320 men with 1,100 in the army (in three infantry battalions), 120 in the navy, and 100 in the air force. In addition, there were two Ninja paramilitary units. In April the garrison in Kogo was attacked by Equato-Guinean nationals from Gabon, who lost six men in the operation.

About a dozen military men were arrested in Bata in spring 1995 and were accused of plotting a coup d'etat. They later stated and proved before a tribunal that they had been tortured in the basement of the presidential Palacio Africa in Bata and that one of them had succumbed to the injuries he had sustained. Lt.-Col. Pedro Esono Masie and soldier Pedro Masa Mba, a deputy to the Minister of Defense (a cousin of Moto Nsá with two broken arms) were condemned to 12 and 30 years of imprisonment respectively. The others received from 9 to 28 years; one was released. The court was entirely made up of Obiang Nguema's relatives (Lt.-Col. I. Ngomo, chief of headquarters, cousin; Public prosecutor, Cdt E. Nseng, cousin; Capt. R. Mbandongo, relative and aide de camp to the dictator, and members of the clan from Mongomo). Obiang Nguema continued to be more and more distrustful of the army. In April, 140 Moroccan mercenaries returned to supplement the 50 Pretorian guards provided by Rabat. Thirty-three political prisoners including Moto Nsá were pardoned. Some members of the POC warned that the Nguemist army was supported in a large measure by Chinese and North Korean funds and material. In April 1995, the International Committee of the Red Cross gave its first class on human rights, in presence of the Defense Minister and the Chief of Security. Military expenditures for 1995 sum up to 2.5 Mio$.

On April 8, 1996, Captain Eustaquio Nseng Esono Nve, a nephew of Obiang Nguema, was promoted to secretary of state for national defense; his assistant was Melanio Ebendeng Nsomo, minister with special responsibilities for national defense. During the summer of 1996, in Spain, B. Nguema Esono, vice-president of the Republic under Macías Nguema and a relative of Obiang Nguema, declared to the Spanish press agency EFE that the army was tired of Obiang Nguema and that in the 1995 elections, it voted for the opposition. On August 3, 1996—the anniversary of his coup—Obiang Nguema promoted his brother Antonio Mba Nguema from colonel to brigadier general. In November, in Bata, a group of soldiers attacked and wounded the coordinator of the CPDS. On the 18th, 11 junior officers were sentenced to four to 13 years of prison for having organized the coup (July 1996) as well as fines amounting to 59 Mio FCFA. Their identities were not disclosed.

On June 17, 1997, a note from the Armed Forces to Obiang Nguema is handed to the dictator; it denounces disorder, nepotism, the impurity of the presidential guard, the strange death of Pedro Motu (the officer who arrested Macias Nguema), etc. and demands the respect of human rights and free elections. the note also underlines that some parties of the opposition are accomplices of the dictatorship. Tward the middle of June, about thirty soldiers, half of whom are from Mongono, were arrested, and one of them died under torture in Bata at the beginning of July. In 1997, a dozen officers who are members of the popposition and refugees in Cameroon were arrested and imprisoned there, although eight of them benefit of the status of refugee from the U.N. High Comissary.

In January 1998, four soldiers, among them a sergeant, are said to have been killed in Luba by men belonging to the MAIB. In the government of January 21, 1998, Melanio Ebendeng Nsomo remained Vice-Minister of National Defense. Human Rights Watch (NY) reported in 1998 that Equatorial Guinea was among the twenty countries that did not actively participate in the negotiations on the protocol concerning the recruitment of children under 18 in armed conflicts.

As a consequence of Moto Nsá's attempted 1977 coup, the army strength was increased to 2,000 men, and the wages were doubled: a soldier made in 1998 FCFA 50,000 per month (approx. U.S. $90).

In 1998, Equatorial Guinea signed with forty other countires the anti-personnel mines treaty.

See also Aviation; Esono Masie, P.; Eyama Angüe Osa, D.; France; National Security; Navigation; Ndong Ona, A.; Nepotism; Nseng Esono Nve, E.; Petroleum; Salaries.

ARTS. In early 1980, the sculptor Leandro Mbomio Nsue became state secretary for artistic promotion. With UNESCO aid, a Centro para la investigación y desarrollo del Arte negro-africano y bantu (Center for Investigation and Development of the Negro-African Art) was founded in Bata. It only exists on paper.

ARTUCIO RODRIGUEZ, Alejandro. A Uruguayan. Secretary to the International Commission of Jurists for Latin America. Was an observer during the court case against Macías Nguema, in 1979. Replaced Volio Jimenez as reporter to the UN Human Rights Commission for Equatorial Guinea in 1993. In October, Artucio expressed his concern about the human rights situation there. He rendered a terrifying account of the regime. During the term of his December 1993 mission, police stole an envelope delivered to him by an opposition party.

His report, which was discussed in March 1994, spoke of innumerable violations of human rights and of the lack of almost all fundamental rights. Artucio returned to Equatorial Guinea for 15 days in May. His report in June, used by the conference of donor countries, indicated a few slight improvements but stressed the fact that the government had never accepted the previous reports.

In early May 1995, Artucio again returned to Equatorial Guinea for a five-day visit in the capital, avoiding Río Muni. In Madrid, he made light of the Nguemist terror without having really visited the country. On May 17, the UN high commissioner for human rights, Jose Ayala Lasso, rectified his lenient stand by stressing the "grave violations of human rights" in Equatorial Guinea. On May 18, the European Parliament did the same. In June 1995, Artucio demanded the freedom of those civilians condemned by the military tribunals.

He accused the "peripheral authorities" of having committed barbarous acts. Following the success of the opposition in the municipal elections held in September in Santa Isabel, the Bubi Victoriano Bolekia became the first elected mayor of the capital. Just before yet another visit from A. Artucio, the regime freed Bubi political prisoners. Placido Micó suggested that Artucio make an extended visit to Equatorial Guinea in order to prevent the prisons from being filled up again soon after his departure.

Artucio's report to the UN Human Rights Commission (January 1996) and its addendum (March 1996) stress the continuation of torture, election rigging (especially during the presidential elections of February), and the lack of response from the regime to the proposals of the international community. On the occasion of the meeting of the Human Rights Commission, in April, the Nguemist government alleged that Artucio lacked objectivity.

The country's hope for development, based on oil, seems to be limited. The *Annual Report* of the UNDP (August 1996) specified that: "In spite of the thrill and hope generated by the oil production, its impact on the economy is very limited so far. On the one hand, this activity seems unable to create any dynamic impact on the segments of the national economy, all the more so as it does not have any links with other economic sectors." A. Artucio, accompanied by the UN consultant E. Duhalde, carried out a new mission at the beginning of December 1996. The representatives of the opposition denounced once more the violation of democratic rights.

The reports published in 1997 and 1998, although they mention a few improvements—especially concerning freedom of expression—continue to report the violation of most fundmental rights. He attends, at the end of May 1998, the military trial of 117 Bubi, due to the attacks on military quarters in January. After

the death sentence of 15 of them, he asks for clemency and is concerned about the fairness of the trial and the respect of the rights of the defense.
See also Bolekia, V.; Human Rights; Playa Negra.

ASAMBLEA DE LA REPUBLICA (Republican Assembly). Parliament set up in October 1968 with 36 deputies (Fernando Po 15, Río Muni 19, Annobón 2). At the September 1968 elections, the votes were distributed as follows: MONALIGE (A. Ndongo, leader), Fernando Po (F.P.) 5, Río Muni (R.M.) 3; Grupo Macías, F. P. none, R.M. 9; Union Bubi, F.P. 7, R.M. none; MUNGE (Ondo Edu, leader), F.P. none, R.M. 7.

The deputies were elected for five-year terms, but their mandates were terminated in 1973 in order to set up the Asamblea Nacional Popular (Popular National Assembly). In March 1971 a decree by Macías Nguema had modified the Assembly to such an extent that it no longer met. By the end of 1974, four-fifths of the Republican Assembly deputies had been murdered.

ASAMBLEA GENERAL (General Assembly). With Autonomy (1964–1968) the two Diputaciones Provinciales (Provincial Assemblies) merged into one Parliament, with eight deputies from Fernando Po and 11 from Río Muni. The Assembly could legislate, participate in the preparation of the budget, control the Consejo de Gobierno (Government Council), and propose dismissal of ministers to the Spanish government. At the same time, the Consejo de Gobierno was to control the Asamblea General. The first General Assembly met in 1964, presided over by Gori Molubuela. Because of the rotation of the presidency between the two provinces, Ngomo Nandongo of Río Muni became president in 1965. Of 19 deputies of the Assembly, 11 were Africans. With independence, the General Assembly was replaced by the Asamblea de la República (Republican Assembly), with 36 representatives.

ASAMBLEA NACIONAL POPULAR (Popular National Assembly). Parliament born with the "García Trevijano" Constitution of 1973, replacing the Asamblea de la República (Republican Assembly). It is composed of 60 deputies proposed by the PUNT, the single party having the right to dismiss them.

ASECNA (Agency for Security in Aerial Navigation in Africa and Madagascar). A French company for technical management of airports. Carlos Nse Nsuga (from Mongomo) was its Equato-Guinean director. In 1993, ASECNA was said to have installed a radio station for the purpose of jamming broadcasts from Radio Exterior de España, the only source of realistic information on the Nguemist regime.

ASOCIACION DE ANTIGUOS RESIDENTES EN GUINEA ECUATO-RIAL (Association of Former Residents of Equatorial Guinea). It is made up mostly of employees evacuated in March 1969. In 1997, it had 400 members, who demanded indemnities for losses. Its president is Marco Rodriguez Lopez. Seventy-four members received compensation, amounting to 37 Mio pesetas. The others are still waiting. See also Comunidad de Españoles con intereses en Africa.

ASOCIACION DE LA ORGANIZACION DE TECNICOS Y PROFESION-ALES GUINEANOS EN ESPANA (OTEPGE) see Association for the Organization of Guinean Technicians and Professionals in Spain

ASOCIACION PARA LA SOLIDARIDAD DEMOCRATICA CON GUINEA ECUATORIAL (ASODEGUE) see Association for Democracy in Solidarity with Equatorial Guinea

ASSASSINATIONS see also Amnesty International; "Coup d'etat of August 1988"; "Coup d'etat of August 1993"; Elema Borengue, J.; Epam Uri, M. M.; Mba Ondo, C.; Ndowe; Ngomo Mbengono, F. J.; Ngone Maguga, M.-E.; Nguema Esono Nchama, B.; Nguema mba, M.; Obiang Nguema, T.; Santa Isabel; Sibacha Buecheku, A.; Terror; United Kingdom; United States of America; Victims; Witchcraft.

ASSOCIATION OF FRIENDS OF PRESIDENT OBIANG NGUEMA see Seriche Bioko Malabo.

ASSOCIATION FOR THE ORGANIZATION OF GUINEAN TECHNI-CIANS AND PROFESSIONALS IN SPAIN (Associación de la Organización de Técnicos y Profesionales Guineanos en España, OTEPGE). Founded in May 1987, at Valencia, with a view to demonstrating the existence of men and women capable of administrating the country in all fields. Maintains contacts with various international institutions and governments. See also Iyanga Pendi, A.-C.

ASSOCIATION FOR DEMOCRACY IN SOLIDARITY WITH EQUATO-RIAL GUINEA (Asociación para la Solidaridad Democrática con Guinea Ecuatorial, ASODEGUE). Founded in Madrid in March 1993, in the presence of a number of Spanish politicians and trade unionists. Presided by J. M. Bandres. ASODEGUE published an appeal in favor of the professors arrested and tortured in December 1992 in Santa Isabel. Towards the end of 1993, it organized three support-to-the-Equato-Guinean-opposition Days. Since 1994, ASODEGUE has published the bulletin *Voces de Guinea Ecuatorial*.

In the spring of 1995, following the condemnation of its protégé, Moto Nsá, the ASODEGUE accused the Spanish press and the opposition, stating that the criticism against Obiang Nguema was in fact criticism against Spain and the PSOE, which only served to handicap Moto Nsá. See also Joint Opposition Platform.

ASUE OBAMA, Francisco Pasual. In the ministerial reshuffle of January 21, 1998, he became Minister of Public Works and Urban Affairs.

ASUMU, Alejandro. Became vice-minister of public works under the supervision of the new minister, Pedro Nsue Obama Angono, on January 8, 1996. In the ministerial reshuffle of April 8, he was replaced by Micha Nsue Nfumu.

ASUMU MIBUY BIKUI, Francisco. Obuk from Mongomo. Soldier under Macías Nguema who, after the 1979 coup d'etat, went on training in territorial administration to Morocco. He has been governor of Wele-Nzas (Mongomo) and secretary general of the Ministry of Education. He became the government's representative to Niefang. In the April 8, 1996, ministerial reshuffle, he became Director General of Internal Security, an office he kept in 1998. See also Niefang

ASUMU MUM, Anastasio. In the April 8, 1996 ministerial reshuffle, he became chief of ceremonies to the president of the republic with the rank of joint director general.

ASUMU OYONO MEDJA, Guadencio. Fang of Mikomeseng. With independence he became administrator of the Mikomeseng District. In 1969, he was appointed secretary general of the Foreign Office, then secretary to the presidency of the republic.

In 1975 he took refuge in Cameroon. It was he who in 1976 drew attention to the fact that Macías Nguema had sold the islands Conga, Cocottiers, and Mbañe to Gabon in 1974, as well as a zone between Ebebiyin and Mongomo (about 2,000 sq km, or approx. 770 sq mi).

ASUNTOS SOCIALES see Delegación de Asuntos Sociales

ATANGANA, Charles, 1885–1943. Ewondo chief (Cameroon) escaped to Fernando Po with the Germans in 1916. Together with other chiefs he asked the king of Spain to favor the Germans' reinstallation in Cameroon.

ATEBA NSOH, Clemente. Fang. A farmer and founder of the IPGE in 1959. He addressed petitions to the United Nations inviting them to support Guinea's independence. After participating in the Constitutional Conference, he was appointed ambassador to Gabon. In October 1973 he was accused of having close ties with the refugees and dismissed together with other foreign service officers. Some refugee circles, such as Ela Abeme's, maintain that Ateba Nso had in reality never belonged to the IPGE and suspect him of being responsible for the murder of Enrique Nvó.

ATIGE. Recruiting office and labor racketeering, managed by Manuel Nguema. See APEGESA, SONAVI.

ATLANTIC METHANOL PRODUCTION COMPANY (AMPCO). Created in 1998; 45% is owned by CMS and Samedan. The government owns 10%. The factory, which cost 400 Mio $, is located in the outskirts of Malabo. It is going to use 100 Mio m3/d of the Alba gas, for a daily production of 2,500t. of methanol.

ATTEMPTED COUP D'ETAT see Ndongo Miyone, Atanasio

AUTONOMY. The status of autonomy (1964–1967) was prepared with representatives of Guinean authorities (members of the Cortes, provincial deputies, delegates of the Cámara Oficial Agrícola); thus all Spanish proposals were adopted. The head of the Spanish government, Carrero Blanco, was in favor of a separate autonomy of the provinces, whereas the minister of foreign affairs, Castiella, preferred the single status. At the December 15, 1963, referendum, 66% of the voters accepted the proposed single status. During the first months of 1964 municipal elections took place as well as elections for Asambleas Provinciales and Asamblea General. In May the Asamblea General chose the members of the Consejo de Gobierno. The status of autonomy differed from provincialization by the provinces' self-administration for internal affairs. All decisions taken by the Asamblea General could however be vetoed by the Spanish general commissioner, which already forebode the absolute power of Macías Nguema as it was to appear in 1969. With autonomy, Guinea no longer contributed to the Spanish budget.

AVIATION. A link with Libya, via Benin, existed between 1976 and 1979. Iberia's Madrid-Santa Isabel route was shortly cancelled in 1978; about 150 million bikwele from Iberia were frozen in Santa Isabel. Macías Nguema's transfer from Bata to the capital in August 1979 was made in a Spanish Aviocar. The African Development Bank granted $650,000 to Equatorial Guinea for the purpose of modernizing the airport of Bata. In September, the Spanish army lent two C-212 Aviocar aircraft.

Russian pilots and mechanics were present, but Obiang Nguema was distrustful of them. They were made available to the LAGE. In 1980 there were three Russian planes in Equatorial Guinea: a Yak 40, an Antonov [a 22-seater], and a helicopter. The contract for the renovation of the airport of the capital was given to the Spanish company Huarate. There was an Aviocar link between Santa Isabel and Bata.

In August 1981, Río Muni and Fernando Po were to be connected by Lauda-Air, but the project fell through. An Air Morocco link to Santa Isabel was begun.

In July 1982, the nonexistent air force received a unit trained in Spain called the "Apoyo del 4 de Agosto." There was a proposal for a small national airline, Aerolineas de Guinea Ecuatorial (Algesa), to connect Santa Isabel with Douala; the German company Intratex was expected to manage it, but the project failed.

Security was tightened at airports in 1983 to clamp down on currency trafficking. Iberia's officer in charge of stopovers in the country was imprisoned for his refusal to allow his company's incoming luggage to be opened. In just four years Iberia had to pay 150 million pesetas.

In 1984, the Arab Development Bank for Africa granted $4.7 million out of a total of $27.3 million for the renovation of the airport at Bata. In 1985, the aid project of the UTA branch of the company for the development of aerial transport in Africa (Sodetraf) failed. In July, Iberia cancelled its biweekly Boeing 727 flights to Santa Isabel supposedly due to inadequacy of its installations for fire prevention, but, in reality, for political reasons.

The Sociedad Ecuato-Guineana de Avación (EGA) was founded in August 1986, with a Hawker Siddley rented from Air Madagascar; other flights were reserved for Air Cameroon. EGA is a joint-venture with the government holding 70%, and Inter-Gabon 30%. The company enjoys the benefits of French cooperation (FF 3.4 million).

In early 1987, an Aviocar crashed near Bata, killing all crew and passengers including 11 Spanish nationals. The Equato-Guinean ambassador to Madrid put the blame on the Spanish crew, alleging drunkenness, much to Spain's protests. In February, in Libreville, an airport accident grounded the Hawker for four months. In August, the Hawker was again grounded in the capital following a badly handled landing. The EGA airline employed fifty staff, including two French pilots and two Air Madagascar pilots. A Santa Isabel-Lagos link with Nigerian Airways has been established.

From January 1988 onwards, the control of Equato-Guinean airports began progressively to be transferred to the French company ASECNA. In February, the

EGA began a subscription to make up for the losses incurred in 1987 (as a result of nonpayment of their services by the Nguemists).

In 1989, the IBRD continued to term the Bata airport project a "white elephant" as the relaying of roads was much more urgent. EGA continued to incur mounting losses in spite of FF 6.6 million in aid from France. An agreement was signed with Air Africa for biweekly Douala-Bata and Douala-Santa Isabel links.

The EGA went bankrupt in 1990. Concord Airlines, a private Nigerian company, signed a contract that allowed it to reserve the role of national carrier for itself. During the period before finalization of the agreement, a Tchec Turbolet L-410 was leased along with two pilots from Skoda-Air. The agreement collapsed in 1991. According to the U.S. State Department, the official Equatorial-Guinean Airlines (EGA) does not meet international aviation requirements.

Following the arrest in February 1992 of members of the opposition, including dual citizens, Spain ordered the Aviocars not to be used by the Nguemists. Aeroflot flights ceased. Once the EGA was restructured, Armengol Nguema became its director. Towards the end of 1992, the Nguemists grounded the two Spanish military Aviocars, arguing that special permission was necessary for all camouflaged planes.

The ban on the import of foreign newspapers in 1993 was accompanied by threats against airlines and shipping companies to dissuade them from transporting any. The measure was revoked in the summer.

Spain recalled its Aviocar in March 1994. In 15 years and 11,000 missions, Spanish military planes had transported 95,000 passengers and 2,000 tons of merchandise. The air force employed 100 men.In 1995, the army possessed a VIP Yack-40 Codline, three CASA C212 Aviocars, one Cessna F 337, and two Alouette IIIs.

In 1994-95, Río Muni was frequently isolated for lack of flights. The fares were exorbitant. There is a weekly Libreville–Bata return flight. The Aviage company (Aviación Guinea Ecuatorial), which handles ticket sales, practices systematic overbooking.

In June 1997, Teodorín Nguema Obiang received delivery, for his father, on an airplane, a Falcon (14 seats, 15 Mio$). Starting September 25, Madrid and Equatorial Guinea are not only linked by Iberia, but also by a weekly flight provided by *Equato Guineana de Aviación S.A.,* a subsidiary of Spanair. The country was ready to join Air Afrique in the fall of 1998; a cargo flight was to take off on September 1, and the first passenger flight for Europe was scheduled for November 1. At the end of 1997, the following flights were opened: Madrid–Equatorial Guinea with Iberia and Spanir, and Paris–Equatorial Guinea with Air Afrique. Air Gabon opened a flight Libreville–Malabo. France subventioned the construction of the airport in Malabo (inaugurated in 1998).

In 1998, three airlines ensured domestic flights, as well as flights to Douala (Cameroon) and Libreville (Gabon): the official *Equato Guineana de Aviación* (EGA), which flies with two Yak 40s and a Ukrainian crew, the *Compañia Aérea de Guinea Ecuatorial* (COAGE), and *Guinea Equatoriana de Aviación S.A.,* owned by Teodorín Nguema Obiang, eldest son of the dictator and Minister of the Forests and Environment. EGA also has a weekly flight to Madrid, along with Spanair. Iberia still has a weekly flight Madrid–Malabo. *Air Afrique* has a weekly flight Abidjan–Malabo. The private Cameroonian airline *Air Affaires Afrique* (AAA) has flights to Malabo and Bata. Three charter airlines operate in the country: *Air Consul SA* (which sometimes flies to Anobon), the Canadian airline *Eagle Air Service* (helicopters), and the Portuguese airline *Federal Air Guinea Ecuatorial.* Moreover, four charter airlines in Cameroon and Gabon occasionally fly to Equatorial Guinea. During the spring of 1998, Swissair opened a weekly flight Zurich–Malabo. Mobil Oil Corp. and other oil comanies use 2 Canadian and South African helicopters.

Two plane accidents occurred in September 1998; on the 5th, the EGA Yak-40, with a Ukrainian crew, overran the runway in the capital (no wounded, only material damage). On the 22nd, an Air Consul twin-engine plane crashed in the capital's bay and sunk. The two pilots and the only passenger were saved.

According to the U.S. State Department, the official Equatorial-Guinean Airlines (EGA) does not meet international aviation requirements. The Aviage company (Aviación Guinea Ecuatorial), which ensures the ticket sales, practices systematic overbooking.

See also African Development Bank; Annobón; Arab Bank for African Development; Army; Bata; Envoro Ovono, A.; France; Gabon; International Bank for Reconstruction and Development

AYALA LASSO, Jose see Artucio, Rodrigez A.; Human Rights

AYAMIKEN. Locality in the northwestern part of Río Muni, near the Río Campo on the Cameroon frontier. In March 1915 the Germans Lehning and Arm were murdered there by a British agent with the help of a Nsoh-Evan chieftain.

AYEKABA, Maria Jesus. Comes from Mikomenseng, where she was born in 1926. She was appointed counselor to the president of the government for women's integration in January 1994.

AYUNTAMIENTOS (District Councils). Above the Juntas Vecinales (Municipal Councils) were the Ayuntamientos, created in 1960. They replaced the Consejos de Vecinos (Town Councils) and covered a whole district (four in Fernando Po, eleven in Río Muni). The counselors were elected partly by the heads of households and party by economic or cultural organizations, so that Spain could control the decisions. The presidents of the Ayuntamientos were appointed by the civil governor, and those of Bata and Santa Isabel by the head of the Spanish government. After the June 1960 elections, several Guineans had access to these bodies, among whom was W. Jones Niger for Santa Isabel. Seven mayors and counselors were killed between 1969 and 1974.

❖ B ❖

BACALE OBIANG, Celestino see Bakale Obiang, C.-B.

BACA MBA, Silverío see Kogo; Niefang

BAGIELLI see Bayele

BAKALE MBA, Santiago. In the April 8, 1996, ministerial reshuffle, he became director general for commerce.

BAKALE OBIANG, Celestino-Bonifacio. Born April 24, 1957, in Akol-Esawong, district of Niefang. Primary school of Niefang; 1963, Colegio La Salle, in Bata. Baccalaureate in Malabo in 1977. Teaches at the Rey Malabo Institute (Santa Isabel). 1980–1986 studies of engineer at Universidad Politécnica (Madrid).

In 1987, he returned to the country where he was appointed chief of the mine and road department in the Ministry of Mines and Petroleum, run by Juan Olo, brother-in-law to the dictator Obiang Nguema. He left the ministry in 1990 in protest against corruption. The same year, he joined other university graduates disappointed with the Nguemist regime to found the Convergency for Social Democracy (CPDS), which publishes *La Verdad* (of which he is chief editor), and which writes the anti-Nguemist slogans painted on the roads of the capital.

He was arrested along with Placido Mikó in February and March 1992, and tortured in the camp housing the Moroccans. Condemned for "insult to the Head of State" and for "subversive propaganda," he was then released following international protests. He was again arrested in December, along with 12 teachers. Students of the capital marching peacefully, demanding his freedom, were arrested and tortured. Bakale was free on December 29, along with his colleagues.

In early 1993, Bakale fell seriously ill as a result of the torture he had undergone. Convergency remained illegal. Summoned before the Commission for Human Rights in Geneva, he described in detail the methods used in the torture. According to him, the greatest aid Spain could grant would be to convince France to stop supporting Obiang Nguema. With the POC, he organized a boycott of the November 1993 elections.

Being responsible for the CPDS's international relations, he imposed conditions, in the spring of 1994, for the participation of the CPDS in the municipal elections.

On May 27, 1995, Bakale was arrested along with his colleague Andres Esono, who was in charge of information in the CPDS. They were both accused of having published *La Verdad,* which was considered subversive. They were held by Obiang Nguema's brother, Armengol, Ondo Nguema's brother, who was the chief of police of Los Angeles, a neighborhood of the capital. Just a little earlier, the police had arrested Rafael Obiang along with 20 others, for distributing the newspaper *La Verdad.*

On February 16, 1996, during the campaign for the presidential elections, Celestino Bakale was again arrested and tortured, along with other members of the POC, including the mayor of the capital, Victorino Bolekia, Santiago Obama, Julián Ehapo and Gaudencio Asumu. They were released two days later. On April 24, 1996, Bakale was arrested for the fourteenth time and sequestered on the 27th, and was later sent to Bata, where he was released by judges. Until May 13, he was prevented from returning to the capital.

In September 1996 he was able to participate in the meeting of the Socialist International with P. Mikó. Both were received by the American press and by the firm Black, Kelly, Scrugs & Healy, specialized in lobbying, and who had produced Obiang Nguema's propaganda during the electoral farce of February 1996. In Washington, Mikó and Bacale were received by the assistant secretary of state for Africa, William Tuwaddell, who confirmed what the democratic opposition had affirmed for a long time: the election of Obiang Nguema wasn't fair. When returning to his country, he was arrested by a member of the President's Personal Security, Narciso Edu Nsue, and imprisoned from November 15–16, 1996, because the Nguemists wanted to punish him for what he had said on Radio Exterior de España. Bakale was interrogated by police officer José Ndong Ona, a cousin of Obiang Nguema. On the 22th, the minister of defense forbade him to move about in the capital, in retaliation for his refusal to present himself to a military court. He was supported by five parties of the democratic opposition. On Christmas 1996, he fled to Spain. See also Convergency for Social Democracy; Education; Edu Nsue, N.; Joint Opposition Platform; United States.

BALACHA. Locality in eastern Fernando Po. Balachá chief Luba ordered the June 1910 rebellion to protest against forced labor. Three soldiers were killed.

During the November 21, 1993, elections, a nonparticipation rate of 100% was recorded here.

BALAOPI. Prehistoric sites of Fernando Po constituting the two early stages of Carboneras civilization, fishing settlements producing very fragile pottery and thin stone hatchets. Their civilization was replaced by that of Buela.

BALBOA BONEKE, Juan. Half-breed, with a Fernandino father and a Bubi mother. Born in Rebola in 1938. Studied in Santa Isabel at the Escuela superíor indígena and at the Escuela social of Grenade (Spain). A secondary school teacher, he wrote poems in praise of Macías Nguema, and later sought asylum in Spain. Author of a novel and two small volumes of poems, including *Donde estas Guinea?*

In 1985 the Nguemist publisher Ediciones Guinea printed his novel *El Reencuentro: El retorno de un exilado.* He became president's counsellor for information, tourism and culture. The Centro cultural hispano-guineano published his anthology of poems *Sueños en mi selva* in 1987.

In October 1990, he became minister for employment and social security. The opposition considers him one of the regime's barking dogs. As minister for culture, he accompanied Prime Minister Siale Bolekia to the universal exposition in Seville in August 1992. He did not hold any post in the December 1993 government, but he did become the president's cultural advisor.

The Centro Cultural Hispano-Guineano published his *Requiebros* in 1994. In May, he was accused of writing defamatory articles against the government as a member of the MAIB, and was forbidden from flying to Spain to participate in the 1st symposium on Afro-Hispano-American studies in the University of Alcalá de Henares. The US ambassador J. Bennet denounced the fact that Balboa had been publicly interrogated on television.

In February 1995, Balboa Boneque again sought refuge in Spain (Valencia).

BALBOA DOUGAN, Armando Nuñez, d. 1971. Fernandino. Studied modern languages; Spanish wife. As member of the MONALIGE, he participated in the Constitutional Conference and pleaded at the United Nations for the separate independence of the two provinces. The Secretariado Conjunto accused him of being a servant of Spain. Having become first a deputy of the Republican Assembly, then its secretary general, he also held the office of director general of information and tourism (1968–1969). Arrested after the Ndongo Miyone affair in March 1969, he was sentenced to 10 years in prison, beginning in December 1970. He died of gangrene in jail following maltreatment.

BALINGA BALINGA, Benjamin Gabriel. From Mikomeseng. Took refuge in Cameroon under Macías Nguema. In 1979, officer of the government in the Ministry of Foreign Affairs, he later worked in the State Secretariat for the Development Plan. He was involved in a bhanga trafficking scandal, along with the wife of the ambassador in Spain, Evuna Owono Asangono, which led to the recalling of the ambassador and his own arrest. Balinga again sought refuge in Cameroon.

Upon his return in 1992, Balinga became the leader of the Social Democratic Party (PSD). He went into hiding when in July, he was accused of arms trafficking. He was spotted and arrested by the police in August. He was, however, not tortured, and his party was recognized.

As he was returning from Europe with Ebang Mbele in early 1993, he was arrested by the border police. He represented his party at the National Pact negotiations. On October 15, he accused four members of the PSD of high treason and had them expelled from the party for having accepted $9,000 from the government and announced the participation in the November elections, even though the PSD was part of the POC, which was boycotting them; however, in November, the POC also breached the boycott. Balinga has been expelled from the PSD.

In June 1994, he joined the representatives of the UDENA and the PL in demanding that the government stop supporting dissidents. Since 1995 he lived in Spain. He returned to the country in 1997. Unemployed.

BAMA SETEM, Alejandro see Drugs

BANAPA. Cathodic missionary center southwest of Santa Isabel, founded in 1861, to which a priest's training college was added in 1912. Bishop Nzé Abuy and Father Esono were trained in Banapá. Many cocoa plantations were developed with Kru and Fang workers, as well as a vocational school, and in 1903 a printing press was established that published the *Official Bulletin* and *La Guinea Española*. See also Ndongo Miyone, A.

BANCO DE DESARROLLO DE LOS ESTADOS DE AFRICA CENTRAL (BADEAC) see Central African States Development Bank

BANE see Bonkoro

BANEY. A Fernando Po locality. Prime Minister Siale Bilekia comes from here. His family was the only one to participate in the November 21, 1993, elections; the rest of the population stood by the boycott. Bartolome Owono (from Mongomo) is the government's representative here (he entered the president's security service after two years of secondary school and a course in administration in Morocco). The police commissioner of Baney, Juan Engonga, is known for arresting and torturing of schoolboys and mothers with their children.

In the September 1995 municipal elections, Ignacio Bijeri Boko (PDGE) was elected mayor. In January 1996, the governmental delegate seized the keys of the church (built in 1910), accusing the Bubi of holding meetings there. In June 1997, the mayor, Ignacio Biejeri, was beaten by militants of the PDGE. See also Bokokó Boko, D.; Bubi; Children; Oyo Ebule, E.; Oyo Riqueza, E.; Parliament; Siale Bilekia, S.; Terror.

BANKS. In 1942, the Patronato de Indígenas created a limited Crédito Agrícola (credit institution favoring small farmers), but not until independence did the country dispose of a real Crédito Agrícola. Until 1969 the following banks were operating: Banco Exteríor de España, Banco Español de Crédito, Caja Insular de Ahoros de Gran Canarias, as well as a branch office of the Bank of British West Africa. All these institutions endeavored to drain the wealth produced from the colony. The Bank of Bilbao participated in petroleum prospecting operations. In 1968–1969, a group of Spanish speculators (see Profinanco) invited Macías Nguema to create a Central Bank with private capital. After the Emergencia (state of emergency), Macías Nguema found it suitable to create such a bank, but with the assistance of Spain and the IMF. After the foundation in October 1969 of the Central Bank, the National Bank for Deposit and Development (BNDD), the official commercial bank, was founded in 1971 with García Trevijano's assistance. Two luxurious buildings were erected for the Central Bank in Bata and Santa Isabel, by the Société Française des Dragages. In 1969, the Central Bank introduced the Guinean peseta (exchanged at par with the Spanish peseta, but not convertible), changed in 1975 to the ekuele (plural bikuele) also exchanged at par with the Spanish peseta. Since 1972, the BNDD was in charge of activating the cocoa plantations abandoned by the Spaniards, but did not succeed for lack of know-how. Since 1975, Equatorial Guinea has been a member of the African Development Bank. In mid 1976, the director of the Central Bank, Buendy Ndongo, was murdered.

Shortly after the 1979 coup, the African Development Bank granted a loan of US$650,000 for refurbishing the Bata Airport and agreed to provide funds for the rehabilitation of 5,000 hectares of cocoa plantations. In 1985 these loans amounted to some US$10 million.

By the Decree-Law 1 of September 2, 1980, the Banco Popular was established, replacing the Banco Central.

In 1981, the director of the BNDD, Andombe Buanga, was jailed for six months and was replaced by Obiang Nguema's brother-in-law, formerly head of the presidential guard. Also in 1981, the governor of the Central Bank, P. Eka, was dismissed.

In 1982, as a result of various frauds, the Central Bank's funds deposited in Spain were blocked following a court order.

In March 1983, Eyi Nzang, governor of the Central Bank of Guinea, and Nkumu Ela, director of the BNDD, were arrested on charges of illegal currency exports.

Towards the end of 1983 the Arab Bank for African Development granted a US$4.7 million loan for the development of air and road infrastructure. In 1986 France opened branches of the International Bank of West Africa (BIAO) following the introduction of the CFA franc in 1985.

The Guinextebank scandal broke in 1987. The BIAO director confirmed the existence of "political credits" "to powerful men" "that were never repaid." The BIAO then enjoyed a monopolistic position. The IMF suggested that the BIAO limit its operations; this restraint was criticized by the lumberers. Castro Nvono Akele was the president of BIAO—Equatorial Guinea. Spain was looking for a private bank willing to establish itself in Equatorial Guinea with the Spanish administration paying the installation and personnel expenses.

The BIAO was liquidated in June 1990 by its share-holder, the Banque Nationale de Paris, which then acquired 51% of BIAO (Equatorial Guinea), with the Nguemist state getting the rest. The Banque des Etats de l'Afrique Centrale (BEAC) report speaks of official and private withdrawals which were well above the means of the bank. The Nguemists blamed Spanish companies (Suguisa, Los Molinos, etc.) for the bankruptcy of the Guinextebank. One-half of the Guinextebank's loans were written off. In October, the country joined a Convention for the Creation of a Banking Community in Central Africa. Towards the end of 1990, steps had been taken to inaugurate:

- the Guibank, with private local and Spanish capital
- the International Development Bank of Equatorial Guinea Ltd. (BIGDESA), with a capital of $2 million, three-fourths of which were provided by the Brazilian businessman Carlos Rocha. The president of the BIGDESA was said to be Teodorin, Obiang Nguema's eldest son.

Both projects fell through.

In 1991, the Equato-Guinean office of the BEAC was being run by Martin-Crisanto Ebe Mba. The BIAO-Equatorial Guinea was taken over on March 15, partially by Meridian International Bank Ltd (the Cyprio-Zambian Andrew Sardanis's international conglomerate, in Lusaka, whose headquarters were in Bahamas), which had interests in South Africa, and partially by the ITM International group (Luxembourg).

In 1992, the African Development Bank acquired 10% of BIAO-EG's capital, Armengol Nguema possessed a list of all Equato-Guineans holding accounts of more than CFA Fr 1 million. Equatorial Guinea signed a convention for making banking rules in the states of central Africa more uniform.

The Banco de Credito Agrícola de Guinea was founded in May 1993, by Obiang Nguema and his ex-crook ambassador to the UN in Geneva, Engonga Motulu. Teodorin Obiang became its director.

In 1996 two banks were operating in Equatorial Guinea: BIAO-Meridien and CCEI-Bank G.E. The Spanish company AFINSA, linked to the Directorate General of the Postal Service, was involved in negotiating the installation of a Postal Savings Fund (Caja postal de Ahorros) and of automatic cash-vending machines in Equatorial Guinea. At the end of 1996, BIAO S.A., was put into liquidation, for insolvency.

In 1997, Antonio Nve Ngu was the representative for Equatorial Guinea at the Central African Development Bank. M. C. Ebe Mba was the representative at the Bank of Central African States.

There were 3 active banks in 1998: Méridian BIA and La Caisse Commune d'Epargne (The Common Saving Bank). According to the BEAC, these two banks have a precarious balance. In July 1998, the BAD granted 3 Mio $ for a project aiming at improving basic health care: water supplies, training of 50 medical assistants. Since 1978, the BAD has granted 50.6 Mio $ to Equatorial Guinea. The thind bank is the Société Générale de Banque (General Society of Banks, Paris), installated in September: President of the board, Balthasar Engonga Edjo (nephew of Obiang Nguema), executive vice-president, Rafael Tung Ela (Mongomo). Other collaborator: Antonio Ndong Nsobey.

In October 1998, the nguemist regime created a new Bank of Development, the "Banco de Fomento y Desarrollo" (BDF), with a 500 Mio FCFA (U.S. $1 million) capital, in order to "finance development projects and help the population with respect to savings." The bank is entirely national, and its capital is covered 30% by the state, 45% by the Equato-Guinean private sector, and 25% by national financing institutions.

See also African Development Bank; Agriculture; Arab Bank for African Development; Bonkaka Bogeta, V.; Brasil, Concepción; Central Africa States Development Bank; Customs Union of Central African States; Drugs; Engonga Edjo, B.; Fisheries; Gangsterism; Guinextebank; Inestrosa Ikaka, F.; International Bank for Reconstruction and Development; Klitgaard, R.; Malavo, E. Don; Meridien International Bank Ltd.; Ngomo Mbengono, F. J.; Obiang Mangue, T.; Obiang Nguema, T.; Petroleum; Profinanco; Rocha, C.; Roig Balestros, F.; Transports

BAPTISTS see Missions; Saker, A.

BARLEYCORN. Protestant Fernandino family of Nigerian origin, major cocoa plantation owner. A family member participated in labor force negotiations with Liberia in 1927. In 1956 Jeremias Barleycorn became mayor of Santa Isabel. In the 1968 elections, family members ran for Parliament on both the Grup Macías list and that of the opponent, the MUNGE.

BARRERA Y LUYANDO, Angel. Navy officer, captain of the Santa Isabel harbor in 1905, and governor ad interim in 1906–1907. After a stay in Morocco he became gobernador general (governor general) of Spanish Guinea from 1910

to 1918. His paternalistic government favored the Fernandinos. Barrera undertook several expeditions to Río Muni, especially for the recruitment of Fang workers. In 1914, he negotiated a treaty with Liberia for the supply of manpower. During the First World War he was very pro-German and assisted the contraband supply of arms to Cameroon via Río Muni. Under Barrera's government about 50,000 soldiers and civilians of German Cameroon found refuge in Guinea in 1916–1917. His statue was erected in 1916 in front of the Government Palace, but torn down by the crowd during the March 1969 events.

BASILE. About 8 km from Santa Isabel, at an altitude of 450 m, built on the north slope of the Pico de Basilé. After 1860, plantations and a convict prison were created; in 1885, Montes de Oca built his residence in Basilé. In 1885 and 1894 the Concepcionistas and Claretians (see Missions) respectively opened schools for girls and boys. In 1892 Spanish colonists from Algeria attempted to colonize the locality. The country's main radio broadcasting station is based in Basilé. Until 1973 a major chicken farm, the colony's main supplier before independence, was located here. In 1977, the government asked the FAO to send a mission in order to help restore production.

The USA and the Food and Agriculture Organization of the UN have been assisting the rehabilitation of the Basilé poultry farm since 1980.

BASUPO DEL OESTE. Located 14 km southwest of Santa Isabel and connected to the capital by rail via Banapá in 1913. The railroad line was abandoned in 1930.

BATA. Main town of the Continental Province, located in northwestern Río Muni on the Atlantic Ocean. At the end of the 19th century, a French military detachment was stationed there until the signing of the Paris Treaty in 1901. In 1905 the Spaniards moved the small military and trading post of Bata further north. In 1906 Bata had 237 inhabitants, including 37 whites. The French Missionaries of the Holy Spirit stayed in Bata from 1906 to 1919. Several companies had opened subsidiaries in Bata: Holt, Hatton & Cookson; Woermann; Küderling, etc. In 1936 the Frente Popular (Popular Front) was crushed in Bata, after Santa Isabel, by Franco's troops sent from the Canary Islands. In 1960, the city had 3,548 inhabitants, of which 1,426 were whites. Bata had a major hospital, various schools, a thermal power station, barracks, a notorious prison, some mechanical workshops, a company for wood veneering, the headquarters of the Société Forestiere du Río Muni, and a major branch office of the Société Française des Dragages. In February 1969 Macías Nguema ordered the Spanish flags to be taken down, especially from the Spanish Consulate; in view of Spain's refusal they were torn down and Ambassador Duran-Loriga Rodriganez expelled. This was to be the starting point of the flight of 7,000 Spaniards, discouraged by the failure of Ndongo Miyone's attempted coup d'etat in Bata on March 5, 1969.

In 1972, Unesco opened the Centro de Desarrollo de la Educación (CDE0 to train high-school teachers. Mut Macias Nguema's hostility to anything that is "intellectual" ruined the project after a few years.

Since independence the following buildings have been erected in Bata: a hotel, the Presidential Palace, the Central Bank, and a Technical School (Maestria). South of Bata a new harbor was built with a transit capacity of 400,000 tons per year, but it is barely operating in view of the economic stagnation. Since 1975, additional port facilities have been under construction. Up to 1963, the planes from Spain landed in Bata, from which one could reach Santa Isabel by DC-3. Since the construction of an international landing-field in Santa Isabel, traffic operates in the opposite direction but the airstrip needs to be repaired.

The Bata prison has witnessed the disappearance of hundreds of Equatorial Guineans, especially at the time of the attempted coup d'etat of June 1974 and at the time of the Senior Officials Affair in December 1976.

The Italian company CITACO began the construction in 1979 of eight fuel oil reservoirs with financial assistance from the European Development Fund. The Trieste company Grandi Motori subsequently installed two generators in the thermal power station in the town.

In 1981, France opened a cultural center. In February of that year the students of the Carlos Lwanga High School went on strike. In 1981 also, the director of Bata's Radio Ecuatorial died following an attempt on his life.

The military commander of Bata was formerly the driver of Macías Nguema, and on April 2, 1982, distinguished himself by firing on a Spanish aircraft at Bata Airport.

Also in 1981, Obiang Nguema decided to transfer the government to Bata for three or four months each year, but nothing came of this as he did not have the courage to leave his presidential palace in Santa Isabel where he is protected by 600 Moroccan soldiers. In December 1986, the conference of the Customs Union of the Central African States (UDEAC) was held in Bata. However, in order to finance the event, Obiang Nguema had to borrow 5 million naira from Nigeria. This loan also enabled him to pay his soldiers, who had received no money for three months.

A television receiver antenna was installed in 1987. An international telecommunications relay station connecting it to Paris via Douala, built by the company Getesa, was then inaugurated.

In 1988, a Spanish lawyer carried out negotiations in favor of a north-American company for the establishment of a dumping-ground for radon-contaminated earth, near Bata.

In 1989, there was a project for the founding in Bata of a Centro para la investigación y desarrollo del Arte negro-africano y bantu (Center for Research and Development of Black African and Bantu Art). A team of doctors from Cameroon was invited by the Reformed Church for ophthalmological care. The joint venture Promoport Guinea (Trieste/EG), holding a 15-year contract, provided $7 million to increase the capacity of the port installations to 500,000 t/year. 2,000 m^3 of timber was being exported each day from the port. The clash between the Nguemists and the IMF/IBRD over the renovation of the Bata Airport continued. Bata retained the leadership in exports, while Santa Isabel was the leader in imports. In late 1989, the EC adopted the modernization project for the port of Bata. France supported the rehabilitation of the hospital, with an operating theater and a ward to accommodate 40 patients.

In July 1991 the 6th Conference of Ministers of Culture of the CICIBA was held in Bata. Ninety-two political prisoners were estimated to be held in the province.

In 1992, the mayor of Bata, Bibang Abeso Fuma (who was responsible for a financial gap of CFA Fr, 9.5 million) was promoted to governor of the Coastal province. Obiang Nguema's first cousin, Col. Agostin Ndong Ona, became the chief of armed forces in Río Muni and immediately imposed his abusive authority on the Bata police and gendarmerie. Opposition executives were arrested. Teodoro Saez Lasheras, director of the Instituto La Salle, resigned in protest against attempts of infiltration by the Criminal Investigation Department. The students demonstrated on November 23; 40 of them were arrested and tortured; the girls were forced to dance naked before the policemen. They were released on the 26th. Bata is also the place where the Spanish businessmen Hanna and Vilarrasa were imprisoned after being accused of plotting against the regime. Their trial took place in early December. From 1992 to 1994 Luis Oyono was chief of Total/EG in Bata.

In 1993, the traitor Santiago Nvono Avomo was the president of the PDGE for the Coastal region and his brother was the PDGE president for Bata District. In November, the Spanish consul was expelled. Obiang Nguema's first cousin, Agustin Ndong Ona (from Mongomo), was the government's representative. Cayo Ondo Mba (from Mongomo, a policeman and notorious torturer in Macías Nguema's militia, trained in Morocco), was the senior commissioner of Bata until 1993. Following an accident, he was transferred to the capital, and replaced by Julian Ondo Ncumu (from Mongomo), as captain and commissioner. After a series of crazed rampages in his youth, he underwent training with the GEOs, in Spain, and then failed the olice course in Cameroon; being hardly able to speak Spanish, he was posted in Mongomo, and then in Bata. Ondo Ncumu was chief of the Jovenes Antorchas; he joined them in extorting money from foreigners.

In the spring of 1994, the nuns working for the Spanish Cooperation complained that they were being prevented by Nguemist authorities from carrying out their activities. Capt. Ondo Ncumu was notorious among the people as a torturer, drunkard, and drug addict. In May, the hospital received FF 5 million worth of material from France. France mourned the murder of two of its volunteers for cooperation, an economist and a surgeon in charge of the Bata hospital. From 1992 to 1994 Luis Oyono was chief of Total/EG in Bata. The German organization SOS Kinderdorf International grants an aid project in Bata, between 1994 and 2004.

In 1995, Ildefonso Castro was in charge of the Spanish Consulate. The basement of the Palacio de Africe, the presidential residence constructed under Macías Nguema, was being used as the torture room for civilian and military prisoners, under Col. Agostin Ndong Ona. The French hospital project swallowed up tens of millions of FF (approx. $8 million) in six years, but nothing there works. During the September municipal elections, in spite of the city's strong opposition to the Nguemists, the PDGE was declared winner (PDGE 7 seats, POC 5), with Fortunato Nzambi Machinde as mayor. Towards the end of 1995, the population of Bata was estimated to be 45,000.

On November 25, 1996, the regional secretary of the CPDS, Indalecio Abuy Okori, was attacked by four soldiers in uniform; he was saved by his neighbors.

In 1997, a brickyard, which exports to Gabon, was created in Bata.

See also Abeso Fuma, F.; Administration; African Development Bank; Akalayong; Angola; Añisok; Annobón; Arab Bank for African Development; Army; Arts; Aviation; Bibang Abeso Fuma, A.; Bibang Oyee, J.; Bikomo Nanguande, S. P.; Cameroon; Canada; Central Africa States Development Bank; Centro de Desarrollo de la Educación; China, People's Republic of; Convergency for Social Democracy; Korea, North; "Coup d'etat" of August 1988; "Coup d'etat"of the Spring of 1990; Corisco; Cuba; "Democratic" Party of Equatorial Guinea; Democratic Progressive Alliance; Education; Ekong Andeme, P.; Nsue, C.; Ekuku; Elections; Eneme Ovono, S.; Eneme Ovono, J.; Esono Masie, P.; Esono Micka, L.; France; Gabon; Garriga Fuma, F.; Gene, M.; Germany; International Bank for Reconstruction and Development; International Museum for Contemporary Art; Italy; Joint Opposition Platform; Justice; Mafia; Malavo, E.; Martinez Nvo Bikie, J.; Mba Nguema Mikue, A.; Mba Ondo, C.; Mecheba Fernandez, T.; Mecheba Ikaka, J.; Micha Nsue Nfumu, J.; Miko Abogo, P.; Missions; Moto Nsá, S.; Motu Mamiaga, P.; Navigation; Ncogo Eyi, P.; Ndongo Ogüono-Asong, M. M.; Ndowe; Ngolo-Ayop; Ngomo Mbengono, F. J.; Ngore, B.; Ngua Nfumu, S.; Nguema Mbasogo Ondo, A.; Nsue Mokuy, A.; Nve Mbengono, E. E.; Nve Nzeng, A. F.; Nvono Akele Avomo, S.; Nzambi Machinde, F.; Obama Asue Eyegue, F. P.; Obiang Mangue, L.; Obiang Nguema, T.; Oficar Africa S.A.; Oko Ebobo, A. P.; Olo Mba Nseng, J.; Olo Mebuy, A.; Ondo Maye, S.; Ovenga Eyang, Mba, M.; Oyono Ndong Mifumu, M.; Oyono Ntutumo, M.; Parliament; Petroleum; Police; Polytechnic Institute; Post Office; Progress Party; Public Health; Radio; Roig Balestros, F. A.; Rond, S.; Saez Lasheras, T.; Sami Ganet, F.; Sanchez Bustamante, D.; Sima Ngua, A.; Si Ondo, S.; Social Democratic Coalition Party; Social Democratic and Popular Convergency; Spain; Telecommunications; Terror; Timber; Torture; Toxic Wastes; Trade; Transports; Tung, Ela; Customs Union of Central African States; United Nations; United States of America; Victims; Vilarrasa Balanza, S.

BATETE. A Bubi settlement on the outskirts of San Carlos, southwest of Fernando Po. In 1810 the Batete killed British sailors attempting to disembark on the island. The Mission, founded in 1887, was named María Cristina. In 1900, Batete had 300 inhabitants; in 1909 it had 800 inhabitants. Batete, at the time, produced 2,500 bags of cocoa per year.

The town has an agricultural cooperative. The Mission has been deconsecrated since 1969 by the nguemist regime.

The population of Batete was severely harassed by the Nguemists when Obiang Nguema was military commander of Fernando Po.

See also Cayetano Toherida, E. M.; Echeck, S. E.; Muatetema Rivas, C.

BAUXITE. There exist bauxite deposits which could be economically exploitable in the areas of Nzangayong and Ayamiken, with AI230 contents going up to 58.3%.

BAYELE. Pygmy population speaking a Bujeba dialect, colored with ancient words of their own language. They live along the banks of Río Campo, northwest and northeast of Río Muni. In 1922 Pygmies were still reported in the Río Benito region. The original peopling of Fernando Po was assumed to stem from Bubi tribes, but anthropology clearly disproves this assumption. In the Cameroon, the Bayele are known as the Bagielli; they call themselves "Bakos."

BCCK ENGINEERING. Petroleum drilling installation construction company (Midland, Texas). In 1992, it established methane and petroleum separators near the capital. See also Petroleum.

BEECROFT, John, 1790–1854. A half-breed young English civil servant, he arrived in Fernando Po as superintendent with the Owen expedition in 1827. He opened a trading post in Clarence (Santa Isabel) and another one in Bimbia (Cameroon) in 1832, both subsidiaries of Dillon & Tenant. In 1833, after the departure of Nicholls, Beecroft became governor of Clarence City. In 1834, he was appointed governor of the British Establishment of Fernando Po; he bought the Dillon & Tenant Company and administrated the island with the freed slaves living there. When Dillon & Tenant went bankrupt in 1837 it was purchased by the African West Coast Company.

In 1839 Beecroft climbed the Pico de Santa Isabel (Clarence City). In 1840 he was appointed consul and general agent of Her Majesty the Queen for the Benín and Biafra Bay area. After hispanicization of the island by Lerena, in 1843, Beecroft was maintained in office, but the West Coast Company had to cease its activities. Until his death in 1854, Beecroft remained governor of the island, assisted by Lynslager. In 1848 he introduced customs duties on imports and exports. With his little steamship, *Ethiopia,* he extended the British influence in the Niger delta and the Cameroon coast, creating courts of equity. In 1851 he authorized the naval attack of Lagos. He died in 1854 and was replaced by Lynslager.

BEHOLI MALANGO, Lucas. Representative of Corisco at the Constitutional Conference. In the 1968 elections, he supported Macías Nguema and after the 1979 coup he continued to support Nguemist dictatorship. He was also a member of the Akonibé Constitutional Commission, which prepared the constitution that consolidated Obiang Nguema's dictatorship.

BELGIUM. After the fire in 1862 that destroyed the wooden church built by the Jesuits in Santa Isabel, an iron structure was erected on the present site of the cathedral. This church was prefabricated in Belgium. In 1875, King Leopold II of Belgium unsuccessfully entered into negotiations with Spain with a view to purchase some of her colonial possessions. In 1898 new enquiries were made to find out at what price Spain would sell Fernando Po and the Canary Islands.

At the beginning of the twentieth century, Congo Railroad Company, an affiliate of the Thys group, had branches in Bata and at Río Benito. They also operated trading posts at the Senye Falls near Río Benito and at Ekodo in the Utamboni region.

In 1980, the Belgian company Saint Nicolas African Company for consignment and chartering contributed to the creation of the Compañía Guineana de Navegación Marítima, with IBRD financing.

Belgium refused to send observers for the November 21, 1993, "elections" in keeping with the boycott by the EC and the POC.

In 1995, Belgium and Luxembourg occupied fifth place in Equatoguinean imports, with $5 million.

See also Ambassador of Equatorial Guinea in 1998: Aurelio Mbá Oló Andeme; Trade.

BELOBI Island see Borders; Corisco

BENIN (ex-Dahomey). The governor of Fernando Po and Annobón, in 1777, João Manuel de Azambuja, lived in Dahomey. There still exists a fort by his name.

BENIN, Republic of see Aviation; Mba Ondo Nchama, F.; Nguma, M.; Oyono Miguel; Siale Bilekia, S.

BENITO, Río. River running east-west through the center of Río Muni Province.

BENNET, John E. Ambassador of the United States since 1991, after having worked in Latin America. J. E. Bennet replaced Ch. E. Norris (who later became president of Walter Int., which has started the Yankee domination over Equato-Guinean petroleum, with approval of Obiang Nguema). Bennet's contributions on Equatorial Guinea in the State Department's Annual Report to Congress on Human Rights in the World are more explicit than the UN reports.

In early 1993, Bennet received death threats, along with the ambassador of Spain, from a Movimiento Nacional de Guinea Ecuatorial, which claimed a commitment to fight imperialism and colonialism. Bennet was accused of "devilish action" and of "instigating violence." This Movimiento referred to the death of the ambassador of France, shot in Kinshasa in a very Nguemistic style. The USA named Obiang Nguema personally responsible for anything that happened to any American citizen and recalled its 10 Peace Corps members still remaining in the country. The deputy-secretary of state for foreign affairs confirmed to Obiang Nguema Washington's full confidence in Bennet. Bennet's speech in the embassy on July 3 dealt with USA-Africa-EC relations and human rights (he declared that high-ranking Nguemist cadres were playing a major role in the violation of these rights).

Bennet also represents the North American Anti-drug Agency. He revealed that the ex-convict of France V.G. Llansol, Obiang Nguema's economic advisor, was a launderer for Colombian black money. According to him, Equatorial Guinea could succeed Noriega's Panama. In mid-1993, the Nguemists declared Bennet "a noncredible partner in dialogue," and accused him of sorcery. The American petroleum companies were operating in the shadows.

Upon his transfer to Panama in mid-1994, Bennet stressed that Equatorial Guinea was a nonrighteous state, and accused certain high officials of the government quoting a long list of torturers. Bennet was replaced by a chargé d'affaires. In September 1995, a spokesman of the Department of State, Nicholas Burns, qualified the accusation of supporting a coup in 1994 as being "sheer fiction." Bennet left Panama in 1996. See also Balboa Boneke, J.; Diplomacy; Human Rights; Movement for the Autonomy of the Island of Bioko; Norris, Ch. E.; Nve Nzeng, A. F.; Torture; United States of America; Victims.

BERLIN Conference. During the Conference (November 15, 1884 to February 20, 1885), attended by 14 countries, the Spanish representative Count Benomar, assisted by the geographer Coello, claimed 300,000 sq km for Spain of the 800,000 sq km granted by Portugal by the Pardo Treaty. The Conference only conceded

180,000 sq km (approx. 70,000 sq mi) with 200 km of coastline. Shortly afterwards Germany agreed not to extend beyond Río Campo; but France in agreement with Germany decided that her possessions in Gabon would extend as far as Río Campo, which would have eliminated Spain from Río Muni. The Paris Treaty settled the dispute in 1900.

BERNARD, Henri. Ambassador of France from 1969 to 1973.

BERNIKON, Vicente. Fernandino. Catholic priest. On August 25, 1974, after the expulsion of Bishop Gómez Marijuan and the exile of the Bishop Nzé Abuy, he was consecrated bishop. Bernikon died in Spain on September 14, 1976.

BETA ECHUAKA, Marcelo. In the April 8, 1996, ministerial reshuffle, he became general secretary of the Ministry of Planning and Economic Development. He keeps his office after the cabinet reshuffle that occurred in January 1998.

BIAFRA. During the Nigerian Civil War (1967–1969) the International Red Cross carried out relief flights to Biafra from Santa Isabel, starting 1968, a few months before independence. Suspected of weapon transport (in fact these were probably carried out from São Tomé, still Portuguese), Ndongo Miyone ordered them to stop the flights as of January 1969, in order to respect the country's neutrality. Macías Nguema having simultaneously forbidden the Ibo's salary transfers to Biafra, the growing dissatisfaction among Nigerian workers especially in Fernando Po incited Macías Nguema to leave the island for Río Muni. There he started a violent anti-Spanish campaign resulting in the departure of the majority of Spaniards in March. See also Bonny River; Calabar; International Committee of the Red Cross; Nigeria.

BIAHUTE MATEU, Fernando. Secretary-General of the Athletics Federation of Equatorial Guinea. President: Pedro Mabale Fuga.

BIANCAMANO, Price see Italy; Mafia; Obiang Nguema, T.

BIBANG, Roman. Major. Military prosecutor during the trial of the 116 Bubi in May 1998.

BIBANG ABESO FUMA, Aurelio. Born at Machinda (Bata). Uncle of Tito Rafael Eworo Mong, husband of one of the daughters of Obiang Nguema. He worked for several Spanish companies. Mayor of Bata in 1990.

In 1922, he owed the city CFA Fr 540,724, a sum equivalent to unpaid salaries of the municipal staff. He participated in the arrests of members of the opposition. Promoted to governor of the Coastal region. Missionaries considered him a corrupt person par excellence.

In the administrative reorganization of April 8, 1996, he became director general of local corporations.

BIBANG ESONO, Arsencio see Popular Union

BIBANG NTUMU, Santiago (from Mongomo) see Ebebiyin

BIBANG OYEE, Julian. Born at Machinda in 1949. After studies at the Banapa Seminary, he went on to study philology. He taught at Santa Isabel, and then received a scholarship to study at the Conakry Polytechnic Institute.

Upon his return, he taught at the Rey Malabo (Santa Isabel) and the Carlos Lwanga (Bata) High Schools between 1973 and 1980 and later left for Madrid to complete his course in philology. Author of *Estudio fonológico del fang aplicado al hablar de Río Muni.*

Upon his return to the country, he became a school headmaster. In late 1992, along with Celestino Bakale and some others, he was arrested in the capital, tortured, and released, with a dozen other teachers, on December 29, with a broken hand and bruises on his head.

In October 1996 he offered a course on "The sociolinguistic situation in Equatorial Guinea" (in French) for the University of Berlin's Seminar für Afrikawissenschaften.

BICOMO. Locality 13 kms from Bata. The People's Republic of China installed a small hydro-electric power station there in 1984.

BIHAUTE MATEO, Fernando. Sports trainer and coach since 1984. Technical manager of the seven-man Olympic team in the Barcelona Games in 1992. By decree of January 27, 1994, he was confirmed as the director-general of physical education and sports, within the Ministry of Education and Sciences.

BIKO, Captain. Fang from Mongono. At the time of the Macías Nguema regime he was known as Major Bamler. At the trial of Macías Nguema in September 1979 he was sentenced to jail for four years, but only served six months. In October 1981, he was put in charge of the Santa Isabel police, but was evidently arrested in the course of a supposed coup in 1983. He was sent back to the village.

BIKOMO NANGUANDE, Santos Pascal. Called "Akuan." Son of a Nigerian from Lea and a Bisio mother. Born in 1960. Worked as an apprentice-electrician.

He was very actively involved in the youth marching with Macías. He was a criminal investigation agent working with S. Nvono Ivomo at the Instituto Carlos Lwanga in Bata. Upon being dismissed for forging documents and ivory trafficking, he fled to Switzerland. He returned in 1988, then went into exile in Gabon where he brought attention to himself for violence.

He returned in 1992, and became vice-president of the Liberal Democratic Convention (CLD) in November. He stated in December that the Nguemist government was interested in nothing but money.

In March 1993, Bikomo quarrelled with his colleagues and left the CLD. He then founded the Liberal Party (PL), with himself as president and Antonio Nkulu Asumu as secretary. After a brief stint with the POC, the PL allowed itself to be "bought" by the Nguemists and as a satellite party of the PDGE, took part in the November 21 elections, obtaining one seat. After the elections, Bikomo exposed 22 irregularities. The National Council of the party disowned him. In June, Bikomo joined representatives of the UDENA and the PSD in demanding that the government discontinue its support to dissidents. In an interview with *Jeune Afrique Economie,* he called his former party colleagues ambitious men he was forced to get rid of. A member of the PDGE since August 1995. Since 1995, he has been in charge of a government Bureau for countering information about the regime broadcast by the European media, especially Radio Exteríor de España.

In the ministerial reshuffle of January 8, 1996, he became the secretary of state for information and propaganda, as well as spokesman for the government. He was in charge of the filming of the arrest of the mayor of the capital, V. Bolekia and of four of his counsellors. He accused them on television of "preparing a coup d'etat with the help of a foreign terrorist expert." According to *El Sol,* this "terrorist" was the volunteer for cooperation Jacques Ganvril of the French Pedagogical Bureau. Bikomo Nanguande added that the financing of the coup came from the BEAC, the Franco-Guinean SEGESA, and the Lebanese EGTC. Following these declarations, Bikomo Nanguande was summoned to Bata, by Obiang Nguema, who asked him to avoid excesses. The top brass of the PDGE stressed the risk involved in introducing "detractors" in the government. Despite this incident, Bikomo Nanguande retained his portfolio in the April 8, 1996, government.

Dismissed on June 26, 1997—while he was once again in Madrid—replaced by Francisco Pascual Obama, former Minister of Sports. Bikomo then traveled to Pakistan. On his way back, he was arrested on July 6 at the airport of Barajas (Madrid) with 15 kg of heroin in his suitcase. The drug was to be sold in the Spanish market. Twenty-two other people were arrested (Turks, Iranians, Spaniards, and natives of Equatorial-Guinea), three of whom are women. Among the natives of Equatorial Guinea there is a niece of Obiang Nguema and her husband, Joaquín María Alogo Ondo (who pretends he is a minister, hence Doctor). Alogo Ondo lived in a villa at La Moraleja (rent: 600,000 pesetas per month). A printer from Valencia, who helped forge official documents of Equatorial-Guinea, was also arrested. These were seized, as well as an official stamp of Equatorial Guinea Security. In Pakistan, the former Prime Minister Benazir Bhutto asked for a judiciary investigation to clear Pakistani authorities from any ties with drug dealers from Equatorial Buinea.

See also Bolekia Bonay, V.; Government of National Unity; Liberal Party; Nsue Mokuy, A.; Opposition; Press.

BIKUELE see Currency

BINDANG, Monica (Macías Nguema's wife) see Macías Nguema; North Korea

BINDUNG. Locality near Mount Bata, about 15 km from the coast. It is the site of the main concentration camp for political prisoners.

BIOKO see Fernando Po

BIYANG ANDEME, Bonifacio, b. 1925. Fang, from Sacriba. Emancipated, protected by Governor General Ruíz González. Director of First Grade Education from 1964 to 1968 took refuge in Spain, and founded with Nsué Ngomo the FRELIGE. In 1973, U.S. oil interests asked Biyang to participate in a coup d'etat but he was judged inept after tests in the United States.

BIYOGO NSUE, Teodoro. Ambassador Extraordinary and Plenipotentiary to the embassy in Washington, D.C., he works under the orders of Pastor Micha Ondo Bile.

BLACK BEACH (Playa Negra). Blabich in pidgin English. The capital's prison, located in the heart of the presidential domain.
See also Obiang Nguema, T.; Playa Negra.

BLACK, MANAFORT, STONE & KELLY, Public Affairs Company located in Alexandria (VA). It takes care of Obiang's image, as it did with Mobutu and Savimbi.

BLANCO PRIETO, Félix de see Vatican

BOCHONGOLO, Pascual see Convergency for Social Democracy

BODIPO, Eduardo. Ndowe. Protestant theologian. An officer of the World Council of Churches (Geneva), he participated in the creation, in 1972, of ANALIGE.
He was accused of polarizing opposition to Macías Nguema urged by French interests in anticipation of a political change. He is presently teaching at the University of California, Berkeley.

BOKOKO BOKO, Djongele. A Bubi from Baney. Born in 1949. He holds dual citizenship (Spain). Car engineer training in Madrid from 1966; then studied chemical engineering, which he did not complete. He holds a degree in law and fiscal counselling (Centro de Estudios Tecnicos Empresariales, Madrid). He settled in Valencia (Spain).
He has written a number of articles and documents on Bubi civilization and on North-South relations, most of them in *Las Provincias* (Valencia). On the 30th anniversary of independence, he reports that Equatorial Guinea is not part of the majority of international statistics reports. The "Guinea Mejor" (A Better Guinea) proclaimed by Obiang Nguema in 1979 "can only be foound in his pockets and those of his friends."

BOLEKIA BONAY, Victorino. Bubi. Born in 1946 in Basakato de la Sagrada Familia. He was a primary school teacher until 1994.
He was then dismissed by the Nguemist regime, along with many other compatriots, for political reasons. He joined the opposition and became vice-president of the Alianza Democrática Progresista and a member of the POC.
During the September 1995 municipal elections, Bolekia Bonay became the first democratically elected mayor of the capital since 1969. In an interview given to the *Barcelona Avui,* on November 25, 1996, he declared: "In Equatorial Guinea they keep on arresting and torturing members of the opposition, but in a hidden way." See also Democratic Progressive Alliance.

BOLEKIA EJAPA, Anacleto. A Bubi. Born in 1938 at Baney. A secondary school teacher, he trained in Spain to be inspector of police. He became senior police commissioner of Río Muni. Effective 1981, he was made acting governor of the province. Since 1983, he has been minister of labor.
He participated in the International Labor Conference in Geneva as minister of labor, between 1984 and 1988. In 1988, he discussed human rights in the following terms: "For our government, the human subject is the ultimate goal of

the State." According to him, peace and justice were supposed to be the main and constant preoccupations of the Nguemist government.

He no longer held a ministerial post in the January 1992 "transitional" government. On January 19, 1994, he was named president's counsellor for employment and social security.

BOLONDO. A locality of the Río Benito district, on the right bank of the river, close to the ocean. In 1865, the American G. Paull founded a Presbyterian mission. American Presbyterian Reverends Nassau, Clark, Goult, de Heer, as well as Mackey and Clemens (a white, born in Corisco), were among the pastors settled in Bolondo. As early as 1907, Bolondo boasted of a hospital with Dr. Pinney, as well as Drs. Blondon, Lenian, Knyght, and the Catalan José Javier.

At the time of independence, a Methodist mission was still operating in Bolondo. The oil palm plantation María Victoria is situated near Bolondo (formerly owned by Izaguirre). See also Corisco; Djangani, F.; France; Missions; Navigation.

BOLOPA ESAPE, Ricardo María, d. 1969. Bubi. Economist and administration specialist. President of the Río Muni Chamber of Commerce, he was a representative to the Spanish Cortes from 1964 to 1968. He attended the Constitutional Conference, then ran in the elections for the Asamblea de la República (Chamber of Representatives). He was killed in 1969.

BONELLI Y HERNANDO, Lt. Col. Emilio. 1854–1926. Born in Saragossa (Spain) he studied in France and in Italy. He worked in the Sahara, then in Río Muni as a representative of Trasatlántica. He explored the rivers Campo, Benito, and Utamboni in 1887 and 1890 in order to set up trading posts.

BONKAKA BOGETA, Victoriano. A Bubi, born in 1929 at Rebola. Was a cashier in the state treasury under Macías Nguema from 1968 to 1979, and has worked as an official of the BEAC since 1983.

BONKORO. Dynasty of Benga kings. Bonkoro I, also called Bañe, King of Corisco, was followed after his death in 1846 by his son, Bonkoro II, who sent one of his sons to the Saragossa Jesuit College in Spain in 1863. Because of opposition between rivals, the power passed to Munga, Bonkoro II transferring his court to Cape San Juan. After his death in 1874 he was replaced by his brother, Bonkoro III.

BONNELLI RUBIO, Juan María, b. 1904. Gobernador general (governor general) in 1943-44. He studied at the Military Naval School, starting in 1920. His first trip to Spanish Guinea was in 1927 (hydrographical works), then in 1932–1933 he was head of the Meteorological Observatory of Fernando Po. In 1936 he opted for Franco. After being secretary of the Naval Ministry he became governor general at the end of 1943. For having supported the Alvarez García project concerning improvement of African school teachers' salaries, he was suspended in 1947. He was connected with the Banco Exterior de España and the Aggor Company.

BONNY RIVER. An affluent of the Niger River, crossing Port Harcourt. The site was considered Spanish after the trips of Pellón y Rodriguez (1860–1875), but no real occupation ever occurred.

BORDERS. The French protectorate on the coast between the Gabon estuary and Cape San Juan dates back to 1839. After 1842, Franco signed treaties with the local chiefs of Corisco and Elobey Chico without informing Spain, the rightful owner of these territories since the Pardo Treaty of 1778. In 1843 Spain signed treaties with the chiefs of Corisco and the Elobeyes, King Bonkoro surrendering all rights over the Muni to Lerena. In 1845 Guillemar de Aragon and the French commissioner in Gabon implicitly admitted Cape Santa Clara to be the limit between Spanish and French territories. In 1868 the "Vicariat des Deux Guinees" (Gabon) claimed jurisdiction over Fernando Po and the littoral as far as the River Niger, in spite of Spain's strong protest. After 1880 French troops were stationed in Campo, Bata, and Río Benito. Since 1870 nine French trading posts operated in Río Muni.

The Iradier explorations (1875–1877 and 1886) conquered 50,000 sq km for Spain, signing treaties with local chiefs, but no effective occupation of Río Muni, either by Spain or by France, took place. After the Berlin Conference (1884-85) had granted Spain 180,000 sq km (of the 800,000 inherited from Portugal), France announced to Germany in 1885 that it considered Río Campo as the limit between German and French territories, in spite of Spain's protest against its attempted eviction from the continent. This led to a conference in Paris on March 22, 1886, where the Spaniards requested the lands inherited under the Pardo Treaty and France refused to acknowledge Spain's rights, with the exception of the Cape San Juan enclave, pretending that Portugal had assigned only the right to do business on the coasts. Suspended in 1891, the negotiations benefitted in 1892 from the Danish king's arbitration, but the fall of the Spanish colonial empire prevented all meetings. During the Paris Conference in 1900, France took advantage of Spain's recent collapse, granting only 26,000 sq km of the Río Muni. A joint commission drew up the borders in 1901.

In 1970 a Gabonese presidential decree extended the territorial waters up to 12 miles, which enabled Gabon to claim Corisco. Equatorial Guinea protested by a similar decree, on September 24. No agreement having been concluded between Gabon and Guinea concerning the islands of Conga, Cocottiers (Coconut), and Mbañe, Gabonese forces occupied them in 1972. Macías Nguema alerted the United Nations, then accepted arbitration by the OAU. On September 17, 1972, a reconciliation session took place among Presidents Nguabi (Congo-Brazzaville), Mobutu Sese Seko (Zaire), Bongo (Gabon), and Macías Nguema (Equatorial Guinea), which decided to freeze the situation. After a further border incident between Ebebiyin and Mongomo, along the Woleu-Ntem, in 1974, Macías Nguema, according to Asumu Oyono, former secretary general of the presidency, appears to have sold the three islands to Gabon as well as the Kioso zone in the east (about 2,000 sq km in total). While president of OAU, Bongo (Gabon), according to the Spanish press, asked for the help of Spain at the end of 1977 in occupying the Equato-Guinean islands; in turn, he seems to have promised the recognition of the Canary Islands' hispanicization. The Spanish government has denied this.

The border locality of Akalayong to the south of Río Muni was occupied by Gabon for petroleum drilling in 1985.

In January 1993, the Mbañe, Cocoteros, and Conga islands were annexed by a Gabonese presidential decree. However, the Information Guide of the French Ministry for Cooperation declared towards the end of 1993 that the following islands belonged administratively to Río Muni: Belobi, Conga, Corisco, Elobey Grande, Elobey Chico, Mbañe, and Ukoko.

During 1995, negotiations were under way in Calabar for a maritime border agreement with Nigeria, on the basis of the UN Convention of Rights over the Sea. The Equato-Guinean delegation was led by Guillermo Nguema Ela. There was a meeting of a committee of experts in 1996.

In order to settle its disagreements with its neighbors, Equatorial Guinea asked the Multilateral Investment Guaranty Agency (MIGA) of the World Bank to finance a project to settle the issue, with both Nigeria and Cameroon, as well as with Gabon.

In August 1997, borders were closed for an unlimited period. Cameroon accused Equatorial Guinea of allowing armed Nigerians who wanted to destabilize Cameroon to transit on its soil.

In January 1998, the press in Gabon talked of "the growing insecurity at the border with Equatorial Guinea" due to "numerous exactions from soldiers of that country on our territory."

See also Balinga, B.; Customs; Democratic Progressive Alliance; Modu Akuse Bindang, C.; Motu Mamiaga, P.; Nigeria.

BORICO TOICHOA, Roman, d. 1974. Industrial engineer, member of the Unión Bubi, and Consejero de Gobierno (Government Adviser) for Industries and Mines from 1964 to 1968. In 1966 he suggested a separate independence for Fernando Po and Río Muni. In October 1968 he became minister of labor. Imprisoned in Bata in 1973, ill in prison, he took part in the June 1974 attempted coup d'etat and was executed on June 26 with 26 others.

BOSIO DIOCO, Edmundo, 1923–1975. Bubi schoolteacher and cocoa planter, owner of the country's first chocolate factory. A representative to the Cortes from 1964 to 1968, president of the Unión Bubi, and president of the Cámara Oficial Agrícola (Official Agricultural Chamber). Received the Spanish silver medal of the Order of Africa in December 1962. He attended the Constitutional Conference, where he supported the two separate provinces. At the 1968 elections he ran for the presidency of the republic. After Macías Nguema's victory, he became vice-president on October 12, 1968, and minister of commerce. He was arrested, tortured, and executed at the beginning of February 1975 (announced by the Government as having committed suicide on February 9). The note he is said to have left behind has never been published. In F. Forsyth's novel *The Dogs of War*, Bosio Dioco appears under the name of Sir James Manson.

BOSMAN, Willem. Dutch merchant, who visited Corisco, Annobón, and Fernando Po in 1698, leaving a colorful description. Some doubts have been voiced as to the veracity of his trip.

BOUYIGUES. French public works company. Its subsidiary Segasa has been in charge of electricity distribution in the capital since 1990, but later on ran into trouble with the Nguemists.

BRANGER, André. Economist. French volunteer for cooperation. He was murdered in Santa Isabel on February 11, 1993, as he was preparing a book on the Nguemists.

BRAVO CARBONEL, Juan. Spaniard. General Secretary of the Cámara Oficial Agrícola (Official Agricultural Chamber) of Fernando Po under the presidency of Bengoa Arriola. In 1917 he suggested moving the colony's capital to Río Benito. In 1926 he recommended the introduction of banana plantations. The works of Bravo Carbonel remain among the best publications on Spanish Guinea, despite overtones of racism.

BRETON, Francois. French Ambassador since April 1998. He is used to hot spots: Mogandishu, Kigali, Malabo.

BRITISH CONSULS. Established in Clarence City (Santa Isabel) with the Owen expedition since 1827, Beecroft was appointed honorary governor by the British government in 1843, then British Consul for the Benín and Biafra bays in 1849. He remained consul until his death in 1854. The following were British consuls in Fernando Po: John Beecroft (1845–1854), T. J. Hutchinson (1855–1861), R. F. Burton (1861–1864), C. Livingstone (1864–1873), G. Hartley (1873–1878), D. Hopkins (1878–1880), and E. H. Hewett (1880–1882). The British consuls were to further the exploration and commercial expansion in the Niger Basin. They often went beyond their mandates, to such an extent that one could speak of "Consular imperialism." The Santa Isabel Consulate was closed in 1882, but reopened shortly afterward, with Sir Harry Johnston as consul from 1887 to 1888.

BROADCASTING see Radio

BRUNET DE COURSOU, Gérard. Ambassador of France from 1994 to 1998.

BUALE, Emilio. Bubi. Born 1973. Like his parents who fled the Nguemist terror to Spain in 1980, he is of Spanish nationality. Fireman.

He played the role of an immigrant in the Spanish film *Bwana* by Imanol Uribe, presented in 1996 at the International Film Festival of San Sebastian.

BUALE BOKAMA, Esteban. Ndowe from Iduma (Río Benito). In 1963, he joined the Fine Arts School of Las Palmas (Canary Islands, Spain, and in 1964 he attended the Art School of Madrid. A graduate in art, he became a teacher at Bata's high school (1965-1971) and Santa Isabel's High School (1972–1975). He designed the Equato-Guinean peseta in 1969, the ekwele in 1973 and 1979, and took part in the realization of the Equato-Guinean CFA franc. He also drew a number of post stamps, as well as the escutcheons of all the municipalities of the country.

In 1978–79 he became a member of Parliament. In 1979, he was a member of the CMS, technical director of the Ministry of Education, and a member of the House of Representatives of the People. He was also a member of the Central Committee of the PDGE.

Obiang Nguema's official painter, Buale Bokama became Cultural Director in the Ministry of National Education in 1981. He was sent to Madrid in 1987 to have the propaganda material of the "Democratic" Party of Equatorial Guinea printed. He painted the torch symbol of the PDGE, inspired by the Zairian MPR torch. He died in Spain in May 1996. His body was repatriated.

BUALE BORICO, Emiliano. A Bubi, born 1927 in Rebola. Graduate in agricultural engineering from the Swiss Federal Institute of Technology in Zurich (1960). After some time as secretary of the Ministry of Agriculture, he was appointed minister of agriculture in March 1981 and transferred to the Ministry of Health as minister at the end of October 1982. On August 18, 1983, while on a visit to Madrid, he requested political asylum there. Since then he has consistently denounced the terror and corruption of the Nguemist regime.

He published three books between 1984 and 1988: *Africa, resurgimiento y furstración* (Africa: Renaissance and Frustration, (1984); *Guinea Ecuatorial. De la anarquía al laberinto* (Equatorial Guinea: From Anarchy to the Labyrinth, 1988); *Guinea Ecuatorial: Las aspiraciones bubis al autogobierno* (Equatorial Guinea: Bubis Aspirations for Autonomy, 1988).

BUBI. Indigenous population of Fernando Po. The Britisher Kelly appears to be the first to name them this way. The Bubi probably came from the Cameroon coast in several migratory waves. They are racially close to the Fang. They were preceded on the island by the Bolaopi and Buela people, forming the Carboneras culture; the Buela are sometimes called the Old Bubi. The Bubi mark the last neolithic migration to the island. They speak a Bantu language, but because of their fragmented arrivals, four dialects were developed, as well as different anthropological types. In the 15th century, the Portuguese noted the Bubi did not know the use of iron.

Bubi society is divided according to the social function of the individuals and not according to their income: farmers, hunters, fishermen, palm-wine collectors, etc. The supreme chief of the Bubi had his own royal police, the Lojua. The monotheistic Bubi worship the elements, the supreme priest having to protect the sacred fire and to bless the yam plantations. The Bubi are monogamous and matrilineal. For currency they used small round pieces of shellfish (*roiga*) that are no longer used except for jewelry. Iron seems to have been introduced on the island by the Portuguese. The Bubi always refused to mix with foreigners, except Nigerians. Their bashfulness favored the Fernandinos (Creoles) who took greater advantage of the Spanish regime. Decimated by epidemics in the 19th century, the Bubi numbered 12,545 in 1912, but their population rose again from 1940 onwards.

King Moka, who controlled the whole Bubi population during the second half of the 19th century, never accepted going to Santa Isabel. In 1897 Spain's governor general, España y Gómez, paid him a visit in Riabba. Sas Eburea, Moka's successor, refused all contact with Europeans. In 1907, the Bubi refused forced labor in the plantations, which brought about the "Bubi war": in June 1910 Balacha chief Luba offered armed resistance, resulting in the death of three Colonial Guards. Spain controlled the rebellion thanks to the cooperation of M. C. Jones, but did not succeed in imposing forced labor. With Moka's brother Malabo succeeding the usurper Sas Eburea, relations with the Spanish population improved.

In 1943 Governor General Alonso Alonso attempted to become king of the Bubi. An investigation conducted by Carrero Blanco led to his dismissal. In 1960 the first Bubi political activity started with Maho Sikacha. In the 1964 Consejo de Gobierno there were four Bubi ministers for eight seats. In August 1964 and 1966, the leading Bubi citizens gathered together in Baney and Rebola to ask for the separation of Fernando Po from Río Muni. Bubi Torao Sikara brought about the failure of this claim at the Constitutional Conference. The Bubi claim was defended by the Unión Bubi, but did not succeed. In October 1968 Bosio Dioco, president of the Unión Bubi, became vice-president of the republic and minister of commerce.

Bubi victims of Macías Nguema's personal power are innumerable: Borico Toichoa, Torao Sikara, Bosio Dioco, and Gori Molubuela are among them.

The Unión Bubi is known as Partido Nacional (National Party). It remains a national-regionalist movement as it used to be before independence. It disappeared from view when it merged with the shadow party Partido de la Coalición Democrática de Guinea Ecuatorial (PCDGE), led by the Creole Francisco Jones.

In early November 1993, the Elders of Fernando Po wrote to Obiang Nguema demanding autonomy for the island and to confirm plans to boycott the elections (central theme of the Movement for the Self-Determination of the Island of Bioko [Fernando Po], Movimiento para la Autodeterminación de la Isla de Bioko, MAIB,—founded on August 15). On November 21 elections, some localities registered a total boycott (100%). The POC published a paper on "Solidarity with the Bubi people."

In January 1994, Anacleto Bokesa called on Madrid for a more decisive intervention from the Spanish government. During that year, several Bubi localities (Baney, Rebola, Sampaka, etc.) became victims of the Ninjas and of police excesses.

The terror continued in 1995, especially in Basupo, and in Bahó Grande, 74 km from the capital, where 20 youths belonging to the MAIB were held in May for having supported an arrested colleague who had staged a protest against the arbitrary rule under the Nguemists. During and after the September 1995 municipal elections, a number of Bubis were held and tortured.

In February 1996, during the presidential election campaign, the Bubi and first democratically elected mayor of the capital, Victorino Bolekia Bolay, was arrested with his deputies by agents of the police and accused of a conspiracy for having attended a French lesson on the premises of the French Cooperation. All of them were tortured until they bled. In the government of "national unity" there figured five Bubis.

In January 1998, young masked Bubi attacked police and army quarters in various locations on the island of Bioko. Several policemen and soldiers were killed. The nguemist repression was violent and indiscriminate: more than 500 Bubi, of all ages, were arrested and imprisoned in dramatic conditions that led to several deaths. The lawyers could not meet the prisoners. In March, in Nigeria, the minister of Foreign Affairs and the vice-prime minister Miguel Oyono Ndong Mifumu declared that it was a maffia crime and not an attempted coup. The summary legal proceedings started on May 25. Two delegates of AI were present, the special rapporteur of the Human Rights Commission of the United Nations, and six Spanish journalists; the lawyers proposed by various Spanish and European federations were not allowed to attend the trial, among them the representative of the Observatory of the Permanent Commissiion of the General Council of Spanish Lawyers and the vice-secretary Rafael Fernandez. Among the accused there was a deputy of the PDGE, Marcelo Lohoso. On June 1, 1998, 15 death sentences and 55 prison sentences were issued: 26 for 26 years, 19 for 12 years, and 11 for 6 years (among them there is a priest); 46 of the accused were released. Those present agree that the trial showed irregularities and that most of the accused were tortured. The Spanish journalists were expelled after 5 days, accused of insulting the president and the government. The Spanish Council of Lawyers expressed its repulsion. Some lawyers were threatened: they could expect reprisals after the trial. On July 23, the attorney defense of Martin Puye was arrested, accused of "endangering the country's peace and independence," after an interview with the Spanish press. Obiang Nguema, at a conference at the United Nations dealing with the fight against drugs, declared on June 8, 1998, that the weapons used during the Bubi attack were bought with money coming from the drug business. With regard to the sentences issued by the court, he declared "they were sound." On July 24, one of the lawyers of the Bubi was arrested for having criticized the prime minister and the minister of Health regarding the conditions of detention. In September, Obiang Nguema commuted the 15 death sentences to life imprisonment. But AI denounced the appalling conditions of detention in the sinister jail of the capital, Playa Negra.

At the end of November 1998, the Bubi were victims of 35 new arrests after the flight, in a pirogue, of 4 MAIB leaders (sentenced to death in their absensce in May). The prisoners were systematically tortured by security forces to obtain information.

See also Abia Biteo, M.; Artucio, A.; Buela Buepoyo Boseka, P.; Bueribueri, P.-C.; Choni Becoba, V.; Drugs; Movement for the Autonomy of the Island of Bioko; Olo Obano, J.; Popular Union; Public Health; Seriche Dougan, A. S.; Torture.

BUCHANAN, Rubi. A Chilean. Known under the local name of Echama (or Menchaca). Some sources say she is a Venezuelan. United Nations expert on education in Equatorial Guinea. She is said to be one of Obiang Nguema's wives and writes his speeches.

BUECAS URCOILA see Timber

BUELA. Prehistoric culture of Fernando Po, having followed the Bolaopi one, especially in Caraboneras and along the coast. The Buela distinguished themselves with large earthenware and rough unpolished hatchets. They are sometimes named "Old Bubi." See also Carboneras

BUENDY NDONGO, Jesus, 1936-1976. Bubi, born on December 26, 1936. M.A. in economics (Fribourg University, Switzerland), after studying law for two terms. Married to a Swiss woman, who returned to her native country when the situation became critical under Macías Nguema. Remarried to a Guinean woman.

In 1969 he was named director of the Central Bank. Arrested in 1976, charged with the theft of $1 million (71 million pesetas), he seems to have been executed on July 7, together with two officials of the bank and the ambassador's deputy in Spain, Ndongo Nangala. His Equato-Guinean wife was arrested in Río Benito. During her transfer to Bata by helicopter she died in an accident with all other occupants, among whom was the gobernador civil (civil governor) of Río Muni, Ela Ndong. Macías Nguema burnt down Buendy's village, Lea, killing almost all its inhabitants.

BUEPOYO BOSEKA, Pilar. Bubi. A school teacher from Basupu. Born on March 3, 1952. She was appointed secretary of state for women's integration and social affairs on December 2, 1993. She became health minister in the January 8, 1996, government. She became vice-minister for health and the environment on April 8, 1996. She is not part of the 1998 government.

See also Public Health.

BUERIBUERI, Cristino. From Basakato. Born 1949. He studied at the Escuela Superior Indígena. He was a member of the National Democratic Union (UDENA). He took over the leadership of a dissident wing of the UDENA towards the end of 1993, and accepted to participate in the elections with an official funding of 8 million pesetas, thus becoming a satellite of the PDGE. The president of the UDENA, Jose Macheba, remained in the POC with the wing favoring the boycott.

Bueribueri joined a delegation of parliamentary representatives and "members of the opposition," who were visiting Switzerland, Germany, and France in January 1994, for the purpose of glorifying the Nguemist democracy. In April 1995, he was signatory to an anti-Spain document shown on TV, along with other members of the opposition. He participated in the dictator's 2nd Party convention. In the April 8, 1996, government, he was rewarded with the post of minister for culture, tourism, and the francophony. He is not part of the 1998 government.

See also Bubi; Government of National Unity; National Democratic Union; Opposition.

BUJA-BOKOKO see Elema Borengue

BUJEBA (or Bojeba). Name given to the Bisio by the Spanish settlers (in Cameroon they are called Kwasio).

BULLEN. British commodore who arrived in Fernando Po in 1783 with Captain Lawson shortly after the arrival of Argelejos. He returned in 1817 without being able to subject the Bubi to the British crown. He was followed by Robertson, then by Kelly and finally by Owen.

BURGOS TAMARITE, Ciriaco. In 1998, he was the minister of Public Services and Administrative Co-ordination.

BURGOS BIZANTINO, Rodolfo. Born 1960 on Annobón. He undertook diplomatic studies in Spain. In the April 8, 1996, ministerial reshuffle, he became inspector general of Services.

BURKINA FASO. It received an Equato-Guinean mission for the recruitment of labor in 1981. During the November 21, 1993, elections, Burkina Faso was among the few observers, along with Gabon, Togo, and the OUA.

BURNS, Nicolas see United States of America

BURTON, Richard, Sir, 1821–1890. Explorer and philosopher, who started traveling in the far east, and the first white man to discover Lake Tanganyika. He was appointed British consul in Fernando Po in 1861. It was then that he climbed Mount Basilé and Mount Cameroon, and he supervised the British exploration of the Nigerian and Cameroonian coasts. In 1864 he moved to Brazil.

BWITI. Worship developed in Gabon (Mitsogo and Apindji) at the beginning of the 20th century, and adopted by the Ntumu Fang of Río Muni. It is a sect of leopard-men quite similar to the Mau-Mau in Kenya. Of syncretic character, Bwiti is composed of Christian and African tradition with the Creation and the Flight from Paradise clearly recognizable. Bwiti is a reaction to the deculturization due to European pressures. During a long initiation period human sacrifices are made (without any connection to cannibalism). Believed to be xenophobic, Bwiti has been forbidden by the Spaniards as well as by the Republic, but still survives.

During the 1920s, the president-to-be of Gabon, Leon Mba proposed the extension of Bwiti in order to strengthen Fang solidarity. See also Alar Ayong.

❖ C ❖

CABINET see Consejo de Gobierno; Consejo de Ministros

CABRERA Y JAMES, Carlos, d. 1970. Fernandino and manager of the Alada Company. Member of the Diputación Provincial (Assembly) of Fernando Po from 1960 to 1964. As mayor of San Carlos, he became representative to the Cortes from 1960 to 1964. Late in May 1970 he disappeared in a nguemist purge that was aimed also at Ngomo Nandongo, Watson Bueco, etc.

CACAO see Cocoa

CACAWAL. Cocoa farm near the capital, formerly owned by Spanish proprietors, confiscated by Obiang Nguema and sold for $800,000 to Walter Int. The heating oil plant which was installed there produced oil (100 barrels/day) mainly for the vessel *Acacio Mañe,* the army, and for sale in the black market to lumber companies.
See also Petroleum

CALABAR, Old. Nigerian town in the Niger Delta. After Santa Isabel, Old Calabar housed the residence of the British consuls in the Biafra Gulf as of 1872. The Iradier-Ossorío expedition was to occupy the African coast from Old Calabar to Cape Esterias in 1884 but the United Kingdom, Germany, and France had preceded them. It was in Old Calabar that the Anglo-Spanish Employment Agency in charge of labor recruitment was based since 1951.

CAMARA DE LOS REPRESENTANTES DEL PUEBLO. From August 1979, when Obiang Nguema came to power, to the summer of 1983, the country had no parliament at all. However, in October 1982, Elo Nvé, one of the most notorious Nguemists, was nominated as presidential delegate for relations with the Chamber. This body was presided over by Bodieng Ngalo in 1984, with Owono Minang as vice-president. The only function of the Chamber was to rubber-stamp the decisions of the dictator. In May 1985, Nguema Aba Sima, deputy minister of energy under Macías Nguema since 1975, put up a proposal for a return to the one-party system. Thirty-one deputies accepted the proposal, and 29 voted against it. Four of the latter, who had publicly voiced their opposition to the proposal, were arrested.

CAMARA OFICIAL AGRICOLA (Official Agricultural Chamber). Each province has its own chamber. The Fernando Po one specialized in cocoa, but the Río Muni one was turned toward timber and coffee. The Fernando Po Chamber worked hard to market the Guinean products in Spain without taxes or speculation (see also Unión de Agricultores). As of 1952 the agricultural chambers accepted African members, like Jones Niger who presided over the cocoa section of

Fernando Po from 1952 to 1956. From 1960 onwards the agricultural chambers participated in the elections of half of the provincial counselors. Even after independence they maintained the export monopoly for agricultural products and wood.

CAMEROON. The Río Muni Fang are related to those of southern Cameroon; the Ndowe are relatives of Mabea, Douala, etc. Bayele pygmies live on both side of Río Campo. Evidence exists of an exchange between the Mount Cameroon area and Fernando Po since prehistoric times. With the Pardo Treaty the coastal line of Cameroon fell under Spanish authority. In 1860-76 Pellón y Rodríguez urged the hispanicization of the entire region, but Germany and the United Kingdom were faster. During the second half of the 19th century the jurisdiction of the British consuls in Santa Isabel extended as far as the Cameroonian coast.

In 1916–1917 Spanish Guinea took in about 65,000 Cameroonese and Germans, including Governor Ebermaier. The Germans were installed in Santa Isabel, the Africans near Bokoko, in the western part of Fernando Po. In 1919, some 120 exiled Cameroonese chiefs asked the king of Spain to favor their return to a German Cameroon. In 1934 a Franco-Spanish treaty authorized the recruiting of 4,000 Cameroonese for the Fernando Po plantations. Illegal entry of Cameroonese was repressed by the Guardia Nacional (National Guard).

Before independence, Cameroon accepted many Guinean political refugees. The IPGE was founded in Ambam. Ndongo Miyone was strongly influenced by the political ideas of the head of UPC (Union des Populations du Cameroon), Felix Moumié, whose widow he married after Moumié's death, probably by assassination in Geneva in 1960. In 1962, the UPC started to claim annexation of Spanish Guinea. From 1963 up to 1977 the president of Cameroon, Ahidjo, rejected this idea. Since 1968 Cameroon has been granting shelter to about 30,000 Guinean refugees. Some of them were kidnapped by their own embassy, returned to Equatorial Guinea and executed (e.g., Watson Bueco). Equatorial Guinea imports cement from Cameroon. Following up on an official visit to Yaoundé by Obiang Nguema, in January 1980, a return visit was made to Equatorial Guinea by Paul Biya, the then prime minister and future president in August 1980. This was followed in November 1981 by a visit of President Ahidjo. Obiang Nguema returned to Yaoundé in October 1982 to prepare Equatorial Guinea's entry into the Customs Union of the Central African States (UDEAC) and the franc zone. In 1987 observers indicated that Cameroon was the main beneficiary of this operation.

The Presbyterian Church in Spanish Guinea was connected to the Cameroonese District between 1936 and 1960. Esono Abaga Ada was deputy secretary at the embassy at Yaoundé from 1971 to 1973. Some ophthalmologists from Cameroon were invited to Bata, by the Reformed Church in 1989. Imports from Cameroon represented a third of all imports in 1990.

In 1992, Obiang Nguema, who practices sorcery, tried to obtain a chief's skull, said to make one invincible, from the Cameroonian sorcerer Fang Abanda. Abanda is the president's Biya sorcerer-counsellor.

The Equato-Guinean ministers for defence and the interior were said to have sold in Cameroon 32,000 bags of rice offered to their country by Japan (3,500 pesetas a bag). In 1993, Cameroonian Customs carried out checks at certain Equato-Guinean frontier posts, acting as counsellors.

In 1994, Cameroon occupied the top position in exports to Equatorial Guinea (37%). In 1995 Cameroon occupied the second position, behind Spain. Equato-Guineans in Cameroon numbered 30,000 in 1996.

In July 1997, Cameroon closed its border with Equatorial Guinea, and set up two military bases in Olamze and Kye Ossi, under the pretext that its small neighbor would have accepted a Nigerian military base in front of the disputed peninsula of Bakassi. In November 1997, according to military sources, 200 mercenaries were said to have arrived, through Bata, to destroy the military quarters of Ebolowa, the military headquarters for the South province. On November 22, the Cameroonian press announced that six members of the Equato-Guinean police had been arrested because, it seems, they had come to kill politicians and military refugees. A dozen Equato-Guinean soldiers, among whom several officers, members of the opposition, sought refuge in Cameroon in 1997. First stationed at Ebolowa, then under house arrest in Yaounde, they feared they would be sent back, although eight of them had been declared refugees by the U.N. High Comissary for Refugees. After the kidnapping of two FDR leaders in Libreville in November 1997, the soldiers who took refuge in Cameroon feared an operation of Obiang Nguema's secret police. In 1997, Equatorial Guinea exprted 25,000 t of petroleum to Cameroon.

On April 17–19, 1998, Obiang Nguema was on an official visit to Cameroon. In August, it was announced that the twelve officers opposed to the nguemist regime would be sent to Argentina and Spain, France having refused to welcome them. Alfonso Mba Ngoso, former chief of staff,was among them. The French Senate's report N^o #376, concerning Central Africa, mentions that "the relations of Equatorial Guinea are still tense although Cameroon has no reason to feel threatened by that country." See Vatican.

See also Aviation; Balinga, B. G.; Bata; Céline, L-F.; Cocoa; Customs; Dougan, A. S.; Education; Ekong Nsue, C.; Elections; Elephants; Equatorial Guinea Liberation Front; Esono Mika, P. J.; Eyi Mensui Andeme, I.; Fang; Fernando Po; Germany; Japan; Civil Junta for the National Salvation; Kogo; Maho Sikacha, J. L.; Matogo Oyana, J.; Mba Nguema Mikue, A.; Mobo Mba; Mensui Mba, P.; Micha Nsue Nfumu, J.; Miko Abogo, P.; Missions, Modu Akuse, C.; Mukusi Nanga, A.; Navigation; Ndong Ona, A.; Nepotism; Netherlands; Nguema Sema, A. M.; Nigeria; Nsomo; Nve Mbengono, E. E.; Obiang Nguema, T.; Petroleum; Public Health; Riboche, M.; Sneyders, A. L.; Spain; Sports; Trade; Transports; United Kingdom; United Nations; Vatican; Victims

CAMPO, Río (or Ntem). River in the northwest of Río Muni, forming a border with Cameroon before flowing into the Atlantic Ocean. Its basin is peopled with some Bayele Pygmy families. In the race for colonies, France proposed to Germany to adopt Río Campo as the border between their respective possessions, thus eliminating Spain from Río Muni.

At the mouth of Río Campo several trading posts (Holt, Woermann, Jantzen and Thormälen, Küderling, etc.) were installed as well as Protestant missions.

CANADA. The company Damsum Oil was interested in the resources of Equatorial Guinea. Another company, with French involvement, participated in the UN project for the creation of a law on petrol. Tecsult company looked into the possibility of bringing water to the capital and to Bata. In 1990–1991, Canada set aside 960,000 for Equatorial Guinea. See also Eya Nchama, C. M.; Llansol, V.-G.

CANARY ISLANDS. When Spain blocked Equato-Guinean funds in 1982, the fishing boat and freezer "Isla de Annobón" was held at Las Palmas. Towards the end of 1992, entrepreneurs from the Canaries proposed to make commercial and touristic investments. Joint Hispano-Equato-Guinean military maneuvers were held in 1993, with the participation of officers of both countries. Obiang Nguema owns a villa in the archipelago. See also Army; Mikomeseng; Obiang Nguema, T.

CANNIBALISM. Spread by Du Chaillu, the myth of Fang cannibalism has been fought by many Spanish authors. The appropriate word would be necrophagy rather than cannibalism, and refers to "feasts" organized by witchcraft societies during which parts of unburied dead bodies are eaten in order to assimilate the qualities of the deceased. The admission of a new member to such a society is linked to the supply of a corpse. The human sacrifices of the Bwiti have nothing to do with cannibalism. It is the black slave trade which generated the myth. The middlemen of the coast frightened the Europeans as much as the inland population with stories of their respective taste for human flesh, thus avoiding all direct contact between them. And when the missionaries saw skulls of ancestors (called upon as intermediaries with God) in Fang houses, they would attribute this to cannibalism. See also Macías Nguema; Motu Mamiaga, P.

CAPE SAN JUAN see San Juan, Cape

CAPE SANTA CLARA see Santa Clara, Cape

CAPPA. Spanish company owning a palm oil plantation in Senye, on the Campo River estuary.

CARBONERAS, Playa. Prehistoric site, probably pre-Bubi, discovered in 1951 west of Santa Isabel under the coal yards used as of 1862 for British steamers and by other nations later on. The human sediments of Carboneras are as old as 1,300 years (based on carbon 14 dating of palm nuts). The settlement was composed of farmers, living in paved houses, growing yams, oil palm trees, sometimes practicing hunting and fishing; they lived between the 7th and 11th centuries. Three levels are superimposed in Carboneras: Bolaopi I, Bolaopi II, Buela. Similar sites were discovered all around the island. The tools of Carboneras are the Tumbien hoe and the Bamenda type hatchet (Cameroon). Ceramics were found in the Nigerian, Cameroonese and Gabonese settlements and are dated from the 14th century. The numerous neolithic sites of Fernando Po are all of the Buela type.

CARRERO BLANCO, Luis, 1903–1973. Spanish admiral. In 1927 he participated in the survey of the Muni estuary map. In 1941 he was appointed under-secretary of the presidency and ten years later minister and secretary of the presidency, remaining in office without interruption until 1967 when he became vice-president of the government, and in June 1973 president of the government. During many years he was the head of the Dirección General de Marruecos y Colonias. He was killed in Madrid in 1973, by a Basque Independence Movement.

Carrero Blanco owned the majority of the capital of Casas Fuertes, such as ALENA and INASA. He seems to have controlled the Sindicato del Cacao y del Café (Cocoa and Coffee Union), of which he received five pesetas per kilo. In order to bring about the failure of Guinea's independence, Carrero Blanco supported Bubi separatism and the separate autonomy of the two provinces, contrary to Minister of Foreign Affairs Castiella who wished to maintain territorial unity. Carrero Blanco's favorite candidate for the presidency of the republic was Ondo Edu, whereas Castiella supported Ndongo Miyone while Garacía Trevijano prepared the way for Macías Nguema. Carrero Blanco's aversion for Macías Nguema and Macías's hardening anti-Spanish attitudes starting in January 1969 led to the flight of 7,000 of the 8,000 Spaniards living in Guinea, pushed further by the coup d'etat of Ndongo Miyone in early March. Macías Nguema proclaimed the emergencia (state of emergency) and shortly afterwards Carrero Blanco discharged Castiella. Carrero Blanco was said to be the origin of an attempt at overthrowing Macías Nguema by British mercenaries in 1972, but the attempt failed in the Canary Islands. Macías Nguema took advantage of the situation to harden his personal regime. See also Forsyth, Frederick.

CARTER, Chip. Relative of the former president Jimmy Carter. The Carter Foundation refused to send observers to the presidential electoral farce of February 1996. But Chip Carter came bringing his support for the dictator, invited by the South African company Strategic Concepts.

CASA DE GUINEA. Created in 1941 as a continuation of the Unión de Agricultores with headquarters in Barcelona, it grouped especially the Casas Fuertes (ALENA, CAPA, SOCOGUI, CONGUE, Banco Exteríor de España, Comité Sindical, Sindicato Maderero, etc.). Since 1947, it was part of the Junta de Economía Colonial of the Dirrección General de Marruecos y Colonias.

CASAS FUERTES. Name given to large commercial companies and owners of cocoa plantations. They traded Bubi land against pensions of Spanish scholarships for the young Bubi. Maho Sikacha was granted such a scholarship. In reaction against the IPGE and the MONALIGE, the Casas Fuertes favored the creation of the MUNGE under the leadership of Ondo Edu.

CASTELLON NTAYO ERIMOLA, Vicente. An Annobónian school teacher. National Schooling officer since 1982. He became a Supreme Court magistrate in 1990.

CASTIELLA Y MAIZ, Fernando María, 1907–1976. Spanish foreign affairs minister under Carrero Blanco. He presided over the Constitutional Conference in 1967-68 and advocated territorial unity, in opposition to Carrero Blanco's wish to separate the two provinces, supporting Ndongo Miyone rather than Ondo Edu (Carrero Blanco's candidate). In 1969 Ndongo Miyone invited Castiella to put an end to Profinanco's dubious affairs. Irritated by Macías Nguema's excesses, and annoyed by Castiella's support of Ndongo Miyone and his unitary views, Carrero Blanco discharged his minister during the 1969 cabinet reshuffle.

CASTILLO CONZALEZ BARRIL, Manuel, 1932?–1974. An Annobonese, with a B.A. in arts and philosophy and an M.A. in educational science. During autonomy he was the delegate of the Consejo de Gobierno in Madrid. In 1967–1968 he attended the Constitutional Conference. appointed director of education after independence, he was dismissed when Macías Nguema prohibited the use of the word "intellectual." He became head of the Instituto Carlos Lwanga (secondary school) in Bata. In June 1971 he was imprisoned in Bata (because of his pro-Spanish convictions), then placed under house arrest during 1972, and arrested again early in 1974. He was beaten to death with rifle butts in the Bata prison in 1974.

It is rumored that his skull was opened in order to see what an intellectual's brain looks like before his brain was eaten. Castillo Barril wrote several articles on linguistic problems.

CATANEO. Italian businessman. He used to manage a lumber company in Río Muni. Cataneo is believed to have been racketted by Teororín Nguema Obiang, as many others. He seems to have invested 150 Mio pesetas in the (failed) coup d'etat of Spring 1997, led by S. Moto Nsá, against the nguemist regime.

At the end of 1998, Cataneo was in prison in Italy, serving a 20-year sentence (unrelated to the failed coup of 1997).

See Coup d'etat of May 1997; Moto Nsá, S.; Nguema Obiang, T.

CATHOLICISM. In 1998 93% of the inhabitants were Catholics: 3 dioceses, 3 bishops, 39 diocesan priests, 50 diocesan monks, 35 friars, 202 nuns, 50 major seminarists, 1,943 catechists. In 1853 the Saõ Tomé bishopric was extended over Fernando Po. Having become Spanish, the island became an apostolic prefectship in 1855. The Spanish priest Martínez y Sanz was the first prefect in 1856, accompanied by priests (mainly Jesuits), catechists, sisters, and laymen. But, because of illness, the group was obliged to return to Spain in 1856, at the very time when the Jesuits arrived. A decree of 1857 asked the latter to fight against the Protestants on a 6,000-peso annual budget. Starting in 1860, the jurisdiction of the Prefecture is extended to the continental part. On April 25, 1863, the congregation accepted the responsibility of a continental part that extends from the estuary of Río Muni and along the river Utamboni (Mitemele) to Cameroon, with an area of approx. 20,000 km^2 and an estimated population of 235,000 people.The 1868 Spanish revolution caused their departure from Guinea: of 36 missionaries sent, 17 died in Africa. After a short period with army chaplains came the Missionaries of the Immaculate Heart of Mary (the Claretians) in 1883. After 1885, Catholic schools were opened in Corisco, Cape San Juan, and Annobón, in 1887 in Elobey Chico and in San Carlos. In 1888 the Claretians were officially entrusted with education throughout the Spanish possessions, and in 1901 a state budget of 100,000 pesetas was granted to them. Between 1890 and 1900, the Claretin missionaries, in order to create Catholic families and establish Catholic villages placed under their authority, "bought young girls" from families in Fernando Poo and Corisco. Between 1885 and 1903 at the time of the French claims over this Spanish territory, a long dispute opposed the Vicariate of Gabon to that of Spanish Guinea concerning the administration of Río Muni. After the Paris Treaty in 1900, the Vatican settled the dispute in favor of Santa Isabel and in 1904 Father Armengol Coll became the first bishop of the Apostolic Prefectship of Fernando Po. In January 1916 the Santa Isabel cathedral was inaugurated. In 1930 Gómez Marijuan, a Claretian father, who became bishop of Fernando Po in 1958, arrived. He was the last white bishop of the country. Several women missionaries have worked in Guinea, among them Conceptionist sisters and Guinean oblates.

The Congregation of Contemplatives of the mission of St. Pie X was started in 1953. It then had six Spanish sisters. In 1959 the Legión de Maria or "Soldiers of Mary," a secular Catholic movement, was introduced by the Brothers of La Salle.

After provincialization and during Autonomy, the Bishopric of Fernando Po was paired with that of Río Muni, with Bishop Nzé Abuy at the head of the latter. At independence, the Catholic church had in Equatorial Guinea 58 priests, of which 10 were Africans, 19 parishes and 28 religious communities, 2 cathedrals, 4 priests' training schools (Seminarios), 315 chapels, and 16 missionary stations, which means the largest religious substructure in Africa, mainly in the hands of Claretians closely linked to the Spanish State.

The events that followed independence brought about the fall of the Christian churches (Protestant and Catholic). In 1969, Bishop Gómez Marijuan was declared persona non grata, and shortly afterwards Bishop Nzé Abuy went into exile. One hundred and twenty-seven missionaries had to leave the country: 88 nuns of the Immaculate Conception, 34 monks from La Salle, and 5 nuns of the Company of Jesus.

In 1973, in the face of the threatening attitude of Macías Nguema's dictatorship, the three Protestant churches, Methodist, Presbyterian, and Baptist, joined together to form the Reformed Church of Equatorial Guinea. In 1974, a presidential decree obliged all priests to proclaim from the pulpit, "Never Macías, always with Macías. Down with colonialism and the ambitious," and Macías Nguema's portrait was exhibited as being the "only miracle of Equatorial Guinea." At the end of 1974 the PUNT prohibited all religious meetings and processions. The Milicia Popular and the PUNT members had to control the missionaries' "subversive" activities. In January 1976 private religious meetings were forbidden, and priests had to obtain Macías Nguema's personal authorization for traveling. All contacts with missionaries and donations were forbidden. The Protestant church of Santa Isabel was declared a military zone; a Catholic church was changed into an arsenal. The Santa Isabel cathedral was included in the presidential ghetto and deconsecrated, like the Bata one. In June 1976 Bishop A. M. Ndongo, Vicar of the Bata Diocese, was assassinated in the Bata prison, and the priests I. Obama and L. Ondo Mayie were kept prisoners, and apparently liquidated.

During the spring of 1978 six Claretian priests (between 60 and 80 years old) were jailed in Fernando Po. Spain had to pay a ransom of $60,000 for them. Churches were reopened by virtue of Decree No. 2 of August 1979, shortly after the fall of the Macías Nguema dictatorship. In September, however, the American association Catholics for Christian Political Action drew attention to the fact there had not been any real change in the new government's attitude.

In April 1980, the Apostolic Delegate from the Vatican paid a short visit to Santa Isabel. Salesian missionaries also arrived this time; by 1986 their number had risen to 22. In July 1980, the return of Bishop Nzé Abuy from exile was announced. The Claretian missionaries returned in force with funds provided by the International Society of the Claret Missionary Fathers, whose headquarters are in Chicago. In 1982, Nzé Abuy was consecrated archbishop of Santa Isabel while A. Sima was made Bishop of Bata and I. Obama Bishop of Ebebiyin (for details of the Papal visit see Vatican). In the summer of 1986 Franciscan Contemplative Sisters founded a convent in the country. The Salesians inaugurated a vocational school and a youth center at Bata. There were three minor seminaries with about a hundred seminarists. About a dozen Equato-Guineans were studying in the great seminaries of Spain. The seminary at Banapa had 21 seminarists in April 1987.

The following religious congregations were represented in Equatorial Guinea: Monks: Claretians, Salesians, Episcopalians, Brothers of La Salle, Verbum Dei. Nuns: Conceptionists, Saint Angel, Jesus-Maria, Carmelite, Salesians, Saint Ann, Servants of San José, Hospitalarians, Escolapians, Teresianians, Verbum Dei, Daughters of Charity, Augustians, Concepcionist, Daughters of the Christian Doctrine, Missionaries of Maria Immaculate.

On January 1, 1989, the Convent of the Franciscan Contemplative Nuns of Toledo was inaugurated at Akonibe (diocese of Ebebiyin)—it was the 500th Anniversary of their congregation. Equatorial Guinea belonged to the Association of Episcopal Conferences of Central Africa, along with Cameroon, Gabon, the Central African Republic, Chad, and Congo.

In mid-August 1990, Bishop Anacleto Sima Ngua proclaimed Our Lady of the Assumption official patron of the diocese of Bata. The minister for culture, the sculptor Mbomio, announced the founding of a new state religion (in the ex-Macías Nguema style): a religion for "national integration."

In 1991, 25 Equato-Guineans were studying at the Seminarío Mayor at Tenerife. The Seminarío minor at Banapa had 30 students. There were, at that time, only six secular priests, which explained the important role played by the cate-chists. In June, the priest of the archdiocese of Santa Isabel refused to celebrate mass with the archbishop, in protest against the Law on Religious Restrictions. In November, the Claretian Superior at Río Muni, P. Matogo Oyana, was named bishop of Ebebiyin. Religious propaganda was regarded as a violation of the rights recognized by the law, as an illegal form of persuasion. Any allusion to persons and state institutions in the homilies was prohibited, like any questioning of the legitimacy of the acts of the organs of the state.

In 1992, Equato-Guinean novices were studying at the Salesian mission at Lomé (Togo). In February the Conference of FERE was held. On October 12, several priests were threatened for having demanded respect for moral codes; at the Criminal Investigations Department, they were interrogated by the commis-sioner of police at Bata, Cayo Mba Ondo, and the secretary of state for national security, Nguema Mba, brother of Obiang Nguema. They were threatened with being shot, and reminded of the Macías Nguema period, when churches were closed down. In December, two priests were arrested and tortured in the capital.

Towards the end of 1992, a Spanish priest was arrested in Bata. Father Teodoro Saez Lasheras, the Director of Courses at La Salle, resigned because of the arrogance of the Criminal Investigations Department, which tried to infiltrate agents in the establishment. Soon after, a demonstration by students was repressed with arrests numbering 40; the students were imprisoned and tortured. In the capital, the monastery of the Claretian fathers attached to the cathedral was being used as a barracks for the Moroccans.

In early 1993, there were 270 Catholic monks and priests (natives and foreigners). The minister for justice and religion, Mariano Nsue, seized the old mission of the Claretian Fathers, at Concepción (Riaba); the missionaries filed a suit against the minister. In late January, Mgr. Matogo Oyana, the bishop of Ebebiyin, published a document specifying the role of the priest in prophetic denunciation, clearly alluding to the political situation. *La Verdad* (CPDS) stressed that Mgr Matogo was the only sincere prelate; the others were said to be cowardly accomplices of the regime. In August 1993, the priest of Río Benito was forced to go into hiding, due to Nguemist threats, and his father was tortured in Bata. A Salesian was expelled, accused of offensive sermons. On October 4 the first Equato-Guinean (Franciscan) contemplative nun, Rufina Maria, was consecrated in Akonibe.

In 1994, the Spanish Cooperation was being run through the FERE, with 220 volunteers for cooperation (of whom 130 were missionaries), 36 Congregations were involved.

In late April 1995, the apostolic nuncio Abril Castellón (who lived at Yaoundé, Cameroon) delivered a letter from Pope John Paul II to Obiang Nguema requesting clemency for S. Moto Nsá and others condemned. The next day, he received Angel Obama Obiang, a representative of the POC.

In mid-1995, the government authorized the Asociación de Centros Católicos de Enseñaza, supported by the Episcopal Conference and the nuncio of the region. In Río Muni, there was a fresh outbreak of persecutions directed against the church, especially the catechists, by government representatives, and especially in the districts of Mikomeseng, Akonibe et Evinayong. During the municipal elections in September, the missions of the Aesculapius and the Calasancian priests were ransacked at the orders of the provincial governor, in order to find an alleged radio transmitter.

When Obiang Nguema announced the advancement of the presidential election to February 25, the Ministry of the Interior published in mid-January 1996 a document criticizing and condemning the position of the clergy over human rights (and therefore political matters). Rev. José Carlos Esono was arrested and tortured, and accused of opposing the candidacy of Obiang Nguema. On January 27, the bishop of Bata, Anacleto Sima Nguema, addressed a letter to the dictator, protesting against the position of the Ministry of the Interior, and justifying the position of the church for apostolic reasons and threatening to reduce the number of places of worship to 5%. Recalling the closure of churches under Macías Nguema, Sima Ngua demanded the cancellation of measures violating the constitution and the international commitments of the country. In February 1995, following torture by Nguemists, a group of monks and nuns from Bata addressed a communiqué to Radio Exteríor de España denouncing the insults, humiliations, violence, house-arrests, and torture with which the members of all confessions were oppressed. The people organized days of prayer meant to ward off Nguemist terror. The Special Rapporteur of the United Nations Human Rights Commission stressed before the Commission, in March 1996, the numerous violations of religious freedom. On June 28, 1996, the Vatican named archbishop Felix del Blanco Prieto Apostolic Nuncio of Cameroon, with Equatorial Guinea falling within his jurisdiction.

In December 1997, Bosch, a bookshop in Madrid, collected secondhand books, part of which were sent to the Mission of the Sisters of the Holy Family, in Nsork.

On July 23, 1998, three missionaries (two monks and a layman) belonging to the mission of Añisok were expelled and sought refuge in Cameroon. One was a 69-year-old Argentine, a Claretian missionary/doctor who has been in Equatorial Guinea for 11 years; the other was a Spanish Carmelite nun who has been in Añisok for 18 years. The 10 missionaries who were left were not allowed to leave the mission house, even for religious matters. These missionaries take care of a project dealing with autonomous rural development that is supported by the U.S. embassy. The Nunciature and the U.S. embassy have sent letters of complaint to the nguemist authorities. On July 25, 1998, after the Bubi trial and while the trial of the leaders of Fuerza Democática Republicana was being held, the archbishop Ildefonso Obama denounced the fact that "catholic priests and nuns in Equatorial Guinea are victims of persecutions and bad treatment." In Ebebiyin and Mikomeseng (province of Kié-Ntem) priests must ask for authorization to minister their parish and celebrate mass. Some priests were put under house arrest and others were forced into exile. A little earlier, Obama refused to meet with President Obiang Nguema. On August 3, in the cathedral of Malabo, Obama called for "the respect of human dignity." He sent straightforward warnings to Obiang Nguema, and rejected the accusations concerning "the lack of goodwill" addressed to priests by the dictatorship. In the middle of August, the archbishop, while celebrating the feast of the patron of the capital, and in front of Obiang Nguema, asked for "transparency" during the elections at the end of 1998. They must be "fair and peaceful to protect love, peace and unity among all the citizens."

The Salesian missionaries are active in four centers: Bata, Mikomeseng, Malabo and Banapa; the Salesian nuns are present in Bata and Malabo. In Bata, there is Anselmo Perez, a Salesian priest head of Carital for Río Munii, under the direction of father Augustín Hernandez, also a Salesian, for the whole country.

See also Armengol Coll; Committee for Voluntary Return; Obama Obono, I.; Ondo Obiang, F.; Protestantism; Terror; Usera Y Alarcon, J.; Vatican

CATTLE. In the "transitional" government of January 1992, the Ministry of Animal Husbandry and Fisheries fell into the hands of Miguel Oyono Ndong Mifumu, the vice-prime minister. The FAO made no mention of animal husbandry in Equatorial Guinea in 1992, though there most certainly had been 5,000 head of cattle counted within the Moka zone towards the end of the year. In the December 22, 1993, government, the post of minister for agriculture, fisheries and food fell to Daniel Mba Ndemensogo. In the January 8, 1996, government, D. Djoni Becoba was the one to take over the post of minister. He retained it in the ministerial reshuffle of April 8, 1996.

See also Agriculture.

CAUSSE, Marcel. Ambassador of France from 1985 to 1989.

CAYETANO TOHERIDA, Ernesto Maria. A Bubi, from Batete, born 1929. Electrician. Became the director for settlement on March 5, 1981. He was elected deputy of the sole party (PDGE) in 1988.

In the "transitional" government of January 1992, he was the minister for labor and social improvement. In the November elections, he was again elected deputy of the PDGE. He retained his functions in the 1998 Government.

CEGUI (Compañía Española del Golfo de Guinea). Spanish company, financed by the Banco Español de Crédito, owner of an oil palm plantation in Mangola, near Concepción, with 322 hectares (approx. 800 acres) producing 3,600 ton-clusters a year. Besides coffee plantations, it also owned a small cattle ranch near San Carlos.

CEIA see Comunidad de Españoles Con Intereses en Africa

CELINE, Louis-Ferdinand (pseud. Destouches, Louis). A French writer. He stayed in Africa, between 1916 and 1917, with the lumber company Shanga-Oubangui (which he calls in his *Voyage au bout de la nuit* "the Gunpowder company of Little Togo"). He participated in lumber operations in Cameroon at war with the Germans. He would sometimes get away from it all to live in Spanish Guinea.

CENSORSHIP. After the Ndongo Miyone affair on March 5, 1969, censorship of the mass media was enforced. All correspondence is controlled by the Guardia Nacional (National Guard) and the presidency; the foreign press is stopped at the border; the radio no longer broadcasts bulletins, except Macías Nguema's speeches, and schoolbooks are strictly censored. Spanish scientific works on Guinea were burned in public in 1972. Likewise from 1970 to 1976, no information coming from Equatorial Guinea was published in the Spanish press (materia reservada).

During 1980, Spain again imposed censorship on news from Equatorial Guinea, a return to the *materia reservada* of Macías Nguema times.

In 1981, the military government, under the pretext of false reports by the Spanish press, banned the stocking and sale of the Spanish newspapers *Diario 16, Cambio 16,* and *Interviú* under pain of imprisonment and a fine of 100-5000,000 bikwele, as well as expulsion of those found guilty. But it allowed the others in, in order to avoid the isolation not only of Spanish volunteers for cooperation but also Equato-Guinean Hispanophones. All copies already in the country were to be burnt within three days. This censorship was lifted on October 12, after an announcement of Spanish military aid.

In 1992, the government prohibited airlines and shipping companies from delivering newspapers, with a threat of sanctions against offenders. The measure was lifted in mid-1993. During the summer of 1994, State Secretary S. Ngua Nfuma demanded that *La Verdad* and *El Sol* avoid making opinion-based reports. In 1995, a member of the CPDS returning from training in Spain was arrested for possession of newspapers and course notes.

In January 1997, Cosme Nguema, an announcer on national radio and TV, a militant of the party in power (PDGE), and a member of the nguemist regime's political police, was arrested and imprisoned for a month for having reported a student strike. On that occasion, the dictatorship forbade radio and TV reporters to deal with social movements, as well as with any international news. See also Convergency for Social Democracy; Elo Mabale, R.; Joint Opposition Platform.

CENTRAL AFRICAN REPUBLIC. On October 29, 1996, the inauguration of the Zafiro oilfield, exploited by Mobil and UMC, took place in the presence of President A. Patassé.

CENTRAL AFRICA STATES DEVELOPMENT BANK (Banco de Desarrollo de los Estados de Africa Central, BADEAC). Admitted Equatorial Guinea as a sixth member state in 1983. The French-oriented BADEAC granted a special loan of $1.5 million in 1986, for the modernization of Bata's electrical plant and network.

From its entry into the CFA zone until 1991, Equatorial Guinea received FCFA 360 million from the BADEAC.

CENTRO DE DESARROLLO DE LA EDUCACION (CDE) (Education Development Center). After the departure of the Spanish teachers in 1969, the need of training secondary-school teachers became urgent. With the help of UNESCO and the United Nations Development Program (UNDP) a sort of Education Institute was set up in the building of the Teachers' Training College in Bata to train primary, secondary, and vocational teachers, as well as inspectors. Despite Macías Nguema's hostility, a team of experts started the program at the end of 1974 with 80 students. Professors from Cuba, Spain, and France also participated in the training program. But early in 1977 the 60 remaining students were sent to teach in inland schools before the end of their studies, or put to forced labor in Fernando Po's plantations. Thus no students graduated from the school. Several of them live today as refugees in Cameroon and Gabon. After the expulsion of the chief UNESCO expert in 1974, then the assassination of all higher officials of the Popular Education Ministry (Ochaga, Esono, Obiang Mba) in 1976, it is now the accountant of the Ministry for Río Muni who is head of the depopulated CDE, first under the supervision of Health Minister Obiang Alogo Ondo, later that of Macías Nguema himself as "Great Master in Education and Culture." Since 1971 the United Nations (UNDP, UNESCO, UNICEF) have invested about $1.5 million in this project without training one single teacher. In 1977 UNESCO announced its intention of terminating its assistance for lack of concrete results. In December 1977 experts were removed.

CESSION. In 1827 Spain proposed to sell Fernando Po and Annobón to the United Kingdom. In 1839 the British government made an offer of £50,000 (4.5 million reales). Spain refused and claimed £60,000 in 1840 hoping to cover her debts with this sum. The United Kingdom agreed to this amount in 1841 but Spanish public opinion was strongly opposed to the cession and scuttled the project. In 1869 Spain set up a committee to analyze the possible cession of its colony but no report was ever submitted. In 1875, King Leopold II of Belgiium intended to purchase, without results, some parts of Spain's colonial possessions (Fernando Poo, Canary islands). In 1883 the German Colonial Society envisaged buying Fernando Po. New inquiries were made by Belgium in 1889. At the beginning of the 20th century Spain considered the cession of the colony to a private company but the project was short circuited by the Cámara Agrícola de Fernando Po. Conversely, during World War II several Spanish authors suggested occupying Nigeria by Spanish forces.

CHACON Y MICHELENA, Carlos. Frigate commander. First Spanish Governor of Fernando Po and founder of the colony. He arrived in May 1958 accompanied by an engineer, a medical doctor, explorers, Jesuits, a prefabricated hospital, and infantry troops. Catholicism was proclaimed the official religion on the island and the Baptist missionaries were ordered to leave. He improved the access to the Santa Isabel harbor, started to build some roads, and took a census of the population (Santa Isabel: 858 inhab.). He levied a ten-peso passage for each boat using the Muni Estuary (to be collected by the Corisco authorities) in spite of strong protests from France. Chacón left the colony 15 months later, and was replaced by Gandara.

CHAMBER OF REPRESENTATIVES see Parliament

CHEMA MICHERO, Juan. Born 1924 in Musola. Employee of the National Archives since 1944. In 1964 he was elected one of the three heads of families to represent San Fernando. From 1964 to 1982, he was director of the National Library and head of the National Archives. In 1965 he participated in a training course at the Madrid School of Documentalists.

CHEYSSON, Claude. Visited Santa Isabel as French minister for foreign affairs soon after Obiang Nguema's coup d'etat. His brother was said to have had business relations with Macías Nguema.

CHILBO see Timber

CHILDREN. In March 1980 UNICEF participated in the reorganization of health services for children. Tutelary courts for minors were established in May.

The Comite de Apoyo at Niño guineano (Support Group for Guinean Children), which received medicine from the French association Diby-Affouse France-Africa in 1992 and 1993, was presided over by Obiang Nguema's first wife.

In April 1993, a Spanish mission observed the serious state of health, especially of children, in Annobón, whose mortality rate was greater and birth weight less than that of the rest of the country.

In 1996, it was reported that there is an alarming increase in child prostitution. See also Army; Baney; Education; UNICEF.

CHILI. In 1996 the Sipetrol company showed interest in oil exploitation in Equatorial Guinea. See also Buchanan, R.

CHIME, Mount. Summit in the center of Río Muni, north of Evinayong. Altitude: 1,200 m. (approx. 3,800 feet).

CHINA, Nationalist Republic of (Taiwan). Diplomatic relations between Equatorial Guinea and Taiwan were established in 1979. The Taiwanese minister for foreign affairs, Yang Hsi-Kun, visited Santa Isabel in 1980, but in 1991, Equatorial Guinea limited its relations solely to communist China.

In April 1994, investors from Taiwan offered 4 Mio $ to Obiang Nguema. See also China, People's Republic of.

CHINA, People's Republic of. Diplomatic relations were established on October 8, 1970. The Chinese technical assistance concerns particularly the building of a road from N'Kue to Mongomo (225 km), agricultural research, medical assistance with 18 members at the Bata hospital, installation of two printing offices, sports training of the Juventud en Marcha con Macías, and a flat loan of $12.5 million (800 million pesetas) over 50 years for telecommunications, etc. The Guardia Nacional is equipped with Chinese arms and vehicles. Scholarships for sports training have been offered in China. Chinese assistance hardly uses any Guinean personnel. However, the Chinese officers complain about the government's incapacity to offer personnel to be trained. The state-owned shops of Equatorial Guinea sell mainly Chinese goods. Beginning in June 1977 a Guinean commercial mission directed by Esono Ondo visited Peking after visiting Vietnam. During his journey he met President Hua Kuo Feng who announced a slowing down of assistance to Equatorial Guinea. After the 1979 coup, medical aid continued and was supplemented by the construction of the hydroelectric power installation of Bicomo, near Bata. China made loans totalling US $45 million to Equatorial Guinea.

In 1980, the Chinese team comprised 300 members, including nine doctors and medical personnel, in Bata. Other volunteers for cooperation constructed the Nku-Mongomo road, the embassy in Santa Isabel, as well as various elements of the thermal electric power stations in Bata and in the capital. The construction of the hydro-electric power station in Bicomo, near Bata, was going on, along with that of two new radio stations, in Bata and Santa Isabel.

Chinese loans rose to $45 million in 1983. Obiang Nguema visited China in 1984 and inspected a division of the people's army.

In spite of the international boycott in 1990 following the events of Tiananmen Square, Obiang Nguema returned to China, to renegotiate the debt and to ask for an increase in bilateral aid. A technical mission arrived in August to study the feasibility of the Bata-Ebebiyin road project and of the construction of a new 50-bed ward in the capital's hospital. China then became the second biggest donor, after Spain, preceding Italy.

Ambassador Wang Yongcheng represented the People's Republic of China from 1993 onwards.

A delegation from Beijing attended the 1st party Convention of the PDGE in Bata in the spring of 1995. In 1995, the People's Republic of China took third place among the clients of Equatorial Guinea ($14 million), behind the USA and Japan; it did not figure among the five top suppliers. At the end of 1995, the wife of the Equato-Guinean ambassador to Beijing, Lino Sima Ekua Avomo, was arrested in Brazil for dealing cocaine. Sima Ekua was sent as ambassador to France.

In June 1996 the Export-Import Bank of China announced that it was going to grant soft loans to six African countries, of which Equatorial Guinea is one. It appears that this type of loan is aimed at countering the presence of Taiwan. Obiang Nguema traveled to China from September 1–8. He was received by President Jiang Zemin, Prime Minister Li Peng and Minister of Foreign Commerce Mrs.

Wu Yi. A $3 million loan was granted. At the same time as his equivalent in Taiwan, Minister of Foreign Affairs Qian Qichen visited in January 1997 five African states, among which was Equatorial Guinea.

In 1997 an economic and technical agreement was signed during the visit of the vice-prime minister and minister, and Qian Qichen, the minister of foreign affrairs (3 Mio $, for the sectors of electricity, lumber, agriculture and breeding). Qian Qichen is the most eminent Chinese figure to have visited Equatorial Guinea. He expressed his satisfaction with respect to Obiang Nguema's policy of "one single China." The department of health is undergoing changes: Voluntary service from overseas is being replaced by private doctors. In August 1997, the Chinese ambassador Zhang Saxun was replaced by Chen Huailong.

At the beginning of 1998, a mission from Beijing, invited by the PDGE, came to plead the cause of one single China. In June, the civil engineering company China Orient, signed, with the finance minister, an agreement of 300 Mio $ for a housing project. At the end of 1998, the work had not started. Ambassador of Equatorial Guinea: Florencio Maye Ela Mangue.

See also China, Nationalist Republic (Taiwan); Drugs; "Democratic" Party of Equatorial Guinea; Economy; Finances; France; Italy; Justice; Mba Oñana, F.; Nepotism; Nguema Oyono, L.; Obiang Nguema, T.; Public Health; Trade; Transports.

CHI YONG-HO. North Korean ambassador from 1991.

CHOCOLATE, Mount. Summit of the Neifang-Mikomeseng mountain range in west-central Río Muni, 1,100 m high (approx. 3,500 feet), facing Mount Alen. Between both lies the Bata-Evinayong road.

CHOISY, Nicolas. An advocate in Geneva who rounded the company Andromis Ltd., for the export of medicine and medical material to Equatorial Guinea. He was reported, in the press, to be G. Llansol's counsellor. See also Engonga Motulu, M.

CHONI BECOBA, Vidal. Bubi. From Rebola. He was employed by the Spanish business Mora y Mallo. He later became the civilian governor of Río Muni. He was designated mayor of Santa Isabel by Decree 24 of March 5, 1981, replacing Lt. Alonso Rabat Icaca, appointed after the August 3, 1979, coup d'etat.

In the January 8, 1996, cabinet reshuffle, he became minister for agriculture and livestock. He retained his portfolio in the April 8 ministerial reshuffle. In the government of January 21, 1998, he was minister of Industry, Trade and the Promotion of small and medium-sized firms.

See also Mokudi Nanga, A.

CHOURAKI, Francine and Simone (born Lavent). Francine Chouraki is the wife of García Trevijano, Macías Nguema's economic adviser and lawyer in Spain. Her sister, Simone, is García Trevijano's secretary. As such she became in 1972 one of the administrators of Simed S. A., an import-export company created by García Trevijano, attempting to monopolize the external Equato-Guinean trade, like the former Infoge. García Trevijano, the initiator of the Société Forestière du Río Muni, which was looking for a buyer (1976), entrusted Simone Chouraki with the necessary steps in this affair.

CHURCH see Missions; Vatican; World Council of Churches

"CIEN FUEGOS" see Obama Owono Nchama, J.

CIVIL GUARD see Guardia Civil

CIVIL JUNTA FOR NATIONAL SALVATION (Junta cívica de Salvación nacional). This movement was born in Saragoza, Spain, in the period June-July 1983 of the division in the Coordination Council of Opposition Forces (Junta Coordinadora de las Fuerzas de la Oposición) by a group of former members of the Nguemist regime: Moto Nsá, former editor of the newspaper *Ebano* and secretary of state for information; Jones Dougan, the prosecutor at the trial of Macías Nguema; Andombe Buanga, former manager of the Banco de Desarrollo y Crédito. Elected general secretary in August 1983, Alejo Ekube wished for a dialogue with Obiang Nguema. The Junta Civica failed to make any contact with Obiang Nguema. Ekube hinted at possible army intervention from neighboring countries. He proposed an economic embargo. In 1984, a committee of 11 members was announced, which included S. Moto Nsá, J. L. Jones Dougan, G. Andombe Buanga, C. Marqués. They formed a shadow government, and claimed to enjoy support in Cameroon and Gabon, and in Madrid, Barcelona, and Valencia.

In early 1988, A. Mba Ndong, the former Nguemist liaison man with the UN Human Rights Commission, was elected president of the Junta. He demanded that Spain define its policy and make national reconciliation and the return of the refugees conditions for any aid. In 1990, during Moto Nsá's first journey to Santa Isabel, the Junta broke up.

CLARENCE CITY see Santa Isabel

CLARET, Antonio María see Usera y Alarcón, J. M.

COCOA. Imported to Fernando Po by a Fernandino around 1850, then officially via São Tomé in 1854. The first plantations were set up towards 1860. Cocoa spread from Fernando Po to Nigeria, Liberia, and Ghana shortly afterwards. At the end of the 19th century, most planters were Fernandinos and Spaniards. Cocoa production started in 1888. In 1899, Fernando Po was already producing 6,000 tons. In 1902 cocoa exports were 1,200 tons, reaching 10,000 tons in 1922; then it fell to 8,500 tons in 1927. The Casas Fuertes (big companies) traded Bubi land for annual pensions and scholarships for Bubi students. Under the Barrera government, the Fernandinos did well, first because of Fang labor (from Río Muni and Cameroon) and then, Liberian manpower. Fernandino cocoa is often transferred into bags marked Caracas or São Tomé at its arrival in Barcelona to benefit from better prices. The Unión de Agricultores (Farmer's Union), an offshoot of the Cámara Oficial Agrícola (Official Agricultural Chamber) tried to fight against speculation in Spain. With the return of Fangs to Río Muni towards 1926-30, indigenous cocoa plantations appeared along the Bata-Ebebiyin road. The stagnation of Liberian labor starting in 1929 favored the arrival of Cameroonese and Nigerians. As of 1935 the sulphating of trees started, as well as the use of pesticides, which—paired with the progress of indigenous plantations—increased production tremendously. Equatorial Guinea was the world's third largest per capita cocoa producer. Between 1952 and 1956, Spanish Guinea accounted for

2.4% of the world production; at the time of independence it reached 3.8%, of which 90% was produced by Fernando Po in about 50 large plantations. Cocoa plantations covered 60,000 hectares, of which 10,000 were in Río Muni; but many plantations were in need of renewal. At the time of Independence, 75% of Fernando Po's gross national product came from the marketing of cocoa, mainly by the Ambas Bay Company (subsidiary of the United African Company), but also by Spanish and German companies who often did not own any plantations but bought the cocoa from Fernandino landlords or cooperatives. Bosio Dioco, first vice-president of the republic, owned a chocolate factory in Santa Isabel.

The FAO forecast an annual production of 40,000 tons for the first two years after independence, but in 1969–1970 production reached only 28,000 tons. The closing of most Spanish exploitations by Macías Nguema, in March 1969, provoked a new fall in the production despite redistribution of plantations to Fang officials. Through an economic assistance treaty Spain agreed to buy 20,000 tons of cocoa annually; only the surplus was free to be sold to others. This surplus stock generally went to the United Kingdom, West Germany, the Netherlands, or the United States.

In 1970, cocoa represented 27.1% of the gross national product. Since the dissolution of the Comité Sindical del Cacao (Cocoa Trade Union) in 1972, Equatorial Guinea has been looking for a company to take over the marketing of its production. In 1970-71 the Ghanean Allotey and his American wife Tyler sold more than $2 million of Equatorial Guinean cocoa (4,000 tons) to the General Cocoa Company of New York without paying the producers, which led to their arrest in 1973. The 1975–1976 production was bought by the German Democratic Republic: it only reached 8,000 tons against 34,000 in 1968–1969, 22,000 in 1971–1972 and 12,000 tons in 1974–1975; thus it almost fell to the 1950 level. In January 1976, about 26,000 out of 45,000 Nigerians left the country, which augured new drops in production despite the forced labor imposed on 2,500 persons of each district (60,000 in total). Forced labor made it possible to save 8,000 tons of cocoa in 1976–1977, bought by the Soviet Union, the People's Republic of China, and Cuba. In 1973 UNDP recommended the reestablishment of a 30,000-ton level without for the moment considering processing industries. In 1974, Spain granted three annual credits of $780,000 each (50 million pesetas) for the purchase of equipment and fertilizer in Spain.

In 1979, cocoa production did not exceed 4,000 tons a year. By 1985 it had risen to 8,500, but fell again to 5,000 tons in 1987, which was the same tonnage as the 1920 crop. There are about 25,000 hectares of viable plantations in the country. 17,000 hectares of these were acquired by the Swiss citizen Wetzel in 1983.

In 1985, Obiang Nguema auctioned off the Spanish company Chafers plantations near the capital. The BADEA loaned $2.8 million, repayable over 16 years, for the rehabilitation of 7.550 hectares of cocoa plantation (out of the 60,000 hectares planted in 1968). The IDA put $11 million more into the project, and the government $2.2 million. The aim was to produce 800–1000 kg/ha against 300 kg/ha produced elsewhere in Africa. The increase in production costs caused export revenues to fall by 20%.

Production and Exportation of Cocoa (according to FAO)

Year	Production 000 t	Exportations 000 t
1979	6,000	5,587
1980	8,000	6,749
1981	9,900	8,607
1982	7,000	6,859
1983	6,600	9,431
1984	7,000	6,727
1985	8,311	8,280
1986	6,982	8,960
1987	7,903	7,905
1988	7,828	8,432
1989	7,225	7,041
1990	6,670	5,565
1991	5,673	5,640
1992	5,600	4,648
1993	3,900	3,200
1994	2,000	4,000
1995	3,900	4,200
1996	4,200	6,800

Eighty-seven cocoa-related companies were involved in the bankruptcy of the Guinextebank in 1987. An Institute for the promotion of cocoa (Improcao) was founded. The IMF demanded a clarification of the question of ownership rights over the plantations, which had been confiscated by the Nguemists. The Spanish Natra bought one half of the produce in 1988. Equatorial Guinea was admitted as a full member of the ICCO.

In 1985, a kilo of cocoa cost FCFA 500; in 1989, the price was only FCFA 400. The 1988/89 harvest fell by 20% for climatic reasons and due to a lack of materials and the low price caused cocoa smuggling into the neighbor countries: in Cameroon a kilo of cocoa cost FCFA 435 and in Gabon it was selling at FCFA 430. Between 1968 and 1988, production went down by 82%. In spite of efforts at rehabilitation, the country never did recover after the departure of Nigerian laborers in 1976.

The production and export of cocoa between 1979 and 1996 (according to the FAO) are listed above.

In 1989, the IBRD suggested that Equatorial Guinea cancel government funding of production and that production costs be reduced from HFCFA 300 to Fr 250.

A lowering of the quality of the cocoa was obvious from 1991. Less than 15,000 of the 46,000 hectares of plantation was exploitable. Young planters of Fernando Po gave up cultivation as a result of the fall in prices.

In the nineties, Spanish assistance allowed the replanting of 1,200 hectares of cocoa trees. The total planted area with cocoa was 50,000 hectares in 1998.

See also African Development Bank; Agriculture; Arab Bank for African Development; Cacawal; Cooperativas del Campo, Village; International Bank for Reconstruction and Development; Mallo, J.; Mikomeseng; Niefang; Obiang Nguema, T.; Roig Balestros, F. A.; Sampaka; Trade.

COCONUT PALM ISLAND (Cocotiers, Island). Situated near the Gabonese littoral, south of Corisco. The island has been occupied by Gabonese forces in 1972 together with other Equato-Guinean islands (Conga and Mbañe).

Towards the end of 1992, Equatorial Guinea again refused to give up Mbañe, Cocoteros, and Conga to Gabon. Though the island was annexed by a Gabonese presidential decree in January 1993, along with Mbañe, French diplomatic documents continue to consider these islands as Equato-Guinean.

COCOTIERS, Island see Coconut Palm Island

COFFEE. Introduced by a private individual from São Tomé as early as 1800, coffee was officially imported in 1850. However, commercial production only started in 1890, and was subjected to heavy import taxes by Spain. In 1899 the production of coffee at Fernando Po was eight tons. At the beginning of the 20th century coffee exports were insignificant. In 1910 they amounted to 2.5 tons, in 1922, 7 tons, and in 1927, 42 tons. With the return in 1930 of Fang laborers from Fernando Po, Río Muni became the coffee province. From 9 tons in 1917, the Guinean production rose to 2,451 tons in 1939, 9,429 in 1960, of which 7,740 tons were from Río Muni. Production consists of two-thirds Robusta and one-third Liberia. Under the assistance treaty signed with Spain in 1969, the former metropolis was to purchase at least 6,000 tons of coffee; only the surplus was free to be sold elsewhere. From 1965 to 1971 the average production was 6,700 tons of which 75 percent came from small landowners of Río Muni. With the slump following independence, the 1975–1976 production only reached 3,000 tons. Equatorial Guinea is a member of the International Coffee Organization.

In 1978 production dropped below 1,500 tons and after the 1979 coup it dwindled into insignificance. In 1984, total production was still only 500 tons, but in the 1985–1986 season exports rose to 1,000 tons.

The country became the ninth member of the OAMCAF in 1986. The base of exportable coffee was fixed at 20,706 bags of 60 kg.

BBC Guinea, the coffee company, suffered from the bankruptcy of the Guinextebank, in 1987. The cost price fell from CFA Fr. 350 in 1987–1988, to CFA Fr 250 in February 1989. Coffee was being smuggled into neighboring countries in 1988.

COGUISA (Compaña de Guinea, Sociedad Anónima). Company owning an oil palm plantation of 406 hectares (approx. 1,000 acres) in N'Colamvam exploited by ALENA until 1971. Presently the exploitation is no longer profitable.

COGUMADERA see Timber

COLASESGA. French society of civil engineering; part of the Bouyigues group. It built the new French embassy (50 Mio $), the mission of Cooperation, as well as 25 houses for people serving on voluntary service overseas (350 Mio FF).

COLEGIO MAYOR UNIVERSITARIO NUESTRA SEÑORA DE AFRICA see Our Lady of Africa Superior University College

COLOMBIA see Arms Dealing; Drugs

COLOMBITE-TANTALITE see Akonibe

COLONIAL GUARD see Guardia Colonial

COMILLAS, Marqués de. His real name is Claudio Lopez y Brú. One of the 38 grand marquises of Spain, sixth largest latifundium owner, with 23,720 hectares President of the Compañia Trasatlántica. On his incentive, Bonelli and Valero Belenguer (both agents of Trasatlántica) traveled through the Río Muni in 1890 (Ríos Benito and Utamboni) in order to establish trading posts. Comillas made considerable donations for building the Moka church and the Santa Isabel Cathedral.

"COMISARIO Z" see Mbenga Ndong, V.

COMISION PROVINCIAL DE SERVICIOS TECNICOS (Provincial Commission of Technical Services). Since 1960 such a commission has existed in each province. Their purpose was to assist the civil governor in his tasks, but they have practically never been in operation.

COMITE SINDICAL (Trade Union). Following the Spanish example of vertical trade unions, the cocoa, coffee, and timber unions were created between 1936 and 1946, and after two governmental decrees (1952, 1954) were to include a president representing the Ministry of Commerce and Industry, a vice-president representing the Presidency of the Government (Carrero Blanco), five representatives of the planters or foresters, and five representatives of the corresponding Spanish industry. Their headquarters were obligatorily in Madrid. They were to control prices, grant concessions, and credits. All planters or foresters had to join the trade union, the selling of their products being impossible otherwise. The unions were above all instruments of governmental control, defending only European and Fernandino interest as well as those of the Spanish industry. They were dissolved three years after independence.

COMMITTEE FOR THE VOLUNTARY RETURN OF REFUGEES TO EQUATORIAL GUINEA (Comité de Retorno Voluntarío de Refugiados a Guinea Ecuatorial). In 1992, Mokong Onguene was the coordinator of the Returnees' Committee launched in Geneva with the support of Protestant and Catholic churches and the World Council of Churches. The project concerned 64 families settled in Switzerland, Germany and Spain. The committee's president was the professor of theology from Bern, Lukas Vischer, who had been received by Obiang Nguema. Mokong Onguene declared in the press that "if someone were to die, that would be me." See also Mba Ekua Miko, B.; Mokong Onguene, C.

COMMUNICATIONS see Telecommunications; Transportation

COMPAÑIA AEREA DE GUINEA ECUATORIAL (COAGE). In 1998, it had a daily flight Malabo–Bata.

COMPANIA DE GUINEA S.A. see Coguisa

COMPANIA ESPANOLA DEL GOLFO DE GUINEA see Cegui

COMPANIA TRASATLANTICA see Trasatlantica

COMUNIDAD DE ESPANOLES CON INTERESES EN AFRICA (CEIA). (Community of Spaniards with interests in Africa). Since 1970 CEIA has grouped former colonial circles that were stripped of their belongings for various reasons, about 380 companies all told, representing 2.174 million pesetas ($32 million). With the complicity of the former Equatorial Guinean ambassador in Madrid, Nsué Ngomo, an attempt to overthrow Macías Mguema is said to have been prepared in 1970 with the help of British mercenaries and a plan to install W. Jones Niger in the presidency. The plot having been discovered, Equatorial Guinea suspended its ambassador and Spain exiled him to Andorra. In June 1973 CEIA accused the Spanish state of not safeguarding the security of the Spanish companies in Guinea and asked the Banco de Credito Industrial to release 600 million pesetas ($87 million) to favor new economic activities in Equatorial Guinea, but the government disregarded its recommendations.

In 1997, its president was Carlos Fleitas. It has 400 members. They are still waiting for compensation. See also Asociación de Antiguos Residentes.

CONCEPCION. Locality situated on the east coast of Fernando Po, near the heights of Moka. In 1973, the PUNT proposed to call it Riaba. The British had called it Melville Bay during the first half of the 19th century. At the beginning of the 16th century Ramos de Esquivel, a Portuguese, established a trading post and a plantation. In 1885 the consul of Portugal, Diaz de Acunha, owned plantations in Concepción. In 1887 a Consejo de Vecinos, a municipal judge and a Claretian missionary school were established. The church of Concepción was partly financed by M. C. Jones. Since 1900, the Conceptionist Sisters have been running the hospital, and in 1941 they took over the orphanage of the Patronato de Indígenas. Since 1959 junior Oblates have been trained in Concepción. The Seminarío Menor (a priest-staffed secondary school) created in 1956 trained 25 students; it was closed at independence.

In December 1984, the expert sent by the UN Human Rights Commission noted that the civil and military authorities there were almost exclusively Fang.

The Concepción electrical power plant project began in 1986, with a power line to the capital via Musola, financed by the Central Economic Cooperation Fund (Fr 100 million) and the European Investment Bank (Fr 50 million). The power station was inaugurated on August 1, 1989.

In 1993, Marian Sue, the minister for justice and religion, seized the old Claretin mission, which filed a suit against him. In the municipal elections of September 1995, Ireneo Perujo Batajolo (PDGE) was elected mayor; he however died on December 24. See also France; Missions; Public Health; South Africa.

CONCEPTIONIST Sisters (Religiosas de la Inmaculada Concepción). Spanish religious order founded in Barcelona in 1850. The Conceptionists arrived in Spanish Guinea in 1885, settled in Basilé, then in Corisco. Since 1900 they ran the Concepción hospital, since 1906 that of Santa Isabel. In 1941 they took over the orphanage of the Patronato de Indígenas in Concepción. In the same town they started training junior Oblates in 1959, but had to give up in 1969. At the time of independence they owned 12 institutions in Equatorial Guinea: six schools, four hospitals, and two orphanages.

CONCESSIONS. During the 19th century the granting of concessions was rather unorganized. In July 1904 a royal decree attempted to clarify the situation and fixed a price of 30 pesetas/hectare for the lands of Fernando Po, 20 pesetas/hectare for those of Río Muni and 15 pesetas/hectare for Corisco, Elobeyes, and Annobón. The governor general could grant up to 100 hectares, the State Ministry from 100 to 10,000 hectares for 50 years, against an annual tax of three pesetas per hectare in Fernando Po, two in Río Muni, and 1.5 elsewhere. The Spanish Cabinet's agreement was needed for concession over 10,000 hectares. In 1926 large concessions developed in Río Muni, such as Izaguirre (20,000 hectares, or approx. 50,000 acres). Since 1928 the granting of concessions depended on the Dirección General de Marruecos y Colonias. Catholic missions were entitled to 10 hectares free per locality. After the disruption of Liberian workers' arrival, the assignment of concessions was suspended, in 1930, except for the forest concessions, which rose from 2,700 hectares in 1927 to 18,800 in 1941. Between 1944 and 1948 the granting of concessions was clearly reorganized in favor of Europeans, who regularly won at auction sales. Spaniards in general, and all officials, living respectively 10 and 15 years in the colony, could benefit from up to 30 hectares of free concessions; the non-emancipated could only dispose of 4 hectares. The new prices (480–650 pesetas/hectare) favored the large landowners. The provincial governments could grant up to 5,000 hectares, larger ones depending on the metropolitan government. Only with cooperative societies could the de facto monopoly of the large landowners be broken.

In 1971 the French Société Forestière du Río Muni received a 150,000-hectare concession (approx. 375,000 acres), as a guarantee for French loans to Guinea (see Société Francaise des Dragages).

CONCORD AIRLINES. A Nigerian company whose president, Moshood Abiola, signed a contract with Obiang Nguema for domestic flights and flights to Nigeria, in late 1990. Another agreement was signed in June 1991, but the project failed. See also Aviation.

CONGA Island. Situated about 9 km south of Corisco and 2 km south-west of Mbañe. Conga was occupied by Gabonese forces in 1972 in spite of Equato-Guinean protest. Macías Nguema is suspected of having sold the island to Gabon. See also Borders.

CONGO (BRAZZAVILLE). Even before the independence of Spanish Guinea, Congo welcomed political refugees, such as Mba Ovono. The late president Marion Nguabi as well as Mobutu Sese Seko, president of Zaïre, chaired the OAU Reconciliation Commission at the time of the border incident between Gabon and

Equatorial Guinea in 1972–1973, a session of this commission having taken place in Brazzaville. Obiang Nguema allocated 1 Mio Ff to Sasou Nguesso within the context of his coup d'etat. Sasou Nguesso is the godfather of Obiang's twins.

CONGO, Democratic Republic of (ex Zaire). Obiang Nguema sent a letter, dated May 27, 1997, to Laurence Kabila inviting him to reestablish the democratic and political institutions. The same day, he recognized the new regime.

On August 25, 1998, Obiang Nguema called for a cease-fire.

CONGRESO NACIONAL DE LOS PUEBLOS DE GUINEA ECUATO-RIAL (CNPGE) see National Peoples Congress of Equatorial Guinea

CONGUE, Constantino. In 1998, he became minister of Employment and Social Security.

CONSEJO DE GOBIERNO (Government Council). With autonomy, a cabinet of eight members was set up (four for each province), with a president, elected by the Asamblea General (Parliament). The president, nominated by a third of the members, was appointed by decree. Self-administrating, with a role similar to that of the former governor general, the Consejo decided on the bills to be submitted to the Asamblea General, prepared bills and the budget, and supervised the enforcement of the Asamblea General's decisions. By a two-thirds majority the latter could propose the dismissal of a councillor. The first Cabinet of May 1964 was presided over by Ondo Edu and included the following members: from Río Muni: Macías Nguema, Nang Obama, Nsué Nchama, Rondo Maguga, from Fernando Po: Itoha Creda, Watson Bueco, Maho Sikacha, and Borico Toichoa.

The Bubi (6 percent of the population) had four seats. The Cabinet was represented in Spain by Castillo Barril from Annobón. The following participated in the 1967 Constitutional Conference: Ondo Edu, Eñeso Neñe, Maho Sikacha, Nang Obama, Watson Bueco, Macías Nguema, and Castillo Barril. The councilors received a 40,000-peseta salary, a Mercedes car, a house with free personnel, and "gifts" from the Casas Fuertes. Corruption existed openly; Nsue Nchama was discharged in 1966 for misappropriation of funds. The September 1968 elections permitted the replacement of the Consejo de Gobierno by the Consejo de Ministros. Of the nine members of the 1964 Consejo de Gobierno, six—not including Rondo Maguga, who died naturally in 1967—became the victims, after independence, of the Nguemist power and were murdered.

CONSEJO DE LA REPUBLICA (Republican Council-Senate). Composed of six members elected for four years, who assumed the presidency in turn, province by province. Half of the senators were elected by the Consejos Provinciales (provincial assemblies). The senators could sit neither in the provincial assemblies nor in Parliament. The attributions of the Senate included examining the constitutionality of institutional laws, the legality of laws adopted by Parliament, the causes of incapacity or legal impediment of the president of the republic, the arbitration of conflicts between the state and the province, the nominations for Supreme Court judges. Mba Ada was the first president of the Senate. In 1973 it ceased functioning. Most former senators were assassinated or fled abroad.

CONSEJO DE MINISTROS (Cabinet of Ministers). Formed on October 8, 1968, under the guidance of Macías Nguema (who appointed half of its members, the other half being appointed by the Consejos Provinciales), the Cabinet was composed as follows: Presidency and Defense, Macías Nguema (MONA-LIGE/Grupo Macías); Foreign Affairs, Ndongo Miyone (MONALIGE); Interíor, Masie Ntutumu (MONALIGE/ Grupo Macías); Agriculture, Grange Molay (MONALIGE/Grupo Macías); Public Works, Oyono Alogo (MONALIGE); Industry and Mines, Martinez Erimola Yerna (MONALIGE/ Grupo Macías); Vice-President and Commerce, Bosio Dioco (Union Bubi); Education, Nsue Angue Osa (MUNGE/Grupo Macías); Finance, Ikuga Ebombebombe (MUNGE); Health, Ekong Andeme (IPGE); Justice, Eworo Obama (unaffiliated). The confusion between the president of the republic and the head of government, taken over from the Spanish system, rapidly led to conflicts. Besides, with one-third of the ministers, Fernando Po was still overrepresented.

Macías Nguema suspended the Cabinet at the beginning of May 1971, and assumed for himself the right to appoint all ministers by decree. Of 11 ministers of the first government, six were physically liquidated, two live abroad as refugees.

After Obiang Nguema's coup d'etat in August 1979, the country was at first governed by a Supreme Military Council, consisting mainly of Esanguis from Mongomo and close relatives of Obiang Nguema, and thus close relatives of the ex-dictator Macías Nguema. Then on October 18, 1982, the military and the former officers of the youth movement "Juventud en marcha con Macías" on the Council, dropped their uniforms and reappeared as members of a civilian Council of Ministers. Since that date Obiang Nguema has made frequent ministerial reshuffles, either as a result of abortive coups or due to the departure of ministers. In January 1986 a new council, half of whom were from Mongomo, was formed as a result of disorders in the army of Río Muni. In July 1986, several ministers, led by Mba Onana, tried to overthrow Obiang Nguema. Arrested by the Moroccan guards, they were tried by a military court and condemned to 2–18 years in prison, but Esanguis were released in 1987.

See also Coup d'Etat; Government.

CONSEJO DE VECINOS (Municipal council). Called for by a decree of 1880 and composed of seven members, these councils were established in towns with white inhabitants. During colonization they were almost the only existing legislative body. They were directed by Spanish officials and leading citizens and could be dissolved by the governor general. The councils were in charge of collecting taxes (especially those for concessions) and of supplying workers for the plantations. After provincialization in 1960 they were replaced by ayuntamientos.

CONSEJO MILITAR SUPREMO (Supreme Military Council) see Army; Obiang Nguema.

CONSEJO PROVINCIAL (Provincial Assembly). Elected in September 1968 these assemblies never actively met, even though they existed de jure until 1973. Between 1969 and 1974 eight members of the provincial assemblies were executed.

CONSTITUTION. The Constitution drawn up by the Constitutional Conference of 1967–1968 was accepted by referendum on August 11, 1968. All male and female Guineans of African descent over 21 years old were entitled to vote. According to the Constitution, Equatorial Guinea is a unitary indivisible state composed of the Río Muni and Fernando Po provinces; it guarantees autonomy of the provinces and equality between citizens, without discrimination. Regarding the administrative organization, the resemblance to autonomy is evident:

A president, who appoints the vice-president and half of the ministers (one-third at least for each province). He has the right to dissolve the Asamblea de la República (Parliament), suspend basic civil rights during two weeks; he confirms motions of the censor directed against ministers, he has the right to cancel the decision of the Consejos Provinciales after having informed the Supreme Court. The Legislative Assembly is the Asamblea de la Republica (35 deputies). It controls the Executive. The Executive, the Consejo de Ministros, has 12 members. The president of the republic is also chief executive, hence there is a strong concentration of powers in the head of state. The jurisdictions of the state and the provinces are separated but the major part of the power is vested with the state. Each province disposes of a Consejo Provincial (Assembly), elected by universal franchise (eight counselors in Fernando Po, of which one is from Annobón, 12 counselors from Río Muni, of which one is from Corisco and one from the Elobeyes). The decisions of these Councils can be vetoed by the president. Regarding finances, the budget is established every two years; there is a difference between the ordinary budget and the assistance and cooperation budget (assumed especially by Spain).

The Constitution was amended in May 1971, the president assuming the legislative, executive, and judicial powers as well as the parliamentary privileges of the Consejo de la Republica; in October 1971 a decree was published severely punishing contempt of the president.

In July 1972 a new Constitution was proclaimed, written by García Trevijano, which marked a new step towards the personal power that was to culminate with the 1973 Constitution accepted by "referendum" on July 29. It marks a reinforced control of separatism and abolishes provincial autonomy. Following are some of the main features: Art. 1. Equatorial Guinea is a Democratic Republic, sovereign and popular, independent and undivided; Art. 2. All power is vested with the people who exercise it through the party and the state bodies; Art. 4. The PUNT develops the general policies of the Nation; Art. 8. A member of the United Nations and the Organization of African Unity, Equatorial Guinea respects their charters and principles; Art. 42. Election of the President and of the Parliamentarians shall take place every five years; Art. 49. Macías Nguema Biyogo is proclaimed life-time President (article 42 is abolished); Art. 56. The Asamblea Nacional Popular (Parliament) will be composed of 60 members, proposed by the party at secret ballot; Art. 60. The party has the right to dismiss the deputies at all times in case of deviation; Art. 67. The judicial functions proceed from the people and are exercised in its name by the People's supreme court and the other civilian and military courts; Art. 68. All judges are appointed by the President and are removable and responsible. The development since 1968 is tremendous: Art. 1 is characterized by the deletion of the word "free." Forty out of the 46 members of the 1968 Constituent Assembly have been assassinated by the Nguemists.

On April 3, 1980, Obiang Nguema's military government abrogated the July 1973 Constitution and reintroduced that of June 1968. In the spring of 1982, a Nguemist Constitutional Conference was held at Akonibe and elaborated a document that was the subject of a national referendum held in August 1982. No information was given as to what the people were voting for, but it received the expected majority. The International Commission of Jurists, the expert sent by the UN Human Rights Commission, as well as specialists in international law have qualified this Constitution as dictatorial. An additional article appended to the document guarantees Obiang Nguema's tenure for seven years.

The people voted in November 1991 under similar conditions. The new Fundamental Law was amended by the veterans of the regime. The right to go on strike was strengthened, and constitutional guarantees against torture and arbitrary detention were cancelled; however, no texts permitting the application of these amendments were promulgated. In December, the Political Parties Law imposed drastic financial and statutory conditions for those who wanted to join politics. In 1993, UN experts identified 40 antidemocratic articles in the law which comprised 217 articles. See also Ebang Mbele Abang, A.; Equatorial Guinea Liberation Front; Human Rights; Missions; Ndong Ela Mangue, J.; Nve Nzeng, A. F.; Obiang Nguema, T.; Madrid Pact; Presidency; Progress Party; Sima Ngua, A.; Social Democratic and Popular Convergency; Spain; Victims.

CONSTITUTIONAL CONFERENCES. After the investigation by the United Nations Trusteeship Committee in August 1966, and the United Nations General Assembly vote in favor of Spanish Guinea's independence, Spain called a Constitutional Conference to start on October 27, 1967. A delegation of 41 members represented the country's provinces, institutions, and economic bodies, as well as the different political parties such as IPGE, MONALIGE, MUNGE, Democratic Fernandino Union, Unión Bubi, and the Ndowe Union. The delegation was headed by Ngomo Nandong, president of the Asamblea General, and Ondo Edu, president of the Consejo de Gobierno. The Conference was chaired by Castiella, Spanish minister of foreign affairs, who was accompanied by a delegation of 25 members, among whom was Díaz de Villegas, entrusted with the Dirección General de Plazas y Provincias Africanas, representing the presidency of the government (Carrero Blanco). Political, legal, administrative, economic and assistance committees were set up. However, opposition between independence movements brought the Conference to a deadlock, some of them being in favor of maintaining national unity, others of separating both provinces. The Conference was suspended after nine sessions. It resumed on April 17, 1968, debating the subjects mentioned under UN Resolution 2355 of December 1967. All efforts went into the drafting of the Constitution where the unitary views clearly won. The draft Constitution was submitted to the Cortes on June 22, 1968, and accepted on June 24, but 80 delegates signed a declaration stating their apprehensions as to the protection of minorities. The structural organization of the two provinces was worked out only during the summer of 1968. Submitted to the people in August, the Constitution was adopted by 64.3 percent of the voters.

A national constitutional conference was held at Akonibé in May 1982. The constitutional commission was composed of 28 veterans of the Nguemist regime, of whom the most prominent were: Nko Ivasa, Obama Nsué Mangue (Batho), Mensuy Mbá, Elo Nvé, Beholi Melango, and Micha Nsué Nfumu. See also Constitution.

CONVENTION OF BERNE. In 1997, Equatorial Guinea signed this convention concerning the protection of works of art and literature.

CONVERGENCIA SOCIAL DEMOCRATA Y POPULAR (CSDP) see Social Democratic and Popular Convergency

CONVERGENCY FOR SOCIAL DEMOCRACY (Convergencia para la Democrácia Social, CPDS). Founded in 1991, by university graduates returned from Spain, involved in surreptitious actions: slogans on the walls and roads of the capital, distribution of an open letter to Obiang Nguema in April. On May 2, the Nguemists declared a state of emergency. Convergency publishes the *La Verdad* monthly (10–20 pp., photocopied), the only regular periodical in the country; Celestino Bakale is its chief editor and Placido Mikó Abogo its lead writer. The objective of the CPDS is to "make Equatorial Guinea a democratic and righteous State."

In February 1992, Placido Mikó, Celestino Bakale, Jose Antonio Dorronsoro, Arsenio Molonga, and Jose L. Nvumba Mañana were arrested and tortured by the Moroccans. They were forced to work in the President's gardens, while Obiang Nguema flung insults: "Cut the grass, you shit-head intellectuals." In May, the group was condemned for "insults to the head of the State" and for "subversive propaganda." All of them were released following the intervention of the former prime minister of Spain, A. Suarez. Several members of the Convergency, as well as men and women caught possessing *La Verdad,* were arrested and tortured.

Convergency urged the founding of the Joint Opposition Platform (POC). Amancio Nzé Angue (CPDS) was its general secretary. He was the leader of the delegation for the National Pact negotiations in February 1993. Convergency held a public meeting in the capital, before several hundred persons. The American journalist Willy Haywood (*The Boston Globe*), managed to interview leaders of the CPDS in spite of Nguemist threats. In May, several members were arrested in Añisok. Convergency exposed the Nguemists' violation of the National Pact. On July 15, Convergency held a meeting in Rebola, where Nze Angue recalled the decision of 12 parties not to participate in the September 12 elections. Santiago Obama, honorary president of the CPDS and member of its national executive committee, declared that the people were beginning to be less frightened. In August, Nze Angue began a tour of Río Muni. In a communiqué, the population was urged to boycott the electoral census and the elections, which had been postponed to November 21 without consultations. During the summer, the arrests continued. In September, *La Verdad* published a list of persons killed or arrested in Annobón in August. Moto Nsá spread the word that the CPDS may be an agent for French interests. In mid-September, the CPDS held a meeting in the capital in the presence of about a thousand. An open letter to the death squads, the Ninjas, was then distributed. In late September, Julio Ndong Ela Mangue, home minister, Manuel Nguema Mba, secretary of state for security, and Siale Bolekia, prime minister, accompanied by Ninjas, summoned and threatened a CPDS delegation. On the same day, a UN delegation, which had arrived to enquire into the whereabouts of the Ghanian guard of the UNDP who had been arrested for having read *La Verdad*, was insulted and expelled. *La Verdad* was banned. On November 21, the CPDS, along with five other parties, managed to prevent election participation by boycott, bringing it down to no more than 20% in Fernando Po and 30% in Río Muni. Every year the CPDS publishes highly detailed Human Rights Reports, which it forwards to the United Nations. The 1993 report warned that most acts of human rights violations were related to political repression.

On January 13, 1994, the Nguemists again banned *La Verdad*. Upon protests from Reporters Without Borders, the CPDS announced on the 25th that it would continue publication. In May, Celestino Bakale made the participation of the CPDS in the municipal elections contingent on the modification of the Electoral and Census law. He warned that intimidation was the dominant note in Nguemist policy. Between October 7–9, Amancio Gabriel Nzé Angue, Plácido Micó, Victorino Bolekia Banay, and Jose Mecheba Ikaka were arrested and tortured in Santa Isabel and in Akalayong as they were coming back from a conference in Gabon; they were released on October 13. On October 6, three members of the continental committee of the CPDS, Indalecio Abuy (the 36-year-old Río Muni representative studying economics at the UNED and Amnesty International collaborator), Indalecio Eko, and Tomás Nzo were arrested near Niefang and then tortured, in order to prevent them from making an enquiry on human rights in that city. The Constituent Convention, with 110 regional delegates, was held from November 29 until December 2.

In January 1995, Indalecio Abuy, representative from Río Muni, was again arrested and tortured as part of the case against Moto Nsá. Upon his release, Abuy was arrested once more on April 15, along with the CPDS representative in Akonibe, Norberto Mba Nsé, and several observers of the elections, members of CPDS. Abuy was released after two days. During the month of April, the CPDS participated, as part of the POC, in negotiations for the finalization of a single list for the municipal elections. On May 22, Juan Nzó, vice-secretary general in charge of administration and finance in the CPDS, was detained as he was returning from Spain where he had undergone a PSOE course on municipal affairs and accused of introducing materials "of suspicious origin" (journals, course notes). When he tried to retrieve the confiscated materials, he was arrested for his refusal to admit that it was subversive material. Upon his release 48 hours later, he was summoned before a military tribunal, without any mention of justifying causes. He has since been in hiding. His wife was taken hostage the next day and kept for two days from seeing her 14-month-old baby who was all alone at home. *La Verdad* continued to be published under the authority of the secretary for information of the CPDS, Andres Esono Ondo, who held degrees in political science and sociology. But he was arrested with Celestino Bakale on May 27, soon after Rafael Obiang. They were released a few days later upon payment of a fine of FCFA 25,000.

The POC candidate for the presidential election was Amancio Gabriel Nzé; but the president of the PP, Moto Nsá and the UP president, Mba Ada, did not accept the choice and withdrew from the POC. The Election Commission used this to their advantage in order to reject the POC candidate, under the pretext that the POC had disappeared, and had its offices closed. On January 27, 1996, the manager of the CPDS, Abilio Bondjale, was arrested and tortured in the military camp of Yaunde, in Santa Isabel, on the orders of chief superintendent Julian Ondo Nkumu. On February 7, 1996, Antonio Mba Nguema ordered that the headquarters of *La Verdad* and CPDS be closed down due to "their spreading false information during the electoral campaign." During the presidential elections held on February 25, 1996, several members of the CPDS and other opposition parties, including Gaudencio Asumu, Celestino Bakale, Julián Ehapo, and Santiago Obama, all municipal councilors, were arrested in the capital on February 16 and tortured.

In March 1996, *La Verdad* (No. 35), appeared again. On March 16, Amancio Gabriel Nzé and Pedro Ndong Mbale were stripped of CPDS documents near Niefang, while they were on their way to their village. On March 18, upon their return, they were arrested and manhandled. On March 19, they were taken to Bata. Then, while Ndong Mbale was released, Amancio G. Nzé was imprisoned in various military barracks and chained in a cramped cell in the famed miserable prison in the town. He was tortured. During May, the president of the CPDS, Santiago Obama Ndong, was imprisoned at Ebebiyin, for no reason, while he was going to his father's funeral. Towards the end of May 1996, a delegation of the CPDS visited Gabon. It had a number of contacts with the 50,000-strong Equato-Guinean refugee colony in his neighboring country. They met Felipe Ondo and Bonifacio Nguema, of the Republican Democratic Force (RDF), as well as some Gabonese parties, such as Father Paul Mba Abesolo's Woodcutters (Bucherons), and the Gabonese Party for Progress, close to the Socialist International, like the CPDS. On June 2, in the Libreville locality of Nzeng-Ayong, the CPDS delegation held a meeting attended by 3,000 persons. During this time, the dictator Obiang Nguema was in conversation with Bongo, who advised him to move closer to the democratic opposition groups, and obtained the post of director of Elf-Aquitaine Equatorial Guinea for his son Teodorin. After a period of suspension of the POC, the CPDS was the only democratic political group to remain publicly active in the country. In September 1996, C. Bakale and S. Miko participated in the meeting of the Socialist International in New York. They also had press interviews in the USA and with a company that had organized the election of Obiang Nguema in February 1996. In Washington, they were received by the officer for Central African Affairs, J. C. Spiegel, and the deputy secretary of state for Africa, William Tuwaddell, who recognized the irregularities in the election of Obiang Nguema. Miko and Bakale made the secretary of state examine the shameful support which American petroleum companies had been giving to the dictator. On October 21, two members of the CPDS were held prisoners at Niefang by order of the governmental delegate. When returning to his country, Celestino Bakale was imprisoned for three days.

Discharged on the 16th, just before Obiang Nguema's meeting with the Spanish prime minister in Rome, Bakale was put once more under house arrest on the 22nd because he refused to present himself to a military court. On the 25th, the CPDS coordinator for Río Muni, Indalecio Abuy, was attacked by a group of soldiers and hurt in the head. On December 4, the office of the CPDS was investigated and searched by 20 policemen in uniform, commanded by Superintendent Juan Engonga. They were looking for C. Bakale. Several members of the CPDS were invited to Israel to attend various classes and seminars; they had interviews with the National Administration. On Christmas 1996, Bakale fled to Spain. Since 1996, Convergency is a consulting member of the Socialist International. It is also part of the Publishers Association of private Central African presses.

At the beginning of 1997, Plácido Miko, who was in a private meeting with members of the CPDS, in Río Benito, was arrested at the order of Obiang Nguema's cousin, Captain Agustin Ndong Ona.

In 1997–1998, the leaders of the party were very active at the international level. At the beginning of January 1998, militants and leaders of the CPDS were detained at Kogo. The National Radio accused them of practicing the Mbwiti, a forbidden cult. In April 1998, the secretary for Río Muni and a biologist for the European Community's project Ecofac, was arrested, along with 45 members of the CPDS. When José Olo, lawyer of Martín Puye was arrested, the CPDS declared that the government was extremely nervous and has increased its "extra-judiciary arrests." During the end of June and July 1998, the CPDS announced its participation in the November legislative elections. At the end of October, the CPDS informed the international press that the nguemist government had withdrawn 65,000 voters from the electoral lists to be used for the legislative elections, in order to eliminate those it supposed would not vote for PDGE. In the beginning of November 1998, as the probable legislative elections were coming up, several leaders of the CPDS, among them Amancio Nsé, were imprisoned in Bata. A CPDS delegation assisted the Socialist International Meeting in Geneva, November 23–24, 1998. The CPDA person responsible for Río Muni, Nicolas Mangue Mañana, was imprisoned in Niefang, while other members of the CPDS were imprisoned in Nsok-Nsomo and Rio Campo. Among the prisoners was Manuel Owono Obama, who had just bought a mechanical saw for his plantation on Cameroon but was accused of arms dealing. Amnesty International published an Urgent Action on November 30 to alert the international community.

See also Akonibe; Annobón; Bakale, C.; Black, Manafort, Stone & Kelly; Elections; Human Rights; Miko Abogo, P.; National Pact; Ndongo Ogüno-Asong, M. M.; Niefang; Nzé Angue, A. G.; Oyo Awong Ada, S.; Press; Prisons; Reporters without Borders; Río Muni; Social Democratic Union; United Nations; Torture; *Voz del Pueblo*

COOPERATIVAS DEL CAMPO. Among the tasks of the Patronato de Indígenas was that of promoting the development of cooperative farms. In 1910 the Banapa cooperative opened, followed by those of Batete, Moka, and Baríobé, all located in Fernando Po. After World War II, the following cooperatives existed: Moka (potatoes, vegetables, poultry, vacation homes), Batete (cocoa, oil palm), Ayene, close to Mikomeseng (cocoa dryer and warehouse), and Bato Chico (cocoa, oil palm), to which can be added the cocoa cooperatives of Nkomo, Nsie and Oveng, all in Río Muni. In 1944, the selling of cooperative lands was forbidden. During provincialization the Bariobé cooperative produced 117 million pesetas ($1.9 million) worth of cocoa, and owned 44 buildings in stone. After the suppression of the "Patronato," in 1969, cooperatives were placed under the supervision of the Dirección de Agricultura and the "Obra Sindical de Coopera- ción" depending on the Movimiento Nacional. The cooperatives were excluded from the technical and administrative bodies and only served the metropolis' interests thanks to the cheap labor force. In 1962 Río Muni had four cooperatives (2,622 members), Fernando Po 30 (1,610 members). The cooperatives gradually became serious competitors for the large landowners who had to pay for expensive foreign labor. During provincialization the cooperatives participated in the election of half of the deputies of the Deputaciones Provinciales (Assemblies). In 1968 their budgets reached 37 million pesetas ($6 million). By a January 1970 decree, all possessions of the cooperatives became state property.

In January 1980, the U.S. gave the second Nguemist dictatorship US $1 million for agricultural development, half of which was for the cooperatives.

COORDINADORA DEMOCRATICA DE GUINEA ECUATORIAL (CODE) see Democratic Coordination of the Opposition of Equatorial Guinea

COORDINATION OF THE DEMOCRATIC OPPOSITION OF EQUATO-RIAL GUINEA. Founded in July 1998 by Joaquín Elema, president, and Severe Moto, spokesman. On August 3, in Madrid, Elema and Moto denounced the dictatorship, the political oppression, the absence of liberties, and the antidemocratic policy that refuses change. They underlined that the divisions within the opposition reinforce the regime. The democratic opposition needs to be regenerated. The CODE pretends to be "a unique front of the opposition, within and without,"aiming at eliminating the dictatorship and asking for international support: "Obiang Nguema needs to be overthrown."

COPERIATE MUEBAKE, Gaspar, d. 1969. Bubi expert in civil government. A member of the Unión Bubi, he participated in the Constitutional Conference of 1967-68. He was in favor of the separation of the two provinces; he opposed Torao Sikara, also a Bubi, but who was in favor of the country's unity. In July 1968 Coperiate again defended his thesis in front of the United Nations Trusteeship Committee. He became deputy at the Asamblea de la República (Parliament), and was assassinated during the troubles of 1969.

CORISCO Island. Located 16 miles off the Muni estuary, with an area of 5.4 sq miles, the highest point being 35 m (110 feet). It protects the entry to the Muni and Utamboni Rivers, and to the Río Munda. North of Corisco is the small island of Belobi. The geological base of Corisco also includes the islands of Conga and Mbañe. It is part of the Manji Archipelago, with the islands of Elobeyes, Mbañe, Leva, Boko, Mengueamanga, Coga, and Belobi. It consists of 15,32 km, in the bay of Calatrava, facing the cape of San Juan 22 km away from the coast of Equatorial Guinea, 16 km away from the coast of Gabon, and 335 km from the capital. Extension N–S: 6 km, in the narrowest W–E part: 4.5 km. Maximum altitude: 30 m. Crops: manioc, yams, corn, peanuts, coconuts, coffee. Main activity: fishing.

The Portuguese called the Corisco and Elobeyes Islands the "islands of lights" having discovered them during a lightning storm. The island of Corisco was populated in the 18th century by Benga. It seems to have been used as a slave yard by the Portuguese ever since the 15th century. In the middle of the 17th century the Dutch Company of East India occupied it for the same purpose for some years. In 1656, after recovering the island, the Portuguese founded the Corisco Company, which centralized the slave trade between Cameroon and Cape López. After 1724 a Portuguese navigation company set itself up there and exported slaves, via São Tome and Principe, on to Brazil. The Benga were used later as middlemen, quickly taking up the European lifestyle. As early as the 19th century Catalan businessmen settled in Corisco, and opened a hospital. In 1815 an American Presbyterian mission came to the island. In 1836 the United Kingdom showed interest in Corisco and carried out some surveys; it also interposed itself in the slave trade, destroying a Spanish base in 1840. Reverend Clemens, a Corisco-born white, was among the members of the Presbyterian mission in Bolondo during the 19th century. The Reverend Ikenga Ibiya, a Benga from Corisco, was the first convert in the American Presbyterian mission which was founded in 1850 and which continued till 1875. In 1856 three American Protestant schools were operating with 100 pupils (Rev. Mackey and Clemens); however, a real parish church opened only in 1860, shortly after the setting up of a Spanish infantry garrison. In 1858, King Munga (Moonga) became governor of the island. He collected a Spanish anchoring fee of 10 pesos for each boat using the Muni, which highly irritated France. In 1843 Corisco was governed by Bonkoro I. His successor, Bonkoro II, vied for the island with Munga and established himself in Cape San Juan. The Benga of Muni Bay quickly passed under Munga's authority. In 1872 it was Conbeyamango (son of Muele, who governed the south of the Island) who succeeded Munga. The Jesuit mission was established in 1863, by Father Francisco Javier Garcia. It worked until 1868. From 1886 to 1907 the island was under Fernando Otimbo Ijenje's authority, and from 1907 to 1910 under Santiago Uganda's.

In 1848 some 22 ships anchored in Corisco, especially operating for the Theimpson and Duarte trading post. In 1884 a Jesuit school was opened, and in 1885 a Claretian one, followed in 1898 by a Concepcionist school. In 1887 Corisco had 609 inhabitants, of which six were whites. In 1903 the island had 250 inhabitants, but at the beginning of the 20th century business moved to the continent; in 1908 only one Protestant school still existed on the island.

At the 1967–1968 Constitutional Conference, Corisco was represented by L. Beholi Malango. Shortly after independence, in 1968, Gabon started to claim Corisco, putting forward the extension of the limit of territorial waters, to which Equatorial Guinea replied by a similar measure in 1970. Towards the end of 1977, President Bongo of Gabon, according to the Spanish press, invited Spain to favor Gabonese occupation of the Equatorial Guinean islands, but the news was denied by Madrid. With the intensified search for oil in the estuary of the Muni River after 1980 by the French ELF-Aquitaine company and Petrogab, the earlier French designs on the Corisco and Elobey Islands, that had been occupied by Gabon, were revived.

In late 1989, Clarion Petroleum signed a sharing contract for drilling operations around Corisco; Gabon objected to the contract. In 1990, Hamilton Brothers Oil and Enterprise Oil (Brit.) equally shared the drilling at this site. The French ELF-Aquitaine owns 25% of Enterprise Oil.

The January 24, 1992, "transitional" government included a native of Corisco: Inestrosa Ikaka, vice-minister for economy and tourism, who had earlier been finance minister; on December 22, 1993 he became the state secretary for planning and economic development.

The sale of the island had been negotiated with a French company, whose representative was said to be the French consul in Bata, M. Rene. Towards the end of 1993, the French embassy implied in an information guide that Corisco is administratively a part of Río Muni.

See also Bolondo; Borders; Elobeyes; Gabon; Ikenge Ibiya, S.; Inestrosa Ikaka, F.; Missions; Petroleum; Public Health; Simo, B.; Vicente, F.

CORNEE, Pierre. Ambassador of France from 1980 to 1985.

CORNET, Hubert. Ambassador of France from 1978 to 1979.

CORRUPTION. Numerous members and supporters of the clan from Mongomo are known for their corruption. Several bilateral and multilateral projects for technical aid fell through due to the corruption within the Nguemist establishment. Some examples given by Fermín Nguema Esono, ex-magistrate in the Supreme Court:

Agricultural Projects:

* Project for the diversification of cultures and agricultural services (DICSA), $18 million

* Argentinean project for an agro-industrial complex in Mongomo, $5 million

* World Bank Project for the rehabilitation of cocoa farms (IDEPA), $12 million

* U.S. Cooperative League and AID Project for agricultural cooperatives (CLUSA)

Fishing Projects:

* Argentinean project for craft fishing (also Project for an agro-industrial complex

* Italian project for craft fishing, for $10 million

* Japanese project for craft fishing, for $10 million

Other Projects:

* Italian project for Hotel Media Luna (Bata), for $12 million

* Hispano-Equato-Guinean project by the Moulins de Bioko S.A., for $.5 million

In 1994, Freedom House warned that the country had become a place for laundering money and added that Constancia, first wife of Obiang Nguema, had just bought a house in Miami.

A U.S. document of the Department of Commerce, dated June 18, 1998, reports political violence, widespread corruption, and a questionable judiciary system. In September 1998, the opposition reported that a minister had paid people working at polling stations with fake money.

See Alogo Nchama, A.; Angue Ondo, P.; Bibang Abeso Fuma, A.; Commerce; Cyprus; Drugs; Eka Nguema, P.; Elo Ndong, D.; Engonga Motulu, M.; France; Justice; Mangue, R.; Mba Oñana, F.; Modu Akuse Bindang, C.; Navigation; Ndjeng Olo Bahamondes, A.; Ndong Ona, A.; Nguema Esono, L.; Nguemism;

Nsue Nchama, J.; Nve Mbengono, E. E.; Nvono Nka Mañene, C.; Obiang Nguema, Teodorín; Olo Mba, J.; Otogo, R.; Sainz Bayon, J. M.; Siale Bilekia, S.

CORTES (Spanish Parliament). In 1941, under the pressure of public opinion, the Cortes refused to sell Fernando Po and Annobón to the United Kingdom. From the time of provincialization on, Guinea disposed of eight seats at the Spanish Parliament (Esono Nsué, Bolopa Esape, Bosio Dioco, Ekong Andeme, Nsué Angüe, Tomas King, Mba Ada, A. Jones). These men participated in 1962 in working out the autonomy status. Bolopa, Bosio, Ekong, Nsué Angüe and Tomas King participated in the Constitutional Conference of 1967–1968. The latter five were liquidated by Macías Nguema's regime.

COTECO see Timber

COUP D'ETAT see also Plot

COUP D'ETAT OF MARCH 1969 see Ndongo Miyone

COUP D'ETAT OF 1970 (projected) see Union of Spanish Nationals with Interests in Africa

COUP D'ETAT OF JUNE 1974. An escape from the Bata prison was attempted on June 10–11, 1974, but failed because of the treachery of Nvono Akele Avomo: 118 prisoners were shot on the spot. The fugitives had intended to take Bata and then the towns of the interior. The attempt was called "Cruzada de Liberación de Guinea Ecuatorial por Cristo." About 90 conspirators not killed in the massacre and their accomplices from the exterior, among whom were some 20 women, were judged by a military court (June 22–26, 1974) composed of officers of the Guardia Nacional. Twenty-seven convicts were sentenced to death and shot in public in the Bata suburbs on June 26. The execution squad was trained by Russian military experts. After five groups of five convicts had been shot, the labor minister, Bubi Borico Toichoa, together with a 16-year-old Ndowe boy lying on the ground with broken legs, were killed. The other convicts were sentenced to prison for 10 to 30 years. But they appear to have been executed either shortly after the trial in the Bata cemetery, or in 1975 (see United Nations).

COUP D'ETAT OF AUGUST 3, 1979. A palace revolution led by cousins and nephews of Macías Nguema under the command of Obiang Nguema, brought down the first Nguemist dictatorship. By August 6 a Spanish delegation had arrived in the country, followed shortly thereafter by one from the European Economic Community. The old dictator took refuge with some guards in the town of Mongomo. On August 18, however, he was arrested in the forest after most of his guards had deserted. He was tried by court-martial between September 24 and 28 and condemned to death, along with his vice-president and cousin Eyegue Ntutumu and five other minor figures. In order to detract attention from his own participation in Macías Nguema's dictatorship, Obiang Nguema and his accomplices proclaimed their revolt to be the "Coup for Freedom."

Obiang Nguema enlisted the help of professional soldiers sidelined since independence, for his coup. After the coup, these troops were again sidelined.

See also Ayetebe, Iyanga; S. Ela; Maye Ela; Mba Micha; Mansogo, Okenve; Oyó, Tray).

COUP D'ETAT OF MAY 11–13, 1983. An act of vengeance within the clan from Mongomo, the "coup" was given the name "CONO," for Carmelo Owono. It was supposed to have taken place in Río Muni during the inauguration of the electrical power plant in Bikomo. The Moroccans were said to have foiled the plan. According to other sources the "coup" ought to have taken place in the capital in Los Enamorados, one of the clubs frequented by Obiang Nguema. It was said that they were to take advantage of the changing of the Moroccan guard. About a hundred arrests were made. Sgt. Venacio Mikó sought refuge in the Spanish embassy (after the Soviets and the French refused him). Maye Ela denied any involvement in the coup from Latin America and expressed his support for Obiang Nguema.

The Nguemists cut telephone links with Spain. They blamed "certain Spanish sectors." Obiang Nguema offered an ultimatum for the return of Mikó. The Spanish minister of foreign affairs, Moran, took a quick trip to Santa Isabel on May 27. He negotiated an agreement for the return of Mikó, in the presence of the ambassador of France and the Moroccan chargé d'affaires. Obiang Nguema gave his word that if Mikó were to be condemned to death, he would not be executed, but expelled to Spain.

The Spanish press criticized the behavior of the Spanish authorities. Rumors were rife of a plan for military intervention, with paratroopers, 1,500 infantry soldiers, four ships, and a Hercules G-130. Obiang Nguema used this scandal to get rid of his allies, Maye Ela and Ela Nguema, in the 1979 coup.

In the military court, judges and the prosecution were all Esangui. Owono Ndong, Micha Ela and V. Mikó were condemned to death before Chinese and Spanish observers. The first two were executed, while Mikó's sentence was reduced to life imprisonment. The spokesman of the dictatorship, Ochaga Nve, accused some compatriots of plotting to "destabilise the democratic system of the country." See also Miko, V.

COUP D'ETAT OF JUNE 25, 1983 (Hypothetical). A Saharaoui coup d'etat in Equatorial Guinea, said to have been plotted by refugees from Western Sahara and Spanish ex-legionaries to punish Morocco and all those linked to that country. The entire operation was said to have been financed by Libya. The plan was ignored.

COUP D'ETAT OF JULY 1986. On July 14, 1986, Obiang Nguema went to Paris to participate in the French national day celebrations. On his way back he was held up at Douala, Cameroon, on account of disturbances in Santa Isabel. He was able to get back to the capital in the evening of July 19, after the Moroccan presidential guards had arrested a group of officers, ministers, and senior officials who had tried to carry out a coup. This group appears to have been led by his uncle, Mbá Oñana the country's vice-president with the help of Nguema Ela, former minister of finance, Mbá Ondo, former minister of foreign affairs who became Minister of Planning in January 1986. Other members mentioned were Ondo Mañe, director of the Bank of the Central African States in Santa Isabel; Ondo Eyi, secretary of the Ministry of Public Works; Mañe Abeso, formerly minister of education; Ndongo Mba, deputy-minister of defense; Abeso Mondu, member of the Chamber of Deputies; Elo Nve Mbengono, minister with the

Parliament; Ovono Mañana, secretary of the Ministry of Defense; Ndong Ela, secretary of the Office of the President.

A court-martial was convened between August 14 and 18 without any prior announcement, at which Abeso Mondu was sentenced to death and a number of officers were sentenced to 18 to 20 years in jail for failure to provide information about the plot. Friends and relatives of Obiang Nguema were given three to four years of house arrest. Among these were Mba Oñana, Nguema Ela, Mba Ondo, Ondo Eyi, and Mañe Abeso, who were accused of having insulted the head of state. Lt. Col. Ndongo Mba, deputy of defense, was stripped of his rank. A number of others arrested at the time, including several police chiefs were subsequently released. Observers interpreted this family plot as being directed towards the removal from power of the most ambitious elements of the Nguemist power structure.

In France, the press indicated that the coup was either of Spanish or Communist origin, but nothing was said about recent French "conquests" in Equatorial Guinea. In October 1986 Obiang Nguema was raised to the rank of brigadier-general by a representative of the king of Spain.

COUP D'ETAT OF DECEMBER 1987. On December 4, 1987, the minister of the interior and chief of the State Security Services (Seguridad), Eyi Mensuy Andeme, arrested four colleagues: Inestrosa Ikaka, Finance; Mbomio Nsue, Culture, Information, Tourism; Alogo Nchama, Water and Forests; Owono Asangono, Presidential Affairs and Cooperation.

Obiang Nguema was present in Antibes (France) at the Franco-African Conference of Heads of States and of Governments. An argument took place: an alleged maneuver to destabilize him during a series of interviews for the Catalan television TV3. Everybody was detained until December 17.

COUP D'ETAT OF AUGUST 1988. The general secretary of the Progress Party, J. L. Jones Dougan (dual citizen) was arrested in Santa Isabel and imprisoned in Playa Negra, on August 16, 1988. The Nguemists confiscated his passport. He was accused of unauthorized "political activities." A number of other personalities were also arrested in the capital and at Bata.

The repression picked up again after F. Obama Nsue Manque (Mbato), one of the worst members of the regime, was named deputy to the Chamber of Representatives of the People.

The Spanish government protested against the detention of three Hispano-Guineans. The Nguemists refused visiting rights, claiming that they had entered into no agreement concerning dual citizens. The arrests were said to be linked to an attempt to topple Obiang Nguema, so as to prevent him from negotiating with the opposition. More and more information on the treatment meted out to the prisoners was available. Massive detentions began in early August, when a sale of arms by the commander of the Mongomo region was discovered. Obiang Nguema ordered the arrest of members of his own clan.

A War Council met in Bata in September. Accused of endangering the security of the nation, two soldiers were condemned to death: Joaquin Elema Borengue and Francisco-Bonifacio Mba Nguema. These condemnations followed an attempt to assassinate Obiang Nguema. Both of them were pardoned by Obiang Nguema and condemned to life imprisonment. The others got between 15 and 20 years of imprisonment. The verdict was a clear indication of Obiang Nguema's nervousness and his wish to get rid of opponents before the 1989 elections. The Spanish press alleged a self-coup by Obiang Nguema. Soon after, the dictator was received in France by President Mitterrand, R. Dumas, minister for foreign affairs, and J. Pelletier, minister for cooperation. On September 20, a Spanish parliamentary and ministerial delegation went to Santa Isabel and requested a pardon for the two dual citizens. In exchange, the Nguemists demanded the extradition of Moto Nsá, which was refused. At last, Jones Dougan was released at the end of the year, shortly before the previously planned visit of Felipe Gonzalez, the Spanish prime minister.

COUP D'ETAT OF SPRING 1990. Constancia, Obiang Nguema's first wife, and her brother, Juan Olo Mba Nzeng, minister for energy, were accused of plotting to topple the president, and arrested. Constancia was placed under house arrest in her village, while Ola Mba Nzeng was imprisoned in Bata. A presidential decree read on radio and television announced the revoking of Constancia's title of "First Lady of the Nation." Lt.-Col. Alfonso Mbasogo Ntongo, and the captain of the San Carlos garrison, Antonio Angüe, were arrested along with the vice-minister for foreign affairs, Eneme Obono. According to Amnesty International, there were several cases of torture. A little later, the case was referred to as a "domestic scene."

COUP D'ETAT OF AUGUST 1993. In late August, in the midst of the electoral campaign, and in the wake of the ritual assassination of Pedro Motu Mamiaga, nine soldiers were arrested and accused of conspiracy, slander, and insults to the president of the republic. They were said to have planned to raid and loot the Ela Nguema's arms depot in a suburb of the capital, in order to eliminate the president. Their membership in the Progress Party and the Popular Union were noted. A brief court-martial halted the death sentence and condemned them to imprisonment (up to 24 years) or to exile within the country. All of them were discharged.

COUP D'ETAT OF FEBRUARY 1995 (Hypothetical) see Esono Micka, L.

COUP D'ETAT OF JULY 1996. On July 18, 1996, 27 soldiers were arrested by Obiang Nguema's Moroccan guard for an attempted coup d'etat. These included, among others, Inocencio Ngoma Ondo, cousin of Obiang Nguema; colonel, major head of state Agustin Ndong Oná; colonel, inspector of armed forces for Río Muni Valentin Eya Olomo, corvette captain, and his brother Darío Tadeo Ndong Olomo, deputy political administrative secretary of the PDGE; former head of the Jovenes Antorches; minister of Health; Candido Obama Nguema, commissioner of the secret police in the capital Faustino Nve, former customs officer, at Santa Isabel; Salvador Ncogo, Sargent, former bodyguard of Obiang Nguema's first lady.

The minister of foreign affairs, Oyono Ndong, affirmed that it was a matter of an attempt at destabilization by the opposition. According to the latter, the arrested soldiers found themselves in the former Moroccan camp, called Rabat, and in the prison at Black Beach, under the surveillance of Ninjas, and were brutally tortured. On November 18, 1996, 11 junior officers are sentenced to 4–13 years of prison and fines up to 59 Mio FCFA, "for having prepared a coup." They would be relatives and close friends of the former President of Parliament, F. Ondo Obiang, who took refuge in Gabon.

COUP D'ETAT (ATTEMPTED) OF MAY 1997. Revealed by the Cesid (the Spanish secret services), through its information service in Angola. The May 16 inspection of the Russian ship *Sana I,* that had left Pointe Noire to reach Cabinda, revealed 30 Angolan mercenaries, 21 Russians, Italians, and Equato-Guineans, as well as 3 Spaniards (among them a policeman from San Sebastian, driver and member of an information unit, and two other people wanted by the Spanish police). The whole matter was said to have been financed by the Italian lumber company Cataneo, which was misled by Teordorín Nguema Obiang with regard to certain contracts. Cataneo is believed to have invested 150 Mio pesetas. When arrested, it was reported that they possessed 23 guns, 16 loaders, 80 grenades, 23 grenade launchers, pistols, and ammunition, but that the bulk of weapons had not yet been loaded on the ship. The group intended to attack Santa Isabel and Luba, but Moto Nsá would have allowed Obiang Nguema to leave the country.

Moto Nsá and his accomplices were released on June 8—despite the nguemists' demand for extradition—and returned to Spain.

COURTS see Abeso Ondo, A.; Army; Castellon Ntayo Erimola, V.; Convergency for Social Democracy; "Coup" d'etat (?) of May 11-13, 1983; "Coup" d'etat of August 1993; "Democratic" Party of Equatorial Guinea; Edu, F.; Ekong Awong, M.; Elections; Elema Borengue, J.; Eneme Owono, J.; Ensema Mba, S.; Epalepale Evina, F.; Esono Masie, P.; Esono Mbomio, J.; France; International Court of Justice on Animal Rights; Jones Dougan, J. L.; Justice; Maho Sikacha, L. J.; Martinez Nvo Bikie, J.; Mba Mifumu, A.; Micha Nsue Nfumu, J.; Ndong Ela Mangue, J.; Ngomo Ondo, I.; Nseng Esono, Nve, E.; Nsue Nchama, José M.; Ondo Ela Mangue, L.; Plot (1981); Tung Ela; Victims; Vilarrasa Balanza, S.

CPF see Timber

CREOLES see Annobón; Fernandinos

CRIMES (Ritual) see Assassinations; Motu Mamiaga, P.; Murders; Terror.

CRUZADA NACIONAL DE LIBERACION DE GUINEA ECUATORIAL (CNLGE) (National Crusade for the Liberation of Equatorial Guinea). Anticolonial movement created in 1947 by Fangs and Fernandinos. Presided over by Acacio Mañe, the movement really developed in 1958, after Mañe's assassination by the Spanish Civil Guard. MONALIGE and IPGE both derive from the Cruzada. In 1961 the Bubi Maho Sikacha took the leadership of the Cruzada, but he was obliged to flee to Cameroon. Afterwards the Cruzada deteriorated rapidly because of internal disputes.

CUBA. Cubans seem to have arrived in Fernando Po as early as 1834. From 1861 on, several Royal Orders caused the sending of emancipated Cubans, often to reinforce infantry. Most of the time forced recruitment was necessary. Two hundred half-breeds (195 emancipados, 24 foreigners) arrived in July 1862 on "El Ferrol," and were then freed; they helped especially to develop plantations. Ten died before December 1862. Taking in account the deaths and those who escaped in 1867 only 116 were left. From 1866 several arrivals of deported Cubans (100 in 1866, 250 in 1869) are reported. They were put in the buildings of the old English Baptist mission which had been turned into a prison. Several of these Cuban nationalists (medical doctors, writers, journalists, engineers, etc.) died during their transport or upon arrival in Fernando Po. Seventeen escaped in 1869, among whom was Balmesada; he wrote a book on his long journey, published in New York.

Besides their work in the plantations, Cubans also participated in the second Iradier-Ossorio expedition. The founder of the Claretian Order, P. Claret, had been archbishop of Santiago de Cuba before founding the congregation which was to bring Catholicism to the colony. Slavery was abolished in Cuba only in 1886. In 1880 another 267 Cubans arrived, of which only 144 were alive in 1886. After 1875, a half-breed Cuban named Antonio Borgés directed a secular school in Santa Isabel; he was evicted by the Claretians shortly after their arrival (1884).

In 1973 diplomatic relations were established between Equatorial Guinea and Cuba and shortly afterwards some 350 volunteers (professors, foresters, doctors, etc.) arrived in Equatorial Guinea. The Milicia Popular and the Juventud en Marcha con Macias rapidly benefitted from Cuban counselors. The Cubans also advised the presidential guard, as much in Macias's presidential ghetto in Santa Isabel as on his journeys. Most of the civil Cuban counselors left in March 1976, shortly after Nigeria evacuated 25,000 of its nationals. The military personnel (about 300 men) remained in Equatorial Guinea.

By 1976 some 9,000 Cubans had passed through the port of San Carlos on their way to the Angolan front. In 1986, there were still 150 Cubans in Equatorial Guinea.

In the spring of 1995, a delegation from Havana attended the 1st Convention of the PDGE, at Bata.

At the end of 1996, a military delegation participated, in Havana, in the third meeting of the Iberian-American Military Academies.

The vice-minister of education, Teresa Avoro Nguema, visited Cuba in September 1998. She signed an agreement of bilateral cooperation and obtained 8 high school science teachers.

Since 1973 the following Cuban ambassadors have served successively in Equatorial Guinea: Luis González Maturelos, Severino Mansur Jorge, Alberto Suárez Ortega, Floreal Chamon, Juan B. Infante.

See also Army; "Democratic" Party of Equatorial Guinea; Dougan, J.; Esono Masie, P.; Evuna Owono Asangono, A.; Italy; Justice; Micha Ondo Bile; Muatetema Rivas, C.; Ndong Mba Obono, M.; Obiang Ndong, D.; Nguema Bindang, T.; Obama Owono Nchama, J.; Obiang Ndong, D.; Public Health; Simo, B.; Spain.

CULTURE. In December 1981, the sculptor Leandro Mbomio was promoted to minister for culture. In 1988–1989, Spain financed the construction, in Nsogo-Nsogo (near Bata), of a Cultural Center for 1,000 persons, in preparation of a Conference on Traditional Culture in June 1990. In the January 24, 1992, "transitional" government, the Ministry for Culture, Tourism and Handicrafts Promotion went to Juan Balboa Boneque. The December 22, 1993, government included Hilarío Sisa Tores as minister for culture, francophony, and culture. In April 1994, France offered FF 3 million for French teaching.

In the January 8, 1996, ministerial reshuffle, Agustin Nse Nfumu received the post of Minister for Culture and Francophony. Hilarío Sisa Tores became vice-minister for culture. Following criticism received during the presidential election from Nse Nfumu, the April 8, 1996, government added a new minister for culture, tourism, and francophony: Pedro-Cristino Bueribueri. He was assisted by Hilarío Sisa Tores as a minister with special responsibilities.

In the government reshuffle of January 21, 1998, Lucas Nguema Esono became minister of information, tourism and culture; Hilario Sisa Tores became vice-minister.

CURADURIA COLONIAL (Colonial Sponsorship or Guardianship). Created in 1901, its purpose was to take into account the inferiority of the natives. In fact it was a work inspection: it was to develop native civilization, defend the rights and interests of the natives, and in doing so to orient them towards labor and teach them to respect labor contracts. The Patronato de Indígenas was often in opposition with the "curador." Therefore, since 1924, no contract could be signed without the consent of the "Patronato." In 1938 the "Curador" became labor inspector (native), in fact entrusted with maintaining discrimination.

CURRENCY. Traditional Fang currency is the ekule (plural, bikukele) shaped like an iron spearhead; the Bubi used the roiga, small round disks carved in shellfish. After a long reign of the Spanish pesetas, the Guinean peseta was introduced in 1969. It was at par with the Spanish peseta but nonconvertible. In 1974, the Guinean peseta was converted to coins and banknotes called bikuele (sing., ekuele). Following Obiang Nguema's coup in 1979, a new currency was issued bearing the likeness of the new dictator. However, to make the currency convertible and in order to break out of this economic and political isolation, Obiang Nguema turned to France. This led to an agreement on Equatorial Guinea's entry into the Customs Union of the Central African States (UDEAC) and the introduction of the HCFA as the official currency of the country effective January 2, 1985. This meant that Equatorial Guinea, like neighboring Gabon and Cameroon, relinquished control of her monetary policies to the French Treasury. The introduction of this new currency also resulted in a considerable drain of resources towards the other countries of the CFA zone.

On January 11, 1994, Paris devalued the CFA franc by 50%. This decision came about partly as a result of the economic bankruptcy of the Franc-zone countries, and partly due to the apathy of France, which was looking more and more towards the European Union as conceived at Maastricht, while at the same time eyeing Eastern Europe. This devaluation, which the Bretton Woods institutions had been demanding for a long time, resulted in opening the doors wide to American and Japanese businesses. This was particularly obvious in Equatorial Guinea.

See also Petroleum.

CUSTOMS. In the early 1990s, taxes on goods from neighboring countries were prohibitive: potatoes 3%, rice 27%, sugar 78%, toothpaste 98%, beer 105%, beauty cream 118%. In November 1992 an agreement for financial aid was signed with France in order to strengthen customs services. In 1993, there were reports of Cameroonian customs officials carrying out checks at certain Equato-Guinean border posts, posing as technical assistants. By the January 27, 1994, decree, Jose Eneme Obiang was named director general of customs. In June, the parliament adopted a fiscal reform of the customs services. See also Commerce; Oyono Awong Ada, S.; Tabac.

CUSTOMS UNION OF CENTRAL AFRICAN STATES (UDEAC—Union Douanière des Etats de l'Afrique Centrale, comprising Cameroon, Central African Republic, Chad, Congo [Brazzaville], Equatorial Guinea, Gabon). The question of Equatorial Guinea's joining the UDEAC had been mooted since November 1980, at the time of Maye Ela, vice-president and minister of foreign affairs, visit to Yaoundé, Cameroon. Equatorial Guinea was also represented at the 17th summit meeting of the UDEAC in Libreville, Gabon, in December 1981.

In October 1983, eleven heads of state, including Obiang Nguema, founded the Community of Central African States. In November 1982, Mesa Bill and Ndong Ela were in Yaoundé to confirm their country's intention of joining, and on December 17, 1982, the 18th summit meeting of the UDEAC accepted its first Spanish-speaking member. The entry of Equatorial Guinea into the UDEAC was communicated to Spain in October 1982, before the socialists came to power. Joining the BEAC (Bank of Central African States) meant that 85% of the country's currency was to be deposited at the Banque de France. In exchange, France offered a premium of 13% in French Francs. In December Nguema Onguene discussed with the French minister for Cooperation about the UDEAC; on the 19th at Bangui, Equatorial Guinea officially joined. Equatorial Guinea has participated in the creation of the Economic Community of Central African States, and the introduction of the "French" CFA franc in January 1985, replacing the Guinean peseta, was an important step in this process.

On December 2, 1986, Obiang Nguema was forced to borrow 5 million naira from Nigeria in order to finance the 22nd UDEAC summit in Bata in mid-December 1986. Five heads of state and one minister of foreign affairs attended the meeting. The question of a common telecommunications satellite was discussed.

In 1987, *Marchés Tropicaux* wrote: "It was the UDEAC which entered Guinea [Equatorial] and not Equatorial Guinea which entered the UDEAC, said a diplomat."

At the 27th summit, at Libreville, an accusing finger was pointed at Equatorial Guinea for nonpayment of its contribution, i.e., $9.8 million. This posed a problem, as Obiang Nguema was to preside over the summit at Bujumbura, in May 1992. There he denounced the HUDEAC for being slow and for its financial crisis. In October, at the next summit at Bata, France offered FFr 2.3 million for the purchase of vehicles and material, as well as the training of local personnel. Through GE-TOTAL 50 cases of Dom Perignon champagne and 50 cases of whisky were offered. The sum of CFA Fr10 million was deducted from the company's tax dues.

CYPRUS. On February 23, 1998, *Lloyd's List International* indicates that the *Pinner* (6.090 dwt), sailing under the Equato-Guinean flag, was blocked by the Financial Crime Investigation Bureau due to an alleged fake registration. The authorities of Equatorial Guinea were said to have listed 40 ships sailing under the Equato-Guinean flag without authorization. The owner of the ship (a Syrian with Cypriate nationality) declared, in the *Cyprus Mail* of February 25, that the ship was properly registered under the Equato-Guinean flag at Renage Cyprus, a company located in Limasol, and one of the two companies authorized to register ships sailing under the Equato-Guinean flag. However, in July 1997, Renage and the Miami company, managed by Victor Jineo, were no longer authorized to deliver registrations. But the *Pinner* had been registered before that date, which means the registration is perfectly valid. But to avoid trouble, the *Pinner* placed itself under the Belizean flag. According to *Lloyd's List International,* on February 26, 1998, Nathaniel Papageorgiou, superintendent-in-chief of the harbor of Limasol and in charge of the division of financial crimes, reported that he had not received the information he had requested from the Equato-Guinean government via Interpol in December 1997.

❖ D ❖

DECOLONIZATION COMMITTEE. In 1957, two years after Spain's admission to the United Nations, Spanish and Portuguese overseas territories were debated at the UN. The introduction of provincialization in 1960 was judged insufficient by the Afro-Asian group. In 1963 the Trusteeship Council (composed of 17 members at that time) received petitions from Equato-Guinean nationalist movements, to such a point that in August 1963 Spain had to announce the forthcoming autonomy of Equatorial Guinea. In 1966, the Committee of 24 made a fact-finding tour of Spanish Guinea and recommended independence for July 1968. Respectful of its will, Spain organized a Constitutional Conference in 1967 that led to Independence on October 12, 1968.

DELEGACION DE ASUNTOS SOCIALES (Social Affairs Delegation). The Patronato de Indígenas, suppressed in 1960, was replaced by Diputaciones Provinciales (Assemblies), which created delegations to look after native politics. In fact there was only one delegate (Sastre), whose task was especially to investigate the political development of Guinean public opinion. In 1974 the Instituto de Seguridad Social (INESO) was created for these purposes but never became operational and has now disappeared. See also Social Security.

DELEGACIONES GUBERNATIVAS (Territorial Administrations). Called forth by provincialization, the Delegaciones Gubernativas assisted the civil governors at district level since 1960. Chosen by each civil governor, the members' nominations had to be confirmed by the secretario general. The government delegates had to report to the civil governor, who had the right to discharge them with the governor general's consent.

DELMAS-VIELJEUX. A French maritime navigation company gravitating in the orbit of the CFAO. It has connected Equatorial Guinea since 1985.
    See also Navigation.

DEMOCRACY. In October 1988, the Spanish Socialist Party presented before the Parliament resolutions containing an appeal to the Nguemists for cooperation within a democratic framework. The United Left (Izquierda Unida) demanded that the Spanish volunteers for cooperation insist on strict respect of human rights, while it gave its protection to the Hispanic culture of Equatorial Guinea.
    In October 1990, Obiang Nguema spoke of the dangers of a Liberian type of chaos if multipartism were hurriedly instilled, thus disregarding the need for alternatives in democracy. The reporter for the United Nations Human Rights Commission, F. Volio Jimenez, during his interview with the minister of foreign affairs in December 1991, heard the minister exclaim: "What do human rights have to do with democracy?" On October 12, 1992, Obiang Nguema stated that

the democratic process "is not just the President's affair, but concerns all citizens." In November he spoke of a "transition" period until "all those involved in politics understand the meaning of democracy." The Volio-Jimenez Report to the 1993 UN Human Rights Commission was categorical: Equatorial Guinea is a dictatorship; the majority of the people want a change. Several Spanish political parties denounced France's attitude of low solidarity—in contrast with EU decisions—which presented a democratic transition. The press said multipartism was pure fiction, the proof of it being the reluctance of a large majority of intellectuals and professionals among the diaspora to return.

In February 1996, after the electoral farce that renewed the mandate of the dictator Obiang Nguema, the special reporter to the Human Rights Commission once more expressed his doubts over democratization in Equatorial Guinea. Alejandro Artucio showed the subservience of the legislative and the judiciary to the executive power (a principal characteristic of a dictatorship), the excessive powers given to military "justice," the numerous cruel and degrading instances of ill treatment, the torture, the violation of political rights, the irregularities in the presidential elections, the disregard of economic, social and cultural rights, the impunity with which great violations of human rights are committed, the rather low-key efforts of the government towards democratization: in short, serious and repeated violations of fundamental freedoms. Deputy Prime Minister Javier Ngomo Mbengono assured the Commission of the government's commitment to democratization. But the Commission passed a resolution expressing its deep concern at the situation in Nguemist Equatorial Guinea, and exhorted the government to make changes. In his speech to the Commission, the Swiss minister of foreign affairs, Flavio Cotti, put Equatorial Guinea in a single category with three other African countries where "grave problems have been observed."

In April 1996, the State Department Report on Human Rights Practices for 1995 clearly demonstrated the continuation of dictatorship.

Citizens have not had the right to change their government by democratic means. The Constitution nominally provides citizens with the right to change the government peacefully, but in fact there have been no free presidential elections since the independence in 1968. The President exercises complete power as Head of State, commander of the armed forces, and leader of the government party, the PDGE.

Everything is used to allay suspicion. On May 18–22, 1998, Bata held a subregional conference called "Democratic Institutions and Peace in Central Africa."

Every August 3rd, during the commemoration of Macias Nguema's overthrow, the "consolidation of the democratic system" is celebrated in Malabo.

See also Elections; European Union; Human Rights; Mobil Corps; Opposition; Political Parties; Press; Reporter without Borders.

DEMOCRATIC PARTY OF EQUATORIAL GUINEA (Partido Democrático de Guinea Ecuatorial, PDGE). Sole Nguemist party, the successor of Macías Nguema's PUNT. At the end of 1986, with a lack of national political organization capable of promoting political and social development and of making the citizens politically aware, Obiang Nguema planned the imminent creation of the PDGE. This was to be "a party of a democratic nature, open to all Equato-Guineans who would willingly join it." The party "cannot be used as an instrument of terror or of repression," as the PUNT had been. Obiang Nguema also added: "We are going to try to apply democracy in an orderly fashion."

The PDGE was inaugurated on August 3, 1987, on the 8th anniversary of the toppling of Macías Nguema. It was known as the governmental party, and was aimed at ensuring the reelection of Obiang Nguema, in 1989. The emblem of the PDGE is a flaming torch (like the MPR of Mobutu). The actual inauguration of the party took place on October 12, under the supervision of the Nguemist ideologist, Eloy Elo Nve Mbengono.

In October 1988, the first convention was held, in Bata. Obiang Nguema was then elected president of the PDGE. The dictator stressed that after two centuries of merciless colonial exploitation and 11 years of his predecessor's and uncle's dictatorship, the government "was for working for the welfare of the people under the banner of a better Guinea."

On January 13, 1991, Obiang Nguema stated that the party would reject foreign ideologies and opt for an authentic political system. Multipartite democracy was declared to be "an obstacle to the actual process of democratization." A number of purges were carried out, due to irregularities. At the first extraordinary convention in August, various resolutions called upon the government to take short, medium and long term measures towards the creation of other parties and to ensure the freedoms of association and expression. Obiang Nguema was designated the referee and coordinator of the new multipartite process. Out of the 73 members of the central committee, 52 were natives of Mongomo and 38 were military officials; the committee also included 13 members of Obiang Nguema's immediate family.

In 1992, the PDGE inaugurated an occasional journal, which used the title of the periodical published since 1975 by the National Alliance for Democratic Restoration (ANRD): La Voz del Pueblo. In order to expose the trick, the Convergency for Social Democracy (CPDS) exposed it in its monthly La Verdad, using a facsimile page of the ANRD's La Voz del Pueblo's cover page.

In early 1993 the PDGE participated in the negotiations for the National Pact, which was violated by the regime as soon as it was signed, in March. Obiang Nguema cancelled the salary tax, meant for the PDGE. An internal report of the party revealed that it would only obtain six seats if clean elections were held. At the end of September, the minister for the interior (police), the state secretary for criminal investigations, and the prime minister, accompanied by Ninjas, threatened a delegation of the CPDS. La Verdad was again banned from circulation. During the November 21 elections, 70% of absenteeism was recorded in Río Muni and 80% in Fernando Po, as a result of the boycott called by the POC. The PDGE granted itself 68 deputies (out of 80), and the remaining went to three parties of the domestic opposition (CSDP, UDS, PL).

The 2nd convention of the PDGE, which lasted seven days, and was set for December 1994, had to be postponed to February 1995 (Bata), but could not be held and had to be again postponed to March 20, due to a number of internal problems. Members of the democratic opposition were arrested and imprisoned in the suburban presidential palace at Ekuku. On March 26, 1995, Obiang Nguema declared: "I have conquered power. Nobody gifted it to me. If anyone else wishes to have it, he knows how to obtain it!" A delegation of the domesticated opposition parties participated in the convention (UDENA, PSDE, PSGE, CLD), while the POC was absent. Foreign delegations were also present: People's Republic of China, North Korea, Angola, Gabon, Cuba, PSOE). On May 2, Obiang Nguema dismissed Juan Micha Nsue Nfumu, deputy political secretary, and his colleague Carmelo Asumu Obono, both accused of dissidence. They were replaced by Fernando Mabale, secretary of state for mines, and Darío-Tadeo Ndong Olomo, ex-customs official, director general of commerce and coordinator of the Antorchas of the PDGE. According to the POC, the staff of the PDGE were paid from public funds. In August 1995, Armengol Engonga, vice-president of the Partido del Progreso, described the ideology of the PDGE as being communist.

During the municipal elections held on September 17, 1995, the PDGE adjudged itself the winner in Fernando Po, against the views of all observers, with 130 seats (against 79 for the POC), and in Río Muni with 114 seats (against 56 for the POC). But the POC won the capital, with nine seats (PDGE 3, UP 1). Towards the end of 1995, the members of the PDGE circulated a sworn Declaration meant to recruit members, who were called to promise "on god, on my honor and sense of responsibility, never to counter the decisions of the PDGE, and to accept all the decisions that my party may take, and, my faithfulness to its cause is irrevocable. . . . I declare that my vote belongs to the PDGE." All of which was followed by the names of three executives of the dictator's party. F. Mabale stressed during the whole presidential campaign that the public vote "helped avoid dubious situations," and added that the country was in the same condition as during the 1968 Presidential elections, "during which the people encountered persecution, violence and death for having voted in secrecy."

Upon the arrest of the mayor of the capital, V. Bolekia, and his councilors, on February 16, and the fictitious allegations of an attempted coup d'etat by Bikomo Nanguande, some senior executives of the PDGE criticized the "hurried manner in which trust" was given by Obiang Nguema to the floor crossers from the domesticated opposition.

During the presidential elections on February 25, 1996, it was obviously the President of the PDGE, Dictator Obiang Nguema, who after having paralyzed the opposition, claimed victory with 99% of the votes, with the Election Commission being headed by yet another pillar of the clan from Mongomo, Ndong Ela Mangue, minister for the interior (police) (see Elections). In April 1996, the Report of the Department of State on Human Rights Practices for 1995 observed that if

> The Government does not overtly force officials to join the PDGE ... for lawyers, government employees, and others, party membership is necessary for employment and promotion. The party banner is prominently displayed with the national flag in government offices, and many officials wear PDGE lapel pins. Foreign firms are often pressured to hire party members.

It added that: "The President's Democratic Party of Equatorial Guinea (PDGE) controls the judiciary and the legislature, the latter through fraudulent elections."

In May 1996, the Bulletin of the PDGE accused the "radical" opposition of plotting an invasion of the country.

Beginning in 1998, Basilio Ava and Julian Eyapo, first and second vice-presidents of the PP announced on Radio Malabo that they had presented their defection and were joining the PDGE. At the same time, in Madrid, Moto Nsá asked Obiang Nguema to establish a "true democrary," and to give up "the hegemony of a party founded on the fear its militants have of losing their jobs" and to encourage a "state founded on the freedom of spech, the respect of human rights and equality for all." At the end of July, the PDGE, through its spokesman Santiago Ngua, demanded that Spain stop its emission of Radio Exterior de España. Augustin Nsé Nfumu, is secretary general of the PDGE.

See also Abaga Ondo Bindang, A.; Akuakam, Akurenam; Alianza; Angue Ondo; Annobón; Bata; Benito, Rio; Bikomo Nanguande; Buale Bokama; Bueribueri Bokesa; Cayetano Toherida; Democratic and Social Union; Drugs; Ebang Mbele; Ebebeyin, Ebendeng, Nsomo; Ebiaka Nokete; Edjang Angue; Ekong Nsue; Elections; Electricity; Elo Ndong Nsefumu; Engonga Ondo; Envoro Owono; Esono Abaga Ada, J.; Esono Masie; Eyegue Obama Asue; King Somo; Mabala Mba; Mabale Nseng; Mangue Obama Nfube; Masie Ntutumu; Mbale, F.; Mba Ondo Nchama; Mecheba, J.; Mecheba Fernandez; Micha Nsue Nfumu; Mikomeseng; Milam Onvogo; Moto Nsá; Muatetema Rivas, C.; Muñoz Ilata; National Pact; Ndong Mba; Ndong Mbana Obono; Ndong Olomo, D. T.; Nsogo Mbengono; Ngore, B.; Ngua Nfumu; Nguema Esono; Nguema Esono Nichama; Nguema Nguema Onguene; Nguema Mbasogo Ondo; Nguema Owono; Nseng Nve; Nsobeya Efuman Nsue; Nsue Mokuy; Nsue Nchama; Nsue Nguema Nsuga; Nve Mbangono; Nvono Akele, C.; Nvono Akele Avomo; Nvono Nka Mañene; Obama Nsue Mangue; Obiang Nguema; Oko Ebono; Olo Mba Nzen; Ondo Mitogo; Ondo Obiang Alogo; Opposition; Oyono Ndong Mifumu; Oyono Ntutumu; Parliament; Popular Union; Presidency; Press; Ronda, S.; Russia; Seriche Bioko Malabo; Siale Bolekia; Sisa Torres; Social Democratic Party; Social Democratic and Popular Convergency; Socialist Party; Tamarite Burgos; Voz del Pueblo

DEMOCRATIC PROGRESSIVE ALLIANCE (Alianza Democrática Progresista, ADP). Founded in 1992 by Antonio Ebang Mbele Abang, a member of the PDGE committee and former vice-President of the Parliament, deposed in 1990 for his support of multiparties. The ADP, a member of the POC, obtained permission, in 1992, to hold meetings and to open branch offices. In December the police raided its offices in Santa Isabel.

In early 1993, Ebang Mbele, who was just returning from Europe along with other politicians, was arrested at the border. In October, he joined the POC in signing the Institutional Proposal addressed to Obiang Nguema. In early November, Tomas Mba, chief of the youth wing of the party, was arrested, manhandled, and then released. The ADP participated in the election-boycott of November 21.

On October 9, 1994, Victorino Bolekia Bonay, vice-president of the ADP, Jose Mecheba Ikaka, president of the UDENA, and Plácido Micó, one of the directors of the CPDS, were arrested at Akalayong, transferred to Bata and tortured in the city's prison.

In Barcelona, on February 4, 1995, the ADP joined hands with the National Peoples Congress of Equatorial Guinea. Ebang Mbele remained its president,

Francisco Ela Abeme became its general secretary and J. B. Mbia Mbida Essindi the secretary of international relations. A national convention was held to establish the agenda and form the new Committee. Following the September municipal elections, Bubi V. Bolekia became the mayor of the capital.

In early 1996, Ebang Mbele and his Nigerian girlfriend were arrested in Argentina for cocaine trafficking. The POC demanded that Ebang Mbele be expelled from the ADP. At the time of the presidential elections, during a French lesson in February, V. Bolekia and his deputy-mayors, including C. Bakale, were arrested in the French cultural center by Chief Commissioner of Police Julian Ondo Nkumu, and tortured for one whole night. Bikomo Nanguande publicly accused them of plotting a coup d'etat with a French terrorist expert.

The ADP publishes a bulletin: *El Ocho.* In September 1996, V. Bolekia participated in the meeting of the Christian Democratic International in Brussels, accompanied by Moto Nsá (PP).

DEMOCRATIC UNION FOR THE LIBERATION OF EQUATORIAL GUINEA (Reunión Democrática para la Liberación de Guinea Ecuatorial, RDPLGE). Founded by Manuel R. Ndongo, with Pedro Biyogo, in Dakar, towards the end of 1980. Ndongo claimed that four old parties were coming together to assemble 31,000 members.

In 1981, the RDPLGE demanded elections, in an appeal from Dakar, but supported Obiang Nguema's constitutional plebiscite. Biyogo abandoned the boat, accusing Ndongo of playing the dictator. Ndongo, who wished to return to the country, was offered a one-way ticket by Obiang Nguema; Ndongo took fright, and gave up the idea.

In March 1983, in Libreville, and then in Paris, the RDPLGE published a communiqué announcing that it was forming a provisional government-in-exile: the Executive Reorganization Council, following the failure of various efforts at mediation by the CMS; the composition of the government.

In November 1984, Ndongo announced that his RDPLGE was merging with the PSAGE (Partido Socialista Africano), in order to form the Social Democratic and Popular Convergency (CSDP). He claimed to have the support of 80% of Equato-Guinean nationals in exile. He took a stand against the UDEAC and the Franc zone; Secundino Oyono and his wife as well as Sibacha Buecheku, secretary for external relations, were its members. This party has now disappeared. M. R. Ndong later joined Moto Nsa's Progress Party.

DEMOGRAPHY. On December 31, 1965, Spanish Guinea had 254,700 inhabitants, of which 191,000 lived in Río Muni and 63,700 in Fernando Po, but these are only estimations, the official Spanish data changed strongly depending on the issuing administration. On December 31, 1970, the Equato-Guinean administration undertook a census, which showing 1.5 million inhabitants, had to be canceled. In late 1974 the population was estimated (by the World Bank) at 301,000, to which the 120,000 refugees abroad must be added. From 3.4 per 1,000 at the time of independence, the growth rate seems to be only of 1 per 1,000 presently. Maximum population density seems to be 10.7 inhabitants per sq km, or 136 per sq km of cultivated land. In 1968 the death rate was of 7.8 per 1000 against 27 for the rest of tropical Africa; in 1976 the gross death rate seems to

Total population	1997		420,000
projected	2025		798,000
Density, inhab./km^2	1997		15
Population by age (%)	1994	0–14	43
		15–64	54
		65+	4
- 18 years, in %	1996		50
Ubran population in %	1990		29
Projected, in %	2000		45
	2025		68.5
Growth rate, in %	1960–1990		1.5
	1900–2000		2.6
Birth rate, in %	1990–1995		42.4
Death rate, in %	1990–1995		17.3
Fertility rate	1996		5.6
Infant mortality (less			
than 5 yrs), in %	1996		174
Sex ration (men per 100			
women) in pop. aged 60+	1998		73
Life expectancy at birth	1960		36.8
	1998		49.0
	1995–2000		
	Male		48.4
	Female		51.6

have gone up to 21 per 1,000, reaching thus the African average. In 1977 the population was estimated at about 335,000 (taking into account the 25,000 Nigerians who left in 1976). In 1972, only 28% of the population lived in localities of more than 10,000 inhabitants, i.e., Bata (28,000) and Santa Isabel (38,000). Equatorial Guinea can therefore be called a rural country.

In 1981, the Annuario Pontificio indicated 185,000 inhabitants in Río Muni and 72,000 on Fernando Po; with Annobón, the total population reached 270,000 (238,000 Catholics). In April 1982, at the UNDP donors' conference, Obiang Nguema estimated the population of the country to be "between 300,000 and 500,000." The estimates of the Economic Intelligence Unit of London for 1989 put it at 430,000, the UN Report put it at 440,000, of whom 256,000 lived in rural areas, while the UN Economic Commission for Africa put it for 1994 at 389,000 (women: 51.2%).

DENMARK. In 1978 a Danish female journalist, E. Nilsson, visited Equatorial Guinea. In Bata she was sheltered by the Spanish teacher Guarri. Suspected of spying, she was able to go back to Cameroon. Guarri was imprisoned for 41 days, accused of perfidy after a sketch-itinerary he drew for the Danish woman was discovered in his house. E. Nilsson's observations were published in the Danish newspaper *KD* in mid-March 1978. During the 1993 meeting of the United Nations Human Rights Commission in Geneva, the Dane J. Esper Larsen, stressed the continuation of arbitrary arrests and court hearings and torture mainly by the presidential guards. See also France; Río Muni.

DEPARTMENT OF AGRICULTURE see Dirección de Agricultura

DEVELOPMENT PLANS AND PROGRAMS. Created in 1975, this ministry was headed by Abaga Oburu, Vice-Minister, without great authority, all economic affairs being in the hands of Macías Nguema's nephew, Oyono Ayingono Mba.

Some Spanish economists, including Velarde Fuentes, helped Obiang Nguema draw up an economic revival plan, after the August 1979 coup d'etat. Marcos Mba Ondo (from Mongomo) became the military commissioner for the plan. The repatriation of capital was permitted in order to attract foreign enterprises. In December, Mba Ondo was replaced by Mesa Bill. In October 1982, Guillermo Nguema Ela (from Mongomo) became minister for planning and economic development. In October 1990, Marcelino Nguema Nguema Onguene (from Mongomo) became minister for the economy, commerce, and planning. In the January 24, 1992, "transitional" government, Anatolio Ndong Mba was the minister for planning and international cooperation.

In the December 22, 1993, government, F. Inestrosa became secretary of state for planning and industrial development. On December 22, 1993, Ndong Mba became deputy prime minister and minister for the economy and finance. Felipe Inestrosa Ikaka was named the secretary of state for planning and economic development. In the January 8, 1996, ministerial reshuffle, Federico Edjo Ovono took the post of vice-minister for planning and development. But in the ministerial reshuffle of April 8, 1996, these posts were given to A.-F. Nve Nzeng.

In the ministerial reshuffle of January 21, 1998, Anatolio Ndong Mba was named minister of state in charge of planning and international cooperation, and Antonio Fernando Nve Ngu minister of planning.

See also García Barleycorn, F.

DIAZ DE VILLEGAS Y BUSTAMENT, José, 1894–1968. Spanish general, a Francoist, appointed director of the Direccíon General de Marruecos y Colonias in 1944 and director of the "Instituto de Estudios Africanos" in 1945. The right-hand man of Carrero Blanco, Díaz was opposed to the improvement of salary conditions for Guinean schoolteachers in 1945, causing the fall of Governor General Bonelli Rubio and Inspector of Education Alvarez García, which led to the first nationalist movement, the Cruzada Nacional de Liberación de Guinea Ecuatorial. He called Ndongo Miyone a Communist during the Constitutional Conference where he himself represented the head of government.

DILLON, TENANT & CO. Company owning a subsidiary in Fernando Po, of which John Beecroft was a shareholder. From 1833 on, with Beecroft becoming governor of the island, the company became the actual authority of Fernando Po. Having gone bankrupt, Beecroft sold it to the West Africa Company in 1837.

DIPLOMACY. Bruno Esono Ondo has been the ambassador to Spain since 1991. Under him, the embassy was submerged in debts (and the telephone line cut). Spanish authorities pass by the South African embassy, in the same building. In the ambassador's residence, there was no water. The Ministry of Foreign Affairs received bills for clothes, schooling, and also hotel bills left unpaid by the diplomats. Sometimes penniless diplomats, like Vice-Prime Minister Eyi Mensui, even had to be repatriated from Namibia by friendly countries, with Spain's help.

Towards the end of 1991, a note from the diplomatic corps affiliated with the Ministry for Foreign Affairs in Santa Isabel demanded that security forces stop all acts of violence against diplomats and airline flights.

In February 1992, as a punishment to the American embassy and the UNDP for having given asylum to Equato-Guineans persecuted by the army for holding contrary opinions, diplomatic missions and international organizations were subjected to restrictions on their movements and activities, even on their rights to receive their nationals as visitors. Towards the end of 1992, Obiang Nguema accused the opposition of being puppets to the diplomatic corps.

A number of Equato-Guinean diplomats were convinced that drug trafficking and other crimes were rampant. The Equato-Guinean diplomatic passport is widely used to facilitate trafficking.

In early 1993, the Spanish and American ambassadors, Avello and Bennet, received death threats because of their stand on the importance of fundamental rights and the democratic process.

In early 1994, the offices of the embassy in Madrid were closed; there were extremely large numbers of unpaid bills in the commercial sector. The 1994 Report of the Geopolitical Drug Observatory (Paris) warned that Obiang Nguema "has transformed his diplomatic personnel and his family, which are one and the same thing into an international network" of drug traffickers.

In 1995, Minister for External Affairs Oyono Ndong Mifumu presented Nguemism before the General Assembly of the UN as a model regime and denounced the so-called Spanish interference in the country's internal affairs. The UNDP denied the accusation in Santa Isabel.

In the January 8, 1996, ministerial reshuffle, Miguel Oyono Ndong remained minister, with the sinister Batho Obama Nsue Mangue as minister with special responsibility. In the ministerial reshuffle of April 8, 1996, Oyono Ndong retained his post, but Batho was no longer on the list.

In the January 21, 1998 government, Oyono Ndong Mifumu kept his office of Minister of Foreign Affairs and Co-operation, and was appointed first vice-prime minister. Mrs. Teresa Efua Asangono is vice-minister of Foreign Affairs and International Co-operation. See Oyono, Miguel

Equato-Guinean ambassadors in 1998: Belgium, Aurelio Mbá Oló Andeme; China (Popular), Florencio Maye Ela Mangue; France, Lino-Sima Ekau Aviomo; Gabon, José Elá Ebang; Morocco, Eduardo Ndong Oló; Nigeria, Antonio Mba Ndong; Russia, Antonio Javier Nguema Nchama; Spain, Santiago Nsobey Efuman.

See also Abaga Ondo Maye, E.; Argentina; Armenia; Aviation; Balboa Boneke, J.; Balinga, B. G.; Batho (Obama Nsue Mangue, F.); Bennet, J. E.; China, Nationalist Republic of; China, People's Republic of; Coconut Island; Coup d'etat of May 11–13, 1983; Customs Union of the Central African States; Dacosta, M.; Dougan, A. S.; Drugs; Ebang Mbele Abang, A.; Ela Abeme, J.; Esono Abaga Ada, J.; Esono Mika Miha, P. J.; Esono Ondo, B.; European Union; Eyama Angüe Osa, D.; France; Gabon, Germany; Human Rights; Israel; Italy; Japan; Korea, Northern; Korea, Southern; Llansol, V.-G.; Maye Ela, F.; Mba Ekua Miko, B.; Mba Ndong, A.; Mba Nsoro Mban; Mba Oñana; Mbengono Asu Alene, A;, Mensui Mba, P.; Micha Nsue Nfumu, J.; Micha Ondo Bile, P.; Miko Abogo, P.; Mikomeseng, Modu Akuse Bindang, C.; Mokong Onguene, C.; Moto Nsá, S.; Movement for the Autodetermination of the Island of Bioko; National Alliance for Democratic Restauration; National Institute for Social Security; Ndong Abaga Mesian, C.; Ndong Ela Nzang, E.; Ndong Mba, Z.; Ndongo Ogüono-Asong, M. M.; Nepotism; Netherlands; Nguema, L.; Nguema Edu, F.; Nguema Esono, L.; Nguema Sema, A. M.; Niefang; Nigeria; Norris, C.; Nsobeya Efuman Nsue, S.; Nsue Obama Angono, P.; Nsue Nguema Nsuga, M.; Nve Nzeng, A. F.; Nze Nfumu, A.; Obama Nsue Mangue, F.; Nvono Nka Manene; Obiang Mangue, L.; Obiang Ndong, D.; Obiang Nguema, T.; Okenve Mituy, F.; Ondo Ayang, L.; Organization of African Unity; Otero, J. M.; Oyono, M.; Parliament; Petroleum; Platform of Support for Democracy in Equatorial Guinea; Police; Post Offices; Russia; Sanchez Bustamante, D.; Santa Isabel; Seriche Dougan, A. S.; Shinkame, J.; Siale Bilekia, S.; Sima, A.; Sima Ekua Avoma, L.; Sneyders, A. L.; Guinean Gas Company; South Africa; Spain; Switzerland; Terror; Udebeke, E.; United Kingdom; United States; Vakhrameyev, L. A.; Van Boven, T.; Victims; Walter International Inc.; Wang Yongcheng

DIPUTACION PROVINCIAL (Provincial Assembly, General Council). Government body called forth by the 1960 Status of Provincialization, following the example of metropolitan provinces. In each province the Diputación took over the attributions of the Patronato de Indígenas and assumed representation to the Cortes. With ten members for Río Muni and eight for Fernando Po, the Diputaciones, elected for four years, were principally the voice of Spanish administrative, economic, and cultural institutions, the representatives of which formed three-quarters of the members, which was in line with the Falangist plan. As of 1962 the majority of both Diputaciones was African. The decisions were liable to the governor general's veto. All Spanish laws were submitted to the Diputaciones, who could however not adapt them to Guinean conditions before autonomy in 1964, when the two provincial assemblies joined in a single Asambléa General (Parliament).

DIRECCION DE AGRICULTURA (Department of Agriculture). Department supervising all agricultural matters, e.g., pilot farms, young farmers' training, guidance of cooperatives, and the like. It operated in collaboration with the Patronato de Indígenas. With the termination of the latter, the administration of agricultural affairs became separate for each province.

DIRECCION GENERAL DE PLAZAS Y PROVINCIAS see Directorate of Towns and Colonies

DIRECTORATE OF TOWNS AND COLONIES (Dirección General de Plazas y Colonias). Instrument of the Spanish administration in charge of overseas politics placed under the authority of the head of government. Since its creation after Primo de Rivera's dictatorship, by Decree of June 18, 1931, it had been especially in charge of distributing concessions. After Fontan y Lobé (1941–1944), Díaz de Villegas became its director. In 1947 the Dirección set up an advisory Junta Económica Colonial (Committee for Colonial Economy), where the Comité Sindical del Cacao, the Delegación Peninsular del Café, the Sindicato Maderero (timber), and the Casa de Guinea were represented. After 1946, the

Dirección was also responsible for the Colonial Guard. Regarding cultural affairs, it sponsored the Boards of Education Inspection and the Instituto de Estudios Africanos, monopolizing information and research on the African territories. In 1960, by decree of July 21, 1956, it was renamed "Dirección General de Plazas y Provincias Africanas" (Management of Towns and Provinces of Africa). Díaz de Villegas led the delegation of the head of government at the Constitutional Conference of 1967-68. In 1968, after Diaz's retirement, the Dirección became vice-administration headed by Junco Miranda, who attended the celebration of independence of Equatorial Guinea, on October 12, 1968.

DISTRICT COUNCIL see Ayuntamientos

DJANGANI, Fernando. Benga from Río Benito. Born in Bolondo. On January 19, 1994, he was named president's counsellor for judicial affairs.

DJOMBE DJANGANI, Cristina. Benga from Río Benito. School teacher, trained at the Escuela Superior Indígena (Santa Isabel). Graduate in education (UNED, Santa Isabel). In March 1981, she became the secretary of the State Secretariat for Women's Welfare. In the January 24, 1992, "transitional" government, she became the minister for women's welfare. She was not part of the December 22, 1993, government. On January 19, 1994, she was named counsellor to the president of the government for education and sciences. In the April 8, 1996, government, she was confirmed.

DJOMBE DJANGANI DE MBUAMANGONGO, Pilar. Benga from Río Benito. Born 1940. Trained teacher from the Escuela Superior Indígena. Did health studies in the United States and in Spain.

In January 1986, she was appointed vice-minister for health, in which capacity she led the Equato-Guinean delegation to the World Health Conference in Geneva.

In the January 24, 1992, "transitional" government, she was minister for promotion of women and social affairs. In June, she became the WHO representative at São Tomé and Principe.

Upon her return to the country, she became the director of the Teacher's Training School. Towards the end of February 1996, during the presidential elections, she was said to have voted in the name of her students.

DOCTORS WITHOUT BORDERS see Catholicism; Human Rights; Public Health

DOUGAN. Fernandino family, native of Sierra Leone, and important planters. Fr. Dougan, member of the Unión Bubi, participated in the 1967–1968 Constitutional Conference; J. Dougan was on the list of Macías Nguema's Group for the 1968 elections. S. D. Dougan Mendo was an active member of MUNGE. Since 1976, Okori Dougan Kinson has been popular minister of justice, after having been a professor of English in Santa Isabel.

José Dougan, Okori's son, and brother-in-law of Daniel Oyono Ayingono, is Obiang Nguema's cousin and works in Madrid with García Trevijano. Another of Okori Dougan's sons, Beaca Dougan, a member of the ANRD is an official of the UN Human Rights Commission. In 1995, the National Alliance for Democratic Restoration (ANRD) expelled him.

See also Balboa Dougan; Dougan, J.; Dougan Beaca, J. D.; Fernandinos; National Alliance for Democratic Restoration; Ondo Ayang, L.

DOUGAN, Angel Serafin. A Bubi, born in Moka in 1944. Studied at the Escuela Superior Provincial.

As ambassador to Nigeria, he attended the UNDP Donor's Conference, in Geneva, in April 1982. Upon becoming secretary general of the Ministry for Foreign Affairs, he was named ambassador to Cameroon. In the government of January 8, 1996, he was named secretary of state for civil service. During the April 8 ministerial reshuffle, he was named prime minister.

In the ministerial reshuffle of January 21, 1998, he was confirmed as prime minister and head of the government.

DOUGAN, Jose. A Creole, born in Santa Isabel in 1951. Son of Okori Dougan, minister under Macías Nguema; half-brother of Dougan Beaca. Brother-in-law of Daniel Oyono Ayingono. Studied in Cuba, but did not complete his law course. Worked in Macías Nguema's former counsellor, Garcías Trevijano's establishment with Oyono Ayingono, in Madrid. Macías Nguema. Now works as a trader. See also Dougan Beaca; Trevijano Garcia

DOUGAN BEACA, José Domingo. Creole, born 1948. Son of Okori Dougan, minister under Macías Nguema. Half-brother to Dougan, José took refuge in Italy, and then in Switzerland in 1974. Holds a degree in law (University of Freiburg). A founding member of the ANRD, and secretary first for information and later for internal organization. He was replaced in 1983. Employed since 1980 in the Human Rights Division of the UN, in Geneva.

In 1985, Dougan Beaca filed a lawsuit against Liniger-Goumaz and his book, *ONU et dictatures,* and managed to obtain the sales forbidden during 1994, but not the 100,000 Sw. Fr ($80,000) he claimed.

In January 1995, the general secretary of the National Alliance for Democratic Restoration (ANRD), Luis Ondo Ayang, at a press conference in Geneva, commented on the expulsion by the Executive Committee, of Dougan Beaca and Mokong Onguene, on September 4, 1994.

See also National Alliance for Democratic Restoration; Dougan J.; Eya Nchama, C. M.; Jones Dougan; Mba Mombe, S.; Mokong Onguene, C.; Ondo Ayang, L.; Seriche Dougan; United Nations.

DRUGS. In May 1981, the Spanish police caught the ambassador's wife Evuna Owono Asangono (from Mongomo) with a packet of bhanga (Indian hemp). The ambassador was recalled and made secretary general of the ministry of foreign affairs.

In 1982, Carmelo Nvono Nka Mañene, the nephew of Mba Oñana (from Mongomo), ambassador to the United Nations and the U.S., was condemned for trafficking in drugs.

In November 1988, after a drug trafficking scandal with Lucas Nguema (from Mongomo), the chargé d'affaires Francisco Ngua Nguema Edu (from Mongomo), was caught red-handed smuggling tobacco to Madrid. He could leave Spain, thanks to diplomatic immunity.

In October 1990, the ambassador to France, Jesus Ela Abeme (from Mongomo) was arrested along with his wife for heroin trafficking.

In 1991, Sub-Lt. of the Navy David Eyama Angue Osa, military attaché in Lagos, was accused by Nigeria of drug trafficking (32 kg of Brazilian cocaine). The Nigerians demanded that diplomatic immunity be lifted. Obiang Nguema refused and sent his son Teodorín (from Mongomo) to have Eyama repatriated.

In 1993, the Geopolitical Drug Observatory (Paris) warned that Equatorial Guinea was producing cannabis. It added that some of the trafficking was carried out in Obiang Nguema's name. Equatorial Guinea was the link between South America and Europe; money laundering operations were said to be carried out under the direction of Obiang Nguema's economic counsellor, the France-convicted Llansol. Equatorial Guinea was called a new Panama à la Noriega. Armengol Nguema (from Mongomo) was alleged to be the kingpin of all the traffickers. On August 31, 1993, a cousin of Obiang Nguema and wife of the ambassador to Spain, Anita Mbengono Asu Alene, was arrested at São Paulo, with 32 kilos of cocaine. Obiang Nguema allegedly received a payment of $1.5 million, addressed to an International Afrikan Bank, with a commission of 15% for himself. The commission was supposed to have helped found the non-existent Banco de Crédito Agricola de Guinea Ecuatorial. On December 31, the Nguemists denied any truth in the news about their trafficking activities.

The 1994 Report of the Geopolitical Drug Observatory put Equatorial Guinea among the eight African "narco-states." In the autumn of 1994, the third secretary in the embassy in France, Alejandro Bama Setem, was arrested and imprisoned in Bangkok for drug trafficking, which he declared as having been carried out under the orders of the ambassador.

The U.S. Anti-drug Agency maintains that Obiang Nguema is one of the biggest money launderers. According to the NGO Droits de l'Homme sans Frontières (Geneva, December 1995), "the chief of state has transformed his diplomatic personnel and his family, which are in most cases one and the same thing, into an international network, though on a modest scale, in this country of 30,000 km^2 and 400,000 inhabitants."

On December 13, 1995, Corona Atebaso Oyana, administrative assistant to the embassy in Bejing, was arrested in Bolivia with 16.6 kg of cocaine, found in 5 packages wrapped in paper covered with pepper. In spite of her diplomatic passport, she was jailed in Santa Cruz.

The 1997 Report of the International Narcotics Control Board (INCB) published in February, declared that Equato Guinea is one of the nine African states dealing with narcotics. According to Santos Pascual Bikomo, fomer minister of information, drugs arrive in Europe by ships owned by the company Exfosa and by ships carrrying coffee and cocoa (companies Mallo and Arra). According to Bikomo, the dictator used his own private airplane to bring drugs into Europe. For small amounts, the diplomatic bag was used. He published a long list of Equato-Guinean ministers and diplomats in charge of distributing the drugs. Bikomo assumed that Teodorín Nguema Obiang is the main transporter of the drugs (he made a trip to Paris with 40 suitcases).

The European Commission (General Administration, VIII/A72) asked the Geopolitic Drugs Organization (Paris) for a report which was handed over in

September 1997. It recaps the situation concerning local drugs (iboga, cannabis) and international traffic (heroin and cocaine), money laundering, etc.

On October 29, 1997, in the Venezuelan harbor of Guaranao, in Punto Fijo, the national guard stopped a ship sailing under the Malabo Equatorial Guinea flag transporting 2.5 tons of cocaine. The ship's name is *Lady Belle*. It seems it was given away by an anonymous phone call. The ship was coming from the Panama Canal and heading to Miami. In Venezuela, it had to load 200 t of sesame. Ten sailors were arrested (Dominicans, Colombians, and Venezuelans). The cocaine had been loaded in Baranquilla (Colombia). According to Venevision, the drug comes from the Cartel of Cali. It is possible that this ship, as others sailing under the flag of Equatorial Guinea, belongs to international crooks (see Cyprus).

The drug, immediately delivered in Malabo and Bata, is then transported by ships carrying fruit or cocoa to Europe, or else by diplomatic bag and private luggage belonging to diplomats, even by Obiang Nguema and his family. All the ministers caught dealing with drugs have been recuperated by the public sector: Evuna Owono Asangono, former ambassador to Spain; Ela Nguema Buna, former first secretary at the embassy in Madrid; Edjang Mba Medja, former ambassador in Paris (who has become secretary to the minister of foreign affairs); Carmelo Nvono Nka, former ambassador to the U.N. (he has become general secretary of the Minister of Public Works); etc.

Obiang Nguema was present at the U.N. conference in New York dealing with the fight against drugs. On June 8, 1998, when addressing the assembly, he pretended that the weapons used during Moto's failed coup of May 1997, as well as the weapons used by the Bubi in January 1998, were purchased with money coming from the drug business.

In 1998, Equatorial Guinea did not sign the three international treaties dealing with drug control. In September, it was said that a crime had been committed on a probable Equato-Guinean cargo. The news came from Colombia. The victim was a drug dealer already condemned in Spain.

See also Argentina; Bikono Nanguande, S.P.; Democratic Progressive Alliance; Diplomacy; Ebang Mbele Abang, A.; Esono Ondo, B.; Eyama Angüe Osa, D.; France; Maho Sikacha, L.; Mba Ndong, A.; Mbengono Asu Alene, A.; Mikomeseng, Moto Nsá, S.; National Institute for Social Security; Nepotism; Nguema Esono, L.; Nguema Mbasogo Ondo, A.; Nigeria; Nsobeya Efuman Nsue, S.; Obiange Obiang Mangue, L.; Obiang Nguema, T.; Ondo Ayang, L.; Shinkame, J.; Torture; Victims

DUHALDE, Eduardo Luis. UNDP/Human Rights Commission consultant on human rights matters. Participated in watching over the application of the National Pact in 1993. In May 1995, he returned to Equatorial Guinea with A. Artucio.

DURAN-LORIGA RODRIGANEZ, Juan. First Spanish ambassador in Equatorial Guinea, starting October 11, 1968. He was expelled in spring 1969 after the flag incident in Bata (see Bata) and the proclamation of Emergencia (Emergency).

❖ E ❖

EBANG MASIE, Eduardo. Member of the Chamber of Deputies for Añisok. Arrested in May 1985 for insulting the head of state. He was sentenced to 8 years in jail by a military tribunal, but was pardoned six months later.

EBANG MBELE ABANG, Antonio. From Mikomeseng. Of the Nsomo clan (like Enrique Nvó and Bonifacio Ondo Edu). Born 1945. Polygamous (eight wives and more than 30 children). Took part, in 1979, in Obiang Nguema's coup d'etat. Decorated with a bronze medal. As deputy to the Asamblea del Pueblo, for Añisok, and member of the PDGE, he became vice-president of the Parliament.

He spoke in support of multipartyism in 1990; Obiang Nguema expelled him, by decree, from Parliament and from the single party. He was imprisoned and later put under house arrest at Mikomeseng. The International Commission of Jurists showed that Ebang Mbele was stripped of his mandate, in disregard of Art. 123 of the Constitution: "No Representative of the People may be taken into custody or prosecuted for any opinions that he may have expressed in the execution of his duties."

In 1991, Ebang Mbele was refused an exit visa, making him feel endangered. In September 1992, Ebang Mbele obtained provisional recognition for his Democratic Progress Alliance (ADP). In February-March 1993, he led the ADP delegation to the National Pact negotiations. As a member of the POC, his party joined the November election boycott. In Barcelona on February 4, 1995, Ebang Mbele linked the ADP with the Francisco Ela Abeme's National Peoples Congress (CNPGE); the latter became its general secretary, with Ebang Mbele as president. On May 30, he begged for clemency to Moto Nsá on radio and TV.

In early 1996, Ebang Mbele and his Nigerian girlfriend, both holders of diplomatic passports, were arrested in Argentina for cocaine trafficking. The POC demanded that Ebang Mbele be expelled from the ADP. Ebang Mbele and his mistress were still in prison at Buenos Aires in mid-1996.

Ebang Mbele was still in prison at Buenos-Aires at the end of 1998.

See also Argentina; Balinga, B. G.; Democratic Progressive Alliance; National Peoples Congress of Equatorial Guinea; National Pact; Victims.

EBANO. A newspaper. During the colonial period, Ebano belonged to pro-Franco people, who lent their support to Berlin. Under Obiang Nguema, this rather irregular weekly was called *Diario de la Mañana* (Morning Newspaper). From 1985 to 1990 *Ebano* was off the stands, though it was supposed to appear twice a month. Its comeback was made possible by the Spanish volunteers for cooperation who provided machines and materials. In 1997, its publication was interrupted.

See also Press.

EBEBIYIN. There still were political prisoners in 1980. When there was an administrative reorganization in March 1980, Ebebiyin became the county-town of Kie-Ntem county.

Mgr. Ildefonso Obama, was consecrated bishop of Ebebiyin in 1983, and named archbishop to replace Nze Abuy in July 1991. In early 1989, twenty persons were arrested for practicing sorcery. They were tortured; ten were murdered. In November 1991, Reverend Juan Matogo Oyana was consecrated bishop of Ebebiyin.

Three natives of Ebebiyin figured in the January 24, 1992, "transitional" government: Mba Ekua Miko, for Foreign Affairs and Francophony; Ngomo Mbengono, vice-minister for justice and religions; Endjoo Ovono, vice minister for education.

In 1993, J.-C. Okenve was the director of the high school of Ebebiyin. As a member of the Central Committee of the PDGE, presidential security man, parliamentary representative and Obiang Nguema's friend, he caused the departure of Catholic nuns from the high school and of the Peace Corps stationed in the area. On December 24, following elections and the POC boycott, the governor of Kie-Ntem, Santiago Bibang Ntutumu attacked the UP headquarters and imprisoned several militants, whom he tortured. Bibang Ntumu was an ex-truck driver, employed in the presidential gardens. His wife is a faith-healer and practices sorcery. She joined her husband in the torture. On November 10, 1995, Obiang Nguema named Bibang Ntutumu governor of the coastal province.

During the September 1995 municipal elections, a member of the opposition was killed when the army shot at a crowd under the orders of the government's representative, Sr Ediang; Pablo Ondo Eyang (PDGE) was elected mayor.

In 1997–1998, the governor of Kie-Nte (former district of Ebebiyin), Luciano edjang Mba, forbid the meetings of the CPDS. On July 25, 1998, Archbishop Ildefonso Obama denounced the fact that in Ebebiyin and Mikomeseng (province of Kié-Ntem) priests must ask for authorization to minister to their parish and celebrate mass. Some priests are under house arrest, and others are forced into exile. In October 1998, three mayors of the province of Kié-Ntem, among them the mayor of Ebebiyin, were dismissed. These mayors had asked the government to keep the promises it had made during the elections, among which were installing electricity and drinking water.

See also Bibang Ntumu, S.; China, People's Republic of; Edjo Ovono, F.; Education; Eka Nguema, P.; Elections; Eneme Oyono, J.; Engonga Edjo, B.; Esono Masie, P.; Esono Mbomio, J.; France; Kie-Ntem; Mangue Obama Nfube, R.; Martinez Nvo Bikie, J.; Matogo Oyana, J.; Mba Ekua Miko, B.; Mba Mombe, S.; Mba Nsue, J.; Missions; Mokong Onguene, C.; Motu Mamiaga, P.; Ngomo Mbengono, F.; Nvo Bela, E.; Nvono Akele, C.; Okue Moto, M.; Ondo Ayang, L.; Ondo Obiang, V.; Opposition; Ovono Nguema, E.; Oyono Nsue, L.; National Pact; Parliament; Plot (1981); Popular Union; Public Health; Río Muni; Samaranch, C.; Santa Isabel; Transports; United States of America; Victims

EBEMBA, Martín Crisanthos. National director of the BEAC in Equatorial Guinea in 1998.

EBENDENG NSOMO, Melanio. Fang from Niefang. Born January 1, 1942. An army colonel. He owed the failed Guinextebank CFA francs 5,922,000. As a member of Central Committee of the PDGE, he was minister for defence from October 1990. Angered at the rather cool reception he got in Nsoc-Nsomo (Río Muni), in February 1993, he had about fifty opposition members arrested, tortured, and fined. He did not however leave his post in the December 22, 1993, government.

Following Nve Mbengono's accusations of "judicial insecurity" in 1995, Obiang Nguema asked Ebendeng, along with others, to make an enquiry into the state of justice in the country. He also became a member of the board of directors of the Empresa Nacional de Pesca de Guinea Ecuatorial, wholly made up of notorious Nguemists.

In the January 8, 1996, government, he was named minister delegate of national defence, a post he retained in the April 8, 1996, government. He is hated by the army because of his violence. See also Army; Justice; Niefang; Obiang Nguema, T.; Oyono Awong Ada, S.; Plot (1981); Popular Union; Torture; Vilarrasa, S.

EBERMAIER, Karl. Sixth and last German governor of Cameroon, who fled to Río Muni in 1916 and was later transferred to Fernando Po. After the 1914–1918 war, he was sent to Cadiz with some of the German troops, and some Cameroonese, such as Chief Atangana.

EBIAKA MOHETE, Aniceto. Born on June 29, 1956. A Bubi from San Carlos (Luba). Engineer. He was elected PDGE deputy in the November 1993 elections. In the December 22, 1993, government, he became secretary of state for energy and promotion of small and medium-sized businesses, and was the only Bubi in this supposedly "democratic" government. He however did not figure in the 1996 government.

EBONA MAQUINA, Victoriano. Government's representative for the capital. In May 1994, he arranged the arrest of eight UP militants who had not paid their respects to him during the visit of the finca Rosita. See also Santa Isabel.

EBURI MATA, Ceferino. Bubi from San Carlos. In December 1982, he became the director general for public works, environment, and town planning. In the summer of 1985, he became minister for public works, water, and forests. In the January 24, 1992, "transitional" government, he only held the post of vice-minister. In December 1982, he was named director general of Public Works. He lost this function in December 22, 1993.

ECHEK, Salvador Ezekiel. Born in Batete. Farmer. On November 22, 1993, he was elected sole parliamentary representative of the Liberal Party.

ECONOMY AND FINANCES. The 1996–1998 document of strategy of the BAD considered in January 1998 that "the economy of Equatorial Guinea, since the beginning of the oil production in 1992, has shown fast growth, but the population has benefited very little from it. . . . The oil business is still mainly an enclave. Moreover, the county still lacks a reform program accepted by the international community." The 1996–1998 report of the ILO regarding labor in the world feels that Equatorial Guinea "does not meet the requirements as far as macroeconomic stability is concerned."

Main Economic and Financial Indicators, 1995–1998 (Estimated)
In billion of FCFA (unless otherwise specified), according to BEAC and CEMAC

	1995	1996	1997	1998
GNP				
-in current francs	76.5	104.3	202.9	203.6
-oil sector	21.0	36.2	105.4	113.8
-per capita (US$)	391.6	508.8	846.8	807.9
-growth rate in				
effective terms	19.3%	18.1%	53.0%	14.7%
-population (000)	391	401	410	420
Investment rate				
(% of GNP)	84.4	84.6	82.5	80.1
Saving rate (%)				
of GNP)	65.6	-17.6	48.3	21.9

Inflation rate on annual average

11.7%	6.7%	7.0%	6.0%

	1995	1996	1997	1998
Exports, fob	43.1	102.0	281.6	351.7
Exports, oil	18.6	66.3	230.3	304.2
Imports, fob	43.3	112.0	178.6	238.2
State budget				
-total revenues	13.4	30.9	52.3	68.6
-oil revenues	2.3	18.9	29.2	37.5
-total expenditure	20.1	32.8	55.7	44.7
-capital expend.	3.6	8.2	17.4	12.0
-balance in %				
of GNP	-8.8%	-1.8%	-1.7%	11.7%
Exterior debt				
-stock in % of				
GNP	158%	122%	67%	65%
-service	27.8%	7.1%	3.2%	3.8%

ECUAFORSA see Timber

ECUA MIKO MBA. Fang. In 1970 he entered the Ministry of Foreign Affairs in Santa Isabel. In 1972 he was appointed secretary of the Equato-Guinean Embassy in Ethiopia and from 1974 to 1976 he represented his country at the United Nations. On May 6, 1978, he presented his credentials to President Bongo as ambassador to Gabon. He has been replaced at the United Nations by the ambassador's deputy Bibong Aseco Eyang. Ecua Miko was abducted in July 1978 and probably killed.

ECUATO-GUINEANA DE AVIACION (EGA) see Aviation

EDJANG ANGUE, Miguel. Fang fom Niefang. Born 1954, in Nquimi. Related to Obiang Nguema. Holds an elementary Baccalaureat. Armengol Ondo Nguema's brother-in-law. Elected PDGE deputy in November 1993. On December 22, he became secretary of state for autonomous organizations and state involvement. In the January 8, 1996, government, he was promoted to the post of vice-minister for state-run enterprises. He was not part of the government of January, 1998, elections.

EDJANG MANGUE, Benjamin. Fang from Mongomo. Born September 7, 1946. Holds a degree in public administration. He was a secretary in the Home Ministry in 1982. Upon becoming general secretary of his ministry, he was authorized, in 1985, to buy the building housing the Spanish company Frapejo, declared "State property" by the Nguemists, for 5 million bikwele. A professor in the National School for Public Administration (ENAP), he became in the December 22, 1993, government secretary of state for civil services and administrative reform, a post which he still occupied in 1995. He did not hold any post in the January 8, 1996, government. In the ministerial reshuffle of April 8, 1996, he became inspector general of the civil services and administrative reform.

EDJANG MBA MADJA, Pedro. Fang from Mongomo. Studied in Havana and in Spain. He was 1st secretary in the Embassy to the U.S. between 1988 and 1990. He was named ambassador to France in the autumn of 1990, to replace Ela Abeme, who had been arrested for heroin trafficking. During his mandate, in Paris, drug-trafficking scandals were revealed, allegedly under his authorities, especially with a Thai connection. In the April 8, 1996, ministerial reshuffle, he was named general secretary of the Ministry of Foreign Affairs and Cooperation.

See also Drugs; France; Mongomo.

EDJO OVONO, Federico. Fang from Ebebiyin. Born January 26, 1951, in Atut-Efac. Holds a doctorate in physics (USSR). In the January 24, 1992, "transitional" government, he became vice-minister for education, a post he kept in the December 22, 1993, government.

In the January 8, 1996, government, he became vice-minister for planning and development. In the April 8, 1996, government he became counsellor to the president of the government in charge of cooperation affairs with UNESCO, in the Ministry of Education and Science. In June, he was promoted to dean of the National University.

EDU, Francisco. Esangui from Mongomo. Born 1960. Related to Obiang Nguema.

Toward the end of November 1992, he became the prosecutor for the War Council, which condemned the Spanish businessmen Hanna and Vilarrasa, unjustly accused of arms trafficking. He demanded 30 years' imprisonment and a fine of CFA Fr 500 million. The Tribunal decided on 12 years and $550,000. They were later pardoned by Obiang Nguema.

EDUCATION. Since 1839 a school with 120 children existed in Clarence City (Santa Isabel). Between 1840 and 1858 another school in Santa Isabel was run by Baptist missionaries. At their installation in 1858 the Jesuits also opened a school in Santa Isabel, then in Corisco, but the 1858 revolution in Spain put an end to their efforts. In 1870 Primitive Methodists opened a school, too. In 1876–1877 Iradier and his wife taught in a non-confessional school directed by a half-breed Cuban. The massive arrival of Claretians suppressed this school as well as the Methodist one. American Presbyterian Missionary schools existed in Corisco and Río Benito since the beginning of the 19th century. Early in the 20th century, the French Fathers of the Holy Spirit had opened a school with 180 girls and boys in Bata.

The Spanish budget law of 1902 provided for the extension of undenominational schools; this project lasted until 1909, then started again in 1922 in various placed in Río Muni. In 1914 the Escuela Externa (secondary school for day students only) was founded in Santa Isabel, with 600 students in 1920, of which 26 were Europeans. In 1927, a school was opened in Evinayong, in the heart of Río Muni, eventually occupied by the Colonial Guard. Vocational schools were opened, first in 1931 in Santa Isabel, then in 1945 in Bata. In 1935 the Instituto Colonial Indígena was set up to train auxiliary schoolteachers within six months, as well as administrative auxiliaries. The lower secondary courses started in 1942 with the Instituto Cardenal Cisneros (presently Rey Malabo). An English-speaking Methodist school was opened in 1945 but closed in 1973. In August 1943 the Guinean school system was organized for the first time with an education status providing the following stages: elementary and/or preparatory education; primary education; lower secondary; higher vocational education (schoolteachers and administrative auxiliaries); technical and agricultural education; and complementary schooling for natives (men and women).

Toward 1947 Inspector Alvarez García, director of the Instituto Colonial Indígena (changed to Escuela Superior Provincial), proposed to adjust the African teachers' salaries to that of other officials, which led him, as well as Governor General Bonelli Rubio who approved him, to be discharged by Díaz de Villegas.

Free elementary education was intended to generalize the use of the Spanish language and to offer moral, religious and patriotic education. With 90% of its children going to school, Spanish Guinea reached almost the Gabonese level. This percentage is however misleading: most of the children never went beyond elementary school, and three-fifths of the 480 auxiliary schoolteachers were under-qualified. Primary education dealt in particular with the study of Spanish, mathematics, health, civics, religion and manual works. Each child living fewer than five kms from a school had to go to school. In the 25 existing primary schools, there were 2,500 pupils of which only 22% could pass admission to the higher level. The Escuela Superior Provincial offered, at that time, five years of training for elementary teachers and administrators, and a three-year business course, with a level corresponding to European secondary education. In 1963 a Primary Teachers' Training College opened in Bata, training students coming from the Escuela Superior Provincial. The technical schools in Santa Isabel and Bata trained about 300 students at independence. Secondary classical education is given in the Institutos of Santa Isabel and Bata, connected up to now to the Instituto Ramiro de Maeztu of Madrid, which each year sends a jury to examine the level of Equato-Guinean candidates (Revalida). In 1968, 185 primary and elementary schools existed, with 48,000 pupils. The Ministry of Education—in 1973 made the Ministry of Popular Education, Traditional Arts and Culture—has a delegation in Bata to administer the schools of Río Muni. In 1972, 360 primary schools with 578 teachers for 35,902 pupils (45% girls) existed, the teacher-pupil ratio thus being 1 to 62. With Spanish assistance, new secondary school buildings were built in Ebebiyín, Mongomo, Niefang, Añisok, Mikomeseng, but only those of Ebebiyín and Mongomo are being used.

In 1971, UNESCO opened the Centro de Desarrollo de la Educación (CDE) to train high school teachers. But Macias Nguema's hostility to anything "intellectual" ruined the more than 1 Mio$ project after a few years. See Centro de Desrrollo de la Educación.

Early in 1972 a portrait of Macías Nguema was slashed at the entrance of the Instituto Carlos Lwanga in Bata, and anti-Macías leaflets circulated. Some teachers, students and parents were arrested, some liquidated and Minister of Education Eñeso Neñe was killed publicly in May. Since April 1972 military instruction has been compulsory in the schools, followed in April 1975 by political instruction. The dictatorship forbade all private schooling. This resulted in a complete disorganization of the educational system and the dismissal of 600 teachers.

Since 1970 UNESCO and UNDP granted assistance to Equatorial Guinea (professors for secondary level, experts for the Centro de Desarrollo de la Educación). From 1973 to 1976 Cuba sent 30 teachers, as well as Spain (30) and France (2).

Before independence, Guinea had four Catholic seminaries: two "seminarios mayores" (priest training colleges) (Banapa, Nkuefulan), and two "seminarios menores" (priest-staffed secondary schools) (Concepción, Mikomeseng), with some 60 students overall. At the time of autonomy, 100 Guineans held scholarships in higher and technical education in the metropolis.

Among the victims of Macías Nguema's personal power are several officials of education: three ministers, one director general of education, one secretary general, and so on—about 75 persons in all from 1969 to 1976. The use of the word "intellectual" was forbidden, and in 1973 Minister Grange Molay was fined for having used it in a Cabinet session. Since the assassination of Education minister Ochaga Ngomo in December 1976, Obiang Gonsogo, public health minister, had been in charge of the Popular Education Ministry, under Macías Nguema's supervision as "Great Master of Education and Culture."

After the palace revolution of 1979, the education system was slowly put back into operation. Spain has provided a number of teachers and educational material and equipment to Equatorial Guinea, the World Bank has granted finance for educational management, and the UN World Food Program has provided for school canteens. There is, however, still a severe shortage of qualified staff.

Under Obiang Nguema's regime, as in the past, teachers still get arrested on political grounds, while well-known Nguemist supporters get rapid promotion, such as Nvono Akele Avomo, who betrayed the prisoners' uprising in Bata in 1974 and was made the Ministry of Education's representative in 1981 for the whole of the Río Muni province.

Two French cultural centers have been opened, one in Santa Isabel and the other in Bata. In October 1982, Spain announced the opening of a branch of the National University for Correspondence Education (Universidad Nacional de Educación a Distancia, UNED) in the capital. Since 1982, the Spanish Federation of Religious Teachers (FERE) continued the publication of school text books and the supply of personal suited to the needs of the country.

In October 1983 a school for professional training was inaugurated in Santa Isabel with an area of 4,100 m^2. Between 1981 and 1986, several programs designed by young Spanish nationals in Equatorial Guinea were carried out: literacy, reading improvement, hygiene and health, construction of schools, and women's protection.

In 1986, Fortunato Nzambi Machinde became minister for education andsSports. School teachers' salaries went up, depending on the level of specialization, from FCFA 10,000 to FCFA 34,000. Between 1983 and 1989, Spain provided school textbooks, with IBRD credits. In 1987, UN sources estimated the illiteracy rate to be around 35%.

In 1989, 98 Spanish volunteers for cooperation were mobilized for 40 localities. In the capital, the French Institute had 380 students and was managing a small school with 24 students. The USSR offered 13 scholarships. In September, the director of middle and higher education Daniel Mba Ndemensogo stated that Equatorial Guinea was moving towards a bilingual policy, with French being compulsory. In addition to an educational advisor, France offered 5,000 textbooks. A School for Public Administration was opened in November, with UN experts; however, it was not supported by a program. The government made it known that all schools would start teaching democratic principles (but classes mostly deal with lauding Obiang Nguema's regime).

In the October 16, 1990, ministerial reshuffle, Isidoro Eyi Mensuy Andeme was promoted to the post of vice-prime minister in charge of education, youth affairs and sports. In 1990, spending on education represented 1.7% of the GNP (the only countries to be placed lower: Guatemala, Laos, Sierra Leone, Zaïre).

In 1991, religious training was declared optional; some schools replaced it with civic instruction (?). In September, the Bata school complex was full of anti-Nguemist posters. The number of primary school teachers in the country was estimated to be 1,126: 160 teachers with tenure (from the Teachers' training school); 556 degree holders (3 years of studies); 410 non-holders of degrees, for a cohort of 67,000 pupils aged between 7 and 14 years. Though schooling is compulsory, only 55% of the country's children attend. The drop-out rate is very high. Preschool children (3–6 years) are numbered at 42,000. At the secondary level, there are about 30 students to a teacher. Nigeria offered Naira 5 million for the construction of an international school in the capital.

Between 1988 and 1992, the state budget for education went up from 4.8% to 9%. But the problems remained. The country possesess five "higher" institutes:

• National Institute for Health (Bata)
• National Institute for Public Administration (ENAP)
• National Institute for Agriculture (ENAM), Santa Isabel

- The Santa Isabel and Bata Institutes for Teachers' Training
- National Centre for proficiency in teaching (CENAFOD), financed by UNESCO

In the January 24, 1992, "transitional" government, A. P. Oko Ebobo became the minister for education. The literacy rate was then 52% (men 66%, women 38%). Obiang Nguema and his brother Armengol joined the Spanish in founding the company EFUSILA SA, to receive by tender the contract for the construction of the new Secondary School of Santa Isabel (500 million pesetas). In May, the prime minister, Silvestre Siale, instructed the students of the Rey Malabo secondary school not to get involved in politics. He was booed, and forced to leave the school premises; Siale threatened to deliver their dead bodies to their parents. At Obiang Nguema's request, the FERE gave up its proficiency course for Equato-Guinean teachers in the summer of 1992, in order to "ensure the physical safety of the volunteers for cooperation." The university graduate Terencio Luis Ngundi, a Foreign Affairs official and professor at Rey Malabo, was beaten at the Directorate of the Criminal Investigation Department, for some misplaced comments. In November, the Spanish Reverend Teodoro Saez Lasheras, course director at La Salle (Bata) resigned in protest against the intention of the Criminal Investigation Department to infiltrate its agents into the school. A student demonstration ended with the arrest of forty. About twenty Spanish professors were threatened, accused of supporting the students who demanded that the suspension of the contracts of Equato-Guinean professors opposed to Obiang Nguema be lifted. The School La Salle and the Bata Teachers' Training school were closed. In December, several teachers of the Rey Malabo secondary school of the capital were beaten and tortured; about a hundred students, including Professor Celestino Bakale, demanded the release of their teachers after a peaceful demonstration. Bakale and Arsenio Moro were tortured, wounded, and finally freed in late 1992.

On January 11, 1993, the arrested teachers addressed protest letters to the prime minister, the minister for education, the National Commission for Human Rights and the embassies. C. Bakale, allowed to go to Cameroon for medical treatment, appeared before the Human Rights Commission in Geneva in March to denounce the current situation. The adult literacy rate was then estimated at 50%; secondary education was estimated at about 14%. In February, the Spanish government announced the suspension of three aid programs, involving 98 volunteers and 51 employees (125 million pesetas). The measure involved secondary schools and the School of Agriculture, and also implied the closure of experimental farms. Towards the end of July 1993, Equato-Guinean students in Russia (engineers, doctors) were receiving paltry scholarships and even went hungry. UNESCO offered a supplement, but the embassy refused to sign the agreement. The students occupied the embassy. Back in the country, school report cards were printed at the presses of the PDGE. In the December 22, 1993, government, Ricardo Mangue Mbama Nfube became the minister for education and science.

An inventory of the problems facing education, made in 1995 by ASODEGUE, included: the authoritarian and centralist critera, the enormous power vested in the administrative bureaucracy with no real long-term criteria, a lack of training and qualifications among the directors of educational policy, the lack of resources, the lack or, when available, the pitiable state of school buildings, lack of textbooks and teaching methods. During the September municipal elections, 23 teachers from Niefang accused of belonging to the opposition were roughed up and then removed from the educational system.

In the January 8, 1996, ministerial reshuffle, Ricardo Mangue Obama retained the post of minister for education and science, with Lucas Nguema Esono as vice-minister for education, youth affairs, and sports. In the April 8 ministerial reshuffle Mangue Obama retained his post; the post of vice-minister of education was suspended; Nguema Esono remained vice-minister for youth and sports. Lieutenant Eyi Mensui Andeme, cousin of Obiang Nguema's (nicknamed "Mobutu") became general secretary in the Ministry of Education and Science. Education Minister Mangue Mba Nfube accused him of spying and convinced Obiang Nguema, in August 1996, to have him transferred to the Ministry of Transport and Communications. The new general secretary is the unfortunately famous Secundino Nvono Akele Ovomo, who denounced the anti-Macías Nguema patriots shot at Bata in June 1974. During summer 1996 it was announced that an American university will be assisting the country to improve its educational system. The American petroleum company CMS Nomeco supplied instruction manuals. School attendance is very low; only 55% of school-aged children attend primary school. Out of 100 children starting primary school, only 10 finish 5th grade. Due to the poor conditions offered by public schools, the number of private schools is growing steadily. According to UNICEF, the average number of children in first grade is 112 (versus 72 in Burkina Faso, 65 in Ethiopia), 48% of the class rooms have no chalk or blackboards (54% in Tanazania, 51% in Madagascar), 99% of the students have no books.

The professional school in Bata, run by the Salesians, has 120 boys age 16, and more who are part of a training program for carpenters, joiners, tailors, managers, secretaries, and computing. but the equipment is often old and out of order. In the surrounding area of Bata, the Salesians run a School of Agriculture that has 50 students, 15 of whom are women; the school owns 19 cows, 100 sheep, and 60 pigs, but many sheep are bit by snakes. Approximately 250 students have been trained. The school is run by Father Anselmo.

During the inauguration of the Zafiro oilfield in October 1996, P. J. Hoenmans, vice-president of Mobil Corp., announced that his company will donate $150,000 to the University of New Mexico for the training of Equato-Guinean managers.

In March 1997, after the death of Pedro Nve Ada (called Little Peter), who was a history professor and former head of the Instituto Rey Malabo, the students went on strike.

In the government of January 21, 1998, Santiago Ngua Nfumu was minister of education, sciences, and francophony; Edjoo Ovono and Teresa Avoro Nguema were vice-ministers. Mrs. Teresa Avoro Nguema visited Cuba in September and signed an agreement of bilateral cooperation, obtaining eight high school science teachers.

Research done by UNESCO/UNICEF in 1995 shows that 77% of elementary teachers have insufficient secondary school training. With regard to health, the report shows that Equatorial Guinea is among the poorest countries, with 80 students per toilet (the Cape Verde Islands 90, Ethiopia 23).

See also Asumu Bikui F.; Gene, M.; Internet; Mobil Corp.; Petroleum; University.

EDU ENGONGA, Melchior. Fang from Mongomo. Student, medical assistant, acting as consul in Madrid since 1975. He was present at the time of the occupation of the Equatorial Guinean Embassy by fellow students, members of liberation movements, on March 5, 1976. For some time he replaced Ndongo Nangala, the ambassador's deputy assassinated in Santa Isabel in July 1976.

EDU MBUY, Jovino. Fang. Sergeant in the Territorial Guard and the third vice-president of IPGE. He participated in the Constitutional Conference. Macías Nguema's Secretariado Conjunto accused him of being in Spain's pay. He participated in the elections on the MONALIGE list, with Ndongo Miyone for president. After Ndongo Miyone's so-called attempted coup d'etat in March 1969 he fled to Cameroon. He is supposed to have been kidnapped by Abaga Oburu, taken back to Guinea, and liquidated.

EDU NSUE, Narciso. Obuk of Akonibe. In his forties. Active members of the President's security, reports directly to Manuel Nguema Mba (uncle of Obiang Nguema, known for his violence). Edu Nsue is known to torture people. On November 15, 1996, he had Celestino Bakale (CPDS) arrested, accusing him of scandalmongering the dictator. See also Convergency for Social Democracy.

EDU OBA, Bernardino. From Mongomo. Became mayor of Santa Isabel in 1994. In September 1995, he was replaced by the first elected mayor of the capital since 1969, the Bubi V. Bolekia.

EFE. Spanish press agency which in April 1981 opened an office in Santa Isabel, under Jesús Fonseca Escartín. Towards the end of 1994, following threats from the Nguemists, the Equato-Guineen representative of the EFE, Donato Ndongo Bidyogo, sought refuge in Libreville.

EFG see Timber

EFUA EFUA ASANGONO, Teresa. From Mongomo. Born 1957. Studied administration at the Escuela Superior. In the April 8, 1996, ministerial reshuffle, she became director general of international organizations.

In the January 1998 government, she became minister delegate of foreign affairs and cooperation.

EGIDO PANADES, Teodor see Convergency for Social Democracy

EKA NGUEMA, Patricio. From Ebebiyin. Degree holder in economics (Hungary). After Obiang Nguema's coup d'etat, he became Governor of the Banco Central. He was accused of corruption and made to resign in September 1981. He is considered by the diaspora as a scape goat. He was the director of the Caja de Amortización de la Deuda Pública in 1990.

EKO, Indalecio see Convergency for Social Democracy; Niefang

EKOLS SAS see Timber

EKONG ANDEME, Pedro. Born 1941 in Alum, Bata Province. Fang. Refugee in Cameroon before independence and member of the IPGE. He was in favor of Guinea's annexation by Cameroon. Upon his return to Equatorial Guinea he became representative to the Cortes in Madrid from 1964 to 1968. Within the Grupo Macías, he was the only member of IPGE to be named minister in the first government. In October 1968 he became public health minister and in March 1969 minister of industry and mines and as such participated in the creation of the Milicia Popular. In 1971 he had business relations with García Trevijano but never paid for the cement delivered by Trevijano via Simone Chouraki ($60,000). Arrested in April 1973 together with his colleague Momo Bokara, he was accused of conspiracy. He escaped in 1975 to Cameroon (Yaoundé). He is the assumed author of a plan for the annexation of Equatorial Guinea by its three neighbors. In 1979 he returned home, together with several members of Obiang Nguema's family and started up an export-import business. In April 1981 he was arrested but was released in June.

Member of the Executive Committee of the Popular Union in 1993. On January 19, 1994, he was nominated counsellor to the president for culture, tourism, and the French language. A member of the Young Torches (Jovenes Antorchas).

EKONG AWONG (or Ayong), Marcelo. From Mongomo. Corporal. In October 1979, he became deputy military commissioner for finance and commerce, in charge of national banks. Nominated president of the Credit and Development Bank (Banco de Crédito y Desarrollo), he worked as secretary at the military hearing of the April "conspiracy" in June 1981. Became a Supreme Court judge in 1990.

EKONG NSUE, Constantino. Fang fom Bata. Born January 8, 1951. Nephew of Ekong Andeme. Agricultural technician; some sources claim he underwent an apprenticeship as an electrician, which he left incomplete. Exiled in Cameroon, and later in Spain. In a state of destitution, he decided to return to the country in 1992 and to become a member of the PDGE. He is the brother-in-law of Alejandro Envoro, the minister for public works until January 8, 1996. In December 1993 he became minister for labor and social security. In the January 8, 1996, ministerial reshuffle, he became minister for industry and energy. In the April 8, 1996, government, he became the minister for industry and the promotion of small and medium-sized businesses.

In the 1998 government he became minister of agriculture, fisheries, and animal husbandry.

EKUA AVOMO, Lino Sima. On November 2, 1995, he presented his credentials to the French president as Ambassador Extraordinary and Plenipotential.

EKUAGA ESONO, Bienvenido. In the April 8, 1996, ministerial reshuffle, he became a chief official to the President of the government.

EKUA ONDO, Miguel. From Mongomo. Born in Akoa-Kam in 1958. One of Obiang Nguema's brothers. In January 1994, he became general secretary of the Ministry for Industry, Energy, and Promotion of Small- and Medium-Sized Firms. In the April 8, 1996, ministerial reshuffle, he retained his post.

EKUELE. Singular of *bikuele,* traditional Fang currency, shaped like a spearhead. See also Currency.

EKUKU. Coastal village to the south of Bata, the people being principally Kombe, close to the presidential palace. Joaquin Ipúa Ubenga, a native of Ekuku, became a doyen of local administrative agents in 1950. A military academy was founded in Ekuku to allow for more promotions. A number of natives of Ekuku became victims of Nguemist terror tactics. Rio Ekuku is one of the ten protected places under international control.

See also Baca Mba, S.; Bata; "Democratic" Party of Equatorial Guinea; Esono Micka, L.; Justice; Kogo; Motu Mamiaga, P.; Ndong Ona, A.; Victims

ELA ABEME, Francisco Javier. From Añisok district. Born 1945. Former Catholic seminarist. In 1992 he became the general secretary of the National Peoples Congress (CNPGE). In June 1993, he expressed his wish that the country be declared a free-zone, along the lines of Hong Kong. He was of the opinion that Obiang Nguema should be left alone, that there was no use blaming him for anything.

In his book *Guinea. Los últimos años* (Equatorial Guinea. The Recent Years). Ela Abeme seems to lend his support to Obiang Nguema's regime. In February 1995, the CNPGE merged with the Democratic and Progressive Alliance (ADP), of which he became the general secretary.

Lawyer in Tenerife (Canary Islands, Spain).

ELA ABEME, Jesus. Born 1952. From Mongomo. An aeronautical technician, who began his diplomatic career in 1980, in the Escuela de Diplomacia, in Madrid. After being chief of protocol, he went on to become ambassador to France in August 1983, which he remained until 1986.

In 1990 he was arrested, in the capital, for heroin trafficking, according to some. He was imprisoned at Playa Negra, with his wife, Gaudencia, tortured, and later released, with no explanations. Being a committee member of the Popular Union, he was arrested in October 1992, under the Vilarrasa/Hanna case. He was released in November. In the spring of 1994, he became a member of the POC and the Managing Committee of the UP (after the suspension of the general secretary Justino Mba Nsue). His passport was revoked on February 28, 1996, when he was about to travel to Libreville. He is an active member of the democratic opposition (CPDS).

ELA EBANG, José. Ambassador to Gabon in 1998.

ELA NGUEMA, Lino. Born 1954. Esangui from Mongomo. Studied at the Escuela de Diplomáca, in Madrid. In the April 8, 1996, ministerial reshuffle, he became a secretary general of physical education and sports.

ELA NGUEMA BUNA, Pedro. Born 1960. Esangui from Nzang-Ayong (Mongomo). Son of Pedro Ela Nguema, chief of Macías Nguema's civil household. Consul and first secretary at the Madrid Embassy until 1993. In 1995, he entered the administrative council of the Empresa nacional de pesca de Guinea Ecuatorial (National Fishing Co), wholly composed of notorious Nguemists. In the ministerial reshuffle of April 8, 1996, he became director general of cultural and consular affairs.

ELA NSENG, Salvador. Fang from Añisok. Nephew of Macías Nguema. Brother-in-law of Mba Ndong. Was military commander of Río Muni province and director of the infamous Bata prison, the counterpart of the Playa Negra prison in Santa Isabel run by Obiang Nguema. After the 1979 coup, he was appointed second vice-president of the republic. His cousin Maye Ela was first vice-president. Early in 1980 he was replaced in the vice-presidential position by Oyo Riqueza, dispatched by Obiang Nguema as ambassador to Beijing. He was elevated to the rank of Cdt. in 1981. In the latter part of 1979 he undertook a mission to France, which marked the first step in Equatorial Guinea's gravitation into the French currency orbit.

Since 1993 he has been ambassador in Ethiopia and to the OAU.

ELA NSENG, Victoriano. Chief Superintendant of the capital. In 1996–97, the rapporteur of the Commission on Human Rights of the UN observed that he uses torture frequently.

ELA NSUE MEBUY, Rosendo. Born 1932. From Añisok (Wele-Nzas). Teacher trained at the Escuela Superior Indígena. Secretary general of the Instituto Carlos Lwanga (secondary school) in Bata under the Annobónese Castillo Barril (murdered in prison, at Bata, in 1973). After the August 1979 coup d'etat, he taught at the Teachers' Training School at Bata. Member of the Central Committee of the PDGE. In 1991, he became the governor of Wele-Nzas and was noted for his violence. In the ministerial reshuffle of April 8, 1996, he became director general of animal husbandry. See also Mongomo.

ELA OWONO, Federico. From Niefang. Born 1936. Lawyer (studied in Spain). In 1993, he became a judge in the Court of Appeals of Fernando Po. In February, he released members of the opposition accused of resistance against the regime. His post was confirmed in January 1994. Member of the National Election Commission from 1995. See also Elections.

ELA OYANA, José. Fang fom Mongomo. Born 1963. Economist trained in Cuba. In the April 8, 1996, ministerial reshuffle, he became director general of statistics.

ELECTIONS. The House of People's Representatives had 120 members during the early days of Obiang Nguema's dictatorship (75 economic entities, 45 municipalities). Candidates were nominated by the Municipal Councils (consejos de poblados). The president of the republic would appoint the deputies until the economics entities were established.

The House was dissolved towards the end of June 1988. The April electoral law stipulated that only members of the government party (PDGE) were eligible to stand for the July elections. The presidential elections were announced in 1989, as a measure to allow "the finishing touches to reconciliation."

The January 1993 electoral law allows only persons who have resided in the country during the last five years to participate in the elections, which excludes the diaspora. In the National Pact negotiations (February–March), it was decided that the elections, formerly fixed for June, would be postponed to the end of the year. In March, negotiations (February–March), it was decided that the elections, formerly fixed for June, be postponed to the end of the year. In March, the government authorized the entry of foreign experts for the revision of the electoral census. These UN experts declared the Nguemist census inacceptable (as it had been carried out in parallel with the census for PDGE members, implying political pressure). The campaign for the National Pact (15 days) was judged insufficient, as a minimum of 60 days would be necessary. Moreover, out of the law's 217 articles, 40 were considered antidemocratic. The observers stressed the opposition's distrustfulness of the regime. As for the elected representatives' oath of faithfulness and loyalty to the president of the republic, it was declared incompatible with the principles governing all republican states.

The sponsors of the elections (United States, Spain, France, Morocco, EC, and the UNDP) held a meeting with the government, in May 1993 and demanded political guarantees (credible electoral census, and revision of the Electoral Law). The Nguemists demanded $10 million. The UN mission expected the country to effectively collaborate with the Human Rights Commission; and demanded a cessation of arbitrary arrests, a guarantee for the return of the exiled, a revision of legal texts, with opposition participation (amnesty, elections, religious freedom, press, meetings). The Nguemists broke off the discussions. In May, Annobón's Council of Elders repeated its refusal to participate in the elections. Donor countries and organizations refused to finance the elections. France was the only one to donate FCFA 25 million ignoring the need for solidarity with the others. The preparation of the elections was done with the help of the French Mission for Cooperation.

In early July 1993, Obiang Nguema unilaterally fixed the election date as September 12. The dictator rejected American and Spanish observers, and chose about twenty countries, including three with no democratic experience: North Korea, Iraq, and Libya. On August 25, the boycott called for by the POC forced him to postpone the elections to November 21, again a date chosen unilaterally, in total disregard for the terms of the National Pact. The government granted a sum of $16,000 to all parties willing to go to the polls. In mid-October, the seven parties forming the POC addressed an Institutional Proposal to Obiang Nguema who ignored it. The government was of the opinion that if seven other parties went to the polls, it was proof enough that the elections were "free, unopposed and democratic." Burkina Faso, Gabon, Togo, and the OAU alone were willing to send observers. In October, following the example of Annobón's Council of Elders, the Elders of Fernando Po, and a majority of village chiefs of the di trict of Mongomo signed declarations in support of the POC, denouncing Obiang Nguema, his relatives, and accomplices' criminal acts and vandalism, and exposing a bloody dictatorial regime.

Toward the end of October 1993, the leaders of the POC were prevented from travelling within the country. Minister for the Interior Julio Ndong Ela presided over the National Electoral Commission. One week before the elections, the governmental representative for the district of Evinayong, Luis Oyono, assaulted the house of the director of the secondary school, Alberto Nze Mba, member of the opposition. The Madrid Franco-Spanish summit, in November, denounced "the nonpluralistic conditions in which the elections were organised." The six tame parties participating in the elections, and the PDGE, claimed a funding of 75 million pesetas (1% of the national budget) from the French embassy, and threatened that without this aid, they would not participate. On November 21, the following parties participated in the elections with funding from the dictatorship:

- Liberal Democratic Convergency (CLD)
- Democratic Party of Equatorial Guinea (Nguemist, PDGE)
- Democratic and Social Union (UDS)
- Liberal Party (PL)
- National Democratic Union (UDENA)
- Social Democratic Party (PSD)
- Social Democratic and Popular Convergency (CSDP)
- Socialist Party (PSGE)

These opposition parties are said to be tame.

The parties united in the Joint Opposition Platform (POC) applied the boycott:

- Convergency for Social Democracy (CPDS)
- Democratic Progressive Alliance (ADP)
- Popular Action (AP)
- Popular Union (UP)
- Progress Party (PP)
- Social Democratic Coalition Party (PCSD).

Voter turnout was found to be 30% in Río Muni, 20% in Fernando Po (some villages recorded a 100% boycott). These elections had been held on the basis of an electoral census which accounted for not more than 119,000 voters, though in 1989 there had been 170,000 (all potential absentee voters had been eliminated). The extemely high rate of nonparticipation was received by the POC as a victory. As for the results, the PDGE claimed a massive victory: out of 80 seats, it claimed to have won 68, Liberal Party 1, the CSDP 6, and the UDS 5. The American State Department denounced the elections as a "parody of democracy"; the consultant for the United Nations Human Rights Commission referred to "election ma-noeuvring." The POC requested the U.S. to suspend petroleum extraction to cut the monthly income of $250,000 received by Obiang Nguema. In late November the regime's detractors began to be persecuted. On December 22, a new govern-ment with 38 members came into power, without opposition participation. A few Nguemists went out, but were replaced by others (see Obama Nsue Mangue, F.). The persecution of the opposition has continued since December. Road-checks involved compulsory possession of a stamped electoral card, on pain of imprison-ment. Abstentionist government officials were deprived of their December salary.

During the three months following the November 1993 elections, there was information of more than a hundred arbitrary arrests and torture of opponents, apart from innumerable cases of intimidation. The parties which did not participate in the legislative elections and which did not intend to participate in the municipal elections were declared illegal. However, popular resentment forced Obiang Nguema to suspend the October 1994 elections sine die.

In January 1995, the European Union released an aid-budget for electoral registration. France offered FCFA 45 million in February. But after the Moto Nsá problem, it withdrew its support. The POC, following a meeting with donor countries and the UNDP, decided, in March, to participate in the municipal elections. The parliament of Catalonia (Spain) insisted on free elections. In April, even as the hearing of Moto Nsá and 12 military men accused of conspiracy was on, the Nguemists decided on a modification of the Electoral Law: only married and secular Equato-Guinean nationals aged between 40 and 70 years could stand for elections, thus excluding a number of opposition members); a number of categories disallowed were enumerated: those who had been sentenced in court, those who had undergone more than three months' imprisonment, those who had engaged in rebellious activities, those wanted by the police, judges, magistrates. The new electoral rolls listed 250,000 electors, which was twice the number announced for the November 21, 1993 legislative elections. Only 153,000 citizens registered. The UNDP sent in a Nicaraguan expert as early as February to organize the polls. During the preparation of the electoral census, executives of the Progress Party and the CPDS, who joined in the work, were arrested. Toward the end of May, though the electoral census, largely funded by donor countries and the UN had been completed, the date for the municipals was still to be fixed. The opposition alleged that the census had been rigged. During the month of May, Jeronimo Osa Osa Ecoro, director of statistics, threatened his colleagues with sanctions if they exposed any instances of census manipulation. The electoral commission is presided by Minister of the Interior J. Ndong Ela Mangue.

Toward the end of July 1995, Obiang Nguema set the municipal elections for September 17. The August 2 amnesty for political prisoners was meant to allow them to participate. Spain announced its intention to finance all parties. For the municipal elections, the regime manipulated the electoral constituencies, and divided several communes, including Niefang. The POC protested, and also decried the elimination by the Nguemists of the names of those who may vote for the opposition from the electoral lists. In the capital, members of the Jovenes Antorchas terrorized and held members of the opposiiton. Out of 30 observers proposed, only 15 were accepted by the regime. The European Parliament demanded in vain that Obiang Nguema recognize the victory of the POC in the election. At Bata, Akurenam, and Annobón, where the opposition was especially strong, the regime claimed victory. In Río Muni, the PDGE claimed and took 114 seats, the POC 56 (at Bata: PDGE, 7, POC, 5). At Fernando Po, the PDGE obtained 130 seats, and the POC 79. At the national level, UP got 14 seats, and CSDP 3. During these elections, in the Ebebiyin region, one oppos'tion member was seriously injured in a shootout ordered by the government's representative, Sr. Ediang; three others (Miboma hamlet) were killed, under the orders of Elias Osono Nguema, secretary of state for the forest economy. The two Spanish observers, E. Burgos and L. Marcos, in their report, described how their movements had been curbed by the regime and mentioned partiality of those responsible for polling stations and enumerated a number of irregularities. They declared the POC the winner in the elections. The Home Ministry established a report stressing their claims of POC violence. Reuter reported that a number of soldiers had voted twice. A European Parliament (Strasbourg) resolution "condemned the irregularities committed by the government." It appealed against these to the Conseil requesting it to "immediately contact President Obiang and demand that he honor the election results as well as its own commitments to the international community." The UNDP Report on the organization of the municipal elections showed a strong popular participation and the degree of freedom to campaign that the parties enjoyed. But it pronounced a long list of criticisms:

- Irregularities were observed in the majority of polling offices, mainly in the area of secrecy of ballots;

- In several polling booths, only PDGE ballot papers were allowed to be used, with the obligation of exhibiting them;

- A number of voters complained that they did not figure in the electoral lists;

- The members of the polling stations all belonged to the executive, which hardly contributes to impartiality;

- The members of the polling stations were seriously lacking in competence;

- The observers related numerous difficulties encountered in the execution of their functions;

- The report especially stressed the serious fact that the observers did not enjoy freedom of movement and found themselves posted to certain polling stations.

The observers were only able to check on 164 of the 796 polling stations, i.e., 21%. The composition of the team of observers was as follows: Canada 1, Egypt 1, Spain 2, France 2, Gabon 2, Japan 1, Morocco 2, Nigeria 2, UNDP 4. The report made eight recommendations for the improvement of future elections. It was to be noted that during campaign, the opposition parties only had limited access to the radio and the television; 50% of transmission time went to Obiang Nguema. The localities that had offered opposition candidates majority support in the election were punished. Thus, Teguete (Province of Centro-Sur), 43 kilometers from Evinayong, despite 128 members registered in the PDGE only gave 100 votes to the PDGE and 228 to the POC. In reprisal, the installation of the gas facility that had been planned was annulled, as well as the construction of the road between Teguete and Kogo.

The Italian president of the European Union declared on March 7, EU regrets the way the presidential elections were conducted and spoke of a lost chance for democracy.

In its Report on Human Rights Practices for 1995, published April 1996, the American State Department summarized the electoral farce thus: "The government used arbitrary arrest, illegal detention, and beatings in an unsuccessful effort to control a sudden upsurge in opposition political activity. Despite these impediments the opposition parties were able to campaign effectively." In spite of the opposition victory recorded by the observers, "the Government announced the vote totals 11 days later, claiming that it had won control of 18 of 27 municipal councils with a 52 percent overall majority of the vote." Toward the end of 1995, during the Franco-Spanish summit, Paris and Madrid expressed their "disappointment of the Equato-Guinean government's organisation of vote-counting and the announcement of the results." On November 10, Obiang Nguema replaced a number of mayors and other elected representatives and new government representatives (most of whom were ex-militiamen under Macías Nguema), mainly at San Carlos (Luba) and at Niefang.

In his January 8, 1996, report, the special reporter to the UN Commission for Human Rights spoke of the population's lack of faith in the cleanliness of the elections. He also warned that "the reduction in the number of arrests and arbitrary detentions of leaders and workers of political parties which had been observed in May 1995, is no longer observable since the municipal elections of September 17, 1995." In mid-January 1996, the dictator caught the opposition unaware when he announced that he was going to advance the presidential elections from June to February 25. This maneuvering was coupled with a series of decrees aimed at preventing opposition members from participating in the elections (directed against Moto Nsá); minimum age was raised to 40 (a move directed against Placido Mikó), etc. The POC denounced the unconstitutional nature of the election and the continuation of human rights violations. On January 16, the six parties forming the POC coalition announced their participation in the election, with a single candidate. Unanimously, the opposition criticized the so-called electoral census which eliminated sympathizers of the opposition; the list included 30,000 new voters who did not figure on those of September 1995. The National Election Commission, composed only of supporters of Obiang Nguema's, was under the authority of the minister of the interior (and therefore of the police). In preparation of the presidential election, the regime installed a "shock force" of 300 men, charged with minding the polling stations.

The POC chose the architect Amancio G. Nzé of the CPDS (the only candidate fulfilling the criteria of the electoral law) as its candidate for presidency. Moto Nsá, who had been speaking for years of his destiny as a national leader was upset and withdrew the Progress Party from the POC. This attitude made Mba Ada, the president of Popular Union (UP) decide to stand also for elections. The electoral Commission rejected the candidacy of the POC under the pretext that the coalition, having broken up, did not exist any more, and, claiming that it could therefore not present any candidates, shut down the offices of the POC, but accepted the candidacy of Moto Nsá, Mba Ada, and two other minor candidates, to whom the dictator alloted $30,000 for the campaign. Obiang Nguema wished thus to give a democratic facade to his regime. The UN, and the European Union, especially Spain and France, insisted to the Ministry of Foreign Affairs in favor of a demand for cleanliness in the elections.

Towards the end of January 1996, the Nguemist exactions recommenced in dead earnest: opponents, including mayors and municipal councillors, were tortured all over the country, and a Spanish doctor with leanings towards the opposition was expelled from Kogo. Monks were prevented from all movement between January 25 and February 28; a large number of them were arrested, tortured, and even threatened with death. The first democratically elected mayor of the capital and president of the Democratic Progressist Alliance, Victorino Bolekia Bolay, was arrested with his deputies, including C. Bakale, chief editor of the POC's periodical, *La Verdad,* during a French lesson in the premises of the French Cooperation; illiterate agents of the Criminal Investigation Department accused them of plotting a coup d'etat. All of them were tortured, without prior interrogation, and Bolekia Bolay was injured from head to toe; he was seen leaving the premises of the Criminal Investigation Department with his clothes all bloody and being unable to walk.

The American petroleum companies provided Obiang Nguema with a helicopter to facilitate his election campaign. This helicopter distributed telecommunications equipment brought in by the British/South African company Inter-Ocean to all the district capitals in order to facilitate the publication of the election results. Obiang Nguema made inflammatory declarations against Radio Exterior de España, which, he alleged, was dividing the Equato-Guinean people; the director of television, Juan Eyene Opkua Nguema Ocoa, addressed a communiqué to the Spanish media calling the Equato-Guinean opposition a band of "agitators" acting under the orders of their masters, the Spanish democrats.

When in mid-February Mgr. Sima Ngua exposed the torture of the priest Carlos Esono as well as the campaign of intimidation and fear; the special reporter to the United Nations Human Rights Commission, A. Artucio, stressed the facts that military justice continued to handle civil affairs, that torture and ill treatment were common occurences, that the government was not responding sufficiently to the recommendations of the Commission, and that the presidential elections lacked credibility. The Nguemists protested, stating that Artucio was expressing the point of view of exiled opposition members. In his article in *Las Provincias,* the Equato-guinean journalist D. Bokokó Boko termed the February 25 elections a coup d'etat in a country where the laws were only aimed at protecting the dictator.

On February 16, 1996, Obiang Nguema caused the UNDP, the European Union, France, and Spain to refuse to send in observers by announcing drastic restrictions to their freedom, including their assignment to certain polling stations. Simultaneously, the American observers of the Carter Foundation (with the exception of a relative of the American ex-president) also gave up the idea of visiting Equatorial Guinea. Cameroon and Gabon were the only countries to send in observers. They were said by the opposition press in Douala to be "reputed in election fraud." Faced with the obstacles raised to their election campaign, three of the four opposition candidates withdrew from the race, but the Nguemists did not pay any attention to it. Secundino Oyono, president of the CSDP and brother-in-law of Obiang Nguema, was the only one to "face" Obiang Nguema. Shortly before the election, Obiang Nguema declared: "All those who do not vote for me are of low birth."

In order to help his people avoid such misfortune, he began his election campaign with the publication of 100,000 copies of a sworn declaration of membership to his party, which the police carried from door to door and forced the people to sign under the threat of arms. Moreover, he imposed nonsecrecy on the ballot, thus preventing—as the special rapporteur to the United Nations Human Rights Commission stated—free political expression. Apart from a few observers from Cameroon and Gabon, the companies Mobil and Nomeco provided a few "petro-observers."

IFES has given a description of the results of the sophisticated electoral system proposed by the British/South African experts:

The Government spent a reported US $750,000 to supply fax machines and satellite link-ups manned by individual technical experts in each of the 18 districts on the mainland and Bioko. The technician's job was to fax to Malabo the result forms (actas) as they were brought into the district headquarters from individual polling stations. As a backup measure, the president of each polling station was to bring in the original acta, ballots, and all other documentation, to be carried to Malabo for a final verification of the vote count. In Malabo, there were five fax machines standing by to receive the actas as they were sent from all over the country. The results center also had a copy machine where the technicians would make two copies of the original faxes of the acta: one for the electoral Commission to tabulate in order to announce district results on a rolling basis; and one for the Commission to post for easy access by international observers and the media. On paper, this high-tech solution addressed all of the concerns surrounding the transparency of vote transmission and tabulation. But high tech does not mean foolproof.

The portable telephone/fax machine transmitted via satellite to an earth station in Canada, then to a public telephone network on the mainland, then to a microwave link to Malabo, and finally through a local telephone network to the receiving portable telephone/fax machine. Every call went through this process, even a call made from a neighboring town. February 23, however, the earth station in Canada went down, reducing the chances of any call being received to 30 percent, slowing the process considerably.

On February 28, the fax machines were turned off and packed away, with approximately 75 percent of the votes reported. The electoral Commission stopped posting provisional results, explaining that they would wait for results from those areas where the fax technology had broken down. It was not until March 11, fifteen days after the vote took place, that final results were released. With the expensive, high-tech solution, election results took longer to be released than they had in the 1995 municipal elections. Technology can be a boon in the electoral process when it is properly used and understood. But technology cannot be used in a vacuum; it must be accompanied by true political will. With their experience now in the areas of both democracy and technology, the Equatorial Guineans should be in an ideal position to make their next elections (legislative elections scheduled for 1998) free, fair, transparent, and easy. In 1998, the *International Market Insight* of the U.S. Department of State qualified the Nguemist elections as "deeply flawed." The electoral lists of 1998, in anticipation of the legislative elections, resulted in numerous manipulations by the Nguemist regime.

According to F. Ela Owono, president of the Court of Appeals, problems also arose during the counting of the votes: 300,000 votes had been registered for 180,000 registered on the rolls. The "victory" of Obiang Nguema was testimony to the failure of the regime. *El Pais* (Madrid) was of the opinion that "Obiang Nguema has ruled since February 25, 1996, with the same legitimacy as before— none." According to the dictator, his reelection was the culmination of the democratization process. From then on, those who were politically active would be prosecuted. In all future elections, citizens would have to publicly state their choice. While the American observers sent in by Strategic Concepts declared that they had never seen such a high level of rigging, the African Committee of the Socialist International in Ouagadougou, asked the international community not to recognize the election of Obiang Nguema. According to *Africa Confidential,* the election of the dictator with 97.85% of the votes was embarrassing to the American petroleum companies. For the special rapporteur to the Human Rights Commission, a good opportunity to ensure steps towards democracy had been lost. In Spain, the general secretary of the oldest opposition movement against the Nguemist regime, the National Alliance for Democratic Restoration, Luis Ondo Ayang, once again denounced the regime with which he had refused to collaborate ever since its founding.

After the presidential elections, the other parties that had boycotted the election (UP, PP and CSD) addressed a letter to Spain, France, the European Union, the OAU, and the United Nations to expose the rigging and to express their fears of reprisals, and appealed to them to "prevent" all violations of human rights. In spite of the government's protests, the fears expressed were confirmed with the increase in the number of arrests and instances of violence against the opposition. In April 1996, the Report of the American State Department on Human Rights in the world, submitted to the U.S. Congress, was one response to Nguemist protests. The document rectified the lies of the regime and denounced, by enumerating all its exactions, the oppressive regime of Obiang Nguema, as a lesson to the petroleum multinationals.

After his "reelection," the dictator Obiang Nguema formed on April 8 a government of "national unity" with the tame opposition. This government included 33 Fang (of whom 11 were from the district of Wele-Nzas, Mongomo); six posts went to the tame opposition, but the important ministries remained in the hands of the clan from Mongomo. There was one minister for every 277 officials and per 10,000 inhabitants. Angel Serafin Dougan became the new prime minister. The majority of posts of general secretaries and general directors, in all administrations, are entrusted to people from Mongomo or its province (Wele-Nzas).

In September 1996, in Washington, the deputy secretary of state for Africa, William Tuwaddel, expressed to P. Miko and C. Bakale (leaders of the CPDS) his conviction that the election of Obiang Nguema, in February, lacked credibility.

In 1997, the Nguemists tried to change the traditional chiefs, in view of the 1998 elections. On December 1, 1997, upon Artucio's arrival, the government ratified an electoral law forbidding the coalition of nonlegalized political parties.

On March 25, 1998, an agreement was signed between the government and the opposition in order to create a mixed commission in view of the elections. But on April 5 the UP and CPDs denounced "serious violations" of the agreement: increase of police roadblocks, preventing the opposition from carrying out its political activities. The electoral list was launched on June 29, but the opposition was put aside (expatriates and minors were put on the lists). They threatened to boycott: in spite of the agreement, the opposition only has 13 out of 18 districts left. Members of the army worked in making up electoral lists. About 50 UP members of the polling commission in Kié-Ntem were eliminated from the commission. However, Mba Ada insisted on the fact that UP will participate in the election, which it is sure to win if there is no fraud.

During the summer of 1998, UP and CPDS announced their participation in the November legislative elections. It was reported that a minister had paid people making up the polling list with fake money. At the beginning of September, the PDGE again pressured the population to join the party of the dictatorship.

Beginning in October, a so-called Gabinete Político of S.E. (Obiang Nguema) handed over to the dictator a "Draft of the strategy of the PDGE for the parliamentary elections of 1998." These advisors suggested that the government should control electoral lists and electoral tables, replace the untrustworthy members of the Electoral Tribune, prevent the presence of observers from countries that have interests in Equatorial Guinea, such as Spain, and hire, with the extra-budgetary oil revenues, advisors who would be in charge of this control. The arrests of opponents in Río Muni on October 5 was indicative of this PDGE policy. During October, the CPDS reported that the Nguemist government had withdrawn 65,000 voters from the electoral list, that is, those it suspected would not support the PDGE. The CPDS also denounced the existence of illegal polling stations in barracks, schools, and companies. At the same time, three mayors of the province of Kié-Ntem, among whom were the mayor of Ebebiyin, were dismissed. These mayors had asked the government to keep the promises it had made during the elections, among which were installing electricity and drinking water. The government annouonced there would be partial municipal elections on December 13, 1998, in the districts of Río Campo, Corisco, and Nsang, all created in September 1998 by the dictator. On October 27, the opposition threatened not to participate any longer in the elaboration of electoral lists.

On November 10, the Nguemists accused the democratic opposition of "spreading confusion." Many militants of the CPDS, mostly Fang, were arrested and tortured. On November 30 one of the leaders of the FDR, Nguema Ela Angue Ndong, died in the prison of the capital due to torture. On December 4, 35 Bubi were arrested and tortured; the dialogue opposition/dictatorship was broken the very same day.

As of the end of December 1998, the date for the legislative elections had not been set.

See also Administration; Elections; Government of National Unity; International Foundation for Election Systems; Human Rights; Missions; Ndong Ela Mangue, J.; Police; United Nations.

ELECTRICITY. According to the United Nations, the consumption of energy per inhabitant (kg of coal) was at 121 in 1960 and 103 in 1979, at the time of Obiang Nguema's coup. At present, the consumption of electricity is at about 50 kw/year. The capacity of the 12 sites listed totals 2,600 mw. The island of Fernando Po used 15,476 kw from the hydraulic plant of Riaba and the thermal plant in the capital. Technical and other losses in the whole country are substantial: 47%.

Decree 129 of April 7, 1980, regulated the rate for the consumption of electrical energy. China put up an electrical plant at Bicomo, 13 km to the east of Bata. The emergency program of the EDF, in 1980, is to serve in the restoration of the Santa Isabel network; the work was entrusted to the French company Compagnie électro-mécanique (CEM).

In 1981, only the towns of Bata and Santa Isabel enjoyed electrical power. In 1985, the African Development Bank allotted $524,000 for the electrification of 10 towns. The setting up of a new 3.4 Mv plant near Concepción was given to Electricité de France, with financing from the Caisse centrale de Cooperation économique (FF 116 million) and the European Investmant Bank (FF 44 million, i.e., a total of $23.2 million).

The Hispanic-Equato-Guinean monthly magazine *El Patio* (February–March 1997) wrote that they often had power cuts. According to Reporters without Borders, in 1997, the capital's lack of electricity for five months, definitely caused the closing down of the private newspaper *El Sol,* as well as that of the magazine of the party in power, *La Voz del Pueblo.* Once electricity was back, the headquarters of the CPDS and the private residence of Placido Mikó remained several months without electricity.

In October 1987, Obiang Nguema lay the corner stone for the Concepción plant (Riaba). The inauguration took place on August 1, 1989, with a production level of 3.6 Mw. The distribution of power was carried out by the joint electrical company of Fernando Po (Bioko), 51% of the capital of which came from the Compagnie générale d'électricité (France). Discord stemming from the Equato-Guinean side prevented the constitution of this company until 1989. In July 1990, the Société d'aménagement and d'urbanisme pour l'Afrique (Saur-Afrique), part of the French group Bouygues, entered the scene for the creation of the company Segesa. But in December, the government unilaterally lowered the rates by 25%, accusing Segesa of practicing monopolisitc prices. Saur declared the contract null and void, and left the country.

The modernization work at the two electrical plants at Concepción was soon interrupted. The installations that France was to have realized on the Ilady falls were replaced by other less expensive ones, on the Musola River, with a highly erratic flow.

In 1998, Equatorial Guinea had a 5 Mw potential, of which 4 were power stations and 1 hydroelectric. Santa Isabel power station is run by SEGESA, with 5 generators that work during the dry season (consumption: 15,000 l of diesel oil in 24 hours). During the rainy season, Riaba power station provides 3,500 kw. Nevertheless, frequent power cuts occurred in the capital and in Bata. In 1998, the World Bank started financing several projects with U.S. $10 Mio—construction in the capital, by private investors, of a 9 Mw thermic power plant to replace the existing one; it will be run on gas from Alba field—rehabilitation of existing hydroelectric plants and distribution network—technical assistance, training, etc.

On February 13, 1998, the Spanish press agency EFE wrote: "Equatorial Guinea is a country without light, despite the fact that it exports 80,000 barrels of oil per day. The Bubi trial, end of May 1998, could not be concluded on May 28 due to a light shortage that didn't allow the reading of the sentences." See also Introduction; SEGESA.

ELECTRICITY SUPPLIES OF EQUATORIAL GUINEA (Sociedad Electrica de Guinea Ecuatorial, SEGESA). Joint company (62% held by the Nguemist state, 38% by the Spanish company Infisa Int. SA) which manages electrical supplies to Fernando Po. It took over the activities of the French company Saur (Bouygues Group) which abandoned its activities towards the end of 1991. In

1992, M. Ebozogo Ayang became director of the company. Several members of the staff were dismissed under Nguemist pressure.

In 1996, the capital, and especially national radio, underwent frequent power cuts on the part of Segesa. The director general of Segesa, Mauricio Mba Ebosogo, and the president of the Administrative council, Marcelino Oyono, were replaced by Fidel Marcos in the management and D. Elo Ndong as President of the Administrative council. See also Colesesga; Electricity.

ELEMA BORENGUE, Joaquin. Ndowe. Born in Bata, in 1954. Holds a Baccalaureate. Underwent military training in the Spanish Legion. Imprisoned under Macías Nguema, he took refuge in Spain. When he returned after Obiang Nguema's coup, he was sent for military training to Rondo (Spain) until 1985. Upon his return as a noncommissioned officer, he was entrusted with the task of organizing the military police. Named chief of this corps, and coordinator of the Criminal Investigation Department, he realized that Obiang Nguema intended to establish a police state and therefore resigned. He was arrested in relation to the so-called August 1988 coup d'etat, and accused of attempting to assasinate Obiang Nguema. He was tortured by Commander and Presidential Counsellor for Foreign Affairs Santiago Eneme and condemned to death by a summary court-martial, but his sentence was commuted to life imprisonment. He spent four years in a cell, and was tortured several times by the Moroccans. He was released in August 1991, upon UN and OAU intervention, after which he sought refuge in Spain, where he became president of a shadow-party named Union of the People of Equatorial Guinea (UPGE, Left-Centre). He announced, towards the end of 1992, his intention to stand for the presidency of the Liberal Democratic Convergency.

In June 1995, Elema warned, in the press, that if Obiang Nguema were to manipulate the 1996 presidential elections, "then military intervention would be justified." He expressed the wish that his country go back to being "the Switzerland of Central Africa." In May, in Valencia (Spain), Elema, Andombe (Party of the Congress) and Malavo (ex Liberal Party) cofounded a Social Forum for National Reconciliation (Foro Social de Reconciliación Nacional) which, in July, became the Forum for Democracy in Guinea (Foro para la Democracia de Guinea), whose aim was to organize a Peace Conference for Equatorial Guinea. He was elected president. The Spanish national Enrique Millán, formerly first general secretary to the president of the republic and last general secretary of the autonomous government of Equatorial Guinea, Pastor Mateo professor emeritus in constitutional law, Jose Mateo, advocate and former Spanish Civil Governor, Jose Mateo García, regional delegate of the Canovas de Castillo foundation, and Norberto Piñango, degree holder in trade union studies, were all members of its Committee. The Forum had 12 vice-presidents (including six Spanish), who each assumed presidency in rotation, the change coming once every three months. The first president was Buja-Bokokó. After the September 1995 municipal elections, Elema lauded Obiang Nguema's efforts at democratization and urged Spanish investors to return to Equatorial Guinea.

In August 1996 the Spanish minister of foreign affairs, Abel Matutes, gave his support to the Forum for Democracy in Guinea (underwritten by 25 businessmen from Valencia), as well as the rightist politician M. Fraga. Elema wished to create a Hispano-Guinean Fund for Cooperation and Development. Elema proposed amnesty in case of the alternation of power, in order to avoid accountability. On his return from the U.S. he suggested seven points in view of a joint government with Obiang Nguema, among which were respecting the dictator's economic patrimony and amnesty, retaining the presidential guard as well as the Moroccan guard, and the paying of a pension to Obiang Nguema after the elections of 2002.

In July 1998, in Madrid, he created, along with Severo Moto, yet another political party: The Democratic Coordination. In his press conferences he called for the support of the Spanish government and international co-ordination.

Elema is strongly criticized by his compatriots who, at the beginning, had supported his various parties. They think he is not credible. One of Elema's sisters has a child with Obiang Nguema.

See also Coup d'etat of August 1988; Eneme Ovono, S.; Malavo, E.; Nguema Esono, L.; Olo Mba Nseng, J.; Switzerland.

ELEPHANTS. Most of the elephants have been massacred. The scientific community reports contacts between Obiang Nguema personally guilty of abetting elephant poaching. It ordered Cameroon and Gabon to check ivory smuggling.

Lieutenant Colonel Agustin Ndong Ona, representative of Obiang Nguema in Río Muni, is known for loaning village chiefs of the forest zone rifles, in order to hunt elephants. The meat goes to the peasants and the tusks to Ndong Ona.

ELF AQUITAINE-ELF EQUATORIAL GUINEA. French oil company, well-established in Gabon, Nigeria, and São Tomé-Principe, among other countries. Through ELF-Gabon, it seems to have carried out illegal drillings in the south-western part of Rio Muni.

On February 25, 1998, it obtained an offshore area of 6,800 sq km west of Bioko, in Block H. to investigate oil potential. In March 1998, Obiang Nguema announced the participation of ELF-Equatorial Guinea in oil exploitation; the contract was signed in July. Obiang Nguema is said to have granted this contract after President Chirac of France promised to finance the meeting of CEMAC, which was to be held in Equatorial Guinea at the end of 1998.

ELF-EG is presided over by "Patron" Teodorín Nguema Obiang, the eldest son of the dictator. The contract was signed on July 4. It started drilling in 1999 at 1,000–2,700 m. On August 21, Equatorial Guinea said it was "worried" about the "unjustifiable" activities led by the two ELF offshore oil rigs, who operate on its territorial waters "without authorization," coming from Nigeria. ELF must leave. We must wait for the results of the disagreement between Equatorial Guinea and Nigeria, concerning their borders.

ELO AKA, Tomás see Moto Nsá

ELOBEYES ISLANDS. Group of two islands covering about 2 sq km (less than one sq mi). One, Elobey Chico (or Little Elobey), is located southwest of Río Muni, 6 km off the estuary and 1.5 km from Elobey Grande. It is a basaltic plateau of 0.19 sq km. Planted with coconut trees. Before the arrival of the Portuguese at the end of the 15th century, it was depopulated. In 1856 Du Chaillu mentioned lumber deposits but no sign of a settlement. In 1884 there were 521 inhabitants, as well as subsidiaries of German, English, and French companies. In 1886 a Claretian secondary school for boarders was opened. At the beginning of the 20th century subsidiaries of Woermann and Holt, as well as of the Spanish Trasatlántica existed. From 1904 to 1907, Elobey Chico was the seat of the local government of the southern district, which after a brief transfer to Calatrava, returned to Elobey Chico until 1926. In 1950 the island was virtually abandoned (about 10 inhabitants).

Elobey Grande: located one nautical mile from Elobey Chico and 11 nautical miles from Corisco. Basaltic table land of 2.27 sq km, it is 80 m high and has abrupt coastline, to the detriment of its commercial possibilities. A prehistoric stoneware hatchet similar to those found in Ghana was discovered on the island. Elobey Grande was governed successively by Mpapay (1856), Yeli Ibape (1859), and Bodumba (1875), the latter having contacts with Iradier. During the 19th century, France claimed the island. In 1887 a Claretian Missionary School opened in Elobey Grande, paired with a nusery in 1912. Various companies opened subsidiaries: Holt, Hatton & Cookson, Woermann (in 1872), Lübke, Königsdörfer, Trasatlántica, etc. But in the beginning of the 20th century, business moved to Elobey Chico. Presently the island has fewer than 100 inhabitants, mainly Benga.

In 1862, under French pressure, Spain cancelled the navigation taxes for access to Corisco and the Elobey Islands, in vigor since 1843. In 1867, Spain offered France facilities for the establishment of factories, in return for de facto recognition of Spanish jurisdiction over these territories. Towards the end of 1993, an official French document stated that the two Elobeyes belonged administratively to Río Muni. See also Borders.

ELO MABALE, Ricardo. Fang from Mongomo. Holds a law degree (USSR). As joint secretary for information and tourism under Macías Nguema he also worked as joint chief of censorship for the political police. On December 8, 1981, he became national chief for the censoring of information. In 1993, he became director general for justice and penitentiaries. He retained this post under decree 27 of January 1994. In 1996, he was the spokesperson of the "Nguemist" Commission for Human Rights.

He kept this function in 1998.

ELO NDONG NSEFUMU, Demetrio. Fang from Mongomo. Obiang Nguema's relative. Post office official. One of the ambitious opportunists of the Nguemist regime. Appointed in late 1982 secretary of state for telecommunications. In the spring of 1984 he became deputy-minister of health, and in 1986, minister of telecommunications. He received commissions from the Spanish Cooperation. He was a deputy from 1983 to 1993. In the January 24, 1992, "transitional" government, he was appointed political counsellor. He was reelected PDGE deputy in November 1993. He held no posts in the December 22 government. On January 19, 1994, he was appointed the civil cabinet's counsellor to the president for foreign affairs. Along with other Nguemist executives, he participated in the destabilization of the Partido Liberal.

In the April 8, 1996, government, he became the political affairs counsellor to the head of state. He is also the president of the administrative council of the Electrical Company of Equatorial Guinea.

In the government resulting from the ministerial reshuffle of January 21, 1998, he remained Minister Political Adviser of the government. But he also suceeded Julio Ndong Ela Mangue as Minister of the Interior.
See also Mongomo; Nepotism; Post Offices; Transports.

ELO NVE, Eloy see Nve Mbengono, E. E.

EMAGUISA see Timber

EMANCIPATION. A key instrument of Spanish colonial politics, emancipation was granted to natives with higher education, having earned a salary of over 500 pesetas a year for more than two years, being a civil servant beyond the temporary level. In order to become emancipated the native had to adopt Christian habits, have a vocational education, a decent income, and be open to progress: all these clauses were sufficiently vague to allow denial of emancipation to all those thought not favorable to the metropolis. The Catholic missions and the Patronato de Indígenas attributed the emancipation certificates. The emancipated native was no longer obliged to work in European plantations and could appeal to Spanish jurisdiction; the nonemancipated was subject to native justice. The Patronato prohibited all transactions over 500 pesetas with the nonemancipated. This discriminatory institution disappeared with provincialization (1960).

EMERGENCIA (State of Emergency). After Macías Nguema's numerous anti-Spanish speeches, delivered in Río Muni in January 1969, the affair of the flags in Bata and the Guardia Civil's intervention in February 1969, Macías proclaimed a state of emergency on March 3, 1969. Two days later, Ndongo Miyone's coup d'etat took place, followed by the exodus of 7,000 Spaniards. By mid-March Macías suspended the constitution and ordered the liquidation of most Spanish companies.
In view of the void created by the Spaniards' departure, the administrative and economic stalemate and the disorganization of schools and hospitals, the government appealed to the UN and the OAU for expert assistance.

EMPRESA GUINEO-ESPANOLA DE PETROLEOS S.A. (GEPSA). This company was founded in January 1980 by the Spanish concern HISPANOIL in conjunction with the government of Equatorial Guinea, each partner holding 50% of the share capital. The company was granted a concession around Fernando Po and invested US $24 million in the enterprise. The vice-president of the republic, Maye Ela, was made director until 1983. Since 1981, French, American, and other oil companies have been protesting to Obiang Nguema about the special privileges granted to Hispanoil. In April 1984, Hispanoil discovered natural gas and petroleum derivates on the offshore continental shelf north of Fernando Po. See Petroleum.

EMPRESA MIXTA GUINEO-ESPANOLA DE MINAS S.A. (GEMSA). Company founded in 1980, with 55% government capital and 45% from the Spanish company ADARO. The company was established to undertake mining prospecting and research, except for petroleum and radioactive deposits. Its director was Mensuy Mbá. In 1983 the company had collected some 8,500 mineral samples. ADARO had by then invested 340 million Pesetas in the exercise.

EMPRESAS ESTATALES see State-run Enterprises

EMPRESA NACIONAL DE PESCA DE GUINEA ECUATORIAL (EN-PGE). National Fishing Co. Joint Enterprise, mainly composed of important members of the Nguemist regime. ENPGE is free of fiscal and customs obligations. Its president of honor is Obiang Nguema; vice-president: Siale Bilekia; president of the Council: Oyono Ndong; vice-president Nguema Onguene; members (all ministers): A. Alogo Nchama, M. Ebendeng, P. Ela Nguema, R. Mangue, L. Mbomio, M. Micha, A. Ndong Mba, A. Ondo Nguema

EMVELO, Gustavo see Missions; Protestantism.

ENEME OVONO, José (Called "Chele"). Of the Eseng Clan from Bata. Cousin to Fortunato Mba Nzambi, minister for education in 1986. Brother-in-law to the Lebanese businessman Ghabi. Studied at the Ecole National d'Administration in Cameroon. After Obiang Nguema's coup d'etat, he became assistant to the director for technical coordination in the Ministry of Foreign Affairs. He underwent training in the local office of the UNDP. In 1985, he was section head for international organizations in the Ministry of Foreign Affairs.

Upon becoming consul in Douala, he was arrested in December 1989, following the accidental death of a relative of Obiang Nguema's. Held in Bata, he underwent torture. In May 1990, an Ebebiyin tribunal accused him of sorcery; Eneme Ovono confessed under torture. He was condemned to life imprisonment. In December 1991, he received the visit of the expert of the United Nations Human Rights Commission, to whom he stated that he had never received any communication regarding his sentence.

On June 3, 1992, J. Ene Ovono was released, following presidential grace. In 1993 he became a member of Unión popular. From 1994, he joined other Nguemist executives in the domestication of the Liberal Party. In the April 8, 1996, government, he became vice-minister for employment and social security. He then joined the "transitional" government of 1992 as vice-minister for health. On January 8, 1996, he became the minister for health. Eneme Ovono is also personal secretary of the dictator. See also Rola, G.

ENEME OVONO, Santiago. Alias "Alandi" (also called "El Guapo," handsome). From Akua-Kam Esangui (Mongomo). A nephew of Obiang Nguema's. Studied up to grade four of primary school. Member of the Youth Marching with Macías.

In 1988, Eneme received commissions from the Spanish Cooperation. The former chief of the military Criminal Investigation Department Joaquin Elema Borengue, arrested in 1988, said he had been tortured by S. Eneme Ovono, in the presence of other Nguemists. In 1989, Eneme Ovono was promoted to the post of vice-minister for foreign affairs and cooperation. He became minister in October 1990.

Towards the end of 1991, he announced Obiang Nguema's refusal to hold a National Conference (which can only be held in the case of a vacancy in power over government). He denied the existence of a political opposition, even in exile. He protects the Lebanese Rola, who monopolizes the bread market and other mini-markets in Santa Isabel. He did not hold any post in the January 24, 1992, "transitional" government. Since 1994, he works as director general for internation cooperation in the Ministry of Foreign Affairs. His name was mentioned among those involved in the July 18, 1996, coup d'etat.

In 1997, he was ambassador to Cameroon. He was dismissed in July 1998, accused of having organized the theft of Obian Nguema's car (loaded with currency). He is under house arrest in Mongomo.

See also Human Rights.

EÑESO NEÑE, Augustin, d. 1972. Ndowe professor of general education (lower secondary level), holding a B.A. in sociology. Head of the MUNGE from 1964 to 1966. From 1966 to 1968 he was Finance Minister (Consejero), then Minister of Education. He created the Ndowe Union in anticipation of the Constitutional Conference. During the Conference he joined Macías Nguema's Secretariado Conjunto. Teaching in Madrid after independence, he was called back by Macías Nguema to become Minister of Education beginning 1972. In May 1972 he was executed in public and his body exposed, because in April a portrait of Macías Nguema had been slashed at the entrance of the Bata Secondary School and because anti-Macías tracts were circulated in the schools.

ENGONGA EDJO, Baltasar. From Atut-Efac (Ebebiyin). Son of an elder sister of Obiang Nguema's. Has behind him a few years of secondary school. Ex-consul to Madrid. On December 8, 1981, he became cashier of the Bank of Equatorial Guinea in Bata, replacing Nko Ivasa. In January 1986, he was named vice-minister for finance. As vice-minister, he received friendly loans from the Guinexbank. As a member of the Security (Seguridad), he was said to have been responsible for the disappearance of Pedro Moto Mamiaga, in August 1993. During the January 8, 1996, ministerial reshuffle, he was again named minister delegate with special responsibility for the economy and finance. He retained his post during the ministerial reshuffle of April 8, 1996.

In September 1998, he also became president of the board of the French Société Générale de Banque/Guinea Ecuatorial.

ENGONGA MOTULU, Marcelo. Born 1948. From Mbeme-Yengom (Mikome-seng). Called "Maducley," or "law-beater." Studied Law in USSR. Sought refuge in Switzerland in 1981 after fleeing Spain where he left behind him dubious debts. He claims a number of fictitious titles. As a member of the ANRD, he simultaneously claimed to be a representative of the Civic Council National Salvation (Junta cívica de salvación nacional). He moved away from the ANRD and started visiting a "Swiss psychosomatic centre for the teaching of human rights," linked to international extreme right-wingers.

Recuperated by the Nguemists, he was Equatorial Guinea's representative to the UN in Geneva from 1991. He justified Obiang Nguema's refusal to give reentry visas to Equato-Guineans holding dual citizenship.

In 1992, he rejected the Human Rights Commission Report and demanded that the proposed resolution be revoked as it had no relation to existing facts. At that time, he was reportedly involved in sordid affairs, with expatriate Serbs and Obiang Nguema's economic counsellor, the France-convicted V. G. Llansol. In the newspapers of Geneva, he greatly praised the Nguemists. Engonga Motulu was held by the airport police in Paris, in the company of a delegation (MM

Llansol, Bloch, Horwantwaner, Robin, Sanchez, Choisy, Bouchetemble, Romagnoni), as he was travelling to Lagos; the diaspora spoke of the Nigerian Connection.

In the spring of 1993, Motulu and Llansol started the Banco de Guinea Ecuatorial project along with Obiang Nguema and his elder son, Teodorín. In Switzerland, Engonga Motulu accumulated nearly $600,000 in debts. Engonga Motulu was expelled from Switzerland on October 12, 1993, soon after Llansol, for misuse of his residential permit and sordid deals. He returned to Santa Isabel. By Presidential Decree of January 1994, he became director general of international cooperation in the Ministry of Foreign Affairs. He lost this job in 1996. He remains merely a state employee.

See also Banks; Mikomeseng; Ngomo Mbengono, F. J.; Obiang Nguema, T.

ENGONGA NGUEMA, Clemente. Fang from Mongomo. Born 1956. Administrative assistant (Escuela superior of Santa Isabel). By Presidential Decree 19 of January 1994, he became general secretary of the Ministry for Women's Integration and Social Affairs. He retained this post during the April 8, 1996, ministerial reshuffle.

In the January 21, 1998 government, he became vice-minister of the interior (police).

ENGONGA ONDO, Armengol. From Teguete (Prov. Centro-Sur). Born 1947. Emigrated to Spain in 1968. An agricultural technical engineer, and Moto Nsa's right-hand man. From late 1992 he was the vice-president of the Progress Party. His brother-in-law P. J. Esono Miko, also a refugee in Spain, was in charge of the external relations of the PP.

When Moto Nsá was condemned and imprisoned in March-April 1995, Ongonga Ondo created a furor in the press, alleging that "Obiang Nguema's prisons have opponents 'commit suicide.'" Some people thought he was overdoing it. When Moto Nsá was released under the general amnesty decreed by Obiang Nguema on August 2, Engonga stated that "the ideology of the PDGE is communist."

See also Moto Nsá, S.; Progress Party.

ENSEMA, Marcelo. Fang from Mongomo Born 1947. Lawyer. Degree holder in journalism. A poet. Claretian priest since 1973. He has been imprisoned and tortured under Macías Nguema. In 1984 he was appointed provincial head of the Claretians in Equatorial Guinea.

ENSEMA MBA, Salvador. A Catholic priest from Mongomo. Born 1926 in Mongomeyén. Holds a degree in law (Spain). In 1984, a proposal to name him a representative to the UN Human Rights Commission was refused by the Commission. Soon after, he became president of the Supreme Court. In January 1994 he became a member of the Constitutional Court. Ensema Mba praised in some of his writing Obiang Nguema's speeches. See also Siale Bilekia, S.

ENVIRONMENT. According to various environmental organizations (UNCED, 1991; The International Union for Conservation of Nature and Natural Resources, 1991; The World Conservation Union, 1993), the situation is not good. The forest is threatened: the protected areas of the Spanish era were no longer respected, and

THE DICTIONARY-E- / 157

deforestation had seriously increased in the 1980s. Primary forest dropped from 50% to 28%. The coastal area of Mbini had been badly damaged. Itinerant agriculture also played a part, as well as excessive hunting. Result: "The legal regime is inadequate." With deforestation, the biodiversity disappears, drinkable water is lacking, the water sources are polluted, and the deterioration of the environment is harmful to the health and landscape. Moreover, "inadequate deposits from solid waste" have been reported.

The organizations dealing with the protection of nature insisted, in 1998, on the fact that "Equatorial Guinea needs urgent aid for the conservation of nature due to a possible genetic erosion."

See Toxic Wastes.

ENVORO OVONO, Alejandro (called "Alenvoro"). Fang from the Bon clan (Mongomo). Born January 15, 1944. Educated at the Professional School of Bata. In 1975, he worked as a trainee for six months, at the Spanish oil company CEPSA. During the era of Macías Nguema, he was responsible for the national network of hydrocarbon stations, where he made a fortune.

In November 1993, he was elected a deputy of the PDGE. He retained his post in the December 22 government. He founded his own lumber company, after buying materials from the Israeli company Yona. He is the manager of Obiang Nguema's assets. Envoro had several private houses constructed in the capital, in Bata and Mongomo. Envoro Ovono is the president of the administrative council of the oil company TOTAL-GE.

In the 1996 ministerial reshuffle he quit the government, and was replaced by the former noncommissioned officer of the Youth Marching with Macías and member of the CMS, Pedro Nsue Obama.

In 1998 he became minister of civil engineering, construction, and urban affairs.

See also Ekong Nsue, C.; Mongomo; Nsue Obama Angono, P.; Tourism.

EPALEPALE EVINA, Fausto. Ndowe from Río Benito. Born 1929. A reputed pro-Macías Nguema government official. Counsellor to the CMS for Political Affairs from 1979. In January 1981, he further became secretary to the Commission (Ministry) of the Interior, but in fact he actually ran the ministry. In December, he was promoted to vice-minister for justice and religion. In 1990, he became a Supreme Court judge.

EPAM BOTALA, A. A Bubi, born in Rebola. In 1980, he was named technical director of tourism, theatre, and cinema. Member of the Central Committee of the PDGE. After the formation of the "transitional" government towards the end of 1992, he became the director general of tourism and the sea, at Rebola.

EPAM URI, Marcelo Manuel. A Bubi planter. In January 1965 Spain awarded him the silver medal of the Order of Africa. In September 1968 he was elected deputy to the Asamblea de la República (Parliament). As deputy, he joined the Labor Commission. Epam Uri was assassinated under Macías Nguema.

See also Spain.

EQUATORIAL GUINEA LIBERATION FRONT (Frente de Liberación de Guinea Ecuatorial, FRELIGE). Founded in New York in mid-1972 by former members of the MONALIGE. The secretary was A. Bioco. The FRELIGE published an occasional newspaper, *Nkul Ageng* (Warning Tomtom).

The movement published in February 1981, from Malaga (Spain), an appeal for national reconciliation. Its general secretary, the hispanophile Ela Abeme, thought that France wanted to divide Equatorial Guinea between Gabon and Cameroon. He visited the country in the summer, but Obiang Nguema would not receive him. He still had hopes for Obiang Nguema and the future of the nation under him: "Let him be President, as long as he lets us govern," he said. At the FRELIGE Malaga Conference (September 1982), the Spanish cooperation was being wooed and it was made known that Obiang Nguema was embezzling its funds. It was also pointed out that all the ex-tyrants were still in. Ela Abeme stressed in the press on the continuation of Nguemism and threatened to organize guerrilla operations; he recommended the reestablishment of the Constitution of the Independence (1968). Being unable to count either on the USSR, or on France, FRELIGE banked on Spain for help.

In June 1984, Ela Abeme was dismissed by the Junta Coordonadora of Saragoza. In 1989, he published, in his periodical *La Perdiz* (The Partridge), a portrait of the Nguemist theorist Eloy Elo Nve Mbengono, minister for relations with the Parliament, who was called a "grey brain." FRELIGE does not exist any more. See also National People's Congress.

EQUI, Margarita see Moto Nsá, S.

ERI. An ancient name of Fernando Po.

ERIANA POPULAR UNION (Unión Popular Eriana, UPE). Sometimes called Unión del Pueblo de Eri, the old name of Fernando Po. Born of a split in the Unión Bubi; founded on March 19, 1988, by A. Sota Esele, with Solidaridad de Gran Guinea and Grupo nacionalista Bubi 1° de Abril. For want of political vision, this Unión did little apart from hibernating.

ESANG-AYONG. Locality of the district of Mongomo. See Macias Nguema, F.; Obiang Nguema, T.

ESANGUI. One of the 50 or so ethnic groups of the Fang people in the country. The Obiang and Nguema families from the Mongomo region are members of this group. Since 1968 they have held the monopoly of power through the successive dictatorships of Macías Nguema and Obiang Nguema.

ESCUELA SUPERIOR PROVINCIAL. The School "Santo Tomás de Aquino" (formerly, Instituto Colonial Indígena, then Escuela Superior Indígena) trains auxiliary schoolteachers, and assistant administrators. It participated in the elections of half of the deputies to the Provincial Assembly. At independence a large part of the country's higher officials were trained at this school.

See also Education; Alvarez Garcia.

ESON EMAN, Miguel. From Evinayong. Born 1946. Seminarian. Was a refugee in Spain during Macías Nguema's time, secretary general of the MOLIFUGE, and later member of the ANRD; he worked as a secretary to the Madrid Commitee of the ANRD, and then as assistant secretary general, from 1983. Upon his return home, he became an official in the Ministry of Finance. He founded the Popular

Action in January 1992, with C. Masi as president and himself as secretary general. In 1993 he again became a refugee in Spain.

He returned to the country in 1998, but remained Secretary of Popular Action.

See also National Alliance for Democratic Restoration; National Pact; Social Democratic Coalition Party.

ESONO, Jose. 1925?–1976. A Fang and a priest trained at the Banapa "Seminar Mayor" (Priests' Training College) graduating the same year as Bishop Nzé Abuy, bishop of Bata. He was general director of education, inspector of secondary schools, and director of the capital's Instituto "Rey Malabo" since Esuba Machele's disgrace in 1971. Esono was the brain of the Popular Education Ministry. Arrested at the time of the Senior Officials Affair, he was murdered early in December 1976. See also Senior Officials Affair.

ESONO, José Carlos. Catholic priest. Father Esono was arrested and tortured in January 1996, accused of opposing the candidacy of Obiang Nguema for the Presidential elections on February 25. Other priests underwent the same fate. See also Missions.

ESONO ABAGA ADA, Julián. Born in 1946, in Nvulbam (Mikomeseng). From 1971, he was a foreign affairs official and between 1973 and 1975 he was secretary at the embassy at Yaoundé (Cameroon). Upon his return to his country, he became deputy general secretary in the Ministry of Foreign Affairs, in addition to being a roving ambassador. After Obiang Nguema's coup d'etat, in August 1979, he was sent to France as ambassador. He was accused of having misappropriated FFr 1 million (approx. $200,000) and dismissed. He moved in opposition circles for a while, and was then reintegrated into the Nguemist regime. In 1993, he campaigned actively for the PDGE in the Kie-Ntem province.

Since 1995 he has been the head of the distribution of secondhand clothes.

ESONO ABAGA MANGUE, Angel. Fang from Añisok. Born on June 23, 1943. In January 1980 he became director for the Labor Organization (Ordenación laboral). Towards the end of 1981, he became a secretary in the Ministry of Labor. At the end of 1985, he became the vice-minister for industry and commerce. In 1987, he was appointed general secretary of the Ministry of Labour, Social Security, and Women's Rights. In 1993, he became a secretary in the Ministry for Justice and Religions. In the government of December 22, he became vice-minister for the interior.

Since 1995, he has been at the head of the distribution of second-hand clothes.

In the January 8, 1996, ministerial reshuffle, he was appointed minister with special responsibility for the interior. Three months later, he became minister delegate with special responsibilities for the interior and local corporations in the April 8, 1996, government.

He was no longer a member of the government after the ministerial reshuffle of January 1998. See also Police.

ESONO EDJO, Melchor. From Ebebiyin. Born 1960. Economist, trained in Morrocco. In the ministerial reshuffle of April 8, 1996, he became treasurer general of the state. He kept his function during the cabinet reshuffle of January 1998.

ESONO EWORO, Baltasar. In the ministerial reshuffle of April 8, 1996, he was director general of the budget and the state exchequer. He kept his function during the cabinet reshuffle of January 1998.

ESONO MASIE, Pedro. From Okong Oyek (Ebebiyin). Born 1949. Went to military school in Cuba under Macías Nguema. Promoted lieutenant in February 1981. Lt. Colonel, inspector of the armed forces in Fernando Po, he was no more than a decorative figurehead.

Towards the end of 1992, he became a member of the Central Committee of the PDGE. He presided over the military tribunal of Bata, which was charged with the Spanish industrialists Vilarrasa and Hanna's case. He was also a Supreme Court judge and counsellor to the capital's municipal council.

When A. Moíses Mba Ada went to Santa Isabel in August 1993, he had a police station installed before the house where he was staying, in order to spy on the UP president. His grade and duties were confirmed in January 1994. Towards the end of 1994, he was dismissed from the army along with Cdt Pedro Obama Angono, and confined to Okong Oyek.

In January 1995, he was summoned back for reintegration, but was arrested in Bata with other military executives in the Moto Nsá case, which involved some other members of the Progress Party. They were all tortured. Esono Masie was condemned to 30 years' imprisonment.

A refugee in Cameroon, he was arrested with 11 other officers and imprisoned in November 1997. Several humanitarian organizations fear he will be sent back to Equatorial Guinea. The countries of the European Union having refused these refugees, he was finally sent to Argentina with his colleagues.

See also Army.

ESONO MBOMIO, Juan. From Ebebiyin where he was born. Brother of Ponciano Mbomio. Holds a degree from the Soviet Union. Cousin of Ricardo Mangue Obama Nfube, a Judge in the Court of Appeals. Counsellor for Foreign Affairs (1980). In January 1994, he became a judge in the Court of first instance in the district of Santa Isabel.

ESONO MIKA, Leoncio. Armengol Engonga's brother-in-law. Director of the Military Academy at Bata. (Ekuku). In February 1995, he was arrested with 12 other members of the army and accused of plotting a coup d'etat. See also Moto Msá.

ESONO MIKA, Primo José. Born December 16, 1940, in Bisun Esawong (Añisok). Teacher from the Indigenous High School (1956–1960). Married; 10 children. Brother-in-law to Armengol Engonga. A convinced supporter of Macías Nguema. In 1968 he became a deputy on Macías Nguema's list. In 1970 he turned to private economy (Hollando Cy). In 1971 he became permanent representative to the UN in New York. At the end of 1974 he became the ambassador to Spain, and then to Cameroon, and was accredited to six other countries. When he was discharged in 1977, he took asylum in Spain. He has since then taught in a public school in Madrid. After Obiang Nguema's coup d'etat he returned to the scene in 1980 as technical director in the Ministry of Foreign Affairs. He was replaced in 1985 by E. Nzang Beka.

He was imprisoned in 1988 during the coup d'etat of that year, and accused of misappropriation of funds. He was released in 1990. He sought refuge in Spain and joined the Progress Party. He filed a complaint for violation of human rights. The Nguemists, after numerous efforts, responded that Esono Mika infringed on international law. The study completed on his case by a specialist, in *Afrique 200*, in August 1996, concluded that the Nguemist judicial power is directly controlled by the president, and is neither independent, nor impartial. Esono Mika qualified the Nguemist state as "repressive."

From 1993, he worked as secretary for external relations to the Progress Party. In 1995, he underwent dialysis to treat the results of the torture allegedly inflicted on him by Purificación Angue Ondo, Obiang Nguema's sister-in-law, and minister for social welfare.

ESONO NCHAMA, Arsenio see Popular Union

ESONO NDONG, Antimo. Fang from Akok Nsuebot (Ebebiyin). Born 1950. Studied with UNED, in Bata, completed a two-year fellowship in Madrid. Received an M.A. in Philology (Universidad Complutense).

Returned home in 1993. Became secretary general of Democratic and Progressive Alliance (ADP). In 1993 joined Obiang Nguema's "Democratic" Party of Equatorial Guinea (PDGE). In the December 22, 1993, government, he was appointed minister of justice and ritual.

Due to bad health, in the January 8, 1996, ministerial reshuffle, Esono Ndong became vice-minister. In the government of April 8, he remained adviser for social affairs and the condition of women. He died in June 1996.

See also Alene Mba, M.

ESONO NSUE, Felipe, d. 1974. Fang from Evinayong. Chief of the Oyek tribe. Representative to the Cortes from 1960 to 1964 Councillor of the Ayuntamiento (District Council), then mayor of Evinayong from 1969 to 1972. Was awarded the rank of Commander of the Order of Africa in July 1964, by Spain. He was assassinated in, probably, 1974, after Macías Nguema took his wife.

ESONO NSUE, Gaspar see Popular Union

ESONO NSUE NCHAMA, José Luis. Fang from Ebebiyin. Graduated in international relations (USSR). He became an official of the Ministry of Foreign Affairs but was dismissed from his duties in 1994 because he belonged to the Popular Union (UP), a party of the opposition. Later on, he was reintegrated because he boasted, on TV, the advantages of the PDGE, the dictatorship's party. At the ministerial reshuffle of April 8, 1996, he became director general of international cooperation.

ESONO OBAMA EYANG, Pablo. Esangui from Mongomo. Born 1946. Sub-lieutenant of the Youth Marching with Macías. Military training in North Korea. After Obiang Nguema's coup, he became a military commissioner for Health. He was confirmed in his post in 1980, and accompanied the dictator on an official visit to Cameroon.

In February 1981 he was promoted to lieutenant but was soon dismissed for irregularities. In March, he became a counsellor to the mission to the UN (New

York). Recalled in December, he became a secretary to the president of the government. In October 1982, he became director general for agriculture, and soon after, director general of public works. He was arrested for the "coup" of May 1983 and sent to his village, under house arrest.

Since 1983, he has been a member of the road traffic administration. After the ministerial reshuffle of April 8, 1996, he became director general of traffic and road safety.

ESONO OBIANG ENGONE. A Fang of the Eseng group from the village of Mimbaminga in the Niefang district. He is a celebrated player of the musical instrument, the mvett. He is regarded along with the Gabonese Fang, Nsué Nguema Ndong, as one of the greatest exponents of this art.

ESONO ONDO, Andres see Convergency for Social Democracy; Press

ESONO ONDO, Bruno. Fang from Mongomo. Born in Akonibe in 1940. Studied at the Escuela Superior Indígena, in Santa Isabel. Husband to one of Obiang Nguema's cousins, Anita Mbengono Asu Alen. Towards the end of 1991, when he became ambassador to Spain, he systematically rejected Spanish protests at Nguemist exactions. His wife was arrested at São Paulo (Brazil) in 1993, with 32 kg of cocaine, and Esono Ondo was recalled to his country in October.

He wad dismissed from the Ministry of Foreign Affairs in August 1998.

See also Diplomacy; Drugs; Nsobeya Efuman Nsue, S.; Nsue Obama Engono, P.; South Africa; Spain

ESUBA MACHELE, Agustin. Bubi. Doctor of philosophy of the University of Freiburg (Switzerland). In January 1969 he succeeded Mrs. T. Morgades, sister of the assassinated Consejero de la República, as the head of the Instituto of Santa Isabel. As the beginning of 1970 Esuba was in charge of the professors sent by UNESCO after Emergencia. Transferred to Bata in 1971, as director general of education, but actually put aside and fallen from grace, he became director of the Teachers' Training College and the Instituto Carlos Lwanga, replacing Castillo Barrill, who was imprisoned in June 1971 and assassinated in 1974. Because of a medical leave, Esuba Machele was able to take refuge in Spain, where he is teaching in Badajóz.

EUROPEAN UNION (EU). Relations with the European Economic Community (EEC, the ECI's predecessor) were virtually frozen at the time of the Macías Nguema regime, due to the latter's violations of human rights. After the 1979 coup, relations were quickly reestablished. Towards the end of 1985, the regime asked Spain to look after Equatorial Guinea's interests in the EC. But since then it is France that takes the most advantage of the EC projects (electricity, fisheries, telecommunications).

The European Community donated $3.8 milion in 1980. It concluded an agreement with the second Nguemist dictatorship for a series of emergency programs: public health, agriculture, public works, fisheries, electrical energy.

In September 1983, the Fisheries Regulations fixing permissible quantities to be fished were published. In 1985, the European Development Fund (EDF) offered 1.35 million ECUs for agriculture. In 1989, another fishing agreement brought the distance from the coast, authorized for fishing, down from six to four miles.

In 1991, there was a certain deterioration in the country's relations with the EC. Faced with the increase in curbs to fundamental rights, the EC announced that it would stop further aid if democratization remained just verbal. According to the Lomé III Convention, Equatorial Guinea received $69 million aid. In early 1991, Sante Bertagnollo, director of division VIII of the EC, was a member of the astonishing group which awarded Obiang Nguema the so-called Biancamano Prize. The 4th Lomé Convention was signed in November.

In April 1992, the EC, on the basis of Article 5 of the Lomé Convention, again condemned human rights violations. In September, the EC protested against arbitrary arrests and torture. Towards the end of 1992, the EC, Spain, the U.S., France, and the UN again demanded an end to the violence. The EC threatened to suspend cooperation as it did with Zaire, Togo, Sudan, Liberia, and Haiti for systematic and massive violation of human rights. EDF projects then involved more than 12 million ECU. In January 1993, the Nguemists accused the EC representative of inciting violence; the ambassadors of Spain and the U.S. received threatening notes. Several Spainish parties protested against France's lack of solidarity with the other members of the EC as well as the fact that France helping the Nguemists meant blocking democratic transition. The European Parliament adopted a resolution demanding that Obiang Nguema enter into dialogue with the POC. In the meanwhile, it was decided aid would be suspended, as Obiang Nguema showed "zero motivation to install democracy, in the face of elections slated for this year." In early March, the EU denounced arrests, arbitrary trials, and torture before the Human Rights Commission. In September, the EP demanded that Obiang Nguema end his policy of repression and mentioned the "worrisome increase in reprehensible acts against the democratic opposition," acts which led to the massacres in Annobón and the suspicious death of Pedro Motu Mamiaga. The EU and its members joined the USA in the election boycott of November 21, 1993.

On January 20, 1994, the plenary assembly of the EP at Strasbourg demanded suspension of all financial and commercial aid to Obiang Nguema's regime, with the exception of humanitarian aid. One deputy spoke of the "prostitution of democracy" under Obiang Nguema, "which is worse than pure and simple dictatorship." It was demanded that the accounts of the dictator be blocked. In October the EP condemned Obiang Nguema's dictatorship. The minister for foreign affairs, Oyono Ndong, termed the measure an "unfriendly gesture" and expressed the hope that Brussels would "view favorably all that is being done in Equatorial Guinea."

In early 1995, the EU released 980 million pesetas for humanitary aid, and 10.8 million pesetas for electoral census. The EU local representative is the Spaniard Alejandro Montalbán. Another fishing agreement was signed in July. Following the poor organization of the municipal elections in September, the EP insisted, in vain, on the regime's accepting that the POC had won the elections.

In September 1996, the dictator Obiang Nguema called for a return to dialogue and the end of the EU boycott. For this purpose he sent a delegation to Brussels presided over by Marcelino Nguema Onguene. But in December 1996, the *Bulletin d'Afrique Noire* (Paris) recalled that "the persistance in serious human rights violations has made the development of cooperation with Equatorial Guinea very difficult, and since mid 1992, no serious action of cooperation has been carried out."

In 1966, during the joint commission ACP-UE, the ACP prevented the secret vote of a resolution concerning the violation of human rights in Equatorial Guinea. The rapporteur, Ms. Monica Baldi, concluded that the ACP "accept serious violations of human rights." Ambassador in Brussels: Aurelio Mba Olo Andeme.

On November 17, 1997, an EU delegation for technical evaluation arrived in Malabo. They talked to Miguel Oyono, minister of foreign affairs; Marcelino Oyono Ntutumu, minister of economy and finances; Antonio Fernando Nve, minister of planning; Julio Ndong Ela, minister of interior (police); Milam Tang, minister of justice. It was a mission. They met also Mikó (CPDS).

The Guinean biologist Nicolas Mangue, part of the ECOFAC project concerning the preservation of primates, was arrested in April 1998, within the context of the CPDS repression, of which he is the secretary for Rio Muni. After the Bubi trial of May–June 1998, the EP asked for a revision of the trial. Minister of Foreign Affairs Miguel Oyono talked of "intolerable harassment to a sovereign State." ...."our government will not let itself be intimidated." It then granted two months to the EU to restart its projects of cooperation, "if not the country will use its sovereignity." The European Union's representative in Yaoundé: the German Friedrich Nagel; on the spot: Ignacio Sobrino. On October 12, 1998, the EU and the associated countries of Eastern Europe and Cyprus said they were satisfied with the clemency measures taken by Obiang Nguema with regard to the Bubi sentenced to death.

EVINAYONG. Town located in south-central Río Muni, at the foot of Monte Chime. An important crossroads and chief town of the country's largest district. In 1927 an official primary school and inspectorate were opened. In 1931 a Catholic mission school for boys and in 1939 a secondary boarding school for girls were added. An agricultural plant tried to introduce N'Dama cattle and plants such as cloves. In 1969 the missionaries left Evinayong and the Catechist School created by Gómez Marijuan, former bishop of Santa Isabel, expelled from the country. From 1960 to 1964, the head of the Oyek clan, Esono Nsué, a native of Evinayong, was representative to the Cortes in Madrid; from 1969 to 1972 he was mayor of Evinayong. He was liquidated in 1974. Governor General Nuñez de Prado had suggested Evinayong as the colony's capital.

In 1976, during Macias Nguema's dictatorship, a number of citizens of this town who had taken refuge in Gabon since 1972 including Nguema Edu, Mba Nguema, and Eyoma carried out an attack on the garrison at Evinayong armed with shotguns. Despite the amnesty proclaimed in October 1979 by Obiang Nguema, these persons were jailed on their return to the country.

In the January 24, 1992, "transitional" government, there was one minister from Evinayong: Nsue Eworo, minister for health.

Some students were expelled from the local secondary school, in October 1993, for their membership in the Progress Party. Enrique Mesian (from Mongomo), is the government's representative there. Under Macías Nguema, he was initially a government official in the presidential cabinet, and later became a political commissioner. In 1974 he visited Cuba as a journalist. Following the 1979 coup d'etat, he underwent police training in Morocco. As a member of the presidential security, he became the governor of the province of South Fernando Po.

A number of opponents were arrested in 1995, especially members of the Progress Party of Evinayong. The government's representatiave Luis Oyono Mesa attacked one week before elections the home of the secondary school director Albert Nze Mba. Oyono also persecuted the Sunday School teachers of the district. In September, Cristobal Nguema Nfa (PDGE) was elected mayor. The governor of the Centre Sud province is Heriberto Meko, brother-in-law of Armengol Nguema Mbasogo, known for terrorizing the population of Mikomeseng in 1993; his slogan: "Here, I'm the one who rules." His house is decorated with portraits of Obiang Nguema and Mobutu. Acacio Abeso (about 45 years old) is head of presidential security there. In Fang, he publicly proclaimed his hatred of whites. He is the one who threw out of the country three German women and a man in Voluntary Service Overseas, after keeping one of them in jail for three days, in the city police headquarters.

In Evinayong, on the 30th anniversary of independence, October 12, 1998, Obiang Ngucma accused the Western world of looking for new ways of dominating African peoples. Under the pretext of democracy and governance, "the colonial powers want to create linguistic and cultural areas that protect hidden interests and aims." "Obiang Nguema and his family have transformed the country into a private property," adding that not only laymen but the clergy are also victims of nguemist terror.

See also Army; Education; Mbomio Nsue, L.; Mesian, E.; Milam Onvogo, J.; Missions; Ndong, P.; Ndong Micha, A.; Nsue Eworo Micue, A.; Oyono Awong Ada, S.; Progress Party; Sorcery; Transports; Victims.

EVITA ELOY, Leoncino. Born August 8, 1929, in Udubuandolo (Bata). A self-taught man. He took drawing classes by correspondence. Art teacher at the Professional School in Bata. Author, painter, sculptor, he wrote Cuando los combes luchaban (When the Combe fought), the first novel to be written by an Equato-Guinean.

Evita Eloy died in Bata on December 4, 1996.

EVUNA OWONO ASANGONO, Alejandro. Fang, Esangui from Mongomo; relative of Macías Nguema and Obiang Nguema. Born May 25, 1944, in Mongomo. Official trained in the Escuela Superior Provincial of Santa Isabel. Diplomatic training course in Egypt. Skilled government official and noted Nguemist.

Ambassador of Equatorial Guinea to the UN in New York (1978). During the August 30, 1978, meeting at the UN Sub-Commission for the Protection of Minorities, in Geneva, he accused Eya Nchama, the representative of an NGO, of being a member of a terrorist organization (ANRD). The head of the Human Rights division, Mr. van Boven, declared this declaration as nonreceivable, and Pres. Boudhiba closed the meeting. In early 1979, he participated in the 4th Conference of heads of states and governments of non-aligned countries.

Following the 1979 coup, he was appointed ambassador to Spain and Italy. At the sessions of the UN Human Rights Commission in Geneva in March 1980, he refuted accusations about press censorship by saying, "How could there be freedom of the press in a country that does not even have a printing press?" He used this occasion to ask the Commission to provide a printing press. He went on to assert that forced labor had been abolished as salary levels had been increased. At the end of May 1981 the Spanish police found a package of hashish in his wife's luggage. Shortly after this he left his Madrid post and reappeared as secretary-general of the Ministry of Foreign Affairs in Santa Isabel in December 1982.

In December 1987, he became minister for presidency and cooperation. In November 1989, he was promoted to minister and official representative. In 1990, he became a minister of state. He accompanied Obiang Nguema in his travels.

In the January 24, 1992, "transitional" government, he remained minister of state for the government's presidency, and official representative. He tried to undermine the terrifying report of the expert Volio Jiminez, which describes the dictatorship and the general lawlessness, before the UN Human Rights Commission. He threatened the Commission with his country's withdrawal. The Commission responded with one of the most severe resolutions ever voted, showing him wrong on all counts. On December 22, 1992, he was confirmed minister of state for missions.

During the presidential campaign of early 1996, he acted as spokesperson for the PDGE. He retained his duties in the January 8, 1996, as well as the April 8, 1996, ministerial reshuffles. During 1996, the dictator sent him to Spain to negotiate the reopening of relations with Spain. He kept all his functions in 1998. See also Spain.

EWORO NDONGO, Jesús, d. 1970. Fang, sergeant of the Colonial Guard. In 1962 he helped A. Ndongo Miyone to escape from a prohibited meeting of the MONALIGE. In 1964–1965 he attended an officers' training school in Saragossa, Spain. When independence was achieved, he became minister of justice and notary of the republic, not knowing the basics of law. He was placed under house arrest in 1969 and killed in 1970.

EWORO OBAMA, Antonio. Fang. Member of the IPGE. After having become president of the party, he participated in the Constitutional Conference where he joined the Secretariado Conjunto. In the summer of 1968 he was heard at the United Nations in relation to the preparation for independence. At the September 1968 elections he submitted one of the lists of candidates of the Grupo Macías, with Macías Nguema for the presidency and himself for the Asamblea de la República (Parliament). Ever since then, nobody has heard anything of him.

EXIGENSA see Mba Ada; Mba Oñana; Obiang Nguema

EXPULSIONS see Press; Russia; Spain; United Nations

EYAMA ANGUE OSA, David. From Ebibiyin. Born 1942 at Biyabiyan. Frigate sub-lieutenant trained in North Korea. Ranked lieuenant-colonel. In 1991, he became a military attaché at Lagos. He was accused of drug trafficking (30 kg of Brazilian cocaine) and imprisoned in October 1992. Lagos demanded the lifting of his diplomatic immunity. Obiang Nguema sent his son Teodorín to have him freed. According to the Political Drug Observatory, Eyama works for Obiang Nguema.

In 1998, he became an official in the Ministry of Foreign Affairs. See also Drugs.

EYA NCHAMA, Cruz Melchor. Fang, born in Kukumankok on January 6, 1945. Admitted first at the Rural School in 1953, then at the Catholic Mission of Evinayong in 1958, and later at the Instituto Cardenal Císeros in Santa Isabel in 1960. In 1964 he entered the Teachers' Training College in Bata (Magisterio); simultaneously he was chief of the Boy Scout movement. In 1966 he continued his studies in Toledo, Spain, attending the University of Madrid in 1967. The first student to criticize the Nguemist regime, in 1969. He returned to his country in 1969 and left for exile during the Emergencia to continue his studies in educational science. From 1970 to 1972 he taught at a secondary school in Madrid. In 1973 he went to Switzerland. A founding member of the Centro-Ecuato-Guineano grouping Guinean refugee students in Switzerland, he is also a founding member of the ANRD. As ANRD secretary general, he dealt with external relations. In August 1983, Eya Nchama passed on the position of secretary general of the ANRD to Nsomo Okomo.

He participates regularly in the sessions of the UN Human Rights Commission. In several international forums Eya Nchama has declared that "without the civilians, Obiang Nguema would be nothing more than another Macías Nguema" and that if he really had the confidence of the population, he would not have any need for the protection of Moroccan soldiers. At a symposium of the Pax Romana on the subject of refugees in Africa held in Dakar, Senegal, in December 1982, Eya Nchama showed that the Nguemist regime is a derivate of Franco's regime in Spain.

In March 1983, before the Human Rights Commission, he explained the way dictators organize fictitious coups d'etat in order to get rid of adversaries. Eya Nchama recalled the 1503 Resolution to the Commission, which made the Equato-Guinean case a public affair. Furthermore, he asked why the rich countries persist in giving technical assistance to a country which continues to violate human rights.

In 1984, he went on a mission to the United States and Canada. According to the Harvard Law School (Human Rights Internet), "Eya Nchama is one of the most severe critics of dictatorship in Africa." It was thanks to his intervention that Equatorial Guinea was subjected to the confidential process 1503 of the United Nations, an exceptional measure forcing it to publicize the debates.

In 1989, he participated in a conference at King's College in Cambridge on the violation of human rights in Equatorial Guinea. His book *Development and Human Rights in Africa* was published in 1991. Since 1992, Eya Nchama, as a part from the nongovernmental organization UFER, represents the African Association for Education for Development at the United Nations. He participated in the Pan-African Conference on Democracy and the Management of Transition in Africa, at Dakar. He is a member of the Special Committee of International NGOs for Human Rights.

Observers consider Eya Nchama as highly active and competent. He participated in the organization of elections in various countries as a United Nations consultant. In September 1996 he participated in Madrid at the 40th International Congress of Lawyers.

He has been working since March 1997 as coordinator of the UN mission for the observation of human rights in Burundi.

See also Alianza Nacional para la Restauración Democrática (ANRD); Evuna Owono Asangono, A.; Mba Ekua Miko, B.

EYA OLOMO, Valentin. Corvette captain. Arrested with his brother D.T. Ndongo Olomo, during the attempted coup on July 18, 1996.

EYEGUE NTUTUMU, Miguel, 1930?–1976. Fang, and a relative of Macías Nguema. In 1968 he was elected president of the Provincial Council of Río Muni. As such he was briefly arrested at the time of Ndongo Miyone's alleged coup d'etat on March 5, 1969. Shortly afterwards he participated in the creation of the Milicia Popular. In 1970 he became civil governor of Río Muni, then in 1974 vice-president of the republic after the assassination of Bosio Dioco. In 1970 he accompanied García Trevijano and Mbá Ada on a business trip to Europe. The strict censorship in his province is owed to him.

Macías Nguema accused Eyegue's wife, Marguerita Nauzy, in 1975 of planning to poison him and to replace him with her husband. Late in 1975 Eyegue was dismissed with some 20 other persons. He was placed in the Bata prison, where he had himself sent so many compatriots, in December 1976, during the Senior Officials Affair. He was replaced as vice-president by Obiang Nguema's uncle, Nguema Esono, and as civil governor of Río Muni by nephew Ela Nseng. After Obiang Nguema's coup d'etat he was condemned to death with Macías Nguema and executed on September 19, 1979.

EYEGUE OBAMA ASUE, Francisco-Pascual. Fang. A schoolteacher from Kogo, born April 21, 1949. Younger brother of Ildefonso Obama, Archbishop of Santa Isabel, well known for his pro-Nguemist opinions. In the 1970s, he was a highschool teacher in Bata.

In 1980 he was the director of youth affairs, physical education, and sports. He was the secretary of the same Ministry in late 1981, and became minister for industry and commerce in January 1986. In 1992, he became vice-minister for youth affairs and sports in the "transitional" government.

In the November 1993 elections, he became the PDGE deputy for Santa Isabel. In the December 22 government, he became minister and general secretary of the government, a post that he retained until 1996. In the April 8, 1996, ministerial reshuffle, he became minister of state in charge of youth and sports.

In January 1998, he became minister general secretary of the government.

EYENE OPKUA NGUEMA OCOA (or OKWA), Juan. Formerly an announcer on the national radio, and great glorifier of Obiang Nguema in the early 1980s. In 1987, director of Radio Santa Isabel. Was a refugee in Gabon for a while, after which he returned to the country and joined the PDGE. Founder and first director of the National Institute for Social Security (Instituto Nacional de Seguro Social, INSESO). He was director of Radio Malabo since 1995. In March 1996, he addressed a communiqué to the Spanish media, in which he called the Equato-Guinean opposition members a band of "agitators" working for Spanish democrats. He accused the opposition of preventing the Equato-Guinean people from benefiting from the petroleum boom.

As of 1998 he has worked in the Ministry of Information and Tourism.

EYI MENSUI ANDEME, Isidoro. An Esangui, cousin of Obiang Nguema, born 1949 in Mibang Esawong, but comes from Mongomo. Nicknamed "Mobutu." Sub-Lieutenant. Under the Macías Nguema dictatorship he was fanatically anti-Spanish and a well-known torturer. In January 1980 he was appointed deputy-director of the public order brigade of the police force. In 1981 he was appointed chief of security and in October 1982 promoted to secretary of state for security. In June 1983 he was a member of the Akonibé constitutional commission. In January 1986, after having demanded the removal of Spanish police instructor-trainers he was promoted to minister of the interior. He was second-in-command of the Obiang Nguema regime.

In 1985 he was authorized to buy the 521 hectare agricultural estate Esteves-Garcia, not far from the capital. In 1988 he emerged from the bankruptcy of the Guinextebank with 20 million bikwele. In 1988 he became vice-prime minister and right-hand man to Obiang Nguema. In 1990, he retained the post of vice-prime minister. In October, he received the additional post of minister of education, youth affairs, and sport. In November 1991, he was said to have delivered aid milk powder (from international sources, and meant for schools) to yogurt manufacturers in Cameroon.

Eye Mensui did not figure in the January 24, 1992, 'transitional' government. He however remained a part of the Council of Ministers, and asked Obiang Nguema to let him lead it, in order to get rid of what he called "those f... opponents." Obiang Nguema ordered him to receive 50 blows with a stick on the hindquarters. He remained Obiang Nguema's counsellor for security. The Popular Union rejected his candidacy.

On January 19, 1993, he was named president's counsellor for the Home Ministry, but he soon fell from grace. He was attacked by Moroccans under Armengol Nguema's orders, and has since been under house arrest in his native village. In the April 8, 1996, ministerial reshufle, he became general secretary in the Ministry of Education and Science. In August 1996, accused by Minister Mangue Mba Nfube of spying, he was transferred to the Ministry of Transport and Communications. The famous Nguemist Nvono Akele Avomo replaced him at education. In 1998, he became a professor at the University of Equatorial Guinea, after being a trainee for three months in the United States.

❖ F ❖

FANG (or Pahouin, Beti-Pahouin, Pangwe, Pamue). Bantu population which arrived in Río Muni after the Ndowe, in the 15th century. Today they cover most of Río Muni. Their legendary origin is central Cameroon. The theory of the Fang's arrival from the Upper Nile (where they are said to be related to the Azande) is no longer considered correct. The occupation of Río Muni went from northeast to southwest. The Utamboni Basin was not occupied until 1884, and the coastal invasion provoked heavy incidents with the Ndowe. These migrations were presumably due to military pressure by the Hawsa in central Cameroon. The total area of the Fang is about 180,000 sq km from the Sanaga (Cameroon) to the mouth of the Ogoowe (Gabon) and in some areas of Congo and the central African Republic.

The heart of Fang country is situated in the Gabonese Woleu Ntem. At the time of the Spanish occupation of Río Muni in 1926, the Elar-ayong movement was founded in Cameroon and rapidly spread to the entire Fang country. Its purpose was to unite the Fang in one nation. Today Fang country totals over 1.5 million people and extends from the southern part of Cameroon to the northern part of Gabon, including Río Muni.

The Fang are divided into two linguistic areas: Ntumu in the north of Río Benito, Okak in the south. Before the "Pax Hispanica," the various Fang clans were fighting one another.

Regarding their racial origin, the Fang seem to be of paleonegritic stock. They seem to have undergone a great deal of interbreeding with the Pygmies who preceded them in the forest zone. Each clan unit, named Ayong, is composed of

- Etunga-bot (descendance), the set of all the lineages descended from a common ancestor
- Ayom-bot (lineage), the union of several large families, which retain the name of the common ancestor
- Nvogo-bot (general family whose members are descended from a single grandmother), which is usually identical to the village, and which is headed by a chief (midja) and chatting cabin (abá)
- Ndá-bot (family in the strict sense)

Ancestors' experiences remain as legends. Secret trade associations still practice sorcery. The Fang were erroneously called cannibals even though Fang sorcery rules exclude cannibalism (actually it was necrophagy: parts of a dead body would be eaten in order to assimilate the qualities of the deceased). And because ancestors' skulls were kept at home, the missionaries considered them to be leftovers of cannibalistic feasts. Fang art is connected to magic beliefs. The main musical instrument is the mvett guitar. As currency, the Fang used spearheads, called bikuele (singular: ekule); this name was given in 1975 to the Equato-

Guinean monetary unit. A few Fang worked in Fernando Po in the beginning of the 20th century. Having returned to Río Muni in the thirties, they brought with them cocoa and coffee farming on individual plantations.

In order to favor the separation between Fernando Po and Río Muni, the Spanish authorities insisted on the alleged primitive character of the Fang, thus stimulating Bubi nationalism. However, the strong Fang supremacy doomed the project to failure and led to a unitarian state turning rapidly into a nepotic presidential dictatorship (favoritism shown to Macías Nguema's and Obiang Nguema's Esangui relatives).

See also *Historical Dictionary of Gabon,* David E. Gardinier, 1994, pp. 137–141; Oyono Sa Abegue, V.

FEDERACION ESPANOLA DE EMPRESSARIOS ESPANOLES EN GUINEA. Group of 80 Spanish firms with a turnover of 10,000 million pesetas in 1987. This amount represented 90% of the economic activities of Equatorial Guinea.

FEDERAL REPUBLIC OF GERMANY see Germany

FERNANDINOS. Creole community of Fernando Po, located mostly in Santa Isabel, San Carlos, and Concepción, formed by descendants of Liberians, Sierra Leonians, Nigerians and liberated slaves. The Fernandino community has been favored by Spain and constituted the African high society (somewhat like the Creoles of Freetown). Formerly large landowners, the Fernandinos have more and more taken to independent professions. Presently they must number about 3,500. A Fernandino, W. Jones Niger, became the first elected mayor of Santa Isabel from 1960 to 1964. Simultaneously, another Fernandino, Cabrera y James, was a member of the San Fernando local government. In view of the Constitutional Conference, the Unión Democrática Fernandina was created. The Fernandinos were represented at the Constitutional Conference in Madrid (1967–1968) by Grange Molay and Medira Role. Grange Molay joined Macías Nguema's Secretariado Conjunto, which led him to become minister of agriculture in October 1968, then minister of education in 1972 after Eñeso Neñe's assassination. The Fernandino community, being very educated, was one of the favorite targets of Macías Nguema's personal power. In 1975, the Fernandino Okori Dougan Kinson became minister of justice, after the assassination of the Bubi Momo Bokara.

See also Balboa Bonek, J.; Dougan; Dougan, J.; Dougan Beaca, J. D.; Jones Dougan, J. L.; Mokudi Nanga, A.; Popular Union; Seriche Dougan, A.S.

FERNANDO PO (spelled also Fernando Poo). Rectangular island of the Biafra Bay, situated 32 km from Mount Cameroon, covering 2,018 sq km (810 sq mi), at an average altitude of 500 m. Formed by a succession of volcanic cones, with the Pico de Basilé (3,007 m) in the north and a composite southern range with the Pico de Moka (2,260 m) and the Big Caldera of San Carlos in the south. The coastline is rugged and abrupt. Seventy-five out of 105 plant species are endemic. Two central notches harbor the towns of San Carlos and Concepción. Up to 800 m high, the island is covered with forests, widely reclaimed for plantations. At about 1,000 to 1,500 m pastures appear where aralia and araborescent ferns dominate. In 1973 the PUNT proposed to call the island Macías Nguema. In Victoria (today called Limbe, Cameroon), Fernando Po is called "Dikambo."

Fernando Po was discovered about 1471–1472 by Portuguese sailors making business on behalf of the king of Portugal with Gómez de Minha on the Guinean coast, south of Sierra Leone. Tradition has it that the island was discovered by Fernão da Po ("Po" means dust in Portuguese), about whom we know little. The island was first named Ilha Formosa (Beautiful Island). In 1505 Mount Cameroon was called Sierra de Fernão Po and the end of the 16th century, the Wouri estuary (Cameroon) had the same name. Describing his trip to the Congo, Pigafetta indicates that the island in front of the Wouri estuary bears also the name of Fernão Po. In 1777, the Portuguese governor of Fernando Po and Annobón, João Manuel da Azambuja, had his residence in Dahomey.

Since the end of the 15th century, Fernando Po has belonged to the commercial sphere of São Tomé. At the beginning of the 16th century, Ramos de Esquivel established a warehouse and plantations in Concepción. The Bubi were highly irritated by the slave trade and strongly resisted all attempts to occupy the island. In 1787 Fernando Po and the coasts of the Gulf of Guinea were given to Spain by Portugal (see Pardo Treaty). But yellow fever seems to have prevented the occupation of the island for a long time. During the first half of the 19th century, trading posts started to appear all over the coast, prospecting for palm oil. After several unfruitful attempts by the British navy to take foot on the island, the Owen expedition in 1827 founded Clarence City (Santa Isabel), and with the pretense of fighting the slave trade, established warehouses and a school. Beecroft, who was to become governor of the island in 1840, arrived with this expedition. Under his government took place the British explorations of the Niger Delta, the occupation of Lagos, and the progressive occupation of the Cameroon coasts, all lands "legally" belonging to Spain. The project of selling Fernando Po to the United Kingdom in 1841 was rejected by the Cortes due to strong opposition of Spanish public opinion. In 1843 the Lerena expedition was sent to take official possession of the island on behalf of Spain, but for lack of men, Beecroft was confirmed as governor of the island. It is only with the arrival of Chacón, in 1858, four years after Beecroft's death, that the administration of the island became Spanish. From that time on the first cocoa, coffee, and tobacco plantations appeared, in part stimulated by the Cuban exiles. At the same time the first Fernandino dynasties started to prosper. It is with the arrival of the first Claretian missionaries in 1883 that large-scale plantations were started in spite of the hostility of the Bubi working in the European concessions. Thus large estates developed: in 1944 a few hundred Fernandinos and Spaniards owned 36,628 hectares (approx. 91,500 acres) compared to more than 3,000 African planters sharing 14,826 hectares. After using first Fang and Cameroonese workers on the plantations, Liberians and Nigerians were imported. At the time of independence, there were 40,000 unskilled Nigerian workers in Fernando Po, the majority of whom were English speaking and Protestant. About 2.3% of the planters exploited 53% of the 67,000 hectares (approx. 168,500 acres) of developed land.

In the beginning of the 20th century, the foremost trading houses established on the island were: Jerónimo López e Hijo, Antonio Pérez, Lisboa Cunha de Brussaca, John Holt & Co, Ambas Bay, E. H. Moritz, F. Wilson, Manuel Balboa,

Barleycorn, Kinson, Capmany, Prince, Remer, Lolin, Moreno Mora y Co, Roig Piñeiro, Jones, Collins, Antonio Fernández y Ca, Monteiro y Vila, Rius y Torres, Sucesor de Casajuana, Casa y Rodríguez, Sebastián Muñoz, Trasatlátlantica, etc. During the First World War, Fernando Po was the scene of Anglo-German rivalry. The governor of the colony, Barrera, showed a distinct preference for the Germans. British protests in Spain led to his removal in 1918.

At the time of the Constitutional Conference in 1967–1968, the Bubi Unión advocated the separation of the island from the Río Muni province at independence, supported by Carrero Blanco. But the unionist idea succeeded. Despite the great number of Fang in Santa Isabel after independence, the island was almost depopulated early in 1976 with the repatriation of 25,000 of the 45,000 Nigerians after various incidents. In order to save the plantations of Fernando Po, a presidential decree introduced forced labor for 2,000 to 2,500 persons of each district of the country. Almost all traffic has been forbidden on the island since 1976; access to beaches is prohibited or subject to fees. In San Carlos the USSR was building a fishing harbor (in fact, a Soviet naval base).

The Nigerian involvement with Fernando Po seems to be an inheritance of British imperialism. In 1976, the Nigerian press wondered: "Must we annex Equatorial Guinea?"

After the 1979 coup, the military junta renamed the island Bioko. In 1980 the island was divided into two administrative regions, Fernando Po North, that included the capital Santa Isabel, and Fernando Po South, which included the districts of Baney and Concepción (Riaba) as well as San Carlos, which was made the capital of this southern part. Since late 1979, the dictator Obiang Nguema resides in the palace at Santa Isabel, protected by the presidential guard of 600 Moroccan soldiers.

The arrival in 1988 of five South Africans in Equatorial Guinea made Lagos express its anxiety, and to bring the matter up even before the UN. A press campaign reiterated Nigerian claims to Fernando Po. This state of tension led to a general mobilization in Equatorial Guinea. In 1996, the Nguemist's control over the island was effected mainly through more than 200 roadblocks.

See also Aviation; Balacha; Baney; Benin; Bubi; Cocoa, Convergency for Social Democracy; "Democratic" Party of Equatorial Guinea; Ela Owono, F.; Elections; Electricity; Eriana Popular Union; Esono Masie, P.; Evinayong; Fisheries; France; Equatorial Guinea Liberation Front; Germany; International Bank for Reconstruction and Development; Jesuits; Joint Opposition Platform; Justice; Micha Nsue Nfumu, J.; Missions; Moka; Movement for the Autonomy; Musola, Ndong Mba, Z.; Ndong Ona, A.; Nigeria; Norway; Nve Nguema, E.; Organization of Petrol Exporting Countries; Oyono Nsue, L.; Oyo Riqueza, E.; Petroleum; Portugal; Public Health; Sacriba; Sampaka; San Carlos; Segesa; South Africa; Spain; Sports; Timber; Torture; Trade; United Kingdom; Vaz Serra; Village Cooperatives; Walter Int.

FINANCE. Equatorial Guinea's debts reached 246.4 million dollars in 1992. The GNP reached $148.9 million, which is about $430 per capita/year. The IMF and the Nguemists signed a Structural Adjustment Program agreement in February 1993, for the period ending 1996, and for a sum of 412.88 million. In the December 22 government, Anatolio Ndong Mba became vice prime minister, minister for the economy and finance. The budget deficit for 1993 was 8.2% of the GDP, while a surplus of 1.1% had been expected. The per capita debt was the highest in the world.

An economic policy program was signed with the IMF for $134 million in January 1994, supported by the IMF's approval in May of a Structural Adjustment Program. The 1994 budget for CFAFr 29.4 billion against 13.2 billion in 1993, was adopted in March. Income was estimated to be 15.6 billion and the budget deficit 14 billion. In May, Obiang Nguema argued in favor of the adjustment agreements in a television and radio speech. The $134 million was used to finance deficits in current accounts (18 million), for the amortization of the debt (42 million), the settlement of overdue external debts (46 million), the increase in external reserves (25 million). The monetary mass went up, between 1991 and 1994 from CFAFr 2,659 million to CFAFr 7,756 million. The balance of payments for 1994 showed a deficit of CFAFr 11 billion, against a surplus of 0.2 billion in 1993. The objectives for 1993–1995 failed due to a fall in the prices of raw materials and an internal economic crisis that Obiang Nguema blamed on political liberalization.

In the January 8, 1996, ministerial reshuffle, Anatolio Ndong Mba became vice-prime minister and minister of finance, with Baltasar Engonga Edjo as minister with special responsibilities. The country's revenues were ensured mainly by petroleum (more than half) and wood (more than a third). In the April 8, 1996, government, the Ministry of Economy and Finance fell to the hands of Marcelino Oyono Ntutumu, with Baltasar Engonga Edjo as minister with special responsibilities. The Structural Adjustment Program of Equatorial Guinea was described by experts to be a serious failure. The Nguemist government has created a Center for Promotion of Investments to encourage private investments.

AIMF Mission (spring 1996) complained of "total absence of transparency" in government accounting. Another IMF mission, in August, claimed that the Nguemist government showed no interest in the good management of public affairs. According to the UNDP 1996 Report foreign debt is one of the biggest obstacles to development; "it represents a real economic crisis."

The total external debt was the following, according to the IMF:

External Debt (Mio US $)

1990	211.2	1994	261.1
1991	225.5	1995	233.0
1992	221.2	1996	254.4
1993	249.1		

The external debt was the following:

A: Main Bilateral Creditors (Mio US $)

	1992	1993	1994	1995	1996
Spain	60.1	53.3	57.4	41.9	49.2
China	22.7	22.1	23.0	25.2	22.7
(Popular)					
Italy	12.7	13.1	13.7	12.5	15.5
Argentina	6.6	9.1	9.5	10.5	14.3
USSR	5.4	9.1	10.3	5.1	9.8
France	14.4	17.8	18.9	5.6	9.6
Others	4.5	5.1	3.9	4.5	4.2

B: Multilateral (Mio US $)

	1992	1993	1994	1995	1996
IMF	12.7	16.4	19.6	18.5	17.2
ADB		35.6	36.5	38.6	33.3
AIF		47.6	49.4	51.3	51.5
Others		18.3	18.2	18.4	22.2

In 1997, oil represented 58% of the GNP.

In the January 21, 1998, Government, B. Engonga Edjo was minister of economic affairs and finance; M. Abia Biteo was minister delegate.

The 1996–98 document on strategy of the BAD, concerning Equatorial Guinea, observed in January 1998 that "since the failure of the facility for structural adjustment on December 1995, the country still lacks a program of reforms accepted by the international community. The internal and external unbalances of the Equato-Guinean economy still exist."

Fiscal year: April 1–March 31.

See also Banks; Eka Nguema, P.; Economy; Ndong Mba, A.; Petroleum.

FINCAS RUSTICAS (Agricultural estates). In 1985, the Nguemists appropriated around 10 of these big properties, in bikwele, belonging to Spanish families.

FISHERIES. Before independence around 5,000 persons lived on fishing, mainly operating with 10- to 55-ton boats and a crew of 10 to 20. Coastal fishing included tunny, sole, shrimp, lobsters, etc. The seafood was canned in Santa Isabel. To feed the agricultural workers the country imported large quantities of dried cod; this caused the country to become the highest fish consumer of the area (4.7 kg per capita in 1967).

After independence, fishing remained to a large extent in the hands of Spanish companies; AFRIPESCA and Coimpex own huge cold storage warehouses. Macías Nguema having removed almost all pirogues (to prevent escaping abroad), the major part of the fishing in Equatorial Guinean waters was done by the Soviet Union. The Soviets supplied Guinea with ordinary fish and sent the frozen shellfish to the USSR. A fishery project was being carried out in San Carlos by the Russians; however, it was suspected to be of a military nature.

In the 19th century whales could be found as far as the Muni estuary and near Fernando Po and Annobón. The Annobónese were hunting them with self-made harpoons fixed to their small pirogues. Two industrial fishing companies have been established in Gabon and São Tomé e Príncipe. Fish production for 1971–1973 amounted to approximately 4,000 tons. In May 1987 the Committee set about establishing a common fisheries policy for the central African States with a view to becoming self-sufficient. The project funding amounts to 86 million French francs, of which two-thirds have been provided by the European community. Most of its offices will be located in Gabon.

The fishing accord signed with the USSR and broken in 1979 expired in 1980. The Spanish company Afripesca reconstructed its warehouses in 1980. The company Ebana also developed fish-refrigeration installations. The January agreement with the IMF called on the government to stimulate internal production including fisheries. Agreements were signed with Spain for the provision of materials and supervisors. In 1981, fishing agreements were signed with Argentina and Nigeria.

The Nguemists forbade tuna fishing in Equato-Guinean waters, especially by French boats. During Obiang Nguema's official visit to France from September 20–26, an agreement was signed, allowing French boats to operate around Fernando Po. A new prohibition of French tuna boats in the territorial waters of Annobón became effective in August 1982. The Nguemists set the limit of territorial waters at 200 nautical miles. France demanded EC intervention. The press alleged subhuman working conditions for the African personnel of the Spanish company Pescaven. The regulations concerning fishing off Equatorial Guinea signed with the EC was published towards the end of September 1983. The Spanish company Pescanova Ltd. was established in 1884.

Fishing resources were estimated in 1986 to be 11.7% for traditional fishing and 88.3% for industrial fishing. The World Bank complained that EC fisheries were not paying enough for their catch. In June 1989 a three-year agreement was signed with the EC, fixing the permissible quantity of fishing at 9,000 tons/month (tuna, seafood), with 30 licenses. The United States donated the patrol boat *Isla de Bioco* to eject erring fishing boats from the territorial waters (more probably to monitor the fleeing and returning refugees).

In October 1990, the Ministry of Agriculture, Animal Husbandry, Fisheries and Forests was given to A. Ndong Mba. The FAO granted CFAFr 160 million for a nonindustrial fishing project. The catch of French and Spanish boats in Equato-Guinean waters went up in 1989–90 from 3,542 to 4,851 tons, of which 45% was shellfish and other seafood. Nonindustrial fishing accounted for about 150 tons. In 1991, Nigeria managed to have its authorization renewed to fish in Equato-Guinean waters. In the "transitional" government of January 24, Oyono Ndongo Mifumu became vice-prime minister and minister for animal husbandry and fisheries. In 1991, the continental fishing catch increased to 400 tons. During 1992, the deep waters of the territory were opened to Poland, in exchange for naval construction, with unlimited tuna-, crayfish-, and prawn-fishing rights.

In the December 22, 1993, government, A. Mokudi Nanga became the minister for agriculture, fisheries and food. On June 29, 1995, the European Union signed a new agreement on fishing and financial compensation valid from July 1, 1994, to June 30, 1997. A joint enterprise, the Empresa Nacional de Pesca de Guinea Ecuatorial (ENPGE—National Fishing Co), composed wholly of important members of the Nguemist regime, enjoyed fiscal and customs exemptions. Anatolio Ndong Mba was the minister of state for fisheries and forestry in the April 8, 1996, government.

On June 27, 1997, the fishing agreement with the European Union was renewed for three years. It authorized 68 tuna boats to fish in the territorial waters until June 30, 2000, thus allowing a 45% increase of fishing potential. In return, the EU granted, for three years, 960,000 ecus for the control of fishing activities and to support small fishermen.

See also African Development Bank; Agriculture; Alogo Nchama, A.; Annobón; Ebendeng Nsomo, M.; Ela Nguema, P.; European Union; Government of National Unity; Italy; Japan; Mafia; Mangue, R.; Mba Ndemensogo, D.; Mbomio, L.; Micha Nguema Eyang, M.; Mikomeseng; Mokudi Nanga, A.; Navigation; Ndong Mba, A.; Nguema Onguene, M.; Nvono Nka Manene, C.; Obiang Nguema, T.; Ondo Nguema, A.; Oyono Ndong Mifumu, M.; Poland; Presidency; Russia; Siale Bilekia, S.; United States of America; World Council of Churches.

FLAG OF CONVENIENCE see Navigation

FOGUISA see Timber

FONTAN Y LOBE, Juan, 1899–1944. Spanish navy captain, entrusted with repressing the Popular Front in Bata in September 1936. From September 1937 to August 1941 he was gobernador general. From 1941 to his death in 1944 he headed the Dirección General de Marruecos y Colonias. Among his publications, an important African bibliography deserves special mention.

FOREIGN AFFAIRS see Asangons Efue, T.; Diplomacy; Drugs; Nguema Esono Nchama; Ndongo Miyone; Oyono Ndong Mifumu, M.; Gori Molubuela; United Nations

FOREIGN ASSISTANCE. Most of the assistance was given in 1994–1997 by the following (represented in 000 US $):

	1994	1995	1996	1997
Multilateral				
UN Agencies	5.612	6.985	2.890	3.356
European Union	2.011	.737	6.143	7.312
Bilateral				
Spain	6.572	7.750	9.825	6.223
France	9.697	8.683	9.059	2.597

	1994	1995	1996	1997
China				
(Popular)	.699	.774	.598	.719
Japan	—	.15	—	—
Nigeria	1.205	1.827	.35	—
United States	—	.16	—	—
NGO				
World Council				
of Churches	.20	.22	—	—

FOREST, FORESTRY see Timber

FORESTRY INSTITUTE see Instituto Forestal

FORMOSA. Name given in 1471–1472 to the island of Fernando Po (Isla Formosa meaning "Beautiful Island") as well as to the left bank of the Niger mouth (Num and Akasa arms), considered as Spanish in 1875 during the last trip of Pellón y Rodríguez.

FORSYTH, Frederick. British reporter and novelist, established in Dublin. He was reporting for the BBC in Biafra. In 1974 he published *The Dogs of War,* in which he related Fernando Po's occupation by a group of mercenaries. According to the British press, Forsyth, upon his return to Europe in 1970, seems to actually have prepared an attempt to overthrow Macías Nguema and to occupy the island by mercenaries, with British citizen Alex Gay, a former mercenary in Congo (Zaïre) and Biafra, as adviser. With a visa obtained in Yaoundé, Gay made a reconnoitering trip to Santa Isabel, financed by Forsyth, in order to locate possible places for disembarkation.

According to Gay, 12 determined mercenaries and about 50 former Biafran soldiers would be sufficient to control the island. The operation was supposed to cost £50,000. Gay contacted a weapons dealer in Hamburg, who agreed to deliver the goods in Spain (provided with an export license delivered by a Spanish Defense Ministry official and an import certificate for Iraq). Gay then hired 14 mercenaries: nine Frenchmen, one Belgian, one Hungarian (Al Varga), and three British (Scott Sanderson, Ronald Gorman, and Alan Murphy) at a monthly salary of $1,200. A converted fishing boat, the *Albatros,* was rented in Spain (in Fuengirola, near Marbella) from a British expatriate, George Allen, for "oil prospecting." The mercenaries arrived in southern Spain in October 1972. But, in December, the Spanish official refused to deliver the export license for the weapons (the German dealer, however, kept the DM 120,000 despite a trip by Gay to Hamburg). In the meantime the *Albatros,* with three inflatable motorboats aboard, plus food reserves and leopard uniforms, had sailed to Malaga and then to Gibraltar; Gay, who joined them in the Canary Islands (Lanzarote), had to suspend the expedition. But the Spanish authorities arrested and repatriated the group.

According to A. Murphy's written confession, after a stop in the Cape Verde Islands, the group would have picked up 50 Biafran soldiers in Cotonou (Benin), then disembarked overnight in Santa Isabel to occupy first the presidential palace and the Soviet Embassy. In Forsyth's novel, a former Biafran general would be substituted for Macías Nguema. The British *Sunday Times* put forward the name of Chukwuemeka Odumegwu Ojukwu, who denied the information.

Forsyth figures as Shannon in his own novel, with Bosio Dioco as Sir James Manson, the coup's financier. Upon his departure from Santa Isabel in 1973, Forsyth had to submit to the confiscation of his notes; they are said to be held in the Archives of the Ministry for the Interior. See also Carrero Blanco, L.

FORUM FOR DEMOCRACY IN GUINEA (Foro para la Democrácia de Guinea) see Elema Borengue, Joaquin.

FRANCE. After the first Spanish Civil War of 1840–1841, which left the country considerably weakened, Spain abandoned the policing of the ocean off Lower Guinea to France, then favored the establishment of a coal deposit in Fernando Po for the supply of French steamers. The London Treaty of 1845 admitted the establishment of France in the Libreville area. During the second half of the 19th century France started to claim the territories of Río Muni, Corisco and Elobeyes. During the Berlin Conference, Spain could only rescue 180,000 sq km of its initial 800,000 sq km granted under the Pardo Treaty. But France ignored the settlement and agreed with Germany, in 1885, that the River Campo would be the limit between their two territories (Gabon and Cameroon), which amounted to Spain's actual eviction from the continent.

In 1885, the French Libermanian missionaries were established in Sipolo, at the mouth of the Río Benito, with a military post under protection of Senegalese soldiers. They controlled traffic down the river and acted as a counterbalance to the Presbyterian mission of Bolondo. France then extended its territory towards Bata. An 1886 Paris Conference called after Spain's protest and then the Danish King's arbitration starting in 1892 did not settle the dispute. The collapse of the Spanish Empire in 1898 enabled France to take advantage of the situation, and after the Paris Treaty in 1900—and the determination of the Río Muni frontiers in 1901—Spain had only 26,000 sq km of continental territories left. France withdrew its military detachments from Campo, Bata, and Río Benito. But as late as 1900, a French official ordered the burning of the village of Bolondo in view of its inhabitants' refusal to pay taxes to France.

During the 19th century, and until today, the people of Río Muni and Northern Gabon call the French "Falas": cheaters (from the Fang: Fulasi)

Article VII of the Paris Treaty grants France priority in case of total or partial assignment of the Spanish possession. At the beginning of the 20th century two French companies, Société du Haut-Ogooué Société Agricole de Bata, were based in Bata. Since 1906 French missionaries of the Holy Spirit were teaching in Bata (financed by the French Naval Ministry), and left Río Muni only after the First World War. As Spain had, for Fernando Po, France was accused by the League of Nations, in 1930, of recruiting Liberian forced workers for Gabon.

Since 1968, France has been represented in Santa Isabel by nine ambassadors. In 1973, France sent two professors for the secondary level. President Pompidou decided to assist Equatorial Guinea in order to offset Eastern-bloc influence, without however taking the severe interior disorders into consideration. In fact,

France was looking for new markets and trying to monopolize timber exploitation as it did in neighboring Gabon. It granted a $43 million loan to Equatorial Guinea for the building of prestige works to be carried out by the Société Française des Dragages et des Travaux Publics, well introduced in all of French-speaking Africa (having done such jobs as Bata harbor, without any freight to handle, the presidential palace near Bata, the Central Banks in Bata and Santa Isabel, and since 1975 the superstructures of the Bata harbor). As a security for the loan, and upon García Trevijano's intervention, France received forest concessions of 150,000 hectares for the French Société Forestière du Río Muni, which intended to export 1.5 million tons of okoumea and other woods within 10 years. Forestry comes under the direct supervision of the presidency. Acting through S. Chouraki, García Trevijano's secretary, the Sociedad Forestal of J. P. Nouveau was sold to another French timber company, Tardiba, in 1976. In 1975 during the most repressive phase of the Macías Nguema regime the French Cultural Center was opened in Santa Isabel. At the end of 1976, the Chantiers de Bretagne and Alsthom companies tried to obtain the order for a hydrocarbon pumping station in Bata. The French national petroleum company ELF is considering prospecting in Río Muni. After having sold a helicopter to Equatorial Guinea, France lent a pilot and a mechanic to train local personnel from 1972 to 1974. But the candidates having been chosen among the least qualified of the president's circle, France refused to give them a certificate. The French helicopter, destroyed in 1976, has been replaced by two others from the Soviet Union.

In 1975 the Equatorial Guinean ambassador at the United Nations, Ecua Miko, raised a protest against so-called atrocities committed by France in Mayotte (Comores). Since 1976, France is the only Western European country to maintain full diplomatic and economic relations with Equatorial Guinea. The December 1978 issue of *Le Monde Diplomatique* calls Equatorial Guinea a French "zone garde."

After Obiang Nguema's coup d'etat in August 1979, Julian Esono Abaga Ada became the ambassador to France. That is when French Cooperation starts, becoming operational in 1985, after the country had joined the "franc zone." Subsequently France tried to bring the country into its sphere of influence. Experienced French ambassadors posted to Santa Isabel together with various trips to Paris and the provinces by Obiang Nguema resulted in France gradually being granted fishing rights, petroleum and mining prospecting rights, and so forth. In 1982 a second French cultural center was opened in Bata. On July 9, Guy Penne, counsellor to President Mitterrand for African affairs, visited Santa Isabel, accompanied by the journalist Christophe Mitterrand. In May 1983 the negotiations for Equatorial Guinea's entry into the Bank of the Central African States (BEAC) were begun and in December 1973 the country was admitted to the Customs Union of the Central African States (UDEAC). Also at this time a consortium consisting of the French ELF-Aquitaine and the Italian Agip groups and American oil companies was created.

Effective January 1, 1985, the Equatorial-Guinean currency, the Ekwele, was replaced by the CFA franc, signaling the absorption of the country into the French currency zone. French shipping companies, forestry industries, as well as French banks and insurance companies opened branches in the country. In 1985 a section of the French press put out misleading information to the effect that Equatorial Guinea was a democracy.

On June 4, 1985, Obiang Nguema, in the course of an official visit to France, was received by President Mitterrand. At that time there were 83 Frenchmen living in Equatorial Guinea, including 20 advisers. The French newspaper *Le Monde* spoke of a "relative respect" of human rights in Equatorial Guinea. In 1985 France spent about US$1 million for Equatorial Guinea's access to the franc monetary zone and is providing around US $120,000 annually in aid. Shortly after Obiang Nguema's visit to Paris, the Club of Paris rescheduled the country's debt. There was a progressive increase in the number of French companies opening up in the country. Among these were Delmas-Vieljeux (shipping), Moulins de Paris (food and agriculture), and the International Bank of West Africa (BIAO).

In March 1987 there were reports in the Spanish press that France intended that Equatorial Guinea should be absorbed by Gabon or the Cameroon, along the lines of the Senegalese operation in Gambia. Shortly after this, France decorated Leandro Mbomio Nsué as commander of the Order of Arts and Letters. In April, the French society Pullman started to manage the hotels Ureka (Santa Isabel) and Panafrica (Bata) with a 24 million FFr ($4 million) capital for 15 years. The "Caisse Centrale de Coopération Economique" (CCCE) offered a loan of 16 million FF ($2.5 million) for the Concepción power station and 43 million FF ($7 million) to improve the telecommunication network. During Obiang Nguema's participation in the Franco-African Conference in Nice in December 1987, four ministers were arrested by Eyi Mensui Andeme.

In January 1988, France sponsored Equatorial Guinea to the European Development Fund. A joint business firm was founded for the distribution of electricity to Fernando Po. The capital's airport was put into French hands. Obiang Nguema insisted on government officials learning French in order to communicate with the UDEAC, but this fell in the face of popular opposition. Under an agreement for military technical cooperation, France proceeded to reorganize the national police, training of officials, provision of equipment, and created a motorized infantry company and a police academy. The company Getcsa (Guinée-France Cables) was in charge of running the telecommunications center at Bata. The FAC 3rd Convention for FFr 10.9 million dealt with rural development and health in Niefang, the electrical network at Fernando Po, and the airline EGA. The CCCE lent $2.5 million until 1988 for the rehabilitation of the fuel depots of Fernando Po ($3.3 million), with the sum being paid by TOTAL-Equatorial Guinea. In 1988 French aid reached $18 million. France was represented by Edwige Avice, special minister under the minister for foreign affairs, at the 20th anniversary of independence. This rapprochement was called a "choice for friendship."

A convention for budgetary aid of FFr 2.1 million for the EGA company was signed in January 1989. During a visit by Obiang Nguema to Madrid, an agreement was reached to allow Spain to return to its number one position for cooperation, leading to a reduction in contribution from France. The Ministry of National Education decided to introduce French as a compulsory course, in order to promote bilingualism. France offered 5,000 textbooks. Jacques Gazon was named the new ambassador. In December a loan of $2.7 million was given for the modernization of TOTAL-Equatorial-Guinea's installations. The economist Marcos Manuel

Ndongo published a highly critical article about the monetary zone of the franc as well as the FCFA and recommended the intensification of relations with Spain.

In early 1990, the CCCE granted a loan of FCFA 760 million for the rehabilitation of petroleum deposits and the distribution network to Fernando Po and Río Muni, with the help of TOTAL-Africa. The creation of 500 hectares of coffee plantations and vegetable crops was considered. Other French projects included a Cultural Institute for French with 380 students, a French school for 24 pupils, a news bulletin in French on national radio, and a new embassy. French nationals numbered about 150. During the summer, France modified its attitude and demanded democratization. Paris decided to be satisfied with the second place in Equatorial Guinea, and wished to avoid disputes with Madrid. It granted FCFAFr 300 million in budgetary aid. The French mission for cooperation was then being led by Jean-Claude Euxibie. In the autumn the ambassador to France, Jesus Ela Abeme, was arrested for heroin trafficking. He was replaced by Pedro Edjang Mba. Equatorial Guinea received FFr 21.5 million for a company for the exploitation and running of the public electricity service in Fernando Po and for hydroelectric installations in Concepción (Riaba). The trade balance for 1990 indicated a positive figure of FFr 49.9 million in favor of France.

In early 1990, a judge of the Supreme Court of Spain spoke of French "cultural aggression," which he compared to that of the U.S. in the Philippines. In 1990–1991, France was the largest importer of Equatorial Guinean products, especially pearls and precious stones for FFr 9.5 million, which was apparently smuggled goods. However, Franco-Equato-Guinean trade diminished. Towards the end of 1991, France's positive trade balance only amounted to FFr 15.7 million in 1991 (-43.8%).

In 1992, the Presidential Security Forces were being trained by members of the French cooperation. An agreement for financial aid was signed in November: FFr 5.2 million for the customs brigades. France offered FFr 2.3 million on the occasion of the UDEAC summit at Bata, with vehicles, equipment, and training for local personnel. TOTAL-GE "offered" Dom Perignon champagne and whisky, in return for a deduction of FCFAFr 10 million in taxes. France, Spain, the U.S., the EC, and the UN demanded that human rights violations in the country cease. Opposition activists were chased by the Criminal Investigation Department in Renault vehicles offered by France.

In early 1993, the French Association Diby-Affouse France-Afrique offered the Comité de Apoyo al Niño Guineano (Committee to support Guinean children) presided by Obiang Nguema's first wife FCFAFr 25 million; this followed an earlier gift in 1992. A French volunteer for cooperation, André Branger (who was preparing a book on the Nguemists) was assassinated in the capital in February. France contributed to the formation of a militia of Mongomo youth armed to the teeth, the Jovenes Antorchas (Young Torches), as well as a political police force made up of the Ninjas, with Marcel Moreau and René Rodriguez as trainers. These Ninjas wear uniforms provided by Paris. In May, Spain, the United States, France, Maroc, EC, and UNDP, the sponsors of the electoral campaign, demanded political guarantees, but the Nguemists interrupted the discussions; France was then alone in offering FCFAFr 25 million plus a new prison van. In Madrid, the French Minister for Foreign Affairs Alain Juppé stated that "to his knowledge," there was no French military collaboration with Equatorial Guinea. ASECNA installed a jamming station to block out the Spanish broadcasts for Equatorial Guinea. In November, the seven parties participating in the elections, including the PDGE, asked the embassy of France for a funding of 75 million pesetas. France followed the example of the United States and Spain, in refusing to send observers for the November 21 elections. On the occasion of the Franco-Spanish summit, the two delegations denounced the conditions in which the polling was organized, which deprived the elections of a truly pluralistic nature.

A Franco-Spanish meeting of high officials was held in March 1994 in order to coordinate the services of the two countries. France annually contributed about 1,000 million pesetas in aid. In April, it offered FFr 3 million for the teaching of French in secondary schools, the training of teachers and adults; it brought in an added FCFAFr 200 million for the rehabilitation of housing in the capital, the water distribution network, and the construction of public fountains in the capital. The Bata hospital received FFr 5 million. In July 1994, Equatorial Guinea participated, around Paris, in the Second Francophone Games.

The 1994 Report of the Geopolitical Drug Observatory (Paris) indicated that it seemed that "the trafficking President [Obiang Nguema] continued to enjoy the support of France." In June, Obiang Nguema congratulated President Mitterrand for sending troops to Rwanda. Poverty was mounting, with the weakening of the FCFAFr in mid-1994. The Ninjas were supported in 1994 by three representatives of the service for international technical cooperation of the French police (SCTIP). The resentment of the population towards France grew. In July, the French development fund offered FCFAFr 55 million for telecommunications: 22 million as funding for the state and a loan of 33 million for the renovation of the national network and international dialing. In August, a little before his departure, Ambassador Jacques Gazon, was decorated with the Medal of the Great Cross of the Order of Independence, during an interview with Obiang Nguema. On this occasion, he stated his support for the policy of the dictator. He was succeeded by Gérard Brunet de Coursou, formerly posted at Abidjan. Towards the end of 1994, the French volunteer for cooperation Dr. Abdoulaye Keita registered a complaint for three attempts at poisoning him following his denunciation of financial irregularities in the Bata hospital when he succeeded Dr. Gérard Desgranges, who had died in August 1993 of a strange "cardiac arrest." In the capital and at Bata, there are two Cultural Institutes of French Expression with libraries (books, magazines), which also circulate news items from the official television of France, and screen one film per week. At Malabo six technical assistants are allotted to the Ministry of Finance; in Bata two technical assistants work for Financial Planning and for the Customs. All of them seem idle. There are also two French gendarmes for the training of gendarmes, in Bata, and one official from the International Technical Cooperation Service of the French Police allocated to the main police station. Two delegates of Pharmaciens sans Frontières (Chemists without Borders), financed by the Ministry for Cooperation, have been trying since 1994 to establish a pharmaceutical depot and a distribution center, in order to counter generalized corruption and theft of equipment, but in vain. The project for centers for the teaching of French to adults in Ebebiyin, Mongomo, and Niefang also remained suspended. In 1994, four French Mirage aircraft, probably brought in from Gabon, made an unauthorized demonstration of force and flew at a very low altitude. France is the fourth supplier to Equatorial Guinea (9% of imports) and the fifth buyer (8%).

In April 1995, the French Foreign Office summoned the ambassador of Equatorial Guinea, to indicate to him the cancellation of aid for the elections if Moto Nsá remained in prison. Anatolio Ndong Mbá represented Equatorial Guinea at the meeting of Francophone countries in Paris, where he made anti-Spanish accusations. In May, the *Monde Diplomatique* published a letter from two French volunteers for cooperation which denounced human rights violations by "the crazed dictatorship of General Teodoro Obiang" and demanded international pressure. In spite of being well paid, a number of them resigned or asked to be transferred, following harassment, or even physical abuse, as in the case of a volunteer of the National Service, Françoise Vaidie, who was violently slapped in June 1995 in the central police station of Bata; she had already been molested in her home in January. In late July, President Chirac, during his visit to various African countries, extracted a promise from Obiang Nguema, who got himself called at the last minute to Libreville (Gabon), to grant pardon to Moto Nsá. On August 2, Obiang Nguema released about 30 political prisoners, including Moto Nsá. In the minds of a majority of Equato-Guineans, France, Ninjas, and terror are associated as one and the same idea. To this still highly Hispanic population, opposing the dictatorship also means opposing France. In early November 1995, Obiang Nguema again visited France to look for new investors. On November 16, Radio France International's 24-hour relay began, with one hour daily in Spanish, at 11:00 P.M.

But the 1995 Prouteau Report by the president of the Council of French investors in Africa warned that the balance of the zone franc was negative in Equatorial Guinea. At the 9th Franco-Spanish summit in October, Paris and Madrid expressed their "disappointment at the manner in which the Equato-Guinean government had organized the counting of the votes and the announcements of the results" of the municipal elections. France however continued with its military aid to the Nguemists:

Military	**Posts**
1994	4
1995	4
1996	4
1997	4
1998	4
Civilians	
1993	2
1994	2
1998	24 (9 teachers, 15 technicians)

In 1995 France occupied the number three position among the suppliers of Equatorial Guinea ($11 million), but occupied an insignificant place among its buyers.

In the January 8, 1996, ministerial reshuffle, Agustin Nze Nfumu became the minister for culture and the French language. During the presidential elections in February 1996, the chief commissioner of police in the capital, Julkian Ondo Nkumu, along with several henchmen, burst into the Pedagogical Bureau of the French volunteers for cooperation (in a building belonging to Constancia Mangue, the wife of the dictator) and arrested the mayor of the capital, V. Bolekia, and his deputies, during a French lesson given by the volunteer Jacques Ganvril. These men were beaten all night until they bled. The embassy of France expressed its indignation. The Catalan daily *Diari Avui* stated that after the "reelection" of Obiang Nguema, President Chirac lost no time in addressing his congratulations to the Nguemist dictator.

It was Pedro-Cristino Bueribueri who occupied the post of minister for culture, tourism and the French language in the government of April 8, 1996. In 1996, the head of the French cooperation mission was Jean Baptiste Fournier. The main projects included the training of French teachers, the building of a cultural center in Bata, the partial renovation of Bata's hospital, the building of schools, the improvement of the roads in Bata and Santa Isabel, the training of the police, the training and equipment of the Gendarmerie, the Ninjas, etc. During the month of August, Obiang Nguema spent two weeks in France, before his official voyage to the People's Republic of China. The MAIB denounced the French government which had supplied the army and police with material, which reinforced and perfected the methods of Obiang Nguemist repression. In October, Lieutenant-General Obiang Nguema declared in the publicity pages of *June Afrique Plus* (Paris) that "the friendship with France must be situated in the framework of central Africa, where the French presence is far from being negligible." On November 19, 1996, after meeting the Spanish prime minister in Rome, he was greeted in Paris by J. Godfrain, minister of the cooperation; he did not meet President Chirac. New problems occurred between Nigeria and Equatorial Guinea, concerning the limits of territorial waters, in the area where the American Mobil Oil Corporation exploits offshore oilfields, versus the area where the French company Elf-Aquitaine exploits Nigerian offshore oilfields.

In 1996, Mobil contracted Coflexip Stena Offshore SA (Paris) to build several flexible flow lines, at a depth of 570 m. Obiang Nguema was in France during the July 14 celebrations. Chirac met with him in the Elysée. France informed him that it will grant 25 Mio$ (200 Mio FF) in public aid for several years: support to the oil sector, construction of the capital's airport, rural development, assistance to small- and medium-sized firms, electricity companies, stock market, teaching of French in schools. The nongovernmental organization Esperanza Sin Fronteras built 10 public fountains (hand activated) in the capital, a school for 300 students and a clinic of Odontology, run by Seventh-Day Adventist missionaries. In Ela Nguema (San Fernando) the French cooperation had set a polyvalent pavilion within the Salesian missionhouse. Obiang Nguema called on French investors mostly to create infrastructures and develop tourism. He also asked for aid for the security of his country. On September 17, not pleased with the Spanish authorities, Obiang Nguema declared to the minister of foreign affairs, in front of numerous ambassadors, that from now on French is to be the second official language. The Bubi of the island of Bioko refused to abide by such a decision. In November,

Equatorial Guinea participated in the Conference of French-Speaking Communities held in Hanoi, with the prime minister.

According to the 1997 report of the Observatoire des transferts díarmement, France and Equatorial Guinea signed a military cooperation agreement on March 9, 1985. In 1997, four French soldiers were doing military cooperation in the Equato-Guinean army; 700,000 FF (approx. $120,000) were donated to equip the security forces (i.e., Ninjas). In 1996, six Equato-Guinean soldiers trained in French military schools.

In April 1998, Francis Breton was appointed French ambassador. During 1998, the Observatoire des transferts d'armement (Paris) gave details concerning France's military engagement with the nguemists. The French cooperation was made up of 24 civilians (9 teachers, 15 technicians) and 4 military advisers (also in 1996 and 1997). Ambassador of Equatorial Guinea in 1998: Lino-Sima Ekua Avomo.

The French ambassadors were successively: Henri Bernard (1969–1973), Didier Raguenet (1973–1976), Jacques Fournier (1976–1978), Hubert Cornet (1978–1979), Pierre Cornée (1980–1985), Marcel Causse (1985–1989), Jacques Gazon (1989–1994), Gérard Brunet de Courssou (1994–1989), Francis Breton (1998–). The former ambassador to France, Edjang Mba, is secretary general in the ministry of foreign affairs.

Obiang Nguema owns a luxurious flat in Paris.

See also Agriculture; Alar Ayong; Aviation; Bakale Obiang, C,-B.; Bata; Bennet, J. E.; Bueribueri, C.; Geological and Mining Research Bureau; Children; Coup d'etat (?) of May 11-13, 1983; Coup d'etat of December 1987, Coup d'etat of August 1988; Culture; Currency; Customs; Custom Union of Central African States; Democracy; Drugs; Economy; Edjang Mba Madja, P.; Education; Ekuku, Ela Abeme, J.; Elections; Electricity; Elobeyes; Engonga Motulu, M.; Esono Abaga Ada, J.; European Union; Finances; Fisheries; Francophony; Gold; Italy; Joint Oppposition Platform; Justice; L'Hôtel, N.; Liberal Democratic Convention; Llansol, V.-G.; Mangue Okomo Nsue de Obiang Nguema, C.; Micheba Fernandez, T.; Miko Abogo, P.; Morocco; Moto Nsá, S.; National Democratic Union; Ndjoku, J. M.; Nguemism; Nigeria; Ninjas; Norway; Nsue Mokuy, A.; Obiang Mangue, T.; Obiang Nguema, T.; Ondo Nkumu, J.; Ondo Obiang Alogo, F.; Oyono Ndong Mifumu, M.; Parliamen; Petroleum; Police; Public Health; Rasilla, L. de la; Reporters without Borders; Rodriguez, R.; Roussel, Th. (-Onassis); Saur Afrique; Spain; Telecommunications; Terror; Timber; Total; Toxic Waste; Trade; United Nations; United States of America

FRANCO-GUINEAN BUSINESS AND SERVICE COMPANY. Begun in 1995. Director: André Abraham. It represents enterprises of the parapetroleum sector and companies dealing in spare parts for cars.

FRANCOPHONY. In the January 8, 1996, ministerial reshuffle, Agustín Nze Nfumu became minister for culture and French language. In the April 8, 1996, government, Pedro-Chistino Beuriberi occupied the post of minister for culture, tourism, and French language.

In the government of January 21, 1998, Santiago Ngua Nfumu became minister of education, sciences and francophony. Mrs. Teresa Avoro Nguema was vice-minister. On August 11, Obiang Nguema appointed A. Nze Nfumu secretary-general of the PDGE, permanent representative for francophony. On August 24, Obiang Nguemas created by decree a national Commission of Francophony, linked to the presidency, led by the prime minister, with an executive office run by the minister of education.

FRAUD see Corruption

FREE PORT. In the spring of 1983 some Spanish circles wanted to transform Equatorial Guinea into a free port, along the lines of Bahrein. In 1991, some Italian circles, which some sources claimed belonged to the mafia, took over the same idea. See also Biancamano; Price.

FREE UNIONS. In its 1996 report, the International Conference of Free Union (ICFU) reported that Equatorial Guinea is one of the countries that paralyze union structures by preventing their existence (along with Birmany and Saudi Arabia). The Independent Union of public employees, the "Sindicato Independiente de Servicios" (SIS), asked for its recognition the first time in the spring of 1995, in accordance to the rules established by the union laws of 1992. The authorities refused to grant the recognition, in disagreement over the word "independent." A second request was made that same year, but it was also turned down. Soon after, through a letter to the CIOSL, the government denied that the SIS had ever requested recognition, and asserted it had never heard about it. Strikes are forbidden.

FREEDOMS RESTRICTED. All movement needs an authorization by security forces; Moka can no longer be reached, not even by diplomatic personnel; a tax of 150 to 1,500 bikuele was levied for access to the Fernando Po beaches. Religious freedom had also been abolished: since January 1976 all religious meetings and processions were prohibited. Previously, the Protestant ministers and Catholic priests had to place Macías Nguema's picture in the sanctuary and to recite during services PUNT slogans like "Macías, sole miracle of Equatorial Guinea."

Except for some religious freedom, violations of the principal basic rights have continued unabated since the 1979 coup. Various organizations such as the UN Human Rights Commission, Amnesty International, the Christian Democratic International, and the International Commission of Jurists, have attested to this state of affairs year after year. Around 110,000 citizens—virtually the whole of the intelligentsia—are still in exile abroad. Freedom of speech and of assembly are still not guaranteed, and Obiang Nguema protects himself from his citizenry with his 600 strong Moroccan presidential guards, the police, 300 Ninjas, and the Jovenes Antorchas. When some people, even the marionette parliamentarians, dare to voice an opinion, they are arrested on the pretext of insulting the head of state.

FRENTE ANTI-MACIAS (FAM). Small group of refugees in exile in Spain. In October 1978 they published a list of 533 persons tortured and assassinated in Equatorial Guinea, completing the one published earlier by ANRD. Dissolved in 1979.

FRENTE DE LIBERACION DE GUINEA ECUATORIAL (FRELIGE) see Equatorial Guinea Liberation Front

FRENTE DE LIBERACION DEL PUEBLO GUINEANO (FRELINAGE) (Liberation Front of the People of Guinea). Main office in Lagos (Nigeria); formed of exiled students in 1970. No longer in activity.

FRENTE NACIONAL Y POPULAR DE LIBERACION DE GUINEA ECU-ATORIAL (FRENAPO) (National and Popular Liberation Front of Equatorial Guinea). "Socialist" MONALIGE cell founded in October 1964 by J. Mbá Ovono and A. Ndongo Miyone (then in Accra, Ghana). The movement broke up shortly after, for ideological reasons. In March 1965 Ndongo Miyone published the FRENAPO program forecasting FRENAPO as a state party, headed by a collegial board, requesting expropriation without compensation of all European possessions and their transformation into cooperatives and requiring the immediate departure of all officials and Spanish missionaries as well as the seizure of the missions' properties. The IPGE supported this program between 1965 and 1967. The FRENAPO was dissolved in 1968.

FRENTE POPULAR (Popular Front). Socialist party, formed by Spaniards beginning in 1936, with about 150 members. It was specially directed by intellectuals, and was opposed to large landownership and Casas Fuertes, both qualified as "clerical." Troops sent from Spain brought about the fall of the Gobernador General Sánchez Guerra, a socialist, and his supporters from Santa Isabel; then troops under the orders of Fontan y Lobé were sent to Bata where the nationalist troops rapidly crushed the Popular Front, with Vice-Governor M. Porce at its head. Some members of the Popular Front were executed, others exiled to the Canary Islands in November 1936.

FUERZA DEMOCRATICA REPUBLICANA see Republican Democratic Force

❖ G ❖

GABON. The northern part of Gabon is peopled with Fang or other related ethnic groups; the heart of Fang country being the Woleu Ntem situated east of Río Muni. The coasts are partly peopled with Ndowe. In 1834 the Comptoir français du Gabon (French Gabonese Emporium) was created, which was later to become Libreville. From there on, French influence rapidly spread, especially through missionaries, with the Holy Spirit missionaries on the Catholic side, and the American Presbyterians on the Protestant side. Gabon is largely composed of territories assigned to Spain by Portugal under the Pardo Treaty, but confiscated by France, which at the Paris Treaty of 1900 only reckoned a Río Muni no larger than 26,000 sq km to Spain.

In 1990, Gabon imported large quantities of yam from Fernando Po, a 19th-century tradition. The protectionist prices paid by Spain for coffee and cocoa provoked heavy smuggling from Woleu Ntem to Río Muni during the first half of the 20th century. Before and after independence, various Equato-Guinean statesmen (among them, Ondo Edú and Ndongo Miyone) were granted political asylum in Gabon. But Ondo Edú was returned to Santa Isabel shortly after independence, and then disappeared in Guinean prisons. Macías Nguema's and Obiang Nguema's fathers were both natives of the Woleu Ntem.

In 1972 border incidents (islands of Conga, Cocottiers, and Mbañe occupied by Gabonese troops) and the difficulties near Ebebiyin in 1974, seem to have eventuated, according to Asumu Oyono, in the selling of 2,000 sq km to Gabon. During an official visit in Madrid in 1977, President Bongo (OAU president in office), according to the Spanish press, asked Spain's support of Gabon in occupying the Equato-Guinean islands (including Fernando Po); in exchange, Gabon promised to help Spain maintain its domination in the Canary Islands. The Spanish government denied this offer took place.

In 1974, the French lawyer Mignon visited Gabon to carry out an investigation for the International Federation of Jurists on the dramatic internal situation of Equatorial Guinea and on the flow of refugees, of which about 60,000 were living in Gabon and many were working in the Woleu Ntem plantations. Thanks to the intervention of the International Federation for Human Rights (D. Payot), Gabon signed in 1974 and 1981 the Geneva Convention on refugee status. In mid-1976 there took place an attack on Equatorial Guinea by some 30 exiles led by A. Owono Obama. About 10 National Guards were killed or injured; Owono was arrested in Gabon. The forest concession of the Sociedad Forestal de Río Muni touches the Gabonese border and many Equato-Guinean workers seized the opportunity to flee the Macías Nguema regime and take refuge in Gabon. On January 1, 1977, an argument between various factions of Guineans led to several casualties and deportations, without any arrest however and no expulsions. At the end of 1977 Gabon asked the assistance of the UNHCR.

On February 9–10, 1978, some problems opposed Guineans and Gabonese in Libreville. On February 16 police forces took a census of all Equato-Guineans living in Libreville, arresting 17 suspicious persons and distributing identity cards. On March 16, 1978, Gabonese Foreign Affairs Minister Martin Bongo resumed in Madrid the negotiations initiated by President Bongo.

Units of the Gabonese army helped in bringing about the 1979 coup, particularly by occupying the towns of Mongomo, Evinayong, and Nsork. Despite the existence of a joint commission, a certain amount of tension developed between the two countries on account of frontier questions and Gabonese interest in the country's petroleum prospects. In 1979, the High Commission for Refugees of the UN denounced the xenophobia suffered by Equato-Guinean exiles. Bands of Equato-Guinean thieves with connections in the Gabonese underworld were reported in 1982, in Libreville.

In April 1983, Obiang Nguema admitted that a document allowing the transfer of some islands of Río Muni to Gabon had been extracted from him by dubious means. In 1984 Gabon tried in vain to seize the Equato-Guinean coast and the locality of Akalayong in order to facilitate petroleum drilling. The Equato-Guinean Aviation Company (EGA), was founded in 1986, with 70% government capital and 30% from Air Inter-Gabon. Eighty-thousand Equato-Guineans (drivers, workers, laborers, foresters) were living in Gabon in 1988, earning lower salaries than those of the Gabonese. Gabon echoes the 19th century French claims over the then-Spanish islands of Corisco and Elobey. Spanish press reports in 1987 claimed that French diplomacy was planning to carve Equatorial Guinea up between Gabon and Cameroon.

Toward the end of 1989, Gabon protested against Equatorial Guinea granting a petroleum concession over an area of 2,000 sq km around Corisco, to the British company Clarion Petroleum. Equatorial Guinea received $18 million from the International Development Agency for an agricultural diversification project for supplies to Gabon. In November 1992, the Equato-Guineans again refused the transfer to Gabon of the Mbañe, Cocoteros, and Conga Islands.

In 1992, the German firm Gluntz A.G. bought the company Isory, the largest European plywood companyy; in Gabon, it employs about 29 Equato-Guineans.

In January 1993, Gabon unilaterally annexed Mbañe and Cocoteros and Conga by a presidential decree; France continued to consider the islands as Equato-Guinean. On the occasion of the November 1993 elections, Gabon was one of the few countries to send observers, along with Burkina Faso and Togo. Hilaire Mathas is the ambassador to Gabon.On November 3, 1993, Nigerian immigrants were arrested in the suburbs of Libreville, having arrived by boat from Corisco with the help of smugglers. In 1994, four French Mirage planes, probably stationed in Gabon, carried out unauthorized, low-altitude flights over Bata.

Gabon expelled tens of thousands of clandestine immigrants including hundreds of Equato-Guineans in January 1995. Libreville was connected to Bata by a weekly flight. A Gabonese delegation participated in the first convention of the PDGE held that spring at Bata. 1995 began in great tension, as some Gabonese (fishermen, travellers) in Equatorial Guinea were arrested and fishing boats confiscated; Gabonese Minister for Defense I. Ngari Ngari negotiated with Nguemists on October 23. One Gabonese was arrested in Corisco and deported to Bata, along with his fishing boat. In late October, two important dissenters of the PDGE and members of the clan from Mongomo, F. Ondo Obiang and B. Nguema Esono, took refuge in Gabon for a few weeks, fleeing house arrest in Mongomo, and fearing possible elimination by a nephew of Obiang Nguema.

The southern Río Muni frontier dispute begun by Gabon during Macías Nguema's time continued in 1996, and was being examined by an investigating commission. In April, the United Nations Human Rights Commission's resolution aimed at the continuation of investigations in Equatorial Guinea was supported by Gabon. Towards the end of 1995, a delegation of Convergency for Social Democracy (CPDS), led by the general secretary, Plácido Micó, and Jesús Ela, visited Gabon where it held a number of meetings with the colony of 50,000 Equato-Guineans. They had talks with Felipe Ondó Obiang and Bonifacio Nguema, ex-members of the clan from Mongomo, who had sought refuge in Gabon with their party Fuerza Democrática Republicana. Shortly afterwards, Obiang Nguema arrived for talks with President Bongo, as well as personal affairs and negotiations with Elf-Aquitaine, of which his son Teodorín was named director for Equatorial Guinea. In March 1995, the CICIBA organized in Libreville a public conference on the subject: "Promotion of Bantu languages in Equatorial Guinea."

On June 25, 1997, President Bongo spoke of an American plot to throw France out of Africa by destabilizing the French-speaking countries; the sole aim is to control the mineral resources. Obiang Nguema's adversaries, Felipe Ondo Obiang and Guillermo Nguema Ela, refugees in Gabon, were arrested by Col. Mbiga, nephew of Bongo, and deported to Equatorial Guinea on November 5. At first imprisoned, they were released on November 14. Trouble at the southern border of Rio Muni has been reported, and the population of Cocobeach complains aboout insecurity. Fishing boats have been attacked, as well as some villages on the Utamboni; these attacks could have been carried out by Equato-Guineans.

After the 15 death sentences issued at the Bubi trial at the end of May 1998, President Bongo asked for magnanimity.

Ambassador of Equatorial Guinea in 1998: José Elá Ebang.

See also Akalayong; Akurenam; Angue Ondo, P.; Army; Aviation; Bikomo Nanguande, S. P.; Borders; Burkina Faso; Bwiti; Civil Junta for National Salvation; Cocoa; Coconut Island; Convergency for Social Democracy; Corisco; "Democratic" Party of Equatorial Guinea; Elections; Elephants; Equatorial Guinea Liberation Front; Eyene Opkua Nguema Ocoa; Fang; France; Justice; Mbañe, Mikomeseng; Missions; Modu Akuse Bindang, C.; Mongomo, Motu Mamiaga, P.; Nassau, Robert H.; Navigation; Ndong Abaga Mesian, C.; Ndong Mba, Z.; Nguema Edu, F.; Nguema Ela Mangue Ndong, G.; Nguema Esono Nchama, B.; Niefang; Nseng Esono; Nsue Otong, C.; Nve, E.; Obama Nsue Mangue, F.; Obiang Nguema, T.; Olo Mebuy, A.; Ondo Ayang, L.; Ondo Obiang Alogo, F.; Parliament; Petroconsultant S.A.; Petroleum; Popular Union; Public Health; Refugees; Republican Democratic Force; Río Muni; Saharaoui Popular Republic; Sima, A.; Spain; Terror; Toxic Wastes; Trade; Union for Democracy and Social Development

GAESA. Spanish company owning in Maule (Fernando Po) an oil palm plantation of 365 hectares. In 1974 it still produced 3,000 ton clusters per year. The palm-oil factory yields 4,875 tons of oil a year. Formerly Gaesa also owned rice plantations in Musola and a cattle ranch along the road from San Carlos to Concepción with 432 hectares of pastures. In 1969 the herd numbered 1,967 head but has been slaughtered since then.

GANDARA, José de la. Former corporal and gobernador general of Fernando Po succeeding Chacón, in August 1859. He arrived with 128 Spanish settlers and 166 infantry soldiers. Ten months later, only three settlers and half the soldiers were left, because of death and some returning to Spain. Gandara retired from office at the end of June 1862.

GANGSTERISM, GANGSTERS. Robert Klitgaard, World Bank expert for three years, in his book *Tropical Gangsters* (New York, 1991) describes nguemist Equatorial Guinea and the clan from Mongomo as "the worst among the worst."
See also Mongomo; Nguemism; Obiang Nguema; Terror; Torture.

GARCIA BARLEYCORN, Francisco. Fernandino. From Sampaka. Born 1948. Studied at the Escuela Superior Indígena, in Santa Isabel. He was named technical director of finance in 1981. He joined the commission that conceived the principles of the Nguemist regime in Akonibe in 1982. This helped him become the secretary of state for planning and economic development.

GARCIA MINAUR. Spanish shipowner associated with the company owned by the widow of Besora y Escuder y Galliana. After the Transmediterranean company had refused to ensure regular sailings to Santa Isabel and Bata in accordance with the agreements signed with Madrid, this company took over the service and has the monopoly of shipping to and from the former colony. In November 1985, Equatorial Guinea complained about the excessively high rates charged by García Minaur. In 1980, the Spanish press maintained that a vessel of this company had taken arms to South Africa and that some of these arms had been intercepted in Santa Isabel.

GARCIA TREVIJANO FOS, José Antonio. b. 1928. Spanish lawyer, degree in administrative law, married to Francine Chouraki. Former professor at the Universities of Salmanca and Madrid. He became publicly known as economic counselor first to Macías Nguema, then to the Secretariado Conjunto in 1967–68. His draft constitution having been rejected at the Constitutional Conference, he is said to have advised Macías Nguema to campaign against the one adopted by the conference. He seems to have paid some of the Secretariado Conjunto's expenses and also sponsored part of the election campaign of Macías Nguema's group. In 1969 Garcías Trevijano was made Knight of the Order of Independence by Macías Nguema. At this occasion he made his first trip to Equatorial Guinea. In 1970 he participated in the founding of INFOGE, presided over by Mba Ada to monopolize external trade. After the failure of INFOGE, and financial difficulties with Ekong Andeme, Macías Nguema authorized him to set up Simed S.A., of which Simone Chouraki, his secretary and sister-in-law, is an administrator. Since 1975, Simed has suffered from Adoual's competition, sponsored by Macías Nguema's nephew Oyono Ayingono.

In the framework of Spanish internal politics, García Trevijano presided over the Grupo Democrático Independiente (leftist party) that he represented at the Junta Democrática in the political campaign for the post-Franco elections. In 1974, the Francoist government confiscated his passport, and in 1976 he was even imprisoned for two months (since then he travels with an Equato-Guinean diplomatic passport). Also in 1976 the ANRD published a García Trevijano File pointing out his implication—at least moral—in the Macías Nguema terror regime, showing also that García Trevijano manipulated the government of Equatorial Guinea in economic as well as legal matters. Since then the Spanish Socialist Workers' Party boycotted García Trevijano and obtained his exclusion from the Coordinación Democrática, and from the election campaign. During a press conference at the end of 1976, García Trevijano rejected all accusations contained in the "File" published by ANRD.

In 1969, as Equatorial Guinea wanted to launch major constructions and modernization of the telecommunications network, García Trevijano is said to have suggested to Masié Ntutumu, minister of domestic affairs, to contact the French Compagnie des Dragages et Travaux Publics. The company, and France wishing securities for the $43 million loan to finance the constructions, effected the creation of the Sociedad Forestal de Río Muni (headed by J. P. Nouveau and P. Schwarz). Acting through his secretary, S. Chouraki, he negotiated the selling of the Sociedad to the French company, Tardiba, in 1976, as the problem of securing manpower became more and more difficult because many workers fled to nearby Gabon. In 1985, he apparently sold the results of the geological survey he had financed in the period 1969–1971 to the Spanish company ADARO and the French Bureau de Recherches Géologiques et Minières.

At the time of the August 1979 coup d'etat, he declared that Obiang Nguema was the lawful successor to Macías Nguema and that the people had not participated at all in the coup. García Trevijano is the author of several books and pamphlets.

GARRIGA, Tito see Abeso Fuma, F.

GARRIGA FUMA, Fausto. Born in Bata. Son-in-law of Obiang Nguema. A flight lieutenant, trained in the Soviet Union. He belonged to the Nguemist Guard.

GAS see Petroleum

GAY, Alexander. British. Former bank employee in Scotland. Mercenary in Congo (Zaire) and Biafra. With the novelist F. Forsyth, he is supposed to have imagined and organized an unsuccessful invasion of Fernando Po by mercenaries and Biafran soldiers in 1972.

GAZON, Jacques. Ambassador of France from 1989 to 1994, successor to Marcel Causse. On August 25, 1994, he declared his support to the Nguemist regime on Nguemist radio. At his departure, he was decorated with the medal of the Great Cross of the Order of Independence.

GENE, Modesto. A Spanish painter, sculptor, and drawing teacher working in Equatorial Guinea since before independence. He taught in the High School for Teachers in Bata. In 1973, in Bata, he made a statue of Macías Nguema. He died in 1984. The Polytechnic Institute of Bata has been named after him.

GEOLOGICAL AND MINING RESEARCH BUREAU (Bureau de Recherche géologique et minière, BRGM). A French state-run organization. Towards the end of 1983, it ended the third round of prospecting in Río Muni. See also France.

GEPSA see Petroleum

GERMANY. In the 19th century many German companies owned factories in Fernando Po and Río Muni (Moritz, Küderling, Woermann, and others). Until after independence the Wocrmann Line ships served Guinean ports. Since the beginning of the 20th century Hamburg has become the world trading place for okoumea, thanks to Río Muni timber. In 1884 Germans occupied the Cameroon coasts, legally Spanish, but stopped along the Río Campo.

In the early 20th century, the German ambassador to Madrid, Radowitz, declared that in the event of the splitting up of Morocco, Germany would claim compensation from Morocco or Fernando Po. Fernando Po was then a subject of Anglo-German rivalry.

The Germans proved to be extremely active in Fernando Po at the beginning of the First World War. The British government protested to Spain at its sympathy for Germany, in contrast with its policy of neutrality. The Germans ran a powerful shortwave radio station on the island of Fernando Po. The German warships *Ember, Dresden,* and *Stuttgart* were anchored at Santa Isabel in August 1914; the British claimed that Fernando Po had been seized by the Germans, and spoke of Spain's complicity. Military operations in Cameroon began in September. The Germans understood that Fernando Po could be used as a base for arms and ammunition smuggling. Towards the end of 1914, Spanish boats were seized by the British in Lagos, their merchandise confiscated and the Cameroonian staff arrested. The English raised a protest; Barrera asked Luggard to return the Cameroonians. The protests were ignored. Barrera became the Germans' messenger.

Another incident took place in March 1915: two Germans were murdered in Ayamiken, after they tried to return to Bata. The British were involved in the incident, with the help of the Ayamiken chief, Nsho-Evan. The press in Santa Isabel turned highly anti-British. In February 1916, an agreement was signed with Barrera for the imprisonment of the Germans, with the exception of priests and doctors, and for the prevention of smuggling. The European population of Spanish Guinea remained loyal to Germany. At that time, *Ebano* was a journal which received its information from Berlin. After the German defeat of 1916–17, around 60,000 soldiers and Africans took refuge in Spanish Guinea; they were sent home to Europe and Cameroon in 1919. Later on, German foresters settled in Río Muni.

In June 1940, at the time of France's capitulation, former German and Cameroonian settlers who had sought refuge in Fernando Po had some pamphlets proclaiming their imminent return distributed in Cameroonian villages, according to the de Gaulle memoirs. Until 1970, Germany was the second non-Spanish goods supplier for Equatorial Guinea (9.5% of the total supply). In 1970 a German businessman named Pleuger and his wife bought Guinean cocoa but ran into problems with Macías Nguema's government. In 1976 the German Democratic Republic appears to have absorbed the 8,000 tons of cocoa.

In 1979, West Germany signed a normalization agreement with Obiang Nguema. In February 1980, the ambassador of the Federal Republic of Germany

(FRG), Michel R. Engelhard, presented his credentials. The FAO named the German expert Wolfgang Sachers as the representative of the World Food Program; Sachers reported extreme shortages in food. In early 1982, the *Vissilis-D* of the Compañia marítima began its monthly voyages to the port of Hamburg. In July 1990, the new German ambassador was Eberhard Udelbeke, with residence at Yaoundé. The FRG financed several projects, including a farm near Santa Isabel, and a few scholarships.

According to the press, Minister for Agriculture Anatolio Ndong, in May 1992, had the German engineer Friedrich Stennmann hired for a UN project as counsellor for a government lumber company, reserving however for himself 10% in commission. In March 1993, Germany declared its readiness to help the establishment of the democratic process. During 1993, some German entrepreneurs were received by Prime Minister Siale Bolekia, with a view to invite infrastructure investments. Considering the nondemocratic acts of the Nguemists, Germany took part in the election boycott called for by the EC and opposed the sending in of observers for the November 21 "elections." The representative of the German Cooperation, Doris Kocher, was expelled from Equatorial Guinea.

During the last trimester of 1995, three German operatives saw their development project at Teguete fall apart, for political reasons. Two of them were able to leave the country immediately; the third was held three days by Acacio Abeso commissioner for the presidential security for the Center-South province.

On February 28, 1996, *Die Welt* qualified Obiang Nguema's reelection as being "not credible."

Germany imports petroleum from Equatorial guinea. In January–June 1997 it represented 138,000 tons on a total of 56.7 Mio tons.

See also Bueribueri, C.; Committee for the Voluntary Return of Refugees; Evuna Ondo, G.; Liberal Democratic Convention; Pico de Basilé; Pleuger, P. W.; Teguete; Terror.

GHANA. The first cacao beans were imported from Fernando Po by a blacksmith called Tetteh Quashie, in 1879. Ghana has given asylum to many refugees before independence, the most famous one being Ndongo Miyone. In 1964 together with Mba Ovono he founded the FRENAPO in Accra, a Socialist party claiming expropriation of all Spaniards. In 1973 the Ghanian Allotey and his American wife Tyler were arrested in Accra for having sold to the General Cocoa Co. of New York, 4,000 tons of Guinean cacao in 1971-72 without paying the producer.

Since 1982 the Ghanian port of Tema has been linked with Equatorial Guinea by a shipping service known as the Société Africaine de Cabotage, a joint Belgian-Equatorial Guinean company. The April 1996 Report on Human Rights Practices of the U.S. Department of State to the Congress says: "Several thousand citizens of Nigeria and Ghana reside in the country. Most are small traders and business people and are harassed and persecuted by the police."

On September 14, 1998, Obiang Nguema started a three-day visit to Ghana, at President Jerry Rawlings's invitation. According to local television, the two heads of state spoke of "the negative influence of multinationals on the economical and political development" of Africa.

See also Navigation; Nkogo Ondo, E.; Oyono, M.; Sanchez Bustamante, D.; United Nations.

GLOBEX. Oil company. See Petroleum

GOBERNADOR CIVIL (Civil Governor). The civil governor corresponds to gobernador general on the provincial level, being the highest representative of all administrations. In 1974 the civil governor of Río Muni, Eyegue Ntutumu, after the assassination of Vice President Bosio Dioco, was promoted to vice president of the republic but he was then executed by firing squad along with Macías Nguema in September 1979.

GOBERNADOR GENERAL (Governor General). In 1858 this post was given to army officers. Since 1868 it was the chief of the naval station of Santa Isabel who became gobernador general. From 1890 on the governor general had to have the rank of commander, which seems to have been an insufficient preparation for the role of universal arbitrator in the colony. The governor general represented the metropolis and was responsible to the Spanish government. Highest official of Spanish Guinea's executive (Comisario General from 1964 to 1968), he was appointed by decree by the Spanish Government. His main duties were the planning plus supervision of administration all over the colony, responsibility for public order, supervision of civil governors, and maintaining the price level. With provincialization in 1960, his role became more and more representative. Between 1827 and 1858 Fernando Po was headed by British governors (Owen, Nicholls, Beecroft, Lynslager). Chacón in 1858 started the series of Spanish governors: there were 99 through 1968. The most outstanding ones were: Carlos Chacón (1858), José de la Gandara (1858–1862), Pantaleón Lopez de la Torre Ayllón (1858), Jose Montes de Oca (1885–1887), Antonio Moreno Guerra (1888–1889), Angel Barrera y Luyando (1906–1907, 1910–1912), Miguel Nuñez de Prado (1826–1831), Luis Sánchez Guerra Saez (1935–1936), Juan Fontán y Lobe (1937–1941), Juan Maria Boneli Rubio (1943–1949). Faustino Ruíz González (1940–1962), and Pedro Latorre Alcubierre (1964–1968, Comisario General). The biennial rotation instituted in the 19th century was suppressed in 1904. Since independence, the Palace of the Governors General in Santa Isabel has become the main residence of Macías Nguema, located 1973 to 1979 in the heart of the presidential ghetto surrounded by high defense walls. The palace was named the "3 August (1979) Palace" by Obiang Nguema and has been recently restored by an Italian firm.

GOLD. Before World War II, there was a semiindustrial exploitation of gold by the Frenchman Lauzé, with an output of 3 grams per cubic meter. The only mining activity in Río Muni, in 1960, was gold, carried out by Minas del Ecuador and Co. From 1988 onwards, Equatorial Guinea was only allowed to sell its gold to Paris, as a result of its membership in the franc zone. In 1992, the United Nations Economic Commission for Africa provided advice for the improvement and restructuring of the craftmining sector.

In 1998, alluvial gold was exploited in the river Core, between Niefang and Añisok.

GOMEZ DA MINHA, Fernan. In 1469 Alphonso V of Portugal gave permission to this merchant-navigator to do business on the west coast of Africa, south of

Sierra Leone. São Tomé, Príncipe, and Annobón having been discovered in 1473–1474, the discovery of Fernando Po can be dated around 1471–1472.

GOMEZ MARIJUAN, Bishop. Spaniard from the province of Salamanca, "Hijo del Corzón Immaculado de María," Claretian missionary, ordained in 1930. He arrived in Equatorial Guinea in 1931, was a professor at the Priests' Training College of Banapa, director of the publication *La Guinea Española*, and secretary of the bishopric. In June 1958 he was consecrated bishop of Spanish Guinea, and in 1959 he became Grand Officer of the Order of Africa (Spain). After the nomination of Bishop Nzé Abuy in Río Muni in 1964, he remained bishop of Fernando Po. In 1970, Macías Nguema declared him persona non grata for having taken a public stand against presidential decisions. With his departure started the painful series of attacks against the churches of Equatorial Guinea.

GONZALEZ, Felipe. Spanish prime minister. See Obiang Nguema; Spain.

GONZALEZ ARNAU CAMPOS. Ambassador of Spain since October 1997, after J. M. Otero de León.

GORI MOLUBUELA, Enrique, 1924?–1972. Bubi. Seminarist in Banapa for some time, with Ndongo Miyone. Holds an M.A. in jurisprudence and is a member of the International Catholic Movement. President of the Fernando Po committee of MUNGE. Founding member of the Unión Bubi in 1967. Gori Molubuela advocated independence with close ties to Spain. From 1964 to 1968 he was simultaneously president of the Diputación Provincial (Assembly) of Fernando Po, deputy at the Asamblea General (General Assembly or Parliament)—over which he presided in turn with Ngomo Nardongo—as well as representative to the Spanish Cortes. He participated in the Constitutional Conference where the Secretariado Conjunto of Macías Nguema accused him of being devoted to Spain. At the 1968 elections, he became provincial counselor of Fernando Po and simultaneously chief of cabinet of the Foreign Affairs Ministry. After Ndongo Miyone's so-called attempted coup d'etat on March 5, 1969, he was first placed under house arrest then sentenced to 10 years in prison by a military tribunal. In June 1972 his eyes were put out, and he was left to die of gangrene in the Bata prison. He published *Etnología de los Bubis* in 1955.

GORI MOLUBUELA, Gregorio. Born 1950. From Basakato. Son of Enrique Gori Molubela. Studied in Spain. In the ministerial reshuffle of April 8, 1996, he became director general of pharmacies and traditional medicine.

GOVERNMENT see Administration

GOVERNMENT, "TRANSITIONAL." Installed on January 24, 1992.
    See Administration; Alogo Nchama, A.; Bolekia Edjapa, A.; Cattle; Cayetano Toherida, E.; Culture; Democracy; Development Plans and Programs; Djonbe Djangani de Mbuamangono, P.; Ebebiyin, Eburi Mata, C.; Edjo Evono, F.; Education; Elo Ndong Nsefumu, D.; Eneme Ovono, J.; Envoro Ovono, A.; Epam Botala, A.; Evinayong, Evuna Owono Asangono, A.; Eyegue Obama Asue, F.P.; Eyi Mensui Abeme, I.; Fisheries; Inestrosa Ikaka, F.; Kogo; Labor; Mba Ekua Miko, B.; Mba Nsoro Mban, S.; Mikomeseng; Mongomo; National Security; Ndong Ela Mangue, J.; Ndong Mba, A.; Nepotism; Ngomo Mbengono, F.;

Nguema Onguene, M. J.; Niefang, Nsue Eworo Micue, A.; Nve Mbengono, E. E.; Nve Nzeng, A.F.; Obama Asue Eyegue, F. P.; Obama Nsue Mangue, F.; Obiang Nguema, T.; Oko Eboro, A.; Olo Mba Nseng, J.; Olo Mebuy, A.; Oyono Ndong Mifumu, M.; Oyono Ntutumu, M.; Parliament; Post Offices; Presidency; Press; Public Health; Radio; Religion; Seriche Bioko Malabo, C.; Siale Bilekia, S.; Sports; Tamarite Burgos, C.; Telecommunications; Tourism; Trade; Transports.

GOVERNMENT OF NATIONAL CONCENTRATION (Gobierno de Concentración Nacional). A project presented by the POC, on October 21, 1993, in order to facilitate democratic transition. This government for national unity was to be led by an opposition member. The Nguemists alleged an "institutional coup" and rejected the proposal.

GOVERNMENT OF NATIONAL UNITY (Gobierno de Unidad Nacional). After his dubious reelection on February 25, 1996, the dictator Obiang Nguema formed this government on April 8, 1996, after negotiations with parties of the tame opposition, that had begun a week before the election according to the advice of the representatives of the American petroleum companies Mobil, Nomeco, and United Meridian. While the January 8, 1996, government had 39 ministers, the April 8 government was composed of 41 members; it included five Bubis, one Ndowe, one Annobonese and 33 Fang, of whom 11 were natives of the Wele-Nzas district, dominated by Mongomo. In fact, this government remained under the thumb of the clan from Mongomo and the dictator's close relatives. Of 41 posts, 6 went to the tame opposition, with a state minister (C. Modu Akuse Bindang), two ministers (S.P. Bikomo Nanguande, P.-C. Bueribueri), and three secretaries of state or vice-ministers (A. Nculu Asumu, F. Mabale Nseng, A. Nsue Mokuy). All the important ministries remained in the hands of notorious Nguemists: J. Ndong Ela Mangue (Interior), M. Oyono (External Affairs), J. Oló Mba Nseng (Petroleum and Mines), A. Evuna, (Special Missions), A. Ndong Mba (Fisheries and Forests). This government included two women (Margarita Alene Mba, and Pilar Buebuyo Boseka)

In Equatorial Guinea, the army includes 1,345 men; the government has one ministerial post per 277 officials and per 10,000 inhabitants.

GOVERNOR see Gobernador Civil; Gobernador General

GRANGE MOLAY, Augustín Daniel, b. ca. 1920. Fernandino, of Sierra Leone origin. After some years of medical studies in Spain, he returned to manage his cocoa plantations in Fernando Po, dealing especially with the German company Moritz. He owned the funeral undertaking of Santa Isabel. Deputy mayor of the Municipal Council of Santa Isabel. Grange Molay represented the Fernandinos at the Constitutional Conference of 1967–1968 where he rallied the Secretariado Conjunto, Macías Nguema's stepping stone. With Bubi Torao Sikara he opposed the claims for separation of the two provinces, supported by the Unión Bubi and Carrero Blanco. Fernandino member of the MONALIGE, he was named minister of agriculture in October 1968, and after the assassination of Eñeso Neño in June 1972, minister of education. Grange Molay was often put under semi-house arrest in Bata; in 1972 for having pronounced the prohibited word "intellectual" at a cabinet session, he was fined by Macías Nguema. During the same period, he became the assassinated Borico Toichoa's interim at the Labor Ministry. Grange Molay was replaced at the beginning of 1974 by Ochaga Ngomo, general secretary of the PUNT (who was assassinated late in 1976).

GRAULLERA MICO, José Luis. Comptroller of numerous Spanish concerns and manager of the services of the Movimiento Franquista, and under-secretary in the office of the president. In 1976 he was nominated secretary of state for public administration. After the 1979 coup he was appointed Spanish ambassador to Santa Isabel, where he established very close relations with the dictatorship. He was recalled to Spain towards the end of 1981. Once back in Spain he declared that Equatorial Guinea could never develop unless human rights were respected.

GRUPO DE MAYORES. Informal group of the 1970s, gathering exiles over 40 years of age, in Spain, rightists for the most. The group was sponsored by various private sources. The most important members are: Mbá Ada, Nsué Ngomo, Masié Ntutumu, E. Kuba, and Nsué Nguema. Except for members of ANALIGE, the group counted expelled members of ANRD like Mbá Ada and Nsué Ngomo. Most of them are without any clear political definition. Several worked actively in the shoe business.

GRUPO DE ZARAGOZA see Obiang Nguema, T.

GRUPO MACIAS see Secretariado Conjunto

GRUPO NACIONALISTA PRIMIERO DE ABRIL. A Bubi association composed of exiles belonging to the Unión Bubi, the Frelifer, or to the Unión del Pueblo Eri. This group works for the independence of Fernando Po and adopted an anti-Fang policy.

GUARDIA CIVIL (Civil Guard). After the arrival of the navy infantry in 1896 a colonial police was created in 1904 along the lines of the Spanish Guardia Civil. In addition to the police, which became a Guardia Colonial in 1908, the country was controlled by detachments of Guardia Civil.

A secret agreement on October 12, 1968, enabled Spain to maintain two companies of Spanish Civil Guards, a corvette, an escort vessel, and an airplane squadron in Equatorial Guinea. After Macías Nguema's violent anti-Spanish speeches of January 1969, the Spanish Guardia Civil and the other troops occupied all strategic points in the capital and in Bata, in particular the airports. On March 3 Macías Nguema proclaimed the Emergencia (state of emergency), inviting the intervention of the UN and OAU. By the end of March, 7,000 Spaniards had left the country under the protection of Spanish troops. The Guardia Civil left Santa Isabel of April 5, 1969.

GUARDIA COLONIAL (Colonial Guard). In 1908 the local police corps was changed to Guardia Colonial, definitively replacing the old navy infantry. This Guard was modeled on the Spanish Guardia Civil and controlled the respect of law and order, as well as the protection of the territory. In 1910 it had to repress a Bubi revolt protesting against forced labor in the plantations.

In 1926, under the conduct of T. Buiza, the Guardia Colonial occupied for the first time the entire territory of the Río Muni. Spanish officers of the Guard were appointed Delegados Gubernativos (Territorial administrators), which was often detrimental to the quality of administration. Ten percent of the colony's budget went to the Guardia Colonial. Since July 1946 the Guardia Colonial depended directly on the presidency of the Spanish government (Dirección General de Marruecos y Colonias). Towards the end of the colony, it was used especially to repress all desires of independence. With provincialization in 1960, it became the Guardia Territorial with 23 administrator-officers, 44 European noncommissioned officers, and 795 African subordinates. The navy Guard was composed of 12 officers and 94 sailors. The air force consisted of eight officers and technicians and 62 men. After independence, the Guardia Territorial became the Guardia Nacional.

GUARDIA NACIONAL (National Guard). It is one of the two armed forces of the country numbering 1,500 men and intervening particularly for domestic duties. In many ways it is complemented by the Milicia Popular of 2,000 members and the Juventud en Marcha con Macías, both instruments of the PUNT. From 1970 to 1973 the National Guard was trained by Ethiopian officers (with OAU assistance), and since then by Russians, North Koreans, and Cubans. The National Guard participates in the censoring of the mail. Together with the police, it is the only public administration sector to be paid regularly. A large part of its equipment is Chinese. In 1976, refugees from Gabon carried out a successful attack on the National Guard garrison in Evinayong.

From 1969 to 1978, 17 officers and soldiers of the National Guard have been executed for political reasons. After the 1979 coup, Mbá Oñana Nchama, a cousin of Macías Nguema and a former tailor, was nominated inspector-general of the armed forces in 1981. Former members of the youth movement "Juventud en Marcha con Macías" were integrated into the National Guard.

In January 1987, it came to light that Obiang Nguema had not paid the salaries of his soldiers since September 1986. See also Army.

GUILLEMAR DE ARAGON, Adolfo. Spanish consul in Sierra Leone, he accomplished a 40-day mission to Santa Isabel and along the Río Muni coast in 1845. He notified the French representatives in Gabon that Cape Santa Clara was the southern limit of the Spanish possessions. Guillemar changed the English toponymy of Fernando Po into Spanish names, but English names continued to be used until 1858.

GUINEA CONAKRY see Navigation

GUINEAN GAS COMPANY (Sociedad Guineana de Gas, SOGUIGAS). Company for the sale of gas cylinders from the Alba deposit. Its administrative council is composed of relatives of Obiang Nguema's and executives of the Ministry of Mines and Petroleum: Mrs. Juan Ola Mba (minister of mines and petroleum), Pastor Micha (ambassador to the U.S.), Mrs. Mangue de Obiang (the dictator's first wife), and the Spaniards Francisco Maqueada and Javier Garcías Sanmillán.

See also Petroleum.

GUINEO-SPANISH LUMBERING UNION (Unión Guineo-Española de Madera, GUIESMA). Lumber company growing out of the former ALOSA company, set up during the colonial period, with a plant at Niefang. ALOSA had gone bankrupt upon independence. GUIESMA employs about a hundred persons. In

1994 it occupied the sixth place among the lumber companies, with 12,130 cu m being exploited and 2,537 cu m processed in 1994.

GUINEXTEBANK. A bank established jointly in 1980 by the government and the Banco Exterior de España, with each party holding 50% of the capital. After Equatorial Guinea's entry into the franc zone, French business interests aimed to replace this bank with a French institution, namely the International Bank of West Africa (BIAO).

In 1986, the board was composed of well-known Nguemists: director, Nguema Ela; members: Mbá Oñana, Efua Efua, Ondo Mañe, Armengol Nguema (brother of Obiang Nguema). In March 1987, according to Inestrosa Ikaka, minister of finance, a loss of 1,300 million pesetas ($7.2 million) had been reported, due to "political loans." Most Nguemists were involved in the bankruptcy: Obiang Nguema and Mbá Oñana for $250,000 each.

According to Price Waterhouse, 39.46% of loans were to be written off in 1987. An inspection of the Banco Exterior de España led to the same conclusions. A loss of $11.9 million was reported. Most of the losses resulted from political credits. One of the principal debtors was Obiang Nguema (US $589,000). He also had a deposit of FCFAFr 119 million, at 8%.

A whole US $6 million came from Spanish companies, including the Suguisa and Santy groups, which belong to the Spaniard Roig Balestros and to the Lebano-Spanish Hanna, etc.

Towards the end of 1987, the IMF was satisfied with the dissolution of the Guinextebank. In 1988, M. Boyer, ex-minister for the economy, and director of the Banco Exterior de España (Foreign Bank of Spain), admitted that the Guinextebank had been badly run since 1980.

A large part of the archives were destroyed (by water and rats). Four out of the six presidents were imprisoned, and shot; seventy employees were dismissed for misappropriation of funds.

See also Cocoa; Coffee; Ebendeng Nsomo, M;, Engonga Edjo, B.; Eyi Mensui Andeme, I.; Hanna, S.; Inestrosa Ikaka, F.; Mangue Okomo de Obiang Nguema, C.; Mba Oñana, F.; Mensui Mba, P.; Nguea Esono, L.; Nguema Mbasogo Ondo, A.; Nka Esono Nsing, M.; Obiang Nguema, T.; Oficar Africa S.A.; Okenve Edjang, A.; Okue Moto, M.; Olo Mba Nseng, J; Oyo Riqueza, E.; Roig Balestros, F.; Seriche Bioko Malabo, C.; Suministros de Guinea S. A.; United Nations.

❖ H ❖

HANNA, Santiago. Called "Santy." Lebanese naturalized Spanish. Born in 1943. He grew up in Niefang. He went to the same school as Obiang Nguema and was his childhood friend. He lives in Equatorial Guinea.

Hanna owns a bakery, the Variopinto and Commercial Santy stores, the soap factory Injasa (whose administrative council is presided by Obiang Nguema), the shipping company Acemar as well as a large share in the ABM Lumber Company (along with Obiang Nguema). The Spanish businessman Vilarrasa was his associate until 1991. Hanna obtained, thanks to Obiang Nguema, FCFAFr 60 million from the Guinextebank. He was said to be the first private investor in the country.

He was arrested in October 1992, with Vilarrasa, and accused of importing military equipment, which was in reality a certain number of old vehicles from the Dutch army surplus. Certain Nguemists are believed to have tried to expropriate him with a view to grab his wealth. A military council condemned Villarasa and Hanna to 12 years in prison, but they were graced by Obiang Nguema. They left the country towards the end of 1992, but Hanna soon returned to his adopted country.

HANNON'S JOURNEY. Apocryphal account of Carthaginian navigator Hannon's travel along the west coast of Africa. The "very large mountain" spitting rivers of flame and the "divine chariot" mentioned are believed by some to be Mount Cameroon, in front of Fernando Po. However, recent studies, especially by Bouchar, have shown this assumption to be weak.

HATTON & COOKSON. British commercial company that owned warehouses in Spanish Guinea until after independence. Hatton & Cookson still operate in Gabon.

HEALTH see Public Health

HIJAS DEL SOL. A folkloric African duo formed by the two Bubi Paloma Loribo and Apo Piruchi. Their first record was "Sibeba."

HINESTROSA IKAKA, Felipe. Benga from Corisco, born May 17, 1951. Holds a degree in economics and management (Spain). In 1981, he became the director of commerce. In 1982, he became the director general for programming, in the Ministry for Planning and economic Development. He then completed his education in Yaound, at the BEAC. He worked at the BEAC in Santa Isabel from 1985 onwards.

He became minister of finance in January 1986. He signed a receipt for about $180,000 from the Guinextebank budget. Hinestrosa helped install the BIAO, renewed ties with the IMF, liquidated the Guinextebank and the Credit and Development Bank (Banco de Desarrollo y de Crédito), In 1987 he admitted that the Guinextebank had a deficit of 1,300 million pesetas ($7.2 million) due to "political loans." In December, while Obiang Nguema was attending a Franco-African conference at Antibes (France), he was placed under house arrest with three other ministers.

He was relieved of his post in early September 1988, and replaced by A.F. Nve Zend. Upon being sent to Spain, he worked there as Obiang Nguema's informer. Upon his return to the country and as a member of the PFGE, he was named Head of the Commission in charge of reforming the Nguemist Constitution. He became vice-minister for the economy and commerce in the "transitional" government of January 24, 1992. On December 22, 1993, he became state secretary for planning and economic development. In the January 8, 1996, ministerial reshuffle, he was named minister with special responsibility for employment. In the April 8, 1996, government, he became counsellor to the president of the government for the economy and planning. Hinestrosa Ikaka held simultaneously the office of president of the Association of the Friends of Obiang Nguema.

He died in 1997 (poisoned?)

See also coup d'etat of December 1987; Obiang Nguema.

HISPANO-GUINEAN SOCIETY FOR CULTURE AND DEVELOPMENT (Sociedad de Cultura y Desarrollo Hispano-Guineana, SOCUDEGE). Formed mainly of Spanish importers and exporters. Its president was Juan Muro Navarro, with Nicolás Ncong Eba as vice-president. Socudege was connected to Sogedisa.

HISTORY see the chronology and the introduction at the front of this book; Prehistory

HOENMANS, Paul see Mobil Corporation

HOLT, John, 1842–1904. British businessman, secretary to Lynslager since 1862. At the latter's death in 1864, Holt managed the business by himself, bought it in 1867, and started new warehouses in Cameroon and Gabon, shortly after having founded John Holt Ltd., Liverpool. About a dozen warehouses were established in Río Muni. John Holt Ltd. became one of the largest commercial companies in Africa. Today it no longer operates in Equatorial Guinea, but continues to do business in Western Africa.

HOMICIDES. In summer 1996 and 1997, the country was subject to an epidemic of ritual crimes. About 30 mutilated corpses were collected in the large cities. See Assassinations; Terror; Torture.

HUMAN RIGHTS. In the 1968 Constitution human rights are hardly mentioned. With the rapid development of Macías Nguema's personal power, fundamental freedoms were quickly suspended. In 1974 a representative of the International Federation of Jurists confirmed assassinations, the flow of exiles, and the "300,000 domestic hostages." In October 1974, the Swiss Human Rights League called on the OAU to intervene in order to stop torture; after a mission of Me Payot, a Swiss lawyer of the International Federation for Human Rights, the government of Gabon signed the 1951 Geneva Convention on the status of refugees. In 1975 Amnesty International sent a cable to Macías Nguema asking him to put an end to torture. In August 1976 the UN subcommittee for the Prevention of Discrimination and the Protection of Minorities examined the case of Equatorial Guinea, at the very time when the London-based Anti-Slavery Society published a detailed study on forced labor and murders. In March 1977 Amin Data, the Uganda delegate, prevented the ANRD representative from taking the floor at the United Nations Human Rights Commission, in Geneva, but in March 1979, the UN commission resolved to make a study on violation of human rights in Equatorial Guinea, and to appoint a special reporter.

A special UN rapporteur, the Costa-Rican Volio-Jiménez, reporting on a visit made shortly after the 1979 coup, stressed that "the Government of Equatorial Guinea does not appear to pay due attention to the question of the promotion and defense of human rights." Since 1979 the UN General Assembly has regularly requested the secretary-general to keep the situation under review. In the UN Human Rights Commission, Obiang Nguema's dictatorship comes up for discussion year after year under item 12—Flagrant and systematic violations of Human Rights.

In the country, the chief radio and TV announcer, A. Nsué Mekuy, has frequently been summoned by the military government to be told not to broadcast any news about human rights. In March 1984, Obiang Nguema submitted his country's candidacy for membership in the UN Human Rights Commission; this was naturally turned down. Since Amnesty International experienced considerable difficulty in getting any information about the country, their 1985 report makes no reference to it. French and Spanish interests have taken advantage of this by portraying it as a cessation of human rights violations. On August 18, 1986, Equatorial Guinea signed the Charter on Human Rights.

In October 1986, Amnesty International again brought up the question of Equatorial Guinea and cited arrests of members of the Chamber of Deputies in session, on the pretext of their having insulted the head of state. At the end of May 1987, Amnesty International published a detailed report on the military tribunals and the passing of death sentences in Equatorial Guinea. This damning document shows how the dictatorship operates through courts presided over by officers who also held ministerial posts.

The UN Human Rights Commission, in its 1987 session, again expressed its surprise over the continued silence of the government of Equatorial Guinea in the face of the Commission's repeated requests and suggestions since 1982 to pay due attention to the question of human rights. Having received no response, the Commission requested the secretary-general of the UN to keep the question of human rights in that country on the agenda for the 1988 session. In May 1987, before the Commission, M. Malkassian (UFER), calling to mind the alarming situation prevailing in Equatorial Guinea, underlined the negative results of UN aid to the dictatorship. No measures have been taken to apply the UN recommendation.

In early 1990, the UN Human Rights Comission adopted a new resolution on Equatorial Guinea, stating that the government was not fulfilling its obligations as a party to the international treaties concerning human rights. A national commission for human rights composed of Nguemist deputies and officials was formed in September 1990. Towards the end of 1991, Equatorial Guinea's representative to the UN, Damasco Obiang Ndong (Mongomo), declared that his government observed "with sadness and a feeling of helplessness the stress laid [by the United Nations] on human rights issues, to the detriment of other issues requiring high priorities: poverty, hunger and illness."

The Commission's special rapporteur, F. Volio Jimenez, in his February 1992 report, revealed that the minister for foreign affairs, Santiago Eneme Ovono, asked him: "What do human rights have to do with democracy?" In May, the EC published a Declaration condemning Nguemist excesses endangering the process of democratization. It was based on the 4th Lomé Convention of 1991. The U.S. Ambassador, J.-E. Bennet, supported the UN report.

Between 1990 and 1992 the International Commission of Jurists showed that the Nguemist authorities were violating the Constitution by arresting deputies favoring multipartyism. The UNDP's 1992 Report of Human Development placed Equatorial Guinea in the 143rd position in the world (out of 170 countries) and behind all the countries of central Africa. In May, the EC again condemned the excesses of the regime, which were endangering the democratization process. In December, the Spanish government denounced the human rights violations and the ill treatment, and warned that if this state of affairs persists, it would "be obliged" to reconsider the cooperation program.

The UN Human Rights Commission Report discussed in March 1993 states:

23. Political and institutional conditions constitute a significant obstacle to the free exercise of fundamental rights and to the legal protection of these rights were seen to persist in this country.

24. The President of the Republic wields several powers, which he exercises in keeping with the political interest of his regime and to the detriment of the freedom of the citizens.

26. [the] constitution even wilfully places the President of the Republic out of reach of all judicial action which may be aimed at demanding accounts for the abusive exercise of power.

The EC denounced the continuation of the arrests and arbitrary hearings, as well as torture, principally by the presidential guards. The UNDP's Report (April 1993) sets conditions for election aid and demands a credible electoral census, as well as the revision of the electoral law. The U.S. State Department's annual Report to the Congress is even more hardlined. In mid-September, the European Parliament asked Obiang Nguema to see that the "worrying increase in reprehensible acts against the democratic opposition" cease.

In its 1992 report, which was published during 1993, the European Union explained that the "continual serious violations of human rights have made it difficult to develop cooperation with Equatorial Guinea."

Towards the end of 1993, the Human Rights Commission's consultant, E. L. Duhalde, expressed the UN's concern and described the elections as nontransparent. The report of Mr. Artucio, the new special rapporteur, was discussed by the Commission in March 1994, listing generalized violation of fundamental freedoms and rights, and stressed the total lack of independence of the judiciary, and painted a dark picture of an absolute dictatorship. The national commission for human rights does not function. Later, A. Artuccio, as well as the press, indicated that the situation had slightly improved. The United Nations considered financing human rights courses, one for the military, the police and prison staff, and another reserved for political leaders, and a seminar on women's rights. In late September, a human rights activist (Aguado Ndong Nguema) was murdered in Nsok (Niefang) by security forces, and in early October, three human rights activists and members of the Committee of the Convergency for Social Democracy (CPDS) were arrested near Niefang, and tortured.

Artucio stayed in the capital for five days in early May 1995, along with Eduardo Duhalde and Miguel de la Lama. He visited the Playa Negra prison, but did not note any signs of torture. He did not go to Río Muni, which represents 90% of the country's population. Even before submitting his report to the headquarters of the UNO in Geneva, he made soothing declarations to the press in Spain, and was of the opinion that the situation had not gotten any worse for more than a year. On May 17, the United Nations high commissioner for human rights, José Ayala Lasso, corrected this "optimism," also in Madrid, and declared on the basis of his own information that in Equatorial Guinea "severe violations of human rights" had been observed. Ambassador Nsobeya protested and alleged misinformation. On May 18, the European Parliament, in a plenary session, demanded the suspension of aid to the Nguemists, with the exception of humanitarian aid, because no progress had been realized in the direction of human rights. In July, Amnesty International stated that

the number of people arbitrarily detained for having exercised their right to the freedom of expression has increased from year to year since 1992.... Hundreds of political activists have been detained and imprisoned with neither charges nor judgement, under pitiful conditions. The practice of turning members of opposition parties into "opinion prisoners" goes back several years. . . .The political detainees are subjected routinely to torture and ill treatment.

Exit and entry visas are compulsory in the country. On October 12, 1995, Emma Bonino, European commissioner, declared: "Cooperation with Equatorial Guinea has never really started, because of human rights problems."

In its 1996 report addressed to the United Nations Human Rights Commission, the American NGO, Freedom House, placed Equatorial Guinea among the most repressive regimes in the world. Before the same Commission, the Swiss minister for Foreign affairs and acting president of the Organization for the Security and Cooperation in Europe, Flavio Cotti, placed Equatorial Guinea along with Nigeria and Sudan among the African countries where "serious problems have been observed" where democratization and the observance of human rights are concerned. The U.S. State Department, in its April 1996 Report to the Congress on the state of Human Rights in the World (1995), stated that the two successive Nguemist regimes trample on fundamental and

severely restrict freedom of speech. . . the Government . . . effectively limits the right of assembly . . . even as the right of assembly and association is provided for within the Constitution. However, even in private homes, government authorization must be obtained for any gathering of more than 10 persons for discussions that the regime consider political. . . . Despite the formalities of a multipartite form of government, President Obiang [Nguema], in power since 1979, together with his associates, dominates the Government. The President's Democratic Party of Equatorial Guinea (PDGE) controls the judiciary and the legislature, the latter through fraudulent elections. . . .Citizens do not have the right to change their government.

The United Nations special rapporteur confirms the absence of freedom. The bulletin of the PDGE, the *Voz de Pueblo,* stated in May 1996: "It is certain that human rights are not violated any more in Equatorial Guinea than in any other country." In reality, specialists estimate that the Nguemist regime violates about 85% of the articles of the Universal Declaration of Human Rights. In May, the "Nguemist" Commission of Human Rights considered the creation of a National Center for Human Rights. It established a commission in charge of prison visits. In August 1996, an Argentinean expert from the United Nations Commission on Human Rights spent 10 days giving a course on the rights of man. In November 1996, one of the leaders of the CPDS, Celestino Bakale, was imprisoned for three days in the capital, to punish him for what he said on Radio Exterior de España. In December 1996, the French bulletin *d'Afrique Noire* reminded that "the persistence of serious violations of human rights has made the development of cooperation with Equatorial Guinea very difficult; since mid-1992, no serious action of cooperation has been carried out."

At the beginning of the 1990s, the mining engineer and planter Angel N. Oló Bahamonde (born in 1944) was preparing a palm oil project. But during the summer of 1991 he had to flee to Spain. Oló had been arrested several times in 1986 and 1987 for political reasons, and his passport as well as his plantations had been seized. In 1993, the Human Rights Commission of the UN admitted that Oló had been the victim of political discrimination and violations of the Convention on Civic and Political Rights signed by the nguemists. The Commission demanded that his property be given back to him and asked for a financial compensation. Oló is still waiting.

On April 15, 1997, Vice-Prime Minister Francisco-J. Ngomo Mbengono, in front of the Human Rights Commission in Geneva, said that his country has "successfully learnt" to be democratic and respect human rights; human rights are one of the government's priorities. In his 1997 report, the special rapporteur Artucio said that the judiciary system totally lacks independence, that there is evidence of the use of torture and bad treatment, that human rights are repeatedly and seriously violated, and that political parties of the opposition are harassed and repressed. Shortly after, the nguemists demanded that Artucio be replaced.

After the failed attempted coup by Moto Nsá in May 1997, the leaders of the political parties registered in Equatorial Guinea ask Spain not to be fooled by the democratic tricks offered by Obiang Nguema. In Spain, the PSOE refused to "trade human rights against oil." E. Haro Tegglen (*El País,* June 28, 1997) said: "The love of the ancient colonisers for the assassins to whom they handed the power or who obtained power with their help, is without limits. Especially if oil is discovered." The coordinator of the Spanish Committe for Aid to Refugees (CEAR),

Jorge Canarias, qualified Aznar as being "non-presentable," because of his ties with Obiang Nguema. He added (June 24, 1997): "Equatorial Guinea is not a country but the possession of Obiang Nguema and his clan, who shows no respect whatsoever for human rights." Artucio arrived at the same time as an evaluative mission of the UN. Minister of Foreign Affairs Oyono asked him not to be content with the invalidations made by pressure groups or radical opposition. Freedom House (New York), in December 1997, rated Equatorial Guinea in matters of political rights and fundamental liberties at level 7 on a 1–7 scale, number 7 being the least free category. It received the same rating as far as freedom of information is concerned.

In its report of January 30, 1998, the U.S. Department of State reported that:

Serious and systematic violations of human rights have continued, although there has been an improvement in some fields. . . .The main abuses done by security forces include: physical violence against prisoners, torture, beating up prisoners, extortions from prisoners, house search without a warrant and seizure of possessions without trial. The conditions of detention are still dangerous for life. The judiciary system does not guarantee fair trials and is influenced by the executive. . . .Discrimination and violence against women and foreigners is still a serious problem.

As for the special rapporteur of the UN Human Rights Commission, he asked, in his 1998 report, that the authorities immediately stop all form of torture and all other cruel, inhuman, and degrading treatment, and that they find the ones who are responsible, and have them judged and punished by means of disciplinary and criminal law. In his March 1998 addendum (Bubi issue), he says:

A great number [of people] have undergone serious beatings and torture, showing on their bodies (arms and legs) wounds and signs of ill-treatment: this has also been observed on people who were released. . . .The majority remains in solitary confinement in spite of the time elapsed. . . .The lawyers were not authorised to visit them or provide them with technical assistance. . . .The rapporteur must report that the State is to be considered responsible of not having guaranteed the security and integrity of the people who were under its custody.

The 1998 Report of Doctors without Borders confirms that "General Teodoro Obiang Nguema continues to violate human rights." In December1998, the special rapporteur of the UN for human rights, A. Artucio, was on an assignment in Malabo.

See also Artucio A.; Catholics; Democracy; Elections; Esono Mika, P. J.; European Union; Eya Nchama, C. M.; International Committee of the Red Cross; Internet; Mobil Corp.; Ngonde Maguga, M.-E.; Olo Obono, J.; Terror; Torture; United States of America; Yates, J. M.

IBONGO IYANGA, Saturnino, 1937–1969. Ndowe schoolteacher, journalist, and M.A. in Mass communications (Spain). He started a degree in international relations at Columbia University (New York) at the time of independence. Member of the MONALIGE, deputy of the Asamblea General (General Assembly or Parliament), he participated in the Constitutional Conference. Macías Nguema's Secretariado Conjunto accused him of being pro-Spanish. In November 1968 he was appointed ambassador to the United Nations by Macías Nguema "in the country's interest." After Ndongo Miyone's so-called attempted coup d'etat on March 5, 1969, he was lynched at Santa Isabel airport on March 9, 1969.

IDEA POPULAR DE GUINEA ECUATORIAL (IPGE) (Popular Idea of Equatorial Guinea). This movement was set up in Ambam in Cameroon on September 30, 1959, with Nkuna Ndongo as president and Mbá Ovono as secretary-general. It has been erroneously stated that the IPGE had been founded by E. Eworo and C. L. Ateba, who were in fact only candidates to these two posts.

IPGE was prohibited by Spain. It had close ties with the Cameroonese nationalist movements until IPGE's recognition by Spain in 1963. It is said to have been subsidized by the Cameroonese government, one of its wings being in favor of a federation with its northern neighbor. This idea broke up the party at the Ambam Congress, on August 31, 1963; the opponents to the federation with Cameroon, led by J. Seng, founded the Movimiento de Unión Nacional (MUN), which under Ondo Edu was to become the MUNGE. In October 1964 Mbá Ovono and Ndongo Miyone (MONALIGE) founded the FRENAPO, which failed for ideological reasons. After a "communist" domination within the IPGE committee, between 1964 and 1967, the party split up again, the moderate branch creating the ephemeral FERBUBLANC (Fernandinos, Bubi, Blancos). The merging of the other branch with the MUNGE was considered for some time. During the Constitutional Conference, IPGE was represented by Eworo Obama, Edu Mbuy, and Nvo Nguema. The tripartite coalition called Secretariado Conjunto, composed of members from IPGE, MUNGE, and MONALIGE favored Macías Nguema's ascendance but this did not benefit IPGE, which only received the Health Ministry in the first government (Ekong Andeme, exiled in Cameroon until 1979). Like other parties, IPGE was abolished in January 1970 in view of the creation of the PUNT.

IKENGE IBIYA, Saturnino. 1834–1901. A Benga from Corisco, first Christian (Presbyterian) minister of Equatorial Guinea, trained in the United States, in charge of the Corisco parish in 1875. The Presbyterian program was aimed at freeing the African church from its state of financial dependence through commercial plantations and through training in specialized professions. With the help of Rev. Robert H. Nassau (1835–1921), he published *Customs of the Benga and* *their Neighbours* (1875). Upon the Claretians' arrival in Corisco in 1884, he became their Benga teacher, and allowed them to use the books he had in his possession. But the Spanish Claretian missionaries sought to frustrate his missionary work right from their arrival in 1884 and dubbed him the "little clergyman." Ikenge wrote letters of protest to the Claretian authorities in Santa Isabel. This led to his being sued for writing "impertinent letters" and confined to Santa Isabel. Rev. Ikenge Ibiya died on February 28, 1901.

IKUGA EBOMBEBOMBE, Andrés. b. 1916. Ndowe, member of the MUNGE. One of the four members of the Ndowe delegation to the Constitutional Conference of 1967–1968. He did not participate in the 1968 elections. In October 1968 he became the first finance minister of the republic of Equatorial Guinea. In 1972 he was replaced by Nko Ibasa Rondo. On November 12, 1968, he published in the local newspaper *Ebano* a poem comparing Macías Nguema to the Messiah.

ILLEGAL TRAFFICKING see Argentina; Democratic Progressive Alliance; Diplomacy; Drugs; Ebang Mbele Abang, A.; Maho Sikacha, J. L.; Mikomeseng, Moto Nsá, S.; National Institute for Social Security; Navigation; Nepotism; Nguema Edu, F.; Nguema Ela Mangue Ndong, G.; Nguema Esono, L.; Nguema Mbasogo Ondo, A.; Niefang; Nigeria; Obiang Mangue, L.; Obiang Nguema, T.; Ondo Ayang, L.; Shinkame, J.; Torture; United Kingdom; Victims.

INDEPENDENCE (October 12, 1968). The dissatisfaction of the Guinean teachers after the Spanish government's refusal in 1947 to adjust their salaries to those of other officials (proposal submitted by Alvarez García) led to the Cruzada Nacional de Liberación created in 1950 at the instigation of Acacio Mañe with men like Ondo Micha, Enrique Nvó, and Ndongo Miyone. In 1958 Acacio Mañe, supported by his colleagues of the Cruzada, addressed an appeal for independence to the United Nations, after which he had to take refuge in Cameroon where he joined Perea Epota and Ateba Nsoh to found the IPGE. With provincialization appeared the first nationalist parties, e.g., IPGE and MONALIGE, but not being recognized by Spain, their leaders remained in neighboring countries. In 1962, at the Head of State's Conference of the African and Malagasy Union, in Libreville (Gabon) Ndongo Miyone submitted a manifesto proclaiming the creation of the Liberation Committee of Spanish Guinea. In February 1963 the Coordination Bureau for the Spanish-Guinean Movements was set up in Ambam (Cameroon) with Maho Sikacha as secretary general, but ideological conflicts split the movement. In June 1963, eminent Bubi themselves started to formulate nationalist claims, in particular to counter the claims of annexation of Fernando Po by Nigerian trade unions.

Independence of Equatorial Guinea was largely determined by the investigations of the United Nations Trusteeship Committee and the pressures of Afro-Asians, contained by the United States veto. In the course of preparation for autonomy, Spain finally authorized the nationalist parties. Since MONALIGE and IPGE were considered "communist," Spain favored the creation of Ondo Edu's MUNGE, which was more conciliatory towards the metropolis. Before the Constitutional Conference the Unión Bubi and the Unión Democrática Fernandina also appeared. The Unión Bubi was stimulated by the head of the Spanish government in order to encourage separate independence for the two provinces.

During the Constitutional Conference, the unitarian ideology of the Río Muni parties faced the separatist one of Fernando Po. The Secretariado Conjunto, grouping the dissident elements of the MONALIGE, MUNGE, and IPGE, adopted the line of Macías Nguema. The constitution produced by the conference marked the unitarians' triumph. It was accepted by the referendum despite Macías Nguema's opposition, advised by García Trevijano. This attitude enabled Macías to attract public attention and thanks to a well-organized election campaign, he became president after the second ballot. The first government of the republic of Equatorial Guinea took office on October 12, 1968, at midday.

In January 1969 the first executions of the country's educated persons began, with Ondo Edu. After Ndongo Miyone's so-called attempted coup d'etat on March 5, 1969, and the departure of 7,000 of the 8,000 Spaniards living in the country, Macías Nguema after proclaimed the state of emergency (Emergencia), asked for technical assistance by the UN and the OAU. Early in 1970 he outlawed all political parties, creating the PUN (Partido Unico Nacional), which in 1973 became the PUNT (Partido Unico National de Trabajadores), with statutes attributed to García Trevijano. In 1971 the Juventud en Marcha con Macías was changed into a paramilitary force. At the July 1973 PUNT Congress, Macías Nguema was nominated lifetime president, a step that he qualified as the beginning of "total independence." In 1976, the national holiday commemorating independence achieved on October 12, 1968, was changed to March 5, former PUNT holiday and anniversary of Ndongo Miyone's so-called attempted coup.

Ever since independence, Spain has remained the country's major supplier and buyer. After the 1979 coup, however, France rapidly assumed the role of special protector.

INDEPENDENT PARTY (Partido Independiente, PI). A group promoted by lawyer José Olo Obono, ex-CPDS, Acacio Mba Ndong, and Eduardo Medjía, that appeared during the second semester of 1995. Its slogan: "Dialogue, reconciliation, development."

INDUSTRY. In 1997, the Ministery of Industry began a five-year program. In the January 21, 1998, government, Vidal Choni Becoba was minister of industry, trade and the promotion of small- and medium-sized firms. Pedro-Crisitno Bueriberi was vice-minister.

See Mecheba Fernandez, T.

INFOGE see Instituto de Fomento de Guinea Ecuatorial

INSTITUTE FOR DEMOCRATIC STRATEGIES (Virginia) see Internet

INSTITUTO DE ESTUDIOS AFRICANOS (Institute of African Studies). Created in 1945 in Madrid, under the plan of the Dirección General de Marruecos y Colonias, it was directed until 1968 by Días de Villegas. Publisher of the review *Archivos,* the Institute practically monopolized research and publications concerning Spanish Guinea, adjusting them to the line of the Movimiento Nacional. Archives and Documents were taken over by the Archivos Generales de Administración, at Alcala de Henares.

INSTITUTO DE FOMENTO DE GUINEA ECUATORIAL (INFOGE) (Development Institute of Equatorial Guinea). Company created in 1970 with García Trevijano's assistance and Mbá Ada as president, aiming at monopolizing all external trade. Mbá Ada was accused of misappropriation of funds and arrested for some time. Dissolved in 1972, INFOGE made room for Simed S.A. (in the hands of García Trevijano). Both companies were supposed to develop Guinea beyond the Spanish economic sphere, but also to monopolize external trade.

INSTITUTO FORESTAL (Forestry Institute). Created in 1929 after the separation of the Agricultural Department and the Forestry Department and taken over in 1968 by Macías Nguema, who assumed all forestry affairs, maybe because he himself worked in the Forestry Institute as a clerk in 1944. Since 1971 the Institute has been headed by a relative of Macías Nguema, Micha Nguema, himself a former clerk of the Institute, member of the PUNT Central Committee. The Institute was supposed to reclaim a considerable amount of material left behind by the Spanish forest rangers, but appeared incapable of doing so. Reforestation duties have never been used for replanting exploited forests, and during the 1990–1999 decade the forest has been destroyed by Asian companies.

INTERIOR AND LOCAL COMMUNITIES, Ministry of see Police

INTERNATIONAL BANK FOR RECONSTRUCTION AND DEVELOPMENT (IBRD or World Bank). In 1983, the IBRD granted $2.4 million in aid. In 1984, there was a project of developmental strategy for the purpose of financing the services of specialists who had been living in the country for a long time (disregarding the diaspora which was capable of occupying the posts without foreign debts on the part of the country).

In 1985, IDA lent $10 million for the restoration of cocoa plantations. In 1996, this project (IDEPA), for a sum of $12 million had failed due to Nguemist fraud. In 1987, A new Rehabilitation Import Credit, amounting to $10 million, was cofinanced by IDA and the World Bank's Special Fund for Africa.

In 1988, an IBRD expert reported the country's economic development to be extremely negative. This was confirmed towards the end of 1989, by an IMF/IBRD mission. The IBRD continued to oppose the renovation of Bata Airport, as it considered roads as being more important. It demanded the cessation of toxic waste deposits on the island of Annobón, before $10 million was lent for structural adjustments, and reported that each bimonthly consignment of concentrates from the petroleum deposit in Alba (Walter Int., Mobil Oil) brought in $1 million, which never reached the public exchequer. In May 1994, the IBRD put forth a project for environmental protection at Mt. Basile, in Northern Fernando Po and in Annobón, for $5 million.

In 1997, M. Ali Bourhane (Comoros) was executive director of the World Bank for Equatorial Guinea and most French, Lusitanian and Spanish speaking African countries, with Luc-Abdi Aden as alternate.

In 1998, the World Bank started financing several projects in the secor of electricity ($US Mio). See also Corruption; Electricity; United States.

INTERNATIONALE CHRETIENNE-DEMOCRATE (Christian-Democratic International) This organization, which represents most of the world's

Christian Democratic parties, made a formal statement to the UN Human Rights Commission on February 22, 1985, about the violation of civil rights by the Obiang Nguema regime. They repeated denunciations of Nguemist violence in 1992.

INTERNATIONAL COMMISSION OF JURISTS (ICJ). The 1979 report of the ICJ points to a number of procedural aberrations in the trial of Macías Nguema. In the course of the debate in the UN Human Rights Commission in March 1980, the ICJ underlined the continuing risks of deportation in Equatorial Guinea. In 1982, the ICJ was able to expose the dictatorial nature of the Nguemist regime on the basis of an analysis of the August 1982 Constitution that consolidated Obiang Nguema's power.

INTERNATIONAL COMMITTEE OF THE RED CROSS (ICRC). In 1968, shortly before independence, the ICRC started relief flights to Biafra from Santa Isabel Airport. With rumors circulating about weapon transports (in fact these probably came from Portuguese São Tome), Ndongo Miyone asked to stop the flights from Equatorial Guinean territory in January 1969, four months after independence. On January 17, 1969, the ICRC transferred its base to Dahomey (Benin).

The Soviet Red Cross was the only one to have made a donation in 1981 to the second Nguemist dictatorship. As for Spain, a number of "dubious" donations were reported, especially soporifics and weight loss pills, from the Spanish Red Cross. The country also received date-expired penicillin and a lot of spirit.

On July 24, 1986, Equatorial Guinea joined the four Geneva Conventions (1949) as well as the two Additional Protocols (1977), with effect from January 24, 1987. In August, an ICRC mission visited the country. The Swiss Red Cross helped create a national society and took charge of the salaries. Elias Maho Sikacha was named general secretary in May. The government provided a building and approved the statutes.

In 1989, the national society was still not recognized, even though it had 3,500 members. The ICRC began the training of Army officials in the observance of the Geneva Conventions. In July 1993, an information seminar on the principles of the Red Cross and the regulations of humanitarian law were held. The 1993 Report, published in May 1995 specified that "once again, the authorities have refused to give the ICRC the authorization to visit the detention centers placed under the control of the national security services."

On September 28, 1994, the national society for the Red Cross was officially recognized. In April 1995, the U.S. Department of State's Report to the Congress recalled, "The government refused to permit the ICRC to establish an office or visit prisons or detainees." The ICRC gave classes on the rules of war to instructors chosen among officers of the armed forces, of security, and the police. The 1995 Report of the ICRC (published 1996) mentions that President Obiang Nguema will allow visits to prisons.

During the spring of 1995, it took action, along with the National Red Cross and the Swiss Red Cross, to try to repatriate the Equato-Guineans who had been thrown out of Gabon.

In its 1996 report of activities, the ICRC reports its first visit to prisoners in two jails and eight police stations. It also obtained authorization to visit military camps. A distribution of medical items was also organized.

In 1998, the president of the National Red Cross was Elias Maho Sicacha, the vice-president, Jeonico Mitogo Edjang, and the secretary general, Jesus José Mba Nchama.

See also Biafra.

INTERNATIONAL COURT OF JUSTICE ON ANIMAL RIGHTS. Declared Nguemist Equatorial Guinea guilty of abetting elephant poaching and plundering of the African continent, in June 1989 at Geneva. See also Elephants.

INTERNATIONAL FEDERATION OF HUMAN RIGHTS see Gabon; Human Rights

INTERNATIONAL FEDERATION OF JOURNALISTS. The Annuary of the African Press (Brussels, 1996) informs, among other things, that the only alternative source of information in nguemist Equatorial Guinea is *La Verdad,* the magazine of Convergency for Social Democracy. "Its staff and readers have had to pay a heavy price for it." The Annuary concluded:

> Democratisation in Equatorial Guinea is still a fiction, the result of international pressure on the government, which would not remain in power one more day if it were not for foreign assistance, which allows the country to survive. The possibility of the authorities opening up will depend on the international community's desire to put the necessary pressure to have the situation evolve.

INTERNATIONAL FEDERATION OF LIBERAL AND RADICAL YOUTH. In 1993, in Turku (Finland, November 26–28) IFLRY published a resolution against the continuous violation of human rights and condemned Obiang Nguema's regime.

The executive committee of IFLRY, in Kampen (The Netherlands), published in May 1995 a new resolution condemning the psychological and physical brutality used against Moto Nsá. It asked the European Union and Spain to stop their financial aid to Obiang Nguema. It deplored also the Nazi salutation used during the PDGE meeting.

INTERNATIONAL FOUNDATION FOR ELECTION SYSTEMS (IFES, Washington). Carried out with a team of five the observation of the February 25, 1996, presidential election, the first multiparty presidential election to be held. the mission stated lack of many minimal standards: absence of credible voter registration, lack of ballot secrecy, etc. (see Elections). IFES recommended "the complete and thorough reform of elecoral law; the creatio of a new voter register; a national civil education and voter education campaign." In November 1997, IFES sent a two-member assessment team to examine conditions to warrant international assistance in the 1998 legislative elections. The IFES team noted that the government had not adhered to the revised National Pact discussed with 13 political parties. On June 10, 1998, IFES hosted a reception for Obiang Nguema, addressed him with concerns raised in 1997, and heard the dictator about the steps taken in preparation for the November 1998 legislative elections.

INTERNATIONAL FUND FOR AGRICULTURAL DEVELOPMENT (IFAD). In 1985, there existed three projects worth $2.4 million ($90,000 provided by the state), in the north-western part of Rio Muni, for the improvement of local agricultural production: corn, peanuts, yams, and the relaunch of coffee plantations. It involved 3,000 families.

INTERNATIONAL MONETARY FUND (IMF). A mission of the IMF (spring 1996) complained of "a total absence of transparency" in government accounting. Another mission in August noted that the Nguemist government showed no interest in the proper management of public affairs. In June 1998, Obiang Nguema asked once again for the technical assistance of the IMF and the World Bank.

INTERNATIONAL MUSEUM FOR CONTEMPORARY ART (Museo Internacional de Arte contemporáneo). Situated in the presidential palace of Bata. It was the pride of Leandro Mbomio Nsue. The museum looks abandoned today.

INTERNATIONAL SOCIALIST. On February 25, 1996, at Ouagadougou (Burkina Faso), the African Committee requested the International Community not to recognize the "reelection" of Obiang Nguema. C. Bakale, and C. Mbomio (CPDS) participated in the annual meeting in New York, in September 1996.

INTERNET. Since 1998, Equatorial Guinea has an official internet program: "Welcome to the Republic of Equatorial Guinea. Bienvenido" (info@equatorial-guinea.org). Examples of contents:

Education: "Primary school pupils have risen from 65,000 in 1986 to more than 100,000 in 1994. Education is free and compulsory for children between the ages of 6 and 14." UNESCO/UNICEF reported in 1995 that 77% of the less than 500 teachers have insufficient secondary school training; there are 80 students per toilet (Ethiopia 23). See Education.

Human Rights: "With the assistance of the Institute for Democratic Strategies (Virginia), a Center for the Promotion of Democracy and of Human Rights in Equatorial Guinea has been created" in Bata and Malabo. Freedom House (New York), in December 1997, rated Equatorial Guinea at level 7 on a 1–7 scale, number 7 being the least free category. See Human Rights; Terror; Torture.

Petroleum: "President Obiang has pledged to ensure that revenues from oil production will be used wisely to improve the economic situation of all the peoples of Equatorial Guinea." The Document of Strategy 1996–1998 of the ADB considered in January 1998 that "the economy of Equatorial Guinea, since the beginning of the oil production in 1992, has shown a fast growth, but the population has benefited very little from it."

Press: "The Republic of Equatorial Guinea is proud of its rich and vibrant independent media outlets." Examples:

El Sol: publisher expelled in March 1998;

La Gaceta: monthly publication (xeroxed);

La Voz del Pueblo: very occasional publication of the PDGE (party of the nguemist dictatorship).

Foreign newspapers are confiscated at the arrival of the planes.

A 1998 Reporters without Borders report said there is no freedom of press in Equatorial Guinea.

IPUA UBENGA, Joaquin see Ekuku

IRADIER Y BULFY, Manuel. 1854–1911. Basque. A graduate in philosophy and arts, he created the Sociedad Viajera which in 1870 became "La Exploradora." Having been able to collect 10,000 pesetas, he launched an expedition on January 12, 1975. At the end of May he started his exploration from Corisco following the coast to Cape San Juan, then traveling across the Muni estuary and its affluents, especially the Utamboni, visiting Mounts Paluviole and Cristal. Back to Santa Isabel in January 1876, he remained in Fernando Po with his wife, exploring the island, climbing the Pico de Santa Isabel, and teaching in a non-confessional school of the capital. Having returned to Spain, he faced a general lack of understanding, after an 884-day trip and a 1,876-km journey through Río Muni. Together with some friends Iradier prepared a second expedition, helped by the Sociedad de Africanistas y Colonistas. Iradier and Dr. Ossorio Zabala arrived in Santa Isabel on September 28, 1884, two-and-a-half months after Nachtigal had occupied the Cameroon coast on behalf of Germany, and the United Kingdom had taken the Niger zone and Old Calabar. France for its part was about to occupy Río Muni. Iradier's second exploration trip rapidly changed to a territorial conquest. From October 17 to the end of November 1884 the expedition annexed 13,300 sq km (approx. 5,133 sq mi), signing hundreds of treaties with chiefs representing some 50,000 inhabitants. Fallen ill, Iradier had to return to Madrid. He was a well-known and popular explorer. In 1887 Iradier's two volumes of *Africa Tropical* were published, which he improved for a second edition at the beginning of the 20th century. From the 800,000 sq km inherited by Spain from Portugal through the Pardo Treaty, the Berlin Conference only reckoned 180,00 sq km to Spain. From the 50,000 sq km conquered by Iradier, Ossorio, and Montes de Oca, the Paris Treaty in 1900 left only 26,000 sq km.

Iradier died in 1911, without any official celebration. A decree of 1929, ratified under Franco in 1940, granted his son a concession of 1,000 hectares in Río Muni. From 1936 to 1968 Kogo was called Puerto-Iradier.

IRAN. In July 1998, Miguel Oyono, minister of foreign affairs, went to Iran for four days, invited by Teheran, to discuss the possibility of establishing diplomatic relations and cooperation. Iranian companies coould participate in public works or oil projects.

ISLANDS see Annobón; Bañe; Borders; Elobey; Fernando Po (Bioko); Oko; Río Benito; Ukoko

ISORY see Timber

ISRAEL. In 1974, Equatorial Guinea received $1 million from Libya for the "struggle against imperialism and Zionism." In 1985, rumors of the setting up of diplomatic relations with Israel began; Morocco threatened to withdraw its mercenaries. In 1988, Obiang Nguema negotiated to receive Israeli guards, via South Africa, in order to replace the Moroccans. In 1989, the Israeli lumber company Yona International was swindled during the acquisition of the concession for the

French company SEMGE. In 1994, the two countries restored diplomatic relations. Ambassador Moshe Liba, a former university professor, consul, and ambassador in various countries, lives in Yaound (Cameroon). He is accredited to four other Central African countries. At the end of 1996, several members of the CPDS were invited to Israel to attend various classes and seminars. They had interviews with the National Administration.

See also Timber.

ITALY. After the 1979 coup, Italy was awarded contracts for the construction in Bata of fuel oil reservoirs and power stations thanks to funding available through the European Community. In August 1982 an Italian wood-processing plant was set up in Bata and in December 1983, the Italian oil company Agip began prospecting alongside the French Elf-Aquitaine and American companies. A group of architects put up a proposal to the government for the construction of 3,000 dwellings and four hotels. In 1987, Italy offered $5 million for the rehabilitation of the port of Bata, in exchange for wood.

In 1990, Margarita Costa was the Italian ambassador (living in Yaound). Italy occupied the third place, after Spain and China, and before France for cooperation: roads, fisheries, training, maintenance and management of the port of Bata. The port was a joint venture, Promoport Guinea (Trieste/Equatorial Guinea). The law 185 of 1990 forbids the transfer of Italian weapons without the authorization of the government. In spite of this law, radar equipment was sent to Equatorial Guinea. In early 1991, an odd Italian foundation (Mafia-connected?) awarded Obiang Nguema the Umberto Biancomano Prize (after a so-called lord of the middle ages). The people joked, calling it the Obiangcapremio Prize. It seemed to have been financed by foresters, with the support of university graduates. In 1993, the Nguemists contacted Cuba and Italy in order to obtain doctors. Italy wished to write off Equatorial Guinea's debts, following the devaluation of the CFA franc. In 1996, Italian projects for the development of small-scale fishing ($10 million) and the realization of Hotel Media Luna, at Bata ($12 million) had failed due to Nguemist exactions.

The Mafia was said to have its headquarters in Hotel Media Lune, on the road to the Bata Airport. An Italiam firm restored the presidential palace in Malabo, with Italian marble.

See also AGIP; Bata; Cataneo; Centro de Desarrollo de la Educación; China, People's Republic of; Corruption; Dougan Beaca, J. D.; Economy; Evuna Owono Asangono Mba, A.; Finances; Mafia; Obiang Ndong, D.; Obiang Nguema, T.; Oyono Ayingono, D.; Public Health; Telecommunications; Toxic Wastes.

ITOHA CREDA, Aurelio Nicolas, d. 1969. Bubi. Planter. Member of the Diputación Provincial (Assembly) of Fernando Po and a deputy at the Asamblea General (Parliament) from 1964 to 1968. He became Labor Minister in 1967. Member of the Bubi Union, he presented with Maho Sikacha, Borico Toichoa and Watson Bueco, on August 12, 1966, a motion to the Consejo de Gobierno proposing the separation of the two provinces of Fernando Po and Río Muni after independence. He was elected at the Provincial Council of Fernando Po in September 1968, and liquidated in the purge of spring 1969.

IVORY COAST see Navigation

IVILI, Constantino. Secretary of the organization of the Socialist Party (PSGE) in 1993. In November he announced the dismissal of the general secretary Tómas Mecheba, for having announced his participation in the elections, ignoring the boycott called by the party.

IYANGA PENDI, Augusto-Calixto. Ndowe. Born April 20, 1945, at Mbondo (Rio Campo zone). Graduate of the Escuela superior in Santa Isabel. Teacher's Training College in Murcia. Holds a degree and a Ph.D. in philosophy and literature (Valencia). Professor of the theory and the history of education, at the University of Valencia. He presides over the Association for the Organization of Guinean Technicians and Professionals in Spain (OTEPGE). In June 1992, he was part of the Commission for Negotiation with Adolfo Suarez for democratic transition in Equatorial Guinea. He has authored a number of works on the Ndowe. He is on the Committee of the Ndowe Community of Spain.

IZAGUIRRE. Spanish company exploiting since 1926 a forest concession near Río Benito. It also owned in Bolondo (in front of Río Benito) a 778-hectare palm oil plantation that was to become the María Victoria plantation.

❖ J ❖

JAILS. The April 1995 Report of the State Department on Human Rights Practices observes that "Prison conditions are life-threatening." In 1998, before and after the huge Bubi trial, several prisoners died in Playa Negra due to appalling conditions of the detention. See Puye, M.

See also Abaga Ondo Maye, E.; Amnesties; Annobón; Artucio, A.; Aviation; Bata; Benito; Rio Benito; Censorship; Convergency for Democracy; Coup d'etat of May 11-13, 1983; Coup d'etat of August 1988; Coup d'etat of Spring 1990; Coup d'etat of August 1993; Democratic Progressive Alliance; Drugs; Ebang Mbele Abang, A.; Ebebiyin, Edu, F.; Ela Abeme, J.; Elections; Elema Borengue, J.; Eeneme Ovono, J.; Engonga Ondo, A.; Esono Masie, P.; Eyama Angüe Osa, D.; France; Germany; Guinextebank; Hanna, S.; Human Rights; Joint Opposition Platform; Jones Dougan, J. L.; Justice; Kogo; Llansol, V.-G.; Martinez Nvo Bikie, J.; Mba Ondo, C.; Mecheba Ikaka, J.; Miko Abogo, P.; Missions; Modu Akuse Bindang, C.; Morocco; Moto Nsá, S; Motu Mamiaga, P.; Muñoz Ilata, S.; National Pact; Nchama, G.; Nguema Bindang, T.; Nguema Ela Mangue Ndong, G.; Niefang, Nseng Esono Nve, E.; Nve, E.; Nve Nzeng, A. F.; Obiang Nguema, T.; Olo Mba Nseng, J.; Ona Nguema, A.; Playa Negra; Plot (1981); Police; Popular Union; Progressive Party; Public Health; Refugees; Rondo Estrada, T.; Sima Ngua, A.; Social Democratic Party; Socialist Party; Spain; Terror; Torture; United States of America; *Verdad, La;* Victims; Vilarrasa, S.

JAMAICA see Santa Isabel

JANTZEN UND THORMALEN. Commercial company from Hamburg, founded by a former agent of the competing Adolf Woermann. It participated in the occupation of the Cameroonese coasts for the German government's account. It owned several warehouses in Fernando Po and on the Río Muni coast.

JAPAN. In 1980, Japan began diplomatic relations. In 1981, it lent $10 million. In 1991, Japan donated CFAFr 210 million for fisheries. In the spring of 1992, Japan offered Thai rice for CFAFr 208 million. The press alleged that the ministers for defence and for the interior had sold Cameroon 32,000 sacks of rice at 3,500 pesetas. In 1994, Japan occupied the top position in exports to Equatorial Guinea (30%). In 1995 Japan was the number two client, behind the U.S., with $15 million (mostly wood). In 1996, the Japanese project for the development of small-scale fishing, for a sum of $10 million, fell through due to Nguemist frauds.

Professor Hiroto Ueda, from Tokyo University, is in charge of a project on "Spanish in the world (1993–1988)," with an Equato-Guinea participation.

See also Cameroon; Corruption; Currency; Mbana Nchama, J.; Toxic Wastes; Trade.

JESUITS. In July 1857, the island of Fernando Po was entrusted to the Company of Jesus. The Jesuit mission of Corisco was established in 1863, by Father Francisco Javier García. Annobón was visited by Jesuits in 1861, 1864, and 1869. With the revolution in Spain, in 1868, the Jesuits encountered enormous difficulties, like "ruinous government decrees," which reduced the mission to just one parish. They threatened to withdraw. In 1872, they were officially discharged of their duties. See also Missions.

JOINT OPPOSITION PLATFORM (Plataforma de Oposición Conjunta, POC). Presented in Madrid, on November 30, 1991, but effectively inaugurated in the capital only on August 31, 1992. In October, the POC demanded that the Nguemists hold a roundtable conference to discuss the free movement of individuals, the abolition of censorship, a permanent Commission of the International Community to follow the democratization process, the cessation of intimidation and guarantee of political freedom, unconditional legalization of parties, the freeing of all political detainees, and the intervention of the UNHCR. In Brussels, the POC had interviews on the blockage of aid to the Nguemists. The POC demanded the mediation of France and Spain.

In January 1993, Obiang Nguema had an interview with the following organizations: Popular Union (UP), Liberal Democratic Convention (CLD), Progress Party (PP), Democratic and Progressive Alliance (ADP), Democratic and Social Union (UDS), Social Democratic Party (PSD). In February-March, the parties of the POC participated in negotiations with the Nguemists for a National Pact (Pacto Nacional Vinculante). The POC demanded that other strong forces in the country (students, churches) participate in the discussions. It again demanded the liberation of political prisoners, free movement of individuals, and the free exercise of political rights. It also demanded a credible electoral census. For want of trust in the Nguemist partner in the dialogue, they demanded that a notary be in charge of maintaining a diary detailing the discussions. But by March, the POC thought that international pressure was "decisive." Spain granted it a small donation of 15 million pesetas. In April, there were 11 parties (out of the 13 legalized parties). The POC maintained relations with the Socialist International, several African and international leftist groups, including the PSOE. In July, Obiang Nguema unilaterally breached the National Pact by setting the elections for September 12.

The POC organized a boycott; the dictator was forced to postpone the elections to November 21, but again without consultations. After the ritual assassination of Motu Mamiaga by relatives of Obiang Nguema, the POC demanded that the government ensure a transition with no deaths or violence. The spokesperson M. Nsa Bacale stated: "The greatest danger for the opposition is international abandonment." Toward the end of October, the majority of the village chiefs in the district of Mongomo denounced, in a signed declaration, the actions of the Nguemists and supported the POC. In early November, several minor parties let themselves be "bought" by the Nguemists. The POC still comprised six groups: ADP, AP, CPDS, PCSD, PP, UP. They addressed an Institutional Proposal to Obiang Nguema: conscious of their responsibilities, they reiterated their wish for a democratic transition, stated that they were giving up violence, and proposed a government of National Concertation led by a member of the democratic opposition. They wanted free, fair, and transparent elections. The POC appealed to the population to stay calm. The paper was rejected by the minister for the interior. The POC demanded the dissolution of the government (which the spokesperson A. F. Nve Nzeng had just declared null and void). The government qualified the proposal of the POC as an institutional coup d'etat. He claimed the parties of the POC and its leaders were responsible for any disorder that might occur, and called them conspirators. The POC, he said, had no judicial personality. The fact that seven parties had accepted to go to the polls, proved that the elections would be "free, and democratic." Towards the end of October, the leaders of the parties of the POC found themselves forbidden from moving about in the country, and therefore prevented from participating in the electoral campaign. After the elections, the POC demanded a Peace Conference in the name of the king of Spain. The POC suggested to the U.S. government to paralyze the drilling of petroleum by American companies in order to cut off supplies to Obiang Nguema. In December, a manhunt was organized to stop members and supporters of the POC, which was confirmed by A. Artucio's report discussed by the United Nations Human Rights Commission. In August 1994, the POC had an interview with Obiang Nguema, who informed it that his policy of "democratization" enjoyed support from France.

In early 1995, the POC decided to create an organization with unitary coordination and to present single candidates for the impending municipal elections. Following the sentencing of Moto Nsá, in early March 1995, the POC met donor countries and the UNDP, and decided to participate in the municipal elections, with a single list (its symbol being one eye). In April, the second party convention of the PDGE at Bata, though a delegation of the tame opposition did (UDENA, PSD, PSGE, CLD, PCSD). The POC, according to the few international observers, emerged as the winner in the September 17 municipal elections, but the Nguemists adjudged themselves 19 out of 27 municipalities. Finally, the POC obtained 79 seats in Fernando Po (including the capital), and 56 seats in Río Muni. In many localities, reprisals were inflicted because of the POC victory, in particular the suspensions of several public works. Towards the end of September 1995, the European Parliament demanded, in vain, that the POC victory be observed. The POC's appeal, addressed to the Constitutional Court was rejected by it towards the end of November.

In mid-January 1996, following the advancement of the presidential election to February 25, the POC decided to present a single candidate. Moto Nsá, president of the PP who had been proclaiming his suitability for the post of president, not having been selected, withdrew the PP from the POC and stood for the elections; Mba Ada, president of UP, did likewise. The government took advantage of the weakening of the remaining in the Platform. The candidate chosen by the POC, the architect Amancio G. Nzé, of the CPDS, withdrew, leaving Obiang Nguema to face Moto Nsá and Mba Ada, and upon their withdrawal, he was virtually the sole candidate for his own succession. The PDGE noisily predicted the impending demise of the POC. However, in April, the party submitted a detailed report, with a list of 278 persons held, tortured, assassinated, or expelled from their posts for political reasons, to the Human Rights Commission, in Geneva. In May 1996, Mayor Alberto Ngomo, his wife, and their ten-day-old baby, as well as the town councilor Norberto Esono, and all three members of the POC, were arrested. Esono was tortured. In September 1996, C. Bakale and S. Mikó participated in the meeting of the Socialist International in New York. V. Bolekia participated in the meeting of the Christian Democratic International, in Brussels, in the company of Moto Nsa (PP). On Christmas 1996, C. Bakale fled to Spain. Soon after, S. Mikó was arrested for two days in Río Muni.

The year 1996 sounded the death knell of the POC.

See also Elections; Opposition.

JONCOBA see Timber

JONES, Juan Carlos. An athlete who in the 1970s was Spanish and European champion in the 60 m. and 100 m. Died in Spain on February 24, 1997.

JONES, Maximiliano C. Fernandino. Protestant, but educated at a Jesuit school in Spain. In July 1887 he worked as carpentry professor of the Banapa vocational school run by Claretian missionaries. He became foreman on a Spanish plantation and later developed a "finca" (plantation) for himself in Bokoko, southwest of Fernando Po. He was Claretians' providence, lending them his boat, helping to build churches, etc. In 1900 he opened a printer's shop in Santa Isabel. In 1910 he advised the Spanish troops in their repression of the Bubi revolt against forced labor. In 1920 he was the only African among the 10 largest planters of the island. Thanks to him the first thermal power station was built in Santa Isabel in 1925. The family owns a residence in Bilbao (Spain). His seven sons were educated in Spain.

JONES DOUGAN, José Luis. A Creole, born in 1940. Studied in Spain, holds a degree in law. Works as a lawyer. His family owns a number of different businesses in Equatorial Guinea. Once back in his country, he defended the interests of the Spanish who had stayed back. He was the public prosecutor in the trial of Macías Nguema (1979). In 1980, he became the director of the notarial registry in the Ministry of Justice. As a refugee in Spain, in 1983, he joined the Executive Committee of the Civil Council for the Salvation of the Nation (Junta civil de Salvación Nacional), as the secretary of the Progress Party.

In 1988, he returned to the country with Moto Nsá. He was then arrested with several others. He was accused of "irregular political activities" and imprisoned at Playa Negra. The Nguemists refused to legalize his party. He was condemned by the court to 17 years' imprisonment. This was said to be an act of vengeance by Macías Nguema's friends. Spain protested against the arrest of its dual nationals. Under pressure from the EC, Jones Dougan was released in January 1989, before a visit by Obiang Nguema to Madrid. According to the Progress Party, this release was only intended to "Give Obiang Nguema's image a face-lift." Jones Dougan died of cancer in 1993.

JONES NIGER, Wilwardo. Fernandino. Son of industrialist and businessman Maximiliano C. Jones. After completion of his studies in Spain, he worked at the Official Agricultural Department and at the Town Council of Santa Isabel. Around 1945 he became the most important native planter of Fernando Po. From 1952 to 1956 he was president of the cocoa section of the Cámara Oficial Agricola of Fernando Po. He won the municipal elections of June 1960 in Santa Isabel and became the first African mayor to be elected in Equatorial Guinea. From 1960–1964 he was also representative to the Cortes. In 1967 he founded the Unión Democrática Fernandina. In 1968, he militated in favor of Ondo Edu (MUNGE) for presidency of the republic, but his party did not win any seat, neither in Parliament or in government. In 1970, the CEIA (Community of Spaniards with Interests in Africa), with the complicity of Ambassador Nsué Ngomo, seems to have attempted to overthrow Macías Nguema, with the help of mercenaries, in order to replace him by Jones Niger.

In 1969, the Jones family possessed on the hillsides of Pico de Santa Isabel a cattle farm of 170 head, but this farm has been ruined since then. Among Jones Niger's sons, Alfredo José was provincial deputy of Fernando Po, and Representative to the Cortes from 1960–1964; another son has been a professional soccer player in Spain; Francisco Salomé, member of MUNGE, participated in the Constitutional Conference, and was on the list presented by his father for the elections of the Asamblea de la República (Parliament) in September 1968.

JOVENES ANTORCHAS see Army; Young Torches

JOVER Y TOVAR, Pedro. Spaniard, consular officer, head of the Spanish delegation at the Joint Committee for the Río Muni Border Definition in 1901. Witnessing the crumbling of Spanish territories caused him to commit suicide during this return trip to Spain of October 30, 1901.

JUAN CARLOS I, King of Spain. Juan Carlos was enthroned in 1975, after the death of General Franco. Soon after his accession the ruling party, PUNT, in Equatorial Guinea accused him of being a mere marionette. After the 1979 coup he granted Obiang Nguema an audience (April 1980). In return the dictator offered the king an elephant, and made arrangements for a return visit of the King to Equatorial Guinea in December 1980. The king was received in Santa Isabel by Obiang Nguema who referred to the visitor as "our King." This was the first visit in history of a Spanish monarch to Spain's former African possession.

From 1981 onwards, however, the Nguemists demonstrated a growing antipathy towards Spain. On June 24, the Spanish Embassy gave a reception in Santa Isabel in honor of the king's saint day. Obiang Nguema, Maye Ela, and Oyo Riqueza were invited but declined, leaving Mbá Oñana to represent the president. Subsequently in May 1982, Obiang Nguema was received by the king in Madrid but this did not bring any solution to the fundamental questions. Notwithstanding, the king put in a good word for Equatorial Guinea when he visited Gabon and Cameroon in October 1982.

After Equatorial Guinea's entry into the French currency zone, and the abortive coup of July 1986, Obiang Nguema was raised to the rank of brigadier-general by an envoy of the king in October 1986.

JUANOLA, Joaquin. Spanish. Born March 11, 1853. Claretian missionary. He arrived in Santa Isabel in January 1885. Founder of the Catholic Mission in Annobón. In 1885, a German vessel tried to take over the island of Annobón, but failed in the face of the determination of Juanola, who hoisted his country's flag in defiance of the invaders. He died on April 2, 1912, after 27 years of uninterrupted presence in Spanish Guinea.

JUNCO MIRANDA, Eduardo. A Spaniard who in 1968 succeeded Díaz de Villegas at the head of the Dirección General de Plazas y Provinicias Africanas. On October 12, 1968, he attended independence celebrations in Santa Isabel. He is the author of a study on colonial law published in 1945.

JUNTA CIVICA DE SALVACION NACIONAL see Civic Junta for National Salvation

JUNTA COORDONADORA DE LAS FUERZAS DE OPOSICION. Founded in April 1983 by representatives of FRELIGE, the Partido del Progreso, MOLIFUGE, the Group para le Reforma Política, the ANRD, and independent persons. The ANRD, however, withdrew its support in December 1983 as it had only been represented in the junta by a dissident member of little consequence.

This junta was accused by Bubi refugees of being a vehicle for the substitution of Esangui dominance by groups from Mikomeseng and Ebebiyin. Its Secretary-General, Alejo Ecube, let it be known in 1985 that it might be necessary to resort to armed struggle. It also asked Spain clearly to define its policies towards the Nguemist regime and not to sign any agreements with Obiang Nguema without first having a plan for national reconciliation that would allow for the free return of refugees.

JUNTA FOR THE COORDINATION OF OPPOSITION FORCES. Coordonadora de las Fuerzas de la Oposición, Saragoza.

JUNTA VECINAL (Town Council). Lower level of local administration initiated in 1960 at the time of provincialization, in replacement of the Consejo de Vecinos created in 1880. Most of these councils included traditional chiefs and distinguished persons. There were 42 of them in Fernando Po and 146 in Río Muni. The members were elected by the college of "patres familias."

JUSTICE. After the passage of the Lerena expedition in 1843, a Council of Justice was established in Fernando Po for the maintenance of public order and the protection of property. In 1872 Fernando Po was placed under the authority of the Havana Court (Cuba). As of 1880 Santa Isabel had its own municipal judge (later in 1888 Concepción and San Carlos). Since then, the judge of the County Court of Santa Isabel depended on the Las Palmas Court (Canaries). Spanish civil and penal codes, as well as commercial laws, were applied.

Until 1959, the nonemancipated natives were represented in court by the Patronato de Indígenas. At the local level, common law continued to exist as long as it was not contrary to the Spanish law. In the traditional system three courts had been introduced by decree in 1938: District Court (also called Racial Court) headed by the territorial administrator, assisted by the tribal chiefs; Urban Districts Court of Bata and Santa Isabel, likewise based on common law; and the Native Supreme Court. After provincialization these courts were no longer needed and a metropolitan court system was introduced. The Racial Court however remained until independence. For Europeans and for the emancipated, District Courts, a Territorial Court (Madrid), and a Supreme Court of Spain were created. In 1948 a Tutelary Court for nonemancipated under 18 years of age and children of the emancipated under 16 was created. Moreover, a Military Court existed depending on the Spanish system.

At independence, the existing structures were practically taken over. Under the July 1973 constitution, the judicial power "proceeds from the people and is exercised in its name by the People's Supreme Court" and other civil and military courts. All judges are appointed by the president of the republic and can be dismissed by him. Several ministers of justice lost their lives in Macías Nguema's personal power struggle: Eworo Ndongo and Momo Bokara, as well as Nsué Nchama, director general of the Ministry of Justice. From 1975 to 1976 Okori Dougan Kinson was Minister of Popular Justice.

After the 1979 coup, the portfolio of the military commissioner for justice was entrusted to Mensui Mbá. He was succeeded in 1981 by Tomás King Tomás and then in turn by Mansogo Nsi and Ndong Micha. Amnesty International in a 1982 report indicated that foreign companies interested in investing in Equatorial Guinea are frequently fearful of taking the plunge for as long as their investments and their staff are likely to be denied basic legal rights and protection. At the end of 1983, the Spanish press reported that citizens of Equatorial Guinea had been arrested in their country for having spoken to some Spanish persons there. The May 1987 report of Amnesty International on the military tribunals and the passing of death sentences in Equatorial Guinea shows that nothing has really changed since the days of Macías Nguema. The courts are regularly presided over by officers holding simultaneously political positions. The accused and the defense have been given practically no rights at all. There is no question of being able to appeal any decision taken by the tribunals.

In November 1989, Silvestre Siale Bilekia became minister, with José L. Nvumba, as secretary general in charge of penitentiaries, Alfredo Tomas King Tomas, as public prosecutor, Ricardo Mangue Obama Nfube, as president of the Appeals Court. Towards the end of 1990, the Spanish expert J. M. Sainz Bayón, revealed the inadequacy of the judicial personnel mainly composed of nonacademics. Laws and decrees were not published, as there was no official bulletin. In Río Muni, Col. Mba Nguema held his own court, and terrorized the population. Sainz Bayón suggested the transfer of Spanish personnel as well as speeding up of the courts. In 1992, Mariano Nsue Nguema Nsuga was the minister. In 1993, France offered to write up the new legislation and arrange the training of judicial personnel. In the December 22, 1993, government, Francisco Javier Ndongo Mbengono became the minister. In 1993, there were at least four summary executions by security forces.

The Artucio Report, discussed by the Human Rights Commission in March 1994, reported innumerable cases of torture, the total absence of principles of democracy, and widespread violations of human rights. The independence of the judiciary was simply not guaranteed. Laws were not published, and the texts were hardly ever available for reference. Following the denunciation by Eloy Elo Nve Mbengono, in January 1995, of "judicial insecurity" and of "generalized corruption," Obiang Nguema ordered an enquiry by the minister of defense, Col. M. Ebendeng, the minister for relations with the Parliament, Mariano Nsue Nguema, the director general of justice and penitentiaries, Ricardo Ele Obale, the deputy of the "tame" opposition Secundino Oyono. Quick reforms were recommended to the prime minister, S. Siale, and to the minister for justice, F. Ngomo. In the spring of that year, a military court, composed of Obiang Nguema's relatives and other members of the clan from Mongomo, judged Moto Nsá and the military personnel accused of conspiracy. On May 26, Obiang Nguema called the administration and justice officials "incapable, inefficient, ignorant, and ill-intentioned."

Artucio's report addressed to the Human Rights Commission, dated January 8, 1996, presented a number of criticisms: lack of guarantees for the independence and impartiality of judges; no separation of powers; extensive powers attributed to military courts; war councils that did not observe normal procedure; lack of confidence of the population in the fairness of the elections; no visible progress in prison conditions; homicides not inquired into; impunity of violators of human rights; release of political prisoners shortly before the arrival of the special reporter, etc. In the January 8, 1996, ministerial reshuffle, Juan Milam Tang Onvogo became minister for justice and religion, replacing Javier Ngomo, who became minister for labor and social security. Antimo Esono Ndong became the vice-minister. Mariano Nsue Nguema, Minister for relations with the Parliament, continued simultaneously as President of the Supreme Court. On April 8, 1996, Ignacio Milam Tang was reinstated in his posts, with Angel Masié Mibuy as vice-minister.

As for the April 1996 Report of the State Department on Human Rights Practices for 1995, it stressed that "The judiciary is not independent; judges serve at the pleasure of the President and are appointed, transferred, and dismissed for political reasons. Corruption is rampant." As a consequence: "The judicial system does not ensure due process and is subject to executive influence." Along with all the obvious excesses, there are however a few honest judges.

In the January 21, 1998, government, Ruben Maye Nsue Mangue was minister of justice and religion. Mrs. Evangelina Oyo Ebule was vice-minister. At the end of May 1998, a summary military trial was held in Malabo against 117 Bubi accused of being involved in the attack of army quarters in January. President of the court: Col. Santiago Mauro Nguema (trained at Zaragoza). About 50 imprisonment sentences (going up to 30 years) and 17 death penalties were issued. The witnesses from AI, the Human Rights Commission, and the Spanish press denounced the irregularities of the trial and the visible signs of torture they witessed on the accused. The accounts of the legal proceedings were never published (not even handed over to the lawyers). It was a parody of justice. In July 1998, the head of *La Gaceta de Guinea Ecuatorial,* Torribio Obiang Mba, flew into a temper because the population was worried about the impunity of the judiciary system. After the arrest of lawyer José Olo, defender of the late Martin Puye, all the lawyers of the capital resigned but two who had ties with the Nguemists. On July 14, 1998, Miguel Oyono, minister of foreign affairs, affirmed that only those condemned to death could ask for pardon. Ponciano Mbomio, a lawyer, complained that the defense attorneys did not receive the text of the sentences and therefore cannot act.

The furniture for the Supreme Court was supplied by Nigerian aid.

See also Army, Bolekia Edjapa, A.; Concepción; Courts; Democracy; Ebebiyin, Ebendeng Nsomo, M.; Elections; Ele Obale, R.; Elephants; Elo Mabale, E, R.; Epalepale Evina, F.; Esono Abaha, A.; Esono Mbomio, J.; Esono Mika, P. J.;

Esono Ndong, A.; International Court of Justice on Animal Rights; Jones Dougan, J. L.; Maho Sikacha, L. J;, Mangue Obama Nfube, R.; Masie Mibuy, A.; Mba Ondo, C.; Miko Abogo, P.; Milam Onvogo, J.; Milam Tang Onvogo, I.; Missions; Modu Akuse Bindang, C.; Moto Nsá, S.; Muatetema Rivas, C;, Ndjoku, José M.; Ndong Ela Mangue, J.; Ngomo Mbengono, F. J.; Nguema Esono, F.; Nseng Esono; Nsue Nchama; Nsue Nguema Nsuga, M.; Nve, E.; Obiang Nguema, T.; Olo Obono, J.; Ondo Esono, L.; Oyono Awong Ada, S.; Oyo Riqueza, E.; Police; Sainz Bayon, J. M.; Siale Bilekia, S.; Social Democratic Union; Tomas King Tomas.

JUVENTUD EN MARCHA CON MACIAS (Youth Macías) or Juventudes Azules (Blue Youth). Youth movement of the PUNT, created on February 22, 1969, and institutionalized on February 12, 1970. By its excesses, it contributed in February/March 1969 to provoking the departure of 7,000 Spaniards. In 1971, under the direction of R. Obiang Gonsogo, the Juventud was turned into a paramilitary force. Used as a repressive instrument, it participates for example in road controls and more generally in internal security. It is given intensive sports training by the People's Republic of China and military training by Cuban and North Korean experts.

After the 1979 coup, Vice-President Maye Ela admitted to the special rapporteur of the UN Human Rights Commission that the Juventud had been engaged in terrorizing the population. The cadres of the Juventud were integrated into the regular army in 1981. It was the former Juventud militiaman, the Esangui Nsué Ela, who was responsible for the breach of diplomatic privilege in opening the Spanish diplomatic pouch in the Ministry of Foreign Affairs in Santa Isabel in 1981.

❖ K ❖

KELLY. British naval captain who founded Concepción in 1821, then chose the location of future Clarence City (Santa Isabel). He seems to be the first one to have used the word *Bubi*.

KIE-NTEM. Formerly district of Ebebiyin.

KING NSOMO, Manuel Enrique. Creolo, b. December 19, 1944. Holds a degree in banking. Until the end of 1993, he was the director general of budgets and the state treasury, in the Ministry of Economy. In the November 1993 elections, he was elected in Luba as a deputy for the PDGE. On December 22, he became vice-minister for economy and finance. He did not figure in the January 8, 1996, government.

KING TOMAS, Alfredo Tomás see Tomas King Tomas, Alfredo

KIOSI. Locality in Río Muni, at the border of Woleu Ntem, occupied in 1974 by Gabonese forces. According to Asumu Oyono, former secretary general of the presidency, the Kiosi zone, as well as the Islands Conga, Cocotiers, and Mbañe (occupied in 1972 by Gabonese forces), were sold to Gabon by Macías Nguema.

KIWANIS. In 1996 they granted $103,000 for the elimination of iodine deficiency (goiter and cretinism).

KLITGAARD, Robert. American. Associate professor of public policy at Harvard's Kennedy School and special assistant to Harvard's president. Consultant in 22 developing countries. He worked in Equatorial Guinea from 1986 to 1989 for the World Bank. His book, *Tropical Gangsters: One Man's Experience with Development and Decadence in Deepest Africa,* is a description of the horror and insanity of the Nguemist regime.

After teaching in South Africa, he is now dean of Rand Graduate School, Santa Monica, CA.

KOCH-LUSCHER, Walter F. Honorary consul of Equatorial Guinea to the Federal Republic of Germany, with residence in Dusseldorf. In 1981 he provided funds for Equatorial Guinea's exhibit at the Berlin Trade Fair.

KOGO. Locality situated on the right bank of the Muni estuary, 12 km from the Atlantic Ocean, at the junction of Río Kongue. In 1990 a private boat of 40 tons plied between Kogo, Akalayong, and Cocoabeach. Former main town of the Southern District, it was named from 1936–1968 Puerto Iradier. A good natural harbor, Kogo was especially used for timber exportation and fishing. In the 19th century various German, English, French, and Spanish warehouses were established there. Not to be mistaken for Uermakogo (confusion with Woermann-Kogo and Oguermakok, village located at the entrance of the Utamboni). Bishop Nze Abuy was a native of Kogo.

In September 1995, Salvador Obama Sima Eyang (PP/POC) was elected mayor. In late January 1996, the government's representative in Kogo, Enrique Mesian Abaga, expelled a Spanish doctor for his leanings towards the opposition. In May, he put members of the CPDS in jail. See also Akalayong; Army; Elections; Evinayong; Eyegue Obama Asue, F.-P.; Navigation; Ndongo Ogüono-Asong, M.; Niefang P.; Nsue Otong, C.; Obama Asue Eyegue, F. P.; Ondo Mitogo; Parliament; Petroleum; Public Health; Spain; Transports; Victims.

KOMBE MADJE, Manuel. Ndowe. medical doctor. In 1968 he was a member of the Electoral Committee for the Constitutional referendum. After independence, he became technical director of the Ministry of Health. Arrested in May 1972, at the same time as Eñeso Neñe, Watson Bueco, and Cabrera y James, he was in the Bata prison at the time of the June 1974 attempted coup d'etat. Sentenced to death by a military court, he was shot on June 26, 1974.

KOREA, NORTH. Diplomatic relations started in 1970. North Korea keeps an embassy in Santa Isabel. Cooperation is limited to assistance by 60 military experts to the National Guard, and some scholarship for the Military Academy of North Korea. In July 1977, Monica Bindang, Macías Nguema's wife, paid an official visit to Pyongyang, accompanied by Oyono Ayingono. After Obiang Nguema's coup d'etat in August 1979, his half-brother, Sub-Lt. Antonio Mba Nguema Mikuke, trained in USSR and North Korea, became the president's principal private secretary for military affairs. After the execution of Macías Nguema, Monica Macías Bindang and her three sons sought refuge in North Korea. She returned in 1980, leaving one of her sons behind, for military training. As a successor to Li Chong Zeng, Eni Sok Chai presented his credentials in February 1980.

In 1984, Pyongyang granted technical aid. In 1990, four North Korean members of Parliament visited the country, leading to strengthening of relations between the countries. In 1991, the ambassador was Chi Youg-Ho. In 1992, Obiang Nguema stayed for two weeks in North Korea; officially, the visit was for the purpose of attending the 80th anniversary of Kim Il Sung, and to sign a lumber agreement; but in fact, the purpose was to obtain a Pretorian-Korean guard as well as arms. Soon after, dozens of Koreans arrived in Equatorial Guinea to work in the lumber activities of the Chilbo enterprise. According to the opposition, they were lodged under subhuman conditions. During the legislative elections of 1994, the dictator rejected American and Spanish observers, but chose 20 other countries, including North Korea. A North Korean delegation participated in the 1st Convention of the PDGE in Bata, in the spring of 1995.

See also Akalayong; Army; Elections; Eyama Angüe Osa, D.; Eyegue Obama Asuekogo, F.-P.; Navigation; Ndongo Ogüono-Asong, M. M.; Niefang; Obama Asue Eyegue, F. P.; Ondo Mitogo, P.; Parliament; Petroleum; Public Health; Spain; Transports; Victims

KOREA, SOUTH. In 1990, Ambassador Nan Cha Hwang, who lived in Yaound, presented his credentials. The Korean cooperation provided the administration with a few vehicles. The South Korean oil company Youkong Ltd. joined in the exploitation of a part of the Zafiro site. See also Petroleum; Timber.

KROHNERT, Otto. German, established in Río Muni after the German defeat in Cameroon. He started a 339-hectare oil palm plantation at Akom, near Mikomeseng, which at present is no longer profitable. His daughter, Frida Krohnert Oyana, a medical auxiliary, was the wife of Felipe Ondo Nkunu (from Rio Benito), first general director of Security, killed by Macías Nguema. In 1981, the second dictator, Obiang Nguema, appointed her a director in the Ministry of Health. In 1998 she worked as ATS in Las Palmas de Gran Canarias.

KRUMEN. The Kru are a population originating from the Ivory Coast and Liberia. They are excellent navigators, specializing in the loading of timber boats. In the 19th century, they were the preferred labor force in the Gulf of Guinea under the name "Monrovias." There were 467 Krumen living in Santa Isabel in 1869. Some Kru mixed with Bubi. Others, as well as Sierra Leoneans and Nigerians, gave birth to the Creole population called Fernandinos. See also Labor; Liberia.

KUKUMANKOK. Locality founded in 1930, in south-central Río Muni. A semi-industrial exploitation of gold with an output of three grams per cubic meter was founded by the Frenchman Lauzé. In 1940 a Catholic mission was established in Kukumankok. Since 1955 an official school has been operating there also. A public dispensary was added in 1963. In 1974 the locality had 2,500 inhabitants. Near Kukumankok were the installations of the Société Forestière du Río Muni. Kukumankok is the place of origin of Heya Nehama, secretary general of ANRD until 1983.

KUWAIT. Obiang Nguema made an official visit to Kuwait in April 1982, in order to obtain economic aid. The Kuwait Arab Development Fund (KADF) granted Equatorial Guinea KD 1.1 million for the development of transports, in 1989–1990. In 1995, the Nguemist Maximiliano Ovenga Eyang Mba spoke of Equatorial Guinea as the future Kuwait of Africa. See also Obiang Nguema, T.

KYE River. Affluent of the River Campo, it skirts the eastern border of Río Muni Province, a few kilometers inside the Gabonese Woleu Ntem. The Joint Committee for the definition of the Río Muni border, in 1901, did not consider fixing the eastern limit of the continental province along the Kyé River. In 1926, a verbal agreement between Lieutenant Buiza of the Guardia Colonial and the Governor of Woleu Ntem set the border along the Kyé. But Paris never confirmed this agreement.

❖ L ❖

LABOR. The lack of manpower is a constant fact in Equatorial Guinea's history. During the 19th century as the Bubi refused to work on European plantations, Krumen from Liberia, Sierra Leoneans, Nigerians (the Lagos), Spanish, and Cuban political prisoners were used. In 1894 the Claretian missionaries initiated the Fang flow towards Fernando Po, but the Fang returned to Río Muni around 1930 and started local cocoa and coffee plantations of their own.

In 1904 the Patronato de Indígenas and the Curaduría Colonial were created to assist unskilled Guinean manpower largely made up of the nonemancipated (see Emancipation). Before the First World War, the Nigerian authorities protested against the illegal recruitment of labor by Spain, and qualified their methods as slavery. In 1927 came the Liberian workers affair: a League of Nations inquiry, provoked by Firestone Tire Company, gave proof that bribes were paid to local suppliers of manpower, and was considered as forced labor. Having called upon the Cameroonese before the Second World War, Spanish Guinea then hired Nigerians, mainly Ibo of Biafra.

Because of the bad treatment undergone by its citizens, the Nigerian government removed 26,000 of the 40,000 Nigerians working in Equatorial Guinea, in January 1976. The lack of manpower and the economic crisis caused the PUNT to introduce forced labor. Since March 1976, each district had to supply 2,500 workers to the Fernando Po cocoa plantations. Boricho Toichoa, first popular labor minister after independence, was shot in 1974.

After the 1979 coup, the forced labor plantation workers in Fernando Po and Río Muni, believed that they had been set free. The coup took place on August 3, but by August 25, all the workers were drafted back into the plantations. In November 1979, the mayors of Niefang and Añisok as well as the secretary of the military government in Río Muni, all confirmed to the special rapporteur of the UN Human Rights Commission that forced labor continued to be practiced.

In 1980, Oyo Riqueza, second vice-president of the republic, was appointed minister of labor. There was an acute shortage of manpower in the country, but all attempts to recruit laborers from Nigeria, Upper Volta (Burkina Faso), or Burundi met with failure. At the Conference of African Trade Unions held in Mogadishu, Somalia in October 1980, Equatorial Guinea was requested to allow trade unions to operate in the country. Despite Equatorial Guinea's admission to membership of the International Labor Organization (ILO) in 1981 nothing has been done in this respect. In December 1981, Oyo Riqueza lost his position as Vice-President but retained that of minister of labor. On many occasions, Obiang Nguema appealed to the populace to work harder, but to no avail as the go-slow movement that grew up under the Macías Nguema dictatorship continued to operate. In October 1982 Oyo Riqueza was replaced by Ndong Micha in the Ministry of

Labor, who is in turn replaced by Bolekia Ejapa in June 1984, former police commissioner in Santa Isabel and thereafter governor of Bata.

In February 1985, some 200 Nigerian workers were evacuated from Fernando Po after one of their members had been murdered. The Nigerian press accused the regime of practicing slavery. In 1987, the basic wage was 20,000 CFA francs per month, but a bottle of beer costs 500 CFA francs. In June 1985 the ILO noted the ratification of five conventions by Equatorial Guinea: no. 1, on working hours in industry; no. 14, on weekly leave in industry; no. 30, on working hours in commercial enterprises and offices; no. 100, on equality in remuneration; no. 103, on maternity rights; no. 138, on minimum age limit.

In June 1988, before the International Labor Conference, Bolekia Edjapa chose the subject of human rights: "For our government, humanity is the ultimate goal of the State." In late 1989, Antonio Pascual Oko Ebobo became minister of labor and social welfare. In the Statistical Labor Directory 1945–1989, published by the ILO, Equatorial Guinea is absent. In October 1990, Juan Balboa Boneque became the labor minister. During the visit of the president of Nigeria, General Babangida, the Nigerian delegation expressed interest in sending in labor. In the "transitional" government of January 24, 1992, the minister for labor and social welfare was Ernesto Maria Cayetano Toherida.

In the December 22, 1993, government, Costantino Ekong Nsue became minister for labor and social security. On April 8, 1996, Carmelo Modu Akuse Bindang, a member of the tamed opposition, became minister of state in charge of labor and social security.

A 1995 law established minimum monthly salaries:

Agriculture/Forestry workers	23,000 FCFA (US $40)
Others	41,250 FCFA (US $70)
Petroleum Sector	109,000 FCFA (US $170)

Equatorial Guinea ratified the following Conventions up to December 31, 1997:

Ratification 6/12/85

C001	Hours of Work (Industry), Convention, 1919
C014	Weekly Rest (Industry), Convention, 1921
C030	Hours of Work (Commerce, Offices), Convention, 1930
C100	Equal remuneration, Convention, 1951
C103	Maternity protection, Convention (revised), 1952
C138	Minimum age, Convention, 1973 (minimum age specified: 14 years)

Ratification 4/23/96

C068	Food and Catering (Ship's crews), Convention, 1946
C092	Accommodation of crews, Convention, 1951.

Equatorial Guinea is practically nonexistent in the annual reports of the Commission of Experts of the ILO for the application of Conventions and Recommendations. The 1997 and 1998 reports mention the absence of the government of Equatorial Guinea, which is among the only 13 countries that are members of the ILO that have not provided the commentaries of the conventions signed.

With the ministerial reshuffle of January 21, 1998, E. M. Toherida became once again minister of labor and social security.

The job and laboring racketing agencies APEGES, ATICE, and SONAVI require the books of the PDGE to hire staff and keep 60% of the wages billed to companies, particularly in the oil sector.

In the 1996–1997 ILO Report on Labor in the World underlines that Equatorial Guinea "does not meet the requirements in matter of macroeconomic stability." See also Apegesa; Atige; Sonavi; Trade Unions.

LANDER, Richard Lemon, 1804–1834. British subject, servant of the explorer Clapperton. After the latter's death, he continued the exploration from the Niger delta to Sokoto. Returned to Western Africa at the request of the British government, with his brother and Commander Allen, he was taken prisoner by the Ibo, then freed and taken to Santa Isabel by Beecroft. Injured in 1834 during the business trip on the Niger River, he died shortly afterwards in Santa Isabel, where he is buried.

LANGUAGES. The various languages spoken in the country are the following:
Spanish: official
French: official (since 1996)
Vernacular languages:
  Annobonian (Fa d'Ambu) 1.5%
  Bubi 9.7%
  Bujeba 1.5%
  Fang (Ntumu and Oca dialects) 82.8%
  Ndowe 3.7%
  Others 0.8%

LEBANON. At the end of the 19th century, there were eight Syrian commercial companies established in Fernando Po. Several Lebanese families practiced trade in the country under Macías Nguema. In 1984, the only restaurant-discotheque in the capital was run by a Lebanese, Ghadi, who was close to certain Nguemist ministers. From 1988 onwards, there were large number of Lebanese who returned. A supermarket in Santa Isabel was being run by the Lebanese, Hanna. In 1992, Equatorial Guinea opened its embassy in Beirut. The Lebanese company Equato-Guinea Trading Co. (EGTC) has been dealing in retail trade since 1995; its partners are Haidar Daher and Mouhamed Abdelallah. A number of other Lebanese enterprises were present (e.g., Pizza Place, Restaurante Club Naútico, Gabby Suggar, etc.).

LEPER see Mikomeseng

LERENA Y BARY, Juan José de. Royal plenipotentiary Commissioner of Spain and head of the Lerena expedition, he arrived in Santa Isabel on February 23, 1843, proclaiming Spanish sovereignty in an island managed since 1827 by the British, and changing the name of Clarence City to Santa Isabel. At the same time, because of a lack of Spanish staff, he confirmed Beecroft as governor of the island. He ordered the closing of the West Africa Company that exported the lumber of the island. In Corisco, on March 15 he obtained the obedience of about 500 Muni chiefs, the whole coast as far as Cape Santa Clara coming under Spanish domination. On March 17 he granted Spanish nationality to the Ndowe. On May 19, the expedition reached Annobón where Spanish sovereignty was also proclaimed before the expedition's return to Spain.

L'HOTE, Nicolas. Bishop in the Orthodox Apostolic Church for Spain, metropolitan for France and Africa, titular bishop of Saint Catherine d'Alexandrie, 134th successor to Saint Peter, by Holy See of Antioch. At Obiang Nguema's wife's request, he attended the second Convention of the PDGE, at Bata, in March 1995. He awarded the dictator the Grande Croix du Grand Prieuré des Chevaliers du Christ. He spoke glorifying Obiang Nguema the constructor, and then blessed the grandstand. He considered opening of an orthodox church in the capital and at Bata.

LIBERAL DEMOCRATIC CONVENTION (Convención Liberal Democrática, CLD). Sometimes called Social Democratic Convention (Convención Social Democrática). Founded by members of the Nguemist system: Alfonso Nsue Mokuy, the number one announcer on Nguemist Radio-TVGE, and Nkulu Nsue Oye, an officer of the civilian cabinet of the president of the republic. Claims to be center right. Legalized in June 1992. Several internal disputes. The first party to be legalized by the dictatorship, it is openly aligned to the principles of the dictatorship. The democratic opposition calls Nsue Mokuy a puppet. The CLD did not observe the boycott declared by the opposition in the summer of 1993 against the Nguemist elections. In late August 1993, Nsue Mokuy publicly condemned the Spanish government for its "interference in the political affairs of Equatorial Guinea." The CLD did not win a single seat in the August 22 elections.

In January 1994, the CLD joined the parliamentary delegation of tame opposition representatives who were given the task of explaining Obiang Nguema's system of democracy to Germany, France, and Switzerland. In the April 8, 1996, government, Nsue Mokuy was rewarded with the post of secretary of state for housing and urbanism.

LIBERAL PARTY (Partido Liberal, PL). Founded on March 23, 1993, by Santos Pascual Bikomo, ex-leader and founder of the Liberal Democratic Convergency, with Nsue Mokuy. Bikomo presented the legalization file, in the capacity of President. Secretary: Antonio Nkulu (also of the CLD, but he had left it due to rivalry with Nsue Mokuy, and moved to the PP). Nkulu claimed to have quit the PP after it merged with the Popular Union. Nkuklu appeared to be in the regime's pay. As a result: he breached the POC boycott of the November 21 elections. He received $16,000 for participating in the elections. After the elections, Bikomo Nanguande denounced 22 poll irregularities; he was dismissed by the national council of the PL. S. Ezequiel Echeck was the one to be elected to a PL seat on November 21. On November 27, Antonio Nculu declared himself president of the PL. The PL published a bulletin: *Cambio 93.*

In January 1994, the PL participated in the parliamentary delegation of representatives of the tame opposition in charge of explaining Nguemist democracy to Europeans and to the UNO. Shortly afterward, the government shut down the party headquarters. S. E. Echeck declared that the president of the Election Commission (minister of the interior) will be the one to nominate the heads of opposition parties. Several Nguemist executives helped divide the PL: D. Elo Ndong, E. Mercader, J. Eneme, T. Garriga.

In 1995, the PL continued to figure among the opposition parties "tamed" by the Nguemists, under the leadership of Bikomo Nanguande. In the April 8, 1996, government, S.-P. Bikomo Nanguande was rewarded with the post of minister for information. He retained this post in the April 8, 1996, government.

LIBERIA. At the beginning of the 19th century the lack of local manpower and the refusal of the Bubi to work in European plantations caused the Spaniards to hire Liberian Krumen. Later the Kru were engaged in the naval infantry. Around 1900, the German companies Humplmayr and then Wiechers and Helm monopolized the recruiting of Liberians. The Liberian government later broke this monopoly by also granting an authorization to the Woermann Company. In 1905 a Spanish-Liberian Convention on manpower supply was signed, providing minimum contracts of one year and maximum contracts of two years. But the convention was frequently violated by forced extension of contracts or refusal to pay complete salaries. The Liberian public opinion feared especially these violation in "Nanny Po" (Fernando Po). The Liberian under secretary of state, Sharp, ordered an inquiry which did not prove evidence of forced labor in Fernando Po. Therefore, on May 22, 1914, Gobernador General Barrera and the future president of Liberia, King, signed a new Convention on recruitment, under the supervision of the Spanish consul in Monrovia and the Curador Colonial in Spanish Guinea. See Labor; League of Nations

LITORAL, Province of see Bibang Ntutmu, S.

LITOR-WELE. Company founded to take care of customs with regard to the petroleum industry. Its Administrative Council included: Sisiano Mbana, Juan Olo Mba, Miguel Abia Biteco, Dario Tadeo Ndong Olomo. See also Petroleum.

LLANSOL, Victor-Guy. Frenchman, born in 1945. Claims to be a gem merchant. In 1977, he was condemned in France to five years imprisonment, for robbery with aggravating circumstances, and incarcerated at Montpellier. He was newly arrested in 1982 for forgery and possession of stolen goods. He was again accused of forgery and circulation of fake dollars in 1983. Llansol met with Obiang Nguema in Canada and became his economic ambassador, with a diplomatic passport. The press regards him as a money launderer for the Medellin cartel. He was expelled from Switzerland in June 1993 when he went to Geneva on business. Llansol then returned to Santa Isabel. In 1979 he worked through the Groupe Financier 611 SA (registered at Caracas) and the Société financière pour la Communauté Economique Européenne (SFCE), in Panama. See also Engonga Motulu, M.

LOJUA see Bubi

LOPETE LOPETE, Manuel see Popular Union

LOPEZ, Cape. Contraction of Cabo Lopo Gonzalves, name of the Portuguese adventurer who, with Fernando Poo, discovered the island named after the latter.

Cape López is the westernmost tip of Gabon, north of Port Gentil, which marked the limit of Spanish possessions under the Pardo Treaty.

LOPEZ DE LA TORRE AYLLON, Pantaleón. A former corporal, and governor general from 1862 to 1865. He strongly advised the Spanish government to immediately occupy the coasts between Bonny River and Cape Esterias, but his efforts were in vain.

LOPEZ Y BRU, Claudio see Comillas, Marqués de

LOTERIA NACIONAL DE GUINEA ECUATORIAL (National Lottery of Equatorial Guinea - LONAGE). Established in October 1996, supported by French businessmen and gaullist politicians, under the umbrella of Obiang Nguema's brother Armengol Nguema Mbasogo Ondo.

LOUIS, Marceau, b. 1914. Ex-director of education in Haiti, Louis became adviser to the Guinean Ministry of Education in 1970, and United Nations Development Program (UNDP) representative in Equatorial Guinea in 1972. In July some suspicious documents were said to be found in his office, and the government requested their restitution. In view of the diplomat's refusal, the government expelled Louis and his family, as well as his international collaborators. His driver, an Equato-Guinean hired by the UNDP, was arrested and mixed in the June 1974 attempted coup d'etat in the Bata prison. Sentenced to life imprisonment, the driver was released in 1979.

LUBA, d. 1910. Chief of the Balacha Bubi. In June 1910 he directed the rebellion against forced labor in the European concessions, incorrectly named the "Bubi war." The Spanish repression helped by Fernandinos was harsh, and Luba died shortly afterwards. In 1973, the PUNT proposed to change the toponym San Carlos for "Luba."

LUBA, Loc see San Carlos

LYNSLAGER, James, d. 1864. British businessman of Dutch origin. Beecroft's assistant. After Beecroft's death he was named British consul in 1854–1855, and governor of Fernando Po in 1854–1858 at the arrival of Gandara. His consultative council included Samuel Brew, Peter Nicoll, Samuel Johnson, and Mr. Scott. Lynslager's secretary, J. Holt, after Lynslager's death in 1864, took over his affairs and extended them to all coasts of the Gulf of Guinea, especially in Río Muni.

❖ M ❖

MABALE MBA NOMO, Fernando. Fang from Akurenam. Born January 4, 1941. A schoolteacher. In November 1993, he was elected deputy of the PDGE. In the government, he became state secretary for mines, a post he retained in 1995. In April 1995 he replaced Micha Nsue Nfumu as administrative and political secretary of the PDGE. In the April 8, 1996, government, he got the post of minister with special responsibilities for civil service and administrative reform. He keeps these functions in the 1998 government.

MABALE NSENG [or Nzang], Francisco. From Mbini. Secondary school in Santa Isabel. Towards the end of 1992, he was among the leaders of the Social Democratic Party. He participated in discussions for the National Pact with Balinga Balinga et Ondo Obiang. In October 1993, having accepted $9,000 from the government and announced on Spanish television that he would participate in the November 21 elections, he was expelled from the PSD, along with some others, for "high treason"; the PSD belonged to the POC and was boycotting the elections. In return for his participation in the elections, he obtained a post with the Electricity Company of Equatorial Guinea (Sociedad de Electricidad de Guinea Ecuatorial); Tomas Mecheba (UDENA) also obtained a similar post. In April 1995, he joined other members of "tame" opposition parties in signing an anti-Spanish document presented on TV. He attended the 2nd Convention of the PDGE, with other members of the tame opposition. He was rewarded with the post of secretary of state for energy in the April 8, 1996, government. He was not a member of the government after the ministerial reshuffle of January 1998.

MACIAS NGUEMA BIYOGO NEGUE NDONG, Francisco, b. 1924. Fang, born of a Gabonese father, sorcer in Nfenga (Nsork) on January 1, 1924, brought up in Esang-Ayon, district of Mongomo. Married three times, his latest wife is Monica Bindang, whose two children he adopted and with whom he had a son. Macías attended Catholic primary school in Mongomo. His inferiority complex in front of foreigners and educated persons and his arrogance towards modest persons were noted very early. He changed his real name, Masié (or Mez-m), to the more Spanish sounding one Macías. Macías is generally described as a paranoid, cruel megalomaniac.

In 1944 he entered the colonial administration, first as a clerk in the local government of Bata. In 1944 he was named administrative assistant, decorated with the "Mérito de Guinea," then he turned to the Forest Department of Río Benito, afterwards to the Public Works in Bata. Between 1947 and 1951 he was on leave of absence to work in his own coffee plantations. In 1950 he became emancipated. In 1951 he was hired as assistant-interpreter at the Racial Court of Monogo. Spain awarded him the grade of commander of the Order of Africa in

April 1961. During provincialization he was appointed mayor of Mongomo and soon received the medal of commander.

On the political scene he distinguished himself only in 1963, when joining the IPGE party freshly authorized by Spain. But he left the IPGE rapidly to join the MUNGE, Ondo Edu's party. In this capacity he was sent to Spain in order to pay tribute to Franco upon his 25th anniversary in power. A second trip to Spain enabled him to participate in the preparation of the status of autonomy. Macías Nguema then switched over to the MONALIGE led by Ndongo Miyone, which was opposed to the autonomy government. In 1964 he was a member of the Diputacion Provincial (Assembly) of Río Muni and deputy of the Asamblea General (Parliament) until 1968. Also a member of the Consejo de Gobierno (Cabinet), he was in charge of Public Works. Since 1967 it became evident that he was striving for the presidency of the republic. During the Constitutional Conference, he was assisted and advised by García Trevijano. Since June 1968 the latter invited him to campaign against the Constitution. The Secretariado Conjunto formed around Macías Nguema during the Conference (dissidents of IPGE, MUNGE, and MONALIGE), became the Grupo Macías, and grew more and more violently opposed to other statesmen, in particular to Ndongo Miyone.

At the September 1968 elections, Macías Nguema won at the second ballot, beating Ondo Edu, after a campaign supposedly financed by Garcia Trevijano (which the latter denied in 1976) with slogans such as "En Marcha con Macías" (Progress with Macías), and a lot of posters and leaflets, coming from Madrid, with promises to all and sundry. In October, he kept the War Department portfolio for himself as well as that for Forestry. A month later, through false promises he obtained the return of Ondo Edu exiled in Gabon. But under house arrest, Ondo Edu was killed in January 1969, inaugurating a long list of political assassinations. After violent anti-Spanish speeches in his January 1969 trip to Río Muni, and the intervention of Spanish armed forces, Macías Nguema proclaimed the state of emergency (Emergencia) on March 3; two days later he was confronted with Ndongo Miyone's coup d'etat; he then asked for UN and OAU assistance in order to help replace some of the 7,000 Spaniards who left the country in March, and suspended the fundamental constitutional guarantees. His electoral slogan, "Macías siempre cumple con sus palabras" (Macías always keeps his promises), took on a dramatic aspect.

From October 1968 to March 1969, a few Spanish speculators (Armijo, Novais, Paesa) urged Macías to create a Central Bank with private funds (relying on the fictitious Profinanco). Macías used this affair as a means of extortion to obtain 426 million pesetas from Spain to cover his budget deficit caused by an oversized and politicized administration. After liquidating first Ondo Edu and Ndongo Miyone, then the ambassador to UN, Ibongo Iyanga, then the president and the secretary of the Asamblea de la República (Parliament), Torao Sikara and Balboa Dougan, and several others, his well-known hatred for educated people caused him to prohibit the use of the word "intellectual." Grange Molay, minister of education, promptly got fined for having pronounced the forbidden word at the Cabinet meeting. In August 1971, after his return from Congo-Brazzaville, Macías accused the United States of having set up an attempt against his life, provoking a new series of liquidations (Bubi, Fernandinos). One of his portraits having been slashed in the Bata Secondary School and anti-Macías tracts having circulated early in 1972, teachers, students, and parents were arrested, and in May, Eñeso Neñe, minister of education, was assassinated. In August 1972, Gabonese forces occupied the Guinean islands of Conga, Mbañe, and Cocottiers. Macías accepted OAU mediation (presidents Mobutu and Nguabi) and went to Kinshasa and to Brazzaville, meeting Gabonese president Bongo. Two months later the Forsyth affair started. In July 1974 the occupation of a border area between Ebebiyin and Mongomo by Gabonese armed forces led to a meeting of Bongo and Macías during which, according to the former secretary general of the presidency, Asumu Oyono, Macías Nguema appears to have sold the three islands and the Kiosi zone to Gabon.

In 1970, Macías Nguema charged the Société Française des Dragages with the building of a $12 million (840 million peseta) presidential palace near Bata, with wood and marble coming from Europe. The presidential bed alone cost $4,400 (300,000 pesetas). More and more concerned about his security, Macías Nguema created a presidential ghetto around his palace in Santa Isabel (former residence of the Gobernadores Generales) after having displaced all people in the area and neutralizing the cathedral; the whole area is now surrounded by high walls topped with electric wire. Macías Nguema retired more and more to Río Muni, in particular Mongomo, fortified by major military installations. At the OAU extraordinary summit in January 1976, the national holiday celebrating Independence Day was changed from October 12 to March 5, PUNT Day and a commemoration of the failure of the coup d'etat of Ndongo Miyone. April 1976, Macías Nguema announced to the population that they were given six months to change their Christian names into African ones, for a return to authenticity; he himself returned to his original names Masié Ngueme. On October 31, 1976, rumors of conspiracy against Macías Nguema spread, but they were quickly denied by the Madrid Embassy. The president was said to have taken refuge in Mongomo. Towards the end of 1976, shortly after the Senior officials' Affair, he fell from the rostrum in Ebebiyin, while delivering a speech, and in view of the lack of reactions from those attending, his Cuban guards had to help him on his feet again.

In July 1977, his wife paid an official visit to Pyongyang (North Korea) accompanied by Oyono Ayingono. Macías Nguema himself paid an official visit to Vietnam on September 18–19, 1977, then to the People's Republic of China from September 20 on, where Hua Kuo Feng informed him of the reduction of China's technical assistance to Equatorial Guinea. After having liquidated the secretary general of the presidency, his former minister and personal friend Alogo Oyono, in December 1976, Macías Nguema's government became restricted to three of his relatives: Obiang Nguema, chief of the National Guard, B. Nguema Esono Nchama, minister of foreign affairs and vice-president, and D. Oyono Ayingono who held five ministries. Besides the Military and Forestry Departments, Macías had also taken over the Department of National Security and Popular Constructions after the assassination of Nsué Micha late in 1976. From 1969 to 1976 the list of victims of the lifetime president and "sole miracle of Equatorial Guinea" included 600 men, women, and minors, not mentioning the more than 120,000 exiles.

On National Day, October 12, 1978, Macías Nguema ordered 32 new executions.

After the 1979 coup led by Obiang Nguema, the first dictator, Macías Nguema, was forced to flee into the forests in his native Mongomo region, where he was captured by P. Motu Mamiaga and some peasants on August 18. He was tried by court-martial and sentenced to death and executed in September along with five other prisoners among whom was Vice-President Ntutumu. They were all executed by firing squad without witnesses, by Moroccan soldiers. This detail gave rise to the story that Macías Nguema is still alive somewhere in Africa.

Monica Macías Bindang, who had taken refuge with her three children in North Korea, returned in 1980, leaving her children there. She was troubled in Santa Isabel during August and had to flee the crowds in a military vehicle.

On August 3, 1981, Obiang Nguema who had faithfully served his uncle from 1968 to 1979, speaking at Bata described him as "an envoy of the Devil and president of sorcerers." An ex-wife of Macías Nguema's Frida Krohnert Oyana, was named director of health for the insular region. In 1985, the Spanish press stated that Macías Nguema had traded with a Cheysson brother to the former French minister Claude Cheysson. After the ritual assassination and cannibalistic end of Pedro Motu Mamiaga in August 1993, similar treatment was said to have been meted out to Macías Nguema, whose tomb had never been revealed. After Obiang Nguema's coup d'etat, the vessel *Macías Nguema* (5,000 tons) was renamed *Acacio Mañe Ela*.

Every August 3, Malabo celebrates the Feast for the Overthrowing of Macías Nguema and "the consolidation of the democratic system." Under Macías Nguema, almost 10% of the population was murdered.

See also Cacawal; Esono Mika, P. J.; Obiang Nguema, T.; Nguemism; Spain.

MACISM see Nguemism

MACKEY, James Love, 1820–1867. American Protestant missionary (Presbyterian) and linguist. He founded the Corisco Mission in 1850 where he served as minister and teacher, visiting a large part of western Río Muni. He is the author of the first scientific study on the Benga.

MADENCO see Timber

MADRID see Occupation of the Madrid Embassy

MADRID PACT FOR DEMOCRACY AND THE SELF-DETERMINA-TION OF EQUATORIAL GUINEA (Pacto de Madrid para la Democracia y Autodeterminación de la Guinea Ecuatorial). Platform resulting from the union of Spanish parties and of representatives of movements opposing the Nguemists, in Madrid, in December 1988.

On March 15, 1989, the Pact was signed by:

- For Equatorial Guinea: National Alliance for Democratic Reconstruction, FRELIGE, MOLIFUGE, Progress Party, Eriana Popular Union, Annobónese community; Cultural Associations: Organization of Equato-Guinean technicians and professionals (Organización de técnicos y profesionales), Cultural Association of the Equato-Guineans of Spanish Levante (Asociación cultural de Guineanos de Levante), Rhombe Cultural Association (Asociación cultural Unión de la Hispanidad).

- For Spain: Centro Democrático Social, Convergencia Democrática de Cataluña, Euskadiko Ezquerra, Izquierda Unida, Partido Nacional Vasco, various non-governmental organizations; the press; the PSOE remained an observer. Its primary aim: the struggle for the rightful return of the diaspora. In April a permanent secretariat was created.

In March 1990, the Declaration of Madrid announced the setting up of various sections: Human Rights, Follow-up Commission, Technical Commission (problems of exiled people and their return), Working group on the conservation of nature. The Pact addressed an official demand to Felipe Gonzalez to support the return to democracy. In October, several members spoke of the possibility of an armed solution. Since July 1991, the Pact has been null and void, mainly due to splits and the maneuvers of Jones Ivina, thrice elected to be president. In its place the Coalición Democrática was created.

MAELE. A singer. Discography: Ayong (The tribe), Paris 1980; Esa mwan (The lost son), Paris, 1986; Abóme (The abduction), Paris, 1988. He made several records glorifying the nguemist regime and Obiang Nguema. Since 1998, he is provincial delegate of the Ministry of Information and tourism, in Rio Muni.

MAFESA. Spanish lumber company born in 1980 out of the company SENFESA, founded in 1969 by Jose Ferreira Perez. It operated two concessions of a total of 23,000 ha. between Bata and Añisok. 50% of the production was exported in the form of bark and 50% sold to A.B.M. MAFESA owns furniture manufacturing workshops for the local market. See also Timber.

MAFIA. In 1990, some Italians awarded Obiang Nguema the Biancamano Prize, promising to pay the external debt during a period of ten years, in addition to 1,500 hospital beds with mattresses, as well as medicines. In return, this group obtained authorization for the founding of a bank, a fishing enterprise, a lumber company and a mining company. The capital was to become a free zone. The Italian Minister for Foreign Affairs knew nothing of the Prix Biancamano. According to certain members of the press, the Biancamano group was said to have ties with the Mafia. The Mafia was said to have its headquarters in Hotel Media Luna, on the road to the Bata airport. Most of the 1990 promises were not kept.

MAKUBA BUAKI, Myriam see Convergency for Social Democracy

MAHO SIKACHA, Elias Manuel. A Bubi from Riaba, and brother of José Luis. Holds a degree in medicine and surgery. During 1980–1981, he was health director for Río Muni. In 1990, he was named mayor of the capital. He is also the president of the National Red Cross Society.

MAHO SIKACHA, José Luis. A Bubi from Riaba and brother to Sikacha (above). Born 1940 (?). Lawyer who studied in Spain thanks to a Casa Fuerte scholarship. Returning to the country in 1960, he became head of the Cruzada Nacional de Liberación de Guinea Ecuatorial in 1961. After six months he had to flee to Gabon, where he met with Ndongo Miyone. Together with Ndongo he submitted a memorandum at the Conference of Head of States of the African and Malagasy Union. In Libreville, in September 1964, asked for assistance for Guinea's independence. Maho's disputes with Ndongo Miyone caused the failure of their venture; Maho left for Douala (Cameroon). In February 1963, he became the president of the Coordination Office of the Liberation Movements in Ambam, which already split in June. In October 1963, Maho gave up the Cruzada and joined the IPGE. Maho asked for immediate independence, rejecting autonomy. He therefore became a member of the MONALIGE, then returned to IPGE where he was offered the presidency. At the beginning of 1964 he joined MUNGE, and in May became a member of the Consejo de Gobierno (Cabinet), in charge of the Department of Information and Tourism. With Itoha Creda, Watson Bueco, and Borico Toichoa he presented a motion to the Cabinet, on August 12, 1966, in view of the separation of Fernando Po and Río Muni at independence. Maho participated in the Constitutional Conference. At that time a member of the Unión Bubi, he did not run in the 1968 elections, but in October 1968 he became president of the Supreme Court.

In 1980 he became director for justice. He was also a judge in a court of first instance, but the Nguemists quashed some of his judgments. In 1982 he was the president of the tribunal that condemned Mba Ndongo and Nvono Nka Manene for drug trafficking. He was still a judge in the Supreme Court in 1993.

MAKING EBONA, Victoriano see Santa Isabel

MALABO, d. 1937. Legitimate successor of Bubi king Moka, he was evicted in 1898 by Sas Eburea. At the latter's death in 1904, he became king. Under his leadership the Bubi revolt occurred against compulsory labor, directed by Luba. Malabo died an alcoholic in Moka in April 1937 and was replaced by his brother Alobari who in turn was succeeded by Oriche.

MALABO. Village of the Moka Valley, headed in 1965 by Gabriel Boari.

MALABO. Name proposed in 1973 by the PUNT for the town of Santa Isabel. See Santa Isabel.

MALAVO, Estanislao. A Bisio from the district of Mbini (Río Benito), born April 13, 1963. Nephew of J. Buendi, the first governor of the Central Bank, who was shot to death under Macías Nguema. Primary and secondary schooling in Bata; studied French in the French Cultural Center at Bata (1978–1981). A scholarship holder to the English Language Institute (University of Alabama), after which he studied at the University of San Diego. Graduated in economic sciences, in 1990.

Upon his return to Equatorial Guinea in 1991, he was employed by the UNDP, until 1993. He participated in the installation of the American petroleum company Walter Int. (1991–1992). In 1992 he cofounded the Liberal Democratic Convergency. He toured Europe as part of a mission for the Joint Opposition Platform (POC). Upon his return, he was arrested and tortured. He sought asylum in Spain. In 1994, he planned to found a shadow party, the Reformist Party (Partido Reformista, PR).

In May 1995, along with Elema Borengue, he founded a nonoperational Social Forum for National Reconciliation, which later became the Forum for Democracy (Foro para la Democracia), involving the support of some Spanish nationals. In 1998 he was a tradesman between Valencia (Spain) and Libreville (Gabon).

MALAYA see Timber/Shimmer

MALLO, Joaquin. A Spanish owner of plantations. He trades alcohol against coffee and cocoa. He is an associate of several Spanish companies, including Roig Balestros, Ebana, Escuder y Otero, Esteller y Ferris. He belongs to what the Spanish press calls the "Spanish lobby." In 1989, the IBRD accused the Casa Mallo of parasitism.

MAÑE ELA, Acacio, d. 1968. Fang of Cameroonese origin. Planter from the village of San Joaquin de Njakom, 40 km from Bata. In 1950 he presided over a meeting of rebellious teachers after the refusal of Spain to improve their salaries as proposed by Alvarez and Governor General Bonelli. They then founded the Cruzada Nacional de Liberación. Pretending to recruit laborers, Mañe traveled through Río Muni, campaigning for the Cruzada. In 1952 Ndongo Miyone joined the movement, which under his impulse was to become the MONALIGE seven years later. Shortly after Spain's admission to the United Nations, Mañe co-signed with E. Nvo and Ndongo Miyone a memorandum to the United Nations accusing Spain of usurpation of the Guinean territory. Mañe always refused to go into exile; he was denounced to the civil guard on November 20, 1958, by Father Nicolas Preboste, the Superior of the Catholic mission in Bata and was arrested. He was assassinated in Bata and his body was thrown into the sea. His death triggered off the beginning of provincialization and thus, after autonomy, independence. After independence, Acacio Mañe was proclaimed a national hero and a martyr of independence.

MANGUE, T. see Nsue Ngomo Abumengono

MANGUE OBAMA NFUBE, Ricardo (called Ricardin). Fang from Nsomo, born February 6, 1960, at Aton-Nzomo (Ebebiyin district). Attended secondary school in the country, and then studied in University in Spain to receive a master's degree in political science and sociology, as well as a degree in law. A member of Youth Marching with Macías.

He occupied various posts in the administration and in the department of justice. After having been a Judge in the Court of Appeals, he became general secretary to the president on January 23, 1992. As a member of the presidential security and escort, he is said to be behind a number of repressive operations as the thinking brain of Armengol Nguema Mbasogo Ondo.

In the November 1993 elections, he was elected deputy of Ebebiyin under the banner of the PDGE. As he seemed to be assuming too much power, Obiang Nguema named him minister for education and sciences on December 22, 1993, in order to remove him to some distance from the decision makers of the regime. In 1995, he entered the administrative council of the Empresa nacional de pesca de Guinea Ecuatorial, wholly composed of Nguemists.

He retained his ministerial post in the January 8, 1996, ministerial reshuffle. He did not take up any responsibilities within the PDGE. In August 1996, he persuaded Obiang Nguema to transfer the secretary of his ministry—whom he accuses of spying—to the Ministry of Transport and Communications. The new secretary of education is the famous Nguemist Nvono Akele Avomo. In 1996, R. Mangue Obame Nfube participated, as minister of education, in the Iberian–

American Conference on Education, held in Buenos-aires. On January 21, 1998, Mangue Obama again became minister of education and sciences.

MANGUE OKOMO NSUE DE OBIANG NGUEMA, Constancia. From Mongomo. Sister to the pistolero Efa Mba and to Olo Mba Nzeng, minister for mines and energy. First wife of Obiang Nguema. In 1985, she obtained loans from the Guinextebank, for business purposes. In 1987, she became the president's counsellor for health and social affairs, a post she lost in 1990, following a brief family problem. On January 19, 1994, she was confirmed to the post of counsellor to the Civil Cabinet of the President of the Republic for Social Affairs. One of the buildings she owns in the capital houses the Pedagogical Bureau of the French Cooperation.

See also France; Obiang Nguema, T.; Terror.

MANTEROLA, Nicholas de. Commander. After Guillemar de Aragón, he arrived in Fernando Po on Christmas Day 1845 to notify the French authorities to Gabon of the extension of the Spanish territories until Cape Santa Clara, which then was admitted without objection, but was later strongly objected to by France. Manterola confirmed Beecroft as governor of Fernando Po.

MAQUEADA, Francisco. Spanish proprietor of the company PAJE. A friend of Obiang Nguema's. He held a seat on the Administrative Council of SOGUIGAS.

MARIA VICTORIA see Izaguirre

MARTINEZ (NVO BIKIE), Jose. Born in 1933. Fang from Ebebiyin district. His primary education was in the district. From 1947-1954 he worked as an office clerk. In 1954 he enrolled in voluntary military service and pledged allegiance to Spain on July 18. He later fled to Cameroon where he was accused by his compatriots of being a Spanish spy. In 1965 he joined MONALIGE. An enthusiastic supporter of Macías Nguema, he became consejero provincial in Río Muni on the Grupo Macías list.

After participating in the setting up of the Milicia Popular, then of the PUNT, he became president of the Consejo de la República (Senate) in 1972. minister of economic affairs and markets (Ministry of Trade) in September 1975 after Julio Bonoko Eye, who had shortly succeeded Vice-President Bosio Dioco after the latter's assassination. Martinez Nvo was regularly sent abroad in order to liquidate all opposition to Macías Nguema. In 1976 he was erroneously declared dead in a fire accident.

A friend of Idi Amin Dada's, who later became his eldest son's godfather. This son trained to be a pilot at Kampala. Belonging to the top brass of Popular Union, Martinez Nvo Bikie was arrested at Ebebiyin in May 1992, along with Pedro Motu Mamiaka, Marcelino Asumu, and others, and accused of insulting the head of the state and the government, following a meeting held in Nsok Nsomo. On October 26, all of them were declared innocent by the judge of the Appeals Court at Bata, Tadeo Ela, except Martinez Bikie, who was condemned to six months imprisonment and a fine of FCFA 200,000. The general secretary of the UP, Domingo Abuy, stressed that the accusations were groundless, as Martinez, as provincial delegate, had acted within the framework of the law on meetings and demonstrations.

Since 1993, Martinez Nvo Bikie has been working under the orders of Obiang Nguema in the Ministry of Public Works, Town Planning and Transports. He was again arrested on May 6, 1995, and imprisoned at Playa Negra. He was quickly released. He joined the UP, of which he was a member of the national management in 1998. Tradesman in Bata.

MARINE PROTECTED AREAS. In 1990, four areas were made protected: the Rio Muni estuary (70,000 hectares.); the Ntem (Rio Campo) estuary (20,000 hectares); the island of Annobon (1,700 hectares); and South Fernando Poo (60,000 hectares).

MARTINEZ PELAYO ERIMOLA YEMA, Ricardo, d. 1969. Bubi, member of the Union Bubi, elected at the Asamblea de la República (Parliament) in September 1968. In the first government he became minister of industries and mines. He was liquidated at the end of March 1969 and replaced by Ekong Andeme.

MARTINEZ Y SANZ, Miguel. Spaniard. Chaplain of *Queen Isabel II,* he arrived in Santa Isabel as its first Apostolic prefect in May 1856. He established catechists in Corisco where thus far only American Presbyterian missionaries had been preaching. He invited the Spanish government to send prisoners and outlaws to Fernando Po and stimulated settlement of liberated blacks of Sierra Leone and Liberia on the island: the King, Jones, Dougan, Atkins, Collins, and other families, all Fernandinos, are descendants issued of these immigrants. Martínez returned to Spain in 1857.

MARTYRS see Women Martyrs

MASA MBA, Pedro see Army

MASI, Casiano see Popular Alliance

MASIE MIBUY, Angel. From Mikomeseng. Born 1952. Son of Angel Masié Ntutumu, minister for the interior under Macías Nguema. Public school in Equatorial Guinea and Spain. Law studies in Cuba. In charge of the youth wing of the Popular Union; he struggled for the rejuvenation of the leadership, which was then suffering from acute gerontocracy. He left the UP in September 1994 and moved to the dictator's party, the PDGE. In February 1995 he acted as the prosecutor of the president of the Progress Party, Moto Nsá, during its first hearing. Moto Nsa's wife is a cousin to Angel Masié Mibuy. In the April 8, 1996, government, he became vice-minister for justice and religion. In the governmental reshuffle of January 21, 1998, he was replaced by F.-J. Ngomo Mbengono.

MASIE NTUTUMU MANGUE, Angel. Fang from Mikomeseng district, first cousin of Macías Nguema. Father-in-law to Moto Nsa. Educated in social and administrative sciences in Santa Isabel around 1965. A member of the MON-ALIGE, he did not participate in the 1968 elections. In the first government, he was named home secretary (Ministro del Interior), where he remained until 1976. He is said to be responsible for a great number of death sentences, especially those of Ondo Edu, Mbá Micha, and Ndongo Engonga. At the so-called coup d'etat of Ndongo Miyone, of March 5, 1969, he is supposed to have been briefly arrested.

Masie Ntutumu participated in the creation of the Milicia Popular. Through García Trevijano, he was able to contact French business interests resulting in a $43 million loan for major constructions (Société Française des Dragages), against a large forest concession (150,000 hectares) as guarantee: the Société Forestiere du Río Muni. In 1972, Masie Ntumu participated in Bern (Switzerland) in an international telecommunications conference. This is probably where the postage stamps affair started (see Post Office). Having become under secretary of state (to the presidency of the republic) Masie Ntutumu took refuge in Spain in November 1976 shortly before the Senior Officials Affair, after having evacuated his family and belongings. He lived in Barcelona, and he is mentioned as being a member of the informal Grupo de Mayores. Some accuse him of being a spy among Equato-Guinean refugees.

After the 1979 coup, he returned home and set himself up as an importer-exporter. He was under arrest between April and June 1981 in connection with the supposed plot led by Mba Oñana. Member of the central committee of Nguemist PDGE since 1987. As part of the "democratization" of the country, he left the PDGE. He was briefly behind bars in 1991 and 1993, as a member of the Popular Union for having written to President bongo (Gabon) asking him to intervene in the democratization of Equatorial Guinea. He was arrested once again in 1993. In 1998 he was a member of the national management of the UP. He lives in Spain (Torrejón de Ardoz).

MATECO, Pastor see Elema Borengue.

MATEO, Jose see Elema Borengue.

MATERIA RESERVADA see Censorship

MATOGO OYANA, Juan. From Ncué (Mikomeseng). Provincial superior of the Claretians for Río Muni. In November 1991, he became the bishop of Ebebiyin in the presence of Obiang Nguema. According to the press, the journey to Ebebiyin was made by the dictator in order to meet the Cameroonian Fang sorcerer Abanda, from whom he was expecting advice about his anxiety due to mounting pressure for democracy.

In 1993, Mgr. Matogo Oyana published a document clearly alluding to the disastrous political situation. The priest has to adapt to his audience and practice biblical denunciation. In September, *La Verdad* spoke of the bishop of Ebebiyin as the only member of the Catholic hierarchy who still resisted the regime. In October of that year, Matogo consecrated the first Equato-Guinean contemplative nun, Rufina Maria, in Akonibe.

MATROGUISA see Timber

MAURO NGUEMA, Santiago. Colonel trained in Zaragoza. He presided over the military trial against the Bubi held in Malabo at the end of May 1998.

MAYE ELA, Florencio. Member of the Mbon Clan of Mongomo. He was one of the second wave of people sent for training in Spain in the immediate pre-independence period. After entering into employment he was sent on a six-month training course in the USSR. When his uncle Macías Nguema became president, he was promoted to the rank of naval captain and stationed in Bata.

He joined forces with his cousins Obiang Nguema, Ela Nseng and uncle Mba Onana in the palace revolution of 1979. While retaining his naval command, he was made vice-president of the republic and second to Obiang Nguema, the President. In August 1979 he told representatives of the United Nations that it was imperative to maintain the system of forced labor in the cocoa plantations in the interests of the national economy. Addressing the UN General Assembly in September 1979, he led his audience to believe that the military government had created the necessary conditions for the return of exiles.

He is known to be very pro-French. On January 22, 1980, he was appointed minister of foreign affairs, replacing Ela Nseng, who was posted as ambassador to Peking. He has a number of European business connections and became particularly well known for his association with the Spanish businessman Manuel Ferris from Valencia and the importation of meat that the press described as being of unacceptable quality.

By the end of 1980 Maye Ela came to be regarded as the strong man of the second Nguemist dictatorship, since Obiang Nguema was virtually a prisoner of the Moroccans. In the spring of 1981, Maye Ela undertook an official tour of Latin America and the U.S.A. While in Chile he invited General Pinochet to visit Equatorial Guinea. A "plot" discovered while Maye was on his tour, enabled Obiang Nguema to arrest 30 naval officers and numerous officials of the Ministry of Foreign Affairs, including Mba Ndong, who was acting as the liaison with the UN Human Rights Commission. The arrests were actually carried out by Mba Oñana who was jealous of his nephew Maye Ela, whom he described as "a whale."

In 1981 Maye Ela took over the chairmanship of the joint Spanish-Equatorial Guinean oil company GEPSA. In February 1981, he took part in the ministerial conference of the Organization of African Unity, accompanied by Mba Ndong, who had just been released from prison. In the summer, in the company of Obiang Nguema, he went to Nigeria to obtain some labor, but was met with a refusal. On December 8, 1981, he was removed from the vice-presidency and also lost his Foreign Affairs post. He was then posted to New York as ambassador to the United Nations. In the summer of 1983 he lost the directorship of GEPSA but continued to receive emoluments from Hispanoil.

In 1988, he was said to have gotten in touch with British companies for the dumping of toxic wastes. He was an ordinary official in the Ministry of Foreign Affairs. On January 19, 1994, he was named counsellor to the president's civil cabinet for diplomatic affairs and protocol. In 1998, he was ambassador to Popular China.

MAYE NSUE MANGUE, Rubén. Obuk, born at Mongomo. Training in USSR. In the April 8, 1996, ministerial reshuffle, he became director general of justice and penitentiary institutions. Public prosecuter of the republic, he lauds in November 1997 the collaboration with the Constitutional Spanish court. In the January 21, 1998, government, he became minister of justice.

MBA, Tomas. Chief of the youth of the Democratic and Progressive Alliance (ADP). He was arrested shortly before the November 21, 1993, elections, beaten up, and then released. His party called for the boycott of the elections.

MBA ADA, André Moíses, b. 1928. Fang from the Mikomeseng district. A corporal in the Guardia Colonial, he later became an office clerk with a company of Santa Isabel. With the certificates of emancipation, he returned to Río Muni in 1959 to take care of his plantations. In 1960 he became vice-president of the Diputacion Provincial (Assembly of Río Muni). Between 1964 and 1968, he was also representative to the Cortes. Father to Antonio Mba Mifumu. His nephews, Enrique and Fortunato Matogo Oyana, took refuge in Germany. When Enrique returned in 1979, he became the director of the central services of the CMS.

He participated in the Constitutional Conference as counselor of the Movimiento Nacional of Equatorial Guinea (Francoist). Not elected in September 1968, but a member of the Grupo Macías he became Consejero de la república and presided over the senate. He was at the time the only person who could make known Macías Nguema's incapacity to assume the presidency of the country. In 1969 he was named president of INFOGE, created at García Trevijano's instigation. In 1970 he accompanied Eyegue Ntutumu and Garcia Trevijano on a business trip to Europe. Accused of having misappropriated 50 million pesetas ($750,000), he was imprisoned and Macías Nguema closed INFOGE. Mba Ada was able to flee to Cameroon, from there to Switzerland and then to Spain. He had entered the ANRD in 1974, but was excluded from the movement on April 15, 1976, for inefficiency and for his close contacts with Spanish interests (CEIA). He is mentioned in the Grupo de Mayores, but he considers himself politically uncommitted. In January 1965 he was named officer of the Order of Africa by the Spanish government.

Mba Ada returned home in January 1980 along with Nsue Ngomo where they set up the import-export company EXIGENSA in Bata. While on a trip to Madrid in April 1981, Mba Ada is accused by Mba Oñana of hatching in conspiracy after a cache of arms had been discovered in Ebebiyin. This resulted in some 50 arrests. In reality, the whole affair was an invention of Mba Oñana to avoid paying for a truck that he had bought from Mba Ada. The equipment belonging to the EXIGENSA company was confiscated by Mba Oñana while Obiang Nguema took charge of the company itself making his son, still a minor, the principal shareholder. The supposed conspiracy was brought before the courts and one soldier was condemned to death. Mba Ada was sentenced, in absentia, to 20 years in prison and 15 others got 15-year sentences.

In Madrid, in May 1982, Obiang Nguema tried unsuccessfully to obtain the extradition of Mba Ada to Equatorial Guinea; he was, however, jailed at Carabanchel in Spain but was released at the end of June thanks to intercession by the ANRD with the Spanish authorities. Since February 1993, Mba Ada has been president of Popular Union (UP). He returned to the country on August 21. The next day, following the ritual assassination of Pedro Motu Mamiaga, an eminent member of the UP, he held his tongue. In November, he asked the population to boycott the elections.

In 1996, he briefly ran for the presidency but withdrew after the opposition's boycott. Ever since, he has been living in Spain. In July 1998, Mba Ada announced the participation of the UP in the legislative elections.

See also Elections; Esono Masie, P.

MBA BELA, Jesus. Esangui. Born 1948, at Mongomo. No professional training. Son-in-law to Obiang Nguema upon marriage to Nnang, a cousin of the dictator's. Obiang Nguema's chief of protocol. His brother, Angabi, was a member of the Youth marching with Macías. He was a member of the Nguemist Criminal Investigation Department under the orders of Armengol Nguema Mbasogo Ondo, the dictator's brother and PDGE deputy. In the April 8, 1996, ministerial reshuffle, he was confirmed in his post as chief of protocol to the president of the republic, with the rank of joint director general, an office he kept in 1998.

MBA EKUA MIKO, Benjamin. Of the Obadjom clan (Ebebiyin). Born 1948. Protestant. Under Macías Nguema he was ambassador to the United Nations, in New York, and later Ambassador in Gabon. In 1979, during the Conference on Refugees in Africa, Mba Ekua Miko tried to have the secretary general of the ANRD, representative of an NGO and member of the Human Rights Commission (UFER) Eya Nchama, expelled. The Conference repudiated him.

In the early stages of Obiang Nguema's regime, he worked for the Reformed Church. In this capacity, he frequently visited the World Council of Churches in Geneva. There he met Protestant compatriots from Ebebiyin,who had taken refuge in Switzerland and Germany and negotiated for their return (former workers of Nguemist Foreign Affairs were among them; see Mokong).

In 1981, Mba Ekua Miko became the ambassador to Cameroon. In late 1982, he was named director general of International Organizations and Cooperation, in the Ministry of Foreign Affairs and Cooperation. In 1988 he became minister for public health.

In early 1992, he became the minister for foreign affairs and the French language in the transitional government. Following discussions with the Madrid Pact, Mba Ekua Miko announced pluralistic legislative elections for 1993, even though no opposition party had been registered, and in spite of the arrests and tortures of opponents. The natives of Ebebiyin, mostly Protestants, who had settled in Germany and Switzerland set up a Committee for the Voluntary Return of Refugees (Comité de Retorno Voluntario de Refugiados).

In 1993, Mba Ekua Miko raised his voice against the denunciations of Nguemist terror by members of the Parliament and the Spanish press, as well as the opposition. He termed the blocking of a part of the Spanish aid as "intolerable interference." As part of the legislative elections, he was sent by the dictator to make the Kie-Ntem (Ebebiyin) population conscious of Nguemism. He does not figure in the government of December 22. On January 19, 1994, he was named president's counsellor for Foreign Affairs and Cooperation. Since 1994, he has been a member of the central committee of the PDGE.

MBA MABALE, Fernando. Member of the hardcore wing of the PDGE. State secretary for mines. In May 1995, he became the administrative secretary of the PDGE, to replace Juan Micha, dismissed by Obiang Nguema.

MBA MIFUMU, Antonio. From Mikomeseng. Born in 1950. Son of André-Moïses Mba Ada. Secondary studies in Bata. Layer trained in a private institution in Spain. He became a counsellor for public works and a member of the constitutional Tribunal in January 1994.

MBA MOMBE, Samuel. From Ebebiyin. Born 1953. Doctor in medicine, trained at Patrice Lumumba University (USSR). Became a refugee in Germany (Berlin). General Secretary of the ANRD after the death of Nsono Okomo, in August 1985. During his mandate, internal dissent in the ANRD, caused by Nguemist infiltrators continued. In 1989, during the presidential election, Mba Mombe declared that ANRD militants continued to "feel Spanish and that Equatorial Guinea only existed through Spain." In 1993, the expulsion of Mokong Onguene and Dougan Beaca by the National Alliance for Democratic Restoration (ANRD) brought order back into the party. Mba Mombe became joint secretary, while Luis Ondo Ayang became general secretary. Mba Mombe resigned from ANRD in 1996. He published an occasional bulletin, *La Diaspora,* under the cover of a so-called Comunidad Guineo-Ecuatoriana en el extranjero.

MBA NDEMENSOGO, Daniel. Fang from Niefang. Born on November 11, 1940. Protestant. Studied in Romania. Holds an M.A. in philosophy and letters. After the 1979 coup he was nominated secretary of the Ministry of Education and Culture. In December 1981 he was made director of higher and vocational education, which was a demotion. He was replaced in the Ministry by an Esangui, Ochaga Nve. In May 1982 Mbá Ndemensogo spent some time at the International Bureau of Education (IBE) in Geneva. Since 1984 he has been director of the Santa Isabel teacher training college.

In 1989, he declared that Equatorial Guinea was becoming bilingual with the compulsory teaching of French. In 1993, he was director of Francophony in the Ministry of National Education. In the December 22 government, he became vice-minister for agriculture, fisheries and food. He died in 1996.

MBA NDONG, Antonio. From Mongomo. Born 1949 in Oveng-Esambe, Ebebiyin district, married to Victoria Nchama Obiang. Brother-in-law to Salvador Ela Nseng Abegue, former vice-president of the republic, and ambassador to Ethiopia. Foreign Service officer. Member of the National Alliance for Democratic Restoration. After the 1979 coup he was with the Ministry of Foreign Affairs. On October 16, 1979, he met the director of the UN Human Rights Division in New York, C. van Boven, to arrange for the visit of a special rapporteur to Equatorial Guinea (see Volio-Jimenez). He was later promoted to become advisor to the Supreme Military Council on Diplomatic Questions and Foreign Affairs. He took part in the conference of nonaligned nations in Havana, Cuba, as well as the Ministerial Conference of the Organization of African Unity, together with Maye Ela.

Mbá Ndong was arrested in connection with the "plot" of April 1981 (see Mbá Oñana) after having tried to seek refuge in the French Embassy. He was accused of being a co-conspirator with Mbá Ada. Mbá Ndong was released shortly after his arrest but was relieved of his post. On March 30, 1982, he was arrested again, with his wife, and sentenced to six months in prison and fined 200,000 ekwele for drug trafficking. This was organized by Mbá Oñana who wanted to neutralize both Maye Ela and Mbá Ndong out of jealousy. Mbá Ndong was, however, released on August 3, 1982, after intervention by Amnesty International, whereupon he took refuge in Cameroon.

He returned to the country in the late 1980s and joined the administration again. In the autumn of 1994, Mba Ndong was named ambassador to the OUA, Addis Abaeba. In the ministerial reshuffle of April 8, 1996, he became general secretary of the Ministry of National Defense. Since the end of 1996, he has been ambassador in Nigeria. He belongs to the few ANRD members who were lured by the nguemists.

MBA NDONG, Roberto. From Mongomo. Born in Akoa-Kam. Cousin to Obiang Nguema. Studied in the USSR. Lt. commander, and later a naval commander. Under Obiang Nguema, he became a judge at the Appeals Court and a warrant officer in the military camp; Mba Ndong, acted as the dictator's aide-de-camp. In the ministerial reshuffle of April 8, 1996, he became general secretary of the Ministry of National Defense.

MBANA, Sesino. Fang from Mongomo, born in 1940(?). Primary school education. Towards 1980, minister of public health, and later on ambassador in Morocco. In 1995 he was head of the harbor of the capital. In 1998 he was head of personnel of Total-Equatorial Guinea.

MBANE Island. Situated 6 km southeast of Corisco and 2 km northeast of Conga, geologically part of Corisco, known as a rat's nest. Despite the presence of Spanish missionaries in Corisco since 1886, France tried to annex Mbañe in the same year. In 1896 the French set up a marker cairn carrying the French tricolor flag close to the island. The Spanish missionaries had it removed by the Spanish deputy-governor.

In 1955, the French made a further attempt to gain control of this island by planting the French flag on it again. It was removed by a Spanish gunboat. The French authorities in Gabon apologized, saying that the marker was only intended to indicate dangerous rocks for shipping. The Spanish authorities replied that a Spanish flag would have served the same purpose.

In 1972 Gabonese forces occupied Mbañe, Conga, and Cocotiers. After first verbal protests, Macías Nguema appears to have sold the disputed territories to Gabon. In late 1992, in Libreville, a delegation refused to give up the Cocoteros, Conga, and Mbañe islands to Gabon.

In early 1993, Gabon annexed these islands by a presidential decree, to the advantage of the French Elf-Aquitaine (via Elf-Gabon). The Nguemists maintained silence on the issue as Obiang Nguema was said to have accepted the matter in a secret accord. An official French document of November 1993 stated, however, that Mbañe and a number of other islands of Río Muni were administratively a part of Río Muni.

See also Borders; Coconut Island; Gabon; Obiang Nguema, T.

MBANE River. Flows into the Utamboni on its right bank. It was explored by Iradier.

MBA NGUEMA MIKUE, Antonio. Esangui. Born 1951 in Akoa-Kam (Mongomo). Half-brother to Obiang Nguema. Sub-lt. trained in the USSR and in North Korea. In 1979, member of the CMS. Chief of the president's military cabinet. After the August 1979 coup d'etat, he was a member of the Supreme Military Council. January 22, 1980, he is named joint secretary for information, press, radio, télévision and tourism. January 24-26, 1980, he accompanied Obiang Nguema during his official visit to Cameroon.

On February 3, 1981, he was promoted lieutenant. As joint commissioner of information and tourism, he participated in the Conference of Donors of the UNDP, in April 1982, in Geneva. He refused to see M. van Boven, director of the Human Rights Division. In December 1982, he replaced Mba Oñana as inspector general of the armed forces in the ministry of national defense. In the capital, he ran over a Bubi infant, and two others, with his car. His punishment was to be transferred to the ministry of justice. He mistreated a bureaucrat, but it didn't shorten his sanction. At the end of the 1980s he was responsible for the army of Río Muni. At Bata and in the rest of the province he spread terror at the head of the band called Odoville. He most notably tortured Gaspar Mañana Okiri Avoro in 1988. Mañana himself was the one who informed the expert of the United Nations Human Rights Commission, in late 1991, that they had seen the minister for foreign affairs among the torturers. Mba Nguema threatened some of the arrested persons to shoot them off on the spot. In 1989, he benefited from the generosity of the Israeli lumber company Yona Internationa. See Timber.

He figured among the counsellors of the INSESO, and earned a monthly sum of CFA Fr. 150,000.

In 1992 he became a colonel, and was made inspector general of the armed forces of Río Muni, and therefore the absolute military head of the province, where he held his own jurisdiction. Obiang Nguema sent him to Cameroon in order to try to obtain a Fang chief's skull, supposed to have the power to render Obiang Nguema invincible, from the sorcerer Abanda, a counsellor to President Biya. In February, he arrested 40 members of Popular Union and tortured a member of the Progress Party. He also tortured Ecori Nzang, close to its Progress Party. Obiang Nguema recalled him to Santa Isabel and named him director of the Criminal Investigations Department.

During the ministerial reshuffle of April 8, 1996, he became director general of national security. On August 3, at the 17th anniversary of the coup d'etat which brought Obiang Nguema into power, he promised his brother a promotion from colonel to brigadier-general. In the 1998 governmental reshuffle of January 21, he succeeded his uncle Manuel Nguema Mba as Secretary of State for National Security.

MBA NSE, Norberto see Akonibe; Convergency for Social Democracy

MBA NSUE, Justino. Fang. From Ebebiyin. Born in 1943. In 1963-64, with Eñeso Neñe, he directed the MUNGE until Ondo Edu took over the movement, when he became secretary to the Executive Committee. During the Constitutional Conference he quarreled with Ondo Edu and joined Macías Nguema's Secretariado Conjunto. Above all a businessman, he took refuge in Spain, as soon as he noted Macías Nguema's many excesses, pretending health problems. He now owns a shoe business. A founding member of the ANALIGE, he joined ANRD in 1974, but was excluded at the same time as Mbá Ada, Nsué Ngomo, and Nsué Angué, because of his close ties to Spanish circles. He is said to be a member of the Grupo de Mayores. His adviser is supposed to be the Spanish economist J. Velarde Fuentes.

Mbá Nsué returned to Equatorial Guinea following the amnesty proclaimed in 1979. He then set up an import-export business. During his exile, it was said that he would take up offers from any quarter. A political tourist. Has connections with the Spanish extreme rightwing, and claimed, in the 1980s, to run a Political Reform Group (Grupo de Reforma política). He is said to be close to García Trevijano. In early 1980, he founded Exigensa Co, with the Spaniard José Rovira Alepuz and Andrés Moises Mba Ada. During the Obiang Nguema period, he belonged successively to Popular Action, the Progress Party, and the Popular Union. On April 12, 1994, the National Executive Committee of UP suspended him following an accusation of "personalistic policy." He was readmitted in 1995 and has been Secretary General ever since. He lives in Madrid. See also Exigensa.

MBA NZE, Norberto ("Tito") see Akonibe; Convergency; Torture

MBA OLO ANDEME, Aurelio. In 1996, ambassadorin Brussels. He kept this function at the end of 1998.

MBA OÑANA NCHAMA, Fructoso. An Esangui from Mongomo, a cousin to Obiang Nguema on his father's side. A tailor by trade. Joined the army and spent some time in Spain and the USSR. Together with his nephews, Obiang Nguema and Maye Ela, he took part in the successful 1979 coup, after which he was designated commander of the land forces and military governor of Río Muni. In November 1979, he refused to receive the special rapporteur of the UN Human Rights commission. When this rapporteur was involved in a car accident between Bata and Evinayong, he only very reluctantly made available a vehicle to take the UN personnel to the hospital in Bata. It was Mba Oñana who gave orders for refugees returning after the 1979 amnesty to be beaten up.

At the end of January 1980, he was posted to New York as counsellor to the ambassador to the United Nations—after having diverted to his own profit, food destined for civilians in Bata. He returned home at the end of 1980, as it was reported he had committed acts of aggression against his nephew the ambassador, Nvono Nka Manene. It is also reported that on his return, he killed a man near the telecommunications center in Santa Isabel, claiming self-defense. In 1981, Mba Oñana was promoted to lieutenant-colonel and became second in command in the military government, taking precedence over vice-president Maye Ela, of whom he was jealous. In March he was appointed inspector-general of the armed forces. Shortly after this, news broke of a "conspiracy" involving the arrest of a number of naval officers and officials of the Ministry of Foreign Affairs, all dependent on Maye Ela. They were accused of taking part in a subversive movement led by Mba Ada. In reality Mba Oñana did not want to pay for a truck and some equipment he had bought through the EXIGENSA company and these arrests enabled him to seize all the assets of that company and resulted in Obiang Nguema becoming the principal shareholder.

In December 1981, Maye Ela was out-posted to the UN in New York, sealing Mba Onana's victory. In April 1982 he went to North Korea on an official mission, and in October he was nominated vice-president with special responsibility for national defense and inspection of the armed forces. He was concurrently manager of the transport company OFICAR. In January 1986, following rumors of dissatisfaction in Río Muni, he was transferred to the Ministry of Public Works as minister, while retaining his vice-presidential position. He was arrested in connection with the attempted coup of July 1986 and sentenced in August 1986 to two years of house arrest, but released in October 1987.

Mbana Oñana was involved in the bankruptcy of the Guinextebank. In early 1987, his wife Leocadia Manguinde owed FCFA 17,514,000; he himself FCFA 14,924,000, and his company Oficar Africa SA FCFA 42,084,000. Mba Onana was involved in the "coup" of August 1988 and he was arrested with Guillermo Nguema and Pancracio Bee, military commander for the region of Mongomo. In 1992, Mba Oñana was named ambassador to China. On the eve of his departure, following a dinner with Obiang Nguema, he died at the hospital.

MBA ONDO, Cayo. Born at Mongomeyen (Mongomo). Named militia police for Macías Nguema. Mba Ondo became a notorious torturer and deputy to the bloodthirsty Ondo Ela in the Playa Negra prison. He later trained in Morocco. After Obiang Nguema's coup d'etat, he became the chief of customs in the capital; he distinguished himself by his excesses, repressions, and tortures. Mba Ondo became senior commissioner of Bata until 1993, the year in which, following an accident, he was transferred to the capital as chief senior commissioner of police.

On January 28, 1995, along with two deputies, he assassinated Martin Obama Ondo, farmer and uncle to minister and government's spokesperson, A. F. Nvée, along with two deputies, both natives of Akonibe (Wele-Nzas). Obama Ondo's brain and genitals were cut off, placed in a boot, and the body was delivered to the capital's hospital. Under pressure from the opposition, and especially from *La Verdad* (the periodical of CPDS), he was brought before justice and condemned on May 21 to two years and four months of military imprisonment and a fine of FCFA 1,000,000 for the victim's family. These sentences were not fully carried out.

Under his orders, nine opponents to the regime were arrested and tortured at the end of June 1997. Among them: Alberto Ondo Ncogo (secretary of the PP), elected mayor of Nkimi.

MBA ONDO MBUY, Marcos. A native of Mongomo. Born 1950. Military training in USSR and North Korea. Cadet in the land forces. In August 1979 he took part in Obiang Nguema's coup d'etat. On September 15 he became a military commissioner for planning. On January 22, 1980, he became military commissioner in charge of the Secretariat of State for Planning and Economic Development. In the December 8, 1981, ministerial reshuffle, Mba Ondo moved to Foreign Affairs, in order to replace Maye Ela. In April 1982, as minister for foreign affairs, he attended the donor conference of the UNDP, in Geneva. In late October, he became secretary of state for the economy and finance.

On July 19, 1986, he was arrested for the coup d'etat attempted by Mba Oñana. On August 18 he was condemned along with five others to two years and four months of house arrest for insult to the head of the state. Obiang Nguema pardoned him on October 12, 1987, along with Mba Oñana, Nguema Ela, and Ondo Mañe. He remained under house arrest until 1991. In 1993 he became a counsellor to the company ENERGE (founded after the 1979 coup d'etat) for the distribution of electricity to Río Muni. In the April 8, 1996, ministerial reshuffle, he became director general for energy. During the summer, 1996, he was involved in an attempted palace revolution between Nguemists. Dismissed from his duties, he was put under house arrest in Mongomo. In 1997, he was appointed general manager of the French telecommunication company GETESA.

MBA ONDO NCHAMA, Felix. An Esangui from Mongomo. Junior-lieutenant in the "Juventud en Marcha con Macías" youth organization. After the 1979 coup, he was made minister of the interior. In the spring of 1980 he was responsible for the recruitment of forced labor for the plantations in Río Muni and was one of the persons who prevented the special rapporteur of the UN Human Rights Commission from having free access to the population in Santa Isabel and in the provinces. In December 1981, he took over from the former vice-president Nguema Esono as ambassador to Ethiopia. He was dismissed from this post in 1983 and took refuge in the Greek Embassy, recalling that one of his predecessors, Nsue Angue Osa, had been assassinated by the nguemist regime. He made a public statement against Obiang Nguema and then took refuge in Gabon.

He returned to Mongomo in 1988. In 1990 he took refuge again in Gabon. In 1993, upon his return, he joined the Populat Undion. Feeling once again threatened, he quickly went into exile in Benin. During the spring of 1998, Manuel Mba tried to have him expelled.

MBA OVONO, Jesus. Fang from Mikomeseng. Founding member of the IPGE during his exile in Congo-Brazzaville in 1959. He rapidly became the leader of the radical branch of this party. Later on he joined the MONALIGE. In 1964 together with Ndongo Miyone in exile in Accra (Ghana) he founded the FRENAPO, a socialist movement, the program of which included nationalization of Spanish belongings in Equatorial Guinea. At the 1968 elections, Mba Ovono ran on the MONALIGE list. He seems to have been arrested in Cameroon in July 1968. He died in Barcelona (Spain) in 1996.

MBA OVONO, Marcelino. From Mongomo. At the ministerial reshuffle of April 8, 1996, he was director general of customs.

MBA OYONO AYINGONO see Oyono Ayingono Mba.

"MBATO" see Obama Nsue Mangue, F.

MBEE NSUE, Marcelo. Captain of the cargo ship *Acacio Mañe.* See also Spain.

MBELA, Gustavo. Kombe. Protestant minister. After Ibongo's assassination in March 1969, Mbela became the United Nations representative for Equatorial Guinea. He resigned in 1970 and took refuge in the United States.

MBENGA NDONG, Vicente. From Niefang. Inspector of police, known for his excesses under Macías Nguema. Also called "Comisario Z." From March 1981, he was senior commissioner of police in Río Muni. He was involved in the Modu Akuse/Esteller scandal.

MBENDENG see Ebendeng

MBENGONO ASU ALENE, Anita. Born in 1947. Cousin to Obiang Nguema. Wife of the ambassador to Spain, Esono Ondo. She was arrested in July 1993 at São Paulo, for trafficking 32 kilos of cocaine. See also Drugs.

MBIA MBIDA-ESSINDI MBEZELE, Juan Benedicto see Democratic and Progressive Alliance

MBINI see Rio Benito

MBO MBA. Mythical Fang, war lord of the early 20th century, known for his intelligence, who put together the Fang empire, which extended from Cameroon to Congo. His skull was said to have the capacity to render people carrying it invulnerable. In 1992, Obiang Nguema tried in vain to lay hands on it. He failed, as the relic belonged to the Nsomo tribe, enemies of Obiang Nguema's Esanguis.

MBOMIO, Ponciano. From Aton-Somo (Ebebiyin). Born 1946. Studied at the Escuela Provincial at Santa Isabel. An administrative agent. In the early 1970s, he worked in the Planning Department of the Ministry of Education, in the company of the Haitian UNESCO expert, Marceau Louis. In the late 1980s, he became a lawyer, after studying at the UNED, where he was one of the few degree holders. In 1995 he became the secretary of the National College of Lawyers.

See also Esono Mbomio, J.; Moto Nsá, S.

MBOMIO NSUE, Leandro. Born in 1949, in Evinayong. A Fang from Mbe-Nsomo, Niefang district, sculptor. Studied at the Vocational School of Bata, then, from 1960 on, at the Ceramic School and Fine Arts School in Spain. Holder of a fellowship in Germany, he later made various trips to Africa, Europe, and America. Mbomio's first masterpieces in terra-cotta and wood date back to 1955. He also paints and works with bronze.

In 1969, he directed the artistic delegation of the OAU at the Pan-African Festival in Algiers. He was one of the few refugees to return after the announcement of the amnesty in October 1979. He was appointed director of culture and art in the Ministry of Education. In December 1981, he was promoted to minister of education and culture. In October 1982, however, he was demoted to secretary of state for artistic development. In 1985 he reappeared as minister of information, culture and art. In January 1986 he was nominated minister of information and tourism. In April 1987, he was made commander of the Order of Arts and Letters. In late 1987 he was placed under house arrest, along with other ministers during the time Obiang Nguema attended the Franco-African Conference at Antibes (France).

In 1990, he became the minister to the president for culture, tourism and artistic promotion. Faced with the protests of the Catholic Church regarding the government's policy, he answered that a new state religion was going to be created (Macías Nguema style): "a religion for national unity." During the awarding of the so-called Biancamano Prize to Obiang Nguema (see Italy; Mafia) in 1991, he spoke in great praise of the dictator.

In 1992, he was president of the Council for Scientific and Technological Research (Consejo de Investigación Cientifica et Tecnologica) in a country that did not have a small center for higher technical education; he was also named joint commissioner for the International Exposition at Seville (Spain). He stated that Equatorial Guinea wished to have its Academy for the Spanish Language (Academia de la Lengua Española). In 1995, he entered the administrative council, wholly composed of important members of the regime, of the Empresa nacional de pesca de Guinea Ecuatorial. In 1998, Leandrp Mbomio received honorific citizenship from Dade County, FL (USA).

See also Coup d'ctat of December 1987

MBUAMANGONO, Tomas see Popular Union

McCORMIC, S. H. Director for Africa of the National Security Council for Africa, at the White House. See United States.

MECHEBA FERNANDEZ, Tomas. From Bata. Born in 1962. Arrived in Spain in 1984. Studied medicine but left it incomplete. He returned to the country in 1992. In 1993 he became general secretary to the Socialist Party (PSGE). In November, being penniless, he announced his candidacy for the elections, The secretary for organization in the PSGE, Constantino Ivili, announced his dismissal. In exchange for his participation in the elections, T. Mecheba obtained a post in the Electricity Company of Equatorial Guinea (Sociedad de Electricidad de Guinea Ecuatorial), a grant on the part of the dictator.

In January 1994, he was part of the delegation of 10 members of Parliament, from the tame opposition, to France, Germany, Switzerland, Spain, and the U.S. In Washington, he informed those in charge of the IMF, IBRD, and the American government on the internal situation. He observed that in the view of these authorities, the Obiang Nguema government was discredited. His party had no representative in parliament.

In April 1995, he co-signed, with several representatives of other parties of the tame opposition, an anti-Spanish document shown on TV. He attended the 2nd Convention of the PDGE, as part of a delegation of this opposition. He was proposed for the post of secretary of state for industry in the April 8, 1996, government, but he refused. He became a tradesman in Malabo.

MECHEBA IKAKA, Jose. Ndowe. An official of the territorial administration. Became its director in December 1982. In January 1986, was appointed minister in charge of civil service.

Founding member of the liberal group National Democratic Union (UDENA) in 1992. In 1993, president of the UDENA. In November, Pedro Bueribueri took the leadership away from him, breached solidarity with the POC, and formed a satellite-wing of the PDGE, with 8 million pesetas in grants, in order to participate in the elections, but did not win any seats. With another wing, Mecheba remained a member of the POC and applied the boycott of the elections. On October 9, 1994, Mecheba Ikaka, while he was returning from a conference at Libreville, was arrested in Akalayong, along with Placido Mikó (CPDS) and Bolekia Bonay (ADP); he was transferred to Bata and tortured in the city's prison.

MEDA SERICHE, Clementino. In the ministerial reshuffle of April 8, 1996, he became director general of the cabinet of the prime minister and head of government.

MEKO, Heriberto see Mikomeseng; Evinayong

MEÑE ABESO ADIGHA, Tarsico. An Esangui from Mongomo. Lieutenant in the "Juventud en Marcha con Macías" youth organization and subsequently integrated into the regular army. In January 1980 he was made military commissioner for education and culture. In December 1981 he was posted to Yaoundé (Cameroon) as first secretary in the embassy there. In 1998, he was a state employee in the Ministry of Foreign Affairs.

MENSUI MBA, Policarpo. From Nsork. Son-in-law to Clemente Ateba. Notorious Nguemist. Junior lieutenant in the "Juventud en Marcha con Macías" youth organization, subsequently integrated into the regular army. After the 1979 coup, he was made military commissioner for justice. He was promoted to the rank of lieutenant in February 1981. He was under arrest for a short time in connection with the alleged plot of April 1981 orchestrated by Mbá Oñana. On December 8, 1981, he was appointed minister of industry and power. In May 1982 he was one of the members of the Akonibé constitutional commission that consolidated Obiang Nguema's dictatorship. At the end of October 1982 he is transferred to the Ministry of Forestry and Water Resources. After the minister of health, Buale Borico, had gone into exile, he took over that position in August 1983. In that capacity he took part in the 38th World Health Assembly in Geneva in May 1985. In 1986, he owed the Guinextebank FCFA 11,638,000. Soon after, he was named ambassador to Cameroon. From 1993, he was ambassador to Moscow. In 1998, he was living in Equatorial Guinea as a member of the Political Bureau of the PDG.

MERCADER, Enrique. A half-breed, born 1956. Since 1985 he has organized various private companies: the Nora bakery, SODISA import-export. Along with other Nguemist executives, he participated in the break-up of the Liberal Party. On March 27, 1994, he was named president of the Chamber of Agriculture and Commerce of Malabo by presidential decree.

MERIDIEN INTERNATIONAL BANK Ltd. Belongs to Andrew Sardanis, in Lusaka, with its headquarters in the Bahamas. In 1991, it absorbed the BIAO-Equatorial Guinea. The control was effected via Meridien BIAO SA, in Luxembourg. The African Development Bank takes 10% of the capital. At the end of 1996, BIAO S.A., was put into liquidation, for insolvency.

MESA BILL CONGUE, Federico. From Douala, Cameroon. He claims to be a Fernandino. He was an administrative official under Macías Nguema and was appointed in the spring of 1979 director of the central services of the presidency. In January 1980 he accompanied Obiang Nguema on his official visit to Cameroon. In December 1981 he was nominated minister of planning and international cooperation. He took part, in that capacity, in the UN-organized donors' conference in Geneva in April 1983. In October he became minister of public administration and administrative reform. At the end of 1982 he returned to Cameroon with Ndong Ela, to prepare Equatorial Guinea's entry into the Customs Union of the Central African States (UDEAC).

Did not figure in the list of ministers from 1986 onwards. In 1993, Mesa Bill Congue was the president's counsellor, chancellor of the National Order of the Republic. The decree of January 15, 1994, put an end to this post, which was given to Victor Ondo Asi.

MESI EDU, Casiano see Popular Action.

MESIAN, Enrique (Mongomo) see Evinayong; Ndong Abaga Mesian

METHODISTS see Protestantism

MEXICO. In 1997, the State University of Equatorial Guinea signed a Convention with the University of Cuernavaca. In July 1998, S. Ngua Nfumu, secretary for press, radio, and TV, had talks in Mexico about a project concerning professional training for radio and TV.

MICHA NDONG, Natán. Born 1958, at Akonibe. Son of Juan Micha Nsue Nfumu, former general secretary of the PDGE. Training in Morocco. At the ministerial reshuffle of April 8, 1996, he was director general of youth.

MICHA NGUEMA EYANG, Maximiliano. A Fang Obuk from the district of Mongomo. Born 1943, at Mongomo. Director of the Instituto Forestal of Río Benito since July 1971. Dedicated supporter of Macías Nguema, member of the PUNT Central Committee, chief of the security in the Río Muni Province. He was known for his violence. After Ntutumu Eyegue's nomination as vice president of the republic, he assumed briefly the interim of the gobernador civil (civil governor) until the nomination of Ela Ndong. Micha showed himself incapable at the Instituto Forestal of recovering the materials left over by the Spanish forest rangers.

Until the end of 1993, he was the general secretary of the Ministry of Animal Husbandry and Fisheries. President of the National Committee for the Protection of the Environment.

By decree dated January 17, 1994, he became the director general of civil services and administrative reform. In 1995, he became a member of the administrative council, entirely Nguemist, and the Empresa nacional de pesca de Guinea Ecuatorial. In the January 8, 1996, government, he was promoted to vice-minister for forest economy. Since the ministerial reshuffle of April 8, 1996, he became secretary general of the Ministry of Fisheries and Forests.

MICHA NSUE, Alejandro. From Akonibé. Studied law in Morocco. In the April 8, 1996, government, he was promoted to the post of secretary of state for public works. He is no longer a member of the government after the January 21, 1998, reshuffle.

MICHA NSUE NFUMU, Juan. Of the Obuk clan to which Obiang Nguema's first wife belongs. Brother-in-law to Obiang Nguema. Studied at Bata. Lieutenant. An official in various administrations. He later took courses at the high school for officials for three years in Madrid. Father of Natán Micha Ndong.

After the 1979 coup, he was appointed chargé d'affaires in the Embassy to Cameroon. In 1980 he was appointed ambassador to Nigeria. In 1982, he took part in the Akonibé Constitutional Commission, which consolidated Obiang Nguema's dictatorship.

He was recalled to the country to become an ambassador in charge of a mission and parliamentary secretary. Since 1987, he has been political and administrative secretary of the PDGE. He was sent to Annobón with a number of policemen for inspection and sensitivization. The Annobón people tore a PDGE flag. Micha Nsue Nfmu represented the PDGE in the negotiations for the National Pact (February-

March 1993). He was the one to organize the PDGE Convention at Bata, in early 1995.

On May 3, 1995, he was pulled out by Obiang Nguema, along with the joint secretary Carmelo Asumu Obono, for being favorable to leniency towards the opposition. He was replaced by Fernando Mbale, of the hard core of the party, while Asumu Obono was replaced by Dario T. Ndong Olomo, who came from the Young Torches (Jovenes Antorchas). But Micha Nsue Nfumu remained a member of the national political bureau and of the central committee of the PDGE. His son José Maria Nsue Nchama is a judge in the Court of First Instance in Fernando Po.

MICHA ONDO BILE, Pastor. From Mongomo. In February 1990, he was director of mines and petroleum, and went on a mission to Houston for discussions with Walter International. By decree dated January 19, 1994, he became general secretary in the Ministry for Mines and Petroleum. From May 1995, he was the ambassador to the USA and Cuba. According to Obiang Nguema, Micha Ondo and the embassy were financed by the Mobil Oil Co. Micha Ondo's wife holds a seat on the administrative board of SOGUIGAS. Pastor Micha holds a seat on the administrative board of APEGESA. Ambassador in the U.S.A., he declared to the *Washington Post* (1997): "We have a loving country of peace and freedom." On July 17 of the same year he became ambassador in Argentina.

See also Petroleum.

MIKO, Fernando see Moto Nsá

MIKO ABOGO, Placido. From Kogo. Born in 1960, in Egombegombe (Río Benito). Holds a degree in chemistry from the University Complutense, Madrid (1986). Upon his return to the country, he taught mathematics within the framework of the UNED.

In early 1991, he founded, with some others, the Convergency for Social Democracy (CPDS), which covered the roads of the capital with slogans and published the only regular periodical of the country, *La Verdad,* for which he wrote the editorials. Some soldiers and Moroccans arrested him with several colleagues in early 1991, and accused them of sending copies of *La Verdad,* declared subversive, to Europe. Some of the arrested opponents were accused of practicing Kong sorcery. Mikó was tortured under the orders of Lt. Fausto Garriga Fuma, son-in-law to Obiang Nguema, and the Moroccans: there were fractured cheeks, feet, and hands. He has since suffered from a cardiac murmur. He was accused of having attacked the forces which had arrested him. Mikó was also threatened by Armengol Nguema Mbasogo Ondo, chief of the Criminal Investigations Department and brother to Obiang Nguema. A joint protest by the ambassadors of the U.S., France, Spain, the UNDP, and the EC was addressed to the government.

Mikó Abogo was condemned in May 1992 for "insulting the Head of the State" and for "subversive propaganda," and then released in early June, following pardon from Obiang Nguema, on the occasion of his fiftieth birthday. Mikó, though he could avail of health assistance from Amnesty International, a ticket from the Red Cross, and though he had relatives in Spain, was refused an exit visa. He fled by pirogue, via Cameroon. Once in Madrid, he revealed his experience of torture "of the Ethiopian kind." He wished to return to the country as soon as the medical treatment ended. According to him the nguemist government was violating all its promises of democratization; unfortunately, the opposition was divided by personal ambitions. Mikó Abogo's epic struggle was published as a "terrible testimony" by La Lettre de Reprorters sans Frontières (October 1992).

Mikó represented the CPDS along with Nvumba Mañana and Nzé Angue, in the negotiations for the National Pact (February-March 1993). He was invited in August by the French Socialist Party to a conference, at Bangui, but he was refused an exit visa. He joined the election boycott called by the POC. He now has one paralyzed arm.

On October 9, 1994, as he was returning from a conference at Libreville, along with Victorino Bolekia Bonay, vice-president of the ADP, and José Mecheba Ikaka, president of UDENA, Plácido Mikó was arrested at Akalayong and transferred with them to Bata where they were tortured in the city's prison. In an Urgent Action, Amnesty International stated that the reasons for the arrest were not known. From November 29 to December 2, the Constitution Assembly of the CPDS, with its 110 regional delegates, elected Plácido Mikó general secretary with 80% of the votes. He also became the No. 1 of the POC.

In the summer of 1995, P. Mikó received the 1st Leon Felipe Award 1995 from the Organization International Solidarity, for his courageous defense of human rights, justice, and fundamental liberties. He was very active during the September municipal elections. But for the manipulations made by the regime, the POC would have run away with the elections, if one went by the remarks of the foreign observers and the POC. In late October, the police came for Mikó to the headquarters of the CPDS, following a radio interview given to Radio Exterior de España, during which he requested Madrid to continue to watch over the process of democratization. Not finding Plácido Mikó, the police arrested his brother.

During the presidential elections in February 1996, the nguemists formulated an electoral regulation that excluded candidates less than 40 years of age, (therefore excluding P. Mikó) and those not having lived in the country during the last five years (thus excluding Moto Nsá). After the electoral farce that brought Obiang Nguema back to power, Plácido Mikó, in agreement with the other leaders of the CPDS, refused Nguemist offers for the constitution of a "government of national unity." "We are not going to talk with such an absurd government," he declared. In May, Obiang Nguema summoned Mikó's parents and insisted that their son call him Mr. President and not Mr. Obiang. In September 1996, he participated with C. Bakale in the meeting of the Socialist International, in New York. Both men were received by the American press and by the company Black, Manaforth, Stone & Kelly, who specialized in lobbying, and who provided the propaganda for Obiang Nguema on the occasion of the fraudulent presidential elections. In Washington, Mikó and Bacale were received by the secretary of state for Africa, William Tuwaddel, who confirmed what the democratic opposition had affirmed for a long time: the election of Obiang Nguema was irregular.

At the beginning of January 1997, Plácido Mikó, who was having a private meeting with members of CPDS, in Río Benito, was arrested by order of Agustin Ndong Ona, cousin of Obiang Nguema.

On October 6, 1996, when Plácido Mikó returned from Spain, he had several copies of the newspapers *ABC, El País, Le Monde,* and *Le Monde Diplomatique* seized.

In January 1997, Colonel Ndong Ona, cousin of Obiang Nguema, imprisoned P. Mikó for two days after a meeting with members of the CPDS in Rio Benito. During the year, the capital's lack of electricity for five months stopped the publication of *La Voz del Pueblo* and other newspapers. Once electricity was back, the headquarters of the CPDS and the private residence of Plácido Mikó remained several months more without electricity. On November 17, an EU delegation for technical evaluation arrived in Malago and met with Mikó.

In November 1998, Mikó came to Europe with a CPDS delegation to assist the Socialist International meeting in Geneva.

See also Bakale, C.; Convergency for Social Democracy; Elections; Electricity; Press; United States.

MIKO OBIANG, Venancio. Born 1950 at Elansok (Mongomo). Electrician, trained in the USSR. Sergeant in the territorial army. He was accused of having taken part in an attempted coup in May 1983. He took refuge in the Spanish Embassy which gave rise to tension with Spain. Miko was eventually handed over to the Moroccans by the Spanish embassy after the latter had been promised he would not be executed. He was held in the courtyard of the Spanish company Frapejo, which was used as a Moroccan billet and then transferred in the Playa Negra prison where he was still seen at the end of 1987. He is the father of five children.

In 1988, Mikó was introduced to the press. In August 1989 he was granted amnesty and his sentence reduced to six years. In August 1991, shortly before the Spanish Prime Minister's visit (which was cancelled) to Equatorial Guinea, Mikó was released. He withdrew to his village and took care of cultivation.

MIKOMESENG. District and town along the Bata-Ebebiyin road, in north-central Río Muni, 5 km from the Cameroonese border, in the heart of cocoa and coffee plantations. Until independence, a priest-staffed secondary school existed (Seminario minor). In 1938, the Spanish authorities built a leprosarium about one kilometer outside the town. Modern buildings were added in 1950, up to 3,000 patients were cared for there, but by 1968 the number had dwindled to only 313. The lepers were cared for by the Sisters of Charity. The decrease was due to the patients being progressively moved to the new leprosarium at Kie Osi near Ebebiyin.

Spanish assistance was used to build school buildings, which have been empty since 1972, for lack of teachers. Mikomeseng disposes of a large lepers' hospital that counted 3,000 patients in 1955. Mbá Ada, Masié Ntutumu, and Asumu Oyono are natives of the Mikomeseng district. A number of citizens of Mikomeseng and Ebebiyin were arrested in connection with the spurious coup of April 1981. In 1983, the Bubi refugees in Spain accused the Fang people of Mikomeseng and Ebebiyin of wanting to take over power from the Esangui of Mongomo. In the eighties, the leper-house was financed by the Sovereign Order of Malta.

In the "transitional" government of February 24, 1992, there figured two ministers from Mikomeseng: Oyono Ndong Mifumu, vice-prime minister and minister for animal husbandry and fisheries, and Olo Mibuy, vice-minister for culture, tourism and promotion of crafts. Heriberto Miko, ex-consul at las Palmas, and later government's representative to Mikomeseng, was appointed ambassador to Nigeria. Towards the end of 1992, a chapel in the town was closed because the catechist refused to obey the orders of the PDGE.

Engonga Motulu, expelled from Switzerland in June 1993, and dismissed from the ANRD for financial misappropriation is from Mbeme-Yengom (Mikomeseng). In the December 22, 1993, government, Oyono Ndong Mifumu was minister of state in charge of foreign affairs and the francophony.

The church was rebuilt under the control of three Salesians. The leper house is run by Spanish nuns. Only the serious cases are treated there. The leper house has no running water. In 1994, 300 children died in that area due to severe diarrhea.

The government's representative was Heriberto Meko from Niefang, born 1960, who had a few years of senior baccalaureate. Named consul at Las Palmas (the Canaries) he indulged in drug trafficking and he was transferred to Mikomeseng. He drew attention there by arresting political opponents). Surname: "Heriberto el malo" (the bad). In 1993 he terrorized the population of Mikomeseng. His slogan—"Here, I'm the one who rules." Meko was transferred in 1995 to Evinayong. In September 1995, Andrés Ntutumu (PDGE) was elected mayor of Mikomeseng.

In 1997–1998, the governmental delegate Francisco Mba Mandama had members of the opposition imprisoned and asked for a ransom.

See also Ayekaba, M. J.; Balinga, B. G.; Engonga Motulu, M.; Esono Abaga; Ada, J.; Kogo; Matogo Oyana; Mba Mifumu; Modu Akuse Bindang, C.; Moyos Esacunan; Nguema Esono, L.; Olo Mba Nseng, J.; Olo Mebuy, A.; Oyono Ndong Mifumu, M.; Parliament; Plot (1981); Press; Río Muni; Santa Isabel; Sima, A.; Transports; Victims

MILAM ONVOA, Juan. Fang from Evinayong. Born July 17, 1946. Technician in central administration of the state. He has been a deputy of the PDGE since 1983. In November 1993, he was reelected from Evinayong, again for the PDGE. In the December 22 government, he became vice-minister for industry, energy and promotion of small and medium-scale enterprises. On April 8, 1996, he became counsellor for administrative affairs at the general secretariat to the president of the government. In the government of January 21, 1998, he became vice-minister of the relations with Parliament and Juridical Affairs.

MILAMTANG, Ignacio. Fang from Evinayong. Born 1940. Studied in the Escuela superior Indígena, in Santa Isabel. President of the National Soccer Federation. In 1981, he negotiated for affiliation with the International Olympic Committee and to the FIFA. Towards the end of 1982, he became the director general for administrative coordination to the president. In 1992, he became director general of financial supervision. He retained this post by decree no. 27 dated January 1994. On April 8, 1996, he became minister for justice and ritual. In the government of January 21, 1998, he was minister of sports and youth.

MILICIA POPULAR (Popular militia). Paramilitary unit of the PUNT created in 1969, trained by Russian, Cuban, and North Korean Instructors. It was founded by members of the Grupo Macías from the Secretariado Conjunto inspired by García Trevijano. Originally all ethnic groups belonged to this militia. Various founding members of the militia were given high offices: Asumu Oyono, Nsué Ngomo, R. Obiang, Momo Bokara, etc. Progressively as the initial group disintegrated (exile, assassinations), the militia passed into the hands of fanatics and tribalists, while Macías Nguema's personal power grew stronger. The militia counted about 2,000 men and women and represents a typical political police. Following Obiang Nguema's coup in August 1979, the militia was integrated into the army and several of their officers now hold important executive and administrative posts in the government.

MILLAN, Enrique. The last general secretary of the autonomous government of Equatorial Guinea and first general secretary to the president of the republic. With Elema Borengue, he cofounded in Valencia (Spain) the Forum for Democracy in Guinea (Foro paral la Democracia de Guinea), whose aim was to organize a peace conference for Equatorial Guinea.

In March 1996, Millan addressed an "Open letter to the Equato-guineans and to Spaniards residing in Guinea" in the periodical *El Sol,* in which he complained of his articles being rejected by the Spanish press, and accused the Spanish Socialist government of cynicism, incompetence, and corruption.

See also Elema Borengue, J.

MINAS DE ECUADOR S.A. A Spanish gold mining company that operated in various districts in the area of Evinayong between 1950 and 1968. See also Gold.

MINES. Except for the rather amateurish exploitation of alluvial gold, there are no exploited mines in the country. Traces of rutile (a titaniuim compound), copper, uranium, and oil exist. In 1969 the American Steel Company was refused the right to prospect in the country because it requested a monopoly position and offered insufficient royalties. The geophysical aerial mapping carried ouot in 1970 by "Hunting Geology and Geophysics Ltd." for Chevron pointed to some concentrations of iron iin the south of Bata. The oil prospecting does not seem to have yielded any results so far. Among the Mines and Industry ministers since 1964, Martinez Pelayo and Borico tiochoa were assassinated and Ekong Andeme fled to Cameroon. Since 1976 the Ministry of Natural Resources and Electricity has been entrusted to Nguema Ada with the title of vice minister.

After the 1979 coup the joint Spanish-Equatorial-Guinea company GEMSA was set up with Mensuy Mbá as its director. The Bureau Français de Rescherches Géologiques et Minières (BRGM) also opened offices. In 1982 the GEMSA took some 8,500 mineral samples in the country and drew up a geophysical map. The GEMSA and BRGM apparently purchased from García Trevijano the findings of the geological studies he had financed in 1971

The minister of mining and petroleum resources, Joan Olo Mba Nseng, brother-in-law to Obiang Nguema, appointed in October 1982, was made secretary of state in the Ministry of Planning. He is pro-French and is seen as a possible successor to Obiang Nguema.

Mining law by decree of June 12, 1981: All mineral resources are the propertyof the state. The maximum exploitation areas are of 150,000 hectares, for three years, with two possibilities of extension of one year each. The contract of participation is limited to 25 years. The technical equipment can be imported exempt from taxes. The production is subject to 5% royalties and to a 20% fee on profits, until recovery of the initial investment. There is a 50% tax.

Geological investigations are mostly done on the Rio Muni, and have shown that gold, diamonds, tin, tentalite, colombite, iron, and most probably nickel and bauxite can be found.

According to the Mining Forum of the EU, the terms of a Mineral Development Agreement (1998) are the following:

1. 7 year term
2. 25 years development
3. Area covered by a progessively reduced permit
4. Minimum required works are negotiable
5. Tax base 30% (on gross income, minus costs and expenses)
6. Taxes not exceeding 20% on expatriates' wages
7. Rental charges: $0.25/hectare for prospecting areas; $1.0/hectare for producing areas
8. Royalties: 3% on gold; up to 5% on all other minerals
9. Management charges on profits abroad for foreign companies
10. Exemption of duties on imports by foreign companies
11. A company can divide the covered area of the prospecting area into a maximum of five parts

MISSIONS. Catholicism was introduced by the Portuguese and Spaniards. Spanish missionary action for the Gulf of Guinea goes back to 1460–1480, with the Nunciatura Castellana de Guinea, whose headquarters was in Tenerife (Canary Islands). Protestantism arrived with British and American missionaries. In 1998, the country had 93% Catholics, 4% Protestants, and 19% Animists.

See also Catholicism; Protestantism; Religions; Terror.

MOBIL Corp. American petroleum company (Fairfax). Lucio A. Noto, chairman; Paul Hoenmans, executive vice-chairman. Mobil is the biggest of the American petroleum interests in the Nguemist regime since 1995.

The compay is called Mobil Equatorial Guinea Inc. (MEGI). Art Green is the head of production.

The Government Relations Representative of the Mobil Business Resources Corporation (New York) answered Spanish protesting political parties and humanitarian organizations, in May 1996, that

Mobil conducts its operations worldwide according to high ethical standards, which include protection of the environment and respect for human rights and workers rights. We operate according to agreements and concessions entered into between Mobil and these governments, which generally are proprietary. From time to time, we may inform the public about a specific country in which we operate, describing our activities and what we hope to accomplish. We understand your interest in Equatorial Guinea and we appreciate your bringing your concerns to our attention. However, we believe these concerns are best addressed between your government and the government of Equatorial Guinea.

That is, the Nguemists. In May 1996, the PDGE's *Voz del Pueblo* insisted on the petroleum benefits for the Equato-Guinean people. October 9, 1996, in 16 pages of pro-Nguemist propaganda in *Jeune Afrique* (Paris), Mobil Corporation, under the title "A Ray of Sunshine" took two of the pages to proclaim that "We are happy to work with Equatorial Guinea and to tie the knot with her in a long collaboration." On October 29, the oil field of Zafiro was inaugurated in the presence of Mobil Vice-Chairman Paul Hoenmans and President A. Patassé of the Central African Republic. *The Financial Times* reported that "opponents maintain Mobil is merely feeding a dictatorship which echoes the very worst of General Franco's legacy." The Mobil Foundation, supported by Mobil and UMC, made a donation of $150,000 to fund a program to train Equato-Guinean educational professionals at the University of New Mexico.

At the end of 1996, the company said it is giving aid to Equatorial Guinea: roads, bridges, electric plants, school books. In 1997, it invited the director of the British Council to Younde to visit Malabo and to organize English classes.

In February 1998, negotiations for an increase in royalties were held in London between Mobil and the Nguemists. Mobil finances the embassy in Washington and the representation at the UN. It also takes care of tarring the roads of the capital. In June–July 1998, it organized a reunion with videos and reports to present its activities in Malabo and Madrid, where it was trying to find Equato-Guinean managers willing to return to their country in spite of their fear of the Nguemists. After 10 days of rain during the middle of July 1998, and the destruction of the highway bridge linking Malabo to the airport, Mobil had a metal bridge measuring 45 m per 5 m brought to the city. In August, Mobil announced an increase in production in Equatorial Guinea, especially in block B, that it exploits (71.25) with Ocean Energy (23.75%), the state owning 5%. At the end of 1998, Mobil carried out a project to bring drinkable water to nine villages of the south of Bioko (from Ruiche to Borcoricho).

On September 5, 1998, when visiting Ghana, Obiang Nguema declared that the neocolonial heritage had to be destroyed. Obiang Nguema and Rawlings, when they met on the 15th, evoked: "The negative influence of multinationals on the economic and political development of the African continent."

Mobil Oil criticizes the attitude of the U.S. government with regard to dictatorships in a document entitled "Africa" (1998): "The United States sometimes tries to force it viewpoint throuogh unilateral trade sanctions. Such sanctions simply don't work, even with the best intentions. By undermining a country's economy, they often hurt the local citizens. Sanctions inhibit the very thing that will foster democracy and encourage political engagement—free trade between nations." Mobil Oil estimates implicitly that violation of human rights, among them terror and torture, do not matter.

The European Commissioner for Humanitarian Action, Emma Bonino, underlined in December 1998 (*Nigrizia,* Verona) that "the warriors and strategists of today could not care less about the moral principles and international conventions directed at prosecution of crimes against humanity, so as to strengthen their objectives...A sort of moral desert. . . ."

See also Democracy; Elections; Government of National Unity; Micha Ondo Bile, P.; Noble Affiliates Inc.; Obiang Nguema, T.; Petroleum; Saudi Arabia; United States of America.

MODU AKUSE BINDANG, Carmelo. From Mikomeseng Born in 1938. Has never studied. A trader from the colonial period. After independence, he became the director of the company Amilibia S.A. He sought refuge in Cameroon under the dictatorship of Macías Nguema in 1969. He returned to the country after Obiang Nguema's coup and plunged into the import-export business.

Towards the end of 1976, the Spaniard A. Esteller was said to have been swindled in Cameroon by Modu Akuse, out of a sum of 76 million pesetas. His representative at Santa Isabel was then José Luis Jones Dougan. In early 1981, Modu was named vice-president of the Chamber of Commerce of Río Muni. In March, he was arrested with a number of pillars of the Macías Nguema regime. Upon release, he found himself encumbered with a lawsuit filed by Esteller. On May 22, 1982, he was condemned and his assets were sealed. Modu then contacted some Nguemist friends; Esteller was summoned to the Criminal Investigations Department by the chief of frontier police Mbenga Ndong and declared persona non grata. The governor of the Banco de Guinea did not execute the embargo on credits, letters of credit etc, ordered by the committee, which would have allowed Esteller to retrieve his assets. Two cargo loads from Spain addressed to Modu were then detained at Las Palmas. In 1985, Modu Akuse was condemned to 10 years' imprisonment for forging Banco de Crédito y Desarrollo checks. He managed to flee the country. He was based at Valencia, Spain, where he did business, thanks to the Banco Exterior de España, making significant profits with home appliances.

Toward the end of 1990, Modu founded the Democratic and Social Union (UDS) at Lisbon, with Secundino Oyono; he was its generl secretary. He claimed to enjoy support among Venezuelans and to have 160,000 members. According to a document dated December 28, 1990, published by various media and signed by the Equato-Guinean ambassador to Gabon, Crisanto Ndong Abama Mesian, an assassination attempt on Modu Akuse was said to have been organized. Ali Asumi, Ndong Biken, Mve Mba, and Monolito Mba were mentioned in the document.

Modu returned in 1992, but in November 1992 the members of the UDS expelled him from the party, fearing that he would assume too much power. He strayed into Popular Union, and was then accepted back.

In 1993, the UDS was torn into two rival factions. The party breached the boycott called by the POC, joined the tame opposition, and participated in the November 21 elections, obtaining five seats. In fact, Obiang Nguema practiced blackmail: participation in the elections, or completing his 10-year prison sentence. Modu Asjuse was elected deputy from Mikomseng in November 1993. In exchange for his participation as a tame opponent, he was named vice-president of the Empresa Nacional de Petróleos.

In 1995, along with other parties of the tame opposition, he signed an anti-Spanish document shwn on TV. In the April 8, 1996, government, after the farce that was the presidential election, he was rewarded by the dictator with the post of minister of state in charge of labor and social promotion.

In the January 21, 1998, ministerial reshuffle, he was replaced by Ernesto Maria Cayetano Toherida.

See also APEGESA.

MOBUTU SESE SEKO. Zaire's dictator was a member of the OAU arbitration commission in the 1972 border conflict between Equatorial Guinea and Gabon.

In 1997, Obiang Nguema was a member of the Central African heads of state who tried to arrange the conflict between Mobutu and Kabila.

MOICHE ECHEK, Apolinar. Bubi from Riaba. A translator and interpreter, trained in Egypt. After Obiang Nguema's coup, he became chief of protocol for foreign affairs. In this capacity, he received the special reporter of the Human Rights Commission of the United Nations, F. Volio Jimenez, in November 1979, following the defection of B. Mba Ekua Miko.

On January 22, 1980, he became technical director for African, Asian, and Middle and Far Eastern Affairs, in the Ministry of Foreign Affairs. None of the demands that the special reporter for Human Rights addressed to him were acted upon. On December 8, 1981, Moiche Echek became state secretary in charge of international cooperation, and diplomatic counsellor to the president of the government. He remained in his post in the October 1982 ministerial reshuffle.

He was arrested in Santa Isabel in early December 1983, with two officials, for having delivered diplomatic passports to two North Koreans who were to accompany Obiang Nguema to Morocco. In 1994, he became an official in the Ministry of Foreign Affairs. In the April 8, 1996, ministerial reshuffle, he was named director general for foreign policy.

MOKA, King, 1794?–1898. Chief of the Bubi, successor of Lorite during the first half of the 19th century. He lived an isolated life in Riaba, and accepted his first contact with Europeans only in 1887. Moka set up a police, the Lojua, first in charge of administering justice, but it later became a regular royal guard. At his death, "Prime Minister" Sas Eburea usurped power, which returned to the legitimate heir, Malabo, in 1904.

MOKA. Locality situated in south-central Fernando Po, at 1,500 m height. In 1904 the Trasatlántica created a cattle farm that covered at independence 3,000 hectares and numbered almost 2,500 head. Since 1940 a cooperative farm produced potatoes, European vegetables, eggs, and poultry. In 1958 a Geographic Institute was established to register the variations of the magnetic field (World Geophysical Year). Since 1980, thanks to the EC, the horticultural cooperative was again functional. See also Seriche Bioko, C.

MOKONG ONGUENE, Carmelo. Fang from Ebebiyin. Protestant. Born in 1945. Trained in the USSR. Ex-secretary in the embassy in the USSR. He later worked at the Ministry of Foreign Affairs. He was a refugee in Switzerland in 1984. He joined the National Alliance for Democratic Restoration (ANRD). Having managed to infiltrate the central committee, he got himself named president, a post that had not been provided for in the statutes.

In August 1992, he claimed to be the coordinator of a committee for voluntary return, founded in Geneva with the support of churches. Sixty-four families, settled in Switzerland, Germany, and Spain, started preparing to return. The president of the committee, professor of theology Lukas Vischer, was received by Obiang Nguema (while the special reporter to the UN, Volio Jimenez, was not), and he obtained a lot of promises. Mokong declared: "If anyone is to die, it will be me." He was a Popular Union activist in Equatorial Guinea. In April 1993, the ANRD published a communique, dismissing Mokong "for dishonest behavior and negligence of his responsibilities."

In 1998 he was secretary of international relations of the UP.

See also Dougan Beaca, J.; Ngomo Mbengono, F.

MOKUDI NANGA, Alfredo. A Creole from Santa Isabel, born on August 4, 1935 (of Cameroonian parents). He went to secondary school in the capital. A farmer. He entered the administration, and became the president of the Chamber of Commerce (which was involved in the marketing of cocoa); he occupied the post for 11 years. After Obiang Nguema's coup d'etat, he was named to the Parliament as a representative of the Chamber of Commerce. He retained his seat there for five years as second vice-president. On December 22, 1993, he became minister for agriculture, fisheries and food. In the January 8, 1996, ministerial reshuffle, he left the government and was replaced by Djoni Bekoba. He was appointed deputy. He is a member of the Asociación de Amigos de Obiang Nguema (Assocation of the Friends of Obiang Nguema).

MOMO BOKARA, Expedito Rafael, d. 1974. Bubi. Administrative technician. Deputy at the Asamblea General (Parliament), from 1964 to 1968, member of the Unión Bubi, he became gobernador vivil of Fernando Po in 1968, then minister of justice, succeeding Eworo Ndongo, who had been assassinated. In 1969 he participated in the creation of the Milicia Popular. Arrested in March 1973 and charged with conspiracy, he was imprisoned in Bata where he was mixed up in the attempted coup d'etat of June 1974. The plot failed and Momo Bokara officially "committed suicide."

MONGOMO. Locality situated in east-central Río Muni, close to the Gabonese border (Woleu-Ntem), along the Ebebiyin–Nsork road. The locality is connected to Gabon by a bridge over the Kié. From 1936 to 1968 it was called Mongomo de Guadalupe. Born of a Gabonese father in the district of Nsork, Macías Nguema was brought up in Mongomo. In 1944 he became administrative assistant in Bata; in 1951 assistant interpreter at the Tribunal de Razas, and from 1960 to 1964 mayor of Mongomo. In the immediate preindependence period, the place was called Mongomo-Mbá Ndong. The Nguemists Obiang Nguema, Mbá Oñana, Oyono Ayingono, etc. are dubbed "Mongomists." The People's Republic of China recently built the road from Mongomo to Nkué—i.e., 225 km connecting Mongomo with the Bata-Ebebiyin road. Macías Nguema spent more and more time in Mongomo, which was encircled by important military safety devices. With the suppression of almost all the elite (except for the exiled), Macías Nguema is surrounded more and more by people from Mongomo, such as B. Nguema, T. Nguema, L. Ela, D. Oyono Ayingono, and M. Oyono Asangono. Shortly after the 1979 coup led by the Esangui from Mongomo, it was the Esangui, Salvador Ndongo Ela, who was appointed government representative in Mongomo. In March 1984 the dictatorship unsuccessfully tried to get Father Ensema Mbá from Mongomo nominated as delegate to the UN Human Rights Commission.

In 1985, a number of members of the clan from Mongomo bought agricultural estates confiscated from Spanish nationals, with unconvertible bikwele: they included Alogo Nchama, Edjang Mba, Engonga Nguema, Eyi Monsui Andeme, Ndong Mba (2), Nguema Nguema Onguene, Nka Esono Nsing, Nko Ivassa Ronde, Ondo Ondo, and Owono Ovono Menana.

In the January 1992 "transitional" government, of 35 members, 12 ministers and secretaries of state, as well as the president, were from Mongomo and its region. In May, the press informed that Obiang Nguema indulged in sorcery in the forests of Mongomo. Not having managed to obtain the skull of the famous Fang chief, Mbo-ba, he considered himself obliged to practice ritual sacrifice, to substitute the powers of the skull. During 1992, a three-star hotel financed by Obiang Nguema, via A. Envoro Ovono, was inaugurated in Mongomo. Rosendo Ela Nsue (from Mongomo), was the commissioner of police in Mongomo. He actively prevented the members of the opposition from reaching the locality.

In February 1993, two French teachers, Marcel Moreau and René Rodriguez, were training the Young Torches (Jovenes Antorchas, Obiang Nguema's Juventud) composed of 300 youth from Mongomo (qualified by the media as death squads). During the summer and autumn of 1993, arms were distributed in Mongomo. In October a declaration of the majority of the village chiefs of the district of Mongomo, expressing their "revulsion at all the criminal acts and political vandalism of Teodoro Obiang Nguema, his family and accomplices in his dictatorial and bloodthirsty regime," was published. They supported the POC and the call for election boycott. In the December 22 government, some persons from Mongomo, including Elo Nve Mbengono, Elo Ndong Nsefumu, and Nguema Onguene, figured no more, but some monsters of the Macías Nguema period, like Mbato (Obama Nsue Mangue) appeared on the scene.

The summary trial in April 1995, of Moto Nsa and a dozen other military men, before judges who were relatives or friends of Obiang Nguema's, proved that the clan from Mongomo still holds the country hostage.

The U.S. State Department Report on Human Rights Practices for 1995 (April 1996) stated: "The government does not overtly limit participation by ethnic minorities, but the monopolization of political power by the president's Mongomo subclan of the Fang ethnic group persists." In September 1995, Martín Nguema Nsue (PSGE) was elected Mayor.

The January 8, 1996, ministerial reshuffle again increased the number of members of the clan from Mongomo in the government. In the April 8, 1996, government, the Mongomists represented more than a fourth of the ministers, not including the dictator. Whenever one looks, the administration is packed with natives of Mongomo.

- Board of Directors of the Cabinet of the Private Secretary of H.E., the President of the Republic: Eneme Obama, José

- Joint Board of Directors of the Cabinet of the Private Secretary of H.E., the President of the Republic: Ncogo Abegue, Braulio

- Joint Board of Directors of the Cabinet of Personal Affairs of H.E., the President of the Republic: Olomo Nve Nsang, Domingo

- Chief of Protocol of the Presidency of the Republic: Mba Nguema Mikue, Antonio

- General Inspection of the Services: Nguema Mbasogo Ondo, Armengol

- Joint Board of Presidential Security: Ndong Obiang, Pedro, and Olomo Nve Nsang, Domingo

- Spokesman of the PDGE: Evuna Owono Asangono, Alejandro

- Counsellor for Political Affairs for the Chief of State/President of Electricity supplies of Equatorial Guinea: Elo Ndong Nsefumu, Demetrio

- Joint General Inspection of the Services: Akieme Molungua, Ignacio
- General Secretariate of the Ministry of Foreign Affairs and Cooperation: Edjang Mba Madja, Pedro
- General Director for Protocol: Ndong Monsuy Francisco Javier
- General Director for International Organizations: Efua Efua Asangono, Teresa
- General Director for Cultural and Consular Affairs: Ela Nguema Buna, Pedro
- General Secretary of the Ministry of National Defense: Mba Ndong, Roberto
- General Director of Internal Police: Asumu Bikui, Francisco
- General Director of National Security: Mba Nguema Mikue, Antonio
- General Director of Justice and Penitentiary Institutions: Maye Nsue Mangue, Rubén
- General Secretary of the Ministry for Fisheries and Forests: Micha Nguema Eyang, Maximiliano
- General Director for Energy: Mba Ondo Mbuy, Marcos
- General Director for Petroleum and Gas: Ondo Angue, Miguel
- President of the Administrative Council of Equatorial Guinea - Total: Envoro Ovono, Alejandro
- General Secretary of the Ministry of Economy and Finance: Nguema Ela Mangue Ndong, Guillermo
- General Director for Taxes: Osa Osa Ecoro, Jeronimo
- Director of Fiscal Control: Owono Edu, Marcelino
- Director of Statistics: Osa Osa Ecoro, Jeronimo
- General Director of Post and Telecommunications: Nguema Ndong, Joaquin
- General Director of Traffic and Road Security: Esono Obama Eyang, Pablo
- General Secretary of Health and Environment: Obama Eyene Bindang, Jacinto
- General Secretary of the Ministry of Education and Sports: Eyi Mensui Andeme, Isidoro
- General Secretary of the Ministry for Social Matters and Women's Integration: Egonga Nguema, Clemente
- General Secretary of the Ministry of Information: Nka Esono Nsing, Martin
- General Director for Physical Education and Sports: Ela Nguema, Lino
- General Director of the National School for Administration: Ndong Nsi, Agustin

Moreover, many senior executives come from Wele-Nzas (that is, the province of Mongomo).

May 12, 1996, F. Jiminez Losantos opined in the Spanish daily *ABC* that soon one wouldn't call it "Equatorial Guinea," but "Mongomo Guinea." In June, Doctors without Borders points out that the dictatorship of Obiang Nguema and the Mongomo Clan is becoming more powerful.

In the government of January 21, 1998, the presence of the Fang of Mongomo and of the province of Wele-Nzas largely prevailed, namely with the arrival of

Teororin Nguema Obiang, eldest son of the dictator and minister of forestry and environment. The January 30, 1998, report of the Department of State describes the dictatorship as follows: "The President has full power as Head of State, commander of the armed forces, and leader of the PFGE, the governmental party. The key positions in the government are usually limited to the president's clan and to his closest supporters. Although there is an elected Chamber of Deputies, it is not representative and is controlled by the government."

See also Abaga Ondo Bindang; Akonibe; Akurenam; Andeme Ela, M.; Angue Ondo; Anisok; Antorchas; Army; Asencna; Asumu Bikuy; Baney; Bata; Evebiyin; China People's Republic; Coups d'etat; Development Plans; Drugs; Edjang Mba Madja; Edu, F.; Education; Edu Oba, B.; Efua Efua Asangono, T.; Ekong Awong; Ekua Ondo; Ela Abeme, J.; Ela Nguema, L;, Ela Nguema, P.; Ela Nguema Buna, P.; Ela Nsue; Ela Oyana, J.; Elections; Elo Mabale; Elo Ndong; Nsefumu, Enemo Obama, J.; Eneme Ovono, J.; Eneme Owono, S;, Engonga Nguema; Ensema Mba; Envoro Owono; Esono Ondo, B.; Evinayong; Evuna Owono Asangono; Eyi Mensui Andeme; France; Gangsterism; Gangsters; Human Rights; National Institute for Social Security; Young Torches; Justice; Mangue Okomo Nsue; Maye Ela, F.; Maye Nsue Mangue, R.; Mba Bela, J.; Mba Ndong, A.; Mba Ndong, R; Mba Nguema Mikue, A.; Mba Nsoro Mban, S.; Mba Onana, F.; Mba Ondo, C.; Mba Ondo Mbuy, M.; Mba Ondo Nchama; Mesian, E.; Micha Nguema Eyang, M.; Micha Ondo Bile; Miko Obieng; Mongomo Mba; Motu Mamiaga; Ncogo Abegue, B.; Ndong, D.; Ndong, J.; Ndong Abaga Mesian; Ndong Ela Mangue; Ndong Ela Nzeng; Ndong Mba, Z.; Ndong Mba Obono; Ndong Monsuy, F. J.; Ndong Obiang, P.; Ndong Olomo, D.-T.; Ndong Ona; Nepotism; Nguema Edu; Nguema Ela Mangue Ndong, G.; Nguema Emaga Eyui; Nguema Esono Nchama; Nguema Mba; Nguema Mbasogo Ondo; Nguema Ndong, J.; Nguema Nguema Onguene; Nguema Mbasogo Ondo; Niefang; Nka Esono Nsing; Nseng Nve; Nve Nguema; Obama Eyene Bindang; Obama Owono Nchama; Obiang Mangue; Obiang Ndong, D.; Obiang Nguema; Okenve Edjang; Olo Mba Nzeng; Olomo Nve Nsang, D.; Ondo Ela Mangue; Ondo Mane Ondo Avang; Ondo Nkumu; Ondo Obiang Alogo; Osa Osa Ecoro, J.; Owono, B.; Oyono Ayingono; Parliament; Police; Sorcery; Torture; Tung Ela, R.

MONGOMO MBA, Telesforo. From Mongomo. Born in Yenvam-Melen, Mongomo. Administrative assistant (Escuela superior). Does not hold a degree. Took a course in law. In January 1994, he was confirmed as a judge in the Supreme Court.

MONKEYS see Primates

MOROCCO. Moroccan soldiers arrived in Equatorial Guinea a few hours after the beginning of the coup of August 3, 1979, that brought Obiang Nguema to power. Since then, he has been protected by 600 Moroccan soldiers, in exchange for Equatorial Guinea's refusal to give diplomatic recognition to the Saharoui Democratic Republic. Obiange Nguema was described by the Mauritanian press as an ignoramus and guilty of insulting the Mauritanian people after he had publicly declared that historically, Morocco stretched from the Mediterranean to the river Senegal. The ANRD maintains that Equatorial Guinea has become a

Moroccan protectorate. It seems that already, by 1981, the army of Equatorial Guinea was exasperated by the presence of this soldiery.

At the time of the UN Decolonization Committee's vote on the independence of the Saharoui people, Equatorial Guuinea was one of the seven countries voting against it, along with El Salvador, Gabon, Morocco, Senegal, Zaire, and the U.S. In 1983 the Spanish press intimated that the Moroccan soldiers were being paid out of Spanish aid funds. It was evidently the Moroccan guards who thwarted the coup attempt of July 1986 led by Mbá Oñana.

In 1987, Moroccan veterans from the Sahara were stationed in Bata and Santa Isabel, where they guarded all the official buildings, the political prisoners (the Equato-Guineans took care of common law), and indulged in violence and arbitrary arrests; some of them specialized in torture. To Equatorial Guinea, they introduced methods unknown before 1979. The UN confirmed this. They used the building belonging to the Claretian Fathers as barracks.

During 1990, discussions with Angola involved the possibility of replacing the Moroccans with Angolans. In 1991, in Spain, the opposition parties demanded police protection due to the presence of a commando of Moroccan agents.

During the debates in the UN Human Rights Commission in March 1993, Béatrice Fauchère responded, in the name of the World Labor Confederation (WLC), to the protests of the Nguemist Minister of State Evuna Nvono Ayingono, stating that a regime that required the support of Moroccan soldiers to protect itself from its own people could never be trusted. She also asked if, after the occupation of ex-Spanish Sahara, Morocco would not be busy colonizing black Africa. The Moroccan mercenaries left the country in August, at the insistence of the U.S., except for the praetorian guards, numbering 50. They were replaced by the Young Torches and Ninjas. In return for its help, Morocco obtained a huge lumber concession in Northwestern Río Muni. France was able to reinforce its influence over the country for several years through Moroccan presence.

On April 29, 1995, Moroccan mercenaries returned, as Obiang Nguema began to distrust the Ninjas. Hamed Ghoul, Moroccan inspector, chief of Obiang Nguema's presidential guard, recruited military instructors for Bata at the beginning of 1996. In July 1996 a new elite unit of Moroccan guards arrived to protect the dictator.

At the end of 1998, there were only 30 Morocans left, having been replaced by the Ninjas. Ambassador of Equatorial Guinea in 1998: Eduardo Ndong Oló.

See also Administration; Akurenam; France; Germany; Israel; Mba Nsoro Mban, S.; Mba Ondo, C.; Miko Abogo, P.; Missions; Moto Nsá, S.; Motu Mamiaga, P.; Nguema Mba, M.; Nguema Mbasogo Ondo, A.; Niefang; Nsue Nchama, J. M.; Obiang Nguema, T.; Public Health; Saharaoui Popular Republic; Santa Isabel; Seriche Dougan, A. S.; Sibacha Buecheku, A.; Socialist Party; Torture; Tung Ela, R.

MORO MALONGA, Arsenio see United Nations (UNDP)

MOSWI m'ASUMU, Buenaventura see Social Democratic Coalition Party

MOTO NSA, Severo. From Acok-Esanguong (Niefang), the Esawong clan. Born in 1943. The third of 11 children. From 1958, he studied in seminaries in Spain (Cervera/Lerida, Barbastro/Huesca) and became a novice at Na Sa del Pueyo. In

1964 he gave up priesthood and returned to his country where he studied to become a teacher at the Teachers' Training School at Bata. In 1967, he studied journalism at the Leon XIII Foundation, at Madrid.

In 1971 he became director of Ebano, in Santa Isabel. Between 1976 and 1979 he was said to be in prison. After Obiang Nguema's coup d'etat, he again took charge of Ebano and entered the first government of the second Nguemist regime under Obiang Nguema, as secretary of state for information and tourism. In 1980 he became a local representative of the Spanish press agency EFE. He is married to one of Masié Ntutumu's daughters, with whom he has four children.

His Progress Party (PP) returned in 1988, with protection from journalists, deputies of the European Council, and from the lawyer José Luis Jones, party secretary. The people were prevented from getting close to them. The director of the Criminal Investigations Department, Armengol Nguema Mbasogo Ondo, and the minister for the interior refused to permit the setting up of the party. Moto Nsa returned to Europe in late June. In August, Jones Dougan was arrested in Santa Isabel. In October, Moto Nsa claimed to have been threatened with expulsion from Spain and asked not to have any more Equato-Guinean political activities. He accused Spanish Prime Minister Felipe Gonzalez of becoming an accomplice of Obiang Nguema.

In June 1990, Moto Nsa returned to Santa Isabel, and accused the Obiang Nguema government of practicing military dictatorship like Macías Nguema. He demanded the legalization of the PP as well as democratic liberalization. He announced his candidacy for the post of president, and was severely criticized by the National Alliance for Democratic Restoration (ANRD).

In 1991, after the announcement of the impending introduction of multiparty-ism, the embassy at Madrid refused him a visa, as he held dual nationality.

In May 1992, Moto Nsa arrived in Santa Isabel without a passport, along with Vice-President T. Bueichecu and some journalists, and was received by 200 persons. Soon after, the impending arrival of A. Suarez, the Spanish mediator accepted by Obiang Nguema, was also announced. In early September, Moto Nsa was arrested with 23 members. He was released after long sessions of interrogation at the headquarters of the Criminal Investigations Department, while the others were tortured and imprisoned at Playa Negra. Moto Nsa cosigned the POC's communiqués along with Pablo Ndong Nsama. On October 16, the PP was legalized. Upon return to Madrid, he demanded the departure of the Moroccans, and declared that Spain "has to endure the Guinean government for a few months," in order to avoid "civil war." Moto Nsa denounced increasing gallicizing of Equatorial Guinea. In March, under the aegis of the Spanish Partido Popular, the PP merged with Justino Mba's Popular Union, thus creating the Popular Progress Party (PPP). Moto Nsa and Masié Ntutumu were thus to be grouped under the same party. But the representatives of the PP in Equatorial Guinea, including T. Bueichecu, rejected this "improper alliance," and the project failed.

In November 1993, the Progress Party joined the POC in the election boycott. In April 1994, just as he was returning home, Moto Nsa stated that in Spain Equato-Guinean affairs remained "classified material" (meaning censored), for economic reasons. In August, four of his nine brothers were arrested and tortured, following a nephew's suicide, in order to indirectly threaten Moto Nsa. His brother

Santiago was condemned to 20 years in prison. In late November, Moto Nsa went to Washington; he then boasted of American promises to fight Obiang Nguema's narco-traffic.

In late January 1995, Moto Nsa was condemned to house arrest in Santa Isabel, under the orders of Judge J. M. Nsue Nchama, who was close to Obiang Nguema, after army men had raided the headquarters of his party. Along with other leaders of the PP, he was accused of defamation committed against Obiang Nguema. The organizational secretary of the PP, Ona Nguema, accused Moto Nsa, on television and upon being tortured, of plotting the kidnapping of Obiang Nguema with Spain and the USA during a coup d'etat. The interrogatory was directed by Manuel Nguema Mba, Obiang Nguema's cousin, in the presence of his younger brother, Armengol; they were respectively state secretary and director general of security. Moto Nsa was defended by three lawyers: Celestino Obiang, Fernando Miko, Ponciano Mbomio. The prosecutor, Nazarin Oyono, was a jurist who had studied in Uzbekistan (USSR). On March 6, the court of appeals condemned Moto Nsa to 18 months in prison for abetting the subordination of a police commissioner, and for slander against Obiang Nguema. He was also condemned to pay a fine of FCFA 50 million (approx. $100,000). Further, he was declared ineligible for elections for a period of 18 months, which excluded him from the September municipal elections and from the first pluralist presidential election in 1996. Tomas Elo Aka, secretary for Finance, was also condemned for corruption. The 12 journalists who requested a visa to attend the trial were turned back. Moto Nsa was confined to a camp with 300 other prisoners, near the prison of Playa Negra; he was sent out of there only to be forced to clean the houses of noted military men.

In late March, he was accused by the Nguemists of participation in plans for a coup d'etat, along with several officers, arrested in February, including Leoncio Esono Micha, director of the Military Academy of Bata, and brother-in-law to the vice-president of PP, Armengol Engonga. The regime rejected pressure from the group of donors (Spain, United States, France, Nigeria), from Spanish political parties, and from King Juan Carlos I for the release of Moto Nsa. From March 6, Moto Nsa was at Playa Negra. On April 11, the "confessions" of Moto Nsa were aired by Equato-Guinean television. In May, Moto Nsa's wife, Margarita Equi, attended the meetings of Aznar's Partido Popular in Spain in order to collect money to pay the lawyers. She declared that the policy of the Progress Party and the Partido Popular were very close. In June M.-E. Ngonde Maguga (UDENA) accused Moto Nsá of having ties with the two Nguemist dictatorships and of indulging in political assassinations. On July 22, Obiang Nguema was called to Libreville by French President J. Chirac, who asked him "firmly but in a friendly manner" to liberate Moto Nsa. On August 2, during a television speech, Obiang Nguema granted pardon to 33 prisoners (of whom 18 were at Bata). Moto Nsá was released with the army personnel who had been condemned with him. He declared that he would be a candidate for the municipal elections (in the capital, like Chirac in Paris) before standing for presidency in 1996. In mid-August, Moto returned to Madrid for a week, but extended his stay for medical reasons. Under pressure from leaders of the Progress Party, he was persuaded to give up his plans for the municipal elections. In Madrid, Moto Nsa threatened to leave the POC if he was not selected as a candidate for the presidency. A number of opponents, including some from the PP, judged Moto Nsá too ambitious and incapable of adjustment. Others accused him of dividing the opposition. His own entourage alleged an anti-Moto Nsa conspiracy.These accusations were repeated during the February 25, 1996, presidential election. The press stressed the "personalism" of Moto Nsa, who systematically divided the opposition to the advantage of the dictator. Having given up plans for candidacy, Moto Nsa made the surprising proposal about an Equato-Guinean government whose key posts would be occupied by Spaniards. In September 1996, Moto Nsa participated with V. Bolekia (ADP) in the annual meeting of the Christian Democratic International, in Brussels. A short while later, the major Madrid daily newspaper El País, evoked Moto Nsa, noting "his talent not very different from that of Obiang" Nguema.

By the end of May 1997, he was being held prisoner at Cabinda (Angola) along with Spaniards and Equato-Guinean members of the PP—Luciano Ndong Esono and Aniceto Okenve Osono—as well as the Soviet crew of the Sana I, who were transporting weapons meant to be used for a coup (23 guns, 16 loaders, 80 grenades, 23 grenade launchers, pistols, and various ammunition). He was released on June 8 in spite of the nguemists' demand for extradition. The minister of foreign affairs, Miguel Oyono, said in Bata that the government had known about the conspiracy since March. It is said to have been planned by the Italian lumber company Cataneo, formerly an ally of the government, but who now wished a change in power to suit its interests. It is also believed that besides the Italian company, three Spanish contractors also financed the project. See Nguema Obiang, T.

At the end of June 1997, the Spanish government said it agreed, as requested by Obiang Nguema, to deport Moto Nsa as long as the Angolan government could present acceptable proof. The Spanish press participated in the debate on whether Moto Nsa should or should not be allowed to keep his refugee status. On July 7, Moto announced that he would settle in Africa to continue his fight against Obiang Nguema: "One must die of something." On July 11, Moto Nsa was destituted by the Permanent Committee of the PP National Council. In August, the court condemned him to 101 years of imprisonment for "high treason." His lawyers were Reginaldo Egido and Rafael Maria Nsé. In September, in an interview given in his African hideaway, Moto denied participating in a coup in Angola, but corrected himself in an interview given at the end of September, in which he comfirmed his desire to fight against Obiang Nguema (or for himself), no matter how. He still wants to be president of the country; the oppositiion accused Moto of megalomania. The Spanish government continued to grant him his refugee status. Besides the accusations against the Spanish PP, which would be financed by Obiang Nguema, Moto Nsa said that Obiang Nguema is finished.

On February 1998, the National PP Committee on Discipline relieved Moto Nsa of his duties and appointed Mocache Meinga president. The PP representation in Spain was dissolved. On February 16, Moto accepted his dismissal and congratulated the new administration of the party. In July, he created a new party in Madrid, with Elema Borengue: Democratic Coordination of the Democratic Opposition of Equatorial Guinea. On November 18, along with four other people, he presented in Madrid, to the Audiencia Nacional (Supreme Court) a denunciation of Obiang Nguema, accusing him of national and international terrorism. The minister of the interior, Julio Ndong Ela Mangue, and the minister of planning, Antonio Fernando Nve Ngu, were also denounced. They are also accused of the murders of members of the opposition and Spanish managers, as well as of numerous ritual crimes. Obiang Nguema is also accused of drug dealing. On November 23, the Nguemist regime asked Spain to extradite Moto Nsa after Miguel Oyono, minister of foreign affairs and vice-prime minister, had declared that he was surprised that the Spanish government kept on protecting dangerous criminals.

See also Amnesty International; Elections; Masie Mibuy, A.; Mba Nze, N.; Mba Ondo Nchama, F., Ndong Mba, A.; Progress Party; Rwanda; Vatican

MOTU MAMIAGA, Pedro. Born in 1945 at Odjit-Mongó (Ebebiyin). After independence, he was named director of Radio Ecuatorial (Bata). He was then sent by Macías Nguema to the Military Academy of Ekuku (near Bata), where he became a lieutenant of the Nguemist militia.

In August 1979, he was the leader of the patrol that arrested Macías Nguema. A month later, he was declared persona non grata, accused of having killed a number of members of the clan from Mongomo, and sent into internal exile to his village. He fled to Gabon. He returned in 1991, and joined the Popular Union. He was arrested in December 1991, in Santa Isabel, for having declared himself favorable to multipartyism, and then released as part of a general amnesty. He was again arrested in late February 1992, after he refused to return to his village (another internal exile). He was imprisoned in the camp of the Moroccans, and then brought back by force to Río Muni. In early 1993, he was arrested by the frontier police for missing papers, as he was returning from Europe along with other opponents.

During the night of August 22–23, 1993, he was arrested in Santa Isabel, at hotel Ureca, while he was having a discussion with Moïses Mba Ada, president of Popular Union, who had just returned from Spain. He was killed in prison. The Nguemists alleged "suicide." There were converging testimonies in favor of a ritual Esangui assassination, with the heart and the genitals having been torn off. Manuel Nguema, Obiang Nguema's uncle and his trusted man, Tito Garriga, were said to have committed the act. It was in fact said to be an act of ritual cannibalism. UP President Mba Ada failed to protest. The rapporteur of the Human Rights Commission stated in his report debated on in March 1994 that, in order to escape criticism, the government cooked up a conspiracy, arrested old army personnel, condemned them in September 1993, but granted them amnesty on October 12.

MOVEMENT FOR THE AUTONOMY OF THE ISLAND OF BIOKO (Fernando Po) (Movimiento para la Autodeterminación de la Isla de Bioko, MAIB). A Bubi group, launched in August 1993; in November it addressed a Manifesto to Obiang Nguema. MAIB publishes a secret newspaper: *Bojuelo,* and demands autonomy for the island.

In February 1994, the dictatorship threatened the MAIB, calling it an "illegal and clandestine pseudo-movement." When he departed, the American ambassador Bennet denounced the public interrogation, on TV, of several members of the

MAIB. In April 1995, the MAIB confirmed its boycott of the electoral census. Its spokesman is Umberto Riochi.

In August 1996 the MAIB denounced the French government as giving the army and the police material that allowed the reinforcement and perfection of the methods of repression of Obiang Nguema. In October, three Bubi merchants gave an account to the Spanish press of their arrest and torture, the three being accused of separatism. At the end of November 1996, members of the MAIB were once again arrested.

MAIB is based on the same arguments held by the former Bubi Union. It demands a ngeotiation concerning the future of the island, under Spanish and UN control, the aim being a referendum on self-determination. But the MAIB is hostile to the Bubi who are not members (namely Bokekia Boney, the mayor of the capital, elected on POC lists). In June 1997, the MAIB declared that Moto Nsa's megalomania makes him worse than Obiang Nguema.

After the assault on soldiers in Luba at the beginning of 1998 by young masked Bubi, and the massive arrest of Bubi, among them Father Eduardo Losoha, responsible for Caritas in the capital, and the protestant minister Samba Momesori, the MAIB asked all Bubi, on February 11, to resign from the administration. The Nguemists accused the Spanish nongovernmental organization Vererinarians without Borders, in Biscaya, of having financed the terrorist actions. The headquarters of the NGO in Barcelona were flabbergasted: there has never been a Veterinarians without Borders office in Biscaya.

See also Bolekia, V.; Bubi.

MOVEMENT FOR THE SUPPORT OF OBIANG NGUEMA (Movimiento de Apoyo a Obiang, MAO). According to the Spanish newspaper *Diario 16,* a group of forced sympathizers of General Obiang Nguema, which takes care of the cleaning up of the capital. It is mainly made up of Spanish executives who are working in the country. It is said the dictator called a meeting of the members ("Maoists") at the beginning of February 1996 asking them to finance his campaign. It is said he demanded $100,000 and gave the number of the bank account.

MOVEMENT OF WELL-WISHERS OF OBIANG NGUEMA see Seriche Bioko

MOVIMIENTO DE LIBERACAO DO SÃO TOME Y PRINCIPE (MLSTP) (Liberation Movement of São Tomé and Príncipe). The leaders of this movement, presently at the head of the republic, benefitted until spring 1971 from Equato-Guinean hospitality (first President Manuel Pinto d'Acosta and second President Miguel Trovoada). Then Macías Nguema expelled them for fear of their political activism.

MOVIMIENTO DE LIBERACION Y FUTURO DE GUINEA ECUATO-RIAL (MOLIFUGE) (Movement for Liberation and Future of Equatorial Guinea). Founded in 1972 in Spain, deep-rooted among the workers' youth, but without a clear ideology other than African nationalism. Organized on a military-type structure, with strong internal discipline. It collaborated briefly with URGE. Its first secretary general is Miguel Esono, former driver of the Equato-Guinean ambassadors in Spain. In 1978, Macías's agents attempted to kidnap the MOLI-

FUGE leader, but they were arrested by the Spanish police. The Spanish press considers MOLIFUGE an instrument of García Trevijano. In October 1978, M. Esono and some of his friends clandestinely recorded in Madrid several conversations with Obiang's minister of health, about Macías Nguema's removal, and then published them in a Spanish newspaper. The exercise was called "Operación Ebano" (Operation Ebony). Representatives of MOLIFUGE have been arrested in Cameroon in 1978 and expelled after the discovery in their luggage of plans for an attack of Equatorial Guinea.

MOVIMIENTO DE UNION NACIONAL (MUN) (National Union Movement). Founded after the IPGE Ambam Congress (Cameroon) at the end of October 1963, by J. Nseng, former secretary of the IPGE opposed to the idea of a federation between Equatorial Guinea and Cameroon. Later on, the MUN became the MUNGE.

MOVIMIENTO DE UNION NACIONAL DE GUINEA ECUATORIAL (MUNGE) (National Union Movement of Equatorial Guinea). Before 1963, some of its founding members revolved around the Camcroonese nationalist parties (IPGE, MUN, MUPGE). The creation of the MUNGE was encouraged by Spain and the Casas Fuertes, first under the leadership of Eñeso Neñe and Mbá Nsué, then, since 1964, under Ondo Edu, who freed the movement from its Cameroonese influence. He turned it into a national party but its center of gravity clearly remained in Río Muni. A moderate movement, the MUNGE bore the Spanish government's confidence. With autonomy, Ondo Edu was named chief of the autonomous government (Consejo de Gobierno). His party requested independence but with close ties with Spain. Before the United Nations Trusteeship Council, Ondo Edu estimated however in 1966, that independence was untimely. He became Carrero Blanco's candidate for the presidency of the republic. The MUNGE was represented at the Constitutional Conference by J. Mbá, E. Nsué Ngomo, E. Nkuba, F. S. Jones, and Ondo Edu being in the delegation of the Consejo de Gobierno. During the conference, the marginal elements of the MUNGE joined Macías Nguema's Secretariado Conjunto, which later became Grupo Macías. At the September 1968 elections, the MUNGE obtained seven seats of the Asamblea de la República (Parliament), and in October, two ministers and a representative at the Consejo de la República (Senate), Ondo Edu having been defeated at the first and second ballot by Macías Nguema for the presidency of the republic. Shortly after independence, Ondo Edu took refuge in Gabon but Macías Nguema succeeded in having him extradited by making false promises. Ondo was accused of a plot and liquidated in January 1969 with other members of the MUNGE. The MUNGE, like all other parties, was abolished in January 1970, in view of the creation of the PUN.

MOVIMIENTO DE UNION POPULAR DE LIBERACION DE LA GUINEA ECUATORIAL (MUPGE) (Popular Liberation Union Movement of Equatorial Guinea). Founded in 1963 by Ondo Edu in Gabon. Ondo Edu addressed an appeal to the United Nations in view of his country's independence. With the coming of autonomy, the MUPGE was reorganized and in association with the MUN, became the MUNGE.

MOVIMIENTO NACIONAL (National Movement). Francoist movement, resembling a fascist state party, that played an important role in Spanish Guinea because of its influence on officials and on the army, as well as on the trade unions. During autonomy the Movimiento de Guinea Ecuatorial was organized, composed of elements from the neocapitalist bourgeoisie, officials, small merchants and planters, more in favor of the status quo than of independence. At the Constitutional Conference the Movimiento Nacional was represented by M. Mbá Ada.

MOVIMIENTO NACIONAL DE LIBERACION DE GUINEA ECUATO-RIAL (MONALIGE) (National Liberation Movement of Equatorial Guinea). Founded in 1959 under the leadership of S. Ebuka, P. Torao Sikara, A. Ndongo Miyone, and since 1960 Maho Sikacha. Spain did not recognize any nationalist movements until 1963 when preparations for autonomy started. In 1963 Ndongo protested against the overly strong authority of the Comisario General in the future status of autonomy. A leftist party, the MONALIGE was divided into different ideological cells. Thus, at the end of 1964, Ndongo Miyone (having taken refuge in Ghana) and Mbá Ovono created the FRENAPO, requesting immediate independence and nationalization of Spanish belongings. Simultaneously, Torao Sikara defended the Bubi's particular interests. Initially a member of the MUNGE, Macías Nguema moved closer to the MONALIGE; with Ndongo Miyone he wrote a manifesto given to Spain in view of Guinea's self-determination.

In 1967, members of the MONALIGE went to the United Nations announcing that without immediate independence they would start an armed struggle. The leader of the MONALIGE youth, Balboa Dougan, reported in 1968 to the Fourth Commission of the United Nations. The MONALIGE participated at the Constitutional Conference with Ndongo Miyone. Torao Sikara, Balboa Dougan, and Ibongo Iyanga, adopted a centrist position and supported the draft Constitution presented by Spain and opposing the separatist projects of the Unión Bubi and the Secretariado Conjunto. Macías Nguema openly opposed Ndongo Miyone during the conference, challenging his representativeness and exhibiting letters from supporters of his own policy from various local Río Muni committees. On March 30, 1968, an open letter published by the Grupo Macías was circulated in Bata discharging Ndongo Miyone and Torao Sikara. The MONALIGE countered with a meeting in the Bata Stadium, on August 3. At the elections from the Asamblea de la República (Parliament) in September 1968, the MONALIGE proved to be the strongest party, being able to place six ministers out of 12 in the government, after Ndongo Miyone had withdrawn in favor of Macías Nguema at the second ballot in the presidential elections. Ndongo Miyone became minister of foreign ffairs. On March 5, 1969, an attempted coup d'etat by Ndongo Miyone took place in Bata, in which Ndongo Miyone as well as several other members of the MONALIGE lost their lives. On January 19, 1970, the Cabinet abolished all political parties, among them the MONALIGE, in view of the creation of the PUNT.

MOVIMIENTO PRO-INDEPENDENCIA DE LA GUINEA ECUATO-RIAL (MPIGE) (Pro-Independence Movement of Equatorial Guinea). Founded in 1962 by Torao Sikara. After Maho Sikacha's defection from the Cruzada Nacional de Liberación, Sikara supported the MPIGE from his exile in Douala

(Cameroon). After the splitting up in June 1963 of the Coordination Bureau of the Equato-Guinean Movements (created in Ambam in February), Maho and his followers left the MPIGE, which afterwards disappeared from the political scene.

MOVIMIENTO SOCIALISTA GUINEANO (MSG) (Guinean Socialist Movement). Movement founded in Madrid by Zamora Segorbe and some other refugees, in 1972. MSG disappeared in 1974.

MOYOS ESACUNAN, Loc see Terror

MUATETEMA RIVAS, Candido. Bubi from Batete. Born 20 February 1960. Studied at Havana (Cuba). Holds a degree in finance and accounting. He returned to the country in 1990 and soon became a member of the PDGE. On December 22, 1993, he became secretary of state for youth affairs and sports. In 1995 he became the coordinator of the Jovenes Antorchas of the PDGE. In the ministerial reshuffle of April 8, 1996, he became counsellor for transports and communications.

MUNGA (King of Corisco) see Bonkoro; Corisco Island

MUNI, Río. Name given to the estuary of the Utamboni, in the southwest of the continental province. In the 16th century, the estuary was named Angra and later the English gave it the name of River Danger. The mouth of the estuary is 1,700 m wide and 33 m deep, then after 15 km splits into two arms with numerous affluents. The province was partly penetrated via the Río Benito and the Utamboni, in particular by Iradier. In the 19th century, various warehouses were established along its banks. Kogo, 20 km from the mouth, was for a time seat of the local government of the southern part of the continental province. See also Río Muni.

MUNICIPAL COUNCIL see Consejo De Vecinos; Junta Vecinal

MUNOZ YLATA, Segundo. Annobónese, born on the island. A government official, after studying at the Escuela superior at Santa Isabel. In 1988, he underwent a raid of his home in Annobón, carried out by prisoners confined to the island. In October 1990, he became minister for territorial administration and communication. In 1993, he became the president's counsellor for criminal investigations. During the Annobón scandal, in August, he exposed his compatriots, who had settled in the capital, and who had been imprisoned at Playa Negra. In the November election, he was elected as a PDGE deputy for Annobón. On January 19, 1994, he was named counsellor to the president for transports and communications.

He was replaced by C. Muatetema Rivas in the ministerial reshuffle of April 1996.

MURDERS see Annobon; Assassinations; Bata; Branger, A.; Ebebiyin; Germany; Human Rights; Obiang Nguema, T.; Ondo Obiang Alogo, F.; Parliament; Terror; Unicque National Workers Party

MURPHY, Alan, 1935–1978. British citizen and a mercenary from 1963 to 1978 (Congo, Biafra, etc.). According to his personal diary, he was an active participant in F. Forsyth's project of occupying Fernando Po in 1972. He committed suicide during a police control of his London flat in March 1978.

MUSIC. In some regions groups of women play tunes as they walk into a river up to chest level. They form a circle and beat the surface of the water with calabash bowls of various sizes, making a strange noise. See also Maele, Hijas del Sol.

MUSOLA. A Fernando Po locality, which had an agricultural cooperative before independence. It possesses a 500 kw hydroelectric plant that mainly supplies San Carlos (Luba). The army founded an academy for training and reorientation, in 1993; it houses 80 trainees. See also Army; Concepción.

MVETT. Musical instrument, a kind of harp-zither made of three gourds, the stem of a leaf of the raphia plant and cords made of vegetable fibers. The word also applies to the sagas of the Fang people. A Fang institution, Order of the Bebom-Mvett, is the custodian of the national saga the "Cycle of Legends of Engong" which is a kind of Old Testament for the Fang nation. The best known mvett players in Equatorial Guinea are Esono Obiang Engone, Nkoa Alu, Tsira Ndong, Ntutume, Mve Megue, Minto'O Mi Esawong, Eyi Nko Ase and Zeng Akwe.

❖ N ❖

NAN CHA HWANG. He was the ambassador of South Korea from 1990.

NANG OBAMA ONDO, Antonio Candido, b. 1934. Fang from Bata. Businessman. Member of the MONALIGE, member of the Diputación Provincial (Assembly) of Río Muni and deputy at the Asamblea General (Parliament) from 1964 to 1968. In the Consejo de Gobierno (Cabinet) he was first responsible for Labor, then Education after Rondo Maguga's death. Nang Obama participated in the Constitutional Conference but did not participate in the elections. At independence, he became director of the ministry of agriculture, then he was attached to the Ministry of Justice. In 1973 he left the administration for the private sector. He died in 1997.

NANDONGO NGUEMA, Antonio. From Ebebiyin. Born 1947. Press technician. In December 1981 he became the director of *Ebano.* He also took on the post of director of *La Voz del Pueblo,* the PDGE bulletin. In early 1993 he published a document showing the democratic opposition as being to blame for civil war in the name of neocolonial forces. In the April 8, 1996, ministerial reshuffle, he became director general for the press. He kept this office in the January 1998 cabinet reshuffle.

NASSAU, Robert Hamilton, 1835–1921. American linguist, medical doctor, folklorist, and Presbyterian missionary. He arrived in Río Muni with his wife Mary Cloyd in 1861. They first lived in Corisco, then created the Río Benito Mission, exploring the coast and some parts of Río Muni inland. Mary Cloyd died at sea, in 1870, during her transfer to a Gabonese hospital. From 1874 to 1898 R. H. Nassau worked in Gabon. It was with his help that the Reverend Benga Ibea Ikenga wrote a history of the Benga people. R. H. Nassau left Río Benito in 1871. He left behind a Benga translation of the Bible, and a number of historical manuscripts about the Fangs, Galoa Bakale, and Benga. Rev. Nassau died in the United States on May 6, 1921.

NATIONAL ALLIANCE FOR DEMOCRATIC RESTORATION (Alianza Nacional para la Restauración Democrática, ANRD). This movement has grouped members of the MUNGE, MONALIGE, and the Bubi Union since August 1974. It has committees in the neighboring countries of Guinea, Spain, Switzerland, and the U.S. ANRD publishes *La Voz del Pueblo* (The People's Voice). Among its leaders is Eya Nchama, responsible for international relations. ANRD strives to obtain improvement of the living standard of Equato-Guinean refugees and to alert them, as well as their countrymen within Equatorial Guinea, to the existing problems. At the 1976 Congress ANRD expelled several members who seemed connected with the CEIA: Mbá Ada, Nsué Ngomo, Nsué Angue, Balboa Boneque, and Olo Mibuy. At the end of 1975, ANRD asked EC to exclude Equatorial Guinea from the Lomé Convention. In 1976, they presented a "García Trevijano File" blaming the Spanish lawyer's collusion with Macías Nguema and created the Organisacion de la Mujer de Guinea Ecuatorial for the defense of the Guinean women. In March 1977, at the United Nations Human Rights Commission in Geneva, the representative of ANRD was prevented from expressing himself by the Ugandan delegate. At the end of January 1978 ANRD proclaimed a general alarm after Spain's decision to grant Spanish nationality to refugees and after alleged declarations by President Bongo in Madrid concerning possible annexation of Equato-Guinean islands by Gabon. On August 21–23, 1978, the central committee of the ANRD held its third meeting. At the end of 1978 the ANRD rejected firmly Nsue Ngomo's (Frelige) freakish proposals made in Madrid regarding a front for the "Salvación de Guinea Ecuatorial." Between 1974 and 1979, the ANRD obtained about 100 scholarships for many of their members.

In August 1979, at the time of the installation of Obiang Nguema, the ANRD made it quite clear that the dictatorship would carry on as before. This has proved to be the case. The ANRD is represented in several international bodies where they remonstrate against the support given by certain countries and institutions to the second Nguemist dictatorship. Between 1982 and 1983, several communiqués put out by the ANRD criticized the pope's visit to Santa Isabel and Bata, the adoption of a new dictatorial constitution, etc.

The periods of office of the secretaries-general of the ANRD have been as follows: Nsué Ngomo, 1974–1976 (expelled); Oyono Sa Abegue, 1976–1978; Eya Nchama, 1978–1983; Nsono Okomo, 1983–1985; Mba Mombe, 1985–1992; Ondo Ayang, 1992– . Since 1984 the organization has been torn by internal dissention and regional tensions. According to reports circulating in Spain it seems the ANRD has been infiltrated by agents of Obiang Nguema.

Martin Nsono Okomo died in August 1985. He was replaced by Samuel Mba Mombe. In 1990, Samuel Mba Mombe, stressing the inoperative nature of the Pact of Madrid, insisted on the participation of the Spanish government (especially the PSOE). He termed Moto Nsa's journey to Santa Isabel "suspicious," and accused Felipe Gonzalez of supporting the dictator. He however signed the pact.

In 1991, the PDGE began to publish its periodical, named, like the ANRD's, the *Voz del Pueblo* (People's Voice). *La Verdad* (CPDS) published a facsimile of the ANRD's magazine.

In 1992, the dissident Miguel Esono Eman became general secretary of the Popular Party, while the "crook-diplomat" Mokong Onguene became active within the Popular Union, at Santa Isabel. In April 1993, the ANRD published a communiqué washing its hands of Mokong Onguene "for dishonest behavior and for neglect of his responsibilities."

Luis Ondo Ayang succeeded Mba Mombe as secretary general in 1992, and Mba Mombe was relegated to the post of vice-secretary. The emblem of the ANRD is a white dove carrying a red rose, with the motto Liberty and Justice. In September 1993, ANRD published *Learn to Understand ANRD* (Conozca la ANRD), which stated its objectives as being:

• to fight this and all future dictatorships;

- to restore the people's sovereignty in order to allow citizens to participate freely in political decision making;
- to restore the dignity of the citizen through the principles of liberty and justice;
- to restore and consolidate democracy with a view to preventing all future abuse of power, etc.

The document reiterates the principles and codes of behavior adopted at the Third Convention (Geneva, 1976):

- faithfulness and unwavering commitment to democratic principles;
- purposeful dialogue with other democratic forces;
- to resist manipulation by all Nguemist regimes;
- never to establish any secret contacts with members of the nguemist regime, etc., except on neutral terrain.

In early 1994, the ANRD complained of lack of support from the Spanish government. In its 20th anniversary communique, the ANRD reaffirms its long-standing commitment to fight the regime. On September 4, in the wake of Mokong Onguene's expulsion and for similar reasons, Dougan Beaca was expelled from the National Alliance for Democratic Reconstruction by an executive committee decision. In a press conference held in Geneva in January 1995, Luis Ondo Ayang, general secretary, enumerated the allegations against Dougan Beaca. Answering questions for Radio Exterior de España in April, he expressed the need for a sovereign national conference, as the Nguemist laws did not constitute an adequate legal framework. The Nguemist regime was declared one with "a legal system lacking in legitimacy." Of course, he said, "Elections do not solve the problems of a nation, but what really counts is the will of the people and the attitude of the opposition."

Using its own publishing house, Claves para el futuro (Keys to the Future), the ANRD published *Africa y las Democracias descencadenadas: El Caso de Guinea Ecuatorial* in 1994 and *Guinea Ecuatorial y el ensayo democrático: La conquista del Golfo de Guinea* in 1996.

In April 1996, Ondo Ayang qualified the petroleum economy of Equatorial Guinea as a personal business of Obiang Nguema's before the Human Rights Commission in Geneva. After the meeting in Madrid of the central committee of the executive committee of the ANRD in August 1996, Ondo Ayang convened the other opposition parties in order to study the national pact violated by Obiang Nguema on March 13, 1993.

In 1997, in Madrid, ANRD held a meeting with leaders of the PSOE, to whom they handed over a report concerning its structure and a proposition on how to achieve a transition in Equatorial Guinea without traumas. The management of the ANRD, led by Secretary General Luis Ondo Ayang, also met with leaders of Izquierda Unida (IU), to whom they handed over a document describing the problems of Equatorial Guinea, the misadventures of the opposition, and the need for a national conference as the only efficient way to achieve democratization.

In 1998, the secretary of the Organization and Mobilization of Masses of the Executive Council met with the regional and provincial delegates of the interior of the country to inform them of the aims and projects of the party. During 1998, ANRD increased its numbers, owing to the fact that dissidents of the USD joined the party.

See also Dougan; Dougan Beaca, J. D.; Elections; Engonga Motulu, M.; Eya Nchama, C. M.; Joint Opposition Platform; Mba Ekua Miko, B.; Mba Mombe, S.; Mikomeseng; Mokong Onguene, C.; Moto Nsá, S.; Nsono Okomo, M.; Okenve, C.; Olo Mebuy, A.; Ondo Ayang, L.; Opposition; Oyono Awong Ada, S.; Popular Union; Press; *Voz del Pueblo, La.*

NATIONAL DEFENSE see Army

NATIONAL DEMOCRATIC UNION (Unión Democratica Nacional, UDENA). Party with conservative ideology, created in 1992 by Jose Mecheba Ikaka, formerly Obiang Nguema's minister for public administration. The POC's communiqués were co-signed in the name of this group by Mecheba Ikaka, an official in the Ministry of the Interior (and therefore of the police).

UDENA was legalized in May 1993. In October, UDENA signed the Institutional Proposal addressed to Obiang Nguema by the seven members of the POC. But in November UDENA broke up: under the leadership of Pedro-Cristino Bueribueri, one wing broke away from the POC and participated in the elections becoming a satellite party of the PDGE, in return for funding. The other wing, under the leadership of Jose Mecheba, remained in the POC.

In January 1994, P.-C. Bueribueri joined the delegation of parliamentary representatives and representatives of the tame opposition given the job of praising the Nguemist democracy in Germany, France, and Switzerland.

In June, Mecheba Ikaka, along with representatives of the PL and the PSD demanded that the government discontinue its support to dissidents who breached the election boycott in November 1993. The UDENA had no deputies in the National Assembly. In 1995, P.-C. Bueribueri attended the 2nd Convention of the Democratic Party of Equatorial Guinea in the name of the UDENA, which was presided over by the dictator Obiang Nguema. On April 8, 1996, P.-C. Bueribueri was rewarded with the post of minister for culture, tourism and the French language.

In the ministerial reshuffle of January 21, 1998, P.-C. Bueribueri disappeared from the government; he was replaced by Anacleto Olo Mibuy as Vice Minister of Culture, Tourism, and Crafts Promotion.

See also Ngonde Maguga.

NATIONAL GUARD see Guardia Nacional

NATIONAL INSTITUTE FOR SOCIAL SECURITY (Instituto nacional de Seguridad social, INSESO). In 1980, Francisco Salomé Jones became the director for Employment, Provident Fund and the Institute for Social Security, in the Ministry of Labor. In 1992, the former ambassador to Madrid, Nguema Esono, expelled for drug-trafficking, became the president of the Administrative Council. Several natives of Mongomo are counsellors for the INSESO. Each of them received FCFA 100,000 per month. See also Nguema Esono, L.

NATIONAL MOVEMENT see Movimiento Nacional

NATIONAL PACT (Pacto Nacional). A meeting between the Nguemists and ten political parties recognized by the government took place in the capital in February-March 1993. The participants were:

Government: S. Siale Bilekia (Bubi), prime minister, president; R. Mangue Obama Nfube, minister general secretary to the president (Ebebiyin); J. Ndong ela Mangue, minister for territorial administration and local bodies (Mongomo), and of the interior; A.-F. Nve-Ngo, spokesperson-minister.

Parties: Convergency for Social Democracy (CPDS): A.-G. Nsé Angue, J.-L.; Nvumba Mañana, P.; Micó Abogo; "Democratic" Party of Equatorial Guinea: J. Micha Nsué Nfumu; Democratic and Progressive Alliance (ADP): A. Ebang Mbele Abang; A. Esono Ndong Maye; Democratic and Social Union (UDS): J. Nzé Obama Ovomo, T.; Mitogo Mba Mangue, A.; Mico Alo; Liberal Democratic Convention (CLD): A. Nsue Mokuy; Popular Action (AP): C. Masi Edu, M. Eson Eman; C. Mba Bakale; Popular Union: D. Abuy Elo Nchama; Progress Party (PP): T. Boicheku Boneke; P. Ndong Ensema; A. Nkulu Asumu; Social Democratic Coalition Party (PCSD): B. Moswui m'Asumu; N. Massoko Elonga; N. Siboko; Social Democratic Party (PSD): B.-G. Balinga Balinga Alene; F. Mabale Nseng; Social Democratic and Popular Convergency (CSDP): S. Oyono Ada; F. Abaga Ndong; M. Owono Obama Alene.

Under discussion of the Pacto Nacional vinculante (Compulsive National Pact) were: the release of political prisoners, the legalization of parties without exceptions, the liberalization of means of communication, the cessation of all forms of intimidation of the population, the funding of parties, total exemption from taxes for the import of vehicles and working material of parties, etc.

One month later, a negotiating commission, composed of 17 persons, was constituted, representing the entire opposition as well as the government and the PDGE. Nothing came of it, as the Nguemists not only refused the recommendations of the UN experts on the electoral law, but unilaterally fixed the elections for September, without consulting the opposition. See also Elections.

NATIONAL PARKS. One-tenth of the national territory is national park. Here chimpanzee, drill, mandrill, sea turtles, manatee, gorillas, and elephant are protected.

NATIONAL PARTY FOR DEMOCRACY, DEVELOPMENT AND CIVIC EDUCATION (Partido Nacional para la Democracia, Desarrollo y Educación Civica, PANDECA). The Spanish government hoped, in March-April 1980 to receive the support of this elitist group. Some of its members returned to the country and the edifice of the PANDECA crumbled, just like the URGE and the MOLIFUGE.

NATIONAL PEOPLES CONGRESS OF EQUATORIAL GUINEA. (Congreso Nacional de los Pueblos de Guinea Ecuatorial, CNPGE). On February 4, 1995, in Barcelona, Ebang Mbele linked the ADP with Francisco Ela Abeme's Congreso Nacional de los Pueblos; Ela Abeme became its general secretary with Ebang Mbele as president. This party never functioned. See also Ela Abeme, F.

NATIONAL PETROLEUM COMPANY (Sociedad Nacional de Petroleos) see Petroleum

NATIONAL SECURITY (called Territorial Administration/Interior, and Presidential Criminal Investigations Department = Police). In the April 4, 1996, ministerial reshuffle, Eyi Monsuy Andeme (Mongomo) became state secretary in charge of the Criminal Investigations Department.

In October 1990, Muñoz Ilata from Annobón became minister for territorial administration and communication. In the January 24, 1992, "transitional" government, the state secretary for national security was Manuel Nguema (Mongomo), former chief of the military cabinet, and Obiang Nguema's cousin. The premises of the Directorate General of the Criminal Investigations Department were frequently the scene of torture sessions. On November 16, T. Saez Lasheras, director of courses at La Salle (Bata), resigned in protest at the attempts of the Criminal Investigations Department to infiltrate his establishment. A demonstration by students, on November 23, ended with 40 arrests and torture. A dozen counsellors of the INSESO were also agents of the presidential Criminal Investigations Department.

In 1993, Muñoz Ilata remained presidential counsellor for matters regarding the Criminal Investigations Department. In 1995, Manuel Nguema mainly persecuted those holding copies of *La Verdad,* the periodical of the CPDS. In July the periodical reported that "the entire population was at the mercy of the Criminal Investigations Department. The security forces were not answerable to anyone for their acts and only obey their own desires, which is their law. . . ." "The security forces embody the law." The periodical also reported that the Criminal Investigations Department "included a large number of civilians—including members of the PDGE, officials of the government and members of the judiciary."

In the January 8, 1996, ministerial reshuffle, Julio Ndong Ela Mangue remained minister of the interior, with Obiang Nguema's cousin, Manuel Nguema Mba, as state secretary for national security.

In the ministerial reshuffle of January 21, 1998, national security was once again monopolized by Esangui parents of the dictator and members of the clan of Mongono: Demetrio Elo Ndong Nsefumu (Mongono), minister of state for interior and local corporations; Julio Ndong Ela Mangue (Mongomo), minister of territorial administration and local government, as well as minister political adviser to the government; Antonio Mba Nguema Mikue (Mongomo, half-brother of Obiang Nguema), secretary of state for national security.

See also Army; International Committee of the Red Cross; Mba Nguema Mikue, A.; Police; Terror; Torture.

NATIONAL SOCIAL SECURITY FUND (Caja Nacional de Seguridad Social). Launched in 1973 with the help of the ILO. The press stated in 1992 that Obiang Nguema had imposed taxes on this fund for personal benefits (FCFA 6 million).

NATURAL RESOURCES AND ELECTRICITY. This ministry was held successively by Ekong Andeme (now a refugee in Cameroon), Obiang Gonsogo (first minister of public health, 1969–1973), and Nguema Ada (vice-minister since April 1976). See also Mines.

NAVIGATION. In 1859–1860, the bay of Santa Isabel harbored 200 ships (90 of which were military) of the following nationalities: United Kingdom (115), France (23), Spain (22), United States (16), Germany (3), etc. In 1980, along with the IBRD, the Nguemists founded the Compania Guineana de Navegación Maritíma SA (state 51%), in association with the Belgian Société africaine de consignation et affretement Saint-Nicolas and its subsidiary the Sociedad Africana de Cabotaje, Consignacion y Afletamente (Douala). The general agent for Europe is the Maritime Chartering and Liner Shipping Co NV (Antwerp). The first departure took place in August 1980, with cargo for the ports of Hamburg, Rotterdam, and Antwerp.

From 1985, the French shipping company Delmas-Vieljeux served Bata and Santa Isabel. In 1987 a regular tramping link between Equatorial Guinea, Gabon, São Tomé and Principe was established with a 200-ton coasting vessel, the *Pagne.* In 1988 the EC helped in the planning of the modernization of the port of Bata (dredging and removal of wreckage). This port is larger than the one in the capital, with a capacity of 126,000 tons against 29,000 tons. The United States donated the patrol boat *Isla de Bioco,* in order to chase away illegal fishing boats from the country's territorial waters (in fact, it was to monitor the return of refugees to neighboring countries).

The EDF facilitated the purchase of a ferry boat for the Bolondo–Río Benito (Mbini) link; this became operational in April 1990, and remained so until the reconstruction of the port of Sendje (around 1996). Also, a ferry link between Akalayong and Kogo is being considered, along with one between Cocoabeach and Gabon. The link is made by private 40-ton boats. On July 14, 1990, following the sinking of the *Trader,* a ferry boat of the Equato-Guinean shipping lines shortly after departure from Douala, 6 were registered as dead and 20 had disappeared. The boat was carrying rice, beer, cement, and a number of passengers. Overloading was named as the cause of tragedy.

In the spring of 1992 an embarkation tax of $1,727 was introduced; students and sick people were exempt. In early 1993, Obiang Nguema prohibited the import of foreign newspapers and threatened shipping and aviation companies which may allow these to enter the country. The cargo *Acacio Mañe* (captain: Marcelo Bee Nsue), was run by the national company AMGESA, which ran Domingo Efa Mangue since 1993. The majority of the sailors on *Acacio Mañe* are Chinese. In May 1994, the *Acacio Mañe* was anchored at Gibraltar; the police observed that it was used in the trafficking of various animals. The navy included 100 men and had four patrol boats of less than 100 tons.

On July 24, 1997, Equatorial Guinea signed the UN Convention on the Rights of Sea. On December 15, the American Offshore Company was selling a dry cargo ship built in 1990 in Russia (tonnage: 355 tons, length: 42.05, width, 7.60, depth: 3.5; registered under Equato-Guinean flag; price: $360,000).

The *Acacio Mañe* burnt in the waters off the Ivory Coast, on its way back from a shipyard in Poland. Its skeleton is still in Abijan. The crew was sentenced to several years in jail for carelessness. In order to provide the sea link Malabo–Mata and Malabo–Annobon, the Agencia Marítima de Transporte de Guinea Ecuatorial S.A. contracted, in 1998, for two years, the transporter *Odoragushin* (from Guinea Conakry); with a capacity of 1,000 passengers, it carries goods, but cars are not accepted. The crew is made up of Nigerians and natives from Cameroon and Ghana. The ship should have a weekly roundtrip Malabo–Bata–Balabo (price 15,000 FCFA). But the *Odoragushin* did not receive authorization to carry out activities (the technical and safety standards were insufficient). At the end of 1998, the country still had no sea link between Malabo, Bata, and Annobon.

See also Cyprus; Spain.

NAVIGATION COMPANY OF EQUATORIAL GUINEA. (Compañia marítima de Guinea Ecuatorial, COMAGE). Directed by "Angabi," the brother of Obiang Nguema's director general of protocol and Obiang Nguema's brother-in-law, Mba Bela (from Mongomo), in 1992. See also Navigation.

NBA NCHAMA, Pablo. Fang, born in 1926 in Biyabiyang. Presbyterian minister trained in Bolondo (Río Benito) and Bimbia (Cameroon). Since 1960 secretary general of the Evangelical Church of Equatorial Guinea. From 1961 to 1963 he studied at the Barcelona Protestant College (Spain). With independence he became Consejero de la República. Father of nine children, he fled to Cameroon in 1975.

NCHAMA NVO, Balbina. Daughter of the national hero Enrique Nvo. Teacher. She had a child by Macías Nguema. Also very close to Obiang Nguema. On December 22, 1993, she became minister for the integration of woman and social affairs. She held that post in the January 8, 1998, ministerial reshuffle. But she disappeared from the government in the April 8, 1996, ministerial reshuffle, replaced by Margarita Aleva Mba.

NCOA-BIDOLO see Akurenam

NCOGO, Salvador. Ex-bodyguard to the first wife of Obiang Nguema's. See Coup d'etat of July 18, 1996.

NCOGO ABEGUE, Braulio. Fang from Mongomo. Studied in the USSR. In the ministerial reshuffle of April 8, 1996, he became joint director general of the Personal Affairs Cabinet of H. E. the president of the republic.

NCOGO EYE, Pedro. From Bata. Holds a degree in philosophy and literature. A Claretian, in charge of the parish of the Claret Sanctuary, in the capital. In 1980, he became the director of higher, middle, and vocational education. In 1987, he became the director general of primary education. He was arrested and tortured towards the end of 1992, along with Father Ondo Maye and about a hundred professors and students demanding the release of Celestino Bakale. In 1993, he continued his resistance to Nguemism, refusing to baptize a child to whom Manuel Nguema Mba, was to be the godfather, as the minimal conditions fixed by the Church were not satisfied.

NCOGO ONDO, Carmelo see Río Benito

NCUL OYOE see Nculu Asuu, A.

NCULU ASUMU, Antonio. From Niefang. Born 1956. Studied in the Escuela superior indígena, in Santa Isabel (administration). Brother of Nculu Oye, secretary general to the Ministry of Interior, member of the PDGE. Secretary general of the tame Liberal Progressive Party (PLP). In the April 8, 1996, government, he became vice-minister for agriculture and animal husbandry. He is no longer a member of the government after the ministerial reshuffle of January 1998.

NDJENG OLO MBA see Mines

NDJOKU BONDJALE, José Manuel. Benga from Bata. Born in Punta Mbonda. An official in the Ministry of Justice. In January 1994 he was appointed a member of the Constitutional Court. Shortly before his appointment, he went on a national tour with the Jovenes Antorchas.

NDJUNGA BELICA, E. see Río Benito

NDONG, Damaso. From Mongomo. A seminarist, who later studied in Catholic University in Rome. After Obiang Nguema's coup d'etat, in August 1979, he became the director of international organizations in the Ministry of Foreign Affairs. In 1985 he became chief of protocol. From 1990, he was a representative to the United Nations, in New York. There he acted as a defender of Nguemism and attacked the UN. He was recalled to his country in the summer of 1993.

NDONG, Demetrio Elo. In the January 21, 1998, cabinet reshuffle, he replaced Ndong Ela Mangue as minister of the interior (police).

NDONG, Joaquin. From Mongomo. Obiang Nguema's nephew. Called "El matute." Captain of the militia. A reputed torturer. Aide-de-camp to Obiang Nguema. As captain of the naval forces, he was posted in Rio Benito in 1991, and put in charge of the surveillance of coastal Río Muni in order to prevent landings by opponents. He was among the 12 counsellors of the INSESO. In this capacity he earned FCFA 100,000 each month.

NDONG, Petra. "Sorceress" from Evinayong. She lived in the presidential palace.

NDONG ABAGA MESIAN, Crisantos. Fang from Mongomo. Born 1942(?). Until the end of 1981, he was first secretary at the embassy in Moscow. Towards the end of 1982, he became director general of state-run companies to the president of the government. At the end of the 1980s, he became the ambassador to Gabon. In 1991, the Spanish media revealed that towards the end of 1990, as the ambassador to Gabon, Ndong Abaga addressed a letter to some compatriots (Ali Asumu, Manolito Mba, Marcelo Mve Mba, and Ndong Biken) confirming an offer of money for the assassination of Modu Akuse and for the destruction of his archives. Since 1993 he has been counsellor for foreign affairs. In August 1998 he was dismissed from the Ministry.

NDONG AYONG, Santos Pascual see Press

NDONG ELA MANGUE, Julio. A Fang from Mongomo. Born March 1946 in Nkedjoen-San Carlos (Mongomo). Brother to Lorenzo Ondo Ela and Guillermo Nguema Ela Mangue Ndong. Went to the missionary school at Bata, and later studied to be a teacher at the Escuela Superior Indígena, in Santa Isabel. He belonged to the hard core of the clan from Mongomo.

In 1969–1970, he went to the School for Administration at Madrid and returned with the title of an officer of justice. He was named administrative secretary at the prefecture at Mongomo. He then became president of the tribunal at Bata, and finally the prefect of the district of Bata. He was at that time one of the political commissioners of Macías Nguema. After Obiang Nguema's coup in 1979, he became the director of central services of the CMS. In May 1982, he took part in the Akonibe constitutional commission, which consolidated the Obiang Nguema dictatorship. In October, he became secretary of the office of the president with ministerial rank.

At the end of 1984 he was designated minister for presidential affairs. He was arrested in connection with the attempted coup of July 1986. In 1988 he returned as joint secretary to the president. In 1989 he was among the Nguemists who created a new made-to-order constitution for the dictator. In 1991, he was promoted to president of the Supreme Court.

In the January 24, 1992, "transitional" government, he became the minister for the interior (territorial administration and local bodies). He was still president of the Supreme Court.

As the president of the National Electoral Commission, he was a member of the government delegation for the National Pact (February–March 1993). In September, he prohibited La Verdad. It is true that this journal had just revealed he was involved in the circulation of forged banknotes. In the December 22 government, he was the minister of state in charge of the interior. In January 1994, he again banned La Verdad, but the measure was accompanied by death threats against the leaders of the CPDS. Reporters without Borders made a firm protest.

In 1995, he was the president of the Electoral Commission of the municipal elections, and then of the presidential elections of February 1996. After the observation of a number of irregularities by the observers who were few and far between, and after denunciations by the POC, he had a report made which stressed the violence the POC indulged in.

In the January 8, 1996, ministerial reshuffle, he remained the minister of state for local corporations and the interior. In the April 8, 1996, government he retained his posts as minister of the interior and of local communities. Rumor had it that he could be an alternative to the dictator Obiang Nguema.

Obiang Nguema started to suspect him more and more because he is the brother of Guillermo Nguema Ela, one of the leaders of the Republican Democratic Force, which is made up of natives of Mongomo (former Nguemists who had returned to more democratic convictions). Julio Ndong Ela disappeared from the government in the ministerial reshuffle of January 21, 1998, and was replaced by Demetrio Elo Ndong Nsefumu. In November, Moto Nsá and a few others accused him, along with Obiang Nguema and Nve Ngu, in the Spanish Audiencia Nacional (High Court) of national and international terrorism, murders, and ritual crimes.

NDONG ELA NZANG, Eduardo. From Alonibe. Born 1947. Employed in the company Afripesca. Called "Gordi." Ambassador to Spain from late 1986; in fact, he was the dummy of the embassy. In 1987, Moto Nsa accused Ndong Ela—who had been his student—of lying about the internal situation of Equatorial Guinea. He returned to the country in 1991, as an official in the Ministry of Foreign Affairs. Ambassador in Morocco since 1995.

NDONG MBA, Anatolio. Fang from Río Benito. Born July 3, 1946. Called "Abuglu." After his baccalaureate, he obtained a scholarship to Cairo. He studied there to be an agricultural engineer. During his stay in Cairo, he taught at the Institute for International Cooperation and was also an announcer on Radio Cairo, for broadcasts to Latin America. He returned to the country after Obiang Nguema's coup d'etat. In the Ministry of Agriculture he was in charge of the rehabilitation of the agricultural estates. In early 1980, he was named director of animal husbandry and fisheries, in the Ministry of Agriculture. Towards the end of 1982, he became general secretary in the Ministry.

In 1984 he became the coordinator of development programs. In 1986 he was reinstated as the general secretary of the Ministry of Agriculture. On August 15, 1989, he was named minister for agriculture, animal husbandry, fisheries and forests. The expert of the Israeli company Yona International told him: "You [the Nguemists] are not only beggars, but thieves too"; he was expelled for his insolence.

In the January 24, 1992, "transitional" government, he became minister of state in charge of planning and international cooperation. The press stated that he was using funds from UN projects for personal ends. He had a German engineer hired for a salary of 35 million pesetas for counseling a government lumber company; the contract had provisions for a commission of 10% for the minister. His task was also to make the people of Río Benito conscious of Nguemism.

In 1993, he threatened government officials, as a result of some leaks. In the November 1993 elections, he was elected PDGE deputy for Río Benito. In the December 22 government, he was vice prime minister, minister for the economy and finance. In the spring of 1994, Ndong travelled to Paris, shortly before Obiang Nguema, to request economic aid, following the devaluation of the CFA franc. In the spring of 1995, he protested at the attitude of the Spanish government in the Moto Nsa case. In April, he represented the country at the meeting of francophone countries, where he made accusations against Spain.

With a number of other noted Nguemists, he became a member of the administrative council of the Empresa nacional de pesca de Guinea Ecuatorial. On January 8, 1996, he was confirmed as vice-prime minister, minister for the economy and finance, while Siale Bilekia remained prime minister. Ndong Mba was a member of the political committee of the PDGE. In the April 8, 1996, government, he became minister of state for water, forestry and fishing, and director general for protocol.

In the 1998 government, he became minister of state planning and international cooperation.

NDONG MBA, Zakarias. From Mongomo. Born around 1946. A male nurse trained in Conakry Guinea (who passes himself off as a doctor). In February 1980, he became the director of health for Fernando Po. He was dismissed for irregularities, but returned in December as joint secretary in the Ministry. Shortly afterwards, he became director of health for Río Muni, and then secretary of state for health. He spread terror in the hospital at Bata. In the late 1980s, he became ambassador to Gabon and then to Morocco. He died in 1976.

NDONG MBA OBONO, Melchior. From Mongomo. Born in 1959. Obiang Nguema's cousin. A sub-lieutenant of the Youth Marching with Macías. Shipping captain trained in Cuba. Was promoted to the rank of captain by Obiang Nguema in 1979 and became military commissioner for labor. In 1980 he was appointed military governor of Fernando Po. After spending some time in the technical secretariat of the Ministry of Defense, he was made deputy-minister of defense in October 1982. He was arrested in connection with the attempted coup of July 1986. In 1983, he was the president of the war council dealing with V. Mikó. In 1985 he was authorized to buy the 96 hectare agricultural estate in the Bay of Venus, for FCFA 4,723,384, and Pedro García Amilivia, in Santa Isabel, for FCFA 5,776,168. In late 1987 he was found to be an orderly to the director general of the Criminal Investigations Department, aide-de-camp to the president, and member of the central committee of the PDGE. Shortly afterwards he was sent to his village. In 1991 he was reinstated as general secretary of the Ministry of Labor. He was appointed colonel. Died in 1996.

NDONG MIBUY, Benjamin Pablo. Fang from Kogo. Born March 31, 1946. Responsible for industrial training. On December 22, 1993, he became vice-minister of public works, environment and town planning.

NDONG MICHA, Adolfo. From Evinayong. Born July 3, 1946. Holds a degree in law (Spain). Member of the Akonibé constitutional commission in May 1982. Nominated minister of justice and religion in January 1986. He later became director general of the notarial registry, in the Ministry for Justice and Religions. He was confirmed in this post on January 27, 1994. He was a judge in the Supreme Court. Since the ministerial reshuffle of April 8, 1996, he remained director general of the national registry. He kept this function in 1998.

NDONG MICHA MIA, Angel. From Añisok. Born 1945. Holds a diploma in administration. Shortly after Obiang Nguema's coup, he became secretary of the Ministry of Public Works. In 1982, he was promoted to minister for labor, social security and women's welfare. In 1984, he became minister for justice and religion. From 1993, he held the post of secretary general. In the ministerial reshuffle of April 8, 1996, he became general secretary of the Ministry of Public Works, Housing and Town Planning.

NDONG NSI, Agustín. Born in Mongomo. Studied in Cuba. Former delegate of the government in Malabo. In the ministerial reshuffle of April 8, 1996, he became director general of the National School for Administration.

NDONG OBA, José see Bakale, C.; Nepotism; Obiang Nguema

NDONG OBIANG, Pedro. Born in Mongomo. Trained in Cuba. In the ministerial reshuffle of April 8, 1996, he became joint director general for presidential security.

NDONG OGUONO-ASONG, Marcos Manuel. Born in Sipolo, Río Benito, in 1948. Studied in missionary schools in Río Benito and Kogo, and later with the La Salle brothers at the Instituto Nacional de Enseñanza Media "Carlos Lwanga" (Secondary School) at Bata. In 1970, he studied at Bilbao. Holds a degree in economic and commercial sciences (1976). Licensed to be a pilot at Cuatro-Vientos (Madrid). Sought asylum in Spain, and became an inspector of the Cooperative Industrial Credit Fund, and then became administrative head of Industrias Jofe SA and Covex SA. From 1980 to 1982, he was the commercial attaché at the embassy at Madrid.

As director general for planning, in 1982, at Santa Isabel, he also taught at the UNED from 1989. In *Africa 2000*, he published a highly critical article about the franc zone and the CFA franc. He appealed to hispanophone countries, and proposed a significant collaboration with Latin American countries. He resigned in 1990 and returned to Spain. In 1993 he became the external coordinator of the Convergency for Social Democracy. Shortly after the Constitutive Convention of the CPDS, from November 29–December 2, 1994, the Nguemists accused him of relations with terrorist organizations. He lives as a refugee in Spain.

NDONGO, A. M. Died 1976. Fang. Vicar of the Bata diocese. Imprisoned with several other priests and murdered in 1976 in the Bata prison.

NDONGO, Manuel Ruben. A Fang, born in 1950. Native of Kukumankok (Evinayong district). A former seminarist and member of the MUNGE (Movimiento de Unión Nacional de Guinea Ecuatorial), he has been a refugee in France since 1968. Cofounder, in 1982 with a friend, of a Democratic Association for the Liberation of Equatorial Guinea, which claimed to group together four older parties, which appears to have been manipulated by France. After having flattered Obiang Nguema and received his permission to return to the country, he took flight and went to Calabar, Libreville, and Dakar and settled finally in Paris. In December 1984 he founded the Convergencia Social Democrática with a so-called Socialist and African Party of Equatorial Guinea. S. Oyono also belonged to this group. In November 1984, he accused Obiang Nguema of having set up a network of informers among the refugees in Gabon.

In 1998 he published *L'Afrique sud-saharienne au 21e siecle* (L'Harmattan, Paris). See Democratic Union for the Liberation of Equatorial Guinea.

NDONGO BIDYOGO, Donato. Fang from Niefang. Born in 1950 in Niefang. Journalist and novelist. In 1975, in Spain, secretary of the Allianza Nacional de Restauración Democrática (National Alliance for Democratic Restoration), but excluded from the movement on April 15, 1976, with Mba Ada and some others.

He published in 1977 the first historical work on Equatorial Guinea written by an Equato-Guinean: *Historia y Tragedia de Guinea Ecuatorial*. He collaborates with various Spanish newspapers, including *El País* and *Mundo negro*. He has been assistant director of the Our Lady of Africa University College in Madrid. He is a member of the Associación para el Progreso de Guinea Ecuatorial founded in early 1985. At the end of 1985, he was appointed deputy-director of the Hispano-Guinean Cultural Center in Santa Isabel and adviser to the minister of information, culture, and art. He also represented the Spanish News Agency EFE in Santa Isabel.

In early 1987, he launched the journal *Africa 2000* with help from the Spanish Cooperation. In 1986 he became president of the Guinextebank. During the same year, he was arrested and accused of complicity in the attempted coup d'etat by

Mba Oña. In 1988, *Mundo negro* published his first novel: *Las tienieblas de tu memoria negra.* Obiang Nguema granted him pardon in 1987.

In 1993, Ndongo Bidyogo was counsellor to the president for economic affairs. He ran the EFE agency at Santa Isabel until 1994, after which he was again forced to seek asylum abroad. Since 1995 he has collaborated with the journal *Mundo negro,* in Madrid. In early 1996, he exposed the electoral maneuvering of the "eternal candidate" Obiang Nguema in the journal.

In 1998, he published the second novel of his trilogy, which began in 1997: *Los poderes de la tempestad* (The Powers of the Tempest).

See also Mba Oñana, F.

NDONGO ENGONGA, Antonio, d. 1969. Fang. Administrative technician. From 1960 to 1964 he was a member of Parliament during autonomy from 1964 to 1968. After the Constitutional Conference he ran for elections for Parliament, of which he became vice-president in October 1968. Shortly after the arrest of Ondo Edu, who had been extradited from Gabon, Macías Nguema denounced a so-called plot and ordered the arrest of Ndongo Engonga, M. Mbá Micha, and S. Ngomo. Ndongo and Mbá were liquidated without trial in the Bata prison, Ondo Edu and Ngomo in the Santa Isabel one.

NDONG OLO, Eduardo. In 1998, ambassador of Equatorial Guinea to Morocco.

NDONG OLOMO, Darío-Tadeo. Fang from Mongomo. Born 1960. Intern of customs officials in Cameroon and in the Central African Republic. Joint political administrative secretary of the Partido Democratico de Guinea Ecuatorial, and leader of the Jovenes Antorchas. He chaired the Administrative Council of Litor-Wele. On April 8, 1996, he entered the government as minister for health and the environment. On July 18, he was arrested for an attempted coup d'etat.

See Coup d'etat

NDONG ONA, Agostin. From Mongomo; first cousin to Obiang Nguema. Did not finish his baccalaureate. A captain trained in Cameroon. In charge of security of the president, and assistant to Armengol Nguema, military chief of Fernando Po. Strongman of the praetorian guards. One of the 12 counsellors of the INSESO; in this capacity, he earns FCFA 100,000 per month.

In late 1992, he became director general of the Criminal Investigations Department. He then became lt.-col. and found himself appointed Obiang Nguema's representative for Río Muni. Apart from the army, he supervised the police and the gendarmerie.

Upon being appointed colonel, he was the one to lead 200 men in the repressive operation against Annobón in August 1993. Beyond the violence, he is reputed to have lent rifles to village chiefs of the forest zone of Río Muni, for them to hunt elephants: the villagers keep the meat and Ndong Ona keeps the tusks.

He was briefly arrested for participation in the July 18, 1996, coup d'etat. At the beginning of January 1997, he had the leader of the CPDS, Placido Mikó arrested for two days. The latter was having a meeting with party members in Río Benito.

NDONGO MIYONE, Atanasio, d. 1969. Fang from Río Benito. Educated at Banapa Priest School, which he left after a student strike to take refuge in Gabon, where he became a member of the constabulary in Libreville and married one of Léon Mba's daughters (Mba became president of Gabon in 1961). Ndongo Miyone spent several years as a refugee in Cameroon, where he met the socialist leader Felix Moumié. A member of the Cruzada Nacional de Liberación, he started to campaign in the border districts in 1961, especially in Mongomo and Ebebiyin. In 1962 he caused the Cruzada to change to MONALIGE, of which he rapidly became the chief. Threatened by Spain, he fled to Gabon, welcomed by his father-in-law, President M'ba. In Libreville in September 1962, together with Maho Sikacha, he submitted a memorandum at the Heads of State Conference of the African and Malagasy Union announcing the creation of a Liberation Committee of Spanish Guinea. But the rivalries between Ndongo and Maho upset the conference, which neglected the Equato-Guinean problem.

In Ambam (Cameroon), in February 1963, he became secretary general of the Coordination Bureau of Spanish Guinean Movements (which, however, split up in June). Refusing to cooperate with the autonomous government under Ondo Edu, he founded the FRENAPO in Ghana, with Mbá Ovono, requiring immediate independence and nationalization of Spanish belongings. Ndongo stayed in exile until 1966 (Ghana, Algeria, Cameroon). During this period, he married the widow of Felix Moumié (who seemed to have been assassinated in Geneva by a French secret service agent).

Back in his country, he took part in the Constitutional Conference during which Macías Nguema strongly protested his representativity. In Equatorial Guinea he was maligned by an open letter of the Grupo Macías (former Secretariado Conjunto, advised by García Trevijano), distributed on March 30, 1968, in Bata. He was accused of bribery, compromising with Spain, nepotism, etc. Ndongo Miyone answered on Radio Ecuatorial and during a meeting at the Bata stadium, accusing his adversaries of demagoguery. Weakened by its dissidents, who passed to the Grupo Macías, the MONALIGE, with a too intellectual Ndongo Miyone, faced the September 1968 presidential elections as only the third force. Having taken the third position in the first ballot, after Macías Nguema and Ondo Edu, Ndongo Miyone withdrew in favor of Macías because of Ondo Edu's uncompromising stand.

A. Ndongo Miyone is the author with Jesus Mitogo, of the national anthem:

Caminemos pisando las sendas

De nuestra inmensa felicidad
En fraternidad, sin separación
¡Cantemos Libertad¡
Tras dos siglos de esar sometidos
En fraterna unión sin discriminar

¡Cante Libertad¡
¡Gritamos Viva, Libre Guinea¡

Y defendemos nuestra Libertad
Cantemos siempre, Libre Guinea

Y conservemos siempre la unidad
¡Gritamos Viva, Libra Guinea

Y defendamos nuestra Libertad
Cantemos siempre Libre Guinea
Y conservemos,Y conservamos

La independencia nacional Y conservamos,
Y conservamos,

Ahead let us go on the pathways
Where to us great happiness belongs
In brotherhood, ever undivided,
Sing we now Freedom's song
The ended colonial domination
As one in brotherhood, with no discrimination
Sing we now Freedom's song
Let us cry: Long live, long live free Guinea
And let us all defend our Libery
Let us sing always of our free Guinea

And let us keep intact our unity
And let us cry: Long live, long live free Guinea.

And let us defend our Liberty
Let us sing always of our free Guinea
And let us keep now, And let us keep now
This country independent, free
And let us keep now, And let us keep now
This country independent, free.
(Trans. by T. M. Cartledge)

In the first government, Ndongo Miyone became minister of foreign affairs. In January 1969 he negotiated in Washington with Secretary of State William Rogers, and had discussions in New York with UN Secretary General U Thant regarding the civil war in Biafra. Back in Santa Isabel, he ordered the interruption of the International Red Cross relief flights. Macías Nguema had just liquidated Ondo Edu and his political friends. Violent anti-Spanish speeches had alerted the Spanish Guardia Civil, which still remained in Equatorial Guinea. Macías proclaimed the State of Emergency (Emergencia) on March 3, 1969, while 7,000 Spaniards were about to leave the country. On March 5 Ndongo Miyone, according to official information, attempted a coup d'etat in Bata that Macías Nguema, informed by senior officials from Madrid, was able to thwart. Ndongo Miyone appears to have been thrown out of a window at the governmental residence. Macías Nguema's former Spanish counselor declared that having been beaten by the PUN Youth (later PUNT), Ndongo had died without assistance in the Bata prison. Ndongo's death was followed by a purge in which the chief of Cabinet,

Gori Molubuela, the secretary general of his ministry, Mitogo Osa, the Equatorial Guinean ambassador at the United Nations, Itoha Iyanga, and several others perished. Ndongo Miyone was a cousin of Bishop Nzé Abuy.

In 1976, the Independence Day Celebration (October 12) was moved to March 5, in commemoration of the failure of the so-called Ndongo Miyone coup d'etat.

NDONGO NANGALA, Laureano, d. 1976. Fang. First secretary of the Guinean Embassy in Madrid in 1975–1976. On March 5, 1976, the Guinean students in Madrid occupied the embassy (see Occupation). Santa Isabel accused Ndongo Nangala of complicity with the Central Bank director, Buendy Ndongo, and called him back to Santa Isabel. He was taken to an unknown destination, leaving his wife and children in Madrid. He was replaced by Edu Engonga.

NDONGO NSOBEYA, Antonio. Fang from Añisok, brother of S. Nsobeya Efuman Nsue. Named vice-president of the Asamblea Nacional Popular (Parliament) by presidential decree beginning 1974 while Nso Ndong Akele was president. A famous syclist in his country. He works in the French Cosiété Générale de Banque (General Society of Banks), in the capital.

NDOWE. Name given in the strict sense to all populations speaking Kombe and in the wider sense also to Benga, Bapuku, Bujeba, Balenke, Baseke, i.e., the Bantu of the coast, improperly called Playeros. The Ndowe can be classified in two ethnic groups: the boumba (Banga and Bapuku) and the bongue (Kombe, Bomoudi, Asangon, Muiko, et al.). They seem to have arrived on the coast around the 14th century, after having stayed on the Ubangui where they met the Fang, who in the 19th century were to push them to the sea.

The social organization of the Ndowe is like the Fang, with four levels: family, village, lineage, clan. The Ndowe live on cassava, malanga, plantain, banana ,and corn. The Ndowe very early had close contacts with Europeans, merchants, and missionaries. In 1967 the Ndowe Union was constituted and directed by Eñeso Neñe, who participated in the Constitutional Conference. The Ndowe have particularly suffered from the excesses of the Nguemist dictatorship.

A number of them have been assassinated: Jorge Oma, A Eñeso, ex-minister, H. Engura, an official, A. J. Nchuchuma, provincial counsellor. The mayor of Bata, Alejandro Mbuña, belongs to this ethnic group. In Catalonia, there exists the Rhombe Cultural Association, founded in 1988 by the Ndowe community. Its general secretary since 1994 is the journalist D.M. Bendje Ngongolo. Prof. A. Iyanga Pendi, of the University of Valencia, published a number of studies about the Ndowe. In October 1994 the Organization of the Ndowe Community in Spain was founded, with M. E. Ngonde Maguga as president.

After the uprising of the Bubi of Biolo in January 1998 and the violent repression, the Council of the Elderly of Biko and Ndowe denounced, in February 1998, the confiscation of the ancestral lands by the Nguemists, and wondered if after the repression of the Annobonians and the Bubi, they are not next.

See also Annobon; Bubi; Djombe Djangani de Mbuamangongo, P.; Epalepale Evina, F.; Government of National Unity; Iyanga Pendi, A.-C.; Civil Junta for National Salvation; Ngonde Maguga, M.-E.; Madrid Pact.

NEPOTISM. Since 1968 several members of the Macías Nguema family have been part of the government: Eyegue Ntutumu, civil governor of the Río Muni, then vice-president of the republic (but murdered in 1976) and Masié Ntutumu, Home Secretary who sought refuge in Spain in 1976, are both cousins of Macías Nguema. In 1977, except for a few vice-ministers, the country is practically dominated by the Macías Nguema clan.

Macías himself is president of the republic, defense minister, national security and popular constructions minister, and forestry affairs minister. His cousin Bonifacio Nguema Esono Nchama is Foreign Affairs Minister and Vice-President since 1977. His nephew Teodoro Obiang Nguema is chief of the army.

Daniel Oyono Ayingono Mbá, another nephew, has recently been Finance Minister (replacing Nko Ibasa, murdered in 1976). Industry and Trade Minister (replacing Bosio Dioco, murdered in 1975 and Nvo Bikie, murdered in 1976). Under Secretary of State to the Presidency (replacing Asumu Oyono, in exile since 1975). Chief of Protocol, Director General of Information, Director General of National Security (replacing Masié Ntutumu, in exile since 1976), and Commissary for the State Companies. Oyono Ayingono fled to Spain in January 1978.

After the 1979 coup of Obiang Nguema, the Esangui from Mongomo continued to hold the monopoly of power as ministers, senior officials, or members of the diplomatic service. The most well-known of these were Obiang Nguema, Mbá Oñana, Micha Nsué, Abaga Ondo Maye, Frida Krohnert, Masié Ntutumu, Ngomo Ndumu, Nguema Ela, Obiang Alogo, Nsué Ela. This has given rise to the regime being known as Nguemist or Mongomist. Macías Nguema's nephew, and Obiang Nguema's cousin, Juan Micha Nsué, was sent as a chargé d'affaires to Cameroon. On Janaury 22, 1980, he was replaced by Okenve Mituy, along with the first secretary F. Obama Nsue Mangue, the famous torturer called Mbato. Micha Nsue became ambassador to Nigeria; uncles Mba Oñana and Nguema Esono respectively became ambassador to the United Nations and ambassador to the OAU; Ela Nseng became ambassador to China. Mba Oñana was said to have been distanced due to misappropriation of supplies delivered by Spain, and Ela Nseng for breach of trust. After the new territorial organization of Río Muni, 80% of the country's leaders came from the district of Mongomo, and a large number were Esangui.

On March 21, 1981, Frida Krohnert, Macías Nguema's former wife, was named the technical directress of health for Río Muni. But on March 16, Obiang Nguema removed Eusebio Abaga Ondo Maye, the husband of a cousin, from his post as secretary for information and tourism. That summer, in order to replace Evuna Owono Asangono, ambassador to Spain, removed from his post following a drug trafficking scandal, the Nguemists proposed Felipe Obiang Alogo Ondo, minister for agriculture and later for health and education under Macías Nguema, famous for having led the anti-Spanish campaign and as a member of the central committee of the PUNT. Spain refused him, and likewise refused Macías Nguema's former vice-president, B. Nguema Esono. The former ambassador of Spain Graullera explained that "Macism" [Nguemism] was merely abuse of power and injustice. The army was busy with what did not concern it and it was Obiang Nguema who commanded it. One of his brothers-in-law, Constanza's brother, was promoted in September to the post of deputy director of the Banco de Crédito y Desarrollo, and joint chief of the Presidential guards. In December, the natives of

Mongomo hurried to ensure the continuation of the leadership of the country. A typical example of these natives is the man named Bote, one of the chiefs of Obiang Nguema's security. A native of Mongomo, he was a militiaman with the Juventud en marcha con Macías. He was the one who violated the Spanish diplomatic bag on January 23, 1982, under the orders of Nsue Ela, in the Ministry of Foreign Affairs.

In 1983, the new ambassador to Spain was Luis Obiang Mangue, an accomplice in a bhanga (hashish) trafficking scandal, also an Esangui.

The members of the clan from Mongomo drew attention to themselves by constant corruption. Some of them were: Obiang Nguema and his son Teodorin, Demeterio Elo Ndong, Santiago Eneme, Francisco Nguema, Juan Olo Mba, Angel Ndjeng Olo Bahamondes, Agostin Ndong Ona, Lucas Nguema Esono Nseng, etc., etc. The delegation accompanying Obiang Nguema to Madrid in January 1989 was almost entirely from Mongomo.

Since the January 1992 "transitional" government, Mongomo and Wele-Nzas have retained the upper hand. Thus Manuel Nguema Mba, in the January 8, 1996, ministerial reshuffle, became the secretary of state for national security, and then in the April 8, 1996, government, went on to become vice-minister for national security. More than a fourth of the 41 ministers in this sham of a government of national unity came from Mongomo and its surrounding areas. On August 3, on the 17th Anniversary of the coup, Lieutenant-general Obiang Nguema being in power, he promoted his brother from colonel to General Brigadier. The elder son of Obiang Nguema entered the government as a counsellor for forestry and fishing affairs in January 1998.

See also Engonga Edjo, B.; Evuna Owono Asangono, A.; Government of National Unity; Justice; Mangue Obama Nfube, R.; Mongomo, Nguema Esono, L.; Nguema Eyi, D.; Nguema Mba, M.; Nguema Obiang, T.; Obiang Mbasogo Ondo, A.; Nguemism; Nsue Obama Angue, P.; Obiang Nguema, T.; Olo Mba Nseng, J.; Oyono Ntutumu, M.

NETHERLANDS, THE. In 1980 the ambassador, Abraham L. Schneyders, dean of the diplomatic corps, presented his credentials. He lived in Cameroon. From August 1992, Rotterdam was served once a month by a vessel belonging to the Société africaine de cabotage (an Equato-Guinean/Belgian company). In 1995 the Netherlands took fifth place among the clients of Equatorial Guinea (above all because of wood imports) at $5 million. See also Addax BV Rotterdam.

NGOLO-AYOP. A locality to the east of Bata. Under Macías Nguema, this was where opponents of the regime were eliminated. Obiang Nguema constructed the conference building, there, using North Korean labor.

NGOMO MBENGONO, Francisco Javier (called Paco). Fang from Ebebiyin. Born August 2, 1951. Son of Federico Ngomo, deputy from Bata and representative in the Spanish Parliament before independence, and later inspector at the Central Bank (assassinated in 1970). Holds a degree in law. Married to a Spanish woman.

In the January 1992 "transitional" government he was the vice-minister for justice and religion. In November, he became the third vice-president of the regional African Conference at Tunis, preparatory to the World Human Rights

Conference in Vienna (1993). He was accompanied by Engonga Motulu. In March 1993, he attended the meeting of the Human Rights Commission along with Engonga Motulu, in Geneva, where he met with Dougan Beaca. In November 1993, he was elected PDGE deputy for Ebebiyin. On December 22, 1993, he became minister for justice and religion. He was replaced in 1995 by F. Ngomo. In the January 8, 1996, ministerial reshuffle, he became minister for labor and social security. He was replaced in the ministry of Justice and Religions by Juan Milam. On April 8, 1996, he became deputy prime minister, minister of civil service and administrative reform.

In Geneva, in April 1997, in front of the Commission on Human Rights, he lauded the Nguemist democratization, saying there are no political prisoners and that Equatorial Guinea is a state of law. "The country is learning to become a democracy."

During the January 1998 cabinet reshuffle, he became vice minister of justice and religious affairs.

NGOMO NANDONGO, Federico, 1929–1972. Fang from the Ebebiyin district. Business diploma. President of the Diputación Provincial (Assembly) of Río Muni from August 1963, secretary of the Asamblea General (Parliament) from 1964 to 1968. At the same time he was Representative to the Cortes. He participated in the Constitutional Conference but not in the September 1968 elections. In 1970 Macías Nguema appointed him chief auditor of the Central Bank. Removed in 1971, he was put under house arrest in his village. Arrested at the same time as Cabrera James, Oma Ekoka, Watson Bueco, he was transferred to the Bata prison where a warden decapitated him with a machete.

NGOMO NDUMU ASUMU, Simon, d. 1969. Gobernador civil (civil governor) of the Río Muni province from 1964 to 1968, and from 1968 to 1969. After Ondo Edu's arrest in January 1969, S. Ngomo was also arrested with Ndongo Engonga and Mbá Micha, and liquidated in the Santa Isabel prison.

NGOMO NVONO, Jesus. In the April 8, 1996, ministerial reshuffle, he became director general for military cooperation. During the ministerial reshuffle of January 1998, he became general director of military instruction and teaching.

NGOMO ONDO, Inocencio. Obiang Nguema's nephew. A navy sergeant, trained in the U.S. and the former USSR. On February 3, 1981, he was promoted as sub-frigate lieutenant. In 1992, he became lt.-col., chief of headquarters. In the trial of Moto Nsá and about a dozen soldiers in April 1995, he was vice-president of the tribunal. He was arrested for participation in the July 18, 1996, coup d'etat. See also Army; Justice; Mongomo; Moto Nsá, S.

NGONDE MAGUGA, Martin-Endje. An Ndowe schoolteacher. In 1962 he visited Spain. After his return in 1969, he sought asylum in Spain. Holds a degree in law (1983), is a lawyer, an official in the fiscal administration at Barcelona. In October 1994, he was elected president of the Organisación de la Comunidad Ndowe en España. In 1995 he simultaneously became President of the Liga guineana de los Derechos del Hombre, with headquarters in Madrid. In May, following the Moto Nsá scandal, he demanded international intervention, in order to avoid civil war. In June, before the press, he described Moto Nsá as being close to the two Nguemist dictatorships and of having "participated in political assassinations." He was said to have links with the UDENA.

NGONG ELO NZANG, Eduardo. Appointed ambassador to Spain on November 27, 1986. In January 1987 he accused the Spanish pilots of being responsible for the accident to the aircraft at Bata airport on January 2, alleging it was due to New Year festivities. The Spanish government entered a protest.

NGORE, Bernabe. Ndowe from Punta-Mbonda (Bata), born April 14, 1947. A gynecologist. Member of the PDGE. On December 22, 1993, he became minister for health and the environment. He left the government in the January 8, 1996, ministerial reshuffle. In the 1998 government, he became minister for health and environment.

NGUA EDU, Francisco. From Mongomo. Former head of Macías Nguema's military escort. Member of the CMS. Military Commander from Mongomo after Obiang Nguema's coup. He protested against the special rapporteur to the Human Rights Commission, who questioned frontier Gabonese near Nsork in 1979. In 1981, he was named lieutenant and became joint secretary in the Ministry of Defence. In 1983, he accompanied Seriche Bioco to Madrid in order to have the passage to the franc zone "digested."

In 1988 he turned up as the chargé d'affaires, number two counsellor at the embassy at Madrid, replacing Lucas Nguema Esono, who had been expelled for drug trafficking. Shortly afterwards, he was caught in his car selling cigarettes under diplomatic franchise. He was in turn expelled. Shortly afterwards, he was named to the Nguemist Commission of Human Rights. He died in June 1998, soon after an interview with Obiang Nguema.

NGUA NFUMU, Santiago. Fang from Bata. Born February 18, 1956. Member of the Youth Marching with Macías. Holds a degree in information sciences. In November 1993, he was elected PDGE deputy for Bata. On December 22, 1993, he was named secretary of state for information. In the summer of 1994, he demanded that the editor of *El Sol* and *La Verdad* "avoid opinion journalism." In 1995 he was the national director for the IEC Project/Population of UNPAP. He did not figure in the January 8, 1996, government.

In the January 1998 government, he is Secretary of State for Press, Radio and TV. At the end of July, he went to Mexico to talk about a project concerning professional training for radio and TV.

NGUEMA ADA SIMA, Alberto. Fang from Niefang. In 1968 he became director general of the health department, then governmental delegate in Niefang, and since 1973 in Río Benito. In 1975 he was promoted to vice-minister in charge of natural resources and electricity. He remained vice-minister until the August 1979 coup. Obiang Nguema sent him as ambassador to Gabon. He was called back two years later and settled in Niefang as one of Obiang Nguema's sorcerers.

NGUEMA BINDANG, Teonesto. Macías Nguema's son. Obiang Nguema's cousin. He underwent military training in Cuba. An officer. He lives in Equatorial Guinea and is involved in business. It was said that it was in order to prevent Teonesto from succeeding his father that Obiang Nguema seized power in August

1979. On September 16, 1988, following the coup of August 1988, Teonesto was arrested and condemned to a prison sentence.

NGUEMA ELA MANGUE NDONG, Guillermo. Born 1953. An Esangui from Mongomo. Studied in Spain and the USSR. Civil engineer. Appointed technical director of public works in January 1980. In October 1982 he was appointed minister of planning and development. In 1985 he moved to the Ministry of Finance as minister. In this capacity he took part in the World Bank-International Monetary Fund meetings in Seoul flanked by French experts. In January 1986, he was relieved of his post within the framework of a ministerial reshuffle. He was arrested in connection with the attempted coup of July 1986 and sentenced to two-and-a-half years in jail, but released in October 1987.

In August 1988, he was again arrested, along with Mba Oñana and Pancracio Bee, military Commander from Mongomo, accused of arms-trafficking from Gabon. In September, a war council condemned him to two years in prison. In 1993 he became an advisor to the president for economic affairs. In January 1994, by decree 19, he became general secretary of the Ministry for the Economy and Finance. During 1995, he negotiated with Nigeria, at Calabar, for a maritime frontier agreement.

In the ministerial reshuffle of April 8, 1996, he remained general secretary of the Ministry of the Economy and Finance. During the same year, he founded Fuerza Democrática Republicana (FDR) with Felipe Ondo Obiang; both blamed Obiang Nguema for his poor management, his nepotism, and the fact that he does not wish to establish a democracy. The government refused to legalize the party. The leaders of FDR sought refuge in Gabon in 1997 and asked the UNHCR to protect them. Nguema Ela and his colleagues were arrested and deported to Equatorial Guinea on November 5, 1997. They were released for some time and then referred to Playa Negra carcel.

The trial of the two FDR leaders started on July 23, 1998. They were accused of "false accusations and offences" against the head of state. At the end of August 1998, Nguema Ela and his colleagues were sentenced to two years imprisonment and heavy fines.

See also Borders; Republican Democratic Force.

NGUEMA EMAGA EYUI. Fang from Mikomeseng. Sought asylum as a very young man in Barcelona. An ex-seminarist. With his wife, he created the journal *Tam-Tam,* for which he was chief editor. He also ran an Inter-African Center for Cultural Initiatives (Centro Interafricano de iniciativas culturales). This center organized a 1st Convention on "Equatorial Guinea: Past, present, future" in 1992. In 1994, the journal *Tam-Tam* stopped appearing.

In the January 21, 1998, government, he became minister of information, tourism and culture. During the Bubi trial at the end of May 1998, he demanded that Spanish journalists deal only with the trial. He owns a company that imports sportswear.

NGUEMA ESONO, Fermin. A Fang, born in 1948 in Nfene-Yepuo (Nsok-Nsomo district, Ebebiyin). Ex-Claretian seminarist. Holds a degree in law (Murcia). He worked as a lawyer in Murcia from 1976 to 1985. Upon his return to the country in 1985, he taught law at the UNED, became a district judge in a court of first instance (Ela Nguema, a suburb of the capital) and prosecutor at the Appeals Court, and then in 1990 a magistrate at the Supreme Court. In 1993, he especially defended Tobias Nguema, accused of participating in an attempted attack on Nguema Ela's ammunition depot, in August. He entered Popular Union (UP) where he became secretary for organization in the executive committee. After some conflicts, especially with Justino Mba Nsue, he resigned in 1994 and sought asylum in Madrid. Since 1995, he has been a magistrate in one of the tribunals of Zaragoza. In 1996, he published *La Transición de Guinea Ecuatorial Historia de un fracaso* (Transition in Equatorial Guinea: The Story of a Failure) with Juan Balboa Boneke. He has been living in Spain (Almerias) since 1997. See also Popular Union.

NGUEMA ESONO, Lucas. Called "Luquito." Fang, born September 10, 1959, at Akong-Yebivein (Mikomeseng). No professional training. An industrialist. Family friend of Obiang Nguema who ran some of his businesses, including discotheques. Agent of the Nguemist Criminal Investigations Department. In late 1986 he owed the Guinextebank FCFA 6,236,000.

In 1988, he became first secretary at the embassy at Madrid. He was caught for drug-trafficking: 18 kgs of marijuana and 340 g of heroin. He was expelled. Shortly afterwards, he took part in a torture session inflicted on Joaquin Elema Borengue. He was the president of the Administrative Council of the INSESO, with more than FCFA 100,000 in honorariums. In the November 1993 elections, he became a PDGE deputy for Mikomeseng. On December 22, 1993, he was promoted to vice-minister for labor and social security.

In the January 8, 1996, government, he became minister delegate for education, youth and sports. He was also ooordinator of the political police and political secretary in charge of the organization of the PDGE. On April 8, 1996, he was confirmed in his ministerial posts. In the 1998 government, he became minister of information, tourism and culture.

NGUEMA ESONO AFANG, Faustino. Born in 1946. Fang from Evinayong. A schoolteacher trained in the Escuela Superior Indigena at Santa Isabel. In September 1979, he became first secretary at the embassy in Spain and a consul, with ambassador Evuna Owono Asangono. In 1984, he became ambassador to Nigeria. From 1986 until 1988 he was ambassador to France. He signed the accord on the EGA aviation company with Paris. In 1993, he became joint secretary in the Ministry of Foreign Affairs. In the ministerial reshuffle of April 8, 1996, he was ambassador in charge of missions.

NGUEMA ESONO NCHAMA, Bonifacio. Fang of the Obue clan from Mongomo, but belongs to Akurenam. Cousin to Macías Nguema. Married to Rosa Abeme Otong (born in 1947). In 1969 he became technical secretary general of foreign affairs, after the elimination of Ndongo Miyone as minister, Gori Molubuela as chief of Cabinet and Motogo Osa as secretary general. Since 1971 he was deputy minister of the presidency and minister of exterior relations and friendship with peoples. Since the beginning of the party he has also been a member of the PUNT Central Committee. In 1975 he traveled to Cameroon in order to negotiate the expulsion of the 30,000 Equato-Guinean refugees. But

Cameroon told him that this was against African hospitality. He is one of the beneficiaries of the presidential nepotism.

In 1976 he was appointed vice-president of the republic. With Obiang Nguema, he helped purge the administration of elements external to the clan from Mongomo. After traveling to Yaoundé, with Nguema Esono, A. Nzue, chief of Protocol, took refuge in Cameroon, in February 1979.

Obiang Nguema informed him of his plan to topple Macías Nguema, and promised him the post of president of the republic. But Obiang Nguema only gave him the post of ambassador to the Organization of African Unity. In December 1981 he was replaced by Mba Ondo Nchama. He was proposed as ambassador to Madrid, but Spain refused, as a result of his past with Macías Nguema. He then became the mayor of Mongomo, but he soon fell from grace. As a representative of the Popular Union at Mongomo, he lived there under rustic conditions.

In August 1995, in preparation for the presidential elections in September, he founded a new opposition party, Fuerza Democrática Republicana, along with F. Ondo Obiang and E. Elo Nve Mbengono, also of the clan from Mongomo. He was arrested in the capital on October 4, with Ondo Obiang; both of them were placed under house arrest at Mongomo. In late October, fearing assassination by a commando led by Obiang Nguema's nephew, Eustaqui Nseng Nve, they sought asylum in Gabon. In summer 1996, in Spain, B. Nguema Esono declared to the Spanish press agency EFE, that the army had left Obiang Nguema, and the legislative elections of 1995 saw them largely vote for the opposition. At the end of 1998 he lived in Spain.

NGUEMA EYE, Diosdado. Obiang Nguema's relative. In 1996, he was senior chief of the Nguemist police, at Bata. A notorious torturer. See also Police.

NGUEMA MBA, Manuel. Fang Esangui, born December 25, 1953, at Eba-Enug (Mongomo). Uncle to Obiang Nguema (Eba parents). Studied until the second year of secondary school. Known for his violence. Called "El Nervio" (the nerve).

A militiaman under Macías Nguema, who later became a policeman after the 1979 coup d'etat. Commander of the national police, trained in Morocco. An expert in torture. He is noted for his hatred of Spanish and intellectuals. From 1991 he belonged to the death squads in charge of eliminating those opposing the Nguemists.

Secretary of state for national security (Criminal Investigations Department). In 1992 he was one of the counsellors of the INSESO, and earned FCFA 100,000 per month. He was the one who led the arrest of professors and students in the capital, and it was under his command that they were tortured.

Along with his trusted man, Tito Garriga (see F. Abeso Fuma), he participated in the ritual assassination of Motu Mamiaga, on August 22, 1993. Towards the end of September, he summoned and threatened a CPDS delegation, along with Ndong Ela Mangue and Siale Bilekia; the next day, *La Verdad* was banned.

In December 22, 1993, he remained secretary of state for the National Criminal Investigations Department. His advisors were Narciso Edu and Mr. Pierre. In 1995, he continued the persecution of the publishers of *La Verdad,* the periodical of the Convergency for Social Democracy. He also attacked the public prosecutor, Eloy Elo Nve Mbengono, as a result of his criticism of the regime.

In the January 8, 1996, ministerial reshuffle, he remained state secretary for national security. In the April 8, 1996, government, he became vice minister for national security.

In the ministerial reshuffle of January 21, 1998, he left his job to his nephew and Obiang Nguema's half brother, Antonio Mba Nguema Mikue.

Following the example of Olo Mba Nzeng, minister of mines and hydrocarbon, also from Mongomo, and manager of the APEGESA agency for job recruitment and labor racketing, Manuel Nguema manages a similar company, ATIGE, whereas his nephew Armengo Nguema, younger brother of Obiang Nguema, manages the agency SONAVI.

During the spring of 1998, Manuel Nguema went to Benin to negotiate, without success, the expulsion of the opponent Felix Mba, as well as the expulsion of other exiles friendlly with Moto Nsá.

NGUEMA MBASOGO ONDO, Armengol. Called "El Mono" (the monkey). Born in Akoakam-Esangui (Mongomo). Obiang Nguema's younger brother. He was illiterate in 1979. His brother had lessons given to him. He cannot read fluently. He was sent for three-months of military training in Morocco.

From 1981, he led the repression along with his cousin Mba Oñana. He became chief of presidential security, a member of the Board of Directors of the Guinextebank and deputy director of the Banco de Credito y Desarrollo. He began to hold the business circles to ransom. He was said to have made off with cash from the aviation company EGA. He exercised repression against agents of imaginary conspiracies.

In 1992, he became director general of the State Criminal Investigations Department, which is to say, the political police. He was the one who granted exit visas, and who, in case of refusal, confiscated the passports. Along with Obiang Nguema and some Spaniards, he founded Efusila SA, for receiving the contract for the construction of a new secondary school in the capital. The arrests and torture of professors and students continued, under his leadership. He was a member of the Board of Directors of the INSESO and earned FCFA 100,000 each month.

The Spanish press portrayed him as a drug trafficking don, with Epifanio Ngomo, Lucas Ngue Edu, Luis Obiang, Fortunato and Demeterio Ondo Nguema as runners. He was said to be "incapable of understanding an administrative text." In Bata he constructed a tower valued at FCFA 250 million.

In 1995, he became a member of the Board of Directors of the Empresa nacional de Pesca de Guinea Ecuatorial along with some important Nguemists; its president of honor is his brother Teodoro Obiang Nguema. At the ministerial reshuffle of April 8, 1996, he remained director general for presidential security. In October, he headed a group of French businessmen in order to create the National Lottery of Equatorial Guinea. He manages the job and labor racketing company SONAVI.

NGUEMA NCHAMA, Antonio Javier. In 1998, ambassador in Russia.

NGUEMA NDONG, Adolfo. From Akonibe. Born 1969. Holds a degree from the Soviet Union. In January 1994 he became a magistrate at the Appeals Court of Río Muni. He was still the head of presidential security at the end of 1998.

NGUEMA NDONG, Joaquin. Born 1952 in Mongomo. Studied in Cuba and Spain. At the ministerial reshuffle of April 8, 1996, he became director general of Post and Telecommunications.

NGUEMA NFA, Cristobal see Evinayong

NGUEMA NGUEMA ONGUENE, Marcelino. Fang Esangui, born in Mongomo. A government official, and later a scholarship holder at the Lumumba University in Moscow. Studied medicine. His wife, Eulalia Nvo Bela, also from Mongomo, holds a degree in law (Soviet Union), and is a judge at the Supreme Court.

Nguema Onguene returned to the country after Obiang Nguema's coup d'etat. In January 1980 he became secretary for health. In 1982 he took part in the Akonibé constitutional conference. In October he was appointed secretary of state for foreign affairs and negotiated the entry of Equatorial Guinea into the Customs Union of the Central African States (UDEAC).

In 1985, he was authorized to buy the 105 agricultural estate Hacienda Navidad, at Basile, for FCFA 8,876,572. In January 1986 he was confirmed as minister of foreign affairs. In 1988, he delivered a message to President Babangida (Nigeria) in order to defuse the scandal caused by the country's new relations with South Africa. In late 1989, he became General secretary to the President of the Republic. On October 16, 1990, he became minister for the Economy, Commerce and Planning, a post he retained in the January 24, 1992, "transitional" government. In 1992, he became minister of State in charge of Foreign Affairs. He is known to be anti-Spanish.

In November 1993 he was elected as PDGE deputy for Mongomo. He did not figure in the November 22 government. Member of the Central committee of the PDGE. On January 19, 1994, he became advisor to the president of the government for health. On October 29, following the dismissal of the president and vice-president of the Parliament by Obiang Nguema, Nguema Onguene was named president of the Parliament, with Secretary Toribio-Micha Ela Mangue.

In 1995, he also became vice-president of the bold council of the Empresa nacional de pesca de Guinea Ecuatorial, made up of notorious Nguemists. In the summer of 1996, Nguema Onguene led a delegation to the European Union, in order to obtain an end to the boycott of his country for violation of human rights. In the 1998 government, he became minister of economy and commerce.

NGUEMA NSUE ABEME, Martin. Born 1965. Elected mayor of Mongomo in September 1995.

NGUEMA OBIANG MANGUE, Teodoro. Called "Teodorín." Born in 1968 at Akoakam-Esangui (Mongomo). Beloved son of Obiang Nguema. No education. A number of study periods in France proved useless. During his stay in Paris, he often rented a plane to go and parade in luxury spots. Various sources call him a drug addict. The International Bank for the Development of Equatorial Guinea SA (BIDGESA), planned by the Brazilian financier Carlos Rocha, in 1990, was presided over by Teodorín.

In 1991, he was caught at the Miami Airport with a suitcase containing $10 million. In 1992, his father sent him to Lagos to free the military attaché at the embassy, D. Eyama Angüe Osa, who had been arrested for drug trafficking (30 kgs of cocaine). In 1993, he was associated with his father in several enterprises in the capital and in Bata. He drove around in the capital on a Harley-Davidson motorcycle. Since 1994, Teodorín is the owner of a huge lumber company with the Italian familyCataneo. The numerous French and Spanish lumberers of Río Muni complained about this racket which affected them. In 1995, he was named advisor to the minister for fisheries and forest resources. As it was during Macías Nguema's times, the forest remained a family preserve. In early 1996 he was named director of Elf-Equatorial Guinea. In the April 8, 1996, government, he became advisor to the president of the government for fisheries and forests.

Angry at Teodorín, the Cataneo financed an attempted coup by Moto Nsa during the spring of 1997.

In January 1998, his father appointed him minister of environment and forests in the new government. He is the main shareholder of the private airline GEASA that flies alternately with the national airline EGA. GEASA flies abroad under EGA colors. He is also sector secretary for social and working issues of the Specialized Organization for Workers, of PDGE.

According to Joan Roig, a Spanish expert on Equatorial Guinea, Teorodín is addicted to alcohol and drugs; he has difficulties expressing himself and has problems conjugating verbs. He is also said to have declared in certain "speeches" that he would kill with his gun "those that destroy this country." He also threatened to dismiss state employees and politicans who are opposed to him. After racketing lumber companies in Río Muni (see Cataneo), many firms are said to be leaving the country, thus leading to a crisis due to lack of companies who are ready to rescue the business.

Besides his office as minister, he is also secretary of state of forestry affairs, which allows him to have a double income. In 1997 he trained 45 days at the American Military Academy "Interarmas," in Ekuku, near Bata, and obtained the rank of captain. In 1998 he became a commander. He goes about Río Muni dressed in combat uniform, surrounded by about 20 guards, and sees himself as the heir to his father. Often called "El Niño" (The Boy), Teodorín Nguema Obiang is president of the "Association of the Sons of Obiang" (Hijos de Obiang, AHO), and has himself called Hermano mayor (Eldest Brother) or Hijo modelo, "The Model Son." He sees himself more and more as the heir to his father. His personal radio station, Asonga, transmits in Río Muni, from Bata, thus allowing him to spread his personal propaganda. In Malabo he lives in the residential compound of Abayak, built by his father on 3 km of the airport road, where the offices and accommodations of the Mobil Oil staff are also located. The Abayak residential houses are guarded by the Ninjas.

Since 1998 Teodorín has demanded to be called "Patron" (Master). In Paris, Teodorín usually goes to the hotel George V. The staff has labeled him "Dody al Fayed." The French Television "M6" broadcasted, at the beginning of 1998, under the motto "Zone interdite," a very suggestive film on "El Niño."

NGUEMA OBONO, Manuel, d. 1970. Fang from the Ebebiyin district. Medical doctor. Member of the MUNGE, he became deputy at the Asamblea de la República in September 1968. He was a member of the Constitutional Conference in Madrid in 1967/68. He disappeared at the end of the May 1970 purge, along with Watson Bueco, Cabrera y James, and others.

NGUEMA OKUA (or OCOA), Juan. From Ebazok-Yebekon (Mikomeseng). Sunday school teacher at the Catholic mission at Nkue, and later a school teacher at Ayactan. In the 1968 elections, he was a candidate on MUNGE's list. It was with him that Nicolas Abeso, the priest, wanted to found a pro-Nguemist party, Unión democrática cristiana.

In October 1982, he became director for the coordination of information in the Ministry of Communication, Information and Transports. In 1993, he was a teacher in the central military camp in Bata. During the ministerial reshuffle of April 8, 1996, he became director general for labor and employment.

NGUEMA ONDO, Inocencio. Esangui from Mongomo. Corvette lieutenant trained in the USSR and in the U.S. Appointed captain in 1981, he became commander of the armed forces in Río Muni. Since 1983 he has been a member of the central committee of the PDGE.

In 1993 he was chief of headquarters with the grade of lieutenant-colonel. In 1998, he became colonel and chief of staff.

NGUEMA OVONO, Salomon. Fang from Mongomo, born on December 12, 1954, at Yebemveiñ. A doctor trained in the USSR. A member of the Ninjas. In the November 1993 elections, he was elected a PDGE deputy for Añisok. In the December 22 government, he was the vice-minister for health and environment. In the January 8, 1996, ministerial reshuffle he retained his post of minister. In the April 8, 1996, government he also became government secretary general. In the government of January 21, 1998, he became minister of public health.

NGUEMA SEMA, Alejandro Moíses. Called "Nanuco." Cousin of a half-brother of Obiang Nguema's. Member of security. In July 1993, at Niefang, he raped a doctor of the Spanish Cooperation (Doctors without Borders) under the threat of a weapon. Shortly afterwards, he was transferred to the embassy in Cameroon.

NGUEMISM. Philosophy of the Nguema family (Macías Nguema, Obiang Nguema, etc., formerly called Macism) belonging to the Esangui ethnic group. In this philosophy, Equatorial Guinea is seen as the private family domain; violence, torture, terror, "suicides," rape, and ransom are the means used to perpetuate this dominance. It is also frequently referred to as "Mongomism" on account of the locality from which the family comes (the clan from Mongomo).

In a clear statement of February 22, 1985, the Christian Democratic International, along with a number of other organizations roundly condemned Nguemism, which derived its inspiration from Franco's regime in Spain. This was also the view expressed in a symposium of the Pax Romana held in Dakar (Senegal) in December 1982. See Eya Nchama.

In May 1987, a damning document published by Amnesty International shows up the machinations of Nguemist justice operating through military tribunals—even for civilians—and through death sentences. This form of justice has been in operations since 1969 under Macías Nguema as well as Obiang Nguema.

The following definition of the Nguemist system comes from Agustin Nsé Nfumu, a longtime minister for culture, who in April 1996, was counsellor to the president of the government for diplomatic and protocol affairs: "The degree of power an individual holds in Equatorial Guinea is proportional to his capacity to infringe the law without any consequences."

See Corruption; "Democratic" Party of Equatorial Nguema; Drugs; Esono Mikla, P. J.; European Union; Human Rights; Klitgaard, R.; Macías Nguema, F.; Mangue, R.; Mba Ondo, C.; Mongomo; Nepotism; Ndong Mba, A.; Nguema Mba; Nvono Akele Avomo, S.; Obiang Nguema, T.; Ondo Ela, S.; Ondo Obiang Alogo, F.; Otogo, R.; Oyono Ndong Mifumu, M.; Terror; Torture; Victims

NGUNDI, Aniceto. Bisio, born December 20, 1937. Architectural technician. In the December 22 government of 1993, he became secretary of state for environment and town planning. He did not figure in the government set up on January 8, 1996.

NGUNDI, Terencio Luis see Education

NICHOLLS, Edward. British, colonel of the Royal Marines, he accompanied the Owen expedition in Fernando Po, in 1827. In 1829, he became governor of Clarence City (Santa Isabel). He left the island in 1833 and was replaced by Beecroft.

NIEFANG. Town situated at the former order between Fang and Ndowe country divided by the Río Benito, 50 km east of Bata, at 400 m height. After the Francoist triumph of 1936, it was baptized Sevilla de Niefang. A commercial and administrative center and main town of the district, Niefang has a College of Oblate Sisters. In 1960, Niefang distinguished itself at the municipal elections by its 100% participation of the patres familias. It was in Niefang in February 1969 that the Cabinet made the decision to found a movement that was to become the Juventud en Marcha con Macías. The former mayor of the town, P. Ondo Nsí, was, it is believed, assassinated in 1976. The church at Niefang was used as a training ring for boxers during the Macías Nguema dictatorship, at a time when Obiang Nguema was commander-in-chief of the army.

The mayor of Niefang, Angel Nguema Azin, told the special rapporteur of the UN Human Rights Commission on November 8, 1979, of the thousands of people who had fled from the area on account of political repression, torture, and assassination or conscription into forced labor camps. There were still political prisoners in the Niefang jail.

In 1988 the French cooperation set up a project for health, another for rural development, and a project to resume the marketing of coffee and cocoa. In 1989, the Spanish doctor R. Vila Montlleo, of the Spanish Cooperation, carried out research on filariasis in the district of Niefang. In the January 24, 1992, "transitional" government, there figured two ministers from Niefang: Obiang Bengono, agriculture and forests; Ebendeng Nsomo, vice-minister for national defense.

In early June 1993, a Spanish doctor belonging to Doctors without Borders was raped at Niefang, under threat of a pistol, by Alejandro M. Nguema Sema, a relative of Obiang Nguema's. The nongovernmental organization withdrew from the region. In December, about 30 sympathizers of the POC were arrested at

Niefang. The government representative was Francisco Asumu Bikui, from Mongomo, who was a militiaman under Macías Nguema, and after the 1979 coup d'etat underwent training in territorial administration in Morocco. He has been governor of Wele-Nzas and general secretary in the Ministry of Education. The mayor of Niefang was Gaspar Ndong Ela, former cigarette vendor imposed by the regime, and having studied for three years in primary school. Involved in various kinds of trafficking, he was caught red-handed trying to sell Gabon a truckload of milk powder, which had come in through international aid.

In early October 1994, three members of the committee of the Convergency for Social Democracy for Río Muni were arrested at the entry to Niefang by the government's representative, the chief of police, gendarmes, and soldiers; Indalecio Abuy, Indalecio Eko, and Romás Nzo were tortured.

In January 1995, the French rural development project was attacked by armed men. Following protests from the embassy, Col. Agostín Ndong Ona had seven local employees imprisoned, tortured, and sent into forced labor with no judgment. During the municipal elections in September, 23 schoolteachers, accused of belonging to the opposition, were brutally beaten and expelled from the teaching profession. Benjamin Obama Ngomo (PP/POC) was elected mayor. On November 10, Obiang Nguema named Silverio Baka Mba, ex-militiaman under Macías Nguema and judge at Kogo known for his violations of human rights, as the government's representative.

On October 21, 1996, after Eyi Mensui's transfer to the Ministry of Transport and Communications, Nvono Akele Avomo became general secretary of the Ministry of Education. The same day, Baka Mba arrested two members of the CPDS. See also Abeso Ondo, A.; Convergency for Social Democracy; Ebendeng Nsomo, M.; Edjang Angue, M.; Education; Ela Owono, F.; Elections; Esono Mika, P. J.; France; Hanna, S.; Human Rights; Kogo; Mba Ndemesogo, D., Mbenga Ndong, V.; Mikomeseng; Moto Nsa, S.; Ndongo Bidyiogo, D.; Nguema Esono, F.; Nguema Sema, A. M.; Nkuku Oye Nsue, A.; Nsue Mokuy, A.; Ondo Esono, L. A.; Parliament; Progress Party; Public Health; Sima, A.; Sports; Terror; Guineo-Spanish Union of Lumberers; Victims.

NIGERIA. Contacts between Fernando Po and Nigeria have existed since prehistoric times. Under the Pardo Treaty (1778) the whole Niger Delta belonged to Spain, in particular Bonny River and Río Gallinas. Various British expeditions left from Fernando Po to conquer Nigeria-Laird, Lander, Oldfields, and later in 1851 the Conquerors of Lagos under Beecroft. From 1860 to 1875, Pellón y Rodríguez still confirmed that a large part of the Niger Delta belonged to Spain, but like Germany and France farther south, the United Kingdom evicted Spain during the second half of the 19th century. During the Second World War, some Spanish authors suggested Spain annex Nigeria.

At the end of the 19th century, Nigerian laborers (the "Lagos") worked in Fernando Po cocoa plantations. Before the First World War, the Nigerian authorities accused the Spanish of organizing slavery, through the illegal traffic of labor, leading to patrolling by the British Admiralty of the seas between Fernando Po and Nigeria. Under Governor Barrera during the Second World War, the British imposed a blockade of Fernando Po and Río Muni, as Madrid's neutrality seemed suspicious to them. Nigerian claims over Fernando Po seemed to be an inheritance of British imperialism.

After the interruption of the Liberian manpower supply, in 1930, the arrival of Nigerian workers was resumed together with that of Cameroonese. But in 1941, Spanish Guinea recruited 10,000 laborers from Nigeria. In 1942, an agreement was signed between Spain and the British administration of Nigeria for the supply of manpower, with 36-month contracts. Since 1951 the British-Spanish Employment Agency in Calabar was in charge of this recruiting. In 1957, a Nigerian delegation visited Fernando Po. The mass arrival of Nigerians (English speaking, Protestants) strongly modified the social structure of the island.

In 1960, at the time of their country's independence, the Nigerian workers' agitation caused about 20 expulsions. Since then various Nigerian trade unions have been claiming the annexation of Fernando Po by their country. During the Biafra war, Santa Isabel was used from 1968 to 1969 as an air base for relief flights of the International Red Cross. But at the end of January 1969, a few months after Equatorial Guinea's independence, Foreign Affairs Minister Ndongo Miyone ordered the interruption of these flights to preserve his country's neutrality. The Ibo workers' dissatisfaction, increased by the suspension of their salary transfers ordered by Macías Nguema, caused major upheavals in the Nigerian colony, and this caused Macías Nguema to remain in Río Muni for some time.

At that time he started his violent anti-Spanish campaign that provoked the departure of 7,000 Spaniards. In 1970, about 70,000 Nigerians lived in Equatorial Guinea. Between 1970 and 1971, at least 95 of them were murdered in Fernando Po for having dared ask for their overdue salaries. On December 30, 1971, a new labor convention was signed in replacement of the 1963 one, including salary improvements. Within the framework of OAU assistance plans to Equatorial Guinea, Nigeria sent television and radio technicians. In 1972, about 20,000 Nigerians left Equatorial Guinea, but the same year a new convention brought in 15,000 new workers. Due to bad treatment, the recruiting of laborers was suspended in 1975.

In September 1975 some staff members of the Nigerian Embassy were bothered in public by the Juventud en Marcha con Macías. On January 8, 1976, National Guard soldiers killed 11 Nigerians in the embassy gardens. The withdrawal of Nigerians started as of January 11 by air and by sea, directed by Col. Garba, federal commissar for foreign affairs. About 26,000 Nigerians were transferred to camps created for them in the River State. Fernando Po was quite paralyzed and its cocoa economy severely hit. In Nigeria, the Trade Union Congress pushed the government to annex Fernando Po. In 1976 the Nigerian government granted $300 million (Nigerian) for the reinstallation of the Nigerian workers returning from Guinea; each of the country's 19 states was invited to put 3,000 hectares at their disposal.

Obiang Nguema's and Maye Ela's attempts to obtain some manpower from Nigeria after the 1979 coup were met with a categorical refusal by the Nigerians, who insisted that compensation would have to be paid to the 26,000 Nigerians who had to be evacuated in a military operation in 1976 before any discussions on this question could be begun with Equatorial Guinea. These negotiations suffered a further setback in August 1981 after an official of the Nigerian Embassy in Santa Isabel had been beaten up by the security services. In November 1981, however, agreement was reached on fishing rights in the territorial waters of both countries. The Belgian "Société Africaine de Cabotage" began a shipping service between Equatorial Guinea, Port Harcourt, and Lagos in August 1982 with twice monthly sailings.

On October 12, 1982, the Nigerian vice-president, Alex Ekwueme, attended the 14th Independence Day celebrations in Santa Isabel and opened a Nigerian consulate in Bata. In 1985 some 500 Nigerians were still working in Equatorial Guinea, but in February of that year again had to resort to an evacuation exercise repatriating 200 workers from Fernando Po. The Nigerian News Agency (NAN) stated in February 1985 that Nigerians worked in Equatorial Guinea like slaves. In December 1986, the nguemist government borrowed 5 million naira from Nigeria (US $750,000 approx.) to help finance the conference of the UDEAC countries to be held in Equatorial Guinea. There is still an undercurrent of irredentism in Nigeria in respect of Fernando Po. In February 1987, Nigeria and Equatorial Guinea signed a military assistance treaty.

In May 1988, the arrival in Equatorial Guinea of five South Africans led to rumors of military intervention against Nigeria. A violent press campaign in Nigeria again mentioned its claims over Fernando Po. This escalation of tension led to troop displacements from Río Muni to Fernando Po. The minister of foreign affairs, M. Nguema Onguene, visited Lagos in order to defuse the situation. The forces present were as follows: Equatorial Guinea, 2,000 troops; Nigeria, 90,000 troops.

Nigeria offered Equatorial Guinea a Polyclinic of 52 beds in the capital, a school with 11 classes, and 13 university scholarships in order to replace South African aid. Nigeria was mainly trying to contain French expansion. Towards the end of June 1988, Equatorial Guinea protested to the United Nations, accusing Nigeria of interference in its internal affairs.

In November 1989, Nigeria opened a credit of $1.3 million, over 10 years, for trade with Nigeria. In December, 35 Equato-Guinean students entered Nigerian higher institutes.

In October 1990 a contract ensuring all internal flights in Equatorial Guinea as well as flights to Lagos and Calabar for Concord Airlines was signed by Obiang Nguema and Moshood Abiola, President of the Nigerian company. But the project fell through. On December 11, President Babangida paid an official visit to the country. In 1991, Nigeria was Equatorial Guinea's second largest client. Another agreement was signed with Concord Airlines; this one failed too.

In 1992, Heriberto Mikó was named ambassador to Lagos. In March, the ambassador of Nigeria, John K. Shinkaiye, protested at the arrest of about 20 nationals, and at the cases of torture. In March, Obiang Nguema and his wife paid a private visit to Nigeria. Interviews with General Babangida took place at Abuja. Nigeria announced various educational and health projects. But the final communiqué remained silent over the question of labor, which the Nguemists want to discuss. Shortly afterwards, the military attaché David Eyema Angüe Osa was arrested at Lagos for trafficking 32 kgs of cocaine. Nigeria demanded the lifting of his diplomatic immunity. Obiang Nguema refused. He sent his son Teodorin, who brought him back to the country. In 1993 the construction of housing for Nigerian technical assistants was begun in the capital.

Border talks with Equatorial Guinea—which were taking place in Port Harcourt—were coming to an end in mid-1996. But the tension started again at the end of 1996. One must not forget that along with the Equato-Guinean offshore oilfields, exploited by Mobil, there are the Nigerian oilfields exploited by the French Elf Aquitaine.

In August, 16 Nigerians carrying false passports made in Equatorial Guinea (probably obtained from the police mafia in Malabo) tried to emigrate to Spain through the Iberia flight. Malabo refused to take them back, and they finally were sent to Lagos. This affair led Spain to decide thereafter to refuse visas from Equatorial Guinea.

The Report on Human Rights Practices of the U.S. Department of State to the Congress (April 1996) stated: "Several thousand citizens of Nigeria and Ghana reside in the country. Most are small traders and business people who are harassed and persecuted by the police." Since 1996, the Nguemist Mba Ndong has been ambassador to Nigeria.

The two countries agreed to settle their problems on the basis of the Convention on the Rights of Sea of the UN (1982). As for the border issue between the two countries, EG obtained the mediation of the Multilateral Investment Guarantee Agency (MIGA) of the World Bank. On August 31, 1996, the negotiations between the two countries were over but still needed to be ratified by the two governments. In September 1997, two Nigerian tradesmen were killed in their pirogue by coast guardsmen. Other Nigerians were killed in 1992 and 1995. The president of the Association of Nigerians in Equatorial Guinea, Cosmas Tanko Ogbudu, asserts that his compatriots were badly treated, despised, and treated as slaves, although Nigeria granted important technical aid: International School, Añisok Hosptal, 10 Peugeots, furniture for the Supreme Court, military training, etc.

Due to the attacks on soldiers by young masked Bubi in the beginning of January 1998, which was said to be the work of Nigeria, many Bubi were arrested on the island of Fernando Po. On February 10, 1998, the News Agency of Nigeria (NAN) announced that several hundred Nigerians had been arrested in Equatorial Guinea, information that was published by the *Lagos Daily Champion,* which spoke of 700 bodies buried in a communal grave. On the 12th, the Nguemist government denied this charge. The Nguemist consul in Calabar was Antonio Bibang Nchuchuma. In September 1998, Obiang Nguema discussed regional security matters and bilateral issues with General Abubakar.

Since 1984, Nigeria has trained 1,800 officers, of whom 180 trainees were from EG, Niger, and Zimbabwe.

Ambassador of Equatorial Guinea in 1998: Antonio Mba Ndong.

See also Akonibe; Aviation; Biafra; Bikomo Nanguande, S. P.; Borders; Cocoa; Concord Airlines; Customs Union of the Central African States; Dougan, A. S.; Drugs; Education; Engonga Motulu, M.; Eyama Angüe Osa, D.; Fernando Po; Fisheries; Germany; Labor; Micha Nsue Nfumu, J.; Mikomeseng; Moto Nsá, S.; Navigation; Nepotism; Nguema Ela Mangue Ndong, G.; Nguema Nguema Onguene, M.; Obiang Nguema, T;, Okenve Mituy, F.; Oyono Nsue, L.; Petroleum;

Police; Radio; Rwanda; Shinmkame, J.; South Africa; Spain; Teibiale Sipoto, J.; United Kingdom

NINJAS. Obiang Nguema's political police. These 300 men wear black uniforms and weapons provided by France. Various opposition groups announced that after the elimination of Nguemism, the Ninjas would be judged. The population calls them "the guards of the beast."

The ninjas are often recruited when they are very young, as early as 13. They have partially replaced the majority of Moroccan troops that were the presidential guards, and live in the Moroccan military camp named Rabat. But they also guard some of Nbiang Nguema's properties, such as the residential compound of Abayak, close to Malabo, where the staff of Mobil Oil and Theodorín Nguema Obiang live.

See also Army; Convergency for Social Democracy; "Democratic" party of Equatorial Guinea; France; Nguema Owono, S.; Police; Post Offices; Refugees; Siale Bilekia, S.; Terror; *Verdad, La;* Young Torches

NKA ESONO NSING, Martin. Born 1945. Fang from Mongomo. He is said to be anti-Spanish and Obiang Nguema's handy man. In 1985 he was authorized to buy the 451-hectare agricultural estate Liviano Vaz Serra, at Sacriba, for FCFA 8,743,437. In 1986, he owed the Guinextebank FCFA 8,019,000. On October 16, 1990, he became joint general secretary to the president with ministerial rank. At the ministerial reshuffle of April 8, 1996, he became general secretary of the ministry for information.

NKA MANENE NVONO, Carmelo. An Esangui from Mongomo. Ambassador to the United Nations, New York, from 1980 to 1983.

NKILI NZE, Nemesio. From Ebebiyin. Journalist trained in Spain in 1976. He was secretary of state for information in 1980–1982, and then director of the national radio in 1983–1984. In 1984–1985 he was director of television. He was named delegate for information, tourism and culture for the continental region in 1986. From 1987 he again became director of television. On April 8, 1996, he was named secretary of state for information. He is no longer a member of the government after the ministerial reshuffle of January 1998.

NKIMI. Locality in the Central-South Province of Río Muni. See Ngomo Nfumu, N.

NKOGO, Salvador. Sergeant. By summer a sometimes bodyguard of the first lady of Obiang Nguema. Arrested in the attempted coup d'etat of July 18, 1996.

NKOGO ONDO, Eugenio. From Bibás (Akonibe). Born 1944. Ph.D. in literature (Complutense University, Madrid) and postdoctoral studies at the Sorbonne (Paris). Professor at the University of Ghana (1979–1980), and researcher at the Universities of Delaware and Georgetown (Washington, D.C., 1980–1981), and later associate professor at the University of León (Spain, 1981–1982). As a philosophy teacher, he worked in the teacher's training school of the University of León. Upon the closure of this school, he moved to the "Padre Isla" secondary school in León. He continued his research activities. In 1993, he publicly suggested that the OAU or the UN help replace Obiang Nguema. He has published several books on philosophy and one novel.

NKO IBASSA RONDO, Andrés. Combe from Rio Campo (Punta Mbonda). Born in 1930. Participated in March 1969 in the creation of the Milicia Popular (Popular Militia). Named minister of economy in 1972, succeeding Kuga Ebombebombe, he was deprived of his office in 1976, charged with helping the director of the Central Bank, Buendy Ndongo, to misappropriate a million dollars. He was imprisoned along with the cashier of the National Treasury, Victor Bonkaka, and another high official of the bank, M. Nkoui. In September 1979 he was nominated director-general of the Central Bank. On December 8, 1981, Obiang Nguema promoted him to minister of finance, that is, the position that he had held under Macías Nguema. As one of the pillars of Nguemist power, he participated in the Akonibé constitutional commission that consolidated Obiang Nguema's dictatorship. In addition to this he was made personal adviser to Obiang Nguema in 1985 for finance and economic planning. In late 1985 he acquired the Pradesa Company's agricultural estate. In 1986 he was replaced as the head of the Ministry of Finance. In 1998, he was retired and living in the village.

NKUE. Locality situated along the Bata-Ebebiyin road, 103 km from Bata. China finished building a road from Nkué to Mongomo. Since 1929 the Oblate Sisters have been working in Nkué taking care of orphans and lepers. Since 1963, Nkué is the headquarters of the Oblates' general government. Until the Emergencia a priests' training college existed in Nkué.

NKULU OYE NSUE, Antonio. Fang from Bebewele-Eseng (Niefang). Born in Yebekoan. Cousin to Antonio Nkulu Asumu, director of the central services of the president of the executive, secretary to the National Electoral Committee, and a leading member of the PDGE. An official in the civil cabinet of the president. In 1991 he underwent training in public administration in Argentina. In radio interviews, he made Nguemist propaganda. Upon his return, he became secretary of the PDGE in the capital.

In March 1993, he became secretary of the new Liberal Party led by Bikomo Nanguande. Shortly afterwards, he joined the Partido del Progreso, and then the Liberal Democratic Convention of Nsue Mokuy. In January 1994, by decree 19, he became general secretary of the Ministry of the Interior. During the ministerial reshuffle of April 8, 1996, he became general secretary of the Ministry of Public Administration and Administrative Reform.

NOBLE AFFILIATES Inc. American petroleum company (Ardmore). Owns Samedan of North Africa Inc. It holds 30% of the Mobil consortium for the Alba deposit. See also Atlantic Methanol Production Corp.; Petroleum.

NOMECO (US CMS Energy Nomeco). This company furnished the Nguemist state with schoolbooks and financed anti-malaria campaign.
See also Petroleum.

NON-AGGRESSION PACT. In 1996, such a pact was signed between Congo, Cameroon, RCA, Gabon, Equatorial Guinea, and Sao-Tomé–Principe (but it will only become effective when it has been signed by a seventh country).

NORRIS, Chester, Jr. Ambassador of the United States from 1987–1991. President of the petroleum company Walter International. Obiang Nguema received him several times from 1994 and received several gifts from him. See also Petroleum.

NORWAY. From 1993 Den Norske Stats Oljeselskap AS joined Walter International, British Petroleum, CONOCO, in a pool for the exploitation of the petroleum resources of Fernando Po. United Meridian Co. collaborated with the drilling companies Wilring (Norway) and Sedco-Forex (France). But Norway had just withdrawn from Equatorial Guinea, in a show of disapproval for the dictatorial Nguemist regime. The Norwegian Church Aid assists the Council of Protestant Churches in Equatorial Guinea.

NOSTI NAVA, Jaime. Spanish agricultural expert, who has headed the Dirección de Agricultura in Equatorial Guinea since the Second World War. He is an outstanding expert in Guinean agriculture and in natural and human environment. Between 1940 and 1961 he published some 75 books and articles on agriculture, economy, and society in Equatorial Guinea.

NOTO, Lucio A. see Mobil Corp.

NOVAIS TOME, José Antonio, b. 1925. Spanish journalist and writer, former correspondent of the French newspaper *Le Monde*, correspondent of *Diario de Noticias* (Lisbon and *Oestado* (Brazil). He criticized García Trevijano's activities around 1968–1969. The latter reported on Novais's participation in the group of speculators who had created the fictitious Profinanco in order to convince Macías Nguema to create a Central Bank with nonexistent private funds. At the end of 1968 Novais prepared a document for Macías Nguema entitled "Promotion Campaign of the Equatorial Guinean Republic before international opinion and of its President H. E. Don Francisco Macías Nguema." Novais seems to have assisted the International Red Cross Committee in Equatorial Guinea at the time of the Biafra affair. Threatened with death by rightist movements around 1970, he was a victim of assault and battery in Madrid, on December 9, 1977.

NSANG ANDEME, Jose Antonio. Fang from Mikomeseng. Born February 2, 1967, in Akam-Oyec (Ebebiyin). Secondary studies in Malabo. University studies at the Universidad Complutense (Madrid). Graduate in political sciences in 1992. He earned a master's degree in international cooperation in 1996. Subject of his thesis: "Democracy and Human Rights in the Politics of Cooperation for the Development of the European Union and Spain with Equatorial Guinea" (in Spanish). From 1992 to 1994, a civil servant in Equatorial Guinea for the Program for Structural Adjustment. In 1993–1994, professor of law at the Law School of the UNED, in Santa Isabel.

In January 1996, he got a scholarship for research work from the Universidad Complutense, and trained in the International Cooperation Section of the Spanish Ministry of Foreign Affairs. As of September 1996, he has been a member of the follow-up team at Price Waterhouse.

NSANGAYONG (Esang-Ayong). Locality of the district of Mongomo. See Marías Nguema, F.; Obiang Nguema, T.

NSE NFUMU, Agustin. Fang from Anisok. Born May 18, 1949 (of a Cameroonian soldier who was with German troops during the First World War). Trained in Cairo to be a diplomat under Macías Nguema. Chief of protocol of Foreign Affairs since 1974. After six months in exile in Cameroon, he returned to his post under Obiang Nguema, from August 1979. In 1980 he became director of protocol. In the January 24, 1992, "transitional" government, he became vice-minister of foreign affairs, in charge of the French language. As a member of the Administrative Council of the INSESO, he earned 150,000 FCFA per month. Since December 22, 1993, he has been minister for culture, tourism and the French language. In October 1995, he entered the managing committee of the Association of Obiang Nguema's well-wishers.

In the January 8, 1996, ministerial reshuffle, he retained his ministerial post along with the post of government's spokesman. During the February 25 Presidential election, he acknowledged rigging, but later went back on his word and denied it.

At the ministerial reshuffle of April 8, 1996, he became the director for diplomatic and protocol affairs. In May, he simultaneously appeared as the president of the publishing company (Sogedisa) of a new periodical: *La Gazeta de Guinea Ecuatorial.*

He was secretary general of the PDGE, commissioner for the Lisbon Exhibit of 1998. The assistant-commissioner was Candido Muatemémá Rivas (Equatorial Guinea did not participate in the exhibit). In the 1998 government, he became minister of culture, tourism and francophony.

On August 11, 1998, Obiang Nguema appointed him permanent representative for Francophony.

This definition of the Nguemist system is attributed to Nse Nfumu: "The degree of power an individual holds in Equatorial Guinea is proportional to his capacity to infringe the law without any consequences." See also Seriche Bioko.

NSENG ESONO NVE, Eustaquio. An Esangui, born in Nzang-Ayong (Mongomo), nephew to Macías Nguema and cousin to Obiang Nguema. Commander, trained in Zaragoza, just like his cousin. Member of the clan from Mongomo.

In late November 1992, at the trial of the Spanish nationals Vilarrasa and Hanna, he was the prosecutor of the military court. Apart from his attacks against the Spanish Cooperation and the consulate, he demanded 30 years imprisonment and a fine of FCFA 212 million. He was promoted to commander.

Upon becoming a judge of the Supreme Court of Justice, he was one of the two prosecutors at the summary trial of Moto Nsa and a dozen military personnel, in a court composed mainly of members of the Clan from Mongomo, in April 1995. During the second trial against Moto Nsa, he again was a prosecutor. In November, F. Ondo Obiang and B. Nguema Esono, members of the clan from Mongomo, but dissidents of the PDGE, made it known that Nseng Esono Nve, at the head of a commando unit, had been ordered to liquidate them. Ondo Obiang and Nguema Esono briefly took refuge in Gabon. In the April 8, 1996, government, he became secretary of state for national defense. He was said to continue to belong to the Supreme Court of Justice. He is no longer a member of the government since the ministerial reshuffle of January 1998.

NSE NSUGA, Carlos see Asecna

NSE OBIANG, Gabriel, Cap. see Army

NSI MBA, Manuel. Fang. Since 1975, vice-minister of the Youth Department and of departments directly depending on the head of the republic. He was executed in 1976 along with Father José Esono and Buenaventura Ochaga in connection with the arrest of a hundred senior officials by Obiang Nguema.

NSOBEYA EFUMAN NSUE, Santiago (sometimes spelled Zue Beya Fuman). From Añisok. Fang; brother of A. Ndongo Nsabeya. A consular official, trained in Egypt. Under Macías Nguema and Obiang Nguema, he was joint chief of protocol of foreign affairs. In 1981, he became director general of protocol. In 1993, he became ambassador to the president for protocol missions. He is a member of the Administrative Council of the INSESO, with FCFA 150,000 in monthly earnings. The same year, he became a chargé d'affaires in Madrid. He was interim ambassador after the recall of ambassador Esono Ondo who was involved in a drug scandal. On November 21, he was elected parliamentary deputy, as a member of the PDGE. Since then, he has been writing letters to the Spanish press to protest against "derogatory" information about the Nguemist regime. On September 27, 1994, he was named ambassador to Spain.

Upon the arrest of the secretary of the CPDS, in late March 1996, and the torture inflicted by the senior chief of police at Bata D. Nguema Eyi who was a relative of Obiang Nguema's, Nsobeya protested by fax to the Spanish minister of foreign affairs and to the press at their presentation of this affair. He kept his function in 1998.

NSOK NSOMO (loc.) see Nsomo

NSO MANGUE, Maria Carmen see Convergency for Social Democracy

NSOMO. Fang tribe in Cameroon and Equatorial Guinea. It possesses the skull of the mythical Fang warrior chief, Mbo-ba, which was said to have the virtue of rendering its possessor invincible. Mbo-ba was known for his intelligence; he formed a Fang empire extending from Cameroon to the Congo. In the spring of 1992, Obiang Nguema—fearing for his power—negotiated with the Nsomo chiefs for obtaining this skull. It was refused to him.

The government's representative to Nsok Nsomo, Lucio Anseme, was almost illiterate. An automobile driver, he was married to a relative of Obiang Nguema's and entered presidential security. His violence against the opposition was well known. In the municipal elections of September 1995, Vicente Obama Ondo Ada was elected mayor (PDGE)

NSONO OKOMO, Martin. From Ebebiyin. International lawyer, trained in the USSR and married to a Russian. Member of the ANRD. He was elected its secretary-general at the 4th extraordinary Congress in Madrid in August 1983, succeeding Eya Nchama who had been secretary-general since 1978. Under his mandate the ANRD was torn by internal dissention. Nsono Okomo died in Paris in August 1985. He was replaced by S. Mba Mombe.

See also Dougan Beaca, J. D.; Mokong Onguene, C.; National Alliance for Democratic Restoration (ANRD).

NSUE, Manuel, Dr. see AIDS

NSUE ALENE, Hilario. From Nsok-Nsomo. Brother of Segismundo Nsue Alene. Minister for planning and development of Obiang Nguema. In 1994, Obiang Nguema benefited from the demands for structural adjustments to liquidate government officials who were also political adversaries, including Hilario Nsue Alene, Enrique Matogo, minister for civil service, Manuel Nse Nsogo, director of presidential protocol, as well as a number of professors and doctors, mostly Bubis.

NSUE ALENE, Segismundo. Born 1946, at Nsok-Nsomo. Studied in Spain, in 1974. Younger brother of Hilario Nsue Alene, former minister for planning and development. Head of Obiang Nguema's press bureau in 1995. At the ministerial reshuffle of April 8, 1996, he was appointed director general of presidential press relations.

NSUE ANGUE OSA, José. Fang Ntumu from Ebebiyin. Born in 1928 (?). Social worker. Member of the MUNGE, he was a member of Parliament during autonomy. Simultaneously he sat in the Spanish Cortes and took part in the Constitutional Conference where he was part of the Secretariado Conjunto. In the October 1968 government he was named minister of national education. Early in 1972 he was replaced by Eñeso Neñe. Named ambassador to Ethiopia in 1973, he had been poisoned by Macías' sbirros at the end of 1976. In March 1981, his widow, María, was appointed technical director of the State Secretariat for Women's Affairs. However, by December of that year she was relieved of the post. Thereafter, she went to Madrid to study journalism and is becoming known for her poetry and a novel, *Ekomo*.

NSUE ELA EYANG, Pedro. An Esangui from Mongomo. In 1978 he was posted to the embassy in Madrid as counsellor. Exile circles suspect him, in collaboration with Oyono Ayingono, of being responsible for the disappearance of 2,500 gold coins from the Madrid Embassy. It is also alleged that he made a lot of money through the sale of whiskey.

In 1980 he was put in charge of the European desk of the Ministry of Foreign Affairs at Santa Isabel. It was at this time that he disclosed the drug scandal involving the wife of the ambassador to Spain, the Esangui Owono Asangono. On January 23, 1983, he witnessed, without any qualms, the breach of diplomatic privilege in the opening of the Spanish diplomatic pouch in the ministry. In December 1982 he was put in charge of cultural and consular affairs. He is persona non grata in Spain for having threatened a Spanish police officer at the Barajas Airport in Madrid and for having attacked a Spanish journalist in Santa Isabel.

NSUE EWORO MICUE, Anselmo. From Evinayong. Holds a degree in pharmacology. Formerly of the URGE. Chief of the central pharmaceutical services in the Ministry of Health, and from late 1981 onwards, he was director of public health for Río Muni. In late 1982 he became director general of pharmacies and traditional medicine in the Ministry of Health, and in 1988, director of public health and sanitary planning. In the January 24, 1992, "transitional" government, he was minister for Health. He no longer figured in the December 22, 1993, government. In 1994, he became vice-minister for health. In the January 8, 1996, ministerial reshuffle he was replaced by Salomon Nguema Owono. He lives in Bata, where he runs a drugstore with his brothers.

NSUE MICHA, Norberto, d. 1976. Fang from Ebebiyin. He was a member of one of the first groups of Equatorial Guineans sent for military training in Spain in 1960. He was trained as a pilot. From 1968 to 1969 director general at the Department of Justice, he was then called upon to replace Oyono Eyanga as director of national security after the so-called attempted coup d'etat of A. Ndongo Miyone on March 5, 1969. At the beginning of 1972 he became civil governor and interim of Río Muni Province, during Eyegue Ntutumu's illness, then returned to security. In 1975 he became vice-minister of the popular constructions. In 1976, he was imprisoned in Malabo, then released. He was arrested again during the coup of Obiang Nguema and condemned to life imprisonment during the trial of Macías Nguema, in September. He was pardoned by Obiang Nguema soon after.

In 1998, he was a leading member of Union Popular.

NSUE MICO, Salvador. Fang of Añisok. Elected to the Río Muni Consejo Provincial on Macías Nguema's list in 1968, he later became ambassador to Spain. Recalled to Equatorial Guinea in 1973 he was imprisoned several times before being appointed vice-minister of soil cultivation in replacement for Ondo Alogo in 1975. He suffered a new arrest in 1978 after youngsters cleared a cocoa plantation to establish a soccer ground. Member of the PP.

NSUE NCHAMA, José Maria. Fang from Akonibe-Obuk. Son of Juan Micha Nsue Nfumu (political secretary of the Nguemist Partido Democrático), of the Obuk clan to which Obiang Nguema's wife, brother-in-law, and Eloy Elo Nve Mbengono belong. Holds a degree in law from Morocco. Claims to be an advocate, but does not hold the degree. Agent of the Criminal Investigations Department and member of the Nguemist militia.

In January 1994 he was lawyer judge at the Magistrate's court of the insular region. He was the one who had the president of the Progress Party, Moto Nsá, arrested in early 1995. The Obuk Eloy Elo Nve Mbengono, who had recently been dismissed as public prosecutor for having spoken on TV about corruption among judges, was arrested apparently for having mentioned J. M. Nsue Nchama.

NSUE NCHAMA, Rafael, d. 1969. Fang. Secondary school teacher. During autonomy, he was provincial deputy of Río Muni and deputy to the Asamblea General (Parliament). At the same time, he held the office of agricultural counsellor (minister). He was deprived of office in 1966 for having misappropriated several million pesetas and was replaced by Nvé Ondo Nchama. He was murdered along with his successor at the time of the Ndongo Miyone affairs, in March 1969. In September 1961, Spain decorated him with the grade of commander of the Order of Africa.

NSUE MOKUY, Alfonso. Fang born in 1948 at Mebe-Welel-Eseng (Niefang). Qualified to be a radio announcer in Spain. Appointed director of the press, radio and television service on March 16, 1981, under Moto Nsa. He was the main announcer on national radio and television programs. He was frequently summoned to the Nguemist authorities to prevent him from disseminating news about human rights or any references to democracy.

From 1992, Nsue Mokuy led an "opposition" satellite party of the PDGE, the Liberal Democratic Convergency (CLD). In May, the CLD was recognized by the regime. Nsue Mokuy co-signed the communiqués of the POC. The Spanish press portrayed Santos Pascual Bikomo as chairman; Nsue Mokuy became the counsellor for information, ideology and propaganda. In December, on TV, Nsue Mokuy accused the members of the POC of sabotaging democratization and of proposing violent action.

In late August 1993, Nsue Mokuy joined the Nguemists in condemning the Spanish government for interference in the political affairs of Equatorial Guinea. The opposition accused him of being a "puppet" of the regime. In October, his party, as well as the PL, UDS and the PP demanded that the government increase its financial support for the electoral campaign. All these groups breached the boycott of the POC, which Nsue Mokuy accused of delaying the democratic process. In the November 21, 1993, elections, the CLD did not obtain any seats.

In January 1994, Nsue Mokuy was part of the delegation of parliamentary representatives and leaders of the tame opposition given the task of informing France, Germany and Switzerland. In April 1995 he co-signed, along with other tame opposition parties, an anti-Spanish document presented on TV. He attended the second convention of the PDGE, at Bata, where he made a speech.

On April 8, 1996, he was named state secretary for housing and town planning. In the ministerial reshuffle of January 21, 1998, he was replaced by Ceferino Eburi Matta.

NSUE NDONG, Baltasar. Known to be an entertainment singer. At the ministerial reshuffle of April 8, 1996, he became the director general for Ibero-American culture. He proposed that the government hold, in 1997, a First International Convention for Artists and Writers for Peace.

NSUE NGOMO ABUMENGONO, Esteban, b. 1930. Fang from Añisok, Ebebiyin district. Trained as an administrative assistant at the Escuela Superior Indígena, he worked in various services of the colonial administration, then was named governmental delegate first in Mikomeseng in 1964 then in Evinayong in 1966. Founding member of the MUNGE, National delegate of the Youth Movement within the party, he joined Macías Nguema's Secretariado Conjunto during the Constitutional Conference and turned out to be a friend of García Trevijano. In 1968 he became president of the Consejo de la Republica (Senate) and simultaneously Macías Nguema named him governmental delegate in Bata. It was he who was entrusted with Ondo Edu's repatriation from the Gabonese border. After having participated in the creation of the Milicia Popular (Popular Militia), he was promoted to ambassador to Madrid in November 1969. Recalled for consultation in August 1970 he took flight and remained in exile in Spain where shortly afterwards he founded the FRELIGE with J. Mbá and B. Biyang, connected with former Spanish interests in Guinea. With the CEIA he allegedly participated in an attempt to overthrow Macías Nguema, which is why he was deprived of office and exiled to Andorra by Spain where, in 1972 he founded the ANALIGE with Bodipo, Mbá Nsué and J. Mangue. In 1974, he made a trip to Cameroon, with J. Mangue, in order to contact the exiles. Arrested at his arrival in Cameroon, he escaped to Switzerland with the help of the United Nations. Mangue was sequestered by Macías Nguema's agents, led to Equatorial Guinea, tortured and assassinated. Nsue Ngomo took up contacts with the Circulo Ecuato-Guineano and the Swiss Human Rights League.

Having participated in the creation of ANRD in 1974, he was however excluded from this movement in 1976 for inefficiency and for his connections with Spanish business groups. His three wives and 13 children live miserably in Madrid, according to his own statements to the press in 1977. Nsué Ngomo is mentioned as a member of the informal Grupo de Mayores. In 1978 he tried to found in Spain a front called Salvación de Guinea Ecuatorial. Its goal was the integration of all liberation movements (obliging each to abandon its individual activities) and the constitution of a government in exile. The main movement, the ANRD, has categorically refused any participation. In late 1979, he confirmed the existence of forced labor to the rapporteur of the Human Rights Commission.

At the time of the signing of the National Pact, on March 19, 1993, he made a speech in the name of the entire opposition, referring to the democratic transition as one "which will lead Equatorial Guinea to becoming the little Switzerland we have been dreaming about for years."

He was very active in the Protestant church of his country. In spring 1996 he was arrested by the governmental delegate of Mikomeseng, and tortured. Freed, he made his way to Madrid, to be taken care of. He died there October 6.

NSUE NGUEMA NSUGA, Mariano. Fang from Akurenam. Born December 12, 1937. Holds a degree in law, a degree in classical literature, and a master's in social security. A diplomat by career. Returned from exile after Obiang Nguema's coup.

In 1980 he was named director for European and American affairs in the Ministry of Foreign Affairs. In early 1981, he became the dean of the Order of lawyers, but he was relieved of his post in March. In December, he became joint secretary in the Ministry of Foreign Affairs. In late 1982 he became general secretary in the Ministry of Labor. In 1988, he became director of foreign affairs.

In 1989 he became general secretary in the Ministry of Foreign Affairs and Cooperation. On January 24, 1992, he became minister for justice and religion in the "transitional" government. In the November 1993 elections, he was elected deputy of the PDGE. In the December 22 government, he became minister with special responsibility for relations with the Parliament and for legislative coordination.

In early 1995, he was put in charge, along with M. Ebendeng, minister for defense, of the inquiry into the accusation of "judicial insecurity" made by Nve Mbengono. In June he replaced Eualalia Nvo Bela as the president of the Supreme Court. In the January 8, 1996, ministerial reshuffle, he retained his ministerial post, while remaining president of the Supreme Court. In the April 8, 1996, government, he was replaced in the ministry by A.-P. Oko Ebobo.

NSUE OBAMA ENGONO, Pedro. An Esangui from Añisok. Born 1946. Sub-lieutenant of the Juventud en marcha con Macías (Youth Marching), from

1979. Member of the CMS. He was entrusted with the post of commissioner for industry, mines and energy. In 1981 he was promoted to lieutenant. In 1991–1992 he had become a military attaché in Madrid. In 1992, his residence was sequestered by court decision, for nonpayment of mortgages. In 1993, he became a press attaché in Madrid, but was recalled to the country along with Ambassador Esono Ondo in October. Shortly afterwards he became a counsellor to the president.

In the January 8, 1996, ministerial reshuffle he became minister of public works, housing and urbanism, replacing Alejandro Envoro Ovono. In the April 8, 1996, government, he retained these posts.

Member of the nonlegalized party FDR, composed mainly of Esngui opponents, Nsue Obama Engono was arrested, and then was killed at the end of November 1998 in the Prison of Playa Negra, after severe torture. See Nguema Ela Mongue; Republican Democratic Force; Terror.

NSUE OTONG, Carlos, Fang born in Mbini, 1952. Holds a degree in literature from the Omar Bongo University, in Libreville (Gabon). He proved to be highly supportive of the Nguemists. He was hired by the CICIBA (Libreville) but was soon replaced by A. Olo Mibuy. He then became an opponent of the regime and tried in vain to obtain asylum in Switzerland.

He founded several nongovernmental organizations, which were never known to be active in any way. Upon becoming political secretary of the Social Democratic Convergency, he immediately proclaimed himself the coordinator of the entire Equato-Guinean opposition living in Gabon.

Since 1992, he has passed himself off as the president of the Gabon League for Human Rights in Equatorial Guinea. In this capacity, he participated in the first Convention on Equatorial Guinea organized in October in Spain by the journal *Tam-Tam*. He has now become a member of Obiang Nguema's PDGE, while simultaneously teaching in a high school in Libreville. He was dismissed in June 1998 for refusing an appointment in Bitam. He works as a tradesman.

NTEM see Campo, Río

NTUMU see Fang

NUNEZ DE PRADO, Miguel. Spaniard. Under the dictatorship of Primo de Rivera he became governor general from 1926 to 1931 at the time the Dirección General de Marruecos y Colonias started operating in Madrid. Thanks to a considerable special budget, he could start to occupy the whole of Río Muni since 1926, and to build roads after having introduced compulsory personal taxes.

NVE, Faustino. Ex-sergeant of customs, in the capital. See Coup d'etat of July 18, 1996.

NVE MBENGONO, Eloy Elo. Born 1944. His father was an Obuk. Was married to a Cameroonian. A lawyer. After the 1979 coup, he was nominated council for the defense at the trial of Macías Nguema in September and legal adviser to the Supreme Military Council. A fanatical opponent of democracy. In October 1982 he became minister responsible for legal affairs. Since May 1982 he had been a member of the Akonibé constitutional commission that drew up Obiang Nguema's dictatorial constitution. At the end of 1982 he was nominated presidential representative for parliamentary affairs. He was confirmed in this position in January 1986 with the rank of minister. He was arrested after the attempted coup of July 1986.

He is the father of the "Democratic" Party of Equatorial Guinea (PDGE), an imitation of the Francoist National Movement and of Macías Nguema's PUNT. According to him, Francoism is the ideal solution for Africa. In 1988, he praised Francoism in the Spanish press. According to the FELIGE, he was the worst of Obiang Nguema's enemies and that of the people, due to his antidemocraticism. In the January 24, 1992, "transitional" government, he was minister of state to the president of the government, in charge of relations with the Parliament and judicial affairs. Upon dissolution of the Parliament, he praised multi-Nguemism.

He did not figure in the December 22, 1993, government. Since January 1994 he has been attorney general. In January 1995, he exposed "judicial insecurity" and "generalized corruption," especially of judges, on TV. He was threatened by Manuel Nguema Mba, and removed from his post. It was in fact revenge for sanctioning the magistrate José María Nsué Nchama, a security agent and member of Obiang Nguema's militia, for corruption. In April, he was prohibited by Nguema Mba, under the threat of arms, from flying to Cameroon and Bata. After being placed under house arrest, he managed to flee to Cameroon, by canoe. Upon his return to the country, he tried to launch a new party (Fuerza Demócrata Republicana), but the Nguemist administration opposed it.

At the end of May 1997, when coming back from Spain, his passport was seized. He describes Obiang's regime as "a ferocious military dictatorship."

He is married to Regina Mañe. She was elected mayor of Bata on December 21, 1997. But Obiang Nguema did not allow her to carry out her office and asked her to be municipal advisor.

Since 1998, the couple have been refugees in Barcalona, Spain.

See also Justice; Fuerza Demócrata Republicana.

NVE NGU, Antonio Fernando. Fang, born on May 21, 1947, at Akonibe (Wele-Nzas). Went to secondary school in Bata. In 1964 he left for Spain for commercial studies in Murcia. He worked in Spanish companies until 1980. Professor of commerce studies and qualified in the field of management and administration of enterprises.

In 1980 he returned to the country and became administrative director of ENERGE. He was simultaneously director for International economic relations and cooperation. Between 1985 and 1986 he was the director of financial controls, and then worked at the BEAC. In 1987 he became director general of financial control and statistics. In September 1988 he replaced F. Inestrosa as minister for the economy and finance.

On August 15, 1989, he became minister with special responsibilities for economic affairs and finance. He belonged to the commission that prepared a new made-to-order constitution for Obiang Nguema. In the January 1992 "transitional" government, he was minister and spokesman. He accused the embassies of granting asylum to detractors, and the priests of inciting public unrest.

The Spanish government announced in early 1993 the suspension of three educational programs. Fearing denunciation of the Nguemist regime by the UN

Human Rights Commission, in Geneva, Nvé Nzeng announced the release of all political prisoners. He was part of the government delegation to the National Pact (February–March). In October, he admitted that the transitional government was null and void. The POC referred to this declaration to address an Institutional Proposal to Obiang Nguema.

In the November 1993 elections, he was elected PDGE deputy. On December 22, 1993, he became minister of state for transport, information and communications, and was also spokesman of government. In February 1994, Nve Ngu addressed threats to the Movement for the Self-determination of the Island of Bioko (Bubi). In March, following Obiang Nguema's denials of his declarations against Ambassador Bennet, he was given support.

Still as a spokesman of the Nguemist regime on March 2, 1995, Nve Ngu announced on TV, at the time of Moto Nsa's trial and two weeks before the Convention of the PDGE, that the United States and Spain were planning to invade Equatorial Guinea and to eliminate the 5,000 delegates of the party. Spain was said to be sending the aircraft carrier *Principe de Asturias*. The authorities and the Spanish press protested, and spoke of confabulations. In the January 8, 1996, ministerial reshuffle he remained the minister of state for transport, information and communications. In the April 8, 1996, government, he became minister of state for planning and economic development.

In 1997 he represented his country at the Central African States Development Bank.

In the government of January 21, 1998, he was minister of planning. Direct collaborator of Obiang Nguema, the opposition describes him as one of the pillars of Nguemism. In November, Moto Nsa and a few others accused him, along with Obiang Nguema and Julio Ndong Ela Mangue, in the Spanish Audiencia Naciional (High Court) of national and international terrorism, murders, and ritual crimes.

NVE NGUEMA, Eustaquio. Fang from Mongomo. Born in 1958, at Nzang-Ayong. Underwent military training at the Saragozza Academy. Commander of police. Joint chief of headquarters in the Ministry of Defense. In January 1994 he was named a judge in the Appeals Court of Fernando Po.

NVE ONDO NCHAMA. Augustin, d. 1969. Fang planter. From 1960 to 1962 he was a member of the Diputación Provincial (Assambly) of Río Muni. During autonomy he was minister of agriculture and forests, after the removal of Nsué Nchama in 1966. He did not take part in the 1968 elections. He was liquidated during the Ndongo Miyone affair in March 1969.

NVO BELA, Eulalia. From Ebebiyin. Born in Esabok-Eyeiñ. Holds a degree in law (Soviet Union). Wife of Marcelino Nguema Onguene, ex-minister for the economy and commerce. She was named Supreme Court judge and counsellor to the president of the government for health. From January to June 1995 she presided over the Supreme Court, after which she was replaced by Mariano Nsue Nguema.

NVO BIKIE MARTINEZ, José see Martinez Nvo Bikie, José

NVO MBOMIO, Fermin see Press

NVONO AKELE, Casto. From Ebebiyin. Born in Bikum-Eté. Administrative assistant (Escuela Superior). In the November 1993 elections, he was elected a PDGE deputy for the capital.

See also Banks.

NVONO AKELE AVOMO, Secundino. Fang from Bata. Born in 1947. A school teacher. A traitor, who denounced the attempted coup against Macías Nguema, in 1974, at Bata, which led to the execution of 27 patriots. Promoted director of the Instituto de Bata. In 1981, he was the regional delegate for primary and middle education for Río Muni.

In 1993, he became president of the PDGE for the coastal province. His brother, José Ncogo Mba, was president of the PDGE for the district of Bata. In January 1994, by decree 19, he became General secretary of the Ministry of Transports, Information and Communication. He retained this post in 1995. In the ministerial reshuffles of April 1998 and January 1998, he was confirmed in his post.

NVONO NKA MANENE, Carmelo, b. 1937. Fang from Amegong (Ebebiyin). Ambassador's deputy in Madrid in 1974-75, he publicly denied the existence of so-called victims of Macías Nguema's personal power and affirmed that there were no more than 15 prisoners in the country, which seems correct if one considers the incredible number of "suicides." He accused Catholic missionaries of subversion.

After assassination of Ateba Nsoh, ambassador to Gabon until May 1977, he was replaced by Ekua Miko. From June 1977 to August 1979, ambassador to Communist China. Since August 1979, member of Foreign Affairs Commission. From November 1981 to March 1982, ambassador to U.S. In March 1982, A. Mbá Ndong and his wife were condemned for drug trafficking. Shortly afterwards, Nvono was named general secretary of the Ministry of Industry and Commerce. He was later dismissed for embezzlement.

In 1992 he was a member of the central committee of the PDGE and General secretary of the Ministry of Industry and Mines. In January 1994, by decree 19, he became General secretary of the Ministry of Agriculture, Fisheries and Food.

During the ministerial reshuffle of April 8, 1996, he became general secretary of the Ministry for the Interior and Local Bodies. During the cabinet reshuffle of January 1998, he became secretary general of the Ministery of Employment and Social Security.

NVONO OKOMO see Nvono Akele Avomo, S.

NVO OKENVE, Enrique. Fang from Mikomeseng. Cofounder of the Cruzada Nacional de Liberación. After a Mañe's assassination by the Spanish Civil Guard, he fled to Cameroon. He was assassinated there by elements in Spain's pay, on November 21, 1959 (however, some sources say it was in Gabon). According to Ela Abeme, he was assassinated by his co-religionaires, Ateba Nsoh and Antonio Eworo. He was declared a national hero, with A. Mañe, and Martyr of Independence, in 1971. In 1973 the third PUNT Congress decided to erect a monument to him. The old ship *Romeu* given by Spain to Equatorial Guinea in 1972 was rebaptized *Enrique Nvó.*

NZAMBI MACHINDE, Fortunato. Native of Bata. Arrested for a short time in 1981, when he was working in the Ministry of Agriculture. He was moved in 1982 to become minister of industry and power. In 1986 he was appointed minister of education and sport. On January 10, 1985, he was authorized to buy the agricultural estate "Luis Sanz Escaned," at Basupo del Oeste, for bikwele 4,202,137. He did not figure in later governments. He is technical director of the lumber factory of the A.B.M. Company, of the Santy group, at Bata. In the September 1995 municipal elections, he was elected mayor (PDGE).

NZANG BEKA, E., Born 1946. From Mikomeseng. Studied at the Escuela Superior Indígena. In the ministerial reshuffle of April 8, 1996, he became director general for administrative coordination. First secretary of the embassy in Spain in 1983. Recalled to the country, he became technical director of administrative and consulor affairs of the Ministry of Foreign Affairs, replacing Primo Esono Mika. As of 1986 he was first secretary in the embassy in Moskow.

NZE ABUY, Rafael. Fanag, born September 1924 in Rio Benito. Ph.D. in missionology (University of Propaganda Fide, Rome). Became a member of the Claretian congregation in 1950. Trained with the José Esono Obama group in the Banapa Seminary and ordained on May 2, 1954. He is a cousin of Ndongo Miyone. On December 12, 1965, he was consecrated bishop and took over the Bata Diocese (Río Muni) on June 2, 1966, leaving the Santa Isabel Diocese (Fernando Po) to Gómez Marijuan. In 1972, Mgr. Nzé Abuy at the Vatican's request, left Equatorial Guinea for health reasons. He took refuge first in the Federal Republic of Germany, and recently in Rome (Italy). After a trip to the United States, he was named president of the nonprofit Friends of Equatorial Guinea Refugees, Inc. It was I. Obama who replaced Bishop Nzé Abuy as the senior church official in the country. After the 1979 coup, the Vatican asked him to return to Equatorial Guinea where he arrived on June 26, 1980. In 1982 he was named archbishop of Santa Isabel. A. Sima was made bishop of Bata and I. Obama bishop of Ebebiyin.

On December 8, 1986, he consecrated Mary Immaculate as the patron saint of Equatorial Guinea. In 1988, Nze Abuy was considered by the Spanish press as a mediator between the opposition and the government. During a sermon in the capital's cathedral in June, he hinted that he did not approve of the intrusion of the French language. In May 1991, a declaration of the Assembly of People's Representatives, read before Obiang Nguema and Nze Abuy, accused some priests of using the altar to criticize the political action of the government with destructive intentions. Obiang Nguema claimed that some priests were receiving funds from Spain in order to attack the government. Archbishop Nze Abuy qualified these accusations as "totally false and groundless." Being highly upset, Nze Abuy died in Madrid, following an attack of hepatitis on July 7, 1991.

NZE ANGUE, Amancio Gabriel. Fang born in 1953. From Akurenam. Architect after studies in the Polytechnic University of Madrid. General secretary of the Convergency for Social Democracy. Arrested and tortured several times. In April 1995 he was a candidate for the post of mayor of Bata.

As the sole opposition leader to fulfill the conditions of the electoral law, A. G. Nzé registered as a candidate for the February 25, 1996, presidential election.

The Electoral Commission run by the Minister of the Interior gave him a limited number of votes. In mid-March he was arrested and sent to the prison at Bata. On March 21 he was tortured for several hours by the chief commissioner of police, Diosdado Nguema Eyi, Obiang Nguema's nephew. Nguema Eyi prevented Nzé Angue from receiving any food. A relative who had just fed him received 50 cane strokes on his feet. Toward the end of March, Nzé Angue was released. His Toyota Landcruiser was confiscated and never returned.

When Placido Miko was arrested in Río Benito at the beginning of January 1997 by order of Obiang Nguema's cousin, Ndong Ona, Amancio Nzé declared: "This regime must not be judged on what it says, but on what it does."

In 1997 and 1998, Amancio Nzé suffered numerous humiliations by nguemists. At the beginning of November 1998, several leaders of the CPDS, among them Amancio Nzé, were imprisoned in Bata.

See also Convergency for Social Democracy.

NZE MBA, Alberto see Elections; Evinayong

NZENG, Eustaquio. Commander of police. In January 1994 he became a member of the Constitutional Court.

NZE OBAMA ANGONO, Pedro. On April 8, 1996, he was designated minister of public works, housing and town planning. In the ministerial reshuffle of January 21, 1998, he was replaced by Francisco Pascual Asue Obama, with the title of minister of public work and urban affairs.

NZI BINDANG, Salvador. Fang. Lawyer, until 1977, he seems to have signed on Macías's behalf the numerous death sentences. Actually refuged in Spain.

NZO, Tomás see Convergency for Social Democracy

NZO MANGUE, Maria Carmen see Convergency for Social Democracy

NZO ONDO, Juan see Convergency for Social Democracy

❖ O ❖

OBAMA, Cándido. Police commissioner in the capital. See Coup d'etat of July 18, 1996.

OBAMA OBONO, Ildefonso. Fang. Brother of Pascual Obama Asue. Claretian priest, trained in Banapa together with J. Esono and R. Nzé Abuy. He was secretary of the Bata bishopric, and after Nzé Abuy's exile he was frequently put under house arrest. He seems not to have left the Bata prison since June 1976, when he was imprisoned at the same time as his colleague L. Ondo Maye while Mgr. A. M. Ndongo was assassinated in prison, shortly after his arrival.

After the 1979 coup, he spent some time in Spain. In 1982, he was appointed bishop in Ebebiyin by the Vatican. Upon the death of Mgr. Nze Abuy, in 1991, I. Obama was promoted to archbishop. Since then, Mgr. Obama has distinguished himself with the silence he maintains over matters of human rights violations, and especially over the Nguemist exactions against priests and churches during the presidential elections in February 1996.

After the Bubi trial and while the trial of the leaders of Fuerza Democática Republicana was being held, Archbishop Ildefonso Obama refused to meet with President Obiang Nguema. On July 25, 1998, he denounced the fact that "catholic priests and nuns in Equatorial Guinea are victims of persecutions and bad treatment." In Ebebiyin and Mikomeseng (province of Kié-Ntem) priests must ask for authorization to minister their parish and celebrate mass; some of them are under house arrest and others are forced into exile. On August 3, in the cathedral of Malabo, Mgr. Obama called for "the respect of human dignity," and sent straightforward warnings to Obiange Nguema, rejecting the accusations concerning "the lack of goodwill" addressed to priests by the dictatorship. In mid-August, the archbishop, while celebrating the feast of the patron of the capital, and in front of Obiang Nguema, asked for "transparency" during the elections at the end of 1998. They must be "fair and peaceful to protect love, peace and unity among all the citizens."

OBAMA ASUE EYEGUE, Francisco Pascual. Fang from Kogo. Brother of Idefonso Obama Obono. A gymnastics teacher. After Obiang Nguema's coup d'etat he was appointed technical director of youth, physical education and sport, and at the end of 1982 became secretary-general of sport. In January 1986 he was appointed minister of trade and industry. In early 1987, his wife and his four sons died in an accident with a Spanish Hercules, at Bata. Towards the end of 1990 he was replaced by S. Obiang Bengono.

In the January 24, 1992, "transitional" government, he returned to power as minister for youth affairs and sports. He did not figure in the December 22, 1993, government. In 1994, he became minister general secretary to the president. In the

January 8 ministerial reshuffle, he retained this post. In the April 8, 1996, government he became minister of state in charge of youth and sports. At the end of June 1997, he replaced S. P. Bikomo Nanguande, who was dismissed as minister of information and propaganda.

In the January 21, 1998, government, he became minister in charge of civil engineering, housing and urbanism, and secretary general of the government.

OBAMA ELA, Antonio Maria. Born 1958 (?). From Añisok (Wele-Nzas). Aeronautical engineer trained in the USSR. Member of the CSDP, which allegedly expelled him in November 1995. Second vice-president of the Parliament. At the ministerial reshuffle of April 8, 1996, he became director general for transports and civil aviation. In the cabinet reshuffle of January 21, 1998, he became general director of transports and civil aviation.

OBAMA EYENE BINDANG, Jacinto. Fang from Mongomo. Born 1946, in Yenvam. Technician in territorial administration. In October 1982, he became general secretary of the Ministry of Justice and Religion. In the April 8, 1996, ministerial reshuffle, he was reinstated in this post.

OBAMA NDONG, Santiago see Bakale, C. ; Convergency for Social Democracy

OBAMA NSUE (alias Ncoá-Bidoló) see Akurenam

OBAMA NSUE MANGUE, Feliciano (also called Batho, a nickname he received due to the cruelty he practices, in bludgeoning victims; see Senior Officials Affair). Fang Esangui from Mongomo. Born on December 14, 1945, at Mongomeyen. Electrician by trade. As member of the Youth marching with Macías movement, he participated in the World Youth Congress, in New York, in 1974. Mbato was responsible for a number of rapes during his service with the organization.

In 1975 he was appointed state secretary for security within the Directorate-general of the Ministry of Justice and worked under the Creole Minister Okori-Dougan. He was subsequently made head of the internal policy section of the National Security, and was concurrently head of the PUNT, after the arrest and assassination of B. Ochaga on orders of Obiang Nguema. On the occasion of the senior officials' arrests in December 1976, he became notorious for the numerous executions also carried out on the orders of Obiang Nguema. He usually carried a cane with which to strike people, which gave rise to his nickname M'Batho, or stick.

In the spring of 1979 he became secretary-general in the Ministry of Foreign Affairs and director of the Security Service. Under Macías Nguema's dictatorship he was one of the principal torturers. Obiang Nguema, on coming to power, also nominated him as a member of the electricity commission. In January 1980 he was posted as first secretary to the embassy in Yaoundé, Cameroon, and was promoted to ambassador in March 1981. In May 1982 he took part in the Akonibé constitutional commission that laid the basis for Obiang Nguema's dictatorship. Some sources in the Spanish media maintain that he is aiming to overthrow Obiang Nguema.

In 1988 he was appointed deputy. On being sent to Annobón for some time, he drew attention to himself through violence and rape. In 1991, he lost his position as deputy and became a representative of the PDGE in Wele-Nzas. In the January 24, 1992, "transitional" government, he occupied the post of vice-minister to the president. He was also in charge of the central bureau of the party in the capital.

On December 22, 1993, he became vice-minister for foreign affairs and cooperation. In October 1975, he entered the managing committee of the Association of Well-wishers of Obiang Nguema. In the January 8, 1996, ministerial reshuffle, he was confirmed as minister with special responsibility for foreign affairs and cooperation. In the April 8, 1996, government he became counsellor to the president of the government for territorial administration in the Ministry of the Interior (in fact the Police). At the end of 1998, he kept his office.

See also Seriche Bioko.

OBAMA OBIANG, Angel see Convergency for Social Democracy

OBAMA OWONO, Nicolas see Akonibe

OBAMA OWONO NCHAMA, Jaime. From Mongomo. Born 1940. Sub-lieutenant trained in North Korea and Cuba under Macías Nguema. Also called Cien fuegos (hundred shots), because of his trigger-happiness. In 1981, he was promoted as lieutenant. In 1982, he became director general of materials and equipment in the Ministry of National Defense, in charge of ammunition. In 1990, he was promoted to colonel.

Decree 27 of January 1994 confirmed him as director general of logistics in the Ministry of National Defense. At the ministerial reshuffle of April 8, 1996, he retained this duty. He kept his office at the end of 1998. He is now called "Mil fuegos" (One thousand shoots).

OBIANG, Rafael see Social Democratic and Popular Convergency; Press

OBIANG ABOGO, Victorino. From Añisok. Holds a degree from the Soviet Union. In early 1994 he was named judge in the Court of Appeals of Río Muni.

OBIANG MANGUE, Luis. An Esangui from Mongomo, born in 1945. Nickname: Ebo Aki Kub (rotten egg). A schoolteacher. In 1983, Obiang Mangue became ambassador to Spain. He drew attention to himself with his vulgarity, especially with regard to the press. He was replaced in November 1986.

In 1993, he became a secretary in the Ministry of Foreign Affairs. By decree 17 of January 1994, he became director general of international organizations. Having become deputy of the PDGE in 1995, he was dismissed from his duties by Obiang Nguema in April 1996, and replaced by the minister of civil engineering, A. Envoro Ovono. Obiang Mangue publicly expressed his indignation.

In 1998, he remained deputy of the PDGE.

OBIANG MBA, Job, 1934?–1976. Fang from Ebebiyin district and a schoolteacher trained in Bata, then in Spain. He taught in Ebebiyin and from 1969–1976 was secretary general of the Ministry of Education. He was one of the rare educated persons of this ministry. An active member of the PUNT, he was among those arrested at the beginning of December 1976 in the Senior Officials Affair. He was killed in the Bata prison, along with practically all other educated persons of his ministry, including Minister Ochaga Ngomo, secretary general of the PUNT.

OBIANG MBE MEYE, Toribio. From Mongomo. Journalist trained in Spain. During Macías Nguema's dictatorship, he remained in Spain. Member of the rightist opposition party Pandeca. Back to his country after Obiang Nguema's coup, he became director of the revue *Ebano,* in May 1980. In December 1981, he was promoted director general for tourism in the Ministry of Industries, Commerce and Tourism. In May 1996, he became the director of a new periodical: *La Gaceta de Guinea Ecuatorial,* with Anacleto Olo Mebuy as a deputy.

OBIANG NDONG, Damaso. From the Ndong ethnicity, born in 1947. Diploma in political science. Diplomat trained in Italy. License in politics. Director of economic relations in the Ministry of Foreign Affairs.

In 1982, he became director of international organizations and of cooperation in the Ministry of Foreign Affaiars. In 1989, he became ambassador to Cuba. In 1991, he succeeded Maye Ela as a representative to the United Nations. The following quote was attributed to him and was made before the General Assembly and indicates the Nguemist attitude: "we have noted with sadness and a feeling of helplessness the importance accorded here to the human rights problems, in detriment of what should be, in our opinion, a priority and an imperative: poverty, misery, hunger, and sickness, from which nearly half the people of the world suffer." Towards the end of 1993, he was recalled to fulfill other functions in the Ministry of Foreign Affairs. He was dismissed in August 1998.

OBIANG NGUEMA MBASOGO, Teodoro. Born 1942. First of ten children. Fang Esangui from Acoa Kam, Mongomo district. Nephew of Macías Nguema. His father, like Macías Nguema's, was a Gabonese national. Obiang Nguema's father was born in Koss Esangui, and his mother at Abam Ebea, in the Gabonese district of Oyem. They came to Spanish Guinea in order to flee the poll-tax and settled down first in the village of Nanama Esangui, and later 6 km from Mongomo in a place he baptized with the fictitious name of Akoa-Kam Esangui. Obiang Nguema's mother was an Ebea, while Macías Nguema's was an Obuk. Obiang Nguema married Constancia Mangue Fang from Akuakam) in 1968. He attended secondary school in Bata, but completed his secondary education through evening classes (without results). From 1963 to 1965 he underwent military training at the Saragossa Military Academy, Spain. He returned with the rank of junior lieutenant. He then joined the territorial guards and was rapidly promoted to lieutenant. Once his uncle was elected president of the republic, Obiang Nguema was appointed military governor of Fernando Po and director of the Playa Negra prison. He then became directly involved in political repression and the expulsion of the representative of the UN Development Program, Marceau Louis, in 1973. In 1975 he was promoted to lieutenant colonel and became the aide-de-camp of the dictator Macías Nguema.

In 1976, he impotently witnessed the evacuation of 26,000 Nigerian laborers in a Nigerian military operation. In that year he was also responsible for the arrest of the last remaining cadres in the country, whom Macías had asked him to eliminate. At that time there was no money left in the treasury, but Obiang Nguema was able to live off the profits of the Hotel Bahia in Santa Isabel. At this time he told his cousin Oyon Ayingono that he was afraid of being lynched by the populace if Macías Nguema were to be overthrown. In the spring of 1979 one of his brothers was among the officers executed on orders of Macías Nguema; it was then that he began to prepare a coup with his cousins Maye Ela, Ela Nseng, and Mbá Oñana with military help from Morocco and Gabon. He was also assured of some diplomatic sympathy from Spain, France and the U.S.A. In July 1979, he evacuated his second wife and her children and on August 3, he overthrew Macías Nguema in what he described as the "Coup for Freedom." After the execution of Macías Nguema at the end of September, he proclaimed an amnesty for all political refugees overseas, implying that being a refugee was in itself a crime. In any event, very few refugees trusted Obiang Nguema's amnesty. He was in fact, accused of numerous crimes and particularly of having regularly attended torture sessions in the Playa Negra prison where some of his relatives were employed. From then on, Obiang Nguema governed with his relatives and his close relations, members of the army, at the head of a Supreme Military Council (Consejo Militar supremo, CMS, qualified by the population as "Con Mongomo Siempre," Always with Mongomo).

On October 11, 1979, he was sworn in as the second Esangui dictator-president. In December he received the King of Spain, Juan Carlos I, referring to him as "our King," though only the month before he had gone to Paris on a working visit which was the beginning of the country's absorption into the French orbit.

Obiang Nguema protects himself with 600 strong Moroccan guards. Between 1979 and 1980 he undertook trips to Cameroon, Gabon, and Spain. Besides chairing the Supreme Military Council, he concurrently holds the portfolio of defense, and military commissioner of Finance, as well as military commissioner and state secretary for information and tourism.

In April 1980, the 1973 constitution was abrogated and the 1968 constitution reinstated. However, in May 1982, Obiang Nguema set about drawing up a new constitution with the help of a group of old Nguemist hands under the chairmanship of the same Minister of Finance who had served under both Macías and Obiang Nguema. A referendum on this new document was held on August 15, 1982, which was approved by 139,777 votes with 6,149 against. The voters, however, had not been informed what the referendum was really about, nor that the proposed constitution had been condemned by international specialists and that an additional article made Obiang Nguema president for a further seven years. The International Commission of Jurists, as well as university professors, stressed that this new constitution paved the way for a new dictatorship.

Most of Obiang Nguema's ministers are Esangui and former officers of the "Juventud en Marcha con Macías" youth organization. In June 1980, he participated for the first time in the Franco-African conference in Nice. At home he rarely leaves his palace; when he does he is always accompanied by a strong armed escort. He made numerous appeals to the population to work hard in order to improve the economy, but the passive resistance that began under his uncle's earlier regime continued unabated. He obviously laid all the blame for the various evils on his uncle and sought to disengage himself from any responsibility for the genocide committed in the years 1969 to 1979. All those who know the situation well, however, see Obiang Nguema merely as the executor of Macías Nguema's old policies.

On January 31, 1981, the vice-president, Oyo Riqueza, decorated Obiang Nguema with the military Order of Merit in the name of the Supreme Military Council. In the spring of 1981, he used the fictitious coup orchestrated by Mba Oñana to gain control of the Exigensa company founded by Mbá Ada and others, and made himself the principal shareholder. In August 1981, while on a visit to Nigeria, he endeavored to persuade the Nigerian government to supply him with laborers, but they set a number of conditions, including the compensation due to the 26,000 Nigerian workers who had to be evacuated from Equatorial Guinea in 1976. In 1981 also, in a speech at Bata, he described his uncle Macías Nguema as an "envoy of the Devil, son of Lucifer, President of sorcerers." Shortly thereafter, he pardoned 29 Nguemists who had been sentenced at the same time as Macías Nguema. At that time the Spanish press let it be known that Obiang Nguema was aiming to have himself elected president for life, following in the footsteps of his uncle.

In early 1982, Obiang Nguema requested Spain to give him the skull of the Fang chief taken in the 19th century by Montes de Oca, and deposited in the Ethnological Museum of Barcelona. A delegation gave it to him on the occasion of the national holiday, October 12. In April, the dictator went on a tour of Kuwait, Saudi Arabia and Morocco, in order to obtain economic aid. He undertook also a series of missions to Paris, Rabat, and Yaoundé as well as to the Vatican. In a rating given by the French-language magazine *Jeune Afrique* of the 66 heads of state in the Third World, Obiang Nguema appeared in 53rd place. In that same year, Obiang Nguema purchased an apartment in Paris and built a villa in the Canary Islands.

In February 1983, Obiang Nguema advised the population to learn French. In August a former minister of agriculture and of health, Buale Borico, revealed, after having taken refuge in Spain, that Obiang Nguema had deposited large sums of money in Switzerland. Then, in June 1984, Obiang Nguema declared in a press interview that Equatorial Guinea was one of the countries that did not appear in the list of violators of human rights. However, the following year and again in 1986, the UN Human Rights Commission described the country as one where there were "flagrant and repeated" violations of human rights.

Following the precedent set by Macías Nguema, he took over the Ministry of Defense in January 1986 after having moved the incumbent Mbá Oñana to public works as minister. In July 1986, Mbá Oñana led a coup attempt against Obiang Nguema at a time when the latter was attending the July 14, national day celebrations in Paris (see Coup d'etat of July 1986).

On October 12, 1986, Obiang Nguema was promoted to the rank of brigadier general in Bata by the commanding general of the Spanish Military Academy of Saragozza in the name of the king of Spain. The total number of servicemen in the army, navy , and air force in Equatorial Guinea is around 1,550. On December 2, 1986, Obiang Nguema obtained a loan of 5 million Naira from Nigeria to finance the annual conference of the UDEAC that was held in Bata on December 18, since the treasury was empty and the government was not even able to pay the armed forces for the previous four months.

In May 1987 Amnesty International published a damning report on the activities of military tribunals and the passing of death sentences, which clearly showed the importance of the judiciary. The lack of separation of powers is confirmed by the fact that the courts are always presided over by military officers who concurrently hold ministerial positions in the Obiang Nguema government. In July, Obiang Nguema designated his first wife, Constancia Mangue, as presidential councillor for social affairs. On October 12, he liberated his relatives condemned after the 1986 coup d'etat to 28 months in prison. He created the Democratic Party of Equatorial Guinea, a unique party like former PUNT. Obiang Nguema and wife are involved in Guinextebank bankruptcy for $250,000. Obiang Nguema participated in the Franco-African Conference, in Nice, in December 1987; in the meantime, four ministers were arrested in Santa Isabel.

In June 1988, in an interview entitled "The people want me to continue," Obiang Nguema rejected multipartyism. He denied that citizens had fled the country for political reasons. "We recognise no Equato-Guinean as an opponent to the government, and cannot recognise any oppostion party." Those who had organized such parties outside the country did so, he claimed, to obtain grants from the ICRC or from Amnesty International. In September, at Paris, Obiang Nguema proposed to President Mitterrand that Equatorial Guinea enter the community of francophone countries. Upon his return, the dictator insisted that his officials learn French in order to be able to deal with the UDEAC. In late September, it was learnt that he made $60 for each of the 720,000 tons of toxic wastes deposited in Equatorial Guinea by a North American company. In October, he specified before the Spanish parliament that his request for entry into the group of francophone countries did not imply the abandonment of Spain. On the 20th anniversary of independence, in Bata, Obiang Nguema was elected president of the PDGE; at the closing of the first convention of the single party, he declared that Equatorial Guinea "was experimenting for the first time with her freedom, after eleven years of dictatorship" and "almost two centuries of indiscriminate and merciless exploitation by Spain." . . ."The Government of the Third [?] Republic was for the good of the people, and its motto was for a better Guinea." Some Spanish university graduates compared Obiang Nguema to Pinochet. The Donovan Report (IMF) considered Equatorial Guinea as "the second most corrupt country in the world," and thus converged with the opinion of Robert Klitgaard (World Bank), about the Nguemists, the Tropical Gangsters. In November, Obiang Nguema accused French and Spanish volunteers and traders of getting rich at the expense of the country. Obiang Nguema did business with the Santy Company, belonging to the Lebanese from the Canary Islands, S. Hanna. With his help, Hanna obtained FCFA 60 million from the Guinextebank.

In early 1989, Obiang Nguema returned to Spain. He obtained a 30% reduction of the debt, equipment and military advisors, as well as a promise to introduce a private bank. He accused the business circles in Equatorial Guinea (especially Fr. Roig Ballestros) of being adventurers responsible for a whole 1,500 million pesetas in external debt. In June the presidential election was held. All meetings of more than four people were prohibited. The Spanish press spoke of "self-proclamation." In his speeches, the dictator rejected "scientific materialism" and argued in favor of "capitalism" and the "Bantu civilisation;" but proposed neither a real political nor economic program, apart from a few promises. As the sole candidate, Obiang Nguema was reelected with 99.96% of the votes and asked the opposition to return and collaborate for reconstruction. He compared his reelection to the Soviet perestroïka. In early August, he declared amnesty for 15 political prisoners. In November, he held discussions with a Soviet delegation on the way to make a single party democratically credible.

In February 1990, Obiang Nguema sold land meant for the installation of a crude oil processing plant to Walter International. Shortly afterwards, his wife, Constancia Mangue, and his brother-in-law, Olo Mba Nzeng, minister for mines and energy, were arrested, accused of conspiracy. Constancia was placed under house arrest in her village; the national radio announced the withdrawal of the title "First Lady of the Nation." Olo Mba Nzeng was sent to the prison at Bata. This state of affairs did not last, as Olo Mba Nzeng returned each time in various governments—the ones in late 1990, in early 1992 and in late 1993 until 1998. In April, Obiang Nguema visited China, in defiance of the international boycott following the violence at Tiananmen Square. He renegotiated the debt and requested an increase in bilaterial aid. In June, he attended the 2nd Conference of the PMA. On August 4, he pardoned 13 prisoners. In early September, he went on a private visit to Nigeria. He was received by President Babangida, at Abuja. The discussions touched upon topics like the peace force in Liberia and bilaterial commercial relations. Upon his return, Obiang Nguema asked Spanish Prime Minister Felipe Gonzalez for help in finishing his law studies in the Autonomous University of Madrid; he was upset, because, having studied courses in the UNED, in Santa Isabel, the organization refused him its degree, as he had not passed the baccalaureat. On October 12, 1990, the dictator declared that "the monolithic system" is "the most viable political system" for his country. On October 16 a ministerial reshuffle took place. On October 29, in Bata, Obiang Nguema signed the contract giving domestic flights to the Nigerian private company Concord Airlines, which also received flights to Nigeria and the task of training of personnel (the contract was still nonoperational in 1993). In December, several of the Nguemist top brass were arrested. The Bank Bidgesa planned with the Brazilian financier Carlos Rocha, was supposed to be managed by Teodorín, the dictator's eldest son.

In early 1991, an unknown Italian foundation awarded a so-called Umberto Biancamano Prize to Obiang Nguema (supposedly named after a medieval lord). People in Santa Isabel mocked, saying: Obiangcapremio. The ambassador of Italy, living in Cameroon, refused to attend this farce. In March, at Libreville, Obiang Nguema presided over the seventh summit of the Economic Community of the States of Central Africa. In mid-June, he paid an official visit to Rabat. At the same time, it was said that he had begun militarizing the capital following the appearance of slogans on the roads, claiming democratic liberalization (see Convergency for Social Democracy). A number of arrests were made. In the face of these "threats," the regime resuscitated the Youth marching with Macías through the Young Torches, composed of 300 youth from Mongomo and its province Wele-Nzas, who were trained by French military counsellors. In July, he undertook a tour around the country, and declared: "The time has come to make way for freedom of expression," adding: "Political parties are not bad; what is bad is the lack of education and information." He made threats against those who may take political initiatives. In late August, the minister for foreign affairs, Santiago Eneme Obono, declared in Libreville that Obiang Nguema was refusing to hold a national conference. The conference was supposedly only to be called in case of a vacancy in power, which is not the case. He denied the existence of any political opposition in exile. In September a new advertisement appeared in *Jeune Afrique* (Paris) boasting about his regime and the "Biancamano Prize"; the sponsors of the dictator paid FCFA 60 million. On the occasion of the visit of Felipe Gonzalez, the Spanish prime minister, to Equatorial Guinea, between November 22-24, Obiang Nguema announced that before political pluralism, "the country has to satisfy certain conditions for the development of its political culture. The introduction of multi-partism always produces negative political effects which lead to disorder and convulsions." He maintained silence on the question of respect for human rights, and so did Gonzalez. Obiang Nguema stressed principally the increased level of Spanish aid. Obiang Nguema announced that there would soon be a general amnesty (the third in his region), "which will allow more than a thousand Equato-Guineans exiled abroad to return." Obiang Nguema compared himself in public to Adolfo Suarez and Valéry Giscard d'Estaing. Before Gonzalez, the dictator criticized Amnesty International and claimed that his praetorian guard from Morocco was indispensable, as he did not trust his entourage. But he added: "I am a charismatic leader of this people, and in myself a part of its [Equato]-Guinean heritage." Gonzalez declared that he had not come to give any advice. During the press conference, Obiang Nguema read a text on democratization, while leaflets with the questions to be asked circulated among the journalists. The press of Madrid stressed Obiang Nguema's talent at manipulating the Spanish authorities. In December, Obiang Nguema organized a second constitutional referendum, whose additional measure—ignored by the public—declared:

> Given that President Obiang Nguema has led the country for 12 years to an optimal level of political, economic, social and cultural development in an atmosphere of peace, justice, unity, tranquility, order, agreement, fraternity and national reconciliation, we hereby constitutionally decide that Obiang Nguema cannot be prosecuted, judged or called as witness before, during and after his mandate.

One again sees the influence of Pinocheist Chile. Moreover, the article necessitating at least 10 years of uninterrupted stay in the country for candidacy to the presidential election was rewritten, thus excluding the diaspora. With the new seven-year mandate, Obiang Nguema will have been in power for 19 years. The new constitution sets no age limit for the president; death alone can necessitate his replacement. In late November 1991, the Spanish professor of constitutional law Jorge de Esteban showed that "the regime of [Equatorial] Guinea is destined to function in a dictatorial manner with a constitutional facade; it is in fact an attempt to consolidate a judicial pantomime." The dictator's grip over the country remains total. Obiang Nguema explained that the dual nationals were not forbidden, but their Equato-Guinean passport was declared null and void, unless they gave up Spanish nationality. And he accused Amnesty International of publishing false information on torture. In order to divide the opposition, he incited deputies and functionaries of his clan to form parties.

In early 1992, it was said that Obiang Nguema had seized the cocoa plantation at Sampaka, formerly in the possession of the Mora Co, expropriated and seized by Mba Oñana, vice-president and minister for defense (who died in the meantime). His heirs were said to have given it to Obiang Nguema. The press continued to term Obiang Nguema a megalomaniac who sees enemies everywhere (not unlike his father-uncle). Thanks to some relatives of Obiang Nguema, it was learnt that he practiced sorcery in order to cling to power. He tried to lay hands on the skull of the mythical Fang warrior Mbo-ba, held by the Nsomo tribe, the possession of which has the powers to make one invincible. The dictator, whenever he has problems to solve, resorts to the old traditions. He sent his brother A. Mba Nguema, in charge of the armed forces in Río Muni, to Cameroon, to the sorcerer Abanda, the counsellor to President Paul Biya. The question he asked the sorcerer: What is to be done to remain in power like Biya? The sorcerer answered that he wished to talk in person with Obiang Nguema. So a meeting was organized in Ebibiyin, on the occasion of the consecration of the new bishop Juan Matogo Oyana. The sorcerer suggested to Obiang Nguema that he walk naked for several nights in the forests and procure the skull of the warrior Mbo-ba to acquire its benefits; he would then become invincible. The dictator continued to covet the skull, but the Nsomo were hostile to the Esangui. The refusal of the Nsomo became Obiang Nguema's biggest problem. It was not enough to seize the skull; a ceremony had to be organized so that the spirit would follow. Faced with the refusal of the Nsomos, Obiang Nguema sent his brother Mba Nguema to the deep forests of Nsok-Nsomo, in order to negotiate, under the cover of the inauguration of a local market. This new attempt at obtaining the skull also failed. Obiang Nguema left with a convoy of eight vehicles from Bata to Mongomo, to participate at an Esangui council. It was hinted that the dictator would frequently disappear into the forest, a sign of his loss of composure (Bata and Santa Isabel). Some persons even accused him of murders, especially of a little girl. According to some sorcerers, in order to obtain the skull of Mbo-ba, one had to commit 10 assassinations and cut off heads of women, as well as some of men.

In April 1992, Obiang Nguema went to North Korea for two weeks with Minister for Defense M. Ebendeng Nsomo. The trip ended in the signing of a lumber agreement. In fact, it was about recruiting North Korean mercenaries to form a new praetorian guard. In May, the Spanish press stated that Obiang Nguema was making a fortune, racketing the companies of the country, as well as some social institutions like the National Social Security Fund, with a tax of 3% supposedly "for his party"; he was said to have drawn FCFA 6 million from the Social Security Fund. That spring, the American magazine *Africa Report* published a declaration of a British journalist, attributing the following slogan to Obiang Nguema: "Unfair order is better than unfair disorder." In the president's gardens, prisoners belonging to the CPSD, including the engineer Celestino Bakale and José L. Nvumba were made to work. Obiang Nguema hurled abuse at them saying: "You are dirty intellectuals, you may have learnt about democracy in Europe, but here we are in Africa, and I am not Noriega." Obiang Nguema aimed mainly at dividing the opposition. During 1992, Obiang Nguema and his brother Armengol founded the company EFUSILA SA with a few Spaniards in order to award himself the construction of the new instituto (high school) at Santa Isabel, estimated to cost 500 million pesetas. The dictator also signed the contract for founding the lumber company A.B.M. On August 3, in the speech made on the anniversary of his coup d'etat, Obiang Nguema denounced foreign interference in the democratic process. Various political groups were provisionally authorized. In a televised speech, on the occasion of the 24th anniversary of independence, Obiang Nguema announced the suppression of a deposit of $120,000 demanded as legalization fee for political parties. "Multipartyism has already become a reality" he proclaimed, leaving out the other aspect of democracy, alternative government. The Spanish press stated that Obiang Nguema resisted all attempts to introduce democracy and was reproducing all the errors of fascism. The time had come for Spain to treat him as such. On November 16, during a press conference in Bata, Obiang Nguema claimed that the "transition" period will continue "till all political actors assimilate the true meaning of democracy." In late November, he threatened to expel the counsul of Spain, accusing him of circulating false information. In Bata, about 20 Spanish teachers of the Instituto Carlos Lwanga were summoned and threatened, so that they stop student demonstrations aimed at cancelling the suspension of the contracts of some of their teachers, regarded as detractors. Towards the end of 1992, Spain underwent several humiliations while in the capital and in Bata students and teachers as well as priests were increasingly being arrested. In his year-end speech, the dictator criticized the economic reprisals of Spain and the international organizations; the consequences of these reprisals "will affect the defenceless people." According to him, the opposition is composed of puppets and acolytes of the diplomatic corps. Towards the end of 1992, the people of Annobón burned the PDGE flag, as election promises were not being kept; Governor Ondo Nze left the island. Amnesty International warned that "since the introduction of multipartism, in January, hundreds of people have been arbitrarily detained . . ."almost all those detained in 1992 have been subject to bad treatment and tortured, while some suffer from serious injuries."

On January 5, 1993, during the closing session of the Chamber, Obiang Nguema declared: "I am not President for life." A new electoral law was adopted, unanimously, without amendments, prohibiting the participation of all those who have not lived in the country during the last five years in the legislative elections. This again excludes the majority of the dictator's opponents, who had been forced into exile. On January 21, the European Parliament unanimously adopted a resolution of the European Popular Party asking Obiang Nguema to enter into discussion with the Joint Opposition Platform (POC). In the meantime, the EC decided, its aid to the country will be interrupted. The situation in Equatorial Guinea was considered as being "very serious," Obiang Nguema showing "zero desire for democracy in the perspective of the forthcoming elections" in 1993. While the PDGE practiced intimidation to obtain members, members of the POC were arrested in Bata. Obiang Nguema accused Madrid of wanting to program Equato-Guinean democracy, but kept silent over the report of the special rapporteur of the UN Human Rights Division which, in February–March, repeated its observance of the total absence of fundamental liberties. While the ambassadors of Spain and the United States received death threats, Obiang Nguema, by a secret accord, seemed to have abandoned the Cocoteros and Mbañe isles to Gabon, which represent an illegal transfer of national territory. Gabon absorbed the Equato-Guinean islands by presidential decree, during January. On March 20, in Libreville, the EO commisioner for development and cooperation, M. Marín, explained to the dictator the reasons for the withdrawal of EC aid. On March 29, following the signing of the National Pact with the opposition parties, Obiang Nguema decreed the liberation of political prisoners. In March, the dictator insisted, at the military camp Acacio Mañe Ela (Santa Isabel) that the army—which he did not trust, as he declared to Felipe Gonzalez—had to use arms to keep the civilian population respectful. He wanted the help of the UNHCR to arrange for the return and the relocation of the exiled. But once again, the majority of the intelligentsia refused to return.

After 15 days in France, in April, and a reception hosted by Mitterrand, Obiang Nguema returned, expressing his satisfaction at France's cooperation. During this time, the Geopolitical Drug Observatory (Paris) revealed that the National Drug Law Enforcement Agency of Nigeria had it publicly made known that some traffickers were working for Obiang Nguema. The contributions to the "4th Day of Reflection on Equatorial Guinea," organized in May 1993 by the Colegio Mayor Universitario Our Lady of Africa, in Madrid, and especially the words of the Swiss Africanist Max Liniger-Goumaz on Radio Exterior de España, troubled the Nguemists so much so that Vice-Prime Minister Oyono Ndongo Mifumu expressed his preoccupation to the press on May 14, as the dictator was just beginning another stay in France. At the same time, the countries and international organizations willing to help in the holding of democratic elections demanded "political guarantees" before discussing the $20 million that Santa Isabel wanted. On May 20, the Round Table of Donors (Spain, United States, France, Morocco, EC, UNDP) was suspended, due to the reluctance of the Nguemists with regard to the minimal conditions required. Obiang Nguema's government replied on June 17, by partly prohibiting the transport of 40 tons of supplies and medicines by planes belonging to the Spanish Cooperation to famine-hit Annobón; on the other hand, the use of the roads around the capital, especially around the airport and the port was prohibited to foreigners, for reasons of "national security."

In January 1993, the European Parliament observed that Obiang Nguema, faced with legislative elections, was showing "zero desire for democracy." During his electoral campaign in Río Muni, in the spring of 1993, he claimed several times before the population that he held a power "which comes fromm God." In reality, the promises to respect human rights were not kept. Terror reigned in the country, while France and Morocco supported Obiang Nguema's tyranny. The 1993 Report of Amnesty International, proved the felony of Obiang Nguema who declared in August 1979 that he had toppled his father-uncle "at the request of the people." In early July, Obiang Nguema announced the dissolution of the Parliament and the legislative elections for September 12, in violation of the National Pact agreement signed on March 18. Before Parliament, he stressed the talent with which he claimed to have led the country to sociopolitical balance, peace, and progress. On July 10, the POC, unhappy with the dictator's refusal to reform the electoral law and carry out a credible census, proclaimed an election boycott "until the conditions of liberty, justice and fairness were fulfilled"; they were supported by the countries and international organizations willing to help the process of democratization; they hinted that there is "no real will on the part of the government" to introduce democracy." The first half of 1993 was characterized further by several banking manipulations (see Banks), especially with a so-called International Bank of Malabo, concocted by the Frenchman Pierre Marie Bord, with Obiang Nguema as honorary president. There was also talk of the founding of a Bank of Equatorial Guinea, registered at Santa Isabel on May 14, 1994, by Engonga Motulu and the France-convicted Llansol, with Obiang Nguema and Teodorin, with the technical support of a company from Luxembourg, the International Company for Finance SA. Llansol therefore started a new bank with a Swiss firm, and French articles of association. Obiang Nguema and his son Teodorín were involved with Llansol's projects as well as those of a group of Serbs who planned to found a company, Codis SA (with 25% belonging to Obiang Nguema and 10% to Teodorín), but it fell into bankruptcy on the day of its establishment in Geneva.

Multi-Nguemism was at its height: the majority of recent opposition groups fell into the trap laid by Obiang Nguema (decorated with a few thousand dollars). In late August 1993, when the election boycott called by the POC had forced the dictatorship to postpone the polls to November, political assassinations (disguised as suicides, as under Macías Nguema), mass arrests and torture began again. In a document dated late August 1993, the ANRD made a "summary of the action of General Obiang Nguema": systematic violation of human rights—crumbling of the administrative and productive structures—frightening increase in insalubrity—unreasonable levels of external debts—patrimonialization of the state and of private property—blockage of external financing—social tension, tribal government, separatistic tendencies and constant refusal to have a dialogue—total rejection of Obiang Nguema by the people—isolation and international discrediting of Equatorial Guinea, as a consequence of fooling the United Nations and the nonfulfilment of the Plan of the Human Rights Commission. The Guinean tragedy reached the level of a nightmare: 25% of the population lived outside the country, 85% of the executives and the intellectuals were in exile. Rumor had it that Obiang Nguema was the puppet of his brother Armengol and his uncle Manuel. In his 25th anniversary speech, Obiang Nguema spoke of an irreversible democratic process; but the prohibitions, especially with regard to *La Verdad,* continued. The Spanish press observed a Francoist style.

The European Parliament, in Strasbourg, denounced in January 1994 the "prostitution of democracy" by Obiang Nguema, and demanded the suspension of aid and the blocking of the dictator's bank accounts. The American government considered an official visit by Obiang Nguema to the USA as untimely. In March, the dictator visited Paris, in order to ask for economic aid following the devaluation of the CFA franc. The 1994 Report of the Geopolitical Drug Observatory stated that Obiang Nguema "has transformed his diplomatic personnel and his family, which are often one and the same thing, into an international network" for drug-trafficking . . ." it seems that the trafficking President continues to enjoy the support of France." In late April, before the Parliament, Obiang Nguema recognized errors in the writing and the application of the Constitution and of the Electoral Law and promised reforms. Further, to stress the division of powers, he asked the ministers elected deputies in November 1993 to give up their seat to an alternate.

In the spring of 1995, Obiang Nguema was accused of again making up stories when he alleged yet another coup d'etat and other subversive acts, as the Nguemists always do before election time (in this case it was the presidential election). On March 28, on state radio, the dictator accused donor countries (Spain, France, U.S.) and the UNDP of "preparing an electoral fraud to favour the opposition against the PDGE," by "clandestinely giving it electoral notebooks." As early as March 20, at the opening of the 1st Convention of the PDGE, in Bata, Obiang Nguema accused foreign countries of interference in the internal affairs of the country to advance their expansionistic aims. He then criticized the IMF and the World Bank in equally strong terms, and accused them of not keeping their promises. One of his relatives, Lieutenant-Commander Roberto Mba Ndong, acted as his aide-de-camp. The torturer and assassin Cayo Ondo Mba had the same post before his arrest in the spring of 1995. Obiang Nguema claimed that mercenaries were being trained in Spain in order to annex the country. Therefore, on April 29, he brought in a reinforcement of 140 Moroccan mercenaries, which was three times the number of the Moroccan praetorian guard that was still present on the spot. On August 2, during this televised speech for the 16th anniversary of his coup d'etat, Obiang Nguema pardoned 33 political prionsers including Moto Nsa and 11 military men under the effect of international pressure (also from the French president Chirac, whom he hurried to meet at Libreville in mid-July). During all of August, the dictator, along with a sizeable escort, toured Río Muni to praise the merits of the PDGE. During this time, the *New York Times* published a whole page glorifying the dictator. After the fraudulent municipal elections on September 17, which were garnished with all kinds of violence, Obiang Nguema again visited France in early November in order to invite investments. In October, at the Non-Aligned Summit in Columbia, the dictator accused Spain of perpetrating discord by financing the opposition. In his country, Obiang Nguema became vice-president of the Empresa Nacional de Pesca (National Fishing Co.), mainly run by big shots of the Nguemist regime.

On January 8, 1996, Obiang Nguema had Siale Bilekia carry out yet another ministerial reshuffle. It was a minor reshuffle that helped maintain the upper hand of the clan from Mongomo over the executive. A week later, the dictator announced that he was advancing the presidential election from June to February 25, catching the opposition unawares. Addressing an election rally in Bata, Brigadier General Obiang Nguema, surrounded by posters proclaiming "Obiang—today, tomorrow and always," said it was time to forget about any more ballots. With help from American petroleum companies and from American and South African public relations companies, and also by intensifying terror tactics, the dictator managed to eliminate all rivals even before the election and to renew his mandate for seven years with more than 97.85% of the votes cast (99.29% at Santa Isabel, 99.69% in Bata; the level of participation was 86.12%; the ballot was not secret). The election, unnacceptable to the POC, was declared valid by the Constitutional Court, even though it was well known that the conditions for the observation of the elections were not in conformity with international rules. The cruelty endured by the clergy of all religions during the presidential campaign led the priests, especially those of Río Muni, to publish a communiqué in which they stated that whoever did not venerate "Papa Obiang" was putting himself in danger. According to the journalist-historian D. Ndongo-Bidyogo, "The spirit of Macías [Nguema] is reincarnated and again governs at Malabo [Santa Isabel]" (*Mundo negro,* April 1996). On April 8, the dictator appointed a new government of "national unity," with more than a fourth of the members belonging directly to the clan from Mongomo, plus five leaders from political parties of the tame opposition. In this manner, any pressure from American petroleum companies (led by Mobil) for democratization of the regime were satisfied. The Nguemist democratorship continues.

It was in April 1996 that the Country Report on Human Rights Practices for 1995, by the U.S. State Department of the members of the U.S. House of Representatives and the U.S. Senate was published. It was recalled that

> Equatorial Guinea is nominally a multi party constitutional republic, but in reality, power has been exercised by President Teodoro Obiang [Nguema] through a small subclan of the majority Fang tribe which has ruled since the country's independence in 1968. Despite the formalities of a multi party form of government, President Obiang [Nguema], in power since 1979, together with his associates, dominates the Government. The President's Democratic Party of Equatorial Guinea (PDGE) controls the judiciary and the legislature, the latter through fraudulent elections. . . .President Obiang [Nguema] exercises control over the police and security forces through the Minister of Interior. The security forces committed serious human rights abuses. . . . Serious human rights abuses continue. After some progress in 1994, the human rights situation deteriorated in 1995.

On May 27, 1996, the dictator visited Libreville for discussions with President Bongo, the company Elf-Aquitaine, and various other matters. On this occasion, his son Teodorín was named director of Elf-Aquitaine Equatorial Guinea. Obiang Nguema was said to have discussed with Bongo the inefficiency of his government of national unity, constituted with the tame opposition; the Gabonese president was said to have advised him to have closer ties with the democratic opposition. On August 1, 1996, Obiang Nguema was promoted to general-in chief (general-mayor) by a decree signed by himself. On September 1–8 Obiang Nguema was in China where he had an interview with President Jiang Zemin, Prime Minister Li Peng, and the Minister of Foreign Trade, Miss Wu Yi. He received a credit loan of $3 million. On his return he made stops in France, then Morocco, where he was able to meet with the Spanish prime minister, Aznar. During that time, in Washington, the deputy secretary of state for Africa, William Tuwaddel, said to P. Miko and C. Bakale (high officials in the CPDS) that he was convinced that the election of Obiang Nguema, in February 1996, was irregular. The dictator proposed for the end of October 1996 that a National Economic Conference be held, to explain to "all active forces" his petroleum policy. The leader of the CPDS, C. Bakale, is questioned by Obiang Nguema's cousin José Ndong Oba. On November 19, 1996, after meeting the Spanish prime minister in Rome, he is greeted in Paris by J. Godfrain, minister for cooperation; he did not meet President Chirac. Before coming back to his country, he met with King Hassan II, in Morocco, as he does since then every year.

Obiang Nguema owns a luxurious flat near the Porte Dauphine in Paris, a new villa at Las Palmas in the Canary Islands, a sumptuous residence near Miami (Florida), a palace at Acoakam, his native village. According to the Spanish press in 1993, he has 1,500 million pesetas in Canarian banks. According to historian D. Ndongo-Bidiyoge (*Mundo negro*) Obiang Ngucma's fortune would amount to $200 million, hidden in French, Spanish, Argentine, Swiss, and American banks.

The dictator goes by the following nicknames: "El Fundador," "El Tigre" (Nse Ebere ekum: The tiger at source = the dictator).

Various sources claim that he suffers from a split personality. This kind of paranoia leads him to regularly imagine, like Macías Nguema, strange plots to eliminate him, which also explains his disproportionate security service. According to *El Mundo*, the former president of the Spanish government, Adolfo Suarez, called Obiang Nguema mentally ill, wily, cowardly, and unscrupulous.

The informers frequently stressed his sexual obsession. The population calls Obiang Nguema's political police, the Ninjas, "the guards of the beast." Obiang Nguema's twins, Justo and Pastor, now call themselves Hassan and Husein.

During the 27th anniversary of independence, on October 12, 1995, he appointed himself major general. His brother Antonio Obiang Nguema, minister of national defense and head of national security, was promoted to brigadier general.

On December 2, 1996, Obiang Nguema attended, in Brazzaville, the summit of African heads of state of countries that are members of the Consultative Committee of the UN for African Security.

In his New Year address in 1997, Obiang Nguema reiterated the idea of a National Economic Conference. Carlos Carnero González (*El País,* March) mentioned the fact that "Obiang Nguema never keeps his promises"; Baltasar Porcel (*La Vanguardia*): "The gloomy dictator Obiang (Nguema) sucks blood wherever he can." In the beginning of June, Teodorín received delivery of a Falcon for his father. In September 1997, Obiang Nguema participated in the summit in Libreville on the crisis in the Congo (Zaire), as he had previously participated in the commission of reconciliation between Mobutu and Kabila, of Zaire. It is said that Obiang financed the war in Congo-Brazzaville with 1 Mio FCFA, by credit transfer via Meridien-BIAO to Sassou-Nguesso.

In 1997, when the twins of Obiang Nguema made their first communion, the dictator emptied the fish market GUINACO in Malabo (of which he is a shareholder), leaving the population without food.

In January 1998, Obiang Nguema dissolved the government and appointed a new one, still run by Dougan. His son Teodorín holds the office of minister of environment and forests. In April he paid an official visit to Cameroon, then to Morocco, where he underlined the excellent relations his country has with Spain. In June, Obiange Nguema participated in a Forum on African Development (World Bank), in Dakar (Senegal), and in a conference dealing with the fight against drugs in New York, soon after the Bubi trial. On June 8, 1998, on the platform, he said that the weapons used during Moto's failed coup, as well as those used during the Bubi attack, were bought with money from the drug traffic. Obiang Nguema declared in Accra, during the September 14–16, 1998, visit to Ghana that the neocolonial heritage must be destroyed. During the meeting of the 15th between Obiang and Rawlings, both discussed "the negative influence of multinationals on the political and economic development of the African continent." Just as Macias Nguema used to do, Obiang Nguema eliminates those who are culturally superior to him.

In Evinayong, on the 30th anniversary of independence, October 12, 1998, Obiang Nguema accused the Western world of looking for new ways of dominating African peoples:

> Presently it is required from African countries that they respect new modern political concepts as a priiority, as a "sine qua non" condition to obtain the help and assistance from developed countries: the democratization of the human rights of their peoples; governability and good management; globalization in international economic relations, etc. These concealed plans aim at swerving African reality, its marginalization by western economic organizations and powers, as well as a penalization of their peoples to destabilize and disinherit its children.

Equatorial Guinea will maintain the relations of friendship and cooperation with all countries, "within the context of a scrupulous respect of the sovereignity and independence of Equatorial Guinea." He did not give a date for the elections. The CPDS released a statement in which it underlined that after Macias Nguema's tyranny, "Obiang Nguema and his family have transformed the country into a private property," adding that not only laymen but the clergy also are a victim of Nguemist terror. Toward the middle of October 1998, Obiang Nguema went on an official visit to São-Tomé-Principe. The Economist Intelligence Unit observed that President Obiang Nguemas increasingly looks

> to cultivate an image as an international statesman. . . .Under pressure from oil companies already present in Equatorial Guinea, and in the hope of attracting further foreign direct investment in the future, Mr. Obiang is anxious to overcome the lingering image of his regime as corrupt, incompetent, unaccountable and occasionally brutal. Instead, he would prefer to project a more modern, less isolationist picture of a small country adapting quickly to international norms. . . .President Obiang's grip on power, however, is likely to remain formidable.

Obiang Nguema has been married five times. Four of his wives have an office in the government (education, presidency, agriculture, interior). One of his sons studies in Venezuela. The godfather of Obiang Nguema's twins, Hassan and Husein, is President Sassou Ngueso, from Congo Brazzaville.

Another of his sons, who is about 30 years old (from the second wife of Obiang Nguema, of São-Tomean origin) came back from the U.S. in 1998 with a degree in mining engineering and now works for Mobil Oil. The dictator lives in a residence close to Punta Europa, toward the northwest area of the capital. His neighborhood is surrounded by walls and barbed wire, as was Macias Nguema's presidential ghetto.

The Equato-Guinean historian D. Ndongo-Bidiyogo, one of the most serious observers of his country, estimated in 1998 the dictator's fortune to be $270 million

(U.S.), whereas the country's external debt comes up to $260 million (U.S.), without taking into account the interest on capital.

See also Abeso Fuma, F.; Akurenam; Army; Bacale, C.; Bokoko Boko, D.; Buchanan, R.; "Democratic" Party of Equatorial Guinea; Elections; Elo Ndong Nsefumu, D.; Ekua Ondo, M.; Esono Mbomio, J.; Eyi Monsuy Andeme, I.; Garriga Fuma; Maquada, F. K.; Mba Oñana, F.; Moto Nsa, S.; Nepotism; Nguema Esono, I..; Nguema Mba, M.; Nguema Mbasogo Ondo, A.; Nguemism; Obiang Mangue, T.; Olo Mebuy, A.; Ondo Nkumu, J.; Oyo Riqueza, E.; Petroleum; Press; Terror; Venezuela.

OBIANG NSOGO, Rafael. Fang from Rio Benito. Medical doctor. In 1968 he became minister of justice, then public health minister, succeeding Ekong Andeme in March 1969. He participated in the creation of the Milicia Popular (Popular Militia) and in March 1971 was among the initiators of the Juventud en Marcha con Macías. In 1973 he became minister of industries and mines, after Ekong Andeme's arrest. In 1976 he had to give up his office to Nguema Ada with the title of vice-minister, and became again minister of health and hygiene. In 1977, he paid an official visit to the U.S.S.R. In October 1978 he represented Equatorial Guinea at the General Assembly of the United Nations in New York. During his trip he stopped in Madrid where Miguel Esono and other members of the MOLIFUGE recorded secretly several conversations held with him on the subject of Macías Nguema's dismissal, and then had them published in a Madrid newspaper. Obiang Gonsogo, called also "Colonel Bangala," admitted to being the holder of a bank account in the Canary Islands that could help to finance an action against Macías Nguema. Presently a tradesman.

OBIANG NZO MBENGONO, Severino. Fang from Niefang. Born on August 7, 1946. Industrial technical engineer and holds a diploma electronics. In December 1993 Obiang Nzo was confirmed as minister for industry, energy and promotion of small and medium-scale enterprises. Obiang Nzo supported a project for the elimination of heads of the opposition, with Father Efong, the Nguemists devoted priest, and brother to Mgr. Obama Obono, the bishop of the capital. Ever since the municipal elections of 1995, he has been mayor of Bata.

OBLATES see Missions, Catholic.

OBSERVATOIRE DES TRANSFERTS D'ARMEMENT (Paris) see Army; France

OCCUPATION OF THE MADRID EMBASSY. On March 5, 1976, about 200 Equato-Guinean students occupied the Madrid Embassy after celebrating a funeral ceremony honoring the victims of Macías Nguema's personal power. The students belonged to ANALIGE, URGE, MOLIFUGE, and ANRD. After Ndongo Nangala and Edu Egonga, respectively deputy ambassador and consul parleyed with them, the students left the embassy without incident. Ndongo Nangala was recalled to Santa Isabel, accused of complicity with Buendy Ndongo, and murdered.

OCEANEERING Int. (Houston). Cooperates with Mobil, thanks to a 26,000-ton tanker, transformed in 1995, in South Africa, into a floating oil tanker with a capacity of 1.2 million barrels. In 1997, Mobil hired it to increase the extracting possibilities in Zafiro to 120,000 b/d, by means of gas and hot water injection system.

In 1997, the company sold its share in Zafiro field to Mobil. See Petroleum.

OCEAN ENERGY. American oil company. It merged with United Meridian Corp. in April 1998. In August, it announced that three wells were working in Block B (Jade). In Block B, the East Opalo well 1 and 2 are also producing 24,365 b/d. It has been planned that the Zafiro well production will be increased to 120,222 b/d in the year 2000. Also in Block B, they keep on drilling Turmalina, Beriliio, and Plata. In Block D, they are still investigating by means of various drills (Estaurolita, Aapatito, and Zirconia).

OCHAGA NGOMO ABESO, Buenaventura, 1929?–1976. Fang from the Ebebiyin district. Since independence he was director general of internal affairs, then secretary general of the PUNT since 1969, simultaneously heading the Milicia Popular. Towards the end of 1973 he succeeded Grange Molay in the Ministry of Popular Education, making it a point of honor to have the Centro de Desarrollo de la Educación in Bata operate despite Macías Nguema's reluctance. Late in 1976, during the Senior Officials Affair, he was arrested with all other high ranking persons of his ministry and a hundred other officials. Imprisoned in Bata, he was assassinated on December 6, 1976 (having committed "suicide" according to the government). He has been replaced by Macías's cousin Feliciano Oyono as permanent secretary of the PUNT.

OCHAGA NVE BENGOBESAMA, Constantino. Born 1943. An Esangui from Nsangayong. A cousin of Obiang Nguema. Educated at the Banapa Seminary and then proceeded to a degree in philosophy and letters in Spain in 1966 (geography/history) of the Universidad Complutense (Madrid). He went into exile in Spain and was one of the founders of the PANDECA movement, which had close links with Spanish authorities.

After the 1979 coup he returned to Equatorial Guinea and was appointed headmaster of the "Instituto Rey Malabo" high school in Santa Isabel. In March 1981, he was nominated director of higher education, technical and secondary education in the Ministry of Education; by December he had been promoted to secretary-general of the ministry. In May 1982 he took part in the Akonibé constitutional conference, which laid the groundwork for Obiang Nguema's dictatorship. In October 1982, he became the official government spokesman and at the end of the month he was appointed minister of communications, transport and tourism. In a number of public statements he accused various opponents of threatening the process of "democratization" that the Nguemist regime was engaged in.

After the attempted coup d'etat of May 1983, it was Ochaga Nve who on the national radio accused the opponents of "derailing the democratic process." Shortly afterwards he became the deputy director of the UNED in Equatorial Guinea. He was one of the barking dogs of the regime. In 1985, Ochaga Nve published *Semblanzas de Hispanidad,* as well as *Guinea Ecuatorial: Polémica y Realdad* in Nguemist Ediciones Guinea. In 1986, Ochaga Nve was replaced by Eloy Elo Nve Mbengono. He died in 1991, at Moscow. His death remains unexplained. See also Bibliography.

ODOVILLE see Mba Nguema Mikue, A.

OFICAR AFRICA S.A. Urban transport company in Bata (1981) which also monopolized transport within Río Muni. The company belongs to Manuel Moreno, president of Anetra, a road transport company in Spain. Mba Onãna was its president. In 1986, Oficar owed the Guinextebank FCFA 42,984,000. Towards the end of 1987, Oficar fell within the authority of Hinestrosa Ikaka, minister for finance.

OIL see Petroleum

OIL PALMS. Until the First World War only indigenous production existed. With the introduction of the power press around 1935, industrial plantations started. Just before independence, Equatorial Guinea had 8,200 hectares of palm groves, of which 7,000 were in Río Muni, more than half owned by large companies (Casas fuertes). In 1977, the main plantations (although abandoned) were Cape San Juan (SOCOGUI), with 1,678 hectares; Bolondo (María Victoria), with 778; Sendye (Juan Jover), 666; Bolondo (San Cristobal), 650; and Rio Mbaña (AGGOR), with 500 hectares.

Village palm groves represent about 2,000 hectares. At independence, eight factories transformed the oil (into soap, washing powders, edible oil). The exportation of palm oil and palm nuts rapidly developed since 1950, reaching a total of 3,092,000 tons of palm oil and 2,795,000 tons of nuts in 1960 and 3,686,000 tons of oil and 2,365,000 tons of nuts in 1968. The neglect of plantations at the Spaniards' departure in March 1969 caused production and trade to collapse. A United Nations Commission suggested the reopening of 7,000 hectares, of which 3,600 now belong to the state. But so far nothing has been done.

OKENVE EDJANG, Adolfo. Fang from Mongomo, born 1943. Studied at the Escuela Superior Indígena. Internship in administration at Madrid in 1980. Director of Obiang Nguema's civil cabinet. He is also called Obiang Nguema's "nurse."In April 1982, he attended the Donor Conference of the UNDP, in Geneva. In late October 1986, he owed the Guinextebank FCFA 9,117,000. He was still director of Obiang Nguema's civil cabinet after the April 8, 1996, ministerial reshuffle.

OKENVE MITUY, Fortunato. Fang from Mikomeseng. Born in 1926. Captain of the National Guard. Secretary general of the Popular Armed Forces until 1976. Following the attempted coup d'etat of June 1974, he became President of the Military Court set up in Bata on June 22, 1974, whence he proclaimed 27 death sentences. Since the occupation of the Madrid Embassy, in which his son participated, Fortunato Okenve Mituy has been under house arrest. Shortly after the 1979 coup he was rehabilitated and nominated ambassador to Cameroon early in 1980. His son, who was living in exile in Spain where he was one of the founding members of the URGE movement, returned to Equatorial Guinea at that time. In February 1981, he was promoted to commander and returned to his country. In 1988, he figured again as ambassador to Nigeria. In 1993, he became an official in the Ministry of Foreign Affairs. Since, he has become a tradesman owing to a 15 Mio FCFA loan by Obiang Nguema.

OKENVE NDO, Celestino-Nvo. Fang. Son of F. Okenve Mituy. An aeronautical engineer. In charge of external affairs of URGE in Spain, where he is a refugee; he participated, on March 5, 1976, in the occupation of his country's embassy in Madrid with about 200 other students, in order to protest against the Macías and Obiang Nguema dictatorship. In 1991, he became general secretary of the Coalición Social Democrática (CSD). He wished to be the external spokesperson of the POC, in Madrid, but the nine parties present preferred another candidate. Okenve then returned to the country. In 1996, professor at the Universidad Politécnica, Madrid.

OKO. Little Equato-Guinean island to the southwest of Río Muni. See Borders.

OKO EBOBO, Antonio Pascual. Kombe from Bata. Born in 1947. A schoolteacher. Holds a degree in law from the UNED. In 1987, he became general secretary in the Ministry of Information, Tourism and Culture. Towards the end of 1989, he became minister of labor and social welfare. In June 1990, he attended the International Labor Conference, in Geneva. He became minister for education in the "transitional" government of January 24, 1992. In the November 1993 elections, he was elected deputy under the PDGE. He did not figure in the December 22 government. In the April 8, 1996, government he became minister in charge of relations with Parliament and legislative coordination. At the end of 1998 he kept his function.

OKORI DOUGAN KINSON, José see Dougan

OKUE MOTO, Melchor. From Ebebiyin. Born in 1947. Studied at the Escuela Superior Indígena, and then studied commerce in Spain. Football player at Cordoba (Spain). Deputy director of the Guinextebank. Towards the end of 1986 he owed his bank FCFA 2.5 million. A representative of the workers at the International Labor Conference, in Geneva, in 1987. He owns a flour trade and a bakery at Santa Isabel. Since 1996, he has been president of the Olympic Committee of Equatorial Guinea.

OLD BUBI see Buela

OLO, José. Fang. Lawyer. Defense attorney for the Bubi ideologue Martin Puye during the May 1998 trial. He talked of "the state of anarchy" of Equatorial Guinea. He was arrested in July, accused of "endangering the country's independence and peace," after an interview with the Spanish press. He was released on August 21 but later tried for insulting the authorities.

OLO MBA NSENG, Juan. Fang Esangui, born on June 23, 1947, at Angong-Obue (district of Mongomo), like Purificación Angue Ondo. He is Constancia Mangue Nsue's, Obiang Nguema's first wife's brother. Went to primary school in Mikomeseng. In 1962 he returned to the little seminary at Banapa. After four years, he went to the Rey Malabo Secondary School at Santa Isabel, where he took the baccalaureate. Member of the clan from Mongomo.

In 1971 he obtained a scholarship for studies in the USSR. He received a degree in international law and in maritime law from the University of Kiev. Deeply anti-Spanish. Called "El mudo" (the Mute).

In 1977 he entered Macias Nguema's government. After Obiang Nguema's coup d'etat, he became staff-officer to the president of the republic. In 1979, he became secretary general for the diplomatic representation at the UN in New York. In 1980, he was employed as an official in the supreme Military Council. In December 1981, he was made state secretary for trade and in October 1982, minister of mining and petroleum resources. He retained this post after the January 1986 ministerial reshuffle.

He received money out of the budget of the Spanish cooperation. In May 1985, he became secretary of state for planning and cooperation. In 1988, the surveys of the French BRGM continued, in spite of the difficulties in terms of means of communication.

In 1986 he owed the Guinextebank FCFA 21,042,000. The experts considered his debt unrecoverable. In the autumn of 1988, he was present at the torture inflicted on Joaquin Elema Borengue, in the capital. In November 1989, Olo Mba Nseng ordered the Spanish company Gepsa to give up its petroleum concession at Alba (Repsol also decided to stop costs, as it considered the deposits nonprofitable). Olo Mba Nseng was arrested in early 1990, at the same time as Obiang Nguema's wife, Constancia Mangue, accused of conspiracy. He was imprisoned at Bata. But in October he became minister in charge of mines and petroleum.

Olo Mba Nseng was back in the same post in the "transitional" government appointed on January 24, 1992, as well as in the government of December 22, 1993. In November 1993, he was elected PDGE deputy. Mrs. Olo Mba Nseng held a seat on the administrative council of SOGUIGAS. Juan Olo Mba Nseng holds a seat on the administrative council of APEGESA and LITOR-WELE. In the January 8, 1996, ministerial reshuffle, he retained the Ministry of Mines and Energy, a post which went to him once again in the April 8, 1996, government. His deputy for energy was Francisco Mabale Nseng, and for mines, it was Miguel Abia Biteo, both secretaries of state.

In mid-1996, United Meridian Corp. signed an agreement for mining for gold (in some granite formations), diamonds (near Nsork), bauxite, and tantalite in Río Muni.

See also Apegesa; Litor-Wele; Mbale, F.; Nepotistm; Petroleum.

OLO MEBUY, Anacleto. Fang from Kam (Mikomeseng). Born in 1951. Baccalaureate at the school of La Salle at Bata. Went to seminary at Nkue, and later at Albacete (Spain), and finally to the Pontifical University, at Rome. Holds a degree in philosophy and theology, and a diploma in social communication. Married to a Kenyan. He became a member of the ANRD in 1974, and was the secretary for information. But he was expelled, along with some others, in 1976.

In 1977, he completed a degree in anthropology at the University of Freiburg (Switzerland). Upon his return, he not only taught history at the Carlos Lwanga Secondary School at Bata, but was also the deputy director of the periodical *Ebano*. He wrote poetry critical of the Macías Nguema period. From 1987 he worked as department head in the Museum of the CICIBA, a Libreville (Gabon). In the January 24, 1992, "transitional" government, he became vice-minister for culture, tourism and promotion of handicrafts. He did not figure in the December 22, 1993, government. On January 19, 1994, he was appointed counsellor to the president for social affairs. On April 8, 1996, he was appointed counsellor for culture,

tourism and francophony and was simultaneously joint director of a new periodical: *La Gaceta de Guinea Ecuatorial.*
In May 1996 he was replaced by Toribio Obiang Mba. In the government of January 1998, he was minister of culture, tourism and craft promotion.

OLOMO NVE NSANG, Domingo. From Mongomo. Born 1941. Nicknamed "Bote." Military training in the USSR. At the ministerial reshuffle of April 8, 1996, he became joint director general of the president's Civil Cabinet.

OLO OBONO, José. From Bata. Born in 1955 (?). A lawyer. Secretary at the College of Lawyers of Equatorial Guinea. In 1991, he was prevented by the Nguemists from attending the Conference of Jurists at Barcelona. Member of Convergency for Social Democracy (CPDS). In the autumn of 1992, he was in charge of the defence of the Spanish businessmen Hanna and Vilarrasa, accused of conspiracy against Obiang Nguema (the advocate C. Ndong had been arrested). As for GE-Total legal advisor, he was dismissed by the president of the bold council, A. Nvoro Obono, for political reasons.
One of the founders, in August 1995, of the Republican Democratic Front, not legalized by the Nguemists.
During the May 1998 Bubi trial, he was defender of a leader of the Movement for Self-Determination of Bioko Island, Martin Puye (liquidated in prison in July). Obono was arrested on July 21, 1998, and incarcerated in Playa Negra prison after conducting a radio interview in which he criticized the conditions of detention in the prison of the capital and mentioned the death in prison of Puye, as a consequence of ill-treatment and lack of medical care. On September 17, the Appeals Court of Malabo sentenced Oló Obono to five months imprisonment on charges of "insult." The charges did not specify who had been insulted. The court rendered its decision despite the fact that the public prosecutor had withdrawn the charge against Obono. In the opinion of the NGO Lawyer-to-Lawyer, Obono's prosecution appears to be motivated by his role as a defense lawyer in the Bubi summary and unfair trial of May. "His conviction [says Lawyers-to-Lawyers] is seen in Equatorial Guinea as a warning by the government to critics of its human rights record." See Human Rights; Republican Democratic Front; Terror.

OMA EKOGA, Jorge, d. 1972. From 1960 to 1968 he was a member of the Diputación Provincial (Assembly) of Río Muni, and from 1964 to 1968 simultaneously deputy of the Asamblea General (Parliament). Member of the MUNGE, he was elected to the Provincial Council of Río Muni in 1968. Oma Ekoga disappeared in the end of May 1972 purge, at the same time as Eñeso Neñe, Watson Bueco, Cabrera y James, and others.

ONA NGUEMA, Agapito. An Esangui. Born in Niefang in 1944. Studied at the Escuela Superior Indigena, at Santa Isabel. Joint Secretary for organization in the Progress Party. His clumsy declarations were the cause of the Moto Nsa case. In the spring of 1995, he was arrested and tortured by Commissioner Ondo Ncumu and Lieutenant-Colonel Agustin Ndong Ona, and condemned to 20 years in prison. The Progress Party expelled him in April 1995. See also Moto Nsá, S.

ONDO ANGUE, Miguel. Fang, born 1951, in Niefang. Studied in the Santa Isabel High School. Stepbrother of Armengol Nguema, brother of Obiang Nguema. In the ministerial reshuffle of April 8, 1996, he became director general for petro-chemicals.

ONDO ASI, Victor. Fang from Mikomeseng. Civil servant. Appointed secretary in the Ministry of Foreign Affairs in January 1980. He drew attention to himself by making a number of statements against democracy. He led the Equatorial Guinean delegation to the UN Human Rights Commission in Geneva in 1981. Effective March 1981, however, he was demoted and posted as a junior official to the town of Nsork. By decree 16 of January 1994, he replaced Mesa Bill as chancellor to the president for the National Orders of the Republic.

ONDO AYANG, Luis. From Ebebiyin. Born May 19, 1955. Sought refuge in Gabon, and joined the National Alliance for Democratic Restoration (ANRD) in 1975; he earned a degree in literature and humanities at the University of Libreville. He then obtained a degree in philosophy and literature at the Autono-mous University of Madrid, (1990), where he also studied law. He taught literature and history at the Instituto Rey Malabo(high school) in Santa Isabel in 1979–1980.

He returned to Spain and attended a course in the School for Diplomats (1981), where he received the degree. It was at that time that he was falsely accused of drug trafficking by colleagues from Mongomo. In 1983, he was elected to the Executive Committee of the Central Committee of the ANRD as a secretary for organization and for the mobilization of the masses.

Once the divisive operation benefiting the Nguemists that the ANRD accused some of its members of carrying out became known, he became the general secretary of the ANRD, in the spring of 1993. On September 4, in Madrid, he was elected by the representatives of nine opposition parties as external spokesman of the POC, but he declined this post.

In January 1995, in Geneva, in a press conference, Ondo Ayang explained the reasons for the expulsion of Dougan Beaca from the National Alliance for Democratic Restoration, a year after Mokong Onguene.

In April 1996, Luis Ondo Ayang addressed the Human Rights Commision, in Geneva, and the petroleum economy of Equatorial Guinea as a personal business of Obiang Nguema's. He added commentaries on the reelection of the dictator of 99%.

In 1997, the ANRD invited to Madrid nine political parties of the interior and the diaspora. Luis Ondo Ayang told them about the need to celebrate a National Sovereign Conference, this being the only way to efficiently and truly domacratize the country. His proposal of a transitional electoral calendar was accepted by all the parties, but was blocked and boycotted by the dictatorship.

In 1998, a delegation of four members of the national management of the ANRD, led by L. Ondo Ayang, was received by members of the Spanish govern-ment in the Moncloa (Madrid). They produced a document asking for more active intervention in Equatorial Guinea for its democratization. By means of Radio Exterior de España, the secretary general of the ANRD addressed the people of Equatorial Guinea several times, informing them of the maneuvers of Obiang Nguema in order to remain in power forever and of his total absence of desire to democratize the country.

See also Bangha; Dougan Beaca, J. D.; Elections; Joint Opposition Platform; Mba Mombe, S.; Mokong Onguene; National Alliance for Democratic Restoration; Okenve, C.

ONDO EDU, Bonifacio, d. 1969. Fang from Evinayong. Studied at the San José of Evinayong mission. Planter and Catholic catechist. After A. Mañe's assassination in 1958, he took refuge in Gabon, where he created the Unión de Guinea Ecuatorial. Back in his country, he became mayor of Evinayong from 1960 to 1961. In 1963, assisted by Spain, he founded the MUNGE. President of the party, Ondo Edu became in 1964 chief of the autonomous government (Consejo de Gobierno). Before the United Nations Trusteeship Committee, he declared in 1966 that it was still too early for independence. Thanks to Ondo Edu, the MUNGE was represented at the Constitutional Conference of 1967–1968 as a government party. Ondo Edu became Carrero Blanco's favorite candidate for the presidency of the future republic. But at the 1968 elections, he was beaten by Macías Nguema in the first and second ballot, not having wanted to enter an agreement with Ndongo Miyone after the first ballot, the latter then withdrawing in favor of Macías Nguema. But two of Ondo Edu's main supporters, Ndongo Engonga and Mba Ada, became vice-president of the Asamblea de la Republica (Parliament) and president of the Consejo de la Republica (Senate), respectively. After the celebration of independence, Ondo Edu, knowing his life was in danger, again sought refuge in Gabon. With Macías's assurance that Ondo Edu had nothing to fear in his country, Gabon authorized his extradition in November 1968. Rapidly Ondo Edu was placed under house arrest, charged with conspiracy, and murdered in January 1969 with Ndongo Engonga, Mba Micha, S. Ngomo Ndumu, etc. Ondo Edu's wife, Edelvina Oyana, was also murdered.

ONDO ELA, Salvador. An Esangui from Mongomo. A cousin of Obiang Nguema. During the Macías Nguema regime, he was in charge of the prison and torture chamber of Playa Negra prison in Santa Isabel. He was notorious for the torture inflicted with the help of his dog. His assistant was Cayo Mba Ondo. Ondo Ela was condemned to death in the trial of Macías Nguema in September 1979, and was said, by the International Commission of Jurists, to have been executed. However, he reappeared miraculously on October 8, 1981, joining the army that same day. In 1983 he was designated government delegate in Mongomo. In 1983, he became a government representative to Mongomo. He died in 1990.

ONDO ELA MANGUE, Lorenzo. Fang from Mongomo. A cadet, promoted on February 3, 1981, to the grade of sub-lieutenant. Brother to J. Ndong Ela Mangue, minister for the interior. In December 1982 he was named director general for military cooperation in the Ministry of Defense. In the military trial of April 1995, he was a member of the tribunal that judged Moto Nsá and a dozen other military men. In August 1998, he was expelled from the army (due to the actions of his brothers Guillermo and Julio Ela Mangue).

ONDO MANE ONDO AVANG, Damian. An Esangui from Mongomo. Governor of the National Bank under Macías Nguema. After the 1979 coup he was made private secretary to Vice-President Maye Ela and a director within the Supreme Military Council. He is reputed to be the strong man in the national banking system. In 1984, Obiang Nguema nominated him director of the Bank of the Central African States in Santa Isabel upon accession of Equatorial Guinea to the French franc zone. He was arrested in July 1986 after the abortive coup led by Mbá Onaña and sentenced to 28 months imprisonment for having "insulted the Head of State." He was released in October 1987 with other Nguemists. In 1992 he was found to be a barman at Mongomo.

ONDO MAYE, Serafin. Holds a degree from the Soviet Union. In January 1994, he became judge in the Court of Appeals at Bata.

ONDO MBA, Cayo see Mba Ondo, C.

ONDO MICHA, Lucas, 1939?–1974. Fang from the Nsork district. Primary school teacher trained in Bata, then in Spain, just as Obiang Mbá. With A. Mañe Ela and others, he took part in the Cruzada Nacional de Liberación de Guinea Ecuatorial. After teaching in several schools of Río Muni, he became economic delegate of the Education Ministry in 1969 in this province. Arrested and imprisoned in 1973, he was the mainspring of the attempted coup d'etat of June 1974 by the Bata prisoners. He was sentenced to death by a military court and executed on June 26, 1974, with 26 other democrats.

ONDO MITOGO, Pedro. Fang from Kogo. Born on April 20, 1953. Holds a diploma in administration and communication. In 1993 he became director general of postal services. On September 11, he was present with his minister at the confiscation and the searching of postal bags. In November, he was elected a PDGE deputy. In the December 22 government, he became secretary of state for post and telecommunications. He did not figure in the government of January 8, 1996.

ONDO MONDO, Antonio see Popular Action

ONDO NGUEMA, Armengol see Nguema Mbasogo Ondo, A.

ONDO NKUMU, Julian (Mongomo). Cousin to Obiang Nguema. See Bata; France; Krohnert; Santa Isabel; Terror; Torture.

ONDO OBIANG NCHAMA, Vicente. Fang from Ebebiyin. Went to secondary school at Santa Isabel. Studied economics in the USSR. Along with E. Engonga Nguema he was authorized in 1985 to buy the 134-hectare agricultural estate Vista Legre at Basupo del Oeste, for FCFA 14,789,322. A member of the PSD led by Balinga, he was expelled, accused of treason for having accepted, along with three others, to contest the 21 November 1993 elections in return for $9,000 received from the dictatorship. He became a member of the central committee of the PDGE, as well as financial controller and head of studies and projects of the National Society of Electricity (EGA).

ONDO OBIANG ALOGO, Felipe. Fang from Mongomo. Born in 1940. A schoolteacher (Escuela Superior Indígena). Reputed to be very anti-Spanish. Under Macías Nguema, member of the PUNT. Well known for his dubious declarations: before students, he termed Christ a "disgusting worm hung up on a Cross"; as for King Juan Carlos I of Spain, he called him "an indecent bastard."

From 1972 to 1975, minister of soil cultivation, succeeding Grange Molay, then replaced by Nsué Miko in 1975. He then became public health minister, following Rafael Obiang. In 1981 he was designated secretary with the Ministry of Foreign Affairs. In June he was put forward as a replacement for the Esangui Owono Asangono, as ambassador to Spain, but the Spanish government refused to accept him on the grounds that under Macías Nguema he had conducted violent anti-Spanish campaigns. At the end of 1982, he was appointed minister of education and culture.

Since 1988, he has been PDGE deputy and counsellor to the president. In November 1993, he was again elected PDGE deputy. In December, he was named president of the Parliament.

In January 1994, he led a delegation of 10 parliamentary representatives and leaders of the "opposition" to praise Nguemist democracy in France, Germany and Switzerland, and to the UN. But in December, he was dismissed from his post as president of the Chamber of Representatives of the People, for having criticized the Human Rights situation in the country.

In August 1995, with Bonifacio Nguema Esono and Eloy Eyi Mbengono (also from the clan from Mongomo), he formed FDR: Fuerza Democrática Republicana. He was arrested along with his colleagues in the capital on October 4, and transferred to house arrest in Mongomo. In late October, Ondo Obiang and Nguema Esono sought refuge in Gabon and informed the resident representative of the UN and the High Commission for Refugees that at Mongomo, a commando led by Commander Eustaquio Nseng Esono Nve was in charge of eliminating them.

In the spring of 1996, Radio Exterior de España broadcast an interview with Ondo Obiang, descrediting information about a so-called desire for democratization in Obiang Nguema. This interview had great repercussions among the 50,000 Equato-Guineans who had sought refuge in Gabon. At the beginning of September 1996, it is said he was victim of an attempted murder by an agent of the Nguemist security, arrested in Oyem. On November 18, 11 junior officers were sentenced to 4–13 years of prison and fines up to FCFA 59 mio having prepared a coup in July. They would be relatives to Ondo Obiang.

ONDO OBIANG MUKUY, Saturnino. At the ministerial reshuffle of April 8, 1996, he became director general of the central services and the high officials of the president of the republic.

O'NEILL, Joseph. In October 1995, the U.S. closed its embassy and only a chargé d'affaires, J. O'Neill remained in spite of the protests of the Nguemists.
See also United States.

ONVA ONDO, Crispín (named Ngueguer Nguru). Born 1950 in Ebebiyin. Following the path of the UNED. At the ministerial reshuffle of April 8, 1996, he became director general of secondary education. One of the leaders of UDS.

OPERACION LEON see Obiang Nguema, T.

OPPOSITION. With the exception of some credible groups, there is an opposition said to be "tame," pro-Obiang Nguema, made up of satellite parties of the

PDGE. In 1995, the FRELIGE stressed the need for the opposition to stop infighting.

On April 26, 1995, it published a strongly anti-Spain document, accusing Felipe Gonzalez of creating artificial tensions. This document was signed by the Liberal Party (Alfonso Nsue), UDENA (Pedro Bueriberi), Social Democratic Coalition Party (Francisco Mabale), Socialist Party (Tomas Mecheba). A delegation of this "opposition" attended the 2nd Party Convention of the PDGE (Bueribueri, Mabale, Mecheba, Moswi). During the municipal elections in September, the Jovenes Antorchas spread terror in the capital, while local authorities in various localities of Río Muni had opponents shot (Ebebiyin region) and arrests and raids on houses increased. On October 20, the police raided the headquarters of the CPDS to arrest Placido Mico; not finding him there, they arrested his brother Inocencio, who was imprisoned for one week. Towards the end of 1995, offices of opposition parties in all the provincial towns and villages were closed down.

The Nguemist regime referred to opponents of Obiang Nguema as Mikó. It also used the expression "moderate opposition" for the "tame" parties, and calls the effective opposition "radical," as he does the ANRD. In March 1996, after Obiang Nguema's "reelection," the director of television, Eyene Opkua, addressed a communique to the Spanish media, in which he referred to opponents as "agitators" acting for the benefit of Spanish democrats and accused the opposition of preventing the people from benefiting from petroleum revenues. The so-called "government of national unity" of April 8, 1996, included several leaders of the domesticated opposition as ministers or secretaries of state (in particular Bikomo Nanguande, Modu Akuse Bindang, Nsue Mokui, etc.). In its May 1996 bulletin, the PDGE accused these parties of plotting an invasion of the country. On June 28, 1996, the Nguemist law and order forces killed an opponent and arrested dozens of others in the village of Moyos Esacunan (Mikomeseng district). In August under the presidency of Luis Ondo Ayang, general secretary of the National Alliance for Democratic Restoration, ten opposition parties reunited at Madrid, in an effort to revive the national pact violated by Obiang Nguema. When returning to his country, he was arrested by a member of the president's personal security, Narciso Edu Nsue, and imprisoned from November 15–17, 1996, to punish him for what he had said on Radio Exterior de España. End of 1996, other members of the CPDS and MAIB were arrested, and some of them wounded. The authorities wanted to force C. Bakale to present himself to a military court. He refused, supported by the CPDS and five other parties of the opposition. On December 4, 1996, 20 policemen in uniform invaded CPDS's headquarters without a search warrant.

At the end of May 1997, the walls of the capital were scribbled with "Kabila, come." Throughout the country, repressive measures were taken against the opposition after the announcement of Moto Nsa's attempted coup in June 1997. In his 1997 report, the special rapporteur of the UN Commission for Human Rights confirmed that political parties of the opposition were harassed and repressed. On June 17, 1997, a note from the armed forces to Obiang Nguema underlined that some parties of the opposition were accomplices of the dictatorship. A dozen officers, members of the opposition, took refuge in Cameroon; they were arrested and imprisoned there, although eight of them benefitted from the status of refugees from the UN High Commissary. In 1997–1998, the government delegate in Mikomeseng, Francisco Mba Mandama, had members of the opposition imprisoned and asked for a ransom.

On March 25, 1998, an agreement was signed between the government and the opposition in order to create a mixed commission in view of the elections. But on April 5, the UP and CPDS denounced "serious violations" of the agreement: increasing of police roadblocks and preventing the opposition from carrying out its political activities. The electoral list was launched on June 29, but the opposition was put aside (expatriates and minors were put on the lists). They threatened to boycott: in spite of the agreement, the opposition had only 13 out of 18 districts left. On July 8, 1998, Union Popular denounced the preparation of fraudulent massive elections. On July 14, 1998, the Nguemists denounced "the lack of maturity of the leaders of the opposition, who want to create an atmosphere of turpitude." Members of the army worked in making up electoral lists. About 50 UP members of the polling commission in Kié-Ntem were eliminated from the commission. However, Mba Ada insisted on the fact that UP will participate on the ballot, which it is sure to win if there is no fraud.

In September 1998, the opposition reported that a minister had paid people working at polling stations with fake money. The PDGE put growing pressure on the population to join the party of the dictator. More than 50 opponents were arrested in Rio Muni and in Fernando Po during the last trimester of 1998, thus showing the popular resistance. On October 9, the opposition accused the government of dismissing mayors who were members of the opposition. On the 13th, the democratic opposition announced a transition pact in view of the legislative elections. On the 26th, they threatened not to participate any longer in the elaboration of elector lists. On the 28th, the government withdrew 65,000 electors from the electoral lists (opponents).

On November 10, the Nguemists accused the democratic opposition of "spreading confusion" and arrested some 20 militants, among them the secretary general of CPDS, Amancio Nzé. At the end of November, a delegation of the CPDS travelled to Switzerland in order to participate in the Socialist International meeting.

On December 3, the mixed commission of the government and the opposition concerning the legislative elections failed.

See also Elections; Human Rights; Joint Opposition Platform; Missions; Moto; Ndong Ona, A.; Political Parties; Refugees; Terror; Torture.

ORDEN DE AFRICA see Spain

ORGANISACION DE LA MUJER DE GUINEA ECUATORIAL. Movement set up in 1975 by ANRD to defend the situation of Equatorial-Guinean women.

ORGANIZATION OF AFRICAN UNITY (OAU). Established in May 1963 "to promote the unity and solidarity of the African and Malagasy States," the organization groups some 50 countries. The Equato-Guinean referendum on the Constitution in August 1968 was supervised by an OAU commission. After the March-April 1968 events (Emergencia), the OAU agreed to send technical personnel to Equatorial Guinea. Of the 63 experts required, they offered 16 (doctors, engineers, administrators, military advisers). Most of these technical advisers have left the country of their own free will or were expelled. Whereas various members of the OAU strongly criticized the Uganda regime. Equatorial Guinea has been treated with "brotherly silence." It is the only country that did not attend the OAU Khartoum summit in 1978.

In early 1980, the former vice-president of the republic under Macías Nguema and Uncle Obiang Nguema's, Donifacio Nguema Esono, was sent as ambassador to the OAU and Ethiopia, in Addis-Ababa.

In late January 1981, General Secretary Edem Kodjo attended in Santa Isabel the ceremony promoting Obiang Nguema to colonel and Mba Oñana to lieutenant-colonel. In December, Nguema Esono was replaced by F. Mba Ondo Nchama. In October 1993, OAU first refused to provide observers for the November "21 elections," stating that the request had come too late. It however sent some, in spite of the international boycott. In November 1995, Equatorial Guinea, and nine other countries were deprived of their right of vote and participation in the OAU, as a result of $1.6 million in delayed contributions.

ORGANIZATION OF PETROL EXPORTING COUNTRIES (OPEC). Towards the end of 1987, OPEC lent $1 million to support the balance of provided support for the balance of payments four times. In 1991, OPEC again offered aid for $1.5 million, for a project of agricultural diversification; this was a gift that was renewed two years later. In 1995, a new agreement for $2 million for the improvement of educational infrastructure on the island of Fernando Po was concluded. See also Petroleum.

OSA ADUGU, Simón. Born May 15, 1961, in Andok Eseng (Ebebiyin). Secondary school in Ebebiyin and Bata. In 1987 began studies at the University of Las Palmas (Canary Islands, Spain). In 1993, studied maritime engineering. Since February 1994, director general of fisheries. At the ministerial reshuffle of April 8, 1996, he remains in charge of this function.He kept his office at the end of 1998.

OSA MONGOMO, Diosdade, Sergio. In the April 8, 1996, ministerial reshuffle, he became director general of agriculture.

OSA OSA ECORO, Jeronimo. Born 1957. Fang from Mongomo. Internship in statistics at Yaounde. In 1994, director general of statistics. In this capacity, he threatened his colleagues with sanctions if they exposed any instances of census manipulation. At the ministerial reshuffle of April 8, 1996, he was director general of taxes. He kept his office at the end of 1998.
See also Elections.

OSONO NGUEMA, Elias see Timber

OSSORIO ZABALA, Amadeo. Spanish doctor. Founding member of the Sociedad de Africanistas y Colonialistas (Society of Africanists and Colonialists) that supported Iradier. Ossorio participated with 5,000 pesetas in the financing of the second Iradier expedition, joining it in September 1884. He explored the Río Campo and Utamboni basins, even after Iradier and Montes de Oca, fallen ill, had given up. From 50,000 sq km placed under Spanish authority by Ossorio, Iradier and Montes de Oca, the Paris Treaty left only 26,000 sq km in 1900. In 1901

Ossorio was a member of the Mixed Commission for delimitation of the Río Muni frontier. He wrote six major works on Spanish Guinea.

OTERO DE LEON, José Maria. Ambassador of Spain since 1995. In the Moto Nsa case, he was highly criticized by the Equato-Guinean opposition and the Spanish press, and accused of strengthening the Nguemist regime. In June 1997, he was sent to Senegal and replaced by Jacobo González-Arnao Campos.

OTOGO, Rosendo. Auditor general of the Guinextebank. He favored his friends with loans. In 1986 he owed the Guinextebank two loans which he granted himself, for a total of FCFA 7,926,000. In 1992 he became director of GE-Total and was among the counsellors of the INSESO. In this capacity, he earned FCFA 100,000 per month. In 1996, according to the former judge of the Supreme Court, Fermin Nguema Esono, the Guineo-Spanish project to finance the Moulins de Bioko SA ($5 million) had failed due to Nguemists frauds (in this case, those of R. Otogo and R. Mangue).

OUR LADY OF AFRICA SUPERIOR UNIVERSITY COLLEGE (Colegio Mayor Universitario Nuestra Señora de Africa). A college in the Madrid University campus founded in 1964. Equato-Guinean students have been residing there since before independence, along with other Africans and a few Europeans. L. Beltrán was its director in 1985, after which he was succeeded by Olegario Negrín Fajardo, and on June 12, 1998, by Carlos Robles Fraga, with Basilio Rodriguez Cañada as sub-director.

OVENGA EYANG MBA, Maximiliano. In the spring of 1979, he became director general of the Foreign Affairs bureau. Towards the end of 1982 he became administrative secretary of the Ministry of Defense.

Since 1991, he has been personal advisor to Obiang Nguema and director general of radio, press and TV. Towards the end of 1993, he closed down Radio Africa 2000, as reprisal for the Spanish sanctions in protest against the undemocratic elections in November. Towards the end of 1995 he compared the petroleum economy of Equatorial Guinea to Kuwait.

OVONO NGUEMA, Elias. Fang from Ebebiyin. Born on October 30, 1962. Nephew of Obiang Nguema. An auditor. On December 22, 1993, he became state secretary for the forest economy. In the January 8, 1996, government, he was promoted to vice-minister of post and telecommunications. In the April 8, 1996, government, he became minister for transports and communications. At the ministerial reshuffle of January 21, 1998, he was succeded by Marcelino Oyono Ntutumu.

OWEN, Fitz-William, 1774–1857. British captain in the Royal Navy. Seeing that Fernando Po had been abandoned by Spain at the end of the 18th century, several British expeditions, in particular the Kelly one, tried to occupy the island. In 1827 it was Captain Owen's expedition that attempted occupation pretending to establish the Anti-Slavery Tribunal transferred from Sierra Leone. In 1826 Owen had participated in Great Britain's fight against the Ashanti in Nigeria. In Fernando Po he founded Clarence Port and Clarence City (Santa Isabel). A few months after the expedition's arrival three-quarters of the members had died. From 1827 to

1833 Owen was superintendent of the island, with Captain Harrison as civil governor (1827–1830) and Colonel Nicholls as governor of Clarence. Owen had under his authority a young half-breed, John Beecroft, who was the intendant of the expedition and who later became governor of Fernando Po. Owen left Fernando Po in 1833 with the Warren expedition, which had come to rescue the survivors of several previous expeditions.

OWONO, Bartolomé. From Mongomo. An agent of Presidential security. See also Baney.

OWONO ASANGONO, Evuna see Evuna Owono Asangono, A.

OWONO MANANA, Felipe. Fang native of Mongomo. Junior lieutenant. Appointed minister of the interior in December 1981, then minister of territorial administration in October 1982. He was arrested in connection with the coup attempt of July 1986. Died.

OWONO MITUY, Damian see Plot (April 1981)

OWONO NGUEMA ONGUENE, Marcelino see Nguema Nguema Onguene

OWONO OBAMA, Antonio. Fang from the Evinayong district. Teacher, trained in the Escuela Superior Indígena from 1950 to 1955. After a training period in Spain as town hall secretary, he became, in 1964, governmental delegate of the Evinayong district. A refugee first in Cameroon, then in Gabon, he attempted in 1976, with about 30 compatriots, an armed attack on the frontier-post close to Akurenam, killing and injuring about 10 National Guards. He was arrested by Gabonese authorities.

During the elections of 1993, he became vice-president of the National Assembly on the PSD list. In 1998 he joined the PDGE.

OYO EBULE, Evangelina. From Baney. Holds a degree in law (Madrid). Since 1989 she has been a judge at the Supreme Court.

OYONO, Luis see Evinayong

OYONO, Nazarino. Holds a degree in law from the University of Tachkent (Uzbekistan, USSR). In 1995 he acted as the prosecutor at Moto Nsa's trial.

OYONO ALOGO, Jesus Alfonso, 1920?–1976. Fang from Ebebiyin. Member of the MONALIGE and former close comrade of Macías Nguema. In October 1968 he became minister of public works. Late in 1970 he went to the U.S.S.R. and North Korea, to initiate diplomatic relations. In 1974 he became minister to the presidency of the republic. During the Senior Officials Affair he was assassinated in the Bata prison, together with his colleague Ochaga Ngomo and many others. It is Nguema Esono Nchama who was taken over his office at the presidency, with Oyono Ayingono Mbá as under-secretary of state.

OYONO AYINGONO MBA, Daniel, b. 1940. From Mongomo. Born in 1938. Nephew to Macías Nguema. Preparatory baccalaureate from Madrid. He then studied in Italy, but did not complete his course. He boasts of imaginary degrees. He was brought back to Equatorial Guinea by his father and sent to Cairo for training (six months) for the foreign service which was paid for by his uncle Macías Nguema. On his return he was made chief of the presidential protocol department, and from 1971 he was put in charge of the President's household.

After the disappearance of several political and administrative leaders, Oyono Ayingono has become the government's man Friday since October 1975: i.e., under-secretary of state to the presidency, chief of protocol, general director of information, commissioner of empresas estatales (state-owned shops), finance minister, responsibile for merchant marine, head of national security. Through the Adoual Company (Canary Islands) he monopolized the import business and competed with García Trevijano's SIMED S.A. In 1976 he openly published "El Balle de los Malditos" (The Dance of the Damned), composed of manipulated excerpts from the June 1974 coup d'etat trial. In mid-1977 he accompanied Monica Bindang Macías during an official visit to North Korea. At the end of January 1978, according to the Spanish press, he took refuge in Spain with Monica Bindang, the director of the Central Bank and a North Korean officer. In fact they have all gone back to Santa Isabel via Libya.

After the 1979 coup, he took refuge in Gabon, but returned shortly thereafter to take up his earlier functions again. Maye Ela was, however, jealous of him and wanted to take over his residence, and at the same time he left for Paris, where he made accusations that Maye Ela had been implicated in murders and torture, and Obiang Nguema and Maye Ela, both cousins of his, were usurpers. He later went to Spain to work with García Trevijano and José Dougan. He tried to found an antidictatorial movement and was spreading defamatory statements about the ANRD.

Oyono Ayingono was feared, among the refugees, as a Nguemist spy. Towards 1980, he founded a Council for Revolutionary Command of Guinean Socialist Patriots and Executives (CCRCGS); the council does not have any known activities. Since 1980, he has been a tradesman in African objects in the suburb of Madrid (Mostoles).

OYONO AWONG ADA, Secundino. From Evinayong. Nephew to Ondo Edu. Brother-in-law to Obiang Nguema. A lawyer. He attended the meeting of refugees in April 1983, at Saragossa, for a so-called ANRD (Accion Nacional de Reforma Democratica), which misused the acronym of the National Alliance for Democratic Restoration (Alianza Nacional de Restauración Democrática, ANRD).

In 1984–1985, he was an ally to Ruben Ndong in Paris. His wife and he were both members of the Committee for the Democratic Union for Liberty in Equatorial Guinea. In mid-1990, he founded the Democratic and Social Union (Union democrática y social, UDS) with the businessman Modu Akuse, a refugee in Lisbon. Well known for his lack of political commitment.

The UDS joined the POC; but it breached the election boycott of November 21, 1993, and turned into a satellite party of the PDGE. In the elections, the UDS obtained 5 seats out of 80. Oyono Awong was elected deputy from Evinayong. Disappointed at not receiving a ministerial appointment, Oyono had to be happy with a small post as a customs official. His colleague Francisco Abaga returned unhappily to Spain.

In January 1994, S. Oyono was a part of the delegation of parliamentary representatives and representatives of the "opposition" who were to praise the

Nguemist democracy in Europe and to the UNO. After accusations of "judicial insecurity" made by the prosecutor Nve Mbangono, in January 1995, Oyono Awong was part of an enquiry commission appointed by M. Ebendeng Nsomo, minister for defense, under the orders of Obiang Nguema. On May 9 he was received by the dictator, to discuss the political situation.

During the presidential elections in February 1996, S. Oyono Awong was the only candidate of the "opposition" left, as all the other representatives of the democratic opposition parties had withdrawn. He did not campaign, and did no more than accompany the dictator on his movements. During the negotiations for the "government of national unity" (February–March 1996), Obiang Nguema tried to force him to become minister for justice and religion. He refused. Oyono Awong then proposed the founding of a Democratic Front for National Salvation (Frente Democrático de Salvación Nacional, FDSN) which was said to be composed of parties he called "moderate," i.e., those of the tame opposition (CLD, CSDP, PSD, PL, PSGE, a faction of UDENA) and, obviously, the PDGE.

See also Elections; Social Democratic and Popular Convergency.

OYONO MASA, Luis. Fang born in Bisogo-Nsomo (Evinayong), in 1944. Trained in the secondary school, in Bata, with Alejandro Envoro Ovono (from Mongomo). In 1975 Envoro Ovono became responsible for the national network of hydrocarbon stations; he then hired Oyono Masa. From 1992 to 1995, Oyono became director of GE-Total in Bata.

Since 1995 Oyono Masa is delegate of the government for the district of Evinayong. He practices the Bwiti cult, and regularly uses iboga. He is thought to have been leader of the attack against the former headmaster of the secondary school "B. Ondo Edu," in Evinayong, Alberto Nze Mba, a week before the municipal elections of September 1995.

OYONO NDONGO MIFUMU, Miguel. Called "Olobot" (the robot). A Ntumu Fang from Mikomeseng. Returned to the country in 1975, and became a technician in the Ministry of Agriculture, and later chief of the chemistry laboratory (food administration). He obtained a scholarship to study in Brazil, from where he returned just before the coup d'etat of August 1979. On January 22, 1980, he became joint secretary of the Ministry of Agriculture. On May 16, 1981, he became technical secretary in the Ministry. In October 1982, he became minister for agriculture in the civil government, replacing Buale Borico, who had fled to Spain.

In July 1983 he accompanied Obiang Nguema to Madrid; he was involved in various scandals. In January 1986, Obiang Nguema had him replaced by Abeso Nvono. He was posted at Libreville, as the Director of the Department of Agriculture and Industry of the EEAC. On January 22, 1992, Oyono Ndong became vice-prime minister and minister of state to the president of the "transitional" government, in charge of Livestock and Fisheries. That summer, he led a delegation to the EC, Spain and France, which was rejected almost everywhere. He suggested hiring an expert in communication in order to counter the so-called defamation campaigns.

In March 1993, Oyono Ndong was sent to Felipe Gonzalez, in order to make peace. He was willing to expel all the Spanish volunteers for cooperation. In

November, he was elected PDGE deputy for Mikomeseng. On December 22, he was appointed minister of state in charge of foreign affairs and cooperation, a post with which he ferociously defended the regime. The Spanish press termed him illiterate.

On October 11, 1995, before the UN General Assembly, Oyono Ndong accused political circles and the Spanish media of interference in the internal affairs of the country by supporting defamation campaigns and distortion of facts. He presented the Nguemist regime as a model regime.

In the January 8, 1996, ministerial reshuffle he retained his post of minister of state in charge of foreign affairs and cooperation, with Feliciano "Mbato" Obama Nsue Mangue as vice-minister. Being a confirmed Nguemist, he retained his ministerial post in the April 8, 1996, government. While Equatorial Guinea had just come before the UN Human Rights Commission, in Geneva, he denounced the paper of the special reporter, A. Artucio, whom he accused of lacking objectivity.

In the government of January 1998, he kept his office of minister of foreign affairs, but also became vice-minister. An obsessed Nguemist, he wanted the government to be recognized internationally. In July, he denounced the disapproval of the Spanish government (and of the international community) of the Bubi trial, and blamed the authorities of Madrid for criticizing Obiang. In August 1998, he discreetly threatened the Spanish cooperation. *El País* mentioned that during a conversation with the newspaper, Oyono invited international observers to come and check the conditions of the prisoners in Playa Negra, known to be "one of the most sordid prisons in Africa." The next day, he had changed his mind, accusing the newspaper of "informative terrorism." Soon after, he went on an African tour (Benin, Togo, Ghana) to thwart the "systematic denigration campaign" by Radio Exterior de España and other media of democratic countries, and to "report on the real situation of the country, with respect to the systematic campaign of denigration carried from the exterior."

On the 30th anniversary of the republic, October 12, 1998, while justifying the fact that an official Spanish delegation has not been invited, he declared that the Nguemist regime has managed to put in place a free marked economy and a stable democracy showing constant improvements.

See also Agriculture; European Community; Spain.

OYONO NSUE, Lucas. From Ebebiyin. A captain. In 1988 he was the military attaché to Nigeria. He tried to soothe the Nigerians with regard to the settling of South Africans in Fernando Po. He was arrested in the so-called coup attempt of August 1993, as a member of the Unión Popular. In an Urgent Action, Amnesty International said it feared his disappearance. He was expelled and was sentenced to three years of house arrest.

OYONO NTUTUMU, Marcelino. Fang from Bata. Born in 1952. Brother-in-law to Obiang Nguema. A trader. Called "Abigui." In the January 24, 1992, "transitional" government, he became minister for transports, post and telecommunications. With Obiang Nguema he held the GETESA to ransom, via the BIAO. In November 1993, he was elected PDGE deputy for Bata. But when he was accused of favoring the opposition, he did not figure in the December government.

On January 19, 1994, he was named adviser to the president of the government for the economy and finance. In the April 8, 1996, government, he was promoted to minister for the economy and finance. In the January 1998 government he became minister of transport and commerce.

OYONO SA ABEGUE, Valentin. A Fang born July 16, 1946, in Ndjong-Nsomo (Evinayong). Holds a Ph.D. in economics (Lyon, France). Founding member of the ANRD. From 1974 to 1976 he was coordinating secretary of the organization's executive committee: from 1976 to 1978 secretary-general; 1978-81 secretary for ideological orientation. He is the author of a noteworthy economic history of Equatorial Guinea and the best researched analysis to date of Fang society (see Bibliography).

OYO RIQUEZA, Eulogio. A Bubi; born in 1941 at Baney. Junior lieutenant trained in the Saragozza Military Academy, Spain. In the transitional period before Independence he was promoted to lieutenant, and after independence, to captain. Under Macías Nguema, Oyo Riqueza presided over court-martials. After the 1979 coup he was made a member of the Supreme Military Council and governor of Fernando Po. In September 1979 he was presiding judge at the military court that passed judgment on Macías Nguema. He was one of the few Equatorial Guineans to have witnessed the execution of Macías Nguema and his accomplices by the Moroccan firing squad. In September 1979 he was also made head of the Chamber of Agriculture in Santa Isabel.

In January 1980, he undertook a mission to Annobón. On February 4, 1980, he replaced Ela Nseng as second vice-president of the republic (the latter being posted as ambassador to China in Beijing) and was concurrently made responsible for trade and finance. In February 1981 he was promoted to major after having decorated President Obiang Nguema with the Order of Merit on January 31 in the name of the Supreme Military Council. At the end of May 1981 he was relieved of his vice-presidential post, but retained the labor portfolio. He was relieved of this latter post in October 1982.

In April 1982, he attended the donors conference of the UNDP in Geneva. He disappeared from the list of ministers of the cabinet in October of the same year. Towards the end of 1986, he owed the Guinextebank FCFA 51,761,000. In 1993, he declared himself a faithful servant of the Nguemist regime, but the top brass remained wary of his ambition. He was sent as a commercial attaché to the embassy in Cameron. He kept his office in 1998, and is also a tradesman.

❖ P ❖

PACT OF NON-AGGRESSION see Non-Aggression Pact

PAGALU. Name proposed in 1973 by the PUNT for the island of Annobón; in recollection of the rooster (galo in Portuguese) symbol used during 1968 elections. Macías Nguema was called Papa Gallo (Father Cock), shortened to Pagalú. After 1979 coup d'etat, the islanders forced the second Nguemist dictator, Obiang Nguema, to revert to the name Annobón. See Annobón.

PALACIOS, José. Claretian priest, at Annobón since 1980. He was alone for five years, until he was joined by Brother Manuel Pampillón, in 1985.

PANADES, Teodoro Egidio see Convergency for Social Democracy

PARDO TREATY. Signed on March 24, 1778, in confirmation of the San Ildefonso Treaty, between Maria I of Portugal and Carlos II of Spain. Under the 13th clause, Spain obtained, in addition to the islands, the African coast between the mouth of the Niger and that of the Ogoowe (Cape Lopez). No European state protested against this treaty. Three weeks after its signing, the Argelejos expedition was sent to take possession of these territories representing about 800,000 sq km.

See also History.

PARIS TREATY (also called Muni Treaty). Spain requested the acknowledgment of 300,000 sq km in the Gulf of Guinea (of the 800,000 sq km inherited under the Pardo Treaty), but the Berlin Conference only granted 180,000 sq km. By the end of 1885, France and Germany agreed to set the limit between their two territories, Gabon and the Cameroon, along Río Campo, which meant Spain's eviction from the African continent. The Spanish protests led to the establishment of a Franco-Spanish Commission in 1886, but the latter only recognized the status quo and entrusted arbitration to the king of Denmark. Arbitration could however not take place because of the collapse of Spain's empire in the Americas and Asia. Meanwhile France set up military posts in various places of Río Muni, and French warehouses were established. From February to June 1900 Franco-Spanish negotiations took place in Paris, which by the Paris Treaty left 26,000 sq km between the Campo and Utamboni Rivers to Spain, with the eastern border on 10° 30' Greenwich. A joint committee determined the borderline in 1901. In 1903 the Vatican, relying on the Paris Treaty and against the Gabonese vicariate's wishes, entrusted jurisdiction over Río Muni to the vicariate of the Spanish Church of Fernando Po, which in 1904 became the apostolic prefecture.

PARLIAMENT. Under Obiang Nguema, in October 1982, Elo Nve Mbengono, a Nguemist fascist ideologist, was named delegate to the President for relations with the House of Representatives of the People.

In late 1984, the president of the House was F. Boddien Ngalo, and the vice-president Owono Minang. In 1985, A. Sima proposed the creation of a single party. Upon voting there were 31 ayes and 29 nays (a remarkable result in an assembly whose members were named by the dictator). Several members supporting multipartyism were arrested. In the January 24, 1992, "transitional" government, Elo Nve Mbengono retained his post.

On December 10, 1993, the new Parliament was opened by Obiang Nguema. Out of 80 deputies, 68 belonged to the PDGE, 6 to the CSDP, 5 to the UDS, 1 to the PL. All of them swore loyalty to the president, a procedure that had been judged nondemocratic by the UN experts. The ambassadors of Spain, France and USA were not present at the session. The Parliament was presided over by Felipe Ondo Obiang (of the clan from Mongomo), with Oko Ebobo as vice-president. The regional composition of the house was as follows:

Akonibe	3	Luba	4
Akurenam	4	Mikomeseng	4
Anisok	3	Mongomo	7
Annobón	3	Niefang	4
Baney	3	Nso Nsomo	3
Bata	8	Nsork	3
Riaba	2	Río Benito	3
Ebebiyin	7	Santa Isabel	9
Kogo	3		

Decisions are taken by consensus in order to "avoid opposition among the deputies."

In January 1994, a croup of 10 parliamentary representatives and leaders of the "opposition" made a two-week journey to France, Germany, and Switzerland (mainly to the UN Geneva) to praise Nguemist democracy. The delegation was led by F. Ondo Obiang. In October, Obiang Nguema dismissed F. Ondo Obiang (according to him, he resigned) and Oko Ebobo, and named Marcelino Nguema Onguene as president of the Parliament. The deputies earn a monthly salary of FCFA100,000 (average salary of a schoolteacher: FCFA 30,000) and during the two sessions of 60 days, a per diem of FCFA 20,000.

In late 1995, Ondo Obiang and Nguema Esono, briefly took refuge in Gabon, fearing murder by Cdr. Eustaqui Nseng Nve, Obiang Nguema's nephew. Considering the lack of an Official Bulletin, the decisions of the Parliament were not published.

In the April 8, 1996, government, the Ministry in Charge of Relations with the Parliament and Legislative Coordination was given to Antonio-Pascual Oko Ebobo. The April 1996 Report of the Department of State on Human Rights for 1995, presented to the Chamber of Representatives and to the Senate stressed that the President's Democratic Party of Equatorial Guinea (PDGE) "controls the judiciary and the legislature, the latter through fraudulent elections." As a consequence: "While there is an elected Chamber of Representatives, it is not representative and is dominated by the Government." . . ."In practice, authorities do not uniformly respect the Constitution and laws passed by the Chamber of Deputies." In the government of January 1998, A. F. Nve Ngu is Minister of State at the Presidency, in charge of Relations with the Assemblies and Legal Matters.

See also Army; Asamblea de la Republica; Asamblea General; Asamblea Nacional Popular; Baney; Camara de los Representantes; Cayetano Toherida; Censorship; China (Popular); Convergencia; Coup d'etat; Ebiaka Mohete; Echek, S.E.; Ebang Mbele Abang; Edjang Angue; Elections; Elo Ndong Nsefumu; Envoro Owono; Epam Uri; Esono Miko Miha; Eyegue Obama Asue; Francophony: Human Rights; International Federation; Labor; Mabale Mba; Mangue Obama Nfube; Mecheba Fernandez; Milam Onvogo; Modu Akuse Bindang; Muñoz Ilata; Ndong Mba, A.; Ngomo Bengono; Ngua Nfumu; Nguema Esono, L.; Nguema Nguema Onguene; Nguema Onvono; Nsé Nfumu, A.; Nsobey Efuman Nsue; Nsue Nguema Nsuga; Nve Nzeng; Nvono Akele; Obama Nsue Mangue; Oko Ebono; Olo Mba Nzeng; Ondo Mitogo; Ondo Obiang Alogo; Opposition; Oyono Awong Ada; Oyono Ndongo Mifumu; Oyono Ntutumu; Progress Party; Radio Exterior de Espáa; Seriche Bioko Malabo; Siale Bilekia; Sima, A.; Sisa Torres; Tamarite Burgos; Young Torches.

PARLIAMENT OF STRASBOURG see European Union

PARTIDO DE LA COALICION SOCIAL DEMOCRATA (PCSD) see Social Democratic Coalition Party

PARTIDO DE LA CONVERGENCIA PARA LA DEMOCRACIA SOCIAL see Social and Popular Convergency

PARTIDO DEL PROGRESO DE GUINEA ECUATORIAL (PP) see Progress Party

PARTIDO DEMOCRATICO DE GUINEA ECUATORIAL see "Democratic" Party of Equatorial Guinea (PDGE)

PARTIDO INDEPENDIENTE (PI) see Independent Party

PARTIDO LIBERAL (PL) see Liberal Party

PARTIDO NACIONAL PARA LA DEMOCRACIA, DESARROLLO Y EDUCACION CIVICA (PANDECA) see National Party for Democracy, Development and Civic Education

PARTIDO POPULAR DE PROGRESO (PPP) see Popular Progress Party

PARTIDO SOCIAL DEMOCRATA DE GUINEA ECUATORIAL (PSD) see Social Democratic Party

PARTIDO SOCIALISTA DE GUINEA ECUATORIAL (PSGE) see Socialist Party

PATRONATO COLONIAL DE ENSENANZA MEDIA. "Cardenal Cisneros" (Colonial patronage of junior high school). During colonization, only children of colonists and a few children of the emancipated could attend this secondary school of Santa Isabel, that depended on the Instituto (high school) "Ramiro Maeztu" of Madrid. With provincialization it became Patronato Provincial and accepted children without discrimination; however severe discipline was requested from young Africans. In 1962 the school became the Instituto Nacional and the Spanish Education Ministry sent qualified professors whereas so far the Dirección General de Plazas y Provincias Españolas used officials, officers, priests, whoever was locally available. Presently the school is named "Rey Malabo." Its head from 1963 to 1969, Trinidad Morgades, was dismissed at the beginning of independence after her brother's assassination (he was counsellor of the republic). Esuba Machele who succeeded Mrs. Morgades fell in disgrace, and became head of the Instituto (High School) "Carlos Lwanga" of Bata; thanks to a medical leave, he could seek refuge in Spain. Father Esono, director general of education, who succeeded him, was assassinated in December 1976 during the Senior Officials Affair.

PATRONATO DE INDIGENAS (Patronage of the Natives). Created in 1904 and headed by the apostolic vicar (Armengoll Coll from 1904 to 1918). Theoretically it was created to protect the Bubi. It was a consultative body for the Curador Colonial, but as early as 1926 no labor contract could be signed without the Patronato's agreement. Modified in 1928, then in 1938, the Patronato was based on the principle of the natives' mental inferiority, and was to develop their culture and their moral sense and to reinforce their support of Spain. After evidence of good behavior, the natives could obtain cards of emancipation. With Francoism, the Patronato became an institution and could acquire and own properties, and besides education handled savings banks, cooperatives, and legal assistance to the unemancipated. The "patrocinado" had no appeal whatever against the Patronato. A Junta de Patrones of 14 members included the governor general, the Apostolic Vicar, represenatives of the administrations, and two emancipated blacks representing the natives of the two provinces. The Patronato levied a tax on each kilo of cocoa and/or coffee that left the colony, which was supposed to be used to finance schools, orphanages, hospitals, cooperatives, etc. With provincialization, since 1960, the Patronato de Indígenas became null and void, the distinction between the emancipated and the unemancipated being no longer legal.

PAULL, George. American Presbyterian missionary, arrived in Corisco in 1864. In 1865 he founded the Mbade mission, on the Río Benito estuary that was to become Río Benito Mission. He died in May 1905.

PAYOT, D. Swiss lawyer. International Federation for Human Rights expert. See Gabon; Human Rights.

PEACE CORPS see United States

PELLON Y RODRIGUEZ, José. Commissioned by the Spanish government to inspect Fernando Po between 1860 and 1875, he visited the colony serveral times and had the opportunity of exploring the coasts of Nigeria, Cameroon, and Gabon, long before the British, German and French did. This permitted the determination of the limits of the Spanish possessions:
  (a) Punta Malimba, at the mouth of Río Cameroon (Wouri);
  (b) left bank of Río Bimbia (i.e., the whole Cameroon Bay);
  (c) left bank of Bonny River, in the Biafra Bay, near New Calabar;

(d) zone between Old Calabar and Cross River;
(e) Cape Formosa, i.e., the eastern part of the Niger Delta;
(f) Río Muni Province, from Rio Campo to Cape Santa Clara.
The 12 volumes of his geographical studies have strangely been lost by the Colonial Section of the Spanish State Ministry. They had caused no reaction from the Spanish authorities concerning the effective occupation of these territories.

PEOPLE'S REPUBLIC OF CHINA see China, People's Republic of

PEREA EPOTA, José. A merchant who lived a long time in Chad. During provincialization he sought refuge in Cameroon, where he participated in the foundation of IPGE and then assumed its presidency. IPGE had its headquarters in Ambam; Ateba was secretary. In 1962 Perea Epota presented a petition to the United Nations for his country's independence. In February 1963 he became president of the Coordination Bureau of the Spanish-Guinean Movement constituted in Ambam.

PEREZ, Melchor see Viyil

PEREZ GOMEZ, Joaquin see Spain

PESCAVEN see Fisheries

PETROCONSULTANTS S.A. Canadian power consultants with head offices in Geneva, Switzerland. Publishes an annual review of prospecting and drilling operations, including maps. The company was awarded a contract with Equatorial Guinea financed by a $2.4 million credit from the World Bank's International Development Association. The company is also involved in frontier questions with Gabon.

PETROLEUM. Oil prospecting in the region started in Gabon in 1931, and later in Nigeria with the Gulf Oil Company. Gulf Oil Spain began drilling in Spanish Guinea. In 1960, apart from Spanish interests, Mobil Spain proved to be very active. From 1966, the following companies have prospected in Equatorial Guinea: Gulf, associated with Minas de Río Tinto; Mobil, associated with the Spanish firm Cipsa; and the Banco de Bilbao; then Chevron Oil, Continental Oil, etc. Royalties yielded about $15 million (1 billion pesetas between 1960 and 1970) to Equatorial Guinea and more than $5 million between 1971 and 1976 (350 million pesetas). After independence in 1968, Chevron Oil began aerophysical readings; it received several concessions to the southwest of Río Muni. Shortly after, it conceded its rights to Continental Oil. The Gabonese claims over Corisco became more pressing. Some Spanish companies were active around Fernando Po. The deposits to the northwest of Fernando Po are part of the geological formation of Que Iboe.
    In 1972 the Gabonese military occupations of the islands of Mbañe, Congo, and Cocotiers along the Río Muni shore gave a strong sense of petroleum interest. The world oil crisis since 1973 has strongly affected Equatorial Guinea, which had to ration gasoline and domestic petroleum. Late in 1974 the U.S.S.R. supplied oil, but later these supplies were stopped because of delays in payments.
    In June 1979 eight petroleum tanks were inaugurated by the Société Française de Dragages and de Trauvaux Publics in Bata. The Italian company Citaco, of the

IRI-Finsider group, carried out the work. These reservoirs have since been managed by Total-Guinea Ecuatorial. After Obiang Nguema's coup, there developed an intense rivalry for the control of Equatorial Guinea's petroleum and gas resources. The protagonists were the Empresa Guineo-Española de Petroleos S.A. (GEPSA) on the one hand and the French Elf-Aquitaine and Total companies on the other. Up to 1983, GEPSA was directed by Maye Ela. Petrogab, under Elf-Aquitaine, suggested drilling in the maritime frontier zone to the Nguemists. Obiang Nguema refused, but the Gabonese managed to get his signature after getting him drunk. OPEC made an interest-free loan to Equatorial Guinea for balance-of-payment support.

A Hispanic-Equato-Guinean convention (1980) founded the joint undertaking Empresa Guineo-Española de Petroleos S.A. (GEPSA), with 50% participation from the Equato-Guinean state and 50% from Hispanoil. France accused Spain of monopolizing the market.

Gabon also has eyes on the country's oil resources and has hardened its line on the question of boundary agreements between the two countries. The Franco-Spanish competition proved to be a veritable war game. A petroleum law was passed with the assistance of the World Bank. The area granted to each contractor was limited to 1,650 sq km. Seventy offshore blocks were offered for five years, extensible to eight. The first serious signs of petroleum were noted in 1981. Some American companies requested licenses to drill: Exxon,Texaco, Mobil, Atlantic Richfield, Gerry, apart from the two French companies Elf-Aquitaine and CFP. But Hispanoil was already well established.

In early 1982, Obiang Nguema aproved the petroleum law. He managed to expel Maye Ela from the management of Gepsa, with help from Mba Oñana. The IBRD announced that the petroleum administration was using an IDA loan of $2.4 million. Explorations to the Northwest of Fernando Po revealed the existence of light petroleum of excellent quality, of a quality of 39 API. The deposits were situated at a depth of 60 meters, in a sandy zone over largely clay strata. The IBRD entrusted the realization of the administrative infrastructure for the petroleum business to the Société generale Pétroconsultant SA, in Geneva.

In early 1983, drilling by Elf-Aquitaine/Petrogab took place at Corisco. Hispanoil protested and obtained the intervention of Madrid. In December, the consortium composed of Elf-Aquitaine-Agip-Ultramar-Murphy—with the French company being the chief operator—concluded an offshore petroleum drilling contract to the Southwest of Río Muni, over 3000 sq km.

Seismic studies were carried out by the GSI's Black Seal: one for the Elf group and the other for the Getty group. The zones of exploitation were distributed, on December 31, 1984, as follows:

Agip (with ELF), Getty/Total	1,968 sq km
Elf	2,232 sq km
Government, Gepsa	1,973 sq km
Murphy, Odeco, Ultramar	2,160 sq km
ELF-Pecten, Total-Ultramar	
Total	8,333 sq km

In early 1985 the French company Total reserved for itself the distribution of petrol in Equatorial Guinea in the place of the National Enterprise for Petroleum (Empresa Nacional de Petróleo). Negotiations continued in the OAU over the question of sovereignty of Corisco, in an ad hoc committee. Seismic studies were being conducted by the US Geco. The project, with Clarion, extended over five years, to be annually extended three times. ELF-Aquitaine-Equatorial Guinea enjoyed a 25% participation from UK Britoil, Agip, and a consortium of American petroleum firms. All of these had their licenses renewed in January 1989. The drilling in the gas deposits around Fernando Po was conducted by the Spanish company Repsol (formerly Hispanoil) for Empresa Guineo-Española de Petroleos (Gepsol). In November, Minister Olo Mba Nseng asked GEPSA to surrender its concession. As for Repsol, it considered the Equato-Guinean deposits unprofitable and abandoned them. In late 1989, Clarion Petroleum (UK) signed a sharing contract over 2,000 sq km for drilling around Corisco. Gabon protested, contesting the concession for border reasons.

In the 1960s, Mobil had drilled a promising well in Alba-1. In Río Muni, drilling had been done in 1968–1972, 1985–1992, in the coastal locations of N'Dole, Benito, Matondo, Ewondo, etc. Between 1983–1990, six seismic soundings were performed.

In early 1990, the director for mines and petroleum, Pastor Micha, negotiated with Walter International at Houston. He signed a secret accord for $800,000, which provided for the location of a domain belonging to Obiang Nguema near the capital for the installation of a crude-treatment and stocking plant, the agricultural estate Cacawal, confiscated by Obiang Nguema from Spanish proprietors. The FCFA 600 million set apart for the deal were deposited in American banks; Washington blocked the funds in protest of the violation of human rights by the dictator. In June, GEPSA was dissolved by the Nguemist government. A contract was signed in April with Walter International as an operator with 25% and a production agreement including US Mc Moran International (25%) and Samedan Oil Co. (25%). The contract involved 100,000 hectares, over a period of five years, and 30 years if the petroleum was exploited, or 50 years in case of discovery of gas. The government retained 60% of the profits. The wells of Walter International were situated at a depth of 75 m, at 1.5 km to the 1984 GEPSA well. It was planned to drill up to -3,000 m. An oleoduct was planned leading to Fernando Po, rather than toward Cameroon. The reserves of the Alba site (18 miles to the north of Santa Isabel) were estimated at 68 million barrels of condensates (9.3 million tons) and 1.3 billions cu m of gas. The deposit was situated at a depth of 74 m, 36 km from the coast of Fernando Po and 20 km from the deposits of Limbe (formerly Victoria, Cameroon). In 1994, Alba provided 6,800 barrels a day of condensates.

In early 1991, 18 drillings were under way in Río Muni, but ELF announced that it had found nothing. The 1984 agreement with Venezuela became concrete: Venezuela would train a supervisor for the Ministry of Energy and Mines. The three American companies involved with the Alba site embraced a fourth company, US Name Oil & Gas, a division of US CMS Energy, with a promise of 20%. The operator remained Walter International, associated with a Venezuelan company through its local subsidiary, Walter International Equatorial Guinea. The drilling at Alba 2 run by Walter International was considered sufficient to produce 4,000 barrels/day over 10 years. The condensates were to be pumped, and it was planned to install a flotilla for the separation of gas from petroleum. Production was expected to begin in October. The drilling was carried out over 30 days by Reading & Bates Jack-up C. E. Thornton, detached from the fields of Pecten in Cameroon. The reserves of Alba 2 were estimated at 68 million barrels, exploitable at the initial rate of 2,000 per day, with an increase of up to 5,000 b/d. Walter International signed a contract with Oceaneering International, with a view to provide and install an offshore loading station for the condensates, subcontracted to Omega Maring and Nomeco Oil and Gas, which took 20% of the consortium led by Walter.

Since 1992, the Alba deposit produces 10,000 b/d of condensates, as well as 70–90 million cubic feet of gas. These are stocked near the capital (a capacity of 300,000 barrels). The operation of Alba falls mainly to NMS Nomeco. The reserves are estimated at a trillion cubic feet. Drilling has been given to the American First Exchange Corp., a subsidiary of First Seismic Exchange (Houston and Denver), already involved in drilling in Senegal. The pipeline of the Alba deposit at Santa Isabel is being prepared by the American Offshore Pipeline International. The installations for the separation of petroleum from gas have been installed by US BCCK Engineers (Midland, Texas). In April the first petroleum platform was inaugurated at Punta Europa, filling up the first reservoir, in the presence of Prime Minister Siale Bolekia, a number of ministers, and the ambassador of the United States. In 1992, 124,345 tons were exported.

In January 1993, Gabon, by presidential decree, annexed the Cocoteros and Mbañe Islands, to the advantage of Elf-Aquitaine. Out of about 75 Americans present, about 30 worked for petroleum companies. A new petroleum pool began to get interested in Equatorial Guinea: United Meridian Corporation. According to Petroconsultant, the country holds a reserve for 18 years. Drilling under way near the frontier with Gabon is being carried out by Hamilton Oil and Enterprise Oil. Exploitation will only begin when the border dispute is settled. Moreover, one part of the zone, granted to Hamilton by Equatorial Guinea, has been allocated by Gabon to Elf-Aquitaine. On the Fernando Po side, Walter International is working with the United Meridian Corp. (Houston), Conoco, British Petroleum, Den Norske Stats Oljeselskap. UMC was finishing a seismic program of $4 million and planned to drill in the Dorado zone in late 1994, at 6,750 feet. In late 1993, 140 wells were explored (mainly at Punta Mbonda/Rio Campo and Co-risco/Kogo), of which 30 proved to be positive. Petroleum exports in 1993 totaled 1.6 million barrels, representing $23.9 million. The natural gas reserves are estimated at 37 million cu m (i.e., half those of Congo).

Spain has poured more than 10 billion pesetas into Equatorial Guinea for the search for petroleum, but the deposits have been worked by France and the U.S. Walter International amortized its works and installations in 1996 and planned to organize a consortium for the liquefaction of gas with Gas Corporal (Colorado), Globex International (Texas), Nomeco (Michigan), Samedan (Oklahoma), and Mobile Oil (Texas). Mobil is participating, along with United Meridian, and the government has a sharing contract (PSC) on block B of 547,000 acres to the southwest of Alba. UMC hoped to earn 65% interest. This contract will only come into force after covering investment costs.

The drillings were carried out with the Norwegian company Wilring and Sedco-Forex of the French group Schlumberger. The boss of the Equato-Guinean subsidiary of UMC was William Van Goidtnoven. He directs a team of 88 on the platforms and 11 in the offices, including four expatriates. In February 1994, Chester Edward Norris, president of Walter International (ambassador of the U.S. from 1987–1991), was received by Obiang Nguema. In 1994, 90,000 b/d were extracted, 10,000 for Walter and 80,000 for United Meridian. The French publication *L'Etat du monde 1995* states that the income from the petroleum deposit at Alba did not reach the public treasury, even via the fiscal system. In 20 years, production is expected to reach 10,000 b/d. The government hopes to cover 30% of its budget with petroleum revenues; the IMF expects 18%. The condensates extracted by Walter are bought by ADDAX (Geneva). Of $73.3 million in petroleum products exported, Walter was said to have paid a total of 10% to Equatorial Guinea. In 1994, petroleum produced more than half the resources of the country. Some 241,568 barrels were exported. From 1992-94, Luis Oyono was director of GT-Total in Bata.

In February 1995, the rights of Walter International were absorbed by US CMS Energy Nomeco. In parallel, Mobil—which was also growing in the Ivory Coast—and United Meridian reported another petroleum deposit at San Carlos (Luba), off the island of Fernando Po (Bioco, Zafiro deposit, near the Nigerian border, 65% Mobil, 35% United Meridian); Amoco did likewise for a deposit off the coast of Río Benito. In April, Amnesty International asked Mobil to intercede with Obiang Nguema to prevent Moto Nsá and several military personnel from being sentenced to death. In May, four representatives of Obiang Nguema, who had come to negotiate a petroleum contract in the U.S., were prevented from contacting all members of the Clinton administration. In mid-1995, production reached 10,000 b/d. Mobil and United Meridian wanted to produce 40,000 b/d from 1996 in Zafiro (some sources cited 150,000 b/d). The two American companies were associated with the South Korean company Yukong Ltd. (for blocks C and D in Zafiro). In August, Samedan of North Africa increased its participation in the Alba deposit, of which it then held 34.39%. Alba then delivered 7,000 b/d. In late November, a subsidiary of Oceaneering International signed a three-year contract with Mobil Equatorial Guinea, Inc., for the exploitation, stocking, and loading of block B in Zafiro. A 2,680,000-ton tanker ($70 million) was transformed for this purpose, to receive the production of six wells (from 400–1,700 m.); this tanker can store 1.5 million barrels. It left the zone with its first shipment in October 1996. The Nguemist regime was to take 60% of the profits, more than $100 million/year (12,000 million pesetas). From 1996 petroleum revenues were expected to represent $3,000/per capita/year, in a country with an annual per capita income of $290. But in late 1995 some Equato-Guinean economists writing under pseudonyms believed this would not be the case because of the "clandestine nature of the exploitation." The gas from the deposit at Alba was sold (from August 1994) in cylinders by the Sociedad guineana de gas (SOGUIGAS), managed by relatives of Obiang Nguema and executives of the Ministry of Mines and Petrochemicals at a price greater than the one current in Spain. In five years, the petroleum companies were able to repatriate up to 90% of their investments. In 1995, 318,639 tons were exported. In late 1995, the government promised the following salaries in the petroleum sector for 1996: engineers FCFA 450,000–500,000; technical personnel FCFA 200,000–320,000; workers FCFA 150,000–250,000. The minimum salary in the petroleum sector was fixed at FCFA. 100,000. The investments of Mobil totalled about US $130 million, of which 30% was covered by Noble Affiliates and 25% by United Meridian. These investments also concerned the French company Schlumberger for the renovation of sanitary services in the capital and Xenel, a Saudi Arabia-based company, for the renovation of the port of Luba. In the spring of 1996, Mobil and United Meridian extracted 11,055 b/d and 3.2 million cubic feet of gas from the new deposit at Topacio-1. This deposit, located three miles from Zafiro 1, became operational in late 1996. In mid-1996, five offshore deposits had been explored around Bioko (Fernando Po). Production for 1996–1997 was estimated to be 8.8 and 17 million barrels, respectively. Mobil and UMC estimate that the Zafiro and Topacio-1 fields, when under full-scale production, are going to furnish 40,000 b/d. A second phase of drilling, with 30 additional wells, should, according to the government, raise production to 80,000 b/d. In June 1996, one of the directors of United Meridian, John Brock, announced that drilling in the Topacio-2 deposit offered the greatest petroleum and gas reserves in the region (at a depth of 6,000 feet).

According to Prime Minister Siale Bilekia, petroleum revenues were reaching the treasury. According to Vice Prime Minister Ndong Mba, these resources were not included in the state budget, but in an economic and social development fund, blocked for "future generations." On October 21, 1996, the minister of foreign affairs, M. Oyono, confirmed the existence of such a program. Olo Mba Nseng, minister for mines and energy, gave yet another version of the use made of the petroleum revenues: support for (1) the state budget, (2) social activities, (3) future generations. Petroleum revenues were said to be paid by check to Minister Juan Olo Mba Nzeng. The treasurer-general of the state was Melchor Esono Edjo, Lieutenant-General Obiang Nguema's nephew. The company Litor-Wele was founded for customs affairs for petrochemicals. The IMF provided the following statistics and forecasts (in millions of US dollars):

Year	Exports (A)	Profits (B)	% B/A
1992	17.1	4.1	23.0
1993	24.0	12.2	50.8
1994	0.9	18.5	59.9
1995	35.5	22.8	64.2
1996	39.8	23.7	59.5
1997	40.6	23.6	50.1
1998	41.5	12.6	30.3

The profits from the companies are evaluated at twice their investments, which should explain their support for the dictator. Until the end of the twentieth century, the country should annually enjoy about $100 million in petroleum revenues.

A daily petroleum production of 40,000 barrels continued to be announced for 1996 (some sources estimated it at only 8,000). But the petroleum sector remains an enclave in a famished national economy. The director of television, J. Eyene Opkua, in a communiqué to the Spanish media, stated in March 1976 the "agitators of the Equato-Guinean opposition were preventing the people from enjoying the petroleum manna." A new law on petroleum has been in effect since April 1996. The companies deal directly with the Ministry of Mines, that is, with some members of the government, in the absence of a national petrochemical company. On April 24, various Spanish political parties wrote to Mobil Oil in Madrid to demand the publication of data on petroleum production in Equatorial Guinea. Mobil was also asked to openly express its observance of democratic practices. Some experts think that before the year 2000 the country will be producing 100,000 barrels/day, worth about $2 million.

Equatorial Guinea possesses about 13,000 sq km of land rich in petroleum. Some parts of this territory are, however, disputed by Nigeria and Gabon. To the southwest of Río Muni, the continental platform has been divided into seven blocks: ML 1-17, OL 1-5. ML 7 has been explored since 1995 by Petroinet Co. (Cayman Islands). The other blocks are under discussion.

During the summer of 1996, a new hydrocarbon law and petroleum legislation were under preparation. In 1996, oil production reached 60,000 b/d. The contract with the petroleum majors is a production sharing contract (PSC): the companies keep the production just until recovering their initial investments ($160 million, according to Mobil), after which they share it with the state. August 12, Equatorial Guinea became the twelfth member of the African Petroleum Producer Association (APPA). Mobil and UMC announced that the drilling at Amatista 1, between Zafiro and Topacio, was successful. At the end of August exploratory drilling began at Azurita 1, around 25 km from Amatista 1. In October 1996 Obiang Nguema announced in *Jeune Afrique Plus* that he had asked the prime minister to convene a national confederacy on the use of petroleum revenues: "A program of priority investments will thus be decided in transparency and the government will behave itself with all responsibility before the people. The rule ought to be to mobilize every cent provided by petroleum for the improvement of the level of living and the creation of jobs. But we do not anticipate. We are in an initial phase." On October 21, Minister of Foreign Affairs M. Oyono confirmed the existence of this program. Secretary of State for Mines and Energy Miguel Abia Biteo Borico, declared in the *Financial Times* that by the year 2000 production should be around 500,000 b/d.

UNDP's Annual Report (August 1996) specifies that "in spite of the hope created by the oil production, its impact on the economy is still very weak. On the one hand, this activity does not seem to be able to create any dynamic impact on other sectors of national economy, mostly because there exist no links between the oil production and other activities." In October 1996, the *Financial Times* said that "opponents maintain Mobil is merely feeding a dictatorship which echoes the very worst of General Franco's legacy." On October 25, the two CPDS leaders, C. Bakale and P. Miko, were greeted at the White House by S. H. McCormick, director for Africa of the National Security Council. He promised to convince American oil companies to change their attitude toward the Nguemist dictatorship.

On October 29, the Zafiro oilfield was inaugurated in the presence of Paul J. Hoenmans, Mobil's vice president, and A. Patassé, the president of the Central African Republic. Only 18 miles separate Zafiro field from Edop field (Nigeria). Since 1996, the ports of the capital and Luba have become insufficient to handle the heavy traffic of materials linked to petroleum exploitation. According to an IMF mission (September 1996), the GDP of $434 million in early 1996 went up to $677 million in late 1996, reaching $1,300 million in 1997. Oil represents 70% of the GNP.

The government relies on naphtha reserves of about 44 million tons. Oceaneering Int. bought the tanker *M.T. Swift* from Mobil Shipping & Transportation Co.; it was newly named *Zafiro Producer.* It is the second largest naphtha stocking ship in the world. In 1996, Mobil hired Coflexip Stena Ofshore SA (Paris) to built several flexible flow lines, at a depth of 570 m. On July 23, 1996, Equatorial Guinea signed the international agreements concerning damages due to oil. The organization Oilwatch believed that

> the Brigadier Teodoro Obiang Nguema Mbasogo has established a dictatorial regime and one of violation of human rights. Many members of the opposition are imprisoned or have been tortured. . . .The exploitation offshore along the coasts of the Gulf of Guinea not only represent a danger to the environment, but it is also believed that the profits from the oil business only help to increase the fortune of Obiang Nguema's family. The people who will be affected are the inhabitants of Fernando Po, that includes Bantu (Bubi), Ibo immigrants from Nigeria, and several colonies of half-caste who have arrived in the last years.

The 1996 production was shared between Mobil (58%) and Nomeco (42%). The crude production has evolved in the following way (in million tons):

1993	0.20	1996	1.74
1994	0.32	1997	3.98 (estimate ECA)
1995	0.42		

In January 1997, CMS Nomeco Oil & Gas Co. announced it was setting up a factory for the liquefication of Alba gas (1,700 b/d, which they intended to increase to 2,400 b/d and 400 b/d of concentrate). In April, Mobil said it had reached its production goal of 80,000 b/d. With UMC it announced that the oilfield of Serpentina #1 (6,155 b/d), at 2.5 miles northwest of Jade #1, and 5 miles northeast of Zafiro-Opalo, corresponds to block B. UMC and Mobil drilled a new well: Turquesa #1. On block D, UMC worked with Yukon Ltd. (25%). CMS Nomeco also participated in the drillings of blocks 1 and 6 of the Douala field (located between Douala and Kribi), in Cameroon, with Globex and the National Society of Hydrocarbons.

Exports of Crude Petroleum (according to the BEAC)

	000 t	*Mil FCFA*	*Mil $US*
1992	125.7	4'657	28.2
1993	222.9	8'000	29.3
1994	243.3	16'090	29.0

1995	301.6	18'562	37.8
1996*	822.0	66'325	126.6
1997*	2'949.0	144'698	241.6
1998**	4'147.4	316'516	512.2

* = estimate
** = provision

During the economic conference in Bata in September 1997, it was fouond out that the government receives 10% of the oil incomes. The Western Geophysical (a subsidiary of Western Atlas International) signed, with the minister of hydrocarbons and mineral resources, an agreement to carry out offshore seismic drillings starting on the fourth trimester of 1997 (over approx. 500 sq km). The French company Elf-Aquitaine exploits, in Rio Muni, the offshore field of Moho (-800 m); the American Triton Energy obtained in August 1997, to fully manage blocks F and G offshore, which occupy half of the central coast of the Rio Muni (approx. 4,800 sq km). Five fields were drilled, but for the time being they were insufficient. Oceaneering's contract was signed on a sharing basis and authorizes the exportation of the totality (minus the needs of Equatorial Guinea). In October, the capacity of the Zafiro deposit was increased to 120,000 b/d. In 1997, Cameroon bought 25,000 t of petroleum from Equatorial Guinea.

At the beginning of February, Mobil announced that it wanted to invest an additional $2 million in Equatorial Guinea. The company discussed in London the government's desire to increase its benefits. For the time being, Equatorial Guinea only received 10% of royalties. A major U.S. company sold, at the beginning of 1998, the oil from Zafiro to a refinery in the Gulf of Mexico, at 90 cts below the Brent price. The various companies operated with the assistance of Baker Hughes Canadian Helicopter. The latter, as well as the companies Mobil, CMS, and UMC, helped in the project for the protection of the monkeys of Bioko.

Indicators of Economic Importance of Petroleum
(according to the World Bank)

Indicators	1993	1994	1995	1996	1997
GIB (Mil US$	152	126	164	259	401
GIB, without petroleum (MilUS$)	135	103	135	151	161
Petroleum sector/GNB	11	18	42	42	58
Total GIB per capita (US$)	407	426	410	631	949

Indicators	1993	1994	1995	1996	1997
GIB per capita without petroleum (US$)	360	266	337	367	397
Real growth of total GIP (%)	6.3	5.1	13.3	29.1	76.1
Real growth of non-petroleum GIP (%)	4.0	6.5	10.8	11.5	25.7

In 1998, the proven reserves increased to 12 million barrels. Jade produced 10,000 b/d, and Opale (2 wells) 24,000 b/d. The March 1998 discussions between Mobil, Ocean Energy, and the government led to the following sharing of profits: government 5%, Mobil 71.25% (before 75%), Ocean Energy 23.75 (before 25%). The nongovernmental organization Oilwatch said, in 1998, that the profits from the oil industry only benefit the oligarchy. According to a diplomatic source, Equatorial Guinea received 10% of the value of extracted oil. Experts believed that in the next 20 years, oil companies will invest between $40 to $60 billion in the Gulf of Guinea. According to the American Energy Information administration, the oil reserves of Equatorial Guinea were 160 million barrels, and the gas reserves 1.3 billion cubic feet. As for production, at the beginning of 1998, it represented 90,000 b/d. According to the American workers, the rules to protect the environment did not correspond to those requested in the U.S. The UN's 1995 Large Marine Ecosystems Project stated that the beaches are covered with pieces of tar. The French company Total had created Total-Equatorial Guinea, 50/50 with the government. In June 1998, Total buys up to 80% of the company, because it wants to consolidate its position in Africa. Total's installations consist of 2 terminals in Malabo and Bata, 2 oilfields representing a total of 22,500 cu m, 1 oilfield to fill up jets in Malabo, and 16 petrol stations.

Severo Moto Nsá, former member of the Obiang Nguema government and a refugee in Spain, reported at the end of August 1998 that the dictator had declared several times that "the oil of Equatorial Guinea belongs to me and to my family." On November 4, Obiang Nguema called for international tenders for oil in deep offshore (until March 1999).

The 1996–1998 Document of Strategy of the ADB considered in January 1998 that "the economy of Equatorial Guinea, since the beginning of the oil production in 1992, has shown a fast growth, but the population has benefited very little from it. . . .The oil business is still mainly an enclave."

See also Akalayong; Apegsa; ASECNA; BCCK Engineering; Bennet; Borders; Cacawal; Elections; ELF; Envoro Owono, A.; Finances; France; Gabon; Germany; Litor-Wele; Modu Akuse; Nigeria; Opposition; Organization of Petroleum Exporting Counties; Petroconsultants S.A;, São-Tomé-Principe; Switzerland; United Kingdom; United States of America.

PHILIPPINES. During the nineteenth century, Philippino members of the independence movement were deported to Fernando Po. American oil companies employ Philippine staff on their platforms off Fernando Po.

PICO BASILE (Mt. Basilé, 3008 m., also called Wassa, Clarence Peak, or Pico de Santa Isabel). In 1860, the German naturalist Gustav Mann climbed it five times. During his stay in Fernando Po in 1876, Manuel Iradier y Bulfy climbed the Pico de Santa Isabel. In 1884, the Polish adventurer Stephen Rogozinski also climbed Pico de Santa Isabel, with his wife, the first woman ever to climb it.

On January11, 1940, the German naturalist H. Eidman and his team reached its summit.

In 1967–1968 Spain set up one of the highest transmitters in Africa at the summit of Pico de Basilé. See Television.

PINANGO, Norberto see Elema Borengue, J.

PLATFORM IN SUPPORT OF DEMOCRACY IN EQUATORIAL GUINEA (Plataforma de Apoyo a la Democracia en Guinea Ecuatorial). Founded in early 1995, in Madrid, by the following groups: PSOE, Partido Popular, Izquierda Unida, Partido Nacional Vasco, etc., as well as the trade unions CCOO and Unión General de Trabajadores and ASODEGUE, with the participation of the POC and the MAIB. The Equato-Guinean Embassy termed intolerable its involvement in the internal affairs of the country.

PLATAFORMA DE OPOSICION CONJUNTA (POC) see Joint Opposition Platform

PLAYA CARBONERAS see Carboneras, Playa

PLAYA NEGRA (Black Beach). Prison in Santa Isabel (Malabo) under the two Nguemist dictatorships. Well known for the excesses committed there. In April 1996, the Report of the State Department on Human Rights Practices for 1995 was presented to the House of Representatives and the Senate; it stated that "During the September [1995] election campaign, a guard at the former U.S. embassy was arrested by police and beaten. Police released him after high level diplomatic intervention. His late uncle, a political opponent of the regime, had been beaten to death in Malabo's Blackbeach Prison 2 years before [1993]."

See also Coup d'etat of August 1988; Ela Abeme, J.; Human Rights; Jones Dougan, J. L.; Martinez, Nvo Bikie, J.; Moto Nsá, S.; Muñoz Ylata, S.; Olo Obono, J.; Police; Republican Democratic Front; Ronda Estrada, T.; Social Democratic Party; Torture.

PLEUGER, Friedrich. German diplomat sent to Ghana during the 1970s, connected with Hamburg-based food companies. In 1970, his wife Irmagard bought 2,732 tons of Equato-Guinean cocoa in exchange for German goods. The cocoa seems to have been of inadequate quality, as were the German supplies, and as a result Macías Neugema imprisoned Mrs. Pleuger, accusing her, as well as her Spanish associates, of treason and giving her a 4 million peseta fine ($57,600).

The affair was settled after a campaign in the international press. Mrs. Pleuger was set free after supplying a dozen Mercedes-Benz vehicles. In 1972 Mrs. Pleuger published the German-language book *Das verrückteste Jahr Meines Lebens* (The Craziest Year of My Life). Friedrich Pleuger died that same year.

PLOT (April 1981). Took place while Maye Ela was on an official trip to Latin America. He made statements in Mexico denying all involvement. Fifteen Equato-Guinean soldiers and four Moroccan mercenaries were killed. Thirty officers of the navy and several natives of Mikomeseng and Ebebiyin were arrested and accused of possessing knowledge of an arms cache in Ebebiyin. The junta blamed the plot on Mba Ada, who was alleged to have employed mercenaries with the support of foreign powers. Mba Ada managed to obtain asylum in Madrid, but Mba Nsue, his partner, was arrested. The repression was orchestrated by Mba Oñana and Armengol Nguema. Obiang Nguema alleged a conspiracy. The capital's prison was full after 180 arrests, and commercial warehouses were requisitioned. Among those detained there were three ministers, including one of Macías Nguema's vice-ministers, one director general of central services, and one director general of the Banco de Crédito y Desarrollo. The plot led to the strengthening of military protection to the presidential palace and in the roads of the capital, as well as telecommunications centers. People spoke of "Obiang Nguema's cleverly organized provocation."

A military court (with Melanio Ebendeng Nsomo's participation) condemned a 32-year-old soldier, Damian Owono Mituy, to death. He denied the charges and claimed to have made statements of guilt under torture. He was shot on June 19. Seven subofficers and four government servants received prison sentences of 30 years. Navy officers and subofficers got six months. A number of relatives and friends of Obiang Nguema were released. On August 14, Obiang Nguema pardoned some of the main pillars of his regime.

See also Bubi; Coup d'etat; Justice; Moto Nsá, S.; Moto Mamiaga, P.; Nguema Oyono, L.; Obiang Nguema, T.; Olo Mba Nseng, J.; Olo Obono, J.; Progress Party; Senior Officials Affair; Siale Bilekia, S.; Spain; Union of Spanish Nationals.

PLOT OF JULY 1996. According to some opposition circles, on July 18, 1996, 27 military men were arrested by Obiang Nguema's Moroccan guards for an attempted coup d'etat. Many men of the establishment were said to be involved, among whom were: Indocencio Ngomo Ondo, second cousin of Obiang Nguema, colonel, chief of headquarters, Ndong Oná, from Mongomo was inspector of the armed forces for Río Muni; Dario-Tadeo Ndong Olomo, joint administrative political secretary of the PDGE, former chief of the Antorchas and minister for health; Candido Obama, police commissioner in the capital; Faustino Nvé, ex-sergeant of customs in Santa Isabel; Salvador Ncogo, former bodyguard to Obiang Nguema's first wife.

The name of Santiago Eneme Ovono ("Alandi"), Obiang Nguema's nephew and ex-minister for Foreign affairs, was also mentioned. The minister for foreign affairs, Oyono Ndong, denied this information, stating that it was actually the opposition's attempt at destabilization. The latter stated that the arrested army men were in the former group of Moroccans, called Rabat, under the surveillance of

Ninjas, and had been tortured. The case seemed to be closed by familial settlements.

POLAND. During 1992, the deep seas of Equatorial Guinea were opened to Poland in exchange for naval construction, with unlimited rights in the harvesting of tuna, lobster, and prawn. See also Navigation.

POLICE. After Obiang Nguema's coup in August 1979, the interim military commissioner for the interior was sub-lieutenant F. Mba Ondo Nchama (Mongomo). The brigade of police for public order, he fell under the Directorate of the Criminal Investigations Department, whose director was A. Nguema Ndje; his deputy was I. Eyi Mensui Andeme (Mongomo).

In June 1980 the organization of public order institutions was fixed. The senior commissioner of police of Río Muni, A. Bolekia Ejapa, became interim governor of the coastal province, and inspector V. Mbenga Ndong was named senior commissioner of police for Río Muni. Fifteen Equato-Guineans were under military training in the Academy for Special Intervention Groups (Academia de los Grupos Especiales de Operaciones, Geo's), at Guardalajara, Spain, and were preparing to train Obiang Nguema's personal guards. In November 1980, Equatorial Guinea joined Interpol. Of 400 Spanish volunteers for cooperation, 100 were military and police personnel.

In March 1981, Eyi Mensui (from Mongomo) became the director of police. In August, the Nguemist security services beat up an official of the embassy of Nigeria right in the capital. This incident caused the failure of Obiang Nguema's negotiations with Nigeria for obtaining labor. Out of 356 Spanish volunteers for cooperation, there were 32 policemen. During 1981, the notorious torturer of the prison at Playa Negra (Santa Isabel), Salvador Ondo Ela (Mongomo), who used dogs for torture and was condemned to death with Macías Nguema in September 1979, was "miraculously" returned to the administration as the government's representative to Mongomo.

In late October 1982, Mba Oñana (Mongomo) became vice-prime minister and inspector of national police. The Criminal Investigations Department continued to fall under the State Secretariat for Territorial Administration (Interior), whose director was I. Eyi Mensui.

In 1986 the French cooperation opened a school for the gendarmerie at Bata. The signing of a project for a school for police, again with France, followed in 1988. In 1990, two policemen was condemned to seven and five months of house arrest for having assaulted an official of the IBRD, Andrew Lawson, in the roads of the capital.

In the January 24 "transitional" government, the minister for the interior was J. Ndong Ela Mangue (Mongomo). In the same government, M. Nguema Mba (Mongomo) became state secretary for the National Criminal Investigations Department. In October a French project for support for civil security forces (FF 2.3 million) was announced for Río Muni, to include vehicles, equipment, and the training of local personnel.

On September 11, 1993, F. Edu Ngua, chief of armed police, was party to the confiscation and search of postal bags. In the December 22 government, Manuel Nguema (Mongomo) remained state secretary for the National Criminal Investigations Department. The chief senior commissioner of police in the capital was Diosdado Nguema Eyi, Obiang Nguema's son-in-law.

The founding of a judicial police was announced in 1994 but was not operational in 1995. In 1995, the police were organized in several corps, all armed: National Police, or police for public order, and the Gendarmerie, not to speak of the Ninjas. The army regularly carried out the functions of the police.

In the January 8, 1996, ministerial reshuffle, Julio Ndong Ela Mangue was the minister for the interior, with Angel Esono Abaha as minister with special responsibilities. In the April 8, 1996, ministerial reshuffle, Ndong Ela Mangue and Esono Abaha retained their posts. Manuel Nguema Mba was vice-minister for national security. The minister of the interior presided over electoral commissions in several national polls. In late March, the senior chief of police at Bata, Diosdado Nguema Eyi (a relative of Obiang Nguema) inflicted torture under false charges on the secretary of the CPDS, a former presidential candidate. The magistrate, Juan Esono Mbomio, ordered the immediate release of Nzé in the absence of credible charges.

In April 1996 the Country Report of Human Rights Practices (1995) of the American State Department noted

Principal abuses by the security forces includes: arrests and physical abuses of prisoners in their custody; several extrajudicial killings; torture; beatings of detainees; arbitrary arrests and detention. . . .In January a police commissioner killed a farmer near Malabo [Santa Isabel], then cut open his abdomen and chest to remove several organs used in witchcraft-related rituals. Although the commissioner was tried by a court and found guilty, he was sentenced only to house arrest for 20 years. His movement, however, is apparently unrestricted. . . .Police routinely hold persons in incommunicado detention. The Government arrested political figures and detained them for undeterminate periods. . . .Authorities also continue to hold citizens of Nigeria, Ghana, Gabon, and other countries to secure bribes.

On December 4, 1996, 20 policemen in uniform searched the headquarters of the opposition party CPDS without a warrant. The police reported the presence of a group of common-law criminals who ran away from Punta Negra.

In the beginning of 1997, the municipal police of the capital received new uniforms, given by the city of Barcelona.

In the January 21, 1998, cabinet reshuffle, Ndong Ela Mangue left the government and was replaced by Demeterio Elo Ndong.

See also Artucio, A.; Bakale Obiang, C.-B.; Baney; Bata; Benito; Río Benito; Bolekia Bonay, V.; Bubi; Democratic Progresist Alliance; Drugs; Elections; Elema Borengue, J.; Elo Mabale, R.; Engonga Motulu, K. M.; Esono Masie, P.; Evinayong; France; Human Rights; Mba Ondo, C.; Mbenga Ndong, V.; Miko Abogo, P.; Missions; Modu Akuse Bindang, C.; Moto Nsá, S.; Motu Mamiaga, P.; National Democratic Union; Navigation; Ndong Ela Mangue, J;, Ndong Ona, A.; Nguema Esono, L.; Nguema Mba, M.; Niefang, G.; Ninjas; Nve Nguema, E;, Nzeng, E.; Opposition; Ovenga Eyang; Mba, M.; Press; Río Muni; Ronda Estrada, T;, Santa Isabel; Siale Bilekia, S.; Terror; Torture; United Nations; World Labor Confederation.

POLISARIO see Coup d'etat of June 1983; Morroco; Saharaoui

POLITICAL PARTIES. In 1992, the nguemists demanded $157,800 for the legalization of an opposition party. The following are former and current political groups:

ADP	Democratic and Progressive Alliance
ADSOGE	Social and Democratic Group
ANALIGE	National Liberation Action
ANRD	National Alliance for Democratic Restoration
AP	Popular Action
CLD	Liberal Democratic Convergency
CNPGE	National Peoples Congress
CODE	Coordination of the Democratic Opposition of Equatorial Guinea
CPDS	Convergency for Social Democracy
CSDP	Social Democratic and Popular Convergency
FAM	Anti-Macías Front
FRELIFER	Liberation Front of Fernando Po
FRELIGE	Liberation Front of Equatorial Guinea
FRENAPO	National and Popular Liberation Front
IPGE	Popular Idea of Equatorial Guinea
MAIB	Movement for the Autonomy of the Island of Bioko (Fernando Po)
MN	National Movement (Spain)
MOLIFUGE	Movement for Liberation and Future of Equatorial Guinea
MONALIGE	National Liberation Movement of Equatorial Guinea
MPIGE	Pro-Independance Movement of Equatorial Guinea
MUN	National Union Movement
MUNGE	National Union Movement of Equatorial Guinea
PANDECA	National Party for Democracy, Development and Civic Education
PCSD	Social Democratic and Popular Convergency
PDDSGE	Party [Union] for Democratic and Social Development
PDGE	"Democratic" Party of Equatorial Guinea
PL	Liberal Party
POC	Joint Opposition Platform
PPGE	Progress Party of Equatorial Guinea
PPP	Popular Progress Party
PSD	Social Democratic Party
PSGE	Socialist Party of Equatorial Guinea
PUNT	United National Workers Party
RDPLGE	Democratic Union for the Liberation of Equatorial Guinea
UB	Bubi Union
UDDS	Union for Democracy and Social Development
UDENA	National Democratic Union
UDS	Social Democratic Union
UNDEMO	Fernandino Democratic Union

UP   Popular Union
UPE   Eriana Popular Union
URGE   Revolutionary Union of Equatorial Guinea

POLYTECHNIC INSTITUTE (Instituto Politécnico Modesto Gene). A school constructed by Spain, in Bata, for the training of middle-level technical executives for Maestria. See also Gene, M.

POPULAR ACTION (Acción Popular de Guinea Ecuatorial, APGE). Founded in 1992 by Miguel Eson Eman (dissident of the ANRD, after having been general secretary of MOLIFUGE), secretary general, and Casiano Masi, president, with liberal-conservative leanings (center-right). Legalized in 1993, but in 1995 the constituent congress had still not been held. In 1966: President Antonio Ondo Mondo; Vice-President Casiano Mesi Edu; General Secretary Miguel Eson Eman. President: Mba Bakale.

POPULAR FRONT see Frente Popular

POPULAR PROGRESS PARTY (Partido Popular de Progreso, PPP). Born of the merger of Partido del Progreso (with Moto Nsá) and Unión Popular (with Justina Mba), under the aegis of the Spanish Partido Popular, in March 1993 at Madrid. The members of the PP in Equatorial Guinea denounced this merger, and the affair aborted.

POPULAR UNION (Unión Popular, UP). Leaning toward liberalism, center right. Founded by Ekuka Ebombebombe, minister of finance under Machías Nguema, in 1991. The party functions with a continental committee and an insular committee.

In February 1992, about 400 persons were grouped in this party, but did not manage to have the movement registered. The party was led by Macías Nguema's former Minister of the Interior, A. Masié Ntutumu, a member of the central committee of PDGE, father-in-law to Moto Nsá (PP) since 1987. President of the insular section is the Bubi businessman Sipote. Secretary of the section is Abui Elo Nchama, and Ekong Andeme serves the continental section. Member of the committee, Martinez Bikie, former leader of the Juventud en marcha con Macías. According to the Associación España Pro-Derechos Humanos, the party included former supporters of Macías Nguema. About 40 members were arrested during a meeting at Nsoc-Nsomo and 15 at Mikomeseng. Some received six months' imprisonment and a fine of FCFA 200,000 for insulting the head of the state and the government.

In 1993, UP had a new member in Carmelo Mokong Onguene, ex-secretary at the embassy in Moscow, a refugee in Switzerland who fostered divisions in the ANRD and was expelled by it in April. On February 12, one part of the members of the Unión Democrática y Social, expelled from their party, joined UP. In February again, A. M. Mba Ada became president and G. Esono Nsué secretary general. UP took part in the activities of the POC. At Nsoc-Nsomo, the lack of public enthusiasm during the visit of the minister for defense, M. Ebendeng, led to government's representative to arrest the members of UP, accused of insulting the head of the state. They were undressed, beaten with wires, and imprisoned until a fine of FCFA 521,500 was paid. In March, in Madrid, UP, represented by

Mba Nsue, merged with the PP under the name Popular Progress Party, but the members of the PP at Santa Isabel refused this merger, and the Popular Progress Party was not to be. The division of the Popular Union into two competing groups weakened the group, which lacked a true leader. That summer, UP planned a convention for structuring the party. Mba Ada (who had held responsible posts before independence in the Fascist Francoist National Movement (Movimiento nacional franquiste) and MONALIGE, and was later expelled from the ANRD in 1976, became president of Popular Union. During the night of August 22 and the morning of August 23, P. Motu Mamiaga (lieutenant in Macías Nguema's militia, who arrested the first Nguemist dictator in 1979) was arrested in the capital at the Hotel Ureca while he was in conversation with Moïses Mba Ada, newly arrived from Spain. Motu was killed in prison using methods of ritual cannibalism, in the presence of Manuel Nguema and Tito Garriga. The Nguemist government refused to return the body, claiming suicide, and accused UP of having organized blockades of the roads upon the return from exile of Mba Ada. Mba Ada, who enjoyed Spanish financial support, remained silent. The Nguemists spoke of "suicide." In October, UP co-signed, with six other members of the POC, the Institutional Proposal addressed to Obiang Nguema in order to get out of the political impasse. The party was mainly present in Kie-Ntem. UP joined the boycott of the November 21 elections. In mid-December, the governor of Kie-Ntem, Santiago Bibang Ntumu, led an attack on the headquarters of the UP at Ebebiyin and held six military members of the party.

On April 12, 1994, the general secretary of UP, the veteran Justino Mba Nsue, was accused of "personalist politics" and suspended by the national executive committee. Fermin Nguema Esono, secretary for organization in the executive committee, was named party coordinator with a committee in which Tomas Mbuamangono Melango, Domingo Abui (vice-coordinator and spokesman), Jesus Ela Abeme, Gaspar Esono Nsue, Arsenio Esono Mchama, and Manuel Lopete Lopete were present. The latter spoke of the party's risk of breakup, as Mba Ada had returned to Spain in the autumn of 1993, and due to the lack of respect for the two vice-presidents, who belonged to ethnic minorities. The Bubi, Ndowe, Annobónese, Bisio, and Creole members left the party.

In 1995, Nguemist terror incited several leading members to leave the country, including Lucas Mitogo Nfube. This situation was denounced by the representative of UP to Gabon, Antonio Mengue. UP was split by a dissident faction led by Dominito Abui Eló, with Gaspar Esone Nsué, Jesus Ela Abeme, and Arsenio Bibang Esono. During the September municipal elections, UP obtained 14 seats at the national level, of which one was in the capital.

In mid-January 1996, Genoveva Nchama, member of UP, was imprisoned for several weeks and beaten in prison, following his criticism of the government on Radio Exterior de España. In the February 25 presidential election, Mba Ada, along with Moto Nsá of the PP, breached the coalition of the POC, declared himself candidate and received Obiang Nguema's $10,000 for campaign expenses. Shortly before the deadline, he withdrew from the race in protest of Nguemist obstacles to his campaign.

The representative in Spain, Laurentino Nsue, declared in September 1997 that Obiang Nguema's democratization was a farce.

On April 20, 1998, 200 members were arrested in Río Muni. On July 8, UP protested because 50 members working for the polling lists were expelled, thus violating the agreements signed in the spring when Mba Ada announced the participation of the UP in the November legislative elections.

See also Abago Ondo Maye, E;, Coup d'etat of August 1993; "Democratic" Party of Equatorial Guinea; Ebebiyin; Ebona Maquina, V.; Ekong Andeme, P.; Ela Abeme, J.; Elections; Eyi Mensui Andeme, I.; Joint Opposition Platform; Martinez Nvo Bikie, J.; Masie Mibuy, A.; Masie Ntutumu Mangue, A.; Mba Ada, A. M.; Mba Nguema Mikue, A.; Mba Nsue, J.; Modu Akuse Bindang, C.; Mokong Onguene; Motu Mamiaga, P.; National Alliance for Democratic Restoration; Nchama, G.; Nguema Esono; Nchama, B.; Oyono Nsue, L.; National Pact; Spain; Terror.

POPULATION. The principal ethnic groups in Equatorial Guinea are: the Ambos or Annobónese, the Bayele or Pygmies, the Bisio (and not the Bujeba), the Bubi (or Bahobe), the Creoles (called Fernandinos), the Fangs, and the Ndowes (including subgroups Benga, Kombe, Ona). See also Demography.

PORBEIN, Festis see Nigeria

PORTUGAL. The Portuguese discovered Fernando Po, Annobón, the Río Muni coasts, and the Corisco and Elobeyes Islands between 1471 and 1475. In 1507 Ramos de Esquivel established a trading post and started plantations in the area around Concepción. Under the Ildefonso Treaty, confirmed by the Pardo Treaty (1778), Portugal yielded to Spain the Guinean Gulf coasts from the Niger Delta to the Ogoowe, and the islands Fernando Po and Annobón.

The governor of Fernando Po and Annobón in 1779 was the Portuguese João Manuel de Aruambuja, residing in Dahomey (where there is still a fort named after him). Some Portuguese, however, continued to trade slaves in the region and later opened plantations or directed them as foremen. At the end of the nineteenth century, five Portuguese companies operated on Fernando Po. Among the 7,000 Europeans that fled Equatorial Guinea in March-April 1969 were some Portuguese merchants and foremen. In May 1996 a group of eight Portuguese entrepreneurs carried out an exploratory mission in Equatorial Guinea, principally in the fields of agriculture, fisheries, forest exploitation, and construction.

On January 12, 1998, the Portuguese minister of foreign affairs talked of his positive visit to EG. He signed an agreement on cooperation, especially in economic matters. Portuguese companies will be welcomed without restrictions.

See also Modu Akuse Bindang; Social Democratic Union.

POST OFFICE. Fernando Po's first postage stamps were used in 1860. Afterwards, several postage stamp series were issued for Spanish Guinea in general, but also separate series were printed for Fernando Po, Annobón, Elobeyes, and Corisco, which showed the limited geographical knowledge of the Spanish administration. When the new postage stamps were sent to Spanish Guinea in 1903, there were neither post offices nor postal employees in the country. Today, with 18 post offices (one for every 16,667 inhabitants), Equatorial Guinea is at the lowest level of Central African countries. The buildings left over by Spain are good, but the personnel are insufficiently skilled. Stamps issued by Equatorial

Guinea are not recognized by the Universal Postal Union. A philatelist manufacturer, Dragomire Porodanov, thanks to García Trevijano, was granted exclusive rights to manufacture and sell Equato-Guinean stamps out of the country by Masié Ntutumu. Soon a new concessioner, Juan Carlos Marino Montero, a former diplomat, superseded Porodanov. But of the Montero issues, only the 300 bikuele stamp with Macías Mguema's effigy was put into circulation, the surplus stock ($150,000 = bikuele 10 Mo) being lost. Meanwhile the Porodanov stamps were put into circulation from South America, via his distant cousin Atanas Kesisov, owner of a philatelic agency. In 1973 the Equato-Guinean philatelic service and the Swiss printer Hostettler (Crissier) were fined, the stamps even being impounded. Guinea declared that the issue had been officially entrusted to Porodanov by the national philatelic service. The printer was even prosecuted by Swiss courts for having produced allegedly "gold" stamps that were in fact "gold embossed." The last invention for the marketing of Porodanov stamps—they are not even on sale in Equatorial Guinea—was made by a French cheese brand—"La Vache qui rit"—which offered them as gifts to buyers. The series commemorated the Sdoccer World Cup. All the stamps published in 1972-75 were figured in color in the stamp catalogue *Filanumismatica* (1975).

The Nguemists tried to get rid of the bad reputation and discredit brought to the country over postal stamps. Toward the end of September 1979, Obiang Nguema fixed the new rates. In order to escape past excesses, the releases were again put in the charge of the National Money and Stamp Mint (FNMT, Spain). After the 1979 coup, the state secretaryship for posts and telecommunications was entrusted, effective December 1981, to Captain Celestino Mansogo Nsi until January 1984. In December 1982, C. Mansogo Nsi became state secretary for post and telecommunications, with Elo Ndong Nsefumu as secretary of post and telecommunications. In 1991 a new series of stamps was released: The Olympic Games. As a result of its various abusive releases violating the code of philatelic ethics, Equatorial Guinea was condemned by the International Federation of Collectors, Traders and Catalogue Publishers. In the January 24, 1992, "transitional" government, the Ministry of Transports, Post, and Telecommunications was given to M. Oyono Ntutumu. In late 1991, stamps commemorating the fifth centenary of the discovery of the Americas (the second series on this theme) were released.

On January 19, 1993, nine Spanish parcels were confiscated and sequestered by the Ministry of Foreign Affairs. On September 4, 1993, six diplomatic bags that had arrived in Santa Isabel, and were addressed to the consulate at Bata, were intercepted by the authorities, who demanded that they be opened. The Spanish officials refused; the bags were sent back to Madrid. On September 11, postal bags were confiscated and searched under orders of Minister Oyono Ntutumu, Ondo Mitogo, director general of postal services, J. Nguema, former delegate for postal services, A. Mbuña, general secretary of the ministry, and with the participation of Ninjas. The was the third incident since January. The postal service was run by a joint enterprise, Gecotal.

In the January 8, 1996, ministerial reshuffle, Elia Ovono Nguema became vice-minister for post and telecommunications. In June the Postal Bank Project started, known as the Savings Fund of Equatorial Guinea (Caja de Ahoros de Guinea Ecuatorial) with the collaboration of the Spanish company Afinsa.

PRADESA. Spanish Finca Rústica. In 1985, Nko Ivassa Ronde bought it during the confiscation of Spanish assets.

PREBOSTE, Nicholas. Father Superior of the Claretian missions in Bata in 1958. He betrayed to the Spanish Civil Guard one of the heroes of the independence movement, Acacio Mañe, who was executed shortly thereafter.

PREHISTORY. No traces of paleolithic times have been found in Equatorial Guinea, except for some preneolithic traces of industry (kalino-lupembien) found in Banapa, left by hunting nomads.

The archaeological discoveries found on the island of Bioko show a continuouos ceramics sequence starting in 560 B.C. up to the nineteenth century. Beginning around 6000 B.C. it was possible to cross, on foot, from the continent to the island; this allows the dating of the most ancient sites, at probably 8000 B.C. Along the continental province, the data is scarcer. It seems that the presence of communities from the Iron Age are dated 1200 B.C.

The neolithic period is well represented, in particular in Fernando Po, and is connected to the populations that occupied the area surrounding Mount Cameroon around 1000 B.C.: hunters, stock breeders, farmers. The main stratum is the one of Playa Carboneras, near Santa Isabel (sites of Boloapi and Buela), but various other sites are also mentioned, in particular in the islets Ivelo and Ngande, as well as in Elobey Grande. Fernando Po possesses some small menhirs that seem to have been used for funeral rites. Bubi oral tradition mentions the "Mome," fishermen who are the alleged authors of some rock engravings.

PRESBYTERIAN CHURCH see Alar Ayong; Bolondo; Corisco; Ikenge Ibia; Missions; Protestantism; World Council of Churches; Nassau, R. H.; United States.

PRESIDENCY. On the basis of the 1968 constitution, four parties and political movements presented candidates for the presidential elections: MUNGE with Ondo Edu; MONALIGE with Ndongo Miyone; Unión Bubi with Bosio Dioco; Secretariado Conjunto with Macías Nguema, advised by García Trevijano (with marginal elements from IPGE, MUNGE, and MONALIGE). Macías Nguema won in the second ballot, upon Ndongo Miyone's withdrawal in his favor after the first ballot (not being able to reach agreement with Ondo Edu), with 68,310 votes against 40,254 to Ondo Edu. Since then, Ondo Edu, Ndongo Miyone, Bosio Dioco, and the last vice-president, Eyegue Ntutumu, have all been murdered, together with hundreds of others.

After the 1979 coup, Obiang Nguema was designated president by the Supreme Military Council, effective October 1979. He was the second president from the same family, and the two vice-presidents were cousins of his—Maye Ela and Ela Nseng. The latter was soon relegated to the ambassadorship in Peking and was replaced by Oyo Riqueza. Maye Ela was also relegated later to the ambassador post to the UN.

The Nguemist Constitution elaborated in 1982 and approved by referendum on August 15 enabled Obiang Nguema to hold the office of president for a further seven years. International legal experts have consistently drawn attention to the fact that this constitution perpetuates the dictatorship.

According to the 1982 Constitution, the election of the president takes place under universal suffrage. The president assumes the role of head of state and of the government. In late October, J. Ndong Ela Mangue (Mongomo) became minister and secretary to the president, and Elo Nve Mbengono (Mongomo), delegate to the president for relations with the House.

In 1984, J. Ndong Ela Mangue became minister for presidential affairs. In November 1989, M. Nguema Nguema Onguene (Mongomo) held the post of general secretary to the president. In October 1990, C. Nvono Akele became minister of state. A. Evuna Owono Asangono (Mongomo) became chargé de mission to the president. J. Olo Mba Nseng (Mongomo) and L. Mbomio Nsué were named ministers to the president.

With the revision of the November 17, 1991, constitution, the president is only the head of state, but he continues to share various administrative duties with the prime minister. The party winning the elections (obviously Obiang Nguema's PDGE) proposes the name of the prime minister. In the January 24, 1992 "transitional" government, there was no vice-president of the Republic. A. Evuna Owono Asangono was minister to the president, like Eloy Elo Nve Mbengono. Obama Nsue Mangue, Mbato (Mongomo) was minister delegate to the president, and Mangue Obama Nfube (Mongomo) was minister secretary to the president.

In April 1995, one year before presidential elections, the Nguemists modified the electoral law to stall the opposition. The Council of Ministers announced on January 8, 1996, that Francisco Pascual Eyegue Obama occupied the post of minister and general secretary to the president. On April 8, 1996, he moved to forests and fisheries and was replaced by Salomon Nguema Owono as secretariat to the president of the government.

In the summer of 1998, all mailboxes were renewed, but people wondered if the mail would be collected. See also Elections; Eyegue Obama, F.-P.; Moto Nsá, S.; Ndong Ela Mangue.

PRESS. The country's first printing office was opened in 1875 by the Methodist mission of George's Bay, near Santa Isabel. In 1901, the Claretians set up theirs, which was used for the printing of the magazine *La Guinea Española* and the *Official Bulletin.* Spanish Guinea had a regular daily paper from 1811 (*Voz de Fernando Po*) until 1968 (*Diario de la Guinea Española*), both published in Santa Isabel. Of the various weeklies whose publication started around 1900, *La Guinea Española* lasted the longest (1907–1968). A critical analysis of these publications remains to be made.

During Spanish colonial times, *Ebano* belonged to the Francoists and supported Berlin (also during the Second World War). In 1949 the monthly *El Bantu* appeared; in 1951, the monthly *Ager;* in 1952 the weekly *Potopoto,* with respectively 300, 1,200, and 1,500 copies. In March 1981 the technical director for the press, radio, and television was A Nsué Mokuy. No issues of *Ebano* have appeared since 1963. The only remaining publication in the country is *Potopoto,* which is printed in Bata and not of good quality.

Since independence, sporadic papers appeared that served Macías Nguema's personal worship (*La Libertad, Diario de Guinea, Unidad de la Guinea Ecuato-*

rial, and *Hoja del Lunes*). From 1970 on, all foreign newspapers were prohibited in Equatorial Guinea. Various liberation movements publish periodicals, among which are *La Voz del Pueblo* and *Hoja Informatíva* (ANRD), *Neuva Generación,* (CURGE), *Nkul Ageng* (FRELIGE/USA). While the situation in Equatorial Guinea was deteriorating, Spain introduced censorship on all news coming from its former colony from January 1, 1971 to October 31, 1976. The only trained journalist at independence, S. Ibongo Iyanaga, was murdered in March 1969.

At the time of the 1979 coup, there were no newspapers at all in the country. In March 1980, Spain provided an old printing press that had belonged to the Phalangist movement, so as to permit the publication of the review *Ebano*. Obiang Mbá Meye was then made director of *Ebano* concurrently with his directorship of tourism, cinemas, and theatres, under the orders of Moto Nsá, state secretary for information and tourism. Nsue Mokuy was put in charge of press, radio, and television at the same time. Between May and December 1981 not more than 10 or so issues of *Ebano* appeared, even though it was supposed to be a daily publication. The Spanish printing press soon broke down. In 1981 also, the Soviet press agency TASS was authorized to open an office and window display in Santa Isabel.

In 1983, there were 30 journalists holding the status of government officials and a salary of about FCFA 25,000. Two press agencies were represented, the Spanish EFE and the Portuguese ANGOP. In October 1986, in New York, Obiang Nguema called for assistance at USAID for press, radio, TV, and agriculture.

In early 1987, the magazine *Africa 2000* was founded (printed in Spain by the Hispano-Equato-Guinean Cultural Center in the capital. Its director was Ndongo-Bidyogo. In June the new premises of the governmental weekly *Ebano* were inaugurated, with a printing press offered by UNESCO, along with Spanish technical assistants. As a bimonthly, *Ebano* appeared again in August 1990 (1,000 copies), as the only Spanish magazine in black Africa. The occasional appearance of *Potopoto* (1,000 copies) was in the Fang language. In June the creation of a national news agency was planned with UNESCO.

La Verdad, the monthly founded by the Convergency for Social Democracy (CPDS), appeared from 1991 and exposed the scams of the Nguemists. The "Democratic" Party of Equatorial Guinea brought out its journal, *La Voz del Pueblo,* plagiarizing the name of the periodical being published by the National Alliance for Democratic Restoration since 1975. *La Verdad* therefore published a copy of the cover of *La Voz del Pueblo* of the ANRD, to expose the trick.

In the January 1992 "transitional" government, the secretary of state for the press, radio and television was S. Ngua Nfumu.

Among the indicators of human development of the UNDP, it was reported that the daily circulation of newspapers was 3 for every 1,000 inhabitants. In January 1993, the government prohibited the entry of foreign newspapers, with threats to the airlines and shipping companies that allowed any passengers to disembark with these papers. This censorship was lifted in March. The April report of the UNDP mission posed preconditions to aid for the electoral campaign and especially demanded the revision of legal texts related to the press. In November, the International Organization of Journalists protested the expulsion of foreign journalists. Reporters without Borders protested the torture inflicted on Placido Mikó, editor of *La Verdad*, and the death threat sent in December to the CPDS team. On December 30 the government recognized the first private magazine of the country, the weekly *El Sol*, an independent news organ managed by Antonio Ndong Ayong Nchama.

On January 13, 1994, the Nguemist government banned *La Verdad*. Reporters without Borders protested again. On January 25, the CPSD announced that it would continue publication. During the summer, the secretary of state for information, S. Ngua Nfumu, demanded that *El Sol* and *La Verdad* "avoid opinion journalism."

According to Freedom House (NY), "impertinent" journalists are expelled.

In early 1995, *El Sol* was suspended, with the newspaper and its chief editor being heavily fined, upon being accused of partiality in the Moto Nsá case and of confusing the public. In March 1995, the publisher of *El Sol*, Fermin Nvo Mbonio, was attacked in Mikomeseng by presidential guards who accuse him of taking notes during a speech given by Obiang Nguema. In the beginning of April, the manager of *El Sol*, Antonio Ndong Ayong, was summoned by the minister of information, Santos Pascual bicomo, who accused the newspaper of being nonpatriotic. *El Sol* reappeared toward the end of May. *El Sol* published an extraordinary issue in August–December 1995, dealing mainly with the elections. On May 27, a relative of Armengol Ondo Nguema's and chief of police arrested Celestino Bakale and Andrés Esono, executives of *La Verdad*, shortly after the arrest of Rafael Obiang and about 20 sympathizers, for distributing the periodical of the CPDS. In May 1995 *La Verdad* (CPDS) stopped appearing as a result of government violence. The minister forbid a special edition August–December 1995 of *El Sol* because "it lacks objectivity."

In the January 8, 1996, council of ministers, Antonio Fernando Nve remained minister of state for communication and spokesman of the government. Santos Pascual Bicomo became secretary of state for information and propaganda. In March 1996, *La Verdad* appeared with its 35th issue. On April 8, 1996, Santos-Pascual Bikomo remained minister for information; journalist N. Nkili Nse was named secretary of state for information.

In April 1996, the U.S. State Department's Report on Human Rights for 1995 was presented to the House of Representatives and the Senate, stressing that "The Government severely restricts freedom of speech and the press and effectively limits the right of assembly." As a result, "The country has no press, and foreign publications are not sold. . . . Opposition pamphlets and statements circulate." In May the first issue of *La Gaceta de Guinea Ecuatorial* appeared. Its management and chairmanship included officials of the Nguemist administration: Toribio Obiange Mba, Anacleto Olo Mebuy, Agustín Nse Nfumu, etc. Among its editors was Nnar Nsie, who also edited *El Sol*. This weekly was published by the SOGEDISA company, with the participation of Roberto-Martin Prieto and Hilario Sisa Torres. The magazine claimed to be apolitical and social, for general and cultural information.

In September 1996, Reporters without Borders rated Obiang Nguema as one of the "Top 25 enemies of Freedom of Press," on a scale based on the 185 countries who are members of the UN. On October 6, Placido Mikó, head of *La Verdad* and secretary general of the CPDS, on a return trip from Spain, had several copies of the newspapers *ABC, El País, Le Monde,* and *Le Monde Diplomatique* seized. On November 25, 1996, Reporters without Borders reported that the Canadian journalist Edward Seskus and the Cameroonian journalist Kakmo Piedeu (*Nouvelle Expression*) arrived at Libreville after being arrested on the 23rd a few kilometers from Bata and held for seven hours without justification; moreover, 40,000 FCFA ($80) were taken from them.

In February 1997, the press agency Ceiba was inaugurated. The monthy magazine of the Hispanic-Equato-Guinean center reported in *El Patio* (February-March) that they often have power cuts. On March 23, Francisco Herrera, owner of the printing press Servelt, publisher of *El Sol,* was declared persona non grata and expelled. At the end of June, Bikomo Naanguande was stripped of his power and replaced as minister by Francisco Pasual Obama. Malabo, on August 4–6, held the first seminar on "Press and Democracy in Africa," financed by the U.S. and UNESCO, with about 30 African journalists who flew in from Yaoundé on a plane belonging to the American ambassador (a $35,000 project). A journalist native of Mongomo, and member of the still nonlegalized party Fuerza Democrática Republicana, Sinecio Ngua Esono, was arrested in Bata on August 26, along with a friend who had come to greet him (Francisco Abeso).Both were tortured and imprisoned, without a trial. Amnesty International asked for Urgent Action.

In the January 21, 1998, Government, S. Ngua Nfumu was Secretary of State for the Press, Radio and Television. During the Bubi affair at the end of May 1998, 5 Spanish journalists (plus a few technicians working for TV) were authorised to attend the trial (EFE, *El País, El Haraldo de Aragón,* TVE, *Le Vanguardia*). Accused of insulting Obiang and the government in their articles published in Spain, they were expelled five days later, on May 31. Reporters without Borders protested. In July 1998, S. Ngua Nfumu had talks in Mexico about a project concerning professional training for radio and TV.

The 1998 Report of Reporters without Borders said there is no freedom of press in Equatorial Guinea. On November 5, the minister of Information refused the legalization of a private newspaper.

Noticias de Guinea Ecuatorial, the monthy bulletin of the ASODEGUE, which has been out since January 1998, is necessary to understand the events of Equatorial Guinea. The same is true of the old and daring missionary magazines such as *Mundo Negro* (Madrid) and *Nigrizia* (Verona). Finally, it must be mentioned *Estudios Africanos,* of the Asociación Española de Africanistas (AEA, Madrid), which in 1998 had published vol. XI (22–23).

See also Censorship; Convergency for Social Democracy; EFE; Ndongo Bidyogo, D.; Reporters without Borders; *Verdad, La*

PRIMATES. Beginning in 1997, eight biologists from Beaver College (Glenside, PA), 6 women and 2 men, were doing research on primates on the island of Bioko, and proceeded to a census. They report that these animals are endangered by the population (expensive meat) and unemployment, which leads people to hunt. In collaboration with the Minister of Fishing and Forests, a project for preservation, co-financed by CMS Nomeco, was set up to develop eco-tourism.

PRIME MINISTER see Siale Bilekia; Eyene Opkua; Serich Dougan, A. S.

PRIMO DE RIVERA, Joaquín, 1735–1805. Spanish lieutenant-colonel, second in command to Argelejos during the Montevideo expedition to the Spanish possessions in the Gulf of Guinea, which were obtained three weeks earlier under the Pardo Treaty. Argelejos died between Fernando Po and Annobón, and Primo de Rivera took command. But the crew's dissatisfaction led to a revolt, and Primo de Rivera was taken prisoner. In São Tomé, the Portuguese set Primo de Rivera free and imprisoned the crew. After waiting in vain for new crew members, Primo de Rivera returned to Montevideo, where he arrived on February 12, 1783, putting the rebels at the disposal of the vice-king of Buenos Aires. The meager result of this expedition (as well as yellow fever) explains Spain's lack of interest in its colony during the next 75 years. In 1784 Primo de Rivera became governor of Maracibo, promoted to brigadier. He is the great-grandfather of General Primo de Rivera, Spanish dictator between 1923 and 1930, under whom, thanks to Governor General Nuñez de Prado, Río Muni was effectively occupied by Spain.

PRINCE, G. K. see Santa Isabel

PROFINANCO. The Spanish speculator and escrow Paesa Sancheu de Cabeller set up first a southern bank and then a fictitious company called Profinanco which, with the complicity of Armijo and Novais, tried to convince Macías Nguema to create a central bank with nonexistent private funds. Macías Nguema used this affair to blackmail the Spanish government for a loan of 426 million pesetas, necessary for the financing of administrative inflation. García Trevijano drew Macías Nguema's attention to the fraudulent character of the Profinanco affair. Meanwhile about 7,000 Spaniards had left Equatorial Guinea. The country being "bloodless," Macías Nguema signed a convention with Spain in May 1969 creating an issuing bank with official Spanish aid. Toward the end of 1969, Spain granted the 426 million pesetas.

PROGRESS PARTY (Partido del Progreso de Guinea Ecuatoria, PP). Christian-Democratic party founded in Madrid in 1983 by Moto Nsa (state secretary for information under Obiang Nguema in 1981), with Armengol Engonga as vice-president. One part of the Diaspora spoke of a Nguemist trap aimed at dividing it. The PP presented a seven-point plan that included elections under UN supervision, observance of the Nguemist Constitution of 1982, etc. In mid-1985, the PP was admitted to Demo-Christians International. Moto Nsa visited Equatorial Guinea in April 1988, accompanied by journalists and European deputies.

He returned in 1992 and structured the party. In August, the minister for the interior wrote to Moto Nsa and banned his so-called militia. In early September, Moto Nsa and 31 members of the PP were arrested upon provocation. Most of them were tortured on the premises of the directorate general of the Criminal Investigations Department. Moto Nsa was released after hours of interrogation. Demo-Christians International denounced the violence. In October, the party was legalized. In November, the PP asked Spain to cancel aid to Equatorial Guinea. In December, 3 military men, members of the PP, were condemned to four months imprisonment and 40,000 pesetas in fines for "resistance to authority."

In early 1993, other militants were held. In March, in Madrid, the PP merged with Popular Union under the aegis of the Spanish Partido Popular. The new group was called the Popular Progress Party. The merger failed due to the opposition of the interior section of the PP. Toward the end of August, the Spanish press published confidential official documents stating that Moto Nsa was the puppet of the U.S. and Spain for the presidency of Equatorial Guinea. Moto Nsa claimed sabotage. His party enjoyed official Spanish financial support. In September, the premises of the PP in the capital were broken into. A campaign of exposure against Moto Nsa was led by Ricardo Mangue, minister secretary to the president. In October, the PP signed the Institutional Proposal addressed by the POC to Obiang Nguema. The PP was mainly present at Evinayong, Niefang, and Akurenam. It joined the boycott of the November elections.

In the summer of 1994, Moto Nsa claimed that his party had 40,000 members within the country. Since early August, the regime no longer accepted the presence of the PP in talks with the opposition. The Nguemists tried in August to corrupt the parents of Moto Nsa in order to make him give up politics.

In January 1995, Moto Nsa and several leading members of the PP were arrested at Santa Isabel and Bata and accused of a conspiracy and insults to the dictator. Moto Nsa was condemned in early March to two and one-half years in prison and a fine of $50,000. Tomás Eló was condemned to two years. On March 6, Moto Nsa entered Playa Negra prison and was put into a 3-sq-m cell that had been Macías Nguema's. In early April, "confessions" extracted from Moto Nsa were telecast by Nguemist TV. In April the executive committee of the PP was completely broken up:

In prison: Moto Nsa, president; Agapito Ona, general secretary (tortured); Tomás Eló Aka, financial secretary; Norberto Nkulu, secretary for organization (tortured); Indalecio Abuy, representative for Río Muni. José Ndong, secretary for training (tortured) was released in March. A number of militants were imprisoned.

In exile: Armengol Engonga, vice-president; Pablo Ndong, secretary for international relations; Manuel Ndong, president of the human rights commission.

Sanctioned: Roberto Esono, secretary for international relations, dismissed from his post as a government official

Still free: Basilio Aba, general joint secretary, José Ehapo, secretary for information and propaganda; José Pablo Nvó, joint secretary.

During April, several observers of the elections, members of the PP, and other groups were arrested. Other members left the prison suffering serious injuries following torture. Following the release of Moto Nsa in early August 1995, and his claims to being the presidential candidate of the entire opposition, he threatened to withdraw the PP from the POC.

This happened in mid-January 1996. While the POC had just decided to choose a single candidate fulfilling the requirements of the electoral law—making the architect Amancio G. Nzé, or the CPDS its choice—Moto Nsa withdrew the PP from the POC and declared himself a dissident candidate, receiving the $10,000 offered by Obiang Nguema for campaign expenses. Mba Ada did likewise for the UP. Shortly before the election, on February 25, Mba Ada and Moto Nsa withdrew from the race in protest against the Nguemist obstacles making it impossible to campaign. The Nguemists took advantage of the division arising within the POC and decided to dissolve it. On July 11, the Permanent Council of the National Council of the PP, in Malabo, stripped Moto Nsa of his power; the representation of the PP in Spain was dissolved.In September 1996, Moto Nsa participated with V. Boleikia (ADP) in the annual meeting of the Christian Democratic International in Brussels. On September 10, the police in the capital detained the first vice-president of the PP, Basilio Ava Eworo, and two other persons, on charges of holding an unauthorized political meeting.

In November-December 1997, Moto accused the Aznar government of supporting Obiang Nguema and of being financed by the dictator. According to the vice-president of the PP, Armengol Engonga, Obiang's political program is just a cover-up. According to Moto Nsa, the dictator is trying to justify himself on the international level while continuing to stop the opposition in the interior.

Beginning in 1998, Basilio Ava and Julian Eyapo, prime and secondary vice-presidents of the PP, announced on Radio Malabo that they were resigning and joining the PDGE. At the same time, from Madrid, Moto Nsa asked Obiang Nguema to establish a "true democracy," and to give up "the hegemony of a party based on the fact that its militants fear they might lose their job," and to encourage "a state of law based on freedom of expression, the respect of human rights and equality for all."

See also Akonibe; Elections; Engonga, A.; Esono Micha, L.; Esono Mika, P. J.; Evinayong; Joint Opposition Platform; Liberal Party; Moto Nsa, S.; National Pact; Nsue Mokey, A.; Ona Nguema, A.; Popular Progress Party; Río Muni; Ronda Estrada, T.; Terror

PROMOCION DE LA SOLIDARIDAD DE LOS ESTUDIANTES ECUA-TO-GUINEANOS UNIVERSITARIOS (PSEEU). This movement was founded on April 30, 1983, with the objective of inculcating students with a desire to return and work for the benefit of their country as well as an acceptance of the plurality of the country. It organizes cultural days in the Colegio Mayor Universitarion Nuestra Señora de Africa (Madrid). At the end of 1996, the association funds were embezzled by members of its new committee.

PROMOPORT GUINEA see Envoro Ovono; Italy; Vilarrasa, A.

PROTECTION OF NATURE. The places that must be protected are: the National Park of Mount Raices, the hunting preserve rio Ekuku, the reserves of Mount Alen and Mount Mitra, the Akurenam-Nsok area, the estuary of the Río Muni and Ntem, Pico Basile, and Grande Caldera of Luba, the island of Annobon. See Rio Muni; Timber.

PROTESTANTISM. With the Owen expedition in 1827 arrived the Sierra-Leonean Baptist minister Scott, who built a chapel in Clarence City (Santa Isabel).

The first Jamaican Baptist missionaries (Clarke and Prince) arrived in Fernando Po in January 1841 to buy land in Bocobo and Basupo from local chiefs a few months later. Despite their expulsion, ordered by Guillemar de Aragón, in 1847, the Baptists did not leave Fernando Po until 1858.

The American Presbyterians, established in Cameroon since 1842, installed Corisco mission in 1850; it remained there until 1875. The efforts then turned to Río Benito. The first pastors on the continent were established in Bolondo: Rev. Nassau, Clark, Goult, de Heer, followed by Rev. Mackey and Clemens (a white born in Corisco). The Claretians termed the Protestants "erring missionaries."

In 1875 the Presbyterian Church of Corisco was headed by the Benga Ikenge Ibia, trained in the U.S. At George's Bay (Fernando Po), the Primitive Methodist Mission imported the first printing press into the country. The Presbyterian district of Corisco, created in 1900, was connected to the New Jersey (U.S.) Synod. The American Presbyterian mission in Spanish Guinea lasted until 1924. From 1907, Bolondo had a hospital run by Dr. Pinney and later by Dr. Blondon, Dr. Lenian, Dr. Knyght, and the Catalonian José Javier. The Protestants were also strong in numbers in the district of Ebebiyin.

In 1932 Presbyterian missionary work began again. In 1933, the World Wide Evangelization Crusade (formerly Heart of Africa Mission, Fort Washington, PA) was present in Spanish Guinea.

In 1936 the Presbyterian Church of Spanish Guinea was connected with the Cameroon Synod. At Cameroon's independence in 1960, it passed back to the New Jersey Synod until 1968. There were 14 regular Presbyterian churches and 50 temples in Río Muni, with 5 ministers and 50 African evangelists. Several Guineans studied at Dager Priests' Training School in the U.S. The American missionary couple Ainley traveled all over Río Muni until 1961, with residence in Cameroon, being authorized to establish themselves in Río Muni only that year. In Fernando Po, the Baptist chaplain was authorized in 1945 to open a school for British nationals, partially subsidized by Nigeria. It was the only non-Spanish school in the country and operated until the creation in 1973 of the presidential ghetto, obliging the school to abandon its buildings. In 1944, there was only one Equato-Guinean minister ordained: Gustavo Emvelo. Pablo Mbá Nchama, who became secretary general of the Evangelic Church of Spanish Guinea in 1960, was named a member of the Consejo de la Republica (Senate) after independence. In 1975 he took refuge in Cameroon.

At the time of Obiang Nguema's coup, the secretary of the Reformed Church was Jaime Teibiale Sipoto. In December 1979, some exiled pastors returned to the country. The Protestants had 24 parishes, 100 chapels, and 18 working pastors for about 8,000 followers. In April 1980, J. Sipoto received a mission from the World Council of Churches.

In 1981, the American Baptists arrived via the Foreign Missionary Board (Richmond, VA). In Santa Isabel, an Adventist church was opened by Rev. Ricardo Bul Meni. In 1989, the Reformed Church of Río Muni invited a team of Cameroonian ophthalmologists to Bata.

In January 1991, Mrs. Lois Johnson McNeil died at the age of 92; she was, along with her husband, a Presbyterian missionary in Cameroon and Spanish Guinea until they retired in 1959. In 1991, the Apostolic Church, as well as the Methodists, were awaiting authorization to begin their activities. The Equato-Guinean Protestant Church was then being run by Pastor Samuel Oke Esono Atugu.

In early 1993, there were also about a dozen American Protestant missionaries.

In 1996, non-Roman Catholic Christianity was represented by at least 24 churches and sects:

- Adventist Church of the Seventh Day, founded in 1986; in 1997, it owned 7 churches, with 375 members and 3 ministers, and managed a school and a clinic of odontology built by a nongovernmental French organization

- Baptist Church. Mission reopened in Bata in 1982; the Baptist Seminar of Spain has correspondance courses (language, mathematics)
- Bahaí Center
- Betania Center of Evangelization
- Cherubs and Seraphs. Minister Bienvenido Samba sentenced to death during the Bubi trial at the end of May 1998
- Christianity Ebenezer. Daniela Gómez, prophet
- Deeper Life Bible Church
- Evangelic Association of God. Minister Cristobal Ndong Mikuy
- Evangelic World-Wide Church Enjoyment of Salvation (IEMGS). Brother Bacario Ekoro Mangue
- First Assembly of God. Building churches in Ela Nguema and Sampaka and a Bible College in Bata
- Iglesia Biblica Misionera. Minister Juan Sima; Malabo
- Iglesia Evangelica Mundial "Gozo de la Salvación." Minister Angel Damian, Malabo, Bata, Engolo, Ayactang
- Iglesia Paloma de Christi, Malabo
- Iglesia de las Asambléas de Dios; Malabo, Bata
- Iglesia Biblica de la Vida más profunda; Malabo, Bata, Mongomo
- Iglesia Buenas Noticias para Guinea Ecuatorial. Spanish minister Antonio Amigo; Bata, Ebebiyin
- Methodisst Church. Minister Sipoto Teibale
- Neo-Apostolic Church. In the 1990s, it received 10 tons of medicine, beds, wheelchairs, clothes, and funds to build a school and wells, from the German town of Kirchheim
- Pentecostal Evangelical Church of the World-Wide Missionary Movement. Minister Tomas Obama
- Pentecostal God and Love Church
- Redimita Church
- Reformed Church. Minister Samuel Oke Esono Atugu
- Witnesses of Jehovah

The Council of Protestant Churches in Equatorial Guinea is supported financially by the Board of Mission of the Netherlands Reformed Church, the Norwegian Church Aid, WACC. Budget for 1997: $91,015.

In 1998, it was reported that numerous sects, among them Jehovah's witnesses, are financed by American aid, whereas most groups linked to evangelical churches are principally financed by German aid. See also Catholicism; Elections; Terror; Torture.

PROTOCOL see Foreign Affairs; Presidency

PROVINCIAL ASSEMBLY see Diputación Provincial

PROVINCIALIZATION. After Spain's admission to the United Nations in 1956, international pressure forced Spain to change its colonial policies. In 1960

Guinea became a Spanish territory with two provinces, sending deputies to the Cortes in Madrid. The Dirección General de Marruecos y Colonias became Direccíon General de Plazas y Provincias Africanas. It was in fact a nationalization of overseas territories, having become necessary because of annexationist tendencies that had appeared in Nigeria and Cameroon. With provincialization, the governor general's power increased, only a veto of the head of government (Carrero Blanco) being able to cancel his decisions. The Patronato de Indígenas, principal instrument of native politics, disappeared, and the thesis of the Guineans' mental inferiority was quickly abandoned. After the foundation of the Cruzada Nacional de Liberación, the first appeals at the UN in favor of Spanish Guinea's independence started in 1958. Spain violently repressed nationalistic attempts (assassinating E. Nvo, then A. Mañe); therefore the first parties were created abroad, like IPE in Cameroon. On the administrative level, the Consejos de Vecinos were replaced by the Juntas Vecinales and Ayuntamientos (assemblies) at district level. Each province was endowed with a Diputación provincial (assembly) that took over several assignments of the former Patronato de Indígenas. Simultaneously, each province was called to send three deputies to the Cortes in Madrid. The year 1960 was election year for the town councils, the Santa Isabel town hall (Jones Niger, first African elected mayor), and the appointment of the two presidents of the provincial assemblies (two Europeans) and the six representatives to the Cortes (three Africans). In fact, provincialization was a delusion, the head of government controlling all the important machinery and the governor general having become a mere executive.

PUBLIC DEBT AMORTIZATION FUND. Patricio Eka Nguema was its director in 1990.

PUBLIC HEALTH. Until 1910, Spanish Guinea lacked the most elementary medical and sanitary infrastructure. Santa Isabel was named "death's waiting-room." In 1909 the first health laboratory was finally opened in Santa Isabel. Gradually, hospitals were created in the capital, Bata, Mikomeseng, San Carlos, Kogo, Ebebiyin, and Mongomo, as well as a leper hospital in Mikomeseng. At the time of independence, Río Muni had one doctor for every 9,600 inhabitants. After independence, OAU, WHO, China, and Cuba sent personnel for the two hospitals of Santa Isabel and Bata. A National Health Assistants' School (WHO) existed for a short time in Bata in 1970. The few Equato-Guinean doctors have all been murdered: Dr. Watson Bueco and Dr. Kombe Madje. The Public Health Ministry was directed from 1969 to 1973 by R. Obiang, then by Obiang Alogo, then again by R. Obiang. In 1988, Sisino Mbana Nsoro was minister.

After Obiang Nguema's coup d'etat in 1979, the Chinese doctors of the hospital at Bata continued their activities (radiology and surgery). Morocco offered medicine and supplies. UNICEF released $50,000 for medicine, vaccinations, and equipment. Most of the provincial hospitals were unusable.

In January 1980 public health came under the authority of the military commissioner Sub-lieutenant Esono Obama Eyang. The press mocked the Equato-Guinean doctors trained in the U.S.S.R., such as Nguema Nguema Onguene; their three-year education did not permit them to practice in the U.S.S.R. In February, 40 doctors and 30 Spanish medical assistants arrived at Santa Isabel, but the press in Madrid thrashed them for their lack of training in tropical medicine. UNICEF released $125,000 for setting up a health service for children and aid to the few refugees who had taken the risk of returning to the country. Spain and the U.S. delivered vaccinations and medicine, sold shortly afterward to Gabon. The emergency program of the GDF, of a million ECUs, involved medicines and other supplies, as well as the renovation of the hospitals of Ebebiyin and Mongomo. In May, Equatorial Guinea became a full-fledged member of WHO. Shortly after, the Spanish company Huarte obtained a contract for the renovation of all the hospitals in the country. The density of medical personnel was then as follows:

	1960	1980	1989–1991	1993
Inhabitants/doctor	5,810	58,000	3,570	4,042
Inhabitants/nurse	610	840	2,270	2,590

In March 1981, Capt. C. Seriche Biocho was named military commissioner for health. Macías Nguema's former wife, Frida Krohnert, became director of health for the insular region. Several Spanish doctors were forced to leave the country (like those of WHO under Macías Nguema). In one year, their numbers went down by half. In December, Seriche Bioko was promoted to second vice-president.

In 1982, a strong increase in malaria was observed. The Catholic Committee for Development and the Prevention of Hunger (CCFD, France) provided antimalarial medicine. In late October, E. Buale Borico became minister.

In 1983, a basic vaccination operation of the 350,000 inhabitants was undertaken by the Swiss Corps for Help in Case of Catastrophe. On August 13, Minister Buale Borico resigned during a stay in Madrid and requested political asylum. He accused Obiang Nguema of capital leaks and some health workers of thievery and export of medical equipment. He confirmed the theft of 21 (?) ambulances.

In early 1984, a cholera epidemic hit Fernando Po. Thirteen deaths were registered in March. In May, Spain spent 600 million pesetas for sanitary activities, with 12 doctors and 40 medical assistants. A high number of undernourished children was reported.

In 1985, the ADB allocated Equatorial Guinea $1 million for the health sector. In May, M. Mosuy Mba became minister of state for health. The press stressed the frequency of measles and denounced "the lamentable sanitary state of the population." Spain continued to participate in the renovation of hospitals at Santa Isabel, San Carlos, Niefang, Mongomo, etc. Statistics of sleeping sickness were published; various localities experienced epidemics: Kogo (1907, 1946, 1980); Concepción (1911, 1949); San Carlos (1916, 1982, 1985); Bocoko-Drumen (1918); Utamboni, Río Benito, Rio Campo, Anguma, and Ncoasas. The deterioration was catastrophic due to the disappearance of teams testing for the disease. Statistics for 1986 infant mortality were 20% overall. The principal cause was measles.

In July 1987, S. Mbana Nsoro (Mongomo) became minister for health. Obiang Nguema's wife, Constancia Mangue, became counsellor to the president for health and social affairs. In December, the Swiss mission evaluating the vaccination work begun in 1983 ended as a failure, due to lack of interest in the Ministry of Health. In 1988, Sisino Mbana Nsoro was minister. In 1989, some Cameroonian ophthalmologists were invited to Bata by the Reformed Church. Five percent of the population appeared affected. Dr. R. Vila Montlleo carried out a study of filariasis in the district of Niefang (a sample of 829 persons).

In August 1990, China planned the extension of the capital's hospital (for FCFA 990 million). WHO undertook a new campaign against malaria. In October, A. Masoko Bengono became minister. The Hispanic-Equato-Guinean center for tropical diseases at Santa Isabel worked mainly toward thc eradication of trypanosomiasis.

In 1969, 1980, and 1990, WHO tried, sucessfully, to organize with the government a project aimed at organizing the national service that deals with the decontamination of the environment. In 1990, the evaluation of the sanitary conditions, which have remained unchanged since then, was the following:

> The Republic of Equatorial Guinea must face numerous problems concerning the well-being and development of its population. The sanitary conditions are precarious and, most of the time, health problems are due to the poor conditions of the environment. The main problems are a serious lack of drinking water; an insufficient, inadequate and dangerous elimination of solid and liquid wastes; and alarming proliferation of weakening and sometimes fatal diseases, amongst which the major ones are paludim, schistosomiasis, onchocerciasis, helminthiasis, various diarrheas, etc., as well as cholera, which has been responsible for many deaths in the country in rather recent years.

In 1991 Pilar Mening, known under Macías Nguema as a guard of the prison at Mongomo and for the torture he practiced there, was named an official in the Ministry of Health. After Ethiopia, Equatorial Guinea was the country with the least doctors: 1 for every 62,00 inhabitants.

In early 1992, of 52 local doctors, 28 were dismissed for having leanings toward the opposition. These local doctors reacted in the same manner as those from WHO did under Machías Nguema. The government negotiated with Cuba and Italy. The principal causes of infant mortality were diarrhea and pneumo-bronchitis. In the January 24, 1992, "transitional" government, the Ministry of Health was given to A. Nsue Eworo. UNICEF funded a project to control the quality of potable water (with the United Nations Equipment Fund) of $2 million. In May, there was no running water in the hospitals.

In 1993 UNDP estimated there were 46,420 inhabitants per doctor. In April, a Spanish mission made catastrophic observations in Annobón. Toward the end of August, considering the political tension, and after the rape of a woman doctor from MSF in June by a relative of Obiang Nguema, the government refused to allow the entry of Spanish doctors. In the December 22 government, Bernabe Ngore became minister for health and environment.

There was an epidemic of hemorrhagic dysentery (Shigella dysenteriae type 1) in the districts of Baney, Malabo, Riaba, and Luba, in June 1995: six hundred cases and 104 deaths (according to the 1995 report of the International Red Cross). The Carter Center (U.S.) gives its support for the fight against oncocerciasis (approx. 60,000 cases in Equatorial Guinea). The French nongovernmental international organization Hope without Borders built a school in the capital along with a clinic of odontology run by Seventh Day Adventist missionaries. A. Artucio's report, addressed to the UN Human Rights Commission, spoke of the inadequacy of health centers. In the January 8, 1996, ministerial reshuffle, Salomon Nguema Owono occupied the post of minister for health. In the April 8, 1996, government, Dario-Tadeo Ndong Olono became minister for health and environment. Mme. Pilar Buepoyo Boseka took over the post of vice-minister. In August 1996, the province of Centre-sud experienced a diarrhea epidemic. The American petroleum company CMS Nomeco financed an antimalarial program.

In August 1997, the American Red Cross, abiding by U.S. Food and Drug Administration instructions, refused blood donors that are natives of the following countries: Cameroon, Chad, the Republic of Central Africa, Equatorial Guinea, Congo, Niger, and Nigeria. On December 22, China sent a new medical team.

In the January 21, 1998, government, Salomon Nguema Owono was minister of health and welfare; Mrs. Pilar Buepoyo Boseka was vice-minister. On October 21, 1998, AI sent a Medical Action Letter concerning the lack of medical care in prisons (mostly in Playa Negra, where the Bubi arrested in January and sentenced in May were imprisoned). AI was not given an answer with regard to Martín Puye's death in July. The 11 Bubi prisoners who were pardoned from the death sentence were still in solitary confinement at the end of 1998; they only had one liter of water per day and no medical assistance.

The general sanitary conditions remain deplorable, as WHO reports:

Total national health expenditure as % of GNP, 1990		1
Population with access to safe water, 1996 (%)	Urban	41
	Rural	31
Population with access to adequate sanitation, 1996 (%)	Rural	40
% of population with adequate excreta disposal facilities available, 1994	Urban	22
	Rural	52

20% of households use iodized salt (1992–1996). Several international researchers are investigating paludism. See also Aides; Education.

PUERTO RICO. See Arms Dealing

PUNTA DE LA UNIDAD AFRICANA see Punta Fernanda

PUNTA FERNANDA. Eastern part of the sunken crater around which the city of Santa Isabel is built, in the north of Fernando Po. In 1973 PUNT proposed to call it Punta de la Unidad Africana at the very time when the OAU removed its mission from Equatorial Guinea.

PUYE, Martín. Bubi, born in 1940. MAIB ideologist. He was arrested during the Bubi trial of January 1998. Sentenced to 26 years imprisonment, he was not treated at Playa Negra carcel, and when he was finally sent to the hospital, he died a week later, in the beginning of July. The special rapporteur of the UN, A. Artucio, talked of torture. The body was returned to the family. More than 7,000 people attended his funeral, while the police tried to hold them back. A week later, his lawyer, José Oló, was held prisoner after accusing the prime-minister and the minister of health of the death of Martín Puye. Anmesty International reported inhuman conditions of detention. See Public Health.

PYGMIES see Bayele

❖ R ❖

RACISM. Professing to involve no prejudice against black people, Spanish colonization was based on the idea that *native* meant *underdeveloped,* hence the creation in 1901 of a Curador Colonial and in 1904 of the Patronato de Indígenas (Patronage of the Natives). Spanish literature is full of studies alleging to the mental inferiority of the African except for his manual skills and his social adjustment. The black being considered an underdeveloped minor, emancipation was only granted to the very Catholic and pro-Spanish elite. With provincialization in 1960, the European education scheme was partly extended to Africans, who had previously been considered incapable of assimilating it.

In 1830 Nicholls, British superintendent of Fernando Po, wrote: "The intellect of a Negro is in no way deficient, he is only what all ignorant and savage men are and equally capable of being instructed and enlightened with the rest of the human race. This I know from experience."

RADIO. Each province was equipped with a transmitting station, Fernando Po since 1956 with 5 kW on 41 m, Río Muni since 1953 with Radio Ecuatorial in Bata with 10 kW on 38.2 m. Two private broadcasting stations in San Isabel and Calatrava offered local broadcasting. In 1946 the Compañia de Radiodifusión Intercontinental considered building a commercial transmitting station of 200 kW in Musola (Fernando Po), of which only the first stone was laid. Until 1979, the stations of Santa Isabel and Bata transmitted only traditional music and PUNT slogans, without any news bulletins. The speakers were officials of various administrations.

After the 1979 coup, Jovino Edu Mbuy was named director of the Santa Isabel radio station and Nguema Mangue director of the Bata station, Radio Ecuatorial. Both radio and television were subject to strict censorship. In 1983, the country had 2,000 television sets and 115,000 radio receivers.

In 1987, Radio Ecuatorial (Bata) was run by Jesus Obiang Nguema Ndong, and Radio Santa Isabel by Juan Eyene Opkua Nguema.

In October 1988 Radio Cultural Africa 2000 was started with financing from Spain. The project was led for 10 years by Spanish volunteers for cooperation with the help of RTVE, later becoming the property of the Ministry of Culture. The studios were located in Santa Isabel, in a building constructed especially for them. The personnel included 25 Equato-Guinean professionals and 11 Spanish experts. Three different programs were planned: (1) an educational program; (2) Equato-Guinean news, in Spanish; (3) entertainment. The daily duration of broadcast was nine hours on the following schedule:

1. Radio Africa 2000, short wave (4950 Khz), from 0600 to 2300;

2. Radio Africa 2000 on FM (909 Mhz), from 1330-2300.

The cost of Africa 2000 was $780,000, and the annual functioning cost $430,000. Africa 2000 aimed at ensuring the Spanish cultural presence in the region. The programs extended to Nigeria, Cameroon, and Gabon. Africa 2000 was directed by Matías Navarro.

Since 1989, the national radio aired a news bulletin in French once a day. It was directed by J. Obiang Nguema Ndong. In 1990 there were estimated to be 95,000 radio sets in the country. In 1991, policeman Mbá Ovenga became director general of radio, press, and TV. In January, Spain announced the beginning of a daily one-hour program, in Spanish, from Radio Exterior de España, specially for Equatorial Guinea, at 5:00 P.M. The program was presented by Rafaela de la Torre, Miguel Payo and Pablo Bethencour.

In the "transitional" government of January 24, 1992, Santiago Ngua Nfumu became secretary of state for the press and radio. In February, Spain gave to the minister for foreign affairs, Benjamin Mba Ekua Mikó, the new studios of Radio Santa Isabel (Malabo), for $120,000.

In February 1993, a colonel interrupted the programs of Africa 2000 and carried away a generator. This was a Nguemist warning to Spain and its policy of reduction of aid. Radio 2000 was then being directed by Juan Antonio Martínez. On October 15, the president of the Nguemist government banned the shortwave radio programs on Radio 2000 and accused the Spanish of having deviated from fixed objectives. The agreements had to be revised within seven days, under threat of permanent closure. This ban was disadvantageous to listeners in the continental province and in neighboring countries. Africa 2000 was closed down on December 16 by Mba Ovenga. In 1993, the country had 152,000 radio receivers.

In order to prevent the people from listening to Radio Exterior de España, the regime organized jamming with the help of installations from the French company ASECNA and the American company Pierce International Communications from 1992 to 1994. This jamming, however, was only occasional.

In 1995, National Radio was directed by Juan Eyene Opkua Nguema Ocoa. On November 15 the programs of Radio France International (RFI) at Santa Isabel began as a result of a convention signed between the two countries. RFI made 24-hour broadcasts on 97.5 FM: 23 hours in French, including programs from RFI Africa, and one hour in Spanish, between 11 P.M.-midnight.

In February 1996, Eyene Opkua accused the opposition of being in the pay of Spain and of ruining the country. The daily program of Radio Exterior de España for Equatorial Guinea remained the only means for the people to obtain information that was not blocked out by the regime. The April 1996 U.S. State Department's Report on Human Rights in the world for 1995 confirmed that "the Government withholds even minimal access to broadcasting from opposition parties." During 1996, the national radio suffered numerous power cuts.

Spanish radio amateurs organized various expeditions to Annobon, leaving Gabon by plane: July 6–10, 1971; October 27, 1979, 1982; June 20–July 1986 (boat); November 1989, 1991. They had scheduled an expedition of 13 people to go to Annobon during summer 1997, but 11 of them did not get visas.

In September 1997, the Minister of Foreign Affairs Miguel Oyono denounced the "harassment" by REE. On July 27, 1998, the PDGE, by means of his spokesman Santiago Ngua, asked Spain to stop its program on Equatorial Guinea because it brings discredit upon the government at the international level.

Three religious programs ("Miracle") transmit on 7190 khz SW and 15190 khz SW from Equatorial Guinea (programs last 15 minutes): Radio East Africa: Sunday, 10:15; Radio Africa (Center and West): Tuesday, 10:15; Radio Africa 2 (Southern Africa): Tuesday, 10:15.

"Patron" Teodrín Nguema Obiang has his own radio station in Bata. Radio Asonga allows the "Patron" to spread his personal propaganda in Río Muni.

See also Radio Exterior de España; Sociedad Electrica; Spain; Television.

RADIO AFRIQUE 1. Commercial station located in Libreville. In August 1991, the Equato-Guinean minister of foreign affairs, S. Eneme Ovono, declared on it that Obiang Nguema refused to hold a national conference. Such a conference can only be held in case of a vacancy in the power, which was not the case. Moreover, Eneme denied the existence of any opposition in exile.

RADIO EXTERIOR DE ESPAÑA. The international service of the National Radio of Spain transmits every day at 5 P.M. (central European Time) a daily one-hour special program for Equatorial Guinea and the other countries of the Gulf of Guinea (Cameroon, Gabon, Nigeria, etc., where about 50,000 equatoguinean refugees live). The program is presented by the talented announcer Rafaela (Rafi) de la Torre and permits the democratic opposition to maintain contact with the oppressed population.

When the presidential elections of February 25, 1996, were coming to a close, the Nguemist police seized radio sets from people who were believed to listen to Radio Exterior de España (REE).

In September 1997, Minister of Foreign Affairs Miquel Oyona denounced the "harassment" by REE. On July 27, 1998, the PDGE, by means of its spokesman Santiago Ngue, asked Spain to stop its program on Equatorial Guinea because it brings discredit upon the government at international levels.

RAGUENET, Didier. Ambassador of France from 1973–1976.

RAICES, Mount. Near Evinayong. Natural reserve of 26,000 hectares, with chimpanzees, gorillas, and buffalos.

RAILROAD. At the end of the nineteenth century, Basilé was connected to Santa Isabel by an 8-km Decauville railroad. But only in 1913 was the colony's second railway inaugurated, connecting Santa Isabel to Basupo del Oeste (14 km). The line was to circumscribe the island later, via San Carlos and Concepción, but showing a deficit, the project was ended in 1930, against the planters' wishes. At the same time the building of forest railways (ALENA and AGGOR) for the removal of rough timber started in Río Muni. In 1949 the colony had 207 km of railway tracks, 42 km of which were left in 1962 and none in 1978. The equipment was German (Henschell) or American (Caterpillar). At the beginning of the twentieth century, Almonte proposed a transafrican railway with Río Muni as starting point.

RAMOS DE ESQUIVEL, Luis. Portuguese colonist who established a warehouse and plantations (probably sugarcane) in 1507 in the Concepcíon area. He left the area a few years later due to fevers and Bubi hostility.

RASILLA, Luis de la. Spanish. Former UNED delegate in Santa Isabel during the 1980s. He resigned due to criticism from the Spanish Cooperation. In 1988, he submitted a report to the Spanish Parliament accusing the administration of embezzlement, violation of constitutional rights, and incompetence. Rasilla considered that Spain had to make cooperation with Equatorial Guinea conditional and demand the return of political exiles. He flayed France for its undemocratic behavior. The loss of Hispanity of Equatorial Guinea stemmed from a lack of political will on the part of the Spanish authorities. The debate in the Cortés revealed that the Spanish Cooperation had earned 38 million pesetas, thanks to the black market. Before the Spanish Parliament, de la Rasilla stated that in Equatorial Guinea it was easier to buy a bill than any goods. The diaspora would have to cut all its effort to return to the country and reconstruct it from the inside.

Toward the end of 1988, a commission for Democratic Mediation was founded at Madrid by de la Rasilla, with several deputies and organizations. Obiang Nguema was willing to talk, but in Santa Isabel.

In 1998, he was a professor at the University of La Rabbida (Huelva, Spain).

RASSEMBLEMENT DEMOCRATIQUE POUR LA LIBERATION DE LA GUINEE EQUATORIALE. The founding of this movement was announced by the French agency France-Presse. The two founders were M. R. Ndongo and P. Biyogo, but the latter soon dissociated himself from the former. This association seems only to have existed in the minds of its founders.

REBOLA. Locality on the east side of Santa Isabel where, since 1913, a cooperative has been operating. The first Catholic priest, J. M. Sialo, ordained in 1928, was a native of Rebola. On August 18, 1966, the second meeting of the Bubi leading citizens (after Baney) took place in Rebola, in order to obtain a separate independence for Fernando Po and Río Muni. A motion was presented at the Consejo de Gobierno (cabinet) by Maho Sikacha, Itoha Creda, Watson Bueco, and Bosio Dioco. All were murdered after independence.

In November 1979, the special reporter of the UN Human Rights Commission visited Rebola and received confirmation of the continued practice of forced labor. In the November 21, 1993 elections, almost the entire population boycotted the polls (the one lone voter was Balboa Boneke, the minister for culture). In 1994, the locality was exposed to frequent excesses from the police and the Ninjas. In the municipal elections of September 1995, Gregorio Pancho Bonapa (PP/POC) was elected mayor.

In June 1997, many people were detained because they had refused to participate in a demonstration of support for Obiang Nguema.

After the Bubi issue of January 1998, the mayor of Rebola was dismissed, accused of being a spy. On October 12, 1998, five Bubi students were arrested in Rebola because they had asked for better working conditions.

See also Balboa Boneqke, J.; Bonkaka Bogeta, V.; Bubi; Convergency for Social Democracy; Epam Botala, A.

RED CROSS see International Committee of the Red Cross; Mikó, P.; Switzerland

REDONDO. Spanish agricultural estate at Basakato del Oeste, sold in 1985 to the Nguemist A. Alogo Nchama.

REFUGEES. Before independence, various Equato-Guinean nationalist leaders had to take refuge in neighboring countries because of Spanish repression. They included Maho Sikacha, E. Nvo, and J. Nseng in Cameroon; Mbá Ovono in Congo Brazzaville; Ondo Edu and Ndongo Miyone in Gabon, and many others. During their time in exile these refugees founded political parties, e.g., IPGE, and prepared for independence. After independence, the quick development of Macías Nguema's personal power triggered a considerable flow of exile that in 1979 numbered as many as 120,000—including 65,000 in Gabon (official estimate); 35,000 in Cameroon; 5,000 in Nigeria; and 9,000 in Europe (of which 8,500 went to Spain). Data supplied by the UN high commissioner for refugees are ridiculously low, ignore Nigeria, and contradict those given by the League of Red Cross Societies, even though neither of the two reach the total number of 120,000 given by ANRD. In 1973, PUNT granted a short period to the refugees to return to their country, on pain of losing their nationality and having their passports taken away. In 1975 a delegation headed by Nguema Esono went to Cameroon in order to negotiate the refugees' extradition, but Cameroon replied that this was not only against African hospitality but also a question of brotherhood. Today, more and more Equato-Guineans work in Woleu-Ntem plantations, as stated by the Agricultural Chamber of Libreville. Macías Nguema avers that the refugee affair is part of the American imperialistic propaganda spread by the World Council of Churches in Geneva (see E.. Bodipo).

In March 1976, 200 Equato-Guinean students in Spain occupied their country's embassy to protest the Santa Isabel regime. In mid-1976, refugees in Gabon conducted an attack led by Owono Obama against a frontier post, killing and injuring 10 National guards. After the selling of the French Sociedad Forestal de Río Muni to the French company Tardiba in 1976, the government ordered the suspension of operations in the Kukumankok zone because of the numbers of Equato-Guinean workers fleeing to Gabon. On New Year's Day 1977 disputes between various refugee groups in Gabon led to several casualties. Some refugees were arrested and deported, but there was no extradition. Various parties and movements were born among the refugees, some connected with the former Spanish interests, others, like ANRD, preparing the way for a change with less conservative solutions. ANRD alerts public opinion throughout the world with its publications *La Voz del Pueblo, Supplementos,* etc., calling upon the UN Human Rights Commission, the International Commission of Jurists, etc. A conference organized by Equato-Guinean refugees was held at the end of August 1978 at the headquarters of the World Council of Churches in Geneva.

During the Ministerial Conference of the OAU in Arusha (Tanzania, May 1979), regarding the situation of refugees in Africa, Eya Nchama, secretary general of ANRD, in the name of the International Commission of Jurists, presented an intervention over the principles of "not forcing back refugees" and "economical refugees."

After the 1979 coup and fictitious promises of amnesty in October, very few political refugees returned, other than a few Nguemist natives of Mongomo region. Several of the returnees were beaten on orders of Mbá Oñana or sent to jail. This was confirmed by the special reporter of the UN Human Rights Commission in December 1979. The UN World Food Program and high commissioner for refugees had made provision for the return of some 20,000 refugees, but in fact only a few hundred nonpolitical exiles returned, grateful for the free UN assistance.

In March 1980, around 10,000 Equatorial Guineans were studying in Spain, but were not benefiting from any scholarships; for this reason, they appealed for help from the Spanish authorities. On July 18, 1980, the ANRD protested to the UN high commissioner for refugees about the pressure that Madrid was applying to political refugees to get them to go back into the jaws of the Nguemist dictatorship. In his speech on the occasion of the first anniversary of his 1979 coup, Obiang Nguema maintained that 100,000 refugees had returned, thus indirectly recognizing the extent of the exodus. However, the UNHCR contradicted the dictator by indicating that only around 11,000 had actually returned. The UNHCR reconfirmed these figures in August 1982.

In 1983, Spain had 14,932 Equato-Guinean refugees, including 5,965 naturalized Spanish, plus about 8,000 without papers. Some 3,000 lived in Madrid, and 300 were miners in the Asturias. In 1988, Gabon repatriated about 500 Equato-Guineans. In 1989, the regional associations of refugees in Spain (Coguirespa = Comunidad de Guineano Residentes en España), of which J. L. Jones was general secretary, published an open letter to Obiang Nguema. It accused him of flagrant violation of international pacts on civil, economic, social, and cultural rights signed in 1987.

Before Felipe Gonzalez, who was on an official visit to Equatorial Guinea (November 1991), Obiang Nguema announced an imminent general amnesty allowing the return of more than 1,000 exiled Equato-Guineans. This law, approved by the Parliament in December, was said to be advantageous to all political prisoners (which meant admitting their existence) and would allow the return, especially of leaders. This amnesty had little effect, like the previous ones. The special rapporteur to the UN Human Rights Commission revealed that in December 1991 the prime minister, Capt. Seriche Bioco, had declared that the refugees were "thieves," but that they were authorized to return, thanks to the new law. However, the others, "morons and troublemakers will not be allowed."

In early 1992, Obiang Nguema promulgated newly a law on the program for pluralist liberalization and general amnesty. In August, the UNHRC announced that Obiang Nguema had requested it to facilitate the return of 80,000 national refugees living in Europe. Gabon confirmed that there were 60,000 Equato-Guinean refugees with political or economic grounds. The diaspora therefore numbered about 150,000. A number of exiled returnees were imprisoned and tortured.

The report of the UNDP mission for aid for the elections stated in April 1993 the necessity to seriously amend the laws on amnesty and most of the fundamental liberties.

The belongings of refugees expelled from Gabon in early 1995 were plundered by the customs officials and Ninjas upon their return to Equatorial Guinea. In 1996, the number of Equato-Guineans who had chosen to seek asylum abroad was still estimated to be 110,000, which represents nearly a quarter of the total population. Most of them went into exile, usually under very dangerous conditions.

The nguemist Diplomatic Bureau of Information published on May 21, 1997, a note accusing the exiles of staying outside of the country for reasons of personal comfort, thus "abusing the hospitality of countries that are our friends."

See also Akurenam; Annobón; Balboa Boneke, J.; Balinga Balinga, B. G.; Committee for Voluntary Return; Coup d'etat of May 11-13, 1983; Coup of June 25, 1983; Dougan Beaca, J. D.; EFE; Eleme Borengue, J.; Engonga Ondo, A.; Engonga Motulu, M.; Eson Eman, M.; Fisheries; Gabon; Germany; Kogo; Mba Ekua Miko, B.; Republican Democratic Force; Victims; Visher, L.

RELIGION. The minister for justice is also the minister for religion (worship). In the January 24, 1992 "transitional" government this post was occupied by Mariano Nsue Nguema. In the December 22, 1993, government justice and worship went to Antimo Esono Ndong. In the January 8, 1996, ministerial reshuffle, the ministry of justice and worship went to Ignacio Milam Tang, who retained the post in the April 8, 1996, government.

In the government of January 21, 1998, Ruben Mayé Nsue was minister of justice and religion. Mrs. Evangelina Oyo Ebule was vice-minister. The country counts Catholics, 93%; Protestants, 3%; Animists, 3.93%; Muslims, 0.7%. After the Cape Verde Islands, Equatorial Guinea is the African country with the largest number of Catholics, before the Seychelles, São-Tomé-Principe, Angola, Burundi, Gabon, and theDemocratic Republic of Congo (50%).

See also Army; Catholicism; "Democratic" Party of Equatorial Guinea; Dougan, J.; Esono Masie, P.; Italy; Justice; Missions; Muatetema Rivas, C.; Maye Nsue Mangue, R.; Ndong Mba Obono, M.; Ngomo Mbengono, F. J.; Nguema Bindang, T.; Obama Owono Nchama, J.; Protestantism; Public Health; Simo, B.; Spain; Missions; Vatican; World Council of Churches.

REPORTERS WITHOUT BORDERS. (Reporters sans Frontières, RSF). Organization with its headquarters in Montpellier (France). In *La Lettre,* in October 1992, it related cruelties committed against Placido Mikó, leader of *Convergency for Social Democracy.*

In early 1994, RSF addressed a protest letter to Obiang Nguema about the banning of the CPDS periodical, *La Verdad,* and the death threats from the minister for the interior, J. Ndong Ela Mangue, to the executives of the publication.

In September 1996, Reporters without Borders rated Obiang Nguema as one of the "Top 25 enemies of Freedom of the Press," on a scale based on the 185 countries who are members of the UN. On October 25, Reporters without Borders were informed that a Canadian journalist and his Cameroonian colleague were arrested and that a ransom was demanded; they managed to escape to Gabon.

The 1998 report mentions a seminar on media and democracy held in the capital in August 1997. But "the government has managed, by means of a systemic repression, to eliminate private press from the media. There exists no freedom of press." See Press.

REPRESENTATIVES. With provincialization in 1960, the two Spanish provinces of the Guinea Gulf could send deputies to the Spanish Parliament (three for each province). Among the first representatives were three Africans (Jones Niger, Cabrera y James, Esono Nsué). In 1964 the delegation was entirely African, with Bosio Dioco, Bolopa Esape, King Tomas, Ekong Andeme, Gori Molubuela, and Ngomo Nandongo. Of the nine Guineans who sat in the Cortes from 1960–1968, six were murdered after independence.

REPSOL. Spanish state company for petroleum drilling.
See also Diplomacy; Energy; Petroleum.

REPUBLICAN DEMOCRATIC FORCE (Fuerza Democrática Republicana, FDR). A party founded in August 1995 by dissidents of the PDGE and members of the Clan from Mongomo: Felipe Ondo Obiang, Bonifacio Nguema Esono, Eloy Elo Nve Mbengono. The Nguemist administration refused to register the party under the argument that the district of Mongomo already had its party (the PDGE). The two former, upon being arrested and placed under house arrest in Mongomo and fearing for their lives, took refuge in Gabon in late October 1995.

In 1996, Radio Exterior de España broadcast an interview with Felipe Ondo Obiang, who reported the total absence of democratic intent in Obiang Nguema, a declaration that strongly impressed the colony of more than 50,000 Equato-Guineans who had taken refuge in Gabon.

The two leaders are Ensagui from Mongomo, and therefore very close to Obiang Nguema: Felipe Ondo Obiang, former president of the Parliament, gave up his office in November 1995; Guillermo Nguema Ela, minister of finances until July 1996. Their party had not been legalized.

In August 1997, in Bata, members of the FDR were arrested and tortured. As they felt threatened, they sought refuge in Gabon in 1997, and asked the UNHCR to protect them. But in November 1997 they were kidnapped by Colonel Mbiga, nephew of President Bongo, handed over to Obiang Nguema's secret police, and brought back to Malabo by presidential airplane. This represents a violation of the Geneva Convention and the OAU. The two men blamed Obiang Nguema for his poor management, his nepotism, and the fact that he does not wish to establish a democracy. They were released for a time and then sent to Playa Negra jail.

In 1998, FDR was still a nonlegalized party made up mostly of dissidents of the Mongomo clan. During the cabinet reshuffle of January, the dictator mostly got rid of those in support of the FDR. The trial of the two FDR leaders started on July 23, 1998. They were accused of "false accusations and offences" against the head of state, having denounced his disastrous management, his violation of human rights, and his nepotism. On July 24 the court asked for $83,000 to release them on bail. The military prosecutor asked for a 30-year prison sentence. At the end of August 1998, the leaders of the FDR were sentenced to two years imprisonment and heavy fines. This prevented the party from taking part in the legislative elections at the end of 1998.

See also Elections.

RIABA see Asociación Cultural; Concepción

RIBOCHE, Mastho. A Bubi guitarist who recorded two cassettes in Cameroon. His songs contain a mix of the Bubi and Fang languages.

RIO BENITO (Mbini). Called Wolo by Portuguese navigators and Mbini by the Nguemists. Town of Río Muni, on the Atlantic Coast, at the mouth of the Benito River. In 1973 PUNT decided to name it Mbini.

In the nineteenth century, various European companies had trading posts in Río Benito: Holt, Woermann, Randa-Steindt, Hatton & Cookson, Trasatlántica, etc. Río Benito is the main port for the Río Muni lumber, but as the river is not navigable, timber has to be loaded in the open sea.

Shortly after withdrawal of the French military detachment at the beginning of the twentieth century, the first mechanical sawmill of the Spanish colony was set up in Río Benito. In 1919 the Compañia Forestal de Río Benito arrived, and in 1926, the Izaguirre Company, with a concession of 20,000 hectares. Río Benito was the basis for the American Presbyterian missionaries' exploration of the Río Muni. In 1919–1920, the American Lucius Ernest Smith, a Presbyterian missionary doctor, worked at the Río Benito station. The town has a hospital, a shipyard (abandoned in 1969), a small thermal power station, and an Instituto Forestal (Forest Institute). Ndongo Miyone seems to have left from Río Benito for his failed coup d'etat on March 5, 1969.

After Obiang Nguema's amnesty in October 1979, political prisoners still remained in the prison. In 1988, the Nguemist establishment allowed the dumping of toxic wastes on the coast of Río Benito. Since April 1990 a ferryboat financed by the EC communicated with Bolondo until the bridge of Sendje was reconstructed. An EDF rehabilitation project of the Río Benito-Akalayong road was under discussion.

In 1993, Joaquin Mecheba, president of the PDGE for the district, threatened the Capuchin friar Jose Luis Engono. The government's representative was Carmelo Ncogo Ondo, member of the central committee of the PDGE, known for his torture of opponents. The former head of the Playa Negra prison of Santa Isabel, Judas Mba Sue, was chief of police and practiced intimidation.

In early 1995, an Association of the Former Inhabitants of the District of Mbini (Río Benito) published a letter of three pages protesting the actions of the "new Macías Nguema." The document was signed by the seven committee members, under the chairmanship of E. Ndjunga Belica. In September, in the municipal elections, Jaime Edyaka Gaetjens (CPDS) was elected mayor.

At the beginning of 1997, Plácido Mikó, who was in a private meeting with members of the CPDS in Río Benito, was arrested at the orders of Obiang Nguema's cousin, Captain Agustín Ndong Ona.

See also Akalayong; Djangani, F.; Djombe Djangani de Mbuamangongo, P.; Ekomo Yacure, F.; Epalpeale Evina, F.; France; Malavo, E. Don; Missions; Navigation; Ondo Nguema, A.; Ncogo Ondo, C.; Ndong, J.; Ndong Mba, A.; Ndongo Ogüono-Asong, M. M.; Ovenga Eyang Mba, M.; Parliament; Petroleum; Public Health; Sima, A.; Toxic Wastes; Transports; Victims

RIO CAMPO see Iyanga Pendi, A.; Petroleum; Public Health

RIOCHI, Humberto see Movement for the Autonomy of the Island of Bioko (Fernando Po)

RIO KYE see Kye River

RIO MUNI. The Río Muni Province is a 26,000 sq km (9,459 sq mi) quadrangle bounded by the Atlantic Ocean to the west, Gabonese Woleu Ntem to the east, Cameroon to the north, and Gabon to the south. The Equato-Guinean-Gabonese borders were determined in 1901 after the Paris Conference. The Conga, Mbañe, and Cocotiers Islands are part of Río Muni, but Gabonese forces occupied them in 1972. They appear to have been sold to Gabon in 1974, together with a stretch of land between Ebebiyin and Mongomo, according to the former secretary general to the presidency, Asumu Oyono.

The interior of Río Muni is a peneplain (with an average height of 650 m) of granite and gneiss, with inselberge. The relief originates in Cameroon and continues until Gabon (Cristal Mountains), the highest points being Mitra and Chocolate Mountain and the Piedra de Nzas (between 1,100 and 1,200 m in height). A coastal mountain range 600 m high precedes a coastal plain of tertiary origin that appears to contain oilfields.

Río Muni is almost totally arable. The climate is equatorial, warm and humid all year long, with two short dry seasons. Among various waterways are the three main east-west axes: from north to south Río Campo (or Ntem), Río Benito (coming from Woleu Ntem), and Utamboni (or Mitemele). The province is covered by thick equatorial forest, well cleared in the northern and western parts.

The province is mainly populated by Fang, some Ndowe live along the coast, and some Pygmy-related families (Bayele) along Río Campo. The occupation of Río Muni by the Spaniards has only been effective, except for the coasts, since 1926. German, British, French, Belgian, and Spanish warehouses operated in the province since the end of the eighteenth century, as well as American Presbyterian missions. Roads were built during Primo de Rivera's dictatorship. Río Muni became a coffee and cocoa producer and developed its timber production, especially okoumé. Timber comes first on the list of Río Muni products; agriculture (specially small African planters) is second.

After the 1979 coup, territorial divisions in Río Muni were rearranged into four regions, as follows:

Coastal	capital: Bata
South-central	capital: Evinayong
Kie-Nten	capital: Ebebiyin
Wele-Nzas	capital: Mongomo

At the same time, two new districts were created: Akonibe and Nsok.

Effective March 1980, the nguemist junta started to recruit forced labor again for the cocoa plantations. In Bindung, political prisoners are still held in the concentration camp, as in the Playa Negra prison in Santa Isabel.

In 1980, P. Ondo Nguema, of the Marine Brigade, became military governor. The Ministry of the Interior inspector for Río Muni was Felix Mba Ondo Nchama. The senior commissioner of police was A. Edjapa Bolekia. In March, Mba Ondo Nchama began forced recruitment of labor for the cocoa plantations. During 1981, Hispanoil began to speak of the petroleum prospects for the coast of Río Muni. In 1990, the UN and the EC planned an agricultural diversification project, mainly for supplies to Gabon.

Toward the end of the 1980s, the military commander for Río Muni was Mba Nguema, brother of Obiang Nguema; he held his own jurisdiction there and terrorized the population. In the spring of 1995, the representative of Convergency for Social Democracy was arrested for the ninth time. In June–July, the Mikomeseng-Ebebiyin zone (as well as the capital) were hit by an epidemic of bloody diarrhrea. Hundreds were estimated to have died. WHO sent in chlorine.

Since the beginning of the 1990s, the forest has been destroyed, mostly by Asian companies, leading to a disastrous deforestation.

See also AGIP; Agriculture; Akalayong; Akonibe; Akoakam; Akurenam; Army; Artucio, A.; Aviation; Bata; Bibang Oye, J.; Borders; Convergency for Social Democracy; Cooperativas Del Campo; Corisco; Coup d'etat of May 11-13, 1983; "Democratic" Party of Equatorial Guinea; Ebendeng Msomo, M.; Elections; Elobeyes; France; Gabon; Geological and Mining Research Bureau; Gold; Human Rights; Joint Opposition Platform; Maho Sikacha, E., M.; Matogo Oyana, J.; Mbañe; Mba Nguema Mikue, A.; Mba Ondo, M.; Mbeng Ndong, V.; Missions; Modu Akuse Bindang, C.; Morocco; Motu Mamiaga, P.; Ndong, J.; Ndong Mba, Z.; Ndong Oni, A.; Nepotism; Nguema Ndong, A.; Nguema Mbasogo Ondo, A.; Niefang; Nigeria; Nsue Eworo Micue, A.; Nvono Akele Avomo, S.; Obiang Abogo, V.; Obiang Mangue, T.; Obiang Nguema, T.; Oficar Africa S.A.; Oko (Isla); Petroleum; Police; Progress Party; Protection of Nature; Sanchez Bustamante, D.; Sendje; Sima Ngua, A.; Spain; Television; Terror; Timber; Torture; Transports; University; Wele-Nzas; World Council of Churches.

RIO UTABONI see Utamboni, Río

RIO UTONDE see Utonde, Río

RITUAL CRIMES. In 1997 and 1998, an epidemic of ritual crimes spread throughout the country. During the summer of 1997, at least 17 ritual crimes were committed in the capital. During the first three months of 1998, 30 crimes of this nature were committed, mainly in Bata. The victims, aged 8 to 45, male and female, were all found with various organs amputated: sexual organs, the eyes, the ears, the tongue, the liver, or the heart. These organs are usually used in the context of ritual practices: they are either eaten or integrated into charms ("gri-gri") or fetishes.

See Motu Mamiaga, P.; Nguema Mba, M.; Nguema Mbasogo Ondo, A.; Obiang Nguema Mbasogo, T.; Terror.

RIVAS, Muatetema. From Batete. Born in Luba. In the December 22, 1993, government, he became state secretary for youth affairs and sports.

ROCHA, Carlos. Brazilian businessman. He was said to finance up to 75% of the International Development Bank of Equatorial Guinea S.A. (BIDGESA), at a cost of $2 million, during the 1980s. This project did not succeed.

ROGRIGUEZ, René. French military counsellor. See also France; Ninja; Young Torches.

ROIG BALESTROS, Francisco Alfonso. Spaniard from Valencia, friend of high-placed Spanish political officials. Leader of Industrias Cárnicas Roig and Industrias Cárnicas del Sur. He arrived in Equatorial Guinea toward the end of 1979 and remained there for six years. He founded the company Agropcuaria de Guinea (AGROGUISA) and imported, via licenses from Liechtenstein, products from Sevilla. He was said to have invested 150 million pesetas. He profited from the benevolence of Ambassador Graullera. Roig was associated with companies from the Macías Nguema period: Ebana, Escuder y Otero, Herederos de Magdalena Mora, Esteller y Ferris—which the Spanish press termed the Spanish lobby. He was associated with Vilarrasa and the Lebano-Spanish Hanna. Roig avoided having recourse to the Spanish official credit to escape the checks of the FOCO-EXT. He was said to have traded in food products, especially in meat, which was of poor quality (mainly via his department store Suguisa, founded in 1980 with a loan of FCFA 100 million). With the help of the Bank of Development and Credit (Banco de Desarrollo y Crédito de Guinea Ecuatorial), he modernized the Bahia Hotel.

In 1981, F. A. Roig Balestros wanted to restart a bovine farm in Moka, but part of his livestock was slaughtered. In December 1982 he imported about 20 secondhand military trucks.

The Suguisa empire crumbled in 1983. It was composed of Supermercados de Guinea (Santa Isabel and Bata). Against the 337 million pesetas in deficit ($3 million), the only guarantees were the stores Explotaciones Agrícolas; a cocoa trade, which conformed to contractual risk; and Maderas de Guinea (Magisa), a company mortgaged by the bank. Roig left the country in 1986.

In the bankruptcy of the Guinextebank (1987), the Suguisa group occupied about 21% of the risk portfolio of the bank, which was about $6.3 million. A debt of $1.5 million was personally attributed to F. A. Roig Balestros, which the bank considered as written off. Roig Balestros was said to owe the Banco Exterior de España in Valencia $5.4 million. His elder brother, Juan Roig, the boss of Mercadona, was said to owe 300 million pesetas. Guinextebank blocked his assets.

In 1994, along with former high officials of the PSOE, Roig directed the company Gramisa, founded in 1987 by Solana, the Spanish minister for foreign affairs. Roig was the president of FC Valencia (soccer). In 1998 he still has business in Equatorial Guinea.

ROIGA. Traditional Bubi currency (part of shellfish).

ROKU, Elomba Monongo. At the ministerial reshuffle of April 8, 1996, he became the chancellor of national orders (decorations).

ROLA, Ghadi. Lebanese who dominates the bread market and the minimarkets in the capital. He enjoys the protection of ministers José Eneme Ovono (Mongomo) and F. Mba Nzambi.

RONDA, Saturnino. Annobónese. A deputy of the island to the Parliament and representative of the PDGE. He was arrested by the Jovenes Antorchas in Annobón and was detained in Bata during the events of August 1993, with about 20 others. After being tortured, he was acquitted in September.

RONDO MACOSO, Leoncio. Born approx. 1950. Belonged to the constitutional commission of Akonibe in May 1982.

ROPO URI, Marcos. d. 1975. Bubi from Rebola. A professor, he was the first in 1947 to establish clear requirements in view of independence which later led to the constitution of the Cruzada Nacional de Liberación. At the time of autonomy, he became finance minster, member of the Assembly of Fernando Po, and representative at the Parliament. In 1968 he ran for election on the MUNGE list. Imprisoned in Bata around 1973, he was connected with the 1974 coup with Momo Bokara and Borico Toichoa, sentenced to life in prison, and apparently murdered in 1975.

ROUMANIA. Participated at the donor conference of the UNDP in April 1982 in Geneva.

ROUSSEL, Thierry (-Onassis). Proprietor of the timber company Semge from 1985. He underwent a dubious bankruptcy in 1987 in France. In 1989, the Israeli company Yona International bought the concession. See also Timber.

RUBBER. The first attempts with rubber go back as far as 1864 in Santa Isabel. At that time the colony exported liane rubber from Río Muni. Later rubber trees were used in Fernando Po as a cover in the cocoa plantations. Before independence, a plantation existed in Milagrosa, south of Bata (412 hectares, approximately 1,030 acres).

RUFINA, Maria. First Equato-Guinean contemplative nun, consecrated in October 1993 by Mgr. Juan Matogo, at Akonibe.

RUIZ GONZALES, Faustino. Spanish admiral and governor general from 1949-62 under whom provincialization started. He put an end to administrative instability and stimulated economic development. He gave the name of San Fernando to the new city suburbs of Santa Isabel, named after his hometown in the province of Cadiz, Spain.

RUSSIA. Diplomatic relations were established at the end of 1970 after a visit to Moscow by Oyono Alogo (who was assassinated at the end of 1976). In June 1970 a commercial agreement between the two countries called for the most-favored-nation clause, especially for maritime navigation. All transactions, however, had to be in convertible currency. Russia is authorized to fish in Guinean waters. It supplies Guinea with the common part of the catch, and shrimp and lobster are frozen and sent to Russia. In 1972 a pilot fishery project in San Carlos was set up that some believe to be a submarine base. Annobón serves as a supply base for the Soviet fleet. Agreement on air communications was reached in 1973. Russian technicians partially maintain technical control of Santa Isabel Airport, port of call for the Moscow-Angola connection and departure point of a Santa Isabel-Moscow line since 1974. In 1976 an Aeroflot TU-154 hit the hillsides of the Southern Range of Fernando Po, killing its 11 occupants (see Aviation).

Soviet military advisers participate in the training of the Equato-Guinean National Guard, some operating the radio trucks for interprovincial connection of the presidency. At the execution of 27 prisoners following the coup of June 1974, Soviet advisers were all around the execution squad. The Milicia Popular of PUNT is also trained by Russian counselors. Soviet personnel in Equatorial Guinea in 1977 amounted to approximately 200, of whom 4 were KGB agents—which, considering the number of inhabitants, is the highest proportion of all Central West African counties. In 1971 the U.S.S.R. sold a jet plane to Macías Nguema and sent a Soviet crew paid in advance from the Guinean budget. In 1976 the U.S.S.R. supplied two helicopters for the personal use of the president after the helicopter supplied by France crashed. As a trade-off for landing rights for Aeroflot, Equatorial Guinea also received several armored cars and light weapons. Following the severe oil crisis that also hit Equatorial Guinea, the U.S.S.R. supplied oil as of the end of 1974, but deliveries (as well as supplies of spare parts for weapons) quickly slowed down in 1976 due to delays in payment.

In 1975 a Santa Isabel-Moscow air connection was established in exchange for a "fishing" base at San Carlos. In 1979 the health minister, Obiang Alogo, paid an official visit to the U.S.S.R. A treaty for military assistance was concluded.

After the 1979 coup, the government abrogated the fishing agreement effective January 1, 1980. In March 1980 the Soviet consul was expelled for being too inquisitive. The military assistance treaty between the two countries still stands, and Russian technicians still operate and maintain the Antonov aircraft and the two helicopters. Obiang Nguema refuses to fly in any of these aircraft piloted by Russians.

In April 1981 the Supreme Military Council requested the Soviet Embassy to reduce its staff from 195 to 15. The ambassador refused. Thanks to the opening of a TASS office in Santa Isabel, Russia is assured of a good propaganda base. Russia also offers a number of scholarships for journalists and sportsmen. In September 1982, the embassy's interpreter, Yuri Elimenko, sharply criticized the Nguemist regime. The League of Red Cross Societies reported in 1982 that the Soviet Union was the only country to have provided funds to Equatorial Guinea for emergency relief (the equivalent of $30,000).

From 1988–1991, E. Abaga Maye, the husband of a cousin of Obiang Nguema, was ambassador to the Soviet Union. He had problems with the Equato-Guinean scholarship holders in several universities.

In November 1989, relations between the two countries grew warmer, with the arrival of a mission led by Talbak Mazarov, deputy to the Supreme Soviet and minister for education of Tajikistan. Thirteen scholarships were offered. The discussions with the leaders of PDGE also touched on the question of knowing how a sole party can be adapted to the internationally recognized democratic demands. In October, Obiang Nguema spoke of his political program using the term perestroika. In 1991, Lev Aleksandrovich Vakhrameyev represented Russia in Santa Isabel. In April 1992, the embassy at Santa Isabel was closed for financial reasons.

Ambassador of Equatorial Guinea to Russia in 1998: Antonio Javier Nguema Nchama.

See also Abago Ondo Maye, E.; Economy; Eneme Ovono, S.; Finances; International Committee of the Red Cross; Navigation; Nguema Ndong, A.; Nguema Nguema Onguine, M.; Nvo Bela, E.; Obiang Abogo, V.; Obiang Nguema, T.; Ondo Maye, S.; Oyono, N.; San Carlos; Tung Ela.

RWANDA. In 1980 it received a Nguemist mission for the recruitment of labor, after the refusal of Nigeria. This request also remained without issue. In June 1994, Obiang Nguema congratulated President Mitterand for sending French troops to Rwanda. At his trial in the spring of 1995, Moto Nsá was accused by the prosecutor of wishing to transform Equatorial Guinea into another Rwanda.

See also France; Spain.

❖ S ❖

SACHERS, Wolfgang. Expert of the World Food Program. His 1981 study concluded that the food situation was highly deficient.

SACRIBA. In 1985, a rustic estate in this village in Fernando Po was sold to a member of the clan from Mongomo, Nka Esono Nsing.

SAEZ LASHERAS, Teodoro. Spanish priest. In 1992 he was director of studies at the Instituto La Salle in Bata. On November 16, he resigned because of the arrogance of the Criminal Investigations Department, which tried to infiltrate its agents into the school to supervise the students. Shortly after, a student demonstration was forbidden; 40 students were arrested in late November and tortured.

SAFI see Timber

SAHARAOUI, Popular Republic. Immediately after Obiang Nguema's coup in August 1979, Morocco lent 300 men (which later became 600) as presidential guards, in exchange for Santa Isabel giving up its support to the Front Polisario. Such guards also surround presidents Bongo and Mobutu in Gabon and Zaire. In all the votes over ex-Spanish Sahara at the UN, Equatorial Guinea took the side of Morocco. In November 1981, the UN Commission for Decolonization adopted a resolution that reaffirmed the Saharaoui people's right to independence. Seven countries voted against (Equatorial Guinea, the U.S., Morocco, Gabon, Zaire, Senegal, Salvador); 73 countries voted for the resolution; there were 54 abstentions.
See also Coup d'etat of June 25, 1983; Morocco.

SAINZ BAYON, Juan Manuel. Spanish counsellor in the Ministry of Justice in Santa Isabel since 1981. Toward the end of 1990, Sainz Bayón, in a report on Nguemist justice, revealed the ineptitude of the judiciary personnel composed mainly of nonuniversity graduates, often having studied only up to the primary level. Corruption is less frequent among the judiciary personnel than in other sections. Sainz Bayón proposed the transfer of Spanish personnel, as well as intensive courses. Laws and decrees were not published as a result of the absence of an official bulletin.

SAKER, Alfred, 1814–1880. British Baptist missionary, former carpenter, who arrived in Fernando Po in 1844 after a stay in Jamaica. He developed an important mission school, then left Fernando Po under the Spanish Jesuits' pressure and settled in Douala (Cameroon), from where he shortly returned at the time of the Chacón's arrival and the eviction of the last Baptists. With fellow Baptists, Saker created the Victoria Mission (Cameroon) that generated the city named for it. After 30 years in Cameroon, he returned to England in 1876.

SALARIES. In 1990 the Nguemist government decided to increase the salaries of the private sector by 50%, which caused fury among the Spanish, French, Indian, and Lebanese entrepreneurs. In 1991, the monthly salary of a minister was FCFA 90.000 (approximately $200). In March 1994 the salaries of government officials were increased by 14%. The average monthly salary was FCFA 14,000 (approximately $140), but the basic salary was FCFA 8,000 (approximately $80). According to the BEAC, the index of the cost of living (African type) has evolved in the following manner (Santa Isabel/Bata, base 100: January 1990):

1988	99,7	1992	89,0
1989	105,7	1993	92,5
1990	101,4	1994	132
1991	96,0	1995	156
		1996	185

On December 29, 1995, the government promised a new basis for salaries for 1996, the year of the presidential election (February 25). In the agricultural sector, the increase announced was on average 53%, in the industrial and mining sectors, 50%. In the administration, the officials of levels A-C received raises of 22–50%; orderlies, drivers, and workers were to benefit from a raise of 100%. As for the army, an increase of 22% was announced for the officers and subofficers, 50% for troops, and 100% for guards. See also Petroleum.

SAMARANCH, Carmen. Spanish nun who was assassinated at Ebebiyin. She was killed by two army men. Some sources claim that she had been punished for revealing that 90% of the FAO aid was embezzled.

SAMBA MOMESORI. Bubi Protestant minister. He is one of the many who were sentenced to death during the Bubi trial in May 1998. See Bubi; Movimiento.

SAMI GANET, Fernando. A Bubi from Bariobé. Born in 1930. Does not hold a university degree. In January 1994, he became secretary of the supreme court, and was later a magistrate in the district of Bata.

SAMPAKA. A Fernando Po locality 6 km from the capital, founded in 1906 by Magdalena Mora. Important for cocoa production. Sampaka was given to the Mayo family upon independence. The company employs 500 persons full time. In 1979, the traditional chief was F. Logoba Buericopa, who described to the rapporteur to the UN Human Rights Commission, Volio Jimenez, the terror inflicted on his village by the Nguemist regime. After the elections of November 21, 1993, several Bubi natives were arrested, including Logoba Buericopa, chief of the municipal council, for having recommended the boycott.

See also Bubi; Obiang Nguema, T.

SAN CARLOS. City on the west coast of Fernando Po. The locality was founded in 1821 by a British citizen named Kelly. First called by the British West Bay (the Spaniards said "Oueste"). In 1887 the Claretians landed there, establishing a mission, and at the same time a municipal judge and a Consejo de Vecinos were appointed. Various warehouses were established and important plantations surrounded it, among which was the Vivouor one. In 1904, San Carlos became the seat of local government. A school staffed with Teresian nuns was set up, as well as an electric power station. San Carlos exported a considerable amount of bananas between 1950 and1965. From 1960 to1968 Cabrera y James, a Fernandino, was mayor of San Carlos (he was assassinated in 1970). In 1960 the town had 2,305 inhabitants. In 1973 PUNT proposed to rename the city Luba. Since 1973 Russian experts have developed a fishing harbor, believed by some to be a strategic naval base.

Nine thousand Cubans and their military equipment passed through San Carlos to take part in the war in Angola. They were picked up from San Carlos by MPLA vessels. To the south of San Carlos there is a 2,250 m volcano of the same name. Its crater is 6 km in circumference. After the 1979 coup, the San Carlos hospital, with 280 beds, was abandoned, and the local administration was put into the hands of Nguemists. Upon their departure in 1980, the Soviets were said to have sunk the floating dock out of spite. In 1984 a 20,000-ton oil storage depot was built there.

As part of the new administrative structure, San Carlos (Luba) was the capital of the district of Fernando Po South (Bioko South). In the municipal elections of September 1995, Laureano Ferreira Bela (PP/POC) was elected mayor. On November 10 Obiang Nguema appointed the ex-militiaman of Macías Nguema, Marcelino Asumu Nsue, the government representative of San Carlos.

In 1996, the Xenel Company, based in Saudi Arabia, was entrusted with the renovation of the port by the petroleum consortium. A project for mineral water bottling by the Spanish company Mir Africa failed.

See also Coup d'etat of 1990; Ebiaka Mohete, A.; Eburi Mata, C.; Elections; Musola; Petroleum; Public Health; Russia; Transports; Victims.

SANCHEZ BUSTAMANTE, Diego. Consul of Spain in Río Muni in 1992. He was involved, in October-November, with the two Spanish businessmen Vilarrasa and Hanna, imprisoned in Bata. Sanchez was expelled in November 1993, accused on television of anti-Nguemist attitudes by his former protégé Crispín Onvá (alias Nguen-Gueru, who received a car and cash for approximately CFA Fr. 2 million taken from INSESO funds). Spain dismissed an employee of the embassy at Madrid and, considering the undemocratic elections of November 21, cut off a significant part of the aid budget. In 1994, Sanchez Bustamate became ambassador of Spain to Ghana.

SANCHEZ GUERRA SAEZ, Luis. Governor general in 1935–1936. Member of the Popular Front, Sanchez Guerra came up against the large landowners represented by the Agricultural Chambers, in particular the Río Muni one, on questions of salary increases. Simultaneously he created a forest agency in charge of holding down excessive lumbering and stimulating reforestation. He was dismissed by the Civil Guard in September 1936; shortly after, the Popular Front from Bata fell with Vice-Governor Porcel, under the pressure of Francoist troops led by Fontán y Lobé.

SANCHIS, Manuel. A former international football player who was loaned by the Football Club of Madrid to Equatorial Guinea in January 1980, within the framework of Spanish bilateral aid, to train the national team.

SAN FERNANDO. Town in the outskirts of Santa Isabel. In 1973 PUNT proposed calling it Ele Nguema. It is the first attempt at town planning in Equatorial Guinea, undertaken by Spain shortly before independence. This town was reserved especially for African officials, but was still not finished in 1978. In 1942, San Fernando became a district but was suppressed at independence.

A decree of February 1981 incorporated the municipality of San Fernando into Santa Isabel. In 1975 a large water tower was built there with Spanish funding. In 1985 Spain financed the construction of a water tank meant to improve the water supply. See also Ruiz Gonzales.

SAN ILDEFONSO Treaty. Concluded between Spain and Portugal on October 1, 1977, and confirmed by the Pardo Treaty in March 1778. It settled the Spanish-Portuguese dispute concerning the delimitation of Brazil by Portugal's transferring its rights on the Gulf of Guinea to Spain, in exchange for the colony of Sacramento and the Santa Catalina Island in southern Brazil.

SAN JUAN, Cape. At the southwestern tip of Río Muni, bordering the Bay of Corisco, peopled by Benga. Around 1860, a Presbyterian mission was founded there by Americans. During the nineteenth century, the vicariate of Gabon pressed Spain to hand over Cape San Juan from its jurisdiction, while the French government was doing the same for all of Río Muni. In 1885 the first Catholic missionary school (Claretians) was opened in Cape San Juan.

In 1922 the SOCOGUI settled there too, with oil palm plantations, of which 1,678 hectares presently remain, with an oil mill, everything having stopped operating in 1969.

SANTA CLARA, Cape. Located on the northern coast of Gabon, south of Cape Esterias. In 1843 Lereña received from Bonkoro I, king of the Benga, territories stretching as far as Cape Santa Clara. With the Pardo Treaty, Spanish territories were extended 160 km south of this cape, as far as Cape Lopez on the Ogoowe River. In 1845 a tacit agreement between Guillemar de Aragón and the French Commissary of Gabon settled Cape Santa Clara as the limit between Spanish and French possessions.

SANTA ISABEL. Capital situated in the northern part of the island of Fernando Po, at the foot of the Pico de Santa Isabel. It was founded in 1827 by the British Owen, under the name of Clarence City. With the hispanicization of toponyms, it was called Santa Isabel in 1843. Since 1840, the town was a stocking place for palm oil.

John Clarke, a Jamaican Baptist minister, and Dr. G. K. Prince, landed in Port Clarence in 1841. Confronted by the suspicion of the Bubi (then called Adeeyah), they chose to settle on the continent, in Douala. In July 1844, Alfred Saker, his wife, and several Jamaican settlers (freed slaves) arrived in Port Clarence. They built a school and established the first printing works in the country. In 1858, due to Spanish hostility, Saker settled in Cameroon, where he founded Victoria (today called Limbe). But the Jamaican settlers remained on the island. The fact that Protestantism was forbidden did not prevent clandestine ceremonies.

At the arrival of the first Spanish governor, Chacón, in 1858, Santa Isabel had 858 people, of which 33 were whites. In 1885, the "town" had 1,284 people, of which 170 were whites and 275 female.

Because of its rough climate, the city was called "death's waiting room" until the beginning of the twentieth century. In 1956 the Fernandino Barleycorn was appointed mayor of the town, then, with provincialization, the Fernandino Jones Niger was elected to this post. With the suburb of San Fernando, in 1960 Santa Isabel numbered 19,869 inhabitants, of which 16,997 were Africans. Around the cathedral built in 1916 and the former governmental palace (having become presidential palace—isolated in an area emptied of its inhabitants, and surrounded by defensive walls, the "presidential ghetto"), Santa Isabel could still operate fish meal factories, seafood canneries, a distillery, a carpentry shop, tile works, etc., had these activities not been paralyzed by the April departure of 7,000 of the country's 8,000 Spaniards in March-April 1969.

The harbor, with a transit capacity of 300,000 tons a year, not only has a lack of warehouses, but since independence a lack of freight, especially since the departure in 1976 of about 26,000 Nigerian workers, which has emptied the cocoa plantations and ruined production.

Since 1967 Santa Isabel has an international airport; before then, international flights landed at Bata in Río Muni. A "Mallorca type" town, it has suffered from a lack of maintenance since 1968. The only two constructions since independence are a luxury hotel (almost abandoned) and the Central Bank. The town has seen an inflation of national administrations, with a strong flow of Fang, political clients of Macías Neguema. It is practically impossible to leave Santa Isabel except with authorization of Security. In 1973 PUNT proposed to rename the city Malabo. In 1977, Santa Isabel had a population of 37,237.

After the 1979 coup, the defensive wall surrounding the presidential ghetto remained virtually unchanged. Up to now there are serious electricity shortages in the town, despite the efforts of the French Compagnie électro-mécanique. French concerns were also engaged in rehabilitating the port of Santa Isabel with financing from the European Development Fund. The presidential palace used by Obiang Nguema as his residence is still under the protection of Moroccan soldiers.

Toward the end of 1979, on the occasion of the visit of the king of Spain, Juan Carlos I, the vessel *Ciudad de Pamplona* halted at the port as a hotel for the Spanish. It remained there until August 1980, lodging volunteers and diplomatic personnel. The extension of the airport was entrusted to the Spanish company Huarte.

In 1980, the roads of the capital were still not illuminated. As under Macías Nguema, the capital suffered from a number of power failures. Obiang Nguema continued to occupy the presidential palace, renamed August 3 Palace, and placed under the protection of the Moroccan guards, always within the electrified center. He almost never left the palace. The capital had five discotheques.

In April 1981, a part of the port was burned. The sanitary situation in the capital left a lot to be desired; the population was weakened by malnutrition and illnesses. The French Compagnie électro-mécanique (CEM) was given the creation of the electricity distribution network and public lighting. Financed by the EDF, the work was expected to be done by the end of 1982.

Obiang Nguema is a regular of the Los Enamorados Club. The Nguemists stated that in May 1983 there had been a plot to assassinate the dictator. In October a school for vocational training of over 4,100 sq m, constructed by Spain, was inaugurated in a suburb of Santa Isabel.

In the mid-1980s, the South African company Oprocage opened a restaurant in Santa Isabel in a building belonging to Obiang Nguema's first wife. In 1985, the agricultural estate Esteves García, at the outskirts of the capital, was sold to a member of the clan from Mongomo, the torturer I. Eyi Monsui Andeme. One hundred and fifty apartments and a Spanish high school (Colegio) were built with Spanish bilateral funds.

Toward the end of 1990, the Nguemists received a loan of CFA Fr 760 million (approx. $1.5 million) from the French CCCE for the rehabilitation of the petroleum deposits in the capital. The city had a population of 46,000. The port of Santa Isabel held supremacy in the area of imports, while Bata dominated exports. In 1992 and 1993 there were a number of arrests of opponents who were tortured by the police, the army, or the Moroccans. In 1994, Victoriano Ebona Makina was the government's representative for the capital. He proceeded to arrest opposition members who did not pay him respect. In May–June 1994, the city was deprived of water.

In June–July 1995, like the Mikomeseng-Ebebiyin region (Río Muni), the capital was hit by an epidemic of bloody diarrhea; there were hundreds of deaths. WHO sent in chlorine. In the municipal elections of September 1995, Victorino Bolekia Bonay (ADP/POC) was elected mayor.

On January 29, 1996, the manager of the CPDS, Abilio Bondjale, was arrested by order of Chief Commissioner Julian Ondo Nkumu and tortured with electric wires for an entire week. In February 1996, on the occasion of the presidential election, Obiang Nguema's police, led by Ondo Nkumu, arrested the democratically elected mayor of the capital, V. Bolekia, and his deputies during a French lesson in the cultural center of the French Cooperation. They were tortured until they bled. In April, a hurricane destroyed a part of the municipal market.

See also African Development Bank; Angue Ondo, P.; Annobón; Artucio, A.; ASODEGUE; Aviation; Bakale Obiang, E.-B.; Balboa Boneke, J.; Bata; Benito; Río Benito (Mbini); Bibang Oyee, J.; Bikomo Nanguande; Branger, A.; Cheyson, C.; China Nationalist Republic; China People's Republic; Choni Becoba, V.; Convergency for Social Democracy; Coup d'état of May 11–13, 1983; Coup d'état of August 1988; Democratic Progressive Alliance; Diplomacy; Dougan, J.; Edu Oba, B.; Education; EFE; Eneme Ovono, S.; Engonga Motulu, M.; Engonga Nguema, D.; Esono Masie, P.; Esono Mbomio, J.; Eyegue Obama Asue, F.-P.; Fisheries; Forsyth, F.; France; Gangsterism; Gangsters; Germany; Governor General; Inestrosa Ikaka, F.; Iyanga Pendi, A.-C.; Juanola, J.; Civil Junta for the Salvation of the Nation; Lebanon; Llansol, V.-G.; Macías Nguema; Mba Ondo, C.; Missions; Modu Akuse Bindang, C.; Mokudi Nanga, A.; Moto Nsá, S.; Muñoz Ylata, S.; National Alliance for Democratic Restoration (ANRD); Navigation; Ndong Ela Mangue, J.; Ndong Mba Obono, M.; Ndongo Bidyogo, D.; Ndongo Ogüono-Asong, M. M.; Obiang Nguema, T.; Okue Moto, M.; Olo Mba Nseng, J.; Ondo Ayang, L.; Ondo Ela, S.; Ondo Obiang, V.; Organization of African Unity; Parliament; Petroleum; Police; Popular Union; Post Offices; Public Health;

Rasilla, L. de la; Roig Balestros, F. A.; Russia; Saharaoui Popular Republic; Sainz Bayon, J. M.; Seriche Bioco Malabo, C.; South Africa; Spain; Sports; Summerlin, T.; Television; Terror; Trade; Transmediterránea; Union for Democracy and Social Development; United Kingdom; United Nations; United States of America; Terror; University; Victims.

SÃO TOME. An island that with Príncipe has formed a republic since 1976. Occupied by the Portuguese during the last quarter of the fourteenth century. After 1493 it became responsible for Fernando Po. Its bishopric, created in 1534 by Paul III, extended its jurisdiction to Fernando Po as well as Annobón. In order to convert the inhabitants of Annobón, most of them Bantu of Angola arriving via São Tomé, the canons (chanoines) of the São Tomé cathedral were sent to the island, but they failed in their duty because of the inhabitants' hostility.

In 1866 seeds of cocoa, coffee, and Ficus elastica were sent from São Tométo Fernando Po, which permitted the development of plantations of Spanish soil.

At the time of São Tomé's struggle for independence, Equatorial Guinea accepted the leaders of the São Tomé and Príncipe Liberation Movement, those who are presently leading the country. But Macías Nguema expelled them in 1971, fearing their influence on the Equato-Guineans. In 1978 there were about 300 Equato-Guinean refugees in São Tomé/Príncipe.

President Miguel Trovoada, accompanied by the ministers of foreign affairs, agriculture and fisheries, industry and commerce paid an official visit to Equatorial Guinea between January 25 and 28, 1996, in order to renew an old agreement for cooperation that had never been operational.

In August 1998, discussions were held concerning the maritime borders. Mobil started 18-month offshore investigations with the national company STPETRO. Equatorial Guinea was said to have granted Shell a block to the south of Bioko, which encroaches on NE of the ZEE of São Tome, where the American Environmental Remediation Holding Corp. (EHCR) is working for São Tomé; a second set of discussions was held in September. In the middle of October 1998, Obiang Nguema was invited on an official visit by President Miguel Trovoada. One of the aims of the visit was to settle the problems concerning the delimitation of the respective exclusive areas (mostly for the exploitation of petroleum and fishing).

See also Annobón; Army; Navigation; Obiang Nguema, T.; United Nations; United States.

SARDANIS, Andrew. A Cyprio-Zambian banker. See also Banks.

SAS EBUREA, d. 1904. Prime minister of Bubi King Moka, whose power he usurped in 1899, shortly after Moka's death. He forbade the Bubi from having any contact with Europeans. In 1904, for having encouraged the tax strike, the Spanish Guardia Civil took him to Santa Isabel, where he fell ill and died at the hospital on July 3, not without miraculously having converted himself to Catholicism and having been baptized. The place was therefore vacant for the legal successor of Moka, his brother Malabo.

SAUDI ARABIA. In April 1982, Obiang Nguema made an official visit in order to clinch economic aid. In 1996, the Xenel Company, based in Saudi Arabia, was put in charge of the renovation of the port of San Carlos by the petroleum consortium led by Mobil.

SAUR AFRIQUE. A French company of the Bouygues group specializing in the distribution of electricity. Implanted in the beginning of the 1990s, it failed. Its activities were taken over by the Spanish company SEGESA.

SCHLUMBERGER. French company specializing in drilling oil, presently with 930 sites in about 100 countries, with 53,900 employees and 95 nationalities. Sedco-Forex, Dowell Schlumberger, Measures and Systems are part of the group. See also Petroleum.

SCHOLARSHIPS. In the early days of provincialization, 82 students were granted scholarships to enroll in high and technical education in Spain. The majority were offered by Casas Fuertes. After independence, Equatorial Guinea granted some 30 scholarships, but they were canceled in 1972 when the students refused to return to their country to work on the plantations. In 1972–1973, 224 Guinean students studied abroad, 140 of them in Spain. The People's Republic of China, North Korea, Cuba, and several UN agencies have also been granting scholarships. After Obiang Nguema's palace revolution (1979), most scholarships were given by Spain and France. See also National Alliance for the Restoration of Democracy.

SECRETARIADO CONJUNTO (Joint Secretariat). Also called Group of 23. At the Constitutional Conference, this group intended to be a forum for all parties. Composed of marginal members of IPGE, MUNGE, MONALIGE, it rapidly became a new party which, with García Trevijano's advice, served especially as a mainspring for Macías Nguema. García Trevijano allegedly financed the Secretariado, also called the Grupo Macías, giving him a draft constitution that the conference refused.

Back in Equatorial Guinea, the Grupo Macías militated against the constitution issued from the conference and called Torao Sikara, Balboa Dougan, King Tomas, Ndongo Miyone, J. Edu, Ibongo Iyanga, and others servants of Spain. But at the September 1968 elections, supported by publicity based on posters and leaflets for all categories of the population, the group won both the presidency of the republic with Macías Nguema and the majority in Parliament (Asamblea de la República) and the provincial councils, with the following as "star performers": Primo Esono, Nsué Micó, Eyegue Ntutumu, Owono Obame, Edong Andeme, Mbá Nsué, Nsué Angüe Osa, Eñeso Neóñe, Mbá, Ngomo Nandongo, and others. Of these 10 political friends of Macías Nguema, three were assassinated, six exiled abroad, and only one, Nsué Mico, became a member of the government. After independence, the Grupo Macías no longer had the same reason for existing, but it certainly stimulated Macías Nguema to create the PUNT and to suppress all other political parties, as well as all persons having criticized his concept of power.

SECRETARIADO DE ESTADO A LA PRESIDENCIA (Secretariat of State to the Presidency) see Oyono Avyngono Mba; Presidency

SECRETARIO GENERAL (Secretary General). During provincialization, the office of secretary general was created in order to assist the governor general in his duties. The office remained in existence until the end of autonomy in 1968. Besides replacing the governor general (or the commissar general from 1964–1968) in case of unavailability, the secretary general was head of all departments, with the exception of justice and army, which came directly under the Spanish government's supervision (see Carrero Blanco). The Spanish government appointed the governmental delegates (territorial administrators) of the two provinces.

SEGESA. Joint company (62% held by the Nguemist state, 38% by the Spanish company Infisa International S.A. that manages electrical supply to Fernando Po. It took over the activities of the French company Saur (Bouygues group), which abandoned its activities toward the end of 1991.

SEGU, Ramón. Claretian born around 1895. He worked in Annobón during the time of Macías Nguema, along with Father E. Doce. R. Segu died in 1976, one year after his colleague.

SELF-GOVERNMENT see Autonomy

SEMINARIO. *Seminario menor:* secondary school staffed by priests, as existed in Basilé, Concepcíon, etc. *Seminario major:* training college for the priesthood, such as at Banapa, founded in 1912, and Concepcíon since 1959.

SENATE see Consejo de la República

SENDJE. Locality in Río Muni. See also Navigation; Río Benito

SENG, Jaime. Fang refugee living in Cameroon before independence. He founded IPGE with Perea Epota and C. L. Ateba around 1959. Opposed to a federation of Equatorial Guinea and Cameroon, he split with IPGE after the Ambam Congress in 1963 and founded MUN (Movimiento de Unión Nacional), which generated MUNGE.

SENIOR OFFICIALS AFFAIR (Second). In April 1981, a "plot" was followed by arrests of a number of high-placed officials and military personnel.

SERICHE BIOKCO MALABO, Angel Serfin. Of mixed Bubi-Creole origin. Born in 1940 at Moka. Underwent military training in Saragossa with Obiang Nguema from 1963–1965. Now a Major. He became a member of the Supreme Military Council immediately after the 1979 coup and was appointed military governor of Fernando Po. In January 1980, he was nominated military commissioner for public works, housing, and transport. In May 1981, he acted as public prosecutor at the trial of members of the alleged plot that had been orchestrated by Mbá Oñana in April. The presiding officer at the trial was Oyo Riqueza, second vice-president of the republic, whose position was taken over by Seriche Dougan in December 1981. In that capacity he invited Pope Paul II to visit Equatorial Guinea. The pope spent one day in the country in February 1982.

In March 1982, he refused to allow high-placed Spanish officials in the Equato-Guinean administration. In late October, Seriche Bioko became prime minister. In early 1983, he advised the population to learn French. In late April, he made a visit to Madrid to have the country's plan to enter the franc zone accepted by Spain. In January 1986, he was confirmed as prime minister and minister for public health. In October, he owed the Guinextebank, which was on the way to bankruptcy FCFA, 13 million.

In early August 1989, he resigned with his government. After a short crisis, Seriche Bioko was invited in late August to form the new cabinet, with Eyi Monsuy as vice prime minister. He held no post in the "transitional" government of January 24, 1992.

In 1993, he remained a member of the central committee of PDGE. During the November elections, he became a Santa Isabel deputy and was promoted to vice-president of the National Assembly. On October 9, 1995, he founded the Association of Friends of President Obiang Nguema, which he introduced as apolitical and formed of friends of the dictator who wanted to spread his ideals, his thoughts, and his actions. The directing committee included Nguemists like Batho Obama Nsue Mangue and Agusto Nse Nfumu.

SERICHE DOUGAN, Angel Serafin. Born in Moka in 1944. A Bubi-Creole half-breed descended from the Bubi king Malabo (1904–1937). He belongs to the creole-native "nobility." Studied at the Escuela Superior Provincial. Since 1980, first secretary at the embassy in Morocco, under the orders of Ambassador S. Mbana Nsoro Mban. Highly pro-Spanish.

In late October 1986, he owed the bankrupt Guinextebank FCFA 31,586,000. He indulged in speculation in construction. In private, he admitted Nguemist excesses. As ambassador to Nigeria, he attended the UNDP donor's conference in Geneva in April 1982. In 1993, he was the administrative director of Foreign affairs. Upon becoming secretary general of the Ministry for Foreign affairs, he was named ambassador to Cameroon. By decree 19, he became general secretary of the ministry of Foreign Affairs and Cooperation on January 17, 1994. In the January 8, 1996, government, he became secretary of state for public administration. On April 8, 1996, he was promoted to prime minister, replacing the Bubi Siale Borico. On July 24 he asked Spain to suspend the broadcasts of Radio Exterior that were destined for his country, without success.

He was part of the mediation committee dealing with the quarrel between presidents Lissouba and Sassou Ngueso, from Congo Brazaville. Due to his office, he participated in a meeting in Libreville on June 19, 1997.

During the cabinet reshuffle of January 21, 1998, he kept his office, but Fransisco Ngomo, vice-prime minister, disappeared from the govenment.

SHINKAME, John. Ambassador to Nigeria in 1991. In 1992, he intervened in Lagos so that David Eyama, Equato-Guinean military attaché—convicted of drug trafficking—was released, to aid relations between the two countries.

SIALE BILEKA, Silvestre. Bubi born March 8, 1940, at Baney. A refugee in Switzerland, he obtained a degree in law from the University of Geneva, then sought asylum in Benin in 1978. Upon his return shortly after Obiang Nguema's coup, he was named an official in the Ministry of Justice and later became a prosecutor.

In May 1982 he belonged to the Nguemist constitutional commission of Akonibe. In December, he became director general of the ministry of justice and religion. In March 1984, Obiang Nguema proposed a priest from Mongomo, S.

Ensema Mba, as his country's candidate to the UN Human Rights Commission, with S. Siale Bilekia as his alternate. These candidacies were rejected by the commission. In November 1989, Siale Bilekia became minister for justice and religion. In October 1990, he was confirmed in this post.

In the January 1992, "transitional" government, he became prime minister. In May, Siale visited the high school of the capital (Rey Malabo) and advised the students not to get involved in political affairs. He was booed and left the establishment threatening to return corpses to the parents. On August 18, Siale presided over the Equato-Guinean Day at the international exposition at Seville. That summer, he was chased out of the School of Agriculture by stone throwers when he warned students that they would be the first to be punished in case of disorder. The Spanish press described him as corrupt and a torturer. He was nicknamed Sirena because of his noisy movements using official limousines.

In February–March 1993, he presided over the National Pact negotiations. On September 21, Siale Bilekia participated in the meeting of Nguemist ministers (J. Ndong Ela Mangue and M. Nguema Mba), in the presence of Ninjas, with the representatives of the CPDS, who had received warnings. The next day, Ndong Ela Mangue prohibited *La Verdad*. In his village of Baney, police commissioner Juan Engonga arrested and tortured schoolboys and mothers with children.

During the elections of November 21, 1993, his family was the only one to vote in Baney; the rest of the population observed the POC boycott. Siale Bilekia was elected PDGE deputy for Baney. In the December 22 government, he remained prime minister and head of government.

In April 1995, on the occasion of the Moto Nsá scandal and the so-called military plot, Siale Bilekia summoned the diplomatic corps and accused Spain of blocking the democratic process and financing the opposition.

On January 8, 1996, he proceeded to make a ministerial reshuffle, including four new ministers and various transfers. The executive remained dominated by the clan from Mongomo. Siale Bilekia remained prime minister, with Anatolio Ndong Mba as vice-prime minister in charge of the economy and finance.

After the presidential election, Obiang Nguema replaced Siale Bilekia with a new prime minister, the Bubi-Creole Angel Serafin Dougan. In the April 8, 1996, government, he became counsellor for judicial and administrative affairs to the head of state. He kept this function in 1998.

SIALE DJANGANI see Djangani

SIALO, Joaquin María, d. 1957. Bubi of Rebola. First Equato-Guinean seminarist. As of 1912, he studied at the seminaries of Banapa, Basilé, and Concepcíon, then in Barcelona and the Canary Islands. From 1917–1923, he returned to Banapa. He was the first Guinean to be ordained a Catholic priest (August 25, 1929, in Santa Isabel Cathedral), more than 60 years after Ikenge Ibia, the first Protestant (Presbyterian) minister (who was trained in the U.S.).

SIBACHA BUECHEKU, Antonio. Secretary for external relations of Ruben Ndongo's Social Democratic and Popular Convergency. In the summer of 1990, Sibacha founded the Union for Democracy and Social Development, with Djibelan King Nam. In June 1992, at the Panafrican Conference for Democracy (Dakar), he accused Obiang Nguema of assassinating opponents. He demanded the return of the Moroccans.

SIERRA LEONE. Former British colony where emancipated slaves from North America were settled. During the nineteenth century, several workers from Sierra Leone came to work in Fernando Po. The anti-slavery tribunal in charge of the repression of the slave trade in the Gulf of Guinea, which had to deal severely several times with the slave traders of the Río Muni zone, was established in Freetown. The tribunal's transfer to Fernando Po in 1827 served Owen's expedition as a pretense for occupying the island. Together with Liberians and Nigerians, the Sierra Leonese generated the Creole community of Fernando Po.

SI ESONO, José. 1884–1941. Native of Ebansok. Catholic catechist in Río Muni. He was sometimes called "the saint of the forest," or the first "apostle of the interior of Río Muni," even before being baptized.

SIJIFO see Timber

SIMA EKUA AVOMO, Lino. Born approximately 1952, native of Mongomo. Finished high school, then trained at the diplomatic school in Madrid. Government official in the Ministry of Foreign Affairs.

In the 1980s, he was second secretary at the embassy in Moscow. Later, he became ambassador in Beijing.

After his wife's arrest in Brazil for dealing drugs, he became ambassador to France at the end of 1995. See Drugs.

SIMA ENEME, Alberto (called Albertin). Born 1952. From Niefang. Son of Alberto Sima. Member of Youth Marching with Macias. Noted Nguemist. Trained as a nurse in Russia but claims to be a doctor. Under Macías Nguema, government's representative in Río Benito and then in Mikomeseng, where he drew attention with his brutality.

After Obiang Nguema's coup, he became a deputy. He was considered as one of the ideologists of the single party. In 1992, he became ambassador to Gabon.

Director of the hospital at Concepción (Riaba) and the deputy of the south-central province at the House of Representatives. By Decree 27 of January 1994, he was appointed director general of public health and planning in the Ministry of Health. In May 1985 he proposed the founding of a single party. In Parliament, his proposal received 31 votes for and 29 votes against (which practically means rejection in a totalitarian regime).

Since 1988 he was chief of the section of the Great Endemics. Decree 27 of January 1994 appointed him director general of public health and planning in the Ministry of Health.

During the ministerial reshuffle of April 8, 1996, he became director general for public health and sanitary planning.

SIMA NGUA, Anacleto. Claretian priest. Under Macías Nguema, he spent five years in prisons. Bishop of Bata since 1982. On August 15, 1990, he celebrated the solemn proclamation of Our Lady of the Assumption as head of the diocese. In November 1992, Aurelio Bibang, governor of Río Muni, a prototype of the corrupt person, summoned him to complain against anti-Nguemist comments by priests.

During the presidential elections of February 1996, Mgr. A. Sima Ngua addressed a letter to the dictator or January 27, in protest against the hostility of the Ministry of the Interior toward the clergy, who were fulfilling their apostolic functions. He threatened to reduce the number of places of worship to 5%. Recalling the closure of churches under Macías Nguema, Sima Ngua demanded the cancellation of measures violating the constitution and the international engagements of the regime. Following Nguemist cruelties, the monks and nuns of Bata addressed a communiqué on Radio Exterior de España, denouncing insults, humiliations, violence, house arrests, arrests, and torture, with which priests of all faiths were intimidated. Mgr. Sima still suffers from the violence he endured under the first Nguemist dictatorship.

SIMA NGUEMA ADA see Nguema Ada Sima

SIMED S.A. After the suppression of INFOGE by Macías Nguema in 1972, following the misappropriation of funds that Mbá Ada was accused of, García Trevijano created a new company to monopolize Equatorial Guinea's external trade: Simed S.A. The administrators were Simone Chouraki, sister-in-law and secretary of García Trevijano, and two other assistants of the lawyer. Since 1975 Simed S.A. has been in competition with Adoual, in which Oyono Ayingono Mbá, Macías Nguema's nephew, was an investor.

SIMO, Baltasar. From Ciudadela (Menorca), d. 1877. Trader at Corisco. He left for Cuba around 1834 with his own boat and merchandise. After a journey of more than a hundred days, he arrived in Corisco, where he opened a factory. Upon falling ill, he left his business to his friend Francisco Vicente, from Menorca, also the pilot of a vessel, which arrived by chance in the area. Simó remained at Corisco until English warships burned his factory, then returned to Cuba.

SINDICATO MADERERO (Timber Producer Union). Created in 1936 with headquarters in Río Benito, then in Bata, and with a delegation in Madrid. It represented exclusively the buyers' interest and that of large exploiting companies. It anticipated in the election of half of the deputies of the Diputacíon provincial of Río Muni. Since 1947, the union has been part of the Junta Económica Colonial, consultative body of the Direccíon General de Marruecos y Colonias.

SINDICATOS (Trade Unions). Francoist Spain only had vertical trade unions subjected to the Movimiento Nacional, and these represented the major economic interests rather than the workers. The Unión General de Trabajadores (UCTGE), which in 1966 organized a strike of Guinean officials, has been operating secretly since 1959.

See also Camara Oficial Agricola; Cocoa; Coffee; Comite Sindical; Free Unions; Labor; Sindicato Maderero; Union de Agricultores; Union General de Trabajadores.

SINOSA see Timber

SI ONDO, Sotero. From Bata. Born in Nkog-Ntoma. Holds a degree in law (Spain). In March 1981 he became attorney general for the Republic, a function he exercised mainly during the trial of Mba Ndong and Nvono Nka. In May 1982, he was part of the Nguemist constitutional commission of Akonibe. He was confirmed at his post in January 1994 and also as a judge at the Supreme Court.

SISA TORES, Hilario. From Annobón. Born on October 19, 1960. Principal customs inspector. In November 1993, he was elected PDGE deputy for Annobón. On December 22, he was named vice-minister of Culture, Tourism, and the French language. In the ministerial reshuffle of January 8, 1996, he was confirmed in his post. He retained his function in the April 8, 1996 government.

In the ministerial reshuffle of January 21, 1998, he was replaced by Anacleto Olo Mibuy.

SITOKO BUIYABAN, Teofilo. Member of the Nguemist constitutional commission of Akonibe in May 1982.

SLAVERY. The slave trade started around 1530 when plantations developed in the New World. Between 1642–1648, the Dutch succeeded the Portuguese in raiding the southwest of Río Muni and Fernando Po, driving the Bubi into the mountains. Between 1819–1825, 20 Spanish slave ships were seized by the Royal Navy. At the beginning of the nineteenth century, there was strong competition between English, German, French, Portuguese, and Spanish slave traders, who used the coastal tribes such as the Benga as middle men. After the Vienna Congress (1815), Spain signed a treaty with the United Kingdom for the abolition of the slave trade, but in 1840 the British Navy still had to deal severely in Corisco with Spanish slave traders. Some slaves were freed in Fernando Po. In Cuba, slavery did not cease until 1886 (see also under Cuba and Owen).

In 1986, the Nigerian press accused the Nguemist regime of practicing slavery in their cocoa plantations in Fernando Po with Nigerian workers. See also Nigeria.

SMALL-AND-MEDIUM-SIZED FIRMS. In the government of January 21, 1998, Vidal Choni Becoba was minister of the industry, trade and the promotion of small-and-medium sized firms.

SNEYDERS, Abraham Louis. Ambassador of the Netherlands from February 1980 and don of the diplomatic corps. He lived in Yaoundé (Cameroon).

SOCIAL AFFAIRS see Alene Mba, M.; Delegación de Asuntos Sociales

SOCIAL AND DEMOCRATIC GROUP (Agrupación Democrática y Social, ADSOGE). Nationwide nonseparatist social democratic group founded in Madrid in 1992 by the Bubi Enrique Beaka Belope as an offshoot of the Bubi Union. In 1993 the group was renamed the Democratic and Social Union.

SOCIAL DEMOCRATIC AND POPULAR CONVERGENCY (Convergencia Social-Demócrata y Popular, CSDP). A satellite party of the PDGE, whose president is Secundino Oyono Aguong Ada. He breached the election boycott in November 1993 in return for 8 million pesetas from the dictatorship. In December 1993, the CSDP addressed an inflammatory letter to the CPDS, accusing it of slander in *La Verdad.* Late in 1993, the UDS cancelled a plan to merge with the CSDP because of S. Oyono's close association with the dictatorship.

In January 1994, the CSDP joined the parliamentary delegation of "opposition" representatives who were given the job of praising the Nguemist democratic system to the UN and European Union. In March 1994 S. Oyono Aguong was excluded from the party for his unilateral decision to participate in the November 1993 elections. But Oyono was soon back in the party's fold. In June, at the first convention of the CSDP (in Bata), Oyono called the reduction of 10% in the number of civil servants "a violation of human rights." He also demanded that the country return to the Constitution of October 1968. The CSDP made it known that after the departure of the Nguemists, the Ninjas would be judged.

In 1995, S. Oyono was part of the Enquiry Commission on Judicial Administration. On May 9, he entered into a debate with Obiang Nguema on the political situation. On May 24, Rafael Obiang, one of the leaders of the CSDP, was arrested in his house by the secretary of state for security, Manuel Nguema, a cousin of Obiang Nguema, for possession of copies of *La Verdad,* the CPDS monthly journal. During the September municipal elections, the CSDP won three seats out of about 400. See also Elections.

SOCIAL DEMOCRATIC COALITION PARTY (Partido de la Coalición Social-Demócrata; PCSD). It included the Liberal Party, Popular Action, and Bubi Union. In early 1993, this party had not yet been legalized. In October, it co-signed the Institutional Proposal addressed to Obiang Nguema, with the six members of the POC. With the POC, the PCSD boycotted the elections of November 1993. The PCSD published a bulletin, *Tu Guia.*

In 1995, this group was reported to have been tamed by the Nguemists. In its name, Buenaventura Moswi m'Asumu attended the second party convention of the PDGE in Bata, as part of the delegation of this "opposition." On the occasion of the presidential election of February 1996, B. Moswi presented himself as the "transition president" in a special edition of *Tu Guia.*

See also Elections; Joint Opposition Platform.

SOCIAL DEMOCRATIC PARTY (Partido Social Demócrata de Guinea Ecuatorial, PSD). Founded hastily in June 1990 by a former member of ANRD, M. Mangue Mba, a refugee in Germany, to join the Socialist International under the name of Democratic and Social Union, with Balinga Balinga Alene as general secretary. The PSD was introduced in a brochure with the slogan "motherland, democracy, prosperity." It wished to play the role of a "model party and pioneer democracy," defender of human rights. Article 10 of the statutes deals "With the candidacy for the Presidency of the Republic." A brochure entitled *Project for all Equato-Guineans* was completed with "Our Common Cause." The party drew attention especially to social relations, town-countryside balance, the rational redistribution of resources, access to economic opportunities, and so forth. It foresees the creation of a National institute of economic research for development, with a databank, in order to achieve an autonamous economy. It would support small- and medium-scale industries. A laboratory for research in the field of natural resources and mines was also planned. The PSD stressed the creation of wealth, with development of means of communication being given priority. Upon his return to the country, Balinga Balinga was arrested several times and imprisoned at Playa Negra. He was released without trial or violence.

In June 1991, the members of the Unión Social Demócrata decided to convert themselves into the Partido Social Demócrata (PDS) after several avatars. The party was legalized in 1992. On October 15, 1993, a number of members (including F. Mabale Nseng) were expelled from the party for treason, as each of them had accepted $9,000 from the government for participating in the elections of November 21. The PSD left the POC, which was boycotting the elections. Being of no significance, it obtained no seats. In late March 1995, the PSD participated in the second party convention of the PDGE as part of the tame opposition. In the April 8, 1996, government, Mabale Nseng was rewarded with the post of state secretary for energy.

SOCIAL DEMOCRATIC UNION (Unión Democrática y Social, UDS). Of the center-left, this party was presented at Lisbon in October 1990 as a result of the merger of businessman Modu Akuse Bindang's Democratic and Social Union (in difficulties with the law in Spain) and the Convergency for Social Democracy, one of the many creations of Secundino Oyono. The choice of Portugal was justified by the Portuguese "discovery" of Equatorial Guinea. Modo Akuse claimed to be supported by Venezuelan interests. His aim was to remove Obiang Nguema by free elections.

The statutes from the days of Lisbon, Libreville, and Caracas (1990–1991) showed the Unión as a political organization of the masses that was pluralist and reformist and an instrument of the people for the struggle to obtain political power through democratic means and dialogue. Its fundamental principles are internal democracy, respect for the hierarchy, and transparency. UDS accepts foreigners. Its statutes fix structures and a code of internal discipline. The general secretary should be more than 30 years old and less than 50. Modu Akuse Bindang claimed to have about 160,000 members. He applied to be admitted to the Socialist International.

The party was legalized in October 1992. Toward the end of that year, Modu Akuse Bindang was expelled from the party for taking up too much space, but he was soon reinstated. The UDS joined the POC and participated in the February-March 1993 negotiations for the National Pact. The UDS breached the election boycott of November 21 organized by the POC and transformed itself into a satellite party of PDGE, with a grant of 8 million pesetas. Its members seemed never to have suffered arrest since then. The general secretary is Jesús Nze Obama. In the elections of November 21, the UDS obtained five seats (out of 80). Shortly after, it broke with the Social Democratic and Popular Convergency as a result of the closeness of Secundino Oyono with the regime.

In January 1994, the UDS was part of the delegation of representatives of the "opposition" asked to praise the Nguemist democracy in Europe and before the UN. In 1995, this party was considered as belonging to the opposition tamed by the Nguemists. As a reward, on April 8, 1996, Carmelo Modu Akuse Bindang became minister of state in charge of labor and social promotion.

Modu Akuse did not remain in the government of January 21, 1998, and was replaced by Ernesto Maria Cayetano Toherida.

SOCIALIST PARTY (Partido Socialisto de Guinea Ecuatoria, PSGE). Founded in 1991 and presided over by J. Esono Nsué. He denounced the presence of 600

Moroccan soldiers in Equatorial Guinea and demanded their withdrawal. In 1992, the party was led by T. Mecheba Fernandez. It was legalized in May. Before the EC Parliament in Strasbourg, Mecheba Fernandez exposed the systematic violation of human rights.

In October 1993, the party signed the Institutional Proposal addressed to Obiang Nguema along with the remaining members of the POC. From Lisbon, Tomas Mecheba demanded the cancellation of the November 21 elections and reforms of the electoral census. Upon his return, he agreed to go to the polls in return for funding of 8 million pesetas. The secretary of the organization, Constantino Iviti, announced the expulsion of Tomas Mecheba. In turn, Mecheba exposed Iviti and J. Manuel Ibolo, who were briefly imprisoned. The PSGE did not win any seats.

In January 1994, the PSGE participated in the mission of parliamentary representatives and representatives of the "opposition" to Europe and the UN to praise Obiang Nguema's democracy. In 1995 this party was considered a member of the opposition tamed by the Nguemists. It attended the second party convention of the PDGE, represented by T. Mecheba Fernandez. On April 8, 1996, Mecheba Fernandez was rewarded with the post of secretary of state for industry, but he refused it.

Tomas Mecheba declared during the summer of 1997 that a joint government with Obiang Nguema would have to be accepted until 2003. He strongly insisted on the country's hispanity.

SOCIAL SECURITY. All Europeans were insured through the Seguridad Social de Guinea, depending on the Delegación Provincial de Trabajo. After independence, thanks to an ILO consultation, the Instituto Nacional de Seguridad Social (INSESO) was created. It existed only on paper.

In March 1980, its restructuring was decided upon. In May 1992, the press reported that Obiang Nguema was earning a fortune by racketeering the private and public companies of the countries, including social institutions of the type of the National Social Security Fund, with a tax of 3% (supposedly for his party). He was said to have drawn FCFA 6 million from the fund.

In the 1998 government, C. Congue is minister of employment and social security. During the summer, it was decided that a building for the Equato-Guinean company SEGECO, financed by the INSESO itself, would be built. The building will be finished in the year 2000.

SOCIEDAD COLONIAL DE GUINEA (SOCOGUI, Colonial Society of Guinea). Established in Cape San Juan, where it owned 1,678 hectares of palm oil plantations abandoned since Emergencia, in 1969. The production represented around 22,500 tons of clusters per year.

SOCIEDAD DE AFRICANISTAS Y COLONIALISTAS (Society of Africanists and Colonists). After a section of the Association for the Exploration of Africa had been created in Madrid by the king of Belgium in 1877, a Spanish Society of Specialists on Africa was founded in Madrid in 1883. It supported the efforts of Iradier and Dr. Ossorio for the occupation of the Spanish possessions in the Gulf of Guinea, facing the British, German, and French expansionism that eroded the territories received by Spain under the Pardo Treaty of 1778.

SOCIEDAD DE CULTURA Y DESARROLLO HISPANO-GUINEAN see Hispano-Guinean Society for Culture.

SOCIEDAD FORESTAL DEL RIO MUNI (Forest Company of Río Muni). After the considerable loans granted by France to Equatorial Guinea for the financing of major construction by the Société Française des Dragages since 1970, France received as a guarantee the creation of the Sociedad Forestal, with a 10-year concession of 150,000 hectares of virgin forest in southeast Río Muni. The main installations were in Asog-Abia, near Kukumankok. In 10 years it was forecasted to take out 1,500,000 tons of okoumea and other species. The whole affair was triggered by García Trevijano, who, with J. P. Nouveau, a French businessman living in Switzerland, connected with a French banking group, launched the forestal under the leadership of P. Schwarz, nephew of J. P. Nouveau. The Société Forestière du Río Muni has also tried to obtain a contract for renewing the telecommunications system, but failed because of cheaper assistance offered by the People's Republic of China. J. P. Nouveau allegedly promised García Trevijano that in case of selling of the Forestal, the business would go to a Spanish company, but in 1976, dealings entrusted to Simone Chouraki took place with Tardiba, a French lumber company also working in the Ivory Coast. Shortly after the sale was completed, Tardiba had to abandon exploitation of the concession because the Equatorial Guinean government wished to cut down on the constant flight of Equato-Guinean workers to nearby Gabon. A report in June 1980 by the French Ministry of Overseas Cooperation made no mention of the activities of the company in Equatorial Guinea. See also Timber.

SOCIEDAD GUINEANA DE GAS (SOGUGAS). A company that sells gas equipment for domestic use. It is run by Olo Mba Nseng, Pastor Micha, and Teodorín Nguema Obiang, eldest son of the dictator. Constancia Mangue, first wife of the dictator, controls this company.

SOCIETE D'EXPLOITATION COLONIALE (Company of Colonial Exploitation). Created in 1899 at the instigation of a French merchant, Lesieur, who bought land from the chiefs of northern Río Muni. At the end of the nineteenth century it owned almost the whole northern part of the province. French commercial and transport companies were members of the company. The recognition by France that Río Muni belonged to Spain in 1900, under the Paris Treaty, was detrimental to the company. Since Spain did not recognize the company, it lost all its territories. Lesieur accused the French government, but Paris replied that the purchase of these lands had been done at his own risk. A project of a charter company, extending from the Río Muni province to Río Kye, for indemnity of the company, was refused, which caused its dissolution in 1924.

SOCIETE FRANCAISE DES DRAGAGES ET TRAVAUX PUBLICS. Engineering company well entrenched in all francophone Africa. It had been operating in Equatorial Guinea since provincialization under the name of Dragas y Construcciones, with offices in Madrid. Since independence the Paris headquarters have taken over. Since 1969, thanks to a $43 million loan (3 billion pesetas) from France, they have built mostly prestige projects: Bata Harbor ($28 million or 1,960 million pesetas), without much freight to evacuate, or transit; the presidential palace of Ekuko, near Bata ($12 million, or 1,960 million pesetas); the luxurious buildings of the Central Bank in Bata and Santa Isabel ($3 million or 200 million pesetas). Since 1975, Dragages have been building additional facilities in Bata Harbor. They operate with French executives and non-Equatorial-Guinean workers from Benin, Senegal, etc., under the general direction of Jean Audenis. In about 1975 García Trevijano seems to have filed a legal action because of Dragages's high prices. In a June 1980 report, the French Ministry of Overseas Cooperation made no reference to this company's activities in Equatorial Guinea.

SOCIETE GENERALE DE BANQUES (France) see Banks

SOCIETE GENERALE DE SURVEILLANCE S.A. This Swiss society, with headquarters in Geneva, has been in charge of supervising Equatorial Guinea's foreign trade since 1983.

SOCOGUI see Sociedad Colonial de Guinea

SOFOGE see Timber

SOFONA see Timber

SOGEDISA. Equato-Guinean company that publishes the fortnightly *La Gaceta de Guinea Ecuatorial.* Its president was A. Nse Nfumu, with Robert-Martín Prieto, Hilario Sisa Torres, and A. Olo Mebuy.
    See also Hispano-Guinean Society for Culture and Development; Press.

SOMAVI see Timber

SORCERY. Obiang Nguema publicly called his uncle Macías Nguema an "envoy of the devil, and son of Lucifer, President of all sorcerers." In the spring of 1992, the Spanish press reported Obiang Nguema's use of sorcery to maintain his own power through sacrifices and ritual assassinations.
    In April 1996, the US State Department's report on human rights said that "In January a police commissioner killed a farmer near Malabo [Santa Isabel], and cut open his abdomen and chest to remove several organs used in witchcraft-related rituals. Although the commissioner was tried by a court and found guilty, he was sentenced only to house arrest for 20 years. His movement, however, is apparently unrestricted." A "sorceress," a native of Evinayong, Petra Ndong, lives in the presidential palace at Bata.
    See also Bibang Ntutumu, S.; Ebebiyin.

SOUTH AFRICA, Republic of. Obiang Nguema consistently accuses the United Nations of not doing anything about apartheid, but notwithstanding, he granted a concession to a South African company for the operation, in 1985, of a 3,000-hectare ranch on Fernando Po. A military base has also been established.
    Though Equatorial Guinea did not entertain diplomatic relations with the South African Republic, experts in security and military information arrived in Santa Isabel.
    In 1985 a program of medical aid for $700,000 and road construction was begun. Then a ranch between Concepción and Moka (Fernando Po) was organized.

According to British sources, South Africa wished to introduce a military information and espionage network with the installation of high-frequency listeners of the Omega type used by the USA in Liberia to supervise Western and Central Africa. It was stated that South Africa was going to extend the Santa Isabel Airport to be able to receive the South African C-130, in order to offer a stop to the airline SAA. However, in the United Nations, Obiang Nguema condemned South Africa, complaining of the softness of the UN in the face of apartheid. The South African company Oprocage, managed by Hilton Lack, possessed a restaurant on the premises belonging to Obiang Nguema's first wife in Santa Isabel; wine and other products imported from South Africa were served.

In May 1988, the OUA asked the African countries to "mind their own business" before condemning others for their collaboration with South Africa; this was a criticism aimed mainly at Equatorial Guinea, accused by Nigeria of maintaining relations with Pretoria. The Equato-Guinean personnel of the embassy at Santa Isabel were then arrested. In May again, according to the ambassador to Nigeria, Okenve Mituy, seven South Africans were said to have been expelled. In June, an employee had still not been released, but the return of five South Africans was announced. The Nigerian press, on the other hand, exploded and again brought up the problems of claims over Fernando Po. The minister for foreign affairs, Nguema Nguema Onguene, visited Lagos with a message for President Babangida. The Nigerian protests against the South African presence led to the cancellation of the project for the lengthening of the runway at Santa Isabel (only 3 km).

During the 1990s, the embassy, under the ambassador to Madrid, Bruno Esono Ondo, was submerged in debts (and the telephone line cut). Spanish authorities passed by the South African Embassy, in the same building, to communicate with the Equato-Guinean delegation. Diplomatic relations between the two countries were restored in May 1993. The South African company Strategic Concept was hired to ensure the reelection of President Obiang Nguema, in February 1996. It was this company that invited Chip Carter, a relative of the former U.S. president, as a wellwisher observer of the elections.

SOUTHERN RANGE. A gathering of volcanic cones in the southern part of Fernando Po: the Pico del Condor (1852 m), the Pico de Moka (2009 m), and the Gran Caldera de San Carlos. The mountain range is separated from the Pico de Santa Isabel by the Musola depression. The southern range raises a barrier in front of the Atlantic monsoon (see Ureka). In 1976 a Soviet TU-154 airliner connecting Angola to Moscow via Santa Isabel hit one of the summits. The 11 bodies were not sent to the U.S.S.R. until after payment of $5 million for "damage to the mountain." A Russian expedition liquidated all traces of the accident.

SOVEREIGN ORDER OF MALTA see Mikomeseng

SOVIET UNION see Russia

SPAIN. Spanish colonial policies have always been controlled by the presidency of the government. The basic political concepts relied on the Eurafrican theory, on privileged relations between church and state, and on colonialism as an antidote to communism. Hispanicization was essential, and assimilation was advocated (see Emancipation). In practice, it was nothing but cultural ethnocide. Until 1968, the legal standards included an underlying distinction between Spaniards and non-Spaniards, as well as prejudice concerning the natives' mental capacity.

Between 1819 and 1825, 20 Spanish slave ships were seized by the Royal Navy. It was with Chacón, in 1858, that the Spanish occupation of black African territories started. But it was only in 1888 that Trasatlántica organized the first regular maritime shipping service to Fernando Po. At that time and for a long time after, only Germany and the United Kingdom connected Río Muni to Europe. This explains the encroachments of France, Germany, and the United Kingdom regarding the territories received by Spain under the Pardo Treaty, and the little attention given to Spain's claims at the Berlin Conference. From 1858 to 1910, Spain proved incapable of seriously developing its colony. At the end of the nineteenth century, the Cia Trasatlántica's most important shareholder was Romeo Robledo (minister for overseas colonies). The company made enormous profits as a result of the transfer of troops towards Cuba. Spain's defeat can be explained by the important events of Melilla, the Cuban insurrection, and the war against the U.S.

In 1899, the Ministry of Overseas Colonies was cancelled and the management of African colonies was given to the president of the government. The same year, the Compañia de Fernando Po was founded by Aznar, from Bilbao, and Huelin, from Barcelona. Fifty-seven Spanish commercial firms operated in the colony. It was only in 1926, under the dictatorship of Primo de Rivera, that Río Muni was effectively occupied, thanks to an extraordinary budget of 23 million pesetas. The Dirección General de Marruecos y Colonias, which later became by the July 21, 1956, decree the Directoriate General of Towns and Provinces of Africa (Direccíon General de Plazas y Provincias Africanas), was founded by decree on June 18, 1931.

During the Spanish Civil War, the Popular Front was rapidly swept away in Santa Isabel and in Bata by the Nationalists sent from the Canary Islands. The Dirección General de Marruecos y Colonias, created by Primo de Rivera, assumed more and more importance under Díaz de Villegas, a friend of Franco's, who since 1945 was also the head of the Instituto de Estudios Africanos, monopolizing all research and publications on the Guinean territories. Spain's admission to the United Nations and the pressure of the Afro-Asians signaled the end of the colony.

During the 10 years before independence, a number of Equato-Guineans in the administration and trade found themselves given various ranks in the Order of Africa, including future president and vice-president of the republic, Macías Nguema and Edmundo Bosio Dioco, as well as members of the first Parliament and the first executive:

Silver medal: 6/24/57, Antonio Patoma Bueribueri; 12/4/62, Santiago Engua Ntutumu, Ndong Ndongo, Mbome, Simón Minanga Ngonga, Pedro Osa Ncogo, Salvador Alogo, Oyono Nvo, José Sima Enene, Santiago Ensue Guema, Cirilo Esono Nsue, Rosendo Ela Nsue, Manuel Bokama, Ignacio Nchama, Felipe Nchuchuma, Placido Uganda, Rafael Sime, José María Ondo, Edmundo Bosio; 10/1/62, N. Ndongo Andeme, F. Nguema Nchuchuma, J. Emba Engua; 3/5/63, Don Biyongo Ndongo, Don Ensema Ndongo, P. Abeso Matogo, M. Ndongo Ndong, S. Ondo Ellá, S. Kodo Modinje; 1/6/65, Marcelo Manuel Epam Uri.

Commander: 4/1/61, Francisco Macías Nguema; 9/11/61, Rafael Nsue Chama; 7/18/64, F. Esono Nsue, C. Cabrera James; 1/6/65, Aurelio Nicolas Ithoa, etc. *Officer:* 9/11/61, Agustin Ondo Nchama; 6/18/64, R. D. Sima, Andrés Moíses Mba Ada, etc.

With provincialization from 1960 to 1963, most of the large nationalist movements appeared that were to participate in the Constitutional Conference of 1967–1968 during autonomy. The head of the government (through Carrero Blanco and Díaz de Villegas) in accordance with the Unión Bubi tried to obtain the separation of the two provinces of Río Muni and Fernando Po, but the weight of the Río Muni parties and of Castiella, Spain's minister of foreign affairs, led to the success of the unitary thesis. On October 11, 1968, the first Spanish ambassador to Guinea, Duran-Loriga, was appointed. Independence was proclaimed on October 12, 1968. Macías Nguema rapidly took advantage of the constitution and, advised by García Trevijano, hardened his attitude, requesting greater assistance from Spain and threatening Spain with violent speeches, to such a point that the intervention of the Civil Guard and Spanish troops became necessary and 7,000 of the 8,000 Spaniards left the country. Macías Nguema then closed most of the Spanish companies—further worsening the economic situation. By April or May 1969 a series of agreements on economic and commercial cooperation and on payment (i.e., the creation of a Central Bank and the issuing of a Guinean currency) was signed with Spain. As of January 1971, all news from Equatorial Guinea was censored in the Spanish press (as "Materia reservada"). This measure was lifted at the end of 1976. This way, Spain could continue to supply 80% of Guinean imports and absorb 70% of its former colony's exports, without arousing public opinion. Under the May 1969 agreement, Spain was obliged to buy the major part of the cocoa, coffee, and timber production; only goods in excess of the Spanish quota could be sold elsewhere. Thus, Spain guaranteed prices higher than those of the world market. At the end of 1969 Spain granted financial assistance of 426 million pesetas ($6 million) in order to bridge the budget deficit. Simultaneously Spain paid Guinea's admission fee to the IMF. Under the technical assistance agreement signed at the end of 1969, Spain agreed to assist Guinea in the fields of telecommunication, civil aviation, and maritime navigation. The 1969 agreements were renewed in 1971. Spain presented Guinea with the obsolete ship *Romeu* (renamed *Enrique Nvo*). The Spanish airline Iberia took over the Guinean one ("Lage"). School buildings were financed by Spain, and the Bata Consulate, which had been closed after the 1969 flags affair, reopened. Ever since then payments between the two countries have been stipulated in U.S. dollars. Despite the deterioration of their relations in 1973–1974, Spain agreed in 1975 to grant cultural assistance, again, as well as an important loan in order to supply material for the cocoa plantations. While in Madrid, Guinean students occupied their embassy on March 5, 1976, making political demands. In Bata anti-Spanish public demonstrations against the suppression of the "materia reservada" took place at the end of 1976. After the trip of a Spanish Mission to Equatorial Guinea early in January 1977, Spain announced on January 19 an increase in its assistance in the field of construction (the Bata Airport, water distribution system in Bata, housing schemes and hospitals, etc); all these works had already been arranged for in earlier agreements but had never been executed. After Macías Nguema's violent speeches against the Spanish government and the king, on March 12, 1977, Spain withdrew its ambassador's deputy, without putting an end to it relations and assistance. In 1978 the pilots of Lage, all Spaniards, refused to continue working in Equatorial Guinea. Of the 300 Spaniards that still lived in Equatorial Guinea in 1977, only 60 remained in 1979.

Shortly after the 1979 coup, Obiang Nguema asked Spain for civil guards and for support from the peseta for the ekwele; but Prime Minister A. Suarez refused, citing noninterference in the affairs of a sovereign state and a desire not to practice neocolonialism, as the French were, as reasons. Spain provided the services of 22 teachers, 80 medical doctors and nurses, a football coach, food aid, health assistance, an old printing press, and antiriot gear for the police. A number of joint venture companies were also set up, such as GEMSA, GEPSA, and Guinextbank. The new Spanish ambassador, Graullera, stated that Equatorial Guinea would become a prosperous country within five years. Obiang Nguema and Ela Nguema were received in Spain and a number of Spanish companies began, hesitantly, to reopen businesses.

In October 1979, members of the Union of Spanish radio-amateurs (URE) went to Annobon to establish a radio network with the rest of the world. They discovered no one had been on the island in the last 8 years.

In August 1980, there were 300 Spanish experts in the country, including about 100 military instructors. King Juan Carlos visited the country and was received by Obiang Nguema as "our King." The Spanish Air Force made a DC8 aircraft available to the dictator for his travels. Many commentators regard Spanish assistance as being paternalistic; however, increasing insecurity and corruption made the country unattractive to many Spanish experts.

A number of cases of fraud and drug scandals led to strained relations between the two countries. A five-year treaty of cooperation was signed in July 1981, but Obiang Nguema still banned the entry of Spanish newspapers, which were accused of attacking the dictatorship and slandering him. Between 1979 and 1981 Spanish assistance amounted to 6,000 million pesetas. A military cooperation agreement worth 3,000 million pesetas expired at the end of 1981, despite a further visit by King Juan Carlos (see also under Juan Carlos). At the beginning of 1982, the Spanish diplomatic pouch was opened in the Ministry of Foreign Affairs, in breach of diplomatic privilege. Shortly thereafter the Spanish court decided to freeze the assets of the Central Bank that had been deposited in Madrid, because of a number of frauds perpetrated by Equatorial Guineans. However, in May 1982 Obiang Nguema returned to Madrid and signed a number of technical agreements as well as a new statute for Spanish experts, while at the same time accusing the Spanish press of distorting the situation in his country.

At the conference of donor countries organized by the UN Development Program in Geneva in April 1982, Spain pledged a total of US $21 million of assistance out of a total of US $92 million pledged at the meeting. Early in 1983, the Equatorial Guinean Consul in Bata was physically threatened, and the staff of the Spanish airline, Iberia, was molested. Then in May 1983 a sergeant of the Equatorial Guinean army took refuge in the Spanish Embassy in Santa Isabel in connection with an attempted coup. This greatly strained relations between the two counties, but the soldier was subsequently handed over to the authorities on the express condition that he would not be executed.

By June 1983 the total cumulative amount of Spanish assistance had risen to US $45 million. When Obiang Nguema visited Spain in July 1983, his guards sought to gain access to public buildings, including the prime minister's office, fully armed. By the end of 1983, relations between the two counties had reached a very low ebb and Spain had made a number of cutbacks in its aid package, but Equatorial Guinea was simultaneously making arrangements to join the Customs Union of the Central African States (UDEAC). In 1984–1985 Spain granted 100 university scholarships (48,500 pesetas per month to each).

In 1985, there were 2,500 Spaniards living in Equatorial Guinea, 400 of whom were technical assistance experts, but the figure for Spanish foreign aid had dropped to 1,500 million pesetas. This was an indication that Spain no longer had any illusions about Equatorial Guinea's intentions after her joining the franc zone on January 1, 1985. On the occasion of the visit of the head of Spanish aid programs (State Secretary L. Yañez) to Equatorial Guinea in November 1985, he described relations between the two countries as "fluid." Nevertheless, agreements were signed for a four-year aid program covering education, health, agriculture, public order, and defense. In June 1986 the representative of the Spanish university-level Distance Education Service visited Santa Isabel and expressed his concern that Spanish might disappear in the country by the end of the century. During the same month, Iberia interrupted momentarily its two flights a week to Santa Isabel as a protest against insufficient antifire installations at the airport of the capital.

After the July 1986 coup attempt, the French media insinuated that it was probably hatched either by Spain or the Communist countries. On October 12, 1986, on the occasion of the fourteenth Independence Day celebrations in Bata, the commanding officer of the Military Academy of Saragossa, Spain, decorated Obiang Nguema, promoting him to the rank of Brigadier-General in the name of King Juan Carlos.

During the visit in Equatorial Guinea of Fernandez Ordoñez, Spanish minister of foreign affairs, in March 1987, it was revealed that the Guinextebank (40% belonging to the Banco Exterior de España) had a deficit of 700 million pesetas according the Spain and of 1,300 million pesetas ($7.2 million) according to the Equato-Guinean minister of finance, because of "political loans." In April 1987 there was a real blitz in favor of Equatorial Guinea in Spain. An assocation called Amigos de Guinea Ecuatorial was founded; a motor rally was proposed called "1000 kilometers of friendship" to tour Equatorial Guinea, and a series of lectures on the history of Equatorial Guinea organized.

For 1987, the Spanish aid to Equatorial Guinea rose to 2,000 million pesetas. Between 1979 and 1987, Spain spent 17,000 million pesetas ($95 million) in her former colony. Equatorial Guinea had a $50 million debt toward Spain. In March 1988, 229 Spanish technical assistants worked in the country. According to the Spanish government, most of the assistance went to the airline company.

A Spanish Demo-Christian deputy showed that France was investing 10 times less than Spain, but was obtaining a higher profit. The new action plan planned an increase in aid to 2,000 million pesetas for education, health, and culture. In Paris,

Obiang Nguema declared his intention to join the franc zone. The FERE stigmatized the Spanish politicians' ignorance of Equato-Guinean problems. Radio Cultural Africa 2000 was to be inaugurated in October. In Parliament a debate revealed that the Spanish Cooperation had earned 38 million pesetas in the black market. A report by Obiang Nguema, *Brief Analysis of the Spanish Cooperation since 1981,* informed that of 2,000 million pesetas spent, 95% remained in Spain. Practically all the sectors of the Spanish Cooperation had failed. The ex-minister of commerce, M. Boyer, then the director of the Banco Exterior de España, presented Equatorial Guinea to the deputies as "the most corrupt, disastrous and inefficient country imaginable." But Spain considered aid to Equatorial Guinea as "preferential." The Spanish parties agreed to a possible replacement of Obiang Nguema's Moroccan mercenaries by Spanish forces. Several Equato-Guinean ministers therefore received commissions from the Spanish Cooperation.

In early 1989, in Madrid, Obiang Nguema refused to receive a Spanish Mediation Commission. Spain wrote off a debt of 2,000 million pesetas to Equatorial Guinea, apart from aid in arms, and deputization of instructors for the civil guards. Felipe Gonzalez and Obiang Nguema agreed that Spain would again become number one in its level of cooperation; Santa Isabel would apply brakes to French involvement. The Spanish press stated that Obiang Nguema was just as mad as his uncle. They spoke of the possible breakup of the country, with Fernando Po going to Nigeria and Río Muni to Gabon and Cameroon. In March, the Madrid Pact was signed. Some entrepreneurs and Spanish sailors were expelled. Madrid made it known that the priority objective of Spain was from then on the countries of North Sahara.

In 1990, the budget for the cooperation program was 2,660 million pesetas. The members of the Madrid Pact addressed an appeal to the PSOE for the return of the refugees. Felipe Gonzalez asked Obiang Nguema to ensure sufficient judicial guarantees to Spanish businessmen. France and Spain agreed that quarrelling over Equatorial Guinea was not worth the trouble.

In January 1991, there began a daily broadcast by Radio Exterior de España for Equatorial Guinea, which was also received in neighboring countries where a number of refugees were living. Spain cancelled 35% of the Equato-Guinean debt of $63 million. Obiang Nguema refused to grant a return passport to Equato-Guineans holding dual nationality. He asked for the help of Felipe Gonzalez to finish his law studies in Madrid, after the UNED course in Santa Isabel. The Spanish prime minister again cancelled an official trip due to the international situation. Spain gave Equatorial Guinea TV equipment worth 1,600 million pesetas. In November, a confidential report of the Spanish foreign affairs minister qualified the aid as disorganized. The publication of the exorbitant cost of the UNED, in Equatorial Guinea, which was more expensive than Harvard, only fanned the flames (in nine years, for 140 million pesetas, only five students received degrees). Arturo Arbello became the new ambassador of Spain. The new Equato-Guinean ambassador was B. Esono Ondo. For 1991, the expenditure for cooperation with Equatorial Guinea totalled 2,266 million pesetas. The visit of Felipe Gonzalez in November was to no purpose, as the Spanish prime minister did not make any demands in the area of democratization and allowed himself to be abused by Obiang Nguema. Upon his return to Madrid, Felipe Gonzalez received the representatives of the members of the Madrid Pact. The Spanish Audit Office's Report to the Parliament revealed a number of anomalies in the aid. The intensification of the Nguemist terror brought about the suspension of the meetings of the joint commission.

In early 1992, Obiang Nguema took possession of the new studios of Radio Santa Isabel, at a cost of $120,000.In September, the Criminal Investigations Department arrested about 20 members of the Progress Party, including the president, S. Moto Nsá. He was released following pressure from the ambassadors of Spain and the United States. The arrest, in late October, of the businessmen Vilarrasa and Hanna was interpreted as Obiang Nguema's desire to blackmail Spain. Due to the economic crisis, aid was reduced by 43%. There were 191 volunteers for cooperation and a dozen diplomatic personnel. The Partido Popular and the Spanish Izquierda Unida demanded the suspension of cooperation, the condemnation of the Nguemist regime, and the suspension of aid. In late November, Vilarrasa and Hanna were condemned to 12 years in prison and a heavy fine. Teodoro Saez Lasheras, director of courses at La Salle (Bata), resigned due to the arrogance of the Criminal Investigations Department, which wanted to impose its agents on the establishment. In December, Villarasa and Hanna were pardoned by Obiang Nguema. A number of children of noted Nguemists were studying in Spain. Madrid fixed three conditions for cooperation: democratization, observance of the rights of the Spanish nationals on the spot, and fight against corruption; otherwise it "would be obliged" to reconsider the program for cooperation. Moto Nsá asked Spain to take over governing Equatorial Guinea for a few months, in order to avoid civil war. Aid totalled 1,830 million pesetas.

In the spring of 1993, the ambassadors of the United States, the European Community and Spain received a verbal note that called them agitators and threatened them for their "hostile attitude." While the Nguemists blocked the Spanish diplomatic bags, Spain cut off a part of its program. In December 1993 persecution of opponents, professors, and students of the UNED began: 29 students of the UNED were tortured after a visit to the consulate of Spain at Bata. The Spanish consul in Bata was expelled, and so was a Spanish doctor. Madrid expelled the secretary of the Equato-Guinean Embassy and reduced its aid by half. In reprisal, the Nguemists closed down Radio Africa 2000.

In early 1994, Spain confirmed the cut of 50% of its aid budget, refused to negotiate a new action plan, the cooperation being given to Spanish/religious NGOs. In February, Obiang Nguema declared Spanish an obstacle to the development of the country; in March, Spain withdrew the two Aviocars given to Equatorial Guinea. In reprisal, the broadcasts of Radio Exterior de España were jammed and the personnel of the press agency EFE were persecuted. Obiang Nguema promised to revise the constitution and electoral law. From July, Spain planned a new Convention of cooperation. In 1994, Spain figured in the second position in Equato-Guinean exports (28%).

In early 1995 a Plataforma de Apoyo a la Democrácia de Guinea Ecuatorial (Platform of Support to the Democracy of Equatorial Guinea) was founded by several parties and Spanish organizations. Following the arrest of Moto Nsá, the Nguemists, after torturing one of his colleagues, forced him to "confess" to a conspiracy by the United States and Spain mainly using the aircraft carrier

Principe de Asturias to invade the country and eliminate the 5,000 delegates to the second convention of the PDGE. The consul of Spain at Bata was interviewed on the matter on TV by Lt.-Col. Antoñito. The Spanish government and King Juan Carlos joined the political parties in their appeal for clemency toward Moto Nsá. Upon condemnation of Moto Nsá, ASODEGUE, very close to the PSOE, accused the Spanish press of formulating criticism against Obiang Nguema which was alleged to be in fact directed at the government of Felipe Gonzalez and the PSOE. During the Moto Nsá case and the so-called military conspiracy, the Spanish authorities claimed "confabulation." In March demonstrations in support of Moto Nsá were held in various regions of Spain.

The Partido Popular denounced the attitude of the PSOE and hoped for multilateral pressure. In April, Obiang Nguema alleged that mercenaries were being trained in Spain, in order to attack his country; in late April, there arrived a new contingent of 140 Moroccan mercenaries. In June, the renegotiation of the Equato-Guinean debt (8,000 million pesetas) was placed under the condition of effective democratization. In the Spanish Ministry of Foreign Affairs, Joaquin Pérez Gomez acted as special ambassador for Equatorial Guinea. After the release of 33 political prisoners, following pardon from Obiang Nguema, on August 2, F. Gonzalez congratulated the dictator. During an interview, the Spanish Minister of foreign affairs, Javier Solana, declared that Obiang Nguema had to understand that patience had its limits. Before the UN General Assembly and at the summit of nonaligned countries (Cartagena, Columbia), Obiang Nguema accused Spain of plotting against his regime and of wishing to repeat the Rwanda experience. The Spanish observer, Secretary of State Manuel Dicenta, left the hall. In Paris, Obiang Nguema declared on Radio France International that Spain was jealous of France. But in the 93rd Franco African summit, the two countries agreed to foster the democratic process. However, Javier Solana stated that Paris and Madrid were disappointed with the manner in which the Equato-Guinean government organized the counting of the votes and the publication of the municipal election results in September 1995. In 1995 Spain was the number one supplier of Equatorial Guinea and its number three client. In 1995, the Canary Islands financed projects providing medical aid and assistance to handicapped children.

Upon Obiang Nguema's announcement, in mid-January 1996, of the presidential election for February 25, the Izquierda Unida demanded the end of Spanish Cooperation with the Nguemists. In mid-January, the Nguemists arrested a member of Unión Popular, following his criticism of the government on Radio Exterior de España. In late January, the government's representative to Kogo expelled a Spanish doctor, accusing him of sympathizing with the opposition. During 1996, it was learned from the former judge of the Supreme Court, Fermin Nguema Esono, that the Hispano-Equato-Guinean Project of the Moulin (Mill) de Bioko ($5 million) had been ruined by Nguemist frauds, especially those of Rosendo Otogo and Ricardo Mangue. On July 24 Madrid refused the request of a suspension of broadcasts of Radio Exterior de España, asked by Prime Minister Seriche Dougan.On August 1, 16 Nigerians arrived from Malabo carrying false Equato-Guinean passports. Obiang Nguema refused to accept the return of these persons, and they finally ended up being sent back to Nigeria, but Spain stopped recognizing visas from Equatorial Guinea after August 15.

In October, Spain announced that in 1997 $75 million of aid would go to the Third World. Equatorial Guinea received the largest share of this aid, with $5.6 million in October 1996. Minister of State A. Evuna and Minister of Foreign Affairs M. Oyono brought several proposals before the Spanish government for the improvement of bilateral relations and the elaboration of a new cooperation plan. Spain lifted its sanctions after the affair of the illegal immigrants from Equatorial Guinea. The general director of Foreign policy for Africa, Manuel Alabart, attended celebrations of the 28th anniversary of Equatorial Guinean independence.

On July 6, 1997, one of Obiang Nguema's sons-in-law, Santos Pascual Bikomo Nanguande, former minister of information and propaganda, was arrested at the Madrid Airport with 15 kg of heroin from Pakistan. the EU reported that British bovine meat, exported fraudulently, had been sent to Eastern Europe, but also to Equatorial Guinea, through Belgium and some fictitious Spanish companies. The minister of foreign affairs denounced the alleged incitement to military rebellion by Radio Exterior de España.

According to Mot Nsá, Obiang Nguema's men in the Aznar government are:

Alabart, former ambassador in Equatorial Guinea, general director of foreign policy, Africa, Asia, and the Pacific.

Gil-Casares, director of the Department of the Interior and Defense by the president of the government, at the Moncloa.

In September 1997, Spain granted Moto Nsá his refugee status again. Obiang declared that the relations with Spain were frozen and that French was to become the national language. The director of the Real Academia Española, Fernando Lázaaro Carreter, on September 23, accused the Spanish government of being careless with regard to the teaching of Spanish in EG. Since ambassador Otero was transferred to Senegal, he was replaced in October 1997 by the Marquis Jacobo Gonazalez-Arnao Campos, who came from Vienna. In the beginning of November 1997, IU accused the Aznar government of supporting Obiang Nguema by obtaining a meeting in Brussels with J. Santerre. On December 5, Moto accused the Aznar government of being an accomplice of the "cannibalistic, drug dealing and corrupt dictatorship." According to him, Obiang Nguema finances the Spanish PP. This was confirmed by the PSOE. The money is said to have been brought by Spanish businessmen, members of the Movimiento de Amigos de Obiang (MAO).

In January 1998, the PSOE blamed the Aznar government for its "rambled and incoherent" behavior toward Equatorial Guinea. According to Obiang Nguema, Aznar is more realistic than González. In 1998, Spanish cooperation, behind Latin America, helped Equatorial Guinea and Mozambique. During the summer of 1998, the relationship between the two counties worsened again. Equatorial Guinea wanted a reevaluation of the relationship, and Miguel Oyono, minister of foreign affairs, threatened, in a thinly disguised way, the UNED, the Spanish cultural centers (they enjoy too much freedom) and FERE. Spain was still waiting for Obiang Nguema to establish a state of law. In September, two Spanish doctors (Eva Avira, 28, and Emilio Ledesma, 27), invited by the Equato-Guinean Red Cross for a humanitarian project financed by Mobil Oil, were held prisoner for 11 days in the filthy police quarters of Malabo. They were expelled under the false accusation of having entered the country illegally. On September 15, 1998, the mixed commission Equatorial Guinea/Spain started working in Malabo; it was the first meeting held since the beginning of the Aznar government of Spain. On September 23, 1998, the Spanish government said it would increase the cooperation with Equatorial Guinea if it became a democracy. A secretary of state explained: "The multiparty system confronts itself, in this country, to elements that prevent action and that must disappear." Concerning trade, a new delivery of rotten meat (20 t) from Spainwas sent back to the expeditor.

In the 1990s, Spanish assistance dealt mostly with religious schools and the replanting of 1,200 hectares of cocoa trees. In September 1998, a delegation from the Spanish Agency of International Cooperation stayed in Malabo. But for the 30th anniversary of the Independence, the Nguemists did not invite an official Spanish delegation.

On November 12 Manuel Alabart stressed the doubts the Spanish government had with regard to the Nguemist process of democratization. On November 16, Spanish Prime Minister Aznar had a meeting with Obiang Nguema in Rome. Just before the meeting, the dictator released Bakale, who had been arrested on November 15 and forbidden to move about the capital, whereas more members of the opposition were arrested and harmed. The Aznar government, at the end of 1996, confirmed that it was in favor of democratization and respected human rights for all ethnic groups. It said it wanted proof of goodwill.

In 1997, Spain gave only 6 million pesetas for assistance to Equatorial Guinea.

See also Agriculture; Corruption; Customs Union of the Central African States (UDEAC); Economy; EFE; Elections; Embasa; Engonga Motulu, M.; Esono Mika, P. J.; Evuna Owono Asangono, A.; Fernando Po; Finance; Guinextebank; Joint Opposition Platform; Labor; Maho Sikacha, J. L.; Malavo, E.; Mba Nfumu, A.; Missions; Morocco; Motu Mamiaga, P.; Ndong Mha, A.; Ndong Micha, A.; Ndongo Ogüono-Asong, M.; Ndowe; Nepotism; Ngone Maguga, M.-E.; Nkili Nze, N.; Nkogo Ondo, E.; Nsobeya Efuman Nsue, S.; Nsue Mokuy, A.; Nsue Nchama, R.; Nve Nseng, A. F.; Nze Abuy; Obiang Mangue, L.; Obiang Nguema, T.; Okue Moto, M.; Olo Mebuy, A.; Ondo Ayang, L.; Ondo Ela, S.; Ondo Esono, L. A.; Opposition; Otero, J. M.; Oyono Awong Ada, S.; Oyono Ndong Mifumu, M.; Pact of Madrid; Parliament; Petroleum; Popular Union; Post Offices; Press; Pataforma; Progress Party; Public Health; Radio; Rasilla, L. de la; Río Muni; Sanchez Bustmante, D.; San Fernando; Santa Isabel; Siale Bilekia, S.; Si Ondo, S.; Social Democratic Union; Sports; Suarez, A.; Television; Terror; Torture; Trade; Social Democratic Union; Union for Democracy and Social Development; Unique National Workers Party; United Kingdom; United States of America; University; Zamora, F.

SPANISH LEGION. Between 1960 and 1964 some 50 Equatorial Guinean citizens were sent for training with the Spanish Legion. In June 1983, some ex-legionaries were expected to participate in the toppling of the Nguemist government, along with Saharaouis and some refugees, with Libya financing the operation, as the Nguemists had broken off with that country. In 1993, the press suggested sending Spanish Legionaries to Equatorial Guinea with the UN's approval.

SPIEGEL, J. C. Officer for Central African Affairs, U.S. Department of State. See also Tuwaddel.

SPOKESMEN OF THE GOVERNMENT. In October 1982, Ochaga Nve Bengobesama, minister for communications, tourism, and transport, simultaneously became spokesman for the government. In the January 24, 1992, "transitional" government, the minister-cum-spokesman of the government was A. F. Nve Nzeng. He accused the embassies of giving asylum to detractors, and the priests of creating public unrest. Nve Nzeng retained his post as spokesman in the December 22 government of 1993, in addition to the post of minister of state for transports, information, and communications. In 1995, A. Nze Nfumu took over the post of spokesman, along with that of minister for culture and the French language. In the January 8, 1996, ministerial reshuffle, the tame opposition member S.-P. Bikomo Nanguande became minister for information and propaganda and spokesman for the government. He retained these posts in the April 8, 1996, government. See also Seriche Bioko.

SPORTS. Under Macías Nguema, the church of Niefang became a training hall for boxing. From 1980, Spain sent in the football player Sanchis as a selector and coach for the national football team. In February, Equatorial Guinea played its first match, against Cameroon. That summer, it joined the International Olympic Committee, founded a national Olympic Committee; and also joined FIFA. The president of the Olympic Committee was T. Esono Ava; I. Milam Tang was named president of the Football Federation (soccer).

In 1981, an agreement for cooperation in the field of sports was signed with the U.S.S.R. In July 1992 a sports mission of 22 football players was sent to the U.S.S.R. In 1985 the first football league comprised 11 teams in Fernando Po. A second league had 14 teams, while a third was a student league. Apart from these, there exists a military league. In October 1990, I. Eyi Monsuy Andeme, minister for education, youth Affairs, and sport, simultaneously became vice-prime minister.

In the January 24, 1992, "transitional" government, Francisco P. Obama Eyegue was again minister for youth affairs and sports. The Olympic team for the 1992 Barcelona games comprised seven athletes. In May the first Equato-Guinean athletic championship was held in Santa Isabel, with 26 athletes, including one woman. In July 1994 Equatorial Guinea participated in the Second Francophone Games in Paris. In the April 8, 1996, government, Francisco-Pascual Eyegue Obama Asue occupied the post of minister of state for youth affairs and sports. He was assisted by a minister with special responsibilities for sports, Lucas Nguema Esono. Equatorial Guinea participated in the Olympic Games in Atlanta in 1996, with about 10 athletes.

At the end of June 1997, eyegue Obama became minister of Information and Propaganda, after the dismissal of S. P. Bikomo Nanguande. In the government of January 21, 1998, Ignacio Milam Tang was minister of Youth and Sports.

STAMPS see Post Office

STANLEY, Henry Morton, 1841–1904. The famous journalist-explorer visited Corisco and Fernando Po. In 1874, Iradier submitted to him his plans for exploration of Río Muni; Stanley approved of them but suggested a limitation to make them economically more viable. Stanley later wrote of Fernando Po as the jewel of the ocean, but a jewel which Spain did not endeavor to polish. "Therefore it has no commercial value, and I for one would not pay five crowns for the island in its present state." He suggested a better use of the high lands.

STATE OF EMERGENCY see Emergencia

STATE-RUN ENTERPRISES (Empresas Estatales). They came under the Ministry for Finance and Commerce on January 11, 1980. They were dissolved and transformed into limited companies by Decree 66 of August 1, 1983, with the state being a majority shareholder.

* LAGE (60%)
* Empresa de Energía (55%)
* Empresa petrolífera (55%)
* Empresa de comercio (80%)
* Agencia Marítima Nacional (60%)
* Empresa de Transportes Terrestres de Lujo (55%)
* Empresa Forestal de Guinea Ecuatorial (85%)
* Fabrica Nacional de Ladrillos (70%)

See also Garcia Trevijano; Transports.

SUAREZ, Adolfo. Former Spanish prime minister, named a mediator to facilitate reconciliation between Nguemists and the opposition. In July 1992, Obiang Nguema prohibited flights over the national territory by the Spanish air force, in order to prevent the return of the mediator. The Nguemist spokesperson considered that the role of Adolfo Suarez was fulfilled during his first visit. If circumstances so required, he would be informed. Before the press, Suarez pronounced Obiang Nguema to be mentally ill.

SUGUISA see Suministros de Guinea S.A.

SUICIDES. The colonial period was marked by two famous suicides: Jover y Tovar, head of the Spanish Delegation at the Joint Frontier Commission in 1901, and Bengoa Arriola, manager of the Trasatlántica company in Spanish Guinea and president of the Cámara Oficial Agrícola of Fernando Po. After independence, the numerous personalities that were murdered in prison were nearly all declared by the government to be suicides. Among others were Ndongo Miyone, Ibongo Iyanga, Kombe Madje, Momo Bokara, Ochaga Ngome, Bosio Bioco, Obiang Mbá, J. Oyono, and Eyegue Ntutumu. See also Motu Mamiage, P.; Victims.

SUMINISTROS DE GUINEA S.A. (SUGUISA). Spanish company inaugurated in March 1981, run by F. Roig Balestros, friend of the vice-president of the Spanish government, F. A. Martorell. This company brought together Supermercados de Guinea S.A., Explotaciones Agrícolas S.A., and Maderas de Guinea S.A. Roig was only the visible part of the iceberg in this company. SUGUISA was criticized for the deplorable quality of some food products. In late October 1986, Supermercados SA owed the bankrupt Guinextebank FCFA 346,499,000; Madera de Guinea S.A. owed FCFA 107,000,000.

See also Agriculture; Democratic Union for the Liberation of Equatorial Guinea; Envoro Ovono, A.; Epalepale Evina, F.; Mba Ada, A. M.; Mba Nguema Mikue, A.; Ndong Ela Mangue, J.; Nguema Edu, F.; Nsue Obama Angono, P.; Obiang Ngeuma, T.; Roig Balestros, F. A.

SUMMERLIN, Thomas. In late 1983, Captain Summerlin anchored at Santa Isabel with his vessel the US *Spiegel Grove*. He had talks with Obiang Nguema over the question of bilateral cooperation between the U.S. and Equatorial Guinea. Before the journalists, he spoke of the Americano-Equato-Guinean and friendship ties since 1979.

SUPREME MILITARY COUNCIL. This body was established at the time of coup d'etat of August 3, 1979. It is composed mainly of members of Obiang Nguema's family such as his cousins Ela Nseng, Maye Ela, Mbá Oñana and classmates from the Saragossa Military Academy. Thirty-two of its 35 members come from Mongomo. This has led the population to make the pun on the Spanish acronym for the body, CMS, which instead of representing "Consejo Military Superior" is interpreted as "Con Mongomo Siempre" (with Mongomo forever) which furthermore aped an earlier slogan under Macías Nguema: "with Macías forever."

In January 1981, Obiang Nguema declared that the pressures from democratic circles for more freedom in the country were intended to sabotage the work that the Supreme Military Council was undertaking. Various dissensions within the Council led to its transformation into a civilian government in October 1983. The personalities, however, remained the same, except for a change into civilian clothing. See also Agriculture; Democratic Union for the Liberation of Equatorial Guinea; Envoro Ovono, A.; Epalepale Evina, F.; Mba Ada, A. M.; Mba Nguema Mikue, A.; Ndong Ela Mangue, J.; Nguema Edue, F.; Nsue Obama Angono, P.; Obiang Nguema, T.

SWEDEN. Represented in Santa Isabel by its embassy in Yaoundé (Cameroon). During the 1950s Sweden was one of the main banana buyers of Equatorial Guinea. Consultants from SWEDTEL on behalf of ITU prepared long-term proposals for the development of telecommunications and administrative organization. The French Société Forestiére du Río Muni did not appreciate this Scandinavian "monopoly" and proposed French material. Since then, Chinese technical assistance has taken over.

SWITZERLAND. Represented in Santa Isabel by its ambassador in Cameroon. In 1969–1971, the Swiss Red Cross helped with the restoration of the Santa Isabel Hospital ($250,000 or 17 million pesetas). In 1969–1970 a Swiss expert was sent to train the Guinean diplomats in the Foreign Affairs Ministry in Santa Isabel. The International Red Cross, with headquarters in Geneva, carried out relief flights to Biafra from Santa Isabel Airport in 1968–1969. At the end of 1968, the adventurers of Profinanco (Armijo, Paesa) tried to obtain Swiss capital for their dubious affair of setting up a private Central Bank. Shortly after independence, García Trevijano, accompanied by Mbá Ada and Eyegue Ntutumu, contacted Swiss business circles, in particular Nestlé, about INFOGE. The Société Forestière du Río Muni, despite being French, was established in Switzerland (Commugny, Vaud). In 1976 it was sold to another French company, Tardiba. In 1973 a printer from Crissier (Vaud) was bothered for having manufactured Equato-Guinean postage stamps; it has been established that the affair was a regular one, Guinea having leased its philatelic service to foreigners via García Trevijano. See Post Office.

When King Juan Carlos of Spain visited Santa Isabel on December 13, 1979—just four months after the coup d'etat—Obiang Nguema asked the king to help make Equatorial Guinea "the long hoped-for Switzerland of Africa." In 1980 the UN World Food Program appointed a Swiss, Bigler, to take care of food distribution in Equatorial Guinea. Alfred Rüegg, ambassador in Nigerial from 1981 to 1984, was also accredited for Benin, Togo and Equatorial Guinea (between 1981–1982). In 1981 the Swiss Disaster Relief Organization provided funds for two small field hospitals and assistance to improve the Mikomeseng leprosarium, totalling 599,000 Swiss francs (approx. $1 million).

However, in April 1982 the Swiss Human Rights League felt that it was inopportune to provide assistance to a regime that does not respect human rights. The World Bank awarded a Geneva-based company, Petroconsultants S.A. a contract for the creation of an administrative infrastructure for petrol resources in 1982, to the value of US $2 million. In 1983, the Swiss Disaster Relief Organization was again active and organized a national vaccination campaign with seven volunteer workers. That year, also, the Spanish press maintained that several of the leading personalities in Equatorial Guinea had opened bank accounts in Switzerland. Buale Borico, who formerly held the post of minister of agriculture and of health, and who subsequently went into exile in Spain, denounced the general corruption of the regime and confirmed that Obiang Nguema had placed money in Switzerland. Buale Borico furthermore had completed his training as an engineer at the Swiss Federal Institute of Technology in Zurich. Since 1983, the Swiss Société Générale de Surveillance S.A. (Geneva) supervises the Equato-Guinean foreign trade.

In January 1984, Jacques Rial, Swiss ambassador to Equatorial Guinea, with residence in Yaoundé, Cameroon, presented his letters of accreditation. At this time also, a Swiss citizen, Wetzel, was reputed to be acting as an ecological adviser to Obiang Nguema and to have purchased 17,000 hectares of cocoa plantation. In 1985 there were three Swiss volunteers working in the Ministry of Health, training local staff.

For the 1985–1988 phase, the Swiss Red Cross had an annual budget of Sw. Fr. 149,000 for direct medical aid. In 1985, 9.7% of the tropical wood imported by Switzerland came from Equatorial Guinea. That same year, Obiang Nguema decided on the creation of the national company. In 1987, the National Red Cross had still not been inaugurated, in spite of the setting up of a provisional committee. The journal *Actio* spoke of the "first laborious and sometimes clumsy steps" of the Swiss Red Cross and qualified the population as "little spoilt." Its delegate said he was not very optimistic. In the diplomatic language of the Swiss Red Cross, it meant a true disaster. In December, the evaluation report of the vaccination mission of Swiss Aid for Help in Case of Catastrophe concluded that it was a failure and blamed the Ministry of Health.

On March 19, 1993, during the signing of the National Pact, E. Nsue Ngomo spoke in the name of the opposition and referred to the fraternal dialogue leading to democratic transition, "which will lead Equatorial Guinea to being the little Switzerland we have been dreaming of becoming for years." The oil company ADDAX, of Geneva, marketed petroleum concentrates extracted by Walter Inc. from the Alba deposits. On June 5, 1995, Elema Borengue wished that Equatorial Guinea again become "Switzerland of Central Africa." That same month, Obiang Nguema organized Equato-Guinean Days meant to attract investors.

The Swiss diplomatic delegation has now changed from Yaoundé (Cameroon) to Lagos (Nigeria).

Between 1974 and 1999, the Swiss Africanist, professor at the Swiss Federal Institute of Technology, and former UNESCO expert Max Liniger-Gomaz published his *Bibliografía General de Guinea Ecuatorial,* with more than 30,000 titles.

On June 2, 1998, right after the summary trial of the Bubi ethnic group, Swissair opened a weekly flight from Zurich to Malabo.

See also Addax Co.; Bakale Obiang, C.-B.; Bikomo Nanguande, S. P.; Bolekia Edjapa, A.; Bueribueri, C.; Choisy, N.; Committee for the Voluntary Return; Denmark; Dougan, A. S.; Dougan Beaca, J.D.; Drugs; Education; Elema Borengue, J.; Elephants; Engonga Motulu, M.; Human Rights; International Committee of the Red Cross; Llansol, V.-G.; Mba Ekua Miko, B.; Mechaba Fernandez, T.; Mikomeseng; Liberal Democratic Convention; National Alliance for Democratic Restoration; National Democratic Union; Nsue Mokuy, A.; Nsue Ngomo Abumengono, E.; Obiang Nguema, T.; Olo Mebuy, A.; Ondo Obiang Alogo, F.; Parliament; Petroleum; Popular Union; Public Health; Siale Bikekia, S.; Visher, L.; World Council of Churches.

❖ T ❖

TAMARITE BURGOS, Ciriaco. From Annobón. Born in 1950. Administrative assistant (Escuela Superior Indígena). Training in Argentina. In the January 24, 1992, "transitional" government, he was minister for public services and administrative coordination. In November 1993, he was elected a PDGE deputy for Annobón. But he did not figure in the December 22 government. On January 19, 1994, he was named counsellor to the president of the government for administrative affairs. In the ministerial reshuffle of April 8, 1996, he became counsellor for public administration and administrative reform. He kept this function in 1998.

TARDIBA. A French lumber company first working in the Ivory Coast. In 1976 it repurchased from the Sociedad Forestal de Río Muni, also a French company, the 150,000-hectare concession of the Kukumankok zone, with authorization from the Equato-Guinean government to remove 150,000 tons of timber annually. As the concession touches the border with Gabon in the east and south, a great number of Equato-Guinean workers took advantage of the opportunity to flee the Macías Nguema regime and seek refuge in Gabon. In order to stop this exodus, the government asked Tardiba to transfer its concession from the Kukumankok zone to a new one farther from the border. Tardiba's refusal brought about a suspension of exploitation.

TEIBIALE SIPOTO, Jaime. A Bubi from Batoicopo. Born in 1934. Studied in the United Kingdom and Nigeria. A Protestant pastor. General secretary of the Reformed Church.

TELECOMMUNICATIONS. The first radio-telegraph station was installed in Santa Isabel in 1912. The Primo de Rivera dictatorship permitted, in 1926, the establishment of a radio-telegraph network in the two provinces. In 1947 telecommunications were granted to Torres Quebado S.A., and transferred to the Guinean administration after independence. The departure of the Spaniards in 1970 paralyzed the networks. With the help of cooperation agreements signed in May 1969 with Spain, and in 1970 with the People's Republic of China, telephone and telegraph could be restored, the OAU supplying also television and radio experts. A group of Swedish experts from ITU made some recommendations for a complete reorganization of the telecommunication network. In 1970, nine towns disposed of a manual telephone exchange. Thanks to Chinese material, radio-electric connections became possible. In 1972, there were 115 Guineans employed in telecommmunications, of which only 34 were in the technical branch. Cameroon financed the radio-clectric connection between Santa Isabel and Yaoundé; China signed a cooperation agreement of 800 million pesetas ($112.5 million) permitting the installation of a high-frequency radio-electric system in the 12 districts of Río Muni and in the islands, as well as a connection between Bata and Santa Isabel.

The Société Forestière du Río Muni seems to have tried to attribute these projects to France. In 1976, after the cooling of relations with Spain, telephone connections with the outside world were cut off. After the 1979 coup, China provided assistance for the renovation of the telephone exchanges in Santa Isabel and Bata. These were put into operation in mid-1980. Effective October 1982, the Esangui and former refugee, Ochage Nvé Bengobesama, became minister of telecommunications, tourism, and transport and also acted as government spokesman.

On October 14, 1987, a station for telecommunications by satellite was inaugurated in Bata, with a relay in Douala. This project of the French Caisse Centrale de Cooperation Economique, for FCFA18 million, was financed half by Equatorial Guinea and half by France Cables through the joint company GETESA. In October 1990, the Ministry for Territorial Administration (Interior) and Communication went to S. Muñoz Ylata from Annobón. The same day, Equatorial Guinea was connected to the international telephone network. In 1990, there were 1,400 telephones for the entire country (the smallest number in Africa).

In the January 24, 1992, "transitional" government, it was M. Oyono Ntutumu who became minister for transports, post, and telecommunications. In the December 22, 1993, government, it was A. F. Nve Nzeng, spokesperson for the government, who became minister of state for transports, information, and communications. P. Ondo Mitogo became secretary of state for post and telecommunications. There appeared to have been cases of telephone tapping.

In late 1994, the French Development Fund granted FCFA 5.5 billion for the modernization of the audiovisual media and the telecommunications network. In late 1995, telephones remained entirely manual, with prohibitive prices. The town of Bata had just one public telephone. The company GETESA introduced magnetic cards for the three public telephones in the country (two in the capital, one in Bata). In 1995 there were 1,300 lines for 370,000 inhabitants (a density of 0.35); Equatorial Guinea was thirty-first of the forty-nine countries with a density less than one.

It was Elias Ovono Nguema who held the post of vice-minister of post and telecommunications in the government appointed on January 8, 1996. In June 1996 the setting up of the automatic telephone system, with international connection, started, thanks to France.

TELEFONICA. The network set up by this Spanish company was taken over in 1987 by the French company GETESA.

TELEVISION. In 1967–1968 Spain set up one of the highest transmitters in Africa, at the summit of the Pico de Basilé (3,008 m), with two 300-watt groups, and connected with Santa Isabel by radio relays. Relays on Mounts Bata and Chocolate in the Río Muni province were to be built later. The installations of Fernando Po cost 35 million pesetas ($500,000). Scholarships for 12 technical employees and 6 presenters were offered by Spain in 1967. The presenters were all relations of Consejeros de Gobierno (Ministers), among whom were Macías Nguema's niece Concepción Nguema and her husband Aba Ondo. Inaugurated in July 1968, the installations were used for the election campaign preceding independence. The personnel, almost entirely Spanish, abandoned the installations in

March 1969, and since then everything has stopped functioning, despite the efforts of a few Nigerian technicians supplied by the OAU.

After the 1979 coup, N. Nkili was appointed Director of the television service. He told the Special Rapporteur of the UN Human Rights Commission that governmental control was very strict. In 1979 the Spanish government installed a color television transmitter, but by 1985 the number of receivers did not exceed 1,000. In July 1982, a Spanish TV team was molested by the Nguemist authorities and their equipment was confiscated. In 1985 Spain set up the first TV club in the country at Basilé. It was not until 1987 that a relay station was set up in Bata. In 1987, the television network was run by Saturnino Mbá Elo.

Since February 1988, M. Mba Ovenga has been director of National Television. He was a policeman under Macías Nguema, and well known for his sinister past in Río Muni. National Television is entirely financed by Spain and depends on it for the technology.

In late 1990, Obiang Nguema banned the retransmission of the Spanish telecast "El precio justo" (The Right Price), as it would develop consumerism, bad for populations suffering from all kinds of deprivation. Recorded programs, including soap operas, were brought in once a week by Iberia. Each day, Santa Isabel telecast four hours of programs produced by Spanish TV.

In March 1991, Equatorial Guinea was admitted to the Iberio-American Television Organization, during the Mexico session. The Spanish government paid 1,600 million pesetas for equipment for Equato-Guinean TV. One part of the second four-year plan for cooperation provided for relay antennae for Río Muni, for 12,000 million pesetas.

In the January 24, 1992, "transitional" government, S. Ngua Nfumu became secretary of state for the press, radio, and television. In late 1992, following the Vilarrasa and Hanna case, the Spanish opposition demanded the suppression of financial support for the Nguemist TV, which was only used for anti-Spanish propaganda. Madrid retorted that this support had to be maintained, for the spread of the Spanish language in the region, and because some nonhispanophone countries were lying in wait. In 1993, there were seven receivers per 1,000 inhabitants.

Equato-Guinean television only covered 10% of Río Muni. Competition from television in neighboring countries was very strong. Equato-Guinean TV was run by Nemesio Nkili Nze. In April 1996, the State Department report to the Congress on human rights in the world stressed that the Nguemist government withheld opposition parties' access to the media. In June 1996 the first retransmissions of programs via satellite began. Equato-Guinean TV was run by Hermengildo Moliko Chele.

It is to be noted that Equato-Guinean TV functions in the PAL system, while all neighboring countries (Cameroon, Gabon) function with the SECAM system. Every day, Equato-Guinean TV telecasts one hour of news in regional languages (Bisio, Annobónais, Bubi, Ndowe, Fang).

See also Radio; Telecommunications.

TEODORIN see Army; Nepotism; Obiang Mangue, T.; Terror

TERRITORIAL ADMINISTRATION see Delegaciones Gubernativas

TERROR. After Obiang Nguema's coup d'état in August 1979, the vice-president Maye Ela admitted in December, before the representative of the Human Rights Commission, F. Volio-Jimenez, to the exactions of the Juventud en marcha con Macías (Youth Marching with Macías). The army tolerated them, as the Youth were placed under the direct authority of Macías Nguema. Therefore, the army abetted the Youth. The ambassador of Spain, Graullera, was threatened with a pistol on the temple by an army man at Hotel Ureka.

During 1981, the Spanish diplomatic flag was violated using a machete. In 1984 the refugees in Gabon reported that Obiang Nguema had set up a spy network in order to persecute them. During 1985, the arbitrary detentions were intensified during the vote on the reintroduction of the single party; the 29 opposition parliamentary representatives were arrested and imprisoned, or condemned to individually pay FCFA 2 million and to pass months under house arrest. The regime called Obiang Nguema's opponents Mikoks.

Several times in 1992, in Bata as well as the capital, students, teachers, and priests were arrested, beaten, and in most cases tortured. That autumn, two businessmen, one Spanish and the other Lebanese (Vilarrasa and Hanna), Obiang Nguema's friends, were arrested under the accusation of having imported military equipment, while in fact it was only scrap meant for lumbering activities. In March 1993 the Spanish Eurodeputy, J. M. Bandrés, president of the Asociación para la Solidaridad Democrática con Guinea Ecuatorial, said: "If Equatorial Guinea ill-treats a Spanish industrialist, what will the government do with its own citizens?" In February 1993, a colonel interrupted the Radio Africa 2000 broadcasts, made anti-Spanish threats, and made off with some equipment. In December, 80 opposition members, students, teachers of the UNED, and priests were held in Río Muni and tortured. In the night between August 22–23, in Santa Isabel, Moto Mamiaga was arrested at Hotel Urecka while in discussion with Mba Ada, President of Unión Popular; shortly afterwards he was assassinated in prison using ritual methods, by people close to Obiang Nguema. After the November 21 elections, the arrests of detractors, violence, and torture increased. The editors of *La Verdad* were threatened with death by the Nguemists authorities. The terror was mainly spread by the Ninjas, the overarmed militia dressed in black, and assisted by three representatives of the Service for International Technical Cooperation of the French Police (SCTIP). The anti-French resentment was getting stronger in the population.

Amnesty International announced that since the November 1993 elections, a number of arrests and cases of poisoning hit members of various opposition parties (CPDS, CSDP, PP), as well as some policemen. In late 1993, the ICRC confirmed that prison visits were again prohibited.

Toward the end of September 1994, the forces of public order assassinated Aguado Ndong Nguema in Mosok (Niefang) for having observed the opposition boycott of the government's census.

In 1995, the resumption of ritual murders was reported. Most of them were committed by members of the Nguemist police. During the September municipal elections, the Jovenes Antorchas, the Ninjas and the police spread terror in the capital, and opponents were held all over the country. Numerous cases of unjustified incarcerations and torture were reported. Opposition meetings were machine gunned. At Baney a prisoner accused of abetting robbery was imprisoned and beaten with the breech of a gun; he died in the capital's hospital. In Teguete (prov. of Evinayong, south-center) a German project for development was stopped for political reasons. Two German volunteers were able to escape to Gabon; the third benefited from the hospitality of the police station of Evinayong for three days before being liberated.

In early 1996, civilians possessing arms were estimated at 20,000 (in particular the Young Torches), in a population of 400,000. During the month of January, and in the perspective of the presidential election of February 25, 32 opponents were held and tortured. A Spanish doctor was expelled, being accused of leanings toward the opposition. In February, apart from most priests being placed under house arrest and some of them being tortured, the democratically elected mayor of the capital and his deputies were arrested in the pedagogical bureau of the French cooperation and beaten until they bled.

Cruelty of all kinds was endured by the priests of all religions. In January-February 1996, during the presidential election, they were made to publish a communiqué in which they made it known that whoever did not revere "Papa Obiang" was in danger. The American Freedom House in March 1996 listed Nguemist Equatorial Guinea among "The Most Repressive Regimes." In January 1996, the special rapporteur of the UN Human Rights Commission, A. Artucio, stated that "the declining trend, observed in May 1995, in the number of arrests and arbitrary detention of leaders and workers of political parties has unfortunately been reversed since the municipal elections of 17 September 1995." This sad observation was repeated in the Country Reports on Human Rights Practices for 1995, published by the U.S. State Department in April 1996 and addressed to Congress. In addition it was also observed that "there were several political and extrajudicial killings." On August 28 a member of the Popular Union was tortured and assassinated at Ebebiyin, and 30 youths who sympathized with the Popular Party were found dead on a beach near the capital following ill treatment.

In its report of January 30, 1998, the U.S. Department of State reported that

security forces committed numerous and serious abuses of human rights...Serious and systematic viiolations of human rights have continued, although there has been an improvement in some fields. . . .The main abuses done by security forces include: physical violence against prisoners, torture, beating up prisoners, extortions from prisoners, house search without a warrant and seizure of possessions without trial. The conditions of detention are still dangerous for life. The judiciary system does not guarantee fair trials and is influenced by the executive. . . .Discrimination and violence against women and foreigners is still a serious problem. . . .In November (1977) a series of at least 13 crimes involving mutilations of the victims occurred in Malabo and Bata. . . .These murders are said to have been committed by delinquents protected by the police. It seems many suspects were arrested, but they ran away from prison.

As for the special rapporteur of the UN Human Rights Commission, he asked, in his 1998 report, that the authorities immediately stop all form of torture and all other cruel, inhuman, and degrading treatments, and that they find the ones who are responsible, and have them judged and punished by means of disciplinary and criminal law. In his March 1998 addendum (Bubi issue), he says:

A great number [of people] have undergone serious beatings and torture, showing on their bodies (arms and legs) wounds and signs of ill-treatment: this has also been observed on people who were released. . . .The lawyers were not authorised to visit them or provide them with technical assistance. . . .the rapporteur must report that the State is to be considered responsible of not having guaranteed the security and integrity of the people who were under its custody.

Four Spanish employees of the Cabisuar company were arrested in August 1998 and held prisoner for 30 hours, accused of terrorism. One of them was imprisoned in a humid jail full of rats for eight days. He was then released without a single explanation. The whole thing started on August 9, five days after their arrival to set up prefabricated modules for a shipping company. Their luggage arrived on the same day. The customs officers noticed they had clothes colored kakhi, which is normal for tourists travelling in tropical areas. The minister of foreign affairs also accused them because they had a kind of Swiss army knife. While they were being interrogated, the were asked to give money. The Spanish company has been working for 13 years in various countries. It said: "It is the first and last time we do this."

The large American interests seem to react differently (see Mobil Oil). In 1998, the U.S. Department of State (*International Market Insight*), declared that "the threat of political violence continues to be a possibility in Equatorial Guinea, but it is not likely to target foreign firms or projects." In the fall of 1998, there was a wave of repression, first shown by many arrests of members of the CPDS, mainly Fang, and then, at the end of November, the arrest of about 35 Bubi, in retaliation for the escape of four leaders responsible for the January appraisals, condemned to death in their absence in May. All were tortured. At the end of November a leader of the Republican Democratic front, Nsue Obama, was tortured to death in the prison of the capital. As for the "eldest son," Teororín Nguema Obiang, dressed in combat uniform and surrounded by about 30 praetorian guards, lays down the law in Rio Muni, racketing particularly the lumbering companies.

See also Akurenam; Army; Elections; Evinayong; France; Human Rights; Mba Ondo, C.; Miko, H.; Mikomeseng; Missions; Ndong Ona, A.; Nguema Eyi, D.; Nguemism; Niefang; Ninjas; Nvono Ekele Avomo; Obiang Mangue, T.; Olo Obono, J.; Ondo Ela, S.; Police; Progress Party; Torture; United States; Victims; Watson Breco, G.; Young Torches

TIMBER. Forests cover almost the whole country. They have been exploited since the eighteenth century in the coastal zones. In the nineteenth century, interest went in particular to ebony, okoume, and mahogany. Except for Cameroon and Gabon, Guinea is the only okoume producer. The first large Spanish companies settled in the Río Benito area around 1910–1921. In 1913, the colony exported 12,600 tons of wood (of which 1.5 tons were planks and 193 tons of ebony and palo rojo). In 1915–1917 exports were almost nothing; in 1926 they rose to 28,495 tons (of which 18.7 tons were planks and 996 tons were ebony and palo rojo). The majority of the exports were made in bulk.

In 1941 some 103,000 hectares were exploited. With the okoume crisis during the Second World War, more interest was given to other species so far neglected. At independence the commercialization of a hundred different species was authorized by the Sindicato Maderero (Timber Producers' Union). Since 1948, however, to avoid the depletion of forests, the Spanish government limited the exploitable okoumea allowance to 30%. Progressively, lumbering moved to the interior of the country, with a production of 337,000 tons in 1967. Several companies, one of which was ALENA, owned private railroads for the transportation of rough timber to the coast. With independence and the departure of many Spaniards, lumbering rapidly fell. By an economic agreement, Spain was contracted to absorb 215,000 tons yearly, but production remained under this quota.

In 1971, from the 800,000 tons hectares of lumber reserve, the Société Forestière Río Muni obtained a 150,00 hectare concession for 10 years. Small Spanish companies as well as Cuba have been cutting and exporting Equato-Guinean timber in recent years. In 1976 the Sociedad Forestal de Río Muni was sold to the French company Tardiba, formerly installed in the Ivory Coast. Shortly after the transaction, the Santa Isabel government proposed a new concession, located near the center of Río Muni Province, to try to avoid the mass exodus of Equato-Guinean workers over into Gabon through the bordering Kukumankok concession. Tardiba refused, however, and since then exploitation seems to have ended.

After the 1979 coup, a total of 372,000 hectares of forest concessions were divided among nine forestry concerns, but only three of these were operational. In August 1982 an Italian forestry company was opened in Bata with a plant capable of turning out 20,000 sq m of veneer annually.

In the summer of 1985 the French company Roussel (Onassis) was granted the largest ever concession in Equatorial Guinea—250,000 hectares. There was a precondition that a road be constructed by the company between Evinayong and Kogo. In October 1987, Roussel's Society Semge was granted 90,000 hectares more, near Kogo, and was building a plant in this town. Timber production in Equatorial Guinea rose from 89,500 tons in 1985 to 110,000 tons in 1986.

end of the eightees, Spanish companies still continued to control most commercial enterprises. The timber economy was represented by the following figures from 1987 to 1996 (according to the BEAC, IMF, and the government):

Year	Production* $000\ m^3$	Exports	Product of total timber production Mio FCFA**
1987	228	159	5.129
1988	180	136	4.049
1989	185	137	4.161
1990	192	159	5.432
1991	191	134	4.557
1992	166	133	4.594

Year	Production* 000 m3	Exports	Product of total timber production Mio FCFA**
1993	191	156	4.938
1994	267	217	6.884
1995	464	267	8.243
1996	364	267	9.991

* Saw log and veer log
** At constant prices of 1985

The increase in exports may be explained by the growth of Asian demand, especially from Japan (biggest importer of Equato-Guinean product: 30% of the country's exports).

In 1988, Semge constructed processing installations. As a result of a drop in business, Semge was sold in December to Yona International (Israel). The saturation of the international market reduced the share of okoume (60% of the resources of Río Muni). Production for 1988 was 150,00 cu m (51% of total exports). It was estimated that it would be possible to go up to 300,000 cu m without jeopardizing natural balance. The Italian company for the unrolling of wood, SIEM (an investment of $10 million), closed down following the crisis.

In 1990, A. Ndong Mba became minister for agriculture, animal husbandry, fisheries, and forests. Yona International had to pay $250,000 in taxes unpaid by Semge and said it had been cheated, as the concession only involved 90,000 hectares while Yona had paid for 200,000 hectares. Moreover, access was difficult. An expert of Yona said to the minister: "You are not only beggars, but also thieves." He was expelled. The okoume market remained saturated. The sawn wood went down, too. The timber sector suffered from a lack of bank credits.

Exports of Okoume (in tons)

1987	6.815	1992	44.409
1988	11.968	1993	115.040
1989	53.308	1994	166.443
1990	53.228	1995	180.772
1991	34.718		

Exports of Okoume by Level of Transformation (cu m)
(according to government)

	1995	1996	1997
Rollo	295.161	297.281	570.801
Tablones	3.824	1.369	.217
Chapas	9.336	13.553	17.589
Total	308.321	312.203	588.607

In 1990 and 1991, production was 184,000 tons and 148,000 cu m. The forest was than 46% of the area of the country. In early 1991, A. Alogo Nchama was minister for agriculture and forests. Deforestation went on at a rate of 3,000 hectares/year. Exports reached 130,678 cu m, half of the predicted level. The amount of wood processed was only 17% in weight and 25% in value; the government had hoped to reach 60%. In late 1991, 11 companies totalled 14 concessions over 450,000 hectares in Río Muni; in Fernando Po there are two companies to the south of the island with 40,00 hectares. They evacuated villages by force. The biggest of these companies were: Matransa, 21.1% of the exports; Exfosa, 19.6%; FGE, 17.1%. That is 57.8%, including the new company ABM. (Astimex, Bisa, Matransa), with Obiang Nguema's and the Lebanese Hanna's participation. Mention must also be made of the French company MAFESA of the Isoroy group. Apart from these Spanish companies there are Italian and a Lebanese company. The debts unpaid by the lumberers to two banks in a state of liquidation are worth a tax of 15% on exports. The exports of timber brought in 42 million pesetas in 1991. In the European Parliament at Strasbourg, the EC aid for the lumber economy was attacked due to overexploitation and lack of reforestation.

In late 1992, the FED proposed a lumber project of $5 million for the protection and rational use of forest resources. The minister for agriculture hired a German engineer under a UN contract (35 million pesetas) as a counsellor to a government lumber company. The contract provided for a commission of 10%. On December 22, 1993, Alfredo Mokundi Nanga became minister. Elias Osono Nguema was secretary of state for the forest economy.

Since July 9, 1991, a decree has prohibited the exploitation of forests in Fernando Po, but in 1994 this decree was violated to reduce the timber export deficit. Production of wood for 1994 went up to 266.724 cu m. Seventy-eight % of the forest exploitation was ensured by five enterprises: ABM, Añisok Mangola, Exfosa, Chilbo (a North Korean company installed in Bata since 1992), SOFOGE. ABM ensured 27% of the production (71,033 cu m).

Okoume represents 76% of exports (70% to Asia). The unrolled wood represents 8,424 cu m (corresponding to 16,134 cu m of untreated wood), i.e., 15% of the lumbering production. The value of wood exports in 1994 totalled about $27 million (nearly a third of the exports).

In 1995 there were 2.2 million hectares of forest, of which 400,000 were exploited, 500,000 already had been depleted, 700,000 were protected, and 600,000 were still available. In 1995, the export of wood was worth 17.9 million FCFA. According to the Poste d'expansion économique français, in Cameroon, Equatorial Guinea may produce 400,000 cu m per year, but the installed capacity of enterprises is no more than 240,00 cu m/year.

In the January 8, 1996, ministerial reshuffle, Maximiliano Micha Nguema became vice-minister for the forest economy. In the April 8, 1996, government, he was replaced by Anatolio Ndong Mba. Various studies by experts state that 40% of the usable raw material was being wasted by lumber operations and the sawmills, which represents a heavy loss of jobs and profits. However, the lumber enterprises drew profits of 25–50% of the invested capital.

Between 1991 and 1996, the lumber production had almost tripled. Specialists qualify it as being "a pillaging." Seventy-eight % of the production is mahogany. Five companies extracted 68% of the production, among them the Malaysian company Shimmer,of the group Timbuna Hijan.

Timber Production, by Firms (cu m)
(according to the government)

Firm	1994	1995	1996
Shimmer	0	69.080	321.237
Sofoge	41.772	61.338	80.744
Añisok Mongola	37.772	36.440	50.826
Sijifo	0	0	31.275
Matoguisa	0	0.550	25.890
Ecuaforsa	6.363	21.744	25.319
ABM	74.391	55.819	24.329
Equimasa	1.131	14.887	22.114
Coguimadera	0	3.163	21.474
EFG	8.027	14.987	19.428
Buecas Urcoila	8.216	18.598	16.214
SAFI	11.528	14.262	15.365
Guiesma	10.118	8.578	15.005
Chilbo	17.947	16.014	14.135
Sinosa	0	5.442	11.215
Somavi	23.690	15.922	10.894
Tromad	4.106	10.388	9.040
Sofona	4.211	0.215	4.308
Joncomba	0.827	1.717	3.995
CPF	0	0	2.265
Agroforestal	17.667	1.063	1.109
Mafesa	12.431	16.956	0.564
Madenco	12.509	10.887	0.564
Pilma	0	0	0.127
Mafeso/Shimmer	0	46.256	0
Isoroy	26.167	0	0
Forguisa	4.290	0	0
Emaguisa	0	0	0
Ekols Sas	0	.894	0
Coteco	3.989	0	0
Total	327.152	445.2	757.174

A new lumbering law became effective in 1997: with an annual quota of 450,000 cu m and a new regulation concerning concessions (the companies must prresent a management plan before getting 150,000 hectares, for 15 years). In 1996, 757,174 cu m of lumber were extracted, mostly by Asian companies (Malaysian and South Korean). It is a true plundering.

In June 1998, the opposition reported that a Río Muni lumber company was busy firing 2,000 employees.

The ecological catastrophe that will result from the destruction of the forests since 1991 has been reported by the main organizations that deal with the protection of nature: International Union for Conservation of Nature and Natural Resources and World Conservation Union (Switzerland), World Resources Institute (Washington), United Nations (UNCED). 1991: Equatorial Guinea's "environmental outlook is not good. The economy is based almost exclusively on poorly managed direct resources utilisation (led by timber extraction), . . .a poor macroeconomic outlook coupled with relatively high population growth. . . ." "Primary forest coverage fell from 50% to 28% between 1959 and 1989, and secondary coverage from 10% to 8%. . . .The nation's legal regime is inadequate." 1993: "Equatorial Guinea's highly biodiverse forests are threatened from many sides. The Spanish colonial system of protected areas collapsed subsequent to independance, and hunting devastated wildlife in many regions; deforestation increased dramatically in the 1980s; and economic collapse and population growth have led to interior demand for agriculture land, putting further pressure on forests." No measures to protect the forests have been taken by the two successive Nguemist dictatorships.

On January 21, 1998, Teodorín Nguema Obiang, Obiang Nguema's eldest son, was promoted to minister of environment and forests.

See also A.B.B.; A.B.M.; Agriculture; Alogo Nchama, E.; Añisok-Mongola; Bata; Cacawal; Coup d'etat of December 1987; Eburi Mata, C.; Elections; Finances; France; Gabon; Guineo-Spanish Lumbering Union; Hanna; Israel; Italy; Korea; Lumbering Company of Rio Muni; Mafesa; Mafia; Mba Nguema Mikue, A.; Micha Nguema Eyang, M.; Morocco; Nguema Obiang, T.; Nzambi Machinde, F.; Obiang Mangue, T.; Obiang Nguema, T.; Ovenga Eyang Mba, M.; Ovono Nguema, E.; Petroleum; Roussel, T. (Onassis); State-run Enterprises; Switzerland; Terror; Transports; United Nations; Vilarrasa Balanza, S.; Yona International.

TOGO, Republic of see Oyono Ndongo Mifumu, Miguel

TOMAS KING TOMAS, Alfredo. A Fernandino. Lawyer by profession. Representative to the Spanish Cortes from 1964 to 1969. Legal adviser to the MONALIGE movement. He attended the 1967–1968 Constitutional Conference. He was elected to the Asamblea de la República in the immediate postindependence period, where he chaired the Justice Commission and was a member of the Defense Commission. He acted as defense lawyer at the trial of Macías Nguema in September 1979. After the 1979 coup, he became secretary in the Ministry of Justice and was promoted to minister on December 8, 1981. In May 1982 he took part in the Akonibé constitutional commission that consolidated the dictatorship of Obiang Nguema. In 1984, as president of the Supreme Court, he declared to Human Rights Commission expert Volio-Jiménez that "UN are the sheet-anchor of the juridical power" in Equatorial Guinea. In late 1989, as the attorney general of the republic, he received the representative of the Human Rights Commission, who reported the unavailability of a means to justice. In 1993, he was a member of the Supreme Court.

TORAO SIKARA, Pastor. d. 1969. Important Bubi chief and mayor of Baney. With S. Ebuka and A. Ndongo Miyone, he founded MONALIGE in 1959, of which he became president. In 1962 he also founded MPIGE, with which Maho Sikacha became associated. In 1964 he addressed an appeal to the United Nations for the independence of Spanish Guinea. A fierce opponent of the separation of Fernando Po and Río Muni, he worked for national unity at the Constitutional Conference in 1967–1968. But during the conference Macías Nguema questioned his representativeness as president of the MONALIGE. Back in Guinea, the Grupo Macías accused Torao Sikara of being a servant of Spain. In October 1968 Torao became vice-president and then president of the Asamblea de la Rupública. He was said to have been murdered in 1969 following the coup of Ndongo Miyone, dying of thirst in the Bata prison.

TORO, Gustavo. UNDP resident representative from 1988 to 1991. He worked on an assistance program for $20 million, double the previous one, with the aim of obtaining an efficient administration, the regeneration of forests, and the diversification of agriculture.

TORRE de la, Rafaela (called Rafí). A talented Spanish announcer—with Castillo Meseguer—has had a daily two-hour special program on Radio Exterior de España for Equatorial Guinea, since January 1991.

TORTURE. Under Macías Nguema, priests were tortured on their hands and testicles. At Nazang Ayong a woman, Pilar Mening, was tortured. In August 1979, special rapporteur to the UN Human Rights Commission, Volio-Jiménez, stated that torture and arrests of priests had been on the increase since 1975, that is, since Obiang Nguema took command of the army. In 1980, several members of the government were present at torture sessions, including Juan Oló and Nguema Esono, first secretary of the embassy in Madrid (expelled for drug trafficking). There was no major change with regard to torture after Obiang Nguema took power. Under both Nguemist dictators, torture is a method of government.

During the first years of the second Nguemist dictatorship, many victims, arrested in the capital, were transferred to Bata by a coast guard boat offered by the U.S., and then transferred to the police station by means of a lorry belonging to Afripesca.

The victims are often tortured by Manuel Mba, uncle of Obiang Nguema. The victim is about ten meters away from the presidential table of tortures, where two high officials of the Nguemist regime sit, male or female. The blindfolded victim is surrounded by soldiers, Ninjas, and Moroccans. The "experts" of the presidential table call a soldier, tell him which question should be asked, and according to the answer decide which torture should be applied. The 1982 Constitution specifies that, "The aim of the penitentiary system is to re-educate, rehabilitate and reintegrate into society the accused." See Bibliography (Amnesty International).

In 1992, torture was practiced by the application of chili sauce on the sensitive parts of the body, by submerging heads in soap water, or even by the traditional "Ethiopian method." Amnesty International frequently raised alarms due to the threat of torture weighing on opponents, and especially on members or supporters of the Convergency for Social Democracy or the Progress Party after being arrested by the army, the police, the Criminal Investigations Department, or the Moroccans. After a peaceful demonstration by students of the La Salle Institute and the Teacher Training School at Bata in November, 40 students were arrested, beaten, and some tortured, among them a student who was eight months pregnant. The other young girls had to dance naked before the policemen. Murders by the Security Corps of the president were reported. On December 17 a peaceful demonstration by students and teachers in the capital was violently suppressed, and about 100 persons were imprisoned, including the priests Ncogo Eyi and Ondo Maye. All of them were beaten, and most of them tortured. Amnesty International reported that Celestino Bakale and Arsenio Moro, as well as the priests, were in a serious state.

The former ambassador to Moscow, also arrested and tortured, described the methods used, which consisted mainly of beating the soles of the feet of prisoners with rubber whips after making them lie on the ground. The tired or unconscious victims douched with cold water and the torture recommenced. Like the soldiers, the torturers were mostly unable to count, and often went beyond the 40–60 lashes ordered. Such treatment was generally ordered by Manuel Nguema, uncle of Obiang Nguema. The captain of the gendarmerie at Bata had the reputation of a drunk and drugged torturer.

In February 1993, at Nsoc-Nsomo, about 50 members of the opposition were arrested and tortured under the orders of the government's representative Lucio Aseme, due to their cool reception given to the minister for defense, M. Ebendeng Nsomo. In August, with the postponement of the elections, a number of arrests led to the recommencement of torture. Motu Mamiaga and M. Nseng Bacale were murdered in ritual assassinations in which Manuel Nguema appeared. In the capital several persons were arrested and tortured simply for reading *La Verdad*. After the November 21 elections, a campaign of arrests began, following the triumph of the boycott called for by the POC. On December 10, 29 UNED students were tortured after they left the consulate of Spain in Bata.

In 1994, Nigel Rodley published his special report for the Human Rights Commission of the UN, concerning torture and inhuman treatments. He reported the appalling conditions found in the jail: men and women were not separated, hence many women were raped by prisoners or guards, and the fact that medical assistance is systematically refused. He gave a list of victims. He also reported that many high-school students in Bata and Santa Isabel were tortured in 1992, after pro-democracy demonstrations.

The special rapporteur to the UN Human Rights Commission, A. Artucio, stated in his report discussed in March 1994 that the appeals to the government by the Committee Against Torture received no response. In early March, Amnesty International raised a cry of alarm for Norberto Mba Nze, a mechanic and member of the CPDS and a victim of serious acts of torture at Akonibe. Upon his departure in mid-1994, the American ambassador Bennet gave a long list of military torturers. In early October, in Santa Isabel as well as Bata, several leaders of opposition parties were tortured for no apparent reason: Plácido Mikó, Victorino Bolekia Bonay, José Mechaba Ikaka, Amancio G. Nzé, etc.

In March 1995, several members of the Progress Party and the army were reported tortured. After the September legislative elections, the persecution of opponents started again in Río Muni, Fernando Po, and Annobón.

In January 1996, Rudley published an additional report, with a list of victims. In March and June he called on the government. The latter denied using torture.

During the presidential election advanced by Obiang Nguema to February 25, 1996, numerous acts of torture, aimed at priests as well as laymen, were reported. Among them, the democratically elected mayor of the capital, V. Bolekia, and his deputies. The special reporter of the UN Human Rights Commission provided several examples of tortured persons, including the case of the CPDS militant Jesús Marcial, held for five weeks without being accused, who, being seriously injured after the torture, had to be hospitalized with blood in his urine, a fractured arm, and permanent lesions to the vertebral column. Other persons who had been tortured remained irremediably crippled.

"Torture and Other Cruel, Inhuman, or Degrading Treatment or Punishment..." observed the U.S. State Department in its April 1996 Report on Human Rights addressed to the Congress,

> are serious, frequent, and widespread. The police routinely beat detainees severely, and victims often require hospitalization after release. . . .The Government has not prosecuted or punished any security officials for these abuses. . . .During the September [1995] election campaign, a guard at the former U.S. Embassy was arrested by police and beaten. Police released him after high level diplomatic intervention. His late uncle, a political opponent of the regime, had been beaten to death in Malabo's Blackbeach Prison 2 years before [1993].

At the end of 1996, members from various democratic political parties of the opposition were arrested and underwent torture.

At the end of June 1997, seven people, opponents to the regime, were tortured in Bata, on the orders of Superintendent Cayo Ondo Mba.

Those sentenced to death during the Bubi trial in May–June 1998 underwent psychological torture. In July, AI declared that political imprisonment and torture are still widely used.

About 35 Bubi arrested at the end of November 1998 were systematically tortured by the presidential security forces.

See also Abaga Ondo Maye, E.; Abeso Fuma, F.; Akalayong; Akonibe; Amnesty International; Angue Ondo, P.; Añisok; Annobón; Army; Artucio, A.; ASODEGE; Bakale Obiang, C.-B.; Balinga, B. G.; Baney; Bata; Benito; Bennet, J. E.; Bibang Oyee, J.; Bolekia Bonay, V.; Bubi; Constitution; Convergency for Social Democracy; Coup d'état of spring 1990; Democracy; Democratic Progress Alliance; Denmark; Ebebiyin; Ebendeng Nsomo, M.; Edu Nsue, N.; Education; Ela Abeme, J.; Elections; Eneme Ovono, J.; Eneme Ovono, S.; Esono, J. C.; Esono Masie, P.; Esono Miko Miha, P.; European Union; France; Human Rights; Joint Opposition Platform; Justice; Kogo; Mba Ekua Miko, B.; Mba Nguema Mikue, A.; Mba Ondo, C.; Mecheba Ikaka, J.; Milo Abogo, P.; Morocco; Moto Nsá, S.; Ncogo Eyi, P.; Ndong, J.; Nguema Esono, L.; Nguema Isono Nchama, B.; Nguema Eyi, D.; Nguema Mba, M.; Nguema Mbasogo Ondo, A.; Niefang; Nigeria; Nze

Angue, A. G.; Obiang Nguema, T.; Olo Mba Nseng, J.; Ona Nguema, A.; Ondo Ela, S.; Petroleum; Press; Plot (1981); Progress Party; Public Health; Refugees; Río Benito; Ronda, S.; Ronda Estrada, T.; Saez Lashera, T.; Santa Isabel; Siale Bilekia, S.; Sima Ngua, A.; Spain; Terror; University; *La Verdad;* Victims; Volio-Jimenez, F.; World Labor Confederation.

TOTAL. French oil company. Total has been carrying out oil investigations ever since the 1980s, associated with Agip, ELF, Getty, and other American companies. Since 1985, Total-Guinea Ecuatorial monopolizes the distribution of hydrocarbons over the entire territory (instead of the former Empresa Nacional Petrolífera).

See also Bata; Evinayong; Litor-Wele; Mbana, S.; Oyono, L.; Petroleum; Total-Guinea Ecuatorial.

TOURISM. In early 1981, regulations for the operation of hotels and tourist establishments were laid down. The Spanish Cooperation founded the Miramar hotel school. In March, S. Moto Nsá became secretary of state for information and tourism, replacing Obiang Nguema. Moto Nsá had headed this service under Macías Nguema. In October 1990, the Ministry of Culture, Tourism, and Artisanal Welfare went to L. Mbomio Nsué. In the January 1992 "transitional" government, the minister of tourism and artisanal welfare was J. Balboa Boneque. During 1992 a three-star hotel, constructed by Envoro Ovono for Obiang Nguema, was inaugurated at Mongomo.

In the December 22, 1993, government, Augustín Nse Nfumu became minister for culture, tourism, and the French language. Following his criticism during the February 1996 presidential election, he was replaced by Pedro-Christino Bueribuei in the April 8, 1996, government. It was learned from the former judge of the Supreme Court, Fermín Nguema Esono, that the Italian project for Hotel Media Luna ($12 million), near the Bata Airport, had fallen through due to Nguemist corruption. In 1994, the first tourist guide on Equatorial Guinea was published in Spain (see bibliography).

In 1995, the minister for culture, tourism, and the French language and culture, A. Nsé Nfumu, inaugurated Hotel Ecofac, on Mt. Alen (a gorilla reserve), 95 km from Bata. With UNDP collaboration, Equatorial Guinea identified nine natural reserves, totalling 340,000 hectares, i.e., 8% of the national territory.

Hilario Sisa Tores was vice-minister. Since 1997, an "Office of Tourism and Trade in Italy" opened in Rome.

In the government of January 21, 1998, Lucas Nguema Esono was minister of information, tourism and culture.

See also Balboa Boneque, J.; Bengono Micó, R.; Bueribueri, C.; Corisco, Coup d'etat of December 1987; Culture; Ekomo Yacure, F.; Elo Mabale, R.; Epam Botala, A.; France; Mba Nsue, J.; Mbomio Nsue, L.; Mikomeseng; Moto Nsá, S.; National Democratic Union; Nepotism; Nkili Nze, N.; Nze Nfumu, A.; Oko Ebobo, Antonio P.; Oyono Awong Ada, S.; Sisa Tores, H.

TOXIC WASTES. In 1988, a Spanish lawyer negotiated on behalf of an American company for permission to deposit radon-contaminated earth near Bata. Garbage from New York was sent to the outskirts of Bata in "carefully" packed compressed blocks. A nine-year dumping contract, at $10 a ton, was signed by the Nguemists. These deposits were said to be nontoxic and to conform to the

Basel Convention. Toxic residues were deposited near Río Benito; the Nguemists pocketed $1 million. In June, Obiang Nguema signed a contract for toxic waste deposits on Annobón. Two million barrels of mixed landfill toxic wastes were provided for. A 10-year license was granted, in return for $1.6 million, to the British company Emvatrex (Buckinghamshire) and the American Axim Consortium Group (New York). Another 10-year $720,000 project with Axim and Miele Sanitation Co., for the deposit of wastes at $60 a ton, ensured the Equato-Guinean authorities a revenue of 70 billion pesetas. The Equato-Guinean delegation to the UN admitted that the first consignment to Annobón was sent in August 1988; some wastes were delivered as early as 1987. Annobón has registered one of the highest skin-disease rates in the world.

In mid-1990, the government appears to have refused American radioactive wastes (for $260 million) in return for tourist construction, housing, and communication lines projects. Toxic wastes from the U.S. were also refused by a Panamanian company.

In 1992, France convicted V.-G. Llansol, Obiang Nguema's extraordinary ambassador and counsellor for economic affairs, claiming he was organizing a toxic waste recycling plant in the capital with the help of a Western European company. The project was strongly opposed by European environmentalist parties. Some French, South African, Belgian, Italian, Serb, Norwegian, and Japanese firms began to be interested in the toxic hospitality of the Nguemists. Experts reported mostly formaldehyde, dioxin, heavy metal, cyanide, and chlorophenol wastes. Annobón has now become a time bomb. Since the troops stationed on the island had destroyed all its cats, the rats multiplied and would even attack babies and the elderly, sometimes biting off their fingers. Before the UN General Assembly, permanent representative Dámasco Obiang-Ndong declared in late 1993 that "the developed countries [are] responsible in a large measure for the deterioration of the world ecosystem." See also Annobón; Benito; International Bank for Reconstruction and Development; Maye Ela, F.; Obiang Nguema, T.; Panama; Río Benito; United Kingdom; United States of America.

TRADE. Warehouses were the first sign of international trade in Spanish Guinea and appeared as early as the first half of the nineteenth century. They were frequently engaged in slave trade as well. Portuguese as well as Dutch trading posts are reported since the sixteenth century. During the nineteenth century Fernando Po and Río Muni were dotted with British subsidiaries (Holt, Hatton & Cookson; and Forster), German ones (Woermann, Küderling und Thormälen, Lübke, Panda-Steind, Schulze, Moritz), Spanish ones (Simo, Vincent, Vidal y Rivas, Trasatlántica, etc.), not to mention the Belgian and French ones. The subsidiaries employed traders who traveled by caravan despite the dangers, exchanging goods in the interior of the country for ivory, liana rubber, okoume, palm oil, mahogany, copal resin, etc. In 1894 a royal decree designated Spanish Guinea as a territory of "colonial exploitation." The ships of Trasatlántica, later of Transmediterránia, were only connected with Fernando Po, whereas the ones of the Hamburg Woermann Line and the British Africa Steam were also connected with the Río Muni coast.

In 1960 the Spanish Guinea per capita export index was the highest in Africa: $135 per inhabitant against $112 for São Tomé, $105 for Gabon, $87 for South

Africa, and $48 for Ghana. Totalling 500,000 tons in 1968, the country's external trade fell to 237,000 tons in 1970. It is the country's main income. Independence did not remove Spain from its leading role in commerce: it accounted for 98% of the export trade in 1962 and 91% in 1970. Since 1971 Spanish goods are subject to the same taxes as those coming from other countries. The account currency is the U.S. dollar.

Since independence there have been various attempts to monopolize external trade, in particular by García Trevijano (Simed S.A.) and Oyono Ayingono (Adoual). But the state-owned shops were becoming more and more important, selling mostly goods from the People's Republic of China. From 1968 to 1975 Vice President Bosio Dioco was also the trade minister. He was murdered in 1975. From then on, the trade portfolio has unofficially been in the hands of Oyono Ayingono.

After the 1979 coup d'etat, Obiang Nguema, in addition to the presidency, took over the ministry of Finance and although the trade was freed, the imports were in 1981 reserved specially for the "National Trade Company" financed by the Treasury. Spain is still the first buyer and seller. At the end of 1982, Angel Esono Abaga was appointed secretary of trade; in 1985, he became vice-minister. Since 1983, the Société Générale de Surveillance S.A. (Geneva) has been supervising the foreign trade. Wood, cocoa, and coffee represent 97% of the exports.

The introduction of the CFA franc in 1985 has placed Equatorial Guinea in the commercial dependence of Cameroon and Gabon.

In 1988 and 1989, the deficit in the trade balance respectively totalled $13 and $25 million. All exports of more than FCFA 5,000 required a license. In 1988, the principal export and imports were (in millions of dollars):

Imports		**Exports**	
Food	15.0	Wood	15.6
Petroleum products	2.3	Cocoa	10.9

Traditional exports of yams from Fernando Po to Cameroon and Gabon were resumed. The increase in imports was denounced by the IMF. Retail trade was again dominated by Lebanese and Indians. Since 1989 a reduction in trade with France was recorded (1989–1990: 43.8%; 1990–1991: 33.6%). In 1990, M. Nguema Nguema Onguene became minister for the economy and commerce. Statistics for maritime traffic for the two principal ports show the following values:

	Santa Isabel	**Bata**
Imports	42,804	28,558
Exports	12,659	125,990
Total	55,463	154,548

In the January 24, 1992, "transitional" government, Nguema Nguema Onguene remained minister for the economy and commerce, with F. Inestrosa Ikaka as vice-minister. Since December 22, 1993, successive governments did not include a minister of commerce. In February 1994 a commission for price control was set up, following excesses committed by the traders of Santa Isabel and elsewhere.

1995 Foreign Trade ($ millions)

Imports		Exports	
Spain	74	USA	31
Cameroon	31	Japan	15
France	11	Spain	14
USA	6	China	1
Belgium-Luxembourg	5	Netherlands	5
Total	*145*		*92*

Any property more than FCFA 50.000 is submitted to an import license.

In the government of January 21, 1998, Vidal Choni Becoba was minister of the industry, trade and promotion of small-and-medium sized firms. The U.S. Department of Commerce commented during 1998: "implementation of export/import procedures by the government of Equatorial Guinea officials does not always correspond to written customs laws or codes."

See also Corruption; Customs; Economy.

TRADE UNIONS see Sindicatos

TRADING POSTS see Warehouses

TRAITORS see Corruption

TRANSACCIONES PANAFRICANAS S.A. Company of the Ferris Sanchez group, mainly comprising the Société generale hispano-africaine de commerce et de transports (SOGEHA).

TRANSMEDITERRANEA Company. Since 1934 it has had a monopoly on maritime connection between Spain and Spanish Guinea, and thus an almost complete control of import and export, after 50 years of the Trasatlántica monopoly. In Equatorial Guinea it held the transit companies Aucona and Fortuny. Under the cooperation agreement of July 1971, Spain offered Guinea a monthly connection by a Transmediterránea ship that Spain subsidized in order to offer preferential tariffs. At the same time, Spain presented Guinea with the obsolete ship Romeu, a former steamer belonging to Transmediterránea.

After the fall of Macías Nguema, the Spanish government offered to start regular services again between Spain and Equatorial Guinea with this company. The company, however, demanded a subsidy of 300 million pesetas annually. The government consequently opened negotiations with another company, García Minaur, in late 1979, on the occasion of the visit of King Juan Carlos, and during one part of 1980, the vessel *Pamplona,* of Transmediterránea, halted in the port of Santa Isabel as an onboard hotel.

TRANSPORTS (land). The opening of Río Muni by the Spanish army in 1926 led to the construction of roads, including the Bata-Mikomeseng-Ebebiyin road, along the border with Cameroon. In 1971–1976 the World Bank (IDA) put in $2 million for a road renovation project, via the UNDP. The project never became operational, due to Nguemist obstacles. Under Macías Nguema, the roadways, partly tarred, were no longer maintained and made the transportation of timber difficult. The contracts for lumbering concessions involved the obligation of maintaining roads. After Obiang Nguema's coup, transport was put under the Ministry of Public Works and Environment. The network continued to deteriorate.

In 1980 the number of Mercedes, Peugeot, Volga, Landrover, and Mitsubishi cars in the capital increased, while Bata remained practically empty. In Bata, in April, Oficar Africa SA, run by Mba Oñana, operated urban transports and was later extended to the whole of Río Muni. In 1988, D. Elo Ndong Nsefumu became minister for communications and transports. He earned commissions from the Spanish Cooperation. In August-September 1990, a Chinese mission planned the reconstruction of the Bata-Ebebiyin road. In October A. Evoro Ovono became minister of public works, environment, and transports. In March, in order to facilitate the export of food to Gabon, it was decided that the improvement of the Río Benito-Akalayong-Kogo corridor (65 km) had to be given priority, as some parts were impossible to drive on. The same works were necessary for the Logo-Mitomo and Evinayong-Akurenam roads.

In the January 24, 1992, "transitional" government, M. Oyono Ntutumu became minister for transports, post, and telecommunications. In late 1992 the EDF project for the renovation of the Río Benito-Akalayong road for 1.6 million ECUs was being prepared. In the December 22, 1993, government, A. F. Nve Nzeng became minister of state for transport, information, and communications, and spokesperson for the government. Nve Nzeng retained his post in the January 8, 1996, government. On April 8, 1996, Elias Ovono Nguema became minister for transport and communications.

Ovono Nguema was dismissed at the end of June 1997 and replaced by Fransisco Abaga Ndong.

In the January 21, 1998, government, Marcelino Oyono became minister of communication and transport. José Eneme Oyono was vice-minister. In August, the British Economic Intelligence Unit underlined the "anecdotal evidence of some road development."

See also Aviation; Navigation

TRASATLANTICA, COMPANIA. Maritime shipping company founded in 1850 that was given a monopoly on Spanish connections with Guinea after having mainly operated to and from Cuba. At the instigation of the Marqués de Comillas, agents of Trasatlántica explored business possibilities in Río Muni as of 1887 (Montes de Oca, Ossorio, Bonelli y Hernando, Bengoa Arriola, and others), opening trading posts long after those of J. Holt, Woermann, Hatton & Cookson, and various Catalan traders. Spanish business circles accused Trasatlántica of buying German goods rather than Spanish ones for trading with Guinea. One of the principal shareholders was Romero Robledo, minister of overseas territories in 1892, who made enormous profits in transporting Spanish troops to Cuba. At the beginning of the twentieth century the Marqués de Comillas donated 25,000 pesetas for the building of the Moka church and the Santa Isabel cathedral. The first Trasatlántica messenger steamer arrived in Santa Isabel in 1888, the line having been operated previously by British or German ships only. Second-zone Spanish ships (5,000–6,000 tons) were used for this connection. The company landed only at Santa Isabel and ignored Río Muni. In 1905 Bengoa created the main cattle breeding zone in the Moka heights; during the same period, Trasatlántica bought the plantations and residence of Governor General Montes de Oca, in Basilé, creating also plantations in the region of Concepción. In 1926 Trasatlántica sold the line to Alena, which took over their trading posts, fincas, and cattle farms.

TRAY. Bubi from Rebola. Since 1945 has had a career first in the Colonial Guard, then in the territorial ones. He became commanding officer of the Spanish army. In 1968 he was in charge of the Military House of President Macís Ngtuema. He was shortly thereafter arrested during Ndongo Miyone's coup of March 5, 1969. He is known for having particularly bothered the staff of the Spanish Assistance Program.

Lieutenant-colonel under Macías Nguema. After Obiang Nguema's coup d'etat he returned to his original job as a cocoa planter. Died 1995.

TRITON ENERGY. Oil company; see also Petroleum.

TUNG ELA, Rafael. Born 1950. From Mongomo. Holds a degree from the Soviet Union. Educated in Morocco. In January 1994 he became the prosecutor of the Appeals Tribunal of Bata. In September 1998, he became executive vice-president of the French Société Générale de Banque of Equatorial Guinea (General Society of Banks).

TUWADDEL, William. In 1996, Deputy Secretary of State for Africa. Accompanied by J. C. Spiegel, Officer for Central African Affairs, and Liaison Officer Kent, W. Tuwaddel received in Washington on September 18 the secretary-general of Convergency for Social Democracy (CPDS), Placido Mikó, and Celestino Bakale, responsible for international relations. He assured them of the American will to view the progress of democracy in Equatorial Guinea. He also expressed his conviction that the election of Obiang Nguema in February 1996 was conducted in an irregular fashion. The representatives of the CPDS underlined how much the American petroleum companies had contributed to reinforce the Nguemist dictatorship. See also United States of America.

TWINNINGS, Charles C. U.S. ambassador since May 16, 1996. In the summer of 1998, he was replaced by John M. Yates.

❖ U ❖

UDEBEKE, Eberhart. Ambassador of Germany from 1990 with residence in Yaounde (Cameroon).

U.F.E.R. (International Movement for the Fraternal Union between Races and Peoples) see Eya Nchama, C. M.

UGANDA, Santiago. 1845–1960. Benga king of Corisco. He succeeded to the throne on the death of King Fernando Otimbo Ijenje in 1900. His people called him Tata Bombando. In 1905 he was awarded the Alphonse XIII medal. He died of pneumonia in the Bata hospital at the age of 115.

UGANDA. As of 1978 Uganda was said to have been training Equato-Guinean pilots since 1972. In March 1977 the Uganda delegate to the UN Human Rights Commission in Geneva opposed the intervention of the ANRD representative, speaking then in praise of Macías Nguema's regime.

UKOKO ISLAND see Borders

UKRANIA. The company Sea Factor, Crewing Agency, in Sebastopol, has direct contacts with Sandypool, Ireland, Linksight Shipping Co. It provided 12 crew members for the ship *Bata,* and 12 others for the *Malabo.* See Arms Dealing; Navigation.

UNICEF (United Nations Infants and Children's Fund). After Obiang Nguema's coup of 1979, UNICEF put in $50,000 from its emergency reserves (medicines, vaccinations, medical equipment). In 1980, UNICEF allocated $175,000 for bringing the children's health services back in order. One part of the funds was also meant for some returning refugees following the amnesty of October 1979, in cooperation with the United Nations High Commission for Refugees.

See also Children; Economy; Education; Food; Public Health

UNION BUBI (Bubi Union) see Bubi

UNION DE AGRICULTORES DE GUINEA ESPAÑOLA (Farmers Union of Spanish Guinea). In 1921 a committee of planters and cocoa merchants was constituted in Barcelona and called the Comité de Defensa Agrícola de Fernando Po. It failed, however, through the competition of dissidents in 1923. In 1932 the Unión de Agricultores was created, a kind of official farmers' union. In 1935 a sales association was set up by the Union. In 1937 the Sindicato del Cacao appeared under the Franco regime. The Casa de Guinea handled the Unión de Agricultores.

UNION FOR DEMOCRACY AND SOCIAL DEVELOPMENT (Unión para la Democracia y el Desarrollo Social, UDDS). In 1990, Sibacha Buecheku, an old member of Manuel Ruben Ndong's CSPD, founded the UDDS (headquarters in Gabon) with Djebelan King Nam, an old member of MUNGE. In late 1992, the party demanded that Spain reduce its aid to the Nguemists. At the airport of Santa Isabel, in early 1993, two delegates who had arrived to get the group legalized were deprived of their passports and FCFA 2.5 million.

UNION DEMOCRATICA FERNANDINA (UNDEMO—Fernandine Democratic Union). Political movement created for the Constitutional Conference in March 1967 by W. Jones Niger. He was for independence in a federational setup with Río Muni, while avoiding the overwhelming majority of Fang. UNDEMO did not obtain any seat at the Asamblea General (Parliament) after the September 1968 elections, nor a seat in the Consejo de Ministros. The Fernandino Grange Molay became minister of agriculture as a member of the Macías Group. Like other parties, UNDEMO was dissolved in 1970 at the creation of PUN.

UNION DEMOCRATICA NACIONAL (UDENA) see National Democratic Union

UNION DOUANIERE DES ETATS DE L'AFRIQUE CENTRALE (UDEAC) see Customs Union of Central African States

UNION GENERAL DE TRABAJADORES DE GUINEA ECUATORIAL (UGTGE—General Workers Trade Union of Equatorial Guinea). Created in exile in 1959, it aimed especially at spreading trade unionism not manipulated by the Movimiento Nacional. Of Christian inspiration, the union always remained clandestine; independence under Macías Nguema did not permit them to come out openly. UGTGE signed an agreement allowing it to merge its activities with MONALIGE. Thanks to UGTGE trade union movements were admitted by the Parliament during autonomy, and a strike of Guinean officials for salary increases could be organized on April 22–26, 1966. Trade union freedoms are being violated by the second Nguemist dictatorship as by the first.

The American Department of State, in its Report on Human Rights in Equatorial Guinea, published in January 1998, specifies that although the constitution makes provision for the right to organize unions, the government has not voted on a legislative application. That is why the government did not answer a 1995 petition, made by the employees of the service sector who wanted to create a union in the capital of the continental province, Bata. The report adds that labor regulations include measures aimed at protecting the rights of the workers, but the government usually does not apply them. On March 14, 1998, the Asociación Sindical de Docentes (ASD, teachers union), run by Roque Endama and Carlos Ona, asked for the registration of their association. On April 20, the minister of. labor turned down the proposition. See also ANRD.

UNION GUINEO-ESPANOLA DE MADERA (GUIESMA) see Guineo-Spanish Lumber Union

UNION OF SOVIET SOCIALIST REPUBLICS see Russia

UNION OF SPANISH NATIONALS WITH INTERESTS IN AFRICA (Comunidad de Españoles con Intereses en Africa—CEIA). Since 1970 CEIA has grouped together former colonial circles that were stripped of their belongings for various reasons—about 380 companies all told, representing 2,174 million pesetas ($32 million). With the complicity of the former Equatorial Guinean ambassador in Madrid, Nsué Ngomo, an attempt to overthrow Macías Nguema is said to have been prepared in 1970 with the help of British mercenaries and a plan to install W. Jones Niger as the president. The plot having been discovered, Equatorial Guinea suspended its ambassador and Spain exiled him to Andorra. In June 1973 CEIA accused the Spanish state of not safeguarding the security of the Spanish companies in Guinea and asked the Banco de Crédito Industrial to release 600 million pesetas ($87 million) to favor new economic activities in Guinea, but the government disregarded its recommendations. As late as 1996, repatriated Spanish nationals had not been given compensation.

UNION PARA LA DEMOCRACIA Y EL DESARROLLO SOCIAL (UDDS) see Union for Democracy and Social Democracy

UNION POPULAR (UP) see Popular Union

UNION REVOLUCIONARIA DE GUINEA ECUATORIAL (URGE— Popular Liberation Movement of Equatorial Guinea). The oldest opposition movement to the personal power of Macías Nguema was founded in 1970 in Santa Isabel (it was then called Comitée de Revolucíon Nacional, or CRN). Exiled in Spain, the movement became more radical in 1974 and adopted a socialist stand. In 1976, after a brief period of cooperation with MOLIFUGE that had its climax in the occupation of the Madrid embassy, it merged with the Movimiento Socialista de Guinea (MSG). URGE is one of the more mature opposition movements. It publishes the periodical *Nueva Generación*. In 1974 it presented a "Temporary Draft for an Economic and Social Development Plan," with the participation of cooperative and private enterprises, the state being the primary economic agent. Among its members one should mention C. Okenve, son of the former head of the Equato-Guinean armed forces. On December 24, 1976, Radio Madrid mentioned URGE's activities for the last time.

UNIONS see Free Unions; Human Rights

UNIQUE NATIONAL WORKERS PARTY (Partido Unico Nacional de Trabajadores, PUNT). The PUNT's symbol is an open-mouthed tiger ready to jump, roaring the letters *PUNT* (Macías Nguema's emblem at the 1968 elections was the cock). In December 1968 Macías Nguema started speaking of a single party, and on March 1969, taking advantage of the Ndongo Miyone affair, he publicly promised it, despite the cabinet's opposition. Macías Nguema asked García Trevijano for draft statutes. Starting in 1970, the cabinet abolished the MONALIGE, MUNGE, IPGE, Unión Bubi, Ndowe Unión, and Unión Democrática Fernandina.

The Partido Unico Nacional was proclaimed by a July 7, 1970 decree, and at the third congress in July 1973 became PUNT. All officials, all adult men and women, as well as schoolchildren, have to practice parading once a week (with wooden guns sold by PUNT at 50 bikuele). Since 1975 this practice has been limited to the Juventud en Marcha con Macías. As for the Milicia Popular, it groups fanatic adults with uniforms and real weapons. With the August 1973 constitution, power is exercised by the party in the name of the people. PUNT proposes the 60 deputies for the Asamblea Nacional Popular (Parliament), being able to revoke them any time for "deviationism." At the 1973 Congress, PUNT resolved to institute compulsory labor, to enroll all unmarried women in agriculture, to name Macías Nguema "Tireless and Single Miracle of Equatorial Guinea, Life-Time President, Chief General of the Armed Forces, Great Master in Popular Education, Science and Traditional Culture."

After the attempted coup d'etat of June 1974, the extraordinary PUNT Congress in August decided on the supply by each district of 2,000 to 2,500 persons for compulsory labor in the plantations. Macías Nguema was authorized to nominate traditional chiefs. The building of a Congress Center for 10,000 persons became urgent (15% of the cost to be supported by the militants). In December 1974 Macías Nguema announced the nomination of political commissaries in the schools. Early in December 1976, the secretary general of PUNT, Minister of Popular Education Ochaga Ngomo, was imprisoned during the Senior Officials Affair, and murdered with many others.

In 1977 the PUNT published a brochure: *Linea revolucionaria estudiantil guineana en marcha con Papa Macias*. In it, the king of Spain, Juan Carlos I, was accused of being a puppet and a criminal murderer. The PSOE was similarly accused. The refusal of Equatorial Guinea to belong to the Hispanic community was stressed. "We are African." After Obiang Nguema's coup in August 1979, he dissolved the PUNT. However, in 1985 he requested the government to study the creation of a new one-party system. See also Human Rights; Nguemism; Partido Democratico de Guinea Ecuatorial.

UNITED KINGDOM. From 1783 to 1827 various British expeditions attempted to occupy Fernando Po; they were led by such as Bullen, McWilliam, Robertson, and Kelly. In 1819, two English traders claimed ownership of Fernando Po. In 1825, the Foreign Office recognized Spanish sovereignty over the island, but in 1827 the Owen expedition settled there, founding Clarence City (Santa Isabel) on the pretense of transferring the Anti-Slavery Tribunal from Freetown (Sierra Leone). Owen administered the island with Nicholls and other British officers and turned it over to the half-breed Beecroft in 1833. Until the passage of Lerena in 1843, the island remained entirely British, and in spite of the hispanicization of the toponyms by Lerena, it was not until 1858, with the arrival of Chacón, that an end could be put to the use of English names. Beecroft remained governor until his death in 1854 and was replaced by Lynslager until 1858, with Spain's agreement. In 1856, the *British Royal Yearbook* still mentioned Fernando Po as a British territory.

In 1817 Spain and the United Kingdom signed a treaty for the suppression of the slave trade. Spain's failure to observe the treaty caused the Royal Navy to hail Spanish ships and patrol the seas between Fernando Po and the continent to prevent illegal traffic of labor (Spain was accused of practicing slavery). In 1862–1864 a Spanish royal decree authorized coal deposits for British civil steamers in Fernando Po. Since then Playa Carboneras was found to be the main prehistoric site of the island. A ship of the British Steam Navigation Company brought the first Iradier expedition to Santa Isabel. Until 1888 the British and German fleets were the only ones to regularly connect Fernando Po with Europe. Various British trading posts operated in Fernando Po and in Río Muni: the West African

Company, John Holt, Ambas Bay, F. Wilson, Hatton & Cookson, and others. During World War I, the Spanish governor-general, Barrera, showed much more preference for Germany and facilitated the supply of arms to the then-German colony of Cameroon via Río Muni. For this reason the Spanish vessel SS *Mediterranea,* built in German, was impounded at Calabar on November 24, 1914, as a prize of war. Lord Luggard made no reply to Barrera's protests. Shortly after, a Spanish vessel with merchandise for Cameroon was seized. In March 1915, under the leadership of Lt. R. N. Law, two Germans (Lehning and G. Arm) were assassinated in Ayamiken. The Kribi zone was strongly guarded by the British. The tone of the Santa Isabel press was obviously anti-British. The British were worried over the large number of German refugees in Fernando Po. In spite of the problems created by differences with England, Spain did not replace Barrera until 1918.

In 1943, the Evangelical Publishing House (London) published *God at Work in Spanish Guinea* (75 pp.) by A. Thorne. Until Equatorial Guinea's independence, the United Kingdom was the third largest non-Spanish supplier, after the United States and West Germany, and the first banana buyer. In 1944, when a British military aircraft was downed over Fernando Po, the Spanish suspected espionage. After independence, the United Kingdom sought Guinean cocoa; in 1970 it supplied 61% of the country's non-Spanish imports ($2.5 million, or 170 million pesetas) having superseded the United States and West Germany. In 1970, with the help of British mercenaries, CEIA is supposed to have attempted to overthrow Macías Nguema. Diplomatic relations were established through the British Embassy in Yaoundé (Cameroon).

In 1981, the British ambassador to Cameroon, Bryan Sparrow, was also sent to Equatorial Guinea. The United Kingdom was present in April 1982 at the Donor Conference of the UNDP in Geneva. Beginning in August, the ports of the western coast of Great Britain were visited once a month by a vessel of the Equato-Guineo-Belgian Compagnie Africaine de Cabotage. According to the ambassador of Nigeria, Pobeni, Obiang Nguema had signed a contract with a British company for the deposit of toxic wastes in Annobón. British cooperation between 1986 and 1990 involved annual sums of 50,000 to 100,000 pounds worth of supplies. The United Kingdom did not grant any financial aid.

In 1996, several Equato-Guineans were in the UK to study English and details of the petroleum economy.

In 1998, the head of the British Council was invited by Mobil Oil to visit Malabo and consider setting up English classes there.

See also Forsyth; Teibiale Sipoto, J.

UNITED MERIDIAN CORPORATION (UMC). American petroleum company (Houston) founded in 1987. It had a strong presence in the Ivory Coast and Equatorial Guinea. Associated with Mobil Oil, it increased the drilling in the continental platform between Fernando Po and Cameroon.

At the beginning of the 1990s, UMC bought the rights of the Spanish seismic drills (they were in a basement in Geneva) for $10,000. In 1992, UMC paid $250,000 in royalties for drillings done in three blocks.

In 1996 UMC signed an agreement with the Nguemists for mining searches in Río Muni, especially for gold, diamonds, bauxite, and tantalite. In June 1996, one of the directors of United Meridian, John Brock, announced that the drillings in the Topacio-2 deposits offered the biggest reserves of oil and gas in the region (at a depth of 6,000 feet).

In August 1996, the company announced the extension of the oilfields of Zafiro and Toppacio. At the end of 1996, the Zafiro oilfield, composed of six wells, provided 40,000 b/d, but they intend to reach 80,000 b/d. At the end of 1996 and beginning of 1997, three satellite oilfields were discovered in Zafiro, but have not yet been exploited: Rubi, Jade, Serpentina. The initial investment was $233 million; Mobil had 75%.

Initially based in the U.S. and Canada, UMC's African production rose from 9% in January to 25% in December. UMC's shares on the New York Stock Exchange rose from 42% in 1995 to 161% between January and October 1996.

In January 1997, an explosion due to gas occurred on a platform drilling the well of Tsavorita #1; there were no major accidents. The company announced that the drillings done in Block B, Perla 1 (cost: $5 million) showed that the field was dry; shares dropped, the oilfield was abandoned. But in June, the potential of one of the wells in the oilfield of Topacio was confirmed. So far, 20 wells have been drilled with success. The Board of Directors of UMC approved an increase of $50 million. At the end of 1997, UMC was ready to buy a new area of 4,200 sq km. UMC is also present in Pakistan and Bangladesh.

Until March 1998, UMC had an exclusive permit for the mining prospecting of Río Muni; after it had to give up 75% of the prospected areas. In April, UMC merged with Ocean Energy.

See also Petroleum

UNITED NATIONS. The League of Nations was already dealing with Spanish Guinea at the time of forced labor imposed on Liberian workers in 1929–1930. After Spain's admission to the UN in 1955, various commissions examined the problem of the status of Spanish Guinea, in particular the Committee IV, later called the Committee of 24. Several resolutions of the General Assembly recommended independence for Spanish Guinea (nos. 2067, 2230, 2355). In July 1968, Bubi representatives pleaded in New York in favor of a separate independence for the two provinces, but the Afro-Asians, shaken by the Biafra war, rejected this new separatism. In the September 1968 sessions, a UN commission recognized the regularity of the poll. On November 12, 1968, Equatorial Guinea became the 126th member of the UN.

With the deterioration of Spanish-Guinean relations, Macías Nguema declared a state of emergency (Emergencia) and shortly after, on March 3, 1969, called on the UN and OAU to send experts to replace some of the 7,000 Spaniards who had fled his country. Equatorial Guinea also asked UN troops to replace the Spanish Guardia Civil still in the country, but to no avail, as the UN sent only a personal representative of the secretary-general. Of 87 experts requested, Guinea received 56 (27 teachers, 10 doctors, 7 engineers, 6 financial specialists, and a few others). UNDP was the most important agency, along with UNESCO, ILO, FAO, and UNIDO. WHO carried out projects under its own budget. In 1973 relations between UNDP and the Santa Isabel authorities became strained after the expulsion of the UN representative, Marceau Louis, and his assistants. They were not replaced for a year. Since the beginning of UN assistance, three WHO, one FAO, one World Bank, one UNESCO, and three UNDP experts have been expelled from Equatorial Guinea. Among the UN experts' achievements, despite imperfections due to local conditions, are the Centro de Desarrollo de la Educación, the Instituto de Seguridad Social, and the Medical Training School, but they have been in no position to train the expected personnel. The results of about $6 million spent in Equatorial Guinea between 1970 and 1976 are thus particularly meager. The UNDP budget for Equatorial Guinea for 1977–1981 reached $4.5 million (in 1972–1976 the figure was $3.5 million).

The UN has not taken a position regarding the problem of the 120,000 Equato-Guinean refugees. However, in August 1976, the Geneva-based UN Subcommittee for the Prevention of Discrimination and the Protection of Minorities, at the instigation of the London Anti-Slavery Society, has broken the silence and examined the tragic conditions in Equatorial Guinea. According to the Anti-Slavery Society, Macías Nguema seems to stay in power only with the help of UN programs. In February 1978 the same UN subcommittee resolved that Equatorial Guinea was one of a group of nine countries whose cases it was imperative to study. Equatorial Guinea refused the offer of personal contact between Secretary-General Waldheim and Equato-Guinean authorities in Santa Isabel. In 1968 minister Rafael Obiang explained that he had used the UNDP pouch mail to correspond with Mbá Ada, whom he helped to escape.

After the 1979 coup, a Nguemist, Nvono Nka Manene, represented Equatorial Guinea in the UN. In 1980 his uncle Mba Oñana joined him as counselor, but when he beat up his nephew in the UN building, he was recalled to Santa Isabel. In 1980 the country joined UNESCO and WHO, and in 1981 the ILO. In the summer of 1980, the junta made UNICEF cease its operations in the country and took over the 200 tons of food destined for refugees due to their return to the country. This food was sold by the government in the market. The UN Human Rights Commission sent a special rapporteur to the country in November 1979. He found his work considerably impeded by various members of the second Nguema dictatorship, particularly Mbá Oñana and Mba Nchama, both Esanguis from Mongomo. The successive reports of the UN Human Rights Commission show that the regime of Macías Nguema has in fact continued unchanged, and the UN complained of the lack of cooperation received from Obiang Nguema. Notwithstanding, the IMF provided $22 million in facilities. In April 1982 the UNDP organized a donors' conference in Geneva (the USSR and China did not participate). At this meeting $92 million of assistance was pledged to Equatorial Guinea, of which Spain alone contributed one-quarter. Between 1983 and 1987, the UN Human Rights Commission continued to accuse Equatorial Guinea of flagrant and repeated violations of human rights. It was not surprising that in March 1984 the commission refused to accept the credentials of the delegation that was to be led by the priest Ensema Mba, an Esangui from Mongomo. Equatorial Guinea is categorized as one of the least developed countries. Before independence it had been one of the most prosperous countries in sub-Saharan Africa.

In March 1987, Professor Eya Nchama recalled that the Commission of Human Rights had adopted a public rather than a private procedure, considering the alarming situation in Equatorial Guinea. In May 1987, M. Maalkassian, representative of the nongovernment organization UFER, deplored in front of the commission that no positive results came out of the UN efforts. "Despite the consultative services offered to Equatorial Guinea, the human rights are still violated."

The IMF observed the country in a state of bankruptcy shortly after the failing of the Guinextebank. The economic results showed that the targets accepted by Obiang Nguema had been missed by 45%. A reduction of 40% in the number of government officials was demanded, along with the privatization of public enterprises. In late 1987, the IMF expressed satisfaction with the economic policy and the dissolution of the Guinextebank. But the *Donogan Report* considered Equatorial Guinea "the second most corrupt country in the world."

In 1988, the IBRD committed itself to the rehabilitation of primary education. In April, the representative of WHO praised the "coup for liberty." In November the Round Table of the UNDP was held in Geneva. For 1988-91, 168 projects were planned and $58 million acquired. In December the IMF lent $16 million, of which $3.7 million were immediately given, to accelerate growth.

In January 1989 a project for the restructuring of the debt of $160 million was accepted. The annual service on the debt amounted to $20 million (half of annual exports). Total multilateral aid between 1986 and 1990 was $180 million. In 1989–1990, the recommendations of the IMF were not put into practice, leading to delay in payment of the second part of the structural adjustment facilities. In March, the UN secretary-general, J. Perez de Cuellar, stopped at Santa Isabel. He said that the country had made progress in the area of human rights but urged that the effort be kept up.

During 1990, the UNDP and WHO started a campaign against malaria, with a team of Cameroonian doctors. A British official of the IBRD, Andrew Lawson, was beaten in the capital by two policemen who were given a few months of house arrest as punishment.

In August 1991, the UNDP representative, Gustavo Toro, negotiated for technical assistance of $20 million in New York, double of the previous aid, for an efficient administration, the regeneration of forests, and the diversification of agriculture. Since the suspension of loans by the IMF in December 1989, the UN agencies showed more reserve with the government, which increased its promises but was little disposed to introduce reforms. In late 1991, D. Obiang Ngong (Mongomo) represented the country at the UN. Before the General Assembly, he criticized the stress laid on human rights.

In early 1992, two local employees of the UNDP were arrested by the army under the accusation of "sympathies with the opposition." In May it was learned that the ex-minister for Agriculture, Anatolio Ndong, had used UN funds to hire an expert for a government lumber company, taking a personal commission of 10%. The National Social Security Fund, created in 1973 with the participation of the ILO, was annually taxed FCFA 6 million by Obiang Nguema, for the PDGE or for personal needs. In August 1992, the UN Human Rights Commission stated that Obiang Nguema had solicited it to facilitate the return of 80,000 Equato-Guinean refugees living in Europe. In late 1992, the UNDP again intervened, with Spain, France, the U.S., and the EC, to demand an end to the human rights violations. The POC demanded the intervention of the UN Human Rights Commission, the EC, and the UN peacekeepers to ensure a democratic transition.

The resident representative of the UNDP in 1993 was M. Markku Visapaa. In April a delegation of the UNDP tried to help in the organization of legislative elections. It demanded a serious elector census; the revision of the electoral law; better collaboration with the UN Human Rights Commission; cessation of arbitrary arrest; guarantees for the return of the exiled; and the revision, with the opposition, of legal texts concerning amnesty, freedom of religion, of the press, and of assembly. The UN considered the law on political parties lacking in judicial security and that delays led to too-short elections. The constitutional basis of the electoral process was neither free, fair, nor honest, which condemned future results. The setting up of a civil police was demanded, and it regretted that the electoral law avoided the question of the presidential election. The government refuted the report and condemned it. The UN decided to withdraw from the electoral process. On September 21, 1993, a UNDP delegation sought information from the police commissioner of the capital (see Ela Nseng) regarding a Ghanaian guard of the FAO who was arrested while he was reading *La Verdad*. The group was accused of supporting the opinions of the POC and was thrown into the streets and insulted. The Ghanaian had been beaten in order to obtain a false confession.

In 1993, the UNDP has spent in Equatorial Guinea $1,638,000 (US), and in 1994, $1,021,000.

A. Artucio's March 1994 report on the human rights situation in Equatorial Guinea gave an apocalyptic vision of a country without law. In May, Artucio again stayed in Equatorial Guinea and published a report showing some slight changes. From June 1–3, a donors' conference took place in the capital, presided over by the infamous civil minister of foreign affairs, Batho Obama Nsue. But the round table was cancelled due to differences with the opposition, the government giving priority to dissident factions. The UNDP reported that a political agreement between parties and the government was indispensable for the aid to become effective.

The UNDP resident representative in 1995 was M. Michael Akswith. A. Artucio's 1995 report was discussed in February at the UN Human Rights Commission. Apart from the observation of some local improvements, mainly at Bata and in the capital, the report stressed the persistence of grave violations of fundamental liberties in all areas. The amounts allocated by the UNDP between 1972 and 1996 totaled $36 million.

The resident representative in 1996 was Mansourou Chitou. On December 6, 1996, 20 policemen led by superintendent Juan Engonga surrounded the house of Arsenio Moro Malonga, administrator of the UNDP office, while he was working in the UN office, because Moro is a relative of C. Bakale, one of the leaders of the CPDS.

In 1998, Teodoro Nsue Biyongo, son-in-law of Obiang Nguema, was first secretary of the UN mission.

Here is the evolution of the ranking of Equatorial Guinea concerning human development (UNDP):

Year	Range	Life Expectancy at Birth (years), 1995	Adult Literacy Rate % 1995	Real GDPC/ capita, 1995
1991	137	47	44.9	700*
1992	143	47	50.2	706*
1993	155	47	50.2	700*
1994	150	47.3	51.5	700*
1995	142	48	75.3	700*
1996	131	48.2	76.4	1,800
1997	135	48.6	77.8	1,673
1998	135	49	77.8	1,712

* Estimation. The real GDP per capita in 1996–1998 is purely theoretical, since the country's primary resources (lumber, oil) being monopolized by the very small minority of members belonging to the Mongomo Clan.

See also Artucio, A.; Banks; Borders; Buchanan, R.; Canada; Convergency for Social Democracy; Constitution; Demography; Denmark; Diplomacy; Drugs; Duhalde, E. L.; Education; Elections; Elema Borengue, J.; Eveme Ovono, J.; Engonga Motulu, M.; Esono Mika, P. J.; European Union; Eya Nchama, C. M.; Germany; Gold; Human Rights; Malavo, E.; Mae Ela, F.; Mba Ekua Miko, B.; Mba Ondo, M.; Miko Abogo, P.; Ndong, D.; Nepotism; Nigeria; Nve Nzeng, A. F.; Obiang Ndong, D.; Obiang Nguema, T.; Okenve Edjang, A.; Parliament; Press; Public Health; Refugees; Río Muni; Rumania; Sharaoui Popular Republic; SEDES; South Africa; Toro, G.; Toxic Wastes; Transports; UNICEF; Venezuela; *Verdad, La;* Volio Jimenez, F.

UNITED NATIONS DEVELOPMENT PROGRAM (UNDP) See United Nations

UNITED STATES OF AMERICA. In 1859, Spain authorized the U.S. to establish aa coal deposit in Playa Carboneras, near Santa Isabel, for the supply of civil steamers. From 1850 to 1968 American Presbyterian missionaries arrived regularly in Guinea, in particular in Corsico and Río Benito. In 1927 T. J. Faulkner alerted public opinion in the U.S., revealing forced labor among the Liberian workers, which caused the intervention of the League of Nations and the disruption of recruitment. From 1900 to 1936 the ecclesiastical district of Corsico was connected to the New Jersey synod, later to that of Cameroon, and since 1960 to the New Jersey one again. Since 1933, the Protestant Worldwide Evangelization Crusade (WEC; Fort Washington, PA) directed a mission in Río Muni. From 1961 on, WEC was represented by Mrs. M. O. McDermid, but in 1969 she was obliged to leave the country.

Until independence the U.S. was Guinea's second commercial partner. The first representative of Equatorial Guinea to the United Nations, S. Ibongo Iyanga, started a thesis on international relations at Columbia University; six months later he was assassinated.

Diplomatic relations with the U.S. were begun on November 21, 1968. In January 1969, only a few weeks before Ndongo Miyone's assassination, Secretary of State William Rogers received the minister of foreign affairs concerning the Biafra War. On March 4, 1969, the U.S. evacuated its nationals still in Equatorial Guinea, knowing of the coup planned by Ndongo Miyone. After the departure of the first American ambassador, the U.S. sent only ambassador deputies to Equatorial Guinea. The Santa Isabel embassy was closed after one of the officials, D. J. Leahy, seemed to have been killed with a pair of scissors by his colleague A. J. Erdos, who was charged with murder upon his return to the U.S. on September 4, 1971. At various times Macías Nguema declared he had been threatened by plots hatched with the help of the U.S.. Since 1971 the U.S. embassy in Cameroon has represented the country, paying biannual visits to Santa Isabel and Bata. Except for an expert of the IBRD in 1972–1973, no American citizen has since resided in the country. Diplomatic relations were suspended on March 15, 1976, after Ambassador H. Spiro and Counsul W. Mithoefer, at the end of one of their biannual visits to Equatorial Guinea, received an offensive message declaring them personae non grata.

Between 1963 and 1971 the U.S. paid $30,000 for an anti-smallpox campaign in Equatorial Guinea. But their real interests went to oil prospecting ($15 million, or 960 million pesetas), which has remained unsuccessful (Gulf Oil, Mobil Oil, Chevron, Continental, Valmer). In 1969 the United States Steel Company was refused a general concession for mineral prospecting because of monopoly requirements and the inadequacy of proposed royalties. In 1970 the Chevron Company asked the American Hunting Geology and Geophysics, Ltd. to carry out an aerial geological survey. In 1971–1972 the General Cocoa Company of New York paid a Ghanaian-American couple $2.5 million for Guinean cocoa, which was never paid to Equatorial Guinea. The couple was arrested in Ghana in March 1973. In mid-1972 some Guinean refugees, former members of the MONALIGE, founded the FRELIGE in New York.

The preparations for the 1979 coup d'etat seem to have been known to American authorities. After Macias nguema's desitution, the "Catholics for Christian Political Action" group asked the U.S. government to take note of the fact that the coup had not brought any change in Equatorial Guinea. In January 1981, USAID granted $1 million to assist agricultural cooperatives and a poultry farm. A number of oil companies asked for permission to undertake drilling operations (Exxon, Texaco, Mobil, Atlantic Richfield, Getty, etc.). In December 1981 the first ever visit of a U.S. warship (USS *Kalamazoo*) was made to Santa Isabel. Another visit was made at the end of December 1983 by the USS *Spiegel Grove,* whose Captain Summerlin assured Obiang Nguema of U.S. friendship. From 1983 on, American encouragement was given to Equatorial Guinea's increasing ties with France. The Murphy Oil Company entered into an association with the consortium led by ELF-Aquitaine in December 1983, with a view to undertaking drilling operations in Río Muni.

In October 1986, Obiang Nguema was received by officials of USAID in New York, asking them for assistance (press, radio, television, agriculture). During the same month, the U.S. State Department published the new edition of the *Post Report on Equatorial Guinea* for U.S. foreign service staff, including the following information: "Professional and labor organizations are non-existent"; "The local newspaper is almost never published"; "The educational system is quite poor"; "For a variety of historical and social reasons, Guineans are reluctant to socialize because Government employees frequently require Government permission to accept social invitations." The report underlines clearly that "The country is under absolute rule of the President." In 1986, however, the U.S. delivered a coastal patrol boat.

Edward Norris, Jr., was the ambassador of the U.S. from 1987 to 1991. In September 1987, the U.S. planned to close its embassy as an economy measure, but this did not happen. In November, the counsellor for African affairs of the State Department visited Equatorial Guinea on a mission. William Robertson told Obiang Nguema that President Reagan continued his support of the regime. An agreement on the volunteers of the Peace Corps (32) was signed.

In 1988, a Spanish lawyer negotiated in Santa Isabel on behalf of a North American enterprise for the deposit of radon-contaminated earth near Bata. In 1989, aid reached $1 million. The U.S. delivered yet another patrol boat, the *Isla de Bioco,* meant to chase away illegal fishing vessels in Equato-Guinean territorial waters (in fact it was to prevent the return of the exiled to neighboring countries). Toward the end of the year, the U.S. planned to write off the Equato-Guinean debt. A nine-year contract was signed for the burying, near Bata, of wastes (garbage) from New York that were said to be nontoxic. In 1990, the American Robert Klitgaard, former lawyer of the IBRD and consultant in Equatorial Guinea for one year, published his book *Tropical Gangsters: One Man's Experience with Development and Decadence in Deepest Africa.*

In August 1991, the ECA reported the rejection by Nguemists of a proposal to deposit toxic wastes from the U.S. via a Panamanian company. The State Department's Annual Report to the Congress on the human rights situation still described a disconcerting situation. The chapter on Equatorial Guinea was much more strict in its criticism than the one by the UN Human Rights Commission. Ambassador Chester E. Norris was replaced by John E. Bennet. Chester then became president of the oil company Walter International, which was to ensure Yankee supremacy on Equato-Guinean petroleum before Mobil and others took over. Ambassador John E. Bennett opened his premises to more than 100 students in the evening in order to facilitate their studies and provided seats, tables, and drinking water. For 1988, U.S. aid totalled $850,000.

In early 1992 10 Peace Corps volunteers remained, most in the capital. The director of the Institute of Ebebiyin, an agent of the President's Criminal Investigations Department, Obiang Nguema's friend, deputy, and member of the central committee of the PDGE, José-Cosme, set off the departure of the Peace Corps posted in Ebebiyin after his house was broken into. In late April, Ambassador Bennett attended the inauguration of the first petroleum platform and the filling of the first tanker in Santa Isabel. On July 4 he strongly denounced the arrests and human rights violations and said he was totally in agreement with the report by Volio-Jimenez. On October 15 the embassy published an *Update on Political Detainees,* along with the EC's *Update.* In late 1992, the U.S. again intervened, along with Spain, France, the EC, and the UN, to demand an end to human rights violations.

On Christmas Day 1992, the spokesman for the State Department, Richard Boucher, underlined the American concern regarding the unceasing repression of the political opposition and the hardly hidden violence used on ambassadors and other American citizens, among whom were members of the Peace Corps. Most often, the government does not respect its democratic propositions. since then, cooperation with Equatorial Guinea has been stopped.

In early 1993 there were 75 Americans, including a dozen missionaries and 30 petroleum company employees, in the country. Bennet received death threats, and so did the ambassador of Spain. A mysterious National Movement for Equatorial Guinea, which claimed to struggle against imperialism and colonialism, accused Bennet of "diabolical actions" and of "inciting violence." This was due to the shooting of the ambassador of France at Kinshasa. The American government held Obiang Nguema responsible for anything that may happen to any American citizen and decided to withdraw its last 10 Peace Corps volunteers.

In late May, Obiang Nguema met the Deputy Secretary of State for Foreign Affairs George Moose, who stressed the confidence of the American government in Ambassador Bennet. Toward the end of August, the Spanish press revealed secret official documents stating that Moto Nsá was the puppet of the U.S. and Spain for the presidency of Equatorial Guinea. During the celebrations of the twenty-fifth anniversary of independence, security services tried to take away the camera of the ambassador. The American State Department qualified the November 21 elections as a "parody of democracy." Washington invited the international community to "reconsider collaboration with the regime of Teodoro Obiang" and denounced post-election brutalities. The Nguemists accused Bennet of sorcery when he laid flowers on the tomb of 10 British soldiers who had died in an air crash in 1944; they declared him a "non-credible partner in dialogue." The 1993 State Department Report on Human Rights, published in 1994, described a serious increase in political assassinations. "President Obiang remains the source of political power. Citizens do not have the right to change their government by democratic means. There have been no free elections since 1968. All Government employees—judges, legislators, mayors, civil servants, and security forces—serve at the pleasure of the President."

On January 20, 1994, the U.S. made it known that Obiang Nguema's official visit to the U.S. was not timely. During this time, thanks to the installations of the U.S. Pierce International Communications Company, the Nguemists jammed the broadcasts of Radio Exterior de España. In the State Department, the Desk Officer for Equatorial Guinea was Mary Beth Leonard. Moto Nsá met her in November 1994, along with Arleen Render, director of the Bureau for Central Africa. During 1994, C. E. Norris, president of Walter Int., was received at Santa Isabel by Obiang Nguema, confirming that the huge American petroleum interests were acting without the knowledge of authorities in Washington.

Following the condemnation of Moto Nsá in April, the United States demanded the release of political prisoners under the threat of nonrecognition of the validity of the municipal elections. Four representatives of Obiang Nguema who had come to negotiate a petroleum contract were prevented from making contact with the

Clinton administration in May. From May 1995, the person formerly in charge of mines, Pastor Micha Ondo Bile, from Mongomo, was ambassador to the U.S. In August 1995 a full page glorifying the work of Obiang Nguema appeared in the *New York Times*. The U.S. State Department, in its April 1996 Report on Human Rights, stated that "During the September [1995] election campaign, a guard at the former U.S. Embassy was arrested by police and beaten. Police released him after high level diplomatic intervention. His late uncle, a political opponent of the regime, had been beaten to death in Malabo's Blackbeach Prison 2 years before [1993]." In September 1995, a spokesman of the Department of State, Nicholas Burns, denied the accusation that Ambassador Bennet supported an attempted coup d'etat by calling it "sheer fiction." In October 1995, the U.S. closed its embassy and only left a chargé d'affaires in its place, in spite of Nguemist protests; Joseph O'Neill occupied the post. In 1995 the U.S. took first place among the clients of Equatorial Guinea due to petroleum, and was fourth among its suppliers.

To improve the image of Equatorial Guinea and its regime, the dictator hired public affairs company Black, Manafort, Stone & Kelly for a six-month contract for $56 million, running up to December 14, 1995 (two months before the fraudulent presidential elections). The U.S. embassy was closed in November 1995. After his visit to the US at the end of 1995, Obiang Nguema no longer required American citizens to have a visa. From 1993 to 1997, the U.S. exported to Equatorial Guinea lumber products for: 1993 ($17,000), 1994 ($42,000), 1995 ($22,000), then nothing else since 1996. In 1994 and 1997 several meat preparations were sent: 1994 ($17,000), 1997 ($80,000). In 1994/1995, the U.S. bought hardwood: 1994 (24.041 cu m); 1995 (22.391 cu m), then nothing else since 1996. In 1995, 11 Equato-Guinean trainees worked in the American administration. Since then, the Consular Information Sheets (mostly the one of May 13, 1996) underlined that consular and diplomatic American staff are forbidden to fly with the national airline EGA (Equatorial Guinea Airlines), which does not meet minimum security requirements. Also in May, the U.S. Overseas Security Advisory Council reported that Ninjas, who are often drunk and heavily armed, are extremely dangerous.

According to Obiang Nguema's admission, the Equato-Guinean Embassy in Washington was financed by Mobil Corp. The Carter Foundation planned to send in observers for the presidential election in February 1996. It finally decided not to participate in this "farce," except for sending President Carter's relative, Chip Carter, who was invited by the South African Strategic Concepts. Some "petro-observers" sent in by Mobil and Nomeco also arrived on the spot.

In April 1996, the U.S. Report on Human Rights Practices for 1995 addressed to the Congress by the State Department, gave an apocalyptic vision of Nguemist Equatorial Guinea.

> President Obiang exercises control over the police and security force. . . the security forces committed serious human rights abuses. . . .Serious human rights abuses continue. . .severe restriction of freedom of speech; arbitrary arrests and detention, physical abuses of prisoners; extrajudicial killings; torture; judicial system subject to executive influence; no press and foreign publications; no access to broadcasting from opposition parties; elected Chamber dominated by the government; citizens have no right to change

their Government by democratic means. . .the president exercises complete power as Head of State, commander of the armed forces and leader of the government party. . .the President's Democratic Party of Equatorial Guinea (PDGE) controls the judiciary and the legislature, the latter through fraudulent elections.

Even though Equatorial Guinea is nominally a multiparty constitutional republic, power is actually exercised by the dictator and his subclan from Mongomo. Under the protection of this totalitarian and bloody power, American companies extracted increasing volumes of oil and gas, profits from which did not appear in the nation's budget.

On May 16, 1996, Obiang Nguema accepted the credentials of the new U.S. Ambassador, Charles C. Twinnings. American companies have already invested millions of dollars in projects in Equatorial Guinea, especially Mobil and United Meridian, with more than $250 million. During the summer of 1996, Mobil extracted 40,000b/d. A lamentable information guide called *The Republic of Equatorial Guinea,* disseminated in 1996 by the firm of Black, Kelly, Scrugs & Healy, of Washington, according to which Equatorial Guinea is a paradise of democracy, invites investors to the Nguemist republic. In Washington, Miko and Bakale were received on October 24 by the Officer for Central African affairs, J. C. Spiegel, and the secretary of state for Africa, William Tuwaddel, who confirmed what the democratic opposition had affirmed for a long time: the election of Obiang Nguema was irregular. On October 25 they were greeted at the White House by S. H. McCormick, director of the National Security Council for Africa. He promised to convince American oil companies to change their attitude.

At the beginning of 1997, there were about 30 Americans in the country (excluding diplomatic staff). The ambassador Charles H. Twinning resided in Yaoundé. The U.S. was represented in Equatorial Guinea by consul Kent C. Brokenshire. In June 1997, Lisa Peterson was head of the area of Equatorial Guinea at the State Department. She met Elema. On June 16, the spokesman for the State Department, Nicolas Burns, said to journalists that "in the two and a half years I worked as spokesman, not once was I asked about Equatorial Guinea." Also in June, President Clinton mentioned a "Partnership for Economic Growth and Opportunity." Private investments were encouraged. In the beginning of August 1997, a seminar on "Press and Democracy" was organized in Malabo, financed by the U.S. and UNESCO, with the participation of about 30 African journalists who arrived from Yaoundé with the American ambassador and the American consul, by EGA plane. At the end of 1997, the former ambassador in Equatorial Guinea and Togo, Rush Taylor, vice-president of the Equator Bank, opened an advisory agency specializing in contracts with African presidents. During the first half of 1997, Swiss authorities seized 82 elephant tusks and 6 sculpted ones, belonging to two Americans in transit coming from Equatorial Guinea.

In spite of the warnings given by a few American specialists such as Professors R. Fegley, I. Sundiata, and D. Yates, as well as some very severe criticism of Obiang Nguema's regime by the Department of State in its annual report on human rights, and in spite of the denunciation of Nguemist terror by the Protestant and

Catholic churches, the UN Human Rights Commission, and Amnesty International, the American business world has kept ties with the dictatorship. In January 1997, the Corporate Council on Africa organized a tour of the Ivory Coast, the Congo, and Equatorial Guinea, with representatives of 35 companies and several members of Parliament, including the president of the Budget Commission of the House of Representatives, Bill Archer. The tour was sponsored by Equator Bank and Occidental Petroleum. Ambassador Micha Ondo Bile (from Mongomo) declared to the *Washington Post* in 1997: "We have a loving country of peace and freedom." On July 17 of the same year, he became ambassador in Argentina.

At the beginning of 1998, the South African firm Enviroserve annouonced it was going to dump New York garbage in a nonspecified African country. On January 30, the State Department published the report on Human Rights in the world, with a very severe chapter with regards to Equatorial Guinea. During Obiang Nguema's stay in the U.S. in June, the dictator met high officials of the State Department, as well as members of the Corporation of American Firms in Africa. They signed an agreement on the guarantee of investments. On July 21, President Clinton appointed Melvis Yates as ambassador. He was preceded by the chargé d'affaires Joseph O'Neill.

Among Americans living in Equatorial Guinea there are military councillors of the 3rd Special Forces Group (Fort Bragg, NC), who train infantry Nguemist troops in small unit tactics, on-ground navigation, reconnaissance, and medical assistance.

According to the Americans who work in the oil business in Equatorial Guinea, the measures taken to protect the environment are inferior to those of the U.S.

The sculptor Leandro Mbomio has received honorary citizenship from Dade County, Florida.

D. Yates, of the American University in Paris, declared in 1998 that "The United States are in a situation where they must defend the Equato-Guinean people against a dictator funded by American oil companies. For anyone who has the remotest idea of the relationship between oil and power, the prospect of the United States interfering in Equatorial Guinea seems highly unlikely."

Since 1968, the following diplomats have worked in Equatorial Guinea:

1968–1969: Albert W. Sherer, with residence at Lomé (Togo), accredited on November 21, 1968. The Embassy in Santa Isabel was opened August 1, 1969, with Albert N. Williams as chargé d'affaires during the interim.

1969–1972: Lewis Hoffacker, with residence at Yaoundé (Cameroon), accredited on January 21, 1970.

1972–1975: C. Robert Moore, with residence at Yaoundé, accredited on January 9, 1973.

1975–1976: Herbert J. Spiro, with residence at Yaoundé, accredited on September 1, 1975. On March 14, 1976, he was declared persona non grata.

1979–1980: Mable Murphy Smythe, with residence at Yaoundé, accredited on December 19, 1979.

1980–1981: Hume A. Horan, with residence at Yaoundé, accredited on August 14, 1980. On June 11, 1981, the embassy in Malabo was reopened, with Joanne Thomson as chargé d'affairs during the interim.

1981–1984: Alan M. Hardy, with residence at Malabo, accredited on November 19, 1981.

1984–1988: Francis Stephen Ruddy, with residence at Malabo, accredited on January 27, 1985.

1988–1991: Chester E. Norris, Jr., with residence at Malabo, accredited on March 15, 1988. Chairman of the petroleum company Walter Int.

1991–1994: John E. Bennet, with residence in Malabo, accredited on September5, 1994.

1995–1998: Charles H. Twinning, with residence at Malabo, accredited on May 16, 1996.

1998– :John Melvin Yates, with residence at Yaoundé.

In 1997, the United States set up a military academy in Ekuku, close to Bata, "Interarmas," that trains officers (effective or not, like Teodorín Nguema Obiang). The American staff of Mobil Oil—as well as Teodorín—lives in the residential houses of Abayak, built by Obiang Nguema and located close to the capital.

See also Akurenam; Bennet, J.; Carter, Chip; Catholicism; Currency; Education; Elections; France; Human Rights; Internet; Missions; Mobil Oil; Moto Nsá; Navigation; Nomeco; Norris, C.; Obama Nsue Mangue, F. (M'Batho); Petroleum; Trade; Tuwaddel, W.; Walter International.

UNIVERSITY. In August 1980 Obiang Nguema announced the construction of the first University of Equatorial Guinea, financed by Spain, in Santa Isabel. In fact, only the Spanish University for Distance Education (UNED) was active in Equatorial Guinea, mainly providing law courses for Obiang Nguema. But in 1992 Obiang Nguema had still not received his degree for administrative reasons (lack of a baccalaureate). In nine years, only five students completed their studies, including Ponciano Mbomio (law). The course was more expensive than that of Harvard. On December 1993, as part of the post-election repression, 80 people were arrested and tortured in Río Muni, including students and professors of UNED. In August 1981 the project for the creation of the National University was signed. In June 1996, F. Edjo Ovono was appointed dean of the university. On August 19, 1996, the first stone of the University was laid in the presence of Lieutenant-General Obiang Nguema. Integrated in the University are the National Institute for Agriculture, the National Institute for Public Administration, and the National Institute for Health.

UNED declared in 1998 that Equatorial Guinea is the only country for which voluntary teachers and examiners are needed. Since 1980, there have only been 22 university graduates (8 in law, 14 in sciences of education). In mid-1998, the national university had 165 students enrolled in forestry engineering, agronomy, in the faculties of liberal arts, social sciences, and teacher training. The monthy scholarship amounts to FCFA 70,000, of which 10,000 are given to the student every month, the amount covering school fees.

See also Education.

URBANISM see Nsue Obama Angono, P.; Nsue Mokuy, A.

UREKA. Southernmost locality of Fernando Po, situated in one of the most humid areas of the earth with more than 10 m of rain per year, slightly exceeded by Cape

Debunja, at the foot of Mount Cameroon. A hotel on the road from the capital to the airport is called Ureka. It belonged to the group called Escuder y Galiana.

USERA Y ALARCON, Father Jeronimo Mariano. Born on September 15, 1810. Taught latin in Madrid. His brother Gabriel was surgeon to the crown; his sister Eugenia, wife of Tomas de Corray y Oña, doctor of the queen (he delivered Alfonso XII); his brother Pedro, inspector of the royal gardens. At the age of 14, he entered a Cistercian convent and studied philosophy. He was ordained a priest in 1834. Due to the anti-clericalism of those days, his order was abolished in 1840. Usera gaught latin and greek at the Central University of Madrid. In 1843, Queen Isabel II entrusted to him Ndowe Quir and Yeg, who had arrived from Corisco. He educated them. On July 18, 1845, he left for Fernando Po on the *Venus* and arrived at Christmastime.

Due to his ability in languages, he wrote a catechism, a grammar book, and a Bubi dictionary. He drew a map of the island. After he became very ill, he left on March 25, 1846. During his convalescence, he wrote "Memorias of Fernando Po," then became the priest of Queen Isabel II. He never returned to Africa. In 1848 he was in charge of the cathedral of Santiago de Cuba. After the arrival of Antonio María Claret as archbishop, they became partners. Both received the Order of Isabel the Catholic. Claret founded the Claretins, Usera, the sisters of the Love of God. Both were very respectful of the pope's infallibility. By decree, Isabel II named him dean of the cathedral of san Juan of Puerto Rico in 1853. In 1855, he had to return to Spain because he had contracted yellow fever. In 1960 he met Pope Pius IX. By royal decree, he was authorized to remain in Spain. In April 1864, the first 12 novices of his order were gathered. He died on March 17, 1898, in Havana, in poverty. He is in the process of being sanctified.

The Claretinians are settled down: on Fernando Po at Malabo and Luba; on Annobon, at Palé; in Rio Muni, at Bata, Ebebiyin, Kogo, Niefang, Nzok Nsomo.

The Claretian Congregation presently works in Spain, Portugal, France, Italy, Germany, the Cape Verge islands, Angola, Mozambique, California, Mexido, Peru, Bolivia, Chile, Cuba, Puerto Rico, Dominican republic.

UTAMBONI, Río (or Mitemele). River in the south of Río Muni, running through impressive canyons. Its lower course forms the border with Gabon. It flows into the Muni estuary. Río Utamboni was one of the penetration routes used by Iradier, Bonelli y Hernando, and Bengoa. In 1846, 600-ton steamers proceeded inland on it up to 60 miles. Along the estuary are the localities of Calatrava and Kogo. The riverbanks were dotted with British, German, French, and Catalan warehouses. The Utamboni is a potential producer of about 80,00 kW. See Akalayong; Kogo.

UTONDE, Río. Rather short river of Río Muni, north of Bata. A large forest concession of Alena occupies its banks, with an old timber company's railway track. The region shows major traces of rutile (titania orthobioxyde). A sawmill that was still operating in 1976 is situated near the mouth of the river.

❖ V ❖

VAKHRAMEYEV, Lev Alkeksandrovich. Ambassador from the Soviet Union in 1991.

VAN BOVEN, Theo. Former director of the United Nations Human Rights Division.
See also Diplomacy.

VATICAN. In November 1981, the second vice-president, Seriche Bioco Dougan, invited Pope John Paul II to visit Santa Isabel. The visit took place on February 18, 1982. The pope went both to Santa Isabel and Bata. The pope pleaded for reconciliation, but he made no mention of human rights, although these were often evoked in the case of Poland. In September 1982 Obiang Nguema paid a return visit to the pope. In April 1995, the apostolic nuncio Santos Abril Castellón (who lives in Yaoundé, Cameroon) intervened on behalf of Pope John Paul II to ask Obiang Nguema for clemency for Moto Nsá, The request was qualified as purely humanitarian.

On June 28, 1998, he appointed Felix del Blanco Prieto Apostolic Nonce of Cameroon and Apostolic Nonce of Equatorial Guinea.
See also Catholicism.

VAZ SERRA, Liviano. Finca rústica, in Sácriba (Fernando Po), sold in 1985 to Nka Esono Nsing (Mongomo) for FCFA 8,743,437.

VENEZUELA. In April 1981 Maye Ela visited Venezuela during his tour in Latin America. Venezuela participated in the donor conference of the UNDP in Geneva in April 1982. Businessman Modo Akuse, general secretary of the Democratic and Social Union, stated that he was supported by the Venezuelan economic circles. In 1992, Venezuela signed a petroleum agreement.

On October 29, 1997, in the Venezuelan harbor of Guaranao (Punto Fijo), the national guard stopped a ship (*Lady Belle*), sailing under the Malabo Equatorial Guinea flag, with 2.5 tons of cocaine. It seems it was given away by an anonymous phone call. The ship was coming from the Panama Canal and heading to Miami. In Venezuela, it had to load 200 t of sesame. Ten sailors were arrested (Dominicans, Colombians, Venezuelans). The cocaine had been loaded in Baranquilla (Colombia). According to Venevision, the drug came from the Cartel of Cali.

One of Obiang Nguema's sons studied there in 1997.

VERDAD, La (The Truth). Periodical of the Convergency for Social Democracy (CPDS). It was the only regular monthly in the country (forced to be covertly circulated) to reveal in detail the scams of the regime. A number of readers were arrested and tortured, in addition to the staff. Amnesty International and Reporters without Borders denounced these arrests.

Toward the end of September 1993, Julio Ndong Ela Mangue, minister for the interior; Manuel Nguema Mba, secretary of state for national security; and Siale Bilekia, prime minister, surrounded by Ninjas, summoned and threatened a CPSD delegation. The same day, a United Nations delegation that had come to inquire about the whereabouts of a Ghanaian guard of the UNDP accused of having read *La Verdad,* was insulted and expelled. *La Verdad* was banned, but the CPDS ignored it and published issues on the occasion of the electoral farce in November.

In January 1994, Reporters without Borders protested at the banning of *La Verdad* by the minister for the interior, J. Ndong Ela Mangue, and made death threats. The leaders of the CPDS again announced that they would not obey, as they wanted to play the game democratically. In May 1995, the two editors of *La Verdad,* Bakale Obiang and Andrés Esono, were once again imprisoned. C. Bakale Obiang was again thrown into prison and tortured, with some others, in February and then in April 1996. See also Bakale Obiang, C.; Miko Abongo, P.

VICENTE, Francisco. Merchant of Baleares (Menorca) and shipping captain settled in Corisco around 1834–1835. See also Simo, B.

VICE-PRESIDENCY. The two successive vice-presidents of Equatorial Guinea since 1968 were assassinated: Bubi Bosio Dioco, in Santa Isabel in February 1975; Fang Eyegue Ntutumu, a relative of Macías Nguema, arrested in 1976 and executed in 1979. Bosio Dioco, according to official statements, committed "suicide." The vice-presidency was then given to Macías Nguema's cousin Bonifacio Ondo Obiang. After the 1979 coup two vice-presidents were created. The first was given to Obiang Nguema's cousin Maye Ela and the second to his other cousin, Ela Nseng. Ondo Obiang was then sent as ambassador to Ethiopia. Late in 1980, Ela Nseng was replaced by Oyo Riqueza, the latter being sent to Peking as ambassador. In 1983 Seriche Bioco Dougan took over the first vice-presidency from Maye Ela, who was sent to serve as ambassador to the United Nations. Seriche Bioco was concurrently prime minister. The post of vice-president disappeared in 1992.

See also Bosio Dioco; Ela Nseng; Eyegue Ntutumu; Maye Ela; Mba Oñana; Nguema Esono Nchama; Presidency; Suicides.

VICTIMS. In 1978, some parts of the border with Cameroon, used by citizens fleeing Nguemism, had ditches with sharp stakes. A number of Equato-Guineans were impaled there. These ditches have since been filled up.

In November 1979, before the special rapporteur of the United Nations Human Rights Commission, Volio-Jimenez, Maye Ela, first vice-president and minister of foreign affairs, admitted that the Juventud en marcha con Macias had committed a number of arbitrary acts (rapes, terror) tolerated by the army arguing that the Juventud was directly answerable to Macías Nguema. Volio-Jimenez learned that the arrests and torture of priests had considerably increased from 1975, i.e., since Obiang Nguema was chief of the army. The political prisoners of the Macías Nguema era were not released, except at Bata and Santa Isabel, and remained a large number in Akonibe, Akurenam, Añisok, Ebebiyin, Evinayong, Kogo, Mikomeseng, Niefang, N'sork, Río Benito, and San Carlos.

In August 1990, Amnesty International demanded the release of six prisoners of opinion, and invited the Nguemists to reform the Constitution in order to ban exceptional courts and to obtain impartial judgments. The need to urgently put an end to the tortures was stressed. Amnesty International published its report, *Equatorial Guinea: Torture,* stating that the information on the excesses of the regime were available to it since the earliest days of Obiang Nguema's regime (1979). On September 12, Amnesty International reiterated: "Torture was 'accepted practice' in Equatorial Guinea [Nguemist] and suspects were completely at the mercy of soldiers and guards of the prison." This was followed by the enumeration of the methods of torture. "The government must immediately remind each one that torture will no longer be tolerated." In December, the Spanish jurist J. M. Sanz Bayón submitted a report to the UN Human Rights Commission, in which he observed that the Nguemist state was

nominally republican, it was really an oligarchy in which the real power resided in the so-called "clan from Mongomo". . .No political opposition exists nor are any authorised and so the liberty of expression was eliminated if it involed criticising the government, its acts and its members in any nammer. . . .In police stations, the application of corporal punishment was frequent.

On the 23rd anniversay of independence, October 12, 1991, a report of the Committee for Human Rights in the 86th Conference of the Interparliamentary Union (Santiago, Chile) "spoke of its preoccupation with regard to the regularity of the procedure leading to the loss of the Parliamentary mandate of M. Ebang Mbele Abang [vice-president of the Nguemist Parliament] and to the fact that he had been under house arrest as a result of the opinions he had expressed in the Parliament." It went on to recall "that the situation of M. Ebang Mbele Abang was incompatible with the customary right according to Human Rights."

In October 1992, Reporters without Borderss brought up the case of the chemist Placido Micó, "beaten, tortured till it became unbearable. . ." The report by Amnesty International reiterated its "appeals to the government in favour of the adoption and the application of guarantees against torture, but this request was not responded to." Long lists of political prisoners were published between October and December by the U.S. Embassy, with details on the exactions undergone. This situation led the EC not only to denounce the "violence" on behalf of the members of the opposition, and to express the "preoccupation" of the 12, but also to force Nguemist Equatorial Guinea to respect human rights. On November 27 and December 22, Amnesty International again published urgent communiqués about 150 students and teachers arrested and tortured in the capital as well as Bata. There were some priests among them.

In early 1993, the special rapporteur of the Human Rights Commission, F. Volio-Jimenez, observed in his new report that for many long years,

the Human Rights situation. . .has not changed. One can see the continuation. . .of political and institutional conditions which constitute a significant obstacle to the free exercise of fundamental rights and to the judicial protection of these rights. So the power remains concentrated in the hands of the President of the Republic. . .the situation was worsened by the fact that the government [Nguemist]. . .did not show the necessary will to give up its current repressive policy.

In January, Amnesty International again expressed its fears with regard to torture and the violation of fundamental freedoms. "The Equato-Guinean social situation sometimes moves towards total degradation." Like the uncle-father Macías Nguema, Obiang Nguemas created popular hatred. At the UNO, the minster of foreign affairs/Francophone countries, B. Mba Ekua Mikó demanded that the Third World populations be helped to develop democracy and the fundamental freedoms. It was what the 95 Equato-Guinean students, studying in Russia and abandoned by the government which considered that a scholarship of 200 pesetas per month was sufficient, wished for. An unexpected victim of Nguemism was the U.S. ambassador, John Bennet, who had returned to his post after being recalled for consultation following death threats sent to him. The Nguemists called his July 4, 1993, speech a "series of offences and attacks against the government of Equatorial Guinea." Though he spoke in the name of the American government, the Nguemists were quick to "personalize his words." In a verbal note, J. Bennett responded to the Nguemist accusations, expressed his reservations with regard to the democratization process and his "sadness and indignation at the state of Human Rights." Amnesty International, in a Medical Letter Writing Action addressed the international community in a reaction to the torture inflicted on two industrial engineers of the National Electricity company in July for having read *Le Verdad,* whose condition is now serious. In late August 1993, the assassinations and political "suicides" increased especially among members of the democratic opposition. A member of UP, Pedro Motu Mamiaga—the army man who arrested Macías Nguema—was assassinated in prison on August 23, according to the traditional rite of the Esangui from Mongomo: ablation of genital organs, the heart, and the eyes (see also Nguema, M.). After the November 21 elections, the persecution of opponents and intellectuals was intensified, and was mainly aimed at students and teachers of the UNED. The same disregard for fundamental freedoms and human rights continued before, during, and after the September 1995 municipal elections and the presidential election of February 1996. Victims of another sort: the French, Spanish, and other companies of Río Muni were exacted a ransom by T. Nguema Obiang. Finally, the political disorder created by the nguemists made Equatorial Guinea a country that suffers from cesarism, of which many managers belonging to political groups of opposition are victims, thus ruining any possible chance of democratization.

Indirect victims of the Nguemist terror include persons affected by the drug trafficking of the clan from Mongomo and the foreigners living in Equatorial Guinea who are exposed to various exactions, including armed attacks, robberies, rackets, rape, illegal arrests, unjustified expulsions, and so forth.

See also Abuy, I.; Akalayong; Akonibe; Añisok; Annobon; Bakale Obiang, C.; Baney; Bata; Benito (Río Benito, Mbini); Bibang Oyee, J.; Bolekia Bonay, V.; Convergency for Social Democracy; Ebebiyin; Education; Ela Abeme, F. J.; Elma Borengue, J.; Eneme Ovono, J.; Esono, J. C.; Esono Masie, P.; Esono Mika, P. J.; Evinayong; Human Rights; Joint Opposition Platform; Malavo. E.; Mba Ekua Miko, B.; Mecheba Ikaka, J.; Miko Abogo, P.; Mikomeseng; Missions; Moto Nsa, S.; Nguemism; Nze Angue, A. G.; Ona Nguema, A.; Ondo Maye; Owono Mituy, D.; Police; Press; Refugees; Río Muni; Ronda, S.; Santa Isabel (Malabo); Sima Ngua, A. Mgr; Suicides; Terror; Torture; University; *Verdad, La.*

VILARRASA BALANZA, Salvador. Spanish businessman from Valencia, in the country since 1979, owner of two lumber companies, Matransa and Limitec Guinea, as well as a share in the most recent lumber enterprise of the country, A.B.M., along with Obiang Nguema. Until the summer of 1991, Vilarrasa was associated with the Lebano-Spanish businessman Hanna, a childhood friend of the dictator.

After he and his partner imported two trucks and secondhand military clothes from the Netherlands, they were arrested on October 23, 1992, and accused of plotting a coup. They were judged by a military tribunal presided over by Col. P. Esono Masié. The prosecutor, Capt. Francisco Edu, requested 30 years and a $550,000 fine. The two men were condemned to 12 years in prison with heavy fines. They were pardoned by the dictator on December 2. The minister for defense, Melanio Ebendeng, informed them that they could only leave the country after payment of the fine. Vilarrasa was received by Obiang Nguema, who made him some excuses and reminded him of the seriousness of his crime. Obiang Nguema allowed the two men to leave the country. On March 24, 1993, Vilarrasa returned to Bata.

VILLAGE COOPERATIVES see Cooperativas Del Campo

VISAPAA, Markku see United Nations

VISHER, Lucas. Honorary professor of theology in the University of Bern (Switzerland), former director of the Commission of Faith and Constitution of the World Council of Churches (Geneva). He visited Equatorial Guinea in the summer of 1992 as the president of the Committee for the Voluntary Return of Refugees and was immediately received by Obiang Nguema. In June 1995 he published an article titled "Can One Believe What the Pope Says?" in the *Journal de Genève*.
See also Mba Ekua Miko; Mokong Onguene, C.

VIYIL. Association of Annobóneses (office in Barcelona), whose president is Melchor Pérez. It published the journal *Viyil: Revista de Divulgación cultural.*

VIVOUR, Allen. d. 1900. Fernandino. Methodist of Sierra-Leonean origin, married to Amelia Barleycorn. Major oil palm and yam merchant, then cocoa planter. He helped the Claretians to found the boarding college of Batete. In 1920 his properties passed to the Dougan family. A member of the Vivour family ran for the 1968 elections on the Grupo Macías list.

VOLCANOS. Fernando Po and Annobón are located on the large West African (rift) that stretches from Tibesti to Annobon. Fernando Po had eruptions in 1880 and 1900. The most important peaks in Fernando Po are the Pico de Basilé, and in the southern range the Pico de Moka and the Gran Caldera de San Carlos; in Annobón, the Pico de Fogo.

VOLIO-JIMENEZ, Fernando. Costa Rican professor of constitutional law. Designated in 1979 as special rapporteur of the UN Human Rights Commission for Equatorial Guinea (see Van Boven, L.). He undertook his first mission of two weeks in November 1979. His report was damning and underscored the complete lack of civil liberties other than that of religion. Volio-Jimenez cast doubts on the real motivation of the people in power, most of whom had belonged to the old regime. He also complained of the lack of cooperation from the government, despite the promises made by them. Volio-Jimenez returned to Equatorial Guinea several times in his expert capacity. His successive reports, while recording some minor improvements here and there, still stress the lack of basic civil liberty.

In 1988, the UN Human Rights Commission served notice on Obiang Nguema to reply to its repeated requests for information on the measures proposed to implement the recommendations made by the commission's expert as well as for replies to the UN secretary-general's notes. Since then, Volio-Jimenez makes a visit each year, which is followed by a report to the commission. All the reports spoke of the deterioration of Equatorial Guinea during the worst moments of the Macías Nguema period.

In the February 1991 report, Volio-Jimenez revealed that the minister of foreign affairs, Eneme Ovono (Mongomo) had asked him in so many words: "What do human rights have to do with democracy?" It was learned that once again the expert had not been received by Obiang Nguema. The prime minister, Capt. Seriche Bioco, declared to Volio-Jiminez that the refugees were "thieves," but that they were being permitted to return, thanks to the new amnesty law. The others, "idiots and trouble-makers will not be allowed." The country still does not respect the habeas corpus and the *amparo* demanded since 1979. Volio-Jimenez received a number of precise accounts on the systematic practice of arbitrary arrests and torture.

In February 1992, Volio-Jimenez described Equatorial Guinea as a country that does not respect legal rights. "Everything goes to show that the government, with regard to democratic liberalization, will not go beyond simple rhetoric." The situation is similar to the Macías Nguema period. The observations of Volio-Jimenez confirm the contents of the book *Tropical Bandits* published in 1990 by an American consultant of the World Bank after 1 year in Equatorial Guinea.

Volio-Jimenez stressed that "the new fundamental law or Constitution proclaimed in December 1991, was less democratic than the one in 1982." There was "a negative attitude to human rights" predominant in the government. It was therefore hardly surprising that after the coup that brought Obiang Nguema to power, no reliable system for the protection of fundamental freedoms functioned.

The situation became still worse in early 1992. The laws on amnesty and political parties were very far removed from the promised opening. Volio-Jimenez indicated that on February 17 the diplomatic and consular missions, as well as international organizations, had received an unusual verbal note that restricted their movements and activities. The public discussion about the Volio-Jimenez report gave rise to protests from the number three man of the Nguemist regime, the minister to President Evuna Owono Asangono. According to him, the criticism affected the country's sense of dignity. If continued, Equatorial Guinea will be forced to end its participation in the UN Human Rights Commission.

The report of the UNDP on the electoral law and the electoral campaign stressed the numerous voids and made references to the Volio-Jimenez report. The regime alleged "incorrect and fantastic" appreciation. In the summer of 1993, for health reasons, Volio-Jimenez was replaced by the Uruguayan Alejandro Artucio.

Volio Jimenez died at 71, on May 21, 1996, in San-José de Costa Rica.

VOZ DEL PUEBLO, La (People's Voice). Periodical of the National Alliance for Democratic Restoration (ANRD), published from 1975 (in exile). It spoke of the diaspora's efforts at resistance and of its refusal to have any dialogue with the Nguemist regime. In 1992 the Nguemists, within the framework of the single party, PDGE, brought out a bulletin titled *La Voz del Pueblo,* in order to spread confusion. This maneuver was denounced by *La Verdad,* of Convergency for Social Democracy, with the publication of an old cover page of the ANRD. After an interruption due to the actions of Mokong Onguene and Dougan Beaca, the *Voz del Pueblo* reappeared in August 1995 (sporadic).

See also National Alliance for Democratic Restoration.

❖ W ❖

WALTER INTERNATIONAL. American company for prospecting and exploiting petroleum (Houston). It was at the head of a group in charge of drilling in the fields of Alba, to the north of Fernando Po, according to a five-year agreement signed in April 1990 (40% for Walter, 60% for the state, after amortization). Apart from royalties, the revenues for Equatorial Guinea were only expected in late 1995. The coordinator of Walter Int. in Equatorial Guinea is Tomas Diken, and the director of production is Mike Pavelka. In December 1996 Walter International seems to have invested $50 million.

Walter Int. Equatorial Guinea paid $1 million for each loading of condensates (twice a month). The IMF and the IBRD were conscious that these funds were misappropriated. In late 1993 the POC asked the American government to block the operation of Walter Int. in order to cut off resources for Obiang Nguema. In 1993 the company had exports of $24 million.

In February 1994 Obiang Nguema received Chester Edward Norris, Jr., president of Walter Int, and ambassador of the U.S. in 1987–1991. In 1994 the exports of Walter Int. totalled $28 million.

The French publication *L'Etat du monde 1995* stated that the income from the Alba deposit exploited by Walter "did not reach the public Treasury, even via the fiscal system." In February 1995 Walter was absorbed by US CMS Energy Nomeco, following Nguemist accusations of slackness in the exploitation of the deposits.

See also Abeso Fuma, F.; Norris, E.; Petroleum.

WANG YONGCHENG. Ambassador of the People's Republic of China from 1993 on.

WAREHOUSES. Along with their primary trade, the slave traders also managed warehouses or trading posts, using the coastal tribes, especially the Benga of Corisco, as their middlemen. About 30 warehouses of various nationalities were scattered along the Fernando Po coasts. The most important ones were German and English (Woermann, Holt). Until 1926, occupation of the Río Muni coasts was characterized mainly by the presence of such subsidiaries, accompanied sometimes by a small Spanish or French military detachment. The peak of trade was around 1890: fabrics, alcohol, and weapons were exchanged for ivory, palm oil, okoume, ebony, copal resin, and skins.

WASTES see Toxic Wastes

WATSON BUECO, Gustavo. d. 1969. Bubi medical doctor. In 1958 he cosigned with A. Mañe and Ndongo Miyone a memorandum to the United Nations denouncing the Spanish occupation. He was a member of the Diputación Provincial (assembly) of Fernando Po from 1960–1962 and then of the Conseo de Gobierno during autonomy (public health minister). With Itoha Iyanga, Maho Sikacha, Borico Toichoa, he presented on August 12, 1966, a motion to the cabinet in favor of the separation of Fernando Po from Río Muni at independence, an idea he again defended in vain at the Constitutional Conference. In July 1968, at the UN with Bosio Dioco and others, he attempted a last step that also failed. Appointed ambassador to Cameroon in 1968, he was sequestered by the embassy personnel, brought by force to Santa Isabel in March 1969, and accused of complicity with Ndongo Miyone. He died in prison after having been placed for several days in a barrel full of water.

WELE NZAS. Name given to the district in the southeast of Río Muni, ruled from Mongomo, the fief of the Nguemists, mainly of the Esangui as well as relatives of the Mbon ethnic group.

WEST AFRICA COMPANY see United Kingdom

WITCHCRAFT see Sorcery

WOERMANN, Adolf, 1843–1919. Businessman from Hamburg. His company, created in 1837, appeared on the Cameroonian coast in 1849 and opened many warehouses along the coast as far as Gabon. In the nineteenth century, Hamburg was the first world market for okoume. Around 1870, Johann Thormählen was an agent of Woermann in Cameroon. The Woermann Company helped Nachtigal in his conquest of Cameroon, to the detriment of Spain. During the nineteenth century, this shipping company enjoyed strong footholds in the Reichstag. Toward the end of the century, the Carl Woermann and Jantzen & Thormählen companies were members of the Union for West Africa in Hamburg (Syndikat für Westafrika in Hamburg), founded on October 12, 1884.

Adolf Woermann's brother, Eduard, arrived in Douala in 1884 and helped convince the Douala chiefs to sign the annexation treaty that would lead to the German Protectorate. Woermann supplied his numerous warehouses, especially in Río Muni, with his own steamers, as long as the Spanish Trasatlántica only landed at Fernando Po. In 1903 the Woermann Company signed an agreement with the Liberian government for the supply of manpower to be sent abroad. Like other companies, the employees shamelessly exploited the Liberian workers. At the time of independence in Equatorial Guinea, Woermann still called several times a year at Fernando Po and Río Muni. The line ceased operations in 1972.

WOMEN MARTYRS. A great number of women have followed their assassinated husbands into death, in particular the wives of Ondo Edu, Ngomo Nandongo, Mitogo Esono, Nguema Efua, Eyegue Ntutumu, Buendy Ndongo, and others. Among the women liquidated by the Nguemist regime are schoolteachers, airline stewardesses, and farm women. Among the 120,000 exiles are several thousand women. In August 1976 the United Nations Commission for Human Rights studied the present slavery situation of Equato-Guinean women, particularly the severe sentences of those refusing the sexual advances of government officials.

WORLD BANK see International Bank for Reconstruction and Development

WORLD COUNCIL OF CHURCHES (WCC). The Protestant Church of Equatorial Guinea was a member from 1960. In April 1980 a mission of the WCC visited Río Muni and recommended various projects. In 1983 a sum of $297,650 was set aside for three years for fisheries and agriculture, as well as the training of 7,500 persons by Latin American experts.

The WCC took care of health with Dutch personnel (four) and American Presbyterians (two), and of education through Dienste in Uebersee and Intermedia (NCC/USA). Pain pour le monde (Bread for the World) aided small projects in the areas of agriculture and fishing. The expenses of the church were supported by the Reformed Church of Holland. The representatives of the Reformed Church of Equatorial Guinea considered that the WCC had too much of a tendency to dictate its own decisions.

The WCC supported, by means of Country Programs, the Council of Protestant Churches of Equatorial Guinea, with US $91,015 (1997) and $108,405 (1998). The funds mostly came from the Reformed Church of Netherlands and the Norwegian Church Aid. Main activities: training of local coordinators, of agronomists, of five women in soap making and food conservation, literacy programs, and support to 22 agricultural projects.

See also Protestantism; Visher, Lucas.

WORLD FOOD PROGRAM see Agriculture; United Nations

WORLD LABOR CONFEDERATION. International trade union confederation with its registered offices in Brussels. In 1992 it stated that Moroccan soldiers were policing Equatorial Guinea, preventing free movement within the country, helping the Equato-Guinean authorities to capture and torture its own population, and executing opponents. See also Volio-Jimenez.

X

XENEL Co. see Petroleum; San Carlos

❖ Y ❖

YATES, Douglas Andrew. American. Ph.D. from Boston University (1995) where he was a teaching fellow in comparative politics and international relations. Political scientist who specializes in African studies. Author of *The Rentier State in Africa.* Professor at the American university in Paris. See Bibliography.

YONA INTERNATIONAL. Israeli company for forest exploitation. See also Timber.

YOUNG TORCHES (Jovenes Antorchas). A creation of Armengol Nguema Mbasogo. Called Death Squads or Ninjas en marcha con Obiang (Ninjas Marching with Obiang), by the opposition. A militia armed to the teeth, numbering 300, and composed of the "youth" of Mongomo, including a women's group. They wear black uniforms provided by France.

In 1993 it received France's support, through Marcel Moreau and René Rodriguez, instructors provided by the French Direction des Renseignements Généraux. The secretary of state for the press, radio, and TV, Santiago Ngua, denied the alleged involvement of France. The French minister for foreign affairs, Juppé, did likewise, while observers present in the country stated the opposite.

Some ministers of the January 8, 1996, government were said to be members of the Seguridad and the Ninjas. Dario Tadeo Ndong Olomo led the Young Torches until he was appointed minister of health in April. But Ndong Olomo was arrested for participation in the attempted coup of July 18.

In 1998, Agostino Nse Nfumu, secretary general of the PDGE, was head of this repressive unit.

See also Annobón; Army; Bata; "Democratic" Party of Equatorial Guinea; Ekomo Yacure, F.; Elections; Epalepale, E.; Jovenes Antorchas; Justice; Mba Ondo Nchama; Micha Nsue Nfumu, J.; Mongomo; Morocco; Muatetema Rivas, C.; Ninjas; Obiang Nguema, T.; Police; Rodriguez, R.; Ronda, S., Terror; Youth Marching with Macías.

YOUTH see Eyegue Obama Asue, F. P.; Milam tang, I.; Sports; Young Torches.

❖ Z ❖

ZAFIRO. Offshore oilfield, 40 miles west of Fernando Po, at -140 and -270 m. Eight wells are linked by a floating Production Storage Offloading System (FPSO) set up by Intec Marine Pipelines. Mobil Equatorial Guinea Inc. (MEGI) exploits all of it.

In October 1997, it was announced that Zafiro's capacity will be brought up to 120,000 b/d.

In April 1998, a radar buoy replaced the revolving light buoy. See Petroleum.

ZAMBI MACHINDE, Fortunato see Mba Nzambi

ZAMORA LOBOCH, Francisco. From Annobón. Born 1948. His father was a school teacher. Studied journalism in Spain. Worked as a sports reporter and football (soccer) coach. Published a highly sarcastic work on racism: *Como ser negro y no morir en Aravaca* (How to Be Black and Not Die in Aravaca).

ZARAGOZA see Ela Abeme, F. J.; Junta for the Coordination of Opposition Forces; Modu Akuse, C.; Obiang Nguema; Spain

ZARAGOZA GROUP see Obiang Nguema

❖ BIBLIOGRAPHY ❖

Unlike most other African countries, there are a few general works on Equatorial Guinea or the former Spanish Guinea in English. The isolation in which Spain kept its Guinea Gulf Colony appears also in the information on these territories: most of the articles and books have been published (after 1945) through the Spanish official Instituto de Estudios Africanos, resulting in ideological orientation (glorification of the Movimiento Nacional) and sometimes second-rate quality.

Shortly after the appearance of Equatorial Guinea on the international scene, after Spain's admission to the United Nations and the pressure of Afro-Asians for the independence of the colonial territories, there appeared, in 1961, a dissertation comprising the first major non-Spanish work on the country: *Spanish Guinea: An Annotated Bibliography* (Catholic University of America); in 597 pages, Sanford Berman analyzes about 600 titles and mentions which libraries contain the documents he analyzes. Later on Susan Knoke Rishworth, in her work *Spanish-Speaking Africa* (Washington, DC, 1973) gave 137 titles. Finally, in 1974, 1976, 1978, 1980, 1985, 1987, 1991, 1994, and 1996, the Swiss Africanist Max Liniger-Goumaz published ten volumes of *Equatorial Guinea: Bibliografía Général,* giving a total of 26,746 titles on the country. Recently, the American specialist on Equatorial Guinea, Randall Fegley, published *Equatorial Guinea.* (Denver, CO: Clio Press, World Bibliographical Series 136, 1991). A number of in-depth articles published during the last several years Spanish dailies by S. Aroca and Ana Romero (*El Mundo*), L. A. Ayllón (*ABC*), J. Barajas and Djongele Bokokó Boko (*Las Provincias*), Ana Camacho, M. Josa, R. Lobo and I. Cembrero (*El País*)in *La Vanguardia* may also be consulted.

To approach Equatorial Guinea, it is recommended to consult the following main works:

Amnesty International. *Juicios militares y uso de la pena de muerte en Guinea Ecuatorial.* Doc. AFR 24/01/87/s. London, May 1987. 15 p.

Artucio, A. *Rapport sur la situation des droits de l'homme en Guinée Equatoriale présenté par le Rapporteur spécial de la Commission des droits de l'homme, M. Alejandro Artucio, en application de la résolution 1993/69 de la Commission. 50e session, Point 12 de l'ordre du jour provisoire.* Doc. E/CN.4/1994/56. Geneva, January 10, 1994. 40 p.

_____. *Informe sobre la situación de los derechos humanos en la República de Guinea Ecuatorial presentado por el Relator Espécial de la Comisión, Sr. Alejandro Artucio (Uruguay), de conformidad con la resolución 1995/71 de la Comisiòn de Derechos Humanos y la decisión 1995/282 del Consejo Económico y Social.* Naciones Unidas. Comisión de Derechos Humanos, 52e período de sesiones. Geneva, March 15, 1996. Doc.E/CN.4/1996. 28 p.

_____. *Informe sobre la situación de los derechos humanos en la República de Guinea Ecuatorial presetado por el Relator Espécial de la Comisión, Sr. Alejandro Artucio (Uruguay), de conformidad con la resolución 1995/71 de la Comisión de Derechos*

Humanos y la decisión 1995/282 del Consejo Económico y Social. Comisión de Derechos Humanos, 52e período sesiones. Tema 10 del programa provisional. Cuestión de la violación de los Derechos Humanos y las Libertades fundimentales. Gineabra, 8 enero 1996, 26 p. Doc. E/CN.4/1996/67. Geneva, January 8, 1996.

_____. *Adición [post elección presidencia febrero] al Informe sobre la situación de los derechos humanos en la República de Guinea Ecuatorial presentado por el Relator Espécial de la Comisiòn, Sr. Alejandro Artucio (Uruguay), de conformidad con la resolución 1995/71 de la Comisiòn de Derechos Humanos y la decisión 1995/282 del Consejo Económico y Social.* Comisiòn de Derechos Humanos, 52$ período de sesiones. Tema 10 del programa provisional. Cuestión de la violación de los Derechos Humanos y la Libertades fundamentales. Geneva, January 8, 1996, 5 p. Doc. E/CN.4/1996/67/Add.1. Geneva, March 15, 1996.

_____. *Informe sobre la situación de los derechos humano en la República de Guinea Ecuatorial presentado por el Relator Especial de la Comisión Sr.* Alejandro Artucio (Uruguay), de conformidad con la resolución 1995/71 de la Comisión de Derechos Humanos, 53° período de sesiones. Tema 10 del prorama provisional. Cuestión de la viiolación de los Derechos Humanos y las Libertades fundamentales. Ginebra, March 1997.

Castro Antolín, M., Ndongo Bibiyogo, D., *España en Guinea. Construcción del desencuentro: 1778–1968.* Epilogo de J.U. Martinez Carreras. Ed. Sequitur. Madrid, 1998, 241 p.

Clarence-Smith, W. G. "Equatorial Guinea: Economy." *Africa South of the Sahara.* London, 1993, 1994. 340 p. Statistics, bibliography.

_____. "Equatorial Guinea: Economy." *Africa South of the Sahara.* London, 1993, 1994. 340 p. Statistics, bibliography.

Cronjé, Susanne. *Equatorial Guinea: The Forgotten Dictatorship.* London: Anti-Slavery Society, 1976. 43 p.

Economist Intelligence Unit, The. *Gabon—Equatorial Guinea: Country Report.* London. Quarterly (essential).

_____. *Gabon - Equatorial Guinea. Country Profile.* London. Annual (essential.).

Evita, R. *La evolución económica de Guinea Ecuatorial desde 1850 a 1968.* Unpublished thesis, Howard University, Washington, DC, 1970. 206 p.

Fegley, R. *Equatorial Guinea: An African Tragedy.* New York: American University Studies, XI/39. Peter Lang, 1989.

Fleischhacker, H., "Äquatorialguinea." *Lexikon der Dritten Welt.* Reinback. 1998, pp. 48–50.

Goldman, A., "Rags among the riches. The prospect of petro-dollars has broought prizes and problems for the rulers of Equatorial Buinea." *BBC Focus on Africa.* London, 1998, pp. 34–35, il.

Hornemann-Ray, B. *Spanische Uberseepolitik in Afrika seit 1945 unter besonderer Berücksichtigung Spanish Guinea.* Dissertation. Berlin: 1970. 375p.

Klitgaard, R. E. *Tropical Gangsters: One Man's Experience with Development and Decadence in Deepest Africa.* New York: Basic Books, 1990.

Kobel, Arim Eric. *La République de Guinée Equatoriale.* Neuchatel, Switzerland: Diss, 1976. 623 p. Useful geographic information and economic analysis.

Leguineche, M. *La Tribu* [rev. ed.]. Madrid, 1997.

Liniger-Goumaz, M. *La Guinée Equatoriale: Un pays méconnu.* Paris: L'Harmattan, 1979. 507 p.

_____. *Guinée Equatoriale: De la dictature des colons à la distature des colonels.* Geneva: Les Edition du Temps, 1982. 230 p., ill.

_____. *De la Guinée Equatoriale nguemiste: Eléments pour le dossier de l'afro-fascime.* Geneva: Les Editions du Temps, 1983. 270 p., ill.

_____. *Connaître la Guinée Equatoriale.* Paris-Rouen: Editions des Peuples-Noirs, 1986. 240 p.

_____. *Brève Histoirs de la Guinée Equatoriale.* Paris: L'Harmattan, 1988. 200 p.

_____. "Guinea Ecuatorial," in *La Démocrature: Dictature déguisée. Democratie truquée.* Paris: L'Harmattan, 1992. 364 p.

_____. *Who's Who de la Dictature de Guinée Equatoriale: Les Nguemistes, 1979–1993.* Geneva: Les Editions du Temps, 1993.

_____. *Guinea Ecuatorial es Africa: Temas políticos: La Democracia desencadenada.* Madrid: Editorial Claves para el futuro, 1995.

_____. *Guinea Ecuatorial y el ensayo democrático: La conquista del Golfo de Guinea.* Madrid: Editorial Claves para el futuro, 1996.

_____. *Les USA et le France face à ;a Giomée Equatoriale à la fin du XIXe et du XXe siècle. La continuité de l'Histoire.* Les editions du Temps. Ginebra 1997.

_____. *United States, France and Equatorial Guinea. The "Dubious Friendships."* Three historical synopses. Two bibliographies. (Trilingual). Geneva: Les Editions du Temps, 1997.

_____. *Guinée Equatoriale. 30 ans d'Etat délinquant nguemiste.* L'Harmattan, 1998, 160 p.

Martinez Alcazar, J., Morariega Alcala, F. *Geografía e historia de Guinea ecuatorial.* Universidad Nacional de ecucación a distancia. Madrid, 1982, 124 p.

Ndongo Bidyogo, Donato. *Historia y tragedia de Guinea Ecuatorial.* Madrid: 1977. 307 p.

Nerín i Abad, G., *Guinea Ecuatorial, historia enblanco y negro. Hombres blancos y mujeres negras en Guinea Ecuatorial (1843–1968).* Ediciones Península. Barcelona, 1998, 255 p.

_____. *Los poderes de la tempestad.* Novel. Madrid, 1997.

Ngonde Maguga, M. E. "Informe sobre la situación de los Derechos del Hombre en la República de Guinea Ecuatorial." XXXII Congrese de la FIDH: Crisis y Derechos del Hombre. Madrid, January 13–15, 1995.

Oyono Sa Abegue, V. *L'évolution des structures productives et sociales de l'économie de la Guinée Equatoriale (1858-1968). L'origonalité d'un cas de transition au capitalisme agraire dans un contexte colonial.* Diss. Lyon: Université de Lyon II, 1985. 983 p. A fundamental work.

Programa de las Naciones Unidas para el Desarrollo, Guinea Ecuatorial. Informe 1994–1995. Malabo, August 1966. 138 p., stat.

Sundiata, I. K. *The Fernandinos: Labour and Community in Santa Isabel de Fernando Po, 1827-1931.* Diss. Evanston, IL, 1972. 397 p., maps.

_____. *Equatorial Guinea. Colonialism, State Terror and the Search for Stability.* Boulder, CO, 1990.

UNESCO, Guinea Ecuatorial. *Propuestas para la reconstrucción y el desarrollo de la educación.* Doc. EFM 125. Paris, 1984. 122 p.

United Nations. *Assistance to Equatorial Guinea.* Report of the Secretary General. Doc. A/40/430. New York, August 19, 1985. 26 p.

_____. *Guinée Equatoriale. Octroi de services d'experts dans le domaine des droits de l'homme. Note du secrétaire général.* Geneva: Commission des Droits de l'Homme des Nations Unies, January 16, 1986. 52 p.

Unzueta y Yuste, A. de. *Historia geographica de la Isla de Fernando Poo.* Madrid, 1947. 494 p.

U.S. Department of State, *Equatorial Guinea country Report on Human Rights Practics for 1996.* Bureau of Democracy, Human rights and Labor. Washington, January 30, 1997, 8 p. Annual. Fundamental.

Volio-Jimenez, F. *Situation of Human Rights in Equatorial Guinea.* Commission of Human Rights in the United Nations. Doc. E/CN.4/1439. Geneva, December 19, 1980. 44 p.

_____. *Rapport de l'expert charge d'etudier la situation des droits de l'homme en Guinée équatoriale, etabli conformement au paragraphe 9 de la résolution 1990/57 de la Commission des Droits de l'Homme.* Geneva, December 28, 1990. 4 p., Doc. E/CN.4./1991/54.

_____. *Rapport de l'expert chargé d'etudier la situation des droits de l'homme en Guinée Equatoriale, établi conformément au paragraphe 8 de la résolution 1991/80 de la Commission des Droits de l'Homme.* Geneva, December 17, 1992. 47. p., Doc. E/CN.4./1992/51.

_____. *Rapport de l'expert chargé d'étudier la situation des droits de l'homme en Guinée Equatoriale, en application de la résolution 1992/79 de la Commission des Droits de l'Homme Geneva.* December 31, 1992. Doc E/CN.4/1993/48. 18 p.

_____. *Rapport sur la situation des droits de l'homme en Guinée équatoriale présenté par l'expert de la Commission des droits de l'homme, M. Fernando Volio, en application de la résolution 1992/79 de la Commission.* Conseil Economique et Social des Nations Unies. Commission des Droits de l'Homme. 49e session, Point 12 de l'ordre du jour provisoire. Doc. E/CN.4/1993/48. Geneva, December 31, 1992. 18 p.

The following works, even if not up-to-date, present an excellent basic document:

Bravo Carbonel, J. *Fernando Poo y Río Muni: sus misterios y riquezas; su colonización.* Madrid, 1917. 399 p. Shows what Spain could have made its colony.

Bundesstelle für Aussenhandel-Informationen. *Wirtschaftsstruktur Spanish Guineas/aussenhandel.* Cologne, 1963–67. 5 vols. Describes the preindependence situation.

International Monetary Fund. "Equatorial Guinea." In *Survey of African Economics,* vol. 5, chap. 7 (pp. 314–454). Washington, DC, 1973. Analyzes what was left after three years of independence.

Mitogo. *Guinea: de colonia a dictatura. Cuadernos para el Diálogo.* Suplemento 30. Madrid, 1977. 54 p. Adds to the recent examination of economic disaster that of genocide.

Nosti Nava, J. *Notas geográficas y económicas sobre los territorios españoles del Golfo de Guinea.* Madrid, 1942. 116p.

Perpiñá Grau, R. *De colonización y economía en la Guinea española.* Barcelona, 1945. 422 p. An interesting presentation of the Spainsh colonial system in Central Africa.

Pujadas, T. L. *Geografía e historia de la Guinea ecuatorial.* Santa Isabel, 1969. 112 p. This and the Nosti Nava title both show how the country should be rebuilt.

Roig, J. "Guinea Equatorial: la dictadura enquistada." *Cuadernos Bakeaz.* Bilbao (Spain), December 1996. 12 p.

Simon, W., *Balade africaine.* Novel about "Dictatorial Guinea." Les editions de Rocher. Monaco, 1998.

Sundiata, I. K., *From Slaving to Neoslavery. the bight of Biafra and Fernando Po in the era of abolition, 1827–1930.* University of Wisconsin Press. Madison, 1996, 262 p.

Tessman, G. *Die Pangwe: völkerkundliche Monographie eines westafrikanischen Negerstammes.* Berlin, 1913. 2 vols. On the Fang, still very valid because of resistance to their customs in Río Muni.

_____. *Die Bube auf Fernando Poo: völkerkundliche Einzelbeschreibung eines west-afrikanischen Negerstammes.* Hagen, 1923. 238 p. Bubi civilization has almost completely disappeared under Spanish and Nigerian influences.

Yates, D. "Equatorial Guinea: Oil and Power." *Panafrica.* London, November 1996, pp. 16–17.

_____. "Equatorial Guinea," in "Central-Africa: Oil and the Franco-American rivalry," in *L'Afrique politique 1998.* Paris, January 1998, pp. 225–226, maps.

In spite of certain weaknesses, the Spanish literature on Equatorial Guinea, and in particular various articles of such periodicals as *La Guinea Española* (Santa Isabel), *Africa* (Madrid), and *Archivos del Instituto de Estudios Africanos* (Madrid) deserve the reader's attention. Since 1975, *La Voz del Pueblo,* organ of the ANRD, offers clear orientations on the actual political problems (especially on relations with neighboring countries), and on what the post-Nguemist Equatorial Guinea will be.

The bibliography is broken down as shown here:

GENERAL
   Travels
   Descriptions
   Guides
   Statistical Abstracts
   Bibliography

CULTURAL
   Archeology
   Architecture
   Arts
   Drama
   Linguistics

Literature
Music/Dance
Press/Publishing

ECONOMIC
Economics
Agriculture (Coffee, Cocoa, Palm Oil, Timber, Breeding)
Commerce
Development
Finance
Industry
Labor
Transport/Communications

POLITICAL
Constitution
Government
Law
Political Parties
Race Questions
Foreign Affairs

HISTORICAL
Precolonial
Colonial
Independence

SCIENTIFIC
Geography
Geology
Medicine
Zoology

SOCIAL
Anthropology
Demography
Education
Ethnology
Religion
Sociology

GENERAL

TRAVELS

Bondyck Bastiaanse, J. H. van. *Voyage de la Côte de Guinée dans le Golfe de Biafra à l'île de Fernando Poo, l'île Sainte Hélène et autres îles à bord du Lancier.* The Hague, 1853.

Bosman, W. *A New and Accurate Description of the Coast of Guinea, Divided into the Gold, the Slave and the Ivory Coasts, Written Originally in Dutch and Now Faithfully Done into English.* London: F. Knapton, 1705.

Boteler, T. *Princes, St. Thomas and Anno-Bon Islands, on the Coast of Africa.* London, 1829.

Buff-Thomson, F. W. "A voyage to Fernando Po [extract of the diary of J. C. Clarke, Baptist missionary (approx. 1948)]. *Baptist Quarterly.* Southampton, July 1953, pp. 82–87, 113–121.

Burton, Sir R. Fr. "Benin-Nun-Bonny River to Fernando Po." In J. Holpman. *Travels in Madeira, Sierra Leone, Teneriffe, St. Jage, Cape Coast, Fernando Po, Prince's Island, Etc.* Vol. 1, 2nd ed. London: Routledge, 1840.

Diéz Vilas, J. *Guinea Ecuatorial.* El Viajero independiente. Madrid, 1994, 192 p.

Iradier y Bulfy, M. *Africa; viajes y trabajos de la Asociación Euskara. La Exploradora; primer viaje: exploración del país de Muni, 1875–1877; segundo viaje: adquisición del país de Muni, 1884.* 2 vols. Vitoria: de Iturbe, 1901.

Litvak, L. *El ajedrez de estrellas. Crónicas de viajeros españoles del siglo XIX por países exóticos (1800-1913).* Barcelona, 1987.

Newton, A. "Equatorial Guinea." In *Central Africa: A Travel Survival Kit* (pp. 338–364). Hawthorne, Australia: Lonely Planet Publications, 1994.

Thomas, C. W. "Islands of Biafra." In *Adventures of Observations on the West Coast of Africa and Its Islands* (pp. 250–260). New York: Derby and Jackson, 1860.

DESCRIPTIONS

Arambillet. *Posesiones españolas del Africa occidental.* Madrid: Impr. Revista Général de Marina, 1903.

Arizcun Carrera, E. de, and J. S. Martinez de Pons. *Memoia sobre los territorios españoles de Guinea.* 3 vol. Madrid: n.d.

Bagueña Corella, L. *Guinea.* Manuales del Africa española, 1. Madrid: IDEA, 1950.

Beltrán y Rospide, R. *La Guinea Española.* Manuales Soler 17. Barcelona: Soler, 1901.

Ellis, A. B. *West African Islands.* London, 1885.

Embajada de España. *Spanish Provinces in Africa.* Washington, 1965.

"Equatorial Guinea." *Africa Contemporary Record, 1968–1969* (pp. 479–484). London: Rex Collings, 1969.

"Fernando Po." *West Africa Directory, 1963–1964* (pp. 495-503). London: 1963.

Ferrer Piera, P. *Fernando Poo y sus dependencias, descripción, producciones, y estado sanitario.* Barcelona: López Robert, 1900.

Fisher, P. J. *Island Heritage.* London: Holborn, 1926.

Foreign Office (Great Britian). *Spanish Guinea.* Handbook 125. London: HMSO, 1920.

González Green, J. *España Negra (Una visión de la República de Guinea antes de la explosión).* Relato por un testigo presencial. Sevilla: ECESA, 1968.

Granados, G. *España en el Muni; observaciones hechas en el país.* Prol. de E. Bonelli. Cámara Agrícola. Madrid: Ministerio de la Marina, 1907.

"The Guinea Islands: Spain in Africa." In *The Story of Africa and Its Explorers,* vol. 4, chap. 5 (pp. 70–82). London: n.d.

Gunther, J. "The Spanish Island of Fernando Po, or Poo." In *Inside Africa* (pp. 710–711, 860–862). New York: Harper, 1955.

Gutierrez Sobral, J. *Posesiones españolas en el Africa occidental: Muni, Fernando Poo, Rio de Oro.* Madrid: Impr. de la Revista Général de Marina, 1904.

Howe, R. "Fernando Po." In *Black Africa. Vol I. From Prehistory to the Eve of the Colonial Era.* New York, 1966.

_____. "Spanish Africa." In *Black Africa. Vol. II. From the Colonial Era to Modern Time* (pp. 132–134). New York, 1966.

_____. "Spanish Equatorial Island (Fernando Po)." *Africa Report XI* (June 1966), pp. 48–49.

Hutchinson, T. J. "Fernando Po." In *Impressions of Western Africa* (pp. 173–202). London: 1958.

Ingham, K. "Equatorial Guinea." *Encyclopedia Britannica. Book of the Year, 1972* (p. 291). Chicago, 1972.; Ibid., *1971* (p. 317–318) Chicago, 1972; Ibid., *1970* (pp. 334–335). Chicago, 1971.

Jakande, L. K. (ed.). "Spanish Equatorial Guinea." *West Africa Annual 1966* (pp. 330–339). Lagos, 1965.

Kimble, G. H. T. *Tropical Africa, Vol. II* (pp. 124–125, 269). New York: Twentieth Century Fund, 1960.

Kingsley, M. H. *Impressions of West Africa.* Chap. 12, 13. London: Macmillan, 1858.

_____. *Travels in West Africa.* Chap. 3, "Fernando Po." London: Macmillan, 1858.

_____. *West African Studies.* 2nd ed. (pp. 75–80). London: 1901.

Kobel, Armin. *La République de Guinée équatoriale. Ses resources potentielles et virtuelles et les possibilités de développment.* Diss. Neuchatel, Switzerland: Copy Quick, 1976.

Kramer, M. H. "Aequatorial Guinea (Fernando Poo, Río Muni)." In *Afrika Handbuch für Wissenchaft und Reise, Vol. I.* Hamburg, 1968.

Liberia, Spanish and French Guinea, 1927–1937. Edinburgh: National Bible Society of Scotland, n.d.

López Perea, E. *Fernando Poo y sus dependencias; estudios y observaciones hechas en el país.* Barcelona: J. Miguel, 1912.

Macadam, I. (ed.). "Equatorial Guinea." In *The Annual Register. World Events 1969* (pp. 326–327). London: 1970; 1971, p. 266; 1972, pp. 259–260; 1973, p. 265.

_____. (ed). "Spanish African World Territories." In *The Annual Register. World Events 1963* (p. 334). London: 1964; 1965, p. 323; 1967, pp. 337–338; 1968, p. 33; 1970, pp. 325–326.

Miscellaneous, Equatorial Guinea 1995. "L'essai démocratique" de Teodoro Obiang Nguema Mbasogo. Économie: priorité aux privés. Radioscopie d'un pays en devenir." *Jeune Afrique Économie.* Hors série, Winter 1995, 433 p., ill. (A model in neo-colonial toadying.).

Montfort, M. *La Guinea Española.* Montevideo: El Siglo Ilustrado, 1901. 381 p.

Morgan, W. B., and J. C. Pugh. "The Islands of Spanish Guinea." In *West Africa* (pp. 719–722). London: 1969; "Corisco, Fernando Po, Río Muni," pp. 222, 380–384, 389, 401–402, 410–411, 414, 463, 481, 626, 672, 716.

Moros y Morellón, J. de, and Rios, J. M. de. *Memoria sobre las islas africanans de España, Fernando Poo y Annobón.* Madrid: Companía Tipográfica, 1844.

Nunan, T. J. "Fernando Po." *Manchester Geographical Society Bulletin,* vol. 20 (1904), pp. 29–36.

Pagni, L. "Guinée Equatoriale." *Le Courrier.* Afrique—Caraïbes—Pacifique—Communautés européennes, 107. Paris-Brussels: January-February 1988, pp. 32–43. Ill., map, statistics.

Parker, Fr. "Equatorial Guinea." *The American Annual 1970.* s.l. 1970, p. 281; 1971, pp. 283–284; 1972, p. 274; 1973, p. 280.

Parr, T. "Fernando Po. West Africa." *Journal of the Manchester Geographical Society,* vol. 5 (1989), pp. 20–28.

Pelissier, R. "Equatorial Guinea: A New Republic." *Geographical Magazine* (November 1968).

_____. "Spanish Guinea, an Introduction." *Race: The Journal of the Institute of Race Relations,* vol. 6, 2 (1964), pp. 117–128.

_____. "Les Territories espagnols d'Afrique." *Notes et Documents, 2951.* Paris, 1953.

_____. *Los territorios españoles de Africa.* Madrid: IDEA, 1963; *Boletín de Informaciòn,* 475. Madrid: March 1963.

_____. *Los territorios españoles de Africa* (pp. 39–87). Madrid: IDEA, 1964.

Posesiones españolas en el Africa occidental. Por dos Oficiales del Ejercito. Madrid: Biblioteca del Museo Naval, 1890.

Smith, J. "Fernando Po." In *Trade and Travels in the Gulf of Guinea, Western Africa: With an Account of the Manners, Customs of the Religion of the Inhabitants* (pp. 124, 143, 204, 212). London: Simpkin, Marshall, 1851.

"Spanish Equatorial Guinea." *West African Annual 1966.* Lagos, 1965, pp. 330–339.

Stamp, L. D. "Spanish Guinea." In *Africa: A Study in Tropical Development* (pp. 384–386). New York, 1953; "Equatorial Guinea." New York, 1972.

Stanley, H. M. *"Fernando Poo."* Revista de Geografía Colonial y Mercantil, Vol. 1 (1884), p. 53ff.

Statistisches Bundesamt: Aequatorialguinea. Länderkundebericht. Wiesbaden, 1972.

United States Department of State. *Equatorial Guinea.* Background Notes, 8025. Washington, DC: Office of Media Services, 1968.

_____. Revision, *Republic of Equatorial Guinea.* Washington, DC: Bureau of Public Affairs, April 1971.

_____. *Post Report on Equatorial Guinea.* Washington, DC: October 1986. 6 p., ill.

Vilaro, J. E. *Guinea.* Barcelona, Buenos Aires: Argos, 1950.

Welles, B. "The Spanish Provinces in Africa." *The New York Times* (April 10, 14, 16, 1961).

Woolbert, R. G. "Continental Guinea," *Collier's Encyclopedia,* vol. 5 (p. 637). New York, 1959.

_____. "Corisco." *Collier's Encyclopedia,* vol. 6 (p. 14). New York: 1959.

_____. "Fernando Po." *Collier's Encyclopedia,* vol. 8 (pp. 10–11). New York: 1959.

_____. "Spanish Guinea." *Collier's Encyclopedia,* vol. 9 (pp. 434–435). New York: 1959.

GUIDES

Diez Vilas, J., *Guinea ecuatorial. Guía turistico. El viajero independiente.* Madrid, 1994, 192 p., il.

Guide to Spanish Possessions. London Times (Air Mail ed.), October 31, 1960, p. 10.

STATISTICAL ABSTRACTS

Consejo Superior de Investigaciones Cientificas. Delegación Colonial de Estadística. *Resumunes Negociado de Estadística, 1950–51—1956–57.* Madrid: CSIC, 1953–1958.

Dirección Colonial de Estadística. *Resumenes estadísticos del censo general de población del Gobierno General de los Territorios Españoles del Golfo de Guinea al 31 de diciembre 1950.* Madrid: IDEA, 1952.

Dirección de Agricultura de los Territorios del Golfo de Guinea. *Anuario de Estadística y Catastro.* Madrid, 1944–1964.

Dirección General de Marruecos y Colonias. *Estadísticas del comercio especial de España con los Territorios Españoles del Golfo de Guinea.* Madrid: DGMA, 1942–1959.

_____. *Resumen estadístico de Africa Española.* Madrid: DGMC, 1950–1959.

Dirección Général de Plazas y Provincias Africanas. *Resumen estadístico de Africa Española.* Madrid, 1959–1968.

Gobierno General de la Region Ecuatorial. *Resumenes estadísticos. Provincias de Fernando Poo y Río Muni.* Madrid, 1960–1968.

Gobierno Général de los Territorios y Provincias Africanas. *Negaciado do Estadística, 1941.* Madrid, 1943.

_____. *Resumen estadístico 1948–1949.* Madrid, 1950.

_____. *Resumenes estadísticos del Censo général, 31 de Diciembre 1950.* Madrid, 1952.

Liniger-Goumaz, M. *Statistics of Equatorial Guinea: Data to Explain a Political Disaster— Estadísticas de la Guinea Ecuatorial. Datos para explicar un desastre politico.* Geneva: Les Editions du Temps, 1986.

BIBLIOGRAPHY

Berman, Sanford. *Spanish Guinea: An Annotated Bibliography.* Dissertation. The Catholic University of America, Washington, DC: Multen Library, 1961.

Colegio Mayor Universitario N^a S^a de Africa, Guinea Ecuatorial. *Boletín* [bibliográfico]. Año I, 1992. Irregular.

Dianoux, H. J. de. "Guinée Bissau et Guinée Equatoriale. Bibliographie." *Revue française d'histoire d'Outre-Mer,* 71 (pp. 191–205). Paris, 1984.

España: Guía de Fuentes para la Historia de Africa Subsaharianan. Zug, Switzerland, 1971.

Fegley, R. *Equatorial Guinea.* World Bibliographical Series, vol. 36. Santa Barbara, CA; Denver: Clio Press.

Fernandez Duro, C. *Bibliografía y notas referentes a la Comisión que se reunió en Paris, de la que formó parte, para tratar de los derechos de España a ocupar los territorios en Guinea. Y resumen sobre la question del Muni, 1884–1889.* Madrid: Archivos del Museo Naval. Doc 1, fol. 1–115. Ms 1914.

Granda, G. de. "Bibliografía del Español de Guinea Ecuatorial." *Anuario de Lingüística Hispanica,* 8 (pp. 47–52). Valladolid, 1992.

Hellman, F. A. *List of References on the Spanish Colonies in Africa.* Washington, DC: Library of Congress, 1942.

Hess, R. L., and Coger, D. M. *Bibliography of Nineteenth Century Tropical Africa.* Hoovers Bibliographical Series, 47 (pp. 511–520). Stanford: 1972.

Hornemann-Ray, B. *Spanische Überseepolitik in Africa seit 1975 unter besonderer Berücksichtigung Spanisch-Guineas.* Diss. Berlin, 1970.

Linger-Goumaz, M. *Guinea Ecuatorial: Bibliografía general.* Vol. II. Bern: Commission Nationale Suisse pour l'UNESCO, 1976; Vol. 3. Bern, 1978; Vol. 4. Bern, 1980; Vol. 5. Geneva: Les Editions du Temps, 1985; Vol. 6. Geneva: Les Editions du Temps, 1988.

_____. *Guinea Ecuatorial: Bibliografía general.* Vol. 7. Geneva: Les Editions du Temps, 1991.

_____. *Guinea Ecuatorial: Bibliografía general.* Vol. 8. Geneva: Les Editions du Temps, 1994 (referencias 13 121–17378).

_____. *Guinea Ecuatorial: Bibliografía general.* Vol. 9. Geneva: Les Editions du Temps, 1996 (referencias 17329–22442).

_____. *United States, France and Equatorial Guinea: The "Dubious Friendships."* Three historical synopses. Two bibliographies. (Trilingual). Geneva: Les Editions du Temps, 1997.

_____. *Guinea Ecuatorial: Bibliografía general.* Vol. 10. Geneva: Les Editions du Temps, 1998 (referencias 22443–26746).

_____. *Guinea Ecuatorial. Bibliografía general.* .Vol. XI. Referencias 26746–30000. Les Editions du Temps. 1999, 320 p.

Negrin Fajardo, O. "Fuentes archivísticas y bibliotecarias de Guinea Ecuatorial." *Estudios Africanos* vol. .9, 16-17 (pp. 93–102). Madrid, 1995.

Ochaga Nve, C. *Fuentes archivisticas y bibliotecarias de Guinea Ecuatorial (Guía generall del administrativo, del investigador y del estudiante).* Ediciones Guinea. Madrid, 1985, 414 p.

Pélissier, R. *Africana: Bibliographie sur l'Afrique luso-hiospanophone (1800–1980).* Chez l'auteur. Orgeval, 1980.

———. "Ecrits sur quelques pays sinistrés. Bibliographie sur les anciennes colonies portugaises et espagnoles." *Le Mois en Afrique,* 196/97. Paris, March-April 1982, pp. 138–158.

Rishworth, S. K. (comp.). *Spanish Speaking Africa: A Guide to Official Publications.* Washington, DC: U.S. Government Printing Office, 1973.

CULTURAL

ARCHAEOLOGY

Clist, B. "Nouvelles données archéologiques sur l'histoire ancienne de la Guinée-Equatoriale." L'Anthropologie, 102, n° 2. Paris, 1998, pp. 213–217.

De Maret, P. "Fernando Po and Gabon." In *The Archeology of Central Africa*, F. Noten (ed.). Graz, 1982.

Martín del Molino, A. *Secuencia cultural en el Neolítico de Fernando Poo.* Trabajos de Prehistoria. Seminario de Historia primitiva del Hombre. Universidad de Madrid y CSIC, XVII. Madrid, 1965, 69 p., ill.

Panyella-Gomez, A. "La prehistoria de Fernando Poo." *Archivos del Instituto de Estudios Africanos,* no. 49 (1959).

———. "Primeros resultados de la Campaña de excavaciones del I.E.A. en Fernando Poo." *Archivos del Instituto de Estudios Africanos,* no. 62 (1962).

Perramon Marti, R. *Contribución a la prehistoria y protohistoria de Río Muni.* Santa Isabel: Instituto Clarentiano de Africanistas, 1968.

———. "Notas sobre la archeología de Río Muni." *Guinea Española.* vol. 63, nos. 1606, 1607, 1609 (Sept.-Dec. 1966), pp. 195–200, 224–230, 298–305.

ARCHITECTURE

Fernandez, C. "The Feeling of Architectonic Form: Residual and Emergent Qualities in Fang Cult and Culture." *Geoscience and Man,* vol. 24 (1984), pp. 31–42.

Fernandez, J. W. *Fang Architectonics.* Philadelphia: Institute for the Study of Human Issues, 1977.

Panyella-Gomez, A. "La casa y el poblado fang." *Archivos del Instituto de Estudios Africanos,* vol. 5, no. 16 (March 1951), pp. 7–30.

Segorbe M., and P. Matia. *Bases para la Planificacion estrategica de la "Isla de Annobon" de: Infraestructura, Arquitectura y Urbanismo, Pesca, Sandid y Deporte.* Plan Director. Análisis de necesidades, para su desarrollo. Valencia, June 1994. 15 p.

ARTS

African Folktales and Sculpture. Boligen Ser. 32 (pp. 13, 19, 35, 71–75, 77). New York, 1952.

Arean, C. *Leandro Mbomio en la integración de la negritud.* Madrid, 1975.

Elisfon, E. *Sculpture of Africa* (pp. 160, 164–177). Text, W. Fagg. Prol., R. Linton. Drawings, B. Quint. New York: Thames and Hudson, 1958.

Ibarrola Monasterio, R. "El arte de los pueblos Pamues." *Archivos del Instituto de Estudios Africanos,* no. 41 (1957), pp. 51–60.

Perrois, L., and M. Sierra Delange. *L'art Fang: Guinée Equatoriale.* Paris: Fundación Folch, 1991.

Segy, L. *African Sculpture Speaks* (pp. 75, 192–193, fig. 14, 15, 44, 80–81, 186). New York: 1958

DRAMA

Soria Marcos, B. *Bajo el sol de Guinea.* Comedia dramatica, 4 acts. Barcelona, 1945.

LINGUISTICS

Barrena Moreno, N. *Gramática anobonesa.* Madrid: IDEA, 1957.

Baumann, O. "Beiträge zur Kenntniss der Bube-Sprache." *Zeitschrift für Afrikanische Sprachen (1887–1888),* pp. 143–155.

Bolados Carter, A. *Diccionario español-Paómu y Paómu y Paume-español.* Santa Isabel: Vicariato Apostólico de Fernando Poo, 1990.

Bolekia Bolekia, J. *Aspectos lingüísticos y sociológicos del bubi del noroeste.* Unpublished dissertation, Univ. Madrid, 1986. 496 p.

Castillo Barríl, M. "La influencia de las lenguas nativas en el español de la Guinea Ecuatorial." *Archivo del Instituto de Estudios Africanos,* vol.2, no. 79 (1966), pp. 46–71.

Clarke, J. *Introduction to the Fernandian tongue.* Freeport. Books for Library Press. New York, 1971 (Black heritage Library collection).

Esquerra Guerra, R. "El español en el Africa negra." *Africa 2000,* January-March 1987, pp. 4–8.

Fernández Galilea, L. *Diccionario española-Kombe.* Madrid: IDEA, 1951.

González Echagray, C. "Bibliografía lingüística de los territorios españoles de Guinea." *Archivos del Instituto de Estudios Africanos,* no. 27 (Dec. 1951).

Filología. *Estudios guineos,* vol. 1. Madrid: IDEA, 1959; *Morfología y síntaxis de la lengua Bujeba.* Madrid: IDEA, 1960.

_____. "El método estructural aplicado al verbo en una lengua bantú" (Bujeba). *Estudios ofrecidos a Emilio Alaroc Llorach.* Oviedo, 1985.

Granda, G. de *Estudios de Lingüística afro-romancea.* Valladolid: Universidad de Valladolid, 1985. 225 p.

_____. *Estudios lingüísticos hispanicos, afrohispanicos y criollos.* Madrid, 1978.

_____. "Las lenguas de Guinea Ecuatorial: material bibliográfica para su estudio." *Boletín del Instituto Caro y Cuervo,* vol. 39. Bogota, 1984, pp. 170–193.

_____. "El 'vocabulario fondamental' del criollo portugués de Annobon. Rasgos caracterizadores." *Verba,* 11. Santiago de Compostela, 1984, pp. 25–37.

_____. "Fenómenos de interferencias fonética del fang sobre el español de Guinea Ecuatorial. Consonantismo." *Anuario de Linguística hispanica,* 1. Valladolid, 1985, pp. 95–114.

_____. *Estudios de lingüística afrorománica.* Valladolid, 1985.

_____. "Procedimientos de aculturación léxica en el fang ntumu de Guinea Ecuatorial." *Cahiers de l'Institut Linguistique de Louvain,* vol. 13, 1–2. Louvain, 1987, pp. 15–32.

_____. "Las retenciones lèxicas africanas en el criollo portugués de Annobón y sus implicaciones sociohistoricas." *Verba,* 15. Santiago de Compostela, 1988, pp. 323–337.

_____. *Lingüística e Historia. Temas Afrohispánicos.* Valladolid, 1988.

_____. "Origen y configuración de un rasgo sintacico en el español de Guinea Ecuatorial y e el portugués de Angola." *Anuario de Lingüística hispanica,* 4. Valladolid, 1988, pp. 81–98.

Guthrie, M. "Bube-Benga Group." In *The Bantu Languages of Western Equatorial Africa* (pp. 24–27). London: International African Institute, 1953.

_____. "Makaa-Njem Group." Ibid., pp. 45–49.

_____. "Yaounde-Fang Group." Ibid., pp. 40–44.

Ikuga Ebombebombe, A. *Cómo se habla, se escribe y se lee el Ndowe.* Asociación Cultural Rhombe. Barcelona, 1993, 490 p. [manuscript, 1969].

Iyanga Pendi, A. "Transcripción y escritura de la lengua ndowe (Teoría e Historia)." *Estudios Africanos. Revista de la Asociación Española de Africanistas,* vol. 8, 14–15. Madrid, 1994, pp. 87–96.

Levin, W. B. "Préstamos románicos en batete y en annobonés según le teoría del sociolecto." In *XI Congrese Internacional de Lingüística y Filología Románicas* (p. 177), Madrid: Sept. 1–9, 1965. Madrid, 1965.

Lipski, J. M. *The Spanish of Equatorial Guinea: The Dialect of Malabo and Its Implications for Spanish Dialectology.* Tubingen, 1985.

Livre de Registre de lettres et télérgrammes de l'Administration de Santa Isabel. Archive du Provincial Clarétin de Santa Isabel.

Ndongo Esono, S. *Gramática Pamue.* Madrid: IDEA, 1956.

Nzè Abuy, R. M. *La lengua Fan o Nkobo Fan.* Barcelona, 1986. Id. *Gramática de la lengua fan,* Barcelona, 1974.

Ondo Odjama, S. *El debilitamiiento del español en guinea Ecuatorial en los años sesenta.* Mémoire de maîtrise d'espagnol. Université Toulouse-le-Mirail. toulouse, June 1989.

Pereda, B. *Compendio de gramática bubi.* Barcelona: Impr. Lucet, 1920.

Perez, G., and L. Sorinas. *Gramática de la leguna Benga.* Santa Isabel: Vicariato Apostólico de Fernando Poo y Guinea; Madrid: Corazón de María, edit. Ibérica, 1928.

Piper, K. *Aspektstruktur im Pahouin: zur verbalen Morphologie nord-westlicher Bantusprachen.* Habilitationsschrift. Hamburgo, 1989, 215 p., bibl.

———. "La situación lingüística del Fa d'Ambô," in *Sociolingüistica: Lenguas en contracto. Foro Hispánico,* 13. Rodopi. Ameterdam 1998.

Post, M. "Annobon," in *Seriele werkwoord contructies ind de West Afrins op portugees gebaseerde Kreooltalen.* Diss. Amsterdam, 1988.

Quilis Morales, A., Casaado-Fresnillo, C. *Le lengua española en Guinea Ecuatorial.* UNED. Cooperación Española. Madrid, 1995, 694 p., 6 índexes, 1 CD.

Salvado y Cos, Fr. *Apuntes para las gramáticas Benga y Ambú.* Madrid: Impr. A. Pérez Dubrull, 1891. At the end: "Elementos de gramática Ambú o de Annobón," from I. Vila.

LITERATURE

Alvárez García, H. R. *Leyendas y mitos de Guinea.* Madrid: IDEA, 1951.

Balboa Boneke, J. "Sueños en mi selva." *Antología poetica.* Malaba, Santa Isabel: Centro híspano-guineano, 1987. 93 p.

Bokesa, C. *Voces de espuma.* Malabo, Santa Isabel, 1987. 92 p.

Borico Lopeo, B. *Il villagio racconta. Cultura e tradizione orale del popolo Bubi.* Bologna: E.M.I., 1977. 157 p.

———. "Equatorial Guinea." In *ALA World Encyclopedia of Librarian on Information Service* (pp. 267–269). Chicago, 1986.

Cook, R. *Chromosome 6.* Novel. thorndike Press. New York, 1997, 709 p.

Creus Boixaderas, J. *Cuentos de los Ndowe de Guinea Ecuatorial.* Centro cultural hispano-guineano/Programas de cooperación cultural con Guinea Ecuatorial. *Ensayos,* 6. Malabo [Santa Isabel], 1991.

Creus Boixaderas, J., and A. Brunat Mampel. *Cuentos de los fang de Guinea Ecuatorial.* Centro cultural hispano-guineano. *Ensayos,* 7. Malabo [Santa Isabel], 1991.

———. "Cuentos annoboneses de Guinea Ecuatorial." Centro cultural hispano-guineano. *Ensayos,* 8, 1992.

Creus Boixaderas, J., A. Brunat Mampel, and P. Carulla. *Cuentos bubis de Guinea Ecuatorial.* Centro cultural hispano-guineano. *Ensayos,* 9, 1992.

Evita, L. *Cuando los Comós luchaban: novela de costumbres de Guinea española.* Madrid: IDEA, 1950.

Ilombe, R. *Leyendas guineanas.* Madrid, 1981.

Leguineche, M. *La tribu* [rev. ed.]. Madrid, 1997.

Manfredi Cano, D. *Tierra negra.* Barcelona: Luis de Caralt, 1957.

Martínez García, T. "Leyendas y fábulas." *Guinea Española,* vol. 42, no. 1595–vol. 45, no 1620 (1965–1967).

Ndongo Bidyogo, D. *Antología de la literatura guineana.* Madrid, 1984.

———. *Los poderes de la tempestad.* Morandi. Madrid, 1997, 318 p.

Nkoa ze Lecourt, M. *Le Mvet. Un genre littéraire fang* (Gabon, Sud-Cameroun, Guinée Equatoriale). Mémoire de diplôme. Paris: EPHE, 1973.

Nsué Angüe, María. *Ekomo.* Madrid: Universidad Nacional de Educación a Distancia, 1985. 194 p.

_____. *Ekomo. Au coeur de la forêt [équato-] guinéenne.* L'Harmattan. Paris, 1995, 231 p.

Osubita, J. B., and A. Serrano. "Se habla español. Una introducción en la literatura guineana." *Quimera,* 112–114 (October 1992), pp. 44–49.

_____. "La littérature de Guinée Equatoriale." In *Littératures francophones d'Afrique centrale* (pp. 150–156). Anthologie. Paris: Agence de Cooperation Culturelle et Technique/Nathan, 1955.

Rebollo, E. A. *Estupendos misterios de la Guinea española* (Estampa Novelada). Madrid, n.d.

Rodríguez Barrera, J. *Mobbe, un negro de Fernando Poo.* Barcelona: Impr. Villa, Aleu and Domingo, 1931.

Simon, W. *Balade africaine.* Novel [Nguemist terror]. Editions du Rocher. Paris, 1988, 243 p.

Towo Atangana, G. "Le mvet, genre majeur de la littérature orale des populations pahouines (Buli—Beti—Fang Ntumu)." *Abbia,* nos. 9–10 (July 1965), pp. 163–179.

Zamora, Fr. *Como ser negro y no morir en Aravaca.* Madrid, 1994.

MUSIC/DANCE

González Echegaray, C. "La música en la Guinea española." *Archivos del Instituto de Estudios Africanos,* no. 38 (June 1956), pp. 19–30.

Ibarrola Monasterio, R. "La musica y el baile en los territorios españoles del Golfo de Guinea." *Africa,* no. 142 (Oct. 1953), pp. 15–17.

Norborg, A. *A Handbook of Musical and Other Sound Producing Instruments from Equatorial Guinea and Gabon.* Musikmuseets skrifter, 16. Stockholm, 1989, 477 p. Ill., maps, bibliography, discography. Wallin and Dalhom, Bocktrycjeri, Lund, Suecia.

Sierra Delage, M., and others. "La Danza Ivanga en Guinea ecuatorial (Manifestaciones musicales de los Kombes)." *Estudios Africanos,* 2–3, 1–2 semester 1986, pp. 39–84.

PRESS/PUBLISHING

Africa 2000. Revista trimestrial de cultura. Malabo [Santa Isabel]: (IIa epoca, II ano, 1) 1987–1997.

Ager. Servicio Agronómo de la Guinea Española. Santa Isabel: Dirección de Agricultura, 1951–1956.

Ano, "Equatorial Guinea." *World Press Encyclopedia,* II (pp. 1118–1119). London, 1982.

_____. "Prensa prohibida." *ABC.* Madrid, February 23, 1993, p. 40.

Bantú. Delegación de Asuntos indígenas del distrito insular. Bata: 1949–1951.

Boletín. Cámara Agrícola de Fernando Poo. Santa Isabel: 1907–1922.

Boletín Agrícola de los Territorios Españoles del Golfo de Guinea. Santa Isabel: 1943–1964.

Boletín Oficial de las Provincias de Fernando Poo y Río Muni. Santa Isabel: 1959–1968.

Boletín Oficial de los Territorios españoles del Golfo de Guinea, vols 1–43. Madrid: March 1907–Sept. 1959.

Cámara Agrícola de Fernando Poo. Santa Isabel: 1907–1922.

Cambio 93, Partido Liberal. Santa Isabel, 1993. Sporadic.

EFE, "Obiang Nguema detiene 4 personas por leer prensa opositora." *Levante.* Valencia, July 8, 1993, p. 6.

El Defensor de Guinea. Santa Isabel: 1930–1936.

Delegación de Asuntos indígenas del distrito insular. *Bantú.* Bata: 1949–1951.

El Diario del la Guinea Española. Santa Isabel: 1962–1964.

Dirección Géneral de Marruecos y Colonias. *Boletín Oficial de los Terrirorios españoles del Golftoe Guinea,* vols. 1–53. Madrid: March 1907–Sept. 1959.

Ebano. Santa Isabel: 1939–1941; 1979- . Sporadic.

Eco de Fernando Poo. Santa Isabel: 1900.

España colonial. Santa Isabel: 1928–1930.

La Gazeta de Guinea Ecuatorial. Periódico de información general y cultural. Santa Isabel (Malabo), May 1996-. A weekly. Edited by officials of the Nguemist administration.

Tu Guia. Partido de la Coalicion social-demócrata, Santa Isabel - Madrid, 1993 —.Sporadic.

La Guinea Española. Misioneros Hijos del Inmaculado Corazón de Mariá. Santa Isabel: 1907–1968.

Heraldo colonial. Santa Isabel: 1924–1927.

La Hoja del Lunes. Santa Isabel: 1968–1972.

International Federation of Journalists, "Guinée Equatoriale." *Annuaire de la presse africaine* (pp. 155–156). Brussels, 1996.

La Libertad. Bata 1968–1969.

Liniger-Goumaz, M. "Les rapports d'Amnesty International et la désinformation. Comment la Guinée Equatoriale est devenue le paradis des droits de l'homme, " *Genève-Afrique,* XXIV, 2. Geneva: December 1986, pp. 137–146.

La Luz. Convergencia social-demócrata y popular, Santa Isabel, 1993- . Sporadic.

Misioneros Hijos del Inmaculado Corazón de María. *La Guinea Española.* Santa Isabel: 1907–1968.

Noticias de Guinea Ecuatorial. Publicación mensual editada y distribuida por ASODEGUE. Madrid. N° 1 January 1998- .

El Nacionalista. Santa Isabel: 1937–1939.

Ndongo Bidyogo, D., "Prensa y Desarrolo." *Africa 2000,* V, II, 13. Madrid, 1990, p. 3.

El Ocho. Alianza Democrática y Progresista. Santa Isabel, 1993- . Sporadic.

El Patio. La Revista de la cultura hispano-guineana. N° 0, December 1990, N° 1 January 1991– (July 1997, N° 55).

Poto-Poto. Bata: 1951–1967.

Revisita de la Diputación Provincial. Santa Isabel: 1961–1964.

Romero Gallego, M. *Guinea de provincia a la independencia a través de la presa española. Memoria de licenciatura.* Madrid: Universidad Complutense, 1984.

Servicio Agronómico de la Guinea Española. Ager. Santa Isabel: Dirección de Agricultura, 1951–1965.

Tam-Tam Express. Periódico independiente de Guinea Ecuatorial. Monthly. Malabo-Bata-Madrid, December 1993–August 1995.

La Verdad. Convergencia Para la Democrácia Social (CPDS), monthly. Santa Isabel, N° 00, June 1991, 8 p; 1, July 1991, 10 p. Continued. Interruption between June 1995 and February 1996. No 35, March 1996. According to the International Federation of Journalists, the only alternative source of information available in the country.

Viyil. Revistta de divulgación cultural. Asociación cultural Viyil [Annobón], Barcelona, 1986. Trimestrial.

Voces de Guinea Ecuatorial, Asociación para la Solidaridad democrática con Guinea Ecuatorial (ASODEGUE), 1994– . 6 per year.

La Voz de Fernando Poo. Barcelona, Gerona, Madrid: 1911–1923.

La Voz del Pueblo. Organo de Información de la ANRD. On exile. 1976– . Irregular.

La Voz del Pueblo. Organo del P.D.G.E. [Official paper of the Nguemist dictatorship]. Santa Isabel, 1992– . Sporadic.

ECONOMICS

Ano, "Equatorial Guinea to Enter Oil Ranks (Mobil and United Meridian Plan Oil Development Program for Zafiro Fields on Block B off Equatorial Guinea.)" *Oil and Gas Journal,* vol. 43, October 23, 1995, p. 36.

Banco de los Estados de Africa Central (BEAC), *Nota de conjuntura Económica.* Malabo, February 28, 1995.

_____. "Guinée Equatoriale: Stastiques Économiques." *Etudes et Statistiques,* 190, March 1992, pp. 58–59, 64–65, 73, 75.

_____. "Guinée Equatoriale." *Situation économique, monétaire et financiére des Etats de la Zone d'émission [du franc francais].* Etudes et statistiques, 199, February 1993, pp. 43–87.

Bindang Obiang, M. "Evolution économique de la Guinée Equatoriale de 1985–1993." *Banque des Etats de l'Afrique Centrale. Etudes et Statistiques,* January 1994, p. 518.

Black, Kelly, Scrugs and Healy. *The Republic of Equatorial Guinea.* [ed. Mrs. Levinson]. Washington, DC, July 1996. (A typical neocolonialistic approach: Obiang Nguema's Equatorial Guinea is very democratic).

Bochongolo, P. (pseud.), Nsue, P. (pseud.). "¿Bendición o maldición? La producción de petróleo en Guinea Ecuatorial." *Voces de Guinea Ecuatorial,* 7, October 1995, 8 p.

Bravo Carbonel, J. *Fernando Poo y Río Muni. Sus misterios y riquezas. Su colonización.* Madrid: Impr. Alrededor del Mundo, 1917.

Clarence-Smith, W. G. "The Economic Dynamics of Spanish Colonialism in the Nineteenth and Twentieth Centuries." *Itinerario,* vol. 15, 1. Leiden, 1991, pp. 71–90.

_____. "Ecuatorial Guinea: Economy." *Africa South of the Sahara.* London, 1993, 1994. p. 340.

Comité Nacional de protección del medio ambiente, Informe nacional sobre el medio ambiente y desarrollo. FAO-AGO-EQG/87/7003. *Guinea Ecuatorial.*, September 1991, 194 p.

Economist Intelligence Unit. "Equatorial Guinea." In *EIU Country Report,* 1 (pp. 29–33, Appendix 3). London, 1992. Trimestrial (essential).

Esono Ondo, A., *Impacto Socioeconómico y Medioambiental de las Explraciones forestales en Guinea Ecuatorial.* Malabo, November 1993.

_____. *Equatorial Guinea. Country Profile, 1994–95.* London, 1994, 33 p. Annual.

_____. *Quarterly Economic Review of Gabon, Congo,...Equatorial Guinea,* "Equatorial Guinea: Basic Data. Political Scene. The Economy." Annual Supplement, 1981. London: 1981, pp. 7, 41–46, and following years.

Evita, R. *La evolución economica de Guinea Ecuatorial desde 1850 a 1968.* Unpublished dissertation. Washington, DC: Howard University, 1970. 206 p.

Fa, J. E., and others. "Impact of Market Hunting on Mammal Species in Equatorial Guinea." *Conservation in Biology,* vol. 9, 5 (pp. 1107–1115), October 1995.

Fonds du Koweit pour le dévelopment économique arabe, "Guinée Equatorial." In *28e Rapport d'activité, 1989–1990.* Koweit-City, 1992.

Hodd, M. "Equatorial Guinea." In *The Economics of Africa* (pp. 130–136). London, 1991.

Marek Enterprise's Africa Business Research & Consulting Service, *A Report on American interests in Equatorial Guinea and how that couontry fits into American economic strategy.* Reston (VA), 1998.

Morillas, J. "Para una cronología económica de Guinea Ecuatorial." *Estudios Africanos.* Revista de la Asociación Española de Africanistas. vol. 6, 10–11 (pp. 173–176). Madrid, 1991–1992.

Pagni, L. "Guinée Equatoriale." *Le Courrier.* Afrique—Caraïbes—Pacifiques—Communautés européenes, 107. Paris-Brussels: January–February 1988, pp. 32–43. Ill., map. statistics.

Perpiña Grau, R. *De colonización y economía en la Guinea española.* Barcelona: Labor, 1945.

Servicios comerciales del Estado. Perspectivas económicas del Africa Ecuatorial Español. Serie Divulgación, 23. Madrid, 1960.

Tallón, A. "Francia apunta la colonización económica de Guinea Ecuatorial: Alarmante disminuición de la presencia española en Malabo." *ABC.,* March 28, 1998, p. 3.

United States Energy Information Administration. "Equatorial Guinea," *Oil, Natural Gas & Electricity Profile.* Washington, September 1997, 4 p.

Yates, D. "Equatorial Guinea: Oil and Power." *Panafrica*, November 1996, pp. 16–17. Ill., maps.

_____. "Equatorial Guinea," in "Central-Africa: Oil and the Franco-American Rivalry," in *L'Afrique politique 1998*. Paris, January 1998, pp. 205–226, map.

Wolff, G. "Ein Beitrag zur Wirtschaft von Fernando Poo," *Beiträge zur Kolonialforschung,* vol. I (1942), pp. 93–110.

AGRICULTURE

Agricultura de los Territorios españoles del Golfo de Guinea. Madrid: IDEA, 1948.

Arija, J. *La Guinea Española y sus riquezas*. *Estudios coloniales*. Madrid: Espasa-Calpe, 1930.

Arnal Y Lapuerta, M. de. *Memoria para la fundación de una colonia agrícola y comercial en la isla de Fernando Poo*. Madrid, 1854.

Dirección General de Marruecos y Colonias. *Anuario agrícola de los Territorios españoles del Golfo de Guinea*. Madrid: DGMS, 1941–1959.

Galan, B. B. *Legislación Agropecuaria, Forestal y Pesquera. Guinea Ecuatorial*. Informe técnio. Rome, 1991, 47 p., FAO-LEG-EQG/0052 (a).

Inspección de Colonización. *Informe sobre el estado de los cultivos en la Isla de Fernando Poo*. Madrid, 1901.

International Fund for Agricultural Development. "Equatorial Guinea." In *Report 1990*. Rome, 1992.

Mas Guindal, J. *Datos para el conocimiento de la flora de la Guinea Española, la vegetación espontánea y las plantas cultivadas*. Madrid: Dirección General de Marruecos y Colonias, 1944.

Nosti Nava, J. "La agricultura colonial en Guinea y sus evolución." *Guinea Española*, vol. 42, no. 1213 (February–June 1946).

_____. *Agricultura en Guinea, promesa para España*. Madrid: IDEA, 1948.

Oyono Sa Abegue, V. *L'évolution des structures productives et sociales de l'économie de la Guinée Equatoriale (1858–1968). L'originalité d'un cas de transition au capitalisme agraire dans un contexte colonial*. Diss. Lyon: Université de Lyon II, 1985. 983 p.

Ruiz y Albaya, J. *Descripción de los cultivos que de practican en las llamadas fincas de la isla de Fernando Poo*. Cadiz, 1898.

Coffee

Cámaras oficiales agrícolas de Guinea. *Memoria de la Delegación peninsular para café*. Madrid, 1964.

Delegación peninsular para Café de las Cámaras Oficiales de Agricultura de Guinea. *Memoria, 1954– . Madrid: 1955– .

Dine, J., Chartier, J. C., Simon, D. *Projets de relance de la production et de la commercialisation de café robusta sur la région continentale de la Guinée Equatoriale: rapport d'évaluation*. Min. Coopération. Paris, 1989. 109 p.

Foreign Agricultural Service (FAS), "Equatorial Guines, " in *World Coffee supply and distribution for Producing Countries, Forecast 1996/97*. Horticultural and Tropical Products Division, FAS/USDA. Washington, 2 February 1998.

Nosti Nava, J., and Jimenez Cuende, F. *Como es y como se poda el café "Liberia"* Madrid: IDEA, 1949.

Simon, D. *Projet de relance de la production et de la commercialisation du café robusta sur la région continentale de la Guinée Equatoriale: rapport de supervision.* Min. de la Cooperation et du Développement. Paris, January 1993. 41 p.

Cocoa

Bagueña Corella, L. *Los taladros de cacaoteros, cafetos y otros cultivos en Guinea española.* Madrid: IDEA, 1949.

Clarence-Smith, W. G. "African and European Cocoa Producers on Fernando Pó, 1880s to 1910s." *Journal of African History,* XXXV, 2, 1994, pp. 179–199.

Foreign Adricultural Service (FAS), "Equatorial Guinea," in *Cocoa Beans: Production in Specified Countries, 1992/92–1997/98 (Forecast).* Horticultural and tropican Products Division, FAS/USDA. Washington, 31, March 1998.

Hanish, R., C. Jacobeit (ed.). "Äquatorialguinea," *Der Kakaoweltmarkt,* 2. Hamburg, 1991.

Nosti Nava, J., and J. Alvárez Aparicio. "Características y clasificación de los cacaos de Fernando Poo," *Anuario de los Territorios españoles del Golfo de Guinea,* vol. 4. Madrid, 1942.

Palm Oil

Fickendey, E. "Perspectivas de la explotación del aceite de palma en la Guinea española." *Archivos del Instituto de Estudios Africanos,* nos. 28, 29 (March-June 1954), pp. 23–33, 25–30.

Lejeune Castrillo, J. L. "Aceites de Palma y Palmista. Abaca y otras fibras textiles." *Avance del Informe sobre somera explotación de posibilidades industriales,* vol. 2. Madrid, 1963, pp. 41–43.

Timber

Brown, S., Gaston, G. "Equatorial Guines," in "Use of Forest Inventories and Geographic Information Systems to estimate Biomass Density of Tropical Forests—Application to Tropical Africa." *Environment Monitoring and Assessment,* XXXVIII, 2–3. November–December 1995, pp. 157–168.

Capdevielle, J. M. *El bosque de la Guinea. Exploración y Explotación.* Madrid: IDEA, 1947.

_____. *Tres estudios y un ensayo sobre temas forestales de la Guinea continental española.* Madrid: IDEA, 1949.

Fa, J. E. *Guinea Ecuatorial: conservación y manejo sostenible de los ecosistemas forestales.* IUCN.Tropical Forest Program. Gland (CH), 1991, 232 p., maps, stat.

_____. *The WCMC Closed Moist Troopical forest of Equatorial Guinea (Classification of Forest Types). Dataset documentation.* File: EGUGUIN.E00. Code 121001-001.UNEP-GRID-Nairobi. Roma, s.f.

Fuster Riera, P. *Estudio sobre la constitución y explotación del bosque en la Guinea continental española.* Madrid: Servicio Forestal de los Territorios españoles del Golfo de Guinea, 1941.

Gonzalez Martín, L. *Primera contribución al concocimiento de las maderas de la Guinea continental española.* Madrid: IDEA, 1953.

International Uniion for the Conservation of the Nature (IUCN), "Guinée Equatoriale," in *La conservation des écooystèmes forestiers d'Afrique centrale.* Gland (CH)-Cambridge (UK), 1989, pp. 103–107.

Kometter, R. *Inventario forestal exploratorio, isla de Bioko.* Malabo, 1992. 51 p. Ill, 2 maps 1:100'000. FAO-FO-UTF/EQG/002/EQG—*Estudios de Apoyo a la Preparación del Proyecto Manejo y Conservación de los Recuros Naturales.* Documento de campo 5.

Laporte, N., Justice, C., Kendall, J. "Equatorial Guinea," in "Mapping the Dense Humid Forest od Cameroon and Zaire Using AVHRR Satellite Data." *International Journal of Remote Sensing,* XVI, 6, 1995, pp. 1127–1145.

Lejoly, J., Wilks, Ch., *Seguimento dse los estudios de bioversidad vegetal en los estudios de biodiversidad vegetal en el Parque Nacional de Monte Alen.* ECOFAC. Bruselas, September 1995, 133 p.

Lejoly, J. Issembe, Y., Ayichedehou, M., *Biodiversité végetales de ligneux sur le transect de Monte Chocolate dans le Parc National de Monte Alen.* ECOFAC. Bruselas, Octover 1995, 86 p.

Monzon-Perala, A. *Apoyo y desarrollo intitucional para la Dirección General de Bosque.* Malabo, 1992. 47 p., maps. FAQ-FO-UTF/EQG/002/EQG. *Estudio de Apoyo a la Preparación del Proyecto Manejo y Conservación de los Recursos Naturales.* Documento de campo 3.

United Nations. Evaluación de la capacidad operativa de las empresas forestales. Borrador. FAO/PNUD EQG/92/001. Malabo, April 1995.

Vannières, B. *Situation forestière en Guinée équatoriale.* Rome: FAO, June–July 1969.

Van Paasen, M. *Estudio económico de los recursos forestales se la Región Ecuatorial. Análisis estructural.* Ministerio de Agricultura. Guinea Ecuatorial. Malabo, December 1991. 100 p. FAO-FO-EQG/87/005.

Breeding

Caldwell and Brouwer. *L'élevage en Guinée équatoriale.* Rome: FAO, 1970.

Neches Nicolas, J. "La ganadería en la Guinea española," *Anuario Agrícola de los Terriorios españoles del Golfo de Guinea,* vol. 12 (1944), pp. 93–106.

Fishing

European Union. "Legislation—Regulation on Fishing Agreement with Equatorial Guinea." Spicers Centre for Europe. Reuter Textline, from *Official Journal of the European Community Legislation,* August 18, 1995. 7 p.

Gonzalez Echegaray, C. "Aspecto económico-social de la pesca entre les indígenas de la Guinea Española." *Communiccatión presentada a la V Conferencia Internacional de Africanistas Occidentales. Archivos del Instituto de Estudios africanos,* 44, 1958, pp. 7–19. Ill.

Porto, O. do, Lessi, E. *Informe de misión (julio–agosto 1988), Guinea Ecuatorial. Informe preparado para el proyecto Cursos de Entrenamiento para el Procesamiento Artesanal de Pescado.* Rome, November 1988, 89, p. FAO-FI-ICP/EQG/8351.

Union Européenne. *Réglement No. 114/98, concernant la conclusion de protocole fixant les possibilités de pêche et la compensation financière prévues dans l'accord entre la Communauté économique européenne et le gouvernement de la république de Guinée équatoriale, poour le période du 1er juillet 1997 au /30 juin 2000.* CE/114/98. Brussels, 18 Dicember 1997.

COMMERCE

Arnalte, A. "Noticias sobre comercio español en la costa de Africa a mediados del siglo XIX." *Estudios Africanos. Revista de la Asociación Española de Africanistas,* vol. 6, 10–11, December 1991–92, pp. 35–50.

Brooks, G. E., Jr. "Trade with the Gulf of Guinea and Angola." In *Yankee Traders, Old Coasters and African Middlemen* (pp. 10, 281–290, 316–317, 335, 337). Boston, 1970.

Bundesstelle für Aussenhandel-Informationen (West Germany). *Aussenhandel Spanisch Guineas 1960–1964.* Köln, 1965.

_____. *Wirtschaftsstrucktur Guineas,* vol. 9. Köln: Marktinformationsdienst, 1963.

Lynn, M. "Commerce, Christianity and the 'Creoles' of Fernando Poo." *Journal of African History,* vol. 25, 1984 (pp. 257–278).

_____. "The Fernandinos of Bioko: 1827–1858." In *L'Estat Espanyol y l'Africa negra. Actas de la VIII Setmana d'Estudis Africans,* 1995.

Ministerio de Asuntos exteriores. *Memoria que presenta a las Cortes el Ministro de Estado respecto a la situación política y económica de las Posesiones españolas del Africa Occidental.* Madrid, 1904–1919.

Ndongo Bydiogo, D. "El comercio entre España y Guinea Ecuatorial." Revista MECH. In *Boletín Económico de ICE,* 1771, 3, 1981 (pp. 962–964).

Pozuelo Mascarague, B. "Las relaciones entre España y Africa subsahara: aspectos de la cooperación, comerciales y políticos." In *Portugal, España y Africa en los ultimos cien años.* Merida: UNED Extremadura, 1992.

Velarde Fuentes, J. "Consideraciones sobre las relaciones con el exterior de Guinea ecuatorial." *Informacíon comercial española,* no. 381 (May 1965), pp. 97–124.

DEVELOPMENT

Abaga Edjang, F. *La ayuda externaen el desarrollo de Guine Ecuatorial.* Los libros de la catarata. Madrid, 1997, 223 p.

Alvárez Corugedo, J. "El impacto sectorial del plan de Desarrollo económico de Fernando Poo y Río Muni." *Archivos del Instituto de Estudios Africanos,* no. 71 (1964), pp. 57–78.

Banciella y Barena, J. C. *Rutas de imperio; Fernando Poo y Guinea (su significaión actual y potencial antes las necesidades económicas de España).* Madrid: Victoriano Suarez, 1940.

Barcelo, J. L. *Perspectivas económicas del Africa Ecuatorial Española.* Madrid: 1947.

Bonelli y Rubio, J. M. *Presente y futuro de la economía de Guinea*. Conference. Barcelona: Casa de Guinea, 1945.

Bremón, L. M. *Fernando Poo; su presente y su porvenir; recopiliación de datos y noticias oficiales*. Madrid: Tip. J. Palacios, 1897.

Comisaría del Plan de Desarrollo económico y social de Guinea Ecuatorial. *Plan de Desarrollo económice y social, 1964–1967*. Madrid, 1964.

International Bank for Reconstruction and Development. *The Economy of the Republic of Equatorial Guinea. Recent Evolution and Prospects*. Report AW-37a. Washington, DC: IDA, November 27, 1972.

Jung, U. *Grundlagen einer Entwicklungskonzeption für die Region Teguete [between Evinayong and Kogo]. ASA-Auswertungsbericht über Studienvorhaben "Entwicklungskonzeption Teguete."* Gastland: Äquatorial-Guinea. Berlin, 1995.

Klitgaard, R. E. *Tropical Gangsters: One Man's Experience with Development and Decadence in Deepest Africa*. New York: Basic Books, 1990.

Kobel, Armin. *La République de Guinée Equatoriale. Ses resources potentielles et virtuelles et les possibilitiés de dévelopement*. Diss. Neuchatel, Switzerland: Copy Quick, 1976.

Margallo, B. A. G. "Guinea Ecuatorial ante el Plan de desarrollo," *Africa*, no. 22 (Sept. 1965), pp. 472–475, 475–478.

Ministère de la Cooperation. *Guinée Equatoriale. Dossier d'Information économique*. Paris, June 1980. 100 p.

Negrin Fajardo, O. "Cultura, educación y desarrollo colonial en Guinea española (1949-1959)." *Estudios Africanos. Revista de la Asociación de Africanistas*, vol. 7, 12–13, December 1993.

Programa de las Naciones Unidas para el Desarrollo (PNUD/UNDP), Guinea Ecuatorial. Informe 1994–1995. Malabo, August 1966. 138 p., stat.

Rasilla, L. de la. "La Cooperación con Guinea [Ecuatorial] entre el silencio y le desperanza." *Razón y Fé*, 1063, May 1987, pp. 534–538.

United Nations. *Assistance économique spéciale et secours en cas de catastrophe. Assistance à la Guinée Equatoriale. Rapport du Secrétaire général*. Doc. A/40/430. New York: August 19, 1985. 27 p.

———. *Perspectivas de la Asistencia Técnica en Guinea Ecuatorial*. UNDP. Malabo, 1988.

———. "Equatorial Guinea." *Country Human Development Indicators, 1992*. UNDP. New York, 1992. 4 p.

———. *Propuesta para la formulición del marco estratégico-institucional para un desarrollo humano sostenible*. PNUD. Working Paper. Malabo, 1995.

World Bank. "Equatorial Guinea." In *Trends in Developing Economies, 1990*. Washington, DC, 1990. World Bank Development Services, 102; vol. 2, *Country Analysis*, pp. 187–192.

Yaters, D. "Equatorial Guinea: Oil and Power." *Panafrica*. London, November 1996, pp. 16–17. Ill. maps.

FINANCE

Banco Exterior de España. *Dependencias de los Territorios españoles del Golfo de Guinea. Condiciones generales de y para las Plazas de dichos territorios.* Madrid, 1944.

Banque centrale des Etats de l'Afrique de l'Ouest. "Les institutions monétaires de la République de Guinée équatoriale." *Notes d'Information et Statistiques. Banques et Monnaies,* no. 186. Dakar, July 1971, pp. 1–16.

_____. Banque des Etats de l'Afrique Central. "La situation économique, monétaire et financière de la Guinée Equatoriale à la veille de son adhésion à la zone BEAC." *Etudes et Statistiques,* BEAC, 118, January 1985, pp. 17–32.

_____. "Guinée Equatoriale: Conditions créditrices pratiquées par les banques (en %)." *Etudes et Statistiques,* 190, March 1992, p. 45.

Gard, R. C. *Equatorial Guinea: Machination in Founding a National Bank.* Munger African Library Notes, no. 27. Pasadena, October 1974.

Godeau, R. *Le Franc CFA: Pourquoi la dévaluation de 1994 a tout changé.* Paris, 1996. 218 p.

Gómez Durán, J. *El régimen jurídico-financiero colonial.* Madrid: IDEA, 1946.

International Bank for Reconstruction and Development. "Republic of Equatorial Guinea." Public Expenditure Review. Washington, DC, June 1992.

International Monetary Fund. "Equatorial Guinea." In *Survey of African Economies,* vol. 5, chap. 7. Washington, DC: IMF, 1973.

International Monetary Fund, World Bank. *Documento sobre el marco de política económica y financiera, 1991–1993.* Malabo, 1991.

_____. *Documento sobre el marco de política económica y financeria, 1991–1994.* Malabo, 1991.

_____. "Guinea Ecuatoriale." *Annual Report,* Washington, DC, 1993.

_____. *Economic and Financial Policy Framework Paper, 1994–1996.* Malabo, 1994.

Jauregui, F. "El Banco Exterior de España abandona Guinea [Ecuatorial]." *El País,* October 28, 1987, pp. 1, 3.

Liniger-Goumaz, M. "Guinée Equatoriale et zone franc. Réflexions sur un système monétaire et une récupération." *Genève-Afrique,* XXIII, 2, 1985, pp. 137–146.

Massoud, M. "Guinée Equatoriale," in *Evolution des balances des pairments des Etats de la Zone BEAC en 1989.* Banque des Etats de l'Afrique Centrale. Etudes et Statistiques. Yaounde, January–July 1991, pp. 111–135.

Mbana Nchama, J. "El ekuele y la economía tradicional fang." *Africa 2000,* V, II, 13, 1990, pp. 4–11. Ill.

Mbomio, J. *La zone Franc CFA. L'exemple de la Guinée Equatoriale.* Mémoire. Geneva: Institut Universitaire d'Etudes du Développement, May 1994. 21 p.

Menéndez Hernández, J. *Estudio de la legislación hipotecária de Guinea. Su único procedimiento inmatriculador.* Madrid, 1970.

United States Department of Commerce. "Incomes, High Prices Stable in Spanish Equatorial Guinea." *International Commerce,* vol. 69. Washington, DC, July 15, 1963.

Velarde, G. B. "Una antigua moneda Paume: la Vigüela." *Africa,* no. 147 (1954), pp. 8–9.

World Bank, *Equatorial Guinea: Poverty Note.* Washington, D.C., 1995.

INDUSTRY

Acre, R. *Informe al Gobierno de la República de Guinea Ecuatorial referente a política minera y petroléra.* Santa Isabel: UNDP, September 1971.

Campos Normann, R. "Indústrias de la alimentación." *Avance del Informe sobre somera explotación de posibilidades industriales,* vol. 2 (pp. 34–40). Madrid, 1963.

Canada, E. "Electrificación y posibilidades industriales." *Indústria,* no. 19 (July–August 1964), pp. 48–58.

Carcamo Bredal, E. "Posibilidades de producción de pasta de papel y cellulosa. Derivados de madera. Destilación. Industrialización de la yuca y otros productos agrícolas," *Avance del Informe sobre somera explotación de posibilidades industriales,* vol. 2 (pp. 46–63). Madrid, 1963.

Laorden Jiménez, C. "Asseradorias, Carpinterías y producción de envases, Indústrias químicas." Ibid., pp. 44–45.

Lizaur y Roldan, J. "Minería." Ibid., pp. 32–33.

Novo, P., and F. Chicarro. "Breve reseña geológico-minera de la Guinea continental española." *Boletín de la Sociedad Geográfica Nacional,* vol. 74 (1943), pp. 67–86.

Novo, P., and J. Mendizabal. *Reconocimiento geológico-minero de la Guinea continental española.* Madrid, 1934.

Oficial. "Disposiciones sobre pesca de ballena en Guinea y solicitudes para establecer indústrias derivadas de ella, 1913–18, 1926–32." *Archivos de la Dirección General de Promoción de Sahara.* Madrid. File 185.

LABOR

Dirección General de Marruecos y Colonias. *Legislación del Trabajo de los Territorios españoles del Golfo de Guinea.* Madrid: DGMC, 1946.

International Commission of Inquiry into the Existence of Slavery and Forced Labor in the Republic of Liberia. Report. Monrovia: Sept. 8, 1930. Washington, DC: US Department of State Publications, no. 147, 1931.

International Labor Organization. *Informe al Gobierno de la República de Guinea Ecuatorial sobre la Administración del Trabajo.* Doc. TAP: Guinea Ecuatorial/R1. Geneva: ILO, 1973.

Jones Niger, A. J. *El problema de la mano de obra en Fernando Poo.* Santa Isabel, 1938.

Kloosterboer, W. *Involuntary Labor since the Abolition of Slavery: A Survey of Compulsory Labour Through the World* (pp. 167–168). Leiden: Brill, 1960.

Legislative Council of Nigeria. "Report on Employment of Nigerian Labourers in Fernando Poo." *Sessional Papers,* no. 38. Lagos: Government Print, 1939.

Liniger-Goumaz, M. "Cien años de busqueda de mano obra en Guinea Ecuatorial. La cuestión bracera." *Estudios de Asia y Africa,* XII, 4, no. 74, Oct.–Dec. 1987.

Mezu, S. O. "Nigeria and Fernando Poo: Politics of Indecision." *Nigerian Student's Voice,* vol. 3, no. 2 (Jan. 1966), pp. 68–76.

Official. "Nigeria-Spain Labour Agreement." *Africa Research Bulletin* (Political, Social and Cultural Series), vol. 3, no. 12 (Jan. 1967), p. 691 A; vol. 8, no. 4 (May 1971) p. 2009B; vol. 8, no. 12 (Jan. 31, 1972) p. 2232B.

Perpiña Grau, R. "Mano de obra africana, factor de coste colonial." *Cuadernos de estudios africanos,* no. 3 (1947), pp. 127–144.

Roig, B. *El trabajo a destajo en Fernando Poo.* Santa Isabel, 1912.

Sanz Casas, G. *Política colonial y organización del trabajo en la isla de Fernando Po, 1880–1930.* Barcelona, 1983.

———. "Los finqueros y el uso del trabajo forzado en la agricultura colonial de la isla de Fernando Poo." *Arxiu d'etnografia de Catalunya,* 3. Universidad de Barcelona. Departamento de Antropología cultural. Tarragona, 1984, pp. 121–136.

Sundiata, I. K. "A Note on An Abortive Slave Trade: Fernando Po 1778–1781," *Bulletin de l'Institut Fondamental de l'Afrique Noire,* vol. 35, no. 4 (Oct. 1973), pp. 793–804.

United States Department of State. *Labour conditions in Equatorial Guinea.* Washington, DC: Office of Foreign Labor and Trade, 1966.

Velarde Fuentes, J. "Problema de empleo en la Guinea Ecuatorial." *Revisita de Trabajo,* vol. 26, no. 6 (1964), pp. 141–177.

World Bank. *Equatorial Guinea: Poverty Note.* Washington, D.C., 1995.

TRANSPORTATION/COMMUNICATIONS

"Cameroon-Equatorial Guinea: Telecommunication Links." *Africa Research Bulletin* (Economic, Financial and Technical Series), vol. 20, no. 4 (May 31, 1973), p. 2730C.

Dirección general de Prense. "El problema de las comunicaciones aéreas con Guinea Española." *Boletín monográfico,* no. 64 (1952), 4 p.

Edwards, B. "No Frills Loading Terminal in Operation Off Equatorial Guinea." *Oil & Gas Journal,* vol. 40, 8, February 24, 1992, pp. 54–55.

EFE. "Francia se hace de las comunicaciones de Guinea Equatorial." *El País,* October 10, 1987, p. 19.

García Figueras, T. "Radio y téléfono al servicio de la evolución de Guinea." *ABC* (Dec. 26, 1957), pp. 35, 37.

Llegada de la Fragata de guerra Norteamericana Plymouth a tomar combustible en su recorrido por la Costa Occidental de Africa, 1873. Archivos de la Dirección General de Promoción del Sahara. Madrid: 1858–1910, File 22.

Lloyds. "Equatorial Guinea," in *Maritime guide 1995.* Sect. 2: Ports and Harbours. London, 1995, p. 26.

———. "Equatorial Guinea Bata, Congo, Luba, Malabo, Rio Benito," in *Ports of the World, 1997.* LLP Limited. Colchester (UK), 1997, pp. 26–27.

Official. "Acuerdos entre España y la República de Guinea Ecuatorial." *Revisita de Política internacional,* no. 119 (Jan.–Feb. 1872), pp. 336–367.

Official (USA). *Postal, Express Mail Service: Agreement, with Detailed Regulations, Between the United States of America and Equatorial Guinea, signed at Malabo [Santa Isabel] and Washington, April 9 and May 21, 1991*. United Stateas Treaties. Washington DC: Department of State 1993. 13 p.

Olmos Bullón, J. *El turismo en la Guinea Ecuatorial*. Madrid: Dossat, 1967.

Rio Juan, Fr. del. *El Ferrocarril de Fernando Poo*. Anteproyecto. Madrid, 1914.

Servet, J. L. "El nuevo aeropuerto de Santa Isabel de Fernando Poo." *Africa*, no. 257 (1963), pp. 13–16.

World Bank. *Acronyms from Latin America and Equatorial Guinea = Siglas de los Países latinoamericanos y de Guinea Equatorial*. Terminology Unit. Washington, DC, 1987.

_____. *Equatorial Guinea—Establishment and Management of Protected and Multiple Use Buffer Zones in Bioko and Annobon Island* [5 Mio $]. Project 3 EQGPAO 14. Santa Isabel [Malabo]-Washington, May 1994.

POLITICAL

CONSTITUTION

Aroca, S. "La Constitucion hace a Teodoro Obiang Nguema presidente vitalicio." *El Mundo*, November 24, 1991, p. 80.

Banks, A. J. (ed.). "Equatorial Guinea." In *Political Handbook of the World, 1975* (pp. 94–96). New York, 1975.

"Constitución de la Guinea Ecuatorial." *Documentos Políticos*, no. 10 (1968). 30 p.

Dilg, K. G. "Die Verfassung der Republik Aequatorial Guinea unter besonderer Berücksichtigung der politischen und verfassungsmässigen Entwicklung bis zur Unabhängigkeit im Jahr 1986." *Verfassung und Recht in Uebersee*, no. 2 (1969), pp. 291–303.

"Equatorial Guinea." In *Constitutions of African States*, vol. 1. (pp. 233–256). New York, 1972.

"Establishment of an Unitary State Under New Constitution." *Keensing's Contemporary Archives* (Nov. 5–11, 1973), p. 26185.

Fiallos Oyangurzren, M., and F. Gonzalez-Roura. *Informe de los consultores electorales en Guinea Ecuatorial del 3 al 17 de Abril de 1993, PNUD/NU*. Santa Isabel [Malabo], April 17, 1993. 23 p.

International Commission of Jurists. "New Constitution in Equatorial Guinea." *ICJ Review*, 29, December 1982, pp. 3–6; see also *Une nouvelle constitution en Guinée Equatoriale. Déclaration écrite présentée par la C.I.J. Commission of Human Rights, 39th sessions, Point 12. Doc. E/CN.4/1983/NGO/4*. Geneva: January 31, 1983. 4 p.

Maestre, J. A. *Constituciones y leyes políticas de America Latina, Filipinas y Guinea Ecuatorial* [compiladas por]. Instituto de Cooperación Ibero-americano. Comisiòn Nacional V centenario, t. 1, v. 1: Mexico, Nicaragua, Perú, Guinea. Escuela de Estudios Hispano-americanos. Sevilla, 1987.

Miguel Zaragoza, J. de. "La République de Guinée Equatoriale (aperçu sur la constitution et les droits de l'homme)." *Revue juridique et politique* vol. 23, no. 2 (1969), pp. 213–224.

Official. "Constitution du 13 juillet 1973." *Année Africane,* 1973.

_____. "Constitucion de la República de Guinea Ecuatorial [1968]." *Estudios Africanos. revista de la Asociación Española de Africanistas,* vol. 4, 6, January–June 1989, pp. 95–108.

_____. "Guinée Equatoriale. Nouvelle Constitution." *Bulletin africain des Droits de l'Homme.* African Centre for Democracy and Human Rights Studies, II, 2. Gambia, May-August 1992, p. 7.

Owona, J. "La Guinée Equatoriale et la démocratie: l'astucieux recours à un constitutionnalisme rédhibitoire." *Le mois en Afrique,* 207–208 (April–May 1983), pp. 59–68.

GOVERNMENT

Alvárez Gendin, S. "Guinea: gobierno y administración." In *La administración española en el Protectorado de Marruecos, Plazas de soberanía y Colonias de Africa* (pp. 91–118). Madrid: IDEA, 1949.

Amnesty International. *Guinea Ecuatorial. El historial de promesas incumplidas.* London, July 1995. Doc. AFR 24/09/95/s.

Anon. "Obiang [Nguema] califica de 'relato novelesco' un informe de la ONU. El documento decia no poder garantizar la limpieza y credibildad de los próximos comicios en Guinea [Ecuatorial]." *El Mundo,* February 16, 1996, p. 28.

_____. "Obiang [Nguema] prohibe a los religiosos desplazarse dentro de Guinea [Ecuatorial]." *ABC,* February 16, 1996, p. 48.

_____. "Toda la oposición renunica a participar en las presidenciales de Guinea Ecuatorial. La falta de garantías democráticas deja a Obiang [Nguema] sin rivales en los comicios de domingo." *La Vanguardia,* February 23, 1996.

_____. "Otra farsa de Obiang [Nguema]." Editorial. *ABC,* February 25, 1996, p. 21.

_____. "Farsa en Guinea [Ecuatorial]." Editorial. *La Vanguardia,* February 26, 1996, p. 28.

_____. "Fracaso de Obiang [Nguema]." Editorial. *El País,* February 27, 1996, p. 8.

Armada, A. "La policía de Obiang [Nguema] tortura al primer alcalde democrático de Malabo [Santa Isabel]." *El País,* February 18, 1996, p. 10.

_____. "Los cuatro rivales de Teodoro Obiang [Nguema] en las presidenciales de Guinea se retiran por 'fraude.' El Presidente [ecuato-] guineano se negó a aplazar unos comicios que la oposicion cree 'sin garantías'." *El País,* February 21, 1996, p. 3. Ill.

_____. "Los observadores hablan de prácticas fraudulentas en las elecciónes presidenciales de Guinea." *El País,* February 26, 1996, p. 6. Ill.

_____. "Obiang [Nguema] se atribuye el 99% de los votos. Discrepancias en el Gobierno de Guinea [Ecuatorial] por el nivel de fraude." *El País,* February 27, 1996, p. 5.

Arnalte, A. "El alcade de Malabo [Santa Isabel] sale sangrando de la comisaría. Victorino Bolekia fue detenido y golpeado viernes por la Policia. Horas después, salia de la comisaría sangrando y sin poder caminar." *Diaria 16,* February 22, 1996, p. 30.

Baptist Missionary Society. *Correspondence with Spanish Government Officials: Relations with Spanish Authorities in Fernando Po. 1858.* London.

Bennet, J. E. *Discurso de despedida del Embajador. . .en la Recepción Pública en la Residencia.* Malabo, July 28, 1994. 6 p.

Bokokó Boko, D. "Guinea Ecuatorial: Elecciónes que son un golpe de Estado." *Las Provincias,* February 13, 1996, p. 14.

Brockman, N.C. "Equatorial Guinea: Obiang, Teodoro Nguema Mbasogo (Brigadier General)." *An African Biographical Dictionary* (pp. 90–92). Santa Barbara, CA, 1992.

Buale Borico, E. *Guinea Ecuatorial: De la anarquía al laberinto.* Madrid, 1985.

Department of State (U.S.). "Equatorial Guinea." Country Reports of Human Rights Practices for 1991. Report submitted to the Committee on Foreign Affairs House of Representatives and the Committee on Foreign Relations U.S. Senate. Washington, DC, April 1996, pp. 78–82. Annual (February–March). Fundamental.

Divers. *Manifesto del Pueblo del Distrito de Mongomo al Pueblo Guineano y a la Comunidad Internacional. Con 50 firmas de representantes de 50 poblados.* Mongomo, September 5, 1993. 4 p. In *Boletín Informativo* 5, Asociación para la Solidaridad Democrática son Guinea Ecuatorial. Madrid, November 1993.

_____. "Guinea Ecuatorial. La Farca del cine Marfil [analysis of the nguemist/macist dictatorship]." *Mundo Negro,* May 1995, pp. 8–9.

EFE [Spanish News Agency]. "Fraude general en las elecciónes de Guinea [Ecuatorial], según la oposición. Los guineoecuatoriales acudent en masa a votar en las municipales." *La Vanguardia,* September 18, 1995, p. 10.

I., S. "Toda la oposicion [ecuato-]guineana se retira de las fraudentas presidencialées. La farsa electoral del próxomo domingo tendrá candidato único." *ABC,* February 21, 1996, p. 45.

Gorozope, Iñaki. "La transición política ecuato-guineana." *Crisis,* 2 1993, pp. 65–77.

Liniger-Goumaz, M. "Guinea Equatoriale. Il maestro de [Obiang] Nguema? Pinochet!" *Nigrizia,* July–August 1996, pp. 57–58. Ill.

Mancho Sabau,, R. *El njevo estado de Guinea Ecuatorial. Esina de Liceciatura.* Facultad de Geografía e Historial Universidad de Barcelona. Barcelona, s.f.

McGreal, C. "Obiang [Nguema]: 'Quien no me vote es un mal nacido.' Según el presidente [ecuato-]guinean, es hora de acabar con los procesos electorales porqué no traen más que problemas." *El Mundo* [from *The Guardian*], February 24, 1996, p. 29.

_____. Gobierno Civil de Fernando Poo. *Memoria de gestión correspondiente al año 1965.* Santa Isabel, 1966.

Muñoz y Nuñez de Prado, J. *Los funcionarios en la Guinea Española.* Madrid: Impr. Ciudud Lineal, 1930.

Observatoire géopolitique de la drogue. "Guinée Equatoriale." Rapport 1994. Paris, 1995.

Official (U.S.). *Equatorial Guinea: Background Notes.* Department Travel Information. Washington, DC, December 1993.

Ondo Mba, S. "Guinea Ecuatorial: La gran decepción [despues de la elecciónes municipales]." *Mundo Negro,* November 1995, p. 9.

_____. "Guinea Ecuatorial. Tras el fraude, represallas." *Mundo Negro,* December 1995, pp. 28-33.

Pastrano, F. "Obiang [Nguema] impide la presencia de observadores de la Unión Europea en los comicios presidenciales." *ABC,* February 18, 1996.

_____. "Obiang" Nguema perpetua hoy su dictadura con la farsa de unas elecciónes de candidato único." *ABC,* February 25, 1996, p. 54.

Sanchez, A. "La estructura administrativa del Estado en materia colonial y las posesiones del Golfo de Guinea (1858–1899)." *Estudios Africanos. Revisita de la Asociación Española de Africanistas,* vol. 8, 14–15. Madrid, 1994, pp. 83–100.

United Nations. *Informe sobre la situación de los derecghos humanos en la República de Guinea Ecuatorial presentado por el Relator Espécial de la Comisión, Sr. Alejandro Artucio, de conformidad con la resolución 1994/89 de la Comisión de Derechos Humanos.* Geneva, January 10, 1995, 19 p., Doc. E/CN.4/1995/68.

LAW

Amnesty International. *Juicios militares y uso de la pena muerte en Guinea Ecuatorial.* Doc. AFR 24/01/87/s. London, May 1987. 15 p.

Andrés Andrés, C. "Características económicas y legales de las concesiones petrolíferas en las provincias africanas." *Archivos del Instituto de Estudios Africanos,* vol. 15, no. 59 (July 1961), pp. 85–98.

Cordero Torres, J. M. *Tratado elemental de derecho colonial español.* Madrid, 1941.

Dirección General de Maruecos y Colonias. *Legislación del Trabajo de los Territorios españoles de Golfo de Guinea.* Madrid: DGMC, 1946.

Fraile Roman, A. *Legislación regional de las provincial de Fernando Poo y Río Muni, 1955–1961.* Madrid: IDEA, 1961.

Gómez Durán, J. *El régimen jurídico-financieori colonial.* Madrid: IDEA, 1946.

_____. *Ley tributaria de la Guinea Española.* 2 vols. Madrid: IDEA, 1966.

Martos Avilá, Fr. *Indice Legislativo de Guinea.* Madrid: IDEP, 1944.

Miguel Zaragoza, J. de. *Ensayo sobre el derecho de los Paumes.* Madrid: IDEA, 1963.

Millan López, A. E. *Legislación de Guinea ecuatorial.* Madrid, 1963.

_____. *Legislación de Guinea ecuatorial: Marzo 1967–Abril 1968.* Santa Isabel, 1968.

Miranda Junco, A. *Leyes Coloniales.* Madrid: IDEA, 1945.

Muñoz y Nuñez de Prado, J. *La propiedad en la Guinea española.* Madrid: Impr. Ciudad Lineal, 1929.

Olesa Munido, Fr. F. *Derecho penal aplicable a indígenas en los Territorios del Golfo de Guinea.* Madrid: IDEA, 1953.

Peña y Goyaga, M. M. de la. *Repertorio de la legislación colonial. Territorios Españoles del Golfo de Guinea. Años 1945–1954.* Madrid, 1955.

Sanz Bayon, J. M. *Informe presentado al Magistrado sobre la misión realizada en Guinea Ecuatorial a instancia de los agentes impulsores: Oficina de derechos humanos de las Naciones Unidas con sede en Ginebra y el Instituto de cooperación para el Desarollo de la Agencia espanola de Cooperación Internacional.* Santa Isabel [Malabo], Nov. 16, 1990. Taped. 25 p.

Trujeda Incera, L. *Los Pamues de nuestra Guinea: Estudio de derecho consuetudinario.* Madrid: IDEP, 1946.

POLITICAL PARTIES

Alianza Nacional para la Restauración Democrática (ANRD). *Guinea Ecuatorial Hoy.* Geneva (Jan. 1975).

_____. *Guinea Ecuatorial.* Suplemento *de la Voz de Pueblo.* Geneva (1977).

_____. *La Voz del Pueblo.* Organo de Información de la Anrd on Exile, 1976– .

_____. "Programa político de A.N.R.D." *La Voz del Pueblo.* En exilio, August 1985, pp. 33–57.

_____. *Estatutos generales de la A.N.R.D.* Madrid, 1988. 15 p.

_____. *Conozca la A.N.R.D.* Madrid, September 1993. 12 p.

_____. *Un proyecto para el futuro de Guinea Ecuatorial.* In exile, 1995. 8 p.

Amnesty International. *Equatorial Guinea: Government Opponents Arrested and Tortured in Run up to Elections.* News Service 32/96. AFR 24/02/96. London, February 20, 1996.

Arnolds, G. "Equatorial Guinea." In *Political and Economic Encyclopedia of Africa* (pp. 86–88). London, 1990.

Banks, A. S. (ed.). "Equatorial Guinea." In *Political Handbook of the World: 1994–1995.* (pp. 267–272). Binghamton, NY, 1995.

Divers, *La Razón de un Pueblo* [Bubi]. *La Historia se repite.* L'Hospitalet, Spain: Editional Mey, 1996. 63 p.

Fernández, R. *Guinea: Materia Reservada.* Madrid: Semmay, 1976.

Gorozpe, I. "La oposición a la dictsadura en Guinea Ecuatorial." *Nova Africa,* 1, July 1995, pp. 55–62.

Liniger-Goumaz, M. *Guinea Ecuatorial es Africa: Temas políticos: La Democracia desencadenada.* Madrid: Editorial Claves para el futuro, 1994.

_____. *Guinea Ecuatorial y el ensayo democrático: La conquista del Golfo de Guinea.* Madrid: Editorial Claves para el futuro, 1996.

_____. "Guinea Ecuatoriale: Ostaggion del Clan di Mongomo." *Nigrizia,* 114, March 1996, pp. 12–14. Ill.

_____. "Equatorial Guinea." In *Political Parties of Sub-Saharan Africa.* Westport, CT: Greenwood Press, 1997.

Ondo Ayang, L. "Prefacio." In M. Liniger-Goumaz, *Guinea Ecuatorial es Africa. Temas políticos: La Democracia desencadenada* (pp. 11–18). Madrid: Editorial Claves para el futuro, 1994.

"Prologo." In M. Liniger-Goumaz, *Guinea Ecuatorial y el ensayo democrático. La conquista del Golfo de Guinea* (pp. 5–8). Madrid: Editorial Claves para el futuro, 1996.

"Estrategias, Programas y Proyestos de la Oposición el Exterior: La Alianza Nacional para la Restauración Democrática de Guinea Ecuatorial (A.N.R.D.)" *Africa Negra,* 5, January–February 1996, pp. 22–23. Ill.

Ondo Mba, S. "Guinea Ecuatorial: La oposición desunida." *Mundo negro*, March 1996, pp. 6–7.

Partido de la Coalición Democrática de Guinea Ecuatorial (Acción Popular— A.D.SO.G.E.—Partido Liberal, M.O.L.I.F.U.G.E. (Unión Bubi). *Estatutos generales del Partido*. Madrid, s.f. 26 p. (tapes).

Partido Democrático de Guinea Ecuatorial (PDGE). *La filosofía política del PDGE y su programa del Gobierno*. Santa Isabel [Malabao], 1988. 63 p., Ill.

_____. *Actos del Ier Congreso extraordinario del PDGE*. Bata, 1995. 116 p.

Partido Liberal de Guinea Ecuatorial (P.L.G.E.). *Estados*. Madrid, n.d. 32 p. (taped).

_____. *Programa*. Madrid, s.f., 40 p. (mecanogr.).

Partido Social Demócrata de Guinea Ecuatorial. *Estatutos générals*. S.I., June 1991. 37 p.

_____. *Un programa para todos los Guinea Ecuatorianos*. Nuestra Causa comun. S.I., n.d. 41 p.

Partido Unico Nacional de Trabajadores (PUNT). *Programa del IIo Aniversario de la Proclamación Oficial*. Santa Isabel, July 1974.

_____. *Resoluciónes del IIo Congreso Nacional del PUNT*. Bata, July 14, 1972.

Pélissier, R. "Le mouvement nationaliste en Afrique espagnole." *Le Mois en Afrique*, no. 7, July 1966.

Plataforma de la Oposición Conjunta (POC). *Traducción de Exigencias de la POC al gobierno relativas derechos Humanos*. Santa Isabel, September 23, 1992. 4 p.

_____. Propuesta Institucional [a S.E. Obiang Nguema Mbasogo, Jefe de Estado y Presidente de la República de Guinea Ecuatorial]. Santa Isabel [Malabo], October 14, 1993. 2 p. (signed by 87 Unión Popular, Partido del Progreso, Concergencia para la Democrácia Social, Unión Democratica Nacional, Alianza democrática Progresista, Partido de la Coalición Social, Partido Socialista de Guinea Ecuatorial).

_____. Declaracion institutional [sobre las Elecciónes municipales de 17 de September de 1995]. Coalición Electoral POC. Malabo, September 30, 1995. 6 p.

_____. *Informe sobre la situación política y se los derechos humanos en Guinea Ecuatorial. Con la lista de personas detenidas, encarecladas, torturadas, asesinadasms, expulsadas de sus puestos (278 personas)*. Malabo [Santa Isabel], 13 April 1996, 6 p.

_____. "Political Movements in Spanish Guinea." *African Report* (May 1964).

International Foundation for election Systems (IFES), *1996 Presidential elections in Equatorial Guinea. IFES Observation Report*. Prepared by Pamela R. Reeves. Washington, March 1996, 48 p. Annexes, 195 p.

Unión democrática Social de Guinea Ecuatorial, *Estatutos generales del partido*. Libreville, Lisboa, Caracas, 1990–91. 18 p.

RACE QUESTIONS

Almonte y Muriel, E. de. "Los naturales de la Guinea Española considerados bajo el aspecto de su condición de subditos españoles." Conference. Royal Geographical Society. London, November 8, 1910.

Amnesty International. *Guinea Ecuatorial. Reforma política sin derechos humanos ("¿Que tienen que ver los derechos humanos con la democracia?").* Doc. AFR 24/01/93/s. Madrid: Amnestía Internacional, January 1993. 16 p, Ill.

_____. *Guinea Ecuatorial: El historia de promesas incumplidas.* Landres, July 1995. Doc. AFP 24/09/95/s. 13 p., maps.

Asociación para Derechos Humanos, Guinea Ecuatorial. *Informe sobre la situación politica, económica, social y de derechos humanos.* Madrid, 1978. 40 p., Xerox.

_____. *Estudio analítico de las Jornadas de Reflexíon sobre Guinea Ecuatorial.* Madrid, January 21, 22, 23, 1988. Madrid, April 1988, 87 p.

Bokokó Boko, D. "Represión contra los bubi." *ABC.* Madrid, 17 April 1998. p. 14.

Buell Borico, E. *Guinea Ecuatorial: Las aspiraciones bubis al autogobierno.* Madrid: IEPALA, 1988. 167 p.

Buell, R. L. *The Native Problem in Africa,* vol. 2 (pp. 777–781). New York: Macmillan, 1928.

Canada. "La situación en ,materia de derechos humanos en Guinea Ecuatorial. Proyecto de resolución." United Nations Commission for Human Rights. Doc. E/CN.4/1.1457/Rev.2. Geneva: UN, March 12, 1979.

Castro Antolín, M. I. "Fernando Po y los emancipados de la Habana." *Estudios Africanos. Revista de la Asociación Española de Africanistas,* vol. 8, 14–15, 1994, pp. 7–19. Ill.

Eya Nchama, C. M. "Declaration at the UN Commission for Human Rights." Sub-Commission for the Prevention of Discrimination and Protection of Minorities, 29th Session. Doc. CN.4/Sub.s/SR.760. Geneva: UNO, August 1976.

Nerlín Abad, G. *Guine Equatorial: Historia en Blanc i negra. Estereotips sexo-racials i relacions sexuals interracials a la Guinea Equatorial, 1843-1992.* Memória de licenciature. Barcelona: Universitat de Barcelona, Facultat de Geograffia i Historia, June 1992. 264 p.

FOREIGN AFFAIRS

"Acuerdos entre España entre y la República de Guinea ecuatorial." *Revisita de Política Internacional,* no. 119, Jan.–Feb. 1972, pp. 336–367.

Akinyembe, B. "Nigeria and Fernando Po, 1958–1966. The Politics of Irredentism," *African Affairs,* no. 69, July 1970, pp. 236–249.

Anon. "Equatorial Guinea: Public auction." *Africa Confidential,* 281, January 7, 1987.

_____. "Développement de la présence francaise." *Marches Tropicaux,* August 21, 1987, pp. 2, 231.

_____. "Diplomáticos norteamericanos visitan Fernando Poo." *Africa,* 256, 1963, p. 23.

_____. "Obiang [Nguema] ataca a Radio Exterior [de España] y detiene a quienes hablan en ella." *El País,* February 6, 1996, p. 8.

Aznar Sanchez, J. "Los acuerdos internacionales entre España y Guinea ecuatorial a partir de su indepencia," *Revista española de derecho international,* vol. 28, nos. 1–3, 1975, pp. 57–81.

Becker y González, J. *Tratados, convenios y acuerdos referentes a Marruecos y la Guinea española.* Madrid, 1918.

Bennett, J. E. *Remarks of the Ambassador of the United States of America at Malabo. . .at the Independence Day Celebration in Malabo, July 3, 1993.* Santa Isabel, July 3, 1993. 6 p.

Brooke, J. "South Africa Seeks Allies among Island Neighbors. Foreign Aid Program Brings Cattle and Rumors to Equatorial Guinea." *International Herald Tribune,* October 22, 1987, p. 4 (New York Times Service).

_____. "The Cocoa Slaves of Fernando Po." *The Guardian,* Nov. 21, 1976, p. 7.

"Délimitation et incidents de frontières. Rivières Muny et baie de Corsico," *Gabon-Congo,* vol. 6. Affaires diplomatiques. Files 7, 8, 20, 21. Archives Nationales, 1842–1904. Paris. 4 vols.

EFE [Spanish News Agency]. "El ex embajador norteamericano [J. Bennet] en Guinea [Ecuatorial] niega 'rotundamente' haber conspirado contra Obiang [Nguema]." *Levante.* Valencia, September 20, 1995, p. 7.

"Equatorial Guinea. Developing Economic, Political and Social Ties with Communist China Discussed." *New York Times,* Jan. 31, 1971, p. 2, col. 3.

Eya Nchama, C. M. *Statement at the Ministerial Conference of the OAU on the Situation of Refugees in Africa.* Arusha, Tanzania: International Commission of Jurists, May 7–17, 1979. 3 p.

I., S., "España y Francia piden limpieze en las [elecciónes] presidenciales de Guinea." *El País,* January 25, 1996, p. 10.

J.M.C.T. "Los tratados entre España y Guinea ecuatorial." *Revista de política internacional,* no. 119, Jan–Feb. 1972, pp. 331–335.

Liniger-Goumaz, M. "La ruée sur les Guinées. (I) De petits pays sous influence; (II) Les ambitions secrètes du Plan Gambie." *Journal de Genève,* December 18–19, 1987, pp. 1–2, 5.

_____. "Les relations Gabon-Guinée équatoriale: 1643–1977." In *Africana. L'Afrique d'hier à demain* (pp. 77–94). Geneva: Les Editions du Temps, 1977.

_____. "Journal d'un renversement d'alliances. Guinée Equatoriale, 1983-1985. Titres de presse et histoire immédiate." *Peuples noirs—Peuples africans,* 45, May–June 1985, pp. 8–34.

_____. "Guinée Equatoriale et zone franc. Réflexions sur un système monétaire et une récupération." *Genève-Afrique,* vol. 23, 2, December 1985, pp. 57–78.

_____. "Guinée Equatorial. Rivalités de puissance sur fond d'arbitraire déchaîné." *Journal de Genève,* November 3, 1986, pp. 1, 19.

_____. "Une gueguerre de cent ans dans le Golfe de Guinée." Universidad de São Paulo. *Revisita dop Centro de Estudos Africanos,* vol. 11, 1, 1988, pp. 44–60.

_____. *Guinea Ecuatorial y el ensayo democrático. La conquista del Golfo de Guinea.* Madrid: Editorial Claves para el Futuro, 1996.

_____. "S. M. Hassan II dans ses entreprises africaines. Histoire d'une protection très rapprochée: la Guinée Equatoriale d'Obiang Nguema." *Regards africains,* 28/29, December 1993, pp. 13–15.

———. "De la démocratie en Afrique subsaharienne. Le cas de la Guinée Equatoriale." Newsletter. Bern: Société suisse d'études africaines, 1994.

———. *United States, France and Equatorial Guinea. The "Dubious Friendships."* Two bibliographies. (Trilingual). Geneva: Les Editions du Temps, 1997.

———. "Sinopsos de las relaciones Guinea Ecuatorial—Estados Unidos de America." *Estudions Africanos. Revisita de la Asociación Española de Africanistas,* vol. 10, nos. 18–19, 1997. Bibliography, documents.

———. "Guinea Ecuatorial. diecisiete años de segunda dictadura nguemista (1979–1996). Francia vs España, y algunos intrusos como Estados Unidos de America." *Estudios de Asia y Africa,* 101, September–December 1996.

———. *United States, France and Guinea, the dubious frienships. Three Historical synopsis. Two Bibliographies—Etas-Unis, France et Guinée Equatoriale. Les amitiés douteuses. Trois synopsis historiques. Deux bibliographis: Estados Unidos, Francia y guinea Ecuatorial. Las amistades dudoas. Tres sinopses historicos. Dos bibliografías.* Les Editions du Temps. Ginebra 1997, 288 p.

———. *Les USA et la France face ê la Guinée Equatoriale à la fin du XIXe et de XXe siècle. La continuité de l'Histoire.* Les Editions du Temps. Ginebra 1997, 96 p.

Mangomo-Nzambi, A. "La délimitation des frontieres du Gabon (1885–1911)." *Cahiers d'Etudes africaines,* vol. 9, no. 33, 1969, pp. 34–36, 45–53.

Menendez, M. A. "Plan Mitterrand. Guinea española, provincia del Gabón francés". *Interview.* Madrid, March 4–10, 1987, pp. 83–87.

Ministerio de Asuntos Exteriores, IV. *Reunión de la Comisión mixta Hispano-Ecuatoguineana. Informe sobre la ejecución de los Acuerdos adaptados en la III. Reunión mixta Hispano-Equatoguineana, Madrid, November 1986.* Madrid, 1987. 32 pp., Ill.

Momoh, E. "Mr. Botha's Long Hand." *West Africa,* November 30, 1987, pp. 235.

"Nigerian Exodus." *Africa,* no. 55, March 1976, p. 57.

"Nigerian Union Urges Annexing Neighbour State." *International Herald Tribune,* Jan. 28, 1976.

Nsang Andeme, J. A. *Democracia y Derechos humanos en la Política de Cooperación al Desarrollo de la Unión Europea y de España con Guinea Ecuatorial.* Masters dissertation, Instituto Universitario de Desarrollo y Cooperación. Madrid, October 1995. 108 p.

Pastrano, F. "Guinea prohíbe la presencia de periodistas españoles en los comicios de febrero." *ABC,* February 2, 1996, p. 39.

Rasilla, de la. *España y Guinea Ecuatorial: Refflexiones, denuncias y propuestas por ahora (Recopilación de artículos).* Madrid, December 1988, 87 p.

Ridao, J. M. "Guinea Ecuatorial en perspectiva." *Política Exterior,* vol. 54, 10, November/December 1996, pp. 136–147.

United Nations. *Written statement submitted by International Movement for Fraternal Union among Races and Peoples on the Relations of Equatorial Guinea with South Africa.* Doc. E/CN.4/Sub. 2/1987/NGO/10. Geneva: August 13, 1987. 3 p.

———. *Special Rapporteurs Speak on State of Human Rights in Afghanistan, Iran, Equatorial Guinea.* Press Release. HR/CN/857. Ginebra, 16 April 1998.

_____. *Situation des droits de l'homme en Guinée equatoriale et assistance dans le domaine des droits de l'homme.* Sénégal (au nom du Groupe africain): projet de résolution. Commission des Droiots de l'Homme. Cinquante-quatrième session. Point 10 de l'ordre du jouor. Ginebra, 20 April 1998, 5 p., Doc. E/CN.4/1998/L.104.

_____. *Commission Urges Human rights improvements in Afghanistan, Rwanda, Equatorial Guinea.* Press Release. HR/CN/871. Ginebra 24 April 1998.

_____. *Special Rapporteur Appeals for Clemency in Equatorial Guinea* [Bubi]. Press Release. Geneva 4 June 1998.

Visapaa, M. *Ayuda-Memoria al Embajador de EE.UU. Misión de las Naciones Unidas para la evaluación del entorno para la ejecución del programa del país. Guinea Ecuatorial.* Santa Isabel, April 14, 1993. 14 p.

Volio-Jimenez, F. *Guinée Equatoriale. Rapport à la Commission des Droits de l'Homme, conformement à la résolution 1984/36 de Conseil Économique et Social des Nations Unies.* Geneva, 1985. 35 p. And following annual reports. Fundamental.

HISTORICAL

PRECOLONIAL

Alvarez García, H. R. *Leyendas y mitos de Guinea.* Madrid: IDEA, 1951.

Bagueña Corella, L. "Guinea antes el hombre," *Africa,* no. 210, June 1959, pp. 263–266.

Clist, B. "Nouvelles données archéologiques sur l'histoire ancienne de la Guinée-Equatoriale." *L'Anthropologie,* 102, n° 2. Paris, 1998, pp. 213–217.

Cunha Matos, R. J. de. *Corographia historica des ilhas de S. Thomé, Principe, Anno Bom e Fernando Po.* Porto: Typographia de Revista, 1842.

Howe, R. "Fernando Po." In *Black Africa.* Vol. 2: *From Prehistory to the Eve of the Colonial Era* (pp. 89, 91, 121, 127, 140, 142, 146, 157–177, 180–181, 188, 191). New York, 1966.

Kennedy, R. A. "Grindling Benches and Mortars on Fernando Po." *Man,* vol. 62, Sept. 1962, pp. 129–130.

Martín del Molino, A. *Secuencia cultural en el Neolítico de Fernando Poo.* Trabajos de Prehistoria. Seminario de Historia primitiva del Hombre. Universidad de Madrid y CSIC, XVII. Madrid, 1965, 69 p., ill.

_____. *Etapas de la cultura Carboneras de Fernando Poo en el primer milenio de nuestra era. I. El Neolítico de la selva ecuatorial africana; II. La Cultura Carboneras.* Colección monográfica africana, no. 18. Madrid: IDEA, 1968.

Moreno Moreno, J. A. "Origen y vicisitudes del antiguo reino de Moka." *Archivos del Instituto de Estudios Africanos,* no. 27, Dec. 1953, pp. 7–30.

Munday, J. T. *The Portuguese Discover Central Africa, 1482–1580.* London, 1951.

Nkogo Ondo, E. *La Encerrona (Experiencia pedagógica del maestro Juan Latino).* León: Ediciones de la Creatividad, 1993. 128 p.

Panyella Gomez, A., and J. Sabater. "El poblamiento de la isla de Fernando Poo y el problema de las migraciones africanas." *Archivos del Instituto de Estudios Africanos,* no. 55, July 1960, pp. 31–44.

COLONIAL

Agostinho das Neves. "A reacção dos habitantes de Fernando Pó e Ano Bom a dominação estrangeira." *Studia,* 50, 1991, pp. 199–214.

Aguilar de Campo, Marqués de. *Documentos presentados a las Cortes en la legislatura de 1900 por el Ministro de Estado.* Madrid, 1900.

Arambillet. *Posesiones españolas del Africa occidental.* Madrid: Impr. Revisita General de Marina, 1903.

Arnalte, A. "Una expedición de 3.000 morenos (Un proyecto de colonización de Fernando Poo en 1870)." *Estudios Africanos,* vol. 8, 12–13, 1993, pp. 89–106.

Artom Pasqualini, M. G. *La política della Spanga nei territori di Fernando Poo o del Río Muni dal 1956 all'independenza.* Perugia: Universitá degli Studi, 1971. See also *Annali della Facoltá di Science politiche.* Anni Accademici 1968–1970, no. 10.

Balmesada, Fr. J. *Los confinados a Fernando Poo e impresiones de un viaje a Guinea.* Havana: Antonio Martin Lamy, 1899.

Barrera, Angel, exgobernador general interino de los Territorios del Golfo de Guinea. *Lo que son y lo qur deben ser las Posesiones Españolas del Golfo de Guinea.* Conferencia leida en reunión extraordinaria de la Real Sociedad Geográfica el 20 de junio de 1907. Madrid, 1907.

Batista Gonzalez, L. "Expedición Argelejo: primer intento colonizador de España en Africa colonial." *Revista de Historia Militar,* 32, 1988.

Beltrán, L. "L'Afrique d'expression españole: la région autonome de la Guinée Equatoriale. *Etudes congolaisgnes,* 5, Sept.–Oct. 1967, pp. 45–56.

Berman, S. "Spanish Guinea: Enclave Empire." *Phylon,* no. 17, Dec. 1956, pp. 349–364.

Bonelli Hernando, E. *Guinea Española. Apuntes sobre el estado político y colonial.* Madrid, 1895.

Borrajo Viñas, Emilio. *Demarcación de la Guinea Española.* Conferencia dada en la Real Sociedad Geográfica por el capitan de Estado mayor... el dia 11 de marzo de 1902. Madrid, 1903.

Bravo Carbonel, J. *Fernando Poo y el Muni. Sus misterios, sus riquezas, su colonización.* Madrid: Impr. Alrededor del Mundo, 1917.

Bravo Jenties. *Revolución cubana: los confinados a Fernando Poo. Relación que hace uno de los deportados.* New York, 1869.

Cañamaque, Fr. *La cuestión del Golfo de Guinea.* Madrid: Tip. Manuel Ginés Hernandez, 1891.

Castro Antolin, M. de, Ndongo Bibiyogo, D., *España en Guinea. Construcción del desencuentro: 1778–1968.* Epílogo de J.U. Martín Carreras. Ed. Sequitur. Madrid, 1998, 214 p.

Castro Antolín, M. L. de, and Calle, L. de la. *Orígen de la Colonización española de Guinea Ecuatorial (1777–1860).* Universidad de Valladolid, 1992.

_____. "Fernando Poo y los emancipados de la Habana." *Estudios Africanos. Revista de la Asociación Española de Africanistas,* VIII, 14–15.

Castro Antolin, M. L. de. *La población de Santa Isabel en la segunda mitad del siglo XIX.* Asociación Española de Africanistas. *Cuadernos Monográficos,* 1. Madrid, 1996. 62 p.

Castro Antolin, M. de, Ndongo Bidyogo, D. *España en Guinea. Construcción del desencuentro: 1778–1968.* Ed. Seqiotir. Madrid. 1998. 241 p.

Carrasco González, A. "El proyecto de venta de Fernando Poo y Annobón a G'ean Bretaña en 1841." *Estudios Africanos,* vol. 10, 18–19, 1996, pp. 47–64.

Cerezo Roman, C. E. *La Guinea Ecuatorial española y las relaciones internacionales en la guerra de 1914–1918.* Memoria de Literatura. Madrid: Universidad Complutense, 1981.

Clarence Smith, W. G. "Spanish Equatorial Guinea." in *The Cambridge History of Africa,* 7 (pp. 537–543), 1986.

_____. "Fernando Poo," in *Cocoa Pioneer Fronts since 1800. The role of Smallholders, Planters and Merchants.* Macmillan. Basingstoke, 1996, 250 p.

Coello, Francisco. *La cuestión del Río Muni.* Conferencia pronunciada el 9 de enero de 1889 en reunión pública de la Sociedad geográfica de Madrid.

Coll, Armengol, Padre C.M.F. *Segunda Memoria de las Misiones de Fernando Poo y sus dependencias.* Madrid, 1899.

Colonial Office. *Fernando Po: original correspondence, entry book, 1828–1842.* 12 vols. (C.O. 82). London.

Creus, J. "Guinea Equatorial, 1883–1911: La invenció d'una identitat." In *Estructures agràries i poder polític. Recerques. Historia/Economía/Cultura,* 30, 1995.

_____. *Exploracións centraficans (1887–1901) del P. Joaquim Juanola.* 2o. Premi Preancesc Maspons I Labrós d'estudis sobre l'excursionisme 1995. Agripaciò Excursionista. Granollers, 1995. 32 p., Ill, maps.

Dirección general de Informacíón. *España en el Africa Ecuatorial.* Madrid: DGI, 1964.

Fernández Duro, C. *El derecho a la ocupación de territorios en la costa occidental de Africa. Discutido en la Conferencia internacional de Paris en los Años de 1886 a 1891.* Madrid, 1900. Fundamental.

Fernández Gaitan, J. "Presencia española en el Golfo de Guinea (1778–1858)." *Africa,* May 1964, pp. 51–53; June 1964, pp. 59–61 [from *Revista Général de Marina.* Madrid].

"Fernando Pô: déportations politiques pour les Etats-Unis." *Le Temps,* Oct. 6, 1866, p. 2, col. 4a.

Gandara, J. de la, (gobernador general de Fernando Poo, 1859–1862). *Informe al Gobierno de S. M. Madrid, 13 agosto 1861.* Edición Jacint Creus y Mariano L. de Castro. Ceiba Ediciones. Documentos de la colonización, 2. Vic (Osona), 1996. 77 p.

Grajera Torres, P., and A. M. Maqueada Valbuena. *Informe sobre la colonización de la Provincia de Guinea.* 2 vols. Madrid: Dirección General de Plazas y Provincias Africanas, 1958.

Green, L. G. *White Man's Grave: The Story of West Africa Coast.* London: Stanley Paul, 1954.

Guillemar de Aragón, A. *Opúsculo sobre la colonización de Fernando Poo y revista de los principales establecimientos europeos en la costa occidental de Africa.* Madrid: Impr. Nacional, 1852.

Harrison Church, R. J. "Spanish Guinea: Spain's Last Tropical Territory." *West Africa*, 1960, pp. 519–525.

Hutchinson, T. J. "Fernando Po." In *Impressions of West Africa* (pp. 173–202). London: Longmans, 1958.

Iradier y Bulfy, M. *Viajes y trabajos de la asociación euskara La Exploradora. Fragmentos de un diaro (compendio de ambas obras).* Diputación Foral de Alava. Vittoria-Gasteiz, 1992. 210p., Ill.

Jimenez Redondo, J. C. "Guinea Ecuatorial," in *El ocaso de la amistad entre las dictaduras ibéricas 1955–1968.* UNED—Centro Regional de Extremadura. Mérida, 1996, 258 p.

Lander, R. L., and J. Lander. *Journal of the Expedition to Explore the Course and Termination of the Niger,* vol. 2 (pp. 291–312). New York: J. & J. Harper, 1832.

Ligero Morote, A. "Epítome sobre la evolución sanitaria de la Guinea Ecuatorial durante la colonización (1778–1986)." *Estudios Africanos,* vol. 3, 4–5, 1987–1988, pp. 89–100.

Liniger-Goumaz, M. "Les relations Guinée équatoriale-Gabon, 1643–1977." In *Africana. L'Afrique d'hier à demain* (pp. 77–94). Geneva: Les Editions du Temps, 1977.

_____. "Annobon: l'île oubliée." *Mondes et Cultures. Comptes rendus trimestriels des séances de l'Académie des Sciences d'Outre-Mer,* vol. 44, 4. Paris, 1984, pp. 791–829, 831. Ill., bibliography.

_____. "Cien años de busqueda de mano de obra en Guinea Ecuatorial la cuestión bracera." *Estudios de Asia y Africa,* vol. 12, 4, no. 74, Oct.–Dec. 1987.

_____. *Brève Histoire de la Guinée Equatoriale.* Paris: L'Harmattan, 1988. 200 p.

_____. "150 años de rivalidaded hispano-francesas en el Golfo de Guinea." *Cuadernos Africa-América Latina,* 20, 4/1995, pp. 89–96.

_____. "Guinea Ecuatorial. Diecisiete años de segunda dictadura nguemista (1979–1996). Francia vs España, y algunos intrusos como Estados Unidos de America." *Estudios de Asia y Africa,* 101, September–December 1996.

_____. "Sinopsis de las relaciones Guinea Ecuatorial—Estados Unidos de America." *Estudios Africanos. Revisita de la Asociación Española de Africanistas,* vol. X, Nos 18–19, 1997. Bibliography, documents.

Lopez Perea, Enrique, ex-Subgobernador de Elobey y sus dependencias. *Las posesiones españolas del Golfo de Guinea y datos comerciales del Africa occidental.* Madrid, 1906.

Lucas de Barres, Alfonso de, ex-funcionario colonial. *Posesiones españolas del Golfo de Guinea.* Mexico, 1918.

Lynn, M. *John Beecroft and West Africa 1829–54.* Unpublished dissertation, University of London, 1979.

_____. "Britain's West African Policy and the Island of Fernando Po, 1821–1843." *Journal of Imperial and Commonwealth History,* vol. 18, 2, 1990, pp. 1911–207.

Manga, I. "Variables de peso en la colonización y descolonizacíon de Guinea Ecuatorial." *Africa Negra,* 1, July–August 1992, pp. 18–22.

Madrid, Fr. *La Guinea incógnita; verguenza y escándalo colonial.* Madrid: Edit. España, 1933.

Manuel Segorbe, J. *Guinea Española entre 1939 y 1945.* Memoria de Licenciatura. Madrid: Universidad Complutense, 1982.

Martin del Molino, A. *La Ciudad de Clarence.* Santa Isabel [Malabo]: Centro Cultural Hispano-Guineano, 1994.

Martinez Carreras, J. U. "Guinea Equatorial española en el contexto de la Segunda Guerra Mundial." *Cuadernos de Historia moderna y contemporánea,* V, 1985, pp. 243–255.

Martinez Salazar, A. *Manuel Iradier. Las azarosas empresas de un explorasor de quimeras.* Madrid, 1993.

Mata, José, Padre. *Memoria de las Misiones de Fernando Poo y sus dependencias.* Madrid, 1890.

Mateo Menendez, M.S., de. *Guinea Ecuatorial durante la Primera Guerra Mundial.* Memoria de Licenciatura. Madrid: Universidad Complutense, 1981.

Merlet, A. *Le pays des trois estuaires (1471–1900). Quatre siécles de relations extérieures dans les estuaires du Muni, de la Mondah et du Gabon.* Saint-Maur, France: Editions Sepra, 1991.

Ministére de la Marine. *Report on Spanish Possessions in West Africa: Note on the Number of Troops in the Area.* Paris, 1891.

Misión de María Cristina. Edición, introducción y notas: Jacint Creus. Ceiba Ediciones. Documentos de la colonización, 1. Vic (Osona), 1996. 76 p.

Moreno Moreno, J. A. *Reseña histórica de la presencia española en el Golfo de Guinea.* Madrid: IDEA, 1952.

Móros de Morellon, José de, and Juan Miguel de los Rios. *Memorias sobre las islas africanas de España, Fernando Póo y Annobon.* Madrid: Premiadas por la Sociedad Económica Matritense, 1844.

Muñoz y Gavira, J. *Crónica Général de España: Islas de Fernando Pó, Corisico y Annobón.* Madrid, 1871.

Navarro, J. J. *Apuntes sobre el estado de la Costa Occidental de Africa y principalmente de las posesiones españolas en el Golfo de Guinea.* Madrid, 1859.

Ndongo Bidiyogo, D. *Historia y Tragedia de Guinea Ecuatorial.* Madrid: Cambio 16, 1977.

Negrin Fajardo, O. "El estatudo de Ensenanza de los Terriorios del Golfo de Guinea de 1943. Una lectura crítica." *Africa 2000,* January–March 1987, pp. 35–38. Ill.

Nerin Abad, G. *Guinea Ecuatorial, Historia en blanco y negro. Hombres blancos y mujeres negras en Guinea Ecuatorial (1843–1968).* Ediciones Península. Biblio. Barcelona, 1998, 255 p.

Nfor Gwesi, S., *History of the British Baptist Mission in Cameroon, with beginnings in Fernando Po, 1841–1886.* Bachelor of Divinity. Faculty of the Baptist theological Seminary. Rüschlikon-Zürich (Switzerland), 156 p., taped (Evanston, Unilib, Ill.).

Obregon, E. de. "Historias de Fernando Poo." *Historia y Vida,* XXX, 349. Madrid, April 1997, pp. 118–126.

Owen, R. W. F. *Proclamation Made as a Superintendent of Fernando Po, 1827.* London: National Maritime Museum.

Pasqualini, M. G. *La politica della Spagna nei territorio di Fernando Po e del Río Muni dal 1956 all' independenza.* Perugia 1968–1970, 113 p. Extracto de *Perugia. Universitá Facoltá de Science Politiche,* Annali, n. 10, Academic year 1968/70, pp. 257–369.

Pélisser, R. "Spain Changes Course in Africa." *Africa Report,* vol. 8 (Dec. 1963), pp. 8–11.

_____. "Equatorial Guinea." In *Don Quichotte en Afrique: voyages à la fin de l'empire espagnol.* Orgeval: Chez l'auteur, 1992.

Pereira Rodríguez, T. "Notes sobre el colonismo en el Golfo de Guinea (1880–1912)." *Estudios Africanos. Revista de la Asociación Española de Africanistas,* vol. 1, 1, 2d semester 1985, pp. 92–107.

Puente, J. de la. *¿Debe España conservar nuestras posesiones de Guinea?* Barcelona: Tipografia Iris, 1916.

Pujadas, T. L. *La Iglesia en la Guinea Ecuatorial: Fernando Poo.* Madrid, 1968.

Rdo, P. Procurador de los Misioneros Hijos del Inmaculado Corazón de María, *Memoria de las Misiones de Fernando Póo y sus dependencias.* Madrid, 1889.

Reus, J. "Le 'rachat de jeunes filles africaines' en Guinée équatoriale 1890–1990." *Revue française d'histoire d'Outre-Mer,* LVXXXIV, 315. Paris, 1997, pp. 107–119.

Root, J. W. *Spain and Its Colonies.* London: 1898.

Rouquairol, P. *En marche vers l'autonomie...: la Guinée équatoriale de la colonisation á l'indépendance.* Diss. Besançon, 1986. 603 p.

Rumeu de Armas, A. *España en el Africa Atlántica,* 2 vol., 2nd ed. Las Palmas, 1996. 653 p.

Sánchez, A. "La estructura administrativa del Estado en materia colonial y las posesiones del Golfo de Guinea (1858–1899)." *Estudios Africanos,* vol. 8, 14–15, Madrid 1994, pp. 83–100.

Sanz Casas, G. *Política colonial y organización del trabajo en la isla de Fernando Pó, 1880–1930.* Barcelona, 1983.

Scotter, W. H. *International Rivalry in the Bight of Benin and Biafra, 1815–1885.* Unpublished dissertation. London, 1933.

Slater, S. E. *The British Consulate at Fernando PO: 1854–1870.* Thesis (Master of Arts). University of Calgary. Department of History. Calgary (Alberta), June 1983, 270 p.

Sorela, Lt. *Les possessions espagnoles du Golfe de Guinée. Leur présent et leur avenir.* Paris, 1884.

Sundiata, I. K. *The Fernandinos: Labour and Community in Santa Isabel de Fernando Po, 1827–1931.* Diss. Evanston, IL, 1972.

_____. *From Slaving to Neoslavery: the bight of Biafra and Fernando Po in the era of abolition, 1827–1930.* University of Wisconsin Press. Madison, 1996, 262 p., il, maps, bibl., indexes.

Thorne, A., *God at Work in Spanish Guinea.* Evangelical Publishing House. London, 1943, 75 p.

Unzueta, A., de. *Historia Geográfica de la Isla de Fernando Póo.* Madrid, 1947.

_____. *El Tratado de El Pardo y las expediciones a la Guinea española: aspectos económicos.* Madrid, 1947.

Weatherby, J. N. *Spanish Colonialism in Africa.* Diss. University of Utah, Salt Lake City, 1968. 274 p.

de Wulf, V. "Une étape dans la stratégie missionnaire Clarétine: le déplacement du village principal d'Annobon, Guinée Equatoriale (1892–1895)." *Studia Africana.* Barcelona, 1997, pp. 21–34.

Xavier, Alejandro. *España en Africa, ayer y hoy.* Barcelona: Buenos Aires, 1964.

INDEPENDENCE

AA.VV. *La razón de un Pueblo. La Historia se repite.* Barcelona: Mey, 1995.

Amnesty International. "Equatorial Guinea." *Report 1986.* London: 1986, p. 42.

———. *Guinea Ecuatorial. Torturas.* Madrid, 1990. 43 p.

———. *Guinea Ecuatorial: Una oportunidad perdida para reinstaurar el respecto a los derechos humanos.* Doc. AFR 24/01/94. London, 1994.

———. *Guinea Ecuatorial. El historial de promesas incumplidas.* Doc. AFR 24/09/95/s. London, July 1995.

———. *Guinea Ecuatorial. Violaciónes de derechos humanos tras las elecciónes.* London, January 30, 1996.

———. *Guinea Ecuatorial Una oportunidad para acabar con la impunidad.* Doc. AFR 24/01/97/s. London, July 1997, 3 p.

Anon. "Guinea Ecutorial. La farsa del cine Marfil." *Mundo Negro,* May 1995, pp. 8–9.

———. "Equatorial Guinea. [President Obiang Nguema won over 99 per cent of the vote]." *AED,* March 4, 1996, p. 31.

———. "Guinée équatoriale: Offensive pétrolière. Ce sont les compagnies pétrolières et non les diplomates qui ont pris l'initiative de faire pression sur Obiang [Nguema]." *Africa Confidential,* 225, April 1, 1996, pp. 4–5.

Arnold, G. "Equatorial Guinea." In *Encyclopedia Britannica Book of the Year.* Chicago.

Arson, Fr. "Dossier Guinée Equatoriale." La Lettre du Centre d'Information pour le Développement, 9. Caen, June/July 1998, pp. 2–13.

Artom Pasqualini, M. G. *La política della Spagna nei territori di Fernando Poo e del Río Muni dal 1956 all'independenza.* Perugia: Universitá degli Studi, 1971. Reprint from *Annali delle Facoltá di Science politiche.* Anni Accademici 1968–1970, no. 10.

Asociación para la Solidaridad democrática con Guinea Ecuatorial (ASODEGUE), Guinea Ecuatorial. *Obiang [Nguema] y las Compañias petroléras.* Madrid, 1996. 46 p.

Asociación Pro Derechos Humanos. *Guinea Ecuatorial. Informe sobre la situación politica, económica, social y de derechos humanos.* Madrid, 1977. 40 p., Xerox.

Biarnes, P. "Spain Prepares for Independence of Equatorial Guinea." *Translations on Africa,* no. 453. Washington, DC: US Joint Publication Research Service, Nov. 1, 1966, pp. 63–67.

Bokokó Boko, D., "Guinea Ecuatorial: treinta años de miserias." *Las Provincias.* Valencia, 11 November 1998, p. 5.

Carrascosa, L. *Malabo. Ruptura con Guinea.* Madrid: Mayler, 1977.

Cervera Pery, J. *La Guinea ecuatorial y su régimen de Autonomía.* Madrid: IDEA, 1964.

Chandler, J. A. "The Birth of Equatorial Guinea." *The Journal of African History,* no. 11, 1970, pp. 464–467.

Chao, R. *Après Franco, l'Espagne,* chap. 1. Paris: Stock, 1976.

Clevland, W. A. (ed.). "Equatorial Guinea." *Britannia World Data.* Chicago, 1988. Annual (1985–.).

Colectivo Helio. *La encrucijada de Guinea Ecuatorial.* Incipit. Madrid, 1997, 319 p.

Cronjé, S. *The Forgotten Dictatorship.* London: Ânti-Slavery Society, 1976.

Cusack, I. *Being away from 'home'; the Equatoguinean diaspora, secular pilgrimages and territorial mobility.* University of Bristol, Department of Politics. Department of Hispanic, Portugues and Lating American Studies. Bristol, July 1997, 24 p.

Darbroz, N. "En Guinée équatoriale aussi c'est la terreur. Un émule d'Amin Dada: Francisco Macias Nguema," *La Croix,* April 16–17, 1978, p. 6.

Ekis, C. *Die Diktatur Macías Nguema in Äquatorialguinea 1968–1979, Repräsentation und Reflexion.* Diss. Berlin: Humbold-Universität zu Berlin, 1996, 118 p.

Eman, A. *Equatorial Guinea: During Macias Nguema Regime.* Washington, DC, 1983.

"Equatorial Guinea." *Africa Contemporary Record, 1969–70.* London, 1970, pp. B456–459, and following years.

"Ecuatorial Guinea." *Facts on File,* vol. XXIX. Yearbook 1969 (pp. 66, 138, 290–291, 741, 774, 837). New York: Facts on File, 1970, and following years.

"Equatorial Guinea." *New York Times,* Jan. 9, 17, 23, 24, Feb. 2, March 31, 1969.

España en el Africa ecuatorial. Madrid: IDEA, 1964.

"Fear Enters Another Corner of Africa." *The Times,* May 12, 1971, p. 7b.

Freedom House. *The Most Repressive Regimes of 1996* (pp. 14–16). Washington, DC, March 1996. 51 p.

"Gabon-Guinée équatoriale: le contesté insulaire," *Revue française d'études politiques africaines,* no. 85, Jan. 1973, pp. 223–226.

García Domínguez, R. *Guinea. Macías, la Ley del Silencio.* Madrid: Plaza y Janec, 1977.

García Trevijano, A. *Toda la verdad. Mi intervención en Guinea.* Barcelona, 1997. 151 p.

Gonzalez Echegaray, C. *Guinea Ecuatorial: presente y futuro.* Madrid: Asociación de Profesores jubilados de Escuelas universitarias, 1994. 20 p.

Goldsmith, M. "In Equatorial Guinea, Dissent Often Brings Beating Death." *International Herald Tribune,* Jan. 27 1978.

Gorozpe, I. "Reivindicación política y particularismo en Annobon." In *Transitions líberales en Afrique lusophone. Lusotopie. Enjeux contemporains dans les espaces lusophones.* Paris, 1995, pp. 251–257.

_____. *La Guinea de hoy.* Madrid: IDEA, 1958.

Guinea Ecuatorial. España en Paz. Madrid: IDEA, 1964.

Heinz, W. S. "Aequatorialguinea," in *Ursachen und Folgen von Menschenrechtsverletzungen in der Dritten Welt*. Diss. Sozialwissenschaftliche Studien zu internationalen Problem, 116. Freie Universität, Berlin, 1984, pp. 177–218.

Jacobeit, C. "Äquatorialguinea: schwierige Rehabilitation," *Afrika Spektrum*, XII, 2, pp. III-2–4.

_____. "L'honorable et grand Camarade devient Président à vie d'un Etat unitaire," *L'Année politique et Africaine, 1973*. Dakar, 1974.

Launay, O. "La décolonisation en Africaine noire espagnole." In *L'Histoire Générale de l'Afrique*, vol. 7, chap. 8. Casablanca, 1974, pp. 313–321.

Liniger-Goumaz, M. *La Guinée Equatoriae. Un Pays méconnu*. Paris: L'Harmattan, 1959. 507 p.

_____. *Guinée Equatoriale. De la dictature des colons à la dictature des colonels*. Geneva: Editions du Temps, 1982. 232 p.

_____. *De la Guinée Equatoriale nguemiste. Eléments pour le dossier de l'afro-fascime*. Geneva: Editions du Temps, 1982. 272 p.

_____. "Aequatorialguinea." In *Politisches Lexikon Afrika*. Munich: C. H. Beck, 1984.

_____. "L'ONU et les dictatures nguemistes." In *ONU et dictatures. De la démocratie et des droits de l'homme* (pp. 85–164). Paris: L'Harmattan, 1984. 288 p.

_____. "Guinée Equatoriale." In *ONU et dictatures. De la democratie et des droits de l'Homme*. Paris: L'Harmattan, 1984. 285 p.

_____. "Guinée Equatorial. Réflexions sur des coups d'Etat à répétition." *Le Mois en Afrique*, December 1986–January 1987, pp. 23–44.

_____. *Connaître la Guinée Equatoriale*. Paris-Rouen: Editions Peuples Noirs, 1986. 240 p.

_____. *Brève Histoir de la Guinée Equatoriale*. Paris: L'Harmattan, 1988. 200 p.

_____. *Small Is Not Always Beautiful: The Story of Equatorial Guinea*. London: C. Hurst & Co., 1988; Totowa, NJ: Barnes and Noble Books, 1989, 198 p.

_____. "Equatorial Guinea." In *La Démocrature. Dictature camouflée, démocratie truquée*. Paris: L'Harmattan, 1992.

_____. *Who's Who de la dictature de Guinée Equatoriale. Les Nguemistes, 1979–1993*. Geneva: Les Editions du Temps, 1993.

_____. *Africa y las democracias desencadenadas. El caso de Guinea Ecuatorial*. Madrid: Editorial Claves para el futuro, 1994.

_____. *Guinea Ecuatorial y el ensayo democrático. La conquista del golfo de Guinea*. Madrid: Editorial Claves para el futuro, 1966.

_____. "Guinea Ecuatoriale. Ostaggio del Clan di Mongomo." *Nigrizia*, 114, March 1996, pp. 12–14. Ill.

_____. *United States, France and Equatorial Guinea: The Dubious Frendships*. Geneva: Les Editions du Temps, 1997.

_____. "Guinea Ecuatorial. Diecisiete años de segunda dictadura nguemista (1979–1996). Francia vs España, y algunos intrusos como Estados Unidos de America." *Estudios de Asia y Africa*, 101, January–April 1997.

_____. "Sinopsis de las relaciones Guinea Ecuatorial—Estados Unidos de America." *Estudios Africanos. Revisita de la Asociación Española de Africanistas,* vol. X, Nos. 18–19, 1997. Bibliography, documents.

_____. "Equatorial Guinea." In *The Encyclopedia of Sub-Saharan Africa.* New York: Charles Scribner's Sons, 1997.

_____. *Les USA et le France face à la Guinée Equatoriale à la fin du XIXe et du XXe siècle. La continuité de l'Histoire.* Les Editions du Temps. Geneva, 1997, 96 p.

_____. *Guinée Equatoriale. 30 ans d'Etat délinquant nguemiste.* L'Harmattan, 1998, 160 p.

MacDermot, N. (ed.). "Equatorial Guinea." *Bulletin of the International Commission of Jurists,* no. 13, Dec. 1974, pp. 10–13.

"Macías Nguema Biyogo." In *African Biographies* (n.p.). Bonn-Bad-Godesberg, 1967.

Mackay, M. "Spanish Guinea Now." *West Africa,* nos. 2603, 2604, April 22, 29, 1967, pp. 521–523, 553.

Maneiro, M., "El cuarto oscuro de Obiang [Nguema]" [Informe sobre violencia dictadura Obiang Nguema contra los Bubu]. *Cambio 16.* Madrid, 5 August 1996, p. 39.

Miguez, A. "El rompecabezas [ecuato-]guineao." *Nueva Revisia de Política, Cultura y Arte,* 31, 1993.

Ministère de la Coopération, *Guinée Equatoriale 1993/1994. Collection Guides d'Informa-tion. Ambassade de France a Malabo. Mission de Cooperation et d'action culturelle.* Paris, November 1993. 69 p.

Mitogo. *Guinea: De Colonia a Dictatura.* Suplemento 80. Madrid: Cuadernos para el Dialogo, 1977.

Ndongo Bidiyogo, D. *Historia y Tragedia de Guinea Ecuatorial.* Madrid: Cambio 16, 1977.

"Nguema's Reign of Terror." *Africa,* no. 79, March 1978, pp. 32–33.

Nguema Esono, F., and J. Balboa Boneque. *La transición de Guinea Ecuatorial. Historial de un fracaso.* Madrid: Labrys 54 Ediciones, 1996.

Obama Ondo Ada, V. *La ville de Malabo et les campagnes de l'île de Bioko (Guinée équatorial).* Diss. 3e cycle. Toulouse II. Toulouse, 1982.

"Obiang Nguema Survives Family Plot." *Africa Report,* September–October 1986, p. 50.

Observatoire Géopolitique des Drogues. "Guinée Equatoriale," in *Production, Frafics et consommation de drogues en Afrique centrale.* Rapport, à la demande de la Commission européenne. Direction générale, VIII/A/2. Bruxelles, September 1997, 77–88, maps.

Official (USA). Defense, *International Military Education and Training: Agreement Be-tween the United States of America and Equatorial Guinea, Effected by Exchanging of Notes Dated at Malabo [Santa Isabel] March 9 and 30, 1983.* United States Treaties. Washington, DC: Department of State, 1988.

Ondo Edu, B. "President of the Governing Council of Spanish Guinea Speaks of the Possibilities of the Independence." US Joint Publications Research Service, Transla-tions on Africa, no. 409, Aug. 2, 1966, pp. 57–62.

Pélissier, R. "Equatorial Guinea." *Africa South of the Sahara, 1971* (pp. 284–289). London, 1971 (and the following years).

_____. "Equatorial Guinea: A New Republic." *Geographical Magazine*, Nov. 1968.

_____. "The Nationalist Movement in Spanish Africa." US Joint Publications Research Service. *Translations on Africa*, no. 416, August 17, 196), pp. 40–65.

_____. "Spanish Changes Course in Africa." *Africa Report*, vol. 8, Dec. 1963, pp. 8–11.

_____. "Political Movements in Spanish Guinea." *Africa Report*, vol. 9, May 1964, pp. 3–7.

_____. "Spain's Discreet Decolonization." *Foreign Affairs*, vol. 43, 3, April 27, 1966, pp. 519–527.

_____. "Uncertainties in Spanish Guinea." *Africa Report*, no. 13, March 1968, pp. 16–20.

_____. "Political Executions." *African Recorder*, vol. 14, no. 3, Jan. 29–Feb. 11, 1975, pp. 3896–3897.

Pomponne, M. "La Guinée-Equatoriale sous la botte d'un clan. Sur fond de rivalités franco-espagnoles." *Le Monde diplomatique*, July 1994, pp. 4–5. Ill.

Rodley, N. *Equatorial Guinea. Report of the Special Rapporteur on torture and cruel, inhuman or degrading treatment or punishment.* U.N. Commission on Human Rights. Geneva, 1994. Doc. E/CN.4/1994/31.

Roig, J. "Elections municipales de septembre 1995 en Guinée Equatoriale." *Politique Africaine*, 60, December 1995, pp. 129–134.

_____. *Guinea Ecuatorial: la dictadura enquistada. Cuadernos Bakeaz.* Bilbao, Spain, December 1996. 12 p.

_____. *Régimen autónomo de la Guinea Ecuatorial.* Madrid: IDEA, 1963.

"Republic of Equatorial Guinea." *External Affairs*, no. 20, Dec. 1968.

Sanchez Ruano, Fr. "El frustrado golpe de Estado de Gadhafi en Guinea Ecuatorial." *Historia y vida*, 320, November 1994, pp. 60–67.

Saudinot, E. "Guinea Ecuatorial española: 1. Un territorio del que se habla poco: intereses sobre lo que se habla; 2. La economía de Guinea Ecuatorial; 3. Situación política en Guinea Ecuatorial; 4. El Movimiento social y cooperativo." *Cuadernos del Ruedo Ibérico*, nos. 13–14, July-Sept., 1967.

Servicio Informativo Español. *España en el Africa Ecuatorial.* Documentos Políticos, no. 2. Madrid: SIE, 1964.

_____. *España y Guinea Ecuatorial.* Madrid: SIE, 1968.

_____. *Textos fundamentales de Guinea Ecuatorial.* Documentos históricos, no. 5. Madrid: Ministerio de Informacíon, 1968.

"Spanish Guinea on the Road to Independence." *The Economist*, vol. 209, no. 1251, Dec. 21, 1963.

Stewart, J. "Annobon, Fernando Po, Formosa, Spanish Guinea." In *African States and Rulers* (pp. 16–94, 98–100, 224). London, 1989.

Sundiata, I. K. "Prelude to Scandal." *Journal of African History*, vol. 15, no. 1, 1974, pp. 97–112.

Togores Sanchez, L. E. "La diplomacia española y la formación de funcionarios (nativos) de Guinea Ecuatorial (1965–1981)". *Estudios Africanos*, vol. 7, 12–13, 1993, pp. 129–142.

"Uneasy Head." *The Economist,* vol. 230, Jan. 4, 1969, pp. 20–21.

United Nations. *Report on Equatorial Guinea (Fernando Po and Río Muni).* Special Committee for Decolonization. General Assembly. New York: UNO, 1960.

_____. *La Situación en materia de derechos humanos en Guinea Ecuatorial. Consejo Económico y Social.* Comisiòn de Derechos Humanos (35$ Período). Doc. E/CN.4/L.1457/Rev.2. Canadá: proyecto de resolución revisado; Geneva: UNO, March 12, 1979.

_____. Special Committee on the Situation with Regard to the Implementation of the Declaration on the Colonial Countries and Peoples, Fernando Po, Ifni, Río Muni and Spanish Sahara. Working paper prepared by the Secretariate. Doc. A/AC/109/L144. New York: UNO, 1964.

_____. *Guinée Equatoriale. Question de la violation des droits de l'homme et des libertées fondamentales. . .Services consultatifs dans le domaine des droits de l'homme. Note du Secrétaire général.* Conseil Économique et Social. Doc. E/CN.4/1985/9. New York, January 16, 1985. 51 p., map.

_____. "Situation in Equatorial Guinea." In *Commission on Human Rights Report on the Forty-second session (February 4–March 15, 1986).* Economic and Social Council. Oficial Records, 1986, Supplement no. 2. Doc. E/1986/22-E/CN.4/C.74. Geneva: March 10, 1986. 3 p.

_____. *"La Situation en Guinée Equatorial."* Services consultatifs dans le domaine des Droits de l'Homme. Costa Rica, Pérou: projet de résolution. Conseil Économique et Social. Commission des Droits de l'Homme, 43e session, Point 21. Doc. E/CN.4/1987/L.26. Geneva: February 23, 1987. 2 p.

_____. *Rapport de l'expert chargé d'étudier la situation des droits de l'homme en Guinée équatoriale, F. Volio-Jimenez, établi conformément au paragraphe 9 de la résolution 1990/57 de la Commission des Droits de l'Homme.* Doc. E/CN.4/1991/54. Geneva, Dec. 28, 1990, 4 p.

_____. *Rapport de l'expert chargé d'étudier la situation des droits de l'homme en Guinée Equatoriale, F. Volio-Jimenez, établi conformément au paragraphe 8 de la résolution 1991/80 de la Commission des Droits de l'Homme.* Doc. E/CN.4/1992/51. Geneva, Dec. 17, 1992. 47 p.

_____. *Rapport de l'expert chargé d'étudier la situation des droits de l'homme en Guinée Equatoriale,* F. Volio-Jimenez, en application de la résolution 1992/79 de la Commission des Droits de l'Homme. Doc. E/CN.4/1993/48. Geneva, 31 dicembre 1992. 18 p.

_____. *Informe sobre la situación de los derechos humanos en la República de Guinea Ecuatorial presentado por el Relator Espécial de la Comisión, A. Artucio, de conformidad con la resolución 1994/89 de la Comisiòn de Derechos Humanos.* Doc.E/CN.4/1995/68. Geneva, Jan. 10, 1995. 19 p.

_____. *Situation des droits de l'homme en Guinée équatoriale et assistance dans le domains des droits de l'homme.* Sénégal (au nom du Grouope africain): projet de résolutiion. Commission des Droits de l'Homme. Cinquante-quatrième session. Point 10 de l'ordre du jour. Ginebra, April 20, 1998, 5 p. Doc. E/CN.4/1998/L.104.

"United States Relations with Equatorial Guinea." *The Times,* Sept. 2, 1971), p. 2; Sept. 3, 1971), pp. 6f; Sept. 9, 1971), p. 6g.

Vilar, Juan. "El convenio franco-español de 1900 en los orígenes de la República de Guinea Ecuatorial." *Anales de la Universidad de Murica,* vol. 29, 3–4. Curso 1970. Murcia, 1972.

Wiggins, J. R. "Equatorial Guinea Admitted to the United Nations." *Department of State Bulletin,* no. 59, Dec. 16, 1968, p. 643.

World Council of Churches. "Terror Grips Equatorial Guinea." *One World,* Nov. 1, 1974, pp. 7–9.

Yates, D. "Equatorial Guinea: Oil and Power." *Panafrica,* November 1996, pp. 16–17. Ill., maps.

_____. "Equatorial Guinea. Black Gold, Black Power?" *West Africa.* London-Lagos, 6–26 April 1998, pp. 394–396, ill.

SCIENTIFIC

GEOGRAPHY

Atlas histórico y geográfico de Africa española. Madrid: IDEA, 1955.

Croquís de la Guinea continental española y Lista general de poblados, fincas, establecimientos, etc, con relación de sus tribues, demarcaciones a que pertenece y situación sobre el croquis. Madrid: Instituto geográfico y cadastral, 1947.

Toponimía de la Guinea continental española. Madrid: IDEA, 1947.

Barrena Moreno, N. "La Isla de Annobón." *Guinea Española,* July 10, 1909–June 25, 1911.

Bonelli y Rubio, J. M. "Notas sobre la geografía humana de los territorios españoles del golfo de Guinea." In Díaz de Villegas y Bustamente, J., and others. *España en Africa* (pp. 179–191). Madrid: IDEA, 1949.

Castro Antolín, M. L. de, and M. L. de la Calle Muñoz. *Geografía de Guinea Ecuatorial.* Programa de Colaboración Educativa con Guinea Ecuatorial. Madrid: Ministerio de Educación y Ciencia, 1985. 74 p.

"Change in Place Names." *Keesing's Contemprorary Archives* (p. 26308), Jan. 21–27, 1974.

Cousteau, J.-Y. "Calypso Explores an Undersea Canyon (Romanche Trench) (Annobón)." *Geographical Magazine* (pp. 373–376), March 1958.

García Cogollor, A. *Observatorio Geográfico de Moca, Fernando Poo. Geomagnetismo, año 1958–59.* Madrid: Instituto geográfico y cadastral, 1961.

Guinea Española. Special Issue of *Revista Geográfica Española,* no. 24, 1950.

Juste, J., Cantero, A., *Informe nacional sobre medio ambiente y desarrollo, Guinea Ecuatorial.* UNCED National Reports. World Directory of Country Environmental Studies. Gland, September 1991, 216 p., estadist.

_____. *Zonación ecologica y evaluación del impacto ambiental de los usos actuales en la isla de Bioko* [Fernando Póo]. Malabo, 1992. 98 p., maps. FAO-FO-UTF/EQG/002/EQG. Estudios de Apoyo a la Preparación del Proyecto Manejo y Conservación de los Recursos Naturales. Documento de campaña 2.

Liniger-Goumaz, M. *La Guinée Equatorial. Un Pays méconnu.* Paris: L'Harmattan, 1979. 507 p.

Lizaur y Roldan, J. "Geografía de la Guinea Continental Española." Curso sobre Africa Española, 7. Conference at the Royal Geographical Society. London, Jan. 22, 1945. Madrid: Dirección Général de Marruecos y Colonias, 1944–45.

Martinez Alcazar, J., Morariega Alcala, F. *Geografía e historia de Guinea Ecuatorial.* Universidad Nacional de Educación a distancia. Madrid, 1982, 124 p.

Martínez García, T. *Fernando Poo: geografía, historia, paisaje: La Guinea Española.* Santa Isabel: Instituto "Claret" de Africanistas, 1968.

Official (USA). *Spanish Guinea. Official Standard Names Approved by the U.S. Board on Geographical Names.* Office of Geography, Department of the Interior. Central Intelligence Agency. Washington, DC, 1962.

_____. *Equatorial Guinea.* Maps, 1:3,750,000. Central Intelligence Agency. Washington DC, 1977.

_____. *Africa West Coast, São Tome e Principe, Equatorial Guinea, Gabon, Gulf of Guinea, Cabo San Juan to Cap Lopez.* Combat Support Center. Map 1:300'000. Washington, DC, November 11, 1989.

_____. *Africa. West Coast, Cameroon—Equatorial Guinea, Approches to Doula and Malabo [Santa Isabel].* Defense Mapping Agency Hydrographic/Topographic Center, Combat Support Center, 7th ed. Maps, 1:100,000. Washington, DC, 1990.

_____. *Africa West Coast, Nigeria, Cameroon and Equatorial Guinea, Gulf of Guinea, Bonny River to Kribi including Isla de Bioko [Fernando Po].* Defense Mapping Agency Hydrographic/Topographic Center, 9th ed. Combat Support Center. Maps 1:300,000. Washington, DC, March 23, 1991.

_____. *Equatorial Guinea.* Central Intelligence Agency. Maps, 1:2,550,000. Washington, DC, 1992.

_____. *Africa West Coast, Cameroon-Equatorial Guinea-Gabon, São Tome and Principe, Kribi to Cabo San San Juan, including Principe.* Defense Mapping Agency Hydrographic/Topographic Center, 1st ed. Combat Support Center. Maps 1:300,000. Washington, DC, September 16, 1989.

_____. *Equatorial Guinea.* Consular Information Sheet. State Department Travel Information. Washington, DC, May 11, 1992.

_____. *Tactical Pilotage Chart, TPC. M-2B, Equatorial Guinea.* Prepared and published by the Defense Mapping Agency Aerospace Center. Ed. 1. St. Louis, MO: The Center. USGS Branch of Distribution. Denver, 1992.

_____. *Operational Navigation Chart, [Africa]: Cameroon, Central African Republic, Chad, Congo, Equatorial Guinea, Gabon, Nigeria, São Tome and Principe, Zaire.* Prepared and published by the Defense Mapping. Ed. 6 (N/CG33). National Ocean Service. Denver, s.f.

United Nations System-Wide Earthwatch, *Islands of Equatorial Guinea: Bioko, Corisco, Elobey Grane, Pagalu (Annobon). Island Directory.* New York, 15 September 1990, 4p.

Zamora Loboch, M. *Noticia de Annobón (su geografía, historia y costumbres).* Madrid: Diputación Provincial de Fernando Poo, 1962.

GEOLOGY

Alcaraz Mira, E., and J. M. Sequeiros Bores. "Algunos datos sobre los suelos de la Guinea continental española e la Isla de Fernando Poo." *Boletín del Instituto Nacional de Investigación Agronómica,* no. 22, 1942, pp. 214–235.

Alia Medina, M. *Datos geomorfológicos de la Guinea Continental Española.* Madrid: IDEA, 1951.

Alias Perez, L.-J. *Genesis de suelos y concreciones en Guinea continental española.* Madrid: IDEA, 1958.

Anon. "Equatorial Guinea. Petroleum." *Africa Research Bulletin,* August 16–September 15, 1992, p. 10968.

_____. "[Petroleum liquids production, projection 1990]." *Oil and Gas Journal,* December 4, 1982, p. 2263.

_____. "Oil Raises the Stakes." *Africa Confidential,* vol. 33, 2, January 24, 1992, pp. 2–4.

_____. "Equatorial Guinea." *Petroleum Economist,* August 1993.

_____. "Eyebrow Raised on Oil Revenue." *AED,* September 13, 1993, p. 21.

_____. "Oil Discovered Off Africa's Equatorial Guinea (United Meridian's and Mobil's Discovery Well Odd Equatorial Guinea Tests 10,500 bbl/day Crude Oil and 3,4 nil cu ft/day of Gas)." *Houston Cronicle,* March 21, 1995.

_____. "Equatorial Guinea. Oceaneering's 3-year deal." *AED,* December 18, 1995, p. 31.

_____. "Equatorial Guinea—On the brink of an oil boom." *AED,* March 4, 1996, p. 31.

_____. "Guinée équatoriale: Offensive pétrolière. Ce sont les compagnies pétrolières et non les diplomates qui ont pris l'initiative de faire pression sur Obiang [Nguema] a la présidence." *Africa Confidential,* 255, April 1, 1996, pp. 4–5.

_____. "Production draws near for Equatorial Guinea." *Oil & Gas Journal.* Tulsa (Okl.) June 10, 1996.

_____. "Equatorial Guinea [Mobil has begun offshore oil production at Zafiro field]." *The Financial Times.* London, October 29, 1996.

_____. "Oil has already become the cornerstone of Equatorial Guinea's economic hopes." *Mail & Guardian.* Johannesburg, September 19, 1997.

_____. "Equatorial Guinea: a future oil base?" *Africa Energy and Mining,* 218. Paris, December 10, 1997.

_____. "Troubling the waters. President Obiang [Nguema] wants to be an oil sheikh but this stirs enemies at home and abroad." *Africa Confidential,* XXXIX, 4. London, February 20, 1998, pp. 6–7.

_____. "Equatorial Guinea to get gas-based methanol plant." *Oil & Gas Journal.* Tulsa (Okl.), February 23, 1998, p. 36.

_____. "Equatorial Guinea," in "Oil and Gas. Going with the flow." *Africa confidential,* XXXVIII, 7. London, March 28, 1998.

_____. "Equatorial Guinea [Elf Aquitaine plans to run seismic surveys in 1999]." *The Oil and Gas Journal.* Tulsa (Okl.), July 27, 1998, p. 61.

Arce, R. *Informe al Gobierno de la República de Guinea Ecuatorial referente a política minera y petroléra.* Santa Isabel: UNDP, 1971.

Bev, E. "No Frills Loading Terminal in Operation off Equatorial Guinea." *Oil & Gas Journal,* 90, 1992.

Borico, B. "¿Petróleo en Fernando Poo?" *Guinea Española,* no. 1617, September 1967, pp. 140–144.

Convergencia para la Democrácia Social. "El petróleo, negocio famiciar del presidente Obiang [Nguema]." *La Verdad,* 35, June 1995–March 1996, pp. 3–4.

_____. "Por qué las empresas petrolíferas han apoyado a Obiang [Nguema]." *La Verdad,* 35, June 1995–March 1996, p. 11, cuadro.

_____. "La farsa de Obiang [Nguema]: unas elecciones con olor a petróleo." *La Verdad,* 35, June 1995–March 1996, p. 12.

EMS Limited, *Republic of Equatorial Guinea. Maps: Licensing Round 1993; Block Location; Hydrocarbon Geology—Rio Muni; Seismic Programme Map,* etc. Oxford (Surrey), 1993.

European Union, "Guinée Equatoriale. Profil du pays. Géologie et gisements/Production et compagnies minières." *Mines '96. Forum minier Union Européenne. Afrique de l'Ouest & Centrale,* Bruselas, 1998, 4 p., map.

First Exchange Corp. *Note on the Oil Prospects of Fernando Po, West Africa.* Doc. OC 14000. Houston, 1966.

Fuster Casas. *Estudio petrogénico de los volcanes del Golfo de Guinea.* Madrid: IDEA, 1954.

García Cogollor, A. "Introduction à l'étude gravimétrique de Fernando Po." Diss. Paris, 1963. 64 p., Ill.

Knott, D. "Equatorial Guinea Opens for [Petrol] Business." *Oil and Gas Journal,* June 28, 1993, p. 38.

Madariaga, J. "Chapear, no, 'guru-guru'; Petróleo, para qué?" *Actual,* 20, July 21, 1982, pp. 30–33.

Martinez Torres, L. M., and J. Alonso Ramirez. "Cartografía morfoestructural de la Guinea Ecuatorial continental a partir del análisis de la red de drenaje." *Estudios del Museo de Ciencias naturales de Alava,* 8, 1993, pp. 43–54.

_____. "Geología de Corsico, isla Eloby Grande y Kogo-Puerto Iradier (Guinea Ecuatorial)". *Estudios del Museo de Ciencias naturales de Alva,* 7, 1993, pp. 23–29.

Mateos, J. P., and J. A. Pasual. "Etude de sédiments côtiers de la Guinée continentale." *Deusche Beiträge zur Mineralogie und Petrographie,* vol. 10, no. 2 (1964), pp. 225–229.

Nootebom, U., Menier P. *Zafiro Field Subsea Flowlines and Umbilicals Designed, Manufactured, and Installed in Record Time.* Paper presented to the *1997 Offshore Technology Conference.* Intec Ingeneering, Inc. Houston, 5–8 May 1997.

Nota orientadora sobre posibieidades petrolíferas en España y sus territorios africanos. Madrid: Dirección General de Minas y Combustibles, 1959.

Novo, P., and J. Mendizábal. *Reconocimiento geológico-minero de la Guinea continental española.* Madrid: 1934.

Petroconsultants S.A. *Equatorial Guinea. Annual Review 1984.* International Energy Services. Geneva: January 1985. 13 p., map (1:1,000,000).

_____. *Cartographic Inventory,* 250,000. Geneva. February 1998.

Ross, D., and N. Hempstead. "Geology, Hydrocarbon Potential of Río Muni Area, Equatorial Guinea." *Oil and Gas Journal,* XCI, 35, August 30, 1993, pp. 96–100.

United Meridian Corp. "Equatorial Guinea," in *Third Quarter Earnings Release conference call.* Houston, October 21, 1997, 17 p.

Yates, D. "Equatorial Guinea: Oil and Power." *Panafrica,* November 1996, pp. 16–17. Ill., maps.

Zein, M. "Que será lo que quiere Obiang. El petróleo complica la transición." *El Siglo,* September 10, 1993, pp. 16–17. Ill., maps.

MEDICINE

Center for International Health Information. *Equatorial Guinea Health Statistics Report.* Arlington (VA), 1996, 7 p.

Delmaza Kaufmann, M. S., and J. P. Gonzalez Kirchner. "Patterns of Reproduction Among the Fang of Nsork (Equatorial Guinea)—Pregnancies, Abortions and Child Spacing." *Revista de Biologícía Tropical,*vol. 42, 1–2, April–August 1994, pp. 315–318.

Dirección General de Plazas y Provincias Africanas. *Labor sanitaria en la Provincia de Guinea.* Madrid: DGPPA, 1963.

Doctors without Borders—Spain. *Proyecto de apoyo al sistema de salud de la ciudad y del distrito de Basta.* s.l., February 1996.

Fierro Cueto, J. M. *Manual de cirurgía general para Guinea Ecuatorial.* Asamblea Espiritual Nacional de los Bah'áíss de Guinea Ecuatorial y la Agencia Canadiense de Desarrollo Internaciional. Malabo, 1995, 478 p., bibl.

Gascón Briega, J. "Organización del servicio sanitario en las Provincias de Fernando Poo y Río Muni." *Africa,* nos. 260–261, Aug.–Sept. 1963, p. 413.

Josse, R., and others. "Les maladies diarrhétiques infantiles en Guinée Equatoriale: enquête épidémiologique dans le district de Mongomo, Nsoc-Nsomo et Ebebiyin (zone continentale)." *Bulletin de liason et de documentation de l'OCEAC,* 84, April–June 1988, pp 75–81.

Ligero Morote, A. *La Sanidad en Guinea Ecuatorial, 1778–1968. Evolución del Estado Sanitario de Guinea Ecuatorial a través de la lectura de la Legislación: Logros Sanitarios obtenidos hasta la Independencia el 12 de Octobre de 1968.* Madrid, 1988. 194 p. Available from the author.

_____. "Epítome sobre la evolución sanitaria de la Guinea Ecuatorial durante la colonización (1778–1986)." *Estudios Africanos,* vol. 3, 4–5, 1987–1988, pp. 89–100.

Llaverdo Rodriguez, J. Ruiz Muelas, M. A. "[Nutritional status of the children population in the Annobon island.]" *Revista de Sanidad e Higience Pública,* LXIII, 5–6. Madrid, 1989, pp. 41–47.

López-Motra, C. "Aspectos de la luncha sanitaria en Guinea." *Archivos del Instituto de Estudios Africanos,* no. 9, Aug. 1949, pp. 7–16.

Majo Framis, R. *El pasado de la Sanidad en Guinea como base para la actuación en el futuro.* Colección monográfica africana, no. 17. Madrid: IDEA, 1968.

Martilla y Gomez, V. "Síntesis de la labor sanitaria de España en Africa." *Archivos del Instituto de Estudios Africanos,* no. 74, 1965, pp. 7–28.

Martínez Domínguez, V. *Estudio epidemiológico y clínico de la endemia de la lepra en la Guinea española.* Madrid: IDEA, 1954.

Mas Capo, J. *Prevalencia y distribución geográfica de la oncocercosis en la isla de Bioko* [Fernando Po] (Guinea ecuatorial). Diss. Universidad de Barcelona. Barcelona, 1995.

Modica, R. E., and J. R. Flores. *Hemoglobina anormal en Guinea Ecuatorial.* Santa Isabel: WHO, August 1969.

Molina, R., and others. "Base-Line Entomological Data for a Pilot Malaria Control Program in Equatorial Guinea." *Journal of Medical Entomology,* XXX, 3, May 1993, pp. 622–624.

Roche Royo, and others. "An epidemiological study of Malaria in Bioko and Annobón island (Equatorial Guinea.)" *Annals of Tropical Medecine and Parasitology,* LXXXV, 5. Liverpool, 1991, pp. 477–487.

Roche, J., and others. " Anti-Malaria-Drugs in Equatorial Guinea." *Annals of Tropical Medicine and Parasitology,* LXXXVII, 5, October 1993, pp. 96–100.

Simarro, P. P., and others. "La enfermedad del sueño en Guinea Ecuatorial. Balance de las investigaciones de la cooperación española." *Africa 2000,* III/II/7, 1988, pp. 18–24.

Simarro P. P., and others. "African Trypanosomiasis and S. Intercalatum Infections in Equatorial Guinea: Comparative Epidemiology and Feasability of Integrated Control." *Tropical Medicine and Parasitology,* vol. 40, 2, 1989, pp. 159–162.

_____. "Urban Epidemiology of Schistosoma Intercalatum in the City of Bata, Equatorial Guinea." *Tropical Medicine and Parasitology,* vol. 41, 3, 1990, pp. 254–256.

Simarro, P. P., and others. "Endemic Human Paragoniamiasis in Equatorial Guinea. Detection of the Existance of Endemic Human Paragoniamiasis in Equatorial Guinea As a Result of an Integrated Sanitary Programme." *Tropical and Geographical Medicine,* vol. 43, 3, July 1991, pp. 326–328.

Simarro, P. P., and others. "Effect of Repeated Targeted Mass Due to Schistomatosa-Intercalatum in an Urban-Community in Equatorial Guinea." *Tropical Medicine and Parasitology,* vol. 42, 3, 1961, pp. 167–171.

Simarro, P. P., and others. "Integración de programa de lucha contra distintas enfermedades. Guinea Ecuatorial." *World Health Forum,* vol. 14, 3, 1993, pp. 308–315.

Vallejo, A., and others. "Human T-Cell Leukemia Virus - I/II Infection in Equatorial Guinea." *Aids,* vol. 8, 10, October 1994.

World Health Organisation, "Guinée Equatoriale," in "Dysenterie épidémique." *Aide-Mémoire* 107. Ginebra, marzo 1996, 2 p.

ZOOLOGY

Alers, M. P. T., Blom, A. *Elephants and Apes of Rio Muni.* Unpublished report to Wildlife Conservation International, 1998, 7 p.

Basilio, A. *Aves de la Isla de Fernando Poo.* Madrid: COCULSA, 1963.

_____. *La vida animal animal en la Guinea española.* Madrid: IDEA, 1952.

Baz, A. "Psocoptera From Weaver Bird Nest (Aves, Placcidae) in Equatorial Guinea (West Africa)." *Annales de la Societé entomologique de France,* vol. 26, 1, 1990, pp. 33–38.

Cabrera, A. Catálogo descriptivo de los mamíferos de Guinea Española. *Memoria de la Real Sociedad de Historia Natural,* 16, 1929.

Castelo, R. "Biogeographical Considerations of fish Diversity in Bioko." Biodivisity & Conservation, 3 (9), December 1994, pp. 808–827.

Castroviejo, J., and others. "The Spanish Cooperation Program in Equatorial-Guinea. A 10-Year Review of Research and Nature Conservation in Bioko." *Biodiversity and Conservation,* vol. 3, 9, December 1994, pp. 951–961.

Eisentraut, M. "Die Wierbeltiere von Fernando Poo und West-Kamerun." *Zoologische Monographie,* 3, 1973.

_____. *Im Schatten des Mongo-ma-loba: tropisches Tierleben in Kamerun und auf der Insel Fernando Poo.* Il. Bonn, 1982.

García Yuste, J. E. *Inventario y Censo de las poblaciones de Primates del Parque Nacional Monte Alen.* ECOFAC, January 1995, 99 p.

Gonzalez-Kirchner, Sainz de la Maza, M., *Estudio de la situación actual de las poblaciones de Gorila de costa (Gorilla gorilla gorilla) y del chimpancé común (Pan troglodytes) en la Repúblioca de Guinea Ecuatorial.* Rapport inédit. I.C.D.

_____. "Sticks Used by Wild Chimpanzees : A New Locality in Río Muni." *Folia Primatologica,* 58, 1991, pp. 99–102.

_____. "Primates as Protein Source for Native Human Populations of Equatorial Guinea." *Abstracts,* VIII Congress of the European Anthropological Association, 1992.

_____. "The Diet of Sympatic Prosimians in Equatorial Guinea." *Folia Zoologica,* XVILIV, 1, 1995, pp. 13–18.

_____. "Census of Western Lowland Gorilla Population ini Rio Muni Region, Equatorial Guinea." Folia Zoologica, 46 (1). Basel, 1997, pp. 15–22.

Hearn, G. W., Berghaier R. W. *Census of diurnal primate groups in the Grand Caldera Volcanica de Luba, Bioko Island, Equatorial Guinea.* A report to the Government of Equatorial Guinea. Malabo, January 1996.

Heymans, J.-Cl. *Utilisation rationnelle de la faune sauvage—Elevage de petit gibier.* ECOFAC, September 1994, 66 p.

Jones, C., Sabater Pi, J. "Comparative ecology of Gorilla (Sauvage and Wyman) and Pan troglodytes (Blumenbach) in Rio Muni, West Africa." *Biblioteca primatololgioca,* 13. Basel, 1971, 96 p., il, cuadros.

Jones, P. J. "Diodiversity in the Gulf of Guinea." *Biodiversity & Conservation,* 3 (9). December 1994, pp. 772–784.

Juste, J., Cantero, A. *Informe nacional sobre medio ambiente y desarrollo, Guinea Ecuatorial.* UNCED National Reports. world Directory of Country Environmental Studies. Gland, September 1991, 216 p., stat.

Juste, J., and J. Castroviejo. "Unusual Record of the Spotted Hyena (Crocuta-Crocuta) in Río Muni, Equatorial Guinea (Central Africa)." *Zeitschrift für Säugetierkunde,* vol. 57, 6, December 1992, pp. 380–381.

Juste, J., and C. Ibañez. "Contribution to the Knowledge of the Bat Fauna of Bioko Island [Fernando Po], Equatorial Guinea (Central Africa)." *Zeitschrift für Säugetierkunde,* vol. 49, 5, October 1994, pp. 274–281.

Juste, J., and others. "Altitudinal Variation in the Sub Canopy Fruit Bat Guild in Bioko Island [Fernando Po], Equatorial Guinea (Central Africa)." *Journal of Tropical Ecology,* vol. 11, February 1995, pp. 141–146.

Juste, J., and others. "Market Dynamics of Bush Meat Species in Equatorial Guinea." *Journal of Applied Ecology,* vol. 32, 3, August 1995, pp. 454–467.

Lejoly, J. *Mise en pièce des transects en vue des inventaires de biodiversité à Monte Alen (Guinée Equatoriale).* ECOFAC. Brussels, January 1994, 44 p.

_____. *La biodiversité végétale dans le Parc National de Monte Alen.* ECOFACT. Brussels, December 1994, 75 p.

Ministerio de Agriculture. *Elephant Conservation Plan.* Malabo, 1991, 44 p.

Morales Agacino, E. *Mamíferos de las Posesiomes Españolas del Golfo de Guinea colectados de la expedición de 1933.* Madrid: 1943.

Oficina de Cooperación con Guinea Ecuatorial. *Projecto de investigación y conservación de la Naturaleza en Guinea Ecuatorial.* Ministerio de Asuntos Exteriores, Santa Isabel. Madrid: 1986. 29 p., Ill.

Ortiz de Zárate López, A., and A. Ortiz de Zárate Rocandio. *Descripción de los Moluscos terrestres de la Isla de Fernando Poo (Familia Achatanidae).* Madrid: IDEA, 1959.

Perez del Val, J., *Las aves do Bioko* [Fernando Poo]. Edilesa. León, 1996, 239 p., il, maps.

Roig, B. *Peces del Río Muni. Guinea Ecuatorial (Aguas dulces y salubres).* Barcelona: 1971.

Sabater Pi, J., and Groves, C. "Notes on the Distribution and Ecology of the Higher Primates of Río Muni, West Africa." *Tulane Stud. Zool.,* 14 , 1967, pp. 101–109.

_____. *Gorilas y chimpancés del Africa Occidental.* Ed. Fondo de Culture Económica., 1984.

_____. "Estudio de unos bastones fabricados y usados por chimpanzes de las montañas de Okorobiko en Río Muni (República de Guinea Ecuatorial), Africa occidental." *Anuario de psicología,* II, 39. Barcelona: Universidad de Barcelona, 1988, pp. 67–83.

Schaaf, C. D., Butynski, T. M., Hearn, G. W. *The drill (Mandrillus leucophaesus) and other primates in the Gran Caldera Volcanica de Luba.* Results of a survey conducted March 7–22, 1990. Unpublished report to the Government of equatorial Guinea. Zoo of Atlanta. Atlanta, 1990

Schaaf, C. D., Struhsaker, T. T., Hearn, G. W. *Recommendations for biological conservation area on the island of Bioko, Equatorial Guinea.* Unpublished report to the Government of Equatorial Guinea. Zoo of Atlanta. Atlanta, 1992.

Tatay Puchol, R. *La caza en Guinea.* Madrid: Espasa-Calpe, 1955.

Wolff-Metternich, F., and E. Stresemann. "Biologische Notizen über Vögel von Fernando Poo." *Journal für Ornitologie,* vol. 97, no. 3 (1956).

World Conservation Union, *Equatorial Guinea. Environmental Synopsis.* World Directory of Country Environmental Studies. 1993, 36 p., maps, statistics. Gland, 1996.

World Conservation Monitoring Centre (WCMC), *The Equatorial Guinea protected area coverage.* Washington, October 1997.

SOCIAL

ANTHROPOLOGY

Aranzadi, I. de, y al. *Casas del bosque fang.* Ayuntamiento de Madrid. Catálogo de Ex[psocoón. Parque del Retiro, Madrid, 1998, 223 p., il, glossary.

Beato-Gonzalea, V. *Contribución al estudio del desarrollo somáticomorfológico del niño en Fernando Poo y causas que influyen en su anormal evolución.* Cuestiones de Política Sanitaria Colonial. Madrid: Dirección Général de Marruecos y Colonial, 1942.

Cabezas, J. E. *La persona paume desde el punto de vista biotipológico.* Madrid: IDEA, 1951.

Castillo-Fiel, Conde de. *Notas para un estudio anthropológico y etnológico del Bubi de Fernando Poo.* Madrid: IDEA, 1949.

Creus, J. "La iniciación femenina entre los ndowe: el ndjembé." *Estudios Africanos,* vol. 8, 14–15, 1994, pp. 21–40. Ill.

Fons, Virginia. "Aspectos de marginación social en la ancianidad. El caso de los Ndowe de Guinea Ecuatorial." *Revisita de Gerontología,* vol. 5, 2, June 1995, pp. 102–109.

_____. *Organizació de la procreatción i estructures domèstiques dels ndowes a Guinea Ecuatorial.* Barcelona, 1997.

Juan-Espinosa, M., *Urban and rural people's conceptions of intelligence in Equatorial Guinea.* Paper presented to the International Congress of Cross-cultural Psychology. Pamplona, 1994.

_____. *People's conception of spatial orientation ability in the nungle: the case of "Fang-Okah" hunters from Equatorial Guinea.* Paper presented to the International Congress of Cross-cultural Psychology. Pamplona, 1994.

Mbana Nchama, J. *Las migraciones bantú-fang.* Diss. Madrid, 1994.

Moreno Moreno, J. A. "Formas actuales de antropofagía en los territorios españoles del Golfo de Guinea." *Antropología y Etnología,* 1. Instituto Bernardino de Sahagun. Consejo Superior de Investigaciones Científicas. Madrid, 1948.

Nerín i Abad, G. "El mestissatge, una peculiaritat equto-guineana?" In *Étina i Nació als mons africans* (pp. 189–213). Barcelona, 1995.

Novoa Ruiz, J. A. *A través de la magía bubi. Por las selvas de Guinea [Ecuatorial].* Zaragoza, 1991. Ill.

_____. Iboga. *La Sociedad cescreta del Bueti. Guinea Ecuatorial. Un viaje de investigación al interior de las selvas [ecuato-] Iguineanas en busca de la sociedad secreta de los Bandjns. Sus costumbres, sus ritos y la iniciación en sus cripticos rituales.* Ed. Transglobe films. Madrid, 1998, 265 p., il.

Olo Mibuy, A. "Implicaciones antropológicas de la medicinia (Diagnosis y prognosis bantúes)." *Muntu,* 8, 1st semester 1988, pp. 124–131.

Pons, J. *Impressiones dermopapilares en indígenas de la Guinea española en relación con otras poblaciones; I. Muestras dactilares.* Madrid: IDEA, 1951.

_____. *Impressiones dermopapilares; II. Impressiones palmares.* Madrid: IDEA, 1952.

_____. "La estuaria 'Fang'." In *Revisita del Departamento de Historia del Arte,* 3–4, October 1977, pp. 111–121. Ill.

Relaciones entre grupos sanguíneos y lineas dermopapilares en negros de la Guinea española. Madrid: IDEA, 1957.

Sabater Pi, J. *Etografía africana. Concimientos astronómicos del pueblo fang de Río Muni.* Publicaciones del Centro de Investigaciones Lingüísticas y Etnográficas de la Amazonia Colombiana. Sibundoy, Columbia, 1954, pp. 102–107.

Sabater Pi, J., Oriol Sabater, and J. Coca. *Els tatuatges dels Fang de l'Africa occidental. Art, simbolisme i biologia en una manifestació artística poc conegunda.* Barcelona: Ajuntament de Barcelona, 1992.

Serna Burgaleta, J. de la. *El niño guineano; estudio antropométrico del niño negro.* Madrid: IDEA, 1956.

Veciana Vilaldach, A. de. *Contribución al estudio antropológico del negro africano: los Bujeba de la Guinea Española.* Madrid: IDEA, 1956.

DEMOGRAPHY

Arbelo Curbelo, A., and R. Villarino Uloa. *Contribución al estudio de la despoblación indígena en los territorios españoles del Golfo de Guinea, Con particularidad en Fernando Poo; Campaña sanitaria de 1939–1940.* Madrid: Servicio Sanitario Colonial, 1942.

Caldwell, J. C., G. E. Harrison, and P. Ouiggan. "The Demography of Microstates." *World Development,* vol. 8, 12, 1980, pp. 953–967.

Gobierno Autónomo de la Guinea Ecuatorial. *Reseña demográfica de la Demarcacion (Años 1932–1962). Nomenclator de Entidades y Poblados referidos a 1965.* Bata: Servicio regional de Estadística, 1968.

González Echegaray, A. "Rutas y etapas de los pueblos playeros de la Guinea continental española." International West Africa Conference, 4th. Santa Isabel: 1951: Madrid: 1954, pp. 327–351.

Liniger-Goumaz, M. "Guinée equatorial-Populations. Bibliographie," *Journal de la Société des Africanistes,* vol. 42, no. 1 (1972), pp. 195–206.

Trujeda Incera, L. "El problema demográfico y la política indígena en los Territorios españoles del Golfo de Guinea." *Cuadernos de estudios africanos,* no. 1, 1946, pp. 57–66.

Vila Coro, A. "Natalidad, mortalidad, morbilidad y desarrollo del niño paume en la Guinea continental española." *Revista de Sanidad e Higiene Pública,* vol. 26 (1952), pp. 239–300.

EDUCATION

Action Programs International. *Estudio de requisitos para un proyecto de Educación primera y formación de maestros en Guinea Ecuatorial. Contrato entre Banco Africano de Desarrollo y Action Programs International/Tippetts-Abbett-McCarthy-Shatton.* Washington, DC, February 7, 1984. 146 p.

Altozano Moraleda, H. "El Patronato de Indígenas de Guinea: institución ejemplar." *Archivos del Instituto de Estudios Africanos*, no. 40, March 1957, pp. 49–63.

Alvarez García, H. R. *Historia de la acción cultural en la Guinea Española, con notas sobre la enseñanza en el Africa negra.* Madrid: IDEA, 1948.

Banga, L. "Proverbes et éducation chez les Bubi-Fang-Beti. Une étude des proverbes." Diss. Paris, 1972.

Beato González, V. *Capacidad mental del negro.* Madrid: Dirección General de Marruecos y Colonias, 1944.

Creus, J. "La iniciación femenina entre los ndowe: el Ndjebé." *Estudios Africanos. Revista de la Asociación Española de Africanistas*, vol. 8, 14–15, 1994, pp. 21–40. Ill.

_____. "Sobre héroes, tipos y géneros en la narrativa oral de Guinea." *Estudios Africanos*, X, 18–19, 1996, pp. 18–30.

_____. *La Educación en la Región Ecuatorial de España.* Madrid: IDEA, 1961.

_____. "El problema educativo a través de la colonización española." Junta de abogados de la colonia, Madrid, July 1947.

Fernandez Magaz, M., and others. *Enciclopedia. Guinea Ecuatorial (Religión, Lengua Española, Ciencias sociales, Geografía, Matemática, Ciencias Naturales, Agricultura, Salud, Cocina, Labores).* Madrid, 1993, 391 p.

Negrín Fajardo, O. "La educación de la mujer en los comienzos de la colonización de la Guinea española (1884–1910)." *Actas del VI Coloquio de Historia de la Educación.* Santiago de Compostela, 1990, pp. 482–492.

_____. *Historia de la educación en Guinea Ecuatorial. El modelo educativo colonial español.* UNED. Madrid, 1993.

Ondo, J., *Legislación educativa 1908–1993.* Dirección general de Planificación. Ministerio de Educación. Malabo, s.f.

Sasnet, M., and I. Sepmeyer. "Spanish Africa." In *Educational Systems of Africa.* Los Angeles, 1966, pp. 995–1002.

UNESCO. *Centro de Desarrollo de la Educación.* Doc. 2737 RMO RD/EDS. Paris, Aug. 1972.

_____. *Guinea Ecuatorial. Propuestas para la reconstrucción y el desarrollo de la educación.* Doc. EFM 125. Paris, September 1984, 144 p. Maps, statistics.

Universidad Nacional de Educación a Distancia. *La UNED de España en la República de Guinea Ecuatorial.* Madrid: UNED, 1987, 1255 p.

ETHNOLOGY

Alexandre, P., and J. Binet. *Le groupe dit Pahouin (fang, bulu, beti).* Paris: Presses Universitaires de France, 1958.

Aranzadi, I. X. de. *En el Bosque Fang.* Barcelona: 1982.

Ayemi, A. *Los Bubis de Fernando Poo.* Madrid: Dirección General de Marruecos y Colonias, 1942.

Bagueña Corella, L. "Algunas costumbres pamue." *Archivos del Instituto de Estudios Africanos,* no. 11, Jan. 1950, pp. 81–100.

Boriko Lopes, B. *Il villagio racconta. Cultura e tradizione orale del popolo bubi.* Bologna: Biblioteca Nigrizia, 1977.

Bennett, A. L. "Ethnographical Notes on the Fang." *Journal of the Royal Anthropological Institute,* vol. 29 (1988).

Bravo Carbonell, J. *Anecdotario paume; impressiones de Guinea.* Madrid: Editorial Nacional, 1942.

Castillo Barril, M. "Síntesis valorativa de las culturas autóchtonas de la Guinea ecuatorial." *Archivos del Instituto de Estudios Africanos,* vol. 19, no. 76, 1965, pp. 77–92.

Crespo-Gil-Delgado, C. "Los Bayeles, una tribú pigmea en la Guinea Española." *Africa,* nos. 83–84, Nov.–Dec. 1948, pp. 402–406.

Finlay, C. *Cannibals Were My Friends: Finlay's True Fernandian Tale.* Evesham: Arthur Jamas, 1957.

González Echegaray. *Etnología. Estudios guineanos,* II. Madrid: IDEA, 1964.

Guinea Lopez, E. *En el país de los Bubis.* Madrid: IDEA, 1949.

_____. *En el país de los Paumes.* Madrid: IDEA, 1964.

Iyanga Pendi. *El Pueblo Ndowe. Etnología, sociología e historia.* Valencia: Nau Llibres, 1992. 237 p., bibliography.

Manfredi Cano, D. *Ischulla; panorámica lírica de las costumbres, tradiciónes y artes de los Bubis de Fernando Poo.* Madrid: IDEA, 1950.

Martín del Molino, A. *Los Bubis. Rítos y creencias.* Programa de Cooperación cultural de la Cooperación española con Guinea Ecuatorial. Madrid, 1989. 510 p.

Ombolo, J.-P. *Eléments de base pour une approche ethnologique et historique des Fang-Beti-Boulou.* Yaoundé: University of Yaoundé, 1984. 308 p.

Ondo Mayie, L. M. *Pluralidad de esposas entre los fang de Río Muni y la ética cristiana.* Barcelona, 1972. 74 p.

Osubita, J. B. "Ritos funerarios de los Fang y los Bubis en Guinea Ecuatorial." Diss. University of Paris.

Panyella Gómez, A., and J. Sabater. *Esquema de entología de los Fang Ntumu de la Guinea Española.* Madrid: IDEA, 1959.

Sabater Pi, J., and C. Groves. "The Importance of Higher Primates in the Diet of the Fang of Río Muni." *Man,* vol. 7, no. 2, 1972, pp. 239–243.

Sierra Delange, M. "La danza 'ivanga' en Guinea Ecuatorial (manifestación cultural de los kombes)." *Estudios Africanos,* vol. 2I, 2–3, 1986, pp. 39–84.

Tessman, G. *Die Bube auf Fernando Poo. Völkerkundliche Einzelbeschreibung eines West-afrikanischen Negerstammes.* Hagen: Folkwang Verlag, 1923.

_____. *Die Pangwe. Völkerkundliche Monographie eines West-afrikanische Negerstammes.* 2 vols. Berlin: Ernst Wasmuth A. G., 1913.

Unzueta y Yuste, A. "Etntografía de la Guinea española. I. Los Bengas." *Estudios Geográficos,* vol. 6, no. 19, May 1945, pp. 261–299.

_____. "Etnografía de Fernando Poo: los Bubis." *Estudios Geográficos,* vol. 8., no. 26, Feb. 1947, pp. 155–187.

RELIGION

Anon. "Un obispo [Anacleto Sima Nguea, Bata] acusa a la policía de torturar a un sacerdote católico." *El País,* February 15, 1996, p. 7.

Aranzadi, I. X. de. *La adivinanza en la zona Ntumu.* Madrid: IDEA, 1962.

Armada, A. "El régimen [ecuato-] guineano detiene a varios religiosos." *El País,* February 9, 1996, p. 10.

Assoumu Ndoutombe, D. *Du Mvett. Essai sur la dynastie Ekang Nna.* Paris: L'Harmattan, 1986. 184 p.

Bell, G. *Our Fernandian Field.* London: Primitive Methodist Church, 1926.

Binet, J. "Drugs and Mysticism: The Bwiti Cult of the Fang." *Diogenes,* 86, Summer 1974, pp. 31–54.

Brown, A. J. "Missions in Africa." In *One Hundred Years: A History of the Foreign Missionary Work of the Presbyterian Church in the USA* (pp. 196–290). New York, 1936.

Buff-Thomson, F. W. "A voyage to Fernando Po" [extract of the diary of J. C. Clarke, Baptist missionary (approx. 1948)]. *Baptist Quarterly.* Southampton, July 1953, pp. 82–87, 113–121.

Campbell, P. "The Beginnings of Christian Evangelism and African Responses: American Presbyterians in Equatorial Guinea and Gabon." Paper presented at the 19th Annual Meeting of the African Studies Association, no. 15. Boston, Nov. 3–6, 1976.

Canals, E. *"El Padre Grande" de Guinea* [E. Coll]. Barcelona, 1993.

Coll, Armengol, Padre C.M.F., and the Misión de Mariá Cristina [Fernando Po]. Edición, introduccion and notes by Jacint Creus. Ceiba Ediciones. *Documentos de la colonización,* 1. Vich, 1995, 76 p.

Creus, J. *Action missionnaire en Guinée équatoriale, 1858–1910: Perplexités et naïvetés à l'aube de la colonisation.* Diss. In preparation.

_____. *El padre Joaquim Juanola [1853–1912] i l'inici de la colonització de Guinea Equatorial.* Col-lecció Beques Ciutat d'Olot/2. Patronat d'estudis històrics d'Olot i comarca. Olot, 1998, 158 p., il, maps.

Ensema Nsang, M. *Cien años de evangelización en Guinea Ecuatorial.* Ediciones Claret. Barcelona, 1983.

Fernández, C. *Misiones y Misioneros en la Guinea Española.* Madrid: Editorial COCULSA, 1962.

Fernández, J. W. "Symbolic Consensus in Fang Reformation Cult." *American Anthropologist,* vol. 67, no. 4, Aug. 1965, pp. 902–929.

Fuller, J. J. "Cameroons and Fernando Po." Manuscript, London: The Baptist Missionary Society, 1887.

Gallay, P. "L'Eglise catholique en Guinée equatoriale." *Lumières* (Fianarantsoa/Madagascar, Jan. 17, 1973).

Gwei S. N. *History of the British Baptist Mission in Cameroun, with its Beginnings in Fernando Po: 1841–86.* Unpublished Diss., Baptist College, Zurich, 1966.

Holland, W. *Missionary Work in Oil River and Fernando Po, 1874–1908.* Box 13, File 6. Liverpool: John Holt & Comp. Ltd.

Isisarri, P. J. s.j., *Misión de Fernando Poo, 1859.* Edición: Jacint Creus, Antònia Brunat. Ceiba Ediciones. Documentos de la colonización. Vic (Osonoa), 1998, 85 p.

Martín del Molino, A. *La figura del Abba en la religión de los Bubis,* Madrid: IDEA, 1956.

Montague, L. *Report in Philadelphia Presbytery on the Synod Mission of Twelve Laymen to Río Muni* [1968]. 3 p., Mimeo. Presbyterian Department of History. Philadelphia.

Nassau, R. H. *Corisco Days: The First Thirty Years of the West African Mission.* Philadelphia: Allen, Lane and Scott, 1910.

Nfor Gwesi, S., *History of the British Baptist Mission in Cameroon, with beginnings in Fernando Po, 1841–1886.* Bachelor of Divinity. Faculty of the Baptist Theological seminary. Rüschlikon-Zürich (Switzerland), 156 p., taped (Evanston, Unilib, Ill.).

Olo Mibuy, A. "La concepción de Dios en los Fang." *Africa 2000,* V, II, 13, 1990, pp. 36–41.

Ondo Mba, S. "La Iglesia, perseguida." *Mundo Negro,* March 1996, p. 7.

Reus, J. "Lle 'rachat de jeunes filles africaines' en Guinée équatoriale 1890–1900. *Revue françaaise d'histoire d'Outre-Mer,* LVXXXIV, 315. Paris, 1997, pp. 107–119.

Roe, H. *Fernando Po Mission: A Consecutive History of the Opening of Our First Mission Station.* London: Elliot Stock, 1882.

Teuwissen R. W. "Robert Hamill Nassau, 1835–1921: Presbyterian Pioneer Missionary Equatorial West Africa." Thesis, Louisville Theological Seminary, Louisville, 1973.

Thomas, W. T., and E. B. Faiman. *Africa and the United Presbyterians.* New York: United Presbyterian Church in the USA, 1959.

Thorne, A., *God at Work in Spanish Guinea.* Evangelical Publishing House. London, 1943, 75 p.

Veciana Vilaldach, A. de. *La secta del Bwiti en la Guinea española.* Madrid: IDEA, 1958.

Wheeler, W. R. *The Words of God in the African Forest: The Story of an American Mission in West Africa.* New York: Revell, 1931.

de Wulf, V. "Une étape dans la stratégie missionnaire Clarétine: le déplacement du village principal d'Annobon, Guinée Equatoriale (1892–1895)." *Studia Africana.* Barcelona, 1997, pp. 21–34.

SOCIOLOGY

Alcobe Noguer, S., and A. Panyella Gómez. "Estudio cuantitativo de la exogamía de los Paumes (Fang) de la Guinea continental española." *Archivos del Instituto de Estudios Africanos,* no. 18, 1951.

Bot Ba Njock, H.-M. "Prééminences sociales et système politico-religieux dans la société traditionnelle bubi et fang." *Journal de la Société des Africanistes,* no. 2., 1960, pp. 151–171.

Bulnez Ruiz, A., and others. *Guinea Ecuatorial.* Malaga: Informe Socioéconómico, 1991.

Creus, J. "Guinea Equatorial, 1889-1911: La invenció d'una identitat." In *Estructures agráries i poder politic,* 30. *Recerques. Historia/Economía/Cultura,* 30, 1995.

FAO. *Perfiles nutricionales de los Países. Guinea Ecuatorial.* Rome, 1990. 14 p.

Iyanga Pendi, A. *El pueblo ndowe: etnología, sociología, historia.* Valencia, 1992.

Klinteberg, R. af. *Equatorial Guinea-Macias Country. The Forgotten Refugees.* Geneva: International University Exchange Fund, 1978.

Nerin Abad, G. *Guinea Equatorial: Historia en Blanc i Negra. Estereotips sexoracials i relacions sexuals interracials a la Guinea Equatorial, 1843-1992.* Memória de llicenciatura presentada per. . . .Universitat de Barcelona. Facultat de Geográfica i Historia. Barcelona, June 1992. 264 p., Ill., bibliography.

Nze Abuy, R. M. *Familia y Matrimonio Fán.* Madrid, 1988.

Panyella Gómez, A., and J. Sabater. "Los cuatro grados de la Familia en los Fang de la Guinea Española, Camerones y Gabón." *Archivos del Instituto de Estudios Africanos,* no. 46, March 1957, pp. 7–17.

_____. *Elementos Matrilineares en la organización familiar fang (Guinea Española y Camerones).* Philadelphia: International Congress of Archeology and Ethnology, 1955.

_____. *Estudio del proceso técnico de la ceramica fang (Guinea Española y Camerones) en su relación con la estructura social.* Madrid: IDEA, 1955.

_____. "El indivíduo y la sociedad Fang." *Archivos del Instituto de Estudios Africanos,* no. 46, Sept. 1958, pp. 51–64.

Romero Moliner, R. "Apuntes sobre la estructura social de Fernando Poo." *Cuadernos de Estudios Africanos,* no. 7, 1949, pp. 23–52.

_____. "Notas sobre la situación social de la mujer indígena en Fernando Poo." *Cuadernos de Estudios Africanos,* no. 18, Feb. 1950, pp. 13–16.

_____. "Aspectos sociales de la alimentación en Fernando Poo." *Archivos del Instituto de Estudios Africanos,* 17, June 1951, pp. 23–31.

Veciana Vilaldach, A. de. "La organización familiar de los Kombe." *Archivos del Instituto de Estudios Africanos,* no. 36, Feb. 1956, pp. 83–91.

_____. "La estructura sociólogica del mosaico étnico de la Costa de Guinea (Guinea española)." *Archivos del Instituto de Estudios Africanos,* no. 40, March 1957, pp. 43–48.

❖ ABOUT THE AUTHOR ❖

Max Liniger-Goumaz (Licence en sciences sociales, Licence ès sciences géographiques, Dr. ès sciences économiques, University of Geneva) is a professor of economic geography at the Special Mathematics Center of the Swiss Federal Institute of Technology and the School of Economics and Business Administration in Lausanne. From 1962 to 1979, he served as UNESCO chief technical adviser, IBRD coordinator, and ICRC delegate in Africa. From 1972 to 1974, he directed the establishment of the Centro de Desarrollo de la Educación in Equatorial Guinea. As the principal international specialist on that country, he wrote many books and articles including, between 1974 and 1998, a series of ten volumes of the *Bibliografía General de Guinea Ecuatorial*. Dr. Liniger-Goumaz is a founding member of the Société Suisse d'Etudes Africaines and co-editor of the journal *Genéve-Afrique* as well as a member of the Asociación Española de Africanistas (Madrid), the Société des Ecrivains de Langue Francaise and the Société des Amis de l'Academie des Sciences d'Outre Mer (Paris). Apart from his activities as an Africanist, he is also engaged in work on medieval Switzerland and Europe. He was awarded the Edouard Folliet Prize and the Arthur de Claparéde Prize (marketing, geography, University of Geneva, 1953, 1964) and the William Huber Prize (Société de Géographie de Paris, 1983) for his scholarly contributions to society. In June 1998, Prof. Max Liniger-Goumaz was named honorary member of the Asociación Española de Africanistas (Madrid).